May We Suggest

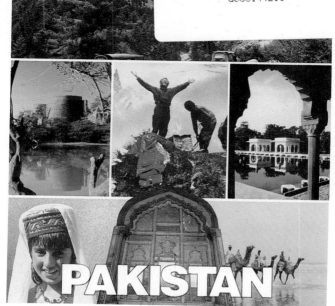

PAKISTAN

As Your Next Destination?

A land where past and present blends into a harmonious culture, where people with a proud heritage welcome you with a smile, adding a special something to your holiday.

PIA is privileged to be the one airline which brings these unrivalled holiday destinations to you. Hospitality and grace, which is the very essence of our nation, is represented by our well trained and experienced staff. So, at any time of the year, PIA invites you to add Pakistan to your itinerary.

PIA
Pakistan International
Great people to fly with

For further information please contact your nearest travel agent or PIA booking office

PIA OFFICES:

London 0171 734 5544 (reservations)
0181 741 8066 (administration)
0181 759 2544 (Heathrow)

Manchester 0161 839 7505/7506
Birmingham 0121 643 7850/7032/5210
Bradford 01274 731705/731804
Glasgow 0141 221 9936
Bristol 01179 290874/290889

PAKISTAN HANDBOOK

Editors **Ivan Mannheim and Dave Winter**
Maps by **Sebastian Ballard**

"All things considered there are only two kinds
of men in the world - those that stay at home
and those that do not."
Kipling

2

TRADE & TRAVEL
Handbooks

Trade & Travel Publications Ltd
6 Riverside Court, Lower Bristol Road, Bath BA2 3DZ, England
Telephone 01225 469141   Fax 01225 469461
Email 100660.1250@compuserve.com

©Trade & Travel Publications Ltd., January 1996

ISBN 0 900751 70 3

CIP DATA: A catalogue record for this book is available from the British Library

In North America, published and distributed by

PASSPORT BOOKS
a division of *NTC Publishing Group*

4255 West Touhy Avenue, Lincolnwood (Chicago), Illinois 60646-1975, USA
Telephone 708-679-5500   Fax 708-679-2494   Email NTCPUB2@AOL.COM

ISBN 0-8442-4903-3

Library of Congress Catalog Card Number 95-71569

Passport Books and colophon are registered trademarks of NTC Publishing Group

**MAPS - Publisher's note: the Government of Pakistan states that "the
accession of Jammu and Kashmir to Pakistan or India remains to be
decided". None of the maps published in this guidebook are intended to
have any political significance.**

**IMPORTANT: While every endeavour is made to ensure that the facts
printed in this book are correct at the time of going to press, travellers
are cautioned to obtain authoritative advice from consulates, airlines,
etc, concerning current travel and visa requirements and conditions
before embarking. The publishers cannot accept legal responsibility for
errors, however caused, that are printed in this book.**

Cover illustration by Suzanne Evans

Printed and bound in Great Britain by Clays Ltd., Bungay, Suffolk

CONTENTS

MAPS	4
THE EDITORS	6
INTRODUCTION	7
INFORMATION FOR VISITORS	10
Before travelling	10
Getting there	16
On arrival	19
Where to stay	25
Food and drink	27
Getting around	31
Communications	37
Media	38
Entertainment	40
Holidays and festivals	43
Further reading	43
Maps	45
HEALTH INFORMATION	47
Before travelling	47
Common problems	48
Other specific problems	52
Other afflictions	55
Returning home	55
Further information	56
ACKNOWLEDGEMENTS	57
PAKISTAN: LAND CULTURE AND HISTORY	59
Land and life	59
Religion	69
Culture	76
History	84
Modern Pakistan	101
SIND	113
Karachi	124
Karachi to Quetta	138
Karachi to Hyderabad via National Highway	139
Karachi to Hyderabad via the Super Highway	143
Hyderabad to Sukkur via the Indus East Bank	150
Hyderabad to Sukkur via the Indus West Bank	156
BALUCHISTAN	166
Quetta	177
Quetta to Loralai via Ziarat	185
Quetta to Dera Ghazi Khan	188
Quetta to Dera Ismail Khan via Zhob	191
Quetta to Sukkur via the Bolan Pass	193
Quetta to Chaman	198
Quetta to Iran	199
Quetta to Karachi	202
The Makran	206
PUNJAB	216
Islamabad	223
Rawalpindi	232
Excursions from Islamabad	239
Islamabad to Murree	247
Islamabad to Peshawar	253
Islamabad to the Salt Range	256
Islamabad to Lahore	264
Lahore	272
Lahore to Sukkur	292
Lahore to Dera Ismail Khan	313
Lahore to Bannu	316
AZAD JAMMU AND KASHMIR	318
Muzaffarabad	324
Neelum Valley	327
Jhelum Valley	329
Poonch and Bagh District	331
Mirpur and Kotli Districts	333
Kotli	334
NORTH WEST FRONTIER PROVINCE	335
Peshawar	347
Southern NWFP	361
Peshawar Valley	371
Swat Valley	379
Chitral Valley	395
KARAKORAM HIGHWAY AND THE NORTHERN AREAS	419
Hazara Section	432
Kaghan Valley	439
Kohistan Section	445
Gilgit District	454
Gilgit to Chitral	468
Baltistan	479
Lower Hunza/Nagar Section	500
Central Hunza/Nagar Section	507
Nagar Valley	515
Gojal (Upper) Hunza Section	516
Khunjerab Pass to China	524
TREKKING	538
URDU WORDS & PHRASES	566
INDEX	569

MAP INDEX

Abbottabad	435	Moenjo Daro	161
Azad Jammu & Kashmir	319	Multan	301
Bahawalpur	305	Murree & the Galis	251
Balakot	440	Murree Town	249
Baltistan	480	Muzaffarabad	325
Baluchistan	167	Naran	442
Besham	448	New Sust	522
Chalt and Chaprot Valley	504	Northern areas	421
Chilas	452	NWFP Province	336
Chitral Town	403	Old Sust	521
Dasu and Komila	450	Pakistan	8-9
Deosai	491	Annual Rainfall, Temperature	
Dera Ismail Khan	370	Regions and Climatic	
Dir	401	Regions	64
Faisalabad	315	Delhi Sultanate in 1236	87
Gilgit		Himalaya Profile	61
District	455	Indus Valley Sites	85
Town	460	Mughal Empire	88
Gilgit to Chitral	469	PIA's Domestic Network	32
Gojal (Upper) Hunza	517	Regional Setting	60
Gulmit	516	Tectonic map	62
Harappa	294	Passu	519
Hazara District	433	Peshawar	
Hunza and Nagar	501	City	348
Hyderabad	145	Old City	350
Islamabad/Rawalpindi area	224	Saddar	353
Islamabad	225	University Town	354
Blue Area	227	Peshawar Valley	372
Kaghan Valley	439	Punjab	217
Kalam	393	Quetta	178
Kalash Valleys	407	Centre	181
Karachi	126-127	Surroundings	186
Centre	132	Ranikot Fort	157
Saddar Bazar	134	Rawalpindi	
Karimabad	511	Cantonment	236
Kashgar	532	Old City	234
Khaplu	497	Saddar Bazaar	235
Khuzdar	204	Rohtas Fort	267
KK Highway	429	Saidu Sharif	385
Kohat	363	Shigar	494
Kohistan District	446	Sialkot	271
Lahore	275	Sibi	196
Fort	278	Sind	114
Museum	284	Skardu	486
Old City	281	Southern NWFP	362
Larkana	165	Sukkur	154
Madyan	389	Sust to Kashgar	524
Makran Coast	207	Swat Valley	380
Mansehra	437	Takht-e-Bhai	374
Mardan	373	Tashkurgan	527
Margalla Hill Treks	240	Taxila	244
Miandam	390	Upper Chitral	415
Mingora	384		

MAP SYMBOLS

Administration

International Border
State / Province Border
Cease Fire Line

Neighbouring country
Neighbouring state

State Capitals □
Other Towns ○

Roads and travel

Main Roads
(National Highways)
Other Roads

Jeepable Roads, Tracks

Railways with station

Water features

River *Indus River*
Lakes, Reservoirs, Tanks
Seasonal Marshlands
Sand Banks, Beaches
Ocean
Waterfall ⑂
Canals
Ferry

Topographical features

Contours (approx),
Rock Outcrops
Mountains
Mountain Pass
Glaciers
Gorge
Escarpment
Palm trees
Deciduous/fir trees

Cities and towns

Built Up Areas

Main through routes
Main streets
Minor Streets
Pedestrianized Streets
One Way Street →
National Parks, Gardens, Stadiums

Fortified Walls ▲▲▲
Airport Ⓚ
Banks Ⓢ
Bus Stations (named in key)
Hospitals ⊕
Market Ⓜ
Police station Ⓟ
Post Office ✉
Telegraphic Office ◔
Tourist Office ⓘ

Key Numbers ❶ ❷ ❸ ❹ ❺

Bridges ⏝

Stupa △ ⌂

Mosque 🕌

Cathedral, church ✝ ✝

Guided routes ....

National parks, trekking areas

National Parks and
Bird Sanctuaries ◆

Hide ⌂

Camp site ⋀

Refuge ⌂

Motorable track - - - - -

Walking track ....

Other symbols

Archaeological Sites ⁛

Places of Interest ○

Viewing point ⚘

THE EDITORS

Dave Winter

Dave Winter, who graduated from the University of London's School of Oriental and African Studies with a first class BA Honours degree in Geography, has spent much of his time travelling. In recent years he has visited Morocco, Egypt, Israel, Syria, Turkey, Iran, India (3 times), Nepal (twice), Sri Lanka, Pakistan (7 times), Thailand, Laos, Vietnam, Singapore, Hong Kong, Macao, China and Australia. Dave speaks Urdu and is a loyal fan of the game of cricket. His travels have given him the opportunity to pursue his other great passion of photography: his work has been displayed in several exhibitions and used in various travel magazines.

Ivan Mannheim

Ivan Mannheim was introduced to the *Handbooks* when he was asked to write a section on the Northwest Frontier for the *South Asian Handbook*. Also a Geography graduate from SOAS and an Urdu speaker, Ivan has travelled extensively in Asia, particularly in China, Nepal, India and Pakistan, the latter having drawn him back half a dozen times over the years to hike and climb in the Karakoram area. He has worked on projects with the Save the Children Fund and has also travelled in the former Soviet Union, Iran and Morocco. In the Caribbean, he worked for a time at the Bitter End Yacht Club in the British Virgin Islands, fulfilling one of his dreams by sailing back to Europe across the Atlantic on a yacht.

INTRODUCTION

Although less than 50 years old, Pakistan has a history that stretches to the very beginnings of human civilization and spans numerous empires. Each has left its legacy; the great Indus Valley Civilization cities of Moenjo Daro and Harappa, the beautiful sculptures of Buddhist Gandhara, the shrines and mosques of early Muslim pilgrims and invaders, the magnificent monuments of the Mughals and the colonial architecture of the British. But brace yourself also for an emerging, dynamic Pakistan, responding as rapidly and diversely as any other country to the challenges of the approaching millennium. The tourist brochures paint a picture of timeless, unchanging traditions, and although life in the rural heartlands may have changed little, in Lahore computer programmers lead the way in software development, while doctors pioneer new surgeries and treatments.

The media paints a bloody picture of violence, danger and fanaticism, but prepare yourself rather for a lesson in human warmth, generosity and hospitality. Despite the wild warring tribesmen image (in places a reality) and the current tragic situation in Karachi, Pakistan is still in many ways one of the safest countries in Asia in which to travel. You are far more likely to find yourself accepting endless invitations to stay or eat in people's houses, or desperately trying to persuade someone you just met on the bus that there's really no need for him to pay for your ticket, than reporting a theft or mugging or trying to get rid of somebody who is after your money. The sheer diversity of peoples, cultures and traditions meanwhile make travelling in Pakistan a continually fascinating experience.

Everyone paints a picture of stunning natural beauty, an almost unbelievable range of landscapes and environments; mighty rivers, huge deserts, fertile plains, thick forests and towering mountains. And for once, nobody has got it wrong. Mountaineers were amongst the first to discover the full glory of Pakistan's magnificent Karakoram, Hindu Kush and Himalayan ranges. Trekkers followed in increasing numbers, and today spectacular feats of engineering have pushed roads through these breathtaking mountains, opening them up to all. But while most people flock to the mountains, the southern half of the country conceals equally magnificent wonders of a different kind.

Pakistan is certainly not the easiest of countries to travel in; if you are looking for an easy, comfortable and predictable holiday, this is perhaps not the place to come. But while travelling huge distances on rickety, overcrowded buses, or dealing with obstructive officials and bureaucrats can be exhausting and frustrating, the rewards are equally great.

Most of all, it is a country full of surprises; travelling through the remotest backwaters of Baluchistan, you might suddenly find yourself the honoured guest in the palacial residence of a local tribal chief (no doubt educated at Oxford or Harvard); just as you are at the end of your tether at the overwhelmingly male-dominated social set-up, you might meet an outspoken Pakistani woman campaigning to promote female education. There is always something or someone around the next corner ready to shatter any simple generalizations or stereotypes you may be tempted to construct for yourself.

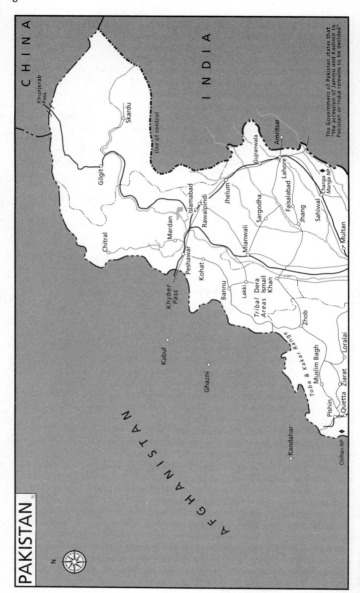

PAKISTAN

The Government of Pakistan states that "the accession of Jammu and Kashmir to Pakistan or India remains to be decided".

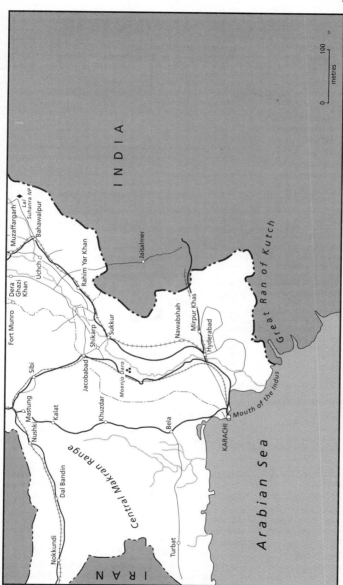

INFORMATION FOR VISITORS

CONTENTS	
Before travelling	10
Entry requirements	10
When to go	14
Health	14
Money	14
What to take	15
Getting there	16
Air; Overland; Sea; Customs	
On arrival	19
Documentation; Customs; Essentials; Etiquette; Safety; Women travelling alone	
Where to stay	25
Food and drink	27
Getting around	31
Air; Train; Road; Car hire; Other land transport	
Communications	37
Language; Postal services; Telephone services; Facsimile	
Media	38
Entertainment	40
Holidays and festivals	43
Further reading	43
Maps	45

Before Travelling

Entry requirements

● **Visas**

Regulations regarding visas are subject to change, so it is essential to check the current situation with the issuing embassy. All foreign nationals require a valid visa for visiting Pakistan, with a few exceptions. Single and double entry tourist visas are valid for a period of 90 days on each visit and must be used within 6 months of the date of issue.

Certain countries have visa abolition agreements with Pakistan, allowing nationals of those countries to visit Pakistan without a visa for periods of between 30-90 days. These agreements in particular are subject to frequent change, so check with your nearest Pakistan embassy.

Cost Visa fees vary according to your nationality, with countries such as Britain being penalized for their draconian immigration policy towards Pakistan. The following fees (£ sterling) were being charged for single entry tourist visas in Nov 1995:

Australia	20
Canada	35
Denmark	Free
France	25
Germany	15
Italy	25
Japan	Free
Spain	10
UK	40
USA	17

Transit Visas are issued *only at the discretion of immigration officials*. Visitors are strongly advised to obtain a full visa beforehand if at all possible; even if a transit visa is issued, the subsequent bureaucracy is extremely time consuming. They are valid for 72 hrs, within which time you must apply for a full tourist visa if you intend to stay on in the country.

Foreigners' Registration Note that all foreign tourists, except nationals of UK, UAE and Australia, are required to register if staying more than 30 days in the country (see below, under On Arrival). See also section on **Permits** for restricted areas.

● **Vaccinations**

Officially you must have a Yellow Fever vaccination certificate if arriving from a country in which Yellow Fever is endemic. In practice this is rarely enforced. Check with a Pakistani embassy regarding any currently enforced regulations in this respect. All foreigners coming to Pakistan for more than 1 year are required to produce a certificate confirming they do not have HIV/AIDS.

● **ISIC**

Anyone in full-time education is entitled to an International Student Identity Card (ISIC). These are issued by student travel offices and travel agencies across the world. In Pakistan they entitle you to a 50% discount on rail tickets. The ISIC head office is: ISIC Association, Box 9048, 1000 Copenhagen, Denmark, T (45) 33939303.

● **Representation overseas**

Australia: 4 Timbarra Crescent, PO Box 648, O'Malley Act-2606, Mawson, 2607 Canberra, T 2901676. Consulates: Sydney T 2677250, Melbourne T 6087153; **Austria:** Hofzeile 13, A 1190, Vienna, T 367381; **Bangladesh:** NE (C) 2, Rd 71, Gulshan, Dhaka, T 885387; **Belgium:** Av Delleur 57, Brussels 1170, T 6738007; **Canada:** Burnside Building, 151 Slater Av, Suite 608, Ottowa, Ontario K1P, 5H3, T 2387881. Consulates: Toronto T 2501255, Montreal T 8452297; **China:** 1 Dong Zhi Men, Wai Da Jie, San Li Tun, Beijing 100600, T 5321217; **Denmark:** Valeursvej 17, 2900 Hellerup, Copenhagen, T 31621693; **France:** 18 Rue Lord Byron, 74008 Paris, T 45610824. Consulate: 10 Blvd Jules Favre, 96006 Lyon, T 78529680; **Germany:** Rheinllee 24, 5300 Bonn 2, T 352004. Consulates: Berlin T 4824448, Frankfurt T 287489, Dusseldorf T 32926566, Hamburg T 23750, Munich T 534880; **Hong Kong:** Rm 3806, 38th Flr, China Resources Building, 26 Harbour Rd, Wanchai, T 8270681; **India:** 2/50-G Shantipath, Chanakyapuri, New Delhi 110021, T 609161; **Indonesia:** 50 Jl Teuku Umar, Jakarta, Pusat, T 3144008; **Iran:** Koocha-e-Ahmed, Eatmadzadeh, Block 1, Jamshedabad Shomali, Tehran, T 394330. Consulates: Mashad T 29845, Zahedan T 23666; **Italy:** Via Della, Camillucia 682, 00135 Rome, T 36301775. Consulates: Genoa T 3628554, Naples T 7532865; **Japan:** 2-14-9 Moto Azabu, 2 Chome, Miato-Ku, Tokyo, T 34544861. Consulate: Osaka T 2262483; **Kazakhstan:** 25 Tulebayeua, Alma Ata, T 331502; **Malaysia:** 132 Jl Ampang, 50450 Kuala Lumpur, T 2418877; **Myanmar (Burma):** PO Box 581, A-4, Diplomatic Quarters, Payay Rd, Rangoon, T 22881; **Nepal:** PO Box 202, Panipokhari, Kathmandu, T 418446; **Netherlands:** Amaliastraat-8, 2514 JC, The Hague, T 3648948; **New Zealand:** Consulate: 251 Kapa Rd, Kohimarama, Aukland 5 N-2, Aukland, T 3072238; **Norway:** Eckersbergsgata 20, 02244 Oslo, T 555197; **Philippines:** Alexander House, 132 Amorsolo St, Legaspi Village, Makati Metro, Manila, T 2776; **Portugal:** Avda da Republic 20-1, 1000 Lisbon, T 3538547; **Russia:** 17 Ul Sadova Kudrinskaya, Moscow, T 2503991; **Singapore:** 20-A Nazim Rd, Singapore 1025, T 7376988; **Spain:** Avda, Pio XII, 11, 28016 Madrid, T 3459138. Consulates: Barcelona T 2574230, Bilbao T 4320845, Seville T 228921; **Sri Lanka:** 211 De Saram Place, Colombo 10, T 696301; **Sweden:** Sergels Tong 12, 14TR 11-57, Stockholm, T 203300. Consulate: Gothenburg T 812124; **Switzerland:** Bernastrasse 47, Ch-3005, Berne, T 3525063; **Tajikistan:** Tajikistan Hotel, Dushanbe, T 275153; **Thailand:** 31 Soi Nana Nua Sukhumvit (3) Rd, Bangkok 10110, T 2532557; **Turkey:** Iran Caddesi No 37, Gazi Osman Pasa, Ankara, T 4271410; **UK:** 35-36 Lowndes Sq, London SW1X 9JN, T 0171 2352044. Consulates: Bradford T 661114, Birmingham T 2334123, Glasgow

T 4295335, Manchester T 2881349; USA: 2315 Massachusetts Av NW, Washington DC 20008, T 9392613. Consulates: New York T 8795800, Los Angeles T 4410167, Boston T 2675555, Chigago T 8537630, San Francisco T 7780677; Uzbekistan: Tchilanzar St 25, Tashkent, T 771003.

● **Tourist offices**
Pakistan Tourism Development Corporation (PTDC) The PTDC head office in Pakistan is at: 13-T/U, College Rd, Markaz F-7, Islamabad, T 816932, F 824173. Apply here also for trekking and mountaineering permits. There are Tourist Information Centres abroad, although they are generally of little help.

● **Travel agents and tour operators**
In Pakistan: Adventure Tours Pakistan, PO Box 1780, Islamabad, T 252759, F 252145, trekking, climbing, jeep safaris, run by Ashraf Aman the first Pakistani to climb K2; **Adventure Travel**, 15 Wali Centre, 86-S Blue Area, Islamabad, T 212490, F 214580, Indus boating, camel safaris, climbing, trekking, jeep safaris, special interest tours (including to Kashgar and Kyrgistan); **Indus Guides**, 24-C II, Gulberg III, Lahore, T 872975, F 5712529, special interest tours, jeep safaris, Indus boating, camel safaris, trekking; **Hindukush Trails**, No 37, St 28, F6/1, Islamabad, T 821576, F 215031, trekking, climbing, jeep safaris, specialising in Chitral, run by Chitral's former ruling family; **Karakoram Treks and Tours**, 1 Baltoro House, St 19, F-7/2, Islamabad, T 829120, trekking, climbing, jeep safaris and special interest tours (Northern Areas); **Nazir Sabir Expeditions**, PO Box 1442, Islamabad, T 853672, F 250293, specialising in climbing expeditions (Nazir Sabir was the second Pakistani to climb K2), also treks and jeep safaris; **Pakistan Tours Ltd**, 24 Flashman's Hotel, The Mall, Rawalpindi T 563038 Ext 24, F 565449, affiliated to PTDC but operating as a commercial concern, full

range of services, able to offer tailor-made packages; **Sitara Travel Consultants**, Sitara House, 232 Khadim Hussain Rd, PO Box 63, T 564750, F 584958, full range of services, including tours of Central Asia; **Trans Pakistan Adventure Services (TPAS)**, Apt 8, 2nd Fl, Muzuffar Chambers, Fazl-e-Haq Rd, Jinnah Ave, Islamabad, PO Box 2103, T 214796, F213426, special interest tours, jeep safaris (including Makran coast), trekking, climbing; **Travel Club**, 29-Raja Centre, Main Market, Gulberg, Lahore, T 874491, F 874491, special interest tours, jeep safaris; **Travel Walji's (Adventure Pakistan)**, Walji's Building, 10 Khabayan-e-Suhrawardy, Islamabad, PO Box 1088, T 214409, F 210762, Pakistan's largest travel agents, full range of services.

Smaller regional companies are listed under Local Information in the relevant towns/cities.

Abroad: Allibert, Agence Chapareillan, route de Grenoble, 38530 Chapareillan, France, T 76452226, F 76452728; **Club Adventure**, 122 Rue d'Assas, 75006 Paris, France, T 4806116; **Encounter Overland**, 267 Old Brompton Rd, London SW5 9JA, UK, T (0171) 3706845, F (0171) 2449737; **Exodus**, 9 Weir Rd, London SW12 0LT, UK, T (0181) 6757996, F (0181) 6730779; **Explore Worldwide**, 1 Frederick St, Aldershot, Hants GU11 1LQ, UK, T (01252) 344161, F (01252) 343170; **Hann Overland**, 2 Ivy Mill Lane, Godstone, Surrey RH9 8NH, UK, T (01883) 744705, F (01883) 744706; **Himalaya Trekking**, Constant Erzeijstraat 49, 3523 Vt Utrecht, Netherlands, T (030) 871420; **Inner Asia Expeditions**, 2627 Lombard St, San Fransisco, CA 94123, USA, T (415) 9220448, F (415) 3465535; **Karakoram Experience**, 32 Lake Rd, Keswick, Cumbria CA12 5DQ, UK, T (017687) 73966, F (017687) 74693; **Mountain Travel**, 6420 Fairmount Av, El Cerrito, CA 94530, USA, T (415) 5278100, F (415) 5257710; **Mountain**

enchanting PAKISTAN

Travel(ExplorAsia), 13 Chapter St, London SW1P 4NY, UK, T (0171) 6307102, F (0171) 6300355; **Sherpa**, 131A Heston Rd, Hounslow, Middlesex, TW5 0RD, UK, T (0181) 5772717, F (0181) 5729788; **Wilderness Travel**, 801 Allston Way, Berkeley, CA 94710, USA, T (415) 5480420, F (415) 5480347.

When to go

Pakistan can be visited at any time of year, the best season varying according to the region to be visited. Very broadly, the southern half of the country (Sind, Punjab, Baluchistan and southern NWFP) is best visited from late autumn to early spring (Nov to Mar) when temperatures are pleasantly cooler. During the summer, most parts of the plains are extremely hot and travelling around is hard work. The northern half of the country (northern NWFP, Northern Areas and parts of Punjab) are best visited from late spring to early autumn (Apr to Oct). During the winter, most of the mountainous N is snowbound, and not easily accessible. The main trekking season in the Northern Areas and NWFP extends from Jun to Sep. For a more detailed analysis of Pakistan's climate, see the Climate sections in the general and provincial introductions.

Health

NB Read the Health section on page 47 for detailed information on health, including vaccinations and immunizations, and common problems.

● Medical services

Excellent health facilities are available in the major cities (Karachi, Lahore, Islamabad, Peshawar, Quetta), but they deteriorate rapidly as one moves to remoter areas. It is well worth taking out medical insurance before you go, as this will give you access to private medical services, which are invariably better than public ones. Details of hospitals and chemists are given for each town.

Money

● Cost of living

The cost of living in Pakistan remains well below that of industrialized countries. Food, accommodation and transport are exceptionally cheap by western standards. Budget travellers can expect to get by on an average of around US$10/day, although this involves staying in the cheapest places and travelling by the cheapest means. Expect to spend considerably more in the main cities. Note that as soon as you start eating and sleeping in slightly better places, costs go up considerably. Likewise, if you are constantly on the move, it gets more expensive.

● Credit cards

Major credit cards are accepted in the five main cities and by most **AL-B** category hotels. They are accepted by most tourist and handicraft shops. American Express card holders can use their cards to obtain either cash or TCs through the Amex offices in Karachi, Lahore, Islamabad and Rawalpindi. Visa card holders can do the same in the five main cities through international banks, although it can be a time consuming business.

● Currency

Pakistani currency is the Pakistani Rupee (as distinct from the Indian Rupee). Notes come in denominations of Rs 1,000, 500, 100, 50, 10, 2 and 1. The Rupee is divided into 100 paise, with coins of 50, 25, 20, 10 and 5 paise. Unlike in India, currency notes are accepted whatever their condition, unless they have been seriously damaged or defaced. Note that obtaining change for larger currency notes can be difficult in remoter areas; it is well worth carrying a good supply of smaller notes.

● Exchange

The National Bank of Pakistan, Habib Bank and United Bank Limited are authorized to change foreign currency and TCs, as well as foreign banks such as ANZ Grindlays, American Express and Citibank. Note that outside of the main towns, Pakistani banks must obtain current exchange rates from their head office; these usually don't arrive until late morning, leaving little time to conduct any transactions. Many of the larger hotels will also change foreign currency, and in some cases TCs, but at considerably lower rates than the banks. US$ are the most widely accepted, followed by £ Sterling. Other European currencies can generally only be changed in the five main cities. US$ have shown the greatest stability recently, while £ Sterling have been subject to significant fluctuations. You must produce encashment certificates in order to reconvert rupees back into foreign currency.

Black market It is illegal to change money through an unauthorized dealer, although this is rarely, if ever, enforced. However black market rates are generally only slightly better than official ones. The best rates are for high denomination US$ and £ Sterling notes. Note that there are plenty of authorized money changers in larger cities, for example around Chowk Yadgar in Peshawar, where it is perfectly legal to change money.

EXCHANGE RATES: NOV 1995

US $1	Rs 34.10
UK £1	Rs 53.79
Aus $1	Rs 25.60
Can $1	Rs 25.08
NZ $1	Rs 22.23
Yen 100	Rs 33.03
DM 1	Rs 24.02
Dutch Gilda 1	Rs 21.45
French Franc 1	Rs 6.96
Spanish Peseta 100	Rs 27.89
Italian Lira 1,000	Rs 21.32

● **Transferring money to Pakistan**
American Express and ANZ Grindlays can make instant money transfers to their banks in Pakistan, but charge a high fee. National Bank of Pakistan and Habib Bank branches abroad charge less, but can take 2-3 days. The cheapest option is to have a bank draft posted out to you personally by priority mail.

● **Travellers cheques (TCs)**
Travellers cheques can be changed in most major towns at the banks listed above. Note that ANZ Grindlays charge a fixed fee, currently Rs 250, for changing TCs. American Express TCs are the best, if only because there are Amex offices in Karachi, Lahore, Islamabad and Rawalpindi, making replacing lost TCs more straighforward. US$ and £ Sterling TCs are the most widely accepted.

What to take

Most travellers tend to take too much. Remember that practically everything is available in Pakistan, at least in the major cities. We have not included a comprehensive list of what to take, but here are a few points worth bearing in mind.

A rucksack is the most practical if you intend to do a lot of moving around (and essential if you intend to trek), but does instantly classify you as 'backpacker' or even 'hippy'. A good compromise is a hybrid backpack/suitcase on which the straps can be zipped out of sight, turning you into a 'respectable' tourist where need be.

Appropriate clothing depends on the season and area in which you will be travelling. In summer, light, loose-fitting cottons are a must (a *shalwar kameez* can be bought very cheaply in Pakistan, off the peg or tailor made, and is ideal in hot, humid weather. It also helps you to blend in a little and draws a warm response from Pakistanis to see you wearing their national dress). Footwear should likewise be as airy as possible for hot weather; comfortable sandals or light canvas trainers are a good bet. In the mountains warm clothing is essential. Note that in winter it gets very chilly even on the plains. It is important for both men and women to dress modestly; shorts, singlets and the like cause a great deal of offence to Muslims. For women a scarf to cover their heads where necessary is very useful. See also the advice for women travellers.

If you are on medication, bring sufficient supplies. It is probably readily available, but brand names may differ and stocks may be out of date. Some medicines deteriorate rapidly in hot conditions. Contact lens cleaning equipment is available only in the main cities. Likewise for tampons and contraceptives. Insect repellents are generally less effective than the stronger western varieties, although good mosquito coils are readily available. Strong sunscreen can be difficult to find away from larger cities.

Lots of spare passport photos are very useful for any bureaucratic dealings. Take photocopies of all important documents, although photocopying facilities are available throughout Pakistan. Photos of family and home are an excellent way of bridging the cultural gap and are always generate great interest. Postcards of home make good gifts.

Budget travellers should bring their own padlock to use in cheaper hotels where doors are usually secured by a padlockable bolt. A cotton sheet sleeping bag is also very useful for when the available sheets are dirty. A secure money belt is the best way to carry money and documents.

Getting there

Air

Pakistan is easily accessible by air from just about any part of the world. The direct flying time from London is around 9 hrs, from New York around 17 hrs, and about 6 hrs from Bangkok. Pakistan is extensively served by its own national airline, PIA, in addition to all the major (and minor) airline companies. Thus, it is possible to find rock-bottom discounted fares, in addition to the luxury associated with the more up-market airlines.

The national carrier, **Pakistan International Airlines** (PIA) serve the following destinations: **Europe**: London (Heathrow), Manchester, Frankfurt, Amsterdam, Paris (Orly), Rome, Copenhagen, Zurich, Athens, Moscow, Istanbul. **North America**: New York (JFK), Toronto. **Middle East**: Abu Dhabi, Dubai, Doha, Bahrain, Muscat, Ras-al-Khaimah, Kuwait, Jeddah, Dhahran, Riyadh, Cairo, Amman, Damascus, Tehran. **Africa**: Nairobi. **South Asia**: Male, Colombo, Bombay, Delhi, Kathmandu, Dhaka. **Central Asia**: Tashkent, Ashkabad, Alma Ata, Baku. **Southeast Asia**: Bangkok, Kuala Lumpar, Singapore, Jakarta, Manila, Beijing, Tokyo (Narita).

International airlines vary in their arrangements and requirements for security, in particular the carrying of equipment like radios, tape-recorders, lap-top computers and batteries. It is advisable to ring the airline in advance to confirm what their current regulations are. **NB** Internal airlines often have different rules from international carriers.

● **Discounts and cheap flights**
The major destination is **Karachi**, although PIA, British Airways, Saudi Airlines and Xinjiang China Airlines also fly to the national capital, **Islamabad**. The cheapest flights are all to Karachi, and it often works out considerably cheaper to fly there, and then buy an onward ticket for a domestic flight to Islamabad upon arrival (see Getting around).

London is probably the cheapest place to pick up a discounted fare to

Karachi. *Trailfinders* of London (T 0171 938 3366), one of the world's biggest agencies, has a range of discounted deals, as do *STA* (T 0171 937 9962). *Campus Travel* offer good discounts to students and have offices in several University cities. The weekly free magazine *TNT* (T 0171 373 3377), found outside London tube-stations each Mon, has a comprehensive list of agencies offering discounted fares. It is possible to fly London-Karachi return for as little as around £300, or £170 one-way. **NB** Many of the minor airlines only fly weekly to/from Pakistan. This can be a headache when it comes to getting home. The Tarom (Romanian) airlines flight back to Europe for example originates in Beijing where it is often overbooked, with the result that passengers are unable to get on in Karachi and have to wait another week.

● **Stop-overs and round the world tickets**

It is possible to include Pakistan as a stop-over on round the world (RTW) and other longer distance tickets. RTW tickets also allow you to fly in to Karachi, and out of another South Asian airport, such as Delhi, Bombay, Calcutta or Kathmandu.

Overland

Pakistan is very much on the overland trail between Europe and Southeast Asia, and beyond. The easing of restrictions on obtaining an Iranian visa, the collapse of the Soviet Union followed by the opening up of the fascinating Central Asian states, and the construction of the spectacular Karakoram Highway (KKH) through the mountains of Northern Pakistan to China have all eased land access into Pakistan. Furthermore, the end of direct Presidential rule in Indian Punjab, and the lifting of the thrice monthly border opening restrictions between India and Pakistan to 365 days a year mean that Pakistan can form an integral part of any overland journey between Europe, Middle East, Central Asia, South Asia, and on to Southeast Asia.

NB Addresses of all Pakistani embassies abroad are given under Representation overseas in this chapter. Addresses of Indian, Chinese, Central Asian, Iranian, Afghan and other embassies are given under Islamabad; Local information (all foreign embassies are located in Islamabad).

● **To/from India**

Despite their long frontier, there is only one recognized border crossing between Pakistan and India, located between Lahore and Amritsar. The border towns are **Wagah** (23 km from Lahore) on the Pakistani side, and **Attari** (39 km from Amritsar) on the Indian side. For much of the 1980s the border crossing was only open for 3 days a month, but it is now possible to make the crossing on any day of the year (check the situation on public holidays). The crossing can be made by train or on foot, although the latter is far quicker. See page 290 for details.

Because of the sensitive nature of relations between Pakistan and India, visas are not issued on the border. In India, Pakistani visas can only be obtained from New Delhi (a 'letter of recommendation' from your own embassy is required by most nationalities). The Pakistani consulate in Bombay has been closed. Indian visas are available in Pakistan from Islamabad ('letter of recommendation' is required). In 1995 visas were being issued in 3-5 days. The office in Karachi has been closed.

NB For those crossing the border with their own motor vehicle it is essential to have the correct documentation. See 'Getting around – Private vehicles' below.

● **To/from China and Central Asia**

For those continuing on to China, it is essential to obtain a visa in advance as they are **not available on the border.**

The Chinese Embassy in Islamabad can issue visas in 1-3 days (**NB** Most nationalities will also require a 'letter of recommendation', plus several passport sized photos). It is **not** permitted to take private vehicles into China. Officially this rule extends to bicycles, for which you need a special permit, although this rule is rarely enforced. The Chinese authorities are now so used to seeing cyclists arriving and departing along the KKH that they no longer attempt to 'encourage' them onto a bus.

If you are arriving in Pakistan from China, it will save a lot of hassle if you already have a visa. Unfortunately, the nearest Pakistani Embassy in China is in Beijing, some 4,000 km away from the Pak/China border! At the time of going to press it was possible to get a Pakistani visa in Uzbekistan (Tashkent), Tajikistan (Dushanbe), Kazakhstan (Alma Ata), and soon from Kyrghizstan (Bishek).

However, for most nationalities it is now possible to get a 15 day visa on arrival at the Pakistani border town of Sust, although this is sometimes subject to the whim of the immigration official in charge. For details of this border crossing see page 523.

● To/from Iran

The only official border crossing between Pakistan and Iran is at Taftan, 84 km from the town of Zahedan in Iran and over 600 km from Quetta in Pakistan. The border opens daily from 1000-1300 and 1600-1800. Trains run between Zahedan and Quetta, although they are very slow (minimum 32 hrs), or you can make the journey by bus which is much quicker (around 15 hrs) but less comfortable. See page 183 for transport details; see page 199 for details of the route between Quetta and Taftan. Note that it is currently very difficult to obtain Iranian visas in Pakistan. It takes a minimum of 1 month, with no guarantee that you will

be granted one. Most nationalities require a 'letter of recommendation' from their embassy. It is far easier to obtin the visa in your own country. American and Israeli passport holders are currently being refused visas. Transit visas are valid for 1-2 weeks depending on your nationality and can usually be extended by a further 1-2 weeks. Tourist visas are valid for 1 month but are only issued to people visiting as part of an organized tour group. The Pakistani embassy is located in Tehran, with consulates in Mashad and Zahedan, although again it is much easier to obtain your visa before leaving home (especially with the limited time available on an Iranian transit visa).

● To/from Afghanistan

At the time of going to press, visas for Afghanistan were only being issued to journalists and aid workers. For a short period following the fall of the Najibullah regime in Kabul, the consulate in Peshawar was freely issuing visas to foreigners (the embassy in Islamabad were more cautious), but this is no longer the case. Tragically, Afghanistan continues to be deeply embroiled in civil war. Although the situation changes from week to week, there appears to be little hope of an end to the fighting in the forseeable future. It is **not** safe for foreigners to visit. Apart from the very real risk of getting caught up in fighting, there is the added danger from several million landmines remaining in the country. The Mine Clearing and Planning Agency report 20-25 'mine incidents' in Afghanistan every day.

Should the situation improve sufficiently, this beautiful country would once again form part of the overland route between Europe and Asia. It would also link Pakistan with the Central Asian republics. The two main border crossings are at Torkham, on the Khyber Pass between Peshawar and Jalalabad, and at Chaman, between

Quetta and Kandahar. Most of Pakistan's border with Afghanistan is however extremely porous. If you are keen to find out about the current situation in Afghanistan, Peshawar is the best place to get information. There are over 100 small NGOs still based there, working with Afghan refugees in Pakistan and across the border in Afghanistan itself. **ACBAR** (Agency Coordinating Body for Afghan Refugees) run **ARIC** (AKBAR Resource and Information Centre), 2 Rehman Baba Rd, University Town, Peshawar, T 44392, which has an excellent library. They issue monthly news summaries of the situation in Afghanistan.

● **Own transport**

For those arriving in their own vehicle, it is essential to have the correct documentation, including a Carnet de Passage (carnet). For further details, see 'Getting around – Private vehicles' below.

Sea

Although Karachi is a major sea-port, there are no regular passenger liners operating to or from Pakistan. Passenger ships do take some *hajj* pilgrims to and from Saudi Arabia, although this is not an option for the casual tourist. There are, however, numerous ships operating between Karachi, the Gulf States and beyond, but your chances of finding a place on one are slim. It may be worth talking to one of the major Karachi based shipping agents, such as Mackinnon and Mackenzie (Mack Volk Building, II Chundrigar, Karachi, T 223041). For those considering booking a passage on a cargo ship travelling to the region, contact the *Strand Cruise and Travel Centre*, Charing Cross Shopping Concourse, The Strand, London, WC2N 4HZ, T (0171) 497 0078.

Documentation

● **Passport**

You should carry your passport with you at all times; this is in fact a legal requirement and you may be required to produce your documents at checkposts, particularly when crossing between provinces, entering tribal or restricted areas and travelling on the Karakoram Highway. If you are applying for other visas and have to submit your passport, make photocopies of all the relevant pages (including the visa page), and get a proper receipt which gives details of the passport number etc.

● **Visa**

Visas can usually be extended or changed from single to double entry, but this is invariably time-consuming and there is no guarantee that extensions will be granted. All such applications should be made in Islamabad (see under Useful addresses in the Local information).

● **Foreigners' registration**

Nationals of Britain, Australia and the UAE are not required to Register. All other foreign visitors must register; on arrival in Pakistan obtain **Form C** – Temporary Certificate of Registration – from Immigration (it is not always offered); those staying less than 30 days should simply hand in the completed form on departure. Foreigners visiting Pakistan for more than 30 days are required to formally register their presence as a 'resident' in the country, before the 30 days are up. This can be done in most towns through the Foreigners' Registration Office or Senior Superintendant of Police (SSP). Bring Form C and two passport size photos and you will be issued with a **Certificate of Registration** and **Residential Permit**. Before leaving Pakistan you must then apply for an **Exit Permit** from the last town you stay in; take your Certificate of Registration and Residential Permit to the SSP office and you will be issued with the Exit Permit.

● **Permits for restricted areas**
Sensitive or unstable areas in Pakistan are designated Restricted Areas and can only be visited with a permit from the relevant authority. These include the Federally Administered Tribal Areas and parts of Sind, Baluchistan, NWFP, and Northern Areas. Details of restricted areas and procedures for applying for permits are given in the relevant sections. However the situation, particularly with regards unstable or 'unsafe' areas in Sind and Baluchistan, changes frequently so check with the police or PTDC. Some areas, including sensitive border areas, are closed to foreigners.

● **Airport departure tax**
Note that an airport departure tax is charged on all international departures. The amount charged in 1995 was Rs 400 for first class passengers, Rs 300 for business class and Rs 200 for economy. A Foreign Travel Tax of Rs 500 is charged on tickets purchased within Pakistan. These charges are not included in the price of your ticket; it is worth setting the money aside for when you leave.

Customs

● **Duty free allowance**
The official list of items which can be imported free of duty by foreign tourists makes for amusing reading ("one electric smoothing iron, one portable electric hot plate, one hair dryer for lady tourists only"). Basically all items which may be reasonably be required can be brought in. Alcohol is forbidden; if found it is usually 'confiscated' by customs officials against a receipt which in theory allows you to reclaim it on leaving; don't count on it. With a little gentle persuasion they sometimes relax the rules; try saying that it is a gift for Christian friends. The official limit on tobacco is 200 cigarettes or 50 cigars or 1 lb of tobacco. Officially, gifts should not exceed Rs 1,000 in value. Cameras and camcorders can be imported free of duty. However, these and other valuable items or professional equipment, including jewellery, laptop computers etc, should be declared to customs and recorded in your passport, and must be brought out again personally.

● **Duty free shopping**
Karachi airport has the reputation of being one of the cheapest places for duty free shopping in the world. If you fly via Dubai, Bahrain or Abu Dhabi, you will also have access to a bewildering range of electrical and other goods. There are duty free shops in the main cities of Pakistan, but they have a very limited selection of goods.

● **Currency regulations**
There are no restrictions on the amount of foreign currency (cash or TCs) tourists can bring in to Pakistan, or take out with them when they leave. However a limit of just Rs 100 of local currency can be brought in or taken out.

● **Export restrictions**
The export of antiquities is prohibited. Jewellery up to the value of Rs 25,000 bought in Pakistan, provided it is not made wholly or mainly of gold, can be exported free of duty, but you must be able to produce foreign exchange encashment receipts up to the value of the jewellery. Other items, including carpets, can be exported up to the value of Rs 75,000 provided you obtain an Export Permit. This is a time consuming process; ask for help from the dealer you bought the goods from, or from PTDC officials. You will need the sales receipt, encashment receipts up to the value of the value of the goods, and photocopies of these and the relevant pages of your passport.

Essentials

● Business hours

There is considerable regional variation in business hours. Timings often differ for winter and summer. The best time to get anything done in Pakistan is 0900-1300. Note that during Ramadam offices are open only from 0800/0900-1200/1300. Generally, the following hours apply:

Banks: Sat 0900-1200, Sun-Thur 0900-1300, 1400-1600, closed Fri.

Post Offices: usually Sat-Thur 0830-1300, 1400-1900, closed Fri.

Central telegraph offices: in most larger towns open 24 hrs/7 days.

Government offices: Sun-Thur 0800-1530, closed Fri and Sat.

Shops: Sun-Thur 0900/1000-1800/1900, closed Fri.

● Electricity

220/240 volts, 50/60 cycle AC. Most plug sockets are of the round 2-pin variety. Some round 3-pin sockets are found in larger hotels. Power cuts or 'load shedding' is common, particularly in remoter areas. Power surges can be a problem; delicate electrical equipment such as laptops should be protected by a surge adaptor.

● Official time

Pakistan is 5 hrs ahead of Greenwich Mean Time (GMT+5). Time is fluid in Pakistan; punctuality is not a widely accepted concept.

● Photography

Major cities are well supplied with fresh stocks of colour negative film, while modern processing labs offer 1-24 hr processing to western standards. Colour transparency film is harder to find, but is available in the major cities. Black and white film is fairly readily available; most of it is produced in Eastern Europe.

NB Photography of military installations, airports, railway stations, bridges and dams is prohibited. Do not take photographs of women without permission.

● Weights and measures

The official system of weights and measures is metric. However, miles are sometimes still quoted on older distance markers and by the older generation. Cloth merchants and tailors still generally work in yards. Locally used weights include the *tola* (around 12 grams) and the *seer* (just under 1 kg).

Etiquette

Pakistan is an extremely hospitable country where visitors are generally treated with great respect. It is important to reciprocate that respect and to show sensitivity towards cultural norms in order to avoid giving offence.

● Bargaining

Bargaining is a widely accepted practice, particularly in bazaars and tourist shops. In many cases it is almost expected, with starting prices way above what a trader will expect to get. It often becomes something of an art, involving long hours spent drinking tea, exchanging small talk and (hopefully) gradually bringing the price down. It is always worth looking around to compare the quality/workmanship of goods, and starting prices. Note that some tourist shops have fixed prices; these can be useful for getting some idea of the going rates for items, although the large tourist shops generally have more expensive (and better quality) goods.

● Begging

Beggars are less common in Pakistan than in India, although they are found in large numbers around bus and train stations. The standard advice is that it is better to give to a recognized charity working with the poor than to make largely ineffectual handouts. This is really a matter of personal judgement. In larger cities, beggars are often exploited by syndicates which cream off most of their daily takings.

● **Conduct**

You will be judged to a large extent by the way you dress; a neat and clean appearance will command more respect and get a better response in any situation. Scanty or tight-fitting clothes cause great offence to Muslims. For their own safety and wellbeing, women need to take particular care over this, although it applies just as much to men. Open displays of affection between couples also causes offence and is not acceptable in public. It is common however to see young men walking around hand in hand; this carries no sexual connotations in Pakistan.

● **Courtesy**

It never pays to be rude or discourteous in Pakistan; doing so will invariably make things more difficult than they might otherwise be. Likewise, direct confrontation is never a good idea and is the surest way of eliminating any hope of achieving your aims in a particular situation. Unfortunately bureaucracy can be a major headache in Pakistan, with reams of red tape surrounding even the simplest of tasks. Bureaucrats are a law unto themselves and can be rude, obstructive and unhelpful. The only way to deal with this is to be patient, polite and firm. Open displays of anger or frustration only serve to delight them.

● **Hands**

The left hand is considered unclean in Pakistan and should never be used for eating. More accurately the rule is that the left hand should not be raised to the mouth. It is perfectly acceptable to hold your *roti* in the left hand and tear bits off with the right. Likewise, avoid offering or accepting things with the left hand.

● **Tipping**

Tipping is generally expected in more expensive restaurants, although many also have a service charge. 10% is considered generous; 5% or rounding off with loose change is perfectly acceptable. Use your discretion. Beware of nodding at waiters as they bring you your change; they are liable to interpret this as an indication that they can pocket the money as a tip.

● **Visiting mosques and shrines**

Non-Muslims are welcome in most mosques and shrines. Always remove your shoes before entering. A thick pair of socks are useful for walking across baking hot marble floors. It is particularly important to dress modestly, not exposing anything more than head, hands and feet. Women should also cover their heads. Never walk directly in front of someone who is praying.

● **Women**

Social etiquette regarding Pakistani women varies enormously. In remote rural and tribal areas women are rarely seen at all and only go out in public with a full *burqa*. In the major cities, upper and middle class women at least are free to move around as they please. They are often well educated and highly westernized. In most circumstances, women do not shake hands with men, and offering your hand is likely to cause confusion and embarrassment. Men should never take photographs of women without their consent, or more importantly that of their male escort. Female tourists are more likely to be given permission to take photos of women but should never take it for granted.

Safety

Many travellers, particularly those arriving from India, are primed with horror stories about the dangers of travelling in Pakistan. Almost always they are very pleasantly surprised. With some notable exceptions, Pakistan is probably one of the safest countries in South Asia for foreign tourists. Basic common sense is the key to ensuring your safety and security in the majority of situations.

● **Confidence tricksters**

These are far rarer than in other countries of South and Southeast Asia. In general people are surprisingly honest and straightforward. If someone offers to help you out or show you round, they are unlikely to be after something in return. However, you must still be on your guard, particularly in larger cities. Lahore has a bad reputation for confidence tricksters.

● **Drugs**

Hashish, or *charas*, is readily available throughout Pakistan, with the exception of the Northern Areas. In many places, including Islamabad, there are profuse quantities of low grade cannabis growing wild. The authorities periodically get embarrassed by this and have it cut down and destroyed.... by burning it in huge bonfires around the city! In many communities it forms an integral part of the social fabric, particularly amongst the Pathans of NWFP and Baluchistan. However, it is also illegal and foreigners should be extremely careful. There is no guarantee that someone offering you hashish will not then go and inform the police. Penalties are stiff and, for larger quantities, generally involve a lengthy prison sentence. Some travellers report instances of hashish being planted on them by corrupt police. If your bags are searched, keep a close eye on what is going on and make it clear that you will not put up with any nonsense. Such occurences are thankfully rare. Don't even consider trying to smuggle drugs out of the country; Pakistan is recognized as a major drug producing country on the international scene and customs officials are generally on the alert.

● **Personal safety**

Certain areas of Pakistan are dangerous for foreigners to travel in or visit. The most notable of these are the Tribal Areas of NWFP and Baluchistan, which are in any case restricted and require permits to visit. Rural Sind was for many years a no-go area due to banditry, although the situation has recently improved. Likewise, remoter parts of Baluchistan, NWFP and even Punjab can be dangerous for foreigners. Note that, up till now at least, Karachi has been safe for foreigners; despite the tragic situation there, violence is restricted to remote suburbs far from the city centre. Detailed information and advice is given in the relevent sections. However, situations can change rapidly so it is always essential to check with tourism officials and/or the police regarding the current situation. Take heed of advice given by locals. If you are heading into a dangerous area or volatile situation, someone will almost invariably materialize to warn you, beg you not to go, or offer you a safe refuge.

When travelling in remoter areas, it is always a good idea to register your presence with the local police and/or the District/Assistant Commissioner. The latter are generally well informed, helpful and speak good English. Women should not travel alone in remoter areas.

● **Police**

The police are something of an unknown quantity in Pakistan. In larger centres they are generally helpful, but in remoter areas they sometimes do not speak any English; wherever you are, they can be corrupt. If you do have anything stolen, report it immediately to the police and be sure to get a copy of the police report if you intend to claim against your insurance. It is a good idea to enlist the help of someone who speaks good English. If you run into problems with corrupt police in remoter areas, insist on being taken to the nearest District Commissioner or Assistant Commissioner.

● **Theft**

"Trust in God, but tie your camel!" The greatest risk of theft is in the cheapest hotels. Never leave valuables and important documents in your hotel room. This applies even to more expensive hotels. If the room is secured by a padlockable bolt, use your own padlock, not the one supplied by the hotel; anyone can stay in the room and get a key cut. Take particular care in crowded bus or railway stations where it is easy for someone to slip away with your bags. Organized gangs and pickpockets do operate in larger cities. When on the move it is a good idea to secure any zips on your bags with a padlock.

Women travelling alone

Travelling in Muslim countries is undoubtedly harder for women than for men, and more so for women travelling alone. Even with a male companion or in a group, women need to be particularly aware of the cultural context. Most Pakistani women never travel alone, and outside of the main cities they are rarely seen in public. Certain remoter and tribal areas are not safe for women on their own; specific warnings are given in the relevant sections. The widely held perception of Western women is based on the images in Western magazines, films and satellite TV, which portrey them as having 'loose' sexual morals. This, along with the fact that in their rigidly segregated society many young Pakistani males openly admit to feeling sexually frustrated, can lead to problems of sexual harrassment. Cases of violent sexual assault are however extremely rare and a firm, unambiguous response will deal with most situations. In public, the best approach is to make a scene. Any form of impropriety towards women is a gross violation of the tenets of Islam and someone is bound to come to your aid; the perpetrator meanwhile will quickly vanish in a cloud of shame. It is worth remembering that a good Muslim would consider it improper to be alone with a female in private, so any attempt to contrive such a situation should set alarm bells ringing.

Many female travellers in Pakistan strongly advise adopting the local dress of *shalwar kameez* (baggy trousers and long overshirt which comes down to the knees) and *dupatta* (scarf) to cover the head in more conservative areas. This is a matter of choice. The important thing is to wear baggy, loose-fitting clothes that do not highlight the lines of your body, and not to expose anything more than head, hands and feet. A scarf is always useful for covering up further if you begin to feel exposed or uncomfortable in a given situation; it is also very good protection against the sun. Some women argue that it makes absolutely no difference to a determined male what you are wearing. However, given that actual harrassment is relatively rare, the main object of dressing modestly is to show respect for Islamic values and not cause offence.

If you are put off the idea of visiting Pakistan by the above, don't be. Plenty of women travel around Pakistan and the majority are very enthusiastic about the country. While it can be very demanding, there are also distinct advantages. Women are generally treated with great respect. Seasoned female travellers in Pakistan argue that they get the best of both worlds. As a foreigner they are generally accorded the status of 'honorary males' in public, while in private they have access to female society, from which men are excluded. Pakistani women, although largely invisible in public life, are a dominant force in family life at home. When invited to a Pakistani household, male guests are usually confined to the guest room while women are whisked away behind the scenes into the 'real' household, where they can meet wives, mothers, sisters and other members of the extended family. Other advantages include getting to sit in the best seats at the front of buses and in special women's compartments on trains, and going straight to the front of lengthy queues.

Where to stay

● Hotels

There is a vast range of hotels across Pakistan, both in terms of price and facilities. The major cities feature international standard hotels, with international prices to match. At the other end of the scale it is possible to find safe and clean accomodation in dormitories for as little as a dollar a night. There are some excellent value hotels in the intermediate and cheaper categories, though quality and cleanliness vary much more.

Outside of the main cities, accommodation at the top end of the market is often more limited, with **C** category often the highest grade of hotel in medium and small towns. This is particularly true of the Northern Areas of Pakistan. The cheapest **E** and **F** hotels can be found in almost all towns, although the variation in quality is enormous. At the end of 1995, the cheapest double rooms with bath generally started from around Rs 100 a night. At the very cheapest end of the hotel scale you may just be offered a *charpoy* (S Asian rope bed on a wooden frame) in a communal area, sometimes at the back of a restaurant.

Air-conditioning Only the larger hotels have central a/c. Elsewhere a/c rooms are cooled by individual units and occasionally 'air-coolers'. These can be noisy and unreliable. When they fail to operate, tell the management as it is often possible to get a rapid repair, or to transfer to another room. Ceiling fans are provided in almost all hotels, even at the cheaper end of the scale.

Insects Very few hotels in Pakistan have mosquito nets, and mosquito screens across doors and windows tend to be full of large holes. Mosquito coils and repellants are widely available in Pakistan, but you should be equipped with your own strong repellant cream or spray (see Health information). At night fans can be effective in keeping mosquitoes off.

In cheaper hotels you may well be sharing your room and bathroom with a whole host of insect life, including cockroaches, ants and geckos (harmless house lizards). Poisonous insects such as scorpions are extremely rare, although they do have a reputation for surprising people in dusty corners in Chitral. Bed bugs are far more common, and should be dealt with by changing room/hotel.

Toilet facilities A major difference between hotel accommodation in Pakistan and India is that, almost without fail, even the cheapest hotels in Pakistan have attached bath and toilet facilities. Obviously there are some exceptions, and on occasion the fact that the toilet is attached can be something of a mixed blessing! In all but the most expensive hotels, toilets tend to be of the Asian 'squat' variety, rather than the Western WC. They are easy to adapt to, and much more hygenic. Many toilets in Pakistan are unable to cope with toilet paper, so a separate waste-paper basket is often provided for this facility. Apart from in **AL** and **A** categories, 'bath' does not necessarily refer to bathrooms with Western bathtubs. It often means a shower, or simply a tap/bucket/scoop combination. In many hotels hot water is only available at certain times of the day, and even then only in buckets. Towels, soap and toilet paper are generally not provided in budget hotels.

Water and electricity supply In many areas you should be prepared for difficulties which are uncommon in Europe, America or Australasia. Power cuts, or 'load-shedding' as it is euphemistically termed, is common across Pakistan, although the situation improves each year. Other areas only have electricity for certain parts of the day. Some hotels have their own generators, but these tend to be extremely noisy. A good torch is recommended.

Erratic or rationed water supply is

HOTEL CATEGORIES

Exact prices for hotel rooms are not quoted; price categories are used instead. Note that categories are based on the cost of a double room, and are not star ratings. Inflation in the tourism industry has been running at around 20-30% over the last few years, although this has been at least partly mitigated by the continuing devaluation of the Rupee. **NB** A Central Exise Duty (CED, currently 12.5%) is charged on rooms in **AL-B** category hotels. Some charge an additional 7.5% Bed Tax.

AL Rs 4,000+ International class luxury hotels, generally part of a multi-national chain and found only in capital city (Islamabad) and regional capitals (Karachi, Lahore, Quetta, Peshawar). All facilities for the business and leisure traveller to the highest international standard.

A Rs 1,800-4,000 International class. Central a/c, rooms with en-suite bathroom, IDD telephone, TV/dish and video channel. Banquetting and conference facilities, often with a business centre. Choice of multicuisine restaurants and coffee shops. All the usual facilities including 24-hr room service, fax/telex, shopping arcade, laundry, foreign exchange, travel counter, swimming pool, and perhaps other sports such as tennis and squash. Often with hairdresser, beauty parlour and health club. Major credit cards accepted.

B Rs 900-1,800 Most of the facilities of A, but perhaps not the business centre, pool and sports, and without the feeling of international luxury. Often with only one restaurant, though still a choice of cuisine. Usually not in top locations.

C Rs 450-900 Often the highest category of hotel in medium and small towns, but not always the best value. The entrance and reception are usually more grand than **D** category hotels, but the quality of rooms is often no better, despite the higher price. Generally have restaurant serving good value meals. Usually with central a/c, TV and attached bath.

D Rs 300-450 Reasonably comfortable. Attached bath, some rooms with a/c and perhaps TV. Restaurant and room service normally available. This is the hotel category where you can get some very good deals through bargaining.

Budget hotels – **NB** Many hotels which charge up to Rs 300 per night for a double room also have much cheaper accommodation, including dormitories for less than Rs 50 per night.

E Rs 150-300 Simple rooms with fan, (rarely a/c), usually a basic attached bath consisting of a shower or bucket and scoop. Limited room service may include meals brought in when no restaurant is available.

F up to Rs 150 Often very basic, generally with attached bath, but sometimes only shared toilet/shower facilities. Cleanliness and hygiene varies greatly. There are some real bargains, pleasantly run and well kept, but also some extremely squalid 'hotels'. Care is essential, particularly in terms of security.

Abbreviations The following abbreviations are used when describing hotel facilities: rm=room; a/c=air-conditioning; TV=television; dish=satelitte television; T=telephone; F=fax; dble=double room; rec=recommended; nr=near to; incl=including; att bath=attached bath/toilet.

another problem that you may encounter. If your bathroom has a bucket, it is recommended that you keep it full at all times so that it is still possible to flush the toilet during water cuts. Few hotel sinks have plugs.

NB It should be assumed that tap water, even in expensive hotels in big cities, is **not** safe for drinking, or cleaning teeth.

● **Off-season rates and bargaining**

In many resort centres, particularly those that are popular with Pakistanis, considerable savings can be made by visiting out of season. In areas such as Murree and the Galis, Swat, and the Kaghan Valley, the price of accommodation can double during the peak season. **NB** 'Peak season' does not necessarily just refer to a time of year; accommodation prices generally inflate at weekends (Thur-Sat) and on public holidays. You will generally have to ask if concessions are available, rather than waiting to see if they are offered. In some areas where hotel supply outstrips demand, eg Karimabad, significant reductions can be had through bargaining, particularly in the intermediate price range.

● **Resthouses and Railway Retiring Rooms**

In many remote areas, most notably in the Northern Areas, NWFP and Azad Jammu and Kashmir, the only accommodation available is in the form of government resthouses. Run by departments such as the 'Northern Areas Public Works Dept' (NAPWD), or the 'NWFP Communications and Works Dept' (CWD), these *Resthouses* or *Inspection Bungalows* are generally small 2 or 3 bedroom bungalows that are used by travelling officials. If available they can be used by tourists. Bookings should be made at the department's regional headquarters, (eg Office of the Executive Engineer, NAPWD, Gilgit, for the resthouses in the Northern Areas), and a booking chit obtained. It should be noted, however, that visiting officials have priority over tourists, even if you have a booking. The resthouses are generally cared for by a *chowkidar* (watchman) who may be able to provide basic meals on request. It is sometimes possible to stay at resthouses

without a prior booking. *Railway Retiring Rooms* are available at most stations for the use of passengers holding a/c and 1st class sleeper tickets. They can be quite good value, although they are extremely popular and can be difficult to book. Blankets and linen are generally not provided.

● **Hostels**

There are a number of Youth Hostels in Pakistan run by the Pakistan Youth Hostel Association (National Office, G/6-4, Garden Rd, Aabpara, Islamabad, T 824866). They are located in Islamabad, Lahore, Taxila, Katas (Salt Range), Bhurban (Galis), Abbottabad, Peshawar, Khanspur (Galis), Balakot, Battakundi, Sharan, Naran, with others under construction at Quetta, Karachi, Pakpattan, Thandiani, Murree and Muzaffarabad. Membership is Rs 40 per year, or through the IYHA. Maximum stay is 3 nights during the season, although many seem to be permanently full of male Pakistani students.

YMCA, YWCA and Salvation Army hostels provide cheap accommodation in many of the larger cities.

● **Camping**

There are few recognized camping sites in Pakistan, although in the more remote areas, most notably in the mountains of the Northern Areas, the potential for camping is unlimited. Some hotels will allow you to pitch your tent in their grounds. In regional trekking centres, eg Gilgit, Skardu, it is possible to purchase second hand camping equipment.

Food and drink

● **Food**

At its very best, Pakistani food can be superb; at its worst, bland and uninspiring. Meat-eaters are particularly well served, with delicious chicken, mutton and beef served in most restaurants. The style of cooking is often referred to as *Mughlai*, hinting at the Mughal and Afghan infuences introduced into the South Asian diet

EATING OUT – FOOD AND MENUS

Pronounce   **ā** as in ah   **ī** as in bee
              ō as in oh   **u** as oo in book
              nasalized vowels are shown as **an un** etc
Note These marks to help with pronunciation do not appear in the main text.

Basic food vocabulary (Urdu)
khana food, to eat (verb)
anda egg
chāwal rice
chini sugar
gosht meat, usually mutton (sheep)
macchli fish
murghi chicken
panīr drained curds
phal fruit
sabzī vegetables
roti bread

Vegetables
āloo potato
baingan aubergine
band gōbi cabbage
bhindi okra, ladies' fingers
dāl lentils
matar peas
piāz onion
phool gōbi cauliflower
sāg spinach

Pulses (beans and lentils)
masoor dāl pink, round split lentils
moong dāl most common form
chanā dāl chick peas
rājmā red kidney beans
Urhad dāl small black beans

Roti – breads
chapāti thin, plain, wholemeal
  unleavened bread cooked on a *tawa*

(griddle), usually made from *ata*
(wheat flour). *Makkai-ki-roti* is with
maize flour
nān oven baked (traditionally in a
  tandoor) white flour leavened bread
  often large and triangular
parāthā ffried bread layered with ghī
  (sometimes cooked with egg or
  stuffed with vegetables)
poori thin deep-fried, puffed rounds
  of flour (in Punjabi *bhaturā*)

Rice
chāwal plain boiled rice
biriyani partially cooked rice layered
  over meat and baked with saffron.
pulaol pilau fried (and then boiled)
  rice cooked with spices and
  vegetables.

Accompaniments
achār pickles (usually spicy and
  preserved in oil)
chutnī often fruit or tomato, freshly
  prepared, sweet and mildly spiced
dahī plain yoghurt
mirch chilli
numuk salt
raita yoghurt with shredded
  cucumber
salat salad, usually onions, tomato or
  cucumber

over a period of 6 centuries. Cream and *ghee* (clarified butter) are favourite cooking mediums, with meat as the main focus of the meal. Dishes are generally less spicy than those found in India, although they are often oilier. Spicy kebabs, meat balls and minced meat are common, as are *Tandoori* dishes – marinated meat cooked in a special clay oven. *Karahi* meals, chicken or meat dishes cooked and served in a thick metal wok with spicy tomatoes and chillies, are very popular in Pakistan, and are being rapidly adopted in the 'curry-houses' of Bradford and London. Although rice is available, wheat is the staple. Most meals are eaten with either *chapatis* or

nan (see Food Glossary). There are regional specialities across Pakistani (eg seafood in Karachi); these are discussed as they occur.

However, many travellers arriving from India find the variety of dishes on offer in Pakistan less inspiring. Vegetarians and vegans are not well served. Although dishes of spinach, potatoes, okra, peas and the ubiquitous *dhal* (lentils) can be excellent when well prepared, all too often they are simply overcooked mush. In many areas, particularly transport stops, all that is on offer is dhal and chapati, okra and chapati, or poor quality mutton and chapati. (see Health information for tips on eating healthily). Snacks such

Methods of preparation

bhoona in a thick, fairly spicy sauce

chargha similar to tandoori (see below)

chops minced meat, fish or vegetables, covered in mashed potato, crumbed and fried

cutlet minced meat, fish, vegetables formed into flat rounds or ovals, crumbed and fried

jhāl frāzi spicy, hot sauce with tomatoes and chillies

karahi (balti) cooked and served in a metal wok, with onions, tomatoes and spices

Kashmiri cooked with mild spices, ground almonds and yoghurt

kebab skewered (or minced and shaped) meat or fish

kīma minced meat (usually 'mutton')

kofta minced meat or vegetable balls

korma in fairly mild rich sauce using cream /yoghurt

Mughlai rich N Indian style

Peshwari rich with dried fruit and nuts

tandoori baked in a *tandoor* (special clay oven) or one imitating it

tikka marinated meat pieces, baked quite dry

Some typical dishes

aloo gosht potato and mutton stew

aloo gobi dry potato and cauliflower with cumin

aloo matar potato and peas in a dryish mildly spicy sauce

bhaji, pakora vegetable fritters (onions, potatoes, cauliflower etc)

deep-fried in batter

bhindi bhaji okra fried with onions and mild spices

boti kebab marinated pieces of meat, skewered and cooked over a fire

chana choor ('Bombay mix') lentil and flattened rice snacks mixed with nuts and dried fruit

chapli kebab spicy burger made with mince, eggs and tomato and served with nan

keema matar minced meat with peas

matar panir curd cheese cubes with peas and spices (and often tomatoes)

rogan josh rich, mutton/ beef pieces in creamy, red sauce

sāg aloo potato and spinach

sāg gosht mutton and spinach

samosa cooked vegetable or meat wrapped in pastry circle into 'triangles' and deep-fried

Sweets

barfi fudge-like rectangles/ diamonds, often with nuts

gulāb jāmun dark fried spongy balls, soaked in syrup

halwa dry sweet made with thickened milk, carrots and spice

kulfi cone-shaped Indian ice cream with pistachhios/ almonds

Drinks

chai tea boiled with milk and sugar

doodh milk

lassi cool drink made with yoghurt and water, salted or sweetened

pāni water

as samosas and good quality biscuits can be found all across Pakistan.

Chinese and Western All the main cities have restaurants offering reasonable imitations of Chinese food. Western 'fast food' is becoming more and more common across the country. In fact, amongst the middle-classes the words 'fast food' are seen more as a style of cuisine than as a derogatory term describing nutritionally poor food. Western style breakfasts are generally available, with the emphasis on fried eggs, boiled eggs or omlette. Porridge and inferior cornflakes can also be found, but those seeking an egg, bacon and sausage fry-up are likely to be disappointed (although some of the large department stores in Karachi and Islamabad that specialize in expensive imported foodstuffs for the expatriate community sell bacon, and non-pork sausages). Reasonable quality Western chocolate is becoming more commonplace, but fans of cheese are recommended to bring their own.

Eating out Almost all hotels, whatever their status or category, have either a restaurant or dining hall, and they can often be very good value. Eating out in Pakistan is far cheaper than in the West, even at the top-end restaurants (although restaurants in 5-star hotels are often priced on a par with the West).

Most restaurants in Pakistan have 'family rooms'; sometimes a separate room, or simply an area partitioned off by a curtain or screen. Pakistani families almost always use this facility, so any travelling couples or females who want to avoid unwarranted attention are recommended to follow suit. Note that children are extremely welcome in even the most expensive restaurants and staff invariably go to great lengths to accommodate them.

In some smaller towns the choice of restaurant and cuisine may be limited to 'meat and chapati' places, where various parts of recently dead animals are hung up outside to tempt you in. In such circumstances it is generally best to follow the example of the local people and select the busiest one. There are also numerous roadside snack-sellers, offering tempting samosas, pakora, burgers etc. Obviously, health risks may well be increased, so it is wise to only eat things that you have seen freshly cooked.

● Drink

Drinking water Public water supplies, even in large cities, are nearly always polluted and unsafe to drink. This applies to both tap water in your hotel room, and water served in a jug at the dining table. Bottled mineral water is now widely available, although not all bottled water is mineral water; some is simply purified water from an urban supply. Check the seal of the bottle when buying, and reject any that appears to have been resealed or tampered with. When disposing of bottles, puncture the neck to prevent misuse, but allowing recycling for storage. Many people begrudge spending 1 or 2 dollars a day on bottled water, but if it reduces the likelihood of illness it must surely be worth it. (See Health information for further information on purifying water). **NB** It is important to use pure water for cleaning teeth.

Beverages and soft drinks Tea, or *chai*, is the universal drink of Pakistan. It is generally made by throwing equal handfuls of tea and sugar into a pot, adding equal parts of UHT (long-life) milk and water, and bringing the whole thing to the boil. It is very sweet, but remarkably refreshing. Ask for chai, or 'Pakistani tea'. If you do not want sugar (*chini*) or milk (*dudh*), you should say so when ordering. Many places offer 'seperate tea' or 'English tea', with a pot of tea, milk and sugar served separately. Chinese-style green tea is available in many areas. Coffee is rarely found outside the bigger hotels, and even then it is generally of the 'instant' variety.

Bottled, carbonated drinks such as 'Pepsi', 'Coca-Cola', '7-Up' and 'Fanta' are found almost everywhere, although prices rise as you move away from the main cities (eg Rs 7 in Islamabad, Rs 10 in Gilgit, or Rs 20 in a 5-star hotel). Cartons of fruit juice, most notably mango, are also widely available. In season, fresh mango, orange and banana shakes are common. **NB** Ice cubes should be considered unsafe because the water source is likely to be contaminated.

Alcohol Pakistan is officially a dry country. Non-Muslim foreigners are, however, permitted to purchase locally produced beers and spirits on production of a special permit. Obtaining the permit does require a certain degree of persistence. The permits are available from the Exise and Tax Department in major cities, although they are only valid for the city or district within which they are issued. You will require your passport, photocopies of the relevant pages and some passport size photographs. Although the fee for the permit is small (Rs 50), it can often only be paid at a certain bank on the other side of town from the permit office. The current allowance is 9 litres per month, which can usually be bought from the more expensive hotels. Some top-end hotels have special bars where guests (and sometimes non-guests) can buy and consume alcohol. Murree Beer, (advertised as being glycerine free!) can be remarkably good, although you do come across the odd rogue bottle. Varieties of whisky, gin, rum and vodka are also available. It is not permitted to bring alcohol into the country, although customs officers generally turn a blind eye to reasonable quantities, or 'confiscate' it against a receipt. (For further information on where to get a drink, see 'Entertainment').

Getting around

Air

Pakistan has an extensive air network, linking all the key cities and major district centres. Internal flights are relatively cheap, often comparing favourably with the price of first class sleeper by rail. It is worth noting that it is considerably cheaper to buy domestic tickets **inside** Pakistan than it is to buy the same ticket overseas. For example, a ticket on a PIA service from Karachi to Islamabad bought in London costs the equivalent of US$180, whereas the same seat paid for in Pakistan will cost around US$75.

Flights to the Northern Areas and NWFP (Gilgit, Skardu and Chitral) are heavily subsidized and very good value. They are also perhaps the most spectacular commercial flights in the world. They are however highly weather dependent and subject to last minute cancellation. They can only be booked in Pakistan. There is also a 'Karakoram sight-seeing' flight available (see Islamabad 'Local Information').

The state-run carrier, Pakistan International Airlines (PIA), operate a comprehensive network of flights across the country (see map), with a fleet of aircraft that range from the latest 747s and Airbuses, to propellar-driven Fokker F27s. PIA publish a small international/domestic timetable which is available from larger booking offices.

Following the deregulation of the airline industry in the early 1990s, three commercial airlines were set up in addition to PIA. **Aero Asia** tend to offer the cheapest fares between the major cities, on planes that are generally leased from the Romanian carrier Tarom. The "travellers' prayer" that is read over the tannoy in a Vincent Price 'Hammer House of Horror' style voice shortly before take-off is not particularly reassuring, especially when it closes with the line, "Remember, we must all return to our creator." Not on this flight, we hope. **Shaheen Air**, an offshoot of the Shaheen Foundation, a welfare foundation for the Pakistan Air Force, also operate services between the major cities. In late 1995, **Bhoja Air** recommenced domestic operations.

All the domestic airlines offer substantial discounts on their 'night coaches', flights that tend to depart or arrive at inconvenient times in the middle of the night, or very early in the morning. Further discounts are sometimes offered if you buy one of the first 50 tickets sold on particular flights. Although extra flights are scheduled to coincide with increased weekend demand (Thur nights, Fri mornings, Sat nights), these services generally sell out first. Most travel agents can issue tickets for all the airlines, although you are more likely to be offered a discount if you go to the airline's own office.

All flight schedules were correct on going to press, although it should be noted that PIA tend to make minor alterations to their timetable on a 4-monthly basis.

● **Airline security**
Security is tight on domestic services, and though foreigners' luggage is rarely inspected at great length, it may have to pass through 2 or 3 X-ray machines. On some flights it is not permitted to take batteries in hand luggage or on your person; this includes the tiny silver oxide batteries used in many cameras.

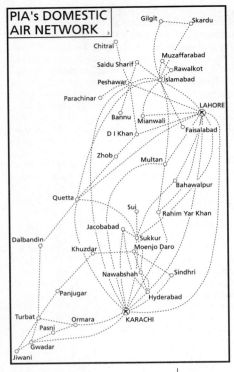

PIA's DOMESTIC AIR NETWORK

Gilgit — Skardu
Chitral
Muzaffarabad
Saidu Sharif — Rawalkot
Peshawar — Islamabad
Parachinar
LAHORE
Bannu — Mianwali
D I Khan — Faisalabad
Zhob
Multan
Bahawalpur
Quetta
Sui
Rahim Yar Khan
Jacobabad
Dalbandin
Sukkur
Khuzdar — Moenjo Daro
Nawabshah — Sindhri
Panjugar
Hyderabad
Turbat — Ormara — KARACHI
Pasni
Gwadar
Jiwani

Train

Like India, Pakistan has an extensive network of railways that can provide a comfortable and fast way of covering large distances, in addition to offering the opportunity to see the countryside and experience a slice of Pakistani society on the move. The main backbone of the system runs in a broad, curving arc N-S between Peshawar and Karachi, via Rawalpindi and Lahore, with an important branch line to Quetta, and various other branches throughout Punjab, Sind and parts of Baluchistan and NWFP. For those intending to travel extensively by train, it is worth purchasing the 'Pakistan Railways Time & Fare Table', Rs 5 from most train stations.

● **Rail information in this book**

Major train services are identified by a name, eg *Khyber Mail*, and smaller ones by their number. The trains listed in the 'Local information' sections of this book tend to be those offering the quickest, most direct daily services between destinations, in addition to all classes of ticket. Where possible, a choice has been offered between morning and afternoon services, although on almost all routes there are more services than those listed.

The train information follows this format: Destination: *Name of train*, Departure time, journey length, eg Lahore: *Shalimar Exp*, 0630, 17 hrs; *Tezgam*, 1630, 19 hrs.

● **Fare structure**

There are three categories of trains in Pakistan, (Express, Mail, Passenger), and six classes of ticket.

A/c Sleeper fares are generally on a par with air travel, although they become very competitive if you obtain a discount (see below). They tend to be quite luxurious, in private compartments sleeping either 2 or 4, and sometimes have private toilets. The a/c can get cold at night, although on occasion it doesn't work at all. A/c Sitter and A/c Lower are seats in the a/c carriage. Tickets for a/c berths and seats can be bought up to 1 month in advance, although they tend to sell out quickly on most journeys.

First Class Sleeper berths are also quite comfortable, and can be reserved up to 15 days in advance. Economy class is basically a reserved first class seat which can also be booked 15 days in

SELECTED FARES FROM KARACHI

Fares are given in Rupees (without discounts) and are exclusive of booking fees (generally Rs 40 per berth or seat for upper classes, Rs 10 per seat for lower classes):

From Karachi to:	Distance (km)	A/c Sleeper	A/c Sitter	1st	Econ	2nd
Bahawalpur	822	725	420	280	140	85
Hyderabad	174	215	125	70	32	21
Lahore	1,260	1,020	590	405	210	130
Larkana	450	455	260	155	80	48
Multan	925	795	455	310	155	95
Peshawar	1,722	1,350	775	535	285	175
Quetta	853	745	430	290	145	90
Rawalpindi	1,549	1,225	705	485	255	155

advance. If you are joining a popular service (eg Karachi to Lahore) halfway through its journey, this may well be the highest class of ticket that you can buy at short notice. You would probably not want to take this class for any journey beyond 8 hrs.

Below Economy is **Second** class, available with reserved or unreserved seats, and sometimes referred to by travellers as 'Livestock Class'. If you are travelling unreserved on long or popular journeys, conditions can be quite miserable. Then again, it is very cheap... The best option in this class is to reserve a sleeper berth for long journeys; only the top berth can be used during the day. Tickets can be bought from 15 days in advance up until time of departure. If you are very lucky, the ticket inspector may be able to upgrade you.

● **Discounts**
Foreign tourists and foreign students who have the patience to deal with a degree of bureaucracy are able to take advantage of some excellent discounts offered by Pakistan Railways. Foreign tourists (except Indians) are elegible for a 25% discount on most fares, whilst holders of an ISIC International Student Card are entitled to a remarkably generous 50% discount. This means that you can travel, for example, the 1,260 km

between Karachi and Lahore for a little over £2, or for £10 in the luxury of an a/c berth.

The proceedure for obtaining these discounts can be quite time-consuming however, sometimes taking the best part of a day. You must first obtain a letter from the local **PTDC** office confirming that you are a foreign tourist or a foreign student (most easily done in the latter case if you can produce an ISIC card). You will need to state which train you intend taking, which class of ticket, and on which date, so a prior visit to the railway ticket office may be necessary to check availability. You should then take the letter along to the **Commercial Department** of Pakistan Railways. These offices are not always located at the train station or at the main ticket office, although directions are given in the text for finding them in cities where they are located elsewhere. (**NB** It is sometimes possible to go directly to the Commercial Dept with your student or tourist ID without first obtaining a letter from the PTDC). The Commercial Dept will then eventually issue you with a certificate stating the date, class, and specific train on which you wish to undertake your journey. This certificate should then be taken to the booking office where the discounted ticket can be purchased. If in the meantime that service has sold out, you have to start all over again. The process must also be repeated every time you want to buy a ticket, in each town you visit.

● **Rail travel tips**

Although it is possible to travel exceptionally cheaply by using the lower classes of rail travel, conditions can become very crowded and quite unpleasant. If your budget can stretch to it, (bear in mind the discounts available), it may be worth moving up a class or two for the sake of your sanity. Having said that, travelling unreserved can be an exhilerating experience; a total immersion in the sights, sounds and smells of Pakistan.

Security, particularly at night, can be a concern. Luggage should ideally be padlocked to the racks, and valuables never left unattended, even for a second. Moneybelts should be worn out of sight, underneath clothing.

Women travelling alone, or in groups, can ask for tickets in women only compartments. If men come into these compartments, demand that they leave.

It is worth asking for upper berths, which offer some protection against theft, and can be used in the day time when the lower seats may all be occupied by sitting passengers.

Always carry plenty of liquid. Bottled water and/or juice and soft drinks in cartons are the safest options. Tea is also widely available, as are snacks and sweets. On many trains, cheap, good quality meals can be ordered from railway catering staff. The drugging and robbing of unwary foreigners by seemingly friendly families offering food and drink is nowhere near as prevalent as in India, although it may be something worth bearing in mind.

If you wish to upgrade your ticket it is worth making a friend of the all important ticket inspector, although generally you will face great competition from other passengers.

Road

● **Long distance buses**

The bus network in Pakistan is extensive, providing a cheap and convenient means of getting around. Each province has its own government-operated service in addition to which there is a multitude of privately run services. There are many different levels of service ranging from the long distance inter-city services, often with a/c and sometimes a video (an experience in itself), down to the ornately decorated 'local' buses that crowd more people inside (and on the roof) than you would think possible, and crawl along at 20 km per hour. Private coach services tend to be more expensive than the government services, although they are generally quicker, more comfortable and with the assurance of a reserved seat. Most long distance and local buses rarely depart before they are full, but in Pakistan they also fill up very quickly. Booking in advance means that you are more likely to get what is termed a 'good seat', and it is not unusual for hospitable Pakistanis to give up the best seats to foreign 'guests'. However, it is difficult to reach that happy compromise between comfort and safety. Seats near the front tend to have greater leg-room, but increase your chances of serious injury in a crash; they also provide uninterrupted views of spine-chilling manouvres that your or other drivers may undertake. Seats nearer to the back tend to have less leg-room, are bumpier, but increase your crash survival chances.

● **Local transport**

Auto-rickshaws Cheaper than taxis, auto-rickshaws are the most convenient way of getting round many towns, although visitors should note that the variety found in Pakistan are even smaller than those found in India, and it is quite

TRANSPORT NOMCLATURE

There is a distinctive nomclature associated with road transport in Pakistan, so it is advisable to have some grasp of the terminology used to describe the various modes of travel. The following terms are used frequently throughout the book.

Inter-city buses are often referred to as **big bus** or **coach**, denoting buses or coaches of varying degrees of comfort designed to seat 50 or so. The degree of comfort is normally denoted by a prefix such as 'deluxe' or 'super deluxe'. Any bus without this prefix, or without reserved, numbered seats, is likely to be cheap, but highly uncomfortable and with little legroom. Such buses are often termed **local buses**. Privately operated buses tend to be more comfortable, are quicker, but you pay extra for this service. They are often referred to as '**Flying Coaches**', although this term of reference is often also applied to minibuses.

The most comfortable form of bus transport in Pakistan is the **Coaster**, somewhere in size between a coach and a minibus. They generally seat around 20, although on some there are fold-down seats in the aisles. Almost all are run by private companies, offering reserved seats and sometimes a/c.

Below the Coasters in size are the **minibuses**, used for shorter inter-city trips, some long distance trips and for around-town transport. In the West, such a vehicle would probably seat 12, but in Pakistan they generally hold up to 18 passengers, plus driver and driver's assistant. Legroom can be a problem; a nightmare on long trips. They are often referred to by their manufacturer's names, eg **Hiace** (Toyota) or **Transit** (Ford).

Smaller vehicles used for transport around town, and for shorter trips between towns, are Suzuki mini-wagons, referred to across Pakistan as **Suzukis** or **wagons**. They too can become impossibly crowded.

In some rural areas, converted pick-up trucks are used as a mode of public transport. They are frequently referred to as **Datsuns**, although most are now manufactured by Toyota, or other Japanese motoring companies.

a squeeze to fit in two adults with backpacks. None have working meters, so it is essential to agree the fare in advance.

Local buses If you are staying in larger towns and cities for only a short time it is unlikely that you will get to grips with the local bus system. Routes are difficult to understand, the buses are often impossibly crowded, and it can be very brutal getting on and off the still moving bus. However, if you are determined, you will generally find someone who will ensure that you are on the right bus.

Minibuses Many towns have minibus or Suzuki services which operate on a fixed route, but pick up and drop passengers on request. They are quicker than local buses, but equally crowded.

Taxis Pakistan's taxi drivers are generally less money-grasping than those in India, and over-charging is less frequent. If you have a good idea in advance of what the fare should be (ask your hotel owner), it is often not necessary to fix the price in advance, although it is best to do so. Do not be afraid to bargain, although you should be realistic; it is unlikely that you will pay exactly the same as a local person. An exception to this general pattern of honesty is to be found at the airports, most notably Karachi, where you may be asked for 10 times the correct fare. In many of the larger towns, there are numerous brand new, comfortable, yellow taxis, most of which have working meters that the drivers are prepared to use.

THE HAZARDS OF ROAD TRAVEL

In theory, vehicles in Pakistan drive on the left! If you drive yourself it is essential to take great care. Pedestrians, cattle and a wide range of other animals roam at will. It can be particularly dangerous when driving after dark because few vehicles are ever lit. The general rule of night-driving in Pakistan seems to be to kill your lights as you approach an on-coming vehicle, and then hit them with the full beam just before you pass! Similarly, use of the indicator lights does not necessarily mean "I am turning right/left"; it can also be read as "Please overtake me to the left/right!".

There is next to no training for would be drivers, and the test is a farce. Licences are invariably obtained through bribery, and as a result there are very real dangers from poor judgement and suicidal overtaking manouvres. The general rule on Pakistan's roads is 'might is right'. These dangers apply to both visitors with their own vehicles, and those travelling on buses and other forms of public transport. Pakistani newspapers are full of stories of buses "turning turtle", followed invariably by the lines "driver is absconding". Accidents often produce large and angry crowds, so if you have an accident it is best to leave the scene and report it to the police as quickly as possible thereafter. It is probably also worth consulting your own embassy.

Tongas Horse drawn carts, or tongas, are still found in many cities, operating on fixed routes, and pulled by mangy beasts usually revealing their entire rib cage.

Other land transport

● Car-hire

Car-hire usually means a car and driver, although it is possible to get self-drive in the major cities. Larger hotels generally have a car-hire desk, with typical fees being around Rs 500 per day plus a per kilometre charge. In more remote areas, most notably the Northern Areas, it is possible to hire jeeps for half, 1 or multi-day trips. Amongst a group these can offer excellent value.

● Cycling

More and more foreign cyclists are to be spotted on Pakistan's roads, particularly on the popular Karakoram Highway route. The majority are travelling on high-tech imported mountain or touring bikes. Another option is to buy a Pakistani or Chinese cycle in Pakistan. These are fairly cheap (around Rs 2,000 new with an almost identical resale value), very solid and can be easily and

cheaply repaired almost anywhere without any worries about finding spare parts. However, they are also very slow and heavy, with cast-iron frames and just one gear (difficult to get going but plenty of momentum once you do!). They are only really viable on the flatter terrain of the plains, although you do meet the occasional determined individual struggling up the KKH.

Although geared bikes are now being imported and manufactured in Pakistan, foreigners on imported cycles still attract a lot of attention, particularly in more remote areas. Keep an eye on your bike during meal and drink stops; adults and children alike are prone to fiddle with gear levers, brakes, and the occasional small hand may find its way into your paniers. Respect for the Islamic sense of decorum should be maintained, and lycra cycling shorts should not really be worn, and certainly not by women.

Almost all buses in Pakistan, including those that make the journey across the border into China, are happy to take cycles on the roof. Make sure that your cycle is properly secured; it will probably sustain more damage being rattled around on the roof than through using it. Expect to pay 50-100% extra on the fare. Many who cycle the Karakoram Highway report unpleasant experiences on the long stretch through Kohistan, from Thakot Bridge to Chilas. Women cyclists should not tackle this stretch of the road alone. It may be worth conserving your energy, taking a bus, and using the time that you have saved to explore the more hospitable valleys further N. In many of the more popular backpacker hotels it is likely that you will meet other cyclists with whom you can exchange information. Look out also for the 'rumour books' at many of these hotels. They often have detailed information written by other cyclists.

There is also endless potential for exploring the southern half of the country on a cycle. Most of the canals that irrigate the plains have good tracks running alongside them which are ideal for cycling and blissfully free of traffic.

Some degree of maintenance competance is required, particularly if you have problems in more remote areas. A tool kit and spares should be carried, especially by those with imported cycles, although local cycle repair shops are extremely resourceful and able to carry out the most unlikely of improvisations.

● **Hitchhiking**

Because public transport is so cheap in Pakistan, the concept of hitchhiking is virtually unknown. One exception is along the Karakoram Highway, particularly in the more northerly parts. Trucks do sometimes give lifts, but they are impossibly slow, rarely averaging more than 40 km per hour. The Western 'thumbs-up' sign is unknown; just flag the vehicle down. Some drivers will expect at least the equivalent bus fare for giving you a lift. Unfortunately, it is not advisable for women to hitchhike alone.

● **Private vehicles**

An increasing number of people are now travelling around Pakistan with their own vehicles, particularly since Iranian visas have become relatively easy to get, reopening the overland trail between Europe and South Asia. There are some spectacular road routes in Pakistan and travelling by private vehicle allows great freedom and flexibility in exploring. However, driving in Pakistan can be very demanding.

If you are bringing your own motor vehicle, a **Carnet de Passage** (carnet) is essential. These are usually available from motoring organizations in your own country (eg AA in England, T 01256 20123).

NB It is currently not permitted to take private cars or motor cycles into China. Vehicle owners continuing on to India should check that they have the right form of carnet (see Lahore 'Transport' section), although in 1995 most carnets were being issued with both the AIT and FIA logos, so the problem may be resolved.

Fuel Both petrol and diesel are widely available. Diesel is normally much cheaper. Petrol is rarely above 92 octane, and tends to be particularly 'dirty'.

Communications

● **Language**

Urdu is the national language of Pakistan and is spoken by most people, at least to some degree. There are four major regional languages; Sindhi, Punjabi, Baluchi and Pashto; and on top of this numerous minor languages and dialects. English is the main language of commerce and business. It is widely spoken and in remote areas there is nearly always at least 1 person (usually the local teacher) who speaks at least a little English.

NB A short glossary of Urdu words and phrases is given at the back of the book. For more information on Pakistan's languages see under Culture in the Introduction.

● **Postal services**

Postal services in Pakistan are on the whole reliable. Note that **PO Box** numbers are frequently used within Pakistan as a way of eliminating 'lost at point of delivery' problems. It is a good idea to take letters to a Post Office where you can hand mail over for franking on the spot. **Poste Restante** facilities are available at most GPOs and mail is held there for up to 3 months. Mail between Europe and the major cities of Pakistan generally takes 4-7 days and to/from North America around 10 days. To/from smaller places in Pakistan takes considerably longer. **Parcels** must be sown up in cloth, however they must also be inspected at the post office; some larger post offices have 'packers' who will do the sowing for you. If not you can get a tailor to partially sow up the parcel and then finish it off yourself. You must also obtain a customs declaration form and attach one copy to the parcel itself. Allow lots of time for sending parcels and check first that the post office has the relevant forms.

● **Telephone services**

The telephone system in Pakistan is undergoing rapid change with the installation of fibre optic lines in many parts of the country. Lines are often busy at peak times. **NB** Telephone numbers within Pakistan change with monotonous regularity; every effort has been made to ensure that numbers are correct, but many will inevitably have changed by the time this book is published. The number for telephone enquiries is T 17 in all the major cities. Standard emergency numbers include: **Police** T 15; **Fire Brigade** T 16; and **Ambulance** T 115, with additional numbers for each city. International Direct Dialling (IDD) is available in most **AL-B** category hotels. International facilities are available in all Central Telegraph Offices and at many Public Call Offices (PCOs).

NB It is not possible to call 'collect' from Pakistan.

● **Facsimile**

Fax facilities are rapidly becoming more widespread in Pakistan, with faxes being installed in many hotels. You can also send faxes from most Telegraph Offices and many PCOs.

Media

● **Newspapers**

There are currently at least five English language daily newspapers available – *The News* (probably the best), *Frontier Post*, *The Muslim*, *The Nation*, *Pakistan Times* – although not all are available nationally (it can be quite difficult to find an English language newspaper in the Northern Areas). Unfortunately, Pakistan's newspapers are a major disappointment. As Emma Duncan points out: "To a visitor picking up the morning's papers it therefore seems mysterious that the journalism produced by a country with a good supply of talented, well-educated people passionately aware of their country's failings should be so poor. The real stuff of journalism, the reporting on corruption and government abuses, riots and bomb blasts, heroin-traders and bank defaulters hardly exists. The news pages are full of reports of chief ministers condoling deaths, announcements of new schemes to benefit the poor, and statements put out by opposition leaders. They are, by and large, boring compilations of press releases." Many visitors to Pakistan see the English language papers merely as a source of amusing instances of the use of archaic English, or 'Inglish' as it is sometimes termed in South Asia. The sports pages also seem to use more photos of Steffi Graf than is probably healthy.

Perhaps the reason for this lack of investigative journalism can be found in the history of Pakistan. Newspapers and their staff have not fared well under martial law in Pakistan. Under Zia's regime, total press censorship was imposed, with papers having to be approved for publication each day by the government. Even when press censorship was lifted in 1982, General Zia warned: "I could close down all the newspapers, say, for a period of 5 years, and nobody would be in a position to raise any voice against it. If they try to organize a meeting or procession, I will send them to jail".

Even under civilian governments, the press have been subject to harrassment from both government and opposition parties, as well as militant groups. According to the Human Rights Commission of Pakistan, in 1994, "three newspapermen were killed, at least one for his professional activity; more than a dozen reporters and photographers suffered harassment at the hands of police or political groups or parties, all but one for professional reasons; seven newspaper offices were attacked by various groups; four Ahmadi journalists were charged under the blasphemy law (which carries a death penalty)". In late 1995, Benazir Bhutto's government suspended a number of Urdu evening papers for supposedly sensationalising the violence in Karachi. Spokesmen for the newspapers countered that they were being victimized because of their sympathies with the MQM.

In the same year, noted Pakistani journalist and renowned human rights activist, Zafaryab Ahmed, was arrested on grounds of criminal conspiracy, sedition, promoting enmity between different groups, and abetment of the Pakistan Penal Code. His crime? Promoting the work of the Bonded Labour Liberation Front (BLLF). For this he has been labelled as "a dangerous Indian Research and Analysis Wing agent,(RAW – the Indian equivalent of the CIA), seeking to sabotage the Rs 3.2bn national carpet industry by exposing it as the largest employer of child labour". Little wonder that Pakistani journalists prefer to keep their heads down.

A further explanation could be the fact that the majority of papers are run as commercial ventures by the large industrial families. Lucrative contracts for government advertising space could be jeopordized by over critical editorials. Other papers are merely party organs, repeating almost verbatim government or opposition press releases.

NB English and American newspapers can be read at the British Council and American Centre respectively. They are also for sale in some of the top end hotels in the major cities, and in some of the bookshops in Islamabad.

● Magazines

For a good summary of the contemporary political, economic, sporting and fashion scene in Pakistan, there are several informative periodicals available. *The Herald* and *Newsline* both appear monthly, covering the political and social scene in Pakistan in some depth. The reporting is of a high standard, and the contributors are not afraid to critisize the government, opposition, or the religious parties. Other interesting magazines include *Pakistan Illustrated* and *Politics and Business*. *Newsweek* and *Time* are available from most bookstands.

● Television and radio

Pakistan's two state-run television stations (Ptv 1 and Ptv 2) have little to offer the foreign visitor. The nightly news in English (at 1900) is very much in the 'what the Prime Minister did today' mould, with very poor coverage of international events (unless the Prime Minister is making yet another trip abroad).

In recent years, however, there has been a truly phenomenal growth in the number of people with access to satellite television stations. Almost all upper and middle class households, all top-end hotels, and more and more restaurants, tea houses and hotels are sprouting satellite dishes. Murdoch's Star TV Network is now beamed direct from Hong Kong in to the remost villages and households. What the long term impacts of this will be is hard to say, but it is now possible to sit in a chai shop in strictly Shia Muslim towns such as Skardu, where it is rare to even see a woman on the streets, and watch uncensored episodes of 'Baywatch'! Foreign tourists, particularly women, may feel very uncomfortable watching 'MTV' etc in such situations.

Although satelitte TV carries both CNN and BBC World Service Television, those who want to keep up to date with news, world affairs and English football results, should consider carrying a short-wave radio (see box below).

Entertainment

● Bars and nightclubs

Pakistan is the wrong country if you are seeking nightclubs and bars. In cities with large expatriate communities, such as Islamabad, Karachi and Peshawar, there are thriving social scenes, although they are difficult to penetrate for the casual, short-term visitor. Legendary nights out in Islamabad include the Thur night swill at the Australian embassy, followed by a trip to *Muddy's Cafe* at the *Marriot Hotel*, where you may see women in sleeveless shalwar kameezes! (see Islamabad 'Local Information').

There's normally a big Tues night drink up at the *Rose and Crown*, the bar at the British Deputy High Commission in Karachi, although it is strictly invitation only. For those desperate for a drink and Western company, contact the *Karachi Hash House Harriers* on a Mon night (see Karachi 'Local information').

● Cinemas

Far more accessible is the key local entertainment centre, the cinema. Pakistan's film industry is based around Lahore ('Lollywood', as opposed to Bombay's 'Bollywood'), and like their Indian counterparts, Pakistani films tend to be a combination of high-octane, non-stop violence, with sloppy love songs and coy love scenes intermittently interspersed. Pakistan does, however, produce some quality dramas, although they are not really accessible to non Urdu speakers. Many cinemas in the larger cities show Western films, although these too are invariably of the 'action' variety. Fans of Arnie, Stallone, Bruce Lee and James Bond are well served.

The atmosphere in a Pakistani cinema is something akin to a boy's night out – which is what it is. You rarely see a woman in a cinema in Pakistan, and consequently Western women (including those accompanied) often feel extremely uncomfortable and intimidated.

SHORT WAVE FREQUENCIES

The BBC's World Service transmissions to South Asia have been greatly enhanced in recent years by the leasing of a relay transmitter in Tashkent. Ironically, the same transmitter had previously been used by the Soviet regime to block out the BBC's services. The frequencies marked in **bold** are the best. Signal strength varies throughout the day, with lower frequencies generally better at night. At times the East Asia Service, and indeed the African Service, are clearer than the South Asia Service. The BBC's nightly 'South Asia Report' offers a good, up to the minute insight into events in the sub-continent. For programme listings contact BBC, PO Box 76, Bush House, London.

BBC World Service (London): 5975, 6195, 7105, **9740**, **11750**, **12095**, 15070, **15310**, 15400, 18080.

Voice of America (VoA): **7215**, **9760**, 11710, **15205**, 21540.

● **Sport**

Pakistan is one of the world's most fanatical sporting nations. Many play sport, even more watch it, but everybody has got an opinion on it. Pakistan is a young state, less than 50-years old, and is still trying to come to terms with its own sense of identity. One of the key collective experiences in Pakistan's nation-build-

ing process came in the field of sport. In a country that was founded on a religious concept rather than an ethnic or nationalist sense of belonging, that has fought and realistically lost three wars with its neighbouring rival, has spent just under half of its independent life under martial law, and where no civilian elected government has ever served its full term, there have been few events

---

1996 CRICKET WORLD CUP

Over Feb and Mar 1996, Pakistan will be co-hosting the cricket world cup with India and Sri Lanka. The final will be played in Lahore on 17 Mar. The teams competing will be: Australia (Aus), England (Eng), Holland (Hol), India (Ind), Kenya (Ken), New Zealand (NZ), Pakistan (Pak), South Africa (SA), Sri Lanka (SL), United Arab Emirates (UAE), West Indies (WI) and Zimbabwe (Zim). Below is the complete itinerary.

Feb 14: Eng v NZ, Ahmedabad (Ind)
Feb 15: SA v UAE, Rawalpindi (Pak)
Feb 16: WI v Zim, Hyderabad (Ind)
Feb 17: SL v Aus, Colombo (SL); Hol v NZ, Baroda or Rajkot (Ind)
Feb 18: Eng v UAE, Peshawar (Pak); Ind v Ken, Cuttack (Ind)
Feb 20: NZ v SA, Faisalabad (Pak)
Feb 21: Ind v WI, Gwailor (Ind); SL v Zim, Kandy (SL)
Feb 22: Eng v Hol, Peshawar, (Pak)
Feb 23: Aus v Ken, Visakhapatnam (Ind)
Feb 24: Pak v NZ, Lahore (Pak)
Feb 25: Eng v SA, Rawalpindi (Pak); SL v WI, Colombo, (SL)
Feb 26: Pak v Hol, Lahore (Pak); Ken v Zim, Patna (Ind)
Feb 27: NZ v UAE, Faisalabad (Pak); Aus v Ind, Bombay, (Ind)
Feb 29: Pak v SA, Karachi (Pak); Ken v WI, Pune (Ind)
Mar 1: Hol v UAE, Lahore (Pak); Aus v Zim, Nagpur (Ind)
Mar 2: Ind v SL, New Delhi (Ind)
Mar 3: Pak v Eng, Karachi (Pak)
Mar 4: Aus v WI, Kanpur (Ind)
Mar 5: Hol v SA, Rawalpindi (Pak)
Mar 6: Pak v UAE, Gujranwala (Pak); Ind v Zim, Kanpur (Ind); SL v Ken, Colombo (SL)
Mar 9: First Quarter Final: Winner Group A v 4th Place Group B, Faisalabad (Pak)
Mar 9: Second Quarter Final: 3rd Place Group A v 2nd Place Group B, Bangalore (Ind)
Mar 11: Third Quarter Final: Winner Group B v 4th Place Group A, Karachi (Pak)
Mar 11: Fourth Quarter Final: 3rd Place Group B v 2nd Place Group A, Madras (Ind)
Mar 13: First Semi-Final: Winners of 1st and 2nd Quarter Finals, Calcutta (Ind)
Mar 14: Second Semi-Final: Winners of 3rd and 4th Quarter Finals, Mohali (Ind)
Mar 17: Final, Lahore (Pak)
Mar 18: Reserve day for final

The latest odds from Ladbrokes on going to press were as follows: 7/2 Pak, Aus; 4/1 WI; 9/2 Ind; 5/1 Eng, SA; 20/1 SL; 28/1 NZ; 1,000/1 Hol; 2,000/1 Zim, Ken, UAE. Watch out for Sri Lanka!

CONTROVERSY IN PAKISTANI CRICKET

A recent feature in a local magazine on the state of Pakistani cricket began with the quote: "Mismanagement, rebellion, lacklustre performances, big money, bloated egos and outright greed... The Pakistan cricket scene, never pristine to begin with, has now sunk so low that it almost mirrors the country's debauched political culture." (*The Herald*, Mar 1995). What could have brought the national game to such a state of affairs?

Pakistani cricket has always been controversial, but is it any more so than in other countries? Much was made in the English press of the revelation by former international captain, and golden boy of Pakistani cricket Imran Khan, that he had on one occasion as a young player used a bottle-top to alter the state of the ball, thus attempting to gain an unfair advantage. Conversely, the famous "dirt in the pocket" incident featuring the England captain was quickly forgotten.

However, controversy does seem to dog the Pakistani national side. The famous Australian fast bowler Dennis Lillie and top Pakistani batsman Javed Miandad once squared up to each other during an international match, and former England captain Mike Gatting alleges in his autobiography that the Pakistani once threw a punch at him on the field. In fact, England's 1987 tour of Pakistan was fraught with allegations of biased umpiring, culminating in the infamous on-field row between Gatting and Pakistani umpire Shakoor Rana. The image of Pakistani cricket took a further bashing with the allegations of drug use during the recent tour of the West Indies, although all those allegedly involved denied the charge, and the evidence seemed dubious.

But the greatest scandal involving the national sport came in 1995 with the allegation by two Australian players that the Pakistani captain had attempted to bribe them to play badly in a match. As The Herald suggests, "Charges of ball tampering and marijuana use were one thing, match-fixing and gambling quite another." Yet allegations of match-fixing in Pakistani cricket are not new. For at least a decade there have been persistent rumours of bookmakers based in Bombay and Karachi 'buying' one, two or even three players in the national side. In fact, many people in Pakistan seriously believe that Pakistan were only knocked out of the semi-finals of the 1987 World Cup because one of their players had been betting against his own team. Imran Khan is said to have once been so incensed with allegations of the national team betting against themselves that he made the side bet their potential victory prize money on a Pakistani win. And prior to the recent tour of Zimbabwe, the entire Pakistani touring party were made to swear on the Qu'ran that they were not involved in satta, or betting.

The Pakistani view of the state of the national game reveals a trait of the national character; as Emma Duncan suggests, "everybody is an amateur conspiracy theorist", and thus revelations about Pakistani cricket in English and Australian newspapers are seen as another excuse for jealous nations to indulge in some 'Paki-bashing'. Because of the failings of the English national side, the press in the UK have to malign the vastly superior Pakistani side. The timing of the Australian revelations against the Pakistani captain was said to have been deliberate, in order to upset Pakistan's defence of the World Cup in 1996. Yet conspiracy theories are really just a useful way of avoiding believing the worst. The BCCP who run the game in Pakistan have recognized this, and are working desperately hard to clean up the game.

that have brought the people of Pakistan as closely together as the rasthe victory of their **cricket** team in the World Cup Final in Melbourne on 25 March 1992. The fact that their opponents were their old colonial masters, the English, made the victory even sweeter. Pakistan will be co-hosting the 1996 Cricket World Cup.

Yet it is not just in the sport of cricket that Pakistan excels. They have won many **hockey** World Championships and Olympic medals, and in Jahangir Khan and Jansheer Khan, Pakistan has dominated world **squash** for the last decade. The World Amateur Snooker Champion is from Lahore, and though Pakistan is yet to make its mark at international level, all the major cities have a thriving football ('soccer' to you philistines) scene. Some claim that the original form of **polo** was first played in the N of Pakistan, as it still is today. The more refined version is played in Lahore. **Golf** is becoming increasingly popular amongst the middle classes, with plenty of opportunities to play in the larger cities. **Horse and camel racing** still take place, though betting is illegal, and **sailing** and **diving** are available off the Karachi coast.

Holidays and festivals

The following is a list of national public holidays and Islamic holy days (also public holidays). Note that the precise timing of Islamic holy days is linked to the sighting of the moon. For details of the significance of the Islamic holy days see under Religion in the Introduction.

Feb: *Eid-ul-Fitr*, 1st of Shawal (20-22) (9-11 Feb 1997) (29-31 Jan 1998)
Mar: *Pakistan Day* (23)
Apr: *Eid-ul-Ajha*, 10th of Zilhaj (29 Apr-1 May) (18-20 Apr 1997) (7-9 Apr 1998)
May: *May Day* (1); *Day of Ashoura*, 9th and 10th of Muharram (29-30) (18-19 May 1997) (7-8 May 1998)

Jul: *Bank Holiday* (1); *Eid-Milad-un-Nabi*, 12th Rabi-ul-Awal (29) (18 Jul 1997) (7 Jul 1998)
Aug: *Independence Day* (14)
Sep: *Defence of Pakistan Day* (6); *Death Anniversary of Qaid-e-Azam* (11)
Nov: *Mohammad Iqbal Day* (9)
Dec: *Birth of Qaid-e-Azam/Christmas* (25); *Bank Holiday* (31)

RAMADAN

During the holy month of Ramadan (or Ramazan) Muslims observe a complete fast during daylight hours. All banks and offices close by around midday. Ramadan last from around 22 January-22 February 1996; 11 January-11 February 1997; 31 December 1997-31 January 1998.

Other important regional festivals include: *Basant*, the kite flying festival in Lahore (late Feb/early Mar); *Nauroz*, a pre-Islamic spring festival popular in the Northern Areas (mid-late Mar); *Baisakhi*, a Sikh holy day centred on the Panja Sahib Gurudwara (temple) in Hasan Abdal (mid Apr); *Shandur Pass Polo Tournament* (late Jul/early Aug); and *Jashan-e-Gilgit* or Northern Areas Independence Day, commemorating the liberation of the Northern Areas (1 Nov). Details of these festivals are given in the relevant sections.

Further reading

● **History**
Allchin, B and R, 1982, "*The Rise of Civilization in India and Pakistan*"; the most authoritative survey of the origins of Pakistani and Indian civilization. Barth, F, 1985, "*The Last Wali of Swat*"; Miangul Jahanzeb's own account of the history of Swat and his period of rule. Caroe, O, reprints, "*The Pathans*"; first published in 1958 and widely regarded as the definitive study of Pathan culture and history. Dani, AH, 1991 "*The History*

of the *Northern Areas*"; the definitive study. Dani, AH, 1995, *"Peshawar; Historic city of the Frontier"*; detailed history of Peshawar and environs. Hassan, MU, 1992, *"Mehergargh; the Oldest Civilization in South Asia"*; concise, readable analysis of the excavations at Merhgarh. Easwaran, E, 1984, *"A Man to Match his Mountains"*; highly readable, if at times a little misty-eyed, account of the life of Abdul Gaffar Khan, the 'Frontier Gandhi'. Robertson, GS, reprints, *"The Kafirs of the Hindu Kush"*; written at the turn of the century and now dated in many respects, but still considered amongst the authoritative works on the Kalasha people. Reprints are available of the *"Imperial Gazetteer of India"* covering most of Pakistan, both at the provincial and district level. Often rich in cultural and historical information, they also provide an interesting insight into British colonial perceptions of the region.

● **'Great Game' and colonial exploits**

Biddulph, J, reprints, *"Tribes of the Hindoo Koosh"*. Durand, A, 1899, *"The Making of a Frontier"*. French, P, 1995, *"Younghusband"*; excellent new biography of this fascinating character. Hopkirk, P, 1990, *"Great Game: On Secret Service in High Asia"*; highly readable account of the Great Game and the history of Central Asia. Keay, J, 1977, *"When Men and Mountains Meet"*; all the great 19th century explorers of the western Himalayas brought to life and placed in historical context; an excellent companion whilst travelling in this area. Keay, J, 1979, *"The Gilgit Game"*; an excellent companion whilst travelling in this area. Knight, EF, 1894, *"Where Three Empires Meet"*; classic colonial writing, including the 1891/92 'Hunza Campaign', unintentionally hilarious. Schomberg, RCF, 1935, *"Between the Oxus and the Indus"*; entertaining, but bigoted, colonial writing.

● **Politics, religion and culture**

Baldick, J, 1989, *"Mystical Islam; An Introduction to Sufism"*. Chaudhry, Mhd Sharif, 1991, *"Women's Rights in Islam"*. Duncan, E, 1989, *"Breaking the Curfew: A Political Journey Through Pakistan"*; one of the best books on Pakistan available, compulsory reading for anyone interested in modern Pakistan. Harrison, SS, 1981, *"In Afghanistan's Shadow; Baluch Nationalism and Soviet Temptations"*; in-depth analysis of Baluch nationalism in its geo-political context. Holt, Lambton, Lewis (Eds), 1970, *"The Cambridge History of Islam"*; (2 Vols). Lamb, C, 1991, *"Waiting for Allah: Pakistan's Struggle for Democracy"*; similar to Emma Duncan's book, though not quite so well written. Mir Ahmed Yar Khan Baluch, 1975, *"Inside Baluchistan; a political autobiography of the Khan of Kalat"*; an interesting insight into the politics of Kalat state, relations with the British and merger with Pakistan. Also gives a traditional history of the Baluch. Wolpert, S, 1984, *"Jinnah of Pakistan"*; the definitive biography of Jinnah, though for a long time versions sold in Pakistan excluded details of Jinnah's penchant for pork sausages. Yousaf, M, and Adkin, M, 1992, *"The Bear Trap; Afghanistan's Untold Story"*; fascinating insight into Pakistan's involvement in the Afghan war from the former head of the Afghan Bureau of the Inter Services Intelligence (ISI). Includes an interesting summary of the various theories surrounding Zia's death.

● **Specialist texts**

Ali, S & Dillon Ripley, S, *"Handbook of the Birds of India and Pakistan"*; available in compact edition, or 5 volumes. Dani, AH, *"Chilas: City of Nanga Parbat"*; excellent guide to petroglyphs found in N Pakistan. Ispahani, MZ, 1989, *"Roads and Rivals; The Political Uses of Access in the Borderlands of Asia"*; includes a fascinating analysis of the politics behind the building of the KKH. Jettmar, K, *"Rock

Carvings and Inscriptions in the Northern Areas of Pakistan"; excellent guide to petroglyphs found in N Pakistan. Khan, Fazle Karim, 1991, "*A Geography of Pakistan*". Messerli, B & Ives, J, 1989, "*Himalayan Crisis: Reconciling Development and Conservation*"; excellent review of the controversial debate over environmental change in the Himalaya. Robinson, F (ed), 1989, "*Cambridge Encyclopedia of India, Pakistan*"; excellent and readable introduction to many aspects of S Asian society.

● **Guidebooks**

Shaw, I and Shaw, B, 1993, "*Pakistan Trekking Guide*"; the only detailed trekking guide available specifically on Pakistan. Carefully researched over 5 years, but as a result parts of it were already out of date even before publication. New edition on its way. Swift, H, 1990, "*Trekking in Pakistan and India*"; well written, with lots of interesting and useful information, although much of it is out of date.

● **Travel writing**

Danzinger, N, 1987, "*Danzinger's Travels: Beyond Forbidden Frontiers*"; highly readable account of travel through Turkey, Iran, Afghanistan, Pakistan, China and Tibet, though rather self-important. Dring, S, 1995, "*On The Road Again*"; book to accompany BBC TV series examining the backpacker phenomenon. Fairley, J, 1975, "*Lion River: The Indus*". Murphy, D, 1965, "*Full Tilt: Ireland to India on a bicycle*". Murphy, D, 1977, "*Where The Indus Is Young: a winter in Baltistan*"; account of a winter spent in Baltistan by the author and her young daughter, though again, rather self-important. Newby, E, 1958, "*A Short Walk in the Hindu Kush*"; one of the best travel books ever written, details a hilarious expedition to Nuristan (in Afghanistan). Paine, S, 1994, "*The Afghan Amulet*"; travels through Pakistan, Iran, Afghanistan, Iraqi and Turkish Kurdistan and Bulgaria in search of the source of an embroidered amulet.

● **Fiction**

Kipling, R, 1901, "*Kim*"; the classic novel that gave prominence to the expression 'Great Game'. Kipling, R, reprints, "*The Man Who Would Be King*"; classic adventure story of two deserters from the British Indian army who find themselves revered as royalty in a remote valley of the NW Frontier. Rushdie, S, 1983, "*Shame*"; bitterly sharp critique of S Asian life. Singh, K, 1956 (reprints), "*Train to Pakistan*"; Khushwant Singh's first novel gives a moving insight into the trauma that accompanied partition.

Maps

Good maps are almost impossible to come by in Pakistan, although some of the major bookshops are currently trying to import them. It is better to bring your own. The most detailed country map available is the Nelles Verlag 1:500,000 Pakistan map (Nelles Verlag also do a Himalaya map covering northern Pakistan, parts of Afghanistan and North India, Nepal, Bhutan, Bangladesh and Tibet). More up to date is the GeoCentre 1:2 million Afghanistan/Pakistan map in the World Map series. If coming overland, the Kummerly & Frey 1:4 million Proche-Orient map is useful, covering Turkey and the Middle East, Iran, Afghanistan, Central Asia, Pakistan and parts of China and India. Major routes are accurately marked.

Survey of Pakistan produce a wide selection of country, regional and town maps, although most are of limited value. The 1:2 million Road Map of Pakistan is one of the better country maps but is difficult to read. Some of the provincial and district maps are good (and quite pretty). Town maps are generally out of date and none too accurate. Survey of Pakistan maps are available from their head office; Murree Rd, Faisabad, Rawalpindi, T 450808, open 0900-1700, closed Fri, Sat. You must select the maps you want from a catalogue at reception and they will be brought down to you. Be sure to keep the receipt and 'authorisation' form to show to customs if neccessary.

PTDC have town plans and maps of most major cities and tourist destinations, although these generally only give an overview and are not sufficient for finding your way around.

Details of **trekking** maps and where they can be obtained are included in the chapter on Trekking.

HEALTH INFORMATION

CONTENTS

Before travelling	47
Common problems	48
Other specific problems	52
Other afflictions	55
Returning home	55
Further information	56

The following information has been compiled by Dr David Snashall, Senior Lecturer in Occupational Health, United Medical Schools of Guy's and St Thomas' Hospitals and Chief Medical Advisor, Foreign and Commonwealth Office, London, with added comments and recommendations specific to Pakistan from Dr Martin Taylor, Kensington Street Health Centre, Bradford, West Yorkshire.

Travellers to Pakistan are exposed to health risks not encountered in Western Europe or North America. Because much of the area is economically underdeveloped, serious infectious diseases are common, as they were in the West some decades ago. Business travellers staying in cities in international hotels, and tourists on organized tours, face different health risks to travellers backpacking through rural areas. There are no absolute rules to follow; you will often have to make your own judgement on the healthiness of your surroundings. With suitable precautions you should stay healthy.

There are many well qualified doctors in Pakistan, most of whom speak English, but the quality and range of medical care diminishes rapidly as you leave the major cities. There are systems and traditions of medicine completely different from the models in the West. If you are in a major city, your embassy may be able to recommend a list of doctors.

If you are a long way from medical help, some self-treatment may be needed and you are more than likely to find many drugs with familiar names on sale. Always buy from a reputable source, and check date stamping. Vaccines in particular have a much reduced shelf-life if not stored properly. Locally produced drugs may be unreliable because of poor quality control and the substitution of inert ingredients for active drugs.

Before travelling

Take out medical insurance. See your doctor or travel clinic for anti-malarial advice and for vaccination. Make sure your health is good. Have a dental check up, and take spare glasses (or at least a glasses prescription) if you wear them. If you have a long-standing medical problem such as diabetes, heart trouble, chest trouble or high blood pressre, get advice from your doctor, and carry sufficient medication to last the full duration of your trip. You may want to ask your doctor for a letter explaining your condition.

Vaccination and immunisation

If you require travel vaccinations see your doctor well in advance of your travel. Most courses can be completed in a minimum of 4 weeks, but as immunity lasts longer than this, vaccination is best done early. Travel clinics may provide rapid courses of vaccination, but are likely to be more expensive.

The following vaccinations are recommended:

Typhoid A single dose injection is now available (*Typhim Vi*) that provides protection for up to 3 years. A vaccine taken by mouth in three doses is also available, but the timing of doses can be a problem and protection only lasts for 1 year.

Polio Protection is by a live vaccine generally given orally, and a full course consists of three doses with a booster every 5 years.

Tetanus If you have not been vaccinated before, one dose of vaccine should be given with a booster at 6 weeks and another at 6 months. 10 yearly boosters are strongly recommended.

Children should, in addition, be properly protected against diphtheria, mumps and measles.

Hepatitis If you are not immune to **hepatitis A** already, then you should consider having *gamma globulin* or vaccination (*Havrix*). A single dose of the vaccine provides protection for at least a year. A booster dose extends immunity to at least 10 years.

If you are not immune to **hepatitis B**, a vaccine is available (three injections over 6 months). This should be considered if you plan to stay in the region for some time.

Malaria For details of malaria prevention, see below.

The following vaccinations may also be considered:

Tuberculosis The disease is still common in the region. Consult your doctor for advice on BCG innoculation.

Meningococcal Meningitis and Diphtheria If you are staying in the country for a long time, vaccination should be considered.

Japanese B Encephalitis (JBE) Immunisation (effective in 10 days) gives protection for around 3 years. There is an extremely small risk in Pakistan, though it varies seasonally and from region to region. Consult a travel clinic or your family doctor.

Rabies Vaccination before travel gives anyone bitten more time to get treatment (so particularly helpful for those visiting remote areas), and also prepares the body to produce antibodies quickly. The cost of the vaccine can be shared by three persons receiving vaccination together.

Smallpox, **Cholera** and **Yellow Fever** vaccinations are not required, although you may be asked to show a vaccination certificate if you have been in a country affected by yellow fever immeadiately prior to travelling to Pakistan.

Common problems

Intestinal upsets

Practically nobody escapes this one, so be prepared for it. Most of the time intestinal upsets are due to the insanitary preparation of food. Do not eat uncooked fish, vegetables or meat (especially pork, though this is highly unlikely in Pakistan), fruit with the skin on (always peel fruit yourself), or food that is exposed to flies (particularly salads).

Tap water should be assumed to be unsafe, especially in the monsoon; the same goes for stream or well water. Bottled mineral water is now widely available, although not all bottled water is mineral water; some is simply purified water from an urban supply. If your hotel has a central hot water supply, this is generally safe to drink after cooling. Ice for drinks should be made from boiled water but rarely is, so stand your drink on the ice cubes rather than putting them in your drink. For details on water purification, see box.

Heat treated milk is widely available, as is ice cream and milk produced by the same methods. Unpasteurized milk products, including cheese, are sources of tuberculosis, brucellosis, listeria and food poisoning germs. You can render fresh milk safe by heating it to 62°C for 30 mins, followed by rapid cooling or by boiling. Matured or processed cheeses are safer than fresh varieties.

Diarrhoea is usually the result of food poisoning, occasionally from contaminated water. There are various causes: viruses, bacteria, protozoa (like amoeba

Common problems

CHILDREN AND BABIES

Younger travellers seem to be more prone to illness abroad, but that should not put you off taking them. More preparation is necessary than for an adult and perhaps a little more care should be taken when travelling to remote areas where health services are primitive. This is because children can become more rapidly ill than adults, although they often recover more quickly.

Diarrhoea and vomiting are the most common problems so take the usual precautions, but more intensively. Make sure all basic childhood **vaccinations** are up to date, as well as the more exotic ones. Children should be properly protected against diphtheria, mumps and measles. Consult your doctor for advice on BCG innoculation against tuberculosis. Protection against mosquitos and drug prophylaxis against malaria are essential. Many children take to 'foreign' food quite happily. Milk in Pakistan tends to be ultra-heat treated (UHT), but not necessarily pasteurized. Powdered milk may be the answer, although you should be certain that the water source is safe. Breast feeding where appropriate is the best option.

The treatment of **diarrhoea** is the same as for adults except that it should be started earlier and be continued with more persistence. Children get dehydrated very quickly in the tropics and can become drowsy and uncooperative unless cajoled to drink water or juice plus salts. Oral rehydration has been a lifesaving technique in children.

Upper respiratory infections such as colds, catarrh and middle ear infection are common-antibiotics should be carried against the possibility. **Outer ear infections** after swimming are also common-antibiotic ear drops will help.

Protect children against the sun with a hat and high factor sun lotion. Severe sunburn at this age may well lead to serious skin cancer in the future.

and giardia), salmonella and cholera organisms. It may take one of several forms, coming on suddenly, or rather slowly. It may be accompanied by vomiting or by severe abdominal pain and the passage of blood or mucus (when it is called dysentery).

How do you know which type you have and how do you treat them? All kinds of diarrhoea, whether or not accompanied by vomiting, respond favourably to the replacement of water and salts taken as frequent small sips of some kind of rehydration solution. Proprietary preparations, consisting of sachets of powder which you dissolve in water (ORS, or Oral Rehydration Solution) are widely available in Pakistan, although it is recommended that you bring some of your own. They can also be made by adding half a teaspoonful of salt (3.5 grams) and 4

tablespoonfuls of sugar (40 grams) to a litre of safe drinking water.

If you can time the onset of diarrhoea to the minute, then it is probably viral or bacterial, and/or the onset of dysentery. The treatment, in addition to rehydration, is Ciprofloxacin (500 mgs every 12 hrs). The drug is now widely available.

If the diarrhoea has come on slowly or intermittently, then it is more likely to be protozoal (ie caused by amoeba or giardia). These cases are best treated by a doctor, as should any diarrhoea continuing for more than 3 days. If medical facilities are remote a short course of Metronidazole (*Flagyl*) may provide relief. This drug is widely available in Pakistan, although it is best to bring a course with you. If there are severe stomach cramps, the following drugs may help: Loperamide (*Imodium, Arret*) and Diphenoxylate with Atropine (*Lomotil*).

WATER PURIFICATION

There are a number of methods for purifying water in order to make it safe to drink. Dirty water should first be strained through a filter bag, and then boiled or treated. Bringing water to a rolling **boil** at sea level is sufficient to make water safe for drinking, but at higher altitudes you have to boil the water for longer to ensure that all the microbes are killed.

Various sterilising methods can be used, and there are propriety preparations containing **chlorine** (eg *'Puritabs'*) or **iodine** (eg *'Pota Aqua'*) compounds. Chlorine compounds generally do not kill protozoa (eg giardia). Prolonged usage of iodine compounds may lead to thyroid problems, although this is rare if used for less than a year.

There are a number of **water filters** now on the market, available both in personal and expedition size. There are broadly two types of water filter, **mechanical** and **chemical**. Mechanical filters are usually a combination of carbon, ceramic and paper, although they can be difficult to use. Ceramic filters tend to last longer in terms of volume of water purifyed. The best brand is possibly the Swiss made *Katadyn*. Although cheaper, the disadvantage of mechanical filters is that they do not always kill viruses or protozoa. Thus, if you are in an area where the presence of these is suspected, the water will have to be treated with iodine before being passed through the filter. When new, the filter will remove the taste, although this may not continue for long. However, ceramic filters will remove bacteria, and their manufacturers claim that since most viruses live on bacteria, the chances are that the viruses will be removed as well. This claim should be treated with scepticism.

Chemical filters usually use a combination of an iodine resin filter and a mechanical filter. The advantage of this system is that, according to the manufacturers' claims, everything in the water will be killed. The disadvantage is that the filters need replacing, adding a third to the price. Probably the best chemical filter is manufactured by *Pur*.

Thus, the lynch pins of treatment for diarrhoea are rest, fluid and salt replacement, antibiotics such as Ciprofloxacin for the bacterial types and special diagnostic tests and medical treatment for amoeba and giardia infections.

Salmonella infections and cholera can be devastating diseases and it would be wise to get to a hospital as soon as possible if these were suspected. Fasting, peculiar diets and the consumption of large quantities of yoghurt have not been found useful in calming travellers' diarrhoea or in rehabilitating inflamed bowels. As there is some evidence that alcohol and milk might prolong diarrhoea, they should probably be avoided during and immediately after an attack. Antibiotics to prevent diarrhoea are probably ineffective and some, such as Entero-vioform, can have serious side effects if taken for long periods.

Heat and cold

Full acclimitisation to high temperatures takes about 2 weeks, and during this period it is normal to feel relatively apathetic, especially if the relative humidity is high. Drink plenty of water (up to 15 litres a day are required when working physically hard in the tropics), use salt on your food, and avoid extreme exertion. When you are acclimitized you will feel more comfortable, but your need for plenty of water will continue.

Tepid showers are more cooling than hot or cold ones. Large hats do not cool you down but do prevent sunburn. Remember that, especially in the mountains and deserts, there can be a large and sudden drop between temperatures in the sun and shade, and between night and day. Dress accordingly. Loose fitting cotton clothes are still the best for hot weather. Warm jackets and woollens are essential after dark at high altitude.

Sunburn and heat stroke

The burning power of the tropical sun is phenomenal, especially at altitude. Always wear a wide brimmed hat and use some form of sun cream or lotion. Normal temperate sun tan lotions (protection factor up to 7) are not much good. You will need to use the types designed specifically for the tropics or for mountaineers/skiers, with a protection factor between 7 and 25 (dependant on skin type). Glare from the sun can cause conjunctivitis, so wear good quality UV protection sunglasses on beaches and snowy areas. There are several variations of 'heat stroke'. The most common cause is severe dehydration, so drink plenty of non-alcoholic fluid. Sun-block and cream is not widely available in Pakistan, so you should bring adequate supplies with you.

Malaria

Malaria is a risk in Pakistan. It remains a serious disease and you are strongly advised to protect yourself against mosquito bites (described under 'Insects' below) and to take prophylactic (preventive) drugs. Recommendations on prevention change, so consult your family doctor or see the further information at the end of this section. However, the current combination of anti-malarial drugs for use in Pakistan requires a daily dosage of *Proguanil* (brands such as Paludrine) and a weekly dosage of *Chloroquine* (various brands). For those unable to use these particular drugs, your doctor may suggest the use of *Mefloquine*, although this tends to be more expensive, less well tried, and more likely to encourage side effects.

Start taking the tablets a week before exposure and continue to take them for 4 weeks after leaving the malarial zone. Remember to give the drugs to babies, children and pregnant women.

The subject of malaria prevention is becoming more complex as the malaria parasite becomes immune to some of the older drugs. In particular, there has been an increase in the proportion of cases of falciparum malaria which is particularly dangerous. Some of the preventive drugs can cause side effects, especially if taken for long periods of time, so before you travel you must check with a reputable agency the likelihood and type of malaria in the areas you intend to visit. Take their advice on prophylaxis, but be prepared to receive conflicting advice. **Do not use the possibility of side effects as an excuse not to take drugs.** In one General Practice in Britain dealing with a lot of travellers to Pakistan, no complications of anti-malarial drugs have been seen in the last 5 years. On the other hand, there have been several cases of malaria, some serious, in travellers who had not taken prevention seriously.

You can catch malaria even when taking prophylactic drugs, although it is unlikely. If you do develop symptoms (high fever, shivering, severe headache, sometimes diarrhoea) seek medical advice immediately. The risk of disease is obviously greater the further you move from the cities into rural areas with primitive facilities and standing water.

Hepatitis (jaundice)

Medically speaking there are two types. The less serious but more common is **hepatitis A**, a disease frequently caught by travellers, and common in Pakistan. The main symptoms are yellowness of eyes and skin, lack of appetite, nausea, tiredness and stomach pains. The best protection is careful preparation of food, the avoidance of contaminated drinking water, and scrupulous attention to toilet hygiene. (For details of vaccinations available, see above).

The other, more serious, version is **hepatitis B**, which is acquired as a sexually transmitted disease, from a blood transfusion or an injection with an unclean needle, or possibly by insect bites. The symptoms are the same as hepatitis A but the incubation period is much longer. (For details of vaccinations available, see above).

You may have had jaundice before or you may have had hepatitis of either type without becoming jaundiced, in which case it is possible that you could be immune to either form. This immunity can be tested for before you travel.

Insects

These can be a great nuisance. Some of course are carriers of serious disease. The best way to keep mosquitos away at night is to sleep off the ground with a mosquito net, and to burn mosquito coils containing Pyrethrum (available in Pakistan). Aerosol sprays or a 'flit' gun may be effective, as are insecticidal tablets which are heated on a mat which is plugged into a wall socket. These devices, and the refills, are not widely available in Pakistan, so if you are taking your own make sure it is of suitable voltage with the right adapter plug. Bear in mind also that there are frequent power cuts in many parts of Pakistan.

A better option is to use a personal insect repellant of which the best contain a high concentration of Diethyltoluamide (DET). Liquid is best for arms, ankles and face (take care around eyes and make sure you do not dissolve the plastic of your spectacles). These are available in Pakistan (eg *Mospel*, *Repel*), although it is recommended that you bring your own supply. Aerosol spray on clothes and ankles deter mites and ticks.

Liquid DET suspended in water can be used to impregnate cotton clothes and mosquito nets.

If you are bitten, itching may be relieved by cool baths and anti-histamine tablets (care with alcohol or driving), corticosteroid creams (great care and never use if hint of infection) or by judicious scratching. Calamine lotion and cream are of no real use, and anti-histamine creams have a tendency to cause skin allergies and are, therefore, not recommended.

Bites which do become infected (common in Pakistan) should be treated with a local antiseptic or antibiotic cream such as Cetrimide, as should infected scratches. Skin infestations with body lice, crabs and scabies are unfortunately easy to pick up, particularly by those travelling cheaply or trekking to mountain grazing pastures. Use Gamma benzene hexachloride for lice and Benzyl benzoate for scabies. Crotamiton cream alleviates itching and also kills a number of skin parasites. Malathion 5% is good for lice, but avoid the highly toxic full strength Malathion used as an agricultural insecticide.

Other specific problems

Altitude sickness

Acute mountain sickness (AMS) can strike from about 3,000m upwards. It is more likely to affect those who ascend rapidly (eg by plane, or by not allowing sufficient acclimitisation time whilst trekking), and those who over-exert themselves. Teenagers seem to be particularly prone. The illness can affect you even if you have not had problems at altitude before.

On reaching heights above 3,000m, heart pounding and shortness of breath, especially on exertion, are almost universal responses to the lack of oxygen in the air. Acute mountain sickness takes a few hours or days to come on and presents with headache, fatigue, dizziness, loss of appetite, nausea and vomiting. Insomnia is common and often associated with a suffocating feeling when lying down in bed. Keen observers may note that their breathing tends to wax and wane at night and their faces tend to be puffy in the morning – this is all part of the syndrome. If the symptoms are mild, the treatment is rest, painkillers for the headache (preferably not Aspirin based), and anti-sickness pills for vomiting. Oxygen may help at very high altitudes but is unlikely to be available.

The best way of preventing acute mountain sickness is a relatively slow ascent and, when trekking to high altitudes, some time spent in the foothills getting fit and adapting to moderate altitude is beneficial. On arrival at places over 3,000m, a few hours rest and avoidance of cigarettes, alcohol and heavy food will help prevent the problem. **Should the symptoms be severe or prolonged, it is best to descend to a lower altitude and to reascend slowly or in stages.** Symptoms disappear very quickly even with a few hundred metres of descent. If a staged ascent is impossible because of shortage of time, the drug Acetazolamide is proven to prevent minor symptoms, but some people experience funny side effects, and it may mask more serious symptoms. The usual dose is 500 mgs of the slow release preparation each night, starting the night before ascending above 3,000m. The drug will not prevent severe altitude sickness.

There is a further, albeit rare, hazard due to rapid ascent to high altitude – a kind of complicated mountain sickness presenting as acute pulmonary oedema or acute cerebral oedema. Both conditions are more common the higher you go. Pulmonary oedema comes on quite rapidly, with breathlessness, noisy breathing, cough, blueness of the lips and possibly frothing at the mouth. Cerebral oedema usually presents with confusion, going on to unconciousness. Anyone developing these symptoms should be evacuated from the mountain as a medical emergency.

Other problems experienced at high altitude are sunburn, excessively dry air causing skin cracking, sore eyes (it may be wise to leave your contact lenses out) and stuffy noses. It is unwise to ascend to high altitude if you are pregnant (especially in the first 3 months), or if you have a history of heart, lung or blood disease, including sickle cell. Do not ascend to high altitude in the 24 hrs following scuba-diving (though the opportunity is unlikely). Rapid descent from high altitude may aggravate sinus and middle ear infections and make bad teeth ache. The same problems are sometimes experienced during descent at the end of a plane flight.

Remember that the mountain ranges of Northern Pakistan are very high, very cold, very remote and potentially very dangerous. Do not travel in them alone, if you are ill, or if you are poorly equipped. Telephone communication can be extremely difficult, mountain rescue all but non-existant, and medical services extremely basic. Despite these various hazards (mostly preventable) of high altitude travel, many people find the environment healthier and more invigorating than at sea level.

AIDS

In Pakistan, AIDS is increasing in prevalence with a pattern typical of developing societies. Thus, it is not wholly confined to the well known high risk sections of the population, ie homosexual men, intravenous drug abusers, prostitutes and the children of infected mothers. Heterosexual transmission is now the dominant mode and so the main risk to travellers is from casual sex. (For most visitors to Pakistan, the chances of casual sex are also minimal.) The same precautions should be taken as when encountering any sexually transmitted disease. Condoms are available in many chemists in Pakistan, though they are not generally prominantly displayed.

The AIDS virus (HIV) can be passed via unsterile needles which have previously been used to inject a HIV positive patient, but the risk of this is very small indeed. It would, however, be sensible to check that needles have been properly sterilized, or better still, disposable needles used. The chance of picking up hepatitis B in this way is much more of a danger. If disposable needles are carried as part of a proper medical kit, customs officials in Pakistan are not generally suspicious.

The risk of receiving a blood transfusion with blood infected with the HIV virus is greater than from dirty needles because of the amount of fluid exchanged. Supplies of blood for transfusion are now usually screened for HIV in reputable hospitals, so the risk may be small. Catching the AIDS virus does not necessarily produce an illness in itself; the only way to be sure if you feel you have been at risk, is to have a blood test for HIV antibodies on your return to a place where there are reliable laboratory facilities. The test does not become positive for many weeks.

Bites and stings

If you are unlucky enough to be bitten by a venomous snake, spider, scorpion, centipede or sea creature, try (within limits) to catch the animal for identification. Failing this, an accurate description will aid treatment. See the information on rabies (below) for other animal bites.

The reactions to be expected are fright, swelling, pain and bruising around the bite, soreness of the regional lymph glands (eg armpits for bites to hands and arms), nausea, vomiting and fever. If, in addition, any of the following symptoms supervene get the victim to a doctor without delay: numbness, tingling of face, muscular spasm, convulsions, shortness of breath or haemorrhage. Commercial snake bite or scorpion sting kits may be available but are only useful for the specific type of snake or scorpion for which they are designed. The serum has to be by injection into a vein, so it is not much good unless you have some practice in making such injections. If the bite is on a limb, immobilize the limb and apply a tight bandage (not a tourniquet) between the bite and the body. Be sure to release it for 90 secs every 15 mins. Do not try to slash the bite and try to suck out the poison because this will do more harm than good. Reassurance of the bitten person is important. Death from snake-bite is extremely rare. Hospitals usually hold stocks of snake-bite serum, though it is important to have a good description of the snake, or where possible, the creature itself. The best precaution is not to walk in snake territory with bare feet, sandals or shorts, and not to touch snakes even if assured they are harmless.

If swimming in an area where there are poisonous fish such as stone or scorpion fish (also called by a variety of local names) or sea urchins on rocky coasts, tread carefully or wear plimsolls. The sting of such fish is intensely painful but can be helped by immersing the stung part in water as hot as you can bear for as long as it remains painful. This is not always very practical and you must take care not to scald yourself. At certain times of the year, coincidental with the best surfing season, stinging jelly-fish can be a problem off the coast of Karachi.

Avoid spiders and scorpions by keeping your bed away from the wall, look under lavatory seats (if you come across any), and inside your shoes in the morning. Dark dusty rooms are popular with scorpions, particularly in Chitral. In the rare event of being bitten, consult a doctor.

FIRST AID KITS

Although pre-packaged first aid kits for travellers are available from many camping and outdoor pursuits shops, it is unlikely that you will ever need to use at least half of their contents. If you are visiting very remote areas, for example if you are trekking, it becomes more important to ensure that you have all the necessary items. However, for most travellers, the majority of items are readily available cheaply in Pakistan. You may want to bring with you a supply of sticky plasters and corn plasters (Band Aid etc), intestinal treatments such as Imodium, and anti-histamine tablets. *Flagyl* can be bought across the chemist's counter in Pakistan, whereas in UK at least, a doctor's prescription is required. Paracetamol is readily available in Pakistan. Pakistan's hospitals and medical centres do not seem to have any shortage of sterile, single-use needles, but if you want to bring your own supply, the standard 'green' size are the most versatile. If you have any specialized requirements, it is recommended that you bring them with you.

Other afflictions

Remember that **rabies** is endemic in Pakistan. If you are bitten by a domestic or wild animal, do not leave things to chance. Scrub the wound immediately with soap and water/disinfectant. Try to capture the animal (within limits). Treatment depends on whether you have already been vaccinated against rabies. If you have (and this is worthwhile if you are spending lengths of time in developing countries) then some further doses of vaccine are all that is needed. Human diploid cell vaccine is best, but expensive; other, older types of vaccine such as that made of duck embyos may be the only type available. These are effective, much cheaper and interchangeable generally with the human derived types. If not already vaccinated then anti-rabies serum (immunoglobulin) may be required in addition. It is wise to finish the course of treatment whether the animal survives or not.

Dengue fever is present in Pakistan. It is a viral disease, transmitted by mosquito bites, presenting severe headache and body pains. Complicated types of dengue known as haemorrhagic fevers occur throughout Asia, but usually in persons who have caught the disease a second time. Thus, although it is a very serious type, it is rarely caught by visitors.

There is no treatment; you must just avoid mosquito bites.

Athlete's foot and other fungal infections are best treated by sunshine and a proprietary preparation such as Canesten or Ecostatin.

Influenza and respiratory diseases are common, perhaps made worse by polluted cities and rapid temperature and climatic changes.

Intestinal worms are common, and the more serious ones such as hookworm can be contracted by walking barefoot on infested earth.

Leishmaniasis can be a serious disease taking several forms. It is generally transmitted by sand flies, which should be avoided in the same way as mosquities.

Prickly heat is a very common itchy rash, and can be avoided by frequent washing and wearing loose clothing. It is helped by the use of talcum powder to allow the skin to dry thoroughly after washing.

Returning home

It is important to take your anti-malaria tablets for 4 weeks after your return. Malaria can develop up to 1 year after leaving a malarious area. If you do become ill, with fever, make sure your doctor knows about your travel. If you have had attacks of diarrhoea, it may be worth having a stool specimen tested in case you have picked up amoebic dysentery, giardiaisis or other protozoal infections. If you have been living rough, a blood test may be worthwhile to detect worms and other parasites.

Further information

The following organizations give information regarding well trained English speaking physicians throughout the world: *International Association for Medical Assistance to Travellers*, 745, 5th Avenue, New York, 10022; *Intermedic*, 777, Third Avenue, New York, 10017.

Information regarding country by country malaria risk can be obtained from: *Malaria Reference Laboratory*, T 0891 600350 (recorded message, premium rate); *Liverpool School of Tropical Medicine*, T 0891 172111 (recorded message, premium rate); *Centre for Disease Control*, Atlanta, USA, T 404 332 4555.

The *London School of Hygiene and Tropical Medicine*, Keppel St, London, WC1E 7HT, publishes a strongly recommended book titled '*The Preservation of Personal Health in Warm Climates*'. The organization *MASTA (Medical Advice Service for Travellers Abroad)*, T (UK) 0171 631 4408, will provide up to date country by country information on health risks.

Further information on medical problems abroad can be obtained from: *Travellers' Health: How To Stay Healthy Abroad*, edited by Richard Dawood (Oxford University Press), recently updated, with good information on travel to more out-of-the-way places. A new edition of the HMSO publication *Health Information for Overseas Travel* is now available.

ACKNOWLEDGEMENTS

This book would not have been possible without the help of numerous people along the way. Thanks first of all to Bob Bradnock for his support, and for allowing us to use sections of text on Taxila, Moenjo Daro and Harappa from the South Asia Handbook. Special thanks are also due to Birgitte Glavind Sperger for contributing an excellent piece on the culture of the Kalasha people of Chitral. We are both particularly indebted to Louisiana Lush who provided us with not only a home in Islamabad, but also a social life and introductions to many very useful contacts, as well as organizing such a successful trek. Khushwaqt-ul-Mulk meanwhile was a wonderful host in Mastuj. Sebastian Ballard deserves special mention having achieved the impossible by getting the maps prepared in time, with help from Curly and Toby. Thanks also to everyone at Trade and Travel for their hard work in pulling everything together; they have been great people to work for.

Dave Winter

At the British Deputy High Commission in Karachi, I would like to thank Peter and Annabelle Scott, Jeremy Hodges, Andy and Corrie Pryce, for revealing a social scene in Karachi that was previously unbeknown to me. Liz and Graham Lambert, as ever, provided great hospitality during my time in Karachi. In Islamabad, I would like to thank Andrea Sessa of UNIDO and Anna of EC for their charming company, and Humaira Usman for the tennis lessons. In Muzaffarabad, Mr Farruk Moghul and Mr Sohail Mirza of the AJ&K Tourism Dept were of great help in dealing with Pakistani bureaucracy, and for information on parts of the state that are closed to foreigners. I am also

extremely grateful for the guided tour of Mangla Dam, arranged by Chief Engineer, Mr Afzal Puri, and conducted so gracefully by Major Azam and Capt Ismail of the WAPDA Security Force. Ayaz Hussain Jafrai proved to be an excellent host in Sukkur, as did Mohammad Farooq in Mirpur and Walthamstow. I am also indebted to Hakeem Sayyid Zaheer ud Daula, descendent of Pir Shah Daula of Gujrat, for the account of his ancestor's life. In the Northern Areas I would like to thank my fellow trekkers for their company and suggestions; Cosmo Lush, Eadie Borman, Mark 'Scorpion' Lloyd, Georgina Palffy and Chloe Gorman. I would also like to thank Annie Harper, Queen of the Northern Areas, and the other staff at the AKRSP in Gilgit, most notably Siobhan Warrington and Abinta Malik. Thanks are also due to Sherrullah Baig and Ali Madad of Altit, Charles Timmis for the George Hayward information, and to James 'five months' Wakefield for his Kashgar comments and observations. I am very grateful to Kevin Hawkins of Bradford for the Mirpur information, and to Martin, Jan and Jack Taylor, also of Bradford. Thanks also to Joe Carter for assisting in procuring expedition equipment, and to Laurence Guillien for putting up with my increasing irritability as deadline approached.

Ivan Mannheim

In Islamabad I am particularly grateful to Sajid and Ibtesam Qaissrani for finding time between two full-time jobs and two full-time children to provide wonderful hospitality, useful suggestions, information and contacts. Ashab Naqvi and Tayyab Nisar Mir at the PTDC head office were particularly helpful and patient in dealing with my endless questions. Mike Semple of Oxfam gave lots of useful information and suggestions. Thanks to Vaqar Zakaria for sharing his extensive knowledge. Rafiq Ahmed Rajput of the Sind Wildlife Management Board provided excellent information on the wildlife of Deosai, and Pakistan in general. In NWFP I would like to thank Salahud-Din, Haroon Rashid, Habib Rahman and Saif Rahman of Daraban Kalan for their hospitality, friendship and extensive information. Zainul Wahab of Mardan Museum introduced me to the Commissioner Mohammad Fareed Khan; between them they ensured that I saw and learnt as much as possible of the Peshawar valley and its history. Khurram Khan of Peshawar helped get me to Parachinar, where the Political Agent, Javed Iqbal, saw to it that I was shown around and well looked after. Mr Qazi of the Swat Serena was helpful and hospitable, while Noor-ul-Amin and friends gave their time to show me round many of the sights of Lower Swat. Saifullah Jan of Rumbur was a fascinating and informative host. In Baluchistan I would like to thank Qamaruddin Mir of PTDC Quetta for his help and support. Yaqoob Shah of CTC provided much useful information, as well as a taste of true Pathan hospitality. Adam Khan of Quetta Serena kindly invited me on their train excursion through the Bolan Pass. Thanks to Abdullah Baluch of the Arts Council for his help and hospitality. Ian Simmons and Jim Fyvie of Halcrow were also very helpful. In the Makran, Sheila Paine and Roland Besenval gave useful information on local culture and the excavations at Miri Kalat. Special thanks to Bakshi Baluch who was much more than just a host in Gwadar, and Ishak Baluch for showing me round and taking me to Jiwani. In Baltistan I am particularly grateful to Anwar Ali who was an excellent guide and all-round fixer. Abbas Qazmi meanwhile was a mine of fascinating information on the history and culture of Baltistan. Finally, thanks and apologies to all at home who have had to put up with me during the writing of this book.

LAND, CULTURE AND HISTORY

LAND AND LIFE

Contents	
Geology and landscape	59
Climate	63
Vegetation, land and wildlife	64

Geology and landscape 59
Climate 63
Vegetation, land and wildlife 64

Basics

OFFICIAL NAME: Islamic Republic of Pakistan (*Islami Jamhuriya-e-Pakistan*)

NATIONAL FLAG: Dark green ground, with white vertical band at the mast. In the centre of the green area is a white crescent and five-pointed heraldic star.

STATE RELIGION: Islam

NATIONAL LANGUAGE: Urdu

KEY STATISTICS: *Area*: 804,000 sq km. *Population*: 128 million (1995 estimate). *Annual increase*: 3.1% (1980-91). *Crude Birth Rate*: 40.6 per thousand (1993). *Crude Death Rate*: 10.6 per thousand (1993). *Infant Mortality Rate*: 95 per thousand (1992). *GDP growth rate*: 5.7% ((1980-94). *Per capita income*: US$ 470 (1992). *Literacy rate*: 37% (1994 Govt estimate).

Geology and landscape

The landscape of Pakistan is one of extraordinary contrasts. To the N lies a mountainous region that features the greatest concentration of high peaks in the world, and the longest glaciers outside the polar regions; to the S is a vast river plain, with a catchment area of over 450,000 sq km. Yet were it not for the complex irrigation schemes that allow cultivation of large tracts in the E and S, 90% of Pakistan would be desert.

The physical geography of Pakistan falls into two major regions, each formed by distinct geomorphic processes: 1) The extensive flat plains of the Indus and its tributaries resulting from the deposition of sediments washed down from the Himalaya; 2) The mountains to the N and W produced by the action of the Indian plate that carries the ancient rocks of the sub-continent, subducting beneath the Eurasian landmass.

Indus Plains

The Indus Plains include most of the provinces of Punjab and Sind. They have been formed by the alluvium laid down by the **Indus** and its major tributaries. The Indus is one of the world's great rivers, stretching 2,880 km from its source at 5,180m in **Manasarovar Lake** in Tibet, to its mouth in the Arabian Sea. From its source, the river runs E-W cutting a deep gorge through the Himalaya and Karakoram ranges, before turning sharply S at Sazli. The Indus makes a tortuous journey through the dramatic gorges of Kohistan before emerging onto the Punjab plains at Attock, still 1,600 km from the sea.

The Indus is joined from the E by five major tributaries; the 'five waters' that give their name to the Punjab. These are the *Sutlej, Beas, Ravi, Chenab* and *Jhelum*, which join together at Panjnad and run together for 72 km before joining the Indus some 900 km from the sea. The natural drainage pattern of this river basin was deeply affected by the partition of the sub-continent at

independence, although the **Indus Waters Treaty** (see page 115) of 1960 successfully resolved the allocation of the waters between Pakistan and India. The most important tributary from the W is the *Kabul*, which joins the Indus just S of Tarbela. The seasonal discharge of the Indus and its tributaries varies greatly, between 25,000 cu secs at the minimum, and 350,000 cu secs at its maximum flow. A number of dams have been built so that stored water can be utilized when the flow is low. The dams also help to a certain extent in controlling flood waters.

The swelling of the Indus and its tributaries during the summer season, when snow-melt from the mountain sources to the N are at a peak, can lead to flooding. The situation can be compounded by monsoon rainfall and thunderstorms, and it is estimated that severe floods occur every 7-8 years. The flood action causes the river to divide, reforming in new beds across the plain. Fertile silts and coarse sands are spread by the river, building the Indus Plains

and giving them their agricultural importance. The gradient of the lower Indus Plains is very gentle, dropping less than 20 cm per km. As the Indus constantly loses water through evaporation and seepage, it is forced to progressively drop its load on the journey to the coast. This results in a network of ever-changing channels meandering through a changing pattern of sandbeds and salt marshes as it approaches the sea.

The Indus Plains can be divided into six main physiographic divisions. The **Active Flood Plains**, known locally as *bet*, are the narrow strips of land running along the side of the Indus and its tributaries. Varying in width between 3 km and 40 km, annual innundation provides rich alluvium, making them important agricultural lands. The **Old Flood Plains** constitute the main agricultural areas of Pakistan, and are located between the active flood plains and the uplands in the N, and at the interface of the *bet* and desert areas in the S. Alluvium deposits are renewed by

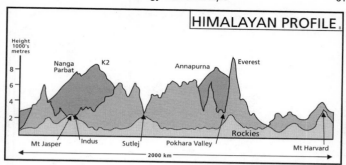

periodic flooding. Oxbow lakes, meander scars, old levees and salt lakes are all common features.

The Indus has a large and active delta at its mouth, constantly expanding and shifting its position. The **Deltaic Plains** are heavily scarred by past and present channels, with tidal channels disecting the extensive mud flats. The deposition of sediment is extending the delta out into the Arabian Sea; about 10 km this century alone.

To the W of the Indus, extensive **Piedmont Plains** have developed in the region between the river and the Sulaiman-Kirthar mountain chain that divides Sind from Baluchistan. These plains have been built on top of alluvial fans, formed from the silt, sand and gravel deposits brought down by small channels running off the mountains. Potentially rich for agriculture, extensive farming is constrained by the paucity of water.

A feature of the Upper Indus Valley are the **Alluvial Terraces**; deposits of 'old alluvium' in the interfluves between the major tributaries. A typical example is the Thal Desert, an alluvial terrace overlain with sand. Recent expansion of irrigation is transforming the area into agricultural land.

Finally, a large area of lower Pakistan is covered by **Rolling Sand Plains and Dunes**. The topography is greatly influenced by wind action, forming large sand plains interspersed with dunes. To the S the dunes are predominantly latitudinal, whereas those to the N are primarily transverse. The desert area has a number of regional names; Cholistan in Punjab, Pat in N Sind and Thar in S Sind. The desert merges imperceptibly across the international border with India to the E, into the Rajasthan Desert.

Mountainous regions

Large areas of Pakistan comprise of mountain systems and plateaux, and though there are great variations in height and extent, the origins of the building process are common to all. The dramatic slow motion collision between the Indian plate and the Eurasian landmass, a process which continues today, resulted in uplift that formed the major mountain chains of South Asia. The process of mountain building has been a relatively recent phenomenon on the geological time scale. Although the Karakoram range may have begun to form 100 million years ago, the core of the Himalayas date to about 35 million years ago, with two further major movements between 5 and 25 million years ago. Sub-Himalayan ranges such as the Siwaliks are even more recent. The rocks at the core of the Himalayas were formed under the intense pressure and heat of the mountain building process.

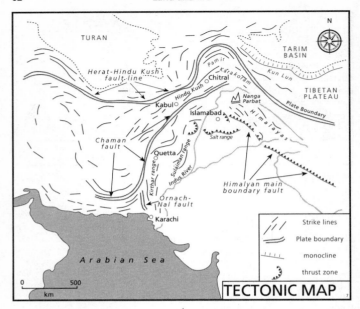

The mountain and plateaux regions of Pakistan can be divided into five main divisions: Mountainous North, Safed Koh and Wazirstan Hills, Suleiman and Kirthar Mountains, Baluchistan Plateau, Potwar Plateau and the Salt Range.

The **Mountainous North** extends across the whole of the Northern Areas, much of North West Frontier Province, and into parts of Punjab. The geological region extends across the international borders into Afghanistan, Tajikistan, China (including Tibet), India and Nepal, and includes most of the world's great mountain ranges. The westernmost extension of the *Greater Himalayas* is marked by the massive Nanga Parbat (8,125m), in the Northern Areas. The chain is dominated by high peaks, many over 4,500m. To the S are the *Lesser Himalayas*, a highly folded and faulted chain that includes Murree and the Galis, the Pir Panjal range in Kashmir,

and much of Hazara District. Heights vary from 1,800m to over 4,500m. The southernmost ranges of the Himalayas are the Siwaliks, or *Sub-Himalayas*. Rising to only 1,200m, they are deeply folded and faulted.

The dominant chain in the Mountainous North is the *Karakoram*, an awesome blend of high peaks, glaciers, plateaus, lakes and river valleys. The Karakoram range, and the various subranges that bifurcate from the main chain, rise to an average height of 6,100m, and include *K2* (8,611m), the world's second highest mountain. The Karakorams are also dominated by glaciers, with approximately double the ice coverage of the Himalayas, and 10 times the coverage of the Alps.

To the W of the Karakorams are the various ranges of the *Hindu Kush*, running E-W along Pakistan's northern borders, before turning NE-SW along the frontier with Afghanistan. The highest peak is *Tirich Mir* (7,690m), near to Chitral. The Hindu Kush are also noted for the number of passes connecting Pakistan to Afghanistan.

The **Safed Koh Ranges and Waziristan Hills** were formed by the same processes as the Mountainous North, but have been subject to later igneous activity. These ranges, rising to around 3,600m and 3,000m respectively, have played a significant role in the settlement pattern of South Asia. Although now forming a boundary between Pakistan and Afghanistan, the ease of access through the passes of the chain, such as the Khyber, has provided a natural route into South Asia for invading armies, traders, new religions and cultures. Further, some of the valleys created by rivers draining off these ranges, eg the Vale of Peshawar, have become the centres of major cultures.

Also formed by the Himalayan mountain building process, but extending N-S in a gently sweeping easterly arc, the **Suleiman-Kirthar Mountains** define the administrative border between Sind and Baluchistan. To the W lies the **Baluchistan Plateau**, an extensive area crossed by a number of low ranges with a number of important basins lying between the upland areas. The E of Baluchistan is occupied by the *Lasbela Plains*, with a narrow coastal plain referred to as the *Makran Coast* to the S.

Another important region is the **Potwar Plateau and the Salt Range** (see pages 264 and 256) in N Punjab. The Potwar Plateau is a highly weathered and eroded landscape, with the Soan River having cut deep ravines into the recently uplifted surface. The region is rich in some of South Asia's earliest settlement sites. The Salt Range, two low parallel lines of rugged hills, is also rich in Palaeolithic sites, and is an important salt mining centre.

Climate

There are three main climatic regimes in Pakistan, although each is modified by factors such as latitude and altitude. The climate over most of the country is predominantly dry, with less than 10% of the land area receiving more than 500 mm of rainfall a year. A narrow E-W belt of land from Lahore to Peshawar experiences a humid subtropical climate, where rainfall totals exceed 800 mm. To the N, the moderating effect of altitude produces a Highland climate, with little rainfall, and arctic temperatures at great heights.

NB For details of the best time to visit, see 'Information for visitors' and regional 'Introductions'.

Rainfall

Much of the southern region of Pakistan, including Sind, Baluchistan and S Punjab receives less than 250 mm per year, with many large areas receiving less than 125 mm. Parts of the central Northern Areas, in the rain shadow of the high mountain chains, also receive less than 125 mm annually, with most of the precipitation at the higher altitudes in the form of snow.

The two main sources of rainfall in Pakistan are the **monsoon**, and the **winter depressions**. Pakistan is at the NW limits of the monsoon, with over half the rainfall on the Indus Plains arriving in the three monsoon months of Jul-Sep. However, much of the rainfall has already been deposited over India, and the secondary monsoon winds that enter S Punjab and Sind have generally lost most of their moisture. The winter depressions, travelling E from the Mediterranean across Iran and Afghanistan, bring some rainfall to the the humid subtropical belt, hilly areas of NWFP and parts of N Baluchistan. The timings of these depressions, generally between Dec-Mar, are highly unpredictable.

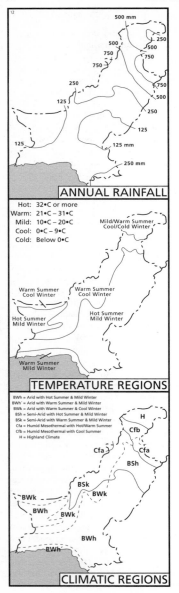

ANNUAL RAINFALL

Hot: 32•C or more
Warm: 21•C – 31•C
Mild: 10•C – 20•C
Cool: 0•C – 9•C
Cold: Below 0•C

Mild/Warm Summer
Cool/Cold Winter

Warm Summer
Cool Winter

Warm Summer
Cool Winter

Hot Summer
Mild Winter

Hot Summer
Mild Winter

Warm Summer
Mild Winter

TEMPERATURE REGIONS

BWh = Arid with Hot Summer & Mild Winter
BWh` = Arid with Warm Summer & Mild Winter
BWk = Arid with Warm Summer & Cool Winter
BSh = Semi-Arid with Hot Summer & Mild Winter
BSk = Semi-Arid with Warm Summer & Mild Winter
Cfa = Humid Mesothermal with Hot/Warm Summer
Cfb = Humid Mesothermal with Cool Summer
H = Highland Climate

H

Cfb

Cfa

Cfa

BSh

BSk

BWk

BWk

BWh

BWk

BWh

BWh

CLIMATIC REGIONS

A further source of rainfall is thunderstorms that often cause catastrophic flooding throughout the entire Indus Basin. These usually occur when the summer high pressure cell, stretching from the Sahara and across Arabia to Pakistan, is replaced by great moist monsoon air masses sweeping across the Arabian Sea.

Temperatures

Pakistan is a country that experiences great extremes of temperature, with figures varying sharply with latitude and altitude. The desert areas of Sind and Baluchistan experience some of the hottest temperatures on earth, with a shade temperature of 52.8°C being recorded at Jacobabad in Jun 1919. By contrast, temperatures of -30°C are not uncommon at altitude in the mountainous N. There can also be great diurnal (day/night) temperature ranges in many areas of the country.

Fazle Karim Khan (1991) identifies four main temperature regions in Pakistan. 1) Hot summer and mild winter: temperature of the hottest month 32°C+, winter temps 10-21°C. 2) Warm summer and mild winter: summer temps 21-32°C, winter temps 10-21°C. 3) Warm summer and cool winter: summer temps 21-32°C, coolest month 0-10°C. 4) Mild summer and cool/cold winter: summer temps 10-21°C and coolest month well below 0°C in some areas, 0-10°C in others.

Vegetation, soils and wildlife

Vegetation

There are around 5,700 different plant species in Pakistan, with 500 of them being listed as endangered. Many are of great value in medicinal terms. However, since the greater part of the country experiences a dry climate, vegetation cover is for the most part scarce. There are also three large desert areas in

Pakistan (Thar-Cholistan, Thal, Kharan), in addition to vast regions of the mountainous N that are under snow and ice, or above the tree-line (approximately 3,800m).

Although parts of Azad Kashmir, Kohistan, Swat Valley, Murree and the Galis, Chitral, Kaghan Valley and Hazara are heavily forested, less than 4% of the land area of Pakistan is under forest. (**NB** This figure excludes the Northern Areas). As in many other parts of the world, figures on forest cover, afforestation and regeneration are highly sensitive and subject to manipulation. Remarkably, current figures suggest that forest cover in Pakistan has actually doubled since Partition, despite the fact that deforestation is seen as a major threat in many areas. In 1995 the Federal Government unveiled an ambitious new campaign to double forest cover within the next generation.

There are seven forest types recognizable in Pakistan. **Alpine Forests** occur above the tree-line in parts of NWFP and the Northern Areas, although the severity of the environment means that they are not extensive. **Coniferous Forests** extend across parts of Baluchistan and NWFP, including Swat, Dir, Malakand, Kohistan and Hazara, plus Rawalpindi District of Punjab, and parts of the Northern Areas. They occur between 1,000 and 4,000m and are dominated by fir (*Abies* spp), spruce (*Picea morinda*), deodar (*Cedrus deodara*), kail (*Pinus excelsa*) and chir (*Pinus roxburghii*). Coniferous forests are often mixed with **deciduous** trees, including oaks (*Quercus*), maple (*Acer*), birch (*Betula*), poplar (*Populas*), walnut (*Juglans*) and juniper (*Juniperus*). Such forests are generally the key source of timber.

Sub-tropical Dry Forests occur in many of the foothill regions of Punjab and NWFP up to 1,000m, and provide mainly a supply of firewood. The key trees are phula (*Acacia modesta*), kao (*Olea cuspidata*) and the main deciduous trees mentioned above. In areas of Punjab and Sind, xerophytic scrubs such as *Acacia* spp are found as part of patchy **Tropical Thorn Forests**, whilst along the banks of the key rivers such as the Indus, there are narrow belts of **Riverain Forests**. The key species here are babul (*Acacia arabica*) and shisham (*Dalbergia sissoo*).

On the coasts, particularly at the Hub and Indus deltas, there are the ecologically important **Mangrove Forests**. These forests act as an interface between the land and the sea, moderating seawater incursions and controlling the overquick export of waste into the sea. These forests are ecologically very sensitive, and are greatly under threat due to over usage of the main species *Rhizophoras* in the charcoal industry.

Finally, there are a number of man-made **Irrigated Forests** in Pakistan, including South Asia's oldest at Chhanga Manga, 68 km SW of Lahore (see Longer excursions from Lahore). Many of these forests form part of national parks, although most are still farmed as sustainable sources of timber and firewood.

In addition to forest areas, there are a number of important **Wetlands** around Pakistan. Amongst the world's most productive environments, wetlands regulate flood levels, purify water, in addition to providing a habitat to many migratory birds. Haleji Lake, near to Thatta in Sind, has recorded as many as 222 different species of birds in the immediate environs.

Soils

The soils of Pakistan are derived primarily from alluvium (river-bourne silt) and weathering action on underlying rocks. The scarce vegetation cover results in soils which are generally rich in basic materials, but poor in organic matter. The topography of the country also has a great role to play, with the nature of the terrain in the mountainous N making it vulnerable to erosion.

Soil erosion is a major problem in Pakistan and is increasingly common in regions subject to deforestation and overgrazing. A further threat to agricultural productivity comes from the twin concerns of **waterlogging** and **salinisation**. These problems are particularly acute in large areas of Sind and Punjab that are irrigated by canals. Many of the canal irrigation schemes begun by the British in the 19th century, and continued ever since, were poorly planned, cutting across natural lines of drainage. As much as a third of irrigation water may be lost through seepage, particularly in schemes where canals are unlined. A further third may be lost through evaporation. Excess water percolating downwards can lead to a rise in the watertable, causing waterlogging. With high temperatures and low humidity causing extremely high rates of evaporation, the static water rapidly dries out leaving a layer of minerals and salts on the surface. The problem is so great in Pakistan that it is estimated that by the middle of the 1970s, over one-third of the irrigated land in Sind and Punjab was moderately to severely affected by waterlogging and salinisation.

Major programmes have been implemented by the Govt of Pakistan in order to combat this problem, including the **Salinity Control and Reclamation Projects** (SCARPS), but the problem is compounded by the fact that large areas of Sind are underlain by severely saline groundwater. The only solution is to drain away the water, at great cost to the programme.

Wildlife

Despite its often harsh environment, Pakistan is home to a surprisingly rich diversity of wildlife. Over 1,000 different species, comprising of 666 bird species, 178 mammal species, 176 reptile species and 16 amphibian species, are found in the country. Five out of six of the **Markhor** species (a type of goat) found in the world occur in Pakistan (the Chiltan, Kabul, Suleiman, Astor and Pir Panjal Markhor). **Wild sheep** species include the Afghan, Punjab and Ladakh Urial, as well as the famous Marco Polo (Great Pamir) Sheep and Blue Sheep (or Bharal). **Himalayan Ibex** and **Sind Ibex** (more correctly the Persian Wild Goat) are also found. Mammals such as the **Indus River Dolphin**, **Chiltan Markhor** and **Suleiman Markhor**, are unique to Pakistan. However, many animals and birds found in Pakistan, including the **Baluch** and **Himalayan Brown Bears**, **Snow Leopard**, and seven different species of **pheasant**, are either rare, seriously endangered or on the point of extinction. Others, such as the **One Horned Rhino** and **Black Buck**, have been completely eliminated from the country, although there are efforts to reintroduce these from remaining stocks elsewhere in the world.

Many migratory birds pass through Pakistan, flying along what is known as the **Indus Flyway** as they migrate from Central Asia to South Asia and East Africa. One of the most important of these is the **Houbara Bustard**, which breeds in Central Asia, mainly in the Kizil Kum Desert region SE of the Aral Sea, before migrating to Pakistan, Afghanistan, Iran and India for the winter. In Pakistan its main habitats are in Baluchistan, Punjab and Sind. Listed as an endangered species, the Houbara Bustard is under serious threat in Pakistan due to excessive hunting. Ironically Sakar Falcons, captured in Chitral (and themselves a threatened species) are used by visitors from the oil-rich Gulf States to hunt the bird. Many endangered duck species, including the **Marble Teal** and **White Headed Duck** also pass through. In Chitral migrating ducks have been hunted for centuries with local people going to great lengths to build artificial ponds alongside rivers in order to encourage the birds to land there.

THE INDUS RIVER DOLPHIN

The Indus River Dolphin or Blind Dolphin (*Platanistan minor*), known locally as *buhlan*, is a unique fresh-water dolphin found only in Pakistan. It is identical in appearance, and closely related to the Ganges Dolphin. Almost completely blind, this highly specialized mammal navigates and hunts in the heavily turbid and silt-laden alluvial waters of the Indus by echo-location, swimming on its side at great speed and snapping up fish in its beak-like jaws. They can be seen in groups at sunset, waiting by the nets of fishermen which are strung across the mouths of canals and by-rivers.

Once it was to be found throughout the Indus river system, from the foothills of the Karakoram and Himalayas down to the sea, and in its main tributaries, the Jhelum, Chenab, Ravi and Sutlej. However since the 1930s, the building of dams, barrages and headworks along these rivers, 18 in all within Pakistan, has restricted the dolphins and their habitat into a series of isolated stretches varying from 48 km to 306 km in length.

The dolphin, which is recognized internationally as an endangered species, was given full legal protection by the Sind Government in 1972. 2 years later the Indus Dolphin Reserve was established on the 170 km stretch of the Indus between the Gaddu and Sukkur Barrages in Sind. More than 400 dolphins, out of a total population of around 500, are restricted to this stretch. Here at least, their numbers appear to be increasing slowly, or at least stable. But numbers above Guddu Barrage, on the Indus as far as Jinnah Barrage and on the Chenab up to Panjnad headworks are critically low and declining. The populations on the Chenab above Panjnad and on the Sutlej above Sulaimanki became extinct in the 1970s. As well as being isolated into a number of sub-populations, the dolphins are still hunted in places, as well as being occasionally caught accidently in the nets of fishermen. The extensive irrigation systems associated with the various barrages and dams have also reduced water levels along the Indus significantly, especially during the low winter discharge months, further threatening the dolphins' habitat.

The apparent success of the Indus Dolphin Reserve in Sind is seen as an excellent example of what can be achieved given a comprehensive programme of conservation involving education and active enforcement. This underlines the need to take urgent action to protect the remaining threatened populations, particularly in Punjab. A nature reserve at Taunsa Barrage is a step in the right direction, but as always, the actual enforcement of protective measures is much harder than the establishing of nominal reserves and sanctuaries.

Conservation

Pakistan is a signatory to the Convention on Trade in Endangered Species (CITES), the Convention on Wetlands of International Importance (Ramsar) and the Convention on the Conservation of Migratory Species of Wild Animals (Bonn). It is also a member of the World Conservation Union (IUCN), World Wide Fund for Nature (WWF), and International Waterfowl and Wetland Research Bureau (WRB), all of which are active in Pakistan. There are a total of 11 National Parks; Kirthar in Sind; Darun, Hingol and Hazerganji Chiltan in Baluchistan; Lal Suhandra, Chinji and Margalla in Punjab; Chitral Gol and Ayubia in NWFP; Khunjerab in Northern Areas; and Matcharia in Azad Jammu and Kashmir. In addition there are more than 100 wildlife sanctuaries, wilderness parks and game reserves.

However, the establishment of National Parks and other protected areas often leads to a conflict of interests with local populations. The Khunjerab National Park in particular was the focus of bitter disputes between park authorities and local people, who resented the outright ban placed on their traditional grazing and hunting rights in the area. Initially the park was a failure, with people continuing to graze their livestock and hunt in the area. Indeed the population of Marco Polo Sheep fell from over 1,000 when the park was established in 1975 to less than 50 by the early 1990s. The experience demonstrated the importance of first gaining the active support and participation of local people. Central to this is the need to raise public awareness and to demonstrate tangible benefits of conservation strategies. The Western concept of protecting wildlife and its environments for largely aesthetic reasons has little relevance in a country where many people, particularly those most affected, are living close to subsistance level.

Subsequent intiatives have been more successful. In the Suleiman mountains of Baluchistan and NWFP, the extensively logged forests of Chilighoza Pine are being increasingly harvested instead for their Chilighoza nut (or pine kernel), which can earn a family around Rs 10,000 (US$330) in a season. In 1990 the people of Bar village N of Gilgit adopted a self-imposed ban on hunting the Himalayan Ibex in the region. As the Ibex population recovered, they were subsequently able to allow limited 'trophy hunting' of the animal, with each one earning as much as US$10,000. Projects to control overgrazing in the high pastures of upper Swat meanwhile have led to the complete recovery of depleted grassland within 3 years.

RELIGION

Contents

Islam   69
Non-Muslim minorities   74

The land which now constitutes Pakistan has a rich history of religions. It gave birth to Brahmanism, which later developed into Hinduism. It saw the flourishing of Buddhism in Gandhara and the establishment of the *Mahayana* school. Prior to the arrival of the British, the Sikhs established their powerful empire which centred on the Punjab.

Today, Pakistan is an Islamic state and 97% of the population are Muslim. Despite its monotheism, Islam displays a remarkable diversity within Pakistan, as well as having its own 'Asian' feel to it, distinctive in many ways from Islam in other parts of the world. This is a reflection of its diverse origins in the region, as well as the many different influences which acted on it.

The *Sufis*, responsible for spreading the faith in much of the country, have left their unique mark, particularly in Sind and southern Punjab. While the Arabs brought the first Islamic contact, it was the Ghaznavids who were responsible for establishing Islamic political power in the region. From the middle of the 13th century, when the Mongols crushed the Arab Caliphate, the Delhi Sultans were left on their own to exercise Islamic authority in the subcontinent, and the main influence came from Persia. Meanwhile, there was a constant process of assimilation and accommodation between the Muslim rulers and local peoples. While the Islamic elites who arrived from Iran or Turkey maintained 'pure' forms of Islam, isolated and less literate communities developed devotional and pietistic forms, incorporating many of their pre-Islamic beliefs, customs and practices. The caste systems for example, completely at variance with Muslim injunctions regarding discrimination, remain a fact of life even today in much of the country.

A number of other religions are also represented in Pakistan, albeit as small minorities; Christian, Hindu, Sikh and Parsee (Zoroastrian) communities are all to be found in different parts of the country.

Islam

Mohammad, the founder of the Islamic faith, was born around 570 AD in the city of **Mecca** in present day Saudi Arabia. His family were of noble descent, members of the house of **Hashim**, belonging to the **Abd Manaf** clan and part of the **Quraish** tribal confederacy of Mecca. The Abd Manaf clan had a semi-priestly status, being responsible for certain functions during the annual pilgrimage to the *Ka'ba* in Mecca (the Ka'ba, the cube shaped building to which Muslims face when praying, predates Islam; Muslims believe that it was established by Adam and revere it as a sanctury where closeness to God can be achieved).

At the age of 40 Mohammad received his first revelations of the *Qur'an* and began preaching his message. He encountered stiff opposition from the powerful Quaish leaders, the temple guardians and the rich traders, and was eventually forced to flee to **Medina**, known then as Yathrib (the famous *Hijra*, or 'flight', which marks the beginning of the Islamic calendar). There he established himself and achieved a position of power, fighting three major battles with the Meccans before finally returning there in triumph 2 years before his death in 632 AD.

In his lifetime he had become recognized as a prophet and founded the Islamic faith. Part of his success was in incorporating many aspects of the ancient Arabian religion, such as the pilgrimage to Ka'ba, as well as aspects of Judaism and Christianity. But his success was not purely in religious terms. He was also an accomplished statesman who laid the foundations for what would later become a great Islamic empire.

Islamic Sects

In the century following Mohammad's death, Islam divided into two major sects. Mohammad left no sons and therefore no obvious heir, and gave no instructions as to who should succeed him. There were two main contenders: **Abu Bakr**, the father of Mohammad's wife, and **Ali**, the husband of Mohammad's daughter Fatimah, and his cousin. In the event Abu Bakr assumed the title of *Caliph* (vice-regent). He died 2 years later in 634 AD and was succeeded by **Omar** who was killed in 644. **Uthman**, a member of the powerful **Umayyad** family, was chosen to succeed him, but proved to be a weak leader and was murdered in 656.

At this point the aggrieved Ali managed to assume the title of Caliph, thus ousting the Umayyads. However **Muawiya**, the governor of Syria and a member of the Umayyad family, soon rose up in revolt. He managed to gain the upper hand; in 661 Ali was murdered (by one of his own supporters) and Muawiya proclaimed himself Caliph. Ali's eldest son **Hassan** set up a rival Caliph in Iraq, but was soon persuaded to abdicate. However, the seeds of the schism in Islam had already been sown; between the Sunnis (those who accepted the legitimacy of the first three Caliphs) and the Shias (those who recognized only Ali as the first legitimate Caliph). Later, when Muawiya died in 680, Ali's second son **Hussain** attempted to revolt against the Umayyads, but was defeated and killed in 681 at Karbala, providing the Shias with their greatest martyr.

Followers of the **Sunni** sect, generally termed 'Orthodox', account for around 80% of Muslims in Pakistan (globally they represent a similar majority). They base their *Sunna* (path, or practice) on the 'Six Books' of traditions. They are organized into four orthodox schools or rites named after their founders, each having equal standing. The *Hanafi* is the most common in Pakistan, and the most moderate. The others are the *Shafii*, *Maliki* and *Hanbali*, the latter being the strictest. Many Muslims today prefer to avoid identification with a particular school, preferring to call themselves simply Sunni.

Followers of the **Shia** sect account for most of the remainder of Muslims in Pakistan. Those that can trace their descent from Hassan bear the title *Sharif*, and those that trace their descent from Hussain, the title *Sayyid*. However there are also many Sharif and Sayyid families in Pakistan who are Sunni. Both lineages hold a position of religious aristocracy in Islam. Aside from the dispute over the succession of Mohammad, Sunnis and Shias do not generally differ on fundamental issues since they draw from the same ultimate sources. However, there are important differences of interpretation which partly derive from the practice of *ijtihad* ('the exercise of independent judgement') amongst Shias, as oppose to *taqlid* (the following of ancient models) as adhered to by Sunnis. Thus Shias divest far more power in their *Imams*, accepting their role as an intermediary between God and man and basing their law and practice on the teachings of the Imams. (**NB** The term Imam is also used more generally by both Shias and Sunnis to refer to the prayer leader of a mosque.)

The majority of Shias are known as *Ithna asharis* or 'Twelvers', since they recognize a succession of 12 Imams.

They believe that the last Imam, who disappeared in 878 AD, is still alive and will reappear soon before the Day of Judgement as the *Mahdi* (One who is rightly guided) who will rule by divine right.

An offshoot of the Shias, and an important minority in Pakistan, are the **Ismailis**. The Ismailis reject the seventh Imam acknowledged by the Twelvers, recognising instead Ismail, the elder son of the sixth Imam. They are also sometimes referred to as *Sab'iya* or 'Seveners'. There was however much dispute amongst themselves as to who was in fact the seventh Imam. The Fatamid Ismailis of Egypt recognized a grandson of the sixth Imam and in turn gave rise to several schismatic offshoots, including the Nizari Ismailis found in Pakistan. The latter recognize the **Aga Khan** as their spiritual head and trace his descent directly to the Prophet Mohammad through his daughter Fatimah. The philosophy of the Ismailis is a largely esoteric one; their theology is based on a cyclical theory of history centred around the number seven, which is considered to be of enormous significance. They are less restrictive in their customs and practice, allowing much greater freedom to women. Likewise, prayers are not linked to a specific formula. The mosque is replaced by a *jamat khana* which also serves as a community centre. Within Pakistan they are found mostly in the Northern Areas and Chitral region, where the Aga Khan Foundation is very active in development work (see page 424).

Various other Muslim minorities are found in Pakistan. Notable amongst these are the **Ahmadis**, another offshoot of the Shias founded by **Mirza Ghulam Ahmad** in 1889. Ghulam Ahmad made a number of claims, including being a recipient of revelations, the Promised Messiah, the *Mahdi* and an *avatar* (incarnation) of Krishna. The Ahmadis believe that Jesus escaped from death on the cross and went to Srinigar where he died and was buried. They split into two main groups, the **Qadiyanis** who hold that Ghulam Ahmad was a Prophet, and the **Lahories** who believe that he was merely a *Mujaddid* or 'Renewer'. The headquarters of the Ahmadis is at Rabwah in Pakistan. Their official periodical, the Al-Fazl, is the oldest surviving in Pakistan. The Ahmadis were declared non-Muslims in Pakistan by General Zia in 1984, making them liable to prosecution (potentially under the blasphemy law which carries a mandatory death sentence) if they adopt any of the religious forms or observances of Islam. Thus they are forbidden to call their place of worship a 'masjid', to recite the formal call to prayers, or display the *Kalim-e-Tayyaba* (the formal declaration of the oneness of God). They have been increasingly persecuted in Pakistan in recent years and in 1994 Zia's ordinance against them was again upheld. There were even demands that a law be passed obliging them to alter the architecture of their places of worship so that they did not resemble mosques.

Another group, the **Zikris** (see page 209), are found mainly in the Makran region of Baluchistan. Like the Ahmadis, they have suffered persecution for their unorthodox beliefs. Attempts to have them declared non-Muslims however have so far been resisted. Their annual pilgrimage to the Koh-e-Murad near Turbat (which replaces the orthodox pilgrimage to Mecca) is the focus for frequent violent attacks and there have been repeated calls to have the Zikri *Baitullah* (house of God) situated there destroyed.

The **Nurbakshi** (see page 484), are a small minority found only in parts of Baltistan. They are closely linked with the Shias and suffer none of the persecution to which the Ahmadis and Zikris are subjected.

Sufism is the mystical aspect of Islam, often described as the "science of

THE FIVE PILLARS OF ISLAM

There are five practices or *Akran*, known as the Five Pillars of Islam, which are generally accepted as being obligatory to Muslims.

Shahada – the profession of faith ("There is no god but Allah..."), which also forms the basis of the call to prayer made by the *muezzin* of the mosque.

Salat – the ritual of prayers, carried out five times a day at prescribed times; in the early morning before the sun has risen above the horizon, in the early afternoon when the sun has passed its zenith, later when the sun is halfway towards setting, immediately after sunset and in the evening before retiring to bed. Prayers can be carried out anywhere, whether it be in a mosque or by the roadside, and involves facing towards the *Ka'ba* in Mecca and prostrating before God while reciting verses of the Koran.

Zakat – the compulsory payment of alms. In early times this was collected by officials of the Islamic state, and was devoted to the relief of the poor, debtors, aid to travellers and other charitable purposes. In many Muslim communities, the fulfilment of this religious obligation is nowadays left to the conscience of the individual. In Pakistan it was enshrined in law by Zia ul-Haq and is still levied today.

Sawm – the 30 days of fasting during the month of Ramadam, the ninth month of the Muslim lunar calendar. It is observed as a fast from sunrise to sunset each day by all Muslims, although there are provisions for special circumstances (see below).

Hajj – the pilgrimage to Mecca. Every Muslim, circumstances permitting, is obliged to perform this pilgrimage at least once in his lifetime and having accomplished it, may assume the title of *Hajji*. The pilgrimage to Mecca involves a massive logistical exercise in Pakistan, where around 90,000 people undertake it each year.

the heart". The word *Sufi* is most probably derived from the Arabic word *suf* meaning 'wool', a reference to the woolen garments worn by the early Sufis. The Sufis do not represent a seperate sect of Islam; rather they aspire to transcend sect, emphasising the importance of personal spiritual development, to be found only through the Koran. The Sufis were instrumental in spreading the Islamic faith in Pakistan, and numerous shrines dedicated to Sufi saints are to be found scattered throughout the country. These shrines still draw large numbers of pilgrims during the annual Urs, or death anniversary of the saint, a testimony to their popularity amongst the people.

Islamic beliefs and practices

The word Islam translates roughly as 'submission to God'. The two central tenets of Islam are embodied in the creed "There is no god but Allah and Mohammad is his Prophet" ("*Lah Illaha illa 'llah Mohammad Rasulu 'llah*") which affirms the belief in the oneness of God and recognizes Mohammad as the divinely appointed messenger of God.

The *Qur'an* (generally referred to as the Koran in English) is Islam's holiest book. The word translates literally as 'recitation' and unlike the Bible, is considered to be the *uncreated* (ie direct) word of God, as revealed to Mohammad through *Jibril* (the angel Gabriel). The text consists of 114 chapters, each known as a *sura*. Each sura is classified as Meccan or Medinan, according to whether it was revealed to Mohammad in Mecca or Medina. Most of the text is written in a kind of rhymed prose known as *saj*, and is considered by Muslims to be inimitable. Each chapter of the Koran

JIHAD – THE SIXTH PILLAR?

Jihad, literally 'holy war' is considered by some Muslims to constitute the sixth pillar of Islam, although it has never been officially elevated to this status. The concept of jihad was the basis for the early expansion of Islam and was carried out very much in the literal sense of the word. A similar concept underpinned the Crusades of Europe's Christians. There are many contemporary examples of jihad. The Afghan guerrillas fighting against Soviet occupation called themselves *Mujahideen*, ie those who wage jihad against the enemies of Islam. Other examples are more controversial. The current situation in Indian held Kashmir is often characterized as a jihad against Hindu domination, while Saddam Hussein, following his invasion of Kuwait, tried to rally support in the ensuing Gulf War by casting it as as a jihad against the evil designs of American infidels.

Many of the attitudes surrounding western perceptions of Islam are based on fears as to the wider implications of the concept. On the other hand, the word actually derives from an Arabic root meaning basically 'to strive', and many Muslims emphasize a less literal interpretation in terms of a personal spiritual striving against sin to attain greater closeness to God.

begins with the words *"Bismillah al-Rahman al-Rahim"* ("In the name of Allah, the Merciful, the Compassionate"), an invocation which can also be heard being uttered by Muslims in numerous everyday situations; when boarding a bus or before eating food for example.

In addition to the Qur'an, there is the *Hadith* body of literature, a record of the sayings and doings of Mohammad and his followers, which forms the basis of Islamic laws (*Shariat*), and precepts. Unlike the Qur'an, the Hadiths are recognized to have been written by men, and are therefore potentially flawed and open to interpretation. Thus they are commonly classified into four major categories according to their trustworthiness; *Sahih* (sound, true, authentic), *Hasan* (fair, good), *Da'if* (weak) and *Saqim* (infirm). The two most revered compilations of Hadiths are those of *al-Bukhari* and *Muslim*. It is in the interpretation of the Hadiths that most of the controversy surrounding certain Islamic laws and their application originates.

While Mohammad is recognized as the founder of the Islamic faith and the principle messenger of God, Muslims also regard him as having been the last in a long line of Prophets, starting with Adam and including both Moses and Jesus. They do not however accept Jesus as the son of God, but simply another of God's Prophets. Both Jews and Christians are considered *Ahl-e-Kitab* ('People of the Book'), the Torah and the Gospels being completed in Islamic belief by the Qur'an.

Nearly all Muslims accept six basic articles of the Islamic faith; belief in one God; in his angels; in his revealed books; in his Apostles; in the Resurrection and Day of Judgement; and in his predestination of good and evil. Heaven is portreyed in Muslim belief as a Paradise filled with sensuous delights and pleasures. The idea of heaven as paradise predates Islam. Alexander the Great is believed to have brought the word into Greek from Persia, where he used it to describe the walled Persian gardens that were found even before the birth of Christ. Hell on the other hand is portreyed as a place of eternal terror and torture, which is the certain fate of all who deny the unity of God.

Islam has no ordained priesthood or clergy. The authority of religious scholars, learned men, Imams, judges etc (referred to collectively as the *Ulema* and individually as *Mullahs* in Pakistan), derives from their authority to interpret the scriptures, rather than from any defined status within the Islamic community. Many Muslims in Pakistan complain that the growing influence of Mullahs interferes with the direct, personal relationship between man and God which Mohammad originally espoused (and was indeed one of the reasons he was driven from Mecca, as it threatened the priveliged position of the temple priests).

The Islamic Calendar

The Islamic calendar begins on 16 July 622 AD, the date of the *Hijra* ('flight' or 'migration') of the Prophet Mohammad from Mecca to Medina in modern Saudi Arabia, which is denoted as 1 AH (Anno Hegirae or year of the Hegira). The Islamic or *Hijri* calender is lunar rather than solar, each year having 354 or 355 days, meaning that annual festivals do not occur on the same day each year, according to the Gregorian calender. The 12 lunar months of the Islamic calander, alternating between 29 and 30 days, are; *Muharram, Safar, Rabi-ul-Awwal, Rabi-ul-Sani, Jumada-ul-Awwal, Jumada-ul-Sani, Rajab, Shaban, Ramadan, Shawwal, Ziquad and Zilhaj.*

To convert a date in the Hijra calender to the Christian date, express the former in years and decimals of a year, multiply by 0.970225, add 621.54 and the total will correspond exactly with the Christian year.

Islamic festivals

New Year 1st Muharram. The first 10 days of the year are regarded as holy, especially the 10th.

Ashoura 9th and 10th Muharram. Anniversary of the killing of Hussain, grandson of the Prophet Mohammad, commemorated by Shi'a Muslims. **NB** Muharram is observed each year by small communities of Shi'a Muslims scattered around Pakistan. As well as involving highly charged processions in which people flagellate themselves with chains and flails to express their mourning for Hussain's death, the festival has also in the past been the focus for violent clashes between Shia and Sunni Muslims. Ashoura also celebrates the meeting of Adam and Eve after leaving Paradise, and the end of the Flood.

Mouloud Birth of Mohammad. 12th Rabi-ul-Awwal.

Leilat al-Meiraj Ascension of Mohammad. 27th Rajab.

Ramadan (or Ramazan) Muslim month of fasting; 21st Ramadan is the *Shab-e-Qadr* or 'Night of Prayer'.

Eid ul-Fitr Literally 'the small feast'. 3 days of celebrations, beginning 1st Shawwal, to mark the end of Ramadan.

Eid ul-Ajha Literally 'the great feast' or 'feast of the sacrafice'. 4 days beginning on 10th Zilhaj. The principal Islamic festival, commemorating Abraham's sacrafice of his son Ismail, and coinciding with the pilgrimage to Mecca. Marked by the sacrifice of a sheep, by feasting and by donations to the poor.

NB For the dates of Islamic festivals, and other holidays, see under Information for visitors.

Non-Muslim minorities

The **Christian** community in Pakistan represents the largest non-Muslim minority, accounting for around 1.6% of the population and numbering nearly 2 million. The majority are found in Punjab, in the NE of the province centred around Lahore, Sheikhupura, Gujranwala and Sialkot. They are divided roughly 50-50 between the Church of Pakistan, which represents an amalgamation of the various Protestant groups, and Catholics, for whom Pakistan represents an archdiocese. **Hindus** are the next largest minority, numbering a little over 1 million, concentrated mainly in Sind, in the E around Tharparkar,

TRAVELLING DURING RAMADAN

The holy month of Ramadan (also referred to as Ramazan in Pakistan) is perhaps the most important in the Islamic calender, and certainly the one period of the year when everyday life is most dramatically affected. All Muslims are required to observe a total fast (which includes liquids and also smoking) between the hours of sunset and sunrise. Exceptions are made for the sick (or very elderly), pregnant women, travellers and young children.

From the point of view of the tourist travelling in Pakistan, it is important to bear in mind the implications of this. Some people advise against visiting Pakistan during Ramadan. Such advice is really overstating the case (although if you are coming specifically for business it may be worth avoiding since offices generally close by midday and significantly less gets done). To begin with, for the next 10 years or so Ramadam falls during the winter months when days are shorter and cooler, making it much less of an ordeal. In the main cities it is always possible to obtain food at any time of day from the larger hotels and restaurants (Chinese restaurants are usually a good bet). Even in smaller towns, many restaurants are happy to serve non-Muslims, who are after all exempt, usually discreetly at the back of the dining hall. However bear in mind that in remote areas smaller hotels sometimes close during Ramadan. Many bus and railway stations provide special facilities in deference to the exemption of travellers. It is always possible to buy fruit from the markets and biscuits, cakes etc from bakeries to take back to your hotel room.

Although it can certainly be more demanding travelling in Pakistan during Ramadan, there are also advantages. For non-smokers, bus and train journeys suddenly become far more pleasant. While tempers can sometimes begin to fray towards the end of the day, the actual breaking of the fast after sunset, which is marked by a snack called *Iftar* (several large meals follow on) is always a warm and friendly moment, with people invariably inviting you to share in their food. Likewise, the end of Ramadan, marked by *Eid-ul-Fitr*, is an occasion for huge celebrations and feasting characterized by outpourings of generosity and goodwill.

Sanghar, Badin and Hyderabad. Karachi also has a number of prominent Hindu temples.

Both Christians and Hindus suffer considerable discrimination, in the latter case aggravated by incidents such as at Ayodhya in India, and the growing atmosphere of animosity between Hindus and Muslims over Kashmir. Human rights groups reported numerous cases of girls, particularly Hindus, being kidnapped, forced to 'convert' to Islam and then married off to Muslims. There is also increasing evidence that Hindus have begun to sell off their properties in Pakistan and migrate to India.

Tiny communities of **Parsees**, descendents of the **Zoroastrians**, are found in Lahore and Karachi where, as in India, they have established themselves very successfully in the business community.

CULTURE

CONTENTS

People and language 76
Architecture 78
Art 79
Literature 80
Music, songs and dance 80
Handicrafts 81

People and language

From the earliest beginings of history, this part of the subcontinent has been a zone of contact. As such, it is not surprising that today there is an enormous diversity of peoples, the result of centuries of new settlement that came with the repeated waves of migrations and invasions, as well as the intermingling of these new arrivals with indigenous populations. Most of the ethnic groups found in Pakistan are descendents of the Aryans, who spread into the region from the NW. This is reflected also in the languages spoken in the country, the majority of which belong to the Aryan branch Indo-European group of languages. These are divided into three further groupings under the Aryan branch; Iranian (Baluchi, Pashto), Dardic (Khowar, Shina, Kohistani, Kashmiri) and Indo-Aryan (Punjabi, Seraiki, Sindhi, Urdu).

Urdu, the official language of Pakistan, was not widely spoken (except amongst the urban Muslim elites) anywhere in the country at Independence. Indeed, it was adopted primarily because of its neutral status in a country where each region had its own dominant languages. Urdu first developed as the common language of the Mughal courts, blending the Persian of the rulers with the local languages of N India. In its spoken form it closely resembles Hindi, the national language of India, though with a greater emphasis on words with Persian and Arabic, as oppose to Sanskrit, roots. The Urdu script in contrast is a distinctive modification of the Arabic script and wholly different from the Sanskrit-based Devanagari of Hindi. Originally, the two languages were identical (referred to as Hindustani by the British), and it was only in the 19th century that they began to diverge along religious lines. Today, Urdu is most widely spoken as a first language in Sind, amongst the **Mohajirs** (migrants) who came from India at Partition. Nationally, it is only spoken in around 8% of households, although it is also widely spoken as a second language throughout Pakistan.

The **Punjabis**, a blend of Aryan and Indian stock, are by far the largest single group, accounting for over half of Pakistan's total population. They dominate public life at a national level, with a disproportionate representation in government, the civil service and army, even given their majority status. They also consider themselves to be the 'cultural heart' of Pakistan; as well as possessing most of the great monuments of the Mughal era, the provincial capital Lahore is one of the main intellectual centres of the country. Not surprisingly, their dominant position is often a source of resentment amongst other groups. Their language, **Punjabi**, is also numerically the most important in Pakistan, being spoken in around 48% of households. There are a variety of dialects and, as one would expect, it is spoken mainly in Punjab province, representing the first language of around 80% of households. There are also significant minorities of Punjabi speakers in Sind, and smaller ones in NWFP and Baluchistan.

The **Seraikis** are an important minority in Punjab, and are also found in adjoining parts of Sind, Baluchistan and NWFP. Their language, **Seraiki**, is spoken by around 15% of households according to the 1981 census, although the true number is disputed. Punjabis generally tend to emphasize the close links with Punjabi, although it also has considerable affinity with the Sindhi language. Seraiki speakers themselves emphasize the uniqueness of both their language and culture. They have campaigned hard for their own province, arguing that they are discriminated against by the majority Punjabis, and in the other provinces where they live. Speakers of **Hindko**, a language which is sometimes grouped together with Seraiki, are found primarily in the Mansehra and Abbottabad districts of NWFP. They are more closely related to Punjabis both culturally and linguistically, with speakers of the two languages being able to understand each other easily.

The next largest group are the **Pathans**, who represent the majority in NWFP and roughly half the population of Baluchistan, where they are concentrated in the N of the province. Fiercely independent and more obviously Aryan in descent with their often fair complexions and green or blue eyes, the Pathans are a formidable people whose social structure is deeply tribal in nature. As an ethnic group, they extend beyond the political boundries of Pakistan, forming an important minority in Afghanistan also (the present border between the two countries was a highly artificial one created by the British and based on strategic rather than cultural considerations). Their language, **Pashto**, represents the first language of around 13% of households nationally. It has numerous dialects, reflecting the fragmented nature of their tribal society.

The **Sindhis** represent a similar percentage of the population as the Pathans. Their language, **Sindhi**, is spoken by around 12% of households nationally and by over half in Sind province. There are many different dialects, including *Vicholi*, the most important; *Lar*, spoken in lower Sind; *Lassi*, spoken mostly in Lasbela district of Baluchistan; and *Thari*, spoken in the Thar desert regions of eastern Sind. The exact origins of the Sindhis are uncertain, although it is clear that as an ethnic group they are the result of centuries of diverse influences, a fact borne out by the diverse roots of their language and indeed the history of the region.

The **Baluch** are another of Pakistan's great tribal societies and, like the Pathans, as an ethnic group they extend far beyond the boundries of Pakistan, in this case encompassing Iran as well as Afghanistan. Their language, **Baluchi**, is the second main language of Baluchistan (after Pashto), being spoken by around 36% of households, the majority being in the southern half of the province, where the Baluch tribes dominate. There are also significant minorities of Baluchi speakers in Sind. Nationally it is the first language of only 3% of households, a reflection mostly of the very low population densities found in this vast province. The Iranian (Persian) influence on Baluchi language is strong, and increases in the dialects spoken to the W. This is often cited as evidence of the Persian origins of the Baluch, although according to their own legends, they are descended from tribes which migrated from present-day Syria. Their nomadic origins are certain; the word 'Baluch' translates literally as 'wanderer'.

The **Brahui** are the third main group found in Baluchistan. Their origins are unclear and the subject of much debate. Their language, **Brahui**, is spoken by just over 20% of households in Baluchistan. It is amongst the very few languages of Pakistan not apparently belonging to the Indo-European group, being generally identified instead with the Dravidian languages of S India. It has however absorbed much of the vocabulary of the Iranian and Indo-Aryan language groups surrounding it. The apparent Dravidian roots of the Brahui language seems to suggest that they represent a remnant of the indigenous Dravidian population which once occupied most of South Asia before being pushed S by successive waves of Ayrans arriving from the NW. This is however disputed by some scholars (particularly Baluch and Brahui), who argue that they are in fact one of the Baluch tribes which migrated from Syria.

The mountainous N of Pakistan displays an enormous diversity of peoples and languages, reflecting the influence of centuries of migration trade along the Silk Routes. Many of the languages of the region are generally identified as belonging to the Dardic group (see above), a blend of indigenous languages with those of the Aryans. **Wakhi**, spoken in upper Hunza, is generally classified as being of the Iranian branch. **Burushaski** however, spoken in central Hunza, defies any such classification and its roots have not been identified. **Balti** meanwhile, spoken in Baltistan, is closely linked with Tibetan.

Architecture

The major styles of monumental architecture found in Pakistan clearly trace the history of the region and its major civilizations, as well as illustrating the many external influences. The great **Indus Valley Civilization** cities of Moenjo Daro and Harappa provide the earliest examples, with their carefully organized layout and clearly defined functional zones around the main citidels.

The excavated remains of the **Gandharan** civilization at Taxila and elsewhere show the succession of Persian, Greek, Central Asian and Indian influences that came with the Greeks (Hellenistic and Bactrian), Mauryans, Scythians, Parthians and Kushans. The

architecture here also demonstrates the fundamental importance of religion, in this case Buddhist, in shaping its forms; remains of the distinctive Stupas of the Buddhists can still be found spread across the Peshawar and lower Swat valleys.

Evidence of the period of Hindu rule in the region can still be seen in the forts and temple remains of the **Hindu Shahis** to be found in the Salt Range, the hills around Dera Ismail Khan and in the lower Swat valley. The styles demonstrate a strong Kashmiri influence as well as replicating the mediaeval architecture of NW India. However, many of the Hindu temples (most of them derelict) date from the 19th century.

The early Arab invaders left their mark on Sind and southern Punjab, and represent the first evidence of the enormous **Islamic** influence on the architecture of Pakistan. They were followed by the Ghaznavids, who arrived from the NW. The magnificent tombs at Multan and Uch Sharif, dating from the period of the Delhi Sultanate which followed, bear witness to the growth of Muslim political power in the region, while the numerous Sufi shrines of Sind and southern Punjab demonstrate the diversity of Islamic influences on the region. The striking Chaukundi Tombs and the massive necropolis of Makli Hill, both in lower Sind, display a remarkable independence from contemporary styles in the region, borrowing more from Rajput and Gujerati traditions than from Persian forms, particularly in the stone structures of the Chaukundi Tombs.

However the most prominent flowering of Islamic architecture in Pakistan dates from the **Mughal** period. It was during this period that the great monuments of Lahore such as Akbar's Fort, the Badshahi Mosque, Jehangir's Tomb and Shalimar Gardens, as well as those of Peshawar such as the Mahabat Khan Mosque, were built and subsequently embellished. Other impressive examples of

Mughal architecture include the massive Rohtas Fort near Jhelum and Attock Fort between Islamabad and Peshawar. **Sikh** architecture meanwhile was based almost entirely on that of the Mughals, although they greatly embellished and adapted the original styles to produce their own distinctive forms. The best known examples are the *samadhs* (funerary memorials) of Guru Arjun Dev and Maharaja Ranjit Singh in Lahore. In some cases, such as the Gurdwara Damdama in Gujranwala, the characteristic Islamic dome is replaced by a tall *sikhara* tower, reflecting the Hindu influence in Sikhism.

The **British** also left a lasting and prominent influence, particularly in the cantonments which they built alongside so many of Pakistan's cities. These existed as entirely separate and self contained areas with wide, spacious boulevards and buildings which generally blended Gothic and Mughal styles to produce some striking pieces of architecture, most noticeably in Lahore and Peshawar.

Modern architecture in Pakistan has tended to rely heavily on foreign architects and be driven by a desire to impress, often seemingly by resorting to designs on a huge scale. It encompasses the extremely ugly, the self-consciously bold, the blatently inappropriate and the inspired. The most prominent examples of modern architecture can be found in the planned capital Islamabad, which in parts succeeds very well in achieving a combination of modern and Islamic styles.

The vernacular traditions represent another important aspect of architecture in Pakistan. These display a diversity as great as the cultural diversity of the country and in terms of design and the building materials used, strongly reflect the social and physical environments in which they have developed. Rural architecture is determined primarily by the availability of building materials; throughout the Indus plains the alluvial soils and clays are used to make sun-dried bricks, often plastered over with mud to give villages and houses a characteristic moulded earth style.

The the fortified stone and mud-built compounds of the Pathans found in the tribal areas around Peshawar evolved in response to the need for defence, the requirements of privacy within family and clan units, and the scarcity of timber for building. Those of northern and central Baluchistan show a similar pattern, though with greater emphasis on mud and straw construction and local stylistic differences.

Further S, and in much of Sind, the scrub vegetation is utilized in wicker fencing and thatching. Many of the houses have distinctive wind catchers built into the roofs to funnel cooling breezes inside. In the valleys N of Peshawar and Islamabad there are rich pine forests, and timber forms a major component of buildings. The Swat valley has developed the richest timber building traditions, with intricately carved decorations to both houses and mosques. Throughout the mountainous N, houses are built around the central fireplace to maximize warmth during the winter.

Art

Early painting in Pakistan was patronized almost exclusively by the Mughals, with their famous minatures depicting scenes of court life, romance and legends. The best sculpture of the region meanwhile emerged during the Gandharan period, displaying an unique fusion of Graeco-Roman and Indian styles. However in modern Pakistan, painting in particular has emerged as an important art form with many excellent artists developing their own unique 'Pakistani' forms and styles. Each of the provincial capitals have a number of art galleries where contemporary works can be seen; regional newspapers give details of the exhibitions and shows.

Literature

There is evidence of a type of pictographic writing from the Indus Valley Civilization, although it has never been deciphered. The Aryan invaders who followed developed a collection of hymns to direct priests in the worship and sacrifices central to their religion. These developed into the **Rig Veda**, the most famous of the Sanskrit Vedas and the forerunner of the great Hindu epics such as the Mahabharata and Ramayana. Like the Vedas, the early literature of Pakistan was essentially sacred in nature. And like the Vedas, it was initially memorized and passed down from generation to generation orally, only being committed to writing later, in some cases not until the 18th and 19th centuries.

The majority of Pakistan's surviving early literature dates from after the arrival of Islam. The Sufis were particularly fond of music and poetry as a medium for their message. The Sufi poet **Kabir** is well known for his treatise attempting to reconcile Hinduism and Islam. Later Sufi poets worked in the regional languages; just a few examples of those whose works still survive today include the Pashto poet **Khushal Khattak Khan** in NWFP, **Abdul Latif Shah** in Sind, **Ghulam Farid** in Punjab and **Mast Tawakali** in Baluchistan. Under the Delhi Sultans, Islamic literature of Persian and Central Asian origin began to be patronized and found new expression within the region. As well as purely sacred literature, the Muslims developed a new emphasis on scholarly literature, particularly in the fields of maths, science, medicine, astronomy and history. Each of the provinces meanwhile developed their own unique literary traditions, expressed in the various regional languages and often centred around ballads and poems recounting the deeds of specific tribes and their genealogies. Many of these have subsequently proved vital in the reconstruction of history at a local level. However, religion and philosophy always remained amongst the most important themes, as did the influence of Sufism. The 17th century saw the birth Sikh holy literature in the **Adi Granth** of Sikhism's founder Guru Nanak. The most respected poet nationally is undoubtedly **Mohammad Iqbal**; his poetry is considered by many to be amongst the finest examples of Urdu literature, while his political works – most notably his espousal of the 'two-nation theory' – formed an integral part of the move toward a separate Islamic state.

Literature continues to be of major importance in modern day Pakistan. There is a wealth of novels, short stories and poetry in Urdu and Punjabi in particular, many of which have been translated into English, and which provide an excellent insight into the psyche of the country. Pakistan has a prolific publishing industry, and in addition to fictional works, there is a bewildering array of books on all subjects. Many are admittedly of variable quality, and those on history are often hopelessly subjective, but there are also some excellent works to be found, and at far lower prices than in the West.

Music, songs and dance

The origins of music in South Asia are often traced to the hymns and chanting of the Rig Veda. These were later supplemented by the *Sama Veda*, or Veda of melodies, and there followed a process of embellishment and refinement; originally it is thought that all the melodies created in the Sama Veda consisted of just three notes, sung in strictly descending order. The religious music of the temples however was restricted to the high caste Brahmins and therefore excluded the vast majority of people, with the result that parallel folk traditions of music developed amongst the common people.

Around the 13th century, the Muslim influence began to make itself felt in the sphere of music. This influence is generally attributed to **Amir Khusrau** who brought with him from Persia what is known as the **Persian Muqaam System**. The 'Hindustani' style of music subsequently developed in N India, influenced strongly by the Sufis, who blended the distinctive folk melodies of the region and their own Persian and Arabic traditions. It was during the Mughal period, under the reign of Akbar, that the classical (Hindustani) music of N India reached its peak, and it is those traditions which form the basis of Pakistan's classical music. Many of the instruments used in Pakistan are identical, or closely related, to those found in India; the *tabla* (small drums, believed to have been introduced by Amir Khasrau), the long-necked *sitar* and related *sarod*, the *sarangi* (a type of violin), the *shenai* (similar to a flute or oboe) and the *tambura* (a harmonium which was introduced later from the West and is now used extensively throughout the sub-continent). Likewise the structure of melodies is based on the *raga*, a framework within which musicians elaborate through improvisation.

Musical ragas provide the basis of both devotional and folk songs. The distinction between song and poetry is anyway a somewhat arbitary one; in Pakistan it is all the more so given that most poetry is freely expressed both to music and in spoken form. Thus the *Ghazal* is basically Urdu poetry sung to music. It first developed in the Mughal courts as a form of light entertainment, although it was subsequently refined into a high art form. During the 1930s and 40s, it was used extensively in films. Within Pakistan it is perhaps the most

popular form of traditional singing. Some of the best known exponents of the art include Mehdi Hasan, Iqbal Bano, Ghulam Ali, Farida Khanum and Abida Parveen. *Tappa*, meaning literally 'stage' or 'halting place' developed amongst the camel traders and the songs are generally divided into four stages, usually recounting a popular love story. It is performed all over Punjab, and in part of NWFP, being sung in Punjabi, Seraiki and Hindko. There are numerous other regional traditions in folk music, and as many famous exponents of the various traditions.

Of the devotional forms of singing, perhaps the best known is the *Qawwali*, generally attributed to the great Sufi poet **Abdul Latif Shah**, who used the form to express his *surs* (religious truths) in musical form. Qawwali is usually sung by a group of up to 12 people with one lead singer. It begins in a slow and measured style, gradually building up to a climax. There are many well known performers of Qawwali, perhaps the most prominent of them being Nusrat Ali Fateh Khan, who has toured extensively in the West in recent years. There are various other branches of Sufi devotional singing. *Vayee* is very close in form to the Qawwali. *Kafi* is generally classified as either 'folk' or 'classical', the former being simpler and in some opinions purer while the latter is far more complex. One of the best known exponents of Kafi was the late Ustad Manzoor Ali Khan. Today his one time students Mohammad Yousif and Abida Parveen keep the form alive. In *Sadarangi* the verses of Sufi poets are sung as ballads, the words of the 'story' conforming to a strict rhythm.

Handicrafts

There is an enormous variety of handicrafts available in Pakistan, reflecting the diversity of cultural traditions. The majority remain of utilitarian importance to local people, not simply aesthetically pleasing items. Some of the workmanship is of extremely high quality, as well as generally being very competitively priced.

Carpets are by far the most important in economic terms, making a significant contribution to export earnings. They are generally handwoven and handknotted and made of wool, silk or a mixture of the two. The main centres of carpet making are around Karachi, Multan, Quetta, Lahore, Faisalabad, Muzaffarabad and Peshawar. Best known amongst the indigenous designs found in Pakistan are those of Baluchistan and lower Sind. The majority of the other designs are borrowed and adapted from other major carpet producing countries such as Iran, Afghanistan and Turkey.

Textiles are found throughout the country and display a huge variety of designs and techniques. *Khaddar* is the simplest cotton weave, used mostly in the traditional shalwar kameez. The *Lungi* is a draped cloth used in NWFP as a turban, and in Sind also as a bridegroom's sash and scarf. The standard pattern is the *charkhana*, made up of small squares. Some of the best examples can be found in Multan. *Sussi* is another popular cotton weave with bright multi-coloured striped patterns. It is found primarily in Sind. *Khes* is a patterned and bound double weave cloth used all over Pakistan for bedcovers and sometimes as shawls. *Bandhni* or *Chunri* is the distinctive tie-dye decoration of cloth, traditionally used by the women of Sind and Cholistan on *dupattas* (long scarves). The most popular form is a pattern of small dots arranged in geometrical designs. In addition to the woven designs, block printing is a popular form, with the *Ajrak* designs of Sind generally considered amongst the best. Designs are invariably brightly coloured, with a traditional emphasis on blues (derived

from the indigo plant) and also reds. The traditional designs include the *kakkar* (cloud), *charkha* (spinning wheel) and *badaam* (almond). *Patti* is a thick woollen cloth usually in a trill or herringbone weave, typically found in the Swat, Chitral and Gilgit areas. Azad Kashmir is famous for its fine *Pashmina* woollen shawls. *Rilli* combines various decorative techniques such as printing, painting, applique and embroidery to produce colourful patchwork quilts.

Embroidery has developed to a fine art, with distinctive regional designs and patterns. The Sindhi *Gajh* is a lavishly embroidered wedding shirt incorporating traditional mirror work, worn by brides. The *Pushk* is found mostly in Baluchistan, with the most intricate examples coming from the Makran coastal region. It is characterized by matching embroidered cuffs and a pouch called a *pudo* in the centre of the lower half of the front of the shirt. *Phulkari*, literally meaning 'flowering', is found all over Punjab, and in the Swat valley and Hazara districts of NWFP. Traditionally, silk thread is used on plain Khaddar cloth. The floral patterns suggested in the name are usually abstracted into geometric motifs, although in Punjab the floral emphasis is retained to a greater extent. Whereas plain areas are usually left, the *bagh* (garden) design involves the entire surface of the cloth being covered in intricate stitching. The gold or silver wire embroidery work on wedding suit and ceremonial clothes is known as *Zari* and probably originated in Mughal times. In the N, the *chunghas* (loose cloaks) of Patti cloth found in Swat, Gilgit and Chitral are often beautifully embroidered around the collars, lapels and cuffs.

Leatherwork is an important craft in Pakistan. Traditionally perhaps the most important product was the leather *mashk* or water bag. Today the main products include items such as jackets, handbags, belts, shoes and sandals.

Shoes and sandals are widely available with each province having its own distinctive designs. Handbags and leather jackets are made to very high standard for export and can be bought very cheaply within Pakistan. There is also an important tradition of leather bookbinding, often intricately decorated and embossed, in centres such as Lahore, Peshawar and Hyderabad.

Jewellery Gold and silver-smiths and jewellers constitute one of the largest communities of craftsmen in Pakistan. Most distinctive is the chunky silver tribal jewellery of Sind, Baluchistan and NWFP. Much of the gold and silver jewellery made and sold in the cities however is intricately fashioned and very delicate. Peshawar's Andarshah bazaar is perhaps the most dazzling place to look for jewellery, although even the smallest towns will have a jeweller where one can see work in progress. Sind, Punjab and Baluchistan are famous for their enamelled silver and for gold and silver inlaid with semi-precious stones. In Baluchistan, NWFP and the Nothern Areas it is possible to find beautiful items of lapis lazuli jewellery, much of it originating from Afghanistan.

Ceramics Clay and terracotta pottery and utensils continue to be of great practical importance throughout Pakistan. Multan and Hala (near Hyderabad) are famous for their glazed pottery employing bright blues and whites. Bahawalpur is famous for its paper-thin *Kaghazi* pottery. Many of the designs of urns, pitchers, bowls and pots seen today are almost identical to those uncovered at Indus Valley sites around the country. Persian and Greek influences meanwhile resulted in distinctive long-necked, narrow-based vessels. A related craft which came also from Persia is that of glazed tile making. Still known in Pakistan as *Kaashi* after the town of Kashan in Iran, the areas most famous for this craft are Sind (Thatta and Hala) and Punjab (Lahore, Multan and Uch Sharif). As in the glazed pottery, blue and white are the most popular colours, with the geometric designs in Sind giving way to a more floral emphasis in Punjab. Distinctive glazed blue tile work is used to decorate many of the great mosques in Pakistan.

Woodwork The Swat valley is perhaps the most famous for its intricately carved architectural woodwork and furniture, although wood carving is common throughout the mountainous N. In Swat, where the craft was undoubtedly most developed, it no longer seems to be practiced, with most items offered for sale having been removed from old houses in the valley. In Sind and the Dera Ghazi Khan and Multan areas of Punjab, brightly lacquered woodwork is popular. These areas, and centres such as Dera Ismail Khan, are famous for their brass and bone-inlaid woodwork.

Metalwork Peshawar is famous for its hammered brass and copper metal work, with a huge range of items including plates, trays, boxes, vessels etc. These can also be found in Lahore and across most of northern Punjab, but the bazaars of Peshawar's Old City are the best place to look.

HISTORY

CONTENTS

Settlement and early history	84
Spread of Islamic power	86
Sikh rule and the rise of British power	89
Independence and partition	90
Post independence	94

Pakistan was born out of the partition of the South Asian sub-continent in 1947 when the British transferred power to the newly independent countries of India and Pakistan. Although the modern state of the Islamic Republic of Pakistan is less than half a century old, the land and the people have far more ancient origins. Indeed, a history of Pakistan is far more than just an appendage to a history of India; for long periods Pakistan has been the "arbiter of India's historical destiny". Over the centuries successive groups have arrived from the W, across the Indus Plains, moving into the South Asian sub-continent. Sometimes these new arrivals are traders, sometimes conquering armies, whilst others are merely agriculturalists seeking new land to cultivate. All have left their mark upon the landscape and culture of South Asia.

However, there is no one single history of Pakistan. In many cases, the history of Pakistan has been shaped by events beyond its borders, in Central Asia, Persia, Europe and India. Further, no single history covers the whole of the country. Numerous dynasties have operated within varying spheres of influences, with contemporary empires frequently having little contact. Thus the following history is just a brief overview of the events that have shaped the modern state of Pakistan. More detailed regional histories are found within the relevant chapters.

Settlement and early history

Prehistory

The territory of the modern Pakistan has always been a frontier zone between settled agriculture and nomadic pastoralism. At the beginning of the Mesolithic period some 10,000 years ago, settled agriculture was developing in the foothills of Baluchistan. At **Mehrgarh**, where the Indus Plains meet the Baluchistan Hills, pottery finds have provided evidence of settled agriculture dating back to 8500 BC; the earliest evidence in South Asia. Settled agriculture began to spread E, supported by the Indus, although nomadic tribes continued to occupy the arid western margins of Pakistan, migrating down to the valleys and plains from their summer pastures in the hills as winter arrived. By 6000 BC farming was widespread on the margins of the Indus Plains, and within 2,500 years agriculture was spread throughout the Indus Plains. This development of widespread settled agriculture represents the origins of the Indus Valley Civilization.

Indus Valley Civilization

The discovery of the two major Indus Valley Civilization sites of **Moenjo Daro** (see page 159) and **Harappa** (see page 293), and their subsequent excavations that begun in the 1920s, have been described as the "most glorious achievement of South Asia's archaeology", fundamentally changing all previous concepts of the origins of South Asian culture. Previously it was believed that the Aryans were the forebearers of South Asian culture.

At its height the Indus Valley Civilization covered an area as great as two other empires with which it maintained

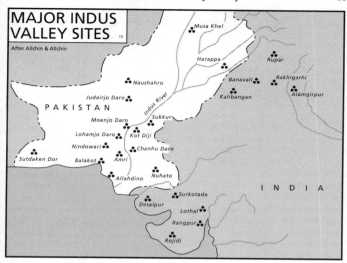

MAJOR INDUS
VALLEY SITES

After Allchin & Allchin

Musa Khel

Harappa

Rupar

Naushahro

Banavali

Rakhigarhi

Judairjo Daro

Kalibangan

Alamgirpur

PAKISTAN

Indus River

Sukkur

Moenjo Daro

Kot Diji

Lohamjo Daro

Nindowari

Chanhu Daro

Sutdaken Dor

Balakot

Amri

Allahdino

Nuhato

INDIA

Surkotada

Desalpur

Lothal

Rangpur

Rojidi

trading links, Egypt and Mesopotamia, and nearly 300 sites of this culture have been discovered. Perhaps the key feature about the Indus Valley Civilization, however, is the fact that the culture developed was distinctively South Asian. Although commerce played a part, the basis of this civilization was the development of urban centres rooted in the agricultural economy of the Indus basin, where local villagers could take their surplus for sale and exchange; a system continuing in much of rural Pakistan today.

Aryan arrival

The Indus Valley Civilization reached its peak around 2500 BC, with the development of great centres such as Moenjo Daro and Harappa, yet by about 1750 BC Moenjo Daro had been deserted and the entire civilization had disintegrated. Many causes of this decline have been presented: environmental change increasing desertification in an already semi-arid landscape, perhaps as a result of a shift in the course of the Indus; internal political decay

accelerating a continuing process of decline; or even the violent arrival of a new wave of immigrants, the Aryans, from the NW. Whatever the causes, the collapse of this civilization precipitated a major shift in the cultural evolution of the South Asian region.

The origins of the **Aryan** invaders are not precisely known, although it is clear that they do not belong to one single ethnic group. Their arrival, however, did open up a route into the frontier regions of Central Asia and Persia. By 1500 BC the Indo-Aryan language had begun to develop, with the centre of population and culture shifting E from the banks of the Indus to the land between the Ganga and the Yamuna. This region became the heart of the Aryan culture, and through the literary traditions of the **Vedas** (such as the *Rig Veda*), laid the foundations of what ultimately became Hinduism.

Ancient empires

In the period that followed the Aryan colonization of large parts of South Asia, a number of empires and dynasties with varying spheres of influence became established in the region of modern Pakistan. The Persian empire of the **Achaemenians** had established itself in the Indus Basin, with **Taxila** evolving as a great cultural centre.

In 326 BC **Alexander the Great** invaded South Asia, marching his armies from Bactria to the N, through modern-day NWFP and Punjab into Sind, and then leaving to the W, along Baluchistan's Makran coast. There are varying interpretations of the impact of Alexander's brief stay in what is now Pakistan. Although the Hellenistic influence did give rise to a distinctive style of Greco-Indian art termed Gandhara that persisted until the 5th century AD, the lands conquered by Alexander, and the vassals that he placed on their thrones, were swiftly defeated and incorporated into other empires shortly after his departure. Indeed, this Hellenistic influence is often traced to the Bactrian Greeks who arrived over a century later (see below).

Within a year of Alexander's retreat, **Chandragupta Maurya** established the first indigenous empire to control most of the South Asian sub-continent. By the middle of the 3rd century AD the **Mauryan** Empire had reached its zenith under the rule of **Asoka**, one of South Asia's greatest kings. Asoka's Empire extended from Afghanistan in the W to Assam in the E, from the Himalayas in the N to Mysore in the S. However, the horrors of the war with the Kalingans left a lasting impression upon Asoka, and though it is not certain as to whether he embraced Buddhism, he certainly embraced many of its pacifist doctrines. He left a series of edicts in the form of inscriptions on rocks and pillars right across the sub-continent, some of which can be seen on three large boulders at **Mansehra** in NWFP. Yet within 50 years of Asoka's death in 232 AD, the entire Mauryan Empire had disintegrated.

In the NW margins of the sub-continent, in the territory of modern Pakistan, a series of invaders from the NW attempted to exert their hegemony over the region. The **Bactrian Greeks**, **Sakkas**, **Parthians** and ultimately the **Kushans** all established empires of varying size. The Kushans controlled a large empire across much of Central Asia, Afghanistan, and the upper reaches of the Indus and Ganges valleys for almost a century. Under the patronage of the Kushans great Buddhist ruler **Kanishka** (around 120 AD, although this date is strongly contested), a famous art and cultural school referred to as Gandharan, flourished in the Vale of Peshawar and the surrounding valleys. It was through these valleys that Buddhism spread into Central Asia and China.

The decline of the Kushan Empire was precipitated by the **Sassasian** invasion and then by the arrival from Central Asia of the **Huns**. Regional kingdoms began to develop as local rulers asserted their influence, and thus the history of the era is highly fragmented.

Spread of Islamic power

Arrival of Islam

South Asia's first contact with Islam came through the Arab traders and sailors using the ancient trade routes through the Persian Gulf into the Indian Ocean during the 7th century AD. However, the mission was commerce and not evangelism, and though some conversions undoubtedly took place, the impact of Islam on the sub-continent was minimal. Even the Muslim conquest of Persia, including the province of Makran, failed to raise the profile of Islam in South Asia.

It was not until the Arab maritime trade routes were threatened that serious attempts were made to establish a comprehensive presence on the land of

DELHI SULTANATE in 1236

Peshawar
Ghazni
Lahore
Multan
Delhi
Mathura
Gwalior
Benaras

Boundary of Delhi Sultanate under Iltutmish

GUJARAT
YADAVAS
ORISSA
KAKATIYAS
HOYSALAS
CHOLA
PANDIYAS

the sub-continent. The harassment of Arab trading vessels off the coast of Sind by Indian pirates, perhaps with the tacit support of the ruler of Sind, precipitated an Arab invasion of Sind. Several unsuccessful punitive expeditions were attempted before the Caliph of Baghdad sent his 17-year-old son-in-law, **Mohammad bin Qasim** to conquer the territory. By 712 AD, the young General's 6,000 strong infantry, supported by a camel corps of equal strength, had conquered most of Sind, plus Multan, the most important town of the Upper Indus Valley. Thus Islam gained its first foothold in South Asia.

However, the impact of the Arab conquest of Sind was more cultural and commercial than religious, and though many learned Islamic scholars arrived to propagate the faith, there was no mass movement towards Islam. In fact, it was almost 300 years before Islam became widely established in South Asia.

Ghaznavid Empire and the Delhi Sultanate

The effective introduction of Islam into South Asia came in the 11th century with the invasion from the NW of the Turks and the establishment of the Ghaznavid Empire. However, once more the mission was not the propagation of Islam, but plunder. **Mahmud of Ghazni**, successor to the Ghaznavid Sultanate of Afghanistan that was established in the 10th century by a former Turkish slave of the Samanids, raided

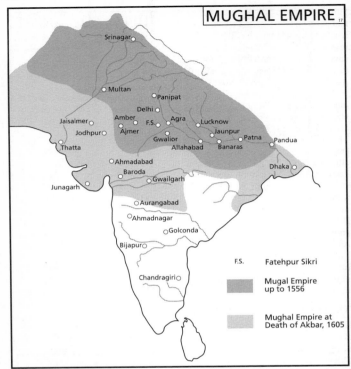

MUGHAL EMPIRE

Srinagar

Multan

Panipat

Delhi

Jaisalmer Amber F.S. Agra Lucknow
Jodhpur Ajmer Gwalior Jaunpur Patna
Thatta Allahabad Banaras Pandua

Ahmadabad

Baroda

Gwailgarh Dhaka

Junagarh

Aurangabad

Ahmadnagar

Golconda

Bijapur

Chandragiri

F.S.   Fatehpur Sikri

Mugal Empire
up to 1556

Mughal Empire at
Death of Akbar, 1605

the Punjab virtually every year between 1000 and 1026, attracted by the agricultural surpluses and the enormous wealth of India's temples. These raids were used to finance his exploits in Central Asia where he maintained an extensive empire.

Mahmud of Ghazni is remembered for his patronage of the arts and learning, and during his period of rule, many Islamic scholars, particularly those of the *Sufi* order, were active in spreading Islam in the region.

Muslim political power in South Asia was consolidated by the raids of one of Mahmud's successors **Mu'izzu'd Din** (referred to in some texts as Mohammad Ghauri), and the defeat of the Rajput

forces at Tarain in 1192. This conquest established a period of Muslim rule in India that was to last 500 years. Mu'izzu'd Din's lieutenant, **Qutb u'd Din Aibak** made further territorial gains and in 1206 the **Delhi Sultanate** was established. At its peak, under the stewardship of **Iltutmish**, another former Turkish slave, the Delhi Sultanate stretched across a huge swathe of N India, from Afghanistan to Bengal.

These early Muslim rulers looked to the Turkish ruling class and to the Arab caliphs for their Islamic legitimacy, and to the Turkish elite for their cultural authority, yet the plundering raids of **Genghis Khan** through Central Asia in the 13th century, all but cut the Delhi

Sultanate off from its cultural, religious and political heritage. As a result, Islam itself underwent major modifications in response to its new social and religious environment, accounting partly for the distinctive form of Islam found in South Asia today.

A succession of dynasties followed including the **Khaljis** and **Tughluqs** before Delhi was sacked in 1398 by the Mongol war-lord **Timur** (Tamerlane). The Delhi Sultanate never really recovered from Timur's murderous attack, although their successors, including the **Lodis** nominally controlled parts of what is now Pakistani Punjab. Meanwhile to the S, in Sind, a series of dynasties that included the **Sumas** (1026-1352), **Samnas** (1353-1520), **Arghuns** and **Tarkhans** (1520-1592) had ruled over much of the Lower Indus Valley. It was not until the **Mughals** came to power, however, that one dynasty actually ruled over the majority of the territory that comprises Pakistan.

The Mughals

The founder of the Mughal Dynasty, **Babur** (The Tiger) defeated the armies of Ibrahim Lodi, last ruler of the Delhi Sultanate, at **Panipat**, 80 km N of Delhi, in 1526. Although the Mughal Empire stretched across much of what is now Pakistani Punjab and NWFP, within 15 years the attentions of the Afghan **Sher Shah Suri** had forced Babur's successor **Humayun** into exile. These northern and central parts of Pakistan returned to Mughal rule following Humuyan's return from exile in 1555.

However, it was not until 1592 that the majority of the Lower Indus Valley joined the Upper Indus Valley as part of the Mughal Empire. **Akbar** took the throne in 1556, and by the mid 1580s had retaken Kabul and established a presence in Kashmir and Baluchistan, whilst establishing his capital at Lahore. Following the defeat of the last Tarkhan ruler of Sind in 1592, the Mughals ruled

the greater part of modern Pakistan. Akbar and his successors, **Jahangir**, **Shah Jahan** and **Aurangzeb** left a lasting impression upon Pakistan, not least in the form of some magnificent Mughal buildings.

Sikh rule and the rise of British power

The Sikhs

Following the death of Aurangzeb in 1707, the Mughal Empire declined rapidly, although nine further emperors did succeed Aurangzeb and continued to rule from Delhi until 1858. However, across the territory of Pakistan a number of rulers began to assert their independence. In Sind the **Kalhoras** and **Talpurs** ruled most of the Lower Indus Valley from the early 1700s until the middle of the 19th century. Meanwhile, much of the Punjab had been subjugated by the Afghan king **Ahmad Shah Durrani**, yet following his defeat at the hands of the Sikh armies in 1764, a fledgling Sikh Empire established itself in the Punjab. Sikh rule was further consolidated in 1799 by **Ranjit Singh** and the empire was to last until the **British** annexed the territory at the conclusion of the Second Sikh War in 1849. 6 years previously the British had annexed Sind.

The British

Although the **British East India Company** had been established in India for 200 years, it was not until the middle of the 19th century that the British began to exercise any form of control over the NW areas of the sub-continent that nowadays form Pakistan. The reason for this was simple. Whereas almost all the previous invasions of South Asia had come through the passes to the W and NW, the British had come by sea, and most of these ports were some considerable distance from this NW frontier region.

The turning point in the history of the British in India was the **Mutiny** in 1857 (or 'War of Independence' depending upon your viewpoint). The Mutiny effected the end of company rule in India, and in 1858 the Government of India Act transfered the empire of the company to the British Crown. Having now acquired this resource rich new colony, the British were keen to hang on to it, and the most pressing concern was to secure the vulnerable and ill defined NW frontier. Although Sind and Punjab had already been annexed, the unpredictable frontier tribes of modern NWFP and the Northern Areas proved to be a major source of anxiety to the British administration. When they weren't raiding into British territory, they were flirting with Britain's imperial rivals across the frontier. This era of the 'Great Game' led to the British annexation of territories such as Hunza and Nagar and the establishment of the Durand Line that remains today as the international border between Pakistan and Afghanistan.

The impact of British colonial rule in the territory of Pakistan is complex. The extension of the railway network into this NW frontier of British India changed patterns of trade and communications, although the tracks were laid primarily to allow the rapid transportation of troops to potential trouble-spots. The British also built an extensive network of canals in Punjab and upper Sind that transformed land-use. However, the use of unlined canals and a degree of poor planning has left a legacy of waterlogging and salinisation. Even the administrative divisions imposed by the British, including the Durand Line, have created problems for the modern state of Pakistan. The unnatural division of contiguous Pathan, or Pushto-speaking communities by an arbitrary line on a map have precipitated calls for an independent, unified Pathan state that the Pakistani government is desperate to resist.

Independence and partition

Birth of the Independence movement

Within 30 years of the Mutiny, the new western educated elite of Indian society were again articulating a demand for greater political rights, and ultimately self-government. The main vehicle for these demands was the **Indian National Congress**, formed in 1885. Although founded as a secular organization, the Congress was viewed with suspicion by the educated Muslim elite of N India, who saw it as a tool of Hindu nationalism. The Muslims sensed a threat to their political rights, even their own identity, with the emergence of a democratic system that would give the Hindus of India, with their greater population and built-in natural majority, significant advantages. Many leading figures within the Muslim community, including Sir Sayyid Ahmad Khan, founding father of the Muslim University at Aligarh, advised Muslims against joining the Congress, and come the turn of the century Muslims made up less than 8% of those attending the party's conferences.

In 1906, with the British Viceroy of India, Lord Minto, announcing planned constitutional changes in India, a delegation of Muslims led by the Aga Khan presented their demands to him for a separate electorate to safeguard their rights and interests. The Viceroy accepted the demands, and following this limited success, the Muslim elite thought it expedient to form an organization that could act as a platform for their views and aspirations. In Dec 1906 the **All-India Muslim League** was founded, and 7 years later it defined its goal for the first time as self-government of the sub-continent.

The demands of the Muslim League were not always opposed to those of the Congress, although great stress was laid upon safeguarding the rights of Muslims in South Asia. In 1916, the League and Congress concluded the **Lucknow Pact** in which the Congress won League support for self-government whilst conceeding the principle of separate electorates for Muslims. The League's demands were presented by its newly elected President, **Mohammad Ali Jinnah**. Although the Secretary of State for India announced in Parliament in 1917 that the British goal in India was the gradual development of self-government institutions within the British Empire, this fell far short of Congress and League expectations.

Independence movement gathers pace

In 1927 the British appointed a Statuary Commission with a view to making recommendations for a new constitution for India. The **Simon Commission** was rejected by both the Congress and the Muslim League because it contained no Indian members. Congress founded their own commission and prepared its own document, referred to as the **Nehru Report**. The report demanded 'Dominion Status' for India, but rejected the Muslim League's demands for separate electorates and reserved seats for Muslims in Punjab and Bengal. The Muslim League countered with their own report, '**Jinnah's Fourteen Points**', setting out the demands of the Muslims, and at the League's annual conference in 1929, a resolution was adopted calling for a federal rather than a unitary structure of government.

The following year, at their annual conference, the Muslim League's President, **Dr ('Allama') Mohammad Iqbal**, articulated the demand for a separate state for South Asia's Muslims: "I would like to see the Punjab, NWFP, Sind and Baluchistan amalgamated into a single state. Self-government within the British Empire, or without the British Empire, the formation of a consolidated North-West Indian Muslim state appears to me to be the final destiny of Muslims at least of NW India." This became known as the '**two-nation theory**'.

Attempts to break the deadlock between the British, Congress and the Muslim League resulted in a series of 'Round Table Conferences' held in London. The deliberations of the conferences led to the ratification of the **Government of India Act of 1935**, a document that envisaged self-government for the people of South Asia. Although both Congress and the Muslim League found fault with the act, it did concede to many of the Muslim demands, including separate electorates, weightage, and a one-third Muslim representation at the centre. The act envisaged a federal structure at the centre, with autonomous governments responsible to the legislature at provincial level.

Both Congress and the All-India Muslim League contested the provincial elections of 1937, but the League performed very poorly, gaining just four of the 11 provinces. A massive re-organization of the structure of the Muslim League took place under the stewardship of its returning President, Mohammad Ali Jinnah, and the party was revitalized. It was in the light of this rejuvenation that Jinnah presented the **Lahore Resolution**.

Lahore Resolution of 1940

On 23 March 1940, Jinnah presided over the annual session of the Muslim League in Lahore. A resolution was passed that called for the partition of India. Jinnah suggested that "geographically contiguous units are demarcated into regions which should be so constituted, with such territorial readjustments as may be necessary, that the areas in which the Muslims are numerically in the majority as in the North Western and Eastern zones of India,

MOHAMMAD ALI JINNAH

The death of Mohammad Ali Jinnah little more than a year after Pakistan gained independence left a vacuum that has never been filled. At the time of his death he was holding three key political posts, Governor General of Pakistan, President of the Muslim League, President of the Constituent Assembly, and had become universally known throughout Pakistan as *Quaid-i-Azam*, or 'Great Leader'.

Much has been written about the personalities involved in the independence movement of the sub-continent, yet almost without fail the part played by Gandhi is vastly overstated, whilst Jinnah's role is diminished. However, in his single-minded drive for Pakistan, Jinnah probably had more impact in the shaping of South Asia's future than any other personality. As Wolpert, Jinnah's principal biographer, points out: "Few individuals significantly alter the course of history. Fewer still modify the map of the world. Hardly anyone can be credited with creating a nation-state. Mohammad Ali Jinnah did all three."

Part of the fascination with Jinnah is the dichotomy between his personal and public persona. Here was a man who called for the establishment of a separate homeland for the Muslims of South Asia, yet had a penchant for fine whisky and pork sausages; the man who married a Parsi girl over half his age (despite the girl's father attempting to get a court injunction to stop the marriage), but disowned his own daughter when she married a Parsi-born Christian. Yet there can be little doubt that without Jinnah's indomitable will, it is unlikely that Pakistan would have come into being.

The 'apparent paradox of Jinnah's strange story', with the 'fascinating complexity of its brilliant light and tragic darkness' can be found in Stanley Wolpert's excellent *Jinnah of Pakistan*, 1984, Oxford University Press.

should be grouped to constitute 'Independent States' in which the constituent units should be autonomous and sovereign." Although Jinnah did not specifically use the word 'Pakistan', this **Lahore Resolution** also became known as the 'Pakistan Resolution'. The 23 Mar is celebrated as 'Pakistan Day.'

Some 7 years earlier, a Punjabi 'student' at Cambridge, **Chaudhuri Rahmat Ali**, had coined a name for a new Muslim state in South Asia – PAKISTAN. This acronym referred to **P**unjab, **A**fghania, **K**ashmir, **S**ind with the suffix *stan*, Persian for country (although the 'stan' is said by some to stand for Baluchistan). By coincidence, 'Pakistan' also means 'land of the pure'.

Independence and Partition

Following the Allies' victory in Europe and the conclusion of the Second World War, the then Viceroy of India, Lord Wavell, convened a meeting in Simla to discuss the future of India. The divide between the viewpoints of the Congress and the Muslim League could not be bridged and the conference ended in failure. In the meantime in Britain, the Labour election landslide had brought Attlee to power with a resounding majority in the House of Commons. With Britain virtually bankrupt following the war, and a new socialist government in power in London, the writing was on the wall for the British colonial empire in India.

A Cabinet Mission arrived from Britain to discuss the future of India, but failed to secure an agreement between the main political parties, and so proposed their own plan. It was accepted by Congress and by the Muslim League, although there were certain reservations, but an interim government was formed.

In 1947, with the gulf between the Hindu and Muslim communities as wide as ever, Attlee, the British Prime Minister, declared that power would be transferred to responsible Indians by Jun 1948 at the latest. In Mar of that year, **Lord Mountbatten** was appointed as Viceroy, to oversee the transfer of power. Mountbatten's plan for the transfer of power envisaged a vote in both the Bengal and Punjab legislative assemblies on the partition of their provinces. On 3 June 1947, the Congress leader Nehru, and Jinnah on behalf of the Muslim League, broadcast their acceptance of the plan. 3 weeks later both provinces vote a resounding 'yes' to partition.

The Indian Independence Bill was passed in Jul 1947, and the date of the transfer of power was brought forward to 14/15 Aug (the 15th was deemed by Indian astrologers to be more auspicious!). Mohammad Ali Jinnah was appointed Governor General of Pakistan, and on **14 August 1947**, Pakistan became an independent nation: two wings, East and West, separated by 1,600 km of potentially antagonistic Indian territory between.

Radcliffe Boundary Commission

When Independence arrived, many questions remained unanswered. Several key Princely States had still not decided firmly to which country they would accede; the most notable being Kashmir, a situation still unresolved today.

The question of the borders, most notably in Punjab and Bengal, was to be resolved by a Boundary Commission headed by the distinguished British barrister, **Sir Cyril Radcliffe**. Radcliffe's main qualification for the job, according to Wolpert, was that he "had never even visited India and expressed no known opinions on its problems." To further complicate a task that was to decide the destiny of millions of Muslims, Hindus and Sikhs, he was given just 5 weeks to complete the task. Many Pakistani historians accuse Radcliffe of bias in his 'awards', particularly of granting two predominantly Muslim tehsils that were adjacent to Kashmir to India. However, it should be noted that it was Jinnah who suggested that Radcliffe head the commission, to the consternation of Nehru.

When the boundary 'awards' were announced on 17 August 1947, the Punjab and Bengal descended into chaos as millions of Muslims, Hindus and Sikhs fled across the respective borders. According to Wolpert: "In and around Amritsar bands of armed Sikhs killed every Muslim they could find, while in and around Lahore, Muslim gangs – many of them 'police' – sharpened their knives and emptied their guns at Hindus and Sikhs. Entire trainloads of refugees were gutted and turned into rolling coffins, funeral pyres on wheels, food for bloated vultures who darkened the skies over the Punjab and were sated with more flesh and blood in those final weeks of Aug than their ancestors had enjoyed in a century." It is estimated that between a quarter and 1 million people died in the massacres that accompanied Partition.

Problems of massive population migration

The result of the movement of 8 million immigrants into Pakistan's towns and cities was a sharp conflict of interests that has remained a fundamental problem for independent Pakistan. In Javed Burki's words, "it was a trauma because it resulted in a clash between two systems based on totally different traditions, beliefs and values. The much older indigenous system was rigidly hierarchical, that imported by the migrants broadly participatory. The first was a tightly organized and stable system with vertical links between different participants; the second was a loosely clustered system of horizontal linkages between members of different social groups who did not owe allegiance to any particular individual." The conflicts of style and interest have dogged Independent Pakistan's political history to the present day.

The Kashmir dispute

This state was given concrete form by the Radcliffe Commission which drew the boundary between India and Pakistan according to the distribution of the Muslim and non-Muslim populations. The main variation from that principle was made in the case of Princely States, where as a result of pressure from Jinnah and the Muslim League the Princes themselves were allowed to choose which country they would accede to. This caused a number of problems, the most difficult being that of Kashmir. On 14 August 1947 the Dogra **Maharaja of Kashmir** had not decided whether to accede to India or Pakistan, and still cherished the hope that Kashmir could remain fully independent of both the new states. Within weeks, however, an uprising of Muslim tribes in the NW threatened to move down into the Vale of Kashmir and to capture Srinagar with Pakistan army support.

Under this pressure the Maharaja asked for Indian help, which Lord Mountbatten insisted should only be given if Kashmir first acceded to the Indian Union. This was done, and the Indian army moved rapidly N to confront the Pakistan army in a war which dragged on until the ceasefire of Jan 1949. From then on the *de facto* border between India and Pakistan has divided Kashmir in two, though legally the whole of the former Princely State is Indian territory.

Post independence

On 11 September 1948, little more than a year since Pakistan became independent, Mohammad Ali Jinnah, the father of the nation, died. In Pakistan today there still remains the feeling that the nation was 'orphaned at birth'. Indeed, Pakistan's lack of political direction and instability is often blamed on Jinnah's early demise. Jinnah left no clear view of his vision of Pakistan; was it to be an Islamic state or a secular one, a theocracy or a democracy? There are numerous reinterpretations of speeches Jinnah gave prior to and post independence, but they are often ambiguous. Jinnah's untimely death was most unfortunate for a nation that needed a strong, honest and well respected hand to guide it through those early, vulnerable days and to lay a solid foundation for the future.

Early years of independence

Following Jinnah's death, **Khawaja Nazim-ud-Din**, Chief Minister of East Pakistan, was appointed as the Governor General of Pakistan, although he acted merely as a constitutional head of state. The real power lay in the hands of Jinnah's long time associate, the new Prime Minister, **Liaqat Ali Khan**. However, Pakistan was yet to frame a new constitution when Liaqat Ali Khan was assassinated in 1951. India had framed its new constitution by the end of 1949 and held its first general elections in 1951, whilst Pakistan was still effectively being governed by the 1935 Government of India Act.

One of the key issues to dominate the political scene in Pakistan during this period was the state of relations between East and West Pakistan. Since independence, the E wing felt it had been getting a raw deal, being treated as a colony of the W. One of the greatest causes of mistrust between the E and W was the language issue. Attempts by the central government to make Urdu the national language of both wings had been fiercely opposed in 1948 by the Bengali speaking E, so attempts to impose the Arabic script for the Bengali language in 1952 were particularly insensitive. The Muslim League were routed in the Provincial Assembly elections held in the E in 1954, but the Ministry was dissolved and placed under Governor's rule.

From 1953 the bureaucracy played an increasingly important role in economic and social policy. In Javed Burki's words "in the 1953-62 period, Pakistan moved from a Parliamentary to a bureaucratic form of government and from an economy dominated by the private sector to an economy guided by the civil service."

The change was partly a result of the **economic crisis** brought on by the end of the Korean War boom. The War had caused a tremendous increase in prices of cotton and jute. The slump produced a major economic crisis, and encouraged the government to take an active hand in industrial policy and management. The Pakistan Industrial Development Corporation, which had been set up in 1950, embarked on a number of projects after 1953. It became strongly allied to the landed families of the Indus plains, for while the wealthy refugee families had liquid capital to invest in industry, the landlords of the Punjab and Sind had most of their capital tied up in the land. If they were to share in industrial expansion they therefore needed support from the government to enable them to become industrial entrepreneurs. They played a prominent role in the PIDC, which by 1959 accounted for 16% of Pakistan's industrial wealth.

The enormous public sector push was highly successful in bringing in new industrial entrepreneurs from the landed class. This group continued to enjoy control of the major share of agricultural land and, most importantly, control of Pakistan's vital irrigation network. Their developing economic power was matched by a transformation of their political significance. The Muslim League, which had been the vehicle for Pakistan's independence, was converted during the 1950s from a party of the Indian refugees into a party reorganized to take account of the interests of West Pakistan's landlords. Party democracy was replaced by a highly centralized party system.

In 1954, despite the objections of the regional assemblies, most notably Sind, the four provinces of West Pakistan were merged into 'One-Unit'. This move undoubtedly helped frame a new constitution, but was probably an attempt to break the dominance in the National Assembly of East Pakistan. On 23 March 1956, the new constitution was drafted and passed (a day celebrated as 'Pakistan Day').

First Martial Law Government

Despite passing a new constitution, a series of weak governments had brought Pakistan to a point of economic and social collapse, with regionalism running rife. On 7 October 1958, the Commander-in-Chief of the Pakistan Army, **General Ayub Khan**, seized power in a bloodless coup and declared martial law stating "there is no alternative except the disintegration and complete ruination of the country". A purge of corrupt politicians and officials was announced, and some 6,000 people were charged.

One of the first acts of the martial law administration was to shift the capital from Karachi to a new site, Islamabad. A decision resented by most Karachites, for many this brand new federal capital was suspiciously close to the army GHQ at Rawalpindi. The second major programme of the Ayub Khan administration was an attempt to introduce a new system of government – **Basic Democracy System** – that was more geared towards Pakistani society. Ayub Khan's object was to give Pakistan the stable government it had so evidently lacked. He decided to create what he termed basic democracies. Every village or town area had up to 400 electors, selected according to criteria such as land ownership or literacy, whose responsibility was to elect a town or village council. These councillors in turn elected councils at a higher level such as the district. They in turn then elected representatives to Provincial councils. Ayub Khan hoped to ensure both limited political answerability down to the village level and political stability.

The 1960s witnessed unprecedented economic growth and a major change in Pakistan's political structure. **Land Reforms** passed in 1959 began to limit the power of the landlords, particularly increasing the power of the middle rank landowners. Ayub Khan also began to curb the bureaucracy, liberalising the economy and dismantling the economic controls that had been imposed through the 1950s. But the rapid economic growth was not without costs. Liberalising the imports of agricultural machinery, for example, has been estimated to have cost 12 jobs for every tractor imported. The cost of 80,000 tractors was thus 1 million rural jobs lost in the course of a decade during which Pakistan's rural population grew by over 10 million.

Ayub Khan also allowed himself to be 'elected' as President of Pakistan, and succeeded in reframing the constitution. In the 1965 Presidential Elections Ayub Khan narrowly defeated Jinnah's sister Fatima, although there were widespread allegations of cheating by the General.

Indo-Pak War of 1965

Some commentators suggest that the Indians interpreted the alleged rigging in the Presidential elections as a sign of weakness on the part of Ayub Khan, and took full advantage by passing a bill that integrated the disputed state of Kashmir into the Indian Union. The result was a full scale war along the Indo-Pak border that was to last for 17 days until a ceasefire was agreed on 23 September 1965. Reading Pakistani newspaper analysis of the war that appears each year on 'Defence of Pakistan Day' (6 Sep), you would get the impression that the war was a great military victory. Impartial observers would suggest that a stalemate is the most generous interpretation of the 1965 war. In 1966, with a degree of Soviet encouragement/pressure, the two side signed an declaration in Tashkent agreeing to settle the dispute through 'peaceful means'.

In 1967, in an action that would have great significance for the future of Pakistani politics, Ayub Khan's Foreign Minister, **Zulfikar Ali Bhutto**, resigned his post and founded the **Pakistan People's Party** (PPP). 2 years later, in 1969, amidst growing unrest in East Pakistan, Ayub Khan stepped down and handed over power to the Commander-in-Chief of the army, **General Yahya Khan**.

Second Martial Law Government

Upon becoming the Chief Martial Law Administrator and President of Pakistan, Yahya Khan swiftly abrogated the constitution of 1962, banned all political activity, and dismissed the central and provincial assemblies. In a popular move he then dissolved the 'One-Unit' of W Pakistan, and scheduled elections for 1970.

General Election of 1970 and the War of 1971

The elections were originally due to be held in Oct 1970 but a devastating cyclone in the E put back the date by 2 months. Whilst the main focus of the PPP's campaign in the W was one of economic reform and Islamic socialism, in the E the main issue was regional autonomy. In the W, the PPP won 82 of the 138 seats, but in the E the **Awami League** won a comprehensive 160 out of 162 seats. The first session of the new assembly, scheduled to be held in Dhaka was postponed at short notice, and it soon became obvious that West Pakistan was reluctant to share power with the East, least of all be ruled by a government from there. Agitations in the East were ruthlessly suppressed by the army, and the country soon dissolved into civil war.

The civil war, and the secession of East Pakistan, is often marked as the most inglorious moment in Pakistan's history. With the Awami League calling for all out secession from Pakistan (the Bangla Desh movement), the Punjabi dominated army was ruthless in its suppression of the insurgency. In fact, most Pakistani historians prefer to gloss over the atrocities committed on civilians by the Pakistan army, or merely suggest "we do not need to go into the details of the army's actions in East Pakistan". Amidst growing atrocities by the Pakistan army in East Pakistan, India lent her mighty force to the Bangla Desh movement, and with such a long supply line to maintain, it is little wonder that the Pakistanis were swiftly defeated. By Dec 1971 Pakistan had been dismembered, and a new nation, **Bangladesh**, was born.

Return to civilian rule

On 20 December 1971, General Yahya Khan handed over control as Chief Martial Law Administrator and President of Pakistan to Zulfikar Ali Bhutto. Bhutto had come into government under the slogan of *roti* (bread), *kapre* (clothes), *makan* (houses/homes), and not surprisingly soon embarked upon a programme of revolutionary land reform. Like many land reform programmes it failed miserably, not least because many of the PPP leaders and politicians were (and still are) major land-owners, and thus this policy was against their vested interests. Further, with no proper land registry, plots above the threshold size were simply divided between family members and re-registered. Additional land reforms were attempted in 1977 but couldn't be implemented because of the elections.

Martial law was lifted on 20 April 1972, and an interim constitution enforced. By this stage Pakistan had lived under 16 years of martial law and five constitutions. Bhutto also sought to normalize relations with India, and in 1972 signed the 'Simla Agreement' with Indira Gandhi, the Indian Prime Minister. The agreement effected troop withdrawals following the 1971 war, and facilitated the exchange of prisoners. In 1974, Lahore was the venue for the Second Islamic Summit Conference that was attended by most of the heads of state from the Muslim world. Although the summit achieved little, the conspiracy theorists in Pakistan would have you believe that Bhutto's efforts to bring the Islamic world closer together is the reason the 'Americans had him hanged'!

Bhutto's main opponents in the 1977 General Elections were the **Pakistan National Alliance** (PNA), an alliance of mainly religious parties, plus the Pakistan Muslim League (PML). In the event, Bhutto's PPP won 155 of the 200 seats in the National Assembly, amidst charges of massive poll rigging. In a deteriorating law and order situation, the PNA contested the result, and on 5 July 1977, the army stepped in once more.

Third Martial Law Government

The army's Chief of Staff, **General Zia ul-Haq**, declared that he had taken over "to enforce Islam in the country". Zia claimed that he had no political ambitions and would return the country to democratic rule through elections within 90 days. His administration was to last 11 years. The 1973 Constitution of Pakistan was suspended, the national and provincial assemblies dissolved, the Prime Minister, cabinet members and leaders of the main political parties arrested and placed under protective custody. Not surprisingly the elections were suspended. Elections were rescheduled for Nov 1979, but in the meantime Zia had started a process of accountability directed primarily against the PPP whilst the PNA joined the martial law administration.

Bhutto's trial and execution

Under Zia, a case against Bhutto dating back to Nov 1974 was reopened. It was claimed that the Federal Security Force (FSF), acting under Bhutto's orders, had opened fire on a car carrying Ahmad Razi Qasuri, a dissident PPP MNA, killing his father. Commenting later on the court proceedings that he had witnessed, Ramsey Clark, former Attorney General of the US noted: "The prosecution case was based entirely on several witnesses who were detained until they confessed, who changed and expanded their confessions and testimony with each reiteration, who contradicted themselves and each other, who, except for Masood Mahmood (Director General of the FSF) were relating what others said, whose testimony led to four different theories of what happened, who were absolutely uncorroborated by an eyewitness, direct evidence, or physical evidence." Bhutto was found guilty, and on 4 April 1979 was hanged.

Zia's Islamization programme

By the end of 1978 Zia had made himself President of Pakistan, but the elections scheduled for 1979 were cancelled. A process of Islamization began with the enforcement of Islamic laws against drinking alcohol, theft, adultery and Qazf. Severe punishments were introduced for those found guilty: for drinking, 80 stripes of the whip; for a first offence of theft (if the goods stolen were valued more than 4.457 gms of gold), amputation of right hand, for a second offence amputation of left foot, for a third offence, life imprisonment; for adultery, stoning to death, for unmarried sex, 100 stripes; for Qazf (false allegation of adultery) 80 stripes. However, despite the uproar in the West over these 'inhumane' punishments, a review of the period suggests that far fewer punishments were actually carried out than first suggested.

The economic system of Pakistan was further Islamicized, with greater emphasis placed on the payment of *Zakat* (tax). The military further took over the judiciary, and in 1981 the High Courts were stripped of their powers of judicial review and writ jurisdiction. The same year saw the formation of the **Movement for Restoration of Democracy** (MRD), involving major parties including the PPP.

In 1984 Zia engineered a referendum that was taken by him as a mandate to remain as President for the next 5 years at least. One of the key reasons for the security of Zia's position was the huge Soviet presence in Afghanistan. Indeed the Soviet invasion of Afghanistan in Dec 1979 is often referred to as 'Brezhnev's Christmas present to Zia'. With both Afghan refugees and Soviet troops on the doorstep, Pakistan received massive quantities of foreign aid, becoming the third largest recipient of US aid after Israel and Egypt. Such was the strength of Zia's position, with the American's fearing the spread of communism, that Zia was able to dismiss a \$400mn aid package from the American President Jimmy Carter as 'peanuts'.

'End' of Martial Law

In 1985 Zia allowed elections to be held, but they had to be contested on a non-party basis. The MRD boycotted the event. Zia was 'elected' President for a further 5 years and **Mohammad Khan Junejo** was appointed as Prime Minister. Amendments were made to the constitution, effectively protecting and justifying all martial law promulgations and laws. On 30 December 1985, Martial Law was lifted, but in name only.

In May 1988 Junejo was dismissed by Zia, who claimed that he had not enforced the Islamic system in the country. In Jul that year Zia promulgated the Shariah ordinance, bringing stricter interpretations of Islamic law. Elections were scheduled for Nov 1988, but on

17 August 1988, Zia ul-Haq was killed in a mysterious air crash at Bahawalpur, Punjab, that also claimed the life of the US Ambassador. The chairman of the Senate, **Ghulam Ishaque Khan**, took over the temporary reigns as President.

National Elections of 1988

General Elections were held in Pakistan on 16 November 1988. The Pakistan Qaumi Jamhoori Ittehad entered into an alliance with, incredibly, 47 other registered parties, but failed to win a single seat! The election was a straight battle for control between the **Islamic Jamhoori Ittehad** (IJI), an alliance of eight parties including the Pakistan Muslim League, and the PPP. Although the PPP didn't enter into an election alliance with any other parties, with the cooperation of the MQM and members from the Federally Administered Tribal Areas (FATA), it was able to form a government. On 1 December 1988, **Benazir Bhutto**, daughter of Zulfikar Ali Bhutto, was sworn in as Prime Minister. Ghulam Ishaque Khan was retained as President.

The government. however, was short-lived, serving just 22 months of its 5-year term. Serious charges of corruption were levelled against members of the ruling party, and Ms Bhutto's husband **Asif Zardari** in particular (so much so that he became labelled 'Mr 10%'). Many charges were false, but the seemingly never-ending scandals involving the people surrounding the Prime Minister caused the people of Pakistan to lose confidence in their government. With Pakistan's history showing short periods of democracy regularly interupted by long periods of military dictatorship, many historians feel that the prevailing attitude of many in government was that this period of democracy would not last, so everyone should make as much money for themselves as quickly as possible. Defenders of the PPP would argue

that with the army constantly peering over their shoulders, effective government was not possible. In 22 months of government, the only legislation passed was the fiscal budget. In Aug 1990 the President dissolved the National Assembly and scheduled elections for 2 months later.

National Elections of 1990

The 1990 elections were won by the IJI alliance, with the Pakistan Muslim League's **Mian Mohammad Nawaz Sharif** installed as Prime Minister. A leading industrialist, Nawaz Sharif's economic policy was based upon increased privatisation, de-nationalisation and de-regulation. Amongst his spectacular failures was the 'Yellow Taxi Fiasco' (see box). During Nawaz Sharif's tenure as PM, a process of accountability was introduced to purge corruption. PPP supporters would view this more as victimisation, with numerous charges being levelled against their members (including the false implication of Asif Zardari in a kidnapping charge). Within 3 years the roles were reversed, with numerous PML members (including Nawaz Sharif) facing corruption charges.

Relations between the Prime Minister and President deteriorated rapidly over, amongst other things, economic policy. In Apr 1993 the government was dismissed, although Nawaz Sharif sought to challenge this in the courts. Eventually the army entered the argument, and both the Prime Minister and President were encouraged to resign. A noted Pakistani economist, **Moeen Qureshi**, was appointed as care-taker PM. In the interim period he undertook a number of economic reforms, including cancelling the yellow taxi scheme. He also published an extensive and damning list of government loan defaulters, and barred them from contesting the forthcoming election.

YELLOW TAXI SCHEME

Nawaz Sharif sought to solve Pakistan's chronic urban transport problem and to reduce massive unemployment in one fell swoop. Enter the 'Prime Minister's Public Transport Scheme', also known as the 'Yellow Taxi Fiasco'. The scheme involved the import of thousands of yellow taxis (and also minibuses) primarily from South Korea. Customs duties were waived, and the vehicles were offered to unemployed men at competitive rates. Only a 10% deposit was required, with the balance paid to the banks by instalment. In addition to virtually draining Pakistan's foreign exchange reserves, the scheme almost bankrupted a number of banks. Few of the taxi-owners ever repaid their loans. Further, it was later found that many of the vehicles imported duty-free ended up in the possession of influential persons who used them for their own personal use. Perhaps the only positive aspect of this affair is the fact that it is now very easy to get a modern taxi in any city in Pakistan.

National Elections of 1993

Pakistani disenchantment with their politicians was illustrated in the remarkably poor turn-out (40%) for the 1993 elections. The PML won 72 seats and the PPP won 86 seats, but Benazir Bhutto was able to form a government with the support of the Junejo faction of the Pakistan Muslim League. A PPP nomination, **Sardar Farooq Ahmad Khan Leghari** was elected President.

The PPP government of Benazir Bhutto has been implementing a monetarist economic policy, whilst coming to terms with a structural adjustment programme imposed as part of a deal with the World Bank. The government continues to face charges of corruption, whilst registering numerous similar charges against the opposition. Talking to many Pakistanis in 1995, the government seemed deeply unpopular with the people, although in fairness, the scenario was much the same during Nawaz Sharif's rule.

MODERN PAKISTAN

CONTENTS

Government, politics and
   institutions 101
Legal system and judiciary 102
International relations 103
Economy 105
Population and settlement 108
Education 110
Health 111

The challenges facing Pakistan at its inception were enormous. Quite apart from the massive upheaval and human trauma that came with partition, the newly created country inherited very little of the administrative infrastructure left behind by the British, and so had to build a new system practically from scratch. Although it inherited much of the canal irrigated agricultural land in Punjab, and all in Sind, it was nowhere near self-sufficient in food grains. It had a minimum of modern factory or heavy industry, while its mineral wealth and power potential were for the most part unexploited. Looking at the problems and shortcomings of the country today, it is easy to forget its achievements.

Government, politics and institutions

Parliament consists of an upper and lower house, the Senate and National Assembly respectively, with the former occupying a largely advisory role (rather like the House of Lords in the UK) while the latter is primarily responsible for the day-to-day business of government. Its ability to formulate policy is however severely restricted. The 1973 constitution is still nominally in force, although it was substantially amended, first by Zulfikar Bhutto, and then by Zia, who in 1985 gave the President (himself at the time) amongst other things the power to dissolve the National Assembly without the prime minister's consent. This clause allowed the dismissal of both Benazir Bhutto's first government, and that of Nawaz Sharif. Thus the president continues to exercise unprecedented power in the country; in 1994 (up till Nov) he was responsible for issuing 81 Presidential Ordinances, while the National Assembly passed just 18 new Acts, all of which, with the exception of the Finance Act dealing with the 1994-5 budget, merely 'regularized' previously issued ordinances.

The constitution provides for a federal democratic structure, with four Provincial governments of Sind, Baluchistan, Punjab and NWFP. In addition there is the Federally Administered Tribal Areas (FATA), a semi-autonomous region governed directly by the Federal government largely according to the model left behind by the British, and the Capital Territory Area (Islamabad). Both Azad Kashmir and the Northern Areas, due to their disputed status, are also administered directly by the Federal government and not strictly speaking constitutionally part of Pakistan. However in the 1980s an elected Northern Areas Council was established, while a package of administrative reforms in 1994 have given the region the basic administrative features of a Provincial government. Azad Jammu and Kashmir meanwhile exists as a 'state' with its own president, prime minister and Legislative Assembly.

One of the most prominent features of Pakistan's fragile democracy is the deep cynicism and disenchantment with which it is viewed. It is not at all uncommon to hear people referring

Modern Pakistan

nostalgically to the days of Zia's Martial Law regime; Pakistan's army, if not perhaps one of the most successful militarily, at least had a reputation for efficiency. Democratic government on the other hand has been characterized by inertia, corruption and patronage. Many people argue that real power remains in the hands of the traditional landlord class (the Bhutto family are one of the largest landowners in Sind), religious leaders (*ulema*), the civil service and the army.

A religious or secular state?

Pakistan is officially an Islamic Republic, and was created in order to provide the Muslims of India with their own homeland. Yet the 1973 constitution, in theory at least, is a secular one, while the legal system was formulated almost entirely on that of the British. This paradox is the source of heated debate in Pakistan. Part of the problem is in defining an Islamic state and many have characterized Pakistan as a country in search of an Islamic ideology with which to underpin its existence. Jinnah, in a much quoted speech to Pakistan's constituent assembly on 11 August 1947, made the following statement:

"You are free; you are free to go to your temples, you are free to go to your mosques or to any other places of worship in this State of Pakistan... You may belong to any religion, caste or creed – that has nothing to do with the business of the State. We are starting with this fundamental principle that we are all citizens and equal citizens of one State... You will find that in the course of time Hindus would cease to be Hindus and Muslims would cease to be Muslims, not in the religious sense, because that is the personal faith of each individual, but in the political sense as citizens of the State."

Equality and freedom of worship were clearly central to his vision, but then most Muslims would argue that these are central features of Islam anyway. Likewise, the socialism which Zulfikar Bhutto

initially promoted so forcefully has many parallels in Islam. Some would argue that the existing democratic system is a purely western model, for which an Islamic parallel exists. But then the country appears to be set against a theocracy on the model of post-revolution Iran; free elections in Pakistan have always resulted in the electorate voting overwhelmingly in favour of secular parties with secular programmes.

Legal system and judiciary

The legal system illustrates many of the problems inherent in reconciling Islamic and secular ideals. Under Zia, a Council of Islamic Ideology was created to bring existing laws into conformity with Islamic injunctions and advise on new legislative proposals. In addition to the provincial High Courts and the Supreme Court, a Shariat (Islamic) Court was established with the power to overrule any law 'considered repugnant to Islam'. Various of the Islamic laws passed during Zia's time, particularly the *Hadood* ordinance, raised great controversy and strong protest from minority rights and women's groups both within Pakistan and abroad. Some, such as the law on the payment of *zakat* (a tax collected for distribution to the poor), highlighted the differing interpretations of Islam; Shia Muslims do not recognize the tax as part of Islamic law. Others, such as those proposing to abolish interest on the grounds that it is un-Islamic, have proved largely unworkable and their implementation remains unresolved.

In 1995 the so called 'blasphemy law' (an amendment to the Penal Code which made the death sentence mandatory for blasphemy) was brought under the public spotlight following a much publicized case in which two Christians were sentenced to death after being charged with writing blasphemous graffiti on the walls of a mosque. A third Christian, also involved in the case, had already been shot dead while returning from one of the court hearings. In a subsequent appeal to the High Court, the judgement was overturned, the judge noting amongst other things that the accused were illiterate. The case served to illustrate the potential for misuse of such laws by extremists and was a source of acute shame for most Muslims. The issue of Shariat law versus 'secular' law meanwhile found dramatic expression in 1994 and 1995 over the 'Malakand episode' (see page 344).

Many argue that disillusionment with the legal system and judiciary is due to its inefficiency and corruption. Even relatively simple cases can drag on for months or years, at prohibitive cost to all but the most wealthy, and with no guarantee of a fair judgement at the end of it. Even more serious at a national and provincial level is the issue of the independence of the judiciary. Effectively, appointments to the judiciary are controlled by the executive (ie the government) and so obviously open to political manipulation and abuse. This was a setup initially inherited from the British, but subsequently reinforced by both Zulfikar Bhutto and Zia-ul-Haq. There have been growing calls and various attempts to seperate the two.

International relations

India Pakistan's international relations are dominated by relations with India, with the **Kashmir Dispute** being the greatest bone of contention. The two countries have gone to war no less than three times over the issue, with both maintaining massive deployments of troops along the Line of Control and regularly shelling each other across it. The current deployment of an estimated 300,000 Indian soldiers within Indian held Kashmir in an attempt to control the insurgency against direct Indian rule there has served to further inflame

what has always been a deeply emotive issue to Pakistanis. The Indian army and government has been widely accused of human rights abuses, while Pakistan has been blamed by the Indians for formenting the current unrest. Officially Pakistan denies any direct involvement, although unofficially it openly admits to supporting the Kashmiri 'Mujahideen' and there are regular calls in the press for the people of Pakistan to rise up in a 'jihad' to aid their brethren in Indian Kashmir. For Pakistani politicians Kashmir is a gift, allowing them to rally populist support and divert attention away from problems at home. The question as to what the people of Kashmir actually want themselves – to remain part of India, join Pakistan or have independence – tends to be ignored. While India blames Pakistan for its problems in Kashmir, Pakistan generally places much of the blame for the problems in Karachi on India. Another less well known and little publicized territorial dispute is over **Junagadh** and **Manavadar** in India's Rann of Kachchh.

The abysmally poor relations between Pakistan and India have their roots in the history of British colonial rule, the Independence movement and Partition. Today those relations continue to have a devastating social, economic and military impact on what would otherwise be a geographically and culturally integrated region. Interpretations and perceptions on both sides remain highly charged and highly subjective, but nobody can deny that there are only losers in the conflict.

Afghanistan Pakistan's involvement in the Mujahideen struggle against the Soviet occupation of Afghanistan was on a massive scale. Mohammad Yousaf, the head of the Afghan Bureau of the Inter Services Intelligence (ISI, akin to the US's CIA) from 1983-87, wrote in his book The Bear Trap; "During my 4 years some 80,000 Mujahideen were trained;

hundreds of thousands of tonnes of arms and ammunition were distributed, several billion dollars were spent on this immense logistic exercise and ISI teams regularly entered Afghanistan alongside the Mujahideen." In the aftermath of the Soviet withdrawal and the continuing civil war in the country, Pakistan never misses an opportunity to reiterate its respect for the sovereignty of other nations and the principles of non interference. But Pakistani undoubtedly remains inextricably involved in Afghanistan. The **Taliban** movement, which initially swept through the eastern and southern provinces of the country so successfully (albeit through Pathan areas sympathetic to its cause), certainly originated from religious schools (*madrassas*) along the Pakistan border and is widely believed to have been funded, equipped and trained, at least to some extent, by Pakistan. Exactly what Pakistan's objectives are in Afghanistan are unclear. The instability of the latter has serious implications for Pakistan's own security, as well as for its ambitions to form close economic links with the newly independent Central Asian States. Most observers agree that there is an increasing likelihood of Afghanistan disintegrating along ethnic lines, in which case the numerically significant Pathans, who are found mostly in areas bordering Pakistan, could well start agitating for an independent 'Pakhtunistan' which included Pathan majority areas inside Pakistan.

Iran and the Middle East Locked in a seemingly intractable dispute with India to the E, Pakistan has traditionally tried hard to forge close links instead with its Islamic neighbours to the W. Iran however is a predominantly Shia country, while Pakistan has a Sunni majority. Relations between the two remain cordial and economic cooperation is developing slowly, but there is little sign of the close links which Pakistan would like to see. On a regional level however,

Pakistan is an active member of the Islamic Organization of Countries (IOC) and a regular participant in regional Islamic Summits. In economic terms, the oil producing countries of the Middle East have been a major source of employment and foreign exchange remittances for Pakistan.

Central Asia The break up of the Soviet Union and the formation of a host of independent states in Central Asia with Muslim majorities was a welcome development for Pakistan. Historical and cultural links with the region are strongly emphasized, and in the recent conference on economic development in the region, Pakistan put forward ambitious (and some would say highly unrealistic) proposals to develop close economic ties in the form of a land route connecting the land-locked states with the sea port at Karachi.

China The old maxim that 'my enemy's enemy is my friend' was perhaps initially the main driving force behind the close relations which Pakistan established with China. While India's border disputes with the latter are still unresolved, having led to war at one stage, Pakistan was only too pleased to agree her international border with China. The building of the KKH meanwhile is the most tangible manifestation of the two countries' close economic links.

USA Relations with the USA are perhaps the most fraught with hypocrisy and contradictions. On the one hand America is held up as the devil incarnate in Pakistan; the embodiment of Western decadence and immorality, an enemy of Islam and worse still, a Zionist stooge. On the other hand, the withdrawal of aid following the Pressler Amendment (a response to Pakistan's apparent possession of a nuclear bomb, or at the very least, the components needed to make one) was felt keenly in Pakistan, which had previously become used to unprecedented levels of US economic and military aid during the

Afghanistan war. In 1995 Benazir Bhutto made a highly publicized trip to America in order to try to have the Pressler Amendment revoked and secure the release of F-16 jet fighters which Pakistan had paid for but never received, as well as to drum up international support for Pakistan's position on Kashmir. Having lost the status of a 'front-line state' in the fight against communism, it seems unlikely however that Pakistan will be able to regain its close relations with the US; indeed, the latter has done much to build closer links with India instead.

Economy

Pakistan's economy has shown remarkable growth in recent years, averaging over 6% since the late 1970s and prompting allusions to the economic miracles of the Southeast Asian 'tigers'. Despite the impressive figures, such comparisons are somewhat far-fetched. Population growth is extremely high and negates most of the benefits of economic growth, while the wealth that has been generated continues to be concentrated in the hands of a tiny minority. The problems of inefficiency, corruption and patronage remain major constaints on economic development, as do political instability in the country.

There have however been concerted efforts, initiated by General Zia and followed up by Nawaz Sharif and Benazir Bhutto, to encourage the growth of the private sector, ease import restrictions, relax bureaucratic controls on investment, stimulate investment in manufacturing and promote exports. In addition, the privatisation of many public sector industries and services was initiated in the early 1990s. More recently, Bhutto's vigorous efforts to encourage foreign investment have produced considerable results on paper at least, although previously Memorandums of Understanding have failed to survive changes

of government in Pakistan. In terms of exports there is still a heavy reliance on a few products with seven major items (raw cotton, rice, cotton cloth, cotton yarn, garments, leather and carpets) accounting for over 60% of the total. This makes Pakistan's economy highly vunerable to changing terms of trade.

Following a debt crisis in 1988, the IMF made loans of US$830mn and since then both the World Bank and IMF have had a significant involvement in economic policy, linking the provision of loans to 'conditionalities' which centre around 'structural adjustment programmes' (SAPs) aimed at achieving improved economic performance and reducing government spending and budget deficits. While such programmes generally benefit the economy as a whole, they are often criticized for their negative impact on the poor and disadvantaged sections of society.

On the other hand, government spending is clearly extremely high, with little of it going to the most needy. The military continues to be a massive burden. Of the 1995 budget, 26.7% was allocated to defence. Debt servicing meanwhile accounted for an even larger 36.5%. Civil government expenditure (administration, law and order, community, social and economic services, grants and subsidies) accounted for 14.4%, with the majority going on bureaucracy and administration. In all, just 22.5% was left for development expenditure.

Agriculture

Agriculture (including forestry and fishing) still dominates the economy, employing 47% of the labour force and accounting for 25% of GDP. This represents a relative decline in economic importance over the years (during the early 1960s it accounted for around 50% of GDP), though this is largely due to the growth of industry. Indeed, growth in agricultural output has kept up with population growth in recent years, to the extent that Pakistan is not only self sufficient in food grains, but like India is also a net exporter of food. The importance of agriculture is demonstrated by the fact that over a quarter of Pakistan's total land area is cultivated. Irrigation meanwhile is crucial to that agriculture, with more than three-quarters of cultivated land being irrigated. The extension of irrigation systems, along with mechanisation, improved seed varieties, fertilizers and insecticides, are together responsible for increased output and higher yields.

Wheat is the most important food grain crop, vital to a diet based around *chapatis* and *nan*, and production has grown steadily over the years. **Rice** has become increasingly important, with production concentrating on high quality *basmati* for export to the Middle East, although other varieties are also grown for home consumption. Other major food grains, which are grown on the unirrigated *barani* lands, include local varieties of winter wheat and other hardy crops such as barley, maize, and pulses. Potatoes, onions, oil seeds, sugar beet, and fruits are the other main crops. The millets *bajra* and *jowar* are primarily grown as animal fodder. By far the most important cash crop and largest agricultural export is **cotton**, of which Pakistan is one of the largest producers in the world. **Sugar cane** is also increasingly important, along with **tobacco**, which is grown mainly in the Peshawar valley.

In a society where meat is central to the diet, the rearing of **livestock** is of considerable significance, particularly in marginal areas. As well as being increasingly important as a source of leather, animals are still vital to agriculture for ploughing and as beasts of burden. **Forestry** is of minimal economic importance at the national level, a reflection mostly of the scarcity of forest cover. However, afforestation schemes focusing on fast-growing species and irrigated tree plantations in the Indus basin could provide a sustainable source of timber and fuelwood, both of which are desparately needed. **Fishing** is an important industry along the coast and a cheap source of protein for many local communities. Shellfish such as shrimps, prawns and lobster are of great commercial value and account for around 2.6% of export earnings. Many of the rivers in the mountains of northern Pakistan were stocked with trout by the British and trout farming is important locally.

Despite the great progress in agriculture since Independence, it still remains highly vunerable to the vagaries of Pakistan's climate, with heavy flooding and droughts regularly devastating harvests. Crop infestations, particularly of cotton, are also a major problem. This vunerability periodically causes major setbacks to the overall economy. The twin problems of waterlogging and salinity leading to the loss of fertile land are also causing increasing concern.

A major constraint on agriculture is the feudal patterns of land ownership which have persisted since Independence, despite attempts (some would say half-hearted) by both Ayub Khan and Zulfikar Bhutto to introduce land reforms. Up-to-date figures are hard to come by, but it was estimated in 1959 that amongst the more powerful *zamindars* (landowners), a mere 6,000 people (0.1% of landowners) held 15% of all cultivated land in holdings of over 208 hectares, while in contrast 3.3 million people (65% of landowners) held an equal percentage of all cultivated land in holdings of less than 2 hectares.

Industry

Manufacturing now accounts for 17.3% of GDP and employs 12.4% of the labour force, a major achievement given its negligable importance at Independence. Growth in manufacturing was greatest in the 1950s and '60s, when it averaged 9% per year. Manufactured goods now account for over 60% of all exports, the bulk of these being processed foods, cotton textiles and garments. The fashion industry goes from strength to strength, with leather garments becoming increasingly important. Many of the designer labels found in western shops are in fact both designed and manufactured in Pakistan. Sports goods are another area of Pakistani expertise; the footballs used in the world cup come from Pakistan, while cricket bats, squash rackets and hockey sticks (all sports in which Pakistan excels) are considered to be of the highest quality.

Heavy industry and large scale manufacturing have grown more slowly, and one of the main criticisms generally made of Pakistan's economy is that it lacks any real 'depth', relying heavily on imports. Nowhere is this more apparent than in the transport sector; the overwhelming majority of vehicles on the roads are Japanese, and although many are now assembled in Pakistan, the country has no indigenous vehicle industry. Pakistan's first integrated iron and steel mill at Pipri, 40 km E of Karachi, was built with Soviet assistance and is now finally fully operational. However, it has yet to achieve sustained profitability and iron and steel remain major imports. With a huge amount of Pakistans industry concentrated around Karachi and Hyderabad, the ongoing violence there is having a significant impact on the overall economy.

Tourism

Tourism in Pakistan remains at a modest level, although it has shown steady growth over the years, notwithstanding the impact of crises such as the Gulf war, when it nose-dived. 1994 and 1995 also saw the violence in Karachi reach new levels, capturing the international media's attention and resulting in a significant slump. Under Nawaz Sharif there

were concerted efforts to promote tourism and in 1995 Benazir Bhutto announced ambitious plans to make it the country's major foreign exchange earner. A package of measures already in force aims to encourage foreign and domestic investment in the tourist industry, while plans are 'in hand' to open up Baluchistan's coastal area and to develop tourist facilities in other parts of the province, as well as in southern NWFP. There is also talk of leasing out government owned PTDC motels to the private sector. However, it remains to be seen how much of this will be translated into action.

Resources and power

By far the most important single resource is **natural gas** which, as well as supplying growing energy needs, provides a raw material for the fertilizer industry. There are 25 fields in operation, concentrated around the Indus plains with the largest, at Sui in Baluchistan, accounting for almost half of all production. Gas is piped from here to both Karachi and Lahore. **Oil** production, although limited, has expanded considerably with a vigerous exploration policy being rewarded by a number of finds. Imports from the Middle East, (Kuwait in particular) are however still the major source of supply. The discovery in May 1992 of a huge **coal** field in Sind's Thar desert boosted known reserves significantly, although most reserves are of a low quality and production remains limited. Non-fuel minerals found in Pakistan include uranium, rock phosphate, gypsum, iron ore, copper, gold, silver, magnesium, chromite, antimony, barite, rock salt, sulpher, percelain, china clays and gemstones. **Hydro-electricity** has been developed as a major power source, with the two largest projects, the Tarbela and Mangla dams, being complemented by numerous smaller schemes. The potential generating capacity from this source

ANYBODY WATCHING?

In 1965 Pakistan signed a Transit Trade Agrement with Afghanistan, whereby this land-locked country could import goods through the sea port of Karachi, and from there by land into Afghanistan, free of any duty. The agreement, still in force today, is automatically renewed every 5 years. However, there are growing calls in Pakistan for its cancellation, due to abuse on a massive scale. Luxury goods are imported into Afghanistan under the agreement and then smuggled back to Pakistan for sale to the growing middle classes. Having bypassed the heavy import duties charged on luxury goods in Pakistan, the smugglers are able to undercut competitors while at the same time raking in huge profits.

Official import statistics on the two countries now make for amusing reading. Thus Afghanistan officially imports more than 10 times as many TV sets as Pakistan, despite having a total population that is nearly one-tenth of the size of Pakistan's, and currently next to no electricity supply outside of Kabul! The Central Board of Revenue has drawn up a list of no less than 15 items ranging from air conditioners to ball bearings for which there is negligable demand in Afghanistan (the 'Negative' list); on aggregate, Afghanistan appears to be importing 14 times more of these items value-wise than Pakistan.

The impact of this smuggling on Pakistan's economy is clearly highly significant (estimates put the annual loss to the exchequer at Rs 7bn; around US$230mn). Although in April 1995 the government banned the import of items on the Negative list under the Transit Trade Agreement, for the most part it is business as usual. Highly influencial vested interests within Pakistan's ruling class make it relatively easy to find ways around the ban, while the more resouciful Afghan smugglers have begun using the Iranian port of Bandar Abbas instead, or chartering planes to fly goods direct from Saudi Arabia to Jalalabad.

has been estimated at 10,000 MW; over a third of this has now been achieved and nearly half of Pakistan's electricity is hydro-electric. Despite rapid expansion of overall electricity capacity, demand still far outstrips supply, making power shortages a major constraint on industrial growth.

Population and settlement

Pakistan's population was estimated (see box) at just over 128 million in 1995, making it the ninth most populous country in the world. Figures for the annual growth rate are placed at between 2.9 and 3.1% (around 3.5 million each year), one of the highest in the world and well above the South Asian average of 2.4%. This reflects a rapidly declining infant mortality rate alongside a much slower decline in the birth rate. The total fertility rate (the average number of children a woman will have in her lifetime) was estimated at 5.4 in 1992 and although this is extremely high (the rate in the UK is 1.9), it is an improvement on the 1981 level of 6.4. Interestingly, Pakistan was one of the first countries in Asia to implement family planning schemes, although today only 12% of married women are estimated to use contraception, and while three quarters of women are aware of a modern contraceptive method, less than half have access to these. Education is seen as a key factor in successful family planning, with women who have had at least some secondary education having significantly fewer children than those with no formal education. The most significant contribution to falling fertility rates is generally attributed to an increase

PAKISTAN – AFRAID OF THE CENSUS?

What is the population of Pakistan? 110 million? 120 million? 130 million? It appears that nobody can say with any degree of certainty. Part of the problem is that a census has not been taken since 1981, yet recent investigations suggest that even this census may have been deeply flawed.

Early reports from the aborted 1991 census show some strange abnomalies. The results of the house enumeration suggested that the population of Pakistan had risen from 81 million in 1981 to 133 million in 1991. However, even at Pakistan's phenomenal reported growth rate of over 3%, the overall population should have been nearer to 110 million. In Sind, it was claimed that the population had risen from 18 million to an incredible 46 million, a staggering decenial growth rate. The census commissioner smelt a rat and the President cancelled the census.

The main reason behind the innaccuracy in Sind lies in the increasing urban-rural divide, with the two communities deliberately inflating their numbers for both political benefits, and to benefit from the distribution of resources between the urban and rural sectors. Censuses are important because they allow governments to plan for the future. They are doubly important in Pakistan because they determine not only the regional representation in the National Assembly, but also the allocation of national resources and federal job quotas to the provinces. Article 51 of the Constitution states: "The National Assembly seats shall be allocated to each province, the Federally Administered Areas and the Federal Capital on the basis of the population in accordance with the last preceding census officially published". It seems that the data on Sind had been deliberately manipulated to show an increase in the population in order to influence the allocation of seats in the National Assembly, jobs in the federal service, and the distribution of federal resources. There had been further manipulation to influence these allocations between urban and rural Sind. If the results of the 1991 census had been accepted, Sind would have gained 26 seats in the National Assembly, whilst Punjab would have lost 22 and NWFP three, in addition to affecting their allocation of resource and job quotas. If this was happening in 1991, did the same occur in 1981?

Attempts by the Punjab and NWFP to de-link the allocation of seats and quotas from the census have been resisted by Sind and Baluchistan, who fear that they may lose out. However, a further problem delaying the rescheduling of the census is the fear that it may reveal the extent of internal divisions within Pakistan. An accurate census may reveal a situation in Sind where the indigenous Sindhi speakers are now outnumbered by an Urdu speaking majority; Punjab's homogeneaity may be challenged by the revelation of the true numbers of the Seraiki community; in NWFP, what will be the impact of Afghan refugees who have managed to obtain Pakistani identity cards? Pakistan desperately needs to hold a census in order to make social and economic planning possible, but it is perhaps afraid of the findings.

in the average age of marriage and in the interval between pregnancies, both of which are linked to education and increased prosperity.

The settlement pattern of Pakistan is highly uneven. The largest province, Baluchistan, which accounts for almost half of the total land area, has a population that is about half the size of Pakistan's largest city, Karachi. The population density of the various regions reflects the nature of the physical terrain, and the climatic conditions. The predominantly mountainous Northern Areas has a population density of just eight persons per square kilometre. Punjab, however, with a quarter of the land surface, has almost 60% of the population (at a density of 230 people per square kilometre), reflecting the easier nature of the terrain and its agricultural potential. Although less than 25% of Pakistan's population is urban, in Sind the urban population stands at around 50%, due almost entirely to the urban primacy of Karachi.

Education

Education remains one of the most neglected sectors in Pakistan, attracting spending of just 2.2% of GNP (the recommended UNESCO level is 4%). Teachers' salaries are abysmal and the profession has low public esteem. Education has also become highly politicized in recent years, with huge variations in statistics, depending on the source. Thus, according to the government's 1994-5 Economic Survey the literacy rate was 37%, a 5% improvement on the previous year and a 'valuable achievement', while recent UNESCO estimates put the figure at around 18%. Part of the discrepancy relates to the governments definition of literacy as merely the ability to read and write one's name.

Whichever sources and definitions are used, the absolute figures also conceal massive variations between men and women and between urban and rural areas. According to the 1994 report of the Human Rights Commission of Pakistan, the literacy rate was more than twice as high for men (48.9%) as for women (23.5%), and likewise between urban and rural areas (57% as against 27.5%). Literacy rates amongst rural women is often as low as 5%. Progress in literacy has also been extremely slow as compared with other South Asian countries; Nepal, which had a literacy rate of just 2% at Independence as compared to Pakistan's 15%, now has 48% literacy.

Although universal and free primary education is enshrined as a constitutional right in Pakistan, it is not compulsory and actual provision of primary school places nowhere near matches the demand. Facilities are generally very basic, particularly in rural areas, and teachers often poorly qualified. There is also widespread evidence of corruption and embezzlement in the system, with many schools existing only on paper in order to draw the relevant government funding.

Less than one-third of children who complete primary education go on to middle and secondary schools; for girls the proportion is one-fifth. Competition for places at secondary level is intense and the private sector now provides a significant proportion of facilities, although these are fee-paying and therefore only accessible to middle and upper class families.

Facilities in higher education are also under exteme pressure. Less than 10% of young people go on to higher secondary (intermediate) level, and as few as 1.6% into technical and vocational education. Only about 3% go from intermediate level into degree courses. There are 21 government-established universities and 774 affiliated colleges, with proposals to establish 20 new universities in the next 10 years. There are however serious administrative and financial problems in all the existing universities. On average teaching staff represent just one-fifth of the administrative and support staff. An investigative committee recently found that the prestigious Peshawar University kept no accounts, had no auditor and considered itself answerable to no-one.

Despite the serious physical constraints on education, the poor quality of services, widespread 'malpractice' and the economic pressures on children and young people to earn a living, one of the most striking things in Pakistan

Examination 'Malpractices'

Those with proud memories of elaborate cheating techniques at school could certainly have learnt a thing or two from Pakistan's students who would appear to have raised the art to startling levels of ingenuity, though one might also be justified in complaining that they have some unfair advantages.

In its 1994 report the Human Rights Commission of Pakistan complains that "The malaise in education is nowhere more remarkable than in the conduct of public examinations at all levels". Dismissing 'common cheating' out of hand, it identifies those active in the business as "staff members of the examining authority, the invigilation staff at examination centres, and groups of professional toughs who either in complicity with or in muscular defiance of the supervision staff ran supply channels to clients in examination halls". It then goes on to give a few of the more memorable examples for the year:

"The Punjab Education Minister disclosed that a gang comprising a headmaster and several senior teachers, later arrested, had contacted select candidates and in return for named sums solved the paper for them. In another raid 348 students were caught cheating and 22 persons substituting for real candidates. One substitute said he had been paid Rs 10,000 [£200] by a headmaster who wanted him to appear for a relative.

A number of rackets of issuance of counterfeit certificates and degrees were revealed. One group in Lahore sold BA degrees for Rs 15,000 apiece, another in Multan rated the Bahauddin Zakria University degrees higher, pricing the BA ones at Rs 25,000 and MA ones at Rs 35,000. Some members of the Gujranwala Board made a speciality of faking matriculation and intermediate certificates.

Eighteen students were, on a tip-off, caught solving F.Sc Physics II paper in a private house in Lahore. The paper and the answer books had been smuggled out to them by some members of the Board of Intermediate and Secondary Education whom they had each paid Rs 100,000. In the English Compulsory A paper, cheating at one of the centres in Lahore was such an open affair that one candidate even brought a mobile phone... There were armed toughs outside warning against any intervention. The superintendent said he could do nothing since the candidates were children of VIPs. One was the nephew of the Education Minister, another the son of the Chairman of the Examination Unfair Means Committee!"

Its not what you know...

is the obvious thirst for knowledge and determination with which people pursue their schooling. Education is widely perceived as the single most important factor in opening up new opportunities and achieving a better standard of living.

Health

Government spending on health is even lower than on education, amounting to just 0.8% of GNP. On average there was estimated to be one doctor for every 1,918 people, one nurse per 5,969 people and one dentist per 50,329 people. However, the majority of facilities are concentrated in urban areas, which account for less than one-third of the population. There were 4,600 Basic Health Units and 500 Rural Health Centres in the country in 1994. These form the basis of health care provision in rural areas, although facilities are often woefully inadequate; more than half have no piped water or sewerage, while staff are often poorly trained. One survey suggested that 70% offered no contraceptive services. Wastage and corruption are major problems throughout the health sector.

However, there has been considerable improvement in facilities over the years, as well as a number of relatively successful immunisation programmes, which have contributed to a 60% drop in infant mortality rates since the 1960s. Nevertheless, the rate is still extremely high; nearly one in 10 children die before their first birthday and a third of these deaths occur within 1 week of birth. A great many deaths amongst infants are as a result of easily treated problems such as diarrhoea and pnumonia. Undernourishment and malnutrition are also widespread. Most women receive no ante-natal care and 85% of births take place at home, often without any trained assistance. Pakistan is estimated to have one of the highest rates of maternal mortality, although this is in part attributable to high birth and fertility rates.

SIND

CONTENTS

Introduction	113
Karachi	124
Karachi to Quetta	138
Karachi to Hyderabad via National Highway	139
Karachi to Hyderabad via the Super Highway	143
Hyderabad to Sukkur via the Indus East Bank	150
Hyderabad to Sukkur via the Indus West Bank	156

MAPS

Sind	114
Karachi	126-127
Centre	132
Saddar Bazar	134
Hyderabad	145
Sukkur	154
Ranikot Fort	157
Moenjo Daro	161
Larkana	165

INTRODUCTION

In recent years, few visitors to Sind have ventured beyond the city limits of the major international air gateway of Karachi. However, Sind has much to offer visitors, including some of the most stunning archaeological sites in South Asia (perhaps the world), in addition to desert adventures, beaches, and the living cultural museums of the state's many Sufi shrines. Whilst travel in the interior has been difficult in recent years, the situation has now changed drastically and no problems were encountered during extensive travels in 1995. However, the situation may change, so it is essential

that you check with your embassy and PTDC, and take advice from other travellers before setting out.

Best time to visit: Winter and spring (Nov-Mar) are very pleasant in Sind, although nights can be chilly, particularly in desert regions. Sind can become very hot in summer, with some of the world's highest temperatures recorded in the state. Sea breezes can have a cooling influence in the S, although humidity tends to be higher.

Land and life

Geography

Sind lies between 23° 30' and 28° 30' N and 66° 42' and 71° 10' E, and represents 17½% of Pakistan's surface area. The name Sind is one of S Asia's oldest regional names, coming from the local name for the Indus River and ultimately giving its name to India. The Province is defined on three sides by natural geographical features, with mountains to the W, the sea to the S, desert to the E, plus the confluence of the five rivers of the Punjab to the N. It is here that some of the earliest examples of settled agriculture in S Asia can be found, as well as the site of one of the world's oldest civilizations.

Sind covers 140,914 sq km, an area almost as large as England. It is bordered by Baluchistan to the W, Punjab to the N, India to the E and the Arabian Sea to the S. The state is approximately 508 km N to S, and 456 km at its widest E-W point. With the exception of the Kirthar Mountains to the W, a small rocky tract W of Dadu, and several insignificant limestone outcrops at

Rohri, Sukkur and Hyderabad, the region is almost entirely flat.

Parallels have been drawn between Sind and Egypt, Lambrick giving a vivid account: "The same 3 parallel tracts, of arid hills, alluvial plain and sandy desert, lie in the same order right to left, the central valley in each owing its fertility not to rainfall but to the annual innundation of a great river. Climatically and geologically, in their characteristic flora and fauna, the affinities between the 2 countries are far more obvious than their differences."

Rivers

Put simply, the **Indus River** dominates many aspects of life in Sind from agriculture and settlement, through history and folklore, to art, poetry, music and architecture. It has been said that "Sind's history is written on the waves of the Indus or is buried beneath its alluvium".

Approximately one third of the Indus' 1,900 km length runs through Sind, and without it the whole region would be desert. The river has changed course so frequently that hardly any part of the plains has not been covered by it at some point. The Indus is one of the world's greatest rivers not only in terms of length, drainage area and discharge, but also by the volume of sediment that it carries. The river valley is underlain by almost 600m of deposited alluvium which has raised the level of the flood plain by 4m in the last 450 years, and extended the delta by 80 km in the last millennium.

The discharge of the Indus has been measured between 5,500 and 6,700 cu secs, 80% of which flows through in the months May to Oct. Upstream uses however, such as construction of dams and barrages, and increased utilization from tributaries in India, have had a profound effect upon the Indus' contribution to land and life in Sind. In fact, some sources argue that the yearly mean flow has fallen by 30% in the last 20 years, resulting in sea water intrusion in the delta, deterioration of the river basin regime and the loss of perhaps 800,000 ha of potential agricultural land.

Indus Waters Treaty Following Partition, the new international border between Pakistan and India cut indiscriminately across the natural drainage system of the Indus. As a downstream neighbour, Pakistan was at the mercy of upstream usage of its key river and major tributaries, and became particularly alarmed by India's plan to stop the flow of the Ravi and Beas into Pakistan by diverting them into the Sutlej. Further plans were also made to divert part of the Chenab, thus depriving Pakistan of water used to irrigate 3.2 million ha of agricultural land.

As a solution to this potentially explosive situation, the World Bank proposed a legal beheading of the Indus River system, dividing the rivers between the two countries. The plan, accepted by both sides in 1960 as the **Indus Waters Treaty**, allocated the three western rivers (**Indus**, **Jhelum**, **Chenab**) to Pakistan, and the three eastern rivers (**Ravi**, **Sutlej**, **Beas**) to India. Technical and financial assistance was also provided by the World Bank and donor countries for construction of dams, link canals, barrages, drainage canals, ancillary works, bridges, roads and railways as part of an integrated development plan.

However, of the five water storage dams that the plan envisaged being constructed in Pakistan by 1995, only two, **Mangla** and **Tarbela**, have been built. Estimates suggest that if a third dam is not built by the year 2000, Pakistan will be forced to import 4 million tonnes of wheat, 2 million tonnes of rice and 3 million tonnes of edible oils to meet the production shortfall. The proposed construction of the third dam at **Kalabagh** in Punjab (see page 263), however, has become a major political issue.

Mountains

The western margins of predominantly flat Sind are defined by the **Kirthar Mountains** that run 240 km N to S in a gently curving easterly arc. The Kirthar Range is topped by Spitangi limestone, between 25 and 50 million years old, and raised from the sea bed as the Indian plate pushed N into the Asian landmass. The highest point in the range is *Kutte-ji Qabar*, or Dog's Grave, at 2,060m in the southern part of the system known as Sindh Kohistan.

Low outcrops of limestone occur at Rohri, Sukkur, Hyderabad and Makli, as well as some isolated granite hills in the SE Nagarparkar area.

Deserts

The E and NE margins of Sind are defined by desert. The **Thar Desert** (see page 147) in the E straddles the international border with India, where it extends into the Rajasthan Desert. To the NE, the Thar extends into the **Cholistan Desert** in Punjab, see page 309. The northern reaches of the Thar are known locally as the *Pat*. The surface configuration of parts of both deserts has been transformed by irrigated agriculture.

Climate

The most noteworthy characteristics of Sind's climate are high summer temperatures, low rainfall and considerable variation in the timing, location and volume of rainfall. Sind stands on the verge of two monsoon systems: the SW monsoon is stopped at Lakhpat in the Rann of Kutch by an inversion layer of warmer continental air, and the NE monsoon passes no further than Karachi in the extreme SW. Climatically, there are great contrasts between Upper (N) and Lower (S) Sind, with the southerly regions modified considerably by maritime influence.

In the N, the hot season can last for up to 7 months, with shade temperatures of 47-50°C not being uncommon. The highest temperature recorded at a Pakistan meteorological station, 52.8°C, was measured at Jacobabad in Jun 1919. In winter (Nov-Mar), temperatures are pleasant although nights can be cold. The S has far greater levels of humidity than regions inland, with cooling sea breezes for 4 months of the year.

A key characteristic of Sind's climate is the variability of rainfall. The state average is approximately 200 mm/year, the coast receiving far more than the desert regions, with rainfall diminishing conspicuously in the N and NW. Almost all the rain falls in Jul and Aug (eg in 1988, all of Karachi's 160 mm, Hyderabad's 328 mm and Nawabshah's 24 mm annual precipitation fell in these 2 months). However, yearly mean rainfall figures can vary significantly (eg at Karachi Airport, 399 mm fell in 1978, 161 mm in 1982, but none at all in 1987).

History

Sind has a unique position in the history of South Asia. The Indus Valley Civilization site of Moenjo Daro represents the major city of South Asia's oldest civilization. Further, with the Arab conquest of Sind in 711/712 AD, it was the region where Islam arrived and became established three centuries before it made an impact elsewhere in the sub-continent.

Pre-history

The earliest remains of human habitation in Sind may date from the late Pleistocene. Despite the lack of fossil or skeletal evidence, rough tools found near Rohri are probably the work of Palaeolithic man. Similar implements belonging to the Chalcolithic, or Bronze Age, have been found throughout Sind, although as Lambrick points out, "it is commonplace ... to find living side by side communities whose standards of civilization are 1,000 years or more apart".

Evolving out of much earlier settlements, the **Indus Valley Civilization** began to reach its height around 2300 BC, prospering for 600 years until 1700 BC when it declined for reasons that are not yet entirely clear. The Indus Valley Civilization is perhaps unique in that it displays a strict cultural uniformity over its entire area of approximately 1.3 million sq km. Of the 1,000 or so sites discovered thus far, 70 have been excavated in this area. The two most important sites are at **Moenjo Daro** in Sind (see page 159) and **Harappa** in Punjab (see page 293).

Pre-Muslim period

Sind's history has been greatly influenced by its geostrategic location. Just to the S of the main line of communication/invasion between the Persian-Afghan plateau and the Indian plains, Sind lies very near to the crossroads of South Asian history.

The **Aryans** are thought to have entered the region c1500 BC, and although there are frequent references to the Indus in the *Rigveda*, it is not possible to deduce anything about conditions in the lower Indus valley.

Between 515-500 BC, King **Darius the Great** sent his general **Scylax of Caryanda** to conquer the region, and incorporate it into the Persian Empire. Scylax organized a fleet, and sailed down the Indus to the sea, continuing on to Egypt.

Partially repeating this feat in 325-324 BC, **Alexander the Great** sailed down the Jhelum, Chenab and Indus, dismantling the Persian Empire, before returning W through the Makran to Karmania. Alexander died the following year, 323 BC, at Babylon, near Baghdad. The region then came under the Buddhist rule of the **Mauryan** kings whose empire was based at Patna in N India. It was the great Mauryan king, **Asoka**, who converted Sind to Buddhism.

Greek influence was reintroduced to the region c175 BC by **Demetrius**, the Greek King of Bactria. Further rulers of varying spheres of influence in the region included the **Scythians**, under whose period of rule Sind was often referred to as Indo-Scythia, before the famous king **Kanishka** incorporated Sind as part of the great **Kushan** Empire (120 AD). A succession of further invaders, including **Sassanians** and **White Huns**, brought further change to the region, until the **Rajputs** established a dynasty that lasted until being usurped by the Brahmin **Chach** in 652 AD. Observations of Sind dating from this period can be found in the travel accounts of the Chinese traveller **Hieun Tsang**, who visited the region c641 AD. The Brahmin Dynasty remained until it was defeated by the Muslim Arab forces of **Mohammad bin Qasim** in 711-712 AD.

Early Muslim rule

Throughout the 6th and 7th centuries, bitter rivalries continued between the Persian, Byzantium and Arab Empires for control of the lucrative maritime trade routes between India and the Mediterranean. As the Arabs gained the ascendency, it became essential for them to control the ports and sea routes along the coast of Sind. Arab dominance in maritime commerce was being challenged by the Hindu merchants of **Debal** (see page 139), who, with the tacit support of the Medes of Sind, encouraged pirates to harass the Arab trading ships. Several punitive expeditions were sent by both land and sea to Sind, though they were largely unsuccessful. In 711 AD, **al-Hajjal**, Governor of Iraq under the **Umayyad** Dynasty sent the 17-year-old Arab governor of Fars to conquer the troublesome region.

Mohammad bin Qasim had made a name for himself at a very young age by suppressing a Kurd rebellion, and subduing the Fars rebels. In 710 AD he left Shiraz with 6,000 Syrian cavalry, joining a further 6,000 armed camel cavalry at the borders of the Makran. Following the siege of Debal in 711 AD, during which six huge catapults were used to deadly effect, and almost the entire population was put to the sword, the Arab armies marched N, taking Nerun (Hyderabad), Siwistan (Sehwan), Brahmanabad, al-Rur (Rohri) and Askalanda (Uch), before crossing the Chenab and taking Multan. Invariably, all men capable of bearing arms were either murdered or forced to accept Islam at the point of a sword, whilst women and children were enslaved.

For the Arab armies, the expedition was an unqualified military and financial success. However, following the death of the Caliph, his successor ordered that Mohammad bin Qasim be arrested and brought back to Iraq. The young Arab conqueror met an ignoble end in a prison dungeon in Wasit, having been tortured to death.

Arab rule in Sind brought a number of cultural developments. **Sindhi** developed as the regional language, and acquired its distinctive **Naksh** script, written like Arabic from right to left. However, although Sind was notionally a province of the Arab Empire, their hold on the region was tenuous, and a number of rulers carved out individual territories for themselves.

Sumras, Sammas, Arghuns and Tarkhans

The Arabs were succeeded by the **Sumra** Dynasty of Muslims from Sind, who loosely ruled the region from c1026 to c1352. During this period of Sumra rule, *Sufi* saints, particularly of the Suharwardiyya order, begun to establish an influence. The last Sumra ruler was defeated c1352, and a new ruling dynasty was established under the **Sammas**, based at Thatta. Under the Sammas, Persian replaced Arabic as the official language, and this era saw the flowering of the mystic *Sufi* movement.

In 1520, the last Samma ruler, **Jam Feroz**, was defeated in battle by **Shah Shuja Beg**, and the rule of Sind passed into the hands of the house of **Arghun**. Descended from Arghun Khan, the great great grandson of Chingiz Khan who was appointed ruler of Persia by Kublai Khan, the Arghuns were eventually succeeded by the **Tarkhans**, a dynasty who also traced their line back to Chingiz Khan.

Many of the Arghun and Tarkhan rulers were noted writers and poets, and it was during their period of rule that attempts were made to record and preserve the rich Sindhi folklore. Indeed, some consider this period of Sind's history as the "Elizabethan age of its literature".

The Mughals

In 1592, the last Tarkhan ruler, **Mirza Jani Beg**, surrendered to the superior forces of **Akbar's** Mughal Empire, led by **Abdul Rahim Khan-e-Khanan**. Ironically, Akbar had been born at Umarkot (see page 148), in Sind some 50 years earlier, whilst his father Humayun had been fleeing from Sher Shah. The Mughals ruled Lower Sind until 1737, when the last Mughal Governor of Thatta handed over power to **Mir Nur Mohammad Kalhora**.

The Kalhoras and the Talpurs

The Kalhora's had already assumed control of much of Upper Sind by the early 1700s, and upon acquiring Thatta from the Mughals, Nur Mohammad Kalhora became regarded as the ruler who made Sind one province. He did, however, continue to pay an annual tribute to the Afghan ruler, **Ahmad Shah Durrani**. The Kalhora capital was initially established at **Khudabad** (see page 159), although this was removed to the new city of **Hyderabad** in 1768 by **Ghulam Shah Kalhora**. His period of rule is remembered as a time of great stability, with progress in agriculture and the flowering of Sindhi literature in the works of **Shah Abdul Latif**, see page 150. However, upon his death in 1772, a period of tyranny ensued as the Kalhora's fought with the **Talpurs** from Baluchistan for control of Sind. Meantime the Afghan kings attempted to extract as much tribute as possible from the two warring factions. Eventually, three branches of the Talpur Dynasty gained a tenuous grip on Sind.

The British

Having become the dominant power in India, two factors attracted the **British** to Sind. Firstly, the British were keen to survey the Indus in order to assess its potential as a trade route. Indeed, when the British completed this survey in 1831, a Sindhi Sayyid, recognizing the implications, remarked "Alas, Sindh has now gone since the English have seen the river". Secondly, Sind became part of the British forward-bloc 'frontier strategy', to counter the perceived threat of Russian expansionism through Afghanistan.

In 1842, **Sir Charles Napier** was appointed British Resident in Sind. A treaty was offered to the Talpurs requiring that a) one side of the coin of

Sind should bear the name of the King of England, b) the Talpurs should surrender Karachi, Shikarpur, Sabzalkot and Umarkot to the British, and c) a strip of land 30m wide on either side of the Indus be given to the British. Historians agree that the British knew these terms would be unacceptable, and in the inevitable resulting war, Napier's forces rapidly defeated the Talpurs.

Napier's actions were strictly against instructions from London not to interfere in Sind, and having accepted the Talpur surrender in Feb 1843, he telegraphed his announcement of the capture with the Latin word *Peccavi* – I have sinned. The annexation came within the background of the disastrous campaign in Afghanistan, and many feel that Napier was looking to restore some military pride to the British army. Indeed, the great Indian adventurer Mountstuart Elphinstone suggested that the British action was "done in the spirit of a bully who has been kicked in the streets and goes home to beat his wife in revenge".

With British rule came changes in the administrative and bureaucratic system, as well as new technology in agriculture, transport and trade. However, the inclusion of Sind within the Bombay Presidency and the decision to pass land holdings to Hindu creditors was a source of much bitterness amongst indigenous Sindhis, and gave rise to a sense of nationalism. It was not until 1935 that agitation by the Sindh Muslim League succeeded in separating the province from Bombay.

Partition

Sindhis are very proud of the fact that they were the first to demand partition of India in 1938, and the first to adopt the Pakistan Resolution of Lahore in 1943. It is also a source of great pride that the Quaid-e-Azam and father of the nation, **Mohammad Ali Jinnah**, was a Sindhi.

Prior to Partition, most of the places in business, education, bureaucracy and trade had been filled by Hindus. At independence, the mass exodus of Hindus was matched by an equally large influx of Muslim settlers from India. Taking advantage of these new opportunities, the immigrants filled the vacuum created by the Hindus, settling mainly in the urban areas of Karachi, Hyderabad and to a lesser extent, Sukkur. Known as **mohajirs**, these recent arrivals brought a whole new culture to Sind, with very different aspirations to the predominantly rural ethnic Sindhis.

The massive influx of mohajirs to the urban areas led to the dramatic growth of cities such as Karachi and Hyderabad, and began to alarm the ethnic Sindhis who now only constituted 48% of the state's population. Because of their traditionally low levels of education and the lack of a middle class, the Sindhis were unable to take advantage of new opportunities created at Partition, particularly in government positions, and felt resentful that these opportunities were being taken by Punjabis and mohajirs.

There was further concern over the threat to Sindhi identity by the dissolution of the individual provinces and the creation of a single administrative unit, West Pakistan, the imposition of Urdu as the national language, the dominance of Punjabis in the army and civil service, and the decision to shift the federal capital away from Karachi to Islamabad. These concerns gave rise to indigenous nationalist movements such as Jeay Sindh and Sindhu Desh.

Culture

People

Because of its strategic location, Sind has had a long experience of influence from outside. Sind is home to more Baluchis than Baluchistan, received more Muslim migrants at Partition than any other state, and due to the urban 'pull' of Karachi, has continued to experience mass internal migration from NWFP, the Northern Areas and the Punjab. In addition, refugees from civil wars and political change in Afghanistan, Iran, Bangladesh, Sri Lanka and India have continued to be drawn to Sind, and Karachi in particular.

Such has been the regularity of incursion of outsiders into Sind, that assessing who were the original inhabitants of the region has become little more than speculation. Lambrick, however, asserts that the majority of Sindhis belong to the Rajputs, themselves the result of a long period of blending between different groupings.

The state is predominantly Muslim, with most followers belonging to the Sunni sect. *Sufi* saints, most of whom arrived in Sind in the 12th to 15th centuries, are particularly revered throughout the state. There are also sizeable Ismaili and Parsi communities in Karachi, whose economic significance is way out of proportion to their numbers.

Prior to Partition, almost a quarter of the population of Sind was Hindu, occupying many of the white-collar, trading, money lending and land owning positions. Following the division of India and Pakistan, most Hindus left the region, although in the Tharparkar region to the SE they still represent a sizeable minority (37%). In the 1981 census, 8% of the state's population were registered Hindu.

Punjabis also represent a sizeable minority within Sind, many of whom were granted land in the state by the British in recognition of their farming skills. This process has continued since independence, with much new agricultural land being gifted to families of the Punjabi dominated armed forces and civil service.

The mohajirs brought with them a culture, attitude and aspirations very much different to the ethnic Sindhis. Their presence, and particularly commercial significance, has led to much friction between the two communities. In turn, the mohajirs feel that they are under represented in the allocation of government job and education quotas, and feel that they deserve greater consideration since they gave up the most to come to Muslim Pakistan.

Language and literature

Although the majority of the population of Sind (52%) have Sindhi as their first language, this does not give a true reflection of the linguistic diversity within the state. In Karachi, for example, 54% have Urdu as their first language, 13% Punjabi, 8% Pushto, with Sindhi a mere 6%. Following the decision in 1971 to make Sindhi the official state language, violent riots occurred that resulted in many deaths. Tensions remain today over the use and teaching of language.

The Sindhi language is linked with Prakitt, Sanskrit, Persian and Arabic, as well as northern Dardic languages, thus emphasizing the history of outside influence in Sind. Sindhi has been written in both Sanskrit and Persian script, although it was the British who backed the use of Arabic as the official written form.

The most important literary works in the Sindhi language are of a religious or devotional nature, and are particularly influenced by Sufism. Sind's foremost mystic poet is Shah Abdul Latif (see page 150), whose 17th century work is revered today.

Modern Sind

Government

Sind re-emerged on the political map of Pakistan in Jul 1970, after the dissolution of the one administrative unit of West Pakistan. The Federal government, in an attempt to arrest the rise of regionalism, had in 1955 dissolved the provincial boundaries of the constituent states of Pakistan, as well as the Princely States, and created the Unified Province of West Pakistan. However, rather than reduce the forces of regionalism, this action increased the sense of regional identity in Sind, and gave impetus to regional movements such as Sindhu Desh and Jeay Sindh.

Politics in Sind has been dominated in recent times by two main parties. Sind has been the traditional power base of the *Pakistan's Peoples' Party* (PPP); a party formed on socialist lines in the late 1960s by Zulfikar Ali Bhutto. However, the party is dominated by the ruling feudal families of Sind, such as the Bhuttos, Zadaris and Legharis, in whose interest the traditional socialist values are in stark contrast. To perpetuate their grip over the peasantry, it is not unusual for the landed families to offer candidates to rival political parties in order to maintain their vested interests.

The second major political party of Sind, the *Mohajir Qaumi Movement* (MQM), represents the overwhelmingly urban mohajir community. The rise of this movement dates to the early 1980s, when disillusionment with access to reserved government job and education quotas prompted the mohajir community to press for greater rights within the framework of Pakistan. More radical members of the community call for the recognition of a mohajir state within Pakistan.

Recent political developments

At the 1988 elections that brought the PPP government of Benazir Bhutto to power, the MQM continued their domination of urban Sind, winning all but one of the seats in Karachi and Hyderabad. They comprised the third largest block in both the National and Provincial Assembly. An uneasy alliance was entered into between the PPP and MQM, aimed at arresting the rapidly deteriorating law and order situation in Karachi and Hyderabad. The alliance was doomed to failure, and by 1989 the streets of Karachi were a free-for-all, with rival student factions of both parties murdering each other with impunity. A crack-down was launched by the Sind government in May 1990, but the one-sided nature of this action perpetuated further the ethnic and political divide.

The army High Command were reluctant to accept a role in Sind that did not grant them full powers to set up military courts and suspend the high court's jurisdiction under Article 245 of the Constitution. The government of Benazir Bhutto, on the other hand, was equally reluctant to allow a martial administration to return to the PPP power base of Sind. The uneasy relationship between the army and the elected government of Bhutto could not withstand the strain of the situation in Sind, and in 1990 the President of Pakistan sacked the Federal government, citing corruption and ineffectiveness as the reasons behind his action.

The political, ethnic and cultural divide within Sind is no better illustrated than in the Oct 1990 general election results. The PPP and allied independent candidates won 60% of the state's seats, with the MQM gaining 33% of the vote. However, the MQM completely dominated the urban areas, winning virtually all of the seats in Karachi and Hyderabad. However, the new Federal government in Islamabad, headed by Nawaz Sharif, were equally unsuccessful in curtailing the cycle of violence in Sind, and in May 1992 the army were given free reign in Sind.

The 30 month military operation that followed, code-named 'Operation Clean-up', at a cost of Rs 730,204mn to the public exchequer, has had mixed results. Whilst travel in interior Sind has been made considerably safer, with a marked reduction in incidents of kidnapping and banditry, the situation in Karachi has if anything, worsened. The arbitrary nature of the army operation has alienated many Karachites, particularly the mohajir community. It is felt that the MQM, Karachi's democratically elected representatives, were the target of the operation, with the army deliberately creating a split in the movement by its outright patronage of the Haqiqi faction of the MQM. Further, it is felt that PPP members with alleged links to criminal and terrorist groups were allowed to continue unchecked, whilst MQM members were imprisoned or driven into exile. Victimization of the opposition by the party in power is a fact of life in the Pakistani political arena, but it seems unlikely that there will be a cessation to the violence in Karachi without the participation of all interested groups.

The Economy

Despite problems of sectarianism, hyper-urbanization, regional inequalities and an uncertain political future, Sind contributes significantly to the economy of Pakistan. Sind accounts for approximately 30% of GDP, 21% of agricultural GDP, 47% of manufacturing GDP and 42% of construction.

Agriculture

Of Sind's total land area of 14.09 million ha, 40% is a cultivable wasteland, and just over one third is used for agriculture. Agriculture is the major economic activity of the state not just in terms of revenue, but also employment.

Most of Sind's agriculture is based on a two season system. The most important summer, or *kharif*, crops are rice, cotton, sugar cane, sorghum and corn. Major winter, or *rabi*, crops include wheat and barley. Sind accounts for almost 50% of Pakistan's **rice** production, although it is suggested that local varieties are more cost-effective than introduced green revolution varieties.

In terms of volume and value, **wheat** is Sind's premier winter crop, account-

ing for 20% of Pakistan's total production. Wheat production has benefitted greatly from the provision of canal irrigation, and now covers 1 million ha of Sind's agricultural land. The major cash crop of Sind is **cotton**, grown over 560,000 ha. Sind's fastest growing crop, however, is **sugar cane**, which has begun to compete with rice and wheat for agricultural land use. Sind produces a third of Pakistan's sugar cane at yields higher per ha than anywhere else in the country.

However, sugar cane aside, agricultural productivity is generally low due to a number of factors. As many as 75% of farmers are *haris* or share-croppers who have little incentive to increase production, and generally use inefficient, traditional systems of agriculture. Further, the system of land inheritance has led to a greater fragmentation of land-holdings into more and more uneconomical sized plots.

Attempts at land reform have been unsuccessful because the *waderas*, or feudal landowners, dominate and control every aspect of political, economic and social life in Sind, with many of the dominant land owning families such as the Bhuttos, Legharis, Syeds, Jatois and Mukhdooms being prominent in Pakistani politics. Ceiling levels of land ownership are circumvented by transferring property deeds into the names of relatives, thus frustrating the objects of equitable land reform.

The comparatively recent development of irrigation in the lower Indus basin has had a major impact upon agriculture in the region, although not necessarily always a positive one. The provision of canal irrigation has greatly increased production, and brought a degree of prosperity to Sind, but the lack of drainage capacity has upset the delicate balance between recharge and discharge of the sub-surface water. As a consequence, the water table has risen by up to 15 m in places, sometimes reaching the surface. The twin problems of

waterlogging and **salinization** are of major concern for Sind's future economic welfare. Of the canal irrigated land, over 1 million ha of the sown land has gone out of production at a rate approaching 40,000 ha/year. The first study into the problem, undertaken in 1956, found that 98% of Upper Sind, 93% of Lower Sind and 27% of the Delta were predominantly poorly drained or waterlogged, whilst 32% of Upper Sind, 50% of Lower Sind and 33% of the Delta were predominantly severely saline.

Attempts have been made to lower the water table through the use of tubewells, but this is considered to be only a temporary measure since the subsurface irrigation water frequently contains more salts than the original surface water, thus perpetuating the problem of salinization.

Resources and industry

Post Partition, Sind has experienced rapid industrial growth and now accounts for 50% of Pakistan's industrial base. However, industrial activity in Sind is so completely dominated by Karachi, that it is threatening to distort the economic, political and social balance of the state. Attempts have been made to encourage industrialists to locate in less developed parts of the state by creating tax-free zones, providing relocation subsidies and introducing planning restrictions in places considered over developed. However, the draw of Karachi, with its large skilled and unskilled labour supply, power generation potential, water supply, transport infrastructure and marketing and financial services, provides a powerful pull to industry. Sind's main industries include textiles, foodstuffs, chemicals, building materials, engineering and electrical goods, pharmaceuticals as well as processing hydro-carbon products.

Natural gas at **Sui** provides a valuable resource, supplying Karachi with power and a raw material for fertilizer. Total production in the 1980s exceeded 2,500 million cu metres of gas. **Oil production** has increased significantly in recent years, rising from 1.7m barrels in 1984 to over 8m barrels in 1991. Sind is also Pakistan's largest single producer of electricity, accounting for 12 billion kW in 1991.

KARACHI

From modest beginnings as the old fishing village of Kalachi-jo-Goth at the mouth of the Indus, Karachi has grown into a mega-city, ranking amongst the greatest metropolis in the world. As capital of Sind Province, and former capital of Pakistan, Karachi represents the country's major commercial, industrial, financial and educational centre, as well as having the premier port and international airport.

Early history

Karachi originated from a collection of small islands – Baba, Shamspir, Keamari and Manora – around a bay that acted as a natural harbour. A harbour at this site is mentioned by Pliny and Ptolemy, writing in the 2nd century. Indeed, Karachi may be the place at which Alexander the Great's admiral Nearchus assembled his fleet in 326 BC to sail to the Euphrates.

Arrival of the British

When the British occupied Sind in 1843, having occupied the Talpur fort on Manora 4 years previously, Karachi was a walled city of 14,000. Although the city walls were demolished in 1846 following a cholera epidemic, the *Kharadar* (Saltwater) Gate to the sea shore and the *Mithadar* (Sweetwater) Gate on the Lyari river bank remain. Sir Charles Napier, Governor of Sind, shifted the provincial capital to Karachi in 1843, and made efforts to develop the town and port. The Karachi Municipal Corporation was formed in 1852, and within the next 20 years, the population had increased three-fold to 57,000 to meet the expansion of commercial activities in the town.

The latter half of the 19th century saw the rapid growth of Karachi's infrastructure, including the opening of the Sind Railway in 1861 and the construction of the Mereweather Pier at the port in 1882. Many early buildings from this period, (Masonic Hall, Frere Hall, Mereweather Tower, Empress Market), can still be seen today. A water supply and underground drainage system was completed in 1894, and electricity was provided in 1914. An aeroplane landed in Karachi for the first time in 1918. The pace of Karachi's expansion and development was enhanced by the city's strategic location during WW2, and by 1941 the population of Karachi was over 350,000.

Partition

The partition of the sub-continent and the emergence of Pakistan dramatically transformed the city. Despite the exodus to India of most of the Hindu population, the massive influx of refugees more than doubled Karachi's population from 420,000 in 1948 to over 1 million by 1951. Over 60% of Karachi's population were immigrants, bringing with them a culture and society quite distinct from both that of earlier Karachi and rural Sind. Known as **mohajirs**, a term

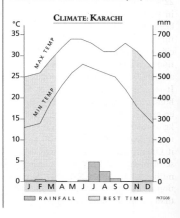

CLIMATE: KARACHI

°C / mm

MAX TEMP
MIN TEMP

J F M A M J J A S O N D

RAINFALL   BEST TIME   PKTG08

associated with the Prophet's flight from Mecca, these refugees continue to dominate political life in Karachi today.

Refugees and migrants continued to flood into Karachi at the rate of 300/day. In 1960, with Karachi's primacy threatening to distort the whole economy of Pakistan (the population doubled to over 2 million in the decade 1951-61 alone), Gen Ayub Khan decided to move the capital to the new city of Islamabad.

Recent history

Despite the selection of Islamabad as the new capital, Karachi continues to attract refugees and internal migrants. Displaced Biharis from the 1971 Bangladesh war, refugees from civil war in Sri Lanka, Iranians, Afghan refugees, Pathans from NWFP, civil servants and skilled workers from Punjab and rural Sindhi migrants all add to the ethnic mix.

Although a census has not been taken since 1981, Karachi's population is conservatively estimated to be some 8 million. By the year 2000 it is expected to exceed 10 million. Nearly 6% of Pakistan's population (some argue 10%), and 22% of Pakistan's urban population live in Karachi. The rapid growth has not been met by the provision of infrastructure and services, leaving Karachi as a city with major problems. The population increases by 6%/year, but the availability of services increases by just 1.2%. It is estimated that only one third of homes have piped water, a quarter sewerage. The city produces over 1 million kg of rubbish daily, yet there are facilities to dispose of less than a quarter of it. Orangi, one of Karachi's largest slum settlements, has a population of over 1 million alone. 25% of Karachi's population are unemployed, and there are more than a million heroin addicts.

Current events

Perhaps the greatest threat to Karachi, however, is the seemingly endless spiral of ethnic, sectarian and criminal violence into which the city has plunged. In 1994, over 1,000 people were killed in violence in Karachi; a further 500 in the first 3 months of 1995. Who exactly is behind the killings is a source of lively debate in Pakistan, filling many column-inches in the newspapers and journals. Conspiracy theories abound, including one which suggests that following the return of Hong Kong to Chinese rule in 1997, mysterious 'Western powers' have selected Karachi as the new regional free-port. The total breakdown of law and order in Karachi will make the city ungovernable, leading to independent status from Pakistan, and thus creating a new Hong Kong.

More realistically, the situation is the culmination of a number of tragic events. Rival political factions have divided the city into small fiefdoms. Although operating under the cover of political parties and factions, they are effectively criminal gangs who rule through terror and extortion. The police, demoralized and poorly paid, are both unable to take effective action, and party to the criminality. The problems are compounded by the ready availability of cheap, high-tech guns (a legacy of the Afghan war), and the drug trafficking mafia who are taking advantage of the deteriorating security situation to enhance huge profits. The PPP government have pinned the blame upon the 'foreign hand', implying that the Indian intelligence agency, RAW, is behind the unrest, in retaliation for Pakistani support for the jihad in Kashmir. In Dec 1994, the Indian consulate was ordered to shut for this reason, although proof of involvement is yet to be produced.

The huge ethnic mix of the city has further exacerbated these problems, with ethnic and sectarian tensions ready

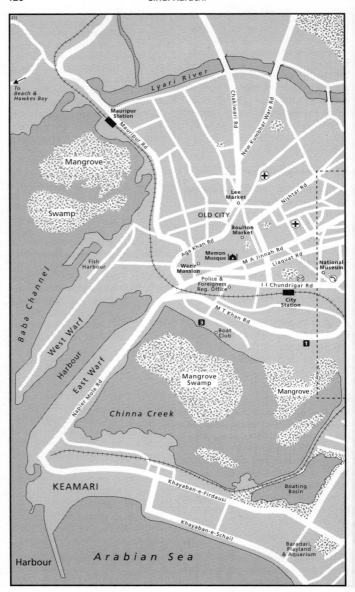

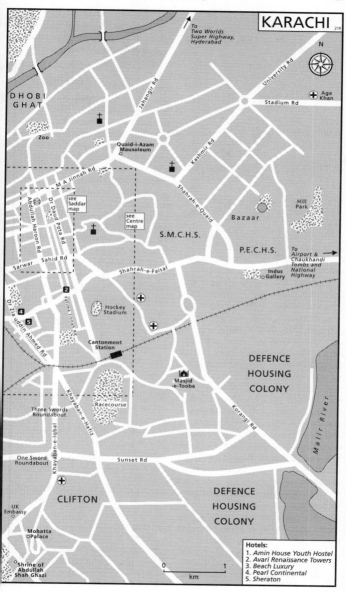

KARACHI 21R

Hotels:
1. *Amin House Youth Hostel*
2. *Avari Renaissance Towers*
3. *Beach Luxury*
4. *Pearl Continental*
5. *Sheraton*

to explode into violence. In 1985, a young mohajir girl was killed in Orangi by a speeding bus driven by a Pathan. In 2 days of rioting that followed, 60 people were killed. The bulldozing by the government of the Pathan squatter settlement of Sorabgoth in 1986, seen by many as the centre of the gun and drugs trade, led to further Pathan-mohajir fighting in which over 200 were killed. Further tensions between Punjabis, native Sindhis, Baluchis, Pathans, Biharis, mohajirs as well as those wishing to exploit the Sunni/Shia split are never far from the surface, and perpetuate the cycle of violence. Add to this Karachi's rapid population growth, high levels of unemployment and poverty, and the future looks bleak.

Despite this, Karachi contributes 15% of Gross Domestic Product, 25% of Federal Revenue, 50% of all bank deposits and 72% of the nation's issued capital.

Warning Despite the levels of violence in Karachi, foreign visitors have been remarkably unaffected. Although two American embassy staff were murdered in 1995, there appears to be no deliberate targeting of foreigners. The British Deputy High Commission in Karachi, however, offers the following safety guidelines.

1. Certain parts of Karachi are considered 'high risk', were the possibility of being caught in indiscriminate firing must be considered. These areas include Orangi, Korangi, North Karachi, Nazimabad, Liaquatabad, Malir, Pak Colony, Pathan Colony and Faisal Colony. Although this list seems extensive, it should be remembered that there is no reason for a tourist to need to go to any of these districts.

2. With car-snatching becoming increasingly common, it is recommended that all vehicles should carry conspicuous as well as hidden security markings (ie sand-blasting engine and chassis numbers on front and rear windscreens). 4WD vehicles appear to be most commonly targetted. Travelling accompanied appears to reduce the risk of attack. If you are involved in a snatch situation **do not attempt to offer any form of resistance**.

Places of interest

City of the Quaid-e-Azam

As the place of Jinnah's birth, Karachi is frequently referred to as the city of the Quaid-e-Azam, and has many buildings associated with his life and death. Jinnah's father, Jinnahbhai Poonja (born c1850), moved to the booming port city sometime in the early 1870s and rented the second floor apartment of the three storey **Wazir Mansion** in Kharadar, one of the oldest residential districts of Karachi. It was in this elegant balconied house on Newnham Rd that Mohammad Ali Jinnah was born. However, prior to 1879, the municipality of Karachi did not issue certificates of birth and death and thus there is some dispute as to his true date of birth. Jinnah was to claim that he was born on Christmas Day 1876, and this day is still celebrated as the Quaid's official birthday in Pakistan. Yet the records at Jinnah's first school register his date of birth as 20 October 1875, and the irony of the significance of the date that Jinnah claimed as his date of birth is not lost on his principal biographer Wolpert. Wazir Mansion is now preserved as a museum and houses a number of Jinnah's personal possessions.

Jinnah attended the first Muslim educational complex to be built in Sind, Karachi's **Sind Madrassa-tul-Islam**, although records show that he was withdrawn after several years due to 'long absences'.

Quaid-e-Azam House Museum, on Shahrah-e-Faisal Rd, opp Avari Towers, is the superbly refurbished former home of Jinnah. It was known as Flag Staff House when occupied by General Gracy.

commanding officer of the British Army in Sind until 1946. Following Partition it became the official residence of Jinnah as first Governor General of Pakistan, although he rarely stayed here. The main building is built of limestone block, with a wooden trussed roof finished with red ceramic Mangalore tiles. Standing in its own grounds, this beautiful Anglo-Indian mansion was opened as a museum in late 1993. The private apartments, bedrooms, study and drawing room of Jinnah and his sister Fatima have been meticulously recreated with original furniture and personal artefacts including the Quaid-e-Azam's Paris-made spat shoes.

Quaid-e-Azam's Mausoleum Situated on a low rise to the E of M A Jinnah Rd, the tomb of the Quaid-e-Azam shows a neat fusion of traditional and modern Islamic architectural styles. Standing on a 54 sq m platform, the white marble mausoleum has high, pointed arches filled with copper grills, in the North African style. The cool and airy interior has a Japanese tiled ceiling, a four tiered Chinese crystal chandelier, and an Iranian silver railing around the cenotaph. There is a regular changing of the guards. Also within the terraced gardens are the tombs of Pakistan's first Prime Minister, Liaquat Ali Khan, and Jinnah's devoted sister, Fatima.

Beaches and harbours

Karachi's proximity to the warm waters of the Arabian Sea has been both a factor in the port's development, as well as being one of the city's prime attractions. West from Karachi, an almost uninterrupted line of beaches stretch for several hundred kilometres along Baluchistan's Makran coast into Iran. Several beaches, **Sandspit**, **Hawkes Bay** and **Paradise Point**, can be reached by car from the town (45 mins) or by bus from **Lea Market** (1½ hrs). Beaches tend to become busy at weekends, and the attention of camel owners, cold drink vendors and

souvenir salesmen can make the experience far from relaxing.

French Beach, at the centre of Hawkes Bay, and some 40 km from Karachi, is for the exclusive use of foreigners and privileged Pakistanis, and offers a greater degree of privacy. The rocky beach and clear water are ideal for snorkelling, although visitors need to bring their own equipment.

Continuing W along Hawkes Bay, you pass **Baleji Beach**, renowned for its snorkelling and diving, past the **Karachi Nuclear Power Plant** to **Paradise Point**. Here, the action of the sea has created a number of stacks, blow-holes and wave-cut platforms. Beyond this point, there are a number of attractive isolated bays and coves.

Warning During the monsoon season from Jun to Aug, currents are strong and the sea is dangerously rough. In May and Jun jellyfish make sea bathing unpleasant.

NB Islamic tradition requires you to dress decently and to avoid unwanted attention it is best to wear bikinis only on hotel or private beaches. Village women in South Asia usually bathe in the sea fully clothed.

During Sep and Oct, giant **Green Turtles** and **Pacific** or **Olive Ridley Turtles** come ashore at Hawkes Bay and Sandspit to lay their eggs, having travelled over 1,500 km. PTDC and various travel agents can arrange night-time turtle watching trips. You can witness the female turtles select a suitable spot above high tide to lay the eggs, before quickly covering them and re-entering the sea, but not before, some say, shedding a tear. With the constant attention of birds and roaming dogs, the mortality rate amongst the young turtles is extremely high.

Clifton Beach is the closest beach to the city, although this very factor makes it polluted and unsuitable for swimming. Developed as a health resort in the 19th century by the British, Clifton is now one of Karachi's most exclusive residential areas. The beach area, however, is where the entire socio-economic strata of Karachi life comes to enjoy itself. The beach is lined with stalls selling snacks, trinkets, shell and onyx souvenirs, and camel owners offering beach rides. *Funland* is an amusement park with roller coasters, dodgems and a bowling alley, and is perhaps Karachi's greatest social leveller. Look out for poor, scruffy young boys terrifying spoilt, rich girls on the dodgems. *Playland*, on the Marine Drive, was originally built as a casino, but is now a restaurant and amusement arcade. Below the arcade is an **aquarium**, with an interesting collection of fresh and seawater fish, and a number of turtles.

Clifton Viewpoint, the yellow sandstone pavilion on the promenade, offers good views of the surrounding area. Also on the promenade is the **Shree Ratneswar Mahdevi Hindu Temple**, known as the Caves of Mahdevi and mentioned in the Ramayana. Inland, 1 km NE, stands the red sandstone **Mohatta Palace**. Built in 1933 in a Mughal-Gothic style with imposing domes and cupolas, the palace was used as the residence of Quaid-e-Azam's sister Fatima, until her death in 1967. It is sometimes known as Qasr-e-Fatima Jinnah. Now all but derelict, it is often used as a location on Pakistani fashion shoots. For a few rupees, the chowkidar may let you in.

On the small hill above Clifton Beach stands the **Shrine of Abdullah Shah Ghazi**, the patron saint of Karachi. A direct descendant of the Prophet, Abdullah Shah Ghazi came to Sind in the 9th century. Legend suggests that his ship was wrecked off the coast and he was one of the few survivors. A noted Muslim mystic and preacher, he gained a large devotional following in Sind that continues to this day. It is suggested that over a thousand pilgrims visit the site daily, and many more at weekends, to join the resident fakirs, medicants, musicians and beggars. On Thur nights *qawwalis*, or devotional songs, are performed and during his *Urs* (20-22 Islamic month of Zilhaj) pilgrims come from all over Pakistan. The square shrine, with a green and white striped dome, is typical of Sufi shrines all across Sind. Beneath the tomb, the sweet water spring that flows from the rock is attributed to the saint's mystic powers.

Gaddani Beach Although strictly speaking in Baluchistan, Gaddani Beach (48 km) can be reached as an excursion from Karachi. Gaddani is famous as the world's largest ship-breakers, where, at high tide, giant supertankers are beached and then reduced to scrap by hand. Although still an impressive sight today, increased taxation on the scrap has made the industry less profitable than in the past, and thus the beach no longer resembles the ship's graveyard that it did at its peak. The main town is set slightly inland. To the W is a small fishing village and a picnic point. To the E is the main centre of ship breaking activity, strung out along the beach. In theory, a Govt permit is required from **Quetta** to visit Gaddani beach. Many foreigners report having reached the beach without the documentation both by private car and public bus, but there remains the possibility of being turned away if you do not have the necessary permit. Regular buses run from Karachi's **Lea Market** as far as **Hub**, 22 km from Gaddani. From Hub there is no regular public transport to the beach.

Keamari Harbour Strategically placed on the Arabian Sea, Karachi has taken advantage of its fine natural harbour to become one of the key ports in the region. Not only is the port critical to the Pakistani economy, it is also the key point of entry for goods in transit to Afghanistan. For the tourist, it is possible to hire boats for **crabbing** expeditions. The best time for crabbing is late afternoon, after the monsoon. Rs 800 should cover an evening's boat hire, including cooking your catch, although you will need to bargain hard. Trips can also be arranged through Karachi travel agents.

From the harbour it is possible to take a ferry launch to **Manora Point**, site of a quiet beach, an old Talpur fort, a couple of British churches and a ruined Hindu temple.

The **West Wharf Harbour** is Karachi's main fishing pier, and is an interesting place to spend a couple of hours. Sea-food represents one of Pakistan's key foreign exchange earners.

Bazaars and markets

In addition to providing excellent shopping, Karachi's bazaars and markets are fascinating places to wander through and absorb the atmosphere. **Saddar** is Karachi's main shopping area, with numerous carpet shops, handicraft centres and jewellers on Abdullah Haroon Rd, Zaibun-Nisa St and Shahrah-e-Iraq. In the lanes between Saddar's main thoroughfares is **Bohri Bazaar**, Karachi's colourful cloth market. To the N of Saddar is **Empress Market**, dominated by the 50m Gothic clock-tower, built in 1889. This covered market sells fruit and vegetables, groceries, fresh meat and fish, and is used by local people. The noise, smells and colourful activity are a typical South Asian assault on the senses. Equally fascinating are the tightly packed bazaars and markets to the N of M A Jinnah Rd, including **Jodia Bazaar**, **Juna Market** and **Khajoor (date) Bazaar**. **Sarafa (jewellers) Bazaar** specializes in heavy, traditional silver jewellery, copper and brass articles.

Mosques and churches

Although Islamabad's Shah Faisal Masjid is Pakistan's best known modern mosque, the **Masjid-e-Tooba** in Karachi's upmarket 'Defence' residential area is an excellent example of modern Islamic architecture. Built in 1969

through subscription from the residents of Defence (sometimes referred to as Defence Housing Society Mosque), the Masjid-e-Tooba's vast, low dome, with a diameter of 72 m, is claimed to be the world's largest. The central hall holds a congregation of 5,000 and has superb acoustics. The mosques single minaret is 70m high.

In a more traditional style, but equally impressive, is the **Memon Mosque** in the W of the city, near Boulton Market. The lofty minarets taper from the cupolas at the top, down to narrow bases at the bottom.

There are also a number of interesting Anglo-Indian churches in central Karachi. These include the 1882 Anglican **St Andrew's Church** on Shahrah-e-Liaquat, **St Patrick's Catholic Cathedral** on Shahrah-e-Iraq, and **Holy Trinity Cathedral** to the S of Saddar.

Other interesting buildings

In addition to the Mohatta Palace and Flag Staff House, Karachi has some of the best examples of Anglo-Indian architecture in Pakistan. Set in the **Bagh-e-Jinnah** (Jinnah Gardens), stands the two-storeyed Venetian-Gothic **Liaquat Hall**. Built in 1865 as the **Frere Hall**, the building has been substantially redecorated in Islamic style by the renowned Pakistani artist **Sadequain**. It houses a library and a permanent exhibition of the artist's work.

Further examples of Karachi's Victorian heritage include the red sandstone **Sind High Court** on Court Rd, complete with cupolas, balconies and pillars. Opposite stands the 19th century **Sind Assembly Building**. Other examples of Karachi's earliest buildings include the **Masonic Hall** (1845), now offices of Sind Wildlife Management Board, and the **Mereweather Tower** (1892), in the heart of the business district.

National Museum of Pakistan

Formerly housed in Frere Hall, the National Museum of Pakistan was moved to this purpose-built building in Burns Garden, Dr Ziauddin Ahmed Rd, in 1970 (open 1000-1700, Rs 4, closed Fri). There are some remarkable exhibits, and efforts have been made to improve the presentation, giving some sense of the dynamism of archaeological research and the significance of recent developments in work on such important themes as the early Indus Valley Civilization.

Pre-and Proto-historic Gallery 5000-1500 BC. Despite some gaps, this period

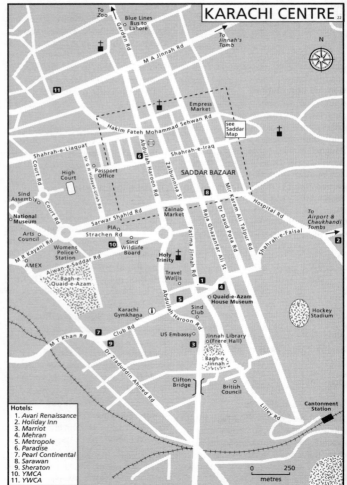

KARACHI CENTRE

To Zoo
Blue Lines Bus to Lahore
Garden Rd
M A Jinnah Rd
To Jinnah's Tomb
N

Empress Market

11

Hakim Fateh Mohammad Sehwan Rd

see Saddar Map

Shahrah-e-Liaquat
Abdullah Haroon Rd
Shahrah-e-Iraq
SADDAR BAZAAR

Court Rd
Sir G H Hidayatullah Rd
6
Zaibunnisa St
Mir Karam Ali Talpur Rd
Hospital Rd

High Court
Passport Office

Sind Assembly

National Museum
Court Rd
Sarwar Shahid Rd
Zainab Market
8
Dr Daud Pota Rd
Shahrah-e-Faisal

To Airport & Chaukhandi Tombs
2

Arts Council
PIA
Strachen Rd
Fatima Jinnah Rd
Raja Ghazanfar Ali St

M R Kayani Rd
AMEX
Womens Police Station
Aiwan-e-Saddar Rd
10
Sind Wildlife Board
Holy Trinity
4

Bagh-e-Quaid-e-Azam
Travel Waljis
1
Quaid-e-Azam House Museum

Hockey Stadium

Karachi Gymkhana
i
Abdullah Haroon Rd
5
Sind Club

7
Club Rd
US Embassy
9
Dr Ziauddin Ahmed Rd
M T Khan Rd
3
Jinnah Library (Frere Hall)
Bagh-e-Jinnah

Clifton Bridge
British Council

Lilley Rd
Cantonment Station

0   250
metres

Hotels:
1. *Avari Renaissance*
2. *Holiday Inn*
3. *Marriot*
4. *Mehran*
5. *Metropole*
6. *Paradise*
7. *Pearl Continental*
8. *Sarawan*
9. *Sheraton*
10. *YMCA*
11. *YWCA*

is very well represented with some remarkable exhibits from Amri (c3500-2200 BC), Kot Diji (c3500-2500 BC), Harappa (c2600-1900) and Moenjo Daro (c2500-1500).

Gandharan Gallery Exhibits from Gandhara sites in Taxila, Peshawar, Swat, Dir, Punjab and parts of Sind, dating from 3rd century BC to 6th-7th century AD. This gallery has a small room attached, displaying some **Hindu** sculptures dating from the 6th to 11th century.

Islamic Gallery Includes ceramics, glass, textiles, metalware and scientific instruments such as globes and astronomical instruments dating from 9th-14th century. Also some impressive pottery, coins and textiles excavated from Banbhore, dating from the 8th-10th century. Exhibits from the late Mughal period include arms and armoury as well as carpets.

Freedom Movement Gallery Photos from events in the life of Mohammad Ali Jinnah, details of the formation and work of the All India Muslim League, the table at which Jinnah presided over the first Govt of Pakistan cabinet meeting, plus some of Jinnah's personal artefacts.

Ethnology Gallery Three dimensional models representing cultural life in different regions of the country, including the Kalash valleys. Handicrafts, jewellery, fabrics, utensils and furniture.

The second floor **Manuscripts Hall** is currently closed to visitors.

Karachi **zoo** on Nishtar Rd is a depressing experience for animal lovers, but a great place for people watching. The 'interesting optical play' of 'half-man half-fox' is worth the Rs 2 entrance fee alone. Wed is ladies-only day and very colourful. About 1 km N of the zoo, on the Lyari River, is the **Dhobi Ghat**, a fascinating giant outdoor laundry stretching for several km along the river bank.

Excursions

Manghopir 30 km N of central Karachi is the shrine to the Muslim saint, **Pir Mangho**. Arriving in Sind from Arabia in the 13th century, he is said to have meditated in a nearby cave until his death at the age of 150. Next to his shrine are two hot sulphur springs, reputed to help sufferers of rheumatism and skin diseases. The Marie Adelaide Leprosy Clinic has a rehabilitation centre nearby. The shrine is guarded by a number of snub-nosed crocodiles, said to have been inadvertently brought to the place in the form of head lice by Pir Mangho. **NB** Reaching Manghopir by public transport requires travelling through some of Karachi's more volatile suburbs.

Local information

HOTEL CLASSIFICATIONS			
AL	Rs4,000	**A**	Rs1,800-4,000
B	Rs900-1,800	**C**	Rs450-900
D	Rs300-450	**E**	Rs150-300
F	up to Rs150		

NB Telephone numbers: unfortunately both private and business telephone numbers change with absurd regularity in Karachi, and although all were correct on going to press, future changes are inevitable.

● **Accommodation**

Karachi has a wide choice of hotels, although prices here are generally more expensive than in other parts of Pakistan. The top hotels are of international standard and advance booking is often required. The moderately priced and cheapest hotels are in the Saddar Bazaar area.

AL *Avari Renaissance Towers*, Fatima Jinnah Rd, T 525261, F 5680310, has all facilities incl pool, tennis, health club, restaurants incl Chinese *Dynasty*, *Shangrila*, and roof barbecue, conference facilities and business centre available, shopping arcade; **AL** *Holiday Inn* (formerly *Taj Mahal*), Shahrah-e-Faisal, T 520211-50, F 5683146, all rooms and suites have satellite TV, and choice of 3 restaurants incl Mexican, business centre plus pool, sauna, jacuzzi and health club; **AL** *Karachi Marriott* (formerly *Holiday Inn*), Abdullah Haroon Rd, T 5680111, F 5681610, popular *Nadia* coffee shop, *Suzie Wong* Chinese res-

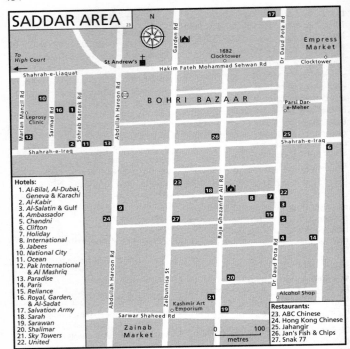

SADDAR AREA

To High Court →

St Andrew's

Shahrah-e-Liaquat

Garden Rd

1682 Clocktower

Empress Market

Clocktower

Hakim Fateh Mohammad Sehwan Rd

Dr Daud Pota Rd

BOHRI BAZAAR

Parsi Dar-e-Meher

Marian Manzil Rd

Sarmad Rd

Sohrab Katrak Rd

Abdullah Haroon Rd

Shahrah-e-Iraq

Shahrah-e-Iraq

Leprosy Clinic

Hotels:
1. Al-Bilal, Al-Dubai, Geneva & Karachi
2. Al-Kabir
3. Al-Salatin & Gulf
4. Ambassador
5. Chandni
6. Clifton
7. Holiday
8. International
9. Jabees
10. National City
11. Ocean
12. Pak International & Al Mashriq
13. Paradise
14. Paris
15. Reliance
16. Royal, Garden, & Al-Sadat
17. Salvation Army
18. Sarah
19. Sarawan
20. Shalimar
21. Sky Towers
22. United

Raja Ghazanfar Ali Rd

Abdullah Haroon Rd

Zaibunnisa St

Dr Daud Pota Rd

Alcohol Shop

Kashmir Art Emporium

Sarwar Shaheed Rd

Zainab Market

0   100
metres

Restaurants:
23. ABC Chinese
24. Hong Kong Chinese
25. Jahangir
26. Jan's Fish & Chips
27. Snak 77

taurant, fitness centre with pool, squash, tennis, business centre plus shopping arcade; **AL** *Karachi Sheraton*, Club Rd, T 521021, F 5682875, superbly equipped, with choice of French cuisine at *Le Marquis*, seafood in *Al-Bustan*, snacks in *Fanoos Lounge* or Italian in *La Mamma* plus sports facilities incl tennis, long-stay guests have access to the *Shalimar Court* suites overlooking the pool, business centre and shopping facilities; **AL** *Pearl Continental*, Club Rd, T 515021, F 5681835, highly rec as best hotel in Pakistan, long-term Karachi residents may apply to use the sports facilities incl pool, tennis, squash and golf, attentive service, and excellent *Chandni Lounge* seafood, *Tai-fan* Chinese and poolside *Marco Polo* restaurants, att mosque.

A *Beach Luxury* (*Avari* chain), MT Khan Rd, Lalazar, T 5611031-7, F 5610674, all rooms face the sea front, there are 4 restaurants, incl a floating dinner buffet and a poolside barbecue (Fri), good value.

B *Mehran*, Shahrah-e-Faisal, T 515061-69, F 515311, restaurants, shops, travel, TV, airport pick-up, overpriced; **B** *Metropole*, Club Rd, T 512051, F 5684301, Karachi's oldest hotel with refurbished Regency floor, rec *Four Seasons* Chinese restaurant; **B** *Sarawan*, Raja Ghazanfar Ali Rd, T 516001, foreign exchange, conference facilities, airport pick-up, good value restaurant; **B** *Sky Towers*, Raja Ghazanfar Ali Khan Rd, Saddar, T 525211, opened 1995, TV, 24-hr coffee shop/room service, *Rubas* restaurant, breakfast incl, credit cards.

C *Airport*, Star Gate Rd, nr airport, T 480141, restaurant, shop, pool; **C** *Gulf*, Daud Pota Rd, Saddar, T 515831-35, F 5682388, some with TV and a/c, overpriced; **C** *National City*, Sarmad Rd, Saddar, T 568003, central a/c, some with TV; **C** *Paradise*, Abdullah Haroon Rd, Saddar, T 5680011, F 5686829, restaurant, central a/c, some TV, along with 'Jabees', popular with Russian women on 'business' trips; **C** *Sarah*, Parr St, Saddar, T 527160, central a/c.

D *Al-Dubai*, Sohrab Katrak Rd, Saddar, T 5685670, some rooms with a/c; **D** *Chilton*, Mir Karam Ali Talpur Rd, Saddar, some with a/c and TV; **D** *Jabees*, Abdullah Haroon Rd, T 512011, F 5682354, central a/c, exchange, restaurant, coffee shop; **D** *Reliance*, Daud Pota Rd, T 516212, some a/c and TV; **D** *Royal City*, Sarmad St, T 5680247, new hotel, some a/c; **D** *United*, Daud Pota Rd, T 515010, F 525611, restaurant and bakery.

E *Al-Salatin*, Daud Pota Rd, T 518454; **E** *Ambassador*, T 514200, att bath; **E** *Holiday*, Daud Pota Rd, T 512082, friendly; **E** *Ocean*, Sohrab Katrak Rd, T 5681922.

F *Al-Kabir*, Sohrab Katrak Rd, T 5683690, att bath; **F** *Al-Sadaat*, Sarmad Rd, T 5688586, F 5680844, good value; **F** *Al-Bilal*, Sohrab Katrak Rd, T 5681176, att; **F** *Chandni*, Daud Pota Rd, T 511487, very cheap but often 'full'; **F** *Geneva*, Sohrab Katrak Rd, T 521754, att bath; **F** *Golden City*, Sarmad Rd, T 5685753, new hotel, reasonable; **F** *Paris*, MK Talpur Rd, Saddar, T 524411, att; **F** *Shalimar*, Blenkin St, off Daud Pota, T 529491, basic.

● **Hostels**

F *Amin House Boy Scout Assoc Youth Hostel*, off Mt Khan Rd, Sultanabad, T 551491, remote, but very cheap, basic dorm; **F** *Salvation Army Hostel*, 78 NI Lines, Frere St, nr Empress Market, T 7214260, dorms and some doubles; **F** *YMCA Hostel*, Strachen Rd, opp PIA, T 5686927, temp 30 day membership fee and Rs 100 returnable deposit, singles, doubles, family rooms, good value; **F** *YWCA Hostel*, MA Jinnah Rd, T 711662, safe, women only hostel in own grounds.

● **Places to eat**

International and Pakistani cuisine is offered at all the major hotels, incl French, Mexican, Chinese, Japanese and Italian. (See Hotel information for details.) Prices are high by Pakistani standards but the quality is excellent.

Chinese restaurants: in Saddar: *ABC Restaurant*, Zaibun Nisa St; *Hong Kong*, Abdullah Haroon Rd, rec. In PECHS: *Kowloon* and *Tung-Nan* on Allama Iqbal Rd, and *Nanking* and *Shanghai* on Tariq Rd. The *Cafe Grand Korean Japanese* nr *Hotel Metropole* serves Chinese and Japanese food, and beer ('frothy tea') is sometimes available.

Cheap restaurants: offering kebabs, grilled chicken, vegetarian curries and dhal can be found in the Saddar area, particularly on Daud Pota Rd (*New Café Subhani* is rec) and around Empress Market.

Fastfood: snacks are readily available around Lea and Empress Markets, and in Saddar. For outdoor barbecue try *Village Garden Restaurant*, opp *Hotel Metropole*, or *Kebabish* inside Funland at Clifton Beach. The all-inclusive Rs 100 buffet at the *Sarawan Hotel* on Raja Ghazanfar Ali Rd, Saddar is rec.

● **Airline offices**

Most of the international and domestic airline offices are located close to the major hotels. At *Avari Towers Plaza*: **American Airlines** and **Canadian**, T 526466; **Biman**, T 514103; **Egypt Air**, T 511109; **Emirates**, T 527044; **Interflug**, T 512235; **Japan**, T 510161. At *Karachi Marriott*: **Air France**, T 520131; **British Airways**, T 516076. At *Karachi Sheraton*: **Kuwait Airways**, T 513272; **Malaysian Airlines**, T 516491. At *Pearl Continental*: **Iberia**, T 529260; **Indian Airlines**, T 522034; **Lufthansa**, T 5685811. At *Holiday Inn*: **Aeroflot**, T 529210. Opp *Holiday Inn*, Shahrah-e-Faisal: **Tajik**; **Taron**, T 7789261; **Turkmen**, T 7783473; **Ukraine**. At *Hotel Metropole*: **Alitalia**, T 511097; **Austrian Airlines**, T 510241; **Cathay Pacific**, T 516525; **Eastern Airlines**, **Royal Jordanian**, T 512026; **SAS**, T 515893; **Swiss Air**, T 512066; **Thai**, T 515893. At Services Club Bldg, Mereweather Rd: **Air Lanka**, T 514421; **Singapore Airlines**, T 521213. **Gulf Air**, Kashif Centre, Shahrah-e-Faisal, T 525231. At PIA Bldg, Strachen Rd: **Air Portugal**, T 510600; **Quantas**, T 513636. **KLM**, Club Rd, T 6637620. At *Mehran Hotel*: **Iran**, T 515001; **Royal Nepal**, T 525683. **Syrian Arab Airlines**, 6 Club Rd, T 5680889.

PIA has an efficient booking office for international and domestic flights on Strachen Rd, T 4572011. **Aero Asia**, for domestic flights, is on Shahrah-e-Faisal, opp *Holiday Inn*, T 7782851. **Shaheen International Airlines**, Avari Plaza, T 513521.

● **Banks & money changers**

Open Mon-Thur: 0900-1300. Sat, Sun: 0900-1200. Fri closed. Banks in II Chundrigar Rd: **Grindlays**, T 2412671; **Muslim Commercial**, T 2414091; **Habib Bank**, T 219111-71. Banks in Shaheen Commercial Complex, Dr Ziauddin Ahmed Rd: **American Express**, T 2630260; **Hongkong Bank**, T 520386. **Foreign exchange** also available to guests at major hotels.

● Cultural centres
Consulates: Arts Council of Pakistan, Strachen Rd. The small AR Afridi Art Gallery has an interesting collection of works by contemporary Pakistani artists. There is also a small reference library and reading room, as well as an exhibition hall, shop selling English and Urdu books, paintings and greeting cards and an open air theatre. Check with the Programme Officer for details of events.

Alliance Francaise, Plot St, 1 Block 8, Sch No5, Clifton, T 5874302; **American Centre**, 8 Abdullah Haroon Rd, T 5685170; **British Council**, 20 Bleak House Rd, T 512036; **Goethe Institute**, 256 Sarawar Shaheed Rd, T 514811; **Islamic Chamber of Commerce**, St 2/A, Blk 9, Clifton, T 5874910; **Japan Cultural Centre**, 233 El Lines, Somerset St, T 516439; **Pakistan American Cultural Centre**, 11 Fatima Jinnah Rd, T 513836; **Pakistan National Centre**, 191 A, SMHS, T 43133.

● Embassies & consulates
Bangladesh, 19 Chowdhury Khaliquzzaman Rd, Clifton, T 514907; **Canada**, 136 Beach Luxury Hotel, T 5687275; **China**, Plot No ST20, Blk 4, Clifton, T 572471; **Denmark**, F50, Feroz Nana Rd, Kehkashan Blk 7, T 535048; **France**, 12/A, Mohammad Ali Bogra Rd, Bath Island, T 5873797; **India**, 3 Fatima Jinnah Rd, T 512542 (temporarily closed by Govt of Pak, 1995); **Iran**, 81, Shahrah-e-Iran, Clifton, T 5874376; **Ireland**, 1-A/1, Saba Ave, Phase 5 Extension, Defence, T 5876955; **Italy**, 85, Clifton, T 531007; **Japan**, 233, Raja Ghazanfar Ali Rd, T 5876955; **Nepal**, 418-419A, Qamar House, 4th Flr, MA Jinnah Rd, T 2416776; **Netherlands**, 4A, Ch Khaliquzzaman Rd, T 526537; **New Zealand**, c/o Commercial Union Ass Co, CU Bldg, 74/1-A, Lalazar, MT Khan Rd, T 551071; **Russian Fed**, 8/26, Flench St, Bleak House Rd, T 512852; **Spain**, 1, 1st Flr, Services Club Extn Bldg, Mereweather Rd, T 510306; **Sri Lanka**, WSA-30, Blk 1, FB Area, T 6326868; **Sweden**, 5/6, Chartered Bank Chamber, Il Chundrigar Rd, T 2415697; **Switzerland**, 98 Clifton, T 5873987; **Turkey**, D264, Blk 5, Kehkashan, Clifton, T 5874194; **UK**, York Place, Runnymede Lane, Clifton, T 5872431; **USA**, 8 Abdullah Haroon Rd, T 5685170.

● Entertainment
Cinemas: there are numerous cinemas on MA Jinnah Rd and Garden Rd/Aga Khan Rd offering the usual diet of all-action Pakistani, Indian and Hong Kong films. For screenings of western or cultural films, see the noticeboard at the British Council or other Cultural Centres.

Clubs: *Karachi Boat Club*, Boat Club Rd, off MT Khan Rd. Founded in 1881, an exclusive members-only club specializing in rowing, with close links with the **Sind Club**, Abdullah Haroon Rd, also members only. Both are proud of their reputation of allowing membership only to those of reputable background, as opposed to money. Other clubs include the **Karachi Gymkhana**, Club Rd and the **Yacht Club**, Grindlays Bldg, Chundrigar Rd.

Nightclubs: there are no western style nightclubs in Karachi, although invited guests may get to visit the '*Rose and Crown*' at the British Deputy High Commission.

● Hospitals & medical services
The best hospital in Pakistan, rec by most overseas missions, is Karachi's *Aga Khan University Hospital*, Stadium Rd, T 4930051. Other well equipped hospitals incl: *Civil*, Baba-e-Urdu Rd, T 7729719; *Holy Family*, Soldier Bazaar, T 718991; *Jinnah Post Graduate Medical Centre*, Rafiqui Shaheed Rd, T 520039; *Liaquat National*, Stadium Rd, T 419612; *Marie Adelaide Leprosy Clinic*, Mariam Manzll, off Shahrah-e-Liaquat, T 5683106.

Other useful telephone numbers: *Edhi Blood Bank*, T 413151; *Edhi Ambulance Service*, T 683432.

● Libraries
Arts Council of Pakistan and the British Council both have libraries. See Cultural Centres above.

● Post & telecommunications
International direct dialling, Fax and Telex facilities at major hotels and Central Telegraph Office. GPO and Central Telegraph Office, Il Chundrigar Rd (incl Poste Restante). Post Offices at top of Abdullah Haroon Rd, Saddar and in *Metropole Hotel* block. Clients' Mail Poste Restante available at American Express to card members and AMEX TCs holders.

Trunk bookings: T 109; Trunk bookings overseas, T 0102.

● Places of worship
Christian: *Holy Trinity*, Zaibun Nisa St; *St Andrews* nr Empress Mkt; *St Patricks Roman Catholic Cathedral*, Shahrah-e-Iraq.

Hindu: *Parsi*, Parsi Dar-e-Meher, Daud Pota Rd, Saddar; *Shree Ratneswar Mahdevi Temple*, Clifton Beach.

Muslim: *Defence Society Tooba Mosque*; *Memon Mosque* nr Boulton Mkt; *Pearl Continental Hotel Mosque*, and countless others.

● **Shopping**

Books: all the major hotels have bookstalls. The *Pak American Book Co* on Zaibun Nisa St, Saddar has a good selection.

Carpets: Pakistan is a top producer of hand-knotted wool and silk carpets. They are woven in the traditional style but are less expensive than the Persian originals. There are numerous carpet shops in Karachi, with the greatest concentration around the southern end of Abdullah Haroon Rd, Zaibun Nisa Rd and around the *Hotel Metropole*. The largest in Karachi is *Afghan Carpet Warehouse*, D/16, Block 8, Chowdary Khaliquzzaman Rd, Clifton, T 532690 with branches at the major hotels.

Clothing: good quality, cheap western clothing is available at **Zainab Market** on Zaibun Nisa St, Saddar. There are a number of boutiques selling good quality Pakistani and western clothes in Saddar, Defence and Clifton.

Duty free: imported goods, incl electrical products, are available at *Karachi Duty Free Shop* on Shahrah-e-Faisal.

Jewellery: all the major hotels have jewellers in their arcades although prices are higher than in other parts of town. There are numerous jewellers in Saddar, on Abdullah Haroon Rd, Shahrah-e-Iraq and Zaibun Nisa Rd. A modern jewellers bazaar is located at *Liaquatabad Shopping Centre*, opp Super Market.

Leather: hand made bags, jackets, coats, shoes and boots are good buys. *Asian Leather Kraft*; *Dice Gifts*; *English Boot House*, Zaibun Nisa St, T 441649; *Mr Leather*, Sheraton Hotel, T 522240 and numerous others on Abdullah Haroon Rd.

Western goods: western food, cosmetics, toiletries, consumer goods etc are available from *Agha Supermarket*, Supermarket Roundabout, Clifton.

● **Sports**

All of the major hotels have sports facilities for the use of guests and long-term Karachi residents can pay to use these facilities.

Cricket: on Fri and evenings, informal games of cricket can be found on any patch of open ground, particularly in Bagh-e-Jinnah Gdns. International matches are played at the National Stadium.

Hashing: for those who want to jog around a Karachi suburb, the very hospitable Karachi Hash House Harriers meet every Mon evening. For details of the 'on-on' and 'down-down' contact the *Pearl Continental* reception on Mon afternoons.

Swimming: easily accessible beaches are within a radius of 30 km. See earlier descriptions of Hawkes Bay, Sandspit, French Beach and Paradise Point.

Watersports: the diving season is from mid-Oct to mid-Mar. **Buleji**, 30 km W of Karachi has some good reef diving and snorkelling suitable even for children at low tide. Contact *Karachi Diving and Salvage Agency*, T 224201.

● **Tour companies & travel agents**

Numerous incl Pakistan's largest, *Travel Walji's*, 13 Services Mess, Mereweather Rd behind *Metropole Hotel*, T 516698. *Sitara Travel Consultants (PVT) Ltd*, Trade Tower, No 105, 1st Flr, Abdullah Haroon Rd, T 5683887, F 5689380. *Raza Khan Tours*, 109 Sheraton Shopping Arcade, Club Rd, T 5682111, offers city tours, crabbing tours, turtle watching trips, plus guided group tours to Thatta/Makli/Chaukundi and to Moenjo Daro. Others located at most top hotels and around Metropole.

● **Tourist offices**

Helpful **PTDC Information Centre** on Club Rd nr Metropole, T 511293. **Sind Tourism Development Corporation**, 114-115, Block C, Sea Breeze Plaza, Shahrah-e-Faisal, T 7782326, for Kinjhar Lake Resort bookings. **Sind Wildlife Management Board**, Strachen Rd, T 523176, can help with information on Kirthar National Park and Haleji Lake.

● **Useful addresses**

Karachi's main **Police Station** and the **Foreigner's Registration Office**, T 2333737, are both on II Chundrigar Rd. For advice on visa extensions contact **Directorate of Immigration and Passports**, T 5681135.

● **Useful telephone numbers**

Fire: T 16. **Police**: T 15.

● **Transport**

Local Bus: like many other South Asian cities, Karachi's public buses are impossibly crowded, routes are confusing, and getting on and off the still moving buses can be dangerous. Taxis and rickshaws are a far more practical way of getting around. Bus No 20 goes from Saddar to Clifton Beach. **Car hire**: most of the major hotels offer car and driver hire. Avis at *Travel Waljis* charge Rs 500+ per km a day minimum with discounts for weekly rates. **Taxi**: most of Karachi's modern fleet of yellow taxis have working meters that the drivers are prepared to use. Otherwise, the fare should be agreed upon before commencing the journey. Outside the central areas, particularly in residential districts, drivers will expect to be directed to the destination. It is worth having the destination clearly written on paper that can be used to ask directions from passers-by. Rickshaws are cheaper than taxis, but more vulnerable in Karachi's chaotic traffic.

Air Karachi's airport is 12 km E of the city centre. The domestic terminal is adjacent to the international one. A taxi to/from the airport should not cost more than Rs 75 on the meter but foreigners rarely get to pay less than Rs 150. Incoming arrivals, however, may initially be asked ten times that amount. Many hotels offer a free airport pick-up service. A crowded local bus, D3, runs from the road outside to Saddar. Several banks inside the international terminal offer foreign exchange, although rates for TCs are poor and commissions high. Security precautions in force in 1995 required check-in 2½ hrs prior to departure, plus photocopy of relevant pages of passport. Cigarettes at the Duty free shop are amongst the cheapest in the world. **PIA**: regular flights daily to **Faisalabad, Islamabad, Lahore, Peshawar** and **Quetta**. Regular flights to all towns and cities served by an airport. International flights to UK, Europe, Middle East, Russia, Central Asia, South Asia, Southeast Asia, North America. **Aero Asia**: Faisalabad, twice daily; **Islamabad**, 3 flights daily; **Lahore**, 6 flights daily; **Multan**, once daily; **Pasni**, once a week; **Peshawar**, once daily. **Shaheen Air**: **Islamabad**, twice daily; **Lahore**, daily, extra weekend flights; **Peshawar**, daily. Most domestic airlines offer considerable discounts on night flights.

Train There are 2 major stations in Karachi: *Karachi City* and *Karachi Cantt*. Reservations should be made in advance at the City booking office, incl trains departing from Cantt. For student and foreign tourist discounts go to the Commercial Dept above the Upper Class booking office. **NB** On some trains, particularly fast services to Lahore, sleepers, AC and 1st Class are often fully booked for 2 weeks ahead. The Pakistan Railways Time & Fare Table, available from all main stations for Rs 5, is a lightweight guide to the entire rail network. The trains to the following destinations are those that offer the most direct daily services, plus all classes of ticket. **Lahore**, *Shalimar Exp* (Cantt), 0630, 17 hrs; *Tezgam* (Cantt), 1630, 19

hrs. **Multan**: *Shalimar Exp* (Cantt), 0630, 12 hrs; *Tezgam* (Cantt), 1630, 14 hrs. **Peshawar**: *Awam Exp* (Cantt), 0730, 32½ hrs; *Khyber Mail* (Cantt), 2145, 32½ hrs. **Quetta**: *Bolan Mail* (City), 1130, 26 hrs; *Sind Exp/45* (City), 0745, 25 hrs. **Rawalpindi**: *Awam Exp* (Cantt), 0730, 28 hrs; *Tezgam* (Cantt), 1630, 25 hrs. **Rohri/Sukkur**: *Shalimar Exp* (Cantt), 0630, 6 hrs; *Sukkur Exp* (Cantt), 2200, 9 hrs. Railway reservations: City, T 2416349; Cantt, T 510178.

Road Bus: **Quetta**: there are a number of coach services operating from Sabzi Mandi on University Rd, opp the *Shahzhob Hotel*, incl *Qalandri Coach*, T 4923721, departing 1600, *Qadri Coach*, T 4938294, departing 0530, 0800, 1730, 1800 (also offices in Sadder, at corner of Daud Pota and Sarwar Shahid Rd, T 524546, and in Lea Market), *Awami Coach*, T 4949065, departing 0600 and 1730. The *Quetta Coach A/C Service* operates from next to the *Lucky Star Restaurant* on Sarwar Shahid Rd, departing 1700. Tickets range from Rs 150-250 for standard, a/c, or 'German coach'. The journey takes approx 12 hrs. *Blue Lines* have temporarily moved their office from opp the *Sheraton Hotel* to Cantt Railway Station, T 529934; services to **Larkarna, Sukkur** and **Lahore**. Other offices at Empress Market, T 7781742, and opp the Bambino Cinema on MA Jinnah Rd run thrice daily services to **Lahore** (0945, 1345, 1945) for Rs 320 (24 hrs). *SRTC* on Aga Khan Rd (Garden Rd) offer regular coach services to **Hyderabad**. Local buses for **Chaukundi/Kinjhar/Thatta/Hyderabad** leave from Lea Market. Local buses to **Mirpur Khas** leave from Boulton Market. Local buses for **Khuzdar** and **Las Bela** leave from Shedi City Rd and Mollah Maddar respectively, both to the N of Lea Market.

KARACHI TO QUETTA

The RCD highway connects Karachi with Quetta, over 700 km away. The road heads NW from Karachi, crossing into Baluchistan at Hub Chowki. The main towns along the route are Bela (182 km), Khuzdar (410 km), Kalat (573 km) and Mustang (667 km). For details of this route, see the section on Quetta to Karachi in the Baluchistan chapter. Details of public transport from Karachi are given under Local Information.

KARACHI TO HYDERABAD VIA NATIONAL HIGHWAY

Travelling through lower Sind between Karachi and Hyderabad gives some idea of the impact that perennial irrigated agriculture has had upon the region. The western route between the two cities, the Super Highway, runs through uncultivated desert, illustrating the bareness of a hot land without water. The National Highway to the E, by contrast, runs through the rich plains of canal irrigated land. The National Highway passes some of Sind's, and Pakistan's, most important ancient settlements, many of which are worth visiting. The total journey is 197 km and takes 3½ hrs.

Chaukundi tombs are located 27 km from Karachi on the National Highway, and are easily visited as a half-day trip. The site is thought to date from the 13th-16th century and is generally attributed to the *Jokhio* and *Baluch* tribes. The superbly carved sandstone tombs are built out of rectangular slabs placed one on top of the other in pyramidal fashion, some reaching 4m high. They stretch for several kilometres along a low ridge with the centrepiece being two large domed mausoleums, although more outlying tombs are simply piles of stones. Women's graves carry carved reproductions of jewellery – bracelets, anklets, earrings while the men's show spears, swords, shields and even horsemen. These style tombs are found only in Sind and Baluchistan, particularly along the Makran coast. The intricate carved designs are still found in textiles, pottery, jewellery and wood carvings in Sind and Baluchistan today.

The tombs can be reached by taking the Thatta or Gharo **bus** from Lea Market (Rs 10), and are situated just to the left of the road past the 26 km marker. There is a small sign in English. To return, simply flag down a passing bus.

Banbhore (64 km from Karachi) is the local name given to an archaeological site near the town of **Gharo**. Ruins from the Scythian-Parthian, Hindu-Buddhist and Arab periods of influence are spread over an extensive area. The remains of a fort with walls and bastions are distinctly traceable, and further excavations have revealed the plan of a well fortified harbour town. It has been suggested that Banbhore could be the site of the ancient Hindu port city of **Debal**, although this remains speculation. The town is thought to have declined rapidly in the 13th century, possibly due to further invasions, although the shifting course of the Indus was certainly a major constraint upon Debal's ability to function as a port.

Debal was the port where the 17-year-old Arab commander **Mohammad bin Qasim** is believed to have landed in 711/712 AD at the head of the forces of the Baghdad Caliphate. The Arab army, having secured the towns of the delta, proceeded N along the Indus, bringing Islam to the sub-continent, and occupying Multan within a few months.

Kufic inscriptions on the Grand Mosque, indicating construction in the 8th century, suggest that it is the earliest known mosque in South Asia, and some of the oldest Muslim coins have been found here. A semi-circular stone mansion and a large mud brick house also date to this period. The most important Hindu remains include a Siva temple. Excavations, begun in 1958, have also revealed 1st century BC pottery, similar in style to that found at **Taxila**, suggesting a link with Alexander. Superb glass and ceramics from Banbhore are displayed in the National Museum in Karachi, and other artefacts are exhibited at the small on-site museum. Open Apr-Sep 0800-1200, 1400-1830; Oct-Mar

0900-1600, closed 1st Mon of month. *Getting there*: take a Gharo or Thatta bus from Karachi's Lea Market.

Haleji Lake Bird Sanctuary (82 km from Karachi), is located to the left of the NH, shortly before **Guju**. As one of Asia's most important waterfowl sanctuaries, Haleji Lake is populated by some 70 varieties of migratory aquatic birds, including flamingoes, pelicans, herons, egrets and pheasant-tailed jacanas as well as marsh crocodiles. Special hides and a Visitor's Centre are provided for bird-watchers. For more information, contact the Sind Wildlife Management Board in Strachen Rd, Karachi, T 5683176. *Dak Bungalows* can be booked through the Chief Engineer, Karachi Water and Sewerage Board which supplies water to Karachi from this reservoir.

Makli Hill, located several kilometres before **Thatta**, is one of the most visually stunning archaeological sites in Pakistan. Covering 15½ sq km and said to contain over 1 million tombs, it is considered to be the world's largest necropolis.

The tombs and mausoleums are seen as the most substantial remains of Sind's greatness between the 14th and 18th centuries, with many belonging to kings, queens, saints, governors, military commanders, philosophers and poets. They are divided into three distinct historical groupings.

The site, on a low ridge, is intersected by the National Highway, with the best preserved tombs on the N (left) side. From the gate the initial group of monuments date from the most recent Mughal period (16th to 18th century). The first major tomb on the right, standing on a high plinth in a courtyard, is that of **Mirza Jani Beg** (d 1599), the last Tarkhan ruler. Octagonal with a domed roof, the tomb shows the use of glazed blue and unglazed brown tiles which are still produced in Thatta today. The next major tomb on the right is that of

Mirza Tughal Beg (d 1679) and has 12 carved sandstone pillars supporting a domed roof.

Perhaps the most imposing tomb on the hill is that of the former Mughal Governor of Sind, **Isa Khan Tarkhan the younger** (d 1644), which stands in a large square courtyard surrounded by a high wall. The chowkidar has the key to the gate. Similar in style to buildings at Fatehpur Sikri nr Agra, the mausoleum comprises a buff coloured square tomb chamber, exquisitely carved inside and out, right up to its domed roof. It is surrounded by a double storey pillared verandah, the upper section roofed by a series of smaller domes. The verandah offers fine views of the whole Makli necropolis.

To the E is a smaller building in the same style housing the tombs of Isa Khan's *zenana* (harem), and carved in a similar fashion to those at Chaukundi. The tomb of **Dewan Shurfa Khan** (d 1638), a little to the NW, is exceptionally well preserved. In its own courtyard, this solid square tomb's exterior is decorated with blue and turquoise glazed tiles whilst the interior is elaborately fashioned in red, white and blue.

The second group of tombs belong to the Arghun and Tarkhan rulers of the 16th century. Sadly many of these carved sandstone tombs are in a poor state of repair, although the squat, octagonal tomb of **Prince Sultan Ibrahim** (d 1559) is an exception.

Between the second and final collection of tombs stands the shrine of the Sufi saint **Abdullah Shah Ash'abi**. Painted in garish colours, the centre piece of the shrine is a marble mausoleum, decorated with mirrored tiles, tinsel streamers and heavy with the smell of incense. The shrine is busy with activity as devotees from all over Sind come here seeking blessings, demonstrating the power of piestic Islam in the region.

The third group of tombs, several kilometres further N, belong to the 14th to 16th century Samma Dynasty, frequently referred to as the Golden Age of Sind. The oldest tomb on the hill with any great historical interest belongs to **Jam Nizamuddin** (d 1508), and has a façade that is very much in the Hindu style. It has been suggested that it was either built with materials from ruined Hindu temples, with idolatrous emblems removed, or that the style is a result of employing Hindu craftsmen in its construction.

• **Accommodation** The nearby *Rest House* appears disused so see under Thatta or Kinjhar. There is a restaurant, *Makli Inn*, nr site entrance.

• **Transport** Makli can be reached as a day trip by local bus from Karachi's Lea Market, or on an organized tour (see Karachi section).

Thatta

The new town of Thatta (98 km E of Karachi) has been identified with the site of both **Debal** and Alexander's **Patala**. It is suggested that Alexander rested his army here following their long march S, whilst his admiral, **Nearchus**, assembled his fleet at the port before sailing down the Indus to the sea. Before that, it is believed to feature in the Hindu epic *Mahabharata*.

Thatta was sacked by Shah Beg Arkhan in 1521, the Portuguese in 1555, and by its own ruler Mirza Jani Beg in 1591 whilst resisting Akbar's forces. Despite its turbulent history, Thatta was described by a visitor in 1699 as a rich and thriving city, and a great artistic centre. At this time it is said to have had 400 schools and seminaries, 'being famous for learning, theology, philosophy and politics'. Within 150 years, however, war, plague, drought, malaria in the surrounding lowlands and the shifting course of the Indus, had led to its decline. Be careful how you pronounce the name of this town because it is remarkably similar to the Urdu word for 'bollocks'.

Places of interest

The **Shah Jahan Mosque**, built between 1644 and 1647, was a gift from **Shah Jahan** in recognition of the hospitality he received in Thatta whilst seeking refuge from his father, Jahangir. A contemporary of one of Shah Jahan's other great buildings, the Taj Mahal, the mosque is built in the form of a great caravanserai, a large court enclosed by a double arcaded corridor of 93 domed compartments. This serves the purpose of carrying the words of the Imam to all parts of the mosque. The decorative turquoise and white tile work is reminiscent of the great Persian mosques of Isfahan and Shiraz in Iran. The gateway at the E entrance was added when the mosque was refurbished in 1959.

The **Dagbir Mosque** on the outskirts of town, one of the earliest examples of this style in Sind, was previously known for its superb tile work but it is now in a poor state of repair. Built by **Mir Khushro Khan** in 1588, it has a superbly sculptured mihrab.

Much of the old mud and brick centre of the town has been bulldozed, although several multi-storeyed houses with carved wooden balconies remain. Many of the old houses use *Munghs*, or 'windcatchers' on their roof to 'catch' and circulate cool breezes into the rooms below. On Fri mornings, on the mud-flats on the edge of town, greyhound races take place, complete with mechanical hare.

Local information
● **Accommodation**
Describing nearby Makli at the turn of the century, Capt Wood suggested "Here neither labour nor expense has been spared for giving the dead better accommodation than the living." The same could be said of Thatta's hotels today. Given the poor accommodation at Thatta, it would seem sensible to visit as a day trip from Karachi, or to stay at Kinjhar Lake.

F *Al-Kadar Muzaffarkhaha*, opp bus stand has filthy doubles with att filthy bath; **F** Unnamed muzaffarkhana along main road next to **E** *Jehan Zeb* (under construction 1995).

● **Places to eat**

Very basic restaurants on main highway. *STDC restaurant* opp Shah Jehan Mosque occasionally open.

● **Transport**

Train Nearest station at **Junvsashi**, 20 km away.

Road Bus: buses from Karachi's Lea Market (2 hrs, Rs 15). Northbound buses from main street.

From Thatta the National Highway turns NE to run up the right or W bank of the Indus. After 22 km a road to the left runs to **Kinjhar Lake**. The richly cultivated fields illustrate the remarkable transformation of the environment that has been produced by controlling the Indus waters.

Kinjhar Lake was constructed for irrigation purposes by linking two smaller lakes, the **Sunheri** and **Kinjhari**. Over 32 km long and 6 km wide, this attractive lake previously supplied water to Karachi, but is now being marketed as a tourist resort. Fishing and boating are available.

● **Accommodation** The **D** *Old Resort* is now all but abandoned, and the **C** *Tourist Resort* is a huge disappointment. There are 8 deluxe and 16 standard split level cabanas, with living area downstairs and rooms and bathroom upstairs, they must have been nice when new, but are now in a very poor state of repair, dirty, with no hot water and non-working a/c, even at reduced weekday rates (Sun-Wed) they are poor value, the restaurant, though nicely situated, is overpriced with little choice and poor service, reservations: STDC 114-115, C Block, Sea Breeze Plaza, Shahrah-e-Faisal, Karachi, T 778236.

● **Transport Local Bus**: from Karachi's Lea Market, or as part of tour (see Karachi).

From Kinjhar the National Highway continues N through Jerruck, a military depot under Napier's command, to the industrial town of Kotri, the bridging point on the Indus to Hyderabad.

The **Kotri Barrage**, built in 1955, provides irrigation water to over 1 million ha of Lower Sind – more than double the area irrigated by former wet season inundation channels. Built upon the recommendation of the 1945 Indus Waters Commission, the Kotri barrage is 1,000m long and comprises 44 spans. Four canals originate from the barrage, one of which feeds Kinjhar Lake.

KARACHI TO HYDERABAD VIA THE SUPER HIGHWAY

The toll road between Karachi and Hyderabad, the Super Highway, offers a quicker alternative to the easterly National Highway route and the 175 km can be covered in 2½ hrs. The Super Highway skirts the lower reaches of the limestone Kirthar Range, crossing some of the southernmost ridges of Sindh Kohistan. Midway between Karachi and Hyderabad is a large industrial estate, taking advantage as the area's status as a tax-free production zone. The road climbs the escarpment before gently descending to the Indus plain. The road crosses the Indus via the Ghulam Mohammad Barrage at Kotri, and enters Hyderabad.

Khadeji Falls, a pleasant picnic spot, can be reached via a short detour off the Super Highway. About 25 km beyond the tollgate, the road climbs a steep escarpment to a small mosque atop the hill. A track behind the mosque leads down to the gorge of Khadeji Falls.

Kirthar National Park

North of the Super Highway, lies the **Kirthar National Park**. There is no public transport to or from the park, and the journey should only really be attempted in a 4WD vehicle. To reach the park, turn off the Super Highway at the marker stone 80 km from Karachi (nr to the cement works and industrial estate). The park is located 72 km N of the Super Highway.

Covering some 3,000 sq km of rolling hills and valleys, Kirthar is one of four UNESCO registered parks in Pakistan. It provides a protected refuge for a number of endangered species including Urial sheep, Sind ibex (wild goat), chinkara and the migratory visitor, the Houbara Bustard. There are also reported to be leopards and desert wolves in the park. The best time to visit is in winter between Nov-Jan. Forest hide-outs are provided, and there are two Visitors' Centres at **Khar** and **Kharchat**.

● **Accommodation** There are a number of basic **E** *Rest Houses* that have running water, cooking facilities and flush toilets. It is also possible to camp. Bookings should be made through Sind Wildlife Management Board, Strachen Rd, Karachi, T 5683176. **NB** Prior to making the trip, it is advisable to check the current security situation with both the PTDC in Karachi and your own embassy, and provide them with your itinerary.

Hyderabad

The site upon which the city of Hyderabad stands has a history of settlement dating back to prehistoric times, when the nearby hills of Ganjo Taka were used as a place of worship. The strategic location of Hyderabad, formerly at the apex of the Indus delta, has been recognized by all invading armies from those of Mohammad bin Qasim in 711, to the British forces of Charles Napier

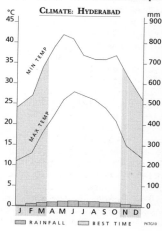

CLIMATE: HYDERABAD

in 1843. Today, Hyderabad is Pakistan's fourth largest city (pop 2 million), and a centre of industrial production. Almost 12% of Sind's urban population live in Hyderabad.

History

Hyderabad traces its origins back to the Hindu ruler Nerun, who built a fort, or *kot*, at the site. The fort at Nerun Kot was occupied by Buddhists when Mohammad bin Qasim conquered Sind in 711/712, and the young Arab General built a mosque on the site of an earlier Buddhist temple. During the 16th and 17th centuries, Nerun Kot was the district headquarters of the Arghun Empire ruled from the nearby city of Thatta, and came to be known as Hyderabad after its founder, **Hyder Quli Arghuni**.

In 1758-59, the changing course of the Indus gave an unexpected boost to Hyderabad's strategic location. Leaving its old bed at a point N of Hyderabad, and turning W, the Indus abandoned almost 150 km of its old course. Not only did this action wash away Narsapur, one of the intended capitals of Mian Muradyab Khan, it also flooded **Khudabad**, the old capital of the Kalhora Mirs in Dadu district. In 1786 **Ghulam Shah Kalhora**, ruler of all Sind, selected Hyderabad as the most eligible site for a large defensible capital. Hyderabad remained the Kalhora's capital until their defeat by the Baluchi **Talpur Mirs** in 1782. The Talpur Mirs occupied Hyderabad until the arrival of the British.

Looking to establish an effective presence in Sind, the British had already forced the rulers of Khairpur and Hyderabad to open the Indus for unrestricted navigation in 1831. In 1843, the British annexed Sind, defeating the Talpur forces at a forest near Hyderabad. In Sep of that year, the British shifted the capital of Sind to Karachi.

Post Partition, Hyderabad experienced a rapid influx of Muslim refugees from India. Like Karachi, Hyderabad has suffered from tensions between the native Sindhi population, and the mohajir community. In Sep 1988, on a day that came to be known as Black Friday, 186 men, women and children were killed and a further 250 wounded as gunmen went on the rampage through the city. A similar incident occurred in May 1990 when, emerging from Hyderabad Fort, crowds of mohajirs fronted by women and children were fired upon by the police. Thirty one people were killed. However, the 30 month military 'Clean-up' operation in Sind appears to have brought a greater degree of stability to Hyderabad than is being experienced in Karachi.

Places of interest

The Fort (Qila) Built in 1768 on the order of **Ghulam Shah Kalhora**, Hyderabad Fort stands on the southern extremity of a rocky limestone outcrop that dominates the surrounding plain. This unique strategic location has been enhanced by the perpendicular extension of the plateau supporting the outer fortification wall.

The fort was occupied as a court by the Kalhora ruler during a period in Sindhi history that is recalled with great pride. Successful improvements in irrigation techniques brought economic prosperity, and Sindhi poetry reached its zenith in the compositions of **Mian Shah Inayat** and **Shah Abdul Latif**. The request on the fort's foundation stone, dating from 1768, "Oh God, Bring peace to this city", appeared fulfilled until Ghulam Shah Kalhora's death in 1772.

The period that followed, however, is recalled as a tyrannical era until the **Talpur Mirs** finally defeated the last Kalhora ruler in 1782 and brought peace to the city. The Talpurs occupied the fort and used it as a palace until their defeat by the British in 1843 at the nearby forest of **Miani**.

Only parts of the 15m high outer wall, a circular tower and the main gate re-

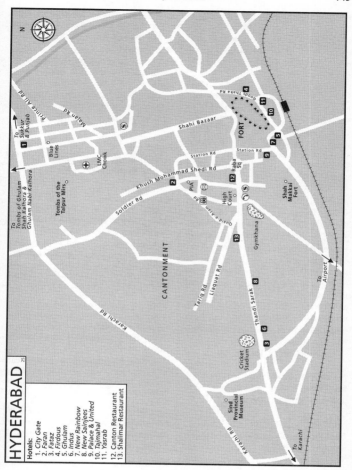

HYDERABAD 25

Hotels:
1. City Gate
2. Faran
3. Fatax
4. Firdous
5. Ghulam
6. Indus
7. New Rainbow
8. New Sainjees
9. Palace & United
10. Tajimahal
11. Yasrab

12. Canton Restaurant
13. Shalimar Restaurant

main intact. Much of the interior section was destroyed during the siege, and many sections fell into disrepair through subsequent neglect. Finally, an explosion in the arsenal in 1906 destroyed much of the *Pukka* (brick built) fort. The small **Museum** has a number of interesting exhibits, including weapons, clothes and portraits from the Talpur period. Open Summer 0700-

1400, Winter 0900-1600. Closed Fri and Sat. It is fascinating to wander through the narrow streets and alleys of the residential area within the fort's walls.

Nearby is the **Shah Makkai Fort** or *Kachcha* (mud built) *Qila*, built in 1771 by Ghulam Shah Kalhora to protect the mausoleum of **Sheikh Mohammad Makkai**. This Muslim saint, born in Mecca (hence the title Makkai) settled in the area some 500 years earlier with his wife, daughter of a Hindu ruler. Although most of the fort is in ruins, the shrine itself attracts devotees from all over Sind, particularly on the saint's *Urs* or death anniversary.

To the N of the city, behind the Central Jail, are the 21 **Kalhora Tombs**. The ornate tombs of the Kalhora rulers are decorated with geometric and floral designs, the most impressive of which belongs to **Ghulam Shah Kalhora**. Despite the loss of the dome, now replaced by a flat roof, the square tomb with an octagonal chamber retains some fine blue and white tile work and carved marble detail.

The **Tombs of the Talpur Mirs**, S of the *Hotel City Gate*, although of better general construction than the Kalhora tombs, are less impressive from an architectural point of view. Located in two compounds, the buildings are covered with glazed tiles which are considered to be poor when compared with older work at Thatta. Built between 1812-1857, much research on the tombs has been undertaken by the Institute of Sindhology at Jamshoro, nr Hyderabad.

Qadam Gah of Hazrat Ali In the centre of the city is the slab of stone with the hand and footprints of Hazrat Ali, the Prophet Mohammad's son-in-law and 4th Caliph of Islam.

Museums

Sind Provincial Museum, Wahdat Colony nr Niaz Stadium and Polytechnic. Well designed, beautifully laid out and clearly labelled. **Section 1**: archaeological display covering whole span from prehistory to the British period; **2**: Sindhi crafts; **3**: children's section.

Talpur House Museum A private museum in a house built between 1860-1864 in 19th century European style. The 2 rm Talpur Harem are furnished with European style period furniture and fittings with original carpets, rugs and European crockery. A particularly good collection of manuscripts brought out on request. Housed in the Bungalow of **Mir Hasan Ali** in Tando Mir Nur Mohammad Khan, a suburb of Hyderabad. Open on application to the family.

Sind University Educational Museum, Inst of Education, Univ of Sind. Sindhi arts and crafts incl needlework, carpets, straw and lacquer work, local musical instruments, costumes, weapons and jewellery.

Excursions
From Hyderabad you can go E through **Mirpur Khas** into the **Thar** desert.

Local information
● **Accommodation**

B *Indus*, Thandi Sarak, T 782397, brand new hotel, central a/c, room service, TV, fridge, 2 restaurants, coffee shop, overpriced.

C *City Gate*, NH opp Central Jail, T 611677, most a/c, room service, TV, laundry, rent-a-car, *Midway* restaurant for à la carte, Chinese and Pakistani, best value in class; **C** *Faran*, Saddar Bazaar, T 780195, central a/c, TV, fridge, restaurant; **C** *Fataz*, Thandi Sarak, T 782125, central a/c, *Naushana* and *Zaushana* restaurants, coffee shop, pool, bank, travel agency, friendly but very run down; **C** *New Sainjees*, Thandi Sarak (sign says Bhitah Gdn), T 782275, some a/c, restaurant, very run down.

Most of the **F** hotels are in the area between the railway station and the fort. Some are reluctant to accept foreigners. **On Goods Naka**: **F** *Firdous*, basic; **F** *Taj Mahal*, T 780592, some a/c, with bath; **F** *Yasrab*, T 28006, fan, with bath, rec. **On Station Rd**: **F** *Ghulam*, basic; **F** *New Rainbow*, with bath. **On Ghazi Abdul Karim Rd**: **F** *Palace*, T 21284, with bath; **F** *United*, basic.

● **Places to eat**
Food in 4 top hotels rec. *Canton* on Ghari Khatta serves generous Chinese and Pakistani dishes; *Shalimar*, Thandi Sarak, opp Gymkhana Club, Chinese, rec, basic restaurants in station area.

● **Airline offices**
PIA in Saddar, 1 block S of Faran, T 28228.

● **Banks & money changers**
National Bank of Pakistan, Ghari Khatta opp High Court offers foreign exchange.

● **Entertainment**

Cinemas: there are many cinemas in the Ghari Khatta area.

● **Hospitals & medical services**

Liaquat Medical College Hospital, LMC Market, Hirabad.

● **Post & telecommunications**

GPO in Saddar, 2 blocks S of Faran. Pak Telecom on Ghari Khatta.

● **Shopping**

The main shopping area is nr the fort, S of town. Shahi Bazaar, at 2 km one of the longest in Pakistan, is a maze of narrow crowded lanes with small shops selling a wide variety of goods incl jewellery, shoes, lacquerware, handloom textiles, Sindhi embroidery and appliqued *Rillis*.

● **Sports**

Cricket: Hyderabad's cricket stadium on Thandi Sarak, to the W of town, is used for 1-day internationals and Test matches.

● **Transport**

Local Hyderabad's streets are choked with rickshaws. Expect to pay Rs 15-20 fare between any two points. **Car hire**: from *City Gate* and *Fataz* hotels.

Air PIA: **Karachi**, daily; **Lahore**, twice weekly; **Sukkur**, 3 flights weekly, incl 1 via **Moenjo Daro**.

Train Karachi: hourly, 2-3 hrs. **Mirpur Khas**: hourly, 1 hr. **Lahore**: *Shalimar Exp*, 0845, 15 hrs; *Tezgam*, 1900, 16 hrs. **Multan**: *Shalimar Exp*, 0845, 10 hrs; *Tezgam*, 1900, 11 hrs. **Peshawar**: *Awam Exp*, 1010, 30 hrs; *Khyber Mail*, 0020, 30 hrs. **Rawalpindi**: *Awam Exp*, 1010, 25½ hrs; *Tezgam*, 1900, 22 hrs. **Rohri/Sukkur**, *Shalimar Exp*, 0845, 4 hrs; *Sukkur Exp*, 0110, 6 hrs.

Road Bus: Hyderabad has no one central bus station, and thus arrival and departure points are spread across the city. *Sind Road Transport Corporation* (SRTC), nr Tayyab Complex, off Quaid-i-Azam Rd, runs Deluxe services via Super Highway to **Karachi**, and hourly Express services via **Thatta**. Northbound buses are said to run from LMC Market, opp *Liaquat Medical College Hospital*. Local buses N towards **Sukkur** run from Pathan Colony, 1 block W of *City Gate Hotel*. Buses E to **Mirpur Khas** run from New Bridge bus stand, although the train is more convenient. *Blue Lines*, Capri Cinema, 1 block S of *City Gate Hotel*, T 61558, run Deluxe services hourly to **Karachi** (Rs 40). Also to: **Larkana**, 0900, 1100, 1300, 1400, 1545, 1830, 2300, 0015, 0045, 0115 (Rs 90); **Mingora**, 1000; **Lahore**, 1230, 1630, 2230 (Rs 320), via **Bahawalpur** (Rs 180), **Multan** (Rs 230), **Sahiwal** (Rs280) and **Faisalabad** (Rs 300); **Sukkur-Shikarpur-Jacobabad**, 1030 (Jacob), 1200, 1330, 1500, 1900, 2330 (Jacob), 0130.

To the E of Hyderabad, the **Thar Desert** defines the eastern boundary of Sind. Running from the Rann of Kutch in the S, the Thar extends N into the Cholistan Desert, and E into India's Rajasthan Desert. The international boundary runs for over 500 km through the Thar, yet prior to Partition, the desert was more of a route than a barrier to trade and movement. Relatively cool winters and the short distances between trading towns on the Indian side make the desert more accessible than the seemingly hostile appearance suggests. In fact, 1½ million people live in the southeasterly Tharparkar division of the desert, at a population density of 53/sq km.

Mirpur Khas

The road E to the district headquarters of Mirpur Khas (65 km), passes through fringes of the Thar Desert that have been transformed by irrigation. The **Rohri Canal** is the chief feeder from the Sukkur Barrage supplying perennial water to the minor canals that irrigate the banana, mango, sugar cane, rice and wheat crops. There is little of interest to tourists in Mirpur Khas, and the nearby Kahujo Daro stupa is in a very poor state of repair.

● **Accommodation** Outside the station are several filthy **F** hotels, such as the *Pakistan Guest House*.

● **Transport Train** Regular train services run to Hyderabad (1 hr, Rs 9). Trains also run to **Khokhropar** (0730, 1550, 6 hrs) on the frontier with India, but the border remains closed. A daily train service runs on a loop line to **Naukot** (0830, 4½ hrs). **Road Bus**: buses run to Hyderabad, to/from Karachi's Boulton Market and to Umarkot (1½ hrs, Rs 20).

The road to **Umarkot** (74 km), the desert town, is rough and dusty, yet the countryside gives little impression of aridity. The region is irrigated by the **Nara Canal**, the easternmost of the Sukkur Canals. Cotton and sugar cane cultivation are particularly prominent, and 6 km E of Mirpur Khas is a major sugar refining plant.

Umarkot

Umarkot stands between the **Marwar** and **Indus Valley**, and the foundation of the town is usually attributed to **Umar**, first king of the Summa Dynasty (1050-1350 AD). In the 13th century it was occupied by the Rajput, **Parmar Soda**, one of whose successors, **Rana Pashad**, played host to **Humayun** during his flight from the Afghan ruler of N India, **Sher Shah Suri**. It was in Umarkot that Humayun's young Sindhi wife **Hamida** gave birth to the future Mughal Emperor **Akbar** (b 1542). 1 km N of the town, a stone marking the birthplace is said to have the wrong date by 6 years.

The town of Umarkot is dominated by the earthen brick fort built by the Kalhora ruler **Nur Mohammad** in the 18th century. The tapering fortification walls are constructed of unbaked bricks, with baked brick semi circular bastions at its four corners and either side of the arched doorway. The central tower offers fine views of the surrounding area. A small one room museum next door has a well labelled collection of Mughal armoury, miniature paintings, coins and various treatise and documents. Winter 0900-1600, Summer 0800-1200, 1400-1700, closed Mon of the month. Umarkot is also renowned locally for its fine embroidery and handloom cloth.

- **Accommodation** The *Circuit House* can be reserved through the Dy Commissioner, Mirpur Khas. The 3 **F** hotels, *Al Hyder, Hotel City Heart* and *Kharoonjhar* are superior to those at Mirpur Khas.

- **Transport** Both Mirpur Khas and Umarkot can be visited by public transport as a day trip from Hyderabad.

Naukot

The real gateway for trips deep into the Thar is **Naukot**, 80 km SE of Mirpur Khas. This small town can be reached by road from either Umarkot or Mirpur Khas, although the road from the latter is in a better state of repair.

- **Transport Train** A daily train also runs on a loop line from Mirpur Khas (0830, 4½ hrs). **Road Bus**: a desert bus service runs from Naukot via **Mithi** and **Islamakot** to **Nagar Parkar**.

NB In recent years, concerns over the security situation in interior Sind has meant that the embryonic 'desert tours' tourist industry that was evolving in Naukot has all but collapsed. Until the market picks up in response to demand, one cannot be certain of being able to hire suitable vehicles in Naukot, and thus vehicle hire should be arranged in Karachi or Hyderabad. It is possible, however, to arrange desert guides in Naukot. It is essential to ensure that your vehicle is mechanically sound, and that you take adequate spares and supplies. Shovels, gloves, water, fuel, cutting tool or axe and a compass are essential. There are no accurate maps of the region. Prior to commencing a journey into the Thar, it is advisable to contact PTDC in Karachi and your own embassy to check on the latest security situation in the region. Where possible, you should avoid travelling by road at night. Basic accommodation is available in **E** *Resthouses* at Mithi, Islamakot and Nagar Parkar, although you should check with the Deputy Commissioner in Mirpur Khas whether it is possible to book them.

Located several km from Naukot, on the road to Mithi, stands the impressive **Naukot Fort**. Built by the Talpurs in 1814, the fort was reoccupied by the Pakistani army during the 1971 war with

India. The desert road continues to **Mithi**, a centre for Thar handicrafts, particularly woollen blankets and embroidery work. The Rajput influence is very much in evidence in this southeasterly corner of Pakistan. In fact, 37% of the population of the Tharparkar administrative district are Hindus, and Mithi has a number of important Hindu temples incl **Temple of Nag Devta** (Snake Temple). There is also a shrine to the 11th century Muslim saint, **Sayed Ali Shah**.

The topography of the land beyond Mithi comprises rough outcrops of wind carved rocks, interspersed with sand blown from the Rann of Kutch. In places, dunes have formed. Xerophytic shrubs and coarse grasses provide the only vegetation. **Islamakot** (40 km) is an ancient Rajput town, and has a predominantly Hindu population. Save The Children Fund have a number of development programmes in the area. To the

N of Islamakot is **Chachro**, a famous peacock centre. It was occupied by Indian troops during the 1971 war, and is now said to be the centre of the cross-border smuggling trade.

The desert road passes the old **Jain Temple of Gori** (45 km), built in the late 14th century, before reaching the last truly desert town of **Virawah** (22 km). Incredibly, the nearby ruined town of **Parinagar** was a flourishing port in the 6th century, at a time when the channels of the Rann of Kutch were still navigable.

Beyond Virawah, the desert gives way to the low, volcanic Karunjhar Hills where Pakistan's most southeasterly town, **Nagar Parkar** stands. Nearby at **Bhodesar**, are the remains of three ancient Jain structures built in 1375 and 1449, and a mosque dating from the same period. The sensitivity of the border with India makes it impossible to travel any further E or SE.

HYDERABAD TO SUKKUR VIA THE INDUS EAST BANK

The National Highway (NH), the main road route to the N of Pakistan, is comparatively fast and dangerous. Might is right on this road, so be prepared to get out of the way as drivers attempt risky overtaking manoeuvres in unlikely places. The tangled wreckage of vehicles beside the road is testament to those overtaking manoeuvres that did not come off. A road widening scheme is underway as far as Ranipur, which may make this journey less nerve-wracking.

The E bank route is far more densely populated than the W bank. It crosses an endless succession of former inundation canals taking off from the right bank of the Indus. Slightly lower than the left bank, the rising waters of the Indus were trained through cuts and led away by canals, making this the granary of Sind.

Miani forest, 10 km N of Hyderabad is the site of the 1843 battle where Napier's forces defeated the Talpur Mirs, ending the 60 year reign of the Baluchis. Napier, who had 2,800 men and 12 artillery pieces, defeated the 22,000 man Talpur army, inflicting over 5,000 fatal casualties. A small memorial remembers the 256 British casualties. There is a *Forest Rest House* and children's park at the site. Connoisseurs of British colonial battles may be interested to find that almost 3 km S of Hyderabad is the dilapidated site of the **Residency** where, in 1843, Major Outram and his escort held out against 8,000 Baluchis of the Talpur Mirs.

40 km N is the turn off for the village of **Bhit Shah**. Holy to all Sindhis, the village houses the shrine of the great poet and Sufi saint **Shah Abdul Latif**. Born in nearby **Hala** in 1689 to a wealthy Hyderabad family, Shah Abdul Latif renounced material comforts for a life of contemplation. He selected a sand dune, *bhit*, as the site of his spiritual environment and spent his life studying both Hindu and Muslim ideas, although the latter became dominant. He is regarded as Sind's (and Sindhi's) foremost poet, and the *Risalo* his greatest work.

Following his death in 1752, Nur Mohammad Kalhora constructed the shrine over his grave. Built in typical Sindhi architectural style, the mausoleum has carved limestone domes and minarets, and is decorated with patterned floors, frescoes and beautiful blue and white tile work. Next to the shrine is a mosque with a superb mirror-tiled ceiling. Each year at the *Urs* anniversary (14-16th of Islamic month of Safar), thousands of devotees come to the shrine of Shah Abdul Latif to listen to his songs and poetry, and to take part in the ecstatic dances of the dervishes, entering a trance like state to the beating of drums.

A small museum near the shrine contains a collection of local handicrafts, paintings and musical instruments. There are also a number of waxworks re-enacting favourite Sindhi stories.

● **Transport Road Bus**: from Pathan Colony, Hyderabad.

Hala (26 km) The town of **Hala** is a famous handicraft centre, particularly renowned for its blue and white ceramics and woven *susi* cloth. The old town was severely damaged during Indus flooding, so a new town, marked by the white and blue tiled archway, was relocated on the National Highway. Hala was the birth place of **Makhdoom Nooh** (b 1505), reputed to have realigned Shah Jahan's mosque at Thatta towards Mecca through the power of a night spent in prayer.

Brahmanabad/Mansura Almost 35 km E of the NH from Hala, via **Shahdadpur**, is a large mass of ruins, the identity of which is a source of controversy. When Mohammad bin Qasim conquered Sind, a fierce battle took place for the Hindu town of **Brahmanabad**. Under Arab rule this town came to be known as **Mansura**, although its exact location is in dispute due to its changing orientation to the shifting course of the Indus. Major Raventry claimed that Brahmanabad stood not on the Indus but on the 'lost river' – **Hakra**. The location of Brahmanabad has also variously been attributed to Kalan Kot, Banbhore and indeed Hyderabad, although in 1854 Bellasis seemed to fix Brahmanabad at this spot. Cunningham has also identified the site with the **Harmateila** of Greek history where Ptolemy was wounded. Excavations have suggested that both a Hindu town (Brahmanabad) and a Muslim town (Mansura) existed at this site. Reasons for the town's decline are uncertain, although earthquake and the shifting course of the Indus have been offered as two possible explanations.

Travelling N, the NH passes through the small town of **Daulatpur**, site of the mausoleum of the Kalhora ruler, **Nur Mohammad**, who made Sind one kingdom.

At **Moro** (110 km) you can cross the Indus via a new bridge to **Dadu** on the W bank. Moro, founded some 350 years ago by **Bazir Fakir** of the Moro tribe, has the modest **F** *Midway Hotel*.

Just S of **Ranipur** (91 km), beside the NH is the **E** *Sajid Hotel*, T 07051.

Kot Diji On a small mound at the side of the NH are the remains of the ancient settlement of Kot Diji. First excavated in 1955, the site stands on one of the rare outcrops of limestone that are part of the Rohri Hills to the N. Dating between 3500-2500 BC, there are two distinct parts to the site. One comprises a citadel and ruling class residency whilst the other is plebeian residency. Excavation

of the upper levels revealed characteristic Harappan pottery whilst the lower levels brought evidence of an unknown pre-Harappan culture, designated as Kot Diji. Distinct forms of pottery were found at this level depicting a new type of ceramic industry. Another interesting feature is evidence of the production and use of sun and oven dried bricks.

On a raised limestone outcrop to the E of the NH stands the magnificent **Kot Diji Fort**. Built between 1803 and 1830 by **Mir Sohrab Khan** to serve as a military stronghold and administrative headquarters, the largely brick built fort dominates the surrounding area. The outer wall runs for over 2,700m and is reinforced by rounded bastions and strategically placed towers. The entrance is in the SE corner on the opposite side to the NH. A steep winding climb passes through three imposing defensive gateways fortified with metal spiked gates to repulse attacks on elephant. At the top stands the Mir's residential quarters, including the plaster floral motif decorated harem. There is a stone pavilion to the N, and a number of cells dating to the period when the fort was utilized by the British as a central state prison. This well preserved structure can also be reached by bus from Sukkur.

Khairpur (24 km) is an important regional centre within Sukkur Division. The town was founded around 1787 by **Mir Sohrab Khan Talpur**, and remained an independent state until 1947. There are a number of impressive tombs of the ruling Talpur princes, the most striking of which is the tomb of **Mir Karam Ali Khan Talpur**, built in 1812. The town was described by a visitor in the 1840s as "the dirtiest, unhealthiest town in Sind".

Khairpur borders the *pat* desert to the E, where impervious clay soils hold up the groundwater. Much of the surface configuration has been changed by the provision of irrigation from the Sukkur Barrage. This has allowed the area under cultivation during the *rabi* (winter) season to be increased by 500%, with the main crop being wheat. A variety of other crops are grown locally, incl rice, sugar cane, oil seeds, dates and mangoes.

However, despite benefiting greatly from the construction of the Sukkur Barrage, the region has experienced severe environmental damage as a result of the raising of the watertable. Despite the efforts of the Salinity and Reclamation Projects, some of the worst examples of waterlogging and salinization can be seen in the region. This phenomenon is particularly striking from the air. The waterlogging has also led to a sharp increase in the incidence of malaria.

Pirjo Goth Several km off the National Highway, W of Khairpur, **Pirjo Goth** is the home town of the **Pagaro Pirs**. The ancestry of this family of hereditary religious leaders dates back to Pir Bakadar Shah, who came to Sind from Arabia. However, it was during the time of **Pir Mohammad Rashdi**, a religious leader who travelled as far as Jaisalmer, Kutch and Kathiawar preaching his message, that the movement really developed. The Pagaro Pirs are not just revered as great religious leaders and teachers, they are credited with supernatural powers.

During the late 19th century, a radical armed faction of the Pir's followers evolved. Known as the **Hurs**, this group waged a 50 year war against British occupation at a time when virtually the whole of Sind had succumbed to British rule. The most revered of the rebel Pirs was **Pir Sibghatullah Shah Saani**, who remained a constant thorn in the side of the British until his arrest in 1930. At his trial, an up and coming young lawyer, Mohammad Ali Jinnah, defended the Pir, although it appears that he abandoned the case when it was obvious that the British were determined to return a 'guilty' verdict (but not before he had charged Rs 100,000 in fees). Sibghatullah Shah spent the next 10 years in and

out of prison for continuing to resist the British until, in 1943, he was sentenced to death and hung. The Pir's two young sons, including **Shah Mardan Shah**, the current Pir Pagaro, were sent to England for a 'proper' education.

Today, Pir Pagaro is a major power-broker in Pakistani politics as well as being credited as the owner of the first television satellite dish in Pakistan! On 27th of the Islamic month of Rajab, thousands of followers gather at the *dargah*, or shrine, to the Pirs in Pirjo Goth. The Pir's residence is the imposing four storeyed red sandstone building, adorned with ornate marble carvings.

Continuing N along the NH, shortly before **Rohri** a road branches left via the 66 span **Sukkur Barrage** across the Indus to the town of **Sukkur**. Prior to the construction of the 1,418m long Sukkur Barrage, agriculture in the whole of Sind was dependent upon the floods of the Indus filling wet season inundation canals. The flow of the river is now controlled by the 66 sluice gates that protect the feeder channels from excessive flooding and regulate the flow of perennial irrigation water. Seven irrigation canals take off from the barrage; four from the W bank (Khairpur E, Khairpur W, Rohri, Nara), and three from the E (Northwestern, Dadu and the seasonal Rice). The total irrigated area dependent upon the Sukkur Barrage is in the region of 2.98 million ha, provided through over 75,000 km of canals. Planned as far back as 1847, the project was inaugurated by the then Governor of Bombay, Sir George Lloyd in 1923 and completed as the Lloyd Barrage in 1932 at a cost of Rs 40.4 million. After the barrage was completed, however, Sind was directly affected by use made in winter of water upstream. Further, the unlined (kachcha) canals of previous irrigation systems have brought problems of increased salinity and waterlogging. There are usual Pakistani photography restrictions at the Barrage.

Sukkur

Sukkur is strategically placed at a crossing point on the Indus where the river cuts through the last outcrop of solid limestone before proceeding to the sea. Sukkur has played a vital part in Sind's history for over 2,000 years. Mohammad bin Qasim took the town during the Arab conquest of Sind, and the military importance of the town was recognized by the British as part of the strategic route to the Bolan Pass in Baluchistan. However, Napier abandoned the town as a military station in 1845 following the outbreak of a terrible form of 'jungle fever' amongst the 78th Highlanders that killed 500 men, women and children.

Places of interest

The Minaret of Masum Shah During the reign of the Mughal Emperor Akbar, **Masum Shah** (1594-1618) was appointed as his Nawab, or Governor, of Sukkur. In 1614 he built the pencil shaped minaret. The tower is 84 ft high, circumference at the base is 84 ft and there are 84 steps leading to the lantern at the top. The spiral staircase is very narrow in places but there are fine views from the top. Sadly, photography is forbidden. At the base of the minaret is the **Faiz Mahal**, an octagonal building with a glazed brick dome, that was built by Masum Shah as a pavilion. Masum Shah is buried in the adjacent tomb.

To the E of the town is the **Mausoleum of Shah Khairuddin Jilani**, the religious scholar and wandering founder of a spiritual dynasty who settled in a nearby cave until his death in 1609 at the reputed age of 116. The shrine was built in 1760, although the blue enamelled dome and tiled façade were restored by Sindhi craftsmen only 40 years ago.

On of the most intriguing places of interest in Sukkur is the active Hindu complex on the island of **Sadhbella**. The symbolism of an outpost of Hinduism in predominantly Muslim Pakistan is not lost on the devotees attending the temples on this rocky island in the Indus. Sadhbella is thought to have emerged as a separate island from Bukkur around 1550 AD. Founded some 150 years ago by **Baba Bankhandi Maharaji**, the complex includes a monastery, an ashram, temples to Hanuman, Siva and Ganesh as well as a library containing Dharmic books in Hindi, Sindhi and English. The first entry in the visitor's book is, surprisingly, by General Zia ul-Haq, former martial law ruler of Pakistan, who visited in 1985.

The main temple contains a shrine to the founder, and is decorated with statues of Hindu deities and scenes from Hindu mythology. It is generally possible to visit the island from the Sukkur riverbank although Muslim visitors may require prior permission. Sadhbella offers fine views of the river.

Excursions

To Punjab There are two routes N from Sukkur into **Punjab**. The W route travels via **Shikarpur** (42 km), **Kandkhot** (64 km), former outpost of the Sind Horse Regiment, **Kashmor** (47 km), famous for its lacquer work and Baluch rugs, onto **Dera Ghazi Khan** (346 km).

The E route passes through the town of **Ghotki** (67 km). The main mosque, built in 1747 by Pir Musan Shah, is one of the largest of its era in Sind. Constructed of burnt bricks, 35m long and 20m wide, it has an extensive courtyard and is surmounted by a cupola covered with glazed tiles.

The NH continues N via **Ubauro** (41 km), site of a mosque built in 1552, onto **Reti**, the last railway stop in Sind. 12 km S of here, on a dry former bed of the Indus, lie the ancient ruins of **Vijnot**. A contemporary of Brahmanabad, this extensive city is believed to have been destroyed by an earthquake. It is also thought to be the 'Pinchen-po-pu-lu' mentioned by the Chinese traveller Hiuen Tsang.

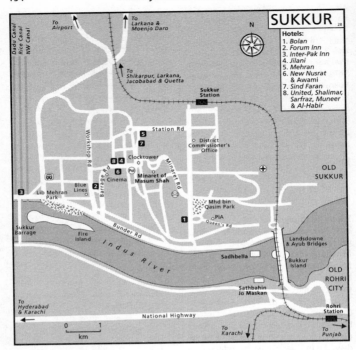

The NH continues N to **Sadiqabad** (29 km), in **Punjab**. For detailed description of routes N to Lahore, see Punjab chapter, page 292.

To Baluchistan From Sukkur it is possible to travel NW to **Quetta**, Baluchistan, via **Shikarpur**, **Jacobabad**, **Sibi** and the **Bolan Pass**. For a detailed description of this route, see Baluchistan chapter.

Local information
● **Accommodation**

C *Forum Inn*, Workshop Rd, T 83011, central a/c, dish TV, *Cherry* restaurant; **C** *Inter-Pak Inn*, Lab-e-Mehran, opp Barrage, T 83051, central a/c, restaurant, balconies with fine views, rec.

E *Al-Habir*, Barrage Rd, T 84359, some a/c, *Taj* restaurant rec; **E** *Bolan*, Mission Rd, nr PIA, T 25087, *Sabrina* restaurant; **E** *Mehran*, Station Rd, T 83792, restaurant, rec; **E** *Nusrat*, Barrage Rd, T 85035, some a/c; **E** *Shalimar*, Barrage Rd, T 83105, some a/c; **E** *Sind Faran*, Station Rd, T 82921, restaurant.

On Barrage Rd: **F** *Awami*, T 85004, att bath; **F** *Jilani*, T 88819, basic; **F** *Munneer*, **F** *Sarfraz*, **F** *United*, some with att bath.

● **Places to eat**

Restaurants can be found at the *Forum Inn*, *Inter-Pak Inn*, *Mehran*, *Bolan* and *Al-Habir* hotels. Basic restaurants can be found around the clock-tower.

● **Airline offices**

PIA, Queen's Rd, opp Mohammad bin Qasim Gdns, T 24547.

● **Post & telecommunications**

GPO: Minaret Rd.

● **Transport**

Local Minivans run from the clock-tower to Rohri (Rs 5). Tongas and rickshaws run between bus stand and town.

Air The airport is 8 km NW of town. **PIA**: Karachi, at least 1 flight daily; Bahawalpur, twice weekly; Sui, twice weekly.

Train Although trains run from Sukkur to Sibi and Quetta, the main railhead for trains N (**Punjab**), W (**Quetta**), and S (**Hyderabad/Karachi**) is at **Rohri**.

Road Bus: the main bus stand is several km W of the town centre, nr the Barrage. There appears to be no advance bookings although *Blue Lines*, Workshop Rd, opp Forum Inn run Deluxe services to **Karachi**, 0830 0930, 1030, 1300, 2000, 2130, 2230 (Rs 110). Buses N run from the NH at Rohri.

Rohri In 1875, Lt Twemlour of the Asiatic Society of Bengal found evidence to suggest that **Rohri** was a flourishing place in neolithic times, making it one of the oldest sites of human habitation in South Asia. Rohri has been a sacred site to Muslims due to the association of Saiyads who settled here, and in 1545 **Mir Mohammad Kalhora** built a shrine – **Mu-e-Mubarak** – to receive a hair of the beard of the Prophet. On 2 Mar each year the sacred relic is displayed to the public.

In the old part of town, a little difficult to find, stands the **Akbari Mosque**, built in 1583 by an officer of the Emperor Akbar. At the S side is a tall, green domed gateway with a blue, green and brown tiled façade. The mosque, a low white building, has a highly decorated mirrored mihrab. A madrassa, or Koranic school, is attached.

Just below the Ayub Khan arch railway bridge, on a raised mound, stands the **Sathbahin Jo Maskan**, a shrine to the legend of seven virgin sisters who locked themselves away and swore never to look upon the face of any man. This attractive site is entered through a small domed gateway. The shrine is 200m long and 50m wide and has a rectangular central raised plinth of red baked bricks. At each corner stands a 5m blue tiled minaret. A number of sandstone tombs, carved with text from the Koran, and similar in style to those at Chaukundi, stand on the plinth. There are fine views across the river to Sukkur, and of the **Ayub Khan** and **Landsdowne Bridges**. Below the bridges, along the W bank of the Indus, reside communities of the **Mohana boat people**, an indigenous ethnic group found in several parts of Sind.

Rohri is reached from Sukkur by crossing the twin bridges via **Bukkur Island** in the centre of the Indus. On the N of this 300m wide limestone island is a simple shrine to **Sadra-u-din Badshah**, a contemporary of **Lal Shahbaz Qalander** whose shrine is at **Sehwan**. The ancient ruined mud fort to the S, occupied by Mohammad bin Qasim, is now a military base so access is denied.

Rohri is an important rail and road junction for Sind, Baluchistan and Punjab.

● **Transport Train** Karachi: 14 trains daily, 6-9 hrs. **Lahore**: *Shalimar*, 1300, 10½ hrs; *Tezgam*, 2335, 11½ hrs. **Multan**: *Shalimar*, 1300, 5½ hrs; *Tezgam*, 2335, 6 hrs. **Peshawar**: *Awam Exp*, 1545, 24 hrs; *Khyber Mail*, 0505, 25 hrs. **Rawalpindi**: *Awam Exp*, 1545, 20 hrs; *Tezgam*, 2335, 18 hrs. **Quetta**, via **Sukkur**, **Jacobabad** and **Sibi**: *Quetta Exp*, 0425, 11 hrs; *Abbaseen Exp*, 2315, 18 hrs.

Alor (or Aror), 8 km E of **Rohri** was the capital of Sind at the time of Mohammad bin Qasim's conquest, but declined with the changing course of the Indus. It is believed that Alexander stopped here during his march down the Indus. The city was also mentioned in the 7th century by the Chinese traveller Hiuen Tsang. The ruins of a Hindu town, a bridge and evidence of the previous course of the Indus can be seen.

HYDERABAD TO SUKKUR VIA THE INDUS WEST BANK

The Indus Highway, running along the W bank of the Indus, passes through some of South Asia's most important proto and prehistoric sites. Despite appearing barren and inhospitable, the hills to the W witnessed the earliest development of settled agriculture in South Asia, some 10,000 years ago. Goats and sheep are known to have been domesticated in the region at least 16,000 ago, and along with the Potwar Plateau in Punjab, the Brahmaputra valley, and the central Indian peninsula around the Krishna and Tungabhadra Rivers, these W borderlands were one of the key South Asian regions at the beginning of the Neolithic period.

Further, the route passes through the heart of one of the world's great pre-modern cultures, the Indus Valley Civilization. From 2500 BC to around 1800 BC, **Moenjo Daro** was the centre of a civilization that embraced the entire plains area of the Indus, and beyond.

Long after the Indus Valley Civilization had collapsed, the region remained the centre of power under a number of dynasties, most notably the **Kushan** Empire. Under their great leader, **Kanishka**, who converted to Buddhism in the 1st century AD, the Kushans spread their power S from the NW passes, building stupas such as that on the citadel at Moenjo Daro.

The great Chinese traveller **Hiuen Tsang** followed this route between 643-44 AD, as did the Arab armies of Mohammad bin Qasim 70 years later.

The road, far quieter than the National Highway on the E bank of the Indus, runs along the flat river plain, skirting the **Kirthar Mountains** to the W. This limestone range runs for 240 km N to S in an eastward curving direction. Although the apparent dearth of vegetation makes the hills look barren, the scrub and grass support the sheep and goats of nomadic tribes, as well as wild ibex and urials. Along streams, and where the soil is rich and irrigated, rice, wheat and oilseeds are grown.

Leaving Hyderabad across the Ghulam Mohammad Barrage to the W, you join the Indus Highway. From the **Sann** crossroads (75 km), it is possible to travel W to **Ranikot Fort**, one of the world's largest, with a circumference of 25 km. Leaving the Indus Highway at the Sann crossroads, the rough jeep track to the fort (32 km) passes through barren hills, dotted with scrub and stunted trees. There is no public transport to the fort, although it may be possible to hire camels in Sann for the trip. **NB** The fort has previously been used as a hide-out by bandits, so it is recommended that you take advice on safety before planning a trip.

Ranikot Fort was first mentioned in 1812 when an older fort, possibly 8th century or even dating back to the Scythians, was refurbished by the Talpur Mirs. Splendid in its isolation, it is assumed that the fort was intended to defend a long since abandoned trade route between Thatta and Central Asia through the Kirthar Hills. The massive defensive walls are visible from several km away, and from the S resemble the Great Wall of China. The battlements near the entrance are sandstone, elsewhere they are shale and limestone, and a sheer limestone rock face protects the northern flank.

You enter through the easterly **Sann Gate**, where the River Rani used to flow out. There are several pools with fish, small waterfalls and a fresh water spring where the river enters the fort through the **Mohan Gate** (W). The others are **Amri Gate** (N) and **Shahper Gate** (S).

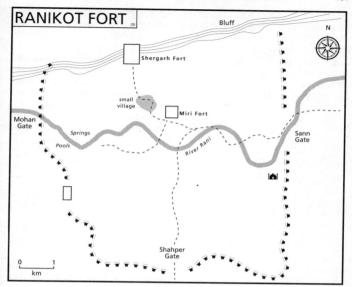

RANIKOT FORT

Bluff

N

Shergarh Fort

small village

Miri Fort

Mohan Gate

Springs

Pools

Sann Gate

River Rani

0   1
km

Shahper Gate

One of two forts within the master fort, **Miri Fort** formerly housed the Talpur Mirs and their harem, and stands on a small hillock in the centre. To the N is the fortified citadel, **Shergarh Fort**. The fort offers excellent views.

Amri Seemingly little more than a mound, made of generations of mud houses built on top of one another, **Amri** (20 km) is in fact an important prehistoric site. In 1929, excavations by the archaeologist NG Majumdar revealed artefacts contemporary with Moenjo Daro. Lower levels, however, revealed a previously unknown ceramic style that extended the period of Amri's occupation from 3500 BC to 2200 BC. Full excavations at the site's three main mounds were not completed until 1962, but revealed three occupations superimposed above one another. Glazed and moulded pottery from the Mughal period were found at the upper level, below which were pieces from the late and mature level of

Harappan occupation. At the lowest level was found pottery that showed no affinity with Harappa or Moenjo Daro and has been named **Amri-ware**. The most important pieces are exhibited at the National Museum in Karachi.

The original inhabitants of Amri predate the Harappan people, and represent a quite distinct culture. As opposed to the predominantly black-on-red style of Indus Valley pottery, Amri-ware typically uses fine buff and pale pink paste in bands around the mouth of the vessels, with geometric patterns infilled with chequered work, chevrons and diamonds. **Potsherds** dating from 3000 BC and also **Indus bricks** of a millennium later have been found.

The absence of a large settlement has led to the belief that the Amri people lived in scattered villages, possibly using a somewhat better placed, larger and more important village as a centre for trading. The pastoral tribes appear to have preferred the hills, with sheltered valleys and springs. They were slowly forced to move from the W through pressure of population on the land and the changes in climate, and were not attracted by the plains of the Indus. Their settlements appear in the valleys along the Sind-Baluchistan border, forming a pattern similar to that of the Baluchis thousands of years later.

The road N from Amri passes close to the foothills of the Kirthar Range at the only point in Sind where Cretaceous rocks are exposed at the surface. A basaltic fissure flow forms the crest of the range, and numerous thermal springs break the surface in the foothills. The four sulphurous springs at **Lakhi Shah Saddar** (10 km) draw people in search of cures for rheumatism and skin ailments. The nearby cave where the Muslim saint Shah Saddar came to meditate is now a shrine. The Indus Highway runs along the foothills until you reach **Sehwan Sharif**.

Sehwan

Formerly known as Siwistan, **Sehwan** may be the oldest continuously occupied town in Sind. The site has been associated with Sindimana, where Sambos, king of the hillmen surrendered to Alexander. The **fort**, whose remains lie across the deep and narrow valley to the N of town, was used by Alexander, and is known locally as the 'Kafir Qila'. The town was later used in the 4th century as the Buddhist capital of Chandragupta II's ascetic brother, and then conquered in the 8th century by Mohammad bin Qasim when the Buddhist population refused to fight. Commanding the Lakhi Pass, Sehwan has been a key strategic location for all invaders in the region.

Sehwan is famous for the shrine of the 13th century Sufi saint **Hazrat Lal Shahbaz Qalander** (Divine Spirit of the Red Falcon). Born in Afghanistan as Sheikh Usman Merwandi, he came from the 11th century **Qalander** order of wandering sufis who gave up everything worldly to devote themselves to propagating a religion free from orthodox rituals. The saint was renowned for his scholarship in Persian and Arabic, and for his miracles. He claimed to be the last direct descendant of the Prophet, helping the local people in times of disaster, and amazing them with his miracles.

The original 14th century **tomb**, decorated with tiles and calligraphy, had a 17th century surround, partly constructed of wood, with beaten silver ornamentation on the railings and spires. However, this was partially destroyed when the original dome roof collapsed, and the shrine has been substantially rebuilt. Almost all pious rulers of Sind or Sewistan have contributed something to the shrine over the years, with the most recent gift being the magnificent gold covered doors at the S gateway, presented by the Shah of Iran. There are plans to entirely rebuild the courtyard, quadrupling its size.

A visit to the shrine is one of the highlights of a journey around Sind, as there is an intense atmosphere charged with piety, devotion and hope. The narrow bazaars leading to the shrine, with their food and souvenir stalls, service the stream of pilgrims, fakirs, miracle-seekers as well as Sehwan's numerous beggars. Indeed, the 1919 Gazetteer of Sind claims "the population is largely composed of beggars". The number of visitors swells on Thur, and peaks during the annual Urs (18th of Shaban). Each evening at 1800, the congregation join in the devotional dance of the dervishes. To the accompaniment of gongs and the rhythmic beating of giant drums, the disciples express their devotion through dancing, music and poetry. The men and women dance separately, reaching a trance-like state, although watching the women can be disturbing. Kneeling on the floor, they swing their heads around and around with remarkable intensity, their long hair sweeping the ground like 'headbangers' at a Heavy Rock concert, before collapsing in a state of exhaustion. The hour of dancing is timed using a **waterclock**, in the form of a pot with a hole which fills and sinks after 15 mins.

● **Accommodation** *Dist Council Rest House*, T 68, reservations: Chief Exec Officer, Dadu, T 342, some a/c. *Irrigation Rest House*, Old Fort, reservations: Exec Engineer, Irrigation, Dadu, T 404. **F** *Indus Rest House*, Station Rd, opp GPO, T 230, some a/c; **F** *Lajpal*, Lajpal Rd, nr mosque, T 444, restaurant, basic.

Across the road, to the W of Sehwan, is the large marshy area covered by **Manchar Lake**, caused by the overflowing of the right bank of the Indus and the drainage of a large area of the Kirthar Hills. Like most major rivers that flow N-S in the N hemisphere, the action of the Earth's rotation causes the Indus to cut into its W bank. The dry season area of the lake, 36 sq km, expands rapidly to 510 sq km when the excess high season flow of the Indus drains off into the lake. As the Indus returns to its low stage during the winter, water starts flowing back to the river from the lake. Effectively, Manchar Lake acts as a great safety valve for the Indus in a similar way that the Tonle Sap acts for the Mekong in Cambodia. However, the effect of upstream dams in reducing the flow of the Indus has lead to the steady deterioration of the lake.

The community of **Mohana** fishermen that live on the lake use traditional methods of catching fish, such as submerged baited lines and driving the fish into nets. They also have an ingenious method of catching herons and water fowl that involves placing a stuffed egret on their heads as a decoy, and then wading neck deep to net their unwary prey. The Mohanas' large, flat bottomed boats characteristically have high prows and usually accommodate a family in two rooms.

You reach the lake by driving from **Bubak** to the embankment of the **Dunister canal** where you can hire a boat or walk the 3 km along the bank.

Continuing N from Sehwan, the National Highway runs through the enigmatic town of **Khudabad**. Built during the rule of **Yar Mohammad Kalhora** (1701-1718), this town became the capital of Sind under the Kalhoras until 1768, when the subsequent changing course of the Indus led to its decline. In 1781 the Talpurs raised the city. In fact, the town is so diminished in size that its two main monuments appear out of place. The huge **Jami Masjid** (Friday Mosque) beside the road is big enough to hold almost 2,000 people. The **Tomb of Yar Mohammad Kalhora** is 2 km off the NH, although it is now in a poor state of repair.

The Indus Highway by-passes the district headquarters of **Dadu** (51 km). This is probably just as well since the forests around Dadu are considered to be Pakistan's "heartland of banditry for 800 years", and prior to the army's anti-bandit drive the police travelled in armoured cars. From Dadu it is possible to cross the bridge at **Moro** to the Indus E bank.

The Indus Highway continues N to Mehar (60 km) from where you turn off via Radhan to **Moenjo Daro** (45 km).

Moenjo Daro

Not only one of the most important archaeological sites of South Asia, for its age, Moenjo Daro is one of the most stunningly restored and preserved prehistoric sites in the world.

Moenjo Daro represented the culmination of a long period of development within the Indus region. In some places early Indus Valley settlements can be traced back to the Neolithic, and the pottery of the whole Indus system may go back to 4000 BC or even earlier. With the development of the Kot Diji style of pottery came also greater uniformity throughout the region, heralding the extraordinary political and cultural unity of the Harappa-Moenjo Daro city culture.

An interesting feature of the civilization is the complete absence of any evidence of warfare; no weapons have ever been found, nor evidence of a warrior class. Some scholars feel that the existence of a specifically non-violent religion was the unifying force which led the civilization to evolve and prosper so successfully. Trade was also extensive, both internally and abroad – with S India, Afghanistan, Egypt and Mesopotamia.

Although the majority of the Indus Valley towns were in what is now Pakistan, there are several important sites in India – the port of **Lothal**, **Rangpur** and **Rojidi** in modern Gujarat, **Kalibangan** in Rajasthan, **Banavli** in Punjab and **Alamgirpur** to the N of Delhi. Yet of all the sites known today Moenjo Daro and Harappa stand out by virtue of their scale and their complexity. The significance of the Indus Valley Civilization is comparable with the two other great ancient civilizations, Egypt and Mesopotamia. The fact that no written records have been discovered and the remnants of the script itself remains undeciphered still leaves the field open to contrasting interpretations of the rise, function and decline of the cities.

Dating the city Both the dating of the city and the causes of its decline remain unclear. Early dating relied on the comparison of objects found in Harappan cities with similar objects found in Mesopotamia, and dated the Indus Valley settlements at between 2500 and 1500 BC. Subsequent analysis, aided in places by radiocarbon dating has suggested an even earlier rise in some parts of the valley, and a decline by 1750 BC at the latest. But what caused the decline is even more speculative than the dating.

The city's decline As you walk back from the lower city past the citadel towards the museum, the fragile nature of the environmental balance is obvious. Any one change might well be enough to tip the balance between success and failure. Probably it was a combination of events. In Lambrick's view, the natural flooding of the Indus may have caused it to move its course massively, resulting in the abandonment of vital agricultural land. Such a change could have been brought about by earthquakes in what is still a highly active earthquake zone.

Flooding itself may have wiped out large parts of the city, or encouraged the spread of disease on such a scale as to decimate the population. Short of further evidence the least likely explanation seems to be the arrival of the 'Indo-Aryan hordes', for there still seems a gap of at least 2 centuries between the decline of the Indus Valley civilization and the first arrival of the Aryans, although new research may change this view. Significantly, unlike Harappa where large graveyards have been discovered, very few skeletons have been uncovered at Moenjo Daro, perhaps suggesting a gradual move away from the area, as opposed to a cataclysmic ending.

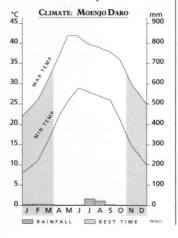

CLIMATE: MOENJO DARO

RAINFALL   BEST TIME   PKTG11

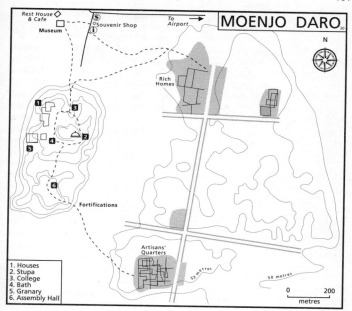

MOENJO DARO

Rest House & Cafe
Museum
Souvenir Shop
To Airport
N

Rich Homes

1. Houses
2. Stupa
3. College
4. Bath
5. Granary
6. Assembly Hall

Fortifications

Artisans' Quarters

53 metres

50 metres

0   200
metres

Inside the entrance is the National Bank of Pakistan, offering foreign exchange, a fixed price Sindhi handicraft shop and the helpful PTDC office. To the right lie the Water and Soil Investigation Laboratory, the *Archaeological Dak Bungalow* (reservations through Dept of Archaeology and Museums, 27-4 Union Commercial Area, Shaheed-e-Millat Rd, Karachi), a canteen and the museum. Even by Mar, temperatures get uncomfortably hot, and as there is virtually no shade on the site, it is essential to take sun-block and water.

The **Museum**, opened in 1967, contains the most important artefacts found at Moenjo Daro. The displays are clearly labelled and well presented, and are set against the backdrop of a stunning artist's impression of the city at its peak. Lambrick surmised that the population of Moenjo Daro may have been about 35,000, but more recent research (taking account of a whole new area of settlement) suggests doubling or even trebling that figure.

The city left behind it abundant evidence of its high quality of life. Many **copper and bronze tools** and decorative objects have been found, the ore probably having come from mines in Rajasthan. Copper and bronze vessels in the late stages of the city show highly developed form, the work of craft specialists.

Gold objects are quite common – beads, pendants and ornaments. Allchin and Allchin argue that the light quality of the gold point to a source as far afield as Karnataka in S India, to the Neolithic settlements that were clustered around the bands of quartz reef gold at Hatti. Silver and other metals were also common for works of sculpture, such as the famous figure of the dancing girl.

The museum also contains seals and sealings, with as yet undecipherable

SAVING MOENJO DARO

At present, approximately one-third of Moenjo Daro has been excavated. The last major excavation was undertaken in 1965 by the American George F Dales, although problems of waterlogging meant that the dig could not be completed. It was soon realized that unless immediate action was taken to reduce the impact of water-table rise and the effects of salinity, the site would suffer permanent and irreversible damage.

It is estimated that the water-table needs to be lowered by some 10m, and for that purpose 27 tube-wells and many cemented disposal channels have been dug to lower the water-table and drain away saline water. Stone pitching has also been introduced to counter seepage from the Indus, just 1½ km away. Cultivation of the traditionally thirsty rice crop has also been banned in the immediate vicinity.

The Water and Soil Investigation Laboratory monitors the water-table level daily, and claims that it has been lowered to the necessary depth. However, during the frequent power cuts, the tube-wells are unable to operate, and the level rises once more. Thus, there is a slight improvement, but not a permanent solution.

Other conservation measures include isolation of structures from saline water by installing damp proof courses, underpinning and mudcapping parts that have already decayed, and providing mud poultice treatment in order to desalinize standing structures.

characters, as well as images of tigers, rhinos, elephants, crocodiles, unicorns and bulls. Terracotta images of animals, some with moving parts, are thought to be toys, and there are also games involving dice and what appear to be chessboards. There are also exhibits from the pre-Moenjo Daro sites of Kot Diji (3370-2655 BC), and Amri, (3660-3360 BC). Open Apr-Sep 0830-1230, 1430-1730; Oct-Mar 0900-1600.

Early excavation Moenjo Daro was first excavated by the Indian Archaeological Survey under Sir John Marshall in 1922 and 1931, and then by Sir Mortimer Wheeler in 1947. Now in the hands of the Pakistan Archaeological Survey, supported by UNESCO, the site is excellently presented.

The main gate is due N of the citadel. It is best to walk up the path and steps to the top of the citadel, now capped by the ruins of a 2nd century Buddhist stupa. From here you get an excellent idea of the layout of the whole city, and can follow a broadly circular path, well marked out with paved footpaths where

necessary, to take you round the main built up areas of the city.

The citadel From the top of the mound you get a commanding view of the citadel below and around the central height. The evidence of town planning, an important feature of the major cities, is all around. Moenjo Daro, in common with Harappa and Kalibangan, has its citadel at the westernmost point of the complex, built up on a mound of bricks. This would have raised the most important area of the city above the floods of the Indus that regularly inundated the town.

The surface level now is more than 10m higher than it was when Moenjo Daro's first houses were being built, and have been submerged under the ever increasing deposits of silt. The 13m high brick embankment here was probably also a defence against flooding. The long axis in all three cities runs N-S. To the E was a lower city – mainly residential houses. The large mural in the museum suggests that the citadel (probably also residential areas) was surrounded by massive brick fortifications. Although the layout of the streets is not absolutely precise, the main pattern is of the wider streets running from N-S and a series of narrower E-W streets. The width seems to be deliberately graded, the widest being twice the second and four times the width of the lanes.

The civic buildings As you walk down from the top through the citadel area immediately to the W of the stupa, you see other features common to the cities: the presence of civic and administrative buildings, **the great bath** (referred to as the 'royal bath', though there is little evidence of the political structure of the society other than that of its buildings and domestic artefacts) and possibly a **granary**.

Whatever the uncertainties of interpretation, the buildings are extraordinarily impressive. The bath, 12m by 7m and 3m deep, with flights of steps into it at each end, has 'changing' cubicles along the side. It may have been used for ritual bathing. If you walk down from the edge of the bath to the level immediately below it you can follow the sluice through which the water was drained away – a beautifully made brick-lined drain, about 3m high. Still further to the W you can see what Sir Mortimer Wheeler argued were **granaries**, 27 blocks crisscrossed with ventilation channels.

All around is the **brickwork** which was one of the hallmarks of Harappan city building. There is a remarkable standardization of size. The most common Harappan brick was 28 cm by 14 cm by 7 cm. At Moenjo Daro sun-dried brick was used mainly for filling, burnt brick for facing and structural work. Special bricks were used for particular purposes: sawn bricks for bathrooms and in the residential area to the E, and wedge-shaped bricks for wells, common in the eastern quarter.

If you walk about 200m S from the stupa mound and the great bath, you cross a shallow valley before climbing to the second main citadel area, with the **Assembly Hall** and **fortifications** at the extreme SE corner. All that remains of this building are five rows of 5-brick plinths, which may have been the bases of wooden columns.

The artisans' quarter The path goes steeply down past the fortifications and across to the SE to a group of 'artisan's houses'. The residential sites in Moenjo Daro show as much evidence of town planning as the citadel. There is a wide range in size, but the archaeologist Sarcina has shown how virtually all the houses in Moenjo Daro conform to one of five basic modules. The main variant is the position of the **courtyard**, and you can still see several of the types in villages in NW India and Pakistan today.

Almost every house had a bathroom (shown by a sawn brick pavement with a surrounding curb). Walking down the narrow streets, drain pipes and vertical chutes for toilet waste disposal are clearly visible. In the lower city are brick drains, covered over with other bricks or sometimes slabs of stone, and in the S zone there are small, barrack-like houses. One of the most remarkable features are the excavated wells which now stand proud of the ground by as much as 4m. The repeated silt deposition was matched by the raising of the brick lining.

The high class residential quarter Walk N again from the southernmost group of houses in the lower city along the broad main street that links the artisans' area with the main higher-class residential area. The remarkable scale of the road suggests it may have been used for triumphal processions. At the top of a slight slope look across the low valley between the S and N settlements to the magnificent view of the upper class residential area in front of you. Houses are superbly preserved, and high walls separate both broad streets and narrow lanes. The main street was probably lined with stalls and shops and inside the buildings to the W of this main street is a series of variously labelled rooms. Wheeler suggested that a building where the stone sculpture of a seated figure was found, was a temple.

● **Transport** Moenjo Daro is easily reached from Karachi by air or by train. From **Karachi** there are 2 flights daily to Moenjo Daro, one departing early morning, and one mid-afternoon. Returning to **Karachi** there is at least 1 flight daily, leaving late afternoon. The flying time is 1½-2 hrs, and the airport is located just outside the main gate. **Train** To Larkana from Karachi (Cantt): *Bolan Mail*, 1140, 10 hrs. From Karachi (City): *Khushal Khan Exp*, 1810, 11 hrs.

From the site, you can continue the 26 km to **Larkana**.

Larkana

Larkana is situated at the place where the Kalhoras first established themselves, and begun to dig canals for irrigated agriculture. The town's location is commercially significant, lying on the route from Karachi to Shikarpur and the Bolan Pass, and under the British it became Sind's greatest grain mart. The town is noted today as the home town of Zulfikar Ali Bhutto, former Prime Minister and President.

The only antiquity in Larkana is the dilapidated remains of a fort that has been used in turn as an arsenal, a jail, a hospital, a store room for the Camel Corps and a lunatic asylum. Larkana is a good base from which to visit Moenjo Daro.

Local information
● **Accommodation and places to eat**
C *STDC Sambara Inn*, Raza Shah Kabir Rd, T 44391, central a/c, restaurant, dish TV, pool, lawn, best in town.

D *United*, 2nd Flr, Royal Rd, T 61863, some a/c, TV, restaurant.

E *Asia*, off Station Rd, behind PIA, T 60007, central a/c, TV, restaurant; **E** *Gulf*, Bunder Rd, T 22282, some a/c, restaurant.

F *Mehran*, Station Rd, T 61077, with bath, restaurant.

In addition to the hotel restaurants, there are basic restaurants on Station Rd. *Indus Bakery*, Station Rd and *Larkana Bakery*, Royal Rd are good for bread, cakes and sweets.

● **Banks & money changers**
Foreign exchange is available at the bank on the Moenjo Daro site.

● **Hospitals**
Almas Medical Centre, Station Rd, T 60303; *Civil Hospital*, Civil Hospital Rd.

● **Post & telecommunications**
GPO and Pak-Telecom are nr Burghry Bazaar on Post Office Rd.

● **Tourist offices**
PTDC is at the Moenjo Daro site.

● **Transport**
Air PIA Booking Office, Station Rd, T 60338. The airport is located at the Moenjo Daro site. For flight details see **Moenjo Daro**.

Train See under **Moenjo Daro**.

Road Bus: *Blue Lines*, nr *Hotel Asia*, run 1 daily Deluxe services to **Karachi** (Rs 110). Buses to **Sukkur** depart from the Stadium Bus Station, N of the train station. Local buses for **Moenjo Daro** run from Bakrani bus stand, nr Attaturk Memorial. Take a Dokri bus which drops you at a junction 5 km from the site (tonga Rs 20).

The road to Shikarpur and Sukkur continues NE from Larkana and passes within 1 km of the Bhutto home village of **Naudero**. Zulfikar Ali Bhutto's tomb is in the family graveyard nearby at Gari Khudabaksh, which is particularly crowded during his Urs (4 Apr). Date palm plantations, orchards and rice fields are prominent in this area, in addition to substantial sugar cane production. The Highway by-passes **Shikarpur**, formerly administered as part of Sibi Province by the Afghan Governor **Ahmed Shah Durrani**, but now greatly reduced from its one-time strategic importance on one of Asia's major trading routes. Between Shikarpur and Sukkur, some of the worst effects of salinization are visible.

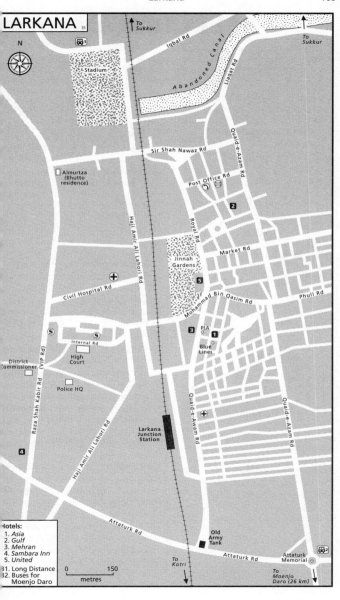

LARKANA

N

To Sukkur
To Sukkur

Stadium

Iqbal Rd

Abandoned Canal

Liaqat Rd

Sir Shah Nawaz Rd

Almurtza
(Bhutto
residence)

Quaid-e-Azam Rd

Post Office Rd

Royal Rd

Haji Amir Ali Lahori Rd

Jinnah
Gardens

Market Rd

Civil Hospital Rd

Mohammad Bin Qasim Rd

Phull Rd

PIA

Blue
Lines

Internal Rd

Raza Shah Kabir Rd (VIP Rd)

District
Commissioner

High
Court

Police HQ

Quaid-e-Awam Rd

Quaid-e-Azam Rd

Larkana
Junction
Station

Haji Amir Ali Lahori Rd

Attaturk Rd

Old
Army
Tank

Attaturk Rd

Attaturk
Memorial

To
Kotri

To
Moenjo
Daro (26 km)

Hotels:
1. *Asia*
2. *Gulf*
3. *Mehran*
4. *Sambara Inn*
5. *United*

31. Long Distance
32. Buses for
    Moenjo Daro

0   150
metres

BALUCHISTAN

CONTENTS

Introduction	166
Quetta	177
Quetta to Loralai via Ziarat	185
Quetta to Dera Ghazi Khan	188
Quetta to Dera Ismail Khan via Zhob	191
Quetta to Sukkur via the Bolan Pass	193
Quetta to Chaman	198
Quetta to Iran	199
Quetta to Karachi	202
The Makran	206

MAPS

Baluchistan	167
Quetta	178
Centre	181
Around Quetta	186
Sibi	196
Khuzdar	204
Makran Coast	207

INTRODUCTION

Baluchistan is in many ways Pakistan's forgotten province. An old saying, variously ascribed to the Pathans or Persians, describes this huge tract of land as "the dump where Allah shot the rubbish of creation". While the saying is a reference to the often barren and inhospitable landscape, strewn with the forbidding mountainous rubble of geological processes, it also neatly encapsulates many people's attitude towards Baluchistan. Despite, or perhaps because of, its strategic significance, it remains amongst the least developed provinces of Pakistan, and the least accessible. Roads, often little more than dirt tracks, are relatively few in number, and there is just one rail link with the rest of the country, while distances are enormous. Yet Baluchistan is also a land of stunning beauty and bewildering contrasts. The hospitality and warm, open friendliness of its people meanwhile make the physical difficulties of exploring this fascinating region all the more rewarding and worthwhile.

Best time to visit: Baluchistan is at its best in spring (Mar-May) when the valleys are carpeted in wild flowers, and autumn (Sep/Oct) when the orchards are heavy with ripe fruit. During both these seasons the days are clear and cool, with chilly nights. Although much of Baluchistan is plateau, and therefore noticeably cooler than the plains during the summer months, it can still get uncomfortably hot. Winters are cold, with snowfall in many places.

> "The mountains are the Baluchi's forts; the peaks are better than any army; the lofty heights are our companions, the pathless gorges our friends. Our drink is from the flowing springs; our bed the thorny bush; the ground we make our pillow."

Land and life

Geography

Baluchistan is Pakistan's largest province. Similar in size to Finland, it covers 347,056 sq km, over 43% of the country's area. It is also the least densely populated with just 5% of the total population. It is bounded on the W by over 800 km of border with Iran and to the N by over 1,150 km of border with Afghanistan. To the N and E it touches the provinces of NWFP, Punjab and Sind.

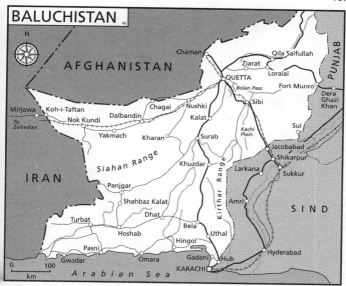

while to the S is over 750 km of coastline along the Arabian Sea. Much of Baluchistan consists of high rugged plateaux and mountains, an extension of the Iranian Plateau to the W.

Mountains

The **Suleiman Range**, with the peak of Takht-e-Suleiman in the N reaching 3,375m, trends N-S marking the eastern border of Baluchistan before swinging E-W towards Quetta. The **Tobar Kakar Range** meanwhile runs NE-SW in a wide arc along the border with Afghanistan. Further W are the **Chagai Hills**, formed of volcanic activity estimated to have occurred just 30,000 years ago, and S of these the peaks of **Ras Koh**, reaching over 3,000m. South of Quetta the **Central Brahui Range** follows on from the Suleimans, running N-S down towards Khuzdar. Further S they continue as the **Kirthar Range**, marking the boundary with Sind, and to the E, the **Pab Range**. In the extreme S are the hills of the **Makran Coast Range**, and

extending N in a series of roughly parallel ranges, the **Central Makran** and **Siahan** Ranges. For the most part, the mountains of Baluchistan consist of bare rocky limestone or conglomerate.

Rivers and lakes

The majority of Baluchistan's rivers are seasonal, being reduced to small streams or dry stony beds for most of the year, but transforming into raging torrents after the short bursts of heavy rain characteristic of the region. In many cases the rivers cut across the main strike of the mountains in deep narrow gorges and drain not into the Arabian Sea, but instead find their way into shallow depressions or *Hamuns*, which are dry expanses of salt flats for most of the year, occasionally forming into shallow lakes. Of these, the major ones are the **Hamun-i-Lora** between the Chagai Hills and Ras Koh, fed by the **Lora River**, the **Hamun-i-Mashkel** S of Nok Kundi, close to the border with Iran, fed by the **Mashkel River** and the **Kap**, to the E of

Panjgur, fed by the **Rakshan River**. The largest river is the **Hingol** in the S, which drains into the Arabian Sea and carries water all the year round. Other major rivers in the S include the **Dasht**, the **Hab** and the **Porali**, while in the N, the **Zhob River** flows into the Gomal before eventually draining into the Indus. In the E the wide Kachhi plains S of Sibi are drained by a series of rivers including the **Mula**, **Bhadra**, **Bolan**, **Nari** and **Teratani**.

Deserts

The largest expanse of desert is in the W, extending across the border into Iran and also N into Afghanistan. Known as the **Sandy Desert**, it is broken only by the Chagai Hills and Ras Koh. In the S, much of the Makran coastal belt is a desert of rolling sand dunes, known as *Lut* or *Dasht-i-Lut*. In the E, the Kachhi plain runs into barren desert to the S, until around Dera Murad Jamali, where it is transformed into fertile agricultural land by irrigation.

Climate

Baluchistan is extremely arid, with an average annual rainfall of just 174 mm. Even its wettest hill areas receive less than 300 mm, while in the deserts to the W, this falls to under 40 mm. Rain, when it does come, arrives in sudden bursts, transforming the otherwise dry river beds into raging torrents. Irrigation is therefore vital to the region, and the *karez* system has been in existence since well before the start of authentic recorded history. Temperatures meanwhile vary enormously according to season and altitude. Sibi, down on the Kachhi plains, has temperatures reaching as high as 52°C in summer and dropping to as low as -2°C in winter, while in Ziarat, just 90 km to the N, it may be a pleasant 27°C in summer and as cold as -19°C in winter.

Flora and fauna

Despite the image of Baluchistan as a barren wasteland, the province contains the largest reserves of **Juniper forests** in South Asia, and the second largest in the world, with two large tracts around Ziarat and Loralai covering approximately 85,000 ha. Other smaller tracts are found around Kalat to the S and in the Suleiman Range to the N. The species found in Baluchistan is *Juniperus excelsa*, known as *Apurs* in Brahui and *Obusht* in Pashto. It is extremely slow-growing, increasing by just 1m in 60 years. The largest trees are estimated to be in the order of 2,000 years old. Due to its slow rate of growth, the Juniper is under severe threat in Baluchistan (as elsewhere in South Asia) where it is cut for firewood and building materials. It is protected under law, although restrictions on the felling of this tree are difficult to implement and the existing tracts continue to decrease in size. As well as their inherent value in providing protection against soil erosion, these forests also harbour a wide range of associated flora and fauna, including many important medicinal plants. Other important trees found in Baluchistan include **pistachio**, **wild olive**, **tamarisk**, **pine** and *Pesh Mazri*, a kind of small palm.

Baluchistan is also home to the **Chiltan Markhor**, a distinct sub-species of wild goat that is now endemic to the province and found only in the Hazerganji Chiltan National Park, just outside of Quetta. The **Baluchistan Black Bear**, related to the Himalayan Brown Bear, is also unique to Baluchistan. Wolves and jackals are found in the hills, as well as foxes, wild ass, wild boar and occasionally leopards. Important birds include the **Chakor**, a distinctive game bird, and several migratory species, including the **Houbara Bustard**, sandgrouse, cranes and various duck which pass through Baluchistan on their way from Central Asia to warmer winter habitats in India and Pakistan. All of these have come under threat from excessive hunting, which despite legislation to control it, remains widespread amongst the elites of Pakistan. The Houbara Bustard in particular is threatened by visitors from the Gulf States, who hunt the bird with falcons.

History

Pre-history

Evidence suggests that Baluchistan's climate was once much wetter, accounting for the high concentrations of prehistoric settlements throughout Baluchistan. **Merhgarh**, the most famous of these, dating back as far as 8500 BC, provides the earliest evidence of settled agriculture in South Asia. Such settlements are thought to have formed the foundations of the Indus Valley Civilization which later flourished in what is now Pakistan.

Ancient history

Despite its prehistoric significance, Baluchistan subsequently remained on the margins of major cultural and political regions. Suzerainty over the various tribal mini-kingdoms of Baluchistan alternated between E and W. The province appears to have been connected with Persia as far back as 5th-6th century BC, when **Darius I** extended his influence over the region, followed by **Cyrus the Great**. After his expedition into South Asia and conquest of Punjab, **Alexander the Great** marched through Baluchistan in 325 BC. His march provides a landmark in the otherwise extremely hazy ancient history of Baluchistan, although he exerted only a minimal influence on the region. He was followed by **Seleucus Nicator** who was defeated by **Chandragupta Maurya**. Under his son **Asoka**, the Mauryan Empire grew to include most of South Asia and around this time Buddhism flourished also in

Baluchistan. Later, the **Graeco-Bactrians**, ancestors of Alexander, exerted some control in the region, before being overthrown by the central Asian hordes of the **Sakas** (Scythians). The **Sassanian Empire** which followed eventually conquered the region around the time of **Nausherwan** (529-577 AD). In 635 AD **Rai Chach** marched from Sind and conquered Makran.

The Coming of Islam

The emergence of Islam and spread of Arab power under the **Caliph Umer** during the 7th century brought major change to Baluchistan. The Arabs carried out a series of expeditions into Makran, and by 664 they had taken Khuzdar and the surrounding country of Jhalawan. Much of Baluchistan was converted to Islam and the Arabs appear to have remained in control until the 10th century, when raids by the **Ghaznavids** under **Sebuktagin** and his son **Mahmud of Ghazni** led eventually to the conquest of Baluchistan, and most of present-day Pakistan. In 1219 Baluchistan was made part of the **Saljuk Empire** for a short period, before the **Mongols** repeatedly attacked it. This period of Persian and Mongol attacks weakened Baluchistan, destroying the stability and prosperity that had developed under the Sassanians and Arabs.

By the 15th century, the various Baluch tribes became united for the first time under a confederacy led by **Mir Chakar Rind**. That unity was however short-lived, and much of his rule was taken up with feuding between his own tribe, the **Rinds** and another Baluch tribe, the **Lasharis**. These battles continued for 30 years between 1490 and 1520 and are the subject of many ballards and legends. Nevertheless, Mir Chakar is regarded as one of the great Baluch leaders and this period is often referred to as the 'Classical Age' of Baluch history, when many of the great traditions of tribal honour and chivalry

ALEXANDER'S MARCH THROUGH THE MAKRAN

In 326 BC, the Greek Macedonian King, Alexander the Great, led his army into the subcontinent through the high mountains of the Hindu Kush, advancing E as far as the river Beas before retreating and turning S to pass through Sind on his way to the Arabian Sea. He then elected to march with his army back to Greece across the wastes of Makran. Sending one of his generals Crateros by a more northerly route via the Mula Pass, Quetta and Helmand, while Nearchus sailed the fleet along the coast, Alexander set off with the remainder of his army, hoping by taking this route to be able to keep his fleet supplied with provisions. Some also suggest that Alexander, by no means ignorant of the difficulty of the route, was inspired by the challenge of successfully leading his army across a country which had reduced the armies of Semiramis and after her Cyrus to a mere handful of people. His ambition was nearly his undoing, The Makran, as for those before him, proved to be a merciless adversary. Alexander's march is described in detail by the historian Arrian:

"The blazing heat and want of water destroyed a great part of the army, and especially the beasts of burden, which perished from the great depth of the sand, and the heat which scorched like fire, while a great many died of thirst. The great distances also between the stages were most distressing to the army... When they traversed by night all the stage they had to complete and came to water in the morning, their distress was all but entirely relieved. But, if, as the day advanced, they were caught still marching owing to the great length of the stage, then suffer they did, tortured alike by raging heat and thirst unquenchable... Thus some were left behind on the road from sickness, others from intolerable thirst... some of the men were overcome by sleep on the way, but on awaking afterwards, those who still had some strength left, followed close on the track of the army and a few out of many saved their lives by overtaking it. The majority perished in the sand like shipwrecked men at sea."

"Many of them besides came by their death through drinking, for, if, when jaded by the broiling heat and thirst, they fell in with abundance of water, they quaffed it with insatiable avidity till they killed themselves... When their provisions ran short, they came together and killed most of the horses and mules. They ate the flesh of these animals, which they professed had died of thirst and perished from the heat... When the army on one occasion lay encamped for the night near a small winter torrent for the sake of its water, the torrent became swollen by rains and came rushing down in so great a deluge that it destroyed most of the women and children of the camp followers, and swept away all the royal baggage and whatever beasts of burden were still left. The soldiers themselves, after a hard struggle, barely escaped with their lives, and a portion only of their weapons."

The portion of the army sailing with the fleet likewise suffered heavily with many dying through disease, malnutrition and lack of water. Crateros meanwhile encountered no major obstacles on his return march. Alexander eventually arrived home to Babylon with a much reduced army. He died shortly after, in 323 BC.

were established. After finally driving the Lasharis out of Baluchistan, Mir Chakar was in turn driven out by the **Arghuns**, and many of the Baluch tribes came to settle in Punjab. Today, many of these tribes, such as the Leghari, Mazari, Khakwani, Gurmani and Dreshik, are still to be found around Multan, Bahawalpur and Dera Ghazi Khan, where they are important landowners.

Kalat State

Meanwhile, the **Brahui** tribes grew in strength. Keen to wrest control of Kalat from the **Sewa** Dynasty of Hindus, they aligned with the Mughals and succeeded in driving them out. Then, during the 15th century the Brahui tribe of **Mirwaris**, with the help of the Dehwars, succeeded in ousting the Mughals and establishing their Khanate. It remained the capital of their successors, the **Ahmadzai Khans** until Independence. Despite its great importance Kalat was never fully independent, being subject to some extent either to Delhi or Kandahar. It reached the height of its power during the 18th century.

Nasir Khan I ruled as the Khan of Kalat for 44 years from 1750 to 1794. He is viewed as one of the great historical rulers by the Brahui, and referred to as Nasir the Great. He gave considerable assistance to **Ahmad Shah Durrani** in his numerous expeditions to Persia, and extended his rule to include Kharan and Makran. In 1758, after Nasir Khan had refused to keep up the heavy tribute and military assistance demanded by Ahmad Shah, the latter attacked Kalat, but was repulsed. Eventually, relations were re-established, with Nasir Khan recognizing Ahmad Shah's suzerainty and agreeing to supply troops, in return for which he received regular payments and munitions, as well as being exempted from the tribute previously paid. The districts of Quetta and Mastung were also ceded to him.

The British period

Following the death of Nasir Khan, there was a long period of instability, during which the extent of Kalat's influence was much reduced. There was widespread disaffection amongst many of the tribal chiefs and on-going intrigues amongst the Khan's ministers. It was against this background that the British became involved in Kalat, becoming deeply, though unwittingly, embroiled in its internal political machinations.

In 1838 the British, having decided to advance into Afghanistan in support of **Shah Shuja**, sent Lieutenant Leech to secure the cooperation of the then Khan of Kalat, **Mir Mehrab Khan**. This he was willing to offer, but unfortunately one of his ministers, **Mulla Mohammad Hasan**, who bore a grudge against him for the death of his father, conspired to create an atmosphere of distrust, alleging that the Khan had siezed and destroyed crops along the route that the British army would take. Later, he went as the Khan's envoy to meet the British army who had arrived in Sind under Sir W Macnaghten, but instead of conveying the Khan's message of goodwill, suggested that he was conspiring against the British. Similarly he relayed to the Khan that the British were intent on attacking Kalat. He also sent letters bearing the Khan's seal to various tribal chiefs, instructing them to attack and harass the British army on its march through Baluchistan. A number of these letters fell into the hands of the Political Agent of Sind, Mr Ross Bell, and as a result Sir Alexander Burnes was sent to Kalat to try to reach a settlement which would put an end to the Khan's supposed hostility. A treaty was negotiated and it was agreed that the Khan should go to Quetta to pay his respects to Shah Shuja. Mulla Mohammad Hasan however managed to convince the Khan that the British were planning to imprison him in Quetta, while at the same time arranging for Burnes to be waylaid and robbed on his way to Quetta. This was easily presented to the British as the treacherous work of the Khan. Subsequently, on the return of Sir Thomas Willshire's brigade from Kabul in 1839, a force was sent to attack Kalat. The Khan and several principal chiefs were killed in the assault, and the treachery of Mulla Mohammad Hasan only exposed afterwards, from various documents discovered at the fort.

In the following decades the British clashed repeatedly with the various Baluch and Brahui tribes and imposed a series of treaties on the Khans of Kalat in which the latter acknowledged allegiance and submission to the British Government. In 1877 the British occupied Quetta permanently, and in 1879 signed the **Treaty of Gandamak**, in which they gained formal control over much of northern and eastern Baluchistan. Sir Robert Sandeman, who became agent to the Governor General of Baluchistan in 1877, did much to consolidate British control over the region, gaining the respect of tribal chiefs through his understanding and sensitivity to the existing power structures, which he successfully manipulated to Britain's advantage. By 1887, the British had gained effective control of much of Baluchistan, developing communications networks, initiating irrigation schemes and ensuring effective systems for the collection of land revenue. As in NWFP however, their control remained indirect, relying on the tribal chiefs to administer the region at the local level.

The struggle against accession to Pakistan

The incorporation of Baluchistan into the newly formed state of Pakistan was far from smooth. While the sardars of 'British' Baluchistan voted to join Pakistan, the Khan of Kalat made clear his intention to claim independence. He argued that Kalat, like Nepal, had a legal status different from that of the other Princely States, having always maintained its treaty relations directly with the British Government in Whitehall, as opposed to the British Indian government in Delhi. On 15 August 1947, a day after the creation of Pakistan, the Khan of Kalat formally declared independence. This was strongly opposed by Pakistan, and it was only under intense pressure that the Khan finally declared the accession of Kalat to Pakistan on 30 March 1948. Later, when the 'One Unit' plan was proposed, in which all the provinces of West Pakistan were to be united into a single entity, the Khan revived his 1947 claim for independence, and along with other Baluch leaders began to organize widespread demonstrations against the One Unit plan. The Pakistan Army was sent into Baluchistan and the Khan arrested in 1958. Immediately afterwards, martial law was declared throughout Pakistan, setting the stage for the establishment of Ayub Khan's military regime.

Culture

People

There are three main tribal groups in Baluchistan; the **Baluch**, **Brahui** and **Pathans**. The term Baluch, literally meaning 'wanderer' or 'nomad', is used very loosely to describe the various tribes inhabiting Baluchistan. In some contexts it is indicative of a class rather than an ethnic group, as in Makran where the Baluch were traditionally a landowning middle class.

The origins of the Baluch are unclear. Their own popular belief, based on their ballads and legends, traces their ancestry back to two tribes, the Baloch and Kurds, who inhabited the Aleppo valley in Syria before migrating slowly eastwards through Persia and finally settling in what became known as Baluchistan. The Kurds arrived first, settling around Kalat, where they still dominate. They were known as the *Brahimi*, after Mir Ibrahim who led them through Persia, which evolved into the *Brahui* of today. The Baluch, who had stayed longer in Aleppo, were finally driven out by the Omyyads and spread out along the sea coast, arriving in Baluchistan later.

Others suggest that the Baluch were Aryans who migrated from northern Iran in the 11th century, or that they are of Arab extraction and arrived shortly before the Arab invasions of the 7th century. The Brahui, meanwhile are considered by some to be of Dravidian origin (see page 77).

The Pathans are now the largest tribal group in Baluchistan, their numbers having been swelled by the arrival of Afghan refugees (also Pathan) in huge numbers. The Pathans are found mostly in the NE of Baluchistan, their traditional home being around Takht-i-Suleiman, although sizeable minorities exist elsewhere in the province, particularly in the E, around Sibi.

The Tribal System There are in effect two tribal systems in Baluchistan. Amongst Pathans it is based on a close kinship amongst groups descended from a common ancestor. The Baluch and Brahui tribes on the other hand represent a confederacy which is more a political entity, with groups of separate origin clustering round a head group or *Sardar Khel*. In Makran, the various groups live independently of each other, with no tribal system uniting them.

Bride Price Amongst many of the Pathan and Baluch tribes of Baluchistan and NWFP, and also in some parts of Sind, the system of bride price is practiced. In contrast to the dowry system practiced in the Punjab, payment is made by the bridegroom and his family to the bride's parents. The money is then used towards the wedding expenses and to

equip the bride appropriately when she moves to her husband's household. Amongst more affluent families, land and other fixed property is often given. Critics of the system point out that the bride price often either comes straight back to the bridegroom's family on their marriage, or is kept by the bride's family and used for other purposes. In a system of arranged marriages, a bride may be 'sold off' to the highest bidder, with no consideration of her interests.

Language

Baluchi, the language of the Baluch, belongs to the Iranian branch of the Aryan sub-family of Indo-European languages. The Farsi (Persian) influence, strongest in the western or **Makrani** dialect, is cited in support of the theory of the Baluch's Iranian origin. Baluchi has also freely absorbed many words from modern Arabic. **Pashto**, the language of the Pathans, is of the same Iranian branch of Indo-European as Baluchi. It differs slightly in Baluchistan from the dialect spoken in NWFP, being softer. The **Brahui** language is intriguing, being apparently of Dravidian origin, with many similarities to S Indian languages such as Telegu. Many Baluchi, Sindhi and Persian words have also been absorbed into it. Other minority languages in Baluchistan include **Lassi** spoken around Bela, **Seraiki**, and **Sindhi**.

Literature

The Baluch and Brahui tribes have a long oral tradition of poetry, folk songs and ballads. These formed the only means by which tribal histories could be handed down from generation to generation. The *Daptar Shah* is a Chronicle of Genealogies in verse form, and much of the early history of Baluchistan is pieced together from such oral traditions. Many ballads date from the Rind era (1400-1600) and relate in colourful detail the epic battles fought between the different tribes, the origins of their feuding and the heroic deeds of their warriors. When not dealing with war, the ballads tell of tragic and passionate romances. During the Ahmadzai period (1600-1850), the poetic literature becomes more complex and introspective, reflecting perhaps the greater stability and safety of the times. It was only towards the end of this period that some of these ballads and poetry began to be committed to writing, partly through the work of various European scholars. Today the literary tradition in Baluchistan remains strong, and there is many a young poet willing to perform his verses in front of appreciative audiences.

Modern Baluchistan

Government and politics

The system of local government in Baluchistan is essentially based on the system which existed under the British. There are six Divisions: Quetta, Zhob, Nasirabad, Sibi, Kalat and Makran, each under a Commissioner, and these are further divided into Districts, of which there are now a total of 26, many of them recently created. Districts are divided into 'A' and 'B' areas, the former being under the direct administration of the Provincial Government, while the latter are tribal areas, governed through the local Sardar and policed by *levies* (locally appointed 'police', drawn from a chief's own tribe).

In the early years following Independence, most of the political parties were united in their opposition to Pakistani control of Baluchistan. Thus the first two parties to emerge, the Astaman Gal (Baluch/Brahui) and the Wror Pushtoon (Pathan) soon united into the National Awam Party (NAP) in opposition to the One Unit plan. The Baluch Students' Organization (BSO) meanwhile, enjoyed popular support from both Pathans and Baluch. In 1970, Baluchistan was raised to Provincial status and elections held, with the NAP gaining the most seats in the Baluchistan Assembly. There followed nearly two decades of effective Martial Law. Elections were again held in 1988, and then in 1990 and 1993. The salient feature of all of these has been the inability of any one party to gain a clear majority, reflecting the fact that politics in Baluchistan has been fundamentally and inevitably shaped by the tribal structure of society. In particular, the major division between Pathans and Baluch/Brahui have been reflected in the affiliations of political groups, which have tended to divide along ethnic lines.

Economy

Agriculture

Baluchistan's arid climate makes agriculture dependent on irrigation. The **karez** system of underground channels to draw water is today supplemented by canals, dams and weirs. Nevertheless, agriculture remains limited with just 10% of suitable land being at present cultivated. **Fruits** are an important crop in Baluchistan, with extensive orchards of grapes, apples, pomegranates, pears, cherries and apricots, as well as almonds, pistachio and walnuts, particularly around Quetta, Pishin and the Zhob valley, while on the plains, limes, mangoes, quinces and guava are grown.

The main spring or *Rabi* crops are wheat, *jowar* and gram and the autumn or *Kharif* crops barley, rice, *bajra*, *makai*, melons, cotton and sugar-cane. **Dates** are an important crop, particularly in Makran, where over 300 varieties are grown, and their significance is reflected in the fact that the Baluchi language has over a hundred words for 'dates', just as it has for 'camels'. In Makran, rice is often planted in the shade of date trees.

The Arabian sea is rich in **fish**, and Pakistan now earns over Rs 300 million from the marine fishing industry each year, much of it along Baluchistan's coastline.

THE BENEVOLENT SEASON

Dates represent the most important crop of the Makran. According to local tradition, the date was introduced into the area at the time of the first Arab invasions in the 7th century AD. However, both Arrian and Strabo mention the presence of date palms in the region when Alexander marched through in 326 BC, suggesting that without them the remnants of his army would surely have perished.

Amen, the date harvesting season, runs from Jul to Sep and is a pivotal point in the agricultural calender when people flock to the main date growing areas of Kech and Panjgur to gather up the rich harvest. The importance of the season is well illustrated by a local story related in the District Gazeteer of Makran.

"A Makrani went to India and heard much of the generosity of a certain king. He enquired whether the king was in the habit of giving food to his subjects, and on receiving a reply in the negative, he laughed and scoffed at such a ruler, saying that in his country there was a chief who visited all parts during 4 months of every year. During his stay he always gave sweet fresh food, not only to all the people of the country, the dwellers in the jungle, the cultivators, the rich and the poor, but also to the camels, the cows, the donkeys, the sheep and the dogs, and his benevolence was so far-reaching that not only during his stay in the country, but on taking his departure, he bestowed on each man sufficient to provide him throughout the remainder of the year. In surprise his listeners asked what chief this could be, and the answer was: 'Our chief is *Amen*.'"

Industry and resources

Baluchistan has little in the way of large-scale industry, the only exception to this being at Hub, where the building of the country's largest oil-fired power station has attracted industrial development from nearby Karachi, particularly cotton processing and textiles. Most industry is at the craft level, with items such as reed screens, matting and traditional Baluch handicrafts.

Baluchistan does however have extensive mineral reserves. The large deposits of copper and lead at Saindak, near the Iranian border, estimated to exceed 350 million tonnes, as well as some gold and molybdenum, are now being exploited with Chinese assistance. Chromite is mined extensively around Muslimbagh, where there are deposits estimated at around 3 million tonnes. Other important mineral deposits include iron, found over a wide area around Dalbandin and Chagai, silica, gypsum, magnesium, marble, limestone, graphite and fluorite.

There are also thought to be extensive oil fields along Baluchistan's western border with Iran, although these have yet to be exploited; one problem is that these deposits are thought to be at a lower level and linked to Iran's main oil fields, and tapping into them would not be good for relations!

TRAVEL IN BALUCHISTAN

In the past, one of the main problems for visitors to Baluchistan has been the tight restrictions placed on travel in the province by the Federal Government. This is due to the perceived threat of kidnapping and banditry in the region. There have indeed been a number of isolated, but highly publicized, incidents involving foreigners over the years. However, most officials, particularly those who actually live and work in Baluchistan, admit that the danger has been vastly exaggerated. The Baluch, Brahui and Pathan tribes of Baluchistan are in fact amongst the most warm-hearted, sociable and hospitable people one could hope to meet, and this is overwhelmingly reflected in most peoples' experience of travelling in the region.

In 1994 the Baluchistan Provincial Government placed a proposal before the Federal Government suggesting that it should be given the discretion to open up different areas of Baluchistan to tourism as it saw fit. Previously, when a foreigner applied for permission to travel in a restricted area, the Provincial Government had first to gain clearance from the Federal Government before granting that permission. The new proposal, which was accepted in early 1995, means that this extra layer of bureaucracy has been removed. While no changes have as yet been made to restrictions on travel, the plan is that all areas should be declared open with the exception of sensitive/unstable areas bordering Afghanistan (particularly around Chaman) and a couple of tribal areas (Marri and Bugti areas – the tract of land between the main highways to Sukkur and Dera Ghazi Khan, and also the area around Zhob) still considered unsafe.

At the time of going to press, the situation regarding travel in Baluchistan for foreigners was as follows:

Open
Quetta to Sukkur via the Bolan Pass

Quetta to Karachi via Khuzdar and Kalat on the RCD Highway

Quetta to Taftan, on the Iranian Border

Quetta to Dera Ghazi Khan via Ziarat or via Quila Saifullah

NB Foreigners are allowed to travel freely along these routes, but not to divert off the main highway.

Restricted
Quetta to Chaman, on the Afghanistan border

The Makran Coast

Quetta to Dera Ismail Khan via Zhob (Fort Sandeman)

Applying for permits
Applications to travel through restricted areas can be made directly to the Home Department of the Provincial Government in Quetta (see under Useful addresses in the Quetta section). You will need to provide a precise itinerary, with dates, and a photocopy of the relevant pages of your passport, including the visa page. They will (hopefully) issue you with a permit, known as a 'No Objection Certificate'. In the case of the route from Quetta to Dera Ismail Khan, you also need permission from the NWFP Home Department, as the route passes through tribal areas in southern NWFP before arriving in DI Khan. **NB** Obtaining permits for restricted areas is significantly easier if you are travelling as part of a package tour. Jeep 'safaris' along the Makran coast for example are perfectly possible if organized through a recognized tour operator.

QUETTA

Quetta, the provincial capital of Baluchistan, with its healthy climate and carefully planned layout, was regarded at the turn of the century as one of the most desirable stations in the N of British India, and was popularly known as 'Little London'. While the wide, tree-lined main boulevards and spacious cantonment still gives a sense of its former atmosphere, today Quetta has been overtaken by heavy traffic and pollution and the image of a city 'refreshed by jasmine scented breezes' is one that is sadly long gone. Nevertheless, at an altitude of 1,676m above sea level, its climate is refreshingly cooler than on the plains. Surrounded by high mountains of bare rock – the steep slopes of Murdar rising immediately to the E, Takatu and Zarghun further off to the N, and Chiltan to the E – its setting is a dramatic one.

Quetta was traditionally one of the major stopping places on the overland route through Afghanistan. With the Soviet invasion in 1979 and the on-going civil war, overland traffic has been much reduced, although there are still a surprising number of independent travellers and groups arriving here via Iran.

The town was almost completely destroyed in the devastating earthquake of 1935. Only the cantonment area to the N of the Habib Nullah survived, while nearly all of the city and bazaar areas to the S date from after this time, its buildings, not more than 1 or 2-storeys high, a legacy to the fear of future earthquakes.

Nearly half the population of Baluchistan live within an 80 km radius around Quetta, with the town itself having a fairly even mix of Pathans, Baluch and Brahui.

History

Known originally as *Shal* or *Shalkot*, Quetta is thought to have existed as a permanent settlement since prehistoric times. The old fort in the N of the city (the name Quetta is derived from 'kwatta', meaning 'fort' in Pashto) is situated on a low mound formed of the debris of continuous occupation, perhaps for 11,000 years. In 1883, the British started excavations to build an arsenal in the fort and unearthed various items, including a prehistoric ringstone and corn crusher made of jasper, and a Greek bronze statue of Heracles, suggesting links with the Graeco-Bactrian Empire. It is also likely that Alexander's general Crateros marched via Quetta on his return to Persia earlier in 326 BC. Just a quarter of the total depth of the mound was excavated and today the fort remains in use by the military. In 1985, during excavation work for the building of the Serena Hotel just 500m away, more items were discovered, including two gold bullocks, alabaster and terracota vases and two semi-precious stones set in gold.

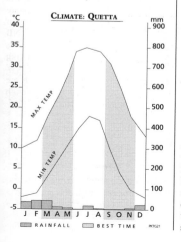
CLIMATE: QUETTA
RAINFALL   BEST TIME

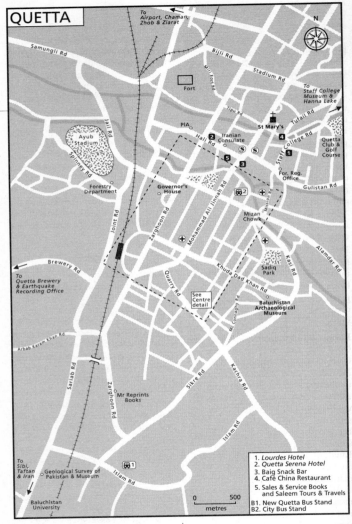

QUETTA

To Airport, Chaman, Zhob & Ziarat

Samungli Rd

Bijli Rd

Stadium Rd

N

Fort

Mirjaan Rd

Tipu Rd

To Staff College Museum & Hanna Lake

Jail Rd

Ayub Stadium

Spinney Rd

PIA

St Mary's

Iranian Consulate

Hali Rd

Staff College Rd

Tufail Rd

Quetta Club & Golf Course

2

5

3

1

4

Forestry Department

Governor's House

Zarghoon Rd

Mohammad Ali Jinnah Rd

For. Reg. Office

Gulistan Rd

B2

Mizan Chowk

Mission Rd

Brewery Rd

To Quetta Brewery & Earthquake Recording Office

Joint Rd

Quarry Rd

Khuda Dad Khan Rd

Sadiq Park

Kasi Rd

Atamdar Rd

See Centre detail

Zarghoon Rd

Qandhari Rd

Baluchistan Archaeological Museum

Arbab Karam Khan Rd

Sariab Rd

Sikre Rd

Kachra Rd

Islam Rd

Mr Reprints Books

To Sibi, Taftan & Iran

Geological Survey of Pakistan & Museum

B1

Islam Rd

Baluchistan University

1. Lourdes Hotel
2. Quetta Serena Hotel
3. Baig Snack Bar
4. Café China Restaurant
5. Sales & Service Books and Saleem Tours & Travels
B1. New Quetta Bus Stand
B2. City Bus Stand

0   500
metres

Until the rise of Brahui power in the 18th century, Quetta's fortunes were closely linked to those of Afghanistan and Persia. It formed part of the kingdoms of Amir Sabuktagin and Mahmud of Ghazni during the 11th century, before passing into the hands of their successors, the Ghorids. Later, Kandahar and with it Quetta was ruled by the Mongols under Ghengis Khan. The

Mughal emperor Hamayun stopped in Quetta on his retreat from India in 1543 and his son Akbar controlled it until 1556, when it was lost to the Persians before being retaken 40 years later.

The British first occupied Quetta between 1839-1842, at the time of the First Afghan War when it formed part of Kalat state, but then abandoned it until 1877 when it was permanently occupied under a treaty between the British and the Khan of Kalat. Despite its strategic importance between the Bolan and Khojak passes, it was not until after this time that Quetta grew into a regional centre of any significance, at the hub of rail and road links with the rest of the empire and its frontiers.

Places of interest

With most of the city dating from after 1935, Quetta has little in the way of historic attractions. The two museums, though very small, are worth a visit. The bazaars meanwhile are colourful and lively, and have some excellent handicrafts, both Baluchi and Afghani (see under Shopping).

Baluchistan Archaeological Museum

Open 0900-1300, 1400-1700, closed Fri. Originally established in 1906 as the McMahon Museum, it was devastated in the 1935 earthquake; many of the exhibits were also destroyed and the rest were transferred to Calcutta. The museum was re-established in 1972 and has been shifted several times. It is now situated in a small rented building off Khuda Dad Khan Rd, although there are plans to find a larger and more permanent home for the collection.

Most interesting are the intricately modelled figurines, beautifully decorated pottery pieces, ceramic tiles and terracotta seals from various sites around Baluchistan, dating back as far as 3500 BC, including some recent additions from Merhgarh and Naushero. Other stone and shell implements date from around 7000 BC. There is also an armoury, with various antique guns and swords, including one sword which was supposedly used to kill a British commander, and a collection of Persian and Arabic manuscripts and Korans, including one written by Aurangzeb.

Command and Staff College Museum

Situated on Staff College Rd in the Cantt area. Open 1500-1730 in winter and 1700-1930 in summer. It is best to arrange your visit with the curator beforehand, T 760 2445. You may be asked for some ID when you arrive. Built in 1905, this was the residence of Col (later Field Marshal) Montgomery, before being inaugurated as a museum in 1979 by President Zia. There is an interesting collection of military regalia, as well as oil paintings, photos, albums and Montgomery's original office furniture. The Command and Staff College still has a high reputation internationally and there are usually officers based here on exchange visits from around the world.

Earthquake Recording Office

Brewery Rd leads W out of town, past Quetta Brewery, and then climbs steeply up to the Earthquake Recording Office, situated on Chiltan Hill with commanding views over Quetta and the surrounding mountains.

Excursions

Hanna Lake and Urak Valley

A popular outing is to Hanna Lake, 10 km E of Quetta. Leave Quetta on Staff College Rd and continue straight on at the roundabout and turning for the museum, taking the next major turning right onto Urak Rd. There are several simple restaurants along the way serving tea, cold drinks and food. Just after a checkpost, fork left (right to Spin Karez) and soon after fork left again (right to Urak valley). The route is well signposted. During summer there are regular buses from City Bus Stand. A taxi is around Rs 400 return.

The lake is surrounded by bare mountains and has been developed into a picnic spot with two cafés, *Lake View* and *Oasis*, offering snacks and drinks. Small picnic huts of dubious aesthetic quality are dotted around the lake. There is a children's playground and boats for hire giving access to a tiny artificial island in the centre of the lake. During the summer it gets very busy, particularly on holidays.

The Urak Valley is particularly beautiful in spring and autumn, when its plentiful orchards are in blossom or laden with fruit. The village of Urak is at the top of the valley and close by is Urak Tangi, another popular picnic spot with a small restaurant, open from Apr to Sep.

Hazerganji Chiltan National Park

Hazerganji (literally 'of a thousand treasures') Chiltan was established as a National Park in 1978. It covers 32,500 acres of hills and valleys in the Chiltan range, including Chiltan Peak (3,264m). Its most important inhabitant is the Chiltan Markhor, a wild goat once fairly common in Baluchistan, before being hunted almost to extinction. Now found only in the park, it is registered as an endangered species and carefully protected. The park is also home to the Straight Horned Markhor, 'Gad' wild sheep, leopards, wolves, Striped Hyena, wild cats, hare, porcupine and the Afghan Tortoise, as well as cobras, pythons and vipers. Birds are also plentiful, the Chukor Partridge, whose distinctive call can be heard throughout the park, is the most common. Others include the Seesee Partridge, warblers, shrikes, Rock Nuthatches and Blue Rock Pidgeons, as well as Golden Eagles, Bearded Vultures, Sparrow Hawks and Peregrine Falcons. Over 200 species of plants have so far been identified. The main trees are Pistachio, Juniper, Olive, Fig, Ash and

Almond. In spring the ground is carpeted in flowering tulips and poppies.

There is a small **Natural History Museum** in the park with various pressed dried flowers and grasses and stuffed birds and mammals. Further on there is an observation post and nearby a small *Resthouse* (3 rm), both of which offer excellent views back down onto the plateau. You must obtain a permit to visit the park from the Forestry Department, Spinney Rd, Quetta. You can also arrange with them to stay in the *resthouse*, well worth it for the splendid views. Allow a full day at the least for a worthwhile visit. Rangers are on hand to show you round and point out the wildlife.

The park is situated 20 km SW of Quetta on the Mustang road. Follow Sariab Rd S past the University and after 8 km take the right fork (left to Sibi). 9 km from the fork, soon after a large sign for the zoological gardens (still under construction in 1995), a signposted gravel track leads off to the right up to the park. To get there by bus, take a Mustang-bound bus from the New Quetta Bus Stand and walk up from here. The track climbs gently for 3 km to the museum. From the road the lower slopes of the park are not readily distinguishable from surrounding areas. Viewed from higher up however the denser vegetation cover of the fenced off area is clearly visible. Further into the park, much of the area is thickly wooded.

Local information

HOTEL CLASSIFICATIONS			
AL	Rs4,000	**A**	Rs1,800-4,000
B	Rs900-1,800	**C**	Rs450-900
D	Rs300-450	**E**	Rs150-300
F	up to Rs150		

● **Accommodation**

AL *Serena*, Shahrah-e-Zarghoon, PO Box 109, T 820071, F 820070, the only international standard luxury hotel in Quetta, tastefully built and furnished to reflect traditional Baluchi architecture, right down to the smallest details

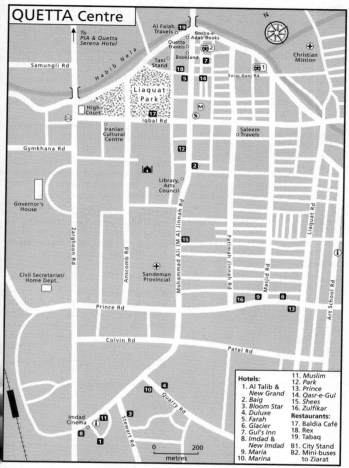

QUETTA Centre

To PIA & Quetta Serena Hotel

Samungli Rd

Habib Nala

Al Falah Travels
Gosha-e-Adab Books
Quetta Travels
Bookland
Taxi Stand
Suraj Ganj Rd
Christian Mission

Liaquat Park

High Court

Iqbal Rd

Iranian Cultural Centre

Gymkhana Rd

Saleem Travels

Library, Arts Council

Governor's House

Zarghoon Rd

Anscomb Rd

Mohammad Ali (M A) Jinnah Rd

Sandeman Provincial

Fatiman Jinnah Rd

Masjid Rd

Liaquat Rd

Art School Rd

Civil Secretariat/ Home Dept.

Prince Rd

Colvin Rd

Patel Rd

Imdad Cinema

Quarry Rd

Stewart Rd

0   200
metres

Hotels:
1. Al Talib & New Grand
2. Baig
3. Bloom Star
4. Duluxe
5. Farah
6. Glacier
7. Gul's Inn
8. Imdad & New Imdad
9. Maria
10. Marina
11. Muslim
12. Park
13. Prince
14. Qasr-e-Gul
15. Shees
16. Zulfikar

Restaurants:
17. Baldia Café
18. Rex
19. Tabaq

B1. City Stand
B2. Mini-buses to Ziarat

of the room decor, centrally located with pleasant gardens and orchards within the grounds, all business and recreational facilities incl conference/function rooms, swimming, tennis and squash, as well as access to the nearby *Quetta Golf Club*, *Loralai Restaurant* (á la carte) and *Ziarat Coffee Shop* (24-hr light meals and buffet), both rec, selection of shops in lobby and Bazaar Court, all usual guest services, as well as baby sitting, special ours to the Bolan Pass by train.

B *Lourdes*, Staff College Rd, PO Box 68, T 829656, F 61463, the oldest hotel in Quetta, with all mod cons and pleasant gardens, air-port service, parking and camping, restaurant, used by many of the overland companies, it can be a good place to find out the latest information on travel in Iran.

C *Gul's Inn*, Ali Bhoy Rd, T 821926, F 63145, a/c, TV/Dish/VCR, hot water, restaurant, also cheaper non a/c rooms; **C** *Qasr-e-Gul*, Suraj Ganj Bazaar, T 825192, a/c, TV/Dish, comfortable, centrally located, restaurant; **C** *Shees*, MA Jinnah Rd, T 822893, a/c, hot water, TV, phone, restaurant, also cheaper non a/c rooms.

D *Bloom Star*, Stewart Rd, T 833350, a/c and non a/c rooms, music, TV/Dish/VCR, parking and pleasant gardens, restaurant.

E *Al Talib*, Jinnah Rd, behind Imdad Cinema, att bath, hot water, fan, heater, pleasant old building with garden, set back from the main road, no phone; the newer, slightly more expensive *New Grand*, T 77781, is adjacent, but has no garden and less atmosphere; **E** *Deluxe*, Quarry Rd, T 831537, fan, att bath, hot water, clean rooms, parking at front, restaurant; **E** *Glacier*, Prince Rd, T 62830, att bath, hot water, fan, heater extra, *Grace Restaurant*; **E** *Imdad*, Jinnah Rd, T 70166, att bath, hot water, fan, a rather imposing but somewhat dilapidated old building; **E** *Marina*, Quarry Rd, T 65099, fan, att bath, hot water, TV/Dish on request, Sarbaan and Mehwash restaurants downstairs, independent of the hotel; **E** *Park*, MA Jinnah Rd, T 75723, att bath, hot water, fan, phone, small rooms, *Anarkali Restaurant* downstairs; **E** *Prince*, Prince Rd, T 825508, att bath, hot water, fan, carpet, clean rooms; **E** *Zulfiqar*, Prince Rd, T 822720, att bath, hot water, fan, quiet courtyard garden, *Al Abid Restaurant*.

F *Maria*, Masjid Rd, T 824364, att bath, hot water, fan, heater extra, restaurant; **F** *Muslim*, Jinnah Rd, T 71857, att bath, hot water, fan, rooms on the 1st floor are lighter and marginally cleaner, courtyard/garden and parking, popular with budget travellers and another good place for picking up current information on overland travel through Iran, PTDC info centre, restaurant; **F** *New Imdad*, Jinnah Rd, T 828065, att bath, hot water, fan, heater extra, restaurant.

● **Places to eat**

Quetta is famous for its lamb, whole legs, known as *Sajji*, are roasted on open fires. Other lamb specialities incl *Roast* and *Joint*. There are a number of simple local-style restaurants offering these preparations. At the top of the range there are the Serena's *Loralai* offering á la carte dinner from 1930 and *Ziarat Coffee Shop* offering breakfast, lunch and evening barbecue buffet. Both are excellent and the buffet is very good value. Many of the other hotels in Quetta also have restaurants.

Qasr-i-Gul's and *Farah's* are rec, the latter particularly for its Sajji; opp the latter is the *Rex*, T 61264; the *Baldia Café* serves Pakistani dishes from 1200-1500 (not Fri) and tea and cold drinks at other times, it has outdoor seating in a pleasant patio garden; the popular *Café China*, Staff College Rd, opp Lourdes Hotel, serves good Chinese food, it can get very busy and it may be worth booking in advance; *Tabaq*, Circular Rd, T 824569, has Pakistani and Chinese dishes.

There are several snack bars at the N end of MA Jinnah Rd and in the streets around Gul's Inn and Qasr-i-Gul Hotel.

● **Airline offices**

PIA Booking Office, 17 Hali Rd, T 820861, efficient service for both domestic and international bookings.

● **Banks & money changers**

Habib Bank, Habib Bank Complex, at the junction of Jinnah Rd and Shahrah-e-Gulistan exchanges cash and TCs quickly and efficiently; **ANZ Grindlays**, opp Habib Bank also has efficient service, but charges a flat rate of Rs 250 for cashing TCs.

● **Cultural centres**

Baluchistan Arts Council (*Idra Saqafat*), MA Jinnah Rd, T 824016, has regular cultural events incl music, theatre and poetry, and is a good source of information on other cultural events in Quetta. Attached to it is an *Art Gallery*, and the *Sandeman Library*; **Iranian Cultural Centre**, Iqbal Rd, opp GPO, T 61373.

● **Embassies & consulates**

Afghan Consulate, 36B Chaman Housing Society, T 834659, will only issue press visas for Afghanistan with authorization from the embassy in Islamabad; **Iranian Consulate**, Hali Rd, T 65210, does not readily issue visas for Iran, it is better to apply at the embassy in Islamabad, though even there it is a lengthy process.

There is no British Consulate, but there is a **British Representative** in Quetta; c/o Sir William Halcrow and Partners Ltd, Chaman Housing Society, T 3354.

● **Hospitals & medical services**

Hospitals: *Sandeman Provincial Hospital*, MA Jinnah Rd, T 62017; *Lady Dufferin Hospital*, McConnaghy Rd, T 65488; *Christian Hospital*, Mission Rd (also known as Mission Hospital), T 75220.

Chemists: there are a number of chemists along Jinnah Rd, most opp the hospital complex. Local newspapers carry details of which ones are open 24 hr.

● **Post & telecommunications**
Area code: 081.

Post Office and **Telegraph Office**: are in the same building on Zarghoon Rd, opp the junction with Iqbal Rd; entry to the Telegraph office (24-hr) is round the corner in Circular Rd, telephone enquiries, T 17.

● **Shopping**
MA Jinnah Rd is lined with shops and the main bazaar is here. Others are Kandahari Bazaar, Shahrah-e-Iqbal, Surajgunj Bazaar, Market Square and Liaqat Rd Market. The Baluchi carpets and embroidery work with mirrors, Afghan carpets, fur coats, onyx carvings, semi-precious stones are good buys. The *Carpet Centre* is on Shahrah-e-Alamda to the E of the town, *Mokham Brothers*, *Carpet House* and *Taj Carpet* are on MA Jinnah Rd. For handicrafts on the same road, try *Chiltan Government Handicrafts Centre*, *Craft Gallery* and *Pakistan Arts and Crafts Centre*. Others are *Pak Handicrafts*, and *Wata Handicraft*, Art School Rd.

Books: there are three good bookshops close to each other along MA Jinnah Rd, *Book Centre*, *New Quetta Bookstall*, and *Bookland*. *Gosha-e-Abab* is on Circular Rd, and its subsidiary *Sales and Service* is nearby, just off Jinnah Rd. *Mr Reprints*, Zarghoon Rd, has an extensive collection on Baluchistan's history and culture.

● **Sports**
The *Ayub Stadium*, off Jail Rd, has a variety of facilities. Check with the CTC for details of major events. The *Golf Club*, Club Rd, off Staff College Rd is part of the *Quetta Club*, which also has squash courts. Foreigners can make use of facilities as the guest of a member. The Serena offers squash, tennis and swimming in summer. There are facilities for boating on Hanna Lake.

● **Tour companies & travel agents**
For special interest tours there are as yet no agencies based in Quetta; see under Islamabad/'Pindi and Lahore. The following are able to book domestic and international flights; *Al-Falah Travels*, Circular Rd, T 63770; *Quetta Travels*, MA Jinnah Rd, T 65350, T 821861; *Saleem Tours and Travels*, head

office Fatima Jinnah Rd, branch office MA Jinnah Rd, T 820995.

● **Tourist offfices**
PTDC Information Centre, Muslim Hotel, Jinnah Rd, T 79519, helpful and friendly staff, able to offer good advice on current travel conditions in Baluchistan; **Culture and Tourism Cell (CTC)**, Art School Rd, T 834575, recently established by the provincial government to promote culture and tourism in Baluchistan. Although still limited in terms of resources. They are very helpful, they operate a number of their own motels and resthouses in Baluchistan and plan to open their own Tourist Information Centre.

● **Useful addresses**
Foreigners' registration: office of Deputy Inspector General (DIG) of Police, Special Branch, Staff College Rd, no phone, open Sun-Thur 0900-1600, Sat 0900-1200, closed Fri.
Police: City Police Station, Liaquat Rd, T 74147.
Political Section II: Home Department, Rm 2, Block 2, 2nd Flr, T 824031, for permits to visit restricted areas, and the latest official information on which areas are restricted. In an emergency they may also be able to help with visa extensions.

● **Transport**
Local Auto-rickshaws: these are ubiquitous in Quetta and the main form of local transport. Perhaps because their engines are not adjusted for the higher altitude, their exhaust fumes are particularly noxious, billowing out in a thick blue cloud. Fares are more or less fixed; some drivers try to charge tourists higher rates, but less so than elsewhere in Pakistan. **Bus**: run from the City Bus Stand is on Circular Rd to Sariab, S of Quetta town. **Taxi/Car hire**: the main taxi stand is at Regal Plaza, Adalat Rd. There are two companies, the **Pakistan Yellow Cab Federation**, T 835371 and the *Taxi Service Stand*, T 821521. The former is slightly cheaper. Both will hire cars (with driver) for long-distance journeys. Fares vary according to road conditions as well as distance. In mid 1995, the following return fares were being charged; Hanna Lake Rs 400, Hazerganji Chiltan National Park Rs 400, Ziarat Rs 1000, Bolan Pass Rs 800, Sibi Rs 1200, Chaman Rs 1200, Airport (one-way) Rs 100. Ask at PTDC for hire of 4WD vehicles.

Air Quetta is served only by PIA. Regular flights to Karachi (up to 3 daily), **Islamabad** (up to 3 daily), **Peshawar** via Zhob and DI Khan (Mon, Wed, Sat), **Lahore** (Mon, Wed, Fri, Sat), **Turbat** (Mon, Tues, Wed, Fri, Sun), **Sukkur** (Mon, Fri), **Panjgur** (Wed, Sun), **Khuzdar** (Fri) and **Dalbandin** (Tues, Sun). Despite its name, there are no international flights from Quetta airport since the discontinuation of flights to Mashad in Iran. **NB** Due to the huge distances involved in travelling to and from Quetta, flights are often heavily booked and reservations should be made well in advance.

Train Enquiries T 65500. **Lahore/Faisalabad**: *Chiltan Exp*, 1230, 30½/34½ hrs. **Rawalpindi**: *Quetta Exp*, 1115, 35¼ hrs. **Peshawar**: *Abbaseen Exp*, 1710, 40¾ hrs. **Karachi**: *Bolan Mail*, 1600, 23 hrs. **Chaman**: *Q-847*, 0830, 4¾ hrs. **Zahidan**: Sat 1205, 29½ hrs, *Q-485*, Wed 1205, 32¼ hrs. **NB** A/c and sleeper tickets should be booked well in advance (up to 2 weeks).

Road Bus: the New Quetta Bus Stand (or General Bus Stand) is S of the main city, close to Satellite Town. Buses from here to Karachi, Sukkur/Jacobabad, DI Khan/Bannu, Peshawar (via Jacobabad), Chaman, Turbat, Panjgur, Nawabshah, Taftan, Loralai, Ziarat. A number of the private coach companies also have offices at the southern end of **Jinnah Rd**, with services to Karachi. Small coaches and Toyota Hiace minivans for Chaman, Zhob, Dera Ismail Khan, Ziarat and Loralai also leave from **Suraj Ganj Bazaar**, in the street running parallel to Jinnah Rd, near Gul's Inn. Some minivans for Ziarat also leave from the **City Bus Stand**. The Balochistan Times prints a bus timetable, but the frequency of most services (especially for Ziarat) varies according to the season and passenger demand, so it is best to check for yourself.

QUETTA TO LORALAI VIA ZIARAT

This route offers a scenic alternative to the route via Muslimbagh and Qila Saifullah to Loralai, passing through the popular summer resort of Ziarat. Although more direct, it is much slower, the road being in poor condition, particularly beyond Ziarat. Follow the route as for Dera Ghazi Khan (see below) as far as Ziarat Mor (52 km), continuing straight at this junction. The road climbs up through barren hills of mud and rock. 50 years ago the area was well wooded, but acute deforestation has exposed the land to heavy erosion, creating what appears in places almost to be a moonscape. At Kach (72 km) there is a checkpost and a few tea shops, overlooked by an old fort up on a ridge.

An alternative route to Kach, on a rough jeep track, leaves Quetta on Staff College Rd. Continue straight on past the turning right to Hanna Lake. The track winds its way past Kach dam, over a saddle between Takatu and Zarghun mountains, down past the village of Gundak and through denuded hills to Kach, 52 km by this route.

2 km beyond Kach, a rough track leads off to the right, passing through **Mangi**, **Khost**, **Harnai** and **Spin Tangi** to eventually arrive at Sibi. Before the British secured the Bolan Pass, this was the route used between Sibi and Quetta. The railway line also originally passed this way, but the terrain proved too unstable and it was re-routed through the Bolan Pass. A branch line still operates between Sibi and Khost. From Mangi there is access to the **Chappar Rift**, a spectacular limestone gorge which cuts through the line of the mountains. This was one of the major obstacles for the railway line and presented a great challenge to the engineers building it. Tunnels were dug through the mountains

either side of the rift, which was spanned by an iron girder bridge. The District Gazetteer describes how the work was carried out ".... by letting down workmen with ropes from the top of the cliff several hundred feet above the point of operation. The first man down had to gain a footing by driving a crowbar into the perpendicular wall; after the first crowbar others were driven in, and then a platform was erected from which blasting operations could begin. So singular and difficult a piece of engineering has probably seldom or never been accomplished before. Six openings were made on one side of the cliff for one tunnel and six on the other, and galleries driven into them until points were reached from where the main tunnel could be constructed right and left, so that the work could be carried on by 14 separate gangs; and in this way the whole tunnel was blasted out in a few months." From Harnai another track branches N through the **Harnai Gorge** to rejoin the main Ziarat-Loralai road at Sanjawi. The route is a breathtaking one, blasted into the side of a precipitous cliff-face. To explore this fascinating area you need your own 4WD transport, and a guide who is familiar with the terrain.

The main road to Ziarat, in poor condition beyond Kach, continues E, following the river past orchards and the small settlements of **Kahan** (27 km), **Verchoum**, **Kawas** (35 km), **Zindra**, **Chena** (42 km) and **Pechi**, to arrive at Ziarat (53 km). The cover of Juniper trees on the hills gradually increases towards Ziarat. Narrow gorges ('*Tangi*') lead off at various points on either side. The most accessible of these are **Kawas Tangi**, N of Kawas, the **Manna Valley**, N of Zindra, **Fern Tangi**, on a track leading S, just past Pechi, and **Sandeman Tangi**, N of the road just before it passes through the crenellated archway

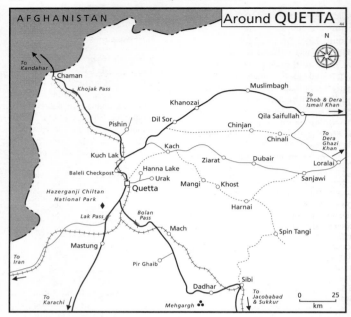

Around QUETTA

marking the start of Ziarat. The latter is the most popular, being easily accessible from Ziarat. All these gorges offer excellent walking and picnic spots.

Ziarat

Ziarat was first developed as a summer retreat by the British. It is the only major hill station in southern Pakistan, and still extremely popular in summer when its climate is pleasantly cool. The season generally runs from Apr to Oct. Outside of these months the resort largely closes down; during winter it is usually completely snowbound. Situated 133 km from Quetta, it is easily accessible by road. Regular minibuses make the journey in around 3 hrs.

The resort itself has a slightly dilapidated atmosphere, though the surrounding hills are a hiker's paradise. The Juniper forests surrounding Ziarat are amongst the oldest in the world, with some of the trees said to be as much as 5,000 years old. Deforestation has however taken its toll, and in places the hillsides have only a thin cover. Under a recent government initiative, gas stoves and subsidized bottles have been distributed amongst the villagers in an attempt to limit the cutting of trees for firewood.

Ziarat was a favourite retreat of Mohammad Ali Jinnah, and the Quaid-e-Azam's **Residency**, in which he spent his last days, has been preserved as a museum, with all the furniture arranged as it was when he died in 1948. Built by the British in 1882, this 2-storey building with wooden verandahs and balconies is situated up on the hillside looking out over the valley. A jeepable track continues up past the Residency to **Prospect Point** (6 km), a massive shoulder of rock which at 2,713m gives spectacular views across the whole valley. From higher up on the ridge behind there are views S toward **Mount Khalifat**, the highest peak in Baluchistan at 3,485m. 3 km further on, the road leads down to the Shrine of Baba Kharwari, known popularly as Baba Mian Abdul Hakim. It is from this shrine, or *ziarat*, that the resort gets its name.

● **Accommodation & places to eat NB** Hotels are often heavily booked in summer so it is worth making advance reservations. Prices in the cheaper hotels can become inflated when it is busy. **C** *PTDC Complex*, T 356, comfortable rooms and villa accommodation, restaurant, book through PTDC, Quetta; **D** *Shalimar*, T 353, clean, comfortable and well-kept, *Juniper Restaurant*, rec, open all year round; **E** *Tourist Rest House*, at E end of town, recently opened, 3 comfortable rm, no electricity in 1995, book through CTC, Quetta; slightly cheaper hotels are around the bus stand, incl the **E** *Grand*, open all year round; and behind it the **E** *Sanobar*, T 308; others incl the **E** *Rising Star*, T 238, and **E** *Ziarat*, T 226.

● **Other services** There are three banks (but no foreign exchange facilities), a Post Office, Telegraph Office and small Hospital.

● **Transport** The frequency of services to and from Ziarat varies greatly with the season and demand. Some minibuses have started operating between Quetta and Loralai via Ziarat on a fairly regular basis.

From Ziarat the road deteriorates considerably, disappearing altogether for stretches as it follows the stony bed of the river. It is 23 km to **Chautair**, a small village with some basic accommodation. During summer this makes a quieter alternative to Ziarat, and is in some ways more beautiful. The surrounding hills are much more densely wooded. Just before the village, a track leads N to **Chautair Tangi**, which gives access to a valley beyond it. The road continues through **Wani**, **Raigora** and **Sanjawi** (62 km). Just before the latter a track leads SW to Harnai (see above). It is a further 28 km to Loralai, on the route to Dera Ghazi Khan (see below).

QUETTA TO DERA GHAZI KHAN

There are two routes E from Quetta to Dera Ghazi Khan. One via Ziarat and the other via Muslimbagh and Qila Saifullah, both joining at Loralai for the remainder of the way. The route via Muslimbagh and Qila Saifullah is longer but the road is better and faster. Head NW out of Quetta on the Chaman road, past the turning for the airport. The road crosses the Chaman railway line and passes through Balel Checkpost. It is 25 km to Kuch Lak, a small town whose population has been swelled significantly by Afghan refugees. Take the right turn in the main bazaar (straight on for Chaman) and continue on a good 2-lane road to the junction known as ZiaratMor (52 km). Turn left here for Muslimbagh (straight on for Ziarat) onto a single lane road. After about 20 km a jeep track leads off to the right, passing through the villages of Chinjan, Zakhpel Dargai and Chinali to rejoin the main road between Qila Saifullah and Loralai.

The main road continues through plentiful orchards of apples, plums, almonds and pomegranates, to **Dil Sor** (79 km), a small settlement with simple restaurants and tea shops. The road crosses and re-crosses the old narrow-guage track, now abandoned, which once connected Quetta with Zhob. **Khanozai** (or Khan Mehtarzai, 96 km) once had the distinction of the highest railway station in Asia at 2,222m. To the N are the mountains of the Toba Kakar range, and beyond the Afghan Border. It is a further 22 km on to **Muslimbagh**, formerly known as Hindubagh. This is the largest village before Loralai, with a reasonable bazaar and an *Irrigation Dept Rest House*, although arranging to stay here may be difficult.

Beyond Muslimbagh, the number of orchards decrease and the landscape gives way to a wide plateau supporting only the meagrest vegetation. To the S, across the plateau, is a large Afghan refugee camp, known locally as the 'Muslimbagh Mohajir Camp'. The road passes through the small village of Nisai and then once again through scattered orchards, to arrive at the small settlement of **Qila Saifullah** (180 km). There is the **E** *Taj* here, offering basic but reasonable accommodation, but little else.

1 km beyond Qila Saifullah, take the turning right (straight on for Zhob) to head S towards Loralai. The road winds its way up through barren hills, emerging onto a plateau and traversing it, passing a *levies* post at Tano. The surrounding scenery is in places quite spectacular, with a distinctive table-topped mountain to the W of the road. It is then a steady gradual descent, past patches of cultivation, to Loralai, 252 km from Quetta.

Loralai

Loralai (4,700 ft), formerly known as Pathan Kot, is the headquarters of Loralai District. It is a small bazaar town with a separate cantonment area which was established by the British between 1890-1897. There is little of interest in the town, which has a vaguely threatening atmosphere to it, perhaps a reflection of the fierce independence of the Pathan tribes which predominate in the area. The complete absence of women is matched only by the abundance of guns and drugs being openly paraded through the bazaar. You may be asked to register with the police if staying overnight.

● **Accommodation & places to eat** There are a limited number of hotels, all fairly basic, along the main bazaar. The two better ones are the **F** *Pakiza*, T 2417 and **F** *Spinza*, T 3403, both with restaurants; more basic is the **F** *Gul*, T 2437 (hotel sign in Urdu only); there is also a *CTC Motel* which should be booked through the Culture and Tourism Cell in Quetta, T 834575, as well as a couple of *Govt Rest Houses* where it may be possible to arrange accommodation – check with the Deputy Commissioner, T 2442 or the Assistant Commissioner, T 2905. As well as the hotel restaurants, there are a number of basic, local-style restaurants in the bazaar.

● **Transport Road Bus**: the various coach companies operate services to Dera Ghazi Khan (8-10 hrs) and Quetta (5 hrs), with several departures through the morning. There is no bus station as such and coaches leave from various points along the main bazaar.

From Loralai to Dera Ghazi Khan the old single-lane road is in poor condition for much of the way, with sections of it having been eroded or washed away. There are several rivers which have to be forded. Repairs and upgrading were in progress in 1995, although the pace of work is very slow; gangs of labourers work with small hammers to break rocks into carefully graded piles of coarse gravel. Known in the past as 'Robbers Road', the British never really managed to subdue the tribes of the surrounding country-side, who, up until very recently, continued to raid traffic along this route.

The road passes through green and fertile countryside with fruit orchards intercropped with wheat, and climbs gently through low hills to **Mekhtar** (79 km), a small village with tea shops and basic food. The road, here very rough, then climbs steeply, passing the tiny village of **Kingri** (139 km), before descending steadily to **Rakhni** (184 km), a small bazaar town. Turn left at the T-junction in the bazaar. The road again climbs steeply, this time into the mountains of the Suleiman range, crossing the border into Punjab, to arrive at the village of Khar (200 km), where a track leads S to the nearby hill station of Fort Munro.

Fort Munro

Founded by Sir Robert Sandeman and named after Colonel Munro, a former Commissioner of the district, this hill station (1,800m) was established by the British as a retreat from the summer heat and remains the only one in south-

ern Punjab. It is situated on what appears from below as a steeply-sided, perfectly conical hill. From the main road a track zigzags its way up the side. During summer, it is busy with visiting officials and tribal chiefs, many of whom have their own summer residences here, while in the winter it is all but deserted. Fort Munro has a peaceful air about it and makes a relaxing place to stop. There are plenty of opportunities for walks in the surrounding area.

● **Accommodation** The only accommodation here is the ideally situated **C** *TDCP Resthouse*, reasonable rooms with att bath, good restaurant and excellent views, open all year round, bookings can be made through TDCP in Lahore.

● **Transport** During the summer there are generally direct bus services between Fort Munro and Dera Ghazi Khan. Irregular buses run to and from Khar on the main road, but out of season you really need your own transport.

The main road continues E from the turning for Fort Munro, descending steadily through spectacular mountain scenery onto the Indus plain, to arrive at Dera Ghazi Khan, 282 km from Loralai and 534 km from Quetta. There are a total of three river fordings along this last stretch. These can be tricky to negotiate after rains, particularly at **Sakhi Sarwar**, site of a famous shrine to a Sufi saint. Bear in mind that even when the weather appears fine, these seasonal streams can be swollen by rainfall occurring a long way off in the mountains.

Dera Ghazi Khan

Known generally by its abbreviated form, DG Khan, this dusty bazaar town is the headquarters of the district of the same name. Originally, the town in fact formed part of Baluchistan and today the people are still predominantly Baluchi or Pathan. However the British, in what was generally perceived to be a politically motivated move to weaken the Baluch tribes, allocated the town and surrounding area to Punjab. This is the home town of the current President, Mr Leghari, although it shows no sign of benefiting from his position of power in terms of its civic amenities. Many of the streets are unpaved, and after rains are churned up into deep mud by the heavy traffic in the town.

● **Accommodation & places to eat** The best hotel in town is the **C** *Shalimar*, Faridi Bazaar, T 62105, a/c, att bath, TV/Dish, Chinese restaurant; **E** *Pakeeza*, Faridi Bazaar, T 63305, has reasonable rooms with att bath and fan, also more expensive a/c VIP rooms, parking, a/c restaurant, good value and friendly. There are several more basic hotels along Faridi Bazaar, incl **F** *New Al-Madina*, T 65665, **F** *Al Marhaba*, T 63522 and **F** *Fourways*, T 62807, all with restaurants. There are a number of basic restaurants in the main bazaars.

● **Transport Road Bus**: DG Khan has no single bus station. There are a number of companies offering 'luxury' coach services, all in Faridi Bazaar; *New Khan Road Runners*, T 62580, to Lahore (1000, 2200, 2300, 9 hrs, Rs 112) and Islamabad/Rawalpindi (0745, 12 hrs, Rs 157). *City Linkers*, T 65692, to Lahore (2200, 8 hrs, Rs 150) and Karachi (1500, 1700, 15 hrs, Rs 200). *Bazanjo Coaches*, to Karachi (1900, 15 hrs, Rs 150). Local buses and minibuses operate services to Muzaffargarh and Multan, as well as to Loralai. There are a number of depots along Faridi Bazaar and a larger one (the nearest there is to a bus station) behind Faridi Bazaar. The only direct service to Dera Ismail Khan is by way of the Bannu bus which departs at 2200. Alternatively, local buses run to Taunsa, from where there are services on to DI Khan. It is quicker to go up the E bank of the Indus, via Muzaffargarh.

From DG Khan a good road continues E, across the Indus River and past Ghazi Ghat, to Muzaffargarh (60 km) and Multan (94 km). See page 297.

DG Khan lies on the W bank route along the Indus. In either direction this road is a narrow single lane, subject to flooding in places. By no means a fast road, it makes a peaceful alternative to the busy National Highway on the opposite bank.

The road S from DG Khan runs through irrigated agricultural land, giving way increasingly to desert as you move further southwards. The main settlements along the way are Jampur (48 km), Rajanpur (114 km), Mithankot (130 km, linked by a bridge of boats with the E bank town of Chacharan), Rohjan (188 km), Kashmor (236 km, just inside Sind, with access to the E bank via the Guddu Barrage), Kandkhot (283 km), and Shikarpur (347 km), on the route between Sukkur and Quetta.

North from DG Khan, the road passes through the small villages of Shah Sadruddin and Shadan Lund (51 km). Just N of Shadan Lund the road forks. Straight ahead takes you across the Indus via the **Taunsa Barrage** on a dual rail/road bridge, to join a quiet road running close to the banks of the Indus, parallel to the National Highway, 4 km N of Kot Addu. The fork left crosses the canal and continues up the W bank to arrive at Taunsa Sharif (70 km).

Taunsa Sharif (literally 'holy Taunsa') is a small town famous for its shrine and mosque to **Pir Mohammad Suleiman Shah**. Built in 1855 by the Nawab of Bahawalpur, this impressive mosque, complete with clocktower, is housed in a large courtyard with a pond. The outside of the dome is decorated with blue tiles and marble from Jaipur, while inside it is lavishly ornate. A passageway leads through to a second building, housing the tomb itself. The annual Urs is held in the first week of the Muslim month of *Safar*.

There is unfortunately no accommodation in Taunsa, other than the extremely basic and best avoided *Café Mahabou Sulaiman*, by the bus stand.

● **Transport** Buses and minivans run services to DG Khan, DI Khan and, via the Taunsa Barrage, to various destinations on the E bank, largely on the basis of demand. The road N of Taunsa is subject to flooding, with a potentially difficult river fording just short of DI Khan.

QUETTA TO DERA ISMAIL KHAN VIA ZHOB

The route NE from Quetta via Zhob to Dera Ismail Khan in southern NWFP is unfortunately still restricted, and appears likely to remain so, despite the fact that it is not particularly dangerous. Locals point out that there have been no incidents involving foreigners along this route. The main difficulty in getting permits stems from the fact that the route passes through tribal areas of both Baluchistan and southern NWFP, so that you need permits from the two Home Departments. Travellers can check the latest situation with PTDC or the Home Department in Quetta. Those travelling by public transport are more likely to be allowed along this route.

The route is a spectacular one. The **Zhob valley**, with an elevation of not less than 1,300m, is relatively fertile with frequent oases supporting vineyards and rich orchards of apples, apricots, peaches, pomegranates, plums, almonds, walnuts and melons. The valley is perhaps at its most beautiful during spring, when it blossoms with wild lavender, tulips, hyacinths, poppies and irises, or in autumn when the weather is pleasant and the orchards heavy with fruit. There is frequently heavy snowfall in winter, while in summer temperatures can reach 40°C. To the N, the peaks of the **Toba Kakar** range rise to over 3,000m, while to the S a range of lower hills expose fantastic patterns of folded rock strata. Here and there ridges rise out of the plain like the backbones of dinosaurs. East of Zhob the road cuts through the northern parts of the Suleiman Range, skirting round the mighty Takht-i-Suleiman. The route is also extremely arduous, particularly once inside NWFP, where there are long stretches where the road disappears altogether and one must follow the course of a stony river bed or rough tracks crossing

country. After rains the road often becomes impassable.

Follow the route for Dera Ghazi Khan as far as **Qila Saifullah** (180 km) and then continue straight on at the junction just E of the town (right for Loralai). The road follows the Zhob River and the old narrow-gauge railway, closed in 1985, passing the settlements of **Tanga** (68 km), **Mina Bazaar** (102 km) and **Badinzai** (120 km), before arriving at Zhob (140 km). There are tea shops and simple restaurants along the way, but little else.

Zhob

Zhob (pronounced 'Jhob') is the headquarters of Zhob district, a combination of tribal and 'settled' areas. The town is an ancient one, known originally as Apozai, and has been a centre for settlement at least as far back as 3000 BC. Excavations were first carried out by Sir Auriel Stein in 1924 and later by Fairservis in 1950, with finds including leaf-shaped arrowheads and female figurines which have been dubbed 'Zhob Goddesses'. The Zhob valley appears to have acted as an ancient caravan route, the Gomal Pass connecting early settlements such as Mundigak in Afghanistan with Indus Valley settlements to the E. Today it is still used by groups of *Powindahs* (literally 'wanderers' or 'nomads'), who migrate between the uplands and plains each spring and autumn.

In 1889 the British captured the town and renamed it Fort Sandeman after Sir Robert Sandeman, the first Agent to the Governor General of Baluchistan. For the British it was an important garrison town, central to their Forward Policy, and they were quick to develop road and rail links with the rest of British India. There are two forts, situated on rocky ridges overlooking the town with its large cantonment area and lively bazaar.

One is still home to the Zhob Militia, founded in 1890 and now part of the Frontier Corps, while the other was Sandeman's Fort, a grand Victorian structure which now houses the Political Agent. The two are supposedly linked by an underground tunnel.

The population is predominantly Pathan and has grown significantly in recent years with the influx of Afghan refugees. Situated close to the Afghan border and linked by road with the tribal areas of South Waziristan, it has also developed as an important market for smuggled goods.

● **Accommodation** There are two basic but reasonable hotels in the town, one close to the bus stands and centre of the bazaar, and the other at the N end of the main bazaar, nr the mosque. There are a few *Government Rest Houses*. If you have a permit, you may be able to stay in one of these.

● **Places to eat** There are a number of simple restaurants in the bazaar.

● **Transport Air** PIA Booking Office, 10A Market Rd, T 2875. Daily flights to Dera Ismail Khan, Peshawar and Islamabad. Three flights weekly to Quetta (Mon, Wed, Sat) and 4 flights weekly to Multan (Tues, Thur, Fri, Sun). **Road Bus**: regular services (bus and minivan) to Quetta (8 hrs); buses for Dera Ismail Khan take approximately 11 hrs, road conditions permitting.

Warning The route N from Zhob into NWFP, passing through **Tanai** (120 km) and **Ramzak** (200 km), before eventually arriving at **Bannu** (326 km), is through the sensitive tribal/border areas of N and S Waziristan, and is strictly off-limits to foreigners.

The main route E from Zhob passes through **Kapip**, surrounded by vineyards, and then starts to climb gradually. Eventually the wide valley begins to narrow and the peaks of the Suleiman range loom up ahead. The road

enters a narrow gorge with walls of sheer rock rising up thousands of metres on either side. **Dhanasar**, on the opposite bank of the river, has a checkpost and small fort. A small steel-girder arch by the side of the road marks the border with NWFP. A little further on is **Mughal Khot** (85 km), a small settlement at the top of the gorge with a checkpost. Here the road abruptly turns to a rough gravel track which descends slowly down the eastern flanks of the Suleiman range, giving spectacular views. A long, difficult stretch follows, often impassable after rains, along the course of a stony riverbed to **Domanda**, where there are tea shops and basic restaurants. From Domanda the road does a wide loop via Drazinda to Daraban. The old British road, which went by a more direct route, is now impassable although there are plans to reopen it. **Takht-e-Suleiman**, the highest peak in the Sulaiman range at 3,375m, previously hidden by a series of ridges, comes slowly into view to the W. There are a few tea shops and basic restaurants in **Drazinda**, and a little further on is a fort and checkpost of the same name. The road then cuts through a ridge of low hills and crosses a wide stony plain to arrive at **Daraban** (167 km, full name Daraban Kalan, to distinguish it from Daraban Khurd, S of DI Khan). From here it is a further 58 km to Dera Ismail Khan, a total of 225 km from Zhob and 545 km from Quetta. The road is single lane and heavily potholed. In 1995 a section of it had been washed away by floods, necessitating a long detour over rough ground. For details of DI Khan and routes from there, see page 368.

QUETTA TO SUKKUR VIA THE BOLAN PASS

The route SE from Quetta, through the historic Bolan Pass and down onto the Kachhi plains has for centuries acted as a thoroughfare for conquerors, traders and nomads alike, providing the easiest access S of the Khyber Pass between the Iranian Plateau and the plains of the Indus. During spring and autumn, nomadic groups with their caravans of camels, horses, donkeys, sheep and goats can still be seen making their seasonal journey between the highlands and the plains. Today, it remains the quickest route to and from Quetta, with a good quality metalled road and a railway line, the only one linking Baluchistan with the rest of Pakistan.

The railway is a spectacular feat of engineering, with a total of 17 tunnels and numerous bridges and culverts carrying it through the Bolan Pass and down onto the plains. On the journey up from Sibi, a second engine is attached to the train to help push it up gradients which reach one in 25 in places. Plans to build a Frontier Railway connecting Quetta with the rest of British India were first drawn up in 1876, when Lord Lytton's Forward Policy was initiated. It was not until 1879 that work began on the first phase, with a line as far as Sibi being completed in 1880. Work on the next phase, known as the 'Harnai Military Road', began in earnest in 1884 and the line as far as Quetta was opened in 1887. This section of the line ran via Harnai, Khost, Chappar Rift and Bostan. Although a branch line still operates from Sibi as far as Khost, further on the terrain proved too unstable after rains, and the route was abandoned in favour of the present route through the Bolan Pass. This second line however proved to be equally problematic. In 1889, just after it was completed, more flooding resulted in substantial subsidence and much of the line had to be rebuilt on a new alignment.

Head S on Suriab Rd, past the University, and after 7 km bear left at the fork (right for the Iranian border and RCD Highway to Karachi). An alternative route from New Quetta Bus Stand joins the Sibi road S of this fork. The main road crosses the wide Quetta plain, running parallel to the railway line, before crossing it and climbing gently to the town of **Kolpur** (25 km), which marks the start of the Bolan Pass. The pass, stretching for 96 km, is in fact more accurately a gorge which cuts through the **Central Brahui Range** giving access to the plains below.

From Kolpur it is a steady descent all the way down to the plains. The road crosses back and forth over the Bolan River, also passing under the railway line several times. Inscribed above the entrance to one of the tunnels, the name 'Mary Jane' is visible from the road, commemorating the wife of the chief engineer who died of an illness while her husband worked on the railway. The occasional tunnels below the railway are remnants of the line which subsided when it first opened.

The road passes the turning left to **Mach**, situated on the other side of the river, clustered around the train station. Mach was at the epicentre of the 1935 earthquake and was completely destroyed. Shortly before the turning there is a stretch of green with date palms on the opposite bank, which was the site of the old town of Mach (in Baluchi, *mach* means 'date'); today it makes a pleasant picnic spot. Beyond Mach, the road descends steeply and then passes numerous simple coal mines cut into the hills on either side. The gorge meanwhile opens out to a wide braided river bed. 25 km from Mach there is a rough track to the right which leads 16 km up to Pir Ghaib.

Pir Ghaib

Permits are no longer required for this short excursion to the hot sulphur springs at Pir Ghaib. The rough track, which has been repaired and is now passable in a 4WD, climbs for 15 km to the rock pools surrounded by shady palm trees, which are dotted around the area. There is a shrine to the Sufi saint from whom the spot gets its name. Traces of an ancient water channel can still be seen, ascribed by locals to the Arabs and constructed of lime and cement, running from Pir Ghaib to Khajuri, about 4 km away. Pir Ghaib makes an excellent picnic place, and with your own transport, is accessible as a long day trip from Quetta. There are plans to further improve access and provide facilities for tourists.

4 km on from the turning to Pir Ghaib is **Bibi Nani Bridge**. In 1986 it was washed away by floods; in 1995 a section of the bridge was again broken and under repair. The road follows the E bank of the river, descending steadily, before crossing again to the W bank. The river, for much of the year a dry stony bed, is up to 15 km wide around here. Further on, around 40 km from Sibi, the **Pinjera Bridge** carries the road back over to the E bank. From here the valley narrows once again to a gorge, passing through a couple of tunnels. At **Bolan Weir** there is a checkpost and traditional mud fort with a mosque inside. The archaeological site of Merhgarh is 10 km from here, on the banks of the Bolan River, N of a track leading to the villages of Sanni and Shoran.

Merhgarh

This archaeological site, first excavated in 1974 by a French team, is one of the most important in Pakistan. As well as pushing back the known dates of settled agriculture in South Asia to around 8500 BC, far beyond anything previously imagined by archaeologists, the site has provided strong evidence to suggest that the great Indus Valley Civilization which later flourished in Pakistan emerged from these first indigenous settlements, as oppose to having been imported by groups migrating from Egypt, Persia or Central Asia. At the same time, finds of turquoise beads suggest that from the earliest period there was trade and contact with far-flung regions.

The earliest part of the settlement, on the high bank of the Bolan River at the N end of the site, was probably a camp of nomadic pastoralists. By 8000 BC there were well developed villages with agriculture and the beginnings of animal domestication, indicating that settled agriculture occurred in Baluchistan at least as early as it did further W in the traditional 'cradle of civilization', the Fertile Crescent of the Zagros mountains. Hunting continued to complement agriculture, with elephants, wild water buffalo and Nilgai deer amongst those killed. Cereals were also introduced remarkably early; a local variety of barley and wheat by 8000 BC and cotton by 5000 BC.

Excavations shifted some time ago from Merhgarh to **Naushero**, 15 km to the W, where the evidence of a transition from the last period of Merhgarh to the Indus Valley period, has been found.

Despite its enormous archaeological significance, a visit to Mehrgarh is only for the specialist or the dedicated. As well as being difficult to reach (your own transport is really needed and the nearest accommodation is at Sibi), there is little to see, apart from the outlines and foundations of buildings. All the pottery and other artefacts have been removed to various museums. The displays at the small museums in Sibi and Quetta, and at the national museum in Karachi, give the best insight into the culture and way of life of these ancient settlements. There are plans to build a hotel near the site.

The road continues past patches of cultivation and then out onto the flat wide **Kachhi plain** before reaching

Dadhar, surrounded by woods and irrigated farmland. There is a stretch of bazaar along the main road, but the town itself is off to the right. Beyond Dadhar the land gives way once more to a barren alluvial plain with a sparse cover of scrub and grass. The road crosses the Nari River and the railway line before arriving in Sibi, 163 km from Quetta.

Sibi

Headquarters of Sibi Division, Sibi is the largest town in Baluchistan after Quetta, with a population now thought to number over 100,000. Although certainly an ancient town, its origins are unclear. There is mention of a tribe known as the Sibi or Sibia in the chronicles of Alexander's expedition to South Asia in 325 BC, perhaps the original inhabitants of the area. Local tradition meanwhile holds that it gained its name from Sewi, a Hindu princess of the Sewa Dynasty. The Brahman king Rai Chach ruled over the area for a period, before it came under the control of the Arab Muslim invaders in the 8th century. Later it was ruled over by Mahmud of Ghazni after he captured Multan in 1004. In 1487 it became the capital of the

short-lived kingdom of Mir Chakar. It was first attacked by the British in 1841 before being captured by them in 1878 during the Second Afghan War and named Sandemanabad after Sir Robert Sandeman. Today it is famous for the **Horse and Cattle Fair**, which is held during the first 2 weeks of Apr each year.

This annual festival originated from the *Shahi Jirga*, a traditional meeting of tribal elders, which was revived by Robert Sandeman in 1882 as a means of encouraging the tribal chiefs of the area to take responsibility for ensuring peace and stability in a region which had been subject to continual and bloody feuds. The Jirga still takes place today as part of the Horse and Cattle Fair, another long-standing institution, to promote agricultural development in the area. The fair attracts politicians and other important figures from all over Pakistan, as well as tribesmen from the surrounding areas, and is an excellent place to shop for local Baluchi handicrafts.

Sibi is also famous, along with Dadhar, and Jacobabad further S, for being amongst the hottest places in South Asia, with summer temperatures sometimes exceeding 50°C. A Persian proverb which runs "Sibi-o-Dadhar sakhti dozakh chira pardakhti", loosely translates as "Oh Allah, having created hot places like Sibi and Dadhar, why bother to conceive of hell?"

Places of interest
Sibi Museum Open 0900-1600, Fri 0900-1200, closed Wed. The small museum is housed in the former Queen Victoria Hall, built in 1903 and later known as the Jirga Hall (it was here that the Jirgas of tribal chiefs organized by Sandeman were held). It has an interesting, well displayed collection of pieces from Merhgarh, Naushero and Pirak, SW of Sibi. The pottery found at Pirak, which dates from 1800-800 BC, is of a different technique and style to that found at Merhgarh and Naushero, being

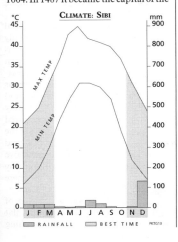

CLIMATE: SIBI

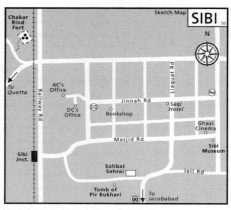

Sketch Map **SIBI** 50

remainder during the Horse and Cattle Fair. A little further down the road, on the opposite side, is the tomb of Pir Bukhari, a famous saint from Bukhara in present day Uzbekistan.

Chakkar Rind Fort A short distance down the road towards the airport, overlooking the railway and river, is the impressive mud fort of Chakkar Rind, dating from the 15th century. Inside the crumbling walls there are two large conical structures which served as grain stores. The fort is within walking distance of the centre of town if the weather is not too hot, or else tongas are readily available. **NB** To the E of the fort is a restricted military area – be careful where you point your camera.

adorned with distinctive geometric designs. It has been suggested that the presence of terracotta toy camels indicates that the inhabitants of this site migrated from Central Asia, the home of the camel during this period. Pirak is also significant in that it has yielded the earliest evidence of double cropping, with the winter crop of wheat and barley being supplemented by a spring crop of rice, sorghum and millet. There is also a small collection of traditional Baluchi jewellery and embroidered clothes, photos of archaeological and historical sites and artifacts from around Baluchistan and photographs and text relating to Baluchistan's relations with Pakistan and Jinnah following Independence.

Sohbat Serai One of several built by the powerful Sardar Sohbat Khan, this impressive *caravanserai* is built in the traditional style with rooms around a large central courtyard shaded by trees and a mosque in one corner. The walls, inside and out, are decorated with glazed blue tiles. During the annual Jirga, the tribal chiefs would stay here, each bringing with them their own entourage of cooks and servants. Today part of the building is given over to a school and government officials are accommodated in the

Local information
● **Accommodation**

There is very limited and basic accommodation in Sibi and it is worth booking in advance. During the Fair you are unlikely to find accommodation unless you have contacts or have booked well ahead. **NB** Foreigners are required to register with the police if staying overnight.

F *Saqi*, Jinnah Rd, T 2428 is the only hotel with reasonable rooms and clean bedding; nearby **F** *Cherry Blossom* is more basic.

There are a number of government resthouses, bookable through the Deputy Commissioner, T 2610. Tourists are unfortunately no longer generally allowed to stay in the Sohbat Serai. It is managed by the Itthad ('unity') Trust, T 3063.

● **Places to eat**

There are a number of basic but reasonably hygienic local style restaurants along Liaqat and Jinnah Rd.

● **Transport**

Train Khost: *Passenger Q-489*, 0630, 5¾ hrs; *Passenger Q491*, 1700, 6 hrs. Quetta: *Bostan Mail*, 0535, 5 hrs; *Abbaseen Exp*, 0625, 4¾ hrs; *Chiltan Exp*, 1130, 5 hrs; *Quetta Exp*, 1220,

5½ hrs; *Passenger 45*, 0235, 5½ hrs. **Lahore**: *Chiltan Exp*, 1745, 25¼ hrs. **Rawalpindi**: *Quetta Exp*, 1630, 30 hrs. **Peshawar**: *Abbaseen Exp*, 2230, 35¼ hrs. **Karachi**: *Bolan Mail*, 2040, 18 hrs. **NB** Other services on the main Karachi-Peshawar line can be accessed from Rohri Junction.

Road Bus: there are regular buses and coaches from the main bus stand to Jacobabad, Sukkur and Quetta. Minibuses arrive and depart from Masjid Rd; significantly faster than the buses, there is usually a hectic scramble for seats on these.

From Sibi, the main road heads SE, following the railway line closely, across the plains of the Kachhi Desert to **Bellpat** (66 km), a small bazaar with food and cold drinks. It is a further 48 km to **Dera Murad Jamali**, a reasonable-sized town with bazaars and very basic accommodation, set in fertile irrigated land. **Jhatpat** is the last village before the border with Sind, marked by the course of a canal. The land around here shows signs of heavy salinization in places. Just across the border in Sind is the town of Jacobabad, 158 km from Sibi.

Jacobabad

The town of Jacobabad is named after **General John Jacob**, the remarkable Political Superintendent of the Upper Sind Frontier Region between 1847-1858. Jacob was responsible for laying out the town, and indeed for transforming the surrounding countryside from virtual desert to fertile agricultural land and bringing an end to the anarchic feuding and banditry which characterized the area. Although his rule was strict and uncompromising, he is still revered as the man who brought peace and relative prosperity to the region. He is also one of only two Englishmen whose name remains attached to a town in Pakistan by popular consent, the other being Abbott of Abbottabad.

Jacob's grave, with an arched gate decorated with blue tiles above it, can still be seen today in a graveyard to the right as you enter the town from the N. His former Residency is now home to the Deputy Commissioner. An ingenious clock, built by Jacob and incorporating lunar and solar calendars, is housed in the building, where it continues to work. The Victoria Tower, a whitewashed stone clocktower, stands nearby in the bazaar. The town itself is today a dusty, somewhat chaotic place with little to indicate the carefully ordered planning which went into its construction.

● **Accommodation & places to eat** With the hottest recorded temperatures in South Asia, even the most basic hotels in Jacobabad have a/c, although this is their only luxury feature. **D** *Palace*, Quaid-i-Azam Rd, T 3395, a/c and cheaper non a/c rooms, restaurant; **D** *Mehran*, basic a/c and non a/c rooms.

● **Useful addresses Deputy Commissioner**: T 2622.

● **Transport Train** Railway enquiries, T 2711. Services as per Sibi, arriving 3¼ hrs earlier/later. Also to **Nawabshah Junction**: *Bedil Exp*, 1445, 6½ hrs. **Karachi**: *Khushhal Khan Khattak Exp*, 1930, 15½ hrs. **Road Bus**: regular services to Quetta, Sibi, Shikarpur and Sukkur.

From Jacobabad it is a further 43 km on to **Shikarpur**, a historically important trading town with an interesting covered bazaar. Founded as a municipal town in 1617, its trading links with Afghanistan and Central Asia go back much further. Traders from Shikarpur travelled very extensively and, before being driven out following the revolution in 1949, were influential in Sinkiang, the westernmost province of China. The road continues through Lakhi to **Sukkur** (42 km), see page 153.

QUETTA TO CHAMAN

The route from Quetta to the Afghanistan border post at Chaman is a restricted one officially requiring permits. Under the proposed changes to restrictions on travel in Baluchistan (see Baluchistan Introduction), it is likely to remain so. There is a large number of Afghan refugees along the border, over whom Pakistani officials have little or no control. Widespread trafficking of weapons and drugs, coupled with periodic feuding between the various tribal groups, do make for a potentially dangerous situation, although the area is on the whole relatively peaceful. In 1995 a number of tourists reported making the trip unofficially and encountering no problems. The best way to visit is with a local guide who is known in the area. An overnight stay is not recommended.

There are regular buses from the Quetta (3 hrs). The train departs daily at 0830, taking 4-5 hrs, and returns at 1430. The railway line, an extension of the Sukkur-Quetta line, follows a dramatic and scenic route. From Bostan it heads NE, climbing gradually as it skirts the northern slopes of **Takatu Mountain**, at one point doing a complete loop to pass over itself. To reach Chaman itself, it passes through a 4 km tunnel, the longest in Asia, under the Khojak Pass. Dug from both ends, the British engineer reputedly attempted suicide when it failed to meet in the middle. It was eventually completed in 1892.

From Quetta the road runs NE, past the turning for the airport and, further on, **Baleli Checkpost**, to **Kuch Lak** (25 km). Continue past the turning right in the bazaar for Ziarat and Muslimbagh. The road winds its way through a spectacular landscape of low mud hills of red and ochre, eroded into outlandish shapes, and past orchards and water channels emerging from underground *karez*.

At **Yaro** a road forks off to the right, towards **Pishin**. The Pishin valley is one of the major areas of karez irrigation and is surrounded by over 5,000 ha of vineyards and orchards, as well as being famous for its duck shooting. During the British period, Pishin was a vitally important cantonment area and the road to the town crosses the abandoned WW2 runway. The town itself has little of interest and is off-limits to foreigners.

The main road passes two large Afghan refugee camps at **Saranan** and **Jungle Piralizai** and crosses the **Lora River**, which flows into the Hamun-i-Lora, to the N of the Taftan road, near Dalbandin. **Qila Abdullah** (78 km) is the last settlement before the pass. The railway enters the tunnel under the **Khojak Pass** shortly after **Shelabagh** station. There is a checkpost here. The road climbs up through bare rocky hills to the top of the pass, which at 2,273m gives excellent views on a clear day across the plains towards **Kandahar**. The hills were once wooded with pistachio trees, but they were cut down during the building of the railway. There is a *Rest House* at the top of the pass, but you are unlikely to get permission to stay here. The road winds its way down to Chaman (113 km), situated at the foot of the pass.

Chaman is a small chaotic bazaar with the atmosphere of a 'wild west' town, Pathan style. The town was established by the British in 1889, replacing Old Chaman, 11 km to the S, which lost its importance with the building of the railway line.

From Chaman it is a further 105 km to Kandahar. In 1995 the situation in Afghanistan remained highly uncertain, and only journalists and aid workers were below allowed entry. Without proper contacts and escorts, visiting Afghanistan remains extremely dangerous.

QUETTA TO IRAN

The route to Taftan on the Iranian border runs through a forbidding, inhospitable and often spectacular landscape, combining wide expanses of desert and semi-desert with barren mountains exposing twisted, folded strata of igneous rock. In summer it is uncomfortably hot, with temperatures reaching well into the forties, and all year round there are frequent dust storms. The route passes through Chagai District in the NW of Baluchistan close to the border with Afghanistan.

Buses and flying coaches make the journey in 13-14 hrs, travelling overnight to arrive at the border in the morning. It is possible to make the journey in daylight by taking local buses, but this is likely to involve an overnight stop along the way. Dalbandin, though the most logical place to stop being roughly half way, has very poor accommodation and is best avoided if possible. Toyota pick-ups operate fairly regular passenger services between the main towns, leaving when full. They are more expensive than the buses, but significantly faster, particularly on the unmetalled sections. The train is more comfortable than the long distance buses but much slower; the quoted time is 24½ hrs to Taftan and a further 7½ hrs through the border and on to Zahedan, although long delays are common.

As far as Nushki the single lane highway is metalled and in reasonably good condition, sections of it having been recently resurfaced and widened. From Nushki to Dalbandin it is for the most part intact, though in poorer condition. Beyond Dalbandin it deteriorates with long sections of rough unmetalled track or heavily potholed tarmac until Nokundi, from where there is a good fast 2-lane highway up to Taftan. This last section is what has so far been completed of a new highway which will one day cover the whole route from Quetta to the border. Inside Iran, road conditions are excellent.

Follow the route S out of Quetta, as for the RCD highway to Karachi. At the bottom of the Lak Pass, bear right at the fork (31 km). The road winds its way through low hills and stony plains with isolated patches of cultivation and small settlements, passing checkposts of the Chagai Force at **Sheikh Wasil** and **Gulandur Post**, the latter with a traditional mud fort on the hillside overlooking the road. Soon after emerging onto a wide desert plain you arrive at Nushki (114 km). Fork right off the main road to reach the town.

Nushki, the headquarters of Chagai District, is a small bazaar town, its population considerably swelled by Afghan refugees. The present town was built by the British in 1899, after they had taken over the administration of the area from the Khan of Kalat. There is a *Resthouse* offering basic facilities, Pakistani-style restaurants in the bazaar and a small bus

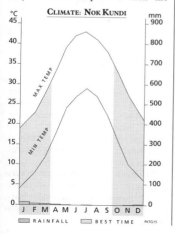

CLIMATE: NOK KUNDI

RAINFALL — BEST TIME   PKTG15

station with local buses to Quetta and Dalbandin.

20 km beyond Nushki a rough track bears off SW, leading eventually to **Kharan**, site of the impressive **Karez Fort**. The fort, just outside the main town, was one of 11 built by Sardar Azad Khan in the 18th century. It is the largest and best preserved, covering over 300 sq metres with thick mud brick walls, a 3-storey building and the remains of four wells.

Originally part of Persia, Kharan emerged as a separate Princely State, home to the **Nousherwani** tribe, in the 18th century. It came under the loose control of Kalat State for a time before turning its allegiance to Afghanistan. **Yacoob Shah**, the Sardar during the period of British expansion in Baluchistan, resisted British control but was killed by his uncle **Nadir Shah** who then accepted a quasi-independent status as a protectorate in 1911. After Independence it maintained its internal autonomy within Pakistan until 1952, when its militia was disbanded and ruler stripped of his power. In 1953 it was made into a separate district. Covering over 36,000 sq km, it is for the most part desert, although there are considerable areas of cultivated land along the Baddo and Mashkel rivers.

Kharan is extremely remote, even by Baluchistan's standards and there are no facilities. To visit it is necessary to organize your own transport, either in Quetta or Nushki. A 4WD and local guide is recommended. With an early start, it is feasible as a day trip from Nushki. **NB** A permit may be necessary. You should register your travel plans with the Commissioner in Nushki or Kharan and check that the road is passable.

The main route to Iran continues across wide open plains and rocky mountains to **Padag** (213 km). Although no more than a cluster of buildings, there is a small, well-kept *Resthouse* here and good water supply. Further W,

roughly half way between Padag and Dalbandin, the shallow seasonal lake of **Hamun-i-Lora** is visible to the N, covering over 600 sq km. For much of the year, it is a dry saline expanse, acquiring a thin sheet of water during the winter months. Green onyx is mined in the vicinity.

Dalbandin (297 km) is the largest town on the route, and since early times was an important staging post on the Seistan Trading Route, though today there is nothing of interest. The bazaar is strung out along the main road, consisting mostly of mechanics' workshops. It has a small airport, but despite this, and its position roughly halfway between Quetta and the border, only the most basic of **accommodation** is available. There is the **F** *Pakistan* and a couple of others; all are very dirty and an overnight stop here is worth avoiding if possible. However a CTC resthouse was under construction in 1995. 30 km N of the town there is a large Afghan refugee camp known as Gardi Jungle.

● **Transport Air** PIA booking office, Alhaman Hotel, T 25519, Airport T 2860, 2 flights weekly to Karachi via Turbat: Tues 1510, Sun 1425, and to Quetta: Tues 1145, Sun 1100. **Road** Toyota pickups and Hiace minivans run to Taftan and Quetta, leaving from the main bazaar when full. Long distance buses in both directions pass through at night, they are best caught at the police checkpost at the edge of town where they are guaranteed to stop, though there is no guarantee of a seat.

Beyond Dalbandin the road is for the most part a rough track running alongside the new highway which is presently under construction. Stony desert stretches for miles on either side, with the volcanic Chagai Hills to the N, barely visible in the distance.

Yakmach (353 km) is a small oasis town with greenery and palm trees relieving the surrounding drab grey and a small *Resthouse* offering reasonable rooms.

Nok Kundi (464 km) is the next town. There is a large cantonment area and a *Resthouse*. A track leads S from here crossing the edges of the Hamun-i-Mashkel, another huge expanse of salt flats over 80 km long and between 12-35 km wide, before eventually arriving at Panjgur in Makran.

From Nok Kundi it is a further 113 km on a good 2-lane metalled road to the Iranian border at Taftan, a total of 606 km from Quetta. Shortly before Taftan, a track leads N to Saindak, now the site of a major mining project which aims to exploit the deposits of copper and lead that are found here.

Taftan is everything one would expect of a remote border post. It is a dusty, ramshackle town with a forlorn, half-built atmosphere. There are a few shops offering a curious range of smuggled goods ranging from plastic kitchenware to tinned food, a couple of very basic Pakistani-style restaurants and the customs and immigration buildings. Money changers wander around armed with plastic carrier bags full of Rials and small pocket calculators.

The border opens from 1000-1300 and 1600-1800. Leave plenty of time for Customs and Immigration formalities which can be very lengthy, especially for private vehicles which are often thoroughly searched, particularly when coming from Pakistan.

There are as yet no hotels, although the CTC is in the process of building one. If you get stuck here, accommodation can be arranged in the Customs House and private vehicles can also park in the compound there.

From Taftan it is a further 84 km on to **Zahedan**, the first major town inside Iran. Regular public transport makes the journey in 1½ hrs, on a road that puts Pakistan's highways to shame. Two trains weekly run from Zahedan to Quetta: *Taftan Express*, Mon 0730, 29½ hrs; *Q486*, Fri 0730, 30½ hrs.

For more information on travel to and from Iran, see the Information for visitors section in the Introduction.

QUETTA TO KARACHI

The RCD Highway (standing for Regional Cooperation for Development) was built as part of a programme initiated in the 1960s to link Turkey, Iran and Pakistan by road. The section between Quetta and Karachi was the only part within Pakistan to be completed. Although when it first opened it provided a good fast route between the two cities, heavy use and extremes of climate, have taken their toll. Today it is being upgraded, with long sections of a new 2-lane highway under construction. In the meantime, although easily passable in a normal car, there are long stretches along rough dirt tracks where work is in progress. Elsewhere, the old single-lane road is in places heavily potholed. The journey can be completed within a day; buses usually take 13-14 hrs. Alternatively, reasonable accommodation is readily available at Khuzdar.

Head S out of Quetta on Suriab Rd, and bear right after 9 km (left to Sibi). The road climbs gradually, past the turning on the right to Hazerganji National Park (13 km), up to the Lak Pass, overlooked by a small mud fort and behind it a modern communications post. From here it descends steeply with good views over the wide plain below. At the bottom the road to Taftan and the Iranian border forks off to the right. The RCD highway continues straight, crossing the railway line for Taftan and passing through orchards and fields to arrive at Mastung (50 km).

Mastung

The small town of Mastung, set in fertile orchards and fields of wheat, is the headquarters of Mastung district. Despite the fertile environment, these are tribal areas, and though generally peaceful, the Deputy Commissioner's house, enclosed by large walls and fortress-like bastions, gives an indication of the potential for trouble. Most of the houses are of mud and straw; there is no hotel and little of interest. The Deputy Commissioner (T 2675) can arrange for accommodation in the government rest house if necessary, although foreigners are not encouraged to stay.

The main road continues S over a wide open plain, through the Kad Khucha section of Mustang division. The scattered settlement of **Manguchar** (105 km) in Kalat division is surrounded by orchards of apples, apricots, pomegranates and almonds. There is a petrol pump, basic restaurants/tea stalls and small shops. It is a further 40 km on to Kalat.

Kalat

Little is known about the early history of Kalat, which is thought to have been inhabited from a very early stage. Known also as Kalat-i-Sewa, after the Hindu **Sewa Dynasty** which is said to have ruled here for a time, it was eventually taken over by Baluch tribes and the State of Kalat established. During the 18th century, Kalat grew to become the largest and most powerful state of

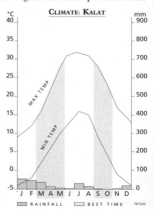

Baluchistan, covering 71,593 sq miles and including the divisions of Sarawan, Kachhi, Jhalawan, Kharan and Makran. The town of Kalat was the seat of power of the influential Khan of Kalat, and under the powerful **Ahmadzais** became an important trading centre on the route between Afghanistan and India. With the arrival of the British and the building of the railway line to Quetta, its importance as a trading centre declined.

The old town of Kalat was almost completely destroyed in the earthquake of 1935 and today there is little to indicate its historic importance. The ruins of the fort and its walls, which enclosed the old town, can still be seen spread out over a low ridge of the Shah-i-Mardan hill. Dominating the town was the citadel or *Miri* of the Khan of Kalat, an impressive 5-storey structure. A Hindu temple to Kali, perhaps a remnant of Sewa rule, stood within the walls which consisted of 10 bastions and 3 gates.

The present town is situated just N of the ridge, on level ground. It is to the E of the main road, across a seasonal stream. Most of the buildings are of traditional mud and straw construction. The new palace of the present Khan of Kalat is situated behind the bus stand. Just S of the town, perched on a small hill to the W of the main road, there is the mosque and shrine of the 11th century Shia saint, **Sheikh Abdul Qadir Gilani**.

● **Accommodation** There is one very basic hotel in the main bazaar, the **F** *Mughal*, or a couple of resthouses, bookable through the Deputy Commissioner (T 417).

● **Places to eat** There are several basic local style restaurants in the bazaar.

From Kalat the road climbs to a low pass and then descends through hills to a wide plateau. In 1995 the old single lane road as far as Khuzdar was upgraded to 2 lanes; where the route still follows the old road, it is in poor condition. Elsewhere, a temporary unmetalled but for the most part good quality track crosses

back and forth over the new highway, which in places is being completely rebuilt. At **Surab**, 70 km from Kalat, a road branches off to the W, leading to Panjgur (320 km) and on to Turbat (598 km), a long arduous journey on rough tracks. The main town of Surab is a short distance down this road. There is a checkpost at the junction, tea shops and fuel. The main route S continues across wide plains with mountains rising up on either side. The rugged and barren landscape is interspersed by small settlements and patches of cultivated land. The road crosses a low pass before arriving at the town of Khuzdar, 163 km from Kalat.

Khuzdar

The town of Khuzdar, set in a wide plain, is the largest settlement on the RCD Highway. A road turns off to the E to the main town. Although it is of little interest, it makes a convenient stopping point being roughly half way between Quetta and Karachi, and has reasonable accommodation. The large cantonment area spreads out to the S, on the other side of the river.

● **Accommodation & places to eat D** *PTDC Motel*, RCD Highway, T 3788, just N of the turning to the main town, clean rooms with fan, att bath, hot and cold water, but overpriced, restaurant; **F** *Prince*, Masjid Rd, T 2516, cheaper and more basic, restaurant; opp is the similar **F** *Holiday*, T 3551, also with restaurant; **F** *Rizwan*, Azadi Chowk, T 3457, clean rooms with fan and att bath, good value, restaurant.

● **Useful addresses DC's Office**: Chakar Khan Rd, T 2633. **PIA Booking Office**: Khoral Rd, T 2225.

● **Transport Air** Weekly flights to Moenjo-daro (Mon) and Sukkur (Fri), and twice weekly to Turbat (Tues, Sat). **Road Bus**: the main bus stand is at Azadi Chowk. There are long distance coaches to Karachi (11-12 hrs, Rs 100), Quetta (8 hrs, Rs 70), Shahdadkot (9 hrs, Rs 90), Panjgur (16 hrs, Rs 170) and Turbat (28 hrs, Rs 200). Also regular minibuses to Kalat, Quetta and Bela. The road E to Shahdadkot in Sind via Karkh, currently unmetalled and very rough, is being surfaced and upgraded.

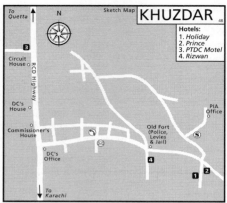

houses still being of mud and straw construction, with wooden beams and simple lattice work. Distinctive open sided chimneys also serve to catch the daytime breezes, ventilating the houses during summer. This was the capital of the old state of Las Bela which was Buddhist during the 7th century, before the arrival of Rai Chach in 631 AD, and later the Arab general Mohammad Bin Qasim. It then existed as a semi-independent division of Kalat, rebelling against it in the 19th century. After independence, Kalat State was divided up and Las Bela became a separate district. The **Lassi**, with their own language of the same name, form the main tribal group around Las Bela. They are thought to have originated from Sind and been converted from Hinduism. As amongst the Makranis, Lassi women are allowed a share in inheritance.

The main road S from Khuzdar passes through terrain which alternates between wide expanses of plateau surrounded by mountains, with occasional patches of cultivated land, and the rough, barren hills of the **Pab Range**. As far as the scattered settlement of Wad (59 km), the road is a good quality 2-lane highway; further S it reverts to a single lane. Urnach, a little further on, consists of a few houses, with tea shops and fuel. At Sunaro, set in an open plain, there are extensive chrome mines. The next settlement is Kohan, consisting only of a few houses and a checkpost. From here the road follows the course of the **Porali River**, with scattered villages and isolated clumps of date palms along its banks, before eventually emerging onto open plains. Shortly before Las Bela, a road, metalled for a short distance, branches off W towards Bedi Dat and Turbat in Makran. The main road bypasses Las Bela (169 km from Wad), which is reached by a left turn soon after the Turbat turning.

Las Bela

The large village of Las Bela is set in fertile surroundings, with plentiful date palms and trees giving the area a tropical feel. The village itself retains its traditional Baluchi character, most of the

Places of interest

The small main bazaar, consisting of a covered street with small wooden shops, is colourful and interesting; good quality embroidered blouses and coarse woven rugs and pannier bags can be found here.

Sandeman's Grave Halfway between the bus station and the bazaar, a track leads off to the E, across a tributary of the nearby Porali River, to the garden and grave of Colonel Sir Robert Sandeman, who died of an illness here in 1892, while on tour as the Chief Commissioner of Baluchistan. The dome over the tomb was built by the *Jam* or ruler, Jamali Khan, who became a close friend of Robert Sandeman, and the shady gardens which he laid out are still well maintained and popular as a picnic spot.

Mausoleum of Gen Mohammad Haroon Just to the N of the village is a domed mausoleum, thought to be that of an Arab General, Mohammad Haroon. The mausoleum is set in a small enclosure and tended by a chowkidar. Inside are five graves, two of them placed together.

Jami Masjid This mosque, built by the Jam Mir Khan in 1866, was unfortunately recently damaged by flooding. Repairs were in progress in 1995. The inside of the main dome still has beautiful intricate glazed tiled work.

Gondrani Caves Approximately 15 km N of Bela, in a narrow side ravine off the main Porali River, there are numerous caves carved into the sheer rock face, thought to date from the Buddhist period. A local legend relates how during the time of Solomon, a king reigned here, whose daughter, Buddul Jumaul, was so beautiful that she attracted the attentions of demons who killed seven of her suitors, all brothers, and tried to carry her off. Saif-ul-Muluk, son of the king of Egypt, arrived there about this time, fell in love with the princess, killed the demons and took her hand in marriage as a reward. The couple then brought peace and security to the area during their reign, and won the loyalty and respect of the people. The story provides an interesting comparison with the legend of Saiful Muluk lake in the Kaghan valley.

Local information
● **Accommodation**
The *Government Rest House* is a classic piece of Colonial architecture set in a pleasant garden and manages to retain much of its atmosphere, reasonable rooms with attached bath and fan, it is necessary to book in advance – contact the Assistant Commissioner, T (002) 3366, a turning W off the main street, opp the bus stand, leads up to the Rest House.

● **Places to eat**
There are basic but reasonable local style restaurants in the bazaar.

● **Transport**
Road The bus stand is to the S of the main village on the road leading off from the RCD Highway. Local buses and minivans operate services N to Khuzdar and S to Uthal. There is also the through traffic from Quetta and Karachi, consisting of both minibuses and large buses/coaches. However the minibuses in particular are often already full. A few jeeps and pick-ups are available for hire from the bazaar.

From Bela the main road continues S through rich fertile land which gives way to increasingly arid plains supporting only low scrub and occasional trees. The road is being repaired and upgraded for most of the way up to Uthal (60 km), with long sections on unsurfaced track or else fairly poor quality single lane road.

Uthal is the headquarters of Las Bela district. There is nothing of interest in the town, which is spread out along the road, although the District Commissioner (T 308, F 252) is based here. The only accommodation is in the Government Rest House.

From Uthal it is a further 115 km to Karachi. After about 20 km, the road passes a turning W, an alternative but little used route to Bela, and then passes within a couple of km of **Siranda Lake**. Further on, a crossroads has turnings W to the dam on the lake and E to the village of Bagh. At the small village of Winder there is a bazaar with tea shops and simple restaurants. Some 7 km before arriving in Hub, there is a turning W to Gaddani Beach (see under Karachi), signposted 'Gaddani Customs House'.

Hub Chowki is a bustling industrial town which has risen to prominence with the building of the Pakistan's largest oil-fired power station here. There are no hotels, although the Government Rest House is comfortable, a/c rooms, bookable through the Deputy Commissioner, T 251. There are several basic but reasonable restaurants in the bazaar.

Just S of the town the road crosses the Hub River which marks the border between Sind and Baluchistan. There is a checkpost here. The last section of the route passes through an increasingly industrialized landscape, before entering Karachi's sprawling suburbs.

THE MAKRAN

History

Despite its forbidding and inhospitable environment, the Makran has always held a historically strategic position as the most direct route between the Iranian Plateau and the plains of the Indus, as well as being strongly influenced by maritime trade and conquest along its coast. The Greeks were the first recorded visitors to the Makran, with the marches of **Cyrus** and **Semiramis** across its arid wastes pre-dating that of Alexander's in 325 BC. The Greeks however never exerted more than a nominal influence over the region, suffering heavily in its harsh desert wastes, as so vividly described by the ancient historian Arrian. **Seleucus Nicator**, Alexander's successor, having marched through Makran and crossed the Indus in 305 BC, was defeated by Chandra Gupta and the region came under the loose control of the Mauryan Empire. The *Shahnama*, written by **Firdousi**, tells of the battles between the Turanian and Iranian kings, and of the conquest of Makran by Ardashir, founder of the Sassanian Dynasty. His grandson, **Khusrau I** is said to have carried out major improvements in agriculture, extending irrigation and establishing orchards. The two karezes in Turbat, known as Kausi and Khusrawi, are probably named after him. Later, **Rai Chach** of Sind extended his influence into Makran for a time.

In the 7th century, the **Arabs** began to exert their influence, arriving both by land and sea, extending maritime trade along the coast of the Arabian Sea and out into the Indian Ocean. Their influence can be seen in the features of the people of Makran, while the distinct communities of African negroes still found in the Makran are thought to have arrived with the Arabs as slaves around this time. To the Arabs, as for the Greeks before them, the Makran was a fearful, inhospitable

place. The first Arab general, sent there in 634 AD, complained of a people so hostile and a country so barren that "If thou hadst a less numerous army there, it would be annihilated and could do nothing; and if thy army is considerable, it will perish of hunger because there are no victuals". Nevertheless, the Arabs were able to establish themselves in the region. **Mohammad bin Qasim**, the famous Arab general passed through on his way to conquer Sind early in the 8th century, and although there is little in the way of historical evidence, the Arabs appeared to remain loosely in control of the Makran up until the 10th century.

There follows a long period of around 7 centuries during which the region appears to have been subject to outside control only for short periods, and even then the succession of foreign dynasties which claimed suzerainty generally did so only on the basis of limited tributes being paid by the indigenous rulers of Makran, who in their turn preserved their effective autonomy. These foreign dynasties included the Deilamis and Seljuks, the Ghaznavids, Ghorids and Mongols. The indigenous rulers, as recorded in local traditions, included the Hots, Rinds, Maliks, Buledais and Gichkis. Early in the 16th century the **Portuguese** began to appear along the coast of Makran as they extended their maritime trade to include India. They never penetrated inland and appear to have been unable to establish anything more than heavily defended military bases at various points. In 1581 they destroyed Gwadar and Pasni, burning them to the ground.

During the 18th century, Makran became linked with the state of Kalat which, under the rule of **Nasir Khan I**, grew to include much of Baluchistan. Half the revenue of Makran was passed over to Kalat, with the other half being divided between the Gichki rulers of the

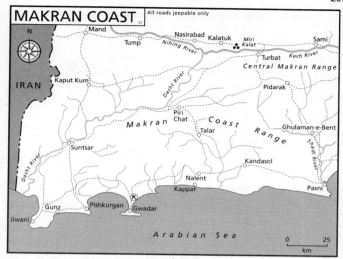

MAKRAN COAST — All roads jeepable only

region. The **Gichkis** however continually agitated against Kalat, briefly regaining full independence during the rule of Mahmud Khan, Nasir Khan's son. Mehrab Khan, the next Khan of Kalat, reasserted control, appointing his own representatives, or *naibs*, to the region. The most influential of these was **Fakir Mohammad**, who remained in place for more than 40 years, marrying a Gichki and establishing effective control over the whole area. Nevertheless, that control was limited to the collection of revenue, with the local chiefs having unlimited power within their own spheres. Even Fakir Mohammad in time became largely independent of Kalat, which had problems of its own much closer to home.

The first British contact with the Makran came during the 19th century. An expedition was sent there in 1838, at the time of the First Afghan War, and full involvement came with the building of the Indo-European telegraph line which passed through Makran. On its completion, Major Goldsmid was posted to Gwadar as Assistant Political Agent in 1863. The British soon became alarmed at the "discovery that the Persians had been showing much activity in these regions ... steadily advancing eastwards". In 1869 Ibrahim Khan, the Persian governor of Bampur, siezed Pishin (in Makran), prompting the British to undertake to establish a firm boundary between Persian and British Baluchistan, eventually agreed in 1872. Makran, like all the largely autonomous borders in the NW of the British Empire, was a source of continuous trouble. Local feuds flared up regularly, and there were frequent attacks on the appointed representatives of the Khan of Kalat, and on the precious Indo-European telegraph line. These in turn prompted frequent British expeditions to restore order, sometimes by negotiation, at other times by force.

Land and life

Geography

Sir Thomas Holditch, Surveyor General of India at the turn of the century, vividly described Makran's "brazen coast washed by a molten sea" and inland the "gigantic cap-crowned pillars and pedestals balanced in a fantastic array about the mountain slopes ... with successive strata so well defined that they possess all the appearance of massive masonry construction ... standing stiff, jagged, naked and uncompromising".

The landscape of Makran is certainly amongst the most outlandish and spectacular in Baluchistan, prompting comparisons with a moonscape, although one might doubt that the moon could possess such bizarre scenery. The region is predominantly mountainous with three parallel ranges running E-W. The southernmost is the **Makran Coastal Range**, a line of low hills rising no higher than 65m. Next is the **Central Makran Range** which reaches heights of over 1,300m, and to the N of this is the **Siahan Range** separating Makran from Kharan.

The coast itself is deeply indented and marked by frequent table-topped promontories and peninsulas of white clay cliffs capped with coarse limestone, as at Gwadar, Pasni and Omara. The coastal belt is a mixture of sand and stony desert with occasional oases supporting the small fishing villages. It is within this coastal belt that the most spectacular scenery of eroded pillars and pedestals occurs. Between the Coastal and Central ranges is the narrow, fertile **Kech valley**, famous as the main growing area of Makran's 300 varieties of dates. North of this, between the Central and Siahan ranges, is the wider but less fertile Rakhshan valley, with Panjgur as the main centre.

All the rivers in Makran are seasonal, being reduced to dry beds with occasional pools during dry weather, and filling rapidly to form fast flowing torrents after rain. The **Dasht River**, formed by the union of the Nihing and Kech rivers, is the largest in the region, draining into Gwatar Bay, just W of Jiwani, close to the Iranian border. The **Kech River**, with its tributaries the Gish and Kil, steadily widens as it flows W through the Kech valley, reaching over 2 km in width at Turbat. The

Shadi River rises close to Jamgwang, S of Turbat, and flows S, E and then S again, fed by various hill torrents and tributaries along the way, to drain into the sea just N of Pasni. Further E the **Basol** winds a tortuous course through the high clay ridges of the Coastal Range before draining into the sea W of Omara. The **Hingol River** is the largest in Baluchistan, although it is not strictly speaking in Makran, flowing for the most part through Jhalawan District and for a short stretch through Las Bela. Its major tributaries are the Mashkai, Nal, Arra and Mar.

Fishing The coastal waters of the Arabian Sea are rich in fish, including tuna, snapper, groakers, grunters, sardines, skate and shark, as well as lobster and shrimp.

Culture

People

Although frequently referred to as Makranis, the people of Makran are essentially Baluch. While they are divided into distinct groups and differentiated according to social status, the absence of a tribal system based on organized political or ethnic units is unique in Baluchistan.

The dominant classes, traditionally wealthy landowners, include the *Gichkis*, *Nausherwanis*, *Mirwaris* and *Bisanjaus*. These family groups maintained their superiority by only marrying amongst themselves. The middle classes, of smaller landowners, consist of a large number of family groups, the more important of which are the *Rinds*, *Rais*, *Hots*, *Kalmatis*, *Kauhdais*, *Shehzada* and *Jadgals* or Jats (meaning cultivators). The lower classes consist of occupational groups and are considered to be the aboriginals of Makran. The *Meds* are fishermen and appear to have much in common with the *Ichthyophagoi* (fish eaters) described by Arrian, although interestingly their patron saint is **Sakhi Tangav**, whose tomb is at Dadhar in Kachhi, suggesting that they originated from that area. The *Koras*, who are sailors, are a branch of the Med. The *Dar-*

zadas are agricultural labourers and although found scattered all over the Makran, they are concentrated around the Kech valley and Panjgur where they are known as *Nakibs*. The *Loris* are traditionally artisans – blacksmiths, carpenters, goldsmiths etc – or else musicians and story-tellers. Many of them are nomadic.

Women occupy a unique position in Makrani society as compared with the rest of Baluchistan. On marriage, as elsewhere, a bride-price is paid by the bridegroom and his family. However, instead of a cash payment to the bride's father, this traditionally consists of land, ornaments and servile dependents, all of which become the personal property of the bride. Women are also entitled to inherit a portion of their parents' property. Thus women are often the wealthy partner in a marriage, with the man being in effect dependent on his wife's wealth. The relatively strong status of women is reflected also in the tradition of attributing the qualities of a child to the mother.

Religion

A sect, known as the **Zikri**, are still to be found in the Makran, particularly around Turbat, where they have established a position of strength in the business community. The Zikri sect is associated to the Mahdevi movement which was started in the 15th century by **Sayid Mohammad Joneri**, who proclaimed himself a *Mahdi* ('one who is rightly guided'). One of his followers, **Mullah Mohammad** is thought to have brought the faith to Makran, perhaps arriving with the Buledais tribe from Helmand. Although they consider themselves to be Muslims, the Zikri are frowned upon by orthodox Islam and there have been attempts by various parties in Baluchistan to have them declared non-Muslims and classified as a religious minority. The all important *Hajj* to Mecca is replaced by an annual pilgrimage to **Koh-i-Murad** ('hill of fulfilment'), near Turbat, where some believe the Mahdi is buried. The term Zikri is derived from the Arabic *Dhikr* or *Zikr*, literally meaning 'remembrance' and more loosely translated as 'litany', in reference to the importance attached to the reciting of the name of God amongst the Zikris. This practice of Zikr replaces the prayers of orthodox Islam.

Local animistic and elemental beliefs, which existed before the advent of Islam, still exert a strong influence, particularly amongst the Meds. Most diseases are considered to be the result of a person being possessed by a spirit or *Gwat*. Patients are first taken to the local *Mat*, somewhat akin to a Shaman, who induces a trance in the patient and speaks through them to the Gwat. Conditions are then agreed for the Gwat to leave the afflicted person, usually involving the holding of a *Leb*, or meeting, at which there is further chanting and induced trances until the Gwat is appeased.

Elsewhere, orthodox Islam has been intermingled with various local beliefs. The most striking example of this can be found in the practice of *shepar-ja*, a type of worship or religious rite. It is confined to people of slave extraction, the patron saint, **Sheikh Farid Shakar** himself having been a slave. The ceremonies, involving frenzied chanting and dancing to the rhythm of drums, have been associated with the fetish worship of Africa, although the songs and chanting are in Urdu and Sindhi.

Language

The main language is Makrani which is basically a dialect of Baluchi with strong underlying Persian influences. Other languages/dialects are Jadgali, a dialect of Sindhi which is very close to the Lassi spoken around Bela, and Lori-Chini which is not so much a language as an invented jargon involving inverted words of Baluchi, Urdu, Sindhi and Punjabi traditionally spoken by the Loris before strangers.

VISITING THE MAKRAN

Permits

In 1995 it was still necessary to obtain a No Objection Certificate to visit the Makran. However, under proposed changes to the restrictions placed on foreigners' travel in Baluchistan, the area would be opened up. Authorities in the Provincial Government were predicting that the restrictions would be lifted "within a year". However, some observers point out that there is talk of opening up the region every year. The political storm in 1995 over allegations that the government had agreed to lease land in Gwadar to the Sultan of Oman, as well as the region's strategic significance close to the Straits of Hormouz and US interest in setting up a surveillance base there, make the area somewhat sensitive. On the other hand, there is also strong pressure, not least from the local population, to see the area opened up. Check with the Home Department of the Provincial Government in Quetta regarding the current situation.

Transport

Air There are airports at Turbat, Jiwani, Qwadar, Pasni and Omara, with regular flights linking these centres to Karachi and Quetta.

Road Distances in the Makran are enormous and the road system all but non-existent. The network of rough jeep tracks are often made impassable by the sudden bursts of heavy rainfall characteristic of the region. A 4WD is strongly recommended, and a guide who is familiar with the area. Some specialist tour operators now run jeep safaris in the Makran and are usually able to offer tailor-made packages; see under Travel Agents in Karachi, Lahore or Islamabad.

The main route from Quetta is on the RCD Highway S as far as Surab (213 km) where it branches SW on a rough track which joins the Rakhshan River valley to eventually arrive at Panjgur (532 km). From here a track leads S again to cut through the Central Makran Range and then follows the Kech River W to reach Turbat (810 km). An alternative, less used route is via Khuzdar and then SW along the Mashkai River to Bedi Dat, on to Hoshab, and then along the Kech River to Turbat.

From Karachi, the main route is N to Bela on the RCD Highway and then W via Bedi Dat and Hoshab. The coastal route branches W earlier, skirting Siranda Lake and Miani Hor, and then bears N along the Hingol River for a while before swinging SW to Omara and continuing W, touching the coast again at Pasni and Gwadar. This latter route is however little used, being extremely difficult and often impassable, particularly between Omara and the RCD Highway.

Bus: long distance buses operate regularly from Quetta to Turbat (min 30 hrs), and from Khuzdar to Panjgur and Turbat. There are regular services from Karachi to Turbat (min 26 hrs), and Pasni and Gwadar, as well as to Panjgur. Services on the coastal route are erratic. **NB** Permits are at present required for all overland routes.

Turbat

Turbat is the Divisional Headquarters for the Makran and has grown considerably in recent years to become an important date processing centre, although the development of industry and enterprise is restricted by the absence of infrastructure, particularly roads, linking it with the rest of the country. The town, of little interest in itself, consists of a dusty bazaar and main street, with most of the new development spread out over a wide area to the S.

● **Accommodation** D *Gul Rang*, Main Rd, T 3002, F 3004, a/c, TV, best hotel in town, good restaurant; E *Mulla Jan*, Main Rd, T 2763, pleasant garden, restaurant; F *Muree*, Main Bazaar, T 2213, basic but relatively clean, restaurant.

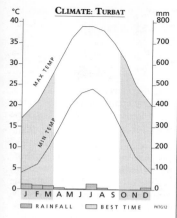

CLIMATE: TURBAT

RAINFALL   BEST TIME   PKTG12

● **Places to eat** The restaurant in the Gul Rang serves good food. *Mulla Jan's* restaurant is also reasonable. The *Muree* hotel has a basic Pakistani style restaurant and there are several other similar restaurants in Main Bazaar and Main Rd.

● **Useful addresses Deputy Commissioner's Office:** T 3202. **Commissioner's Office:** T 3244. **PIA Booking Office:** T 2322 (turn right out of Gul Rang hotel, follow the road round to the left, past a left turn – the road to the airport – and the building is clearly visible on the left hand side). **Police:** T 2222.

● **Transport Air** PIA operates flights to Quetta (Tues, Fri, Sun), Karachi (up to 4 daily), Gwadar (Tues, Thur, Fri), Pasni (Tues, Wed, Thur and Sat), Jiwani (Mon), Omara (Sat), Dalbandin (Tues, Sun), Khuzdar (Tues, Sat) and Panjgur (Mon, Tues, Wed, Fri, Sat). **Bus:** there are long-distance buses to Karachi (via Bela) and Quetta departing from Main Rd. Toyota pick-ups operate passenger services to Qwadar, Pasni and Jiwani on the coast departing from Main Bazaar.

Miri Kalat, situated around 10 km W of Turbat, on the N bank of the Kech River, is an important historical site with the ruins of a large fort perched on top of a high mound. Excavations have revealed evidence of continuous occupation from at least the Harappan period (2700 BC) until around 100 years ago. Little remains of the fort's walls and towers, although it is likely that the high mound on which the fort is situated conceals older walls, perhaps up to 10m high, buildings and artefacts chronicling over 4,500 years of habitation. An Italian team has been involved in excavating the site in recent years, although until there is a comprehensive plan for the conservation and management of the site, it is unlikely to be fully excavated.

To the north of Turbat are the **Zamran** (or Zamuran) hills, the western extension of the Central Makran Range, consisting of a series of very straight and regular parallel ridges forming a wide band running E-W. At the western end of the range there are numerous springs creating fertile patches supporting over 12 varieties of fruit in the intervening valleys.

Turbat to Iran

From Turbat a road runs W along the N bank of the Kech River towards the Iranian border. For the first 30 km the road is metalled, although broken in many places. Beyond, it is a rough track, although work is underway to surface it. The route passes through the oasis of **Kalatuk** where there are the ruins of a mud-brick fort similar to the one at Piderak. **Nasirabad** is the next settlement and further on, after crossing to the S bank, is **Tump**, where there are the remains of another fort of adobe construction. **Mand** (122 km) is the largest settlement on the route, and the last before the border, with a thriving bazaar in smuggled Iranian goods. A track branches S from Mand to Jiwani. It is a further 26 km on to Pishin, on the Iranian side of the border. **NB** The border crossing here is strictly closed to foreigners.

Turbat to Bela (NE-Panjgur)

The route E from Turbat is on a rough unmetalled track following the Kech River and passing through **Sami** and **Hoshab** (95 km). 10 km beyond Hoshab a track leads N across the Central Makran Range to **Panjgur**, a further 173 km. The route E continues on to **Bedi Dat**, 159 km from the Panjgur turning. From here, one track bears NE along the Mashkai River to join the RCD Highway at Surab, 70 km S of Kalat, while the second route cuts across the main strike of the hills to Bela, 182 km N of Karachi.

Turbat to Gwadar

It takes approximately 6 hrs to cover the 190 km from Turbat to Gwadar. The road is an unmetalled jeep track and 4WD is recommended. The track heads S from Turbat through an area of barren rocky hills formed of shales and clay with distinct strata of rock breaking through in vertical ridges. After approximately 20 km it forks; left to **Piderak**, a picturesque oasis with the remains of an old fort, and on to Pasni (115 km), and right to **Suntsar** (150 km), headquarters for the Dasht area, on the route between Mand and Jiwani. Take the right fork, crossing a wide plain and passing through some low hills before bearing E to skirt round the edge of a higher range of hills. After 55 km, just before **Piri Chat** (previously known as Kikki), bear left at a second fork (right to Suntsar). From here it is another 55 km to the coast road. The track bears S to cut through a low point in the hills, and runs parallel to the seasonal Belar River. At the small oasis of **Talar** there are a few buildings and basic facilities for food. The track continues over a wide expanse of open, sparsely vegetated plains with occasional oases and low barren hills before reaching the coast road. From here it is 60 km to Gwadar. The track passes the scattered settlement of **Nalent** and the coastal village of **Kappar** to the S, before crossing the seasonal Karwent River. Here the track passes through a spectacular landscape of low mud hills, heavily eroded into deeply fluted fingers and outlandish shapes. The track then passes a large flat-topped hill to the S, known as **Koh-i-Mehdi**. Soon after is Gwadar airport and from here, for the remaining 12 km to the centre of the town, the road is metalled.

Gwadar

The largest and amongst the oldest of the fishing villages along the coast, Gwadar is spread out along a narrow spit of land extending out to sea, with E and W bays on either side. At the southern tip of the spit, steep cliffs rise up to a wide peninsular platform, known as Koh-e-Bahtil, which fans out into a hammerhead some 10 km long and 2 km wide.

History

Nothing is known about its ancient history. As a maritime port, it was certainly heavily influenced by sea-trade, which from an early period extended throughout the Gulf, Arabian Sea and Indian Ocean region. During the 16th century, Portuguese ships arrived at Gwadar and established a fortified post on top of Koh-e-Bahtil overlooking the town, the remains of which can still be seen today. When they left in 1581, they destroyed the town.

During the 18th century, Makran came under the loose control of Kalat. Nasir Khan, the Khan of Kalat, granted Kalat's portion of Gwadar's revenue, and by implication suzerainty over the port, to **Sayid Sultan**, an estranged brother of the Sultan of Muscat who had taken refuge in Makran. Sayid Sultan subsequently overthrew his brother to gain the Sultanate of Muscat. The exact terms of the agreement between Sayid and Nasir are unclear; some maintain that Gwadar was in effect given as a gift in perpetuity while others argue that Sayid was supposed to relinquish control if ever he regained Muscat. In the event, Gwadar and a considerable area of the surrounding land remained a part of Muscat and later Oman, until it was bought back by the Pakistani Government in 1957. Many of the people retain joint citizenship of Oman and Pakistan, and there are large numbers of Pakistanis from Gwadar working in Oman.

Economic Development

Fishing forms the main source of income, with the waters of the Arabian Sea yealding excellent catches of tuna, *Ghor* and shellfish. Today many of the traditional wooden boats of the Meds are motorized, and a jetty able to handle larger vessels has been built in East Bay. Plans to build a deep sea port have floundered a number of times, although a Memorandum of Understanding (MOU) between Singapore and Pakistan was announced in 1995 to develop port facilities. The Meds meanwhile remain amongst the poorest groups in Makran. For 3 months of the year from May to Jul, the seas are very rough and the fishing poor, forcing many to take loans from businessmen. Loans are then repayed in fish, prices being dictated by the moneylender, with the result that the fishermen are caught in a cycle of debt which renders them in effect bonded labourers.

Places of interest

The old bazaar and fish markets are situated on the East Bay side. From the main square and bus stand a series of narrow alleys lined with old wooden houses and shops lead through to the fish markets. Further along is the new jetty. The Governor's House and many of the administrative buildings are on the West Bay side, as well as the rest house and hotel. The police station, built in the style of a fort, is a good example of the distinctive Omani architecture found in those areas previously controlled by Oman.

Mausoleum of Baba Sheikh Abdullah This mausoleum, situated in a graveyard at the foot of the cliffs represents a piece of architecture unique in the Makran. As well as being constructed of stone in a region where sun-dried bricks are the prevalent building material, it is topped by an onion-shaped dome of a type not found elsewhere in the region. An inscription inside gives the date 1468. However, it is possible that it is much older. One

theory suggests that the mausoleum underwent a major transformation at some stage, having originally been identical in design to the tombs found at Chaukundi in Sind.

Koh-e-Bahtil A link road zig-zags its way up the side of Koh-e-Bahtil. In a depression on top are two small lakes formed by a *band* (dam) which catches all the rainwater run-off from the surrounding area. The origins of the dam are unclear. While local tradition dates it to the period of Portuguese occupation, it has also been suggested that the workmanship is indicative of a much earlier period and bears striking similarities to buildings in Yemen dating from around the time of Christ. Another local tradition tells of a powerful Arabic tribe settled on the Arabian Peninsular, who were forced by political upheavals and ecological changes to abandon their home, and came to settle on Koh-e-Bahtil which they transformed into a fertile orchard. Today the area, shaded by trees and dotted with pools, is a popular picnic spot. To the N, up on the cliffs overlooking the town, are the remains of a stone wall, said to be the ruins of the settlement established by the Portuguese. The best views out over Gwadar can be obtained from here.

Mud Volcano Near to the village of Dhur, to the E of the airport, below the tall cliffs of Koh-i-Mehdi, there is a small mud volcano, known locally by the Persian name *Dharya Chamag*, literally 'eye of the sea' or *Chandra Kups*, 'moon volcano'. It consists of a small pool in the centre of a low mound from which muddy sea water bubbles up at certain times, apparently under the influence of the tides. A number of these mud volcanos are to be found elsewhere along the Makran coast, the largest reportedly being over 100m tall. Nearby, villagers collect sea water in large shallow beds where it evaporates leaving behind deposits of salt which are collected into large mounds. The salt is used in the drying of fish, particularly *Ghor*, which can then be stored for up to 3 years.

Beaches The greatest attraction in this area is undoubtedly the miles of deserted beaches which stretch in both directions from Gwadar. Although generally more exposed, the beaches on the West Bay side are more pleasant, as well as being more easily accessible.

Local information
● **Accommodation**
Hotel facilities are extremely limited, with just two options, both in West Bay, nr the Governor's house. The government's **C** *Fish Harbour Rest House* has a/c rooms but little in the way of character. **D** *Gwadar Tourist Motel*, T 2688, 4 rm, att bath, fan, is much more picturesque, with a pleasant garden and verandah looking out to sea, the restaurant serves excellent fish, rec.

● **Places to eat**
There are a number of basic Pakistani style restaurants around the main square in East Bay.

● **Useful addresses**
District Commissioner's Office: T 2355. **PIA Booking Office**: T 2222 (situated on Airport Rd just S of the main square and bazaar, new premises under construction at the main fork on Airport Rd, N of the town). **Police**: T 2246.

● **Transport**
Air The airport is 12 km N of Gwadar. PIA operate flights to Karachi (up to 3 daily), Turbat (Mon, Tues, Thur, Sat, Sun), Pasni (Mon, Fri), Jiwani (Fri) and Panjgur (Thur).

Road Bus: there are long distance buses to Karachi via Turbat and Bela, as well as irregular local services along the coast, E to Pasni and W to Jiwani. Toyota pick-ups operate regular passenger services to Turbat. **Car hire**: Toyota pick-ups can be hired, with driver, from the main square and provide the most practical means of visiting surrounding areas. A return trip to Jiwani costs around 1,800 Rs, to Pasni around 2,000 Rs.

Gwadar to Jiwani
A 4WD and guide is strongly recommended for this route W along the coast to Jiwani. The road is largely non-existent, with long stretches across open desert and mud flats, marked only by the tyre tracks of previous vehicles.

Head N out of Gwadar, taking the turning W just before the airport. The first few km pass through an area of sand dunes which are liable to drift across the road, making progress difficult. Further on, a track branches off to the right, leading up to the recently completed **Akra Kaur Dam**, which it is hoped, will provide Gwadar with adequate supplies of fresh drinking water. The main track crosses a bridge over the course of the Akra River before emerging onto the wide desert expanses of the coastal belt. The track is at times very rough, passing over deeply corrugated mud flats. Visible to the N are the Garok mountains, and to the S the jagged outline of the Shabi hills. A water pumping station marks the turning S to the fishing village of **Pishkurgan**, also once part of Oman. The levies post here was originally built by the Omanis and closely resembles the police station in Gwadar.

From **Pishkurgan** there is an alternative route W, following the coastline closely. This route, running along the S flank of the coastal hills, gives the best views of their heavily eroded features, which have in places left improbable looking pillars and spires rising out of the desert and huge boulders hollowed by the wind into fragile shells with jagged, pitted surfaces. At the tiny village of **Gunz**, further W along the coast near Jiwani, a definite European/Greek influence is discernible in the features of the people, who also speak a slightly different dialect. The origins of the village's name are also unclear; Gunz is not a Baluchi or Makrani word, and some suggest that it is a corruption of 'guns'.

The main route continues W from the turning to Pishkurgan, across open desert, before bearing gradually SW to reach the village of Jiwani.

Jiwani

Jiwani was an important base for the British during WW2, and the remains of RAF barracks and other buildings can be seen up on the hill behind the village. The nearby officer's mess is now occupied by the Pakistan Navy. The creek or *Hor* behind Jiwani was also used by the navy as a repair yard for ships, which could be sailed in during the spring tides and refloated the following year.

A large graveyard near the village is thought to date from the period of the Arabic invasions during the 7th century. If so, it is interesting as tradition at that time dictated that the dead from an expedition had to be transported home for burial. One theory suggests that the ship returning home with those killed in fighting ran into problems and was forced to land at Jiwani, where the corpses were buried for want of a means to preserve them. One of the gravestones, ornately decorated and surrounded by a border, is inscribed in Arabic, with the names Ibrahim and Mohammad just discernible.

Other graveyards in the villages surrounding Jiwani are thought to have even older origins, with gravestones bearing floral designs, similar to those found near Bela, and thought to date from the time of **Rais Jamu**, ancestor of the Med population in the region. Elsewhere there are shallow vertical graves topped by small cairns in which, according to a local legend, people in ancient times used to entomb themselves, committing suicide in order to escape famine.

● **Accommodation** There are no hotels in Jiwani. The *Government Rest House*, pleasantly located on low cliffs overlooking the bay, is comfortable, though a little run down, it must be booked in advance through the Deputy Commissioner, Gwadar.

● **Places to eat** There are basic restaurants in the bazaar.

● **Transport Air** PIA Booking Office, T 289. PIA operates 2 flights weekly to Karachi: Mon via Gwadar, Fri via Turbat. **Road Bus**: local buses/Toyota pick-ups operate irregular services to Gwadar and Suntsar.

Gwadar to Pasni

The first section of the route from Gwadar to Pasni is the same as for Turbat. Continue E past the turning N for Turbat. The road is never more than a rough track, at times running through wide expanses of sand-dunes. The road passes N of the village of Kandasol and then on to Chakole. Soon after, a track bears off N into the Kalag hills. The main track passes close to the airport before arriving in Pasni, approximately 170 km from Gwadar.

Pasni

The town of Pasni is today the second largest fishing port along the Makran coast after Gwadar. When it was burnt by the Portuguese in 1581, it was described as a 'rich and beautiful city' and at the turn of the century rose in prominence above Gwadar, being closer to the regional centre of Turbat. The mini-port here was completed in 1989 with the help of a German company, and now handles much of the fish catch, some of which is partly dried for export to Sri Lanka, while the rest is taken directly to Karachi for sale or export.

● **Accommodation** There is only one hotel in Pasni, the **E** *Marwi*, T 303, with simple rooms and restaurant.

● **Places to eat** There are some basic restaurants in the bazaar.

● **Useful addresses Assistant Commissioner's Office**: T 529. **PIA Booking Office**: main bazaar, T 501. **Police**: T 515.

● **Transport Air** PIA operates flights to Karachi (up to 2 daily), Turbat (Tues, Wed, Thur, Fri, Sat), Gwadar (Mon, Fri), Omara (Wed) and Panjgur (Sun). **Road Bus**: long distance services to Karachi. Local services/Toyota pick-ups to Gwadar and Turbat.

Omara

The next major settlement E of Pasni is Omara. A large naval base is presently under construction here, and the town is strictly off-limits to foreigners.

PUNJAB

CONTENTS

Introduction	216
Islamabad	223
Rawalpindi	232
Excursions from Islamabad/ Rawalpindi	239
Islamabad/Rawalpindi to Murre	247
Islamabad/Rawalpindi to Peshawar	253
Islamabad/Rawalpindi to the Salt Range	256
Islamabad/Rawalpindi to Lahore	264
Lahore	272
Lahore to Sukkur	292
Lahore to Dera Ismail Khan	313
Lahore to Bannu	316

MAPS

Punjab	217
Islamabad/Rawalpindi	224
Islamabad	225
Blue Area	227
Rawalpindi	
Old City/Murree Road	234
Saddar Bazaar	235
Cantonment	236
Margalla Treks	240
Taxila	244
Murree	249
Murree & the Galis	251
Rohtas Fort	267
Sialkot	271
Lahore	274-275
Old City	281
Fort	278
Museum	284
Harappa	294
Multan	301
Bahawalpur	305
Faisalabad	315

INTRODUCTION

The most populous state in Pakistan, Punjab derives its name from the 'five waters' ('punj' meaning five, 'ab' meaning water) that are tributaries of the Indus. Lying at the crossroads of Asia, the Punjab has seen an endless succession of invaders, all of whom have left their mark on the history, language, religion, culture, literature and architecture of the region. This heritage can be seen by the tourist most notably in the great Mughal and Anglo-Indian buildings of Lahore, the stunningly restored shrines of Multan, and in a string of spectacular desert forts strung across the Cholistan Desert to the SE.

Best time to visit: visiting the Punjab at a suitable time of year will greatly enhance your enjoyment of the state and its attractions. It's not much fun traipsing around the great sights of Lahore and Multan with the temperature in the 40s, and humidity over 90%! Winter (Nov-Feb) is the best time to visit, although Punjab is still pleasant in spring and autumn. Winter nights can be cold, however, and woolens required. Rainfall can be heavy in the monsoonal belt in Jul, Aug and Sep.

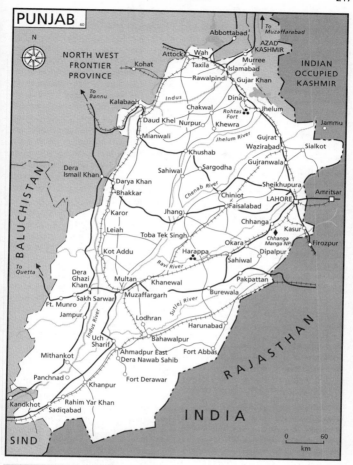

Land and life

Geography

Covering just over 205,000 sq km, Punjab is the second largest state in Pakistan. Prior to Partition, the state of Punjab extended E across the plains towards Delhi. Punjab shares a border with all the other federal states of Pakistan, as well as the international boundary with India to the E. The modern state is the granary of Pakistan, growing most of the country's key agricultural products, as well as having some of the major industrial centres. Much of the state is comprised of the **Upper Indus Plains**, a seemingly featureless terrain sloping gently SW. There are, however, a number of varied and distinctive geographical features within the Punjab.

Rivers

The arbitrary division of the Punjab at independence cut across the natural drainage pattern of the major river basins of the region, leaving the E tributaries of the Indus in India and the W Punjab tributaries in Pakistan. The signing of the **Indus Waters Treaty** in 1960 allocated the eastern rivers (Beas, Ravi and Sutlej) to India, and the western rivers (Indus, Chenab and Sutlej) to Pakistan.

The treaty was part of an integrated development plan that provided for the construction of storage reservoirs on the main rivers. Previously, the irrigation system introduced by the British was based upon huge barrages across the rivers diverting water into a network of irrigation canals. The Indus Waters Treaty initiated the building of two large dams, the **Mangla Dam** (see page 333) on the Jhelum and the **Tarbela Dam** (see page 241) on the Indus, that allowed the improvement and extension of existing agriculture in Punjab. There are plans for a third dam at **Kalabagh** in NW Punjab, see page 263.

Mountains

Although the Punjab is often considered to be a large flat plain, it does in fact have some important mountain features. At its northern margins, the hills of Murree and Kahuta are outlying spurs of the **Himalayas**. Running NE-SW from Mandra to Kalabagh is the **Salt Range** (see page 256), two lines of low rugged hills whose seasonal rivers have carved out deep, colourful gorges interspersed with vibrant, fertile oasis. The range is rich in ancient Palaeolithic sites, and rock salt has been mined here for over 2,000 years. The mine at Khewra is the world's most extensive salt mine, and the second largest in terms of production. In the SW of the state, to the W of the Indus, is the **Suleiman Range**, a line of low, dry and barren hills that separate Punjab from Baluchistan.

In the N of the state is the **Potwar Plateau** (see page 264), an extraordinary landscape covering almost 13,000 sq km. The result of recent uplift, the plateau has deep canyons and gorges carved into the soft rock by ancient rivers such as the **Soan**, and covered by varying depths of loess (wind blown silt). The Potwar is the earliest proven oil producing region in Pakistan, with the country's oldest refinery at Rawalpindi. Despite modest rainfall making it a hard land to cultivate, the Potwar Plateau is rich in ancient sites of some of South Asia's earliest settlements.

The plains of Pakistani Punjab merge imperceptibly with those of Sind to the S and Indian Punjab to the E.

Deserts

In the SE of the state, extending across the international border into the Rajasthan Desert in India, and across the state border into the Thar Desert in Sind, is the **Cholistan Desert** (see page 309). Covering over 25,000 sq km, the Cholistan is the largest desert in Pakistan. Much of Punjab's other great desert, the **Thal**, lying between the Indus and the Jhelum, is undergoing rapid transformation through irrigation.

Climate

Punjab has an inland continental climate, with relatively cool winters and hot summers. Between Nov and Feb, daily minimum temperatures range from 5°C to 10°C, with daily maximum temperatures of 19°C to 27°C. Although humidity is generally low, a narrow belt of N Punjab benefits from winter rains, and depressions moving in from the W can bring a damp chilliness to the air. Summers are hot, with average daily temperatures of 40°C, although 45°C is not uncommon. Total rainfall increases from 100 mm a year in the Multan region to the S, to 800 mm a year at Lahore. Most of the rain falls in the monsoon months of Jul, Aug and Sep, when humidity rates often exceed 90%.

History

Early settlement

Punjab lies on the natural route of any armies marching between Europe, Persia, West Asia and India to the E. It also stands on the N-S route between Central Asia and the Arabian Sea. As a result, the list of conquerors is long and varied. However, there is substantial evidence of ancient settlements in the Punjab that pre-date any known invaders. Stone implements and weapons dating back 400,000 years that have been found on the **Potwar Plateau** suggest colonization of the region prior to the environmental change that now makes this terrain relatively inhospitable.

The N plains have been far more receptive to settlement, allowing the development of large urban civilizations supported by an agricultural surplus. **Harappa**, one of the two major cities of the **Indus Valley Civilization**, developed on the inundated lands along the banks of the Ravi and the Indus between 2500 and 1750 BC.

Perhaps the earliest recorded invaders who passed through Punjab on their way into India are the **Indo-Aryans**, from whom it is believed the Punjabis are descended. The date of their arrival is unclear, with some sources suggesting they precipitated the demise of the Indus Valley Civilization, whilst others claim they arrived at least a century later.

In the 6th century BC, the third Achaemenid Emperor, **Darius I**, claimed possession of **Ghandhara**, an empire including the city of **Taxila**. The site at Taxila has been occupied from at least the Neolithic period, although it was well established as a major centre of learning by the 6th century BC.

Successively it was a centre of Buddhist and Graeco Buddhist influence. In 325-326 BC, **Alexander the Great** briefly passed through the region, and though he certainly visited Taxila, most historians conclude that the Greek influence in this period was slight. Within 15 years of Alexander's departure, **Chandragupta** had established the **Mauryan Empire** that incorporated the whole of the Punjab, and stretched into Afghanistan. His grandson **Asoka**, a Buddhist convert, established an empire that covered most of the sub-continent.

Following Asoka's death in 232 BC, the Mauryan Empire collapsed, initiating a series of invasions to fill the power vacuum in the region. The **Bactrian Greeks**, **Sakas** and **Parthians** successively ruled the area until, about 75 AD, the **Huns** swept across the N plains. Known in the region as the **Kushans**, the great Hun warrior leader **Kanishka** converted to Buddhism, and encouraged the cultural and artistic flowering of the **Gandharan kingdom**.

Muslim period

Following the collapse of the Kushan Empire, there are vast gaps in the recorded history of the Punjab. A succession of tribal chieftains fought for supremacy over various isolated territories within the region, although no one empire attained dominance over the whole of the Punjab.

Muslim influence was first felt in the S of the Punjab when the Arab army of **Mohammad bin Qasim** captured Multan in 712 AD. However, it was not until the raids of **Mahmud of Ghazni** around 1000 AD that Islam made an impression in Punjab, and it was during the period of Ghaznavid rule that Multan and Lahore became centres of Islamic learning.

A succession of Muslim rulers dominated the politics of the region, culminating in the 150 year reign of the **Mughal Empire**. In 1584, **Akbar** made Lahore the capital of the Mughal Empire, and in the years that followed his successors, **Jahangir**, **Shah Jahan** and **Aurangzeb** all left their mark on the Punjab, principally through some fine examples of Mughal architecture.

The Sikhs

During the reign of Aurangzeb, the tenth Sikh Guru, **Gobind Singh**, introduced the series of reforms to the religion that are now universally associated with Sikhism. He founded a new brotherhood called the **Khalsa** (meaning 'the pure' from the Persian word *khales*), and adopted a more militant stance. In 1764 the Sikhs defeated the Afghan king **Ahmad Shah Durrani**, the successor to the Mughal Empire. Sikh rule over the whole of the Punjab was consolidated when the Afghans conceded Lahore to the Sikh warrior king **Ranjit Singh** in 1799. Although Ranjit Singh sided with the British in the **First Afghan War**, his successors fought two wars with the British, until the Sikh defeat at the Battle of Gujrat on 21 February 1849 that led to the British annexation of the Punjab.

British rule

The key feature of the period of British rule in the Punjab was the development of agriculture. The digging of canals and the construction of barrages across the rivers transformed much of what was previously uncultivatable scrub jungle into prime agricultural land. These irrigation projects, along with the establishment of canal colonies, continued from the 1850s right up until independence in 1947.

Partition

The Punjab was one of the states most affected by Partition, with the Radcliffe Boundary Commission literally dividing the state in two between Pakistan and India. It also witnessed some of the worst communal violence that accompanied the announcement of the boundary 'awards'. Ironically, Punjab was one of the last states now in Pakistan to accept the idea of a separate homeland for the Muslims of South Asia. In the elections for Muslim members seats to the Legislative in the years preceding independence, Jinnah's Muslim League party fared badly in Punjab, unable to break the hold of **Sir Sikander Hyat Khan's** Unionist Party. Sir Sikander stood on a platform of Muslim-Hindu-Sikh coexistence, and right up until his death in 1942, was looking for a federal plan with the Indian Congress Party that would allow a federation rather than partition. However, Jinnah's principal biographer Wolpert suggests that Sir Sikander must have realized that his dreams of leading the Muslims of India were effectively ended in 1940, when the Muslim League passed the **Lahore Resolution** that laid the foundation of Pakistan.

Culture

People

Despite a history of invasion by a succession of ethnic groups, Punjab displays greater cultural homogeneity than say, Sind. Most Punjabis are descended from the Indo-Aryans who migrated into South Asia in the 2nd millennium BC. Almost 80% of all households have Punjabi as their mother tongue, with less than 2% of rural and 12% of urban households having Urdu as their first language. Seraiki is a significant minority language in Punjab.

Islam is the principal religion of the state, accounting for 97% of the population. However, there is a considerable Shia Muslim minority within the state. Lahore, Sheikhupura and Gujranwala all have large Christian communities, accounting for 8% of the population in some rural areas. Almost all Hindus and Sikhs left at Partition.

Unlike the mohajirs who migrated from India to Karachi and Hyderabad at Partition (see page 120), most of the migrants who crossed the new international border into Punjab were of the same ethnic group as their new hosts, thus perhaps allowing the Punjab to avoid the ethnic tensions that have dogged Sind.

Literature

Pakistan's most celebrated poet and philosopher, **Mohammad Iqbal**, was a Punjabi, born in Sialkot in 1877. Educated in Lahore, he later taught there before moving to Europe to further his studies. He read Philosophy at the Universities of Heidelberg, Munich and Cambridge, and was awarded a PhD from Munich University.

In addition to his poetry, he was actively involved in politics, and in his Presidential Address at the annual session of the Muslim League in 1930, he proposed for the first time the 'two-nation theory' that envisaged a separate Muslim homeland in the NW of India. He died in 1938 and is buried in a tomb outside the Badshahi Mosque in Lahore. He is usually referred to by the honorific title **Allama**, meaning 'Great Islamic Scholar'.

Government and administration

Although there is an even distribution of seats between the four provinces of Pakistan in the Senate (Upper House) of the legislative assembly, the National Assembly (Lower House) is dominated by the Punjab. Over half of the seats (115 out of 217) in the country's sovereign legislative body are in the Punjab, and although this reflects the fact that half of Pakistan's population live in this state, the other states see it as an attempt by Punjab to dominate the nation. The almost total Punjabi domination of the army, and to a lesser extent Pakistan's powerful civil service, is deeply resented by the other states of the federation, and is seen as a Punjabi plot to exert hegemony over the country.

Recent political developments

Punjab is probably the most stable state in Pakistan, relatively untouched by the ethnic and criminal tension currently gripping Sind, the tribal quarrels affecting Baluchistan and NWFP, and the instability created by the problem of Kashmir.

However, in recent years there has been a significant upsurge in sectarian violence between the majority Sunni sect of Islam and the minority Shia sect. Early in 1994, a new quasi-religious/political party formed to 'protect the rights of their community'. The Shia **Sipah-e-Mohammad Pakistan** (SMP) is considered by many commentators to be the most militant religious organization in the country, responsible for upping the stakes in Punjab's sectarian divide. The SMP, however, argues that it is merely protecting its community from the militant Sunni organization that has 'become a byword for violent anti-Shia fanaticism', the **Sipah-i-Sahaba Pakistan** (SSP). It is a confrontation that the country cannot afford.

The Economy

Punjab's economy is primarily agricultural, although the recent extension of the industrial base now makes a substantial contribution.

Agriculture

Punjab is the heart of Pakistan's agricultural economy, producing over 70% of the country's **wheat** output, almost half of its **rice** (including 95% of *Basmati*), 60% of its **sugar** and nearly 85% of its **cotton**. Livestock rearing is also important in Punjab, accounting for 71% of the country's buffaloes, 50% of the cattle (including some unique Punjab breeds), 53% of poultry, 29% of sheep and 36% of goats. Further, not only is agriculture in Punjab a vital source of foreign exchange earnings, it supplies domestic consumption as well as employing half of the state's labour force.

Recent increases in production have been achieved by introducing **Green Revolution** techniques, such as adopting higher quality seeds and increased use of fertilizer and pesticide. **Mexi-Pak wheat**, cross-bred strains of Mexican and Pakistani wheats, are grown everywhere. There are concerns, however, that intensified production is placing greater strain on the soils, and increasing dependency on fertilizers and pesticides. Further, one estimate suggests that Pakistan's import of tractors in the 2 decades after 1961 cost rural Pakistan 1 million jobs. Had it not been for the intensification of agriculture, however, the pressure of population on resources would have been even greater.

Yet prior to the 1850s, most of the area was scrub jungle, sparsely cultivated and thinly populated. The remarkable transformation of the area, and indeed, the modern history of Punjab, can be dated back to the development of canal irrigation initiated by the British.

The first Punjab canal was the **Upper Bari Doab** canal, dug mainly to offer agricultural land to Sikh settlers at the end of the Sikh wars in 1849. The canals took their names from the rivers between which they flowed – thus Bari was a combination of the Beas and Ravi, 'Doab' meaning two ('do') waters ('ab'). The canals were fed by building a series of major barrages across the rivers, and diverting the waters, thus providing a source of water to the innundation channels in the dry, as well as the high flow wet season. Not only did the barrages allow the growing season to be extended, they also supplied water to land that was previously too high above the river banks to be irrigated. These two factors brought vast new areas under cultivation.

Later schemes included the **Chenab Canal** project of the 1890s, and the **Jhelum Canal**, opened in 1901. Both allowed for the first time, extensive irrigation of the lower E banks of the rivers. Other projects were initiated between 1905-1915, including the **Triple Canals Project** which sought to link the upper Jhelum with the Chenab, in turn feeding the Ravi into the Upper Bari Doab Canal.

All of these schemes were threatened by the partition of the sub-continent which cut across both the natural and the introduced drainage lines. The **Indus Waters Treaty** of 1960 was the solution to this problem (see page 115).

Resources and industry

Although Punjab has a large range of commercially exploitable minerals, most are low value/volume. Fairly large scale productions include coal, limestone, gypsum, rock salt, silica sand, stone and sand gravel. In addition, bentonite, bauxite, China clay, iron ore and milestone marble are exploited on a smaller scale. By the late 1980s Punjab had established itself as Pakistan's most important **oil** producer. Although output of crude petroleum is low at 10m barrels, it represents 60% of the country's total output.

Traditional industries have tended to be small-scale, based on processing agricultural raw materials, although they employ more than 80% of the labour force in the manufacturing sector, and contribute a quarter of value-added. Some industries have expanded rapidly, leading to the rapid growth of towns, such as the evolution of Multan as a major cotton centre, and Faisalabad as the capital of the Pakistani textile industry. A number of towns have evolved specialized export-orientated industries, such as Sialkot, which has a worldwide reputation for its sports goods and surgical instruments. Lahore, and some of the towns to the N on the Grand Trunk Rd, have iron-working, engineering, textiles, chemicals, food processing and shoe manufacture.

ISLAMABAD/RAWALPINDI

The twin cities of Islamabad and Rawalpindi lie at the foot of the Margalla Hills. Islamabad, Pakistan's planned modern capital, was built in the 1960s and arranged in a grid system divided into sectors for government, commerce, residential, recreational and industrial use. It contrasts sharply with Rawalpindi to the SE, a typically Asian town with its old bazaars, cantonment and saddar areas, which has itself grown enormously since the building of Islamabad. The master plan envisages that the two cities will one day form a single urban mass, with Islamabad completely encircling the central core of Rawalpindi.

ISLAMABAD

Islamabad was designated as the modern capital of Pakistan by President Ayub Khan in 1958, and was chosen to act as a counterbalance to the overwhelming economic importance of Karachi, the original capital, and the political dominance of Lahore. A number of planners and architects, including Edward Durrell Stone, Ponti and the Greek firm Doxiadis Associates, were called in to plan the city from scratch.

City layout

Blue Area, running E-W through the centre of Islamabad is the main commercial thoroughfare, with many of the major banks, airlines, tour operators, restaurants and shops located here. The strip consists of three roads, one the central dual carriageway, interspaced by commercial plazas which front onto roads on both sides.

Zero Point was planned as the centre of the city, although the political, administrative and commercial centre of gravity has developed to the N and E. The city is divided into sectors: F-6

through to F10 (also known as Shalimar 6-10) N of Blue Area and G-6 to G-10 (or Ramna 6-10) to the S. Sectors H and I, to the SW of Zero point are being developed.

Each sector has a commercial centre or *Markaz*, with its own name: F-6 is Supermarket, F-7 Jinnah Supermarket, F-8 Ayub Market, while G-6 is Civic Centre or Melody Market and G-7 Sitara Market.

The sectors are further divided into sub-sectors, numbered 1-4 from the bottom left clockwise (eg F-7/1), and streets within these are also numbered. The streets dividing sectors (usually consisting of two parallel roads) and sub-sectors are named. Aabpara, Islamabad's oldest market lies in the southern part of G-6/1, along Khyaban-e-Suhrawardy. Government buildings – the Presidency, Parliament, Secretariat etc, and the diplomatic enclave are situated at the eastern end of the city.

Architecture

Islamabad is home to some of Pakistan's more daring modern architecture, particularly some of the foreign missions in the diplomatic enclave, as well as the

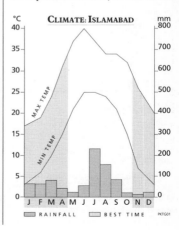

CLIMATE: ISLAMABAD

RAINFALL   BEST TIME   PKTG01

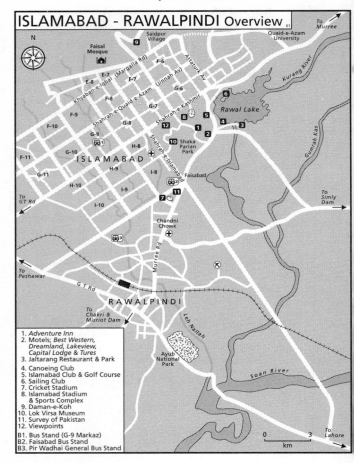

ISLAMABAD - RAWALPINDI Overview

1. Adventure Inn
2. Motels; Best Western, Dreamland, Lakeview, Capital Lodge & Tures
3. Jaltarang Restaurant & Park
4. Canoeing Club
5. Islamabad Club & Golf Course
6. Sailing Club
7. Cricket Stadium
8. Islamabad Stadium & Sports Complex
9. Daman-e-Koh
10. Lok Virsa Museum
11. Survey of Pakistan
12. Viewpoints

B1. Bus Stand (G-9 Markaz)
B2. Faisabad Bus Stand
B3. Pir Wadhai General Bus Stand

government buildings which reflect the grandeur and scale of the city plan, while elsewhere there are some interesting fusions of 20th century post-modernism and traditional Islamic architecture.

Places of interest

Often dismissed as a modern, characterless city, Islamabad has a certain attraction of its own, with its wide tree-lined avenues and parks, gardens and fountains giving it an air of spaciousness and abundant greenery. Its main asset is its setting at the foot of the **Margalla Hills** (see page 239), which dominate the city. Rising up to 1,580m, they are formed of limestone and extend northwards in a series of ridges. Beyond them is Hazara and the lower reaches of the Black Mountains. The area, which covers over 12,000 a, has been designated as a National Park in an attempt to curb the encroachment of quarrying and developers, and to protect the rich flora and fauna. The hills offer numerous opportunities for walks and longer hikes, just minutes from the city centre.

Faisal Masjid

Built with funds gifted by King Faisal Bin Abdul Aziz of Saudi Arabia and

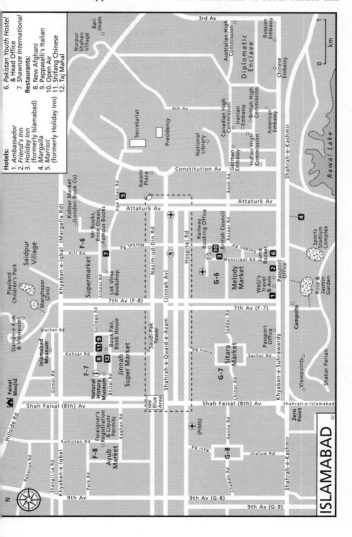

Hotels:
1. Ambassador
2. Friend's Inn
3. Holiday Inn (formerly Islamabad)
4. Margalla
5. Marriott (formerly Holiday Inn)
6. Pakistan Youth Hostel & Head Office
7. Shawnze International

Restaurants:
8. New Afghani
9. Pappasalli's Italian
10. Open Air
11. Shifang Chinese
12. Taj Mahal

ISLAMABAD

designed by a Turkish architect, the mosque is one of the largest in the world, with 88m high minarets resembling rockets. It is said to hold 100,000 worshippers. The main prayer hall is an unique desert tent-like structure with eight faces, rising to 40m. The raised courtyard boasts huge expanses of polished marble. There is a bookshop, library and lecture hall belonging to the Islamic Research Centre, and a restaurant to the rear. Signs state that photography is strictly forbidden, but this is applied only in the main prayer hall.

Daman-e-Koh

The viewpoint at Daman-e-Koh, with its restaurant and snack bars, gives good views over Islamabad and there are a number of short walks around the spur. A road winds its way up to the viewpoint from the N end of 7th Ave, passing the Mini-Zoo below at Marghzar.

Saidpur Village

Situated to the E of Daman-e-Koh and reached by a road leading N from the top end of F-6, this small village, surrounded by mango trees, is a centre for traditional pottery wares. Before Partition it was predominantly Hindu, and the springs in the area were considered holy.

Nurpur Shahan

This small village is situated 3 km to the NE of the Diplomatic Enclave and is famous for the shrine of the 17th century saint, **Hazrat Syed Shah Abdul Latif** or Barri Imam (holy man of the woods), who lived for 12 years in a nearby cave. Pilgrims arrive in large numbers for the annual *Urs* (death anniversary) in May and there is music and prayers every Thur evening. There is a path leading up to the site of his cave, on a hillside to the NE, around 2 hrs' walk.

Islamabad Museum

Islamabad Museum, Hs 41, St 3, E-7, T 223826. Open 0930-1630, closed Wed. This small, recently opened museum has an excellent selection of artefacts with rooms covering the pre-historic Indus Valley, Gandharan, Arabic and Islamic periods. Although no match for the major museums of Peshawar, Lahore and Karachi, the presentation is very good. Well worth a visit, and ideal if you tend to struggle with larger museums.

Shakaparian and Lok Virsa Museum

The low hill overlooking Islamabad, to the S of the main road between Zero Point and Aabpara, has been kept as the Shakaparian Park. There are E and W view points at the top, giving good views of the Margalla Hills to the N, Rawal Lake to the E, Kahuta to the SE (the centre of Pakistan's nuclear technology research programme) and Rawalpindi to the S. It is a very popular area for a stroll, particularly in the evening, when the lights of the city make an attractive sight. There is the *City View Restaurant* T 218254 at the E viewpoint, and some snack bars. The hill is forested and there are various paths giving pleasant walks including around Lotus Lake.

The Lok Virsa Museum is S of the hill, on Garden Rd. It houses an excellent selection of handicrafts, including some beautiful costumes, textiles, jewellery, musical instruments, pottery and carved pieces, displayed according to area, use and motif. Open summer 0900-1900, winter 0900-1700, closed Fri, Sat. There is also a good Library with sound and video archives, an open air theatre and studio. Lok Virsa is Pakistan's National Institute of Folk Heritage. They are active in promoting the tremendous wealth and variety of traditional arts and crafts in Pakistan and have published a valuable range of social research material and reprints of old folk tale collections. The Sound Archive is the largest existing collection of Pakistani songs, ballards, interviews etc, while the Video Archive has films on folk performances, customs and traditions. The Lok Virsa Gallerie and bookshop, where you can buy books and music cassettes, is on the bottom left corner of Supermarket (F-6 Markaz). They also have periodic exhibitions in the gallery upstairs.

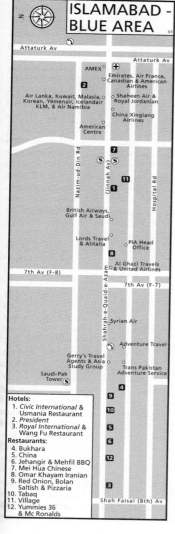

ISLAMABAD - BLUE AREA

Attaturk Av

Attaturk Av

AMEX

Emirates, Air France, Canadian & American Airlines

Air Lanka, Kuwait, Malasia, Korean, Yemenair, Icelandair KLM, & Air Namibia

Shaheen Air & Royal Jordanian

China Xiangiang Airlines

American Centre

Nazim-ud-Din Rd

(Jinnah Av)

Hospital Rd

British Airways, Gulf Air & Saudi

Lords Travel & Alitalia

PIA Head Office

7th Av (F-8)

Shahrah-e-Quaid-e-Azam

Al Ghazi Travels & United Airlines

7th Av (F-7)

Syrian Air

Adventure Travel

Gerry's Travel Agents & Asia Study Group

Trans Pakistan Adventure Service

Saudi-Pak Tower

Hotels:
1. *Civic International* & Usmania Restaurant
2. *President*
3. *Royal International* & Wang Fu Restaurant

Restaurants:
4. Bukhara
5. China
6. Jehangir & Mehfil BBQ
7. Mei Hua Chinese
8. Omar Khayam Iranian
9. Red Onion, Bolan Saltish & Pizzaria
10. Tabaq
11. Village
12. Yummies 36 & Mc Ronalds

Shah Faisal (8th) Av

Rose and Jasmine Garden

The best time to visit is during spring, when the gardens are in flower and there are shows of over 250 varieties of roses and a dozen jasmines. Out of season it is somewhat disappointing.

Rawal Lake

This large lake, formed by a dam across the Kurang River, is the main water supply for Islamabad. There are extensive reed-beds around the northern side of the lake, home to a wide variety of birds and wildlife. There is the *PTDC Jaltarang Restaurant* and various snack bars around a terraced garden by dam, on the S side of the lake. Rowing boats and small motor boats for hire nearby. The Canoeing Club, on the track up to the dam has open membership giving the opportunity to enjoy canoeing on the lake (see Clubs below). There is also a Sailing Club on the N side of the lake, reached from Murree Rd.

Pakistan Museum of Natural History

Pakistan Museum of Natural History is at Jinnah Supermarket, Markaz F-7 (nr PTDC), open 0900-1300, 1400-1700, closed Fri, Sat.

Local information

● **Accommodation**

HOTEL CLASSIFICATIONS			
AL	Rs4,000	A	Rs1,800-4,000
B	Rs900-1,800	C	Rs450-900
D	Rs300-450	E	Rs150-300
F	up to Rs150		

AL *Marriott* (formerly *Holiday Inn*), Aga Khan Rd, Shalimar 5, PO Box 1251, T 826121, F 820648, 5-star international standard hotel, the 24-hr Coffee Shop often acts as an ad-hoc press club, the recently opened *Muddy's Cafe* is a disco/nightclub – Islamabad's first – in all but name, it is worth asking about special off-season packages when making bookings for the hotel.

A *Best Western*, Club Rd, nr Rawal Dam, T 218412, F 218421, situated away from the city centre, a little overpriced; **A** *Holiday Inn* (formerly *Islamabad Hotel*), G-6, Civic Centre, PO Box 1373, T 827311, F 224263, little changed despite the new management, plans to completely refurbish the ground floor with an indoor swimming pool, sauna and health club have yet to be undertaken.

B *Adventure Inn*, Garden Ave, T 212536, F 212540, offices of the Adventure Foundation also located here; **B** *Civic International*, 13 West, Blue Area, Jinnah Ave, T 213740, F 214450, car hire and *Usmania* restaurant, rec, next door; **B** *Dreamland Motel*, Islamabad Club Rd, T 814381, F 815886, *Gul-e-Rukh* restaurant; **B** *Lakeview Motel*, Club Rd, T 821386, F 822394, 24-hr restaurant; **B** *Margala Motel*, 1 Kashmir Highway, nr *Jinnah Sports Complex*, T 813345, F 216982; **B** *President*, 1B Nazimuddin Rd, Blue Area, F-6, T 217142, F 220995, *Aab-o-Dana* restaurant, car hire; **B** *Royal International*, 104E Jinnah Ave, Blue Area, T 223252, F 223258, banquet/conference hall, car rental; **B** *Shawnze International*, Supermarket, Markaz, F-6, T 823703, F 823519, conference facilities available.

Guest Houses (B-C) An alternative to upper range hotels in Islamabad are the privately run Guest Houses in residential areas. They are very good value with the quality of accommodation matching that of **A-B** category hotels (although without the shopping and leisure facilities), often at half the price. Popular with aid-workers and other expats who do not have permanent residences and wish to avoid the more impersonal large hotels. Many are part of the Islamabad Guest House Association and have details of other affiliated guest houses. A selection is listed here, but there are many more: *Best Accomodators*, Hs 6, St 54, F-7/4, T 818574, F 814467; *Drop Inn*, Hs 21, St 88, G-6/3, T 212157; *Dwellers*, Hs 3, St 64, F-8/4, T 857039; *Jacoranda*, 17 College Rd, F-7/3, T/F 223183; *Luxury Inn*, Hs 2, St 30, F-6/1 T 821204, F 823430; *Pearl House*, 22A College Rd, opp Jinnah Super, F-7/2, T 216788, F 218165; *Shelton House*, Hs 11, Kaghan Rd, F-8/3, T 856956; *The Poet*, Hs 35, St 11, F-6/3, T 213587.

C *Ambassador*, Khayaban-e-Suharwardhy, T 824011, F 821320, pleasant garden, well run; **C** *Capital*, Iqbal Hall Rd, T 815091, F 815097; **C** *Capital Lodge*, 2 National Park, Club Rd, T 818411, conference hall; **C** *Friends Inn*, Block 16, I & T Centre (Aabpara), G-6/1, T 222546.

D *Tures Motel*, Club Rd, nr Rawal Dam, T 824503.

F *Islamabad Youth Hostel*, Garden Rd, G-6/4 (nr Aabpara), T 826899, generally clean, good value, maximum stay 3 days in the summer, popular with Pakistani students; **F** *Tourist Camp Site*, opp Rose and Jasmine Garden, nr Aabpara, camping and basic dormitory 'bungalows' (no beds/bedding), for foreigners only, maximum stay 2 weeks, locker storage available, the cheapest budget accommodation in Islamabad, but rather run-down.

● **Places to eat**

There is a good selection of restaurants in Blue Area, most of them between 7th and 8th Ave. Others are located in the main markets at the centre of each sector. All of the larger hotels have good restaurants.

Daman-e-Koh, Daman-e-Koh Viewpoint, in Margalla Hills, offers superb views of Islamabad, buffet is fresher at lunchtime than evening; *Pir Sohawa*,16 km beyond Daman-e-Koh, barbecue.

Blue Area: *McRonalds*, Jinnah Ave, Blue Area, rec for fast food; *Omar Khayyam*, Jinnah Ave, Blue Area, Iranian, rec.

Jinnah Supermarket: *Kabul*; *Kim Mun*, Chinese; *New Afghani*, rec; *Pappasallis*, Block 13e, F/7 Markaz, T 818287, Italian, highly rec; *Shanghai*, Chinese; *Shifang*, Chinese; *Taj Mahal*.

Supermarket: *Heavan Fast Food*, ice creams, pizza, burgers; *Kabul 2*.

There is a rec restaurant complex on 4th St, F 7/3, incl two Chinese, one Pakistani and one American restaurant.

● **Airline offices**

Domestic: Aeroflot, No 7, 80-W Plaza, Jinnah Ave, T 815154, F 824541; **Shaheen Air International**, 33 Buland Markaz, Blue Area, T 813916, F 813964; **Aero Asia**, Block 12-D, SNC Centre, Blue Area, T 219340. It is also possible to purchase tickets directly for all three airlines through many of Islamabad's travel agents, most of them in Blue Area.

International: Aeroflot, No 7, 80-W Plaza, Jinnah Ave, T 815154, F 824541; **Air Canada**, GSA Tradewind Associates, 12 Shahid Plaza, Blue Area, T 824030; **Air France**, GSA Capitol Travels, Shop 6, 1-D Rehmat Plaza, Blue Area, T 218253, F 214563; **Air Lanka**, 12 Shahid Plaza, Blue Area, T 819706; **Alitalia**, GSA Roman Holidays, 3, Block 51, Blue Area, T 214317, F 214349; **American**, 1-D Rehmat Plaza, Unit 4, Block 51, Blue Area, T 217209 F 828844; **British**, GSA Aviona, 10, Block 51

Chaudhry Plaza, Blue Area, T 214070, F 214348; **China Xinjiang Airlines**, Shop 3, Sohrab Plaza, Block 32, Blue Area, T 223446, F 223448; **Emirates**, 1-D Blue Area, T 216302, F 215988; **Gulf**, GSA King Associates, 2/54 W Waheed Plaza, Blue Area, T 210243; **KLM**, 1 Shahid Plaza, Blue Area, T 214542, F 826775; **Kuwait**, 4 Shahid Plaza, Blue Area, T 822727, F 212195; **Lufthansa**, *Islamabad Marriot Hotel*, Aga Khan Rd, F-5, T 814611; **Malaysia**, GSA Muhibah Aviation Services, 4 Shahid Nauroze Plaza, Blue Area, T 213382; **Philippine**, GSA Paramount Aviation, 15 Shahid Plaza, Blue Area, T 821567, F 821568; **Quantas**, GSA Pak Turk Enterprises, 64-E, Marcos Plaza, Blue Area, T 217595, F 217594; **Royal Nepal**, 12 Shahid Plaza, Blue Area, T 218253; **Saudia**, 52 W Modern Plaza, Blue Area, T 210163, F 210179; **Singapore**, GSA Crown Travels, *Islamabad Holiday Inn Hotel*, Civic Centre, T 821555; **Swiss Air**, *Islamabad Holiday Inn Hotel*, T 815255; **Syrian Arab**, *Islamabad Holiday Inn Hotel*, T 811608; **Thai Airways**, GSA Viking Travels, Office 4, 33 Buland Markaz, Blue Area, T 217531; **Turkish**, GSA Pak Turk Enterprises, 64-E Marcos Plaza, Blue Area, T 217595, F 217594; **United**, GSA Val Enterprises, 2 Kulsum Plaza, 42 Jinnah Ave, T 810658, F 220962.

● **Banks & money changers**
American Express, 1E, Ali Plaza, Blue Area, PO Box 1291, T 212425, F 826783 (for client's mail call 823170); **ANZ Grindlays**, Diplomatic Enclave; **United Bank Limited**, UBL Building, Main Civic Centre, G-6.

● **Cultural centres**
American Center, 60, Blue Area, Khayaban-e-Quaid-e-Azam, T 824051; **Asian Study Group**, Malik Complex, 80 West, Sharah-e-Qaid-e-Azam, Blue Area, T 815891, formed in the 1970s by members of the expat community, it now has a wider membership and holds regular lectures and cultural evenings, as well as sightseeing trips and walks in the Margalla Hills, the ASG have published a number of papers and booklets, members can make use of the small library which incl some videos, annual membership Rs 200; **British Council**, No 9, New Melody, T 825265; **French Cultural Centre**, 12, St 88, G 6/3, T 214558; **Gallerie Lok Virsa**, Supermarket, Markaz F6, T 827298, periodic exhibitions of handicrafts etc, selection of tapes and Lok Virsa publications on sale downstairs; **Iran**, 46a, Satellite Town, T 843368.

● **Embassies & consulates**
Afghanistan, No 14, St 83, G 6/4, T 822566; **Australia**, Chancery, Diplomatic Enclave 2, T 214902; **Canada**, Sector G 5, Diplomatic Enclave, T 211101; **China**, Chancery, Diplomatic Enclave, Ramna 4, T 211114; **France**, Diplomatic Enclave G 5, T 213981; **Germany**, Chancery, Diplomatic Enclave, Ramna 5, T 212412; **India**, G 5, Diplomatic Enclave, T 814371; **Iran**, Plots 222-238, St 2, G 5/1, Diplomatic Enclave, T 822694; **Kazakhstan**, No 2, St 4, F 8/3, T 262924; **Nepal**, Chancery House, 506, St 84, G 6/4, T 210642; **Netherlands**, PIA Bldg, 2nd Flr, Blue Area, T 214336; **Russian Federation**, Chancery, Ramna 4, Khayaban-e-Suhrawardy, T 210311; **Sri Lanka**, Chancery, 135c, Khayaban-e-Iqbal, Margalla Rd, F 7/2, T 210286; **Sweden**, 6a, Aga Khan Rd, Markaz Shalimar 6, T 215541; **Syria**, Chancery, 30, Hill Rd, F 6/3, T 211303; **Thailand**, Chancery, No 4, St 2, F 8/3; **Turkey**, Chancery, No 42, St 12, F 6/3, T 821939; **Turkmenistan**, No 22a, Nazurradin Rd, F 7/1, T 214913; **UK**, Diplomatic Enclave G 5, T 822131; **USA**, Diplomatic Enclave, Ramna 5, T 826161; **Uzbekistan**, No 6, St 29, F 7/1, T 820779.

● **Entertainment**
Nightclubs: in the *Marriot Hotel*, Thur, couples only, semi-formal dress, alcohol prohibited. The *Australian Embassy* has a bar night for Australian passport holders (and often other guests) on Thur night, featuring *VB*, *Fosters*, and drunken backpackers.

Video hire: *Radio City*, Supermarket, F/6, T 810471.

● **Hospitals & medical services**
Chemists: there are chemist shops in all the main market centres, in Blue Area (concentrated around the junction with Shaheed-e-Millat Rd) and outside most of the hospitals.

Hospitals: **Private**: *Al-Shifa International*, H-8, T 262830; *Islamabad Hospital*, opp American Express, Blue Area, T 212350. **Public**: *Capital Hospital*, Street 31, G-6/2, T 221334; *Pakistan Institute of Medical Sciences (PIMS) Hospital Complex*, Faisal Ave, G-8/3, T 859511; *Federal Government Services Hospital (Poly Clinic)*, Hospital Rd, G-6/3, T 218300.

● **Libraries**
American Center, 60 Blue Area, Khayaban-e-Quaid-e-Azam, T 824051, periodicals, audiovisual and US Information Service materials;

British Council, 14 Civic Centre, G-6 Markaz, T 822205, F 822670, also has audio-visual section and BBC World TV; *Lok Virsa Heritage Library* is at the museum in Shakarparian; *National Library of Pakistan*, Constitution Ave Building, nr Parliament House, T 812787, open 0900-1700, closed Thur and Fri, European and Oriental languages, Pakistan collection, manuscripts and rare materials, periodicals and newspapers; *PTDC Head Office*, House 2, St 61, F-7/4, T 811011 has a good collection of books on Pakistani regional history and culture.

● **Post & telecommunications**

Area code: 051.

GPO: Civic Centre, Municipal Rd. There are also Post Offices in the major markets.

Central Telegraph Office: Ataturk Ave, Shalimar 5. There is also a Telegraph Office at Aabpara, opp Tourist Camping Site, a Pakistan Telecom Customer Services Centre in Blue Area, just W of 7th Ave, and PCOs in the major markets.

● **Shopping**

Aabpara is Islamabad's oldest market, selling household items, fabrics and spices. Nearby is the *Covered Market* for meat, fruit and veg, and *Juma (Friday) Bazaar*, good for handicrafts. *Kohsar Market*, Shalimar 6 Markaz, has stalls selling handicrafts. There are shopping complexes at the centre of F-6 (*Supermarket*) and F-7 (*Jinnah Supermarket*), both with a selection of chemists, clothing shops, convenience stores, photographic shops, handicrafts, bookshops and restaurants. *Yamood Carpets*, 4 Block G, Upstairs ABL, Supermarket, F/6, T 821515. Rec by Islamabad residents for carpets. *Blue Area* is the main commercial thoroughfair and has some carpet shops and handicrafts.

Books: Islamabad is well supplied with bookshops offering a wide range of books on Pakistan's history, culture, political and economic development etc, many of them not readily available abroad. Most of the guidebooks to Pakistan are available as well as some maps. There are also a number of second-hand bookshops where books can be exchanged. For new books, *The London Book Co*, 3 Kohsar Market, F-6/3, T 823852, has the widest range and a good selection of maps. Others incl *Book Fair* and *The Book House* in Jinnah Supermarket and *Mr Books*, *Famous Books*, *Book Ocean* and *Book City* in Supermarket. Most of the second-hand bookshops are also located in Supermarket and Jinnah Supermarket.

● **Sports**

Adventure Foundation (Pakistan), House 10, St 62, F-8/4, T 852475, or contact at *Adventure Inn*, based on the principles of the Outward Bound Trust, the Foundation aims to offer young people the opportunity to partake in outdoor adventure activities, incl trekking, mountaineering, skiing, boating, sailing, ballooning and gliding; *Islamabad Canoe Club*, Rawal Lake, nr Dam, correspondence c/o Channel 7 Communications, North Portion, 2nd Flr, Block 4B, F-7, Markaz, T 217307, F 219325, membership Rs 210/month, provides a very good value opportunity to enjoy canoeing on Rawal Lake; *Islamabad Club*, Club Rd, with golf course and riding club (non-members can arrange for horse riding outings); *Islamabad Watersports Club*, T 855324; *Islamabad Club*, T 825896, golf, tennis, swimming, membership by application; *Islamabad Sports Complex*, Shakarparian Park, tennis, squash, swimming (women only Fri & Sat), life membership Rs 5,000; *Shaukat Spa*, Supermarket, F/6, pool & spa. *The Gym*, Supermarket, F/6, gymnasium, rock wall.

Flying: *Flying Club*, House 16, St 31, F 6/1.

Golf: *Islamabad Golf Club*, Islamabad Park, T 812637; *Pak Air Force Golf Club*, N of F/10, Khayaban-e-Iqbal, Rs 200 green fees, Rs 100 club hire.

Horse riding: *Riding Club*, H/6, T 831644.

Swimming: also available at *Marriott Hotel*.

● **Tour companies & travel agents**

Adventure Tours Pakistan, PO Box 1780, T 252759, F 252145; *Adventure Travel*, 15 Wali Centre, 86 South Blue Area, T 212490, F 214580; *American Express*, 1-E, Ali Plaza, Blue Area, T 212425, F 814839; *Trans-Pakistan Adventure Services*, PO Box 2103, Apt 8, 2nd Flr, Muzaffar Chambers, Fazl-e-Haq Rd, Jinnah Ave, T 214796, F 213426; *Travel Walji's*, Walji's Bldg, 10 Khayaban-e-Suhrawardy, PO Box 1088, T 214409, F 210762; *Travelwide Services*, 16 Saeed Plaza, Blue Area, T 811457, F 824319.

● **Tourist offices**

PTDC Tourist Information Centre, Room 6 13-T/U, College Rd, Markaz F-7, T 816932 F 824173, well informed and helpful staff applications for mountaineering and trekking permits to the office next door.

Caravans Of Tartary

Waljis opens the doors to the heart of Central Asia .. Samarkand, Bokhara and Khiva; Gengis Khan and Marco Polo; Silks, scents and spices ..
Discover this enchanting and fabled land in the care of Travel Waljis , whose promise of a worry-free and comfortable holiday assures one of the ultimate travel experience.

WALJIS

Pakistan

TRAVEL WALJIS

Walji's Building,
10 Khayaban-e-Suhrawardy,
Islamabad - Pakistan.
Tel: (92-51) 210745-9 (5 lines),
214345, 214409
Fax: (92-51) 210762, 222015

The ultimate travel experience

● **Useful addresses**

Foreigners' registration: Foreigners' Registration Office, nr SSP Office, Markaz F-8 (Ayub Market; if coming by bus ask for Zafar Chowk).

Liquer permits: Central Exise and Taxation Office, Markaz F-8. You need to obtain and fill out an application form, buy court fee stamps (Rs 1/unit/month, available from the lawyers practicing in the square) and submit your application along with photocopies of the relevant pages of your passport. Your passport will be stamped and signed and you will receive a liquer permit. One unit is equal to 1 litre of spirits or around 12 bottles of beer. The permits are valid only for Islamabad, where they can be used at the Marriott Hotel. An additional 'fee' of Rs 10/unit/month was being charged in 1995 – essentially a baksheesh.

No objection certificates: Section Officer, FATA, Ministry of State and Frontier Regions, Room 232, Block S, Secretariat.

Police: the main police station is at Melody Market. Emergency: T 823333.

Travel Permits: **Khewra Salt Mine**, Manager Salt, Pakistan Mineral Development Corporation, Plot 13, H-9, T 855290; **Tarbela Dam**, Section Officer, 4th Flr, Block R, Secretariat, or contact the Protocol Officer, WAPDA, Tarbela Dam Project, Tarbela, T 568941 (sometimes WAPDA will issue permits directly, at other times they require clearance from the Secretariat).

Visa extensions: apply with photocopies of first 3 pages of your passport, + the visa page + 1 passport photo to Interior Ministry at the Secretariat, Block R. Applications between 1100-1200. Closed Fri, Sat. After obtaining a letter of approval go to the **Passport Office**, Aabpara Market, nr National Bank, T 826837. Take another photocopy of passport pages. There is no fee for an ordinary extension, but there is a fee to change a single entry visa into a double entry visa. You may be able to get an extension within a day.

● **Transport**

To & from the airport: taxis are in plentiful supply. Ford and Toyota vans – No 21, with a green stripe on the side – go from near the airport (Airport Chowk) to Islamabad via Faisalabad, Aabpara and the diplomatic enclave, terminating at the Secretariat. Alternatively there are suzuki miniwagons to Rawalpindi.

Local Bus (Intercity): the large brightly coloured Bedford buses run W from Haider Rd in Rawalpindi, looping past Cantt railway station to join Murree Rd, then link Faisalabad, Zero Point, Aabpara, Supermarket, Jinnah Supermarket, Faisal Mosque and F-8 Markaz (Zafar Chowk). They are very slow, stopping frequently and waiting to fill up with passengers. Ford and Toyota vans – Nos 1 and 6, with a red stripe on the side – follow the same route, bearing E at Supermarket towards the Secretariat; No 1 goes via the GPO and No 6 via PIA's main office. They are significantly quicker than the buses. No 3 goes from Raja Bazaar in Rawalpindi to the village of Nurpur Shahan, via Murree Rd, Zero Point, Aabpara and the diplomatic enclave. In addition to the intercity buses, No 120 vans go from G-9 Markaz (known as Karachi Co) to Aabpara via Peshawar Mor (the crossroads W of Zero Point), Zero Point, G-7 Markaz (Sitara) and G-6 Markaz (Civic Centre or Melody), sometimes continuing on to Nurpur Shahan. No 105 follows the same route, but extends as far as G-10 and sometimes F-10. **Car hire**: Avis; Europcar, 10-11 Shahid Plaza, Blue Area, F-6, T 218290, 218291, Honda and Motocorrolas of varying ages, chauffeur driven only. **Taxis**: can be found at all the main markets and cost from Rs 10-15 for short journeys.

Air/Train/Road Are all covered under Rawalpindi below. The railway station is in Rawalpindi, the airport to the E of Rawalpindi, and the main bus stand (Pir Wadhai) is on the NW outskirts of Rawalpindi. There is a bus stand at G-9 Markaz with regular coaster and mini-vans (some a/c) to Lahore, Peshawar, Murree and Abbottabad.

RAWALPINDI

Rawalpindi is a sprawling city, and one of the fastest growing in Pakistan, with three quarters of the capital area's combined population. Although it lacks any major monuments or sites of historical significance, its lively colourful bazaars have plenty of atmosphere.

The British Cantonment area around the Mall, S of the old city, was a separate settlement. It had barracks and spacious residential sections for the military and civilians, its own offices, clubs and churches. Even today it contrasts sharply with the crowded old city centred around Rajah Bazaar to the N. In between is the newer Saddar commercial area with its hotels, restaurants, banks, shops and travel agencies.

History

Archaeological finds of stone implements suggests that primitive man occupied the **Soan Valley** in the Potwar region around 300,000 years ago. The earliest implements named 'Pre-Soan' were made from large pebbles while the later, finer tools of the Palaeolithic period were named 'Early-Soan' and 'Late-Soan'. Neolithic polished stone tools dating from 10,000-5,000 BC have been found in the **Khanpur** area, while Neolithic burial sites have been discovered near **Riwat**.

Later there was a Buddhist settlement here, contemporary with Taxila, which was devastated by Hun invaders. The first Muslim invader, Mahmud of Ghazni, gave the ruined city as a gift to a Ghakkar Chief, but it remained deserted until restored by Jhanda Khan in 1493. The name comes from the village of Rawal.

Rawalpindi served as a strategic base for the Mughal Emperor Jahangir, and later was a 19th century Sikh trading centre. After the Second Sikh War the British gained control in 1849 and established the Army's General HQ for the northern region. Its importance was increased by extending the railways to it and building a large complex of military cantonment buildings there. Today, it is the headquarters of the country's Armed Forces.

Places of interest

Rajah Bazaar

The area around Raja Bazaar is the commercial heart of the old market town of Rawalpindi. Five roads radiate from Fowara Chowk at the centre, and tiny alleys with crowded bustling bazaars and craftsmen practicing their skills wind their way between these roads. It is a fascinating area to explore in and shop around for anything from jewellery, handicrafts and fabrics to smuggled electrical goods. Many of the buildings are extremely old, with intricately carved wooden balconies and windows.

Rai Bahadur Sardar Soojan Singh

This Sikh temple on Ghaznavi Rd, N of Rajah Bazaar, with its air of decaying majesty has some beautiful murals which, though damaged and neglected, are still clearly discernible. It is now occupied by the police and access is restricted.

Ayub National Park

Situated on the GT Rd beyond the Presidency and covering over 900 ha. There is a lake for boating, bridle paths, an aquarium, open-air garden restaurant and theatre, as well as a Japanese garden.

Liaqat Memorial Hall and Gardens

Originally known as Company Bagh but renamed after Liaqat Ali Khan, the first prime minister of Pakistan who was assasinated here in 1951. There is a library here and a large auditorium where art exhibitions, cultural shows and plays are staged.

Army Museum and Library

Iftkhar Rd, open 0800-1400, closed Fri. Various items of military regalia, including paintings, weapons and uniforms, and a collection of books on Pakistan's military history.

Local information

● **Accommodation**
There are over 250 hotels spread over Rawalpindi; a selection of which are given below. The best hotels are along the Mall. Mid-range and cheaper hotels are found in Saddar, in the streets leading off Rajah Bazaar and along Murree Rd, centred around Committee Chowk and Liaqat Chowk. Committee Chowk has developed a good selection of hotels, most of them on 'Hotel Square'. The location is a convenient compromise for both Islamabad and 'Pindi, and also has a bus stand for Peshawar, Lahore, Faisalabad, Sargodha and Multan.

AL *Pearl Continental*, PO Box 211, The Mall, T 566011, F 563972, Continental, Pakistani and Chinese restaurants, cafe, swimming pool, tennis courts, golf and squash by arrangement.

A *Shalimar*, off the Mall, PO Box 93, T 562901, F 566061, choice of restaurants, poolside barbecue, banquet hall, conference facilities.

B *Flashman's* 17-22 The Mall, T 581480, run by PTDC, rooms are overpriced, restaurant, swimming pool, tennis courts, banquet hall, conference facilities, tourist information in Room 59, Pakistan Tours Ltd also in hotel grounds.

C *Akbar*, Liaquat Rd, opp Liaquat Bagh, T 532001, F 557642, central a/c, satellite TV, direct dialling, banquet hall, restaurant; **C** *Al-Baddar*, Committee Chowk, T 502380, F 502330, central a/c, direct dialling, satellite TV, foreign exchange, restaurant, rooftop barbecue, banquet hall; **C** *Al-Nisar International*, Committee Chowk, T 540099, a/c and non-a/c rooms (**D**), upper floors still under construction, restaurant; **C** *Antepara*, Liaquat Rd, T 552716, a/c and non-a/c rooms (**D**), overpriced for standard of rooms, restaurant; **C** *Blue Sky*, Committee Chowk, T 557629, F 501517, central a/c, satellite TV, banquet hall,

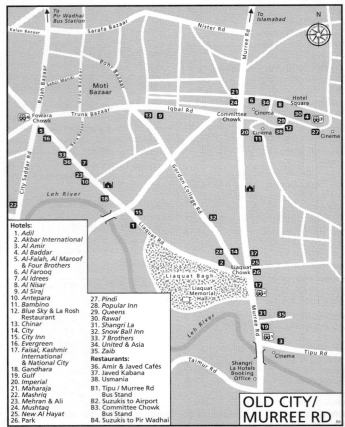

Hotels:
1. Adil
2. Akbar International
3. Al Amir
4. Al Baddar
5. Al-Falah, Al Maroof & Four Brothers
6. Al Farooq
7. Al Idrees
8. Al Nisar
9. Al Siraj
10. Antepara
11. Bambino
12. Blue Sky & La Rosh Restaurant
13. Chinar
14. City
15. City Inn
16. Evergreen
17. Faisal, Kashmir International & National City
18. Gandhara
19. Gulf
20. Imperial
21. Maharaja
22. Mashriq
23. Mehran & Ali
24. Mushtaq
25. New Al Hayat
26. Park
27. Pindi
28. Popular Inn
29. Queens
30. Rawal
31. Shangri La
32. Snow Ball Inn
33. 7 Brothers
34. United & Asia
35. Zaib

Restaurants:
36. Amir & Javed Cafés
37. Javed Kabana
38. Usmania

B1. Tipu / Murree Rd Bus Stand
B2. Suzukis to Airport
B3. Committee Chowk Bus Stand
B4. Suzukis to Pir Wadhai

OLD CITY/ MURREE RD

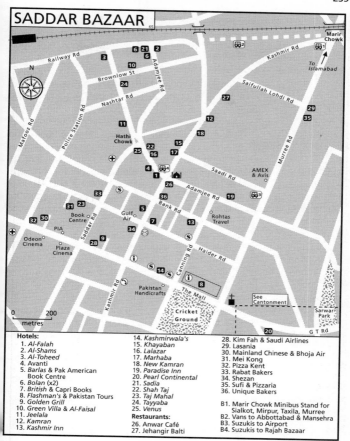

SADDAR BAZAAR

Hotels:
1. Al-Falah
2. Al-Shams
3. Al-Toheed
4. Avanti
5. Barlas & Pak American Book Centre
6. Bolan (x2)
7. British & Capri Books
8. Flashman's & Pakistan Tours
9. Golden Grill
10. Green Villa & Al-Faisal
11. Jeelala
12. Kamran
13. Kashmir Inn
14. Kashmirwala's
15. Khayaban
16. Lalazar
17. Marhaba
18. New Kamran
19. Paradise Inn
20. Pearl Continental
21. Sadia
22. Shah Taj
23. Taj Mahal
24. Tayyaba
25. Venus

Restaurants:
26. Anwar Café
27. Jehangir Balti
28. Kim Fah & Saudi Airlines
29. Lasania
30. Mainland Chinese & Bhoja Air
31. Mei Kong
32. Pizza Kent
33. Rabat Bakers
34. Shezan
35. Sufi & Pizzaria
36. Unique Bakers

B1. Marir Chowk Minibus Stand for Sialkot, Mirpur, Taxila, Murree
B2. Vans to Abbottabad & Mansehra
B3. Suzukis to Airport
B4. Suzukis to Rajah Bazaar

restaurant rec; **C Holiday**, 232B Iftikhar Khan Rd, T 568068, F 583960, central a/c, good value, helpful staff, restaurant; **C Kashmirwala's Tourist Inn**, 2 The Mall, T 583186, F 581554, situated above Union Bank, central a/c, satellite TV, helpful staff, rec restaurant; **C Mushtaq**, Committee Chowk, T 553999, TV extra, restaurant, cheaper rates (**E**) in winter; **C Paradise Inn**, PO Box 1018, 109 Adamjee Rd, T 568594, F 567048, a/c and non a/c rooms (**D**), satellite TV, rec restaurant, rooftop barbecue; **C Park**, Liaqat Bagh Chowk, Murree Rd, T 73284, F 74161, a/c and

cheaper non a/c rooms, restaurant, pleasant old building set slightly back from road, parking; **C Potohar**, N/69-76 Murree Rd, T 559609, central a/c, banquet hall, restaurant; **C Rawal**, Committee Chowk, T 556241, F 552134, central a/c, direct dialling, satellite TV, foreign exchange, banquet hall, restaurant; **C United**, Committee Chowk, T 556205, central a/c; **C Zaib**, Murree Rd, nr Moti Mahal Cinema, T 551447, a/c, TV, phone, cheaper (**D** category) non a/c rooms, restaurant.

D Al-Amir, Tipu Rd, T 500902, a/c and non a/c rooms, clean, reasonably priced but noisy,

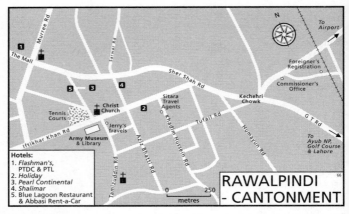

Hotels:
1. Flashman's, PTDC & PTL
2. Holiday
3. Pearl Continental
4. Shalimar
5. Blue Lagoon Restaurant & Abbasi Rent-a-Car

RAWALPINDI - CANTONMENT

restaurant; **D** *Al-Farooq*, Committee Chowk, T 556200, a/c and non-a/c rooms (**E**), banquet hall, restaurant; **D** *British*, GPO Chowk, Haider Rd, T 567377, F 584566, central a/c, somewhat run down atmosphere, restaurant; **D** *Golden Grill*, 7B The Mall, T 512842, F 562230, central a/c, satellite TV, restaurant, flying coach bookings for Gilgit; **D** *Ghandhara*, Liaquat Rd, opp Moti Mosque, T 530279, a/c and non-a/c rooms (**E**), TV, restaurant; **D** *National City*, Liaqat Bagh Chowk, Murree Rd, T 555236, a/c and non a/c rooms, TV/dish, restaurant, friendly staff; **D** *Shangrila* (not part of chain), Liaqat Bagh Chowk, Murree Rd, T 556195, a/c, TV, phone, cheaper (**E** category) non a/c rooms, restaurant.

E *Al-Siraj*, 63E Iqbal Rd, T 550400; **E** *Asia*, Hotel Sq, Committee Chowk, Murree Rd, T 70898, TV on request, restaurant; **E** *Bambino*, Committee Chowk, off Murree Rd, T 557851, simple, fairly clean, rooms a little humid, restaurant; **E** *Barlas*, 51-52 Kashmir Rd, T 567717, pleasant restaurant; **E** *Chinar*, 62E Iqbal Rd, nr Committee Chowk, T 74366, restaurant; **E** *City*, H-12, Gorden College Rd, nr Liaqat Bagh, T 553922, basic but clean and pleasant, courtyard, restaurant; **E** *Maharajah*, Committee Chowk, T 556211, restaurant; **E** *New Kamran*, Kashmir Rd, T 582040, clean rooms, parking; **E** *Pindi*, Committee Chowk, T 558809, upper floors still under construction in 1995 so may be noisy during day, but good value (prices will rise on completion), friendly, helpful staff; **E** *Queens*, Committee Chowk, Murree Rd, T 73240, TV, restaurant; **E** *Snow*

Ball Inn, H-40, Gorden College Rd, T 553327, clean, reasonable, better rooms at front, restaurant; **E** *Taj Mahal*, 32 Haider Rd, T 586802, restaurant; **E** *Tayyaba*, Saddar Bazaar, T 514591, comfortable, good value.

F *Al-Azam*, Hathi Chowk, Adamjee Rd, T 565901, friendly staff but dirty rooms – those without balconies are windowless boxes and best avoided, restaurant, best avoided, restaurant, **NB** the hotel closed down in mid 1995 for a major refit, but may never reopen; **F** *New Al-Hayat*, Liaqat Bagh Chowk, Murree Rd, T 554880, cool quiet building, reasonable rooms, good value, restaurant; **F** *Popular Inn*, G-261, Gorden College Rd, nr Liaqat Bagh, T 531884, beds on dormitory basis, or rent whole room (double), some with attached bath or share, restaurant, simple but well-run hotel, friendly, helpful staff/management, cleanest budget accommodation in Pindi, popular with backpackers, relaxing atmosphere, foreigners only.

Other cheap hotels on Adamjee Rd close to Hathi Chowk incl the **F** *Al-Falah*; **F** *Lalazar*, **F** *Shah Taj*; and **F** *Venus*, T 566501; **F** *Bolan*, Railway Rd, T 563416, has reasonable rooms.

● **Places to eat**

Pakistani: *Jehangir Balti Murgh*, 132 Kashmir Rd, T 563352, good karai, tikkas and kebabs, garden at rear; *Usmania*, Committee Chowk, rec; next door is the *Larosh*. Cheaper Pakistani-style restaurants are dotted around Saddar, Railway Rd and Rajah Bazaar.

Chinese: *Blue Lagoon*, nr Pearl Cont, off the Mall; *Chung Pa*, 163 Bank Rd, T 564577; *Shezan*, Kashmir Rd, T 565743.

Continental: the restaurants in the upper-range hotels offer Continental cuisine.

Fast food: there are numerous fast-food/snack bars, incl a *Pizza Hut* on the Mall and *Burger Express* on Kashmir Rd.

● **Airline offices**

PIA Booking Office, 5 The Mall, T 568071, open 0700-2015, 7 days, outside office hours call airport reservations, T 591071. All the other major airlines have their head offices in Karachi. The following have General Service Agents (GSAs) in Pindi; **British Airways**, Pearl Continental Hotel, The Mall, T 564702, F 567710; **Gulf Air**, King Associates, 53-6 Haider Rd, Saddar, T 584412; **Iraqi**, United Travels, 8 Mobee Plaza, Haider Rd, T 581969; **Royal Jordanian**, World Travel Consultants, T 563242; **Saudi Arabian**, Southern Travels, T 814992.

● **Banks & money changers**

American Express, Rahim Plaza, Murree Rd, T 566001; **ANZ Grindlays**, Haider Rd; **National Bank of Pakistan**, off Bank Rd.

● **Entertainment**

Cinemas: *Ciroz*, Haider Rd, Saddar, *Gullistan* and *Shabistan Cinemas* in Committee Chowk, Murree Rd; *Riaz*, further N on Murree Rd.

● **Hospitals & medical services**

Chemists: most of the chemists are located opp the hospitals.

Hospitals: *Cantonment General Hospital*, Saddar Rd, T 562254; *Rawalpindi General Hospital*, Murree Rd, T 847761.

● **Post & telecommunications**

Area code: 051.

Post Office: GPO, Kashmir Rd, Saddar. Poste restante at rear.

Central Telegraph Office: (Pak Telecom Customer Services Centre), Kashmir Rd, T 580276, open 24 hrs/7 days. There is also a telegraph office for international calls opp the GPO, across the Mall.

● **Shopping**

The main shopping areas are around Saddar and Rajah Bazaar. The streets and tiny alleys around Rajah Bazaar each contain their own smaller bazaars, with the various trades grouped together in traditional Asian style. **Kalan Bazaar** is the main cloth market. **Sarafa**

Bazaar sells intricate hand worked gold and silver jewellery as well as brass, copper and tin utensils. **Moti Bazaar** is the women's market with beads, hairbraids, shawls, make-up etc. **Bara Bazaar**, named after a smuggling town in NWFP nr the border with Afghanistan, is full of smuggled electrical goods and other items. **Bohr Bazaar** contains medical shops, both western and traditional, while **Rajah Bazaar** itself centres around stalls of vegetables, spices and dried fruits and nuts, piled high in colourful arrays.

Saddar has a good selection of antique, jewellery and handicraft shops, some along the Mall, incl *Pakistan Handicrafts*, and others along Kashmir Rd and Haider Rd. On Sun there is a market with handicrafts, second-hand books and numerous other items, which spreads out along Kashmir Rd, centred on the junctions with Haider, Bank and Adamjee rds.

Bookshops: there are several bookshops around Saddar, incl the *Capri* on Haider Rd, the *Pak-American Commercial*, upstairs on Kashmir Rd and *Book Centre*, Saddar Rd, all with a good selection, incl magazines and newspapers. There are also a number of second-hand bookshops.

● **Sports**

Good sports facilities in Liaqat Gardens.

Cricket: Cricket ground off the Mall, although the international Test Match venue is on Stadium Rd, just off Murree Rd (nr to Faisabad).

Golf: there is an 18-hole golf course adjoining Ayub Park and boating on the lake in the park itself.

● **Tour companies & travel agents**

Himalaya Treks and Tours, 112 Rahim Plaza, Murree Rd, T/F 56304; *Pakistan Tours Ltd* (PTL), a branch of PTDC, are situated in the grounds of Flashman's Hotel, they offer a number of package tours and also tailor-made arrangements for groups and individuals, willing to cater for all budgets; *Sitara Travel Consultants*, Sitara House, 232 Khadim Hussain Rd, PO Box 63, T 564750, F 584958, offer a wide range of options, incl tours of Central Asia.

● **Tourist offfices**

PTDC is situated in Room 59 of Flashman's Hotel. PTDC have 2 seats per flight to the Northern Areas (Gilgit/Skardu) reserved for foreign tourists; they will issue you with a letter to present to PIA. Book as early as possible. Selection of brochures etc, PTDC in Islamabad is more helpful/informative; **TDCP** (Tourism Development Corporation of the Punjab), T 564824, is situated on the corner of Kashmir Rd and The Mall.

● **Useful addresses**

Foreigners' registration: Senior Superintendent of Police, Civil Courts, off Willian Rd.

Police: Police Station Rd, Saddar Bazaar, T 564760.

● **Transport**

To & from the airport: there are plenty of taxis available at the airport, many of which now have working meters; the trip should not cost more than Rs 70. There are no buses, but Suzuki mini-wagons costing Rs 4 (very cramped) run from the main road outside the airport to Adamjee Rd in Saddar Bazaar and Fowara Chowk in Rajah Bazaar.

Local Car hire: Abbasi Tours, Masood Akhtar Rd, opp Pearl Continental, T 516733, chauffeur driven cars only, hourly/daily/weekly rates, choice of models. **Bus (Intercity)**: see Islamabad above. **Taxis**: are readily available throughout Rawalpindi. **Tongas** can be hired from Fowara Chowk, Rajah Bazaar, and from Committee Chowk.

Air Islamabad and Rawalpindi share the international airport. PIA, Shaheen Air and Aero Asia all operate from here. Major routes, particularly Lahore, and also Karachi and Quetta, should be booked well in advance. **PIA**: regular flights to Lahore (up to 9 daily), Karachi (up to 8 daily), Peshawar (4 daily), Quetta (Mon, Tues, Wed, Thur, Fri, Sat), Gilgit (up to 3 daily, weather permitting), Skardu (1 daily, 2 Mon), Multan (up to 3 daily), Faisalabad (2 daily), Bahawalpur (1 daily), Dera Ismail Khan (1 daily), Hyderabad (up to 3 daily), Muzzaffarabad (Mon, Tues, Wed, Thur, Sat, Sun), Saidu Sharif (1 daily, 2 Thur, Sat), Sukkur (Tues, Thur, Sun), Zhob (1 daily), Parachinar (Mon, Fri). **Air Safaris** PIA now operate 'air safaris' to K2 and back, leaving at 0900 Sat, weather permitting. **Shaheen Air**: daily flights to Karachi and Lahore. **Aero Asia**: daily flights to Karachi.

Train There is a Pakistan Railways info centre and booking office in Islamabad, at Melody Market, T 827474, as well as at the station, T 555 292. Sleepers and a/c must be booked well in advance. The main booking office for sleepers and upper class tickets is opp Rawalpindi station. Concessions from the Commercial Department. **Havelian (via Taxila)**: *Hazara Exp*, 1730, 3¼ hrs; *R-455*, 0520,

3¼ hrs. **Karachi**: *Tezgam*, 0815, 25¾ hrs; *Awam Exp*, 1215, 29½ hrs; *Khyber Mail*, 0220, 28½ hrs. **Kohat**: *188*, 1630, 4¾ hrs. **Lahore**: *Tezgam*, 0815, 5¾ hrs; *Awam Exp*, 1215, 6 hrs; *Zulfiqar Exp*, 1435, 6½ hrs; *Khyber Mail*, 0220, 6¼ hrs. **Multan**: *Mehran Exp*, 1715, 41¾ hrs. **Peshawar**: *Awam Exp*, 1410, 4 hrs; *Zulfiqar Exp*, 1650, 3¾ hrs; *Chenab Exp*, 0420, 4¼ hrs; *Khyber Mail*, 0310, 3¾ hrs. These often arrive late in Pindi; the *RC-57*, 0715, 3¾ hrs, originating from Pindi is better. **Quetta**: *Quetta Exp*, 0645, 35 hrs; *Abbaseen Exp*, 2215, 36 hrs.

Road Bus: Pir Wadhai, the main bus station, is inconveniently situated on the NW outskirts of Rawalpindi, SW of Islamabad. A taxi is the best way to get there. There are Suzuki minivans from Fowara Chowk in Rajah Bazaar, and regular buses from Faisalabad. There are services to all the major cities and nearby towns. It is a large and chaotic place and locating the correct bus can be confusing. Conductors and touts compete to hussle you aboard their bus. Masherbrum Tours, T 863895 and NATCO (Northern Areas Transport Corporation) T 860283, both of which operate services to **Gilgit**, originate here. **Committee Chowk**: the bus stand here has regular a/c coach services to **Lahore** (Rs 75), **Peshawar** (Rs 40), **Faisalabad** (Rs 100), **Sarghoda** (Rs 75) and **Multan** (Rs 100). TDCP operates a/c bus services to **Lahore** (0900, 1600, 2355, Rs 80) and **Murree** (0930, Rs 20), tickets and departures from their office on the corner of Kashmir Rd and The Mall. *Hameed Travel Service*, Mashriq Hotel, City Saddar Rd, T 73387, has daily a/c coaster services to **Gilgit**, Rs250, 17+ hrs, late afternoon departures. *Sargin Travel*, based opposite Novelty Cinema, nr Fowara Chowk (see map) also operate coasters to **Gilgit**; Rs 250, 17+ hrs, 1500 and 1700. Liaqat Chowk/Tipu Rd *New Flying Coach*, Shangri La Hotel, T 504840, has regular a/c coasters and buses to **Peshawar**, **Lahore**, **Mansehra/Abbottabad** and **Sialkot**. There are several other companies with services to the above destinations, as well as **Sargodha**, **Gujrat**, **Mandi Bahawaldin** and various towns in **Azad Jammu and Kashmir**. Marir Chowk *Hamrhai Travels*, T 565215, has regular Hiace minibuses to **Sialkot**, **Gujranwala**, **Mirpur**, **Chakwal**, **Pind Dada Khan** and **Mianwali**. **Punjab Sarhad Wagon Stand** has Hiaces to **Taxila**, **Wah**, **Attock** and **Murree**.

EXCURSIONS FROM ISLAMABAD/ RAWALPINDI

There are several fascinating excursions from the capital. The Margalla Hills offer some very attractive walks. The famous archaeological remains at Taxila, dating back to the 6th century BC, are just 40 km away. The Tarbela Dam, also easily reached from Islamabad, is a spectacular sight, particularly when full. If you are limited for time, it is also possible to visit the hill stations such as Murree and Thandiani as longer excursions from Islamabad, as well as places further afield to the N and NW.

Margalla Hills

The **Margalla Hills** are also known as the **Islamabad National Park**. Formed of limestone, they cover an area of about 12,000 ha. Numerous nature trails wind around the hills and valleys offering a choice for walkers and hikers of distances covering 1½ km to 15 km (a total length of 110 km), and ranging from heights of 640-1,580m. As well as a wide selection of short walks and half to full-day hikes, there are also longer treks which can take up to 2 to 3 days; go prepared for these with the best maps and a compass. The easy trails can be undertaken in 'trainers' but several are stony and require strong shoes or walking boots. You can start several treks from Islamabad on foot (see below). The best season is Oct-Apr but even in these relatively cooler months, midday can be very hot. Be prepared for heavy rain in Jan and Feb and chilly nights.

Follow the trails, avoid short cuts, as it is easy to get lost (and the thorn bushes can be painful), and carry drinking water with you. In the dry season there is the added risk of fire. The Asia Study Group's *Hiking Around Islamabad* (1992 Revised edition) has very good detailed maps and lists the different possibilities in the Margalla Hills and a few further

N. The Capital Development Authorities *Trekking in the Margalla Hills* is not accurate enough for the longer trails.

The row of hills facing Islamabad is called the '**First Ridge**' with a number of valleys and ravines with pools, springs and water falls, cutting into them from the plains. Some valleys have descriptive names: *Dara Baliman* (Quarry Valley), *Santari* (Banyan Tree Valley), *Nurpur Sara* (Rock Pools Valley), *Rata Hotter* (Leopard Valley) among others. The next row, parallel to the 'First Ridge' and separated from it by the deep *Nilan Nullah*, is known as the '**Second Ridge**'. The only motorable road through the hills is the Pir Sahawa Rd, which starts from the Khayaban-e-Iqbal (or Margalla Rd), near the Zoo, and runs up to the 'First Ridge' eastward. A jeepable track continues E from Pir Sahawa where there is a *Forest Rest House*. Tracks come down to the Nilan Nullah from the Pir Sahawa Rd.

The short walks start near the Zoo (Marghazar), or from Daman-e-Koh or Pir Sahawa. Picnic spots have 'Shades' which can be crowded on Fri. You can reach the highest point in the hills (1,640m) from Pir Sahawa. If you are with children keen on bathing, try the Rock Pools Valley which you can get to by driving up N of Nurpur Shahan village, parking near the Mandiala water works. The longer hikes taking from 4-8 hrs or 2-3 days are described in the Asia Study Group's booklet.

Margalla vegetation The hills have been planted with sub-tropical local as well as non-indigenous ornamental plants with evidence of the primary forest only at the higher levels. The slopes below 1,000m have dry, semi-evergreen vegetation, with acacia and olive predominating. Shrubs protect against soil erosion. On the higher slopes, taller pines are common, particularly *Pinus roxburghii* and also the white oak, *Quercus incana*, which can be a fire hazard. There are numerous other species including *sheesham* and the wild date

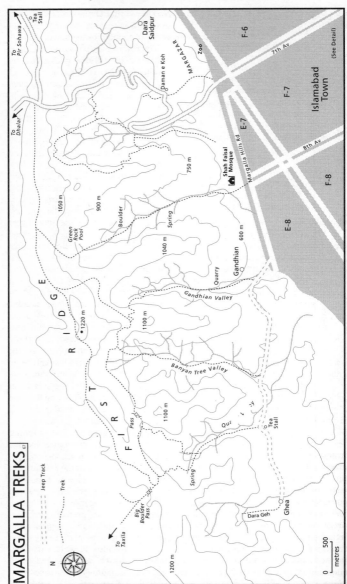

MARGALLA TREKS

- - - - Jeep Track
········· Trek

N

To Pir Sohawa

To Dhalar

Tea Stall

Dara Saidpur

Daman e Koh

MARGAZAR

Zoo

F-6

7th Av

(See Detail)

F-7

Islamabad Town

E-7

8th Av

F-8

750 m

Shah Faisal Mosque

Margalla Hills Rd

E-8

900 m

1050 m

Boulder

Spring

Green Rock Pool

1040 m

600 m

Gandhian

Quarry

Gandhian Valley

RIDGE

•1220 m

1100 m

Banyan Tree Valley

FIRST

Pass

1100 m

Ki

Qui

Tea Stall

Spring

Big Boulder Pass

To Taxila

Dara Geh

Ghea

1200 m

0   500
metres

palm, *Phoenix sylvestris*, the silk cotton tree, *Bombax ceiba*, and the Peepul, *Ficus religiosa*.

Ornamental species include jacaranda, bottlebrush, eucalyptus, amalthus, lilies and chir. In the spring, the plants, strikingly similar to European flora, flower in Mar until mid-Apr when they die down. Then around the beginning of Jul, the barren ground comes to life again with flora of Southeast Asia. A good guide available in Islamabad is *Wild flowers of Rawalpindi-Islamabad Districts* by Nasir and others (1987).

Fauna in the Hills Hunting has been banned and afforestation carried out. Animals and birds now include rhesus monkeys, barking deer, jackal, wild boar, porcupines, mongoose, pangolin (scaly anteater), the rare leopard in the winter as well as black partridges and birds of prey and a large number of butterfly species. Cheer pheasants which had become virtually extinct have been successfully reintroduced. Poisonous snakes include cobra, krait, and Russell's viper. They hibernate in the winter, but take care when walking off the paths in the warmer months. The ASG has published a list of birds by Corfield which supplements the handy *Guide to the birds of the sub-continent* published by Collins. If you are keen to identify butterflies, try *Butterflies of India* by Chas and Antram or *Butterflies of the Himalaya* by Mani.

Tarbela Dam

Tarbela is the world's largest earth-filled dam. Construction work on the dam began in 1968 as part of Pakistan's response to the Indus Waters Treaty of 1960 (see page 218). It was funded in part by contributions from a number of foreign countries (including India), administered by the World Bank and built by an European consortium led by the Italian firm Impreglio. Designed to store nearly 14 million cu metres of water and generate 2.1 million KW of electricity, the dam is still not complete due to unforeseen technical difficulties and design defects. Some experts have criticised it as a dangerous venture in what is an unpredictable earthquake zone. The build-up of silt in the lake, reducing its storage capacity, has proved to be a far greater problem than expected.

The best views of the dam are from its eastern side. From **Ghazi** the road passes through a checkpost and climbs through woods to viewpoints overlooking the two enormous sluice gates. The extensive 'town' of Tarbela which grew up to house the army of technicians and engineers involved in constructing and maintaining the dam is spread across the hillside amongst the woods. Late Aug/early Sep are usually peak flow times, when at least one of the gates are open, unleashing a massive cascade of white water that thunders down before hitting concrete breakers at the bottom and exploding hundreds of feet into the air in a spectacular fountain. The sight is a truly awesome one. The road then passes through a second checkpost and crosses the sluice gates before following the banks of the huge lake created by the dam and descending past more viewpoints to follow the base of the dam across to the other side. The road which runs along the top of the dam is closed to the general public; it may be possible to use it if visiting as part of an official tour.

Visiting the Dam For a guided tour, contact WAPDA's Public Relations Officer in Tarbela (see under Useful Addresses in Islamabad). The staff are not particularly helpful over the phone, and some travellers suggest simply turning up at their office in Tarbela and trying your luck there. You can travel across the dam, from Ghazi to Topi, without a special permit. The viewpoints, and access to the route across the dam, are open only during daylight hours. There are regular buses from Hasan Abdal to Ghazi, and from there to Topi, from where you can either return to the GT Rd at Jehangira or continue W towards Mardan (see page 376). There is also a direct road from Haripur to Ghazi. **NB** No photography in the vicinity.

Taxila

History

The site at Taxila has been occupied from at least the **Neolithic** period. Excavations at **Sarai Khola**, 3 km SW of Taxila city, have shown a succession of occupations, the earliest having several pit dwellings with ground stone axes and burnished pottery. However, until recently it was widely believed that the town first came to prominence when the whole area was incorporated into the **Achaemenid Empire** of **Cyrus the Great** (558-530 BC).

In an inscription of 519 BC the third Achaemenid Emperor, **Darius I**, claimed possession of Gandhara, and soon after of 'Hindush', a region which may well have covered most of the Punjab. By then Taxila was already the centre of a major university, attracting students from as far afield as modern Patna. It occupied a strategically important site on one of the ancient world's most important trade routes. If you stand at the monastery of **Jaulian** today you can still gain a sense of the advantage that its site offered, with the hills behind and the broadening lowlands spreading out below.

Recent excavations by the Cambridge-Pakistan team have produced evidence which supports the finds of Sir Mortimer Wheeler at **Charsadda** to suggest that Taxila was founded possibly as early as 1000 BC. It probably retained a degree of independence throughout the period of Persian rule. When **Alexander the Great** arrived it was certainly still a centre of learning and culture, for Alexander himself is recorded as having philosophical discussions with naked ascetics. However, the Greek occupation

of Taxila was extraordinarily brief, and their influence at this period slight.

They were succeeded around 310 BC by **Chandragupta Maurya**. The contacts with the Greeks were maintained through the reign of his son **Bindusara**, who is recorded as having sent a request to the Greek King Antiochus for "a present of figs, wine and a sophist". According to Basham, Antiochus responded by sending figs and wine, but sent a message to the effect that "Greek philosophers were not for export". During this period Bindusara's son **Asoka**, who was to become one of India's greatest Kings, became the Mauryan Viceroy in Taxila, and the Mauryan influence remained strong throughout his rule.

In the 4th century BC Taxila enjoyed a reputation for learning at least equal to that of Varanasi, with which it was contemporary. However, Taxila was particularly noted for its secular studies. **Caraka**, a master of medicine, **Kautilya**, the Brahman adviser in statecraft to the Emperor Chandragupta and **Panini**, author of the most famous Sanskrit grammar, all worked in Taxila. Throughout this period, the city of Taxila was focused on the area that now is known as the **Bhir Mound**.

From the middle of the 3rd century BC Taxila became the scene of a series of invasions from the NW. Bactrian Greeks under **Euthydemus** gained sufficient independence to break away completely from the Mauryan Empire, establishing a bridgehead for the introduction of western ideas into India. Their widespread coinage gives some impression of the extent and length of their rule, and it seems that Western theories of astrology and medicine, as well as Sanskrit drama, entered at this time. However, by the second half of the 2nd century BC, Bactria was occupied by Parthians and the Greeks in Taxila and its region became isolated. At the beginning of the 2nd century BC the

Bactrian Greeks built a new and quite different city at Taxila, known as **Sirkap**.

Basham suggests that one of the last of the Bactrian kings, **Gondophernes**, may have been the first Indian to have contact with Christianity. "If we are to believe a very old tradition" he writes "the first Christian converts were made by the disciple Thomas himself, soon after the Crucifixion". Gondophernes sent to Syria for a skilful architect to build him a new city, and the envoy returned with St Thomas who told the king of a city not made with hands, and converted him and many members of his court. St Thomas afterwards preached in other parts of India, and died a martyr's death at the hands of a king called in Christian tradition **Misdeos**, who cannot be identified. Many in S India believe that his martyrdom took place at St Thomas's Mount, just outside Madras.

New population movements took place, originating from China, and the **Scythians**, known in India as the Sakas, pressed down from the N into Bactrian lands. By the middle of the 1st century BC the power of the Bactrian Greeks had almost totally disintegrated. The Kushan king **Kanishka** founded the third of Taxila's cities, **Sirsukh**, which was occupied until the middle of the 5th century AD. Shortly afterwards the **Huns** caused widespread destruction, and although the city continued to be occupied for some time it never recovered. The Chinese pilgrim **Hiuen Tsang**, visiting it in the 7th century AD, described it as very decayed.

Visiting the sites

The various sites at Taxila are spread out over a large area. Many visitors return from a tour of the archaeological remains somewhat disappointed; most of the sites are poorly labelled, and for the non-specialist, what are in fact some of the most important excavations in the world, can appear to be no more than an uninspiring pile of old stones. Perhaps the greatest problem is that most tourists come during the summer months, when day-time temperatures often reach well above 40°C. Combined with the lack of shade and the considerable amounts of walking involved, this can make for exhausting work. Visiting in winter infinitely preferable. Otherwise, it is well worth starting as early as possible, perhaps using the hottest part of the day to visit the excellent museum and to rest, and then making use also of the relatively cooler evening hours for more sight-seeing. For the non-specialist, it is also worth being fairly selective as there is a great deal to see; those with a special interest will certainly want to spend more than a day here. The most visually impressive sites are Jaulian, Dharmarajika, Jandial and Sirkap. A possible tour if you have hired a tonga/taxi and have limited time, is to start early at Jaulian, then visit Jandial and Sirkap, send your transport round to Dharmarajika and walk there from Sirkap. Finish with a tour of the museum.

Taxila Museum Open 0830-1230, 1430-1730 in summer (1 Apr-30 Sep); 0800-1600 in winter (1 Oct-31 Mar). Closed first Mon of each month for cleaning. Built during Sir Mortimer Wheeler's time to house the fruits of his exhaustive excavations, this excellent museum is notable for its first class examples of Gandharan sculpture and art, giving some idea of the full splendour of Taxila in its hey-day. There is also an impressive collection of coins and silver ornaments in a small room off the main hall (ask to be shown if the room is locked).

Bir Mound Covering the area of land to the S of the museum, and visible from the road, this is the oldest of the sites, dating from the 6th-2nd centuries BC, and was partially excavated by Sir John Marshall. There is little to see here; the excavations suggest that the settlement was a jumble of unplanned alleys and streets packed tightly together.

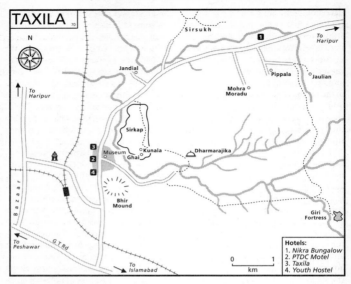

Dharmarajika From the car park at the end of the road, follow the clearly marked path down into a small ravine, across two streams and then up a steep hill that conceals the stupa and surrounding buildings until you are nearly there. The stupa and monastery at the centre of this site possibly date from Asoka's time in the mid 3rd century BC. The main stupa, 15m high, was enlarged after its initial construction and some of the decoration on its E side was added in the 4th century AD.

Originally there was a series of small *votive stupas* (built by wealthy devotees) around the main building, and a series of chapels. If you walk round the stupa to the E side along one of the two processional paths that are a feature of Buddhist stupas you will see the great cut where treasure hunters looked for the relics of the Buddha. When Asoka converted to Buddhism after the great Kalingan War in modern Orissa in India, it is said that he disinterred the

Buddha's remains from their casket at Vaisali and distributed them to eight major stupas across his empire, of which Dharmarajika is one. The best preserved work on this main stupa, the band of ornamental stone carving on the E side of the base, dates from the 4th and 5th centuries.

Immediately to the S of the main stupa is another comparatively well preserved though much smaller stupa, notable for the carvings of a series of Buddhas shown wearing local Kushan style dress. Walking N past the E side of the main stupa you pass a chapel in the NE corner of the compound. There are representations of two of the Buddha's feet, large enough to have supported a statue 11m high. To the N again and on slightly higher ground is the large enclosed space of a former monastery, occupied for as much as 600 years from the 1st century BC. Immediately to the N of the main stupa is a bathing tank, some votive stupas and a building that may have housed an image of the reclining Buddha. Just to the SW of the main stupa, near the entrance to the complex, is an apsidal ended 'chapel'.

Sirkap It is possible to take the path from the NW corner of Dharmarajika, and to walk through a narrow valley up to the stupa and monastery of Kunala on a hill, before going down into Taxila's second city, Sirkap. Alternatively, follow the road N past the *PTDC Motel*; the turning is signposted to the right.

Hiuen Tsang related how the **Kunala stupa** was built on the spot where Kunala, Asoka's son, had his eyes put out at the instructions of his stepmother. As is true of many stupas, the outer shell contains an earlier and much smaller stupa, in this case barely 3m high. The smaller one may date from the 1st century BC, while the larger structure around it dates from the 3rd century AD. You get an excellent view of the city from the stupa.

The remains of Sirkap that have been excavated (just a small part) show a N-S main street, fortified at the N end, and regularly spaced lanes. Most of the buildings come from the beginning of the 2nd century BC through to 85 BC. One feature of the houses is their underground rooms, approached through trap doors.

You need imagination to recapture what Sirkap must have been like when it was occupied. As at Moenjo Daro, the main street at Sirkap was probably lined with shops with 2-storey houses behind them, arranged round courtyards. Halfway down the main street on the E side is the shrine of the **Double-Headed Eagle**, a 1st century AD stupa. Immediately to its S is a small **Jain stupa**. At the extreme S end of the street, again on the E side, is the royal palace, now largely invisible.

Jandial The turning left for Jandial (also signposted) is a little further along the main road from Sirkap. This temple shows obvious signs of its Greek ancestry. It comprised a square inner sanctuary, a meeting hall and a courtyard. Its entrances were flanked by Ionian columns. The existence of a solid tower between the sanctuary and back porch, which would have allowed the rising and setting sun to be observed, have been taken to suggest that this was probably used for **Zoroastrian** worship. It dates from the beginning of the Christian era.

Sirsukh The signposted turning left for Sirsukh is about 1 km further along the main road from Jandial. There is very little to see on the site, which is only partially excavated.

Jaulian It is a short steep climb from the car park to the monastery, but you are rewarded with a magnificent view over the plains below. These are perhaps the most impressive and evocative remains visible today. The site is fully enclosed and there is always a caretaker in attendance.

The entrance is to the lower court leading to the main stupa. This is nothing like the scale of Dharmarajika, but it is far more fully decorated. Some of the surrounding votive stupas have inscriptions in **Kharoshthi** script. Some of the most important sculptures and relics are in the museum. While several of these stupas date from as late as the 5th century, the main monastery to the W comes from the 2nd century. However, the plaster statues of the Buddha are copies of the originals which are in the museum. Surrounding the monastery courtyard are monks cells, originally with plastered and painted walls, rather than the bare stone which now survives.

Local information
● Accommodation & places to eat

C *PTDC Motel*, T (0596) 2344, 3 a/c rm, 2 non a/c (**D** category), comfortable and clean, restaurant, PTDC Tourist Information Centre (phone number as for hotel), gift shop.

E *Taxila*, reasonable rooms with fan, clean, good restaurant.

F *Youth Hostel*, 2 double rm with attached bath, 12-bed dorm (2 toilets, valuables lockers), common room, kitchen, garden (camping), clean, pleasant, well-kept youth hostel, excellent value.

There are two comfortable Archaeological Dept *Rest Houses*, one on the museum grounds, and another, *Nikra Bungalow*, opp the turning to Jaulian. Unfortunately, they are for Archaeological Dept guests only. You could try making a reservation with the Curator of the museum, or with the Director General of Archaeology, Govt of Pakistan, Karachi, at least 10 days in advance.

● **Shopping**

The *Asian Arts* gift shop in the *PTDC Motel* has an wide selection of jewellery, antiques, clothing, souvenirs etc, an excellent (though overpriced) collection of books and their own series of high-quality postcards. There are a number of craft shops selling replicas of Gandharan pieces, as well as traditonal stone pestal and mortars, along from the *Taxila Hotel*. PTDC and the museum kiosk sell booklets and pamphlets about Taxila. If available, *Gandhara, an Instant Guide to Taxila*, is rec.

● **Transport**

Local There are regular public Datsuns and Suzukis plying between the GT Rd and the museum, or you can hire a horse-drawn tonga (about Rs 30). To get around the various sites, which are spread over a large area, you can also hire a tonga, or a taxi, from outside the *PTDC Motel*. A tonga to visit all the main sights (allow at least 6 hrs) should cost around Rs 250; make sure it is clear exactly where you want to go and for roughly how long. A taxi (for around 3 hrs) should cost about Rs 300, but you may have to bargain hard. Organizing transport through PTDC is likely to be a little more expensive, but also more reliable. During winter, a bicycle is an ideal way of getting around, although they are not available for rent in Taxila.

Train The train station at Taxila is within easy walking distance of the museum and hotels. There are 4 trains per day to Rawalpindi, and 4 to Peshawar. Check with PTDC for exact timings as they are subject to frequent minor changes.

Road Bus: frequent buses to Rawalpindi or Peshawar can be caught from the GT Rd, by the junction with Taxila bazaar. Most Rawalpindi-bound buses go to Pir Wadhai, but there are others to Saddar and Rajah Bazaar. Local buses also pass the museum en-route to Haripur.

ISLAMABAD/RAWALPINDI TO MURREE

To the NE of Islamabad, on a series of outlying Himalayan spurs, lie a series of settlements that were developed by the British as hill resorts. Known as 'hill stations', they were used by the British administration and their families to escape the summer heat of the Punjab plains. With their cool summers and brisk winters, they remain popular today with Punjabi tourists and expatriate staff in Islamabad.

The most developed of the hill stations, **Murree**, is 64 km from Islamabad and can be reached by car in under 2 hrs along a good quality, winding alpine road. However, on weekends and holidays the road can be packed with traffic, and drivers should be prepared to encounter suicidal overtaking manoeuvres on the bends.

The toll road passes **Chattar Bagh** (20 km), a tacky picnic spot being developed by TDCP, with mini-zoo, water park, nature trail, children's playground and restaurant. From here, the road gently climbs to the small village of **Tret** (40 km) at an elevation of nearly 1,000m, where pines first appear. Most public buses and minivans stop at **Charra Pani** (18 km) for tea and photos, before continuing to **Ghora Gali** (at 1,600m). Prior to the provision in 1907 of motor transport on this route, this was the point between Rawalpindi and Murree where the carriage horses were changed. Ghora Gali is also the site of the old Murree Brewery. Several km beyond here, at **Bansra Gali**, is the prestigious Lawrence College. Initially established as an asylum for army orphans, it became one of British India's, and now Pakistan's, most reputable education establishments. The road climbs through a sharp S bend at **Sunny Bank** to **Murree**.

Murree

Despite losing its position as summer capital of the British Indian Empire to Simla in 1876, Murree remains the most popular of Pakistan's hill stations. The best season is Apr to Jun, although weekends and holidays remain busy all year round. In summer, Murree can become ridiculously crowded with Punjabi day-trippers taking advantage of the refreshing climate. Yet winter weekends, particularly Jan to Mar, attract equally large numbers of visitors keen to experience their first encounter with snow. You will need light woollens and cottons in summer and heavy woollens in winter.

Places of interest

Despite its ability to draw large numbers of tourists all year round, there are not that many places of interest within the town itself. Beside the views, the main attraction in Murree is a stroll along **The Mall**. Lined with cafes, restaurants and souvenir shops, the Mall is a popular meeting point, as well as being the place to 'be seen'. Although a 1972 ordinance bans motor vehicles from the Mall during summer (with the exception of those carrying the President, Prime Minister or certain VIPs), Murree often suffers from traffic jams of the

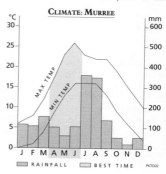

CLIMATE: MURREE

RAINFALL   BEST TIME

SIR FRANCIS YOUNGHUSBAND

Born in Murree on 31 May 1863, Francis Younghusband was destined to become one of Britain's most distinguished explorers and celebrated adventurers. As a young subaltern in the Indian army, he made a name for himself in 1887, when he completed an extraordinary 2,000 km journey across China into India by a route never before attempted by a European.

A Captain in the King's Dragoon Guards at the age of 26, Younghusband became embroiled in the 'Great Game' of espionage and counter-espionage in the high valleys and passes of British India's remote and ill-defined northern margins. Younghusband filled in many of the blanks on the British maps of the Pamir, Hindu Kush, Karakoram and Western Himalayan mountain knot, and in recognition of these solitary travels, he became the youngest ever Fellow of the Royal Geographical Society and a winner of its prestigious Gold Medal. He was to become the first European to reach Karakul Lake, the first to visit Hunza, the first into Chitral, and in 1904, at the head of a British expedition, was the first European to set foot in the holy Tibetan city of Lhasa.

Younghusband's travels in these mountains and amongst their peoples had a profound effect upon him, and within these awesome mountain scenes, he sensed a physical manifestation of the greatness of God. Although he was a committed Christian, Younghusband was fascinated by the teachings of the other great religions with which he came into contact, particularly Buddhism, Islam and Hinduism. He went on to write two books outlining his religious philosophy, "Life in the Stars" (1927) and "The Living Universe" (1933), and in 1936 went on to found the "World Congress of Faiths".

human variety. The vehicle ban does not apply, however, to buggy loads of spoilt, fat, rich children, pushed up the hill by scowling Kohistani youths. It is also possible to take pony and donkey rides.

At the NE point of the ridge upon which Murree stands, **Kashmir Point** offers fine views across the Jhelum River and Pir Panjal range into Kashmir. 7 km along the ridge to the SW, **Pindi Point** overlooks the twin cities of Islamabad and Rawalpindi below. The scene is particularly attractive on a clear night. From Pindi Point, the Wonderland **chair-lift** makes the return trip (Rs 40) to the road several km below. In addition to providing excellent views, the ride gives young Pakistani girls the rare opportunity to flirt outrageously with passengers travelling in the opposite direction. Remarkably, the chair-lift seems to operate in all weathers, but this author can assure you that it is no fun in high winds and driving rain.

Murree does retain a certain colonial air, with its neat bungalows, summer cottages, gardens and churches, but the recent rapid pace of unplanned development is threatening to engulf the town.

Excursions

At almost 2,000m, 16 km from Murree, **Bhurban** has an excellent 9-hole golf course (open May-Oct, members only in high season). It also has one of Pakistan's best appointed hotels, **AL** *Pearl Continental*, T 427082, F 427081, that offers superb views from its a/c rooms, terrace restaurant and even from its swimming pool, the hotel offers shuttle service to/from Islamabad.

19 km from Murree is the TDCP developed attraction of **Patriata**. A chair-lift and then cable-car carries passengers 3½ km to the summit of Patriata Peak (2,187m). Opened in 1990 by Nawaz Sharif, the Patriata 'Skyride' is now one of Murree's prime attractions.

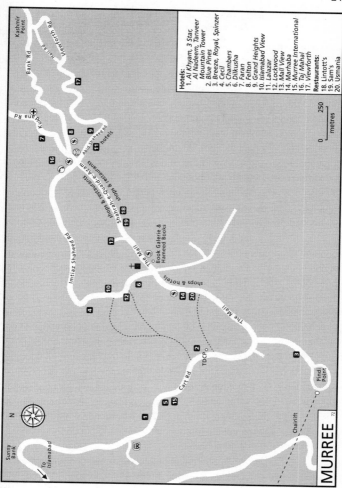

MURREE 72

Hotels:
1. Al Khyam, 3 Star,
   Al Nadeem, Tanveer
   Mountain Tower
2. Blue Pines
3. Breeze, Royal, Spinzer
4. Cecil
5. Chambers
6. Dilkusha
7. Faran
8. Felton
9. Grand Heights
10. Islamabad View
11. Lalazar
12. Lockwood
13. Mall View
14. Marhaba
15. Murree International
16. Taj Mahal
17. Viewforth
Restaurants:
18. Lintott's
19. Sam's
20. Usmania

For Rs 60 return, the chair-lift makes the equivalent of a 250m vertical rise from the base at Gulehra Gali (often referred to as New Murree), before transferring to 8 seater cable-cars for the 209m vertical rise to the summit. The views are magnificent, although getting on and off the moving chair-lift can be brutal, and the whole experience is not recommended for vertigo sufferers. Wandering through the tranquil pine forests at the summit is very relaxing, and the vista across towards Kashmir is superb. For those fully equipped, there is great camping potential. At the base and summit there are restaurants and children's playgrounds. Wagons to Patriata run when full from Murree bus stand.

Local information

● Accommodation

Hotels in Murree are expensive by Pakistani standards, even in the off season. During the high season (Apr-Sep), on holidays, and even at weekends, prices may double or treble. Most hotels do not have the range of facilities to match the price tag, but the almost unlimited choice of accommodation at least gives you a bargaining position. Hotels listed below are categorized according to their **high season** tariff.

B *Cecil*, Imtiaz Shaheed Rd, T 411131, best in town, has more expensive suites, ultra expensive deluxe suites, plus cheaper rooms in the annexe, prices halve in off season, dish TV, phone, tennis, children's park, lawns, conference hall, car rental, restaurant, superb views, given that lesser quality hotels charge similar rates, hotel is good value; **B** *Mall View*, The Mall, T 411111, dish TV, phone, fridge, conference hall, car rental, laundry, but over priced. Other **B/C** hotels on Imtiaz Shaheed Rd incl *Islamabad View*, T 411499; *Lockwood*, T 410270; **B/C** *Felton*, Bank Rd, T 410795, dish TV, phone, car rental; **B/C** *Grand Heights*, Abid Shaheed Rd, T 411711, good views, dish TV, restaurant; **B/C** *Marhaba*, The Mall, T 410184, central, restaurant rec, good value in off season; **B/C** *Taj Mahal*, GPO Chowk, T 411081, dish TV, phone, fridge, conference hall, laundry.

C *Blue Pines*, Cart Rd, T 410230, restaurant, poor value; **C** *Dilkusha*, off Mall, T 410005, good value, especially off season; **C** *Faran*, Kuldana Rd, T 411270, dish TV, restaurant; **C** *Lalazar*, Abid Shaheed Rd, T 410150, TV, phone, restaurant; **C** *Viewforth*, Viewforth Rd, T 411268. There are numerous **C** hotels on the contiguous Abid Shaheed/Viewforth Rd. There are also several **C** hotels at **Pindi Point**, incl *Breeze*, *Royal*, T 411090 and *Spinzer* T 410062, good views, but bleak in winter.

E *Murree International*, Cart Rd, T 410173, attached hot bath.

● Budget hotels

Most of the cheap hotels are on **Cart Road**, nr to the bus stand, incl **E** *Al Madina*, **F** *Al Khyam*, *Al Nadeem*, *Chambers*, *Mountain Tower*, *Tanveer*, *Three Star*.

● Places to eat

The most popular restaurants are along the Mall, although many just serve fast food. *Lintott's*, *Red Onion*, *Usmania* serve Chinese, Continental and Pakistani food. Opposite Holy Trinity Church, below street level, are good value Pakistani restaurants.

● Bars

Despite the proximity to the old Murree Brewery, there are no bars.

● Airline offices

PIA have an office in Sunny Bank.

● Banks & money changers

Habib; Muslim Commercial; National Bank of Pakistan, behind GPO; UBL, The Mall.

● Hospitals & medical services

Tehsil HQ Hospital, Kuldana Rd, down from GPO.

● Post & telecommunications

GPO: is a landmark at top of Mall. Other Post Offices at Pindi Point and Sunny Bank. **Telecommunications**: central Telegraph Office, above Habib Bank, opp GPO.

● Places of worship

Christian: *Holy Trinity*, Mall, English service, Sun 1015. *Catholic Church* on Pindi Point Rd.

● Shopping

Local handicrafts, cloth, furs, caps, woollen shawls, jewellery and some real rubbish can be found in the Mall and the bazaar below.

● Sports

Golf: 9-hole course at **Bhurban** open May-Oct (members only in high season).

● Tourist offices

TDCP, Cart Rd and kiosk on Mall.

● Transport

Buses, wagons and suzukis run when full from main bus stand on Cart Rd to **Ayubia**, **Bhurban**, **Patriata** (New Murree), **Rawalpindi** with several services daily to **Lahore**. A deluxe bus runs at midday to Lahore from Chambers Hotel. Buses to **Muzaffarabad**, on their way from Rawalpindi, pass through **Sunny Bank** just below Murree, and do not come up to the Cart Rd bus stand.

The Galis

North of Murree are the **Galis**, a chain of hill stations that run through Nathia Gali to Abbottabad. ('Gali' is Hindko for 'pass'.) They can be reached by suzuki from Murree bus stand and by less frequent, and slower, buses.

The first village on the road to Abbottabad is **Barian**, on the border between Punjab and NWFP. (Although most of these Galis are within the NWFP administrative sphere of influence, their proximity to Murree makes it logical to include them within the Punjab section.) From Murree, the road climbs steadily to **Chhangla Gali** at 2,762m. **Accommodation E** *Summer Inn*. Several km from here, at **Koza**

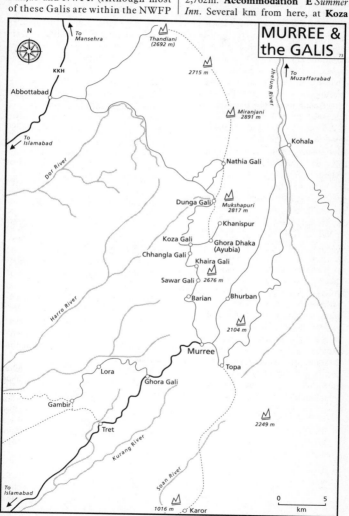

Gali, the road divides, the left fork continuing via Dunga Gali and Nathia Gali to Abbottabad.

The right fork runs 3 km to **Ayubia** (2,416m). Formerly known as Ghora Dhaka, the settlement was renamed after the former President of Pakistan, General Ayub Khan. Ayubia is used as the collective name for the cluster of resorts of Chhangla Gali, Khanispur and Ghora Dhaka, as well as the national park to the E of the road. At Ayubia, a chair-lift (Rs 20) runs to a minor peak, offering good views across the national park. **Accommodation E** *Ayubia Palace*; **E** *Summer Inn*; **F** *Al Madina*.

A 3 km road through the pine forests along the spur offers a pleasant walk to **Khanispur**. Locals speak of tigers and leopards in the hills, although there are certainly packs of rhesus monkeys and grey langurs. There are excellent views across to Kashmir from here. **Accommodation F** *Kashmir View* (follow sign for 'Armour Hut'); **F** *Youth Hostel*.

Nathia Gali To reach Nathia Gali, return to Koza Gali and take the other road fork. Transport to Nathia Gali is more regular from here than Ayubia. There is also a cross-country short cut (6 km) along the 'pipe-line' from Ayubia to Nathia Gali, although this should not be attempted in poor weather or after rain. It is possible to walk the 13 km road to Nathia Gali in about 4 hrs, passing through the hamlets of Toheedabad (2,370m) and Kundla (2,340m). The road is subject to land-slip blockages after prolonged rain, and may be inaccessible from Dec-Feb due to snow. 3 km

before Nathia Gali is the small resort of **Dunga Gali** (2,439m), **C** *Mukshpuri*, **F** *Green Valley*, behind which is 2,817m Mukshpuri Peak.

Nathia Gali (2,500m) is the summer headquarters of the NWFP government, and despite recent unplanned development, is still very picturesque. It retains something of a colonial air, with the wooden St Matthews Church, Governor's House and attractive bungalows. Dominating the view to the NE is the 2,981m **Miran Jani**, which can be climbed in a stiff 3 hrs, following the path N behind the Governor's House. On clear days you can see Nanga Parbat to the N, and across the Jhelum River to the Pir Panjal range. It is also possible to make the 2-3 day hike N to the attractive Gali of **Thandiana** (see page 437), although it is only reachable by road from Abbottabad. There are Resthouses enroute at Palakot and Biran Gali.

The better hotels are on Nathia Gali's upper road. **B** *Greens*, T 868261, F 868244, dish TV, phone, conference hall, skiing (Jan-Feb), restaurant. The **C** hotels, incl *Park Plaza*, *Pines Shangrila*, *Valley View* are all in need of some repair. The budget hotels are down on the lower road, incl **E/F** *Allys*, *International*, *Karachi*, *Madina*, *Marhaba*, *Peshawar*, *Swiss*, although the two best are **E** *Kamran* and **E** *Skyways*. A link road runs from opp Skyways to the upper part of town.

Abbottabad is a further 2-hr drive along the fairly rough road, via the Pak Air Force base at Kalabagh.

The route from Islamabad to Peshawar along the GT Rd is described below. It is a fast but very busy route, lined for much of the way with industrial developments. From Zero point go SW on Shahrah-e-Kashmir for 14 km before turning right onto the main Peshawar GT Rd. A recent fashion in Islamabad for installing old carved doors and windows in new houses has spawned a thriving business in these beautiful artefacts, which are removed from the old houses of Swat Valley, and can be found for sale by the roadside. A short distance on from the junction is the turning left towards Fatehjang, Kushalgarh and Kohat (see page 361). The main road continues on to the Margalla Pass (28 km).

Margalla Pass

The climb up to the Margalla Pass is extremely gentle and the pass itself unimposing, despite its historical importance. Sir Olaf Caroe described it as the real division between Central and South Asia. The pass is marked by a distinctive **granite obelisk** to the left of the road, erected in 1868 "by friends, British and Native, to the memory of Brigadier-General **John Nicholson** CB, who after taking a hero's part in four great wars, fell mortally wounded, in leading to victory the main Column of assault at the great siege of Delhi, and died on 22 September 1857, aged 34". The wars referred to were the two Sikh wars, the First Afghan War and the War of Independence (or Mutiny, depending on your perspective).

The route taken by the GT Rd through the pass is identical to that of the **Shahi road** built by **Sher Shah Suri**, and a walk up to Nicholson's obelisk takes you onto a section of the old cobbled road. This route can be traced back over 2,000 years to the campaigns of Chandragupta Maurya in 324 BC which took the Mauryan Empire onto the soils of modern Afghanistan.

Taxila

The GT Rd decscends equally gently from the pass. After about 1 km there is a turning right signposted 'Taxila Cantonment' which leads directly to the museum and hotels, close to the archaeological remains. This road also leads on to Haripur and the KKH (see page 434). A second turning right for Taxila, which leads through the modern town, is about 2 km further on, marked by a footbridge across the GT Rd. For details on Taxila see above; Excursions from Islamabad.

Immediately after the second Taxila turning, there is a turning right to **Wah Cantonment**, another of the routes taken by traffic heading onto the KKH. **NB** The centre of Wah Cantonment, with its large army ordinance factory is officially off-limits to foreigners. A little further on is a signposted turning left to **Wah Mughal Gardens**. Wah is supposed to have received its name from the exclamation of the Emperor Jahangir – "wah" ('beautiful') – when he saw the beauty of the valley! The gardens were used as one of numerous resting places by the Mughal emperors en-route to Kashmir. The gardens today are somewhat delapidated, though with a little imagination you can get some idea of their former glory. They make for a nice shady picnic spot. A little further on is the town of Hasan Abdal, 48 km from Islamabad.

Hasan Abdal

This town has been an important site for Sikhs, Buddhists and Hindus, as well as Muslims. Gandharan Buddhist remains have been found in the centre of the modern settlement. It is most famous though as a Sikh pilgrimage centre.

The early 19th century Sikh **Panja Sahib Gurudwara** (temple), in the town centre, has a hand cast reputed to be that of **Guru Nanak**, the founder of Sikhism. According to one legend it was through the intervention of the Sikh founder that the temple tank was created. Asking a Muslim saint, Baba Wali, for a drink of water, the mystic simply threw down a huge boulder. Guru Nanak placed his hand on it where it fell, leaving his hand impress on the stone and causing a spring to well up from underneath it. The **Baisakhi Festival** is held here each Apr and still attracts Sikh pilgrims from India. **Baba Wali's Shrine** is on the flat-topped hill overlooking the town, with views in all directions. It takes about 1 hr to walk up to the shrine.

Near the gurudwara are two Mughal tombs. The **Maqbara Haki-man** – the tomb of the *hakims*, or doctors – is at the E end of a platform nearly 40m by 20m. To the W of this platform is a tank, fed by a spring and reputed to remain at a constant level. *Mahseer*, a large species of carp, have been kept in the tank for generations. The tomb was built by one of the Mughal building superintendents, Khwaja Shamsuddin Khawafi. Small bricks were used, covered in lime plaster and then decorated with frescoes. The tomb measures 11m square with a flat outer roof and an inner dome. Most of the plaster has come away.

The second tomb was built for **Khwaja** himself. He died and was buried in Lahore in about 1599. Subsequently Akbar ordered that the tomb be used for **Hakim Abdul Gilani** and **Hakim Himan Gilani**. It served as the secretariat building for Hari Singh Nalwa in the early 20th century and was declared a protected monument in 1923.

- **Accommodation** There are 3 hotels on the GT Rd, by the turning into the main town; the *Frontier*, *Mehran* and *Tourist Rest House*.

Just beyond Hasan Abdal there is a turning right which joins the main road from Wah to Haripur. The GT Rd continues W, crossing the Harro river and passing the town of **Lawrencepur**, named after the 19th Century British Resident of Lahore, Sir Henry Lawrence. Immediately after the town, there is a turning right, the first of three leading up to **Tarbela Dam** (see above, Excursions from Islamabad). Further on there is a turning left to Attock City (marked on some maps by its old name of Campbellpore), then the second turning right to Tarbela, then another turning left to Attock City and the Pak Aeronautical Base of Kamra, followed by the last turning right to Tarbela, signposted for the towns of Shadikhan and Hazro along the way. Finally there is a third turning left for Attock City, before the GT Rd crosses the Indus at Attock itself.

Attock

Historically, this was an important crossing point, along with Hund to the N. **Akbar's Fort** on the E bank, built in the 1580s, dominates the gorge, its rambling walls and large crenallations clearly visible to the S of the road. Today the fort is occupied by the Pakistani military and is closed to the public. **Sher Shah Suri's Caravanserai** is below the fort, right by the road. Attock was also the crossing point for the Shahi Road from Delhi to Kabul, and the large caravanserai served as a resting place for travellers. The walls, with living quarters built into them, enclose a large square courtyard with a mosque inside. Steps lead up onto the walls which are remarkably well preserved, though with some cement repairs to the crenallations, giving good views across the Indus and up to the Fort behind. A signposted track leads up to the caravanserai, just W of the turning up to the Fort, or there are steps leading directly up from the road. The turning S on the W bank of the river leads through the village of Khairabad past the old two-storey road/rail bridge built by the British from 1880-81 (now closed to vehicle traffic), and continues on to Nizampur and Khwala Khel before joining the Islamabad-Kohat road near Kushalgarh. The roads S from Attock City on the E bank are in better condition. **Attock City**, with its railway station and some interesting colonial and pre-colonial architecture, is SW of the bridge crossing, 18 km by road.

● **Accommodation** There is the **D** *Indus View* on the GT Rd, E of the bridge, reasonable rooms, restaurant, friendly staff.

The Indus here marks the boundry between Punjab and NWFP. A little further on is **Jehangira**, where a bridge crosses the Kabul river, the start of the road up to Swabi (26 km) (see page 376). The GT Rd continues W, passing through **Akor Khattack** to arrive at Nowshera.

Nowshera

The town has a large British built cantonment area and is today still an important military base for the Pakistan army. Just before the main town there is a turning N which crosses the Kabul river on a toll bridge and leads up to Mardan (22 km, see page 372) on a good, fast dual carriageway. Civilian traffic is diverted around the cantonment area which is closed to the public. There is little of interest for the general tourist.

● **Accommodation** There are 2 hotels near the bus stand, both with restaurants. **E** *Shobra*, Shobra Chowk, GT Rd, T 3177, some a/c rooms; **F** *Spark*, Cavalry Rd, T 2101.

● **Places to eat** The *Friends Corner* restaurant is nearby, on the GT Rd.

From Nowshera it is a further 44 km on to Peshawar. The road first passes through the town of **Pabbi** and then runs through an increasingly industrial landscape, before entering the suburbs of Peshawar and finally the city itself (see page 347).

ISLAMABAD/RAWALPINDI TO THE SALT RANGE

The Salt Range is formed of two parallel lines of hills running E-W roughly between Jhelum and Mianwali, to the N of the Jhelum River. Geologically the area is fascinating, with the folding of the earth's crust along this thrust zone producing sharp jutting outcrops of rock strata, some dating from 600 million years ago. Archaeologically the area is highly significant, having revealed evidence of a 'Pebble Culture' contemporary to the nearby Soan Culture of the Potwar Plateau (see page 264) dating from the Palaeolithic period. It is also of historical significance, with many Buddhist and Hindu sites dating from the Singhapura Buddhist and Kashmiri Hindu period. Until Partition, much of the area remained predominantly Hindu.

Easily accessible from both Islamabad and Lahore, the Salt Range is a little visited and yet beautiful area. Varying in height between 750 and 1,500m, the climate is noticeably cooler during summer. Much of the area is extremely fertile, supporting a variety of crops and a range of wildlife, including wolves, urial, deer and wild boar. As well as being visually stunning in places, the Salt Range has a number of specific attractions, including the largest salt mine in the world (excellent guided tours available) and a number of old Hindu temples and pilgrimage sites.

NB The Islamabad-Lahore Motorway, presently under construction, passes through the Salt Range close to Kallar Kahar. When complete it will significantly alter communications in the area, particularly around Kallar Kahar.

Chakwal is the largest town in the area. Although of little interest in itself, it gives access to the main places of interest in the eastern part of the Salt Range. There are two hotels, the **E** *Azeem International*, T (0573) 51725,

friendly and reasonable, and the basic **F** *Gulbarak*, T 3071 (hotel sign in Urdu only), both with restaurants.

There are two roads leading to Chakwal; the first (and best) road leaves the Islamabad-Lahore GT road just S of Mandra, running parallel to the railway. The second turning is just NW of Sohawa. There is a signpost in English for Khewra, and in Urdu for Chakawal (72 km) and Mianwali (217 km). Buses run from Rawalpindi and Jhelum or from Mandra, Gujar Khan and Dina. The rail branch from Mandra is now closed.

The Choa Saidan Shah road (31 km) branches S, 2 km E of Chakwal on the road towards Sohawa. The northern slopes of the Salt Range, with its distinctive folded rock strata exposed in sharp jutting outcrops, slowly come into view. 8 km before Choa Saidan Shah, there is a turning to the right, signposted in English, to Dhok Tahlian Dam.

Choa Saidan Shah is named after the saint **Saidan Shah Shirazi** who is reputed to have transformed the area from a desert by causing a spring to emerge (*Choa* meaning spring). The small village is nestled at the foot of a valley and surrounded by orchards of loquat, pomegranate, peach and guava. Roses are also grown and used in the production of perfume and local medicines. The saint's shrine is set back from the main bazaar in a courtyard. The annual *Urs* is held in the first week of Apr.

● **Accommodation** There is a *Civil Resthouse* situated in one of the orchards up on the hillside on the road towards Ketas and Kallar Kahar. It is reserved for officials but if not in use, it may be possible to book it through the Deputy Commissioner in Chakwal, T 2615. The *District Council Resthouse* in the same grounds was being renovated in 1995, while the nearby *Highways Resthouse* serves as the temporary private residence of the Assistant Commissioner. The only other accommodation is the very basic **F** *Hajji*, in the main bazaar.

Daybreak in the village is heralded by a raucous chorus of geese.

The two roads from Choa Saidan Shah, W to Kallar Kahar and S to Khewra, both offer excellent views of different aspects of the Salt Range.

Choa Saidan Shah to Khewra

The road climbs from Choa Saidan Shah, passing the ICI pumping station at Watli Spring, which supplies water to the large ICI Soda Ash factory at **Khewra**, then follows a level stretch of fertile plateau, sown in spring with striking yellow rapeseed, before passing a turning to the right to the ICI limestone quarry at Dandot (4 km). The road then cuts through the main ridge/escarpment of the Salt Range, emerging on the other side to give spectacular panoramic views down onto the wide plain of the Jhelum River. The town of Khewra and the ICI Soda Ash plant are clearly visible. The road winds steeply down off the Salt Range, passing a turning to another limestone quarry at Tober, before reaching Khewra.

Khewra Salt Mine

Situated at the base of the Salt Range, this is the largest salt mine in the world in terms of area. The salt deposits found here stretch in seams up to 90m thick along the whole length of the Salt Range covering over 250 sq km, only a tiny portion of which have so far been mined. The salt found here is a remnant of the Tethys Ocean which evaporated slowly during the Eocene period, some 60 million years ago.

Legend has it that Alexander the Great first extracted salt from the range in 327 BC. Written records suggest that salt began to be mined from around 600 AD with the arrival of the Muslim emperor Sultan-e-Usmania. The local Janjua tribe are also thought to have mined the salt from the 13th century. The Mughuls began larger scale commercial mining in the 15th century and by the 19th century it had been taken over by the British, who called it Yayo Mine. In 1932 electric trains were introduced; before that steam engines were used, and the salt deposits in many of the tunnels are blackened from the soot. Today, 2,300 salt cutters are employed in the mine, which produces around 600,000 kg of salt/day, making it the second largest in the world in terms of output.

Visitors are shown round a small section at ground level where mining has been discontinued. In all, the mine has 17 levels; 5 levels reaching 122m above ground level, and 11 levels reaching 610m below ground level. Each level has a series of four parallel tunnels interconnected at regular intervals. The mine is ventilated by a network of 12 air shafts which also act as a drainage system during the rainy season. Mining is carried out in a series of chambers to the sides of the tunnels in what is known as the 'room and pillar method'. In many of the old chambers, which were dug down to a depth of around 25m, groundwater has seeped in, creating large ponds of salt saturated water, or brine. This brine forms a second important product of the mine, being pumped out to supply the ICI factory with one of the raw materials for the production of Soda Ash (the others are fresh water, from Watli Spring and limestone, from the various quarries in the Salt Range).

The ceiling of the largest chamber, which was mined from the top down, is 72m high, with stairs cut into the walls. The whole chamber was mined by hand and the walls are criss-crossed with the lines of the chiselling work. Today salt is blasted with dynamite.

A small mosque consisting of a low walled enclosure of hewn salt bricks has been constructed in the mine. Lights concealed inside the walls cause the translucent bricks to glow with various hues and shades. Elsewhere, the seepage of water through the ceiling has resulted in the formation of beautiful salt stalactites and stalagmites.

Permits and accommodation To visit Khewra Salt Mine you should apply for a permit to: Manager Salt, Pakistan Mineral Development Corporation, Plot 13, H-9, Islamabad, T 855290. The *PMDC Resthouse* in Khewra can be reserved when arranging a visit. It is clean and well maintained, with a pleasant garden.

7 km S of Khewra is **Pind Dadan Khan**. Named after the Rajput chieftain Dadan Khan who ruled here during the 17th century, this town was once an important centre of trade and was raised to a municipality by the British in 1876. Today its importance has waned, although its old narrow bazaars are still colourful and lively. There are some interesting examples of colonial architecture, including the *tahsildar's* (tax collector's) office and civil administration buildings, built in 1890.

Just before the town there is a road E which passes through Haranpur and Dhariala. From Dhariala there is a road N to Rawal and the cement factory at Gharibwal. To the NE are the remains of a **Mughal gate** at Baghanwala. Beyond that are the ruins of **Nandana Fort** on a huge rock blocking the narrow gorge which formed the ancient gateway to the Salt Range. The main road continues past Jalalpur before crossing the Jhelum River at Rasul Barrage to Rasul. The road then passes through Chillianwalla and Dinga to join the Islamabad-Lahore GT Rd at Kharian.

Choa Saidan Shah to Kallar Kahar

This route follows a wide plateau running along the middle of the Salt Range and is particularly beautiful in late winter and early spring when the fields are bright yellow with the flowering mustard crop. The road climbs from Choa Saidan Shah to **Ketas** (5 km).

Ketas

In the village of Ketas are the extensive **Satghara Hindu Temples**, centred around a large pool and spring. According to legend, the pool was formed of tears from Siva's eye as he wept over the death of his wife Parvati. Tears from his other eye fell near Amjer in Rajasthan, forming a second pool.

The oldest temple, up on the hill overlooking the complex, has a narrow staircase inside which leads up onto the roof, giving good views over the site and surrounding hills. It is thought to date back as far as the 8th-10th century, although the top layer of plasterwork is of a much later date. Lower down there is a fort and next to it a large building which was a Sanskrit language university, where the famous Muslim scholar Al Burani came to study (also with good views from the roof), as well as a bathing and resthouse complex, and various small shrines down by the road.

The complex is now in a state of dereliction, but before Partition used to attract thousands of Hindu pilgrims every Feb. Hindus continued to visit in large numbers until recently, when the Babri Mosque incident at Ayodhya in India soured relations between Hindus and Muslims. One particularly beautiful temple on the other side of the road was destroyed as a result, and has been replaced by a modern white concrete structure. Auriel Stein suggests that the main temple complex may mark the site of the Buddhist university and shrines at the centre the capital of the Singhapura Kingdom that existed in the Salt Range from the 6th-7th centuries AD.

● **Accommodation** Next to the temple complex on the hillside there is an **F** *Youth Hostel*, basic, with no running water, but friendly. If you are on a tight budget, this makes an ideal base from which to explore the Salt Range. In mid-1995, the *TDCP Motel* in Katas, to the N of the road, was still closed pending arrangements for a contractor to operate it.

The tree-lined road continues along the plateau, passing various small coal mining works before descending to Kallar Kahar (28 km). In 1995 traffic was joining the incomplete Islamabad-Lahore motorway for a short stretch before turning off to Kallar Kahar.

Malot

The village of Malot is situated S of the main road between Kallar Kahar and Choa Saidan Shah. Above the village on a large rocky outcrop at the very edge of the Salt Range's southern cliffs, stand the remains of two Hindu temples, built in the Hindu Kashmiri style of the 8th-10th centuries. Standing in such an exposed position, the sandstone temples have been heavily weathered, but the detailed carved reliefs on the sides are still discernible. The larger and better preserved of the two temples has a later Sikh watchtower built on top of it, which replaced the original stepped pyramidal roof. Originally there was a fort here, encompassing the village and temples and covering 5 sq km. It was here that the last of the Hindu Shahi rulers, Raja Mal, was forced to embrace Islam by Mahmud of Ghazni in the early 11th century. Later, in the 16th century, Daulat Khan Lodhi, the last of the Delhi Sultans, was defeated here by the Mughal emperor Babur.

Malot is worth a visit as much for the temples as for the spectacular views from the edge of the sheer cliffs down onto the Jhelum plains. Clearly visible from here is the course of the new Islamabad-Lahore motorway, snaking out of the Salt Range onto the plains and crossing the Jhelum River at Talibwala bridge.

The village can be reached by intermittent public transport from Kallar Kahar in the form of Toyota pick-ups. From the turning S off the Kallar Kahar - Choa Saidan Shah road (this is the first turning coming from Kallar Kahar; there is a tea/snack stall on the corner)

it is 10 km. Follow the road up through the Khandowar Quarry works which supply the Motorway Project, bearing left towards Simbal, Choi and Karoli (signposted). **NB** The road has been re-routed due to the quarrying work and will eventually revert back to its old course. Just after a largish pond on the left, take the turning to the left. After around 6 km the road drops sharply into a small valley, passing some rudimentary coal mines, then climbs again before reaching a fork. Take the right fork which leads to the foot of Malot village. The left fork leads back to the main road, passing another Hindu temple near the village of Dalwal.

Malot village owes its comparative wealth (the stone houses in the village are well built and most have running water, electricity and telephone) to its strong representation in the Pakistan army, with a large number of the villagers occupying high ranks. There are plans to build a tourist rest house here.

Kallar Kahar

The salt lake (from which the village gets its name) and surrounding marshes at **Kallar Kahar** are particularly beautiful at sunrise. The lake is also good for birdwatching, attracting large numbers of migrating birds. At the SW corner there are extensive orchards dating from the 16th century when the Mughal emperor Babur, en route from Kabul to Delhi, was reputedly so taken by the beauty of the lake that he ordered extensive gardens to be laid out. There is a throne cut out of solid rock, the *Takht-e-Babri*, from where Babur is supposed to have enjoyed the view of the lake and addressed his army. Up on the hillside by the road to Khushab is the shrine of **Sheikh Abdul Qadir Jilani**, which offers good views over the lake. Kallar Kahar is also famous for its six springs, which are attributed to the Sufi saint **Baba Freid Ganj Shakar**. Local legend relates how Baba Freid was teased by a woman who refused to give him water from an existing spring, saying that it was contaminated. The saint subsequently cursed the spring, making the water undrinkable. Continually harrassed by petitions of remorseful villagers, he eventually relented and caused the six springs to emerge.

● **Accommodation** There is a **D** *TDCP Resort*, T (0573) 51725 on the S side of the lake, with a comfortable though slightly overpriced

hotel offering rooms with attached bath, far and heater, and a reasonable restaurant, as well as a small playground/fair and boats for hire. There is a forlorn collection of caged birds and monkeys at the entrance.

You can continue round the S side of the lake from the TDCP resort on a rough track to rejoin the road to Choa Saidan Shah via the Islamabad-Lahore motorway. On the right there is a spring amongst a clump of trees, and up on the hillside hidden by scrub, is the cave of Baba Freid

IMRAN KHAN – 'LION OF PAKISTAN'

It is difficult to know what to make of Imran Khan. In cricketing terms it is simple: one of the greatest all-rounders in the history of international cricket, his career statistics (below) speak for themselves. But Imran Khan the person? That is far more complex.

During his playing career he was just as likely to be seen in a newspaper's society pages as its sports pages. As one British newspaper suggested, "hapless English, Australian and West Indian opponents were by no means his only conquests. Newspaper cuttings files bulge with debutantes, film starlets and aristocrats who have been caught by the wickedly handsome Imran." Yet following his retirement, he has sought to present a totally different image. In newspaper parlance, Imran Khan now "goes out to bat for Islam", preferring to wear "baggy shalwar kameez trousers instead of natty suits."

Imran's 'transformation' came on the heels of the controversy surrounding Salman Rushdie's *Satanic Verses*. According to Imran: "People like me who were living in the western world bore the brunt of anti-Islam prejudice that followed the Muslim rejection of the book.... Since I felt strongly that the attacks on Islam were unfair, I decided to fight. It was then I realized that I was not equipped to do so as my knowledge of Islam was inadequate. Hence I started my research and for me a period of my greatest enlightenment."

Imran has also spent time reassessing not only his own identity, but that of the Pakistani nation as a whole. Not surprisingly, some of his statements and syndicated articles have been derided in the Western press, who cry 'hypocrite'. He derides the 'Pukka Brown Sahibs' who imitate their former colonial masters, suggesting that the "elite of Pakistan speak in English, travel to London and New York, attire themselves in western clothing, aspire to western education, and in short, seek to be cosmopolitan in ways that would have pleased the rulers that left this country very recently". This is from a man who was educated at Aitchison College, Pakistan's most prestigious school, and Royal College School, Worcester before attending Keble College, Oxford.

Further, some of the pronouncements regarding Western society that are attributed to Imran, provide excellent material for journalists out to do a hatchet job on him. In a speech in Jhelum, he is quoted as saying "Western values are an evil. The old empire fell because of obscenity and nudity... now the West is falling because of their addiction to sex and obscenity."

The 'Imran debate' received a further airing in 1995 when the 'the world's most eligible bachelor' got married. It had been expected that Imran would marry 'a simple Muslim girl'. Instead he married Jemima, 'the beautiful blond daughter of tycoon Sir James Goldsmith' who is said to be Britain's seventh richest businessman. Not only is Jemima's background Jewish, she is half his age. The press had a field day. Numerous prejudiced

From Kallar Kahar a road leads NE back to Chakwal (22 km) via Bhaun. Another road leads SW towards Khushab. After 38 km there is a turning to the right which leads back N to Talagang (see below), with the possibility also of branching E towards Mt Sukesar (1,522m), the highest peak in the Salt Range. The Khushab road climbs up through the Salt Range to give spectacular views from its precipitous southern cliffs down over the Jhelum plains, before descending steeply onto the plains and arriving at the town of Khushab.

West to Mianwali

From Chakwal you can continue W to Mianwali (144 km) via Talagang (43 km). After around 8 km the road crosses the Islamabad-Lahore motorway. The road runs through flat countryside, for the most part cultivated, occasionally

and stereotyped views were aired on the role of women in Islam, in addition to dreadful puns on the 'bowled his last maiden over' line. Little attention was paid to the fact that Jemima has converted to Islam, and now goes by the name of Haiqa. The couple now live in Lahore's upmarket Zaman Park area.

Even less attention was paid to Imran's greatest achievement to date. In 1985, Imran's mother died of cancer. Had the illness been diagnosed earlier, it is possible that she could have been saved. Realizing the lack of diagnostic facilities in Pakistan, particularly for the poor or those unable to afford treatment abroad, Imran set about raising funds to build a modern yet affordable cancer hospital in Pakistan. In Dec 1994, having raised over £12 million through public subscription and donations, the Shaukat Khanum Memorial Cancer Hospital and Research Centre (named in memory of Imran's mother), was inaugurated. The remarkable fact is that most of the money raised came not from Pakistan's upper and middle class elites, but from the country's poor, with the average donation being around Rs 200. Such is Imran's popularity and trustworthiness amongst his countrymen.

Indeed, Imran is now being touted as a future Prime Minister, and saviour of the nation. Rumours abound, suggesting that he is being manipulated by Lt-Gen Hamid Gul, former head of the ISI (Pakistan's premier intelligence organization), in a plot to topple the government of Benazir Bhutto. One of his main critics is his former Test cricket bowling partner, Sarfraz Nawaz, now working as a 'sports advisor' to the government. But opinions in Pakistan on a political role for Imran Khan are divided. Many wish that the country's greatest sporting hero should stay well clear of the dirty world of politics, avoiding the taint of corruption. Others feel that it is exactly people like Imran that the country needs – a new breed of politicians who don't have this sordid, corrupt past. Imran's views are clear, as he launches a massive literacy programme in Pakistan: "If my objective were power, I'd jump into it (politics) now. But I don't want votes. I'm in a much stronger position to fight for social reform if I stay out of politics." We shall see.

Some career highlights: A genuinely fast bowler, and an aggressive attacking batsman, when Imran Khan retired from international cricket in 1992, he was one of only four men to have scored 3,000 runs and taken 300 wickets in Test cricket. He played in 88 Test matches, captaining Pakistan in 48 of them – the third highest in the history of international cricket. Imran Khan scored 3,807 Test runs, including 6 centuries, at an average of 37.69. He also took 362 Test wickets at a cost of 22.81 each. Prior to the 1996 World Cup, Imran Khan had played in a record 28 World Cup matches, appearing in all of the first five competitions. His greatest sporting moment was captaining his country to victory in the final of the World Cup in 1992, a match in which he top scored with 72 runs.

giving way to grass and scrub and in places heavily eroded. From **Talagang** there is a road S towards Khushab and N towards Islamabad via Fatehjang. There are a couple of hotels near the bus stand in Talagang; the **F** *Bismillah* and the very basic **F** *Iqbal*. Gradually the road to Mianwali approaches the western extremities of the Salt Range, lower here than to the E, but still impressive. The road passes close to the large picturesque **Nambal Lake**, situated right at the foot of the Range, and as it starts to climb you get good views down onto the lake, which attracts large numbers of migrating birds. Emerging on the southern edge of the Salt Range, there are views down onto the plains before the road descends, passing through flat irrigated land planted with rice to arrive at Mianwali.

Mianwali

The town is headquarters of Mianwali District, an area of great agricultural importance, irrigated by a network of canals fed by the water gathered from the Chashma Barrage to the S and the Jinnah Barrage to the N. There is little of interest in the town itself, although it has a claim to fame as the birthplace of **Imran Khan**.

● **Accommodation** The three hotels nr the bus stand on Shahrah-e-Fiazaya are reasonable. All have restaurants and gardens. **E** *Faisal*, T (0459) 30367, a/c and non-a/c; **E** *Sharzad*, T 32706, a/c and non-a/c; **F** *Al-Abbas*, T 31923; nr the railway station there is the very basic **F** *Ghazi Lasani*, T 2978.

● **Transport Train** Karachi: *Khushal Khan Khattak Exp*, 0245, 32¼ hrs. Lahore: *220*, 1845, 11¾ hrs. Mari Indus (Kalabagh): *219*, 0447, 2 hrs; *189*, 2005, 2 hrs. Multan: *190*, 0545, 10 hrs; *180*, 1635, 9½ hrs; *Mehran Exp*, 2325, 8½ hrs. Peshawar: *Khushal Khan Khattak Exp*, 0120, 8 hrs; *179*, 0735, 11½ hrs. Rawalpindi: *RC-145*, 0619, 6¼ hrs; *Mehran Exp*, 2400, 7 hrs. Sargodha: *RC-140*, 0710, 4 hrs. **Road Bus**: there are regular services – a mixture of buses and minivans – from the main bus stand to Lahore, Peshawar, Bannu, Dera Ismail Khan and Multan.

Chashma Barrage

35 km S of Mianwali is the **Chashma Barrage** across the Indus. Follow the Sarghoda road S out of Mianwali and bear right after 8 km at a fork. The road crosses the main canal headworks with three canals branching off it, following the left bank of the southwesterly branch. After 8 km turn right at a crossroads; the road crosses the canal before arriving at Kundian. Turn left and follow the road for around 5 km to the barrage. Alternatively you can follow a track beside the main canal S from Mianwali taking the right hand branch at the headworks. Soon after the narrow gauge railway crosses the canal, there is a bridge over the canal. Turn right on this road and follow it to Khundian.

The Chashma Barrage is one of six spanning the Indus. Completed in 1971 at a cost of Rs 399mn, it created a lake 360 sq km in area. The main headworks with the sluice gates and openings are situated at the western end of the barrage, and have a maximum discharge capacity of 950,000 cusecs.

There is a WAPDA resthouse in the main WAPDA complex on the E side of the barrage, but due to its location next to the Atomic Energy Council complex, they are not keen on accommodating tourists. Contact the Project Director at Chashma, T (045202) 41289. Generally permission must be gained from the head office in Islamabad. There is another resthouse on the W side, up on the hillside with spectacular views looking out over the Indus and the barrage. This belongs to the Canals Dept, and must be booked through their office in Dera Ismail Khan. Again, tourists are not encouraged. It is probably better to visit the barrage as a day-trip from Mianwali. Alternatively there is the basic **F** *Al-Massoum*, T 41006, at Kundian.

From the western end of the barrage you can reach the **Northern Kafir Khot**, 5 km to the N on a rough track. Situated in the Marwat Hills with fine views in all directions, these sprawling ruins of a Hindu Shahi fortress cover a large area, with well preserved walls along the northern ridge and the remains of some Hindu temples inside. The road meanwhile bears S, following the Indus, past the ruins of another Hindu Shahi fortress, to **Dera Ismail Khan**, see page 368.

The road S from Mianwali leads down through the **Thal** desert, parts of which have now been turned into fertile land by the canals feeding from the Jinnah and Chashma Barrages. The road passes the turning W at Dullewala (121 km) across the Indus to Dera Ismail Khan, before eventually arriving at **Muzaffargarh** and **Multan** (282 km).

The road N from Mianwali leads to **Kalabagh** (54 km). Be sure to fork left across the Jinnah Barrage, as the old rail/road bridge across the Indus further on only carries light vehicles. The **Jinnah Barrage** was completed in 1942 but did not provide irrigation to the Thal desert until after Independence in 1947.

Kalabagh

The setting for the town of Kalabagh is a spectacular one. Surrounded by imposing mountains to the N, E and W, the Indus emerges from its narrow gorge here, spreading lazily across the plains to the S. The town itself, nestled on the steep W bank of the Indus, is a tightly packed jumble of old wooden houses, often intricately carved, and narrow bazaars. The hills here are the western extension of the Salt Range and thick deposits of rock salt can be seen along the banks of the river. Old wooden boats ply up and down the river, powered by engines lashed precariously to the side with long propeller shafts reaching down into the water. The old rail/road bridge gives excellent views onto the town. On the opposite bank is Mari Indus, now the terminus for the line from Multan and Mianwali. There are a couple of basic hotels in the town.

From Kalabagh a road leads NW through rugged mountains to join the Bannu-Kohat road just S of Lachi. The route is usually passable in an ordinary car, although there are several fordings where bridges are being constructed or repaired, which can render it impassable after rains.

Another road leads SW to Lakki and then on to join the DI Khan-Bannu road. Buses and minivans for Kohat pass through the town on their way from Mianwali and vice-versa. Buses for **Bannu** (see page 367) can be caught at the junction with the Jinnah Barrage road, a few km to the SW of the town.

KALABAGH DAM

Kalabagh is the proposed site for a controversial new HEP generating scheme on the Indus. Desperate to meet its energy short-fall, the Government of the Punjab has approved the scheme following the completion of feasibility studies and impact assessment reports. However, the project has been blocked by the Sind Government, citing perceived adverse affects on the state's agricultural production due to a reduced flow of the Indus. Further, the NWFP Government has vehemently vetoed Kalabagh as the proposed site fearing the displacement of large communities of the upstream population. Bitter memories remain of broken compensation promises following the construction of the Tarbela Dam. The support by the Punjab Government for the Kalabagh scheme is seen by the other states as a typical example of Punjabi attempts to impose their hegemony over the country.

ISLAMABAD/RAWALPINDI TO LAHORE

The road from Islamabad and Rawalpindi to Lahore follows the historical route of the Grand Trunk Road. First built in the 4th century BC by the Mauryan Emperor Chandragupta, the route was developed by the Mughals in the 16th and 17th centuries to link their major cities of Kabul, Peshawar, Rawalpindi, Lahore and Delhi to Bengal in the E. For over 2 millennium, this route has seen the constant passage of invaders, traders and pilgrims, as well as facilitating the spread of new ideas, technologies and religions. For almost its entire length, including those sections that lie within the borders of India, the route is referred to as the GT Rd.

From Islamabad and Rawalpindi, the GT Rd passes S across the **Potwar Plateau**. The plateau has experienced very recent uplift as a result of the continuing mountain building process on the edge of the Himalayas, with horizontal layers of silt being raised, twisted and bent and new layers of sediment being deposited on top of them. Rivers such as the **Soan** have carved deep gorges and canyons into the soft rock. The overall impression is of a moon landscape, with eroded cliffs and bluffs sculptured out of the weathered alluvium. With modest rainfall (380-635 mm a year), the land is difficult to cultivate, and is one of Pakistan's poorest regions.

This is a region, however, that is rich in the stone tools of South Asia's earliest settlers, and there are several **Palaeolithic sites** that pre-date the most recent mountain folding process.

Crossing the Soan River, the GT Rd passes through the village of **Riwat** (25 km). Several kilometres to the W of the road lie the reasonably well preserved remains of a 16th century **Gakhkhar Fort**. The Gakhkhars were the dominant tribe of the Potwar Plateau, until their defeat by the Mughals. However, their kings were allowed to continue as vassals within the Mughal Empire, and retained a degree of autonomy. Remains of the fort include some of the outside walls, the main gate, a mausoleum and a mosque, but the fort was not secure enough to prevent its capture by **Sher Shah Suri**.

On the banks of the Soan, immediately N of Riwat, is the site of an extraordinary collection of **Middle and Upper Palaeolithic** stone tools, and widespread evidence of settlement by man's earliest ancestors over 100,000 years ago.

The GT Rd keeps close to the railway and after about 8 km passes within 2 km of the **Manikyala Buddhist stupa**, the largest of several stupas in the area, and visible in one of the many clumps of banyan trees. Coins found in the stupa suggest that it dates from the time of **Kanishka's** successor in the 1st century AD, but it may have been rebuilt as late as the 8th century by **Yasovarma** of **Kanauj**, who replaced the relics and included his own gold coins.

The dome of the stupa is over 30m high and 40m in diameter. About 3 km N is another stupa identified by General Cunningham as that referred to by the Chinese traveller Hiuen Tsang as the "stupa of the body-offering". 300m to its S is the 'stupa of the blood offering'. Evidently **Hiuen Tsang** recounted the legend that in a previous life the Buddha had offered his body to ease the hunger of seven tiger cubs. The stupa of the body offering was opened by General Court (a French officer employed by Ranjit Singh) who found three cylindrical caskets made of gold, silver and copper. Four gold coins of the Emperor Kanishka were found in the gold box, seven silver Roman denarii in the silver box dated no later than 43 BC, and eight copper coins, again from Kanishka, were in the copper box.

A further 7 km from here at the village of **Mandra**, a road branches SW of the GT Rd to the **Salt Range** (see page 256). From the junction of GT Rd, buses run SW to **Chakwal** (67 km) (see page 256). Another road leads NE to **Kallar**, headquarters of Bedi Gurbakbsh Singh, spiritual leader of the Potwar Sikhs, and on to **Pharwala Fort**, the former Gakhkhar stronghold. The area is particularly sensitive, and foreigners may be turned back on this road owing to its proximity to the headquarters of Pakistan's nuclear programme at **Kahuta**.

The GT Rd continues S to the large town of **Gujar Khan** (14 km). Formerly a thriving commercial centre, the town has fallen considerably from its position as producer of the Punjab's finest wheat. **Accommodation E** *Jinnah Hotel*, GT Rd, T 2728.

58 km beyond Gujar Khan is the town of **Dina. Accommodation F** *Al Kousar*, GT Rd, T 892, some a/c, restaurant rec, good value; **F** *Iqbal*, GT Rd, T 630624.

From here it is possible to make an excursion W to **Rohtas Fort** and **Tilla Jogian Hill**, or E to **Mangla Dam**.

Excursions

Mangla Dam

Mangla Dam, on the Jhelum River, was completed in 1968 under the provisions of the Indus Waters Treaty (see page 222) to compensate Pakistan for the diversion of water from the E tributaries to India after partition. It was designed to conserve and control the flood waters of the Jhelum, in addition to supplying hydroelectric power to the national grid.

Construction of the dam produced a reservoir, **Mangla Lake**, spread over 160 sq km, with a shoreline over 400 km long, and a gross storage capacity of 5.55 MAF. The project required a massive resettlement programme for the displaced population, including the resiting of 50 villages and the regional headquarters town of **Mirpur** (see page 333), in Pakistani administered Kashmir.

In terms of height, Mangla Dam does not figure amongst the world's highest dams. However, volume-wise, at 65,379 cu metres x 10^3, Mangla is the world's 10th largest (Aswan High Dam is 20th). There are several parts to the dam. To the E is the power house, fed by five 480m tunnels, and capable at peak production of 1,170 mw of HEP. Inside the power house is a stunning 20m by 100m mural, painted in 1967 by the famous Pakistani artist **Sadequain**, and depicting workers from prehistoric times to the 'Sputnik' age. The main dam runs for 3,353m at the crest, and at the centre is a hill surmounted by an old Gakhkhar fort. The viewing area offers panoramic views of the surrounding area and photography is permitted. There is a small cafe and children's play area. The fort houses an aquarium with specimens of fish (including a stuffed 30 kg monster) that are commercially farmed in the lake. At the W end of the dam lie the main and emergency spillways, designed to cope with over 1 million cu secs of excess water. During the major floods of Sep 1992 they were pushed to capacity and the road bridge to the S of the dam was swept away. For full tour of the dam, contact WAPDA Chief Engineer at Mangla.

The dam is located 16 km E of the main GT Rd at Dina, and can be reached by public transport from the main highway. Beyond Mangla Dam it is possible to continue to the Azad Kashmir town of **Mirpur** (see page 333).

Rohtas Fort

Located 7 km off the GT Rd at Dina, the imposing Rohtas Fort is one of the finest castles on the sub-continent. Commanding the gorge of the **Kahan River**, the fort was ordered to be built by **Sher Shah Suri** in 1543 to prevent the return from exile of his defeated enemy Humayun, and to subdue the local

Gakhkhar tribes. The fort also commands a section of the old Grand Trunk Rd. The outer fortification wall runs for over 4 km, following the natural contour of the hill upon which the fort stands, and is reinforced at intervals by 68 bastions and 12 gates.

Legend has it that Sher Shah Suri commanded his architect, Shahu Sultani, to build a massive and impregnable fort in 3 years. Unaware of the grandness of Sher Shah's designs, the fort that Shahu Sultani constructed was considerably smaller than the Emperor had envisaged, and on seeing the completed structure, Sher Shah ordered the architect to be beheaded. As an act of clemency, however, he allowed the architect a further 2 years to build a fort more in keeping with his wishes. In the event, Sher Shah died in battle shortly after, and the fort took a further decade to build. The fort is named after the fort at Rohtas in Bengal, scene of one of Sher Shah's great victories.

In fact, within 10 years Sher Shah's successors had abandoned the fort without it ever seriously being attacked. It is even suggested that far from being impregnable, the fact that some of the gates are remarkably easy access, the construction techniques in places are poor, and that it would require a large army to hold it meant that the fort was something of a military liability. Despite this, Rohtas Fort remains a spectacular sight.

Local charabanc buses run from Dina to Rohtas village inside the fort, entering through the Khwas Khani Gate. Ascertain in advance as to whether you are hiring the whole vehicle ('special'). There are no toilet facilities within the fort, but it is possible to get cold drinks in Rohtas village. Walking around the fort requires some strenuous work, with lots of backtracking as many of the high walkways along the outer walls end in precipitous drops.

The **Sohail Gate** is the most impressive, its image often used to grace Pakistani tourism brochures. Built in typical Pathan style of the era, it stands 20m high and is flanked by two massive rounded bastions. The central gate is topped with seven defensive merlons. Its name is said to derive from the famous saint Sohail Bukhari, although it is argued that the name is taken from the Sohail star that rises above the gate.

Continuing clockwise around the fort's perimeter, you pass through the **Shah Chand Wali Gate** in the wall that divides the inner fort, or citadel, from the outer, main fort. Near to this gate is the shrine of Shah Chand Wali, a holy man who worked on the fort's construction without taking wages right up to his death. The incongruous looking pavilion standing on the small hillock just inside the inner fort is the **Haveli Man Singh**. Built by Man Singh (d 1614), one of Akbar's most famous Rajput generals, the building is made of brick and plaster, rather than the stone used elsewhere in the fort. Its domed roof is topped by a Hindu style lotus emblem. Beyond the haveli is the **Rani Mahal**, the remains of an engraved sandstone minaret.

Immediately to the W of the haveli stands the **execution tower** (*burj*). Built primarily for dealing with rebellious princes and traitors, the execution tower has a raised platform with a hole at its centre through which the unfortunate victims were thrown.

West and SW from the high outer walls lie deep, highly eroded ravines that look set to claim parts of the fort walls. In places the soft sandstone foundations have become worn away, leaving the walls supported only by the durable mortar with which they were constructed.

Continuing along this outer wall, you pass the **Badshahi Gate** and the **Shahi** ('royal') **mosque**, a small prayer chamber standing in a courtyard. Facing Kabul, to the NW, is the striking **Kabuli Gate**. Over 3m wide and flanked by two bastions, a flight of 60

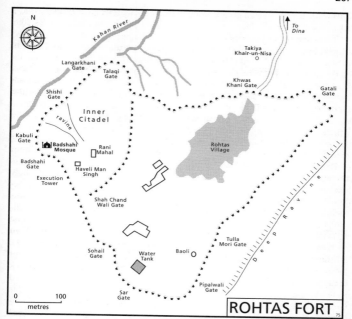

steps leads down to one of the fort's *baolis*, or fresh water wells.

Facing the Kahan River is the **Shishi Gate**, taking its name from the glazed tiles used in the spandrels of the outer arch. Erosion, partly from the river, has greatly cut into the fort at this point. Other gates on the inner fortress include the 15m high **Langarkhani Gate** and the **Talaqi Gate**. Talaqi means 'divorce', although it is sometimes translated as 'condemned', and it is considered unlucky to enter through this gate, following the experience of Sabir Suri who contracted fever shortly after entering through here. On the N wall stands **Mori** or **Kashmiri Gate** (facing Kashmir), and the splendid **Khwas Khani Gate**. The latter was named after Sher Shah's commander, and is the main entrance to the fort as you arrive from Dina. Outside the Khwas Khani Gate, on the road to Dina, is the **Takiya Khair-un-Nisa**, shrine of the daughter of one of Sher Shah's ministers. Khair-un-Nisa was said to have been a warrior of some repute, and she fought alongside her Emperor at a number of battles.

The gates along the E wall, **Gatali**, **Tulla Mori** and **Pipalwala** are smaller and less interesting than those on the S, W and N side.

A further 15 km W of Rohtas Fort is the highest peak in the **Salt Range** (see page 256), the 990m **Tilla Jogian**. On the summit lie the remains of a monastery that may well be one of the oldest religious institutes in the northern part of the sub-continent. Cunningham sees a reference to the place in the writings of Plutarch, relating how Porus' elephant rushed up the hill and implored him in a human voice not to oppose Alexander.

Tilla is further mentioned in numerous folk-tales of the region.

It is believed that Tilla was sacked by Ahmad Shah Durrani in 1748, accounting for the lack of antiquated buildings on this ancient site. There is a shrine on the rocky pinnacle to the W, however, commemorating the visit of the Sikh Guru Nanak. The hill has been used more recently as a summer retreat for British Govt officers. The road to the summit is rough and is best approached in a 4WD vehicle.

Returning to the GT Rd from either Rohtas Fort or Mangla Dam, the main road continues S from Dina. The GT Rd forks right to the new toll bridge over the Jhelum River, or left into **Jhelum** town.

Jhelum

Although a major military town, there is little of tourist interest in **Jhelum**. The town itself is relatively modern, although the ancient mound upon which it stands has provided coins dated to the Greek period, and a lingam (now in the Lahore Museum) that Cunningham dates to the 7th or 8th century.

There are two main axis to the city, meeting at the central Chandni Chowk. The N axis leads to the GT Rd junction, whilst the S axis leads down to the Jhelum River and railway bridge. To the W of Chandni Chowk is the Jhelum Cantt area, including the railway station and all the hotels. To the far W is a 19th century Gothic church, used as a refuge by the families of the British during the 1857 Mutiny. Jhelum's 4 **F** hotels are grouped together in the Cantt area (left out of station and then first right). **Accommodation F** *Faran*, T 3161, restaurant; *Mehwish*, T 2877, restaurant; *Paradise*, T 4267; *Zeelaf*, T 3698, restaurant rec.

To travel N to Islamabad/Pindi, E to Mangla and Mirpur, and to all destinations S, bus services are more regular from Dina. Minibuses to Dina run from just N of Chandni Chowk.

Having crossed the Jhelum River, the GT Rd passes S through **Kharian** (18 km), descending from the broken hills of the Potwar Plateau to the plains. Between Jhelum and Gujrat there are many roadside restaurants, mostly used as meal stops on the Lahore-Pindi Flying Coach services. On GT Rd just N of **Lal Musa** is the **E** *Skyway Motel*, T 2149. The road continues to **Gujrat** (19 km).

Gujrat

The present town of Gujrat probably owes its origin to **Sher Shah Suri**, although it was greatly developed by the Mughals. Akbar built the fort, relying on the Gujjar tribes to guard the town. They were in turn subdued by the Gakhkhars and then the Sikhs. Gujrat was the scene of the final battle of the **Second Sikh War** (21 February 1849) which lead directly to the British annexation of Punjab. Gen Thackwell, present at the battle, describes the fighting courage of the Sikhs: "Sikhs caught hold of the bayonets of their assailants with their left hands and closing with their adversaries, dealt furious blows with their right. ... This circumstance alone will suffice to demonstrate the rare species of courage possessed by these men."

The site of Gujrat has ancient origins, however, and is associated with the 5th century BC capital of the Rajput ruler, Bachan Pal. It is also the scene of the 4th century BC battle in which **Alexander the Great** defeated the Indian king **Puru**, known in Greek as Poros. Alexander is said to have been so impressed by the dignity in defeat of his captive king, that he restored his kingdom as a vassal, and on the retreat of the Greek forces, left Puru as ruler of Punjab. Remains of a fort believed to have been built by Alexander are nearby at Patha Kothi.

In Gujrat there is the shrine of the popular local saint **Shah Daula**. The mausoleum stands in a courtyard just off an alley lined with stalls selling devotional paraphernalia. It is a low white building with a pillared verandah, a green domed roof and eight small minarets. Above the tombs of the saint and his wife, the interior of the dome is decorated with mirrored tiles, inset with intricate geometric designs in red, green, blue and black. The shrine attracts many devotees during the saint's Urs in late Jun.

● **Accommodation** **D** *Faisal*, GT Rd, T 28731, overpriced; **D** *Soufis*, GT Rd, T 28731, restaurant serves Pak, Chinese and Continental food; **E** *Neshaman*, Railway Rd; **E** *New Melody Inn*, Railway Rd, junction GT Rd, T 26037, some a/c, restaurant, good value; **E** *Noor*, opp City Police Stn, T 26133, overpriced.

● **Transport Road Bus**: minibuses run in all directions from GT Rd.

Travelling S from Gujrat, the road crosses the **Chenab** on a new toll bridge. The old Alexandra Bridge, built in 1876 and formerly one of the longest in British India, is now closed. Shortly after the crossing the road divides, with the right fork travelling direct to Lahore.

The left fork passes over the fly-over to the town of **Wazirabad**. Founded in the 17th century by one of Shah Jahan's *Wazirs* or chief ministers, Wazir Khan, the fortified town was rebuilt by the Italian mercenary General Avitabile, then in the employ of Ranjit Singh. The main industry today is metalwork. The road continues 42 km E to **Sialkot**.

Sialkot

Although now one of Pakistan's most important industrial centres, **Sialkot** has ancient roots, and is associated with King Manender's 2nd century BC capital Sagala. During Mughal times, Sialkot's *koftars* were renowned for their fine craftsmanship with swords and daggers. Although their trade declined with the introduction of the rifle in 1857, an unexpected opportunity to modify their craft arose in 1905 when the local American Mission Hospital needed some equipment replaced. High quality stain-

less-steel surgical instruments are now exported from Sialkot around the world. Sialkot is also famous for producing sports goods, including 'Slazenger' tennis racquets and 'Adidas' soccer balls made under licence. The numerous tanneries on the Wazirabad-Sialkot road give a pungent clue to the town's other major industry.

The old part of Sialkot, several km E of the Wazirabad Rd, is a fascinating labyrinth of narrow streets, crowded bazaars and constant donkey cart jams. Down a small side street is the shrine of a local saint **Hazrat Imam Ali ul Haq** (ask for 'Imam Sahib'), who is reputed to have converted the local population to Islam. The path leading to the tomb is lined with numerous beggars, hawkers and prostrating pilgrims. The mausoleum complex is a maze of narrow corridors leading to several shrines of pirs, or holy men. The tomb of Imam Ali is to the right, through a mirrored gateway tiled with Koranic inscriptions and geometric designs. The courtyard is a fascinating place to sit and absorb the atmosphere. To the rear is a small graveyard where drumming, singing and dancing takes place. The market outside is very photogenic, and a large flat roof at the entrance to the shrine offers a panoramic view of the deals being struck.

On a low hill in the centre of town, (behind the Al Sheikh Jinnah Memorial Hospital), are the few remains of an old **fort** where the British took refuge during the Mutiny of 1857. Sialkot was the scene of much looting and rioting during this uprising, although the graves of the 12 British soldiers killed have since disappeared. It is thought that the cemetery caretaker sold the land when his monthly stipend was stopped in the late 1960s. The shrine of Pir Muradala Shah, also on the hill, is said to have exerted a protecting influence on Sialkot during the 1965 war with India.

SHAH DAULA OF BAGHDAD

During the reign of the Mughal Emperor Shah Jahan, the town became home to the saint **Pir Shah Daula of Baghdad**. Known for his good deeds, especially for the poor, Shah Daula established a home, *khan kah*, for invalids. In particular, he gave food, shelter and clothing to sufferers of microcephaly- a condition where the brain does not fully develop and victims have particularly small heads. Due to their appearance these people are known locally as 'mouse'.

During his lifetime, many childless women would come to pray with Shah Daula in the hope of producing offspring. Following his death, a mythology developed that suggested that those praying for children at his shrine entered into a contract in which their first born was to be left at the shrine to serve the community of microcephaly sufferers. For those who reneged on the contract, it was prophesied that their next child would be born with an abnormally sized head.

The descendants of Shah Daula, including those who attend to the shrine today, have done much to dispel this myth, stating that it is not within the teachings of the Pir. Most worshippers at the shrine today, however, are women.

Pakistan's greatest philosopher and poet, **Mohammad Iqbal** (1877-1938), was born and raised in Sialkot and his former residence, Iqbal House, has been turned into a small museum containing some of his personal belongings and work. Another place of interest is the 17th century tomb of the great Muslim scholar, Mian Abdul Hakim (on Khadam Ali Rd nr Saddar Hospital).

● **Accommodation C** *Meryton*, Wazirabad Rd, T 67145, a/c, TV, Chinese restaurant, best in town, but not central; **F** *Mehran*, Wazirabad Rd, nr minibus stand, T 554889, basic and noisy; *Al Farooq*, next door.

Returning to the GT Rd, 34 km S of Wazirabad is the major industrial town of **Gujranwala**.

Gujranwala

Due to its strategic location on the central Punjab plain, **Gujranwala** has had a turbulent history at the hands of advancing and retreating armies on their way to and from India. Although no longer a major garrison town like Jhelum, Gujranwala has a long history of providing army recruits. During WW1, one in 12 of the male population was recruited into service.

Gujranwala was the first district in which Sikh domination of the Punjab was established, following the capture of the town in 1765 by **Charat Singh**. The capital he established here was used by his son, **Mahan Singh**, and his grandson, **Ranjit Singh**, until the capture of Lahore by the latter in 1799. To the SE of the town is the *Samadh*, or octagonal tower, that Ranjit Singh built in memory of his father, Mahan Singh. The tall

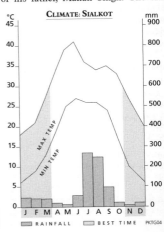

CLIMATE: SIALKOT

MAX TEMP

MIN TEMP

J F M A M J J A S O N D

□ RAINFALL   □ BEST TIME   PKTG04

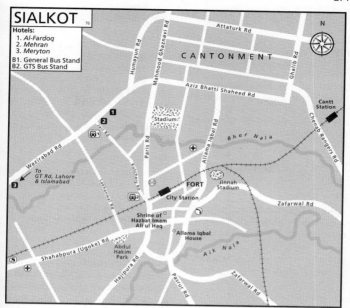

SIALKOT

Hotels:
1. Al-Fardoq
2. Mehran
3. Meryton
B1. General Bus Stand
B2. GTS Bus Stand

pavilion contains a number of Hindu works of art, including scenes from the *Mahabharata*. In 1891, the Dy Commissioner, Ibbetsen, commissioned a marble monument at the site of Ranjit Singh's birth. Another Sikh building, **Qila** (Fort) **Didar Singh**, c 1850, lies 16 km W of the town on the Hafizabad road.

The modern town produces fans, air conditioners, fridges as well as being a centre of steel production.

● **Accommodation** B *Shelton*, opp Gulshan-e-Iqbal, T 259501, best in town, central a/c, dish TV, fridge, restaurant serves Pak, Chinese and Continental dishes; D *Citi Top*, nr Din Plaza, GT Rd, T 42114, some deluxe a/c rooms, Chinese restaurant; E *Gujranwala*, Gondlan Chowk, GT Rd, nr station, T 84679, good value; F *City Gate*, Rail Bazaar, opp station,

T 216372, no English sign, basic but friendly. About 10 km S of Gujranwala, on the GT Rd, is the C *TDCP Motel*.

● **Places to eat** Chinese and Continental food at *Max*, Din Plaza, and *Shanxi*, both on GT Rd.

● **Post & telecommunications** GPO and Pak Telecom opp train station.

● **Sports** *Jinnah Stadium*, just W of the railway line, is the concrete bowl venue for Test and 1-day international cricket matches.

● **Transport Train** Gujranwala City station is on the main Peshawar-Rawalpindi-Lahore-Karachi line. **Road Bus**: buses N and S run from GT Rd.

The GT Rd continues S, after 60 km crossing the **River Ravi** and entering **Lahore** (67 km).

LAHORE

The capital of the Punjab and the state's largest city, Lahore is considered to be the cultural capital of Pakistan. Despite its ancient roots, the golden age of Lahore was during the Mughal period of rule, and today the city contains some of the finest examples of Mughal architecture in South Asia.

History

Early history

Although legend attributes the foundation of Lahore to Loh, son of King Rama, the hero of the epic *Ramayana*, it is not thought that Lahore was founded much before the 1st century AD. No mention is made of Lahore in writings associated with Alexander, although Ptolemy does speak of a town called Labokla that Cunningham has placed 40 km away.

The first recorded history of Lahore probably dates to 630 AD, when **Hiuen Tsang** referred to a large Brahmanical city that he visited on his way to Jullundhur. The city remained in the hands of the Brahmin kings until the end of the 10th century when Jai Pal was defeated by **Mahmud of Ghazni**. To Muslims, the foundation of Lahore dates to 1021 when Mahmud brought Islam to the city.

Shortly afterwards Lahore became capital of the Ghaznavid Empire, although it is the reign of **Zahirud Daula Ibrahim** (1059-1099) that is considered to be the golden period of Ghaznavid rule. It was during this era that the great scholar, and patron saint of the city, **Data Ganj Baksh** came to Lahore from Ghazni, spreading Sufism in the Punjab. This period also produced the first great Persian poet of South Asia, **Masud Saad Salman**, whose mournful songs about Lahore are still considered to be some of the great patriotic songs of Pakistan.

In the centuries that followed Lahore was captured and ruled by the **Ghauris, Khaljis, Tughlaqs, Sayyids**, the **Lodis** of the Delhi Sultanate, in addition to being attacked and occupied by the **Mongols** of **Genghis Khan** and by **Timur** (Tamerlane).

Mughal period

The zenith of Lahore's history, however, dates to the period of **Mughal** rule that effectively began when **Babur** defeated the Sultan of Delhi, **Ibrahim Lodi**, at the first battle of Panipat in 1526. This era marked the construction of some of the finest monuments in the Mughal Empire.

Babur died shortly after this victory (1530) and within 10 years his son **Humayun** had been driven out of the area by the Afghan king **Sher Shah Suri**. Humayun remained in exile for 14 years, but following the death of Sher Shah, he retook Lahore without opposition on 23 February 1555.

Like his father before him, Humayun died shortly after his victory (1556), but under his successor **Akbar** Lahore's fortunes were revived – in 1584 Lahore was made capital of the Mughal Empire. For 14 years Akbar made Lahore his headquarters, directing his campaigns and military operations from there, as well as holding court. Although there are records of an earlier fort at Lahore dating back to 1180, the foundation of the great **Lahore Fort** is attributed to the 12th year of Akbar's reign. He also rebuilt the wall surrounding the old city and the 12 entrance gates, one of which bears his name. Lahore enjoyed a period of economic prosperity under Akbar, as well as great literary achievement in the works of the Persian poets **Urfi** and **Faizi**.

Following Akbar's death in 1605, Lahore continued to flourish under his son **Jahangir**. He was particularly fond of Lahore, adding several buildings to the fort as well as building **Anarkali's Tomb**. Jahangir is buried in the imposing tomb that was built by his son and successor **Shah Jahan** 7 km NW of Lahore. The tomb of Jahangir's wife, **Nur Jahan**, is nearby.

Born in Lahore, Shah Jahan left his mark upon the city in the form of some of the finest buildings and gardens. The most beautiful buildings in the fort, including the **Shish Mahal**, **Naulakha Bunga**, **Moti Masjid** as well as much of the **Diwan-e-Aam** were built by Shah Jahan. The **Wazir Khan Mosque** was also built during his reign, and many of the great Mughal gardens, including the **Shalimar Gardens**, were initiated by Shah Jahan. He was succeeded in 1658 by his son **Aurangzeb**. A great Islamic reformer, in addition to enlarging the fort, Aurangzeb constructed the magnificent **Badshahi Mosque**.

However, in the power vacuum that followed Aurangzeb's death in 1707, Lahore had a turbulent experience, being attacked, lost and retaken by three different Mughal kings, the Sikhs four times, before finally falling after two attempts to the Afghan **Ahmad Shah Durrani** in 1759. In 1799 Lahore was eventually captured by **Ranjit Singh**.

The Sikhs

During the forty year rule (1799-1839) of Ranjit Singh, Sikh power in the Punjab was consolidated. However, although Ranjit Singh added some fine architectural features to the city, including the **Gurdwara of Arjan Singh**, he is best remembered by Muslims as a vandal of some repute. Most of the gardens were neglected, and a great deal of marble and many of the precious inlaid stones were removed to embellish the Golden Temple at Amritsar. Indeed, it is claimed that Ranjit Singh removed enough marble from the Muslim mausoleums in Lahore to build two Golden Temples.

British rule

Following the death of Ranjit Singh, the real victors in the succession struggle that followed were the British. In Dec 1846, a Council of Regency was established, with the real reigns of power in the hands of the British Resident. At the conclusion of the Second Sikh War in 1849, Maharaja Dalip Singh was pensioned off to Norfolk and the city was officially handed over to the British.

The British occupied Lahore for almost a century, during which time they built some fine colonial buildings which combined the Gothic and Victorian with the Mughal style. These include the **High Court**, **Lahore Museum**, **Aitchison College**, the old **University campus**, **General Post Office**, **Tollinton Market** and a number of churches. Restoration work was carried out by the Archaeological Department on many of the Mughal buildings, and those which had been turned into offices, storerooms and living quarters were returned to their original functions.

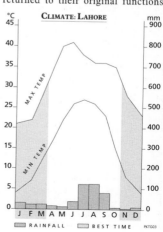

CLIMATE: LAHORE

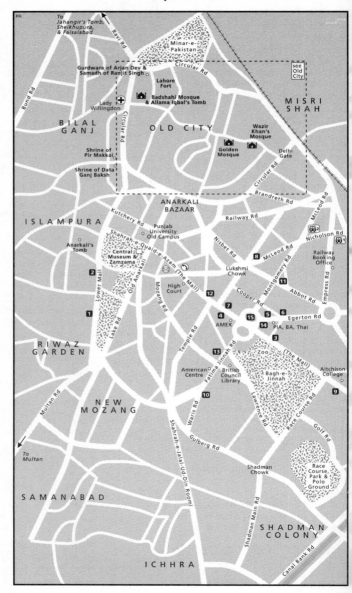

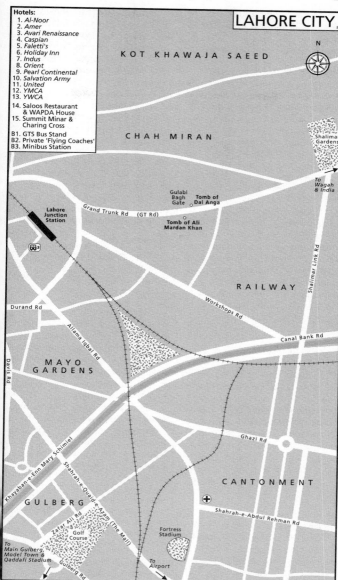

Hotels:
1. Al-Noor
2. Amer
3. Avari Renaissance
4. Caspian
5. Faletti's
6. Holiday Inn
7. Indus
8. Orient
9. Pearl Continental
10. Salvation Army
11. United
12. YMCA
13. YWCA

14. Saloos Restaurant & WAPDA House
15. Summit Minar & Charing Cross

B1. GTS Bus Stand
B2. Private 'Flying Coaches'
B3. Minibus Station

LAHORE CITY

KOT KHAWAJA SAEED

CHAH MIRAN

Shalimar Gardens

To Wagah & India

Lahore Junction Station

Grand Trunk Rd (GT Rd)

Gulabi Bagh Gate

Tomb of Dai Anga

Tomb of Ali Mardan Khan

RAILWAY

Shalimar Link Rd

Durand Rd

Workshops Rd

Canal Bank Rd

Davis Rd

Allama Iqbal Rd

MAYO GARDENS

Ghazi Rd

Khayaban-e-Enn Mary Schimel

Shahrah-e-Quaid-e-Azam (The Mall)

GULBERG

CANTONMENT

Shahrah-e-Abdul Rehman Rd

Zafar Ali Rd

Golf Course

Fortress Stadium

To Main Gulberg, Model Town & Qaddafi Stadium

Gulberg Rd

To Airport

Some adjustments were made to the outer walls of the Badshahi Mosque, however, so that it could not subsequently be used as a fortified base.

Independence

Lahore played a key role in the partition of India and the subsequent creation of Pakistan, but also witnessed some of the worst excesses of this less than amicable divorce. On 23 March 1940, the All India Muslim League met in session at Lahore under the stewardship of Mohammad Ali Jinnah. The conference culminated in the passing of the historic **Lahore Resolution of 1940** that paved the way for the partition of India and the creation of the new state of Pakistan.

Significantly, as Jinnah's biographer Wolpert points out, Pakistan is not explicitly mentioned; rather there is reference to "geographically contiguous units" where "Muslims are numerically in a majority". Nor is it clear whether the two 'zones' of NW India and Bengal are to form two separate autonomous states or one single Muslim state. However, the Indian newspapers referred to the resolution as the "Pakistan Resolution" and the concept has stuck. The day is celebrated as a national holiday in Pakistan.

The decision to divide the Punjab between India and Pakistan was looked upon with a deep sense of foreboding by many observers. The Senior Superintendent of Police, Delhi is quoted as saying several months before Independence Day: "Once a line of division is drawn in the Punjab all Sikhs to the west of it and all Muslims to the east of it will have their -------- chopped off." Right up until the boundary awards were announced, many Sikhs and Hindus in Lahore believed that the city would be 'awarded' to India.

When the awards of the Radcliffe Boundary Commission were announced on 17 August 1947, Lahore descended into anarchy. The city resembled one vast refugee camp, with Hindus and Sikhs abandoning all their valuables in order to dash E in fear of their lives, whilst caravans of plundered and mutilated refugees arrived in Lahore from India. Reports speak of railway carriage doors being opened at both Lahore and Amritsar stations, and pouring out onto the platforms the blood of the slaughtered occupants.

The frustration for the impartial researcher is that almost without exception, all literature on these traumatic events produced in India and Pakistan is so skewered in its bias, it is all but rendered unreadable. Each side seems to blame each other for initiating the slaughter and committing the worst atrocities, when in reality there is little to choose between the two.

Modern Lahore

The modern city of Lahore is considered by many Pakistanis, and certainly most Punjabi's, as the cultural capital of the country. In Punjab University, Lahore has the country's premier educational institute, and the city can also boast that it is the film and fashion centre of Pakistan. Tourist brochures are keen to quote Punjabi proverbs to emphasize Lahore's uniqueness – "Lahore is Lahore" – and its importance – "East or West, Lahore is best", and there is no doubt that Lahore ranks with Agra, Fatehpur Sikri and Delhi as one of the great centres of Mughal architecture. However, the city is changing rapidly, and today represents one of Pakistan's major industrial bases. At Partition it was the most populous city in Pakistan, but has since been overtaken by Karachi.

WARNING Although the city has not experienced the same level of violent political crime that Karachi has suffered from in recent years, Lahore is the city in Pakistan where you are most likely to get tricked, robbed or conned. Levels of crime are far **lower** than in most cities in the West, but there are persistent reports of tourists falling victim to confidence tricksters in Lahore. (**NB** A separate warning about some of the cheaper hotels in Lahore is given in the Accommodation section.) Such scams often involve tourists being approached in the street by bogus policemen (sometimes in unmarked cars) who ask to examine passports, documents or foreign currency, before rapidly disappearing with any valuables that are handed over. As the PTDC point out, there is no reason for any member of the authorities, whether in uniform or not, to need to examine your passport or currency. They recommend that you walk away, making a note of the car registration where applicable, and reporting the incident at a police station or at the tourist office.

Some travellers have also reported having been drugged and subsequently robbed after sharing a 'friendly cup of tea' in the old city. With most Pakistanis being amongst the friendliest and most hospitable people in the world, it is difficult to strike the sensible balance between accepting their overwhelming generosity and paranoia over a small number of incidents that occur each year. It is up to the individual traveller to exercise caution and their discretion.

Places of interest

Badshahi Mosque

Built for the Emperor Aurangzeb in 1673-74, the Badshahi Mosque is Lahore's most striking building. Modelled on the great Jami Masjid in Delhi, it has an impressive 20m high gateway, and a central prayer chamber topped by three large white marble domes that opens onto an enormous 160m square courtyard. It is claimed that 100,000 worshippers can gather in this courtyard, making it one of the largest mosques in the world. At each corner of the courtyard stands a 50m high minaret, although the original cupolas were destroyed in the 1840 earthquake. It is said that the minarets of the Badshahi Mosque and the minarets of Jahangir's Tomb to the NW are so designed that from the top of any one minaret, it is only possible to see three minarets of the other building. Sadly, it is no longer per-

mitted to climb the 204 steps to the top of these towers. The red sandstone from which the bulk of the mosque is constructed was quarried in India. The small museum above the main gate houses some possessions of the Prophet, including his slippers, turban, stick, cloak, pants and some hairs from his beard.

Some argue that the mosque is typical of the later Mughal period in that there is a certain "poverty of detail" and "feebleness of form", although this is ascribed rather to the architect's "orthodoxy than to his bad taste". Nevertheless, Badshahi Mosque remains a remarkable testimony to Mughal architecture. The mosque was used as a powder magazine by the Sikhs, and only returned to the Muslims of Lahore in 1856 after 7 years of British occupation.

Like all mosques in South Asia, the best time to take photographs is early morning when the sun is still in the E.

Hazuri Bagh

Between the Badshahi Mosque and the main entrance to Lahore Fort is a small garden, **Hazuri Bagh**, laid out by Ranjit Singh. At the centre is the marble **baradari** where the Sikh ruler used to hold court. Originally it was a 2-storey pavilion, although the upper storey collapsed in 1932 following a heavy storm and possibly a lightning strike. Many Muslims consider this sweet revenge, since Ranjit Singh considerably vandalized the tombs of Jahangir and Asaf Khan to procure the marble for this baradari.

In the SW corner of the garden stands the **Mausoleum of Allama Iqbal** (1873-1938), Pakistan's greatest poet and expounder of the 'two-nation theory' that led to the creation of the Muslim homeland in South Asia. The red sandstone and marble tomb is built in a mixture of Afghan and Moorish styles, and was paid for by monies raised through public subscription. Following Partition, poor relations between India and Pakistan made it difficult to import the

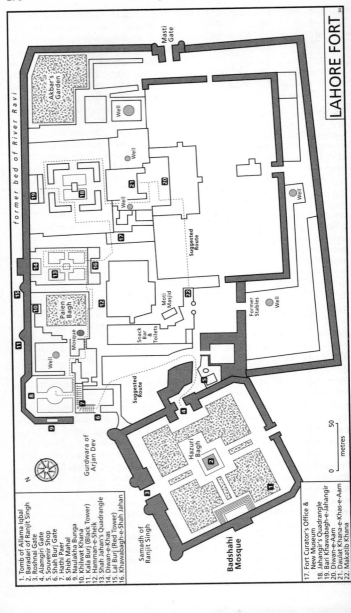

LAHORE FORT

1. Tomb of Allama Iqbal
2. Baradari of Ranjit Singh
3. Roshnai Gate
4. Alamgiri Gate
5. Souvenir Shop
6. Shah Burj Gate
7. Hathi Paer
8. Shish Mahal
9. Naulakha Bunga
10. Khilwat Khana
11. Kala Burj (Black Tower)
12. Hamman-e-Sheikh
13. Shah Jahan's Quadrangle
14. Diwan-e-Khas
15. Lal Burj (Red Tower)
16. Khawabagh-e-Shah Jahan

17. Fort Curator's Office & New Museum
18. Jahangir's Quadrangle
19. Bari Khawabagh-e-Jahangir
20. Diwan-e-Aam
21. Daulat Khana-e-Khas-e-Aam
22. Makatib Khana

0   50
metres

Jaipur sandstone to complete construction, and the tomb lay unfinished for several years. The *ta'weez* of the tomb is of lapis, a gift from Afghanistan, and is engraved with verses from the Qu'ran. The walls of the mausoleum are decorated with couplets from some of Iqbal's *ghazals*.

Gurdwara of Arjan Dev

Just to the N of the Hazuri Bagh is the **Gurdwara of Arjan Dev**, the 5th Guru who completed the *Adi Granth* (the Holy Book of the Sikhs), and initiated work on the Golden Temple at Amritsar. Built by Ranjit Singh, the gurdwara is made conspicuous by its heavily gilded fluted dome, and is a centre of Sikh pilgrimage. The interior ceiling is said to be richly decorated with tracery and inlay, although the complex is only open to Sikhs. Legend suggests that the Guru was swallowed by the waves whilst bathing in the Ravi in 1606, although others suggest that he was executed for supporting Jahangir's rival Khusro.

Also within a walled enclosure is the *Samadh* that holds the ashes of Ranjit Singh. Built in a mixture of Hindu and Muslim styles, the building is also said to have a fine interior. The two buildings are best seen from the vantage point of Lahore Fort.

Lahore Fort

With its counterparts in Delhi and Agra, **Lahore Fort** represents one of the three great forts built by the Mughals. Covering a vast area, some 375m by 300m, the fort contains some of the most impressive secular Mughal buildings in South Asia. Embellished with carved red sandstone, marble, *pietra dura* work, glazed coloured and *kashi* tile work, plus frescoes depicting royal pleasures, it is more a palace than a fort.

It is thought that there have been a succession of earlier forts on this site dating back at least to 1180, although the basis of what we see today was begun during the reign of Akbar. Later additions were made by Jahangir, Shah Jahan and Aurangzeb. The fort was later occupied by the Sikhs and then the British.

The following route takes in all the key buildings. Open daily, summer 0700-1930, winter 0830-1730 (Rs 4).

Enter the fort through the **Alamgiri Gate**. Built by Aurangzeb in 1674, it is a massive gateway flanked by semi octagonal bastions overlooking the Hazuri Bagh. There is a small souvenir shop just inside the gate.

If you walk uphill and then turn **left** down the ramp, you come to the **Shah Burj Gate**. This entrance is credited to Shah Jahan, and was built for the exclusive use of royalty. The Persian inscription dates the gate to 1631-32, and was built under the supervision of Shah Jahan's architect, Mamur Khan. The elaborate *kashi* tile work shows a marked Persian influence, although the painted frescoes are a reminder of the Hindu craftsmanship incorporated into Mughal architecture.

Inside the Shah Burj Gate, to the left, is the **Hathi Paer**, or Elephant Path. The 58 steps provide access for the royal entourage, mounted on elephants, to the private royal apartments.

At the top of the Hathi Paer is the **Shish Mahal**, or Palace of Mirrors. Enclosed in a courtyard with a tank and fountains at its centre, the Shish Mahal was used as the royal residence of Shah Jahan, and is one of the most beautiful buildings in the fort. It is decorated with convex mirror mosaic, known as *aiena kari*, set in arabesque patterns of white cement on the ceiling, walls and spandrels of the arches. The ceiling is supported by six pairs of slender fluted pillars. The fretted marble *jalies*, or screens, are of exceptional craftsmanship.

On the W side of the courtyard is the marble pavilion known as **Naulakha Bunga**, so named because it reputedly cost Shah Jahan 9 lakh rupees (Rs

900,000) to build. It is decorated in a style known as *pietra dura*, inlaid with semi-precious stones such as agate, jade and lapiz.

Continuing along the N wall of the fort, you reach the **Khilwat Khana**, or private sleeping chamber of Shah Jahan. Outside is the **Paien Bagh** (Ladies' Garden), used exclusively by the women of the harem. The paths were said to be lined with fragrance giving flowers, cypresses and dwarf, fruit bearing trees.

Opposite the garden is the **Hamman-e-Sheik**, the royal bath house. The building has a dressing room, **Jama Khana**, a warm room, **Nim Garm**, and a hot room, **Garm**. It is based on the design of a Turkish bath, with an underground heating system.

Shah Jahan's Quadrangle is at the centre of the N wall, and comprises a white marble colonnaded pavilion, **Diwan-e-Khas** (Hall of Private Audience) and the **Khawabagh-e-Shah Jahan**, or private quarters of Shah Jahan. The Diwan-e-Khas was built in 1645, and was used by the king to receive state dignitaries and distinguished guests. Next to the Khawabagh-e-Shah Jahan is the Fort Curator's office, and the new Lahore Fort Museum (summer 0830-1230 1430-1730, winter 0900-1600).

In the NE corner of the fort is **Jahangir's Quadrangle**. Started by Akbar but completed in 1618 by Jahangir, it is flanked to the E and W by carved red sandstone columns. The quadrangle measures 112m by 74m, and has a central tank and fountains. The British built tennis court has long since gone. The main building to the N of the quadrangle is the **Bari Khawabagh-e-Jahangir** that was used by Jahangir as a sleeping chamber, but now houses relics of the Mughal period.

The S side of the quadrangle is completed by the **Diwan-e-Aam**, or Hall of Public Audience. The rear court, or **Daulat Khana-e-Khas-o-Aam**, was built during the reign of Akbar, and has at its centre the **Jaha Roka**, State Balcony. Here, the Emperor held court and granted audience to the nobility. The rest of the Diwan-e-Aam was built by Shah Jahan, and comprises 40 pillars standing on a raised rectangular platform.

Proceeding back towards the main gate, the first major building encountered is the **Makatib Khana**, or Secretariat. Built by Jahangir, it is here that the *muharirs* (clerks) kept the palace records.

The final building of significance is the **Moti Masjid**, so named because of its pearl shaped dome. This white marble mosque, built by Shah Jahan but recently renovated, is in keeping with those at Delhi and Agra.

Next to the mosque are the snack bar and toilets.

The Old City

Most of Lahore's key Mughal monuments are located in and around the **old walled city**. The original 9m high defensive walls were built during the reign of Akbar, and allowed day-time access to the city through 12 large gates. The Sikh ruler Ranjit Singh later strengthened the crumbling walls, and added a defensive moat to the N.

Although only some of the 12 original gates remain, the old city is still very much alive and it is fascinating to wander through the narrow, bustling bazaars. A good route to follow enters through the **Delhi Gate** to the E, although it is almost inevitable that you will get lost at some stage. Immediately inside the Delhi Gate is a useful tourist information centre. Continuing along the narrow bazaar, you come to the **Wazir Khan Mosque** on the left. The mosque was built in 1643 by the physician **Alamud Din Ansari**, a native of Chiniot. History records that he was rewarded for curing Jahangir's wife Nur Jahan of a foot malady, and later rose to the position of *Wazir* during the reign of Shah Jahan, taking the title of **Wazir Khan**. The mosque is renowned for its

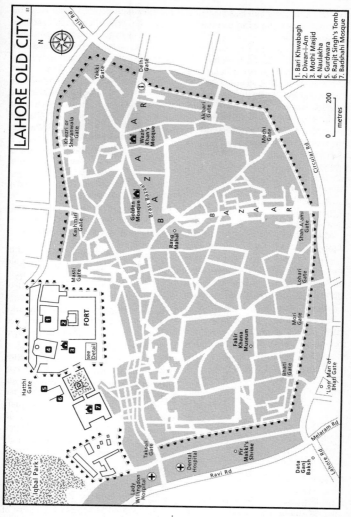

LAHORE OLD CITY

1. Bari Khwabagh
2. Diwan-i-Am
3. Mothi Masjid
4. Naulakha
5. Gurdwara
6. Ranjit Singh's Tomb
7. Badshahi Mosque

0 ____ 200
metres

use and execution of inlaid pottery decoration in the wall panelling. Close inspection reveals that each section of detail is a separate piece of pot or tile, and the work is strictly inlay and not painted decoration. There are also su-

perb arabesque frescoes in the interior. The mosque is divided into five compartments, each surmounted by a dome, and opening onto the courtyard. A tall minaret stands at each corner of the courtyard. For some small baksheesh, one of the small boys will take you on to the roof of the gate for a fine panoramic view of the old city.

Continuing through the bazaar, you come to a fork. The right fork leads to Lahore Fort and Badshahi Mosque, the left leads to the **Golden Mosque**. Built in 1753 by Bikhari Khan, the Golden or **Sunehri Mosque** stands on a raised plinth, and gets its name from its three large gilded domes and gold capped 10m minarets. Legend suggests that Bikhari Khan was a favourite at the court of the former ruler of Lahore, Mir Mannu. However, following the demise of the Mir, his widow had her maid servants beat Bikhari Khan to death with their shoes!

Continuing W, the route passes through the fascinating **Brass Bazaar**, before turning S (left) into the colourful **Shah Alami Market**. It includes the Kashmiri Bazaar, Suha Bazaar, Dabbi Bazaar and Chatta Bazaar where craftsmen still work with copper, brass and silver. You can exit the old city S through the old site of the **Shah Alami Gate**.

Also within the old city walls is the **Faqir Khana Museum**, approached through the **Bhati Gate**. This private museum belongs to the family of Faqir Azizuddin who was Ranjit Singh's Foreign Minister. It is a treasure house of artistic masterpieces including paintings, sculptures, porcelain, carpets and ancient manuscripts. Just outside the Bhati Gate is the self-styled 'Lion man of Bhati Gate', a medical 'quack' who, incredibly, has two fully grown Asiatic lions in a small cage in his shop.

Shrine of Data Ganj Baksh

Located a little to the W of Bhati Gate is the **Shrine of Data Ganj Baksh**, often referred to as the patron saint of Lahore. A renowned Islamic scholar, and author of the classic book on Sufism, 'Kashful Mahjoob', he came to Lahore in the early 11th century and remained there until his death in 1072 (although some recent biographies place his death in 1092).

Although born Abul Hasan Ali, he was given the title Data Ganj Baksh – 'Bestower of treasures' – in recognition of his help amongst the poor and needy. An inscription above the main gate translates: "He who calls at your shrine, Never returns disappointed." Today there are several buildings attached to the shrine which serve the public, such as a dispensary, hospital, an organization to help destitute women, and a public kitchen where food is distributed to the poor.

The shrine is a small octagonal marble building, with white marble supporting pillars and intricately carved screens through which to view the sarcophagus. The original mausoleum was built by the Ghaznavid Sultan, Ibrahim, although later embellishments have been added by Akbar, Aurangzeb and several dignitaries in the employ of the Sikh rulers.

Adjoining the tomb is a large marble courtyard, with arched domed cloisters on the N and S sides. To the W is a splendid modern mosque. The entrance is in black mirrored glass, cut into the shape of three domes, reflecting the image of the shrine opposite. Two tall rocket shaped minarets stand on either side. The carpet inside is in the style of Mughal frescoes, and the mihrab wall has extensive wooden panelling. The basement area is a popular place to read and discuss the Qu'ran.

The shrine is always busy, although visitor numbers peak on Thur evenings, and during the saint's Urs (20th Safar). Suitably dressed visitors are made very welcome.

Shrine of Pir Makki

On Ravi Rd, just to the N of Data Ganj Baksh's shrine, is the tomb of Aziz-uz-Din, a Muslim holy man who came to Lahore in the closing period of Ghaznavid rule. Because he came from Mecca he became known as **Pir Makki**.

Anarkali's Tomb

In the grounds of the Punjab Secretariat on the Lower Mall stands **Anarkali's**

Tomb. Legend has it that Anarkali (literally Pomegranate Blossom) was either a wife of the Emperor Akbar, or a favourite in his harem. Catching a glimpse of a smile pass between Anarkali and his son Prince Salim, later Emperor Jahangir, Akbar suspected them of having an affair, and in a fit of fury, had Anarkali buried alive. When Jahangir later became Emperor, he raised a mausoleum to Anarkali, engraving a mournful Persian couplet on the cenotaph: "Ah, could I behold the face of my beloved once again, I would offer thanks unto God until the day of Resurrection."

Unfortunately this romantic tale has been dismissed as a piece of fiction, originating from Finch, an English traveller who visited Lahore in 1611 on an indigo selling trip. The tomb is thought to contain the body of Sahiba Jamal, a wife of Jahangir.

The tomb is on a hexagonal base, with a domed octagonal tower at each corner, and a huge central dome supported on eight arches. It is now in a poor state of repair, having been previously used as a residence of Ranjit Singh's son Kharak, and later by the Italian General, Ventura, whilst in the employ of Ranjit Singh. The British converted it into an office, and then into the 'Mother Church' of the diocese until the cathedral was completed.

The Mall

Lahore has some of the finest examples of the Gothic-Victorian-Mughal style of architecture on the sub-continent. Many are positioned along **The Mall**, since renamed Shahrah-e-Quaid-e-Azam. The **High Court**, built in 1889, features a central hall, surrounded on four sides by spacious verandahs, and topped by two 30m towers and two 20m towers. Next door is the splendid red brick **General Post Office**, with double storeyed arched verandahs and domed corner towers. On the opposite side of the road is the red brick old campus of

Punjab University, and the Anglican **Cathedral Church of the Resurrection**.

Further E along The Mall is Pakistan's most exclusive school, **Aitchison College**. Set in its own extensive grounds, this classic Anglo-Indian building was established by the British as a Chief's College for sons of local grandees, most of whom were remnants of the Sikh Empire. At Partition, only 42 people were left in the school, including staff. Today there are some 2,500 pupils. Aitchison's most famous recent old boy is Imran Khan.

Another fine colonial building on The Mall is the **Lahore Central Museum**. The museum is the oldest and one of the best in Pakistan. It is superbly housed and excellently maintained. Founded in 1864, it moved to the present building in 1890. The museum's first curator was John Lockwood Kipling, father of Rudyard, who referred to the museum in his classic "Kim" as the 'Ajaib Ghar', or House of Wonders. Some of the collections, notably the Gandharan sculptures, are outstanding.

Open daily except Sat, the first Wed of the month and the following: Eid-ul-Fitr, Eid-ul-Zoha, Eid-e-Milad-un-Nabi, 9th and 10th Muharram, 1 May, 11 Sep. Winter (1 Oct-15 Apr): 0900-1600. Summer (16 Apr-30 Sep): 0800-1700. Times may change without notice. Entry and small camera fee but some exhibits may not be photographed. Free conducted tours and a good printed guide available at the entrance.

The pride of the collection are the **Gandharan** sculptures displayed in Gallery 2, including the famous 'Fasting Buddha'. Centred on the present Vale of Peshawar Gandhara played a significant part in the political and cultural life both of West Asia and of the Indian sub-continent. Brought into the Persian Empire as one of its 42 provinces by the Achaemenid Emperor Darius in the 5th century BC. However the most striking remains of the region today come from its

Buddhist period. Although western influence, through Greek conquests, is evident stylistically in the art of Gandhara from the reign of the Kushan rulers in the early centuries AD, the subjects are almost entirely Indian and Buddhist.

The **Coin Collection** is extremely valuable with some from the period of Alexander the Great, the Guptas and the Buddhists.

Standing on a traffic island in the road outside the museum is the famous

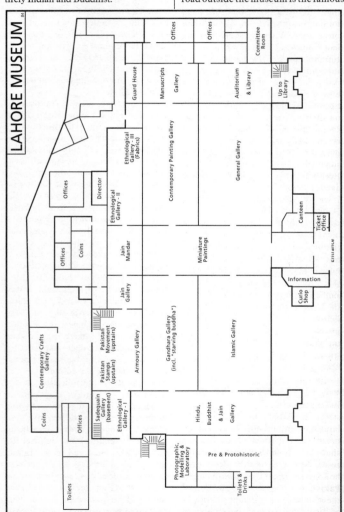

LAHORE MUSEUM

Offices
Offices
Committee Room
Guard House
Manuscripts Gallery
Auditorium & Library
Up to Library
Ethnological Gallery - III (Fabrics)
Contemporary Painting Gallery
General Gallery
Director
Offices
Ethnological Gallery - II
Canteen
Offices
Coins
Jain Mandar
Miniature Paintings
Ticket Office
ENTRANCE
Jain Gallery
Information
Contemporary Crafts Gallery
Pakistan Movement (upstairs)
Curio Shop
Coins
Pakistan Stamps (upstairs)
Armoury Gallery
Gandhara Gallery (incl. "starving buddha")
Islamic Gallery
Offices
Sadequain Gallery (basement)
Ethnological Gallery - I
Hindu, Buddhist & Jain Gallery
Photographic, Modelling & Laboratory
Pre & Protohistoric
Toilets
Toilets & Drinks

Zam zama gun. "He sat, in defiance of municipal orders, astride the gun Zam-Zammah on her brick platform opposite the old Ajaib-Gher – the Wonder House, as natives call the Lahore Museum. Who holds Zam-Zammah, that 'fire-breathing dragon', hold the Punjab; for the great green-bronze piece is always first of the conqueror's loot." (Rudyard Kipling, "Kim", 1901). Immortalized by Kipling in the opening lines of "Kim", this mighty cannon is so named because on firing, it resembles a lion's roar. Cast in copper and bronze collected as public levy in 1757 under the orders of Ahmad Shah Durrani, the gun saw action in the Battle of Panipat in 1761. It was later acquired by Ranjit Singh, and became something of a symbol of the Sikh Empire, although it was badly damaged in the Multan campaign of 1818. It was subsequently retired to Lahore Fort, and then moved to its present site in 1870.

At the E end of The Mall, at its junction with Fatima Jinnah Rd, is the **Summit Minar**. Standing in a small park known informally as **Charing Cross**, this 50m minar was opened in 1977 by Zulfikar Ali Bhutto to commemorate the Islamic Summit held in Lahore in Feb 1974. At the base of the engraved marble obelisk is a small arcade displaying gifts from the participating countries. The small pavilion houses a Qu'ran inscribed with gold leaf.

Parks

In contrast to the densely packed streets of the old city, Lahore has a large number of open spaces and some notable **parks**. To the N of the Badshahi Mosque is **Iqbal Park**, a popular recreational spot on weekends and holidays. At the centre is the **Minar-e-Pakistan**, a 60m tower built to mark the spot where the Lahore Resolution of 1940 was passed. There are fine views of the fort, Badshahi Mosque and the whole city from the top. Using the stairs negates the need to join the long queues for the lift, and also gives access to the less crowded viewing platforms at different levels. In typical Pakistani style, the lift at this national monument is operated by a man sitting on top of the cage, hot-wiring the lift motor.

The **Bagh-e-Jinnah**, formerly the Lawrence Gardens, were laid out off The Mall in 1860. They are a popular leisure spot for Lahore residents. At the centre is the former Montgomery Hall, now the **Jinnah Library**.

Next to the Bagh-e-Jinnah is **Lahore Zoo**. The zoological gardens were laid out on this 8 ha site in 1872, and contain the usual collection of depressed animals that would be better off dead. The Punjab Wildlife Dept who run the zoo are particularly proud of the bear hill and elephant/rhino house that are based on those at London Zoo. Sadly, these style of structures are now considered by progressive zoos as being unsuitable for keeping animals.

The **Race Course Park** to the SE of the Bagh-e-Jinnah is popular with families at weekends, as well as being a venue for **polo** matches (check local press for fixtures). The polo played here is much more akin to the sort that Prince Charles plays in Windsor than to the variety played in the N of Pakistan.

Short excursions

Jahangir's Tomb

Across the river Ravi, 7 km NW of Lahore, is the **Tomb of Jahangir**, the Mughal emperor who ruled from 1605 to 1627. He died at Rajauri in Kashmir, but expressed a wish to be buried in Lahore, and is now the only Mughal emperor buried in Pakistan. 10 years after the emperor's death his son, Shah Jahan, constructed the mausoleum under the supervision of Jahangir's widow, **Nur Jahan**.

Sited in the attractive walled garden **Dil Kusha**, the mausoleum is a single-storey square structure of decorated marble on red sandstone, with four corner minarets and a projecting entrance at the centre of each side. The corner minarets rise to 30m in five stages, are inlaid with zigzag bands of variegated marbles and blocks of yellow stone, and topped with white marble cupolas. Similar in style to the Itimad ad Daulah, built in Agra by Nur Jahan for her father, the disproportion between the height of the base and the minarets gives the tomb an odd appearance – almost as if another storey or a large central dome is missing.

The building is divided into a series of vaulted compartments, with rosettes and arabesques over the arches. The interior is embellished with frescoes, *pietra dura* inlay and coloured marble. In the inner chamber is the white marble sarcophagus, decorated with the black marble inlay, listing the 99 names of God. The Persian inscription reads: "The illuminated resting place of His Majesty, Nur-ud-Din Mohammad Jahangir Badshah AH 1037."

The original edifice of the tomb was far grander, but Ranjit Singh removed the choicest ornaments to adorn the Golden Temple at Amritsar. At one stage it was even used as the residence of Amise, a French general in the Sikh army.

Outside the Dil Kusha garden is the **Akbari Serai**, a Travellers' Rest House of the same period. The open courtyard is flanked by a raised terrace and 180 cells, each fronted by a verandah. The serai has two grand gateways to the N and S, and a red sandstone three domed mosque to the W. In the enclosure beyond the mosque is the **Tomb of Asaf Khan**. Brother of Nur Jahan, and father of Mumtaz Mahal (the lady of the Taj Mahal), Asaf Khan was Shah Jahan's Prime Minister. Following his death in 1641, Shah Jahan built this tomb to house Asaf Khan's remains. Octagonal in shape, with a high bulbous dome, the tomb was one of the main victims of Ranjit Singh's recycling methods.

Further W, across the railway tracks, are the remains of **Nur Jahan's Tomb**. She died in 1645, and was buried in the mausoleum that she had erected for herself. Once richly decorated with floral fresco paintings on lime plaster, most of the embellishments were removed by the Sikhs. The minarets have gone, the marble platform and the sandstone facing are new, and the tomb is little more than a shell.

Buses 6 and 23 from the railway station take about 20 mins to reach the tombs, although it is easier to go by rickshaw or taxi (Rs 50). On a small island in the Ravi, just below the new Ravi Bridge, is the **Kamran Baradari**, a small pleasure pavilion built by Mirza Kamran, son of Babar. It is a popular picnic spot and can be reached by hired pleasure-boat.

Shalimar Gardens

The **Shalimar Gardens** are located 8 km E of Lahore. Open daily: summer 0800-1800, winter 0800-1630. Chilled drinks are on sale in the Sikh guest house which was added in the 19th century. The toilets are near the Turkish Baths. You can reach the gardens by driving E down GT Rd or from Jahangir's Tomb on the Bund Rd. Approx 20 min from the Rly Station on Bus 3, 12 or 17. It is best visited when the flowers are in bloom in Feb and Mar. The shallow niches in the marble wall (a feature of Mughal architecture) were used for hundreds of lamps. The gardens are illuminated on Wed and Sat nights.

The '**Shalimar**' ('abode of love') **gardens** were laid out in 1637 on the instructions of Emperor Shah Jahan. Designed by Ali Mardan Khan, it was a royal pleasure garden. Over 450m long and enclosed within high walls for privacy, with its marble pavilions with carvings, *pietra dura* inlay work and fresco paintings, a marble waterfall, ornamental ponds and over 400 fountains, the gardens provided an alternative residence for the royal family. Sadly they have nothing of their former beauty.

Char baghs The gardens were laid out on the principle of two 'char baghs' (quartered gardens) separated by a terrace in the centre. Water tanks drawing from the canal supplied water up to the height of the highest level, which then cascaded down. The highest 'Farah Baksh', reserved for the royal family, is where you will enter the gardens, although when it was laid out the entrance was at the other end, enabling privacy to be maintained at each higher level. This top terrace is divided into quarters, but the original decorations on the once grand buildings have virtually disappeared.

The Emperor's sleeping chamber Where you enter, the pavilion to house the *harem* and the ladies in waiting to the W and the *Diwan-e-Khas* (Hall of Private Audience) to the E, were the finest buildings of the garden. Steps lead down to the next terrace, about 4m lower, and water was channelled down to the water tank and numerous fountains in the centre. The royal entertainers performed for the Emperor who sat on the marble platform here. To the E are the Turkish Baths. The lowest terrace contained the *Diwan-e-Am* (Hall of Public Audience). The garden was stocked with flowering plants and decorative shrubs from all corners of the Mughal Empire.

The Mughals chose to be 'formal' in their design rather than 'natural', "the aim being to discipline nature and not to imitate it" as Percy Brown puts it. "A regular arrangement of squares, often subdivided into smaller squares to form the favourite figure *char bagh* or fourfold plot."

On the GT Rd on the way to the Shalimar Gardens are a number of other Mughal buildings. To the left, just past the Museum of Science and Technology, is the **Gulabi Bagh Gate**. Constructed in 1655 by the Persian noble, and Admiral of the Fleet, **Mirza Sultan Beg**, the gate stands at the entrance to the long since disappeared **Gulabi Bagh**, or Rose Garden.

Inside the remains of the Rose Garden, to the N, is the **Tomb of Dai Anga**. Known as Zebun Nisa Begum, she was the wet-nurse of Shah Jahan. The tomb is dated to 1671, is rectangular in shape, with a central dome and four corner towers. The decorative mosaic work that adorned the tomb was another victim of Ranjit Singh.

Across the GT Rd is the **Tomb of Ali Mardan Khan**. Formerly Governor of Qandahar under the Safvids, he migrated to India and presented himself at the court of Shah Jahan in 1631. A skilled administrator and engineer, he built a number of canals during his tenure as Governor of Punjab, including the one that feeds the Shalimar Gardens. The mausoleum was built following his death in 1657.

Local festivals

End Oct-early Nov: *National Horse and Cattle Show* is held at the Fortress Stadium. The festival features livestock from all over Pakistan, as well as folk dancing, a military tattoo, displays of tent-pegging, and horse and camel dancing.

Last Sun in March: *Mela Chirghan* (Festival of lights) is held to honour the mystic and folk poet Shah Hussain who died in 1599, and his friend Madho Lal Hussain who is buried with him, the latter having converted to Islam from Hinduism. People from all over Punjab, including peasants and fakirs gather near the Shalimar Gardens on the huge esplanade, where the mausoleum is illuminated with lamps on Shah Hussain's death anniversary. This and the arrival of Spring is greeted with music, dancing, sports and magic shows.

Late March: *Kite Flying Festival* is held to celebrate the arrival of *Basant*, or Spring. It usually takes place in the old city, although religious leaders tried to ban it in 1995 as being un-Islamic!

2nd month of Safar (Muslim calendar): *Urs of Data Ganj Baksh*, death anniversary of the patron saint of Lahore when devotees gather at his tomb. Feasting, dancing and singing marks the occasion which draws famous Qawwali singers.

Local information

HOTEL CLASSIFICATIONS

AL	Rs4,000	A	Rs1,800-4,000
B	Rs900-1,800	C	Rs450-900
D	Rs300-450	E	Rs150-300
F	up to Rs150		

● **Accommodation**

Warning Be very careful of the cheap hotels around the station area, particularly in Brandreth (Nishtar) and McLeod Rd. Persistent reports speak of theft from rooms, sometimes involving drugged food and drinks. Other travellers tell of having to pay large bribes to police after having drugs planted in their rooms. As a very general rule, hotels that send touts to the bus and railway station are **not** recommended. Further, when checking into a hotel, it is useful to memorize all your passport and visa details, so that you don't have to refer to, and reveal the location of, your money belt. Be suspicious of hotel managers that demand to inspect your passport themselves. If, once you're in your room, there are repeated knocks at your door with requests to 're-check your passport', 'check the bathroom's plumbing', 'make sure you have a towel/soap' etc, then it may be time to lock your door, pack your bag, and leave quickly. It may be worth paying slightly more, and staying at a more reputable hotel for the duration of your stay in Lahore. Hotels detailed below are those recommended by PTDC, TDCP and other tourists.

AL *Avari Renaissance*, Shahrah-e-Quaid-e-Azam, T 525261, F 6365367, all facilities of international class hotel; **AL** *Pearl Continental*, Shahrah-e-Quaid-e-Azam, T 6360210, F 6362760, new extension increased capacity to 500 rm, incl Executive and Presidential suites, tennis, pool, gym, business centre, Bok-

hara restaurant, *La Terraza* poolside snack bar, 24-hr coffee shop.

A *Holiday Inn*, Egerton Rd, T 6367879, under construction; **A** *Services International*, Shahrah-e-Quaid-e-Azam, T 870281, F 872363, central a/c, pool, convenient to airport.

B *Amer*, Lower Mall, T 7229971, central a/c, dish TV, fridge, room service, car rental, restaurant, airport pick-up; **B** *Faletti's*, Egerton Rd, T 6364819, fine old colonial hotel, but like its contemporary in Pindi, Flashman's, it has somewhat gone to seed, a/c, foreign exchange, laundry, post office, travel agency, car rental, outdoor barbecue, restaurant, coffee shop, takes credit cards.

C *Caspian*, 73 Shahrah-e-Quaid-e-Azam, T 6363420, central a/c, dish TV, restaurant rec; **C** *Indus*, 56 Shahrah-e-Quaid-e-Azam, T 6302856, a/c, restaurant; **C** *National*, 2 Abbot Rd, T 6363011, central a/c, dish TV, fridge, car rental, restaurant, best value in **C** class; **C** *Orient*, 74 McLeod Rd, T 7223906, some a/c, non-a/c rooms Rs 200 cheaper, no restaurant, but room service; **C** *United*, 1 Abbot Rd, T 6279038, some a/c, dish TV, car parking.

D *Clifton*, Australia Chowk, T 320136, some a/c, TV.

E *Al Noor*, Rewaz Gdns, Lower Mall, T 7233239, some a/c, restaurant, rather run down.

Budget hotels: for years the **F** *Salvation Army Hostel*, Fatima Jinnah Rd, provided a popular and safe place to stay in Lahore, with cheap dorms, a kitchen, camping and a pleasant garden, with several very popular bakeries nearby. However, in mid 1995, the pressing needs of the Salvation Army's basic health and social welfare programme led to the closure of the hostel in favour of office space. **F** *YMCA*, Shahrah-e-Quaid-e-Azam. Often full with long term residents. Cafe open during Ramadan. **F** *YWCA*, Fatima Jinnah Rd. Taking advantage of travellers who turn up in the locality only to find the *Salvation Army* closed, the *YWCA* is now very busy. However, the dorm and family rms are usually occupied by long term Pakistani residents, and all travellers are herded into one large room, where 10 or so bed bug ridden mattresses have to serve as many as 40 people dossing down on the floor. Roll over, and you end up in the arms of your neighbour. Some women justifiably complain that 75% of the guests at this women's hostel are now men. Poor value. **F** *Youth Hostel*, 110 B/3, Gulberg 3, nr Firdous Mkt, T 881505. Inconveniently located.

● **Places to eat**

There is a wide choice of restaurants and fast food outlets, particularly on the Shahrah-e-Quaid-e-Azam and in the upmarket Gulberg area. On Main Blvd, Gulberg: *Gino's Pizza*; *Gulberg Kabana*; *Shanghai Chinese*. In Gulberg 3: *Hong Kong Chinese*, 85-D-1; *Tai Wah Chinese*, 78-E-1; *Xinhua*, 94-C-2. On Shahrah-e-Quaid-e-Azam: *Caspian*, Pakistani, Chinese, Continental, rec; *Cathay Chinese*; *Kim Mun Chinese*, opp Salvation Army; *No 67 Chinese* is reasonable; *Saloos*, WAPDA House. The main hotels all have good, if expensive restaurants.

● **Airline offices**

PIA, Egerton Rd, T 6306411. At Avari Hotel: **American Airlines, Canadian,** T 6279045; **Lufthansa,** T 6365168. At Simla Tower, Davis Rd: **Aero Asia,** T 6360282; **Uzbek,** T 6367067. At Ali Complex, Empress Rd, opp St Anthony's Church: **Aeroflot, Air Lanka, Alitalia, Austrian, Cathay Pacific, Continental, Cyprus, Japan, Kenyan, Oman, SAS, Shaheen, Singapore, Swissair.** At WAPDA: **Air France,** T 6360930; **KLM,** T 6363746. **Gulf,** 25a Davis Rd, T 6377002. **Syrian Arab,** Ambassador Hotel, Davis Rd, T6305484. At Transport House, Egerton Rd, **BA,** T 6301575; **Thai,** T 6312724.

● **Banks & money changers**

On Shahrah-e-Quaid-e-Azam: **American Express; ANZ-Grindlays; National Bank of Pakistan.** On Davis Rd: **Deutsche; Doha; Habib Bank AG Zurich; Muslim Commercial.**

● **Cultural centres**

The **Alhambra Arts Council Hall** cultural centre on Shahrah-e-Quaid-e-Azam is an impressive building of red brick and lime plaster in the British colonial style. **American Center,** Fatima Jinnah Rd. **British Council,** 32 Mozang Rd. **French Centre,** 20 E/2 Gulberg 3. **Goethe Institute,** 92 E/1 Gulberg 3. **Iranian Cultural Centre,** Main Gulberg Rd. **Pakistan National Centre,** Al Fateh, The Mall.

● **Embassies & consulates**

Most of the consulates in Lahore only have 'honorary' status, and will refer you to Islamabad for most matters.

● **Entertainment**

There are numerous **cinemas** around Lakshmi Chowk and on Shahrah-e-Quaid-e-Azam. Lahore's famous **brothels** are in the old city, nr to Badshahi Mosque.

● **Hospitals & medical centres**

Christian Hospital, Gulberg, T 870373; *Dental Hospital,* T 310261; *Edhi ambulance,* T 444460; *Medical Centre,* Gulberg 3, 51-P1-GBG-3, T 881906; *United Lady Willingdon,* Lahore Fort, T 7659001.

● **Libraries**

Jinnah Library in Bagh-e-Jinnah.

● **Post & telecommunications**

Central Telegraph Office: is opp, at 1 McLeod Rd.

GPO: is on Shahrah-e-Quaid-e-Azam. You cannot miss this superb Anglo-Indian building, complete with double-storied arched verandahs, with corner dome towers.

● **Places of worship**

Catholic: *Sacred Heart Cathedral,* Lawrence Rd.

Protestant: *Cathedral Church of the Resurrection,* Shahrah-e-Quaid-e-Azam, English service Sun 0730 and 1800.

● **Shopping**

Bookshops: *Ferozsons* on Shahrah-e-Quaid-e-Azam is one of Pakistan's finest bookshops.

Carpet weaving: Lahore is a centre of carpet weaving, with many retail outlets on Shahrah-e-Quaid-e-Azam, in the main hotel arcades and in the upmarket Gulberg area. Potential buyers should note that the industry in Lahore is a post Partition phenomenon, and carpets offered are unlikely to be antiques.

Duty free: *Duty Free Shop,* Cooper Rd sells imported items, though it's besieged by money-change hustlers.

Fashion: the latest Pakistani fashions can be found in the boutiques on Main Gulberg.

Handicrafts & jewellery: can be found in shops along Shahrah-e-Quaid-e-Azam, incl *Pakistan Handicrafts,* and at *Liberty Market* in Gulberg. Other treasures, as well as modern items and some real junk can be unearthed in *Anarkali Bazaar,* running N from opp the Museum, and from the various bazaars in the walled city.

Slide film: can be found in the *Kodak Products* shop.

● **Sports**

Cricket: the HQ of Pakistani cricket is at the impressive *Qaddafi Stadium* on Ferezpur Rd, venue of the 1996 World Cup Final. Cricket is also played at Bagh-e-Jinnah and Lahore Gymkhana.

Flying: *Lahore Flying Club*, Walton Airport.

Golf: Lahore Gymkhana, Upper Mall; Railway Golf Course, off Shahrah-e-Quaid-e-Azam.

Hockey: National Hockey Stadium, opp Qaddafi Stadium.

Polo: Race Course Park – check local press for fixtures.

● **Tour companies & travel agents**
There are numerous on Shahrah-e-Quaid-e-Azam, at WAPDA House and at main hotels.

● **Tourist offices**
Tourism Development Corporation of Punjab (TDCP), 4-A Lawrence Rd, T 6369687 and 195-B Shadman-2, T 7576826, F 7589097. TDCP run 2 half-day tours lasting 3½ hrs picking up from Faletti's, Services International, Pearl Continental and Avari. **Morning Tour**: 0830. Badshahi Mosque, Lahore Fort, Jahangir's Tomb, Lahore Museum. **Afternoon Tour**: 1430 (1530 1 Apr-30 Sep). Shalimar Gdns, Old City, Wazir Khan's Mosque, Pak Handicrafts Shop. Rs 195 adults, Rs 110 children. TDCP also operate **Winter Package Tours of Southern Punjab**. 6-day tour (incl accommodation, transport, guides, entry fees) visits Multan, Bahawalpur, Uch Sharif, Fort Derawar, Rahim Yar Khan and Bhong Mosque. Departs every Mon, Rs 3,600 pp, min 8 persons. 5-day tour visits Bahawalpur and incl jeep/camel safari in Cholistan Desert. Departs every Tues, Rs 3,000 pp, min 8 persons. Special excursions, eg Harappa or Salt Range, can be arranged. **PTDC** at Faletti's can also book these tours.

● **Useful addresses**
Foreigner's Registration Office: 63 Kutchery Rd, Lower Mall.
Police Station: Montgomery Rd.

● **Transport**
To & from border with INDIA: the land crossing between Pakistan and India is 23 km from Lahore, at **Wagah** on the Pakistan side and **Attari** on the Indian side. The border is generally open from 0900 until 1600 daily. The journey can be made by either train or bus/foot, although the latter is considerably quicker since it can take some 5 hrs for the whole train to clear customs.
Train Lahore-Wagah 0500, 0615, 1100 (Mon and Thur to Amritsar). Wagah-Lahore 0605,

0720, 1325 (Mon and Thur from Amritsar via Attari).

Bus/foot: minibus 12 from Lahore railway station runs to Wagah (although sometimes you may need to change half-way). Leave Pakistani border formalities at Wagah and take a rickshaw to Indian border post at Attari. From there, buses run 39 km to Amritsar.

Private vehicles NB There are two types of **carnet**: AIT and FIA. India (and Nepal) only accept the **AIT**. If you have the wrong permit, you may be turned away at the border or have your vehicle impounded at a later date. AIT carnet is available in Lahore from **Pakistan Automobile Association**, 62 Shadman Market (S of Gulberg and W of canal), T 7588854. You will need your FIA issuers to Fax the Pakistan AA (92-42 7570674) with full details, plus payment of US$120. Open Sat-Wed 0800-1400, Thur 0800-1230. **NB Update** The Carnet de Passage that is currently being issued by most motoring organizations now bears the logo of both AIT and FIA, so this problem may now have been eliminated.

The changing of the guard ceremony on the respective sides of the border is something of a tourist attraction as both countries try to outdo each other in the precision of their troop's drill. The tallest people that you are likely to see in either Pakistan or India are the soldiers participating in this rivalry.

Local Bus: selective minibus routes: 24 Pearl Continental to Lahore Museum via Shahrah-e-Quaid-e-Azam; 1 Salvation Army via Lahore Museum to Fort; 12 Railway station via Shalimar Gdns to Indian border; 34 Qaddafi Stadium via Salvation Army, Charing Cross to railway station; 43 Salvation Army via Charing Cross to railway station. **Car hire**: is available at main hotels and travel agencies. **Taxi/rickshaw**: rickshaw from the station to, say, Salvation Army approx Rs 35.

Air Lahore's airport is 5 km E of the city centre. PIA offer a limited number of weekly international flights to Frankfurt, New York, Toronto, Manchester, Amsterdam, Copenhagen, Bangkok, Dubai, Abu Dhabi, Kuwait, Dhahran, Riyadh and Jeddah. PIA also fly to **Delhi** on Tues, Thur, Sat, Sun 1500. **PIA domestic schedule**: **Bahawalpur**, daily; **DI Khan**, twice weekly; **Hyderabad**, twice weekly; **Islamabad**, 7 flights daily; **Karachi**, 8 flights daily; **Peshawar**, twice daily; **Quetta**, 4 flights weekly; **Rahim Yar Khan**, 5 flights weekly. **Aero Asia**: **Karachi**, 6 flights daily. Both airlines offer considerable discounts on 'night coaches'.

Train Lahore's magnificent main station (known as Lahore Junction) was built by the British in 1860 in Gothic-Mughal style. Complete with towers, turrets and battlements it was obviously built to be defended. The **Railway Reservation Office** for all classes of advanced bookings is 1 km S of the station, behind the Pakistan Railways HQ (large, red sandstone building) on Empress Rd. The concession permit for tourist and student discounts, however, must first be obtained from the rather difficult to find Commercial Office within the main station. Lahore is on the main Peshawar-Rawalpindi-Lahore-Karachi route and the following are just a selection of the quickest trains, offering all classes of tickets and arriving at convenient times. **Karachi**: *Shalimar Exp*, 0630, 17 hrs; *Tezgam*, 1430, 19 hrs. **Multan**: *Shalimar Exp*, 0630, 5 hrs; *Tezgam*, 1430, 5 hrs. **Peshawar**: *Zulfikar Exp*, 0935, 11 hrs; *Khyber Mail*, 2000, 10 hrs. **Quetta**: *Chiltan Exp*, 1045, 28 hrs; *Quetta Exp*, 1245, 27 hrs. **Rawalpindi**: *Rawal Exp*, 0715, 5 hrs; *Tezgam*, 1200, 5$^{1}/_{2}$ hrs.

Road Bus: overcrowded Government buses run to all destinations from the GTS bus yard opp the railway station. 50% discounts are available to student card holders, although for the sake of your sanity it's advisable to use the private bus companies instead. Lahore's main bus and coach transport hub is on the **McLeod Rd/Nicholson Rd** junction, opp the train station. Private deluxe and 'flying coaches' operate on a 'depart when full' policy to all destinations from the numerous bus offices on these roads. A knowledge of Urdu is useful for reading the departure boards, although if you just shout out your destination you will be rapidly propelled in the right direction.

Longer excursions

Jallo Park (27 km E)

Revamped and reopened in 1995, Jallo Park is the pride and joy of the Tourism Development Corporation of Punjab. Covering a 200 ha site, it is now being billed as the 'Pakistani Disneyland'. In addition to the fairground rides and water-park, there are extensive gardens, a children's zoo, a forest research centre, a Japanese garden, a small museum and a boating lake. Despite the heavy crowds at

weekends and holidays, Jallo Park is a pleasant picnic spot. The park is on the GT Rd to the Indian border and can be reached by half-hourly trains from Lahore, minibus 12 from outside the station or by taxi (Rs 200).

Sheikhupura (34 km W)

Formerly known as Jahangirabad, Sheikhupura has a Mughal **fort** that was built by the Emperor in 1619 for use as a hunting lodge. The fort is built of brick rather than the stone more common of Mughal forts, and there are said to be tunnels from the basement to the Hiran Minar (6 km) and to Lahore (34 km)! The fort was later used by the Sikh princess Rani Nakayan, and her private quarters are decorated with superbly preserved frescoes depicting dancing girls, hunts, court scenes and images of the Guru Nanak. The chowkidar claims that the fort was used for 25 years by the Pakistani police as a 'torture cell'. A letter of authorization from the Dept of Archaeology at Lahore Fort is required for entry.

A further 4 km along the Sargodha Rd is the turn off for Jahangir's **deer park** (2 km). The centre-piece to the park is a square artificial lake, with a causeway and arched pavilion in its centre that makes an ideal picnic spot. The tall carved octagonal memorial tower, **Hiran Minar**, was built by the Emperor in memory of his pet antelope 'Maharaj'. The minaret has 99 steps.

Chhanga Manga (68 km SW)

Initially established as a timber plantation in the last century by the British, the 5,000 ha Chhanga Manga National Park is said to be the oldest planted forest in South Asia. The park is now a wildlife reserve and holiday resort, with boating lake and model train ride. TDCP have a **D** *Motel* and restaurant in the grounds, bookable in Lahore. The park is located just off the GT Rd, on the way to Multan.

LAHORE TO SUKKUR

Leaving Lahore S from the Lahore Museum, after several km the Multan Rd joins the National Highway. After 70 km, the road passes to the W of Chhanga Manga (see page 291), passing through classic canal irrigation country. Okara (68 km), named after the *Ukan* (Tamarisk) tree, is a relatively new town, founded in 1915 following the construction of the Lower Bari Doab Canal. Dairy farming is the major industry, with numerous state-run and private dairies on the NH. Accommodation E *Sheesh Mahal Hotel*, GT Rd, T 3465.

A diversion 26 km SE of Okara leads to the ancient town of **Dipalpur**, presumed to be a contemporary of Harappa and Moenjo Daro. Artefacts from the reign of the Scythian kings have been found, and there still remains several Hindu temples, including that of Babu Lal Jas Raj.

Sahiwal

Some 37 km beyond Okara, the NH passes through the Punjab market town of **Sahiwal**, formerly known as Montgomery. The town was originally named by way of what is said to be a doubtful compliment to Sir Robert Montgomery, Lt-Governor of the Punjab between 1859-65. At the S end of Railway Rd is an architecturally bizarre concrete arch that commemorates the occasion in 1966 of renaming the town Sahiwal.

Sahiwal is in the heart of the Punjab's cotton growing belt, as well as having its own breed of milk producing cow and bullocks that are fattened for beef. Less than 100 years ago, however, this land was little more than scrub jungle, but the provision of canal irrigation combined with naturally high soil fertility has made Sahiwal an agriculturally productive area.

The main town lies W of the NH, known locally as GT Rd. Railway Rd, parallel, several km W of GT Rd, is the town's main axis. The GTS bus stand, GPO, PIA office (T 2803) and several hotels are here. At the southern end of Railway Rd is the cricket stadium, used sometimes by touring sides, as well as a 19th century British church.

Sahiwal is a base for exploring Harappa, and has several hotels.

- **Accommodation C** *Modern City*, GT Rd, T 62502, some a/c, restaurant; **D** *Sea Rose*, GT Rd, T 77377, a/c doubles and cheaper non-a/c singles, restaurant rec, good value. On Railway Rd: **E** *Al Habib*, T 778492, some a/c; **E** *Indus*, T 75476; **E** *Montgomery*, T 2885; **F** *Stadium*, T 74656, quiet garden, good value.

- **Transport Road** The most regular buses and deluxe coaches to Lahore, Multan, Bahawalpur, Karachi, Harappa and Pakpattan depart from GT Rd. *Sea Rose Hotel* is booking office for New Khan Rd Runners.

A diversion 47 km SE of Sahiwal leads to the town of **Pakpattan**. A journey along this road gives a good vignette of typical rural life in Punjab. Small hamlets are scattered amongst the wheat and sugar cane fields, and although most have a small mosque, shopping requires a visit to the road side bazaars. Certain plots of land have been laid waste by salinization. Mid-way between Sahiwal and Pakpattan is the massive Ittefaq sugar mill, owned by the family of former Prime Minister of Pakistan, Nawaz Sharif. The mill is a major local employer.

The prime attraction of the town is the shrine of **Baba Farid-ud-din Ganj Shakkar** (1173-1265), a revered holy man from Afghanistan who came to settle here. Indeed, when Tamerlane marched here with his army in 1398, the town was spared out of respect for Baba Farid. The town is now a major pilgrimage centre, particularly during Muharram. Surprisingly, the oldest looking tomb in the complex, a red brick building with white dome roof, is that of the holy man's grandson, Mooj Dira. Baba Farid's tomb is in the more modern, small marble room. A narrow opening in the wall next to the shrine is known as Heaven's Gate, and any males who pass through here are guaranteed entrance into paradise.

Prior to Partition, Pakpattan ('ferry crossing of the pure' – an old crossing on the Sutlej) housed a large Hindu population. On the hill in the centre of town, their tall houses, with carved wooden window frames, can still be seen. Most of the Hindu temples on the hill were destroyed following the bulldozing of the Ayodhya mosque in India in Dec 1992.

From Sahiwal, the NH continues SW towards **Harappa**. The main junction for visiting the site is **Harappa Road** (sometimes known as **Harappa Station**) on the Lahore-Multan Rd. Trains to/from Harappa Station are irregular, so the site is best visited by road. The site is signposted across the rail line and Lower Bari Doab Canal, 7 km away. A tonga costs Rs 30, although there is an irregular bus service.

Harappa

With **Moenjo Daro** (see page 159) in Sind, **Harappa** represents the other key city of the Indus Valley Civilization. Excavations are continuing at Harappa under the auspices of the Archaeological Survey of Pakistan. Today the site is rather poorly cared for, and has nothing of the grandeur of Moenjo Daro, though the total area of the two cities and key features of their basic layout are similar. The ravaging effects of salinization are blatantly evident all across the site.

The single room **Archaeological Museum** at the site entrance contains some of the most interesting artefacts found at the site. These include terracotta figurines and lingums, copper and bronze objects as well as stone tools including blades and plough shares.

There is also a burial reconstruction, showing a female skeleton, complete with bangles, lying supine in a Deodar wood coffin. Below the coffin, pottery vessels are placed in the burial pit, perhaps containing provisions for use in the next life. The museum also contains a male skeleton from Cemetery R-37. Other notable exhibits include painted burial jars from Cemetery H, a model section of Harappa showing the different levels superimposed upon one another, plus a number of artefacts from Moenjo Daro, Amri, Kot Diji and Rohri.

The discovery of the site The existence of the huge mounds, rising nearly 20m above the plain, which comprise the Harappan site was reported by Masson in 1826 and visited again by Cunningham in 1853 and 1876. When the railway between **Multan** and **Lahore** was being built in the 1870s the railway engineers found their apparently inexhaustible supply of ready-baked bricks invaluable for laying the foundations over a distance of more than 150 km, according to Ross, writing in 1882.

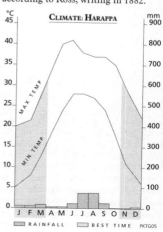

CLIMATE: HARAPPA

MAX TEMP / MIN TEMP

RAINFALL   BEST TIME   PKTG05

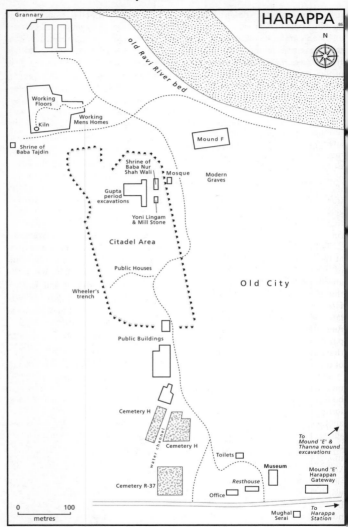

HARAPPA

It was not until the Archaeological Survey started full scale excavations under the Indian Archaeologist **Vats** in 1920, which continued until 1934, that the scale and significance of the buried ruins became clear. Further excavations by **Sir Mortimer Wheeler** in 1946 carried the interpretation of vital features of this Indus Valley city still further. The path across the site is well laid out, and it is possible to walk round the city in about an hour.

The route does not take you past the important sites in chronological order. It starts from the museum at the S edge of the site and passes an area to its left identified as **Cemetery H**, much of which is now grassed over. You get the best view by climbing the path up to the viewing platform and then looking back towards the museum. Cemetery H is a site of vital importance, for as one of the most recent areas of Harappa to be settled it has provided clues to the nature of the last occupants of the town and of the ending of the Indus Valley Civilization. Vats found pottery and other grave goods as well as skeletons, and argued that the **'Cemetery H culture'** was the final stage of the Harappan civilization.

The cemetery contained graves dug at two levels. In the lower (and older) of the two, bodies were buried intact and the pottery was similar to that in the main part of the Harappan city. However, in the upper level disarticulated bones were buried in large urns. As Allchin and Allchin point out, "the painted urns from this site tell us all that is so far known about the beliefs of their makers".

Peacocks are a common decorative motif, in some cases showing hollow bodies with small horizontal human forms painted inside. Bulls and cows are another common motif, one of which shows a pipal leaf springing from the hump. All these features have elements in common with the beliefs of the Rg Veda. Vats pointed to further similarities, including, in Allchin and Allchin's words "two beasts facing each other, held by a man with long wavy hair, while a hound stands menacingly behind one of them; in yet another a little man of similar form stands on the back of a creature which shares the features of a centaur with the Harappan bull-man".

Vats argued that these images bore striking similarities with figures from the Vedas, among them the figure of the hound which he compared with the Vedic God of Death, Yama. Allchin and Allchin suggest that the peacock can be interpreted similarly, "seeing in them the 'One Bird' of the Rg Veda", variously identified with Agni (Fire), Surya (Sun) and Soma.

All these features suggest that there was a continuity in the use of the site between the Indus Valley settlers and the invading Aryans. The pottery of the upper levels shows strong similarities to pottery found in western Iran at a much later period than that of Harappa itself. Although there are as yet no radiocarbon dates available the earliest phase of the Cemetery H culture is put by Allchin and Allchin at around 2000 BC, but the distinctive star and bird motifs on the later pottery is contemporaneous with designs from Iran dating from 1550-1400 BC. They supported the earlier conclusion of Vats that "the Cemetery H culture was the final stage of the Harappan, and continuous with it; but that it must indicate the presence of foreign conquerors or immigrants".

To the S of the Cemetery H area, a path leads to another burial site known as **Cemetery R-37**. Discovered in 1937 by **Shastri**, and further excavated by Wheeler (1946), Mughal (1966) and Dales and Kenoyer (1986-88), 57 graves from the mature Harappan period have been found, with 15-20 pots in each grave, in addition to personal toilet instruments. Over time the area became eroded and the graves exposed, and it is suggested that the cemetery was used as a rubbish site. The graves are generally of a poor order, suggesting it was a burial ground of average citizens ranging from 2600-1900 BC. A male skeleton from Cemetery R-37 is in the site museum.

The citadel From the viewing platform the path climbs N up onto the citadel. This has been far less thoroughly excavated than that at Moenjo

Daro, and far more of the original brick-work has been removed. However, you can see something of the scale of the central city, the outline of some of its roads and its drainage system. The path to the left on top of the citadel leads down to the W edge and overlooks the deep trench cut by Sir Mortimer Wheeler into the fortification wall in 1946. It is possible to scramble down to the bottom and get a good view of the impressive scale of this exterior wall.

The citadel had square towers and bastions, and the widest streets within the citadel ran from N to S, as in Moenjo Daro. The path turns right at the top of the citadel mound and descends through the E wall, following this N. It passes the 17th or early 18th century shrine to **Baba Nur Shah Wali**.

Several myths surround this site and the stones enclosed behind a fence just to its S. The tomb of the saint is exceptionally long, perhaps 9m. If you ask the woman attendant you will hear that the tomb is as big as that because the saint was indeed that length. The stones in front were reputed once to have been gold pestle, mortar and ring. When a thief tried to steal them they turned to stone. Only two are visible today.

Descending from the shrine, the path passes the **Old Mosque**. Originally referred to as the Eidgah, it is thought to date to the Mughal period (1526-1707 AD), and was probably built as a place of worship in honour of a renowned local person (possibly Baba Nur Shah Wali). Measuring 12m N-S, it may have been square, but no evidence of a roof has been found. It is built from reused Harappan bricks, and stands on top of the city walls that date to 2600-1900 BC.

Return to the path and continue N. To the right is another mound with a deep excavation made by Sir Mortimer Wheeler, and across in the distance it is just possible to make out the banks of the **Ravi** (flowing from right to left)

which once brought boats right up to the N edge of Harappa.

The footpath passes through some low trees, and immediately to its E lies the lower town. Walking across this area you can see the great round brick **working floors**, almost certainly used for grinding grain. Wheat and barley chaff were found in the floor's cracks. Beyond and to the S of the round threshing floors is a group of '**working men's homes**' or single roomed barracks, similar to the small houses in Moenjo Daro.

The main path continues N to the remains of what Vats termed the **granary**. It comprises the footings of a series of two rows of six granaries, each 16m by 6m, very close to the old river bank. Allchin and Allchin suggest that the combined floor space was over 800 sq m, similar to that at Moenjo Daro. Although there is no evidence of the superstructure which once covered the brick plinths, their size is still testimony to the sophistication and organization of an urban civilization which both needed and could organize grain storage on such a scale. Evidence of the ever-present problem of increased salinization is particularly prominent here.

Returning to the site entrance, opposite the museum, across the road, are the remains of a 45 sq m caravanserai that was excavated in 1994, and is thought to either date to the Mughal period (1526-1707) or to the rule of Shah Sher Suri (1540-1545).

Another recent discovery at the Harappa site is the **Mound E** and **Thanna Mound**, located E of the museum. The oldest settlement of the early Harappan period covers 8 ha from the NW corner of Mound E to the edge of the Thanna Mound, and has been dated at 3300-2600 BC.

The Harappan settlement on Mound E was enclosed by a city wall made of mud-bricks that stood $5\frac{1}{2}$m wide and several metres high. It enclosed Mound E on the S side, and turned N along the

E ridge of the mound. In 1990 a gateway was discovered in the centre of the S wall, and in 1993 a huge bastion was excavated to the SE. Excavations are continuing.

Continuing SW from Harappa Rd, the NH follows the course of the Lower Bari Doab Canal to the market town of **Khanewal** (121 km). At Khanewal the road forks, the left fork going directly to **Bahawalpur** (103 km), the right fork travelling towards **Multan** (58 km).

Multan

The history of Multan is the history of the sub-continent. Every invader from Alexander through the Mauryans, Kushans, Huns, Arabs, Ghaznavids, Mughals, Afghans, Sikhs, right up to the British, have fought for control of the city. The modern city is developing rapidly as an industrial centre, yet has still managed to retain many important historical and cultural attractions.

History

Early history

Prior to the arrival of the Arabs in the 8th century, little can be said with great certainty about Multan's early history. Cunningham suggests that Multan was a highly civilized centre of population about 800 BC, with others linking it to the Rg Vedic civilization.

The first recorded history of Multan is thought to date to the campaign of **Alexander the Great**, who passed through the district in 326-325 BC. Having crossed the confluence of the Jhelum and Chenab, he is believed to have marched on one of the great cities of the **Malloi** (believed to be the Malavas mentioned in the Mahabharata). It is argued that the original name of Multan was *Malava-Sthana*, or city of the Malavas, which in due course was corrupted to *Mulasthana* and finally Multan. During the battle, Alexander scaled the city walls ahead of his men, and then, in an act of reckless bravado, leapt down alone into the citadel. This action very nearly cost him his life, for as Ptolemy recounts, from one of his wounds air gurgled along with the blood, causing Alexander to swoon and almost lose consciousness. The Macedonians eventually subdued the Malloi, and Alexander later recovered from his wounds. It should be noted, however, that the near impossibility of tracing Alexander's exact route means that identification of Multan with this battle is mere conjecture.

The city was then ruled by the **Mauryans** and **Kushans** up to about 470 AD when it was taken by the **Huns**. They remained until the middle of the 6th century.

Arrival of the Arabs

The next source of the early history of Multan can be found in the writings of the early Arab geographers. When the Arabs first penetrated the region, Multan was in the hands of the Brahmin ruler **Chach**, who had usurped the last ruler of the Rai Dynasty.

It was during the lifetime of Chach that the great Chinese pilgrim, **Hieun Tsang**, visited Multan (641 AD). Referring to the city as *Mulosan Pulu*, he

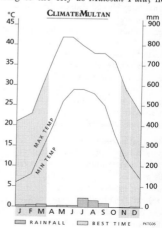

CLIMATE·MULTAN

described in great detail the magnificent golden statue of Mitra in the city's famed **Sun Temple**.

Centuries of Muslim rule began when the Arab commander **Mohammad bin Qasim** captured Multan in 712 AD, although it took several centuries for Islam to establish itself as the dominant religion amongst the populace. (It was not until the saint **Makhdum Syed Mohammad Yusuf Shah** settled in Multan in 1088 that significant numbers of the population converted to Islam.)

By the end of the 9th century, as the Caliphate weakened, Multan became all but independent of Baghdad. At different points the city came under the rule of a number of dynasties, including the **Karmatians** (c 915 AD) and the **Ghaznavides** of Afghanistan (c 1004).

The Ghaznavides
Although Multan passed through the hands of a succession of rulers, it was during the reign of the former Turkish slave **Nasir al-Din Qabacha** (c 1206) that Multan developed as a centre of learning and piety. Families such as the Gardezi Syeds and the Qureshis moved to the area, in search of religious education at centres established by the locally born saint **Hazrat Bahauddin Zakaria**. This period also saw the arrival in Multan of other saints such as **Sham-i Tabriz** from Afghanistan, **Kazi Kutb-ud-din** from Kashan, plus **Baba Farid-ud-din Ganj Shakkar** in Pakpattan (see page 292) and **Jalal al-Din Surkh** in Uch (see page 308). Multan continued to be attacked, besieged and conquered by a succession of invaders until coming under the rule of the greater **Mughal** Empire.

Mughal period
The two centuries of Mughal rule (1528-1752) that Multan enjoyed is regarded as a period of great stability for a city that had experienced so much traumatic upheaval. Coins and documents of the era conferred Multan the title *Dar-ul-Aman* – 'City of Peace' or 'Seat of Safety'.

Afghans and Sikhs
As the Mughal Empire gradually disintegrated, Multan was annexed by the Afghan king, **Ahmad Shah Abdali** (himself born in Multan). Although the Afghans appointed the Governor of Multan, they were only really interested in extracted tribute, so the city was allowed to administer its own internal affairs. This situation continued until 1818 when the Sikh leader, **Maharaja Ranjit Singh**, attacked Multan. During the siege the Sikhs used the famous **Zam zama** cannon (see page 285) that had been used by Ahmad Shah Abdali against the Marathas in the third battle of Panipat, 1761. The battle for the fort at Multan lasted 84 days during which time thousands were killed on both sides, and most of the buildings within the fort were destroyed. Muslim historians look at the period of Sikh rule as Multan's darkest hour, with the suppression of Islam and extortionate tax demands the main complaint.

The British
Following the First Sikh War of 1845, and the appointment of a British Resident in Lahore, the British attempted to replace the uncooperative ruler of Multan, **Mulraj**, with their own choice, **Sardar Khan Singh**. On the morning of 19 April 1848, Mr P A Vans Agnew of the Indian Civil Service and Lt. W A Anderson of the 1st Bombay Fusiliers, rode unarmed into Multan Fort to accept Mulraj's surrender. As they crossed the bridge, one of Mulraj's soldiers, Umeer Chand, thought to be acting on his own initiative, attacked Agnew and severely wounded him. In the ensuing struggle Anderson was mortally wounded. The two Englishmen managed to return to their quarters at the Eidgah, from where Agnew dashed off letters requesting assistance. The following day, deserted by their Sikh bodyguard, the two wounded Englishmen were murdered by a mob instigated by Mulraj.

The British expedition sent to Multan to bring Mulraj to trial captured the fort on 22 January 1849, following a campaign lasting a month. During the battle, a British shell landed on the Jami Masjid in the fort that the Sikhs used as a magazine. The resulting explosion killed 500 of the garrison and destroyed 2,000 kg of powder. At his trial in Lahore, Mulraj was found guilty of complicity in the murder of the two men, although it was established that he had not ordered or encouraged the initial attack. He was taken under house arrest to Calcutta and then to Varanasi, where he died a short time after.

Multan remained under British rule for nearly a century until independence.

Modern Multan

As the district headquarters, Multan is the most important town in southern Punjab. Any literature on Multan quotes the old Persian couplet, "With four rare things Multan abounds, Heat, beggars, dust and burial grounds". Multan, however, is changing fast, with its rapidly developing industrial base and location at the centre of Pakistan's cotton growing belt. Yet the city has managed to retain its status as ancient cultural capital of the region.

Places of interest

The Fort Built on a mound separating it from the city and the dry river bed of the Ravi, the **fort** is a prominent landmark. At its peak the outer walls ran for 2 km, reinforced by 46 bastions and four gateways each with two towers. Much of the fort was destroyed in the siege of 1848-49, although parts of the outer walls and most of the key shrines survived.

The view from the highest point of the fort, the old gun emplacement just inside the **Bohar Gate**, gives a good idea of Multan's size – something that is hard to appreciate as you make your way through the narrow Hassain Agahi Bazaar. In places the gun emplacement looks ready to collapse, plunging unsuspecting sightseers to the ground below. Binoculars can be hired to admire the sights, although most young men use them to discreetly view women! Near to the viewpoint is the **Nigar Khana**, the former armoury that has been turned into a government handicraft shop selling a mixture of beautiful traditional products and pure kitsch.

Within the fort walls are **Qasim Bagh**, a small park offering mini train rides, fairground rides and a children's playground, plus the **Qasim Stadium**, the venue for political rallies and international cricket fixtures. Outside the stadium entrance is a 15m high memorial **obelisk** erected to the memory of Agnew and Anderson. The emotional inscription by Sir Herbert Edwardes tells how Agnew and Anderson "being treacherously deserted by the Sikh escort were on the following day, in flagrant breach of national faith and hospitality, barbarously murdered".

When the Chinese traveller **Hiuen Tsang** visited Multan in 641 AD, he described a stunning **Sun Temple** on the fort mound: "There is a temple dedicated to the sun, very magnificent and profusely decorated. The image of the Sun-Deva is cast in yellow gold and ornamented with rare gems. Its divine insight is mysteriously manifested, and its spiritual powers made plain to all." It was thought to have been destroyed in the 11th century, restored and then finally demolished for good by Aurangzeb. The temple was perhaps replaced by the Jami Masjid that the Sikhs used as the ill-fated powder magazine during the 1848 siege. Cunningham identified the site in 1853 as being just to the W of the obelisk. No trace remains today.

At the northern corner of the fort lie the insubstantial remains of the **Prahladpuri Temple**, dedicated to the man-lion form of Vishnu. Although it survived the battle of 1848-49, its fate since then is unclear. However, many recent guides to Multan confuse its remains near to the shrine of Hazrat Bahauddin Zakaria with those of the long since vanished Sun Temple.

Shrine of Hazrat Bahauddin Zakaria Also known as Bahawal Hakk, **Bahauddin Zakaria** (1182-1266) was born at Kot Aror near Multan and educated in Turan, Iran, Baghdad, Madina and Jerusalem. Having received his doctorate he returned to Multan to preach, in particular spreading the teachings of the **Suhranwardiya Sufi**. The **Khanqah** or University that he founded in Multan became one of the great centres of Islamic learning. He was a great friend of **Farid-ud-din Ganj Shakkar** of Pakpattan (see page 292).

His shrine stands in the NE corner of the fort. Built by the saint himself, the only other similar style of architecture is found at Sonepat in India. The base of the tomb is 15m sq, surmounted by an octagon, and topped by a hemispherical white plastered dome. The façade is decorated with blue tiles and superb frescoes. Although substantially damaged in the siege of 1848-49, it was restored by public subscription. The shrine is particularly busy during the saint's Urs (27th Safar). Several influential members of the Qureshi family, including Nawab Muzaffar Khan, have their graves nearby.

Shrine of Shah Rukn-e-Alam On the W side of the fort, dominating both the fort and the city, is the shrine of the saint's grandson, **Shah Rukn-e-Alam** ('pillar of the people'). The tomb was originally intended for the **Tughluq** family, having been built in 1320 by Emperor Ghiyas ud Din Tughluq, but was given up to the popular Shah Rukn-e-Alam upon his death in 1334.

The shrine is an octagon 15m in diameter inside, with perpendicular walls 12m high and 4m thick, supported by sloping towers at the corners. This is surmounted by a smaller octagon 8m high with a small passage around the lower storey from which the Muezzin calls the prayer. The structure is topped by a dome 18m in diameter, and said to be one of the largest in Asia. The building stands just over 30m high, although the mound upon which it stands raises it to 45m, allowing it to dominate the city. At dusk in the dust laden atmosphere, it seems to rise ethereally above Multan.

The shrine is built of red brick bounded with beams of sisam wood with the exterior ornately decorated with calligraphy and blue and white mosaic tile work. It has been brilliantly renovated, winning an Aga Khan Award for architectural restoration.

Shrine of Sham-i Tabriz 1 km NE of the fort is the tomb of **Sham-i Tabriz**, a Sufi saint born in Afghanistan in 1165. It is said that he raised the dead son of the ruler of Ghazni before coming to Multan in 1202. There are at least three other legends about Sham-i Tabriz (sometimes known as Shams Sabzwari) that associate him with drawing the sun closer to Multan, thus accounting for the city's great heat.

He died in 1276 and the tomb was constructed in 1330, although it was substantially rebuilt in 1780. The main body of the tomb is 10m sq, 8m high and surrounded by a richly coloured carved verandah. It is surmounted by an octagon, topped with a green tiled dome, and the whole building stands just under 20m high. The interior is rather plain.

Shrine of Makhdum Syed Mohammad Yusuf Gardezi A direct descendant of the Imam Hassan, this leading member of the influential Gardezi family settled in Multan in 1088. He was influential in converting much of the population to Islam, as well as having the gift of being able to ride tigers and charm snakes. It is said that for 40 years after his death his hand would occasionally come out of his tomb.

His tomb is in a difficult to find compound to the SW of Bohar Gate. It is a

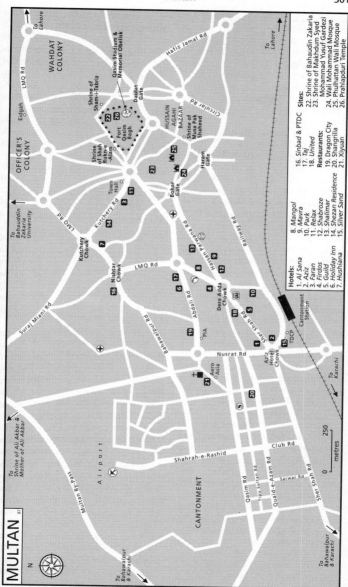

To Lahore

To Lahore

To Karachi

To Bahawalpur & Karachi

To Bahawalpur & Karachi

To Bahaddin Zakaria University

To Ali Akbar & Mother of Ali Akbar

MULTAN

N

WAHDAT COLONY

OFFICER'S COLONY

CANTONMENT

A i r p o r t

Qasim Stadium & Memorial Obelisk

Shrine of Sham-i-Tabriz

Daulat Gate

Fort Qasim Bagh

HUSSAIN AGAHI BAZAAR

Shrine of Musa Pak Shaheed

Shrine of Shah Rukn-e-Alam

Haram Gate

Bohar Gate

Town Hall

Kutchery Chowk

Nishtar Chowk

Dera Adda Chowk

Aziz Hotel Chowk

Nusrat Rd

Aero Asia

PIA

Cantonment Station

TDCP

LMQ Rd

Eidgah

LMQ Rd

Kutchery Rd

Hafiz Jamal Rd

Circular Rd

Railway Rd

Hassan Parwana Rd

Abdali Rd

Bahawalpur Rd

Suraj Miani Rd

Multan By-pass

Shahrah-e-Rashid

Club Rd

Qasim Rd

Tipu Sultan Rd

Quaid-e-Azam Rd

Sarwar Rd

Sher Shah Rd

Sher Shah Rd

metres
0   250

Hotels:
1. Al Sana
2. Aziz
3. Faran
4. Firdos
5. Guild
6. Holiday Inn
7. Hushiana
8. Mangol
9. Mavra
10. Park
11. Relax
12. Shabroze
13. Shalimar
14. Shezan Residence
15. Silver Sand
16. Sinbad & PTDC

Restaurants:
17. Taj
18. United
19. Dragon City
20. Shangrila
21. Xiyuan

Sites:
22. Shrine of Bahaudin Zakaria
23. Shrine of Makhdum Syed Mohammad Yusuf Gardezi
24. Wali Mohammad Mosque
25. Phulhattan Wali Mosque
26. Prahlapduri Temple

rectangular building, with no dome, but exquisitely tiled.

Eidgah To the N of the fort is the **Eidgah**, built in 1735 by the Governor of Lahore, Abdus Samad Khan. It was used by the Sikhs for military purposes and was the scene of the deaths of Agnew and Anderson. It is 72m long, 16m wide, with one central dome and open chambers on either side.

Shrine of Hazrat Ali Akbar Shah Several km NW of the centre of Multan is the 16th century tomb of **Ali Akbar**. Like the nearby tomb of his mother, Ali Akbar's shrine has some of the best glazed tile work in Multan.

Other mosques and shrines There are numerous other interesting mosques and shrines scattered throughout the city, many of which you happen to chance upon whilst wandering through the streets. The following route around the narrow bazaars below the fort takes in some of the most interesting sights.

Enter through the **Bohar Gate**, resplendent with neon Coca-Cola sign, and take the narrow road straight ahead through the cloth market. Above the trader's awnings, it is possible to see some of the old city's many intricately carved wooden houses. Continue more or less straight ahead until the cloth market gives way to other trades, turning right at the first shop selling metal buckets. Take another right turn at the T junction, and after several minutes, you arrive at the **Shrine of Hazrat Musa Pak Shaheed**, to the right. The entrance is marked by an imposing carved stone gateway that leads into a large courtyard. The shrine is the building to the left, with a green dome and blue tiled façade. Musa Pak Shaheed was born in Uch in 1545, and was killed by bandits just S of Multan in 1600. When his successor brought his body here 16 years later, it is said to have not been decomposed at all, and was indeed brought into Multan seated on a horse. He was a descendant of Abdul Kadir Gilani, and

the shrine is popular today with Pathans. The adjacent, low concrete mosque, with three white domes, appears plain from the outside, but has a beautifully decorated mihrab inside.

Returning to the T junction, the left branch leads into a wider square, known variously as Godri Bazaar, Chopar Bazaar or simply Chowk Bazaar. Behind, and to the left, is the **Wali Mohammad Mosque**, built in 1758 by Ali Mohammad Khakwani. The roof is flat, with no dome, but the frescoes on the exterior walls are exceptional. The three doorways have well executed spandrels.

The Chowk Bazaar is dominated by the minaret of the **Phulhattan Wali Mosque**. It is decorated with blue and pink floral motifs to the cupola at the top. The domed ceiling of the entrance gate is tiled with mirrors. Initially constructed by Emperor Farrukh Siyar, the mosque has been substantially rebuilt. The vivid use of tiles is continued in the interior courtyard, but the mirror work above the prayer chamber entrance is too modern to be appealing.

Opposite the mosque is a small Hindu stupa with Sanskrit engravings. A further 50m up the adjacent alley is a stairway leading to the **Girja Ghar Hindu Temple**. The interior is pretty much neglected, but two carvings of Hindu deities can be seen next to the main shrine entrance. The temple is topped by a high stupa. This area of the city has some of the finest examples of the carved wooden balconies and window frames that were a feature of the houses of wealthy Hindus. Prior to Partition, Multan was renowned for its metalwork, particularly jewellery and inlay on gold, silver and copper. Since this trade was primarily done by Hindu craftsmen, it has declined since 1947. Continuing along the Chowk Bazaar will return you to the Hussain Agahi Rd below the fort and Qasim Stadium.

Local information

● Accommodation

NB Multan's hotel pricing policy is quite illogical, with some non-a/c rooms costing more than those with a/c. Some of the **E** hotels offer particularly good value, but all the **F** hotels are very basic.

A *Holiday Inn*, 76 Abdali Rd, T 587777, F 512511, opened 1995, has all facilities incl pool, health club, dish TV, shopping, car rental, business centre, although rooms are smaller than others in the chain, *Heer* coffee shop, *Multan* Pakistani restaurant, pool side barbecue plus Chinese and Continental restaurant, best in town.

B *Shezan Residence*, Kutchery Rd, T 512235, undergoing renovation, central a/c, dish TV, fridge, restaurant, bakery, garden; **B** *Sindbad*, Bahawalpur Rd, Nishtar Chowk, T 72294, central a/c, TV, fridge, coffee lounge, restaurant, bakery.

C *Al-Sana*, Sher Shah Rd, T 32501, central a/c, dish TV, Pakistani, Chinese and Continental restaurant; **C** *Firdos*, Karim Centre, Dera Adda Chowk, LMQ Rd, T 33055, overpriced, restaurant; **C** *Hushiana*, Chowk Kutchery, LMQ Rd, T 43536, central a/c, clean and roomy, restaurant; **C** *Silver Sand*, Railway Rd, T 33061, central a/c, dish TV, fridge, *Whispers* Pakistani, Chinese and Continental restaurant.

D *Mangol*, Nawsan Shahr, LMQ Rd, T 512865; **D** *Relax*, Kutchery Rd, T 31588, some a/c, *Diastar* restaurant, parking; **D** *Shalimar*, Hassan Parwana Rd, T 583245, over-priced, no a/c rooms, restaurant, bakery, parking.

E *Faran*, Kutchery Rd, T 73538, parking, restaurant with dish TV; **E** *Mavra*, Hassan Parwana Rd, T 511822, some a/c, restaurant; **E** *Park*, Azmatwasti Rd, nr Capri cinema, T 514407, good value, restaurant; **E** *Shabroze*, Hassan Parwana Rd (no English sign), T 44224, good value, *Siachin* Chinese restaurant downstairs; **E** *Taj*, Abdali Rd, T 73549, restaurant.

On Sher Shah Rd: **F** *Aziz*, T 30425; **F** *Guild*, T 404651; **F** *United*, T 512088. All pretty filthy, with little to choose between them.

● Places to eat

Pakistani: *Afghan Kabul* and *Multan Chargha Roast*, opp *Sindbad Hotel*; *Restaurant 786*, Karim Centre, LMQ Rd; *Sherington*, Quaid-e-Azam Rd, Saddar; *Taj*, Karim Centre. There are plenty of simple Pakistani restaurants on Sher Shah Rd and in Saddar.

Chinese: *Chinese Dragon*, Abdali Rd opp PIA; *New Tabaq*, Nusrat Rd, although proximity to chicken slaughter houses on either side may influence your choice from the menu; *Shangrilla*, Aziz Shaheed Rd; *Siachin*, Shabroze Hotel; *Xiyuan*, Qasim Rd.

Food Festival, next to *Sindbad Hotel* sells expensive imported food items.

● Airline offices

Aero Asia, Qasim Rd opp Xiyuan rest, T 570182; **Emirates**, Kutchery Rd, T 580727; **PIA**, Abdali Rd, T 570131; **Saudi**, Kutchery Rd, T 580137.

● Banks & money changers

Emirates Int, Jalil Centre, Abdali Rd; **Habib**, Main Cantt; **National Bank of Pakistan**, Kutchery Chowk; **UBL**, Main Cantt.

● Entertainment

Cinemas: *Capri*, Azmatwasti Rd; *Citizan*, opp GTS bus stand; *Starlite*, Firdos Hotel; *Rex*, opp GPO; *Zenith*, LMQ Chowk.

● Hospitals & medical services

Civil, Abdali Rd; *Nishtar*, off Bahawalpur Rd.

● Post & telecommunications

Central Telegraph Office: LMQ Rd, nr Firdos Hotel.

GPO: Hassan Parwana Rd.

● Places of worship

St Mary's Protestant Church, Qasim Rd.

● Shopping

Local crafts & industries: the tradition of *silk textiles* existed before the 8th century, when silk from Bokhara was woven into cloth in Multan and then re-exported. Woollen *carpet* weaving is said to have started when families of weavers settled here during the reign of the Ghauris. The carpets are handwoven on looms and occasionally in addition to pure woollen ones, wool/cotton carpets are also produced. The town is also famous for *painted and glazed pottery*, particularly *naqqashi* designs in the local *Kangri* style. The old blue and white decorative work is seen in the religious monuments, not only in this town but all across the country. The Mughal emperor Shah Jahan is thought to have ordered these tiles specially when the Mosque in Thatta was built and his son Aurangzeb had done likewise for Abu Waraq's shrine. Today you can buy pottery items for everyday use, crafted with the same skill. Multan was once also renowned for metal work especially jewellery making and inlay on gold, silver and copper. Since this was done by the Hindu craftsmen, it has declined since 1947. Multan also produces its particular type of shoes, *khussa*, embroidery work on garments, camel skin articles and lacquered wood. Many of these traditional crafts can be found in the busy bazaars below the fort. Other items can be found in the government handicraft shop inside the fort.

● **Sports**

Cricket: *Qasim Stadium*, inside the old walled city, is the low concrete bowl venue used for international cricket matches. *Multan Cricket Club* is on LMQ Rd.

Snooker: *Hot Shot Snooker Club*, next to Central Telegraph Office.

● **Tourist offices**

PTDC, *Sindbad Hotel*; TDCP, *Silver Sand Hotel*. Southern Punjab tours can be booked from here (see TDCP Lahore).

● **Transport**

Air The airport is several km NW of the town. **PIA**: Faisalabad, 4 flights weekly; Islamabad, 1-2 flights daily; Karachi, 1-2 flights daily; Lahore, 2 flights daily; Quetta, 3 flights weekly; Rahim Yar Khan, twice weekly. Also 4 times a week via Zhob, DI Khan, Parachinar and Peshawar to Islamabad. **Aero Asia** daily to Karachi.

Train Karachi: *Shalimar Exp*, 1135, 12 hrs; *Tezgam*, 2050, 12 hrs. Peshawar: *Khyber Mail*, 1300, 17 hrs; *Awam Exp*, 2330, 16½ hrs. Quetta: *Chiltan Exp*, 1900, 19 hrs; *Quetta Exp*, 2015, 19 hrs. Lahore: *Tezgam*, 0605, 6 hrs; *Khyber Mail*, 1300, 6½ hrs. Rawalpindi: *Quetta Exp*, 0620, 14 hrs; *Awam Exp*, 2330, 12 hrs.

Road **Bus**: minibuses from Sahiwal and Lahore sometimes drop passengers at Officers Colony Chowk, NE of town (Rs 5 wagon to GTS). GTS bus stand is on Sher Shah Rd. Buses serve all locations incl **Dera Ghazi Khan** (2 hrs), **Bahawalpur** (2 hrs), **Sahiwal** (2½ hrs), **Rahim Yar Khan** (7 hrs), **Lahore** (5 hrs), although there appears to be no fixed timetable and buses depart when full. Private minibuses offer quicker, and slightly more comfortable, services to the same locations from yards opp the GTS stand.

From Multan it is possible to continue W towards Baluchistan via **Muzzaffargarh**, **Dera Ghazi Khan** and **Fort Munro** (see page 188).

The road between Multan and **Bahawalpur** (94 km) passes through the flat plains of southern Punjab. Shortly before Bahawalpur, the road crosses the **Sutlej River** via the new bridge.

Bahawalpur

Formerly the capital of the Princely State of Bahawalpur, the modern town was founded in 1748 by Nawab Bahawal Khan Abbasi I, a direct descendant of the Prophet's uncle Abbas. He raised a wall around the villa of Mohammad Panah Khan Ghumrani and proceeded to build a town that he called Bahawalpur after his own name. The foundation of the state is attributed to the Abbasis, who ruled for 2 centuries, although the main seat of the Abbasi family is 55 km SE at Dera Nawab Sahib (see page 310).

The history of the region, however, dates back to pre-Islamic days, although the records are admittedly incomplete. Following the Arab conquest of the region in the 8th century, the Caliphates in Damascus and Baghdad appointed local rulers to represent them. These 'Amirs' continued to rule their princely states under a special treaty signed with the British in 1838.

Entitled to a 17 gun salute, the Nawabs of Bahawalpur were allowed a notional degree of autonomy under the British, until 1903, when the 11th Nawab **Mohammad Bahawal Khan V**, took over the full administrative and legislative duties of the state. Many progressive reforms were undertaken during the rule of the 11th Nawab, including the construction of schools and hospitals.

Upon Partition, Bahawalpur immediately acceded to Pakistan and continued as an autonomous province within the federal state, until the administrative reforms of 1954 merged the Princely State into the Bahawalpur Division of the Punjab.

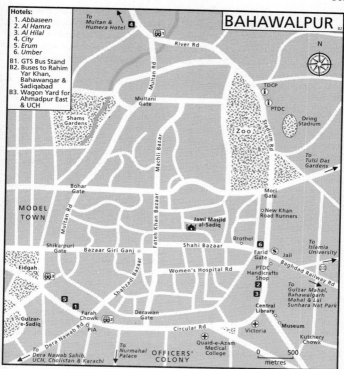

Hotels:
1. Abbaseen
2. Al Hamra
3. Al Hilal
4. City
5. Erum
6. Umber

B1. GTS Bus Stand
B2. Buses to Rahim Yar Khan, Bahawangar & Sadiqabad
B3. Wagon Yard for Ahmadpur East & UCH

BAHAWALPUR

It was near Bahawalpur in Aug 1988 that the plane carrying President **Zia ul-Haq** crashed, killing all on board.

Places of interest

The Amirs built many fine palaces in Bahawalpur before moving out to Dera Nawab Sahib in the 19th century, but sadly most are now occupied by the army and thus off limits to visitors.

Perhaps the finest is the **Nur Mahal Palace** on the SW of town. Completed in 1875 in Italianate style, the palace was originally intended as the residence of the 10th Nawab, Sir Sadiq Mohammad Khan IV, although he chose not to stay there due to its proximity to the Maluk Shah graveyard. It is now part of the

army's Divisional Battle School, and sightseers are turned away sharply. It is perhaps easier to look at the model of the palace in the museum.

The **Daulat Khana**, completed in 1886, was also built for the 10th Nawab but it is now in a very poor state of repair. Other former residences of the Nawabs, the 1876 **Bahawalgarh Mahal** and the 1902 **Gulzar Mahal**, both to the E of town, are also occupied by the military and impossible to visit. The **Emir of Dubai** also has a palace on the outskirts of town that is used as a base for hunting expeditions into the Cholistan Desert.

In a town of low-rise buildings, the stunning **Jamai Masjid al-Sadiq** stands out magnificently, rising above

the bazaar. Built shortly before Partition, the exquisitely carved white stone
mosque compares with any mosque
built in South Asia this century (Shah
Faisal Masjid, Islamabad included). To
the SW of the main bazaar is the **Eidgah**,
whose tall yellow minarets and low yellow wall are a distinctive landmark.

The town has a very open feel, with
many large parks and tree lined avenues.
The **zoo** on Stadium Rd has a representative collection of fauna of the region, plus a successful captive breeding
programme that has supplied amongst
other things, lions to the other zoos in
the country. Opposite is the **Dring Stadium**, one of the country's finest sporting complexes.

The **Museum** (0900-1600, closed Fri)
contains galleries dedicated to the Pakistan Movement, Islamic Arts, Archaeology (incl exhibits from Cholistan,
Gandhara, Moenjo Daro, Harappa,
Derawar, Kot Diji, Amri, Soan and Rohri), Ethnography (incl cloth, jewellery,
pottery from Cholistan, plus Bahawalpur's only cycle rickshaw), and a
room of rare manuscripts and calligraphy.
Next door to the museum stands the
Sadiq Reading Library, whose foundation stone was laid in 1924 by the then
Viceroy and Governor General of India,
Sir Rufus Daniel Isaacs, Earl of Reading.

Despite its limited attractions, Bahawalpur is a pleasant base from which
to visit Uch Sharif, Fort Derawar and
the Cholistan Desert.

Excursions

Lal Suhanra National Park Located 36
km E of Bahawalpur, the Lal Suhanra
National Park has been established on
either side of the Desert Branch Canal
and provides a number of floral and
faunal contrasts. Changing from desert
to forest, with a large lake and grassland,
the park supports a great variety of animal and bird life. Inside the main gate
is a children's playground, and a small
zoo housing deer, antelope, Nilgai, and

gazelles, plus aviaries containing peacocks, falcons, quails, owls, pheasants
and swans, as well as the rare Houbara
Bustard. There are also a couple of miserable rhinos from Nepal. Further into
the park there are black buck, blue bull
antelope and chinkara.

The TDCP has a **D** *Motel* with 6 rm
and restaurant, although it's not possible to book in advance. Further into the
park are two **E** *Resthouses*, that should be
booked at the park office at 3a, Trust
Colony, Bahawalpur, T 3217. The park
is quite peaceful, but you will require
your own transport to explore it fully.
The park can be reached by bus or wagon
from Bahawalpur's GTS bus stand (Rs
11, 30 mins). The bus drops you at Lal
Suhanra Chowk, from where it's a 3 km
(Rs 20) tonga ride to the main gate.

Local information
● Accommodation
C *Abbaseen*, Circular Rd, T 7592, deluxe
rooms with a/c, TV, much cheaper non-deluxe
rooms are very good value, rec, restaurant;
C *Erum*, Circular Rd, T 4730, non-a/c rooms in
E price range, restaurant; **C** *Humera*, Multan
Rd, nr Sutlej Bridge, T 59594, a/c, dish TV,
phone, restaurant, garden, but isolated on
edge of town (5 km).

E *Al Hilal*, Circular Rd, Farid Gate, T 882154,
attached hot bath, restaurant, parking; **E** *City*,
Multan Rd, opp GTS, T 882440, restaurant.

F *Al Hamra*, friendly and good value, rec;
F *Umber*, Farid Gate, very basic.

● Places to eat
The only upmarket restaurant is *Panda Chi-
nese*, quite remote out on Railway Rd. Cheap
Pakistani restaurants inside Farid Gate.

● Airline offices
PIA, Fawara Chowk, Circular Rd, T 4755.

● Banks & money changers
Habib, Muslim Commercial, United, Farid
Gate, Stadium Rd.

● Hospitals
Victoria Hospital, Circular Rd, built in 1906,
resembles a typical turn of the century cottage
hospital. Next door is the huge, modern *Quaid-
e-Azam Medical College*.

● **Libraries**
Bahawalpur has a good record in the provision of education, and the *Central Library* is considered to be one of the best in Pakistan.

● **Post & telecommunications**
GPO: 5 mins' walk E of Farid Gate.

● **Shopping**
Handicrafts: local handicrafts incl '*khussa*' shoes, painted and decorated earthen pottery, embroidery work and reed items such as *morahs* (circular seats). Bahawalpur is also a centre for traditional **Cholistan** handicrafts such as wall hangings and carpets made of camel hair and cotton, *rilli* or *gindi* which are used as blankets, rugs and bedspreads, as well as *changaris*, date leaf baskets. The fixed price PTDC *Pak Handicrafts Centre*, opp Farid Gate, gives an idea of prices to pay in the bazaar.

● **Sports**
The *Dring Stadium* has cricket, football and hockey pitches.

● **Tourist offices**
PTDC, Stadium Rd. The more helpful **TCDP**, Stadium Rd runs tours on demand to Fort Derawar and Uch Sharif. The price is typically Rs 600 guide fee, plus cost of vehicle hire (Rs 1,200 up to 4 persons, Rs 1,800 for 5 or more).

● **Transport**
Air The airport is 11 km E of town. **PIA** flights daily via **Lahore** to **Islamabad**, and twice weekly to **Karachi**.

Train Karachi: *Shalimar Exp*, 1257, 11 hrs; *Karachi Exp*, 2310, 13 hrs. **Lahore**: *Khyber Mail*, 1100, 8½ hrs; *Shalimar Exp*, 1657, 6½ hrs. **Multan**: 9 trains daily, 1½ hrs. **Rawalpindi**: 7 trains daily, 16 hrs.

Road Bus: GTS bus stand is to the N of town. It serves all destinations and buses depart when full. *New Khan Road Runners*, Stadium Rd, T 6363655, run daily a/c coaches to **Lahore**, 0930, 2130, 2215, 2300 (Rs 122) and **Rawalpindi**, 1900 (Rs 162). *Intercity*, City Hotel, T 882132, daily a/c coach to **Lahore**, 0930, 2200, 2330 (Rs 110). Minibuses to **Ahmadpur East** (for **Uch** and **Dera Nawab Sahib**) run from small yard (no English sign) opp Eidgah (1 hr, Rs 10). A/c coaches to **Multan** (2 hrs, Rs 30) and **Rahim Yar Khan** (3½ hrs, Rs 40) run from yards opp PIA on Fowara Chowk and on Circular Rd nr Abbaseen Hotel.

Uch Sharif

Although much diminished from its time as a thriving capital over an extensive area, the town of Uch Sharif contains some of the most beautiful ruined tombs in the country, and represents one of the highlights of a trip to Pakistan.

The etymology of the name is uncertain, but it is thought that the town can trace its origins back to the Buddhist period of rule before Alexander renamed it Askandra (or Alexandria). Following the Arab conquest of Sind and Multan in 711/712 AD, the town came under Muslim influence, but control over Uch was continually contested for the next 7 centuries. The Mughal emperor Akbar eventually annexed Uch to the Delhi Sultanate, and the town developed as an important cultural and literary centre. Indeed, the town reached its peak in the 13th century as a centre of Islamic learning and piety.

The town is variously referred to as Uch, Uchch or Uch Sharif. A very attractive book by Dr Ahmad Nabi Khan is available on the history and architecture of Uch, published by the National Institute of Historical and Cultural Research in Islamabad.

The buildings today There are two distinct groups of religious buildings in Uch. On the one hand is a group of **square** or **rectangular tombs** with low wood-framed flat roofs and timber columns. The second comprise **domed tombs** built on octagonal plans. Tragically many of the buildings have been seriously damaged or even partially destroyed, mainly by the shifting course of the **Chenab**.

By far the most striking monument still standing is the **Tomb of Bibi Jalwindi**. This is one of three such tombs found on the SW edge of the high mound representing the debris of an ancient fortress. Much of the surface comprises a huge graveyard, the earth over the graves standing up sharply from the surrounding baked mud. The earliest of the three mausoleums is that of **Baha' al-Din Uchchhi**, also known as **Baha al-Halim**. Bibi Jalwindi's tomb is next to it and is said to date from 1494. The architect-mason who constructed it is buried in the third of the domed tombs.

If you approach these tombs from the narrow lanes of the town you get the impression that they are still intact. The Tomb of Bibi Jalwindi in particular still suggests the magnificence both of form and decoration which was once the hallmark of the completed structures. The structure is essentially brick built, embellished with stunning glazed tile mosaic.

The mausoleum was erected in three octagonal storeys. The lower storey was supported by rounded and sloping corner turrets, on which a second storey with a narrow gallery for walking round was supported. A hemispherical dome crowned the building. In the W wall is the beautifully carved wooden **Mihrab**. It is one of the finest achievements of Multani style architecture, for which the Rukn-e-Alam and the Baha al-Din Zakaria, built 150 years earlier, had served as outstanding examples. Despite their damaged state these tombs are still among the finest of their kind.

The exterior of the tomb of Bibi Jalwindi is almost totally covered with the glazed tile work which is the hall mark of the style. The spandrel of the arches has a variety of floral patterns, the parapet has a frieze of glazed tiles while the turrets are surmounted with a bunch of broad flowering leaves, unique to this tomb. The first storey rises to a height of 9m, the second storey surmounting it like a drum. The destruction of nearly half of the tomb allows a clear view of the interior decoration, which is equally remarkable. It is well worth scrambling down the slope to the field below to obtain a more distant view, which in the evening light is particularly rewarding.

Next to the Tomb of Bibi Jalwindi is the tomb and mosque of **Jalal al-Din Surkh**. "It was presumed" writes Dr Ahmad Nabi Khan "that the devoted visitor coming to the tomb to offer *fateha* and to pay homage to the personage lying buried there, might like to pray in a nearby situated mosque attached to it". The mosque of Jalal al-Din Sukh belongs to the flat roofed class of tombs and mosques in Uch. It too has suffered damage at various times, an inscription in Persian on either side of the Mihrab records that it was repaired by Mulla Ahmad under the orders of Sheikh Hamid in 1617.

A few minutes walk away stands the tomb of **Jalal al-Din Bukhari**, grandson of Jalal al-Din Surkh. A 14th century saint, he travelled widely to Mecca, Medina, Mesopotamia, Egypt and Persia before settling in Uch, and is credited with popularizing the Sufi Suhrawardiya school in the region. His shrine is a flat-roofed oblong room supported by wooden pillars, with a small room containing a footprint of Imam Ali to the left. It is still visited by pious Muslims today, and is particularly busy during the saint's Urs (10th Zilhaj).

Nearby, and a little difficult to find, is the shrine of **Sheikh Saifuddin Ghazrooni**. A Muslim saint who settled in Uch around 980 AD, his shrine is said to be the oldest Muslim tomb in South Asia, although it is now in a poor state of repair.

As Dr Khan concludes "Today, the dust laden Uchchh Sharif is a small town of little consequence...Its narrow streets and small houses are mostly unsightly. Even its mosques and mausoleums have lost their splendid colour. In fact, the most important ones have sacrificed their halves and much of their original revetment to the ravages of time and tide. Nonetheless, the city is still revered by the devotees of those who are lying buried there. They flock to their tombs and their Khanqahs ceaselessly to offer *fateha* and to seek solace from worldly woes. It seems that the practice will continue for ever."

Wagons run from a small yard (no English sign) opposite the Eidgah in Bahawalpur to Ahmadpur East (Rs 10, 1 hr). From there, buses and wagons run to Uch (1 hr). The best time to visit Uch is late on a spring afternoon, whilst the air is clear and the temperatures not too hot. Some of the shrines are difficult to locate, so it may be worth employing a local person to act as guide.

Some 12 km W of Uch are the **Panjnad Headworks**, the confluence of the five rivers of the Punjab (including the Sutlej and Chenab), before they flow the 50 km S to join the Indus. The place is a popular picnic spot.

Fort Derawar and Cholistan Desert

The **Cholistan Desert** is the largest desert in Pakistan, covering over 25,000 sq km. It extends S into the Thar Desert in Sind, and E into India's Rajasthan Desert. Its name is said to derive from the Urdu verb *cholna* – to walk – although its not clear whether this refers to the shifting sand dunes or the semi-nomadic people who roam the desert in search of water and pasture.

The area has experienced a succession of climatic changes over the last 500,000 years, with a deep layer of red soil below the present sand surface suggesting a much moister environment during the Upper and Middle Palaeolithic periods. The **Hakra River** (known in the Vedas as the **river Sarasvati**, and more recently as the **Ghaggar**) once flowed through the region, supporting a civilization contemporary with Moenjo Daro and Harappa. Over 400 archaeological sites have been uncovered along the dried up bed of the Hakra, in addition to evidence of numerous stone age settlements at the lower levels.

PTDC and TDCP in Lahore, Multan and Bahawalpur can sometimes arrange jeep and camel safaris in the Cholistan Desert.

A series of desert forts have been built to guard the trade route across Cholistan, the best preserved of which is **Fort Derawar**. The present fort at Derawar was built by the Abbasi family in 1733, although it is believed that there have been fortified settlements on the site for several thousand years. Travelling along the desert road, the fort's massive outer walls loom out the desert, visible from some distance away. It is an impressive sight.

The fort remains the property of the Abbasi family and a permit is required to go inside. The permit is available from the seat of the Abbasi family – the splendid 19th century **Sadiq Garh Palace** in **Dera Nawab Sahib**. If travelling as part of a TDCP or PTDC tour, this formality is usually arranged for you. However, the permit is only necessary if you wish to go inside the fort, and since the interior is mostly in ruins, Fort Derawar is still worth a visit even if you do not have the permit.

There is no public transport to the fort but Suzuki mini-vans can be hired easily by asking around in Dera Nawab Sahib. Rates are negotiable, although Rs 500 is the usual day hire fee. The road to the fort has now been tarmaced so a 4WD vehicle is no longer necessary, although the road does deteriorate as you near the fort. Although only 45 km from Dera Nawab Sahib, it takes 1½ hrs to reach the fort. Snacks and cold drinks are available in the village outside the fort, but it is wise to take water and sun-block. PTDC are planning to develop camping facilities at the fort – they have got as far as putting up the sign announcing the project!

Travelling due S from Dera Nawab Sahib, the road to the fort branches right over the irrigation canal, about 10 km beyond the village of Shahi Wali. Continue to the crossroads and then take the left turn at the 28 km marker stone. Recent provision of irrigation has made the area remarkably green, with wheat and sugar cane being prominent. However, about 24 km from the fort, cultivation becomes patchy, with the landscape giving way to dunes and desert scrub.

The deterioration of the sealed road surface coincides with the first view of the fort, some 5 km away. Many drivers elect to drive on the sand flats on nearing the fort, thus romanticizing the approach to this remarkable structure, as well as providing a smoother ride. Mirages of huge lakes are a common phenomenon. The lost in time feel of the place is enhanced by the flocks of wandering sheep and goats grazing on the scrub around the fort, with shepherds keeping watch from the backs of camels. Two famous Pakistani dramas – *Darya* (River) and *Reigzar* (Desert) – were filmed in the ruins of the village at the base of the fort.

The outer walls of the fort rise 30m, out of the desert, and are supported by 40 massive bastions, 10 on each side. The huge defensive tower at the main entrance to the E was added in 1965, during the Indo-Pak war. The fort's defensive walls run for 1½ km, and it is worth walking around the outside of the fort to get a sense of scale.

500m to the E of the fort is the royal cemetery of the ruling Nawabs. Many of the tombs are decorated with marble and blue tile mosaic, although the enclosure is closed to visitors. Nearby is the permanent water-hole from which water is drawn up in goat skin bags. Directly outside the fort, to the E, is the attractive **Sadiq Mosque**. Built in 1849 in the same style as the Moti Masjid in Delhi's Red Fort, a marble slab at the entrance covers the carved signature of **Khewja Ghulam Farid**, a revered Sufi saint. In a small enclosure 500m NW of the fort are the graves of four of the Prophet Mohammad's companions.

Most of the interior of the fort is in ruins, although a few of the modern structures remain. The gates to the ladies' section of the Nawab's quarters and the painted pavilion to the NE are usually locked. There is an extensive network of subterranean passages leading to vaulted chambers, cellars and dungeons beneath the fort, many of which show evidence of being used by trolleys. Locals suggest that there is an underground tunnel from the fort through the desert, to Dera Nawab Sahib, some 45 km away. However, the same locals claim that cannonballs fired from the fort's two cannons once landed on Lahore!

Continuing S from Bahawalpur, the National Highway passes through **Ahmadpur East** (50 km), the junction for **Uch Sharif**, see page 307 (21 km NW), **Dera Nawab Sahib** (4 km S) **Fort Derawar**, see page 309 (45 km S) and the **Cholistan Desert**, see page 309. Much of the old town of Ahmadpur East was destroyed in floods from the Ghara in 1758, and thus a new site was established. Noteworthy shrines include that of Khanagah Akkir Baha-ud-Din, who is said to have practised *chilla* for 8 years without eating or drinking! There is the **E** *Amil Hotel*, T 72827, nr to the bus stand chowk.

The NH proceeds SW to **Khanpur** (67 km). From here, another road leads due S for 109 km to the border with India. The Rajasthan city of Jaisalmer is only 136 km away across the Thar Desert, although the border remains closed.

47 km SW of Khanpur is **Rahim Yar Khan**.

Rahim Yar Khan

District headquarters in the Bahawalpur Division, Rahim Yar Khan lies approximately half-way between Karachi and Lahore. The original site is associated with **Phul Badda**, capital of Phul during the period of Sumra rule over Sind. The present site was laid out in the mid 18th century. It was renamed in 1881 after the eldest son of Nawab Sir Sadiq Mohammad Khan, the Crown Prince Rahim Yar Khan. The modern town is a commercial and industrial centre. The Emir of Abu Dhabi has a palace nearby which is used as a base for hunting expeditions into the Cholistan Desert. He is credited with having financed the construction of Rahim Yar Khan's airport, as well as the huge, modern extension to the district hospital.

● **Accommodation** There are a number of budget hotels in Railway Chowk, Shahi Rd, outside the railway station. The best is **F Paras**, T 72586, the only one with an English sign.

● **Airline offices** PIA is at Iqbal Complex, Town Hall Chowk, T 71132.

● **Services** Most of the utilities (GPO, Pak Telecom, banks) are located E (left) from the station along Shahi Rd towards Town Hall Chowk.

● **Transport Road** Wagons leave from Town Hall Chowk for **Sadiqabad** (for **Bhong Mosque**). Coasters to **Bahawalpur** (3½ hrs, Rs 40) run from the yard next to Punjab Sweet Mart on Shahi Rd. **New Khan Road Runners**, T 73139, opp, run deluxe services to **Lahore** (13 hrs, Rs 152) 1845 1945 (via **Faisalabad**) 2115, 2215. **Manthar Travel**, Shahi Rd (next to Galaxy cinema), T 76925, run a/c coaches to **Karachi** (14 hrs, Rs 180) 1830, 1915.

There are several places of interest in the vicinity of Rahim Yar Khan.

About 10 km to the E are the barely discernible remains of a Buddhist monastery. It stands amongst a number of mounds which are said to represent the remains of the Sumra capital of the 15th century. At its peak the city is said to have covered 160 sq km. Deeper excavations have revealed evidence of a previous civilization, perhaps the ancient city of Pattan Munara. The ruler, **Mousicanus**, was said to have revolted against Alexander and was killed in 325 BC.

Almost 70 km SW of Rahim Yar Khan is the extraordinary **Bhong Mosque**. What is remarkable about this complex is that the relatively insignificant town of **Bhong** (pop 5,000) boasts one of Pakistan's most elaborate and ostentatious mosques. Conceived, designed and financed by a local landlord, (Late) **Sardar Rais Ghazi Mohammad Khan**, the complex comprises two mosques, a library, a madrassa and guest quarters. Construction began in 1932 and continued for 50 years. Essentially, the grand mosque reflects the traditional local style integrated with stylistic elements borrowed from regional Islamic architectural forms, notably from Iran, Spain and Syria. Rais Ghazi also chose to include Western colonial influences. The intention was "to represent as many forms of vernacular craft and Islamic religious architectural features as possible using a combination of traditional and modern materials". Does it work? Cynics may argue that the complex has evolved into something of an Islamic architectural theme park, with the designer choosing to include too many competing styles. However, no one can fail to be impressed by the spectacular interior to the grand mosque. Rais Ghazi chose to use only traditional materials and craftsmanship for the mosque interiors, and this is reflected in the superb use of teak, ivory, marble, onyx, coloured glass, glazed tile work, frescoes, mirror work, gilded tracery, ceramics, calligraphy and inlay. The gold leaf on the mihrab is striking.

The building of the Bhong complex has had a major effect upon the local community. During the fifty year construction period, it is estimated that 1,000 workmen and 200 craftsmen have been employed on the project. Although many workers were brought in from outside – master masons and craftsmen from Rajasthan, from Multan for the glazed tile and mosaic work, from Karachi for painting and calligraphy – most of the unskilled labourers came from the local community. Many of the craftsmen trained in the workshop have subsequently been employed by the government on the restoration of national monuments.

The development of the complex has resulted in the growth of local infrastructure, including provision of electricity, running water, irrigation, transport and a market. Further, prior to the development of secular education in the 1960s, the madrassa was the regional centre for education, attracting at its peak students from Turkey, Afghanistan and Iran. In 1986, Bhong Mosque was awarded the Aga Khan Award for Architecture.

To reach Bhong, take a wagon from Town Hall Chowk in Rahim Yar Khan to Sadiqabad (39 km). From there, local buses run the 27 km (1 hr) to Bhong.

In Rahim Yar Khan you can turn right to cross the Indus by the **Guddu Barrage** to Kashmor (68 km). The barrage, built in 1962, provides water to three canals that irrigate over 1 million ha of agricultural land. However, unlike the canals originating from the Sukkur and Kotri barrages, all the Guddu canals are seasonal, allowing an undiminished supply further south. As a consequence of this arrangement (in accordance with the 1991 Water Appropriations Agreement), the region has become dependent upon the use of some 6,000 tube wells.

The NH goes SW through **Sadiqabad** (39 km), crosses the Sind border to Ubauro (68 km) and goes through Ghotki to **Sukkur** (108 km).

LAHORE TO DERA ISMAIL KHAN

Leaving Lahore to the NW across the Ravi, the road passes through Sheikhupura see page 291 (34 km) and continues W to Faisalabad (96 km), one of Pakistan's most rapidly growing cities.

Faisalabad

Founded in 1890 as Lyallpur, after the then Lt Governor of the Punjab, Sir James Lyall, the town was renamed Faisalabad in 1977 in honour of the Saudi Arabian king. The status of Faisalabad as Pakistan's third largest city belies the town's recent and modest beginnings. Until the construction of the **Lower Chenab Canal** in the 19th century, most of the district was a vast tract of scrub-land known as Sandal Bar. Local tribes, including Bhattis and Virks from Gujranwala, Kharrals from Jhumra and Kamalia, Sials of Jhang and Sayyeds of Rajoa battled for possession of the limited pastures, with a grazing tax, *tarni*, being paid by the lesser tribes to the dominant ones. This system continued until the arrival of the

British. The provision of irrigation that led to the development of the canal colonies established Faisalabad as a centre of cotton production, and provided the catalyst in the town's industrialisation process. As a large agricultural market, the city is known as the granary of the region, and is the site of Pakistan's oldest and foremost **Agricultural University**. Faisalabad is also the centre of the Pakistani textile industry.

It has experienced phenomenal population growth, rising from a population of a mere 72,000 in 1947, to over 420,000 within 4 years of Partition. Today its population is around 1.6 million.

Places of interest

In the words of a local tourism official, "there is nothing of interest to a tourist in Faisalabad"! Locals are fond of referring to the city as "the Manchester of Pakistan", although this does a disservice to the Northern English town.

The original town was laid out on the design of the Union Jack, similar to Khartoum in Sudan. At the centre is the **Clock-tower**, erected in 1905 in 'grateful remembrance of Empress Queen Victoria'. Eight bazaars radiate from this central landmark. Despite recent changes in patterns of land use, a certain segregation of trades can still be discerned between the various bazaars; Jhang (metal utensils), Bwana (shoes), Aminpur (cloth), Chiniot (carpets, embroidered and printed cloth), Kutchery (electrical goods and glass fronted, up-market shops), Rail (cloth and jewellery), Karkhana (agricultural implements and products) and Montgomery (brokers, money lenders and financial services).

Local information
● Accommodation

NB Faisalabad's budget hotels are concentrated in the narrow bazaars around the clock-tower. Few have English signs, and some are difficult to find.

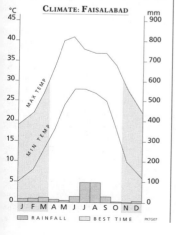

CLIMATE: FAISALABAD

°C / mm scale from 0–45 °C and 0–900 mm

MAX TEMP, MIN TEMP

J F M A M J J A S O N D

RAINFALL · BEST TIME

AL *Serena*, Club Rd, T 30972, F 629235, opened by the Aga Khan in 1987, has all modern facilities in traditional style building, incl pool, squash, golf, tennis, business centre, car rental, shopping arcade, bank and good, though expensive restaurants *Lyallpur*, *Xuelian* Chinese, *Basant Ct* barbecue.

C *Al Amin*, opp Kotwali, Aminpur Bazaar, T 628410, central a/c, dish TV, laundry, airport service; **C** *Rays*, Allama Iqbal Rd, T 620062, central a/c, restaurant.

E *Al Barkat*, Aminpur Bazaar, nr clock-tower, T 634457, rec.

F *Al Javeed*, Kutchery Bazaar, T 34689, best in class; **F** *Mehfil*, Chiniot Bazaar, nr clock-tower, T 635303, basic and unfriendly; **F** *New Kashmir*, Clock-tower Sq, Aminpur Bazaar, T 642089, basic and noisy; **F** *Tower*, Chiniot Bazaar, T 626583, basic but friendly, restaurant.

● **Places to eat**
Beside the upmarket restaurants at the Serena, there are lots of cheap eating places around the clock-tower.

● **Airline offices**
Aero Asia, P-7, Block 8, New Civil Lines, T 677804; PIA, Kotwali Rd, T 640091.

● **Banks & money changers**
Allied, Kotwali Rd; American Express at *Serena Hotel*; Emirates, Kotwali Rd; Habib, Circular Rd, Kutchery Bazaar; Standard Chartered, Railway Rd; State Bank of Pakistan, Railway Rd.

● **Entertainment**
Cinema: *Nagina*, Railway Rd.

● **Libraries**
Allama Iqbal Library, Railway Rd.

● **Post & telecommunications**
Central Telegraph Office: Circular Rd, Chiniot Bazaar.
GPO: Railway Rd.

● **Sports**
Cricket: *Iqbal Stadium* is one of Pakistan's finest international cricket venues. It was also the scene of the infamous face-off in 1987 between England captain Mike Gatting and Pakistani umpire Shakoor Rana.

● **Tour companies & travel agents**
Numerous on Circular Rd, between Chiniot and Kutchery Bazaar, incl *Al Munir*, T 616426 and *Pakland*, T 629797.

● **Tourist offices**
TDCP, 9 Allama Iqbal Rd, T 612375.

● **Transport**
Air The airport is located 9 km W of town on the Jhang Rd. **PIA**: Karachi, twice daily, Islamabad, twice daily. **Aero Asia**: Karachi twice daily.

Train For most long distance train journeys from Faisalabad, it is quicker to go to Lahore and take a train from there. **Lahore**: 9 trains daily, non-stop express at 0635, 1505, 2 hrs; **Karachi**: *Chenab Exp*, 1215, 23 hrs; *Allama Iqbal Exp*, 2120, 23 hrs.

Road Bus: private express and deluxe coaches run from Abdullapur Rd, several km to the N of the city centre. Incl *Farrukh Flying Coach* T 723745, **Lahore** every ½ hr (Rs 35, 2 hrs), *Super Van*, T 723619, **Sialkot, Gujranwala, Sargodha, Jhang, Sahiwal**, depart when full. *Malik Flying Coach*, T 718864, **Islamabad/Pindi** 0930, 1100, 1230, 2130, 2230, 2330, 0030 (Rs 110, 7 hrs); *New Khan Road Runners*, T 710458, **Multan** hourly, **Bahawalpur** 0900 (Rs 150, 10 hrs). *GTS*, local buses to **Lahore** from corner of Railway Rd opp Greyhound Travels. *Greyhound Travels*, Nagina Cinema, Railway Rd, T 641777, **Lahore** every ½ hr (Rs 40), **Islamabad/Rawalpindi** 1000, 2200 (Rs 100), **Sadiqabad** vi **Bahawalpur** and **Rahim Yar Khan** 1900 (Rs 150, 14 hrs).

Leaving Faisalabad to the W, the Jhang Rd passes a number of agricultural research centres and experimental farms attached to the Agricultural University. The town of **Jhang** (79 km) was founded on its present site in 1688, during the reign of Aurangzeb, by a Sanyasi fakir Lal Nath. The original settlement, since lost to the changing course of the Chenab, was founded around 1462 by Mal Khan, a direct descendant of the Sials. Jhang has a large Shia community where the quasi religious/political group Sipah-i-Mohammad is active. **Accommodation** There is one hotel in Jhang **D** *Vicky*, Faisalabad Rd, T 3557, some a/c, restaurant.

The main road continues SW, crossing the confluence of the **Jhelum** and **Chenab** at the **Trimmu Headworks**. The barrage at Trimmu was built at

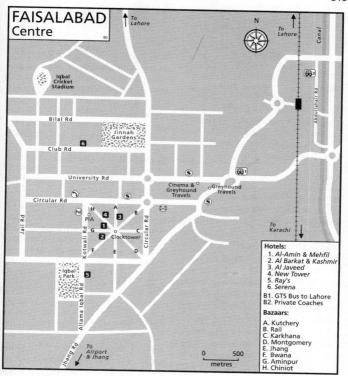

FAISALABAD Centre

90

To Lahore

N

To Lahore

Canal

Abdullahaur Rd

Iqbal Cricket Stadium

Bilal Rd

Jinnah Gardens

Club Rd

6

University Rd

Cinema & Greyhound Travels

Greyhound Travels

Circular Rd

S

Jail Rd

Pol

H   A   B

4   3

PIA   1

2

Clocktower

Kotwali Rd

Circular Rd

E   D

To Karachi

Iqbal Park

5

Allama Iqbal Rd

Jhang Rd

To Airport & Jhang

0   500
metres

Hotels:
1. *Al-Amin & Mehfil*
2. *Al Barkat & Kashmir*
3. *Al Javeed*
4. *New Tower*
5. *Ray's*
6. *Serena*
B1. GTS Bus to Lahore
B2. Private Coaches

Bazaars:
A. Kutchery
B. Rail
C. Karkhana
D. Montgomery
E. Jhang
F. Bwana
G. Aminpur
H. Chiniot

part of the Trimmu-Sindhnai Canal project that allows water to be diverted from the **Chashma Barrage** on the Indus and then channelled through the Jhelum just S of Sargodha to Bahawalpur on the Sutlej. Opened in 1965, the barrage has allowed irrigated agriculture in the **Thal** desert on a massive scale.

Having crossed the Trimmu Barrage, the road then divides in three directions.

The route N passes through **Khushab** (132 km) to **Mianwali** (89 km). See page 317.

The road W, via Nageriwala (96 km) and Darya Khan (40 km) crosses the Indus into NWFP and **Dera Ismail Khan** (22 km). See page 368.

To the SW, the road runs between the Chenab and the Rangpur irrigation canal via Ahmadpur Sial to **Muzaffargarh** (183 km). The road crosses the Indus to **Dera Ghazi Khan** (60 km). See page 189.

Leaving Lahore to the NW across the Ravi, the relatively fast Sheikhupura Rd passes through one of Lahore's major industrial suburbs. The dual carriageway enters Sheikhupura (see page 291) after 39 km. Continuing straight across the main N-S crossroads (Gujranwala-Faisalabad Rd), the road passes through Pindi Bhattian (71 km) to Chiniot (34 km).

Chiniot

Chiniot has ancient origins, with some scholars linking it to a town mentioned in the *Rg Veda*. A town called *Channiwat* is also mentioned in the *Rammayana*, and subsequently by Alberuni in his 'Kitab-ul-Hind', and housed one of the three ancient universities of the Punjab (the other two being at Ajodhan and Taxila). Tradition has it that Chandan, a king's daughter who was accustomed to hunting in a man's attire, visited the spot and was so charmed, she ordered a town, Chiniot, to be built. A later visitor during the period of British rule was less generous about the town's inhabitants, "the townspeople have an unenviable character for forgery, litigiousness and false evidence, and it is said that any old deed that comes out of Chiniot should be looked upon with the greatest suspicion"!

The town is celebrated for its wood carving and masonry, and craftsmen from Chiniot are known to have worked on such artistically renowned monuments as the Taj Mahal, the Golden Temple at Amritsar and the Wazir Khan mosque in Lahore, as well as the more recent Minar-e-Pakistan. Fine wood carving can still be seen on the doors, windows and balconies of the houses in the central part of the old town. The most prosperous days of Chiniot were during the reign of Shah Jahan, and the elegant

Shahi mosque was built during this period. There are no hotels in Chiniot.

Just N of Chiniot, on the Sargodha Rd, is the point where the Chenab cut through the picturesque low rocky out crops. A 2-tier iron bridge (road traffic above, rail track below), crosses the river via a date-palmed island in the middle. TDCP have constructed a restaurant and picnic spot, and it is possible to hire pleasure boats. A bomb case mounted on a plinth beside the Chiniot Bridge is said to have been part of an unsuccessful Indian attempt to destroy the bridge during the 1965 war. The National Highway Authority are constructing a modern road bridge across the Chenab at Chiniot.

As the road to **Sargodha** continues through the jagged, rocky outcrops, the proliferation of quarries gives the impression of a landscape being dismantled piece by piece.

Sargodha

Sargodha (54 km) was established as a colony town in 1903, although its origins are far older. The town's importance today is as a Punjab market town and a Pakistan Air Force base. Legend associates the town with skilled young men in flowing turbans and on white charger "carrying the day in manly sports like tent-pegging and horse riding". Although comprising mainly low rise buildings, Sargodha sprawls over a considerable area. The road from Chiniot enters through the Sargodha Satellite Town, where the main Flying Coach bus stand is located (on College Rd). Buses, wagons and coasters run when full to Mianwali, Khushrab, Chiniot, Chak wal, Faisalabad and Lahore.

● **Accommodation D** *Sargodha*, College Rd, nr Khayyan Cinema (from train station walk along tracks past West Sargodha Cabin, to new road flyover, turn left for hotel), T 60722, some a/c, restaurant; **E** *Malbro*, Court Rd (same directions, but turn right at flyover, walk to main junction and turn left), T 66646, attached bath, some a/c.

● **Airline offices** PIA, College Rd.

The road continues NW through Shahpur (31 km), crossing the Jhelum shortly before **Khushab** (14 km). According to American intelligence sources, Kushab is the site of a heavy-water nuclear reactor that is capable of producing weapons-grade plutonium, a charge denied by Pakistan.

To the N and NE of here run the **Salt Range** (see page 256).

To the W of Khushab, the road runs through the northern reaches of the **Thal** desert region to **Mianwali** (89 km).

Founded in Ghakhar times by Mian Ali, a holy man from Baghdad who was said to have miraculous powers, Mianwali is now best known as home-town of former cricket captain and Pakistan's favourite son, **Imran Khan**.

A further 48 km N of Mianwali is the town of **Kalabagh** (see page 263), commanding the **Jinnah Barrage** on the Indus. It was near to this point that in 1850 an elephant in the train of the Marquis of Dalhousie was engulfed in quicksand during the march to Kalabagh.

Beyond Kalabagh, the road crosses the state border into NWFP and the town of **Lakki** (99 km), and then continues on to **Bannu** (60 km). See page 367.

AZAD JAMMU AND KASHMIR

CONTENTS

Introduction   318
Muzaffarabad   324
Neelum Valley   327
Jhelum Valley   329
Poonch and Bagh District   331
Mirpur and Kotli Districts   333
Kotli   334

MAPS

Azad Jammu and Kashmir   319
Muzaffarabad   325

INTRODUCTION

Lying within the monsoonal belt on the outlying reaches of the Lesser Himalayas, the main attraction of Azad Jammu and Kashmir (AJ&K) is its outstanding natural beauty, in particular the thickly forested valleys. However, the region's beautiful valleys, forests, lakes and mountains have been permanently scarred by a 50-year-old political dispute that shows little sign of being resolved.

Since Pakistan and India became independent of Britain in 1947, Kashmir has been divided between the two nations in a dispute that totally dominates the bilateral relations of the S Asian neighbours. India currently occupies 63% of Kashmir, whilst the rest of Azad ('Free') Kashmir is under Pakistani administration. India and Pakistan have fought three wars over the status of Kashmir, and the current defacto border here between the two countries, the 'Line of Control', is in fact a cease-fire line.

For visiting foreign tourists, the sensitivity of this border means that it is currently impossible to visit some of the region's most attractive spots. Information has been included on these areas (compiled with assistance from the AJ&K Tourism Dept and local sources), in the hope that a resolution to the dispute will allow access to these beautiful areas. In the near future, however, this seems unlikely. Other parts of Azad Kashmir can be visited quite easily, although a permit must first be obtained (details below).

Best time to visit: Northern AJ&K is best visited from Apr-Jun and Sep-Nov, thus avoiding the winter cold and the summer heat (although the higher hill resorts can be pleasantly cool in summer). Southern AJ&K is best avoided in summer (best times Oct-Mar).

Land and life

Geography

The approximate third of Kashmir that Pakistan controls, Azad Kashmir, covers 13,297 sq km. It is bordered on the N by the Northern Areas of Pakistan, to the NW by NWFP, to the W, SW and S by Punjab and to the E by Indian occupied Kashmir. Azad Kashmir is geographically divided into two zones; the hilly and mountainous areas to the N and W, and the lower hills and plains to the S and SW. It is drained by three major rivers, the Poonch, Neelum and Jhelum, the latter providing a major source of hydro-electric power at the Mangla Dam.

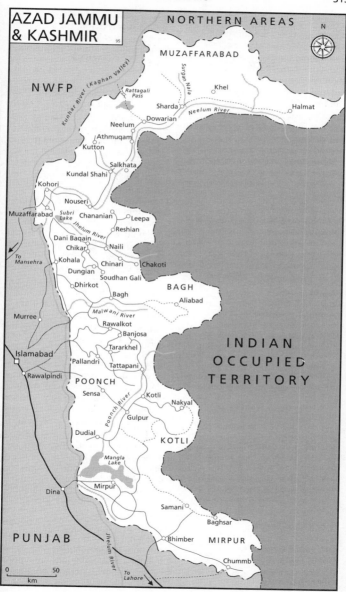

AZAD JAMMU & KASHMIR

95

NORTHERN AREAS

N

MUZAFFARABAD

NWFP

Kunhar River (Kaghan Valley)

Rattagali Pass

Khel

Sharda

Halmat

Neelum River

Dowarian

Neelum

Athmuqam

Kutton

Salkhata

Kundal Shahi

Surgan Nala

Kohori

Nouseri

Subri Lake

Chananian

Leepa

Muzaffarabad

Jhelum River

Reshian

Dani Baqain

Naili

To Mansehra

Chikar

Chinari

Chakoti

Kohala

Dungian

Soudhan Gali

BAGH

Dhirkot

Bagh

Aliabad

Murree

Malwani River

INDIAN OCCUPIED TERRITORY

Rawalkot

Banjosa

Islamabad

Tararkhel

Pallandri

Tattapani

Rawalpindi

POONCH

Sensa

Kotli

Nakyal

Gulpur

Dudial

KOTLI

Mangla Lake

Dina

Mirpur

Samani

Baghsar

PUNJAB

Bhimber

MIRPUR

Chummb

Jhelum River

To Lahore

0   50
km

Climate

Broadly speaking, the climate of Azad Kashmir can be divided into four seasons. These are the winter monsoon (Dec-Feb), the hot weather period (Mar-May), the summer monsoon (Jun-Sep), and the transition period (Oct-Nov). During the winter monsoon, the precipitation over the major portion of the region is in the form of snow, particularly in the higher altitudes. The higher air temperatures that begin in Apr, May and Jun give rise to the snow-melt that sustains the increased flow in the major rivers, most of which reach their maximum in Jun. During the summer monsoon season, the precipitation is concentrated in the southern and western portion of the region and features intense rainstorms. It is these rainstorms, such as those experienced in Sep 1992, that give rise to the sometimes devastating floods which characterise the Jhelum and other rivers of the Punjab.

History

Early rulers

For approximately 600 years, Jammu and Kashmir was a series of distinct and independent kingdoms and fiefdoms, with, almost without exception, Hindu rulers in the predominantly Hindu areas such as Jammu, and Muslim rulers in the Muslim areas. In 1588 the Mughal Emperor **Akbar** conquered the region, largely to gain control of the desirable Vale of Kashmir. Since this time, Kashmir has always been ruled by 'aliens'. Following the decline of the Mughal empire, Kashmir was conquered in 1752 by the armies of **Ahmad Shah Abdali**, thus ushering in an era of Pathan or Afghan rule.

Sikh and Dogra rule

In 1819, after a series of campaigns, the Sikh ruler **Ranjit Singh** eventually succeeded in annexing Kashmir. For the next 25 years or so Kashmir was ruled "quietly, if oppressively" by a Sikh Governor appointed by the court at Lahore. This situation continued until the outbreak of the First Sikh War between the British and the Sikhs in 1845-46. The Dogra Maharaja of the mainly Hindu state of Jammu, **Gulab Singh**, was a very shrewd ruler, and managed to avoid being embroiled in the war. Had his great ally Ranjit Singh been the man fighting the British there is little doubt that Gulab Singh would have entered the war on the Sikh side. Having less respect for Ranjit Singh's successors, however, and having consolidated his own powerbase in Jammu, Gulab Singh remained aloof from the conflict. He was a great opportunist though, and at the conclusion of the war, he acted in the mediations between the British and the defeated Sikhs.

On 9 March 1846, a treaty was signed in Lahore that handed over all Sikh territory, including Kashmir, to the British. When Gulab Singh offered to pay the Sikh war reparations, a sum in the region of Rs750,000, a second treaty was signed at Amritsar one week later. The Treaty of Amritsar stated: "The British Government transfers and makes over for ever, in independent possession, to Maharaja Gulab Singh and the heirs male of his body, all the hilly or mountainous country, situated to the eastward of the river Indus and westward of the river Ravi." Thus Jammu and Kashmir came under Hindu Dogra rule. The name 'Jammu and Kashmir' refers to this administrative district assembled by the British that included not only the Muslim dominated Vale of Kashmir, but the largely Hindu region of Jammu to the S, and Ladakh, the predominantly Buddhist E highlands of the great Himalayan axis. It is interesting to note that in hindsight, the British believed that they made a gross error in separating Kashmir from the Punjab, for had it remained part of the Sikh empire, it would have fallen into British hands following victory in the Second Sikh War in 1849.

Partition

There are two versions of events in Kashmir at Partition; one supported by Pakistan and the other by India. In fact, indigenous accounts of this period of S Asia's history are generally so skewered in their bias that they are rendered unreadable. There is a very fine dividing line between 'law and order' and 'state sponsored terrorism', between 'liberation movement' and 'terrorists'; all terms used regularly by the two sides in the conflict.

Prior to independence, the secular ('Hindu' if you read Pakistani accounts) Congress Party, led by Sheikh Abdullah, had established itself as the leading democratic force in the State of Jammu and Kashmir. As Britain liquidated its empire in the sub-continent, the Muslim League in Kashmir clearly favoured joining Pakistan, whilst the Congress party had a preference for India, or indeed independence. The Hindu Dogra Maharaja **Hari Singh**, ruling a predominantly Muslim state, was still undecided when Pakistan and India became independent in Aug 1947.

What actually happened immediately after independence is vehemently contested by India and Pakistan to this day. According to Indian historians, Pathan tribesmen from NWFP, supported and encouraged by Pakistan, invaded Jammu and Kashmir, attempting to annex the state for Pakistan. Those writing from a Pakistani viewpoint suggest that there was an insurgency amongst the Maharaja's own people, demanding accession to Muslim Pakistan, and the Kashmiris were joined in their struggle by civilian volunteers from across the border. Either way, with the 'rebels' only a few miles from the capital at Srinagar, on 25 October 1947, Hari Singh signed an instrument of accession

to India, and Indian troops were flown into the state. In the meantime, in Gilgit and Baltistan to the far NW of the State of Jammu and Kashmir, the local people rebelled against the decision, declared their independence from Kashmir, and vowed to join Pakistan.

United Nations cease-fire The war in Kashmir between India and Pakistan was one of the first major crisis to be discussed at the United Nations, and remains its longest unresolved dispute. India charged that Pakistan had sent "armed raiders" into the state, and called upon the UN to demand their withdrawal. Pakistan countered that India had used "fraud and violence" to manoeuvre Hari Singh's accession, and demanded that a plebiscite be held under the supervision of the UN in order to settle the dispute. Hostilities between the two countries continued until 30 December 1948 when a UN sponsored cease-fire was agreed upon. The cease-fire line, or 'Line of Control', has been the defacto border between the Indian State of Jammu and Kashmir and the Pakistani administered Azad Kashmir ever since.

The Plebiscite After the war, a plebiscite was agreed to by India on condition that the armies of both parties withdraw from all the territories of the former state, and that peace and normalcy be restored first. These conditions, not surprisingly, have never been met and the plebiscite is yet to be held. In 1957 a bill was passed in the Indian parliament integrating the State of Jammu and Kashmir within the Indian Union. In 1965 Pakistan and India began another brief war over the status of Kashmir, although the war rapidly ground to a stalemate.

The Simla Agreement Following Pakistan's crushing defeat in the 1971 war over Bangladesh, Prime Minister Zulfikar Ali Bhutto was of the opinion that Pakistan could not resolve the issue by military force. In 1972 he signed the

Simla Agreement with the Indian Prime Minister Mrs Gandhi under which both countries recognised the Line of Control, and agreed that the dispute could only be resolved through bilateral negotiations. Many Pakistanis have never forgiven Bhutto for 'selling out' on the Kashmir issue.

The current political situation

With no sign of a resolution to the dispute, the 'Kashmir question' continues to dominate relations between India and Pakistan. In fact, following the uprising, or 'jihad', that began in the Indian occupied part of Kashmir in 1989, there has been a hardening of stances between the two sides. India charges Pakistan with arming, training and funding the 'terrorists', whilst Pakistan insists that it offers just morale support to the 'freedom fighters'. Pakistan further charges India with acts of state terrorism in occupied Kashmir, a charge seemingly substantiated by the reports of independent Human Rights organisations.

In Azad Kashmir the situation remains tense. Much of the state is closed to foreign tourists, with regular reports of firing across the Line of Control. However, as Azad Kashmir becomes more and more integrated within the federal structure of Pakistan, less attention is paid to the voice demanding Kashmiri 'independence'.

Culture

People

The cultural diversity of Azad Kashmir is great, with the population comprising of races descended from Aryans, Persians, Turks and Arabs, amongst others. The cultures of the people to the N show some links to the 'Dardic' races of the Northern Areas, whilst the people of Mirpur and Kotli Districts show a cultural homogeneity with Punjab.

Language

A number of languages are spoken in Azad Kashmir, in addition to the 'official' language of Urdu. **Kashmiri** is influenced by Sanskrit and belongs to the Dardic branch of the Indo-Aryan language group. **Hindko**, related to W Punjabi, is also used in the N and NW, and **Punjabi** is quite common in the S. **Gojri** is the mother tongue of the state's Gujar community. **Pahari** is an indigenous language, literally meaning 'mountaineer'.

Government and administration

Azad Kashmir has a parliamentary form of government with the President as the head of state, and a Prime Minister as the chief executive of the government. There is an elected Legislative Assembly in Muzaffarabad. The Assembly elects the President whilst the Prime Minister is the leader of the majority party in the Assembly. The administrative set-up is similar to the other provincial governments of Pakistan, although the Ministry of Kashmir Affairs and Northern Areas serves as a link between the federal government and Azad Kashmir.

The state is divided into four districts, namely Muzaffarabad, Poonch and Bagh, Kotli and Mirpur. There are plans to divide Poonch and Bagh into two different districts.

Economy

The economy of Azad Kashmir has traditionally been dependent upon agriculture and forestry. There is, however, a substantial flow of savings in the form of remittances from expatriate Pakistanis that has contributed to a rapidly growing private industrial sector. In recent years, a large number of privately funded industrial projects have been initiated, particularly in the Mirpur region. These include a scooter assembly plant, cotton spining mills, a match factory, textile weaving and other small and medium units.

This diversification into industry has been very welcome, and has relieved pressure from the traditional forestry sector. Over exploitation of this resource is a very real threat, affecting not only the long term interests of the timber industry, but also watershed and soil management.

Azad Kashmir also has a degree of mineral wealth, with deposits of bauxite, coal, graphite, limestone and precious stone. Kashmir is renowned for its distinctive handicrafts, including carpets, papier mâché, shawls and wood-carving, particularly in walnut. These crafts have traditionally been centred on the Vale of Kashmir, now in Indian hands, but there has been an attempt to revive these trades in Pakistani administered territory.

Visiting Azad Jammu and Kashmir

Because of the sensitive nature of the defacto border with India, and the very real danger from firing across the Line of Control, certain areas of Azad Kashmir are off-limits to foreigners. Unfortunately, these areas include the two most attractive valleys in Azad Kashmir – **Leepa** and **Neelum** – plus a number of other interesting sites. A permit, or **No Objection Certificate**, is required to visit any other place in the state, although even equipped with this, **you are not permitted to approach within 16 km of the Line of Control**. You will frequently be asked to produce this document, so it is not advised that you attempt to travel around Azad Kashmir without it.

No Objection Certificate

The No Objection Certificate (NOC) should, in theory, be obtained from the Ministry of Home Affairs within the Ministry for Northern Areas, Frontier Regions and Kashmir Affairs at the Secretariat in Islamabad. However, unless you are a journalist working in Pakistan,

it is far more practical to obtain the NOC by going directly to the **AJ&K Home Department** in the **Secretariat** at **Muzaffarabad** (located in the Chattar area, to the S of the town centre, T 4157).

To obtain the NOC you must visit the Home Department (closed Fri/Sat/holidays) and write a short letter explaining the places that you wish to visit, and why. Your letter will then be translated into Urdu, and reproduced into 6 or 7 copies. The various copies will pass through many hands, including those of the police, military intelligence (ISI), Home Secretary and the Tourism Dept, and any sensitive areas will be deleted with bold strokes of a red pen. The whole document will then have to be retyped. This process can take upwards of 4 hrs, allowing plenty of opportunity for endless cups of tea and discussions on the 'Kashmir situation'. Before being given the NOC, you may well be called for interview by the Home Secretary, ISI or both. Freelance journalists will probably be denied the document. If you have any other problems, it is worth enlisting the help of the friendly AJ&K Tourism Dept across the road. There is no guarantee that you will get a NOC.

The NOC, written in Urdu, does not actually list the places to which you can and can't go, although you have to sign a declaration stating that you will **not go within 16 km of the Line of Control, nor photograph bridges or military installations**. Once you have your NOC, you can book AJ&K Tourism Dept *Resthouses* at places you wish to visit.

It is best to obtain your NOC as soon as practical after arriving in Muzaffarabad. It is quite likely that the police or ISI will hear of your arrival in town remarkably quickly, and you may receive a visit at your hotel.

MUZAFFARABAD

Muzaffarabad has retained a strategic importance on the main route between the Punjab and the Vale of Kashmir from at least the Mughal era. However, the town's profile has been raised since the partition of the sub-continent, and the division of Kashmir between Pakistani and Indian control, and Muzaffarabad is now the capital of Azad Kashmir. Ironically, the closing of the trading and communications route along the Jhelum Valley to Srinagar has removed Muzaffarabad's initial raison d'être. Foreigners intending to visit Azad Kashmir are advised to begin their journey in Muzaffarabad because this is the only place at which you can obtain the essential NoObjection Certificate.

The city runs for almost 4 km along the E bank of the Neelum River, from the fort down to the confluence of the **Neelum** and **Jhelum** Rivers. Below the confluence is the area called Chattar, where the AJ&K Legislative Assembly, Secretariat and Tourism Office are located.

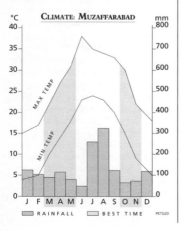

CLIMATE: MUZAFFARABAD

RAINFALL   BEST TIME   PKTG20

Places of interest

Red Fort

Muzaffarabad's sole tourist attraction is the 16th century **Red Fort** located at the northern limit of the town. Begun in 1549, and completed in 1646 by **Sultan Muzaffar Khan** who gave his name to the town, the fort was built as a result of border skirmishes between the Mughal Emperor Akbar and the Chak rulers of Kashmir. Once the Mughal rulers claimed the ascendency, the fort's strategic interest declined, although there was a brief revival under the Afghan Ahmed Shah Durani. The Dogra rulers of Kashmir, **Gulab Singh**, and then **Ranbir Singh**, rebuilt and extended the fort, yet it was abandoned at Partition.

Surrounded on three sides by the Neelum, the impressive red clay outer walls are reasonably well preserved, although the river has caused some damage to the N. The entrance to the compact fort is through the adjacent *Resthouse*, and there are some pleasant gardens and lawns once inside. There is also a small museum. The fort is open until quite late, although the museum closes at 1700. The views across the river to the army stables are impressive during the late afternoon.

Local information

● **Accommodation**

HOTEL CLASSIFICATIONS			
AL	Rs4,000	**A**	Rs1,800-4,000
B	Rs900-1,800	**C**	Rs450-900
D	Rs300-450	**E**	Rs150-300
F	up to Rs150		

B *Sangum*, Secretarial Rd, Domal, T 4194, F 2587, best in town, dish TV, fridge, phone, Oriental and Kashmiri restaurant, rm service, bakery, car rental, banquet hall.

C *Neelum View*, Neelum Rd, opp Fort, T 4733, F 5468, a/C, dish TV, phone, room service, laundry, *Lotus* restaurant.

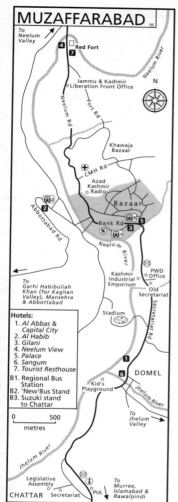

MUZAFFARABAD

Hotels:
1. Al Abbas & Capital City
2. Al Habib
3. Gilani
4. Neelum View
5. Palace
6. Sangum
7. Tourist Resthouse
B1. Regional Bus Station
B2. 'New' Bus Stand
B3. Suzuki stand to Chattar

0   500
metres

D *Tourist Resthouse*, Fort, T 3090, good value government run resthouse, some a/c rooms, quiet garden, good location, meals available, bookings through Tourism Dept, T 4112.

E *Al Abbas*, Secretariat Rd, T 3103, reasonable dbles with attached bath; **E** *Capital City*, Secretariat Rd, (old PIA building), T 4828.

Budget hotels: there are numerous **F** hotels in Muzaffarabad, generally in and around Bank Rd in the main bazaar, and opp the New Bus Station on the W bank of the river. The best in Bank Rd are probably *Palace*, T 3189, (no English sign) with cheap rms, friendly staff, with attached bath and bedbugs, or the *Gilani*, T 3799. The best cheap hotel in town is the friendly **F** *Al Habib*, Abbottabad Rd, opp New Bus Station, T 3282, with good value rms and restaurant.

● **Places to eat**
Not much choice other than the hotel restaurants, although those at the *Sangum* and *Neelum View* are quite good.

● **Airline offices**
PIA is opp Secretariat, Chattar, T 3121.

● **Banks & money changers**
National Bank of Pakistan, Main Branch, Bank Rd, offers foreign exchange, incl travellers' cheques.

● **Hospitals & medical services**
Combined Military Hospital, CMH Rd, T 3666. There are numerous chemists opp the hospital.

● **Post & telecommunications**
Area code: 058.

GPO: is on Secretariat Rd. There is also a Post Office in Chattar. The Telegraph Office is on Bank Rd, behind the National Bank of Pakistan.

● **Shopping**
Although Kashmir is famous for its handicrafts, particularly dyed wools and woodcarvings, they are all distinctly lacking in the main bazaar above Bank Rd. The labyrinth like properties of the bazaar do make it a fascinating place to wander, however.

● **Tourist offices**
Azad Kashmir Tourist Information Centre, opp Secretariat, Chattar, T 4112 (0900-1600, closed Fri/Sat). The helpful office provides essential information to visitors to Azad Kashmir, as well as booking for the various *Tourist Guesthouses*, *Angler's Huts* and *Tourist Cottages*. However, they will not take any bookings until you have your NOC.

● **Useful addresses**
AJ&K PWD Office, Secretariat Rd (first courtyard on left up road opp Kashmir Industrial Emporium), T 3247 (0900-1600, Closed Fri/Sat) for bookings of *PWD Inspection Bungalows* in Chikar, Neelum and Leepa Valley. Inconveniently, those in Soudhan Gali, Bagh and Pallandri must be booked in Bagh.

Divisional Forestry Office: for booking *Forest Resthouses*, is nr Jinnah Bridge in Domal, although it may be about to move to a new site.

Home Department, AJ&K Secretariat: Secretariat Rd, Chattar, T 4157, is the place to obtain your NOC.

Offices of **Jammu and Kashmir Liberation Front** and **Jammu and Kashmir Peoples' Conference** are on Neelum Rd, nr the Fort.

● **Transport**

Local Rickshaw: there is a rickshaw stand on the slope just above Bank Rd. **Suzuki**: see the map for the location of the Suzuki stand N to the Fort and S to Chattar (both Rs2).

Road Bus: the **New Bus Station** is on Abbottabad Rd, on the W side of the Neelum River. There are regular buses and minibuses to **Ghori Garhi Habibullah** (change for **Kaghan Valley**), **Mansehra** (Rs15, 2 hrs), **Abbottabad** (Rs20, 3 hrs) and **Rawalpindi** (Rs 45, 4½ hrs) via **Murree**. **NB** Due to subsidence around the bridge across the Neelum, buses to/from Rawalpindi pass all the way through the town, crossing the river to the N, near the Fort. The new Rs20 million Neelum Bridge is optimistically due for completion in Jan 1996.

The **Regional Bus Stand**, down a side road off Bank Rd, next to the *Gilani* Hotel, has minibuses and large buses serving the Jhelum Valley, incl all stops to **Chakoti** (Rs17, 3 hrs), **Reshian** in the Leepa Valley, and **Bagh** (Rs36, 4 hrs), via **Chikar** (Rs16, 2 hrs) and **Soudhan Gali** (Rs 26, 3 hrs).

NEELUM VALLEY

Considered by many to be the most picturesque of all the Kashmir valleys, the 200 km long Neelum Valley runs in a generally NE direction from Muzaffarabad towards the river's source in the Pir Panjal. The Neelum River, known as Kishanganga prior to Partition, and so marked on many maps, runs for much of its journey through Pakistani administered Kashmir broadly parallel to the Kaghan Valley's Kunhar River. The valley is famous for its scenic beauty, with thick fir and deciduous forests cloaking the hills on either side of the river and affording marvellous trekking opportunities.

Unfortunately, the bad news is that for almost its entire length, the valley runs parallel and adjacent to the Line of Control with India, and is thus strictly off limits to foreigners (even with a No Objection Certificate). Domestic tourists may still visit the area, but the regular Pakistani press reports of Indian firing across the Line of Control suggest that life is anything but normal in the valley. The following details on the Neelum Valley are for information only, hopefully anticipating a time when the valley can be visited.

The road along the Neelum Valley leaves **Muzaffarabad** to the N, past the fort, and is sealed for the first 100 km or so, before becoming a fair weather road, and finally a jeep track. Public buses run as far as **Khel** (155 km), beyond which jeeps and ponies are the only other transport option.

At **Kohori** (marked on some maps as Ghori), 16 km from Muzaffarabad, a trekking route leads N, passing close to Makra Peak (3,885m), and continuing to Shogran in the Kaghan Valley (about 2-3 days). Another trekking route into the Kaghan Valley begins at **Patikha**, 6 km further along from Kohori. Beyond Patikha the road comes within 16 km of the Line of Control, and so tourists are currently not permitted to travel beyond this point.

At **Nouseri** (20 km) the Neelum Valley turns sharply to the NE, the road crossing to the W bank, and continuing up to **Kundal Shahi** (32 km). Here, the Neelum River is joined from the NW by the Jagran Nala, a tributary well stocked with trout. A jeep track goes up the nala to **Kutton** (8 km) where the AJ&K Tourism Dept have several E *Angler's Huts*. Another *Angler's Hut* is located at **Salkhata**, 3 km beyond Kundal Shahi (bookings from the Tourist Office in Muzaffarabad) at a secluded spot close to the trout hatchery.

The road continues NE to **Athmuqam** (84 km from Muzaffarabad), a larger settlement that serves as the sub-divisional headquarters. Just beyond Athmuqam is the village of **Neelum** (9 km), and there is a riverside AJ&K Tourism Dept E *Resthouse* at nearby **Keran**.

A further 13 km from Neelum is the village of **Dowarian**, located at 1,615 m amongst a beautiful conifer forest. There is a E *Resthouse*. From Dowarian it is possible to trek NW across the 4,140m Rattigali Pass onto the Kaghan Valley's Lalazar Plateau (2-3 days). There is excellent camping at the Rattigali Sar, a large alpine lake near to the pass.

The road continues on to **Sharda** (30 km), described by the AJ&K Tourism Dept as being "a breath-taking green spot at an altitude of 1,981m ... a captivating landscape with numerous springs and hill sides covered with trees." The Tourism Dept run a E *Resthouse* and 22 bed *Youth Hostel*. It is possible to trek N, and then NW, along the Surgan Nala and across the Nurinar Pass into the Kaghan Valley.

The main road runs as far as **Khel** (155 km from Muzaffarabad), described as being another picturesque village. Even if Khel ever becomes accessible to tourists, it would probably be too risky to attempt the trek N along the Shounter Nala and across the 4,420m Shounter Pass to the lawless region around Chilas.

Khel is the point at which to hire a jeep or horses for the 49 km journey on to the border village of **Halmat** (**E** *Resthouse*).

The Jhelum Valley runs in a south-easterly direction from Muzaffarabad, and prior to Partition and the subsequent division of Kashmir, provided the main line of communication between Punjab and Srinagar. Today, the Pakistani administered section ends at Chakoti, 60 km from Muzaffarabad. However, because of the proximity to the Line of Control, it is not possible to travel much beyond Dani Baqaian (33 km), the turn off for the chain of hill stations on the road to Bagh District. Thus the beautiful Leepa Valley is off-limits to foreigners, although some information on this valley is included for future reference.

The road along the Jhelum Valley follows the southernmost bank of the river, passing through the small village of Garhi Dopata, before reaching the settlement of Dani Baqaian. The main road continues in a south-easterly direction, towards the turning for the **Leepa Valley** and for the Line of Control at **Chakoti**. Another road turns S at Dani Baqaian, giving access to a string of small **hill stations**, before continuing to Bagh, in Poonch & Bagh District.

The Hill Stations

Chikar

The small town of **Chikar** (13 km) is situated on the crest of a ridge, offering fine views of the terraced wheat and maize fields, leading up to the pine topped hills that surround on all sides. These forests offer some cool and relaxing short walks. A very comfortable **D** *PWD Resthouse* is well sited, just above the main bazaar (no sign). It has 6 large, well furnished rms, with clean attached bath, shady verandah, and pleasant garden. Meals are by arrangement, although there are several basic restaurants in Chikar's bazaar. Bookings should be made in Muzaffarabad. The **E** *Tourist Resthouse*, belonging to the AJ&K Tourism Dept, was under reconstruction in 1995. There are several basic **F** hotels in the bazaar, incl *Al Shabaz* and *Shamsa Barri*.

Noonbagla

To the S of Chikar the road forks. Contrary to some maps, and other guidebooks, the 4 hill stations in this chain are not linked by road on a single N-S axis. The right fork offers a sealed, and then a fair-weather road, to **Noonbagla** (12 km, and sometimes referred to as Loonbagla), a very quiet and relaxing settlement comprising some two dozen or so buildings. There is a very pleasant **E** *Forest Resthouse* just above the bazaar. It offers 2 clean doubles, with attached bath and terrace views, meals by arrangement. Bookings from Muzaffarabad, but they are not always necessary. There are some excellent walks along the pine clad ridge behind the *Resthouse*.

Noonbagla can be reached by Suzuki from Chikar (Rs20, 45 mins), although you should ascertain as to whether you have made a 'booking', or are in a 'service' car.

The fare-weather road continues beyond Noonbagla to **Dungian** (3 km), another tiny settlement surrounded by pine forests, and on to **Soudhan Gali** (13 km). However, there is no regular transport on this route, and following poor weather, the route is often blocked to vehicles. Having said that, it is a very nice walk.

Soudhan Gali

The main route to **Soudhan Gali** (16 km) is via the left fork beyond Chikar. The road drops down to the river below Chikar, before making a slow, tortuous climb up to Soudhan Gali. Public buses

"PROVE YOUR IDENTITY!"

Across the whole of Pakistan, most people are able to recite at least one phrase in English, the ubiquitous "What is your country?" In Azad Kashmir, however, there is an alternative mantra, "Prove your identity!" Obviously the result of the tense security situation in the state, this is a phrase that you may well come to loathe. Its usage is not restricted to police officers and members of the security forces that you may meet; school children, bus drivers, hotel managers, the list is endless. I am sure that my experience in this matter is not unique, and that many other visitors to Kashmir frequently have their breakfast, lunch, dinner, sleep, and any other activity interrupted by someone demanding that you "prove your identity". The irony is that, invariably, those demanding that you prove your identity are unable to prove their own. Those claiming to be members of the police rarely have the documents to substantiate their claim. As a general rule it is advisable that you only show your No Objection Certificate to those in uniform, or in possession of a police or security services identity card. However, you will have to use your discretion. In Soudhan Gali I had to fight my way out of a mob demanding "prove your identity"; and this is in an area away from the sensitive Line of Control. Although it is likely that Indian agents are active in Azad Kashmir, it is unlikely that any are 6 ft 2 in Londoner with fair hair, green eyes and wearing a Leyton Orient football shirt!

Dave Winter

operate on this route from Muzaffarabad (Rs26, 3 hrs via Chikar Rs10, 1 hr), continuing onto Bagh (Rs10, 1 hr). The main bazaar is set just below the pass, at the top of the crest.

Soudhan Gali has a good **D** *PWD Resthouse* situated above the bazaar, but the chowkidar will not let you stay without a booking chit. The booking can only be made at the PWD in Bagh, very inconvenient when you'll have almost certainly come from the direction of Muzaffarabad. There is a reasonable private **E** *Resthouse* located near the hairpin bend on the hill (blue and red verandah, no sign), plus some very basic **F** hotels in the bazaar.

The road from Soudhan Gali gradually descends to the town of **Bagh** (25 km).

Returning to the main route along the Jhelum Valley, beyond Dani Baqaian the road passes through **Naili** (45 km from Muzaffarabad), the turning point for the **Leepa Valley**, before continuing via **Chinari** (6 km) to the border town of **Chakoti** (8 km).

Leepa Valley

All of the literature and brochures from the AJ&K Tourism Dept go to great length to describe the beauty of the **Leepa Valley**, suggesting that it is the most stunning in Azad Kashmir. Unfortunately, most of it lies within 16 km of the Line of Control, and so is off-limits to foreigners. It is open to domestic tourists, however, from May to Nov.

A fair weather road climbs NE from Naili up to the 2,750m **Reshian Pass**. A path leads W from here to the pleasant meadows at **Danna** (AJ&K Tourism Dept **E** *Resthouse*). The main jeep track then drops down into the valley of the Leepa River, a tributary of the Neelum. At the head of the valley the route divides. To the E is **Leepa** (60 km from Naili), a small village at 1,921 m set amongst the rice padi fields, and noted for its typical wooden Kashmiri houses. To the W is **Chananian** (58 km from Naili), located at 2,226 m amongst thick pine forest. There is an AJ&K Tourism Dept **E** *Resthouse* here. Public buses from Muzaffarabad run as far as Reshian, beyond which a jeep will be required.

POONCH AND BAGH DISTRICT

Although not as attractive as the Neelum and Leepa Valleys, Poonch and Bagh District does have some attractive hill resorts, most notably Dhirkot, Banjosa and Tararkhel. Poonch District has a long military history, and is noted for its fighting men. Although there are differing interpretations of events, it is through this area that the 'liberation' of Kashmir was launched following the Maharaja of Kashmir's decision to accede to India in 1947. The region had been under Dogra rule since the British handed over the area to Gulab Singh following the signing of the Treaty of Amritsar in 1846. The Maharaja of Kashmir had, however, found it very difficult to establish his rule in Poonch.

Rawalkot

Rawalkot is the district headquarters, and can be reached from Rawalpindi/Islamabad via Kahuta and Azad Pattan, or via Dhalkot, or from Muzaffarabad via Kohala and Dhirkot. The town is also linked to Banjosa. Tararkhel, Pallandri, Tattapani and Bagh. It serves more as a centre for the communications network than as a tourist attraction itself. There is, however, an AJ&K Tourism Dept **E** *Resthouse*, plus an office at which to book the other *Resthouses* at Dhirkot and Banjosa. *PWD Resthouses* at Pallandri and Tararkhel should also be booked from Rawalkot.

Banjosa

Some 20 km SE of Rawalkot, at Banjosa (1,981m), there is a beautifully situated **E** *Resthouse*, in the heart of the pine forest. There are some excellent walks along the ridge, with fine views of the Pir Panjal, plus boating facilities on a small lake.

Tararkhel and Pallandri

Another pleasantly located hill station, at a similar altitude, is Tararkhel, to the S. There is a small bazaar and an **E** *PWD Inspection Bungalow*, bookable in Rawalkot. Beyond Tarakhel is Pallandri (64 km from Rawalkot), an attractive small resort surrounded by low hills. There is an **E** *Inspection Bungalow*.

Tattapani

Tattapani is situated on the W bank of the Poonch River, a little over halfway between Rawalkot and Kotli, in Kotli District. As well as being an important road junction between the two districts, Tattapani is most famous for its hot sulphurous springs. The AJ&K Tourism Dept have built an attractive hotel around the springs. Unfortunately, Tattapani's proximity to the Line of Control means that foreigners are not allowed to visit.

Bagh

The sub-district headquarters town of **Bagh** is located on either side of the Mahl and Malwani Rivers, at its confluence with a smaller tributary. Unfortunately, Bagh, like Soudhan Gali, is full of people who will keep demanding that you "prove your identity", and there is not much to see in the town anyway.

● **Accommodation** The **E** *PWD Resthouse* is to the W of town, across the main bridge (no sign, but a distinctive red and white surrounding wall), prior booking at the adjacent PWD office is essential. In the same road is the office of the Forestry Department, where you can book *Forestry Resthouses*. There are several grotty **F** hotels in town, although easily the best bet is the excellent **F** *Al Noor*, nr to the hospital, on a hill above the bus stand. It is friendly, with very cheap, clean, carpetted VIP dbles with attached bath, and a restaurant, rec.

● **Transport** On the N side of the river is the main bus yard, with regular buses and mini-buses serving Muzaffarabad (Rs36, 4 hrs) and Rawalpindi (Rs60, 4 ½ hrs). Bagh is connected to Muzaffarabad via the chain of hill stations, and is also connected to Rawalkot to the S.

Aliabad

Aliabad is located 112 km E of Bagh, set amongst a thick forest of deodar and pine. It is reachable by bus and then jeep from Bagh or Rawalkot. It is currently off-limits to foreigners.

Dhirkot

One of the most attractive resorts in the district that foreigners can visit is Dhirkot, on the road between Kohala and Bagh. At 1,676 m the climate is a pleasant change from the summer heat of the Punjab plains. The prime attraction is the location of the **E** *PWD Resthouse* and **E** AJ&K Tourism Dept *Tourist Huts*, set in the heart the deodar and pine forest. The accommodation here is very popular, and booking ahead is essential (in Rawalkot or Muzaffarabad). Access is easy from Islamabad (132 km) via Murree and Kohala (24 km).

MIRPUR AND KOTLI DISTRICTS

Although parts of Mirpur District are hilly, much of the region comprises plains that are geographically and climatically closer to the Punjab than the mountain valleys of the rest of Azad Kashmir. As a result, the district can be incredibly hot in summer.

The district has few tourist attractions (Mangla Dam and Lake are dealt with as an excursion from Dina in Punjab, see page 265), yet has a fascinating background and some remarkable links with the UK. Mirpur district has undergone dramatic transformation since the construction of the massive **Mangla Dam**, including the re-siting of the district headquarters town.

Mirpur

The district headquarters, Mirpur is probably easier to reach from the GT Rd at Dina (on the Islamabad/Rawalpindi to Lahore route) than from other parts of Kashmir. Although there is little of tourist interest beside the Mangla Dam, Mirpur must rate as one of the friendliest towns in Pakistan. Because of the links with the UK, do not be surprised if you are hailed in the street by young Pakistani lads with broad Yorkshire

THE BRADFORD CONNECTION

It may seem incredible, but at least three-quarters of all British Pakistanis can trace their origins to an area no greater than 32 km by 48 km, lying mostly in Azad Kashmir. The overwhelming majority stem from Mirpur district, and parts of southern Kotli district. Mirpuris themselves make up well over half of Britain's Pakistani population, and 75% of the Pakistani population in the northern English town of Bradford.

Although there was a high level of migration from the area as the Mirpuri peasants saw their land disappear beneath the Mangla Lake in 1968, this was actually the culmination of a process that had begun long before the idea for the Mangla Dam was even conceived.

From the closing decades of the last century, Mirpuri villagers began to take jobs as stokers on British merchant ships operating out of Bombay. Britain was reluctant, except in times of war, to recruit subjects of the Maharaja of Kashmir as soldiers in the Punjab regiments, so the Mirpuris found alternative employment with Britain's merchant fleet. As Britain's coal-powered merchant fleet continued to expand rapidly during the early decades of this century, so the demand for labour steadily increased. As seamen, Mirpuris were in an excellent position to keep a close watch on global job opportunities, and some began to seek work ashore.

When acute industrial labour shortages began to emerge in Britain during the Second World War, Mirpuri ex-seamen were eagerly recruited to fill the gaps. As opportunities began to widen further still in Britain's post-war boom, more Mirpuri seamen began to settle. Having established themselves ashore, they began to call their relatives over, initiating a process of chain migration. Many families who received resettlement grants following the construction of the Mangla Dam chose to join relatives in the UK. In many villages in Mirpur District, well over half the population now lives in Britain.

(With thanks to Kevin Hawkins)

accents, halal butchers from Halifax, or if you meet nervous young bridegrooms from Birmingham about to see their future brides for the first time.

Other links manifest themselves in strange forms, such as the ease with which you can direct dial the UK, or the proliferation of new businesses and industries initiated by capital from British Pakistanis.

Local information
● **Accommodation**

C *Jabees*, Allama Iqbal Rd (W end), T 3092, a/c, restaurant, some deluxe rooms; **C** *Kashmir Continental*, Allama Iqbal Rd, T 4303, a/c, dish TV, fridge, direct dialling, fax, car rental, coffee shop, restaurant with Chinese, Pak and Continental food, corporate and group rates, best in town.

E *Roopyal*, Chowk Shaheedian, Allama Iqbal Rd, T 3455, opened in 1992 by Benazir Bhutto, some a/c rooms, very good value, restaurant rec.

F *Nathia Super*, Chowk Shaheedian, Allama Iqbal Rd (E end), very good value doubles with attached bath, rec, run by a Mirpuri from Walthamstow!, downstairs is a 3 table snooker hall. Number of **F** hotels around bus stand incl *Al-Bilal* and *Mir Faisal* (signs in Urdu only).

● **Post & telecommunications**
GPO: is N of Chowk Shaheedian roundabout.

KOTLI

Formerly a sub-district of Mirpur until 1975, Kotli District provides a geographical link between the low hills and plains of Mirpur District to the S, and the more mountainous district of Poonch to the N. There is, however, little of tourist interest in the district.

Kotli town is fairly small, with transport links to Rawalkot, Islamabad (141 km) and Mirpur. It has an **E** *PWD Resthouse* and a number of cheap hotels. About 40 km to the E is the relatively cool hill station of **Nakyal** (1,524m), although this is too close to the Line of Control to be open to foreigners. To the W of Kotli, on the Islamabad road, is **Sensa** (53 km), a good base to explore the nearby chir forests around **Bruhian**. There is a *Forest Resthouse* at Sensa.

NORTH WEST FRONTIER PROVINCE

CONTENTS

Introduction	335
Peshawar	347
Southern NWFP	361
Peshawar Valley	371
Swat Valley	379
Chitral Valley	395

MAPS

NWFP Province	336
Peshawar City	348
Old City	350
Saddar	353
University Town	354
Southern NWFP	362
Kohat	363
Dera Ismail Khan	370
Peshawar Valley	372
Mardan	373
Takht-e-Bhai	374
Swat Valley	380
Mingora	384
Saidu Sharif	385
Miandam	390
Madyan	389
Kalam	393
Dir	401
Chitral Town	403
Kalash Valleys	407
Upper Chitral	415

INTRODUCTION

Measuring more than 600 km in length, NWFP stretches from the Pamir in the extreme N all the way S as far as Dera Ismail Khan, encompassing high mountains, fertile river basins and semi-arid deserts. The mountains to the N, particularly the Hindu Kush, are amongst the most spectacular in Pakistan, offering some of the best (and least visited) trekking and climbing in the world.

The Pathan tribes that dominate the NWFP have for centuries exploited the rugged terrain and thrived on banditry and guerilla warfare, eluding the attempts of invading powers to control and pacify them. During the Colonial period, the frontier grew in strategic importance and the British established their 'Forward Policy', struggling to control the tribal areas as a buffer zone against Russian expansion. Despite the **Durand Line** of 1893, they never gained full control. Even today, nearly a third of the region remains tribal territory with internal autonomy from Pakistani law.

For centuries the region has existed as a turbulent zone of contact between the civilizations of Central Asia and the Middle East on one side and South Asia on the other. Yet the province has a rich cultural history, stretching back to the Indus Valley Civilization. The Peshawar valley and hills of Swat, along with Taxila to the E, were the focus of Gandharan civilization which flourished under the Kushans around the 2nd century AD as one of the most important centres of Buddhism on the subcontinent. Today these areas have the highest concentration of archaeological sites in Pakistan, with some, such as the Buddhist monastery remains at Takht-e-Bhai, remarkably well preserved. Gandharan art, with its distinctive fusion of Graeco-Roman and Indian styles, is famous throughout the world. Peshawar, which became the capital of the Kushan kings, reached its zenith under Moghul rule as a wealthy trading town with lavish mosques, palaces and gardens. Tucked away in the remote valleys of Chitral, the unique Kalasha tribes have existed for centuries in isolation, their colourful, vibrant culture and way of life still surviving today.

Best time to visit: the northern half of the province is best visited from spring through to autumn (Apr-Sep), the length of the season broadly speaking decreasing as one moves further N. The southern half of the province is best visited from late autumn through to early spring (Nov-Mar) when days are pleasantly cooler, but be prepared for cold nights.

Editorial Logic While the district of Hazara, which includes Abbottabad, the Kaghan valley and parts of Indus Kohistan, is administratively part of NWFP, these areas are dealt with in the Northern Areas chapter, since in practical terms they form part of the KKH route.

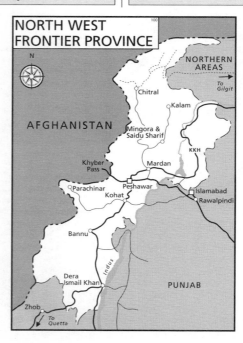

NORTH WEST
FRONTIER PROVINCE

N

NORTHERN
AREAS

To Gilgit

Chitral

Kalam

AFGHANISTAN

Mingora &
Saidu Sharif

KKH

Khyber
Pass

Mardan

Parachinar

Peshawar

Islamabad

Kohat

Rawalpindi

Bannu

Indus

Dera
Ismail Khan

PUNJAB

Zhob

To
Quetta

Land and life

Geography

NWFP covers an area of over 100,000 sq km (including the Tribal Areas). At the heart of the province is the **Peshawar valley**, often referred to as the Vale of Peshawar. Its rich alluvial soils, watered by the Kabul and Swat rivers, make this amongst the most productive agricultural regions in Pakistan. The Peshawar valley divides NWFP into two distinctive parts.

To the S a series of basins proceed in a step-like fashion down to the southern extremities of the region. The Peshawar valley is separated from the **Kohat** basin to the S by the arid Khattack Hills. Next is the **Bannu** basin with its fertile oases and S of this, across the Marwat range, are the semi-arid desert expanses of the **Derajat**. Geologically the area consists of sedimentary rocks from the Tertiary era, part of the Indian Peninsula which broke away from a vast southern landmass of *Gondwanaland* about 100 million years ago.

To the N are the fertile valleys of Swat and Hazara, followed by the high mountains of the Hindu Kush and Shandur. The geological and tectonic processes at work here are closely linked to those responsible for the Karakoram and Himalayas to the West.

Mountains

The rugged and heavily glaciated **Hindu Kush** range (literally 'Hindu killer') raise a formidable barrier along the western and northern border with Afghanistan. Averaging over 6,000m, the highest mountain **Tirich Mir** reaches 7,708m. Further N the **Pamir** mountains with their high plateaux reach over into the Wakhan Corridor and the Central Asian states of the former Soviet Union. The lower **Shandur** range (referred to during colonial times as the Hindu Raj) separates the Gilgit river basin to the N from the hills and mountains of Dir, Swat

and Indus Kohistan. In the S, the **Safed Koh** mountains, averaging 3,600m (the highest peak **Sikeram** reaches 4,760m), run E-W from around the Khyber pass and, along with the **Waziristan** hills to the S, also form a boundary with Afghanistan. The northern extremities of the **Suleiman** range also reach into the province from Baluchistan.

Passes

The mountainous barrier between NWFP and Afghanistan formed by the Hindu Kush, Safed Koh and Waziristan hills is cut by several passes. The most famous is the Khyber, although the Kurram, Tochi and Gomal to the S and the Nama, Dorah and others to the N were equally if not more important in terms of invasion and migration. Internally, the Lowari and Shandur passes are two of the most important, providing the only land routes into the isolated district of Chitral.

River valleys

Five major river valleys dominate the northern half of the province, all running along a roughly NE-SW alignment, the Chitral, Dir, Swat, Indus and Kaghan valleys. The **Chitral valley** is the most remote, situated in the extreme NW of the province. Its river is known as the Yarkhund, Mastuj, Chitral and Kunar at different points along its course. The **Dir valley**, drained by the Panjkora river system which joins the Swat River shortly before it reaches the Peshawar valley, provides a vital access route to Chitral by way of the Lowari Pass. The **Swat valley** is intensively cultivated and densely populated. The Swat River also forms the most important tributary of the Kabul. The **Indus valley** passes through the NWFP, cutting through the wild and desolate Kohistan mountain region before emerging onto the Punjab plains near Attock. The **Kaghan valley**, situated in Hazara District, is the only part of the province E of the Indus. It is drained by the Kunhar River and before the completion of the Karakoram Highway in 1978 provided the main access route to Gilgit and the Northern Areas via the Babusar Pass.

Unlike the rivers of the N which follow the major trends of the mountain ranges, the rivers in the S cut across the grain of the Wazir and Suleiman ranges to reach the Indus. They are also highly seasonal, often only carrying water after severe summer thunderstorms.

Climate

The southern half of NWFP in particular is extremely dry, receiving just 150 mm annually. Temperatures meanwhile vary dramatically both annually and diurnally. From May through to Sep they often reach as high as 45°C in the day, making the summer months an uncomfortable time to travel in this area. In contrast, during the winter, the days are cooler and fresher, while night time temperatures can drop to below freezing, even as far S as Dera Ismail Khan.

The fertile Peshawar basin gets the benefit of rainfall from both the SW monsoon and from westerly depressions, with annual rainfall averaging 350 mm, most of it falling during Aug. Temperatures reflect the pattern to the S, reaching well into the 40s between May and Sep. During Oct and Nov, the weather is clear and settled, and the temperatures mild. Until Apr, daytime temperatures average 14°C, dipping to around freezing at night.

The lower sections of the Swat, Indus and Kaghan valleys receive over 600 mm annually, much in the SW monsoon, and are generally fertile and well wooded. However even certain areas receiving more than 800 mm often seem semi-arid, usually due to acute deforestation and overgrazing. Further N, rainfall averages less than 100 mm and the area is a mountainous desert relying exclusively on irrigation for cultivation. The

higher altitudes give a cooler, more pleasant climate in summer, especially in the Swat and Kaghan valleys where there is more rainfall. Further N however, where the valleys are dry and bare, summer temperatures often reach 40°C during the day. During winter, areas above 1,500m are extremely cold. In Chitral, temperatures of -15°C are not uncommon in Dec and most of the passes are closed by snow from late Nov until early Mar.

Pre-history

The first agricultural communities are thought to have evolved approximately 10,000 years ago on the western flanks of the Indus plain. From these early settlements, the Indus Valley civilisation, centred on the great cities of Moenjo Daro and Harappa, but encompassing much of present day NWFP, developed (see page 159).

Ancient Empires

The **Gandharan** Empire began to evolve from the 6th century BC as a small semi-independent kingdom. Although it remained intact until the 11th century AD, it was continually and fundamentally influenced by invaders who came through the passes to the N and W, and from the Ganges valley to the E. In the 6th century BC, it became the easternmost province of the **Archaemenid** Empire under **Darius the Great**. In 327 BC **Alexander the Great** briefly conquered Gandhara. When he withdrew, the **Mauryan** Empire based in the lower Ganges basin, gained control. **Asoka** promoted Buddhism and his famous Rock Edicts can be found at Shabaz Garhi and Nowsehra in NWFP. After Asoka's death in 232 BC, Gandhara once again came under the influence of Central Asia. The **Bactrian Greeks** built new cities at Taxila and Pushkalavati (present day Charsadda) only to be displaced by the nomadic tribes of the **Scythians** and **Parthians** in turn.

The **Kushan** Empire brought relative stability. By the 2nd century AD it controlled much of the subcontinent. Peshawar became the imperial winter capital, and under **Kanishka**, the most famous Kushan king (AD 128-151), Buddhism flourished again. Monasteries and stupas were built throughout Gandhara, which became an important holy land. Extensive trade with the Roman Empire and China along the Great Silk Route brought widespread prosperity.

By the end of the 3rd century AD, Gandhara had been absorbed by the **Sassanian** Empire. In the 5th century **White Huns** (Hephthalites) invaded from the NW bringing chaos and destruction. Buddhism declined before a resurgent Hinduism, and only survived in the upper Swat valley.

Islam and the Mughals

The earliest evidence of Islam in the NWFP comes from a stone tablet with Arabic and Sanskrit inscriptions (now in Peshawar Museum) dating from 857 AD which was found in the Tochi Valley of Waziristan. However, it was not until the 11th century that **Mahmud of Ghazni** began a series of raids through the province into the Punjab, incorporating the region into the **Ghaznavid** Empire and initiating conversions to Islam. The **Ghorid** Empire ruled by the Turkish Muslims of Ghor in present day Afghanistan followed, and marked the beginnings of the **Delhi Sultanate**.

Islam was also spread by *Shahihs* of the Sufi order. These mystics preached amongst the people, especially in the E and W of the subcontinent, where Islam became the religion of the masses. The greatest challenge to the Sultanate came from the **Mongol** hordes of **Ghengis Khan** who swept through the province reaching the Indus in 1221 and later from **Tamerlane** (Timur the Lame)

who sacked Delhi in 1399. However the Sultanate survived until it fell to **Babur**, the displaced descendant of the House of Timur, and first of the great Mughals, at the beginning of the 16th century.

NWFP was ruled by the **Mughals** until the beginning of the 18th century. Peshawar flourished as a regional capital. However, outside of the Peshawar valley they exercised minimal control over the Pathan tribes. After the death of **Aurangzeb** in 1707, Peshawar was controlled by the **Durranis** of Afghanistan until 1818 when the **Sikhs**, under **Ranjit Singh**, 'the lion of the Punjab', captured the city. He destroyed Babur's Shalimar Gardens and Bala Hisar fort and razed much of the city.

British

By the start of the 19th century the British had not yet extended their empire into present day Pakistan. In the 1820s the NW border ran from Simla along the line of the Sutlej into the deserts of Rajasthan and then down to the Arabian Sea. Punjab and the tribal lands of the NW Frontier were still ruled by the Sikhs; beyond lay the undefined territories of Afghanistan. While the British had established 'satisfactory' relations with the Sikhs, the Afghans (arch enemies of the Sikhs) were an unknown quantity. Moreover, the British were concerned at the perceived threat of Russian expansion into South Asia, and feared that Afghanistan would provide the access route.

Afghan pride had been seriously wounded over the loss of Peshawar to the Sikhs, and **Dost Mohammad**, who was on the throne in Kabul, was keen to regain the city. In 1836 **Alexander Burnes** led a mission to Kabul, hoping to gain the allegiance of Dost Mohammad. His task was however complicated by the fact that the British were undecided on the question of Peshawar; on the one hand they could hardly afford to antagonize the Sikhs by handing

Peshawar back to him, but on the other hand, nothing less would satisfy Dost Mohammad. Sir Olaf Caroe comments that "It has never been sufficiently stressed that the desire to posses Peshawar....was the real cause of the First Afghan War".

In the event, Burnes was outmanoeuvred by the Russians who offered to support Dost if he were to attack the Sikhs. At the same time, Herat to the W (at that time an independent kingdom opposed to Kabul) came under siege from a Persian force supported by the Russians. Burnes's mission had failed and he was forced to return to India. The British opted to install a sympathetic ruler, acceptable to the Sikhs, on the throne of Kabul. In 1838 the **Tripartite Treaty** was signed between the British, Ranjit Singh and **Shah Shuja**, a Durrani and former ruler of Kabul. The British despatched their **Army of the Indus**, invading Afghanistan and installing Shah Shuja on the throne. In 1841 the Afghans got their revenge, killing Shah Shuja and the two British envoys, Burnes and Macnaghten, and triggering a general uprising. The Army of the Indus, still in occupation of Kabul, started its retreat. They were shown no mercy by the Afghans; in what was later described as worst ever defeat of the British army in Asia, just one man, Dr William Brydon, reached Jalalabad alive. "Thus is verified" wrote a civilian captive who was later rescued, "what we were told before leaving Kabul; that Mohammad Akbar would annihilate the whole army except one man, who should reach Jalalabad to tell the tale". A year later the British returned with a second army to seek revenge in Kabul, before marching "as swiftly as terrain and dignity permitted" back to British India.

Meanwhile, the death of Ranjit Singh in 1839 signalled the beginning of the end for Sikh power in the region. Two major wars with the Sikhs, in 1845 and 1848, followed before the British formally annexed the Punjab and NWFP. Initially the whole region was controlled from Lahore, by occupying frontier forts and maintaining military roads between them. Outside the settled areas, agreements were made with the tribes, in an attempt to maintain peaceful relations in return for subsidies and allowances.

In 1893 the **Durand line** was drawn up, dividing British India from Afghanistan. The border cut through the tribal areas of the Pathans and they rose up in series of revolts in 1897, fearing that the British '*Forward Policy*' advocating more direct control of the region would compromise their freedom and independence. 70,000 troops were mobilized in seven military operations to put down the rebellion which led **Lord Curzon** to establish the North West Frontier as a separate province administered from Peshawar in 1901. The British never really attempted to rule the province directly. Instead they allowed the small chiefs of the tribal areas to govern themselves under the watchful eye of a Political Agent. However, force was continually necessary to maintain the status quo. As late as 1937, 40,000 British troops took part in a series of campaigns which ultimately left the tribes of Waziristan "masters of their own house".

Independence

Initially at least, the Independence Movement throughout British India was dominated by the exploits of MK Gandhi, who puzzled, confused and worried the British with his non-violent resistance to Imperial Rule. However, Gandhi was joined also by another, much more improbable champion of non-violence. In the hills of the NW Frontier, another great leader emerged. **Abdul Gaffar Khan**, the son of the Khan of a small village, found Gandhi's non-violence to be deeply compatible with his own Islamic faith. Working amongst some of the most violent and lawless Pathan tribes of the Frontier, he inspired such deep respect and obedience that he was able to raise an army of around 100,000 Pathans committed, under oath, to resist the British through entirely non-violent means.

That the Pathans, whose sacrosanct code of tribal honour requires them to seek revenge, or *badal*, for any insult, should renounce violence in the face of repeated humiliation, and indeed slaughter, at the hands of the British, was incredible. And yet Abdul Gaffar Khan (who became known as the 'Frontier Gandhi'), succeeded in forming such a force, which he named the **Khudai Khidmatgars**, meaning 'Servants of God'.

The British suppressed the Independence Movement in NWFP particularly ruthlessly. The region was seen as being of crucial strategic significance, guarding the 'Gateway of India' from the aggressive designs of Tsarist Russia. They were deeply suspicious of this army of 'non-violent' Pathans; after decades of guerrilla war they saw it as a contradiction in terms. NWFP was ruled by what amounted to draconian martial law and the full extent of the repression hidden from the public eye. Later the Khan wrote "The British feared a non-violent Pathan more than a violent one... All the horrors the British perpetrated on the Pathans had only one purpose; to provoke them to violence".

For all the selfless sacrifice and single-minded determination of Abdul Ghaffar Khan and his followers, they were in the end ignored and discredited. Like Gandhi, Ghaffar Khan opposed the partition of India as demanded by the Muslim League. Indeed NWFP, choosing the Khudai Khidmatgars over the Muslim League, had originally voted to join India. But at the insistence of the Muslim League and in the end Mountbatten, a second referendum was held, and in his desperation to avoid an explosion of communal violence, Ghaffar Khan instructed the Khudai Khidmatgars to abstain. Thus NWFP became a part of an independent Pakistan, ruled by the former Muslim League. Abdul Ghaffar Khan pledged his support for Pakistan, but lobbied hard for an united Pathan province – 'Pakhtunistan' – within Pakistan. The newly founded state of Pakistan, at war with India over Kashmir, arrested the Khan for 'formenting open sedition' (a charge identical to the one repeatedly levelled at him by the British) and sentenced him to 3 years rigourous imprisonment.

As Eknath Easwaran comments, "within less than a year of the night that Mountbatten handed over the reigns of power to India and Pakistan, Mahatma Gandhi had been assassinated by a Hindu who feared he was pro-Muslim and Abdul Ghaffar Khan had been jailed by an Islamic government who claimed he was pro-Hindu".

Post independence

Successive regimes made extensive efforts to integrate the Pathans, initiating generous education and agricultural programmes and encouraging permanent settlements, well connected by roads to market outlets. The aim was to try to persuade the tribesmen to exploit the resources of the frontier rather than its strategic location; to live on the land rather than off it. On the other hand, the system of administration has changed little from the British period, particularly in the Tribal Areas, which maintain a large degree of autonomy from the rest of the province. Development has consequently been slow, with the remotest parts of the province remaining amongst the most backward in Pakistan.

The Soviet invasion of **Afghanistan** in Dec 1979 led to approximately 3 million refugees flooding across the border into some 350 refugee camps, mostly in NWFP. Billions of dollars in foreign aid flooded into Pakistan and the social, political and economic make up of the province was fundamentally changed. Many of the refu-

THE WAY OF THE PATHANS

The **Pukhtunwali** (way of the Pathans) is a strict moral code of behaviour. Hospitality (*Melmastia*) is fundamental to the Pathan code and is extended without question to all strangers and guests. Even the poorest members of Pathan society are expected to adhere to the principle of melmastia, often at great personal sacrifice. Related to this is the concept of *Panah*, by which a Pathan is bound to offer refuge to anyone who asks it. This even extends to protecting a sworn enemy, should they demand it. Once the protected person leaves his host's territory, he once again becomes fair game. Revenge (*Badal*) is the driving force behind the endless cycle of bloody feuding which plagues Pathan society. According to their code, a Pathan must avenge any insult against him or his family or tribe if he is to keep his honour. Traditionally, badal is taken as a result of quarrels over '*zar, zan, zamin*' (gold, women, land). The obligations of badal are shared by all clan members, and can be passed down from generation to generation until they have been fulfilled. The only escape from this cycle is through *Nanawati* (literally 'giving in'), whereby a tribesman or family can go to the aggrieved party and ask them to drop their vow of revenge. Such a request carries with it a connotation of shame, while the other party is under no obligation to accept. It does however provide a mechanism for forgiveness, albeit a rarely utilised one. *Nang*, the Pathan code of honour, is shaped by pride (*Ghairet*), bravery (*Tura*), generosity (*Khegara*) and respect (*Wafa*) and determines an individual's or group's standing in society; failure to uphold these virtues brings disgrace (*Tor*) and ridicule (*Paighor*).

The *Jirga*, or council of elders, is the institution whereby clan decisions are reached, theoretically on a consensus basis. It acts as an executive, judicial and legislative body, and is also commonly used as an instrument of arbitration and conciliation in the case of long-running disputes. The decisions reached at a jirga are binding and cannot be challenged. The jirga also regulates relations with the outside world. Indeed, the jirgas have proved vital in negotiations between the provincial and federal governments and the Tribal Areas. Where a jirga reaches a decision requiring action on a community level, a *Lashkar* may be assembled; essentially a small army gathered from amongst the clans and tribes, entrusted with the task of carrying out the jirga's decision.

The *Hujra* is still very much a feature of Pathan village society. Originally Hujras were established as guest houses by the wealthier members of a village. Later their role broadened to become a focus for the social life of the village; a place where everyone could gather to discuss local matters, exchange views and catch up on news.

gees became integrated into the local economy; in Peshawar for example (and many other cities in the province), Afghans have a virtual monopoly over transport services. Following the Soviet withdrawal in 1992 and the subsequent fall of the Najibullah regime, there were hopes that the refugees would be able to return and start to rebuild their country. However, in the wake of the ongoing civil war between the various factions, few have returned home. Humanitarian assistance to Afghans meanwhile, administered for years on an extensive scale by the UNHCR, as well as numerous NGOs, is now being withdrawn. The implications for the remaining refugees, and for the already strained relations between them and their Pakistani hosts, is not promising.

Culture

People

Approximately 90% of the population are **Pathans** (or **Pukhtuns**). Numbering up to 18 million people and inhabiting North Baluchistan, East Afghanistan and the NWFP, they are one of the largest tribal societies in the world. Divided into numerous sub-tribes and clans, the Pathans are a fiercely independent people constantly feuding amongst themselves and ever hostile to any threat to their freedom. Mughals, Afghans, Sikhs, British and Russians tried to control them, and while those tribes that settled on the plains may have paid taxes and token tribute to their temporary rulers, the semi-nomadic tribes of the hills have never been subdued.

Many Pathan tribes claim a common ancestry from a man called **Quais** who was sent by the Prophet to spread Islam in Afghanistan. One of his sons, *Afghana*, had four sons, who left Afghanistan to settle in different parts of the province as founding fathers of the various tribes. In contrast the **Wazirs** claim to be one of the lost tribes of Israel which migrated E, converted to Islam and finally settled in Waziristan. However it is thought that Pathans originated from an ethnic group in Afghanistan.

The NWFP's non-Pathan populations are mostly in Chitral and Hazara districts. The **Khowar** language of the **Chitralis**, who call their land *Kho*, relates them closely with the nomadic groups of the Wakhan and Pamir regions. Hazara district consists mainly of **Hindko** speaking tribes whose language and culture are closely related to that of the Punjabis to the S. The **Kalash** are a small ethnic group found in the valleys of Humbur, Bumburet and Birir. Their fair complexions led early visitors to liken them to "handsome Europeans, with brown hair and blue eyes" believed to be descendants of Alexander's armies. More probably, they are related to an ancient Indo-Aryan group from Afghanistan.

Language

Pashto, the language of the Pathans, is the most widely spoken language in NWFP. It has evolved into numerous dialects in the isolated valleys of the province. Indeed, the distinction between 'Pathan' and 'Pakhtun', is essentially a linguistic one, with the tribes to the N, such as the Afridis, Orakzais, Shinwaris and Bangash speaking the harder Pakhtu, while those in the S, such as the Durranis, speak the softer Pashto. **Urdu** is also widely spoken, along with **English**, although in remoter rural areas, Pashto dominates. In addition to Khowar and Hindko, mentioned above, **Seraiki** is spoken amongst the Seraiki minority found in parts of southern NWFP, particularly around Dera Ismain Khan. The **Kalash** language is related to the Dardic group of Indo-European languages, suggesting a Central Asian origin.

Literature

Despite their fearsome reputation, the Pathans also have a rich culture which belies their 'savage' image. Their literary and poetical traditions in particular are very strong. **Khushal Khattak Khan** (1613-1689), a powerful chief of the Khattak tribe, is perhaps the best loved and most celebrated of the Pashto poets. He passed on a huge body of poetry, mostly orally, covering the great passions of the Pathan tribal society. He also wrote extensively in Persian on medicine, ethics, philosophy and religion. The '*Tarikh-e-Murassa*', compiled by his grandson Afzal Khan, is an important historical source.

Abdur Rahman (better known as Rahman Baba) a Sufi poet contemporary with Khushal's grandson Afzal, also holds a special place in Pathan poetry. His works are primarily religious and owe their popularity to their direct and simple style.

Modern NWFP

Government and politics

Nearly a third of NWFP is designated Federally Administered Tribal Areas (FATA), consisting of seven Agencies – Bajour, Mohmand, Khyber, Orakzai, Kurram and North and South Waziristan – along the border with Afghanistan which are administered directly by the federal government through a Political Agent (PA). In addition there are a number of tribal areas which are administered directly by the provincial government (PATA). The remaining settled areas are divided into Divisions and Districts administered by a Commissioner and Deputy Commissioner respectively, in the same way as Pakistan's other provinces.

Traditionally the federal and provincial governments have interfered little in the Agencies, being content, like the

---

SHARIAT LAW IN MALAKAND

Malakand Division (encompassing Malakand Agency and the districts of Buner, Swat, Dir and Chitral) is officially designated as a Provincially Administered Tribal Area (PATA). For years this had resulted in a dual judicial system, in some cases based on standard Pakistani law, and in others on the tribal *Jirga* system. In 1989 the Peshawar High Court ruled the jirga system to be in violation of the constitution and banned it. The decision was challenged in the Supreme Court, but finally, in Feb 1994, it was upheld.

The 1989 ruling resulted in a campaign for the introduction of *Shariat*, or Islamic law (seen by many to have been embodied in the banned jirga system), headed by one Maulana Sufi Mohammad, who established the Tehrik-e-Nifaze-e-Shariat-e-Mohammadi (TNSM). In May 1994 the government bowed to pressure from the movement following demonstrations and road blockades and agreed to set up a system of Shariat law. However in Nov 1994 trouble suddenly flared up again, with militants storming a local administrator's office and holding two judges and three other government officials hostage. Word quickly spread of a *jihad* against the government and by the evening the airport at Saidu Sharif had been seized. Later a government minister died trying to escape from the militants. The federal government was quick to intervene, sending in the Frontier Corps and Frontier Constabulary, although order was only restored after prolonged fighting and finally, pleas from Sufi Mohammad himself for an end to the carnage. However, the TNSM's demands were ultimately met, with the passing of what is commonly referred to as the Nifaze Shariat Regulation. Effectively the dual system was restored, with litigants being given the option of taking their disputes before a judge or *Qazi*, to be decided according to Shariat law if they wished.

However, the situation flared up again in June 1995. This time Sufi Mohammad claimed that the Qazis who had been appointed to administer Shariat law were simply government judges under a different name, and demanded that the TNSM be given the right to appoint its own Qazis. Sufi Mohammad is even said to have demanded that all Qazis should have beards! There were isolated outbreaks of violence, although nothing like on the scale of the previous year. This time however the unrest coincided with the height of the tourist season in Swat, and had a devastating impact on an industry which is vital to the livelihoods of many in the valley. The issue of Shariat law in Pakistan remains a delicate one, with many claiming that in an Islamic State it is only right that Islamic law should apply.

British before them, to leave them to manage their own affairs. During the war in Afghanistan the cultivation and production of hashish and opium, already well established, flourished into a major industry and source of income for mujahideen commanders. In recent years the government has come under increasing pressure to control production, leading it into direct confrontation with many of the tribal groups. In 1995 the government arrested a notorious arms and drugs trafficker from Bara in Khyber Agency and later bulldozed his headquarters. The tribes of the area were outraged at what they saw as a government intrusion and violation of their rights, and raised a *Lashkar* of well armed men, threatening to march on Peshawar in revenge. It was only after a series of hastily arranged meetings between the Political Agent and the *Jirgas* of the various tribes involved, that the situation was diffused.

On the whole the province is relatively stable politically. The **Awami National Party**, successors to Abdul Gaffar Khan's Khudai Khidmatgars, are however still agitating for an independent Pathan homeland of **Pukhtunistan** within Pakistan. They are not generally considered to be a major threat, although the situation in Afghanistan certainly gives the government cause for concern. Many observers point out that there is a strong likelihood of Afghanistan fragmenting along ethnic lines, which would almost certainly result in an independent Pathan state just across the border from NWFP, a scenario which could easily destabilize the province.

Education

The overall level of literacy at the time of the 1981 census was estimated at 16.7%, an abysmally low figure even for that time. The disparity between male and female literacy is even more depressing; 25.9% for men and just 6.5% for women. Similarly the disparity between rural and urban areas is equally large; 35.8% in urban areas (47% male, 21.9% female) and 13.2% in rural areas (21.7% male, 3.8% female). Under British rule, education was largely ignored. The tribal chiefs openly opposed education, fearful that it would undermine their authority, and the British were likewise nervous of the consequences of arousing the political consciousness of the population in this sensitive and barely controllable area. Today the greatest obstacles to improving the literacy rate, particularly amongst women, is the resistance from a conservatively tribal and Islamic society. Quite apart from the restrictions inherent in the strict system of Purdah which operates in all but the largest urban centres, the idea of female education remains vaguely threatening in a male-dominated society. In rural areas the problem is compounded by the absence of a system of education relevant to the people it is aimed at. A poor peasant farmer can see little value in sending his children to school when they might be gainfully employed helping him farm his land. If anything education is often seen as being in direct conflict with the interests and needs of rural communities; certainly, in areas where there is little hope of gaining paid employment, its value is easily questioned.

Economy

Agriculture

Agriculture in the NWFP is severely handicapped by the harsh physical environment and is largely dependant on irrigation. Feudal systems of landownership, the fragmentation of land due to population pressure and the loss of fertile land through soil erosion, waterlogging and salinity, have added further problems. Many of the hill tribes in the region are semi-nomadic pastoralists who farm to augment their bare subsistence.

The Peshawar valley, despite its relatively small area, is highly productive due to its fertile alluvial soils and plentiful irrigation water from the Swat and Kabul rivers. The best land is largely devoted to cash crops, in particular **sugar cane** and **tobacco**, and to orchards of oranges, plums, peaches, guavas and pears. On partly irrigated land, the staples wheat and maize are grown as well as some vegetables. Some dairy farming is also practised. The *barani* (unirrigated) land is generally sown with a single *rabi* (winter) crop of wheat.

South of the Peshawar valley, the main crops are wheat, barley, maize, the millets *jowar* and *bajra*, and pulses – a major source of protein. Some rice, sugarcane and fruit are also grown particularly around Bannu. In the Dera Ismail Khan district, farmers use **rod-kohi** or hill torrent cultivation. The seasonal torrents of the Suleiman and Waziristan hills are blocked by temporary dams and the water carefully fed into selected fields below. It is a precarious system, and the dams are often swept away and crops ruined.

In the valleys N of Peshawar agriculture is irrigation based with barley, wheat, millets and pulses, and some rice, vegetables and fruit. The Swat valley however is particularly fertile and intensively cultivated. Maize, a relatively recent import from South America, is the most important crop, followed by rice and barley. The lower Kaghan valley and parts of Hazara district are similarly fertile, receiving adequate monsoon rainfall.

Over the last 15 years or so the Tribal Areas bordering Afghanistan have seen a massive growth in the illegal cultivation of opium. The war in Afghanistan displaced much of the cultivation across the border, and an expanding market in the west and the enormous profit margins have made it an important crop, despite government efforts to eradicate it.

Industry and resources

Industry is extremely limited, mostly related to the processing of tobacco and sugarcane. The redrying plant at **Akora Khattack** near Nowshera, handles 90% of the province's Virginia tobacco crop, mostly for export. Sugar refineries cater for local demand. Cottage industries play an important role, especially in the northern districts, where handwoven woollen cloth is made into shawls, hats, blankets, rugs etc. **Darra**, 40 km S of Peshawar, is the centre for a booming gun making industry. Tourism is relatively undeveloped at present. The picture is starting to change however, with concerted efforts to attract tourists to this fascinating and varied region.

The only mineral deposits of any significance are found in Kohat district on the edge of the Salt Range. Three salt mines, the Bahadur Khel, Jatta and Karak, exist in a 15 km radius around Teri. The industry is an ancient one and the mines are known to have been in operation since recorded history.

There are significant reserves of timber, especially in the Swat and Kaghan valleys, although without proper management, deforestation has become a major problem. The province also has considerable hydro-electric generating potential. The Tarbela Dam, on the border with Punjab, and Warsak Project, to the N of Peshawar, are the two largest in operation although many smaller ones exist.

PESHAWAR

Peshawar, the capital of NWFP, lies on the western edge of the Vale of Peshawar, just 50 km from the Khyber Pass. With the atmosphere of a rough-cut frontier town, and yet also a long and rich history, the name has always been a romantic one. Today it is a large and rapidly growing city, overlain by a succession of influences; the old city with its densely packed bazaars, the spacious tree-lined avenues of the British Cantonment area, the University town, the modern commercial area of Saddar, and more recently, the new residential areas such as Hayatabad and the sprawling refugee camps that sprang up following the Soviet invasion of Afghanistan. On the surface, Peshawar is a chaotic, crowded and polluted city, much like any other in Pakistan, but it has a distinct character of its own, and much of its historical flavour still thrives in the fascinating bazaars of the old city.

History

The city's origins are unclear. The earliest written record, a **Kharoshthi** rock inscription at Ara, near Attock, dated 119 AD, referred to it as *Poshapura* meaning "City of Flowers". The Kushan king *Kanishka* is thought to have moved his winter capital from Pushkalavati to Peshawar, at which time the city became a major pilgrimage centre. Various Buddhist sites have been identified with locations in the modern-day city, the most important being **Shah-ji-ki-Dheri**, site of the Kanishka Vihara, a large monastery and stupa complex. The site was excavated by Spooner in 1907, who discovered the famous bronze reliquary casket of Kanishka, now on display in Peshawar Museum. Nothing remains of the site itself.

After the decline of the Kushans, Peshawar fell to the Sassanians for a period and then reverted to a new dynasty of Kushans, the Kidar (little) Kushans, before being overrun by White Huns in the 5th century AD. They were followed by the Turki and Hindu Shahis in the 6-7th century AD, although little is known about the fate of the city during this period, except that the Hindu Shahis appear to have shifted their capital from Peshawar to Hund on the banks of the Indus. This move appears to have coincided with the spread of Afghan (Pathan) tribes into the Peshawar valley. Later, at the start of the 11th century, Mahmoud of Ghazni invaded, extending the Ghaznavid Empire to include the city of Peshawar. Following the destruction of the Ghaznavid Empire at the hands of the Ghorids, Peshawar found itself on the margins of both the Central Asian and Indian empires, and all but disappeared from historical records.

The city next acquired importance during the Mughal period, when it flourished as a regional capital. The Mughals planted trees, laid out gardens

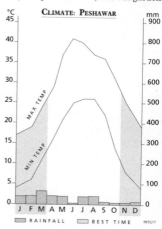

CLIMATE: PESHAWAR

MAX TEMP

MIN TEMP

RAINFALL   BEST TIME

PKTG17

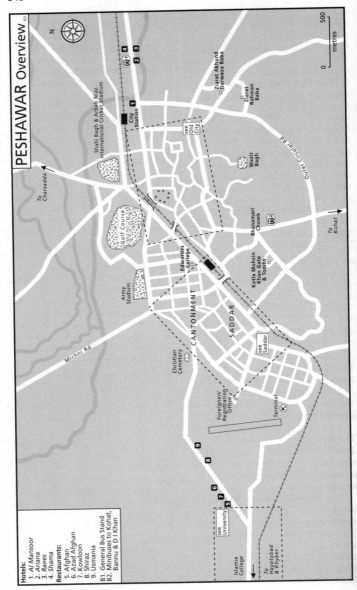

PESHAWAR Overview

N

metres
0   500

To Charsadda

Shahi Bagh & Arbab Niaz International Cricket Stadium

City Station

Ziarat Akhund Darweza Baba

Ziarat Rahman Baba

Wazir Bagh

Outer Circular Rd

Golf Course

Bhanamari Chowk

Kotia Mohsin Khan Gate & Tombs

To Kohat

Army Stadium

Edwardes College

CANTONMENT

SADDAR

see Old City

see Saddar

Michni Rd

Christian Cemetery

Foreigners' Registration Office

Terminal

Islamia College

see University

To Hayatabad & Khyber

Hotels:
1. Al Mansoor
2. Ariana
3. Raees
4. Shama

Restaurants:
5. Afghan
6. Azad Afghan
7. Kowloon
8. Shiraz
9. Usmania

B1. General Bus Stand
B2. Minibuses to Kohat, Bannu & D I Khan

and built forts and mosques; their monuments are amongst the few to have survived the city's long and turbulent history. The present form of the city's name is attributed to Akbar who changed it from the Persian '*Parshawar*' to Peshawar, meaning "Frontier Town". After the decline of the Mughals, the Durranis of Afghanistan gained a firm hold of Peshawar for a time, before being driven out by the Sikh Empire of Ranjit Singh. The city became a major bone of contention between the Durranis and Sikhs, before the British, extending their empire to the N and W, finally brought it under their control.

Places of interest

The Old City

The old city was formerly completely encircled by a wall and centred on a citadel, in traditional Central Asian style. Today the wall and its 16 gates survive for the most part only in name. The **Bala Hisar**, the most imposing landmark, is almost certainly the site of the ancient citadel mentioned by the Chinese pilgrim Hiuen Tsang in 629 AD. This fortified stronghold was the key to control of Peshawar and changed hands many times. When Babur arrived in 1509, he occupied and strengthened the existing fort and laid out the **Shalimar Gardens**.

After the decline of the Mughals, the Durranis of Afghanistan controlled Peshawar until 1818. The fort at this time was in magnificent condition, as described by Elphinstone when he visited in 1809.

"The throne was covered with a cloth adorned with pearls, on which lay a sword and a small mace set with jewels. The room was open all round. The centre was supported by four high pillars, in the midst of which was a large fountain. The floor was covered with the richest carpets, and round the edges were slips of silk embroidered with gold. The view from the hall was beautiful. Immediately below was an extensive garden, full of cypresses and other trees and beyond was a plain of richest verdure."

The Bala Hisar and the Shalimar Gardens were destroyed by Ranjit Singh who later rebuilt the Fort of mud. The present fort was built by the British, who replaced the mud walls with 'pucca' brick. Now occupied by the Pakistani military, it is closed to the public. **NB** No photography in the vicinity.

The Bazaars

The bazaars of the Old City are a kaleidoscope of colours, noise, smells and atmosphere. Crowds of people jostle with cars, bicycles, donkey carts and rickshaws down narrow streets. Narrower alleys lead off from the main streets, concealing even more colourful and atmospheric bazaars with everything from vegetables to ornate gold and silver jewellery. Trades tend to group together on the whole, though less so than in the past. A brief description of the main bazaars is given below, although there are many more; perhaps the best thing is simply wander at will. For the serious shopper, the Old City is a wonderful hunting ground, although it is not for those in a hurry. Deals are negotiated unhurriedly over cups of green tea ('*khawar*') and endless small-talk, interspersed with serious bargaining.

The main route into the Old City from Saddar is over Jail Bridge. Straight on at Shuba Chowk leads to Bajori Rd and **Namak Mandi**, where there are excellent tikka restaurants. Left leads into **Khyber Bazaar**. Most of the street is lined with shops selling electrical goods ranging from air conditioners to hi-fi systems. Towards the end there are the dentists shops with brightly painted signs showing false teeth. Old Kohati Gate is marked by the Kohati Police station. The turning left leads up past Lady Reading Hospital and Bala Hisar

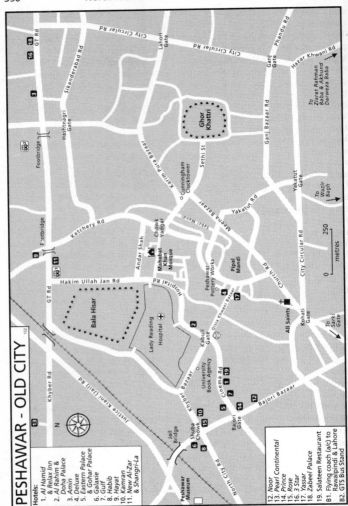

PESHAWAR - OLD CITY

Hotels:
1. Al Hamid & Relax Inn
2. Al Rahim & Doha Palace
3. Amin
4. Deluxe
5. Eastern Palace & Gohar Palace
6. Galaxie
7. Gulf
8. Habib
9. Hayat
10. Kamran
11. New Al-Zar & Shangri-La

12. Noor
13. Pearl Continental
14. Prince
15. Rose
16. 3 Star
17. Yassar
18. Zabeel Palace
19. Salateen Restaurant
B1. Flying coach (a/c) to Rawalpindi & Lahore
B2. GTS Bus Stand

to the GT Rd. Right leads into Cinema Rd and back round towards Namak Mandi. As well as its cinemas and feature bill boards, Cinema Rd is a treasure trove of Indian and Pakistani film-star postcards. Straight on is **Qissa Khawani Bazaar**, or story-tellers bazaar. Here were the '*Khave Khanas*'; tea shops and eating houses where in the past, travellers and traders met to exchange their tales and news of faraway places. Today the tea shops have given way to col-

rink stands, as well as bookshops, lothing, luggage and general stores. urning left at the end, the road runs up ast shops selling **brass and copper-are**. A small turning is signposted to ne left to the *Peshawar Pottery Works*, amous for being twice visited by members of the British royal family. It produces contemporary style items in rong, richly glazed colours. The next urning off to the right is the **Cloth azaar** while straight on is a bazaar elling **tea and spices**. The two streets n parallel, curving off to the right. The ext turning left on either leads up to howk Yadgar. Continuing straight long the Cloth Bazaar takes you past ne bottom of Sabzi Mandi on the left, nen Meena Bazaar and Church Rd to ne left and right, and down towards akatuk Gate. To the S of the cloth maret is **Peepul Mundi**, the main grain holesale area where a peepul tree is elieved to mark the spot where the uddha once preached.

Chowk Yadgar lies at the heart of the ld City. Originally a memorial to Col . C. Hastings, it was replaced by a plaza nd memorial to those who died in the ndo-Pakistani war of 1965. The W side s lined with the shops and stalls of noney changers with their displays of urrencies. An underpass runs under ne plaza from E-W.

Sethi St runs E from Chowk Yadgar. his street was at the heart of the traitional business community and ained its name from the powerful ethi family which at one time conucted highly profitable trade with ussia, China, India and Central Asia. few of the old houses remain, some n precarious states of structural reair, with richly carved wooden doorays and ornate balconies. Inside here are large airy reception rooms nd deep cellars which provided relief rom the summer heat. PTDC's uided tour of Peshawar includes a isit to one of the houses.

The first narrow alley on the left is the **Chappal Market**, selling sandals, followed immediately by the **Vegetable Market**, covered in summer with matting against the heat. Further along is **Cunningham Clocktower**, built in 1900 by Balmukund to celebrate Queen Victoria's Diamond Jubilee, and in honour of Sir George Cunningham who became Governor of NWFP. Around it tanners practice their trade, joined occasionally by fishmongers. **Karim Pura**, the narrow street which forks off left from Sethi St at the Cunningham Clocktower, is also lined with ancient houses with intricately carved woodwork, which are in some ways more impressive, or at least more numerous, than those of Sethi St. The bazaar along here is varied; everything from household goods to meat and spices. Shortly after the clocktower, **Meena Bazaar**(women's bazaar) runs off to the left, where *Burqas* and veils for women are sold along with items of embroidery. If you continue straight this way leads eventually to Kohati Gate and All Saints Church. **Gor Khatri** is at the E end of Sethi St. This large walled compound with its impressive Mughal gateway is today a police headquarters. It is usually possible to wander in and look round, although there is not much left to see. It was originally the site of the '*Tower of the Buddha's Bowl*' where the sacred alms bowl was believed to have been housed. Later it became an important place of Hindu pilgrimage, perhaps as a site for funeral sacrifices or for the initiation of *Yogis*. During the reign of Shah Jahan, his daughter Jahanara Begum converted the place into a *caravanserai* (the existing compound) and built an accompanying mosque. During the Sikh period the mosque was destroyed and replaced with a temple of *Gorakhnath* (Siva) and its subsidiary *Nandi* shrine, the remains of which still stand.

Andarshah Bazaar (meaning 'inner city') runs W from Chowk Yadgar towards Bala Hisar and houses the silver and goldsmiths, selling a wide range of ethnic, antique and modern jewellery. The tiny alleys that lead off to the S from the main street contain many more shops, some with quite rare antique items. About half way along on the N side is an arched gateway into **Mahabat Khan Mosque**. Mahabat Khan was twice governor of Peshawar during the reigns of Shah Jahan and Aurangzeb, and is thought to have built this mosque. It closely resembles the Badshahi Masjid at Lahore, and although much smaller, is beautifully proportioned and an excellent example of Mughal architecture from Shah Jahan's time. During the Sikh period, the two minarets were frequently used as gallows by the Sikh Governor, **Gen Avitabile**, a mercenary of Italian origin who joined Ranjit Singh's court following the Napoleonic wars. The Prayer Hall is decorated with intricate paintwork, aging but still precise and distinct. The fire which swept through Andarshah in 1898 nearly destroyed the mosque but fortunately many of its decorative features were restored.

Other sights around the Old City

All Saints Church Built in 1883 and originally situated in the grounds of the nearby Edwardes High School, this church has a beautiful stained glass chancel window and carved wooden arches. It is open on Sun from 1000-1300, when masses are held. At other times there is a chowkidar in the house opposite who holds the keys.

Ziarat Rahman Baba Situated to the SE of the Old City from Ganj Gate, between Outer Circular Rd and Hazar Khwani Rd, is the shrine of the famous Pashto poet Rahman Baba. There is a new complex here consisting of a library, mosque and shrine, the latter with an imposing white marble dome decorated with blue tiles on the outside and an intricate mirror mozaic on the inside. The much older shrine outside has more character and is a popular meeting place

in the evenings. Just before the turnin[g] right off Hazar Khwani Rd to the shrin[e] there is a small shrine to **Akhund Da[r]weza Baba**, a famous Sufi saint from th[e] Mughal period.

Kotla Mohsin Khan Gate an[d] Tombs Situated SW of Bhanama[n] Chowk, just off Badshahi Rd, this crum[-]bling but impressive gate once forme[d] the entrance to a fortified residence [or] *Kotla*. The identity of Mohsin Khan [is] uncertain. Nearby there are two larg[e] domed tombs; again it is uncertain as [to] who are buried inside. Today they ar[e] home to large numbers of bats.

Cantonment and Saddar Bazaar

British troops first set up camp in wh[at] was to become the cantonment in 184[8]-49. A barbed wire enclosure with 1[6] gates was followed by permanent build[-]ings. Following the classical coloni[al] style, ubiquitous throughout British In[-]dia, a wholly independent town wa[s] built with long wide tree-lined boule[-]vards designed for horse drawn traffi[c] and spacious bungalows set back fro[m] the road, along with all the social infra[-]structure of Government building[s,] schools, churches, clubs etc. The railwa[y] line and station which divides the can[-]tonment from the Old City followe[d.] Today there are still many examples [of] the distinctive Mughal/Gothic architec[-]ture of the British period amongst th[e] more modern buildings, givin[g] glimpses of a bygone age.

Peshawar Museum

Open summer 0830-1230, 1430-170[0,] winter 0900-1600, closed Wed. This clas[-]sic piece of architecture was built i[n] 1905 as the Victoria Memorial Hall. A[ll] the best artefacts from the various stage[s] of Gandharan civilisation, not alread[y] removed from Pakistan, are here or i[n] Lahore Museum. Upstairs are there i[s] an ethnographic section includin[g] wooden carvings from the Kalash val[-]leys. Well presented and worth a visit.

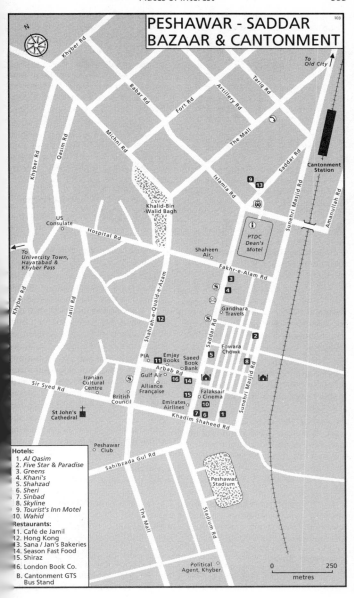

PESHAWAR - SADDAR BAZAAR & CANTONMENT

103

N

Khyber Rd

Babar Rd

Fort Rd

Artillery Rd

Tariq Rd

The Mall

Saddar Rd

To Old City

Cantonment Station

Michni Rd

Qasim Rd

Khyber Rd

Islamia Rd

Khalid-Bin-Walid Bagh

Sunehri Masjid Rd

Amanullah Rd

9

13

US Consulate

Hospital Rd

PTDC Dean's Motel

i

To University Town, Hayatabad & Khyber Pass

Khyber Rd

Jalil Rd

Shahrah-e-Quaid-e-Azam

Shaheen Air

Fakhr-e-Alam Rd

3

4

Gandhara Travels

12

Saddar Rd

2

Fowara Chowk

5

8

PIA

Emjay Books

Saeed Book Bank

11

Arbab Rd

16

14

Gulf Air

Iranian Cultural Centre

British Council

Alliance Française

15

Falaksair Cinema

10

Sir Syed Rd

Emirates Airlines

7

6

1

Sunehri Masjid Rd

St John's Cathedral

Khadim Shaheed Rd

Peshawar Club

Sahibzada Gul Rd

Peshawar Stadium

The Mall

Stadium Rd

Political Agent, Khyber

0   250
metres

Hotels:
1. Al Qasim
2. Five Star & Paradise
3. Greens
4. Khani's
5. Shahzad
6. Sheri
7. Sinbad
8. Skyline
9. Tourist's Inn Motel
10. Wahid

Restaurants:
11. Café de Jamil
12. Hong Kong
13. Sana / Jan's Bakeries
14. Season Fast Food
15. Shiraz
16. London Book Co.

B. Cantonment GTS Bus Stand

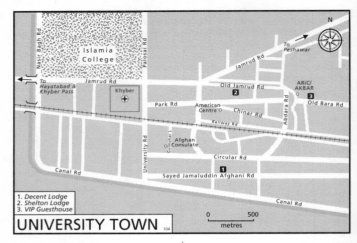

1. Decent Lodge
2. Shelton Lodge
3. VIP Guesthouse

UNIVERSITY TOWN

St John's Cathedral on Sir Sayid Rd, the oldest church in Peshawar (1851-1860), was consecrated by Bishop Cotton of Calcutta. Initially Anglican, it is now Church of Pakistan. Next to it is the **Peshawar Club**, established in 1863 for the British forces in Peshawar (see below), and today living relic of the Raj. **Edwardes College** on the Mall was founded in 1855 by Sir Herbert Edwardes as a school and became a mission college in 1901. **NB** Despite the change in street name nearly 50 years ago, 'The Mall' and 'Sharhah-e-Quaid-e-Azam' are used equally frequently.

Since Independence, the Saddar Bazaar area has grown in size to become the modern commercial centre of Peshawar. The older bazaars are centred on an E-W axis around Fowara Chowk, while Saddar Rd and Arbab Rd have most of the services; banks, restaurants, shopping – both modern consumer goods and carpets, antique jewellery, souvenirs etc – and some hotels.

University Town

Situated 7 km W of Peshawar on Khyber Rd. The impressive **Islamia College** and Collegiate School (1913) was built on a 'parched, barren and uneven tract interspersed by ancient mounds' in Mughal/Gothic style and was followed by the University which was founded in 1930. Today a sprawling residential area of red brick buildings and well kept lawns surrounds the University and various Medical, Engineering, Forestry, Science and Industrial Institutes and Research Councils line the main road.

Further W is the new development of **Hayatabad**, and beyond this, **Smugglers' Bazaar**, selling luxury western goods. At the end of the bazaar is a checkpost which marks the start of **Khyber Agency**. Foreigners are not allowed beyond this point without a permit.

Local information
● Accommodation

Hotel Classifications			
AL	Rs4,000	A	Rs1,800-4,000
B	Rs900-1,800	C	Rs450-900
D	Rs300-450	E	Rs150-300
F	up to Rs150		

There is a wide range of accommodation available both in Saddar and in the Old City. Most of the better hotels are in Saddar/Cantt. Peshawar is relatively expensive for th standard of accommodation. Finding a quiet room is a case of finding a hotel with rooms free at the back, away from the road. The cheaper budget hotels are often extremely basic and far from clean.

Saddar/Cantt: there is little in the way of mid-range accommodation in Saddar. The best in town is the **AL Pearl Continental**, PO Box 197, Khyber Rd, T 276361, F 276456, central a/c, all mod cons, *Marco Polo* restaurant for Pakistani and Continental, *Taipan* for Chinese, terrace barbecue, evening buffet Thur and Fri very good value, the *Gulbar* bar is licensed to serve alcohol to non-Muslims, swimming pool open to non-residents on payment, 18-hole golf course open to guests, conference facilities, shops and services. **A** *Dean's*, 3 Islamia Rd, T 279781, F 279783, a/c normal and deluxe rooms, TV/dish, fridge, real bath, but overpriced, restaurant, open air barbecue, PTDC Information Centre, giftshop, alcohol available to non-Muslims for private consumption, bungalow style in well-kept gardens, parking. **B** *Greens*, Saddar Rd, T 270181, F 276088, normal and deluxe rooms, central a/c, TV/dish, phone, *Lala's Grill* and *China Friendship Restaurant*, *Sehrai* Travel Agents, British Airways Agent, *Ocean Business Centre* for fax, phone, photocopy, printing, stamps and stationary, giftshop. **C** *Khani's*, Saddar Rd, T 277512, a/c, TV/dish, comfortable, also some non a/c rooms (**D** category) and simple rooms on the roof (**F** category), the latter popular with backpackers.

F *Al-Qasim*, Tippu Sultan Rd, T 272052, reasonably clean, good value; **F** *Five Star*, Suneri Masjid Rd, T 276950, noisy, very basic, not rec; next door is the **F** *Paradise*, T 279027, also noisy and basic; **F** *Shahzad*, Saddar Rd, T 275741, hot water in winter, basic but reasonably clean, rooms dark, *Iqbal* restaurant downstairs; **F** *Sheri*, Stadium Chowk, T 278449, basic; **F** *Sinbad*, Saddar Rd, T 275020, hot water in winter, basic but fairly clean, restaurant; **F** *Skyline*, Sunheri Masjid Rd, T 270507, noisy and basic; **F** *Tourists' Inn Motel*, 3 Saddar Rd, T 275632, 3 large dorm rm holding up to 18 beds, 2 double rm, shared bathrooms, hot water, kitchen, common area, parking, popular with backpackers since the closure of Khyber hotel; **F** *Wahid*, Saddar Rd, set back from road, simple but quieter.

Old city: **C** *Galaxie*, Shuba Chowk, Khyber Bazaar, T 212172, a/c rooms, some with TV/dish, hot water in winter, also some non a/c rooms (**D** category), restaurant, parking, centrally located,

popular; **C** *Rose*, Khyber Bazaar, T 250755, a/c, TV, hot water, also non a/c rooms (**E** category), undergoing refurbishment in 1995, *Kababina* restaurant downstairs; **D** *Gohar Palace*, Cinema Rd, T 217562, a/c, reasonable rooms, fairly quiet, also non a/c rooms (**F** category), restaurant; opp is the **E** *Eastern Palace*, Cinema Rd, T 210260, hot water, pleasant/clean, good value; **E** *Habib*, 2 Shoba Bazaar, Railway Rd, T 216219, hot water in winter, also a/c rooms (**C** category), restaurant, small courtyard, parking; **E** *Relax Inn*, Cinema Rd, T 215623, hot water in winter, some TV, clean, good value.

There are lots of **F** category hotels in the Old City. They are basic with little to choose between them. Single women are advised not to stay. **F** *Al-Khaleej*, Ramdas Bazaar, T 216717, basic, hot water in winter, reasonably clean, restaurant, small courtyard, parking; **F** *Al-Rahim*, Hospital Rd, T 211342, basic, jewellery/antique stores in courtyard; **F** *Al-Riaz*, Ramdas Gate, T 210125, hot water in winter, small courtyard, parking; **F** *Doha Palace*, Hospital Rd, T 213437, hot water in winter, basic, small courtyard; **F** *Deluxe*, Qissa Khawani, T 65226, hot water in winter, small rooms; **F** *Gulf*, Cinema Rd, T 210103, hot water, clean/pleasant hotel with balconies, but next to tanners, restaurant; **F** *Noor*, Bajori Rd, T 210916, hot water, clean rooms, some also with a/c and TV (**D** category); **F** *Prince*, Bajori Gate, T 213665, clean rooms, also some a/c (**D** category), restaurant; **F** *Shan*, Khyber Bazaar, T 210668, basic, not very clean; **F** *Shangrila*, Dabgari Gdn, T 210155, basic, hot water in winter, restaurant; **F** *Sharjah*, Dubgari Rd, T 210026, basic, fairly clean, restaurant, small courtyard, parking; **F** *Yassar*, Qissa Khawani, T 21331, very basic.

GT Road: the hotels along GT Rd are generally noisier although there are some good bargains here. **C** *Amin*, T 218215, clean, pleasant rooms, a/c, TV/dish, also non a/c (**E** category), good restaurant, central courtyard, parking, popular with Afghans and local people; **C** *Shangri-la*, opp Firdous Cinema, T 210960, a/c, TV/dish, clean comfortable rooms, restaurant. **D** *Al-Mansoor*, T 213106, F 217608, a/c, hot water, restaurant, courtyard; **D** *Zabeel Palace*, T 218236, a/c and non a/c (**E** category) rooms, clean, good value, courtyard, parking. **F** *Ariana*, opp New Adda, T 252585, basic but reasonable, restaurant, courtyard, parking; **F** *Hayat*, Firdous Chowk, T 218221, set back from main road, also a/c rooms (**D** category), restaurant, courtyard, parking; **F** *New Al-Zar*, opp Firdous Cinema, T 213047, hot water, basic but OK, set slightly back from GT Rd, restaurant; **F** *Raees*, opp bus stand, T 213601, very basic, restaurant; **F** *Three Star*, T 28160, hot water in winter, courtyard with shops on ground floor.

University town/Hayatabad: a long way from the city centre, although Hayatabad is also a centre for NGO offices. A number of very comfortable luxury 'guesthouses' with a/c, TV/dish, fax, phone, catering and airport pick-up have emerged, along the same lines as in Islamabad, mostly serving the NGO community. **B** *Decent Lodge*, 62 D/A Syed Jamaluddin Afghani Rd, T 840221, F 840229; **B** *Shelton House*, 15 B Old Jamrud Rd, T 842087, F 42383; **B** *VIP House*, Old Bara Rd, T 842806, F 843392. **F** *Youth Hostel*, Block B1, Plot No 37, Phase 5 (take the 2nd turning left off GT Rd into Hayatabad, then 1st right, nr water tower and National Bank of Pakistan building), T 813581, several large dorm rooms and some 3-4 bed rooms, kitchen, common room, basic but good value, unfortunately a long way from the centre (walking distance from GT Rd), no shops nearby as yet, small garden, parking, camping.

● **Places to eat**
While Lahore may be the culinary centre of Pakistan, Peshawar is the culinary centre of the Pathans, and one of the best places to sample the Peshawari *Chappli Kebab*, a round, flat burger made with mince, eggs and tomato and served with Naan, puts all western burgers to shame, other meat dishes incl Tikka, karai and 'roast' (usually lamb), vegetarian food is limited to the usual daal and simple vegetable curries, Afghani pilau rice is a good variation but take care as 'veg pilau' does not necessarily mean only veg.

Old City: *Salatins*, Cinema Rd, has rightly gained a reputation for excellent Peshawari food, can get crowded, especially at lunch. Namak Mandi (Bajori Rd) has lots of excellent tikka stalls and restaurants. Other good places for street food incl Qissa Khawani and Church Rd. Lots of cheap places also along GT Rd.

Saddar/Cantt: at the top of the range the *Pearl Continental's Marco Polo* (Pak/Continental) and *Taipan* (Chinese) restaurants serve excellent food, also terrace barbecue, very good value evening buffet Thur and Fri, rec;

Greens Hotel has **Lala's Grill** for Pakistani food and **China Friendship Restaurant** with good selection of vegetarian dishes, rec; *Hong Kong*, 24 D The Mall, T 274504, more expensive, less choice; *Shiraz*, Saddar Rd, good Pakistani food, clean, good service. There are several fast-food places on Arbab Rd, incl *Season* and *Jani*, as well as the *Cafe de Jamil*, 'established 1930 Aligargh', for tea and cakes. There are lots of good cheap Pakistani-style restaurants and food stalls in the older bazaars centred around Chowk Yadgar.

University town: there are several good upper/mid-range restaurants along Jamrud Rd as you approach University Town; *Usmania*, T 43135, a/c, Pak/Continental, good food, good value; *Shiraz*, T 842029, a/c, Chinese/Continental/Pak, more expensive; *Kowloon*, T 44425, a/c, good Chinese food, popular. Cheaper places incl the *Azad Afghan*, T 44152 and *Afghan*, T 42136, both serving kebabs, pilau etc. There are also several fast-food places.

● **Airline offices**
Domestic: PIA Booking Office, Arbab Rd, T 279162, open 0800-1800 7 days; **Shaheen Air International**, 16 Fakhr-e-Alam Rd, Cantt, T 278409, F 278427.

International: Air France, GSA Capitol Travels, Pearl Continental Hotel, T 273386; **British**, GSA Aviona, Greens Hotel, Saddar Rd, T 273252; **Emirates**, 95 B Saddar Rd, T 273744, F 275912; **Gulf**, ticketing – Arbab Rd, Saddar, T 275049, F 275965, reservations – Galaxie Hotel, Khyber Bazaar, T 213171, F 220438; **Saudi**, GSA Southern Travels, Galaxie Hotel, Khyber Bazaar, T 210861, F 217883.

● **Banks & money changers**
ANZ Grindlays, the Mall, opp top of Arbab Rd, fixed fee of Rs 250 to cash TCs, no charge for cash; **Habib Bank**, Saddar Rd, cash/TCs foreign exchange; **Mashreq Bank**, Saddar Rd, will only change US$ (cash/TCs). Cash withdrawal facilities for Visa customers. The money changers around Chowk Yadgar are authorized by the State Bank to deal in foreign currency, both cash and TCs; rates are sometimes better than the banks for cash.

● **Cultural centres**
American Centre, 17-C Chinar Rd, University Town, T 840321. Library/US Information Service; **Iranian Cultural Centre**, 3 Sir Syed Rd, T 279453, library, Audio/Visual, Iranian feature films, Persian language, calligraphy, art,

computing, photography and video classes; **Alliance Française**, 3 Arbab Rd, T 274542. Library, video club, cafeteria, TV, cinema (Sat), French classes; **Peshawar Club**, Sir Sayid Rd, nr the Mall, T 279048, established in 1863 for the armed forces, for members and guests only, but you can look around the library and buildings, facilities include tennis, squash, billiard, gym and swimming pool, foreigners living in Peshawar can apply for temporary membership.

● **Embassies & consulates**

American Consulate, 11 Hospital Rd, Cantt, T 279801, open 0800-1630, closed Fri and Sat; **Afghan Consulate**, 17-C Gulmohar Lane, T 842486; **Iranian Consulate**, 18 Park Ave, University Town, T 41114. Foreigners' visa applications should be made through Islamabad – expect to wait at least 1 month.

● **Entertainment**

Cinema: several in Saddar, including Falasair, and in the Old City, on Cinema Rd.

● **Hospitals & medical services**

Chemists: are located around all the major hospitals, and around Saddar and the Old City.

Hospitals: *Sherpao*, University Town, T 841701 and *Lady Reading*, Hospital Rd, T 210041 (casualty T 214213), are the two largest. *Mission*, Dubgari Gate, T 212371 is the least crowded of the main hospitals. The *Cantonment General*, Sunheri Masjid Rd, T 278153 is alright for minor problems. The *Khyber Medical Centre*, Dubgari Gate, T 211241 is a good private hospital. There are several private practitioners around Dubgari Gate, and also in Doctor Plaza, Saddar Rd, opp Greens Hotel. Opposite the Sherpao there is a free but crowded *Dental Hospital*, or there are private dentists in Saddar Rd.

● **Libraries**

British Council, 35 Shahrah-e-Quaid-e-Azam, PO Box 49, T 273278, reasonable selection of books; newspapers; audio/visual incl video hire, photocopying, education information, BBC World TV.

● **Post & telecommunications**
Area code: 091.

Post office: Saddar Rd, open 0830-1300, 1400-1900, closed Fri.

Telecommunications: **Central Telegraph Office**: (Pak Telecom), 2 The Mall, open 24 hrs, 7 days. Local/international phone, fax, telegram, cable. **Telephone enquiries**: T 17.

● **Shopping**

The bazaars of the Old City are worth visiting (see above). **NB** Closed 1200-1400 Fri for Prayers. For carpets there are many shops around Shuba Chowk, just across Jail Bridge. The Kamran Hotel there is now given over entirely to carpet sellers, and there are several other complexes specialising in carpets. Saddar Bazaar has many tourist shops selling a wide range of jewellery, carpets, furniture, embroidery etc. Prices tend to be higher than in the Old City, although there is plenty of room for bargaining. One or two shops are fixed-price. The *Outlet Venture*, sponsored by the Ockenden Trust, sells high quality rugs, embroidery, jewellery etc, made by Afghan refugees. There are two shops in Saddar, one next to the Falaksair cinema, the other at the E end of Saddar Rd, nr the junction with Sunheri Masjid Rd. You can watch work in progress in *The Afghan Metal Works* off Pagaji Rd.

● **Sports**

Buzkashi: a somewhat riotous variation on the game of polo, in which the wooden ball is replaced by the carcass of a calf, is played at various of the Afghan refugee camps, particularly Khorasan. Ask at PTDC for details of dates and venues.

General: *Arbab Niaz Stadium*, nr Shahi Gardens is Peshawar's international cricket venue, also with polo ground; *Army Stadium*, Khyber Rd, general sports, children's park/funfair outside; *Peshawar Stadium*, Stadium Rd, intercollegiate, provincial and national events, gymnasium and swimming pool open to the public, a large stadium is under construction in Hayatabad; *Peshawar Golf Course*, off Shami Rd (available to guests at Pearl Continental only); *Jans Recreation Centre*, Islamia Rd, snooker hall and swimming pool (Rs 100 or discounted with membership).

Swimming: also available at *Pearl Continental*, Rs 300/day. The oldest and best swimming pool is in the *Peshawar Club*, although it is unfortunately not open to the general public. *Wazir Bagh*, S of the Old City is a good place to watch (and join in) informal cricket, basket ball, badmington, football, Kabadi etc on Fri and Sat evenings.

● **Tour companies & travel agents**

Air Plus, 15 Cantt Plaza, Fakhr-e-Alam Rd, T 272842, F 274947. Domestic and international flights, tours; *Gandhara Travels*, Saddar Rd, T 79653. Domestic and international flights, hotel reservations; *Sehrai Travels and Tours* Greens Hotel, Saddar Rd, T 272085, F 276088. Efficient and helpful, specialising in large group tours, but also offering tailor-made packages for individuals/small groups. International and domestic flight reservation/reconfirmation; *Spinzer Travels*, 2 Islamia Rd, T 278035.

● **Tourist offices**

PTDC Tourist Information Centre, Deans Hotel, 3 Islamia Rd, Saddar, T 279781, F 279783, open 0900-1630 (lunch 1-2), Thur 0900-1330, closed Fri, helpful staff, well informed, ask here for current situation in Khyber Agency and Darra. Can arrange tours; Rates in 1995 for a vehicle for 4 people; Peshawar City, 3 hrs, Rs 500; Peshawar Valley (Charsadda, Takht-i-Bhai, Shabaz Ghari, Nowshera), 6 hrs, Rs 1,200; Darra, 3 hrs, Rs 600. To hire a Land Cruiser for longer journeys is Rs 2,000/day. PTDC have 2 seats/flight to Chitral reserved for foreign tourists; they will issue you with a letter to present to PIA. **Sarhad Tourism Corporation (STC)**, 81 D University Rd, University Town, T 840192. NWFP's provincial tourism corporation, established in 1991 it is responsible for organising events like the Shandur Polo. Useful at present mostly as a source of info on such events, STC is planning to establish a series of local information centres and hopes to see government-owned resthouses in NWFP leased out to the private sector as hotels.

● **Useful addresses**

Police: emergency, T 15; E Cantt, T 279291; W Cantt, T 276215; Faqirabad (Old City), T 273534.

Foreigners' registration: Special Branch, nr Shaheen Camp, T 278165, open 0800-1300, and in theory from 1300-1500, closed Fri and Sat, a morning visit advisable.

● **Transport**

Local Bus: buses are mostly run by Afghan operators. They are plentiful, crowded and often frenetic. The main artery of public transport is between Hayatabad/University Town and the GT Rd general bus stand via Jamrud Rd, Hospital Rd, Sunerhi Masjid Rd and the Old City, crossing the railway either at Railway Colony or Jail Bridge and then up round Bala Hisar. **Car hire**: is available from the major hotels, or can be arranged through PTDC. **Taxis and auto-rickshaws**: are readily available, and also **Tongas**.

Air Peshawar Airport, T 275471. **PIA** has direct international flights to Riyadh, Abu Dhabi, Dubai, Alain and Tashkent, via Lahore to Jeddah and Dharan, and via Karachi to Doha. Regular domestic services to Islamabad (up to 4 daily), Lahore (2 daily), Karachi (up to 3 daily), Quetta (Mon, Sat), Zhob (1 daily except Wed), DI Khan (1 daily), Multan (Tues, Thur, Fri, Sun), Parachinar (Mon, Fri), Saidu Sharif (1 daily) and Chitral (up to 3 daily, weather permitting). **Shaheen Air** and **Aero Asia** have 1 flight each daily to Lahore and Karachi.

Train Enquiries T 117, reservations: City T 274436; Cantt T 274437. Rail services to **Islamabad** are slow and often crowded, and are liable to lengthy searches when crossing into Punjab. The *RC-58*, 1500, 4 hrs, is generally the quietest, being a local service; **Lahore**; any of the services listed below to Karachi/Quetta, and also the *Zulfiqar Exp*, 1010, 10 hrs; **Karachi**; *Awam Exp*, 0800, 33½ hrs; *Khyber Mail*, 2215, 33½ hrs; **Quetta**; *Abaseen Exp*, 1730, 41¼ hrs.

Road Bus: *GTS Saddar*, opp Dean's Hotel, T 272660; buses S to Kohat Bannu and DI Khan in the morning until around 1100. *GTS City*, GT Rd, T 217101; services to Mardan, Mingora, Islamabad/Pindi and Lahore. GTS buses are generally slower. Buses, coaches and Hiace minibuses leave regularly from the **General Bus Stand** on the GT Rd. Services from here to all major towns in Swat, Chitral and Punjab. Airconditioned buses to Islamabad/Pindi and Lahore leave regularly from opp Firdous Cinema on GT Rd, just E of Bala Hisar. There is a bus stand N of Shahi Bagh on Charsadda Rd for local services to Charsadda, Mardan, etc. There are regular mini-buses to Kohat from *Kohat Flying Coach* stand nr Bhanamari Chowk.

Excursions from Peshawar

Khyber Pass

The Khyber Pass has achieved something of a legendary status and remains one of the great attractions for visitors to Peshawar. Its historical significance however has been vastly overstated. Billed as the main invasion route from the W since Aryan times, the first recorded conquerer to pass through it was in fact Babur in the 16th century. For many conquerers before, it was the passes to the N and S that provided routes into the subcontinent. However, to the British it represented the 'Gateway of India', an all important break in the mountainous barrier of their NW frontier.

The pass stretches from Jamrud Fort to Torkham. The Jamrud Rd heads W from Peshawar, passing the University Town, Hayatabad and Smugglers' Bazaar, before entering Khyber Agency. **Jamrud Fort** (18 km) was built by the Sikh General Hari Singh in 1836, provoking an attack by the Afghans, which cost him his life. It is of rough stonework faced with mud plaster, and in 3 tiers; lower and upper forts and a keep. There is also a stone arched gate on the road, the **Bab-i-Khyber**, built in 1964. From the fort, the road zigzags up past viewpoints and watchtowers and there are good views back onto the Peshawar plain. Next is the 1920s British built **Shagai Fort** (30 km). It is now manned by the Frontier Force and closed to the public. In the middle of this pass is Ali Masjid (mosque) and high above it the **Ali Masjid Fort** which defends the narrowest point of the gorge, less than 14m wide.

From here the pass opens out into a wide fertile valley dotted with fortified Pathan villages. Just before Landi Kotal, 15 km from Shagai Fort, there is the **Sphola Stupa**, to the right of the road on a hillock above Zarai. It dates from the 2nd-5th centuries AD and is the last remains (somewhat dilapidated) of an extensive Buddhist monastery. **Landi Kotal** itself is a bustling colourful market town with everything from smuggled electrical goods to drugs. 8 km further on is the border town of **Torkham**.

Visiting the pass Unfortunately, visiting the pass is something of a hit-and-miss affair, as it is frequently closed due to unrest amongst the Afridi tribes controlling the area. A permit is required, from the Political Agent Khyber in Peshawar (see under Useful addresses). Large groups applying for permits are generally referred to the Civil Secretariat of the Home Dept in Peshawar. Bring a photocopy of your relevent passport pages. If the pass is open you will be issued with a permit and assigned an armed guard from the Political Agent's office to accompany you. Foreigners must travel by private transport; the route is easily passable in a normal car.

Khyber Railway Services were discontinued on the Khyber railway some years ago due to insufficient usage (in practical terms it is very slow, prompting most locals to travel by bus). It is still possible however to charter a whole train for the trip up to Landi Kotal (an expensive business at around Rs 60,000). There are a couple of travel agents (*Sehrai Travels and Tours* in Peshawar and *Sitara Travels* in Rawalpindi) which have organized train charters on a number of occasions, catering primarily for the expat population, and there is talk of Pakistan Railways reinstating services on a regular fortnightly or monthly basis.

Built by the British in the 1920s, the railway is a remarkable feat of engineering, with 34 tunnels and 92 bridges and culverts. At one point it climbs 130m in just over 1 km, passing through a series of switchbacks with reversing stations and requiring an additional engine at the back to help push the train up the steep gradient. The journey takes at least $3\frac{1}{2}$ hrs.

Warsak Dam

Situated 24 km from Peshawar on the Michni road the Warsak Dam makes a good picnic spot (also accessible from Jamrud). The dam on the Kabul River was completed in 1960 and created a 42 km long lake upstream. It provides irrigation water to the intensively cultivated Peshawar Valley and generates 160,000 kw of electricity.

Afghan Refugee Camps

Most of the camps are on the GT Rd between Peshawar and Attock, along Jamrud Rd and on the Charsadda Rd. It may be possible to visit these (ask at PTDC) and buy rugs and handicrafts.

Peshawar Valley

The Peshawar valley is rich in historical sites from the Gandharan period; perhaps the most impressive visually is the Buddhist monastery of Takht-e-Bhai. This and many others can be visited as long day-trips from Peshawar. See below, under Peshawar Valley.

Darra Adam Khel

Situated 42 km S of Peshawar on the Kohat road, Darra is the biggest centre of indigenous arms manufacture in the province. Home to the **Adam Afridi** tribe or *khel*, the town consists almost entirely of gunshops where working replicas of anything from pen-guns to Kalashnikovs are meticulously fashioned with only the most primitive of machine tools. These gun-making skills are thought to have arrived here in the 1890s with a Punjabi gunsmith who was wanted for murder and settled in the town, beyond the reach of the authorities.

The town has become something of a tourist attraction in its own right, and negotiations between the provincial government and the Adam Afridis in recent years resulted in an agreement to 'tidy up' the town for tourists; heavy weaponry such as rocket launchers etc, was removed to tribal villages away from the road, and the copious quantities of hashish and opium previously openly displayed for sale began to be traded a

little more discretely. You can still test-fire any weapon of your choice for a small fee, and there seem to be few tourists who return from Darra without having bruised their shoulder on the recoil of a Kalashnikov.

Visiting Darra

It is neccessary to obtain a permit from the Civil Secretariat of the Home Dept in Peshawar in order to visit Darra. Provided there is no trouble in the area, these are generally issued on the spot with a minimum of delay. You can then travel there on public transport without an escort, although you will be met at the town and shown around by a local official who will keep a close eye on you. **NB** The town all but closes down on Fri. Buses are usually searched thoroughly on their return from Darra, particularly if there are foreigners on board; prices may be cheap, but this is probably one of the riskiest places to purchase drugs. Items such as pen guns meanwhile are the stuff of nightmares for airport security and attract stiff penalties.

Transport   Regular buses bound for Bannu (which pass through Darra) leave from the GTS Bus Station opposite Dean's Hotel through the morning up until around 1100. If leaving later, there are mini-buses from Kohat Flying Coach stand near Bhanamari Chowk, to the S of the Old City. On the return journey, any N-bound bus passing through the town is heading for Peshawar.

The southern half of NWFP has poorly developed infrastructure and is little visited by tourists. In summer it can get unbearably hot and dusty during the day. The prevailing image – in places accurately – is of a region beset by tribal feuding and law-lessness. Nevertheless, it does have a certain wild charm of its own, and for the more determined traveller, this is a fascinating and rewarding, if at times demanding, region in which to travel.

The road S from Peshawar, through the districts of Kohat, Bannu and DI Khan, crosses barren semi-arid countryside with hills and mountains averaging around 1,500m and occasional fertile oases. To the W, following the border with Afghanistan are the Federally Administered Tribal Areas of Kurram and N and S Waziristan. The Tribal Areas, or Agencies, are off-limits to foreigners unless they have a permit and escort. The main highway is open to foreigners without a permit as far S as Dera Ismail Khan, although it passes through several pockets of Tribal Areas and you are only allowed to stop in the main towns of Kohat, Bannu and DI Khan. Provided you travel sensibly and take heed of local advice (ask also at PTDC in Peshawar for up-to-date information on travelling in the area), these routes are perfectly safe. Venturing into the Tribal Areas without a permit is however dangerous; this is not an area where the official line on travel restrictions can be ignored. Women travellers are likely to find southern NWFP hard work; travelling alone is inadvisable unless you have some experience of the area. Work is in progress on the Indus Highway Project, which runs along this route and will one day link Peshawar and Karachi by a two-lane highway. The first sections of the highway, as far as Darra, were all but complete in 1995.

From Peshawar, the road passes through the arms manufacturing town of **Darra Adam Khel**, 42 km S of Peshawar. See under Excursions from Peshawar for details. It then climbs up to the Kohat Pass, marked by the Handyside Arch, and descends to Kohat (93 km), set in the wide, fertile Kohat Basin.

Kohat

Kohat developed primarily as a garrison town during the British era, and flourished also as a trading post at the intersection of the E-W route between Afghanistan and the Punjab and N-S along the Indus. Its origins though are much older. Local tradition asserts that the town was founded in the 14th century by the Bangash Pathans, who migrated from the Kurram valley to the E, displacing the indigenous Orakzai. The Khattaks, who are the other main tribal group found here, migrated into the area from the Suleiman mountains to the S in the 15th century. In 1505 the Mughal emperor Babur plundered the town during a raid into the district, but was able to maintain only nominal control. Indeed, throughout its history, it remained for all practical purposes independent, the tribal groups of the area fiercely resisting the control of the Durranis, Dost Mohammad and the Sikhs, until the British firmly established themselves there, though not before undertaking a large-scale campaign against the nearby Mirzanai tribes in 1855. For the British, it formed a vital part of the network of outposts defending the NW border of their empire, and they lost no time in building roads linking it with Peshawar to the N and Bannu to the S.

Today the town's military importance continues, with the large Fort and extensive cantonment area occupied by the Pakistan army. The old city has changed on the surface only and still has many

remnants from British and Mughal times. It is still surrounded by walls and marked by four gates. Inside, the bazaars are packed into narrow, bustling streets. The town had a large Hindu population prior to Partition, and a number of Hindu families still live in Tirah Bazaar, near the Nadria Hotel. This bazaar used to be where the tribes from the Tirah area would come to collect their supplies (they were not allowed into the walled town itself), hence the name. Although in a 'settled' area, Kohat remains a focus for the surrounding tribal areas and still has something of a 'Wild West' feel about it.

Kohat Fort, built by the British, is a large imposing structure overlooking the town, although it is now off-limits to foreigners. The **Deputy Commissioner's residence**, formerly the home of Louis Cavagnari, once British resident in Kabul, is a beautiful white-washed colonial style building with round-topped French windows, set in immaculate gardens. Still in use by the

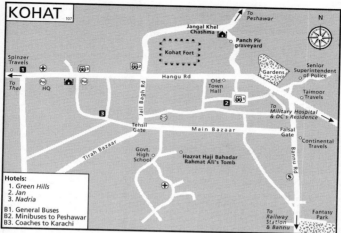

KOHAT 107

Hotels:
1. Green Hills
2. Jan
3. Nadria

B1. General Buses
B2. Minibuses to Peshawar
B3. Coaches to Karachi

DC, getting permission to look around the grounds is difficult, although it is worth trying, if only to see the colourful assortment of tribal chiefs usually gathered here in anticipation of an audience. At **Jangal Khel**, near the fort, there is a large spring-fed water tank next to a mosque, where men and boys come to bathe and wash. Next to it is an old graveyard known as **Panch Pir** or 'five saints', with gravestones dating back to the Mughal period (perhaps casualties of Babur's expedition), and huge shady Banyan trees. In the Old City, the **Tomb of Hazrat Haji Bahadar Rahmat Ali** (also known as Syed Abdullah Shah), a Sufi saint from the time of Aurangzeb, has a beautifully decorated dome. Nearby is the Govt High School for Girls, formerly a Hindu pilgrims' resthouse or *Dharamsala*. The Bazaars of the Old City are also worth exploring in their own right.

● **Accommodation** There is only basic accommodation available; the two best hotels are the **F** *Green Hill*, Hangu Rd, nr Police Line, T 512228, clean rooms, restaurant; and **F** *Nadria*, outside Tehsil Gates, T 513162, reasonable rooms, also some a/c (**E** category). There are a few nr the General Bus Stand, of which the best is the **F** *Jan's*, T 510894, courtyard, restaurant.

● **Tour companies & travel agents** *Taimoor Enterprises*, Hangu Rd, T 510267, domestic sales agent for PIA; *Continental Travel*, Kotal Shopping Centre, Bannu Rd, T 511091.

● **Post & telecommunications Area code**: (0922).

● **Useful telephone numbers Commissioner**: T 510775. **Deputy Commissioner**: T 3527. **Senior Superintendent of Police**: T 4160.

● **Transport Train** A single track narrow gauge railway runs W to Rawalpindi; *187 Passenger*, 0535, 5 hrs. **Road Bus**: regular daily services operate in all directions to major urban centres in the region from the General Bus Stand. Minibuses for Peshawar also depart from nr the Fort. There are long distance buses to Karachi, departing from Hangu Rd (24 hrs).

ROUTES From Kohat a good but narrow metalled road leads E towards Islamabad (175 km). At **Khashalgarh** (50 km from Kohat), the road crosses the Indus on a rail/road bridge into Punjab Province. From Khashalgarh it is 77 km on to **Fatehjang** and a further 47 km into Islamabad, a journey of about 3-5 hrs. The route W to Parachinar is described below in detail, followed by the route SW to Bannu and DI Khan.

West to Kurram Valley and Parachinar

From Kohat a road leads W to Thal and then NE to Parachinar, at the head of the picturesque Kurram Valley. Just beyond Thal is the start of Kurram Agency, a tribal area for which permits are required; apply to the Home Dept of the Secretariat in Peshawar. A sensitive and volatile area during the Afghan war, it has for a long time been closed to foreigners, although it may in the future open up to tourism.

The road as far as Thal is in good condition. Beyond Thal it deteriorates, with long stretches on rough track, although work is in progress on a new two-lane link road between Thal and Parachinar. There are regular 'flying coaches' from Kohat, and slower buses.

The road follows the old narrow-guage railway, now closed, and the river W through mostly arid rocky land with patches of cultivation and the mud walled compounds of families, grouped in village clans. It passes through Nasrat Khel and Sherkot before arriving at the bazaar town of **Hangu**. From Hangu you can take a detour up a rough track to the Samana ridge where there is the **Lockhart Fort** built in 1891 and the Saragarhi Obelisk in memory of those who died during one of the many campaigns against the local *Bangash* tribes between 1897-8. There are spectacular views in all directions from here. Continuing on from Hangu the next town is Doaba, again with a reasonable bazaar. Approaching Thal, the road passes a garrison and large fort, established by the British and now occupied by the local militia, crosses a bridge and enters the town. **Thal** (98 km) developed as an important trading town by the Kurram River, on the caravan route into Afghanistan. Today its importance has diminished although its bazaars are still thriving.

A little further on is **Chapri**, where a stone arched gateway marks the start of Kurram Agency. There is a checkpost and vehicles are stopped. From here the road passes the villages of Manduri, Bagan, Alizai, and Arawali with its fort occupied by the Kurram Militia, before arriving at the bazaar town of **Sadda**.

Upper Kurram

At Sadda, the Kurram River cuts through the main grain of the hills, giving access to Upper Kurram, a wide open valley surrounded on all sides by mountains except where the river enters and leaves. The northern watershed is formed by the Safed Koh or 'White Mountains' (*Spin Ghar* in Pashto), which mark the border with Afghanistan and dominate the valley, the highest peak, Sikaram, reaching 4,755m.

Attracted by its cooler climate, picturesque villages and well wooded hills the British described it as "one of the most beautiful valleys in the province". At that time the hills were well wooded with cedar which is ideally suited to the environment, although the plain was mostly barren. Today it has been reversed; irrigation has brought the fertile land into cultivation and the trees planted by the British along the roads and around villages have matured, while uncontrolled logging of the hills and growing population pressure have left most of the lower slopes bare, although higher up the forest cover still remains in places.

History

According to a local legend, the Kurram valley was once inhabited by demons, or *deos*, who were ruled by a king known as *Safed Deo*, or 'white demon'. Two brothers, Shudani and Budani, then came from the N (from Afghanistan), drove the demons out and settled there. Eventually their descendants were in turn driven out by a fresh wave of migrations from Afghanistan.

The recorded history of Kurram begins in 1148 when Bahram Shah of Ghazni, defeated by Saif-ud-din of Ghor, took refuge in the valley before recapturing Ghazni. The valley then came under the control of the Ghorrids for a while until the arrival of the Mongols in around 1220. It next appears in history during the Mughal period when it was occupied by Hamayun in 1552, prior to his reconquest of India. Mughal control of Kurram was largely nominal and the valley in fact formed one of the chief strongholds of Afghan opposition to Mughal rule. After the break-up of the Mughal Empire, it became part of Afghanistan. The indigenous tribes meanwhile were ousted by the Turis, Shia Muslims of Turkish origin who speak Pashto and are today the main Pathan tribe in the valley. During the British period, the Turis were responsible for repeated raids on villages around Kohat, until an expedition in 1856 under Brigadier-General Neville Chamberlain brought relative peace to the area. In 1878 British forces led by General Roberts marched on Afghanistan through the Kurram Valley, defeating the Afghan forces at Peiwar Kotal and occupying Khost. The Turis sided with the British against what they saw as the tyranny of Afghan rule, providing them with supplies and levies. In 1880, when the British evacuated the Kurram Valley, the Turis petitioned them to stay. However the British opted to leave, and internal feuding quickly spread through the valley. Eventually, at their own request, the British took over the administration of the valley once again in 1892. The British extended the railway line from Kohat as far as Thal and began to set about extending agriculture and irrigation in the valley. Schools and hospitals were established, mostly by missionaries.

People and society

The major Pathan tribes in the area are the Turis, Bangshah, Chamkannis, Ghilzai, Mangals and Orakzai. The Turis form the largest tribe. They are Shia Muslim and comprise around 45% of the population, with the remainder being Sunni. There is also a significant minority of Christians. The Sunni-Shia split has in the past been the source of considerable tension, leading occasionally to violence. After the Soviet invasion of Afghanistan in 1979, Afghan refugees came to outnumber the local population, and being entirely Sunni, upset the existing religious balance. With Afghan border on three sides, the Kurram Valley, and in particular Parachinar, was heavily affected by the war, with fighting and shelling often spilling over into Pakistani territory.

In recent years, the political situation in the Agency has improved considerably. A ban on carrying weapons in settled areas is strictly enforced with the result that the only people one sees armed in Parachinar are levies or Frontier Corps. The steady growth of agriculture, both in extent and productivity, is bringing gradual improvements in the standard of living, which in turn encourages tribesmen to maintain the peace. Officials are hopeful that the region's potential for tourism will soon be exploited; as well as the cool, peaceful atmosphere of Parachinar itself, the surrounding hills, and in particular the Safed Koh, provide endless opportunities for walking and trekking. Much however depends on some modicum of peace and stability being established across the border in Afghanistan.

Leaving Sadda the road crosses a bridge to Balesh Khel, then climbs up the Kurram valley, following the river and passing through increasingly green and fertile land. The next main village is Ghosad. At Shakamal there is a spring and large concrete pool by the roadside, where men and boys come to bathe and wash. Shortly after is Parachinar.

Parachinar

Parachinar is the largest town in the valley and the headquarters of the Agency. At an altitude of 1775m it is pleasantly cooler in summer. Winter can get very cold, with temperatures dropping to below zero. Autumn and spring are the ideal times to visit. The town itself is pleasantly green, with many large Chinar trees – hence the name.

All the administrative buildings, mostly dating from the British period, are up on the hillside to the N. **Chinar House**, built by Capt Ross Keppel, was destroyed by fire in 1990 but has been completely rebuilt in its original style. The **Governor's House** consisting of cottages and bungalows is built in traditional rural English style, complete with bay windows and chimney stacks, but with bright green tin roofs, and set in spacious grounds with well tended lawns. Today it is the home of the Political Agent.

The main bazaar is to the S. Although not particularly large, it has a wealthy atmosphere to it, with more than its fair share of luxury consumer goods smuggled from Afghanistan. There are also Afghan carpets for sale, perhaps for a lot less than in Peshawar.

The Kurram valley around Parachinar is particularly fertile, giving high yields with irrigation and supporting both a spring crop of wheat and barley and an autumn crop of rice, maize and oilseed. There are also orchards of apples, pears, grapes, cherries, pomegranates and peaches. Various Shia shrines are scattered around the valley. The drive from Parachinar up to the roadhead at **Malana** (about 7 km) is particularly beautiful. There is a *Government Rest House* here, beside a weir and irrigation channel where the stream emerges from a narrow gorge. Beyond, the valley climbs up to summer pastures and villages.

Local information
● **Accommodation and places to eat**
There are two hotels in the bazaar, nr to the main mosque. Both are clean and good value. The hotel signs are in Urdu only.

F *Shah Palace*, T 2237, the better of the two; **F** *Agra*, T 2701, simpler but clean. Both have simple restaurants or there are many more in the bazaar.

There is also a comfortable **D** *Circuit House* which must be booked through the Political Agent.

● **Post & telecommunications**
Area code: (0926).

● **Useful telephone numbers**
Political Agent Kurram: T 2511.

● **Transport**
Air There are two flights weekly (Mon, Fri) to Peshawar.

Road Bus: there are regular mini-buses, and slower buses, to Kohat, departing when full.

Southwest to Bannu and DI Khan

At Krappa, SW of Kohat, a new road forks S to Shakadara and then on to Kalabagh, where the Indus emerges from its gorge onto the Indus plain. The road crosses the Indus over the Jinnah Barrage (see page 263). The main road to Bannu crosses the Salt Range passing close to the salt mine at **Jatta**. After

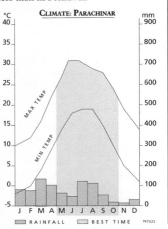

CLIMATE: PARACHINAR

°C / mm scale chart with MAX TEMP and MIN TEMP curves.

RAINFALL   BEST TIME   PKTG22

about 100 km the road winds down from the Kohat and Wazir hills into the Bannu Basin, an almost circular alluvial plain shut in on all sides by mountains and drained by two rivers, the **Kurram** and the **Tochi** (or Gambila). Between them lies a tract of richly irrigated country, densely populated, wooded and crossed by many water courses. This oasis is the setting for Bannu (125 km), refreshingly green and surrounded by palms and shady mango trees.

Bannu

The town (then called Pona), is first mentioned by the Chinese pilgrim Fa-Hien in 404 AD, who describes a Buddhist monastery with 3000 monks. The town grew as a result of its position on the original trading route between Kabul and the Indus, later replaced by the Kurram/Miranzai valley route through Hangu and Kohat.

During the 18th century the Durranis exercised a precarious hold over the area, followed by Ranjit Singh, who built the fort here in 1844. From 1846 the British extended their control over the area through Lieutenant Edwardes, who in turn administered through the

Sikhs. He named the town Dulipshehr after the young Maharaja. In 1899 it was renamed Edwardesabad and in 1903 Bannu. Edwardes gained the respect of the local tribes and exerted considerable influence, even getting many of the surrounding villagers to pull down their fortifications and accept British protection.

The old town of Bannu, with some of its gates still standing, is as crowded, dusty, noisy and chaotic as the cantonment area is spacious, clean, peaceful and ordered; the latter even boasts a small golf course. In the cantonment area there is the **Pennell Missionary Hospital** and school founded at the turn of the century by the British missionary. 11 km SW of Bannu near Barth are the **Akra Mounds** of uncertain origin – a series of low mounds, much reduced by farmers who have excavated them for use as topsoil.

Local information
● **Accommodation and places to eat**

D *Bag-e-Sakoun*, Kohat Rd, T 3868, hotel sign in Urdu, a little out of town (past bus station on road to Kohat), comfortable rooms, restaurant, lovely garden, rec.

E *Inam Palace*, New Lari Adda, nr bus station, T 3241, clean rooms, some with a/c (**D** category), courtyard, restaurant, friendly, good value; **E** *KD's*, Jaman Rd, T 4089, basic; **E** *New Jan's*, Lakki Gate, T 2345, restaurant.

F *Sajjad*, Chai Bazaar, T 2583, basic.

Government Rest House, reservations, Deputy Commissioner. The Mission Hospital takes in guests. As well as the hotel restaurants, there are lots of good Pakistani style eating places in the old town.

● **Post & telecommunications**
Area code: (0928)

● **Useful phone numbers**
Commissioner: T 2299.

Deputy Commissioner: T 2502.

● **Transport**
Air Daily flights (except Wed, Fri) to Peshawar and Islamabad.

Train The narrow gauge railway connecting Bannu with Kalabagh via Lakki no longer operates passenger services.

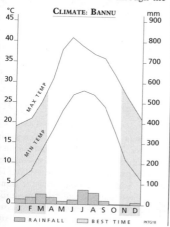

CLIMATE: BANNU

°C / mm graph, axes 0–45 °C and 0–900 mm, months J F M A M J J A S O N D, showing MAX TEMP and MIN TEMP curves.

RAINFALL / BEST TIME

PKTG18

WOMEN ARE NOT ALLOWED

According to a local story, the town of Wana gained its name from a dispute between the British and the local population. Having established their outpost there, the British officers posted to the town began to bring their wives and families to live with them. It was not long before the 'Memsahibs' could be seen wandering around the bazaar, doing their shopping. This raised an outcry amongst the conservative tribal elders, who promptly assembled a jirga in which they voted to ban these immodest white ladies from their town. The British, anxious not to spark a violent confrontation, reluctantly agreed to comply. Subsequently, the town became known by the acronym of Women Are Not Allowed!

Road Bus: regular daily bus services operate in all directions. Buses leave when full.

ROUTES From Bannu one road leads W into the Tribal Agencies of **N and S Waziristan**. These tribal areas can be very dangerous and should non be visited without a permit and escort. Without special connections or a specific reason for visiting, these are not usually granted. The road passes **Razmak** (126 km) with its Army Cadet College, **Wana** the administrative capital of S Waziristan and **Tanai Scout Post** (206 km) with its fort, before crossing into Baluchistan and on to **Zhob** (333 km). At Taudachina just beyond Ramzak and at Tanai there are turnings heading E which converge at Jandola before going on past **Khirgi Post** with its impressive fort, **Dabarra**, centre for the local falcon trade and arriving at **Tank** (110 km). From Tank, one road leads E to join the Bannu-DI Khan road at Pezu, while another leads SE directly to DI Khan.

South to DI Khan

The main road leads S from Bannu following the railway line. After 47 km, there is a turning E to Lakki and Kalabagh (see page 263) while the main road continues S to **Pezu** (82 km). Here there is a turning W to **Tank** (37 km), a large town on the edge of the Tribal Areas and the terminus for another narrow gauge railway which connects with Lakki and Kalabagh by way of Pezu. 6 km W of Tank there is a large mound rich in shards of terracotta pottery and figurines possibly from an *Indus Valley Civilisation* settlement.

From Pezu a path leads up to the nearby peak of **Sheikh Budin** (1377m)

named after the Sufi saint *Sheikh-Baha-ud-din* whose shrine is at the top. The mountain owes its height to a cap of limestone which has prevented erosion. To the SW the snow-clad mountain of **Takht-e-Suleiman** (*Throne of Solomon*), 3,355m, crowns the Suleiman range. The main road continues S from Pezu crossing the W extremities of the Marwat Range before descending on to the Derajat Plain and reaching Dera Ismail Khan. About 22 km before DI Khan is **Rahman Dheri**, an Indus Valley Civilisation settlement dating from 3200 BC. The sight is about 3 km W of the main road, its low mound barely visible from the road. Today nothing remains of the excavations, which once revealed the town layout and ancient brick walls of houses. Numerous pottery shards are still in evidence however, scattered around the site.

Dera Ismail Khan

DI Khan, as it is commonly referred to, the Divisional Headquarters for DI Khan Division, is a prosperous town situated on the W bank of the Indus. Despite being close to restricted Tribal Areas, it is a safe place with a friendly, good natured atmosphere. The old town is encompassed by the Circular Rd and crossed by four main bazaar streets. At the centre is the Chowkala Tower, a freestanding modern brick structure straddling the intersection. DI Khan is famous for its brass inlaid woodwork and the narrow bustling bazaars are a fascinating area in which to explore and shop for these and many other goods, including traditional leather *Chappals*. Many of the houses in the bazaars and in the small alleys running between them have beautifully carved wooden balconies.

The spaciously laid out cantonment area is to the E and S, between the old town and the Indus. The road running along the riverbank forms a pleasant tree-lined promenade, with the Midway Hotel and Restaurant and the Indus View Restaurant both having outside seating by the river's edge; ideal places to relax and enjoy the broad sweep of the Indus, which at this point varies from 10-20 km in width according to the season. The **SS Jhelum**, a now somewhat delapidated paddle steamer which saw service in S Iraq during WWI before being deployed here as a ferry, is moored by the riverbank opposite the Indus View Restaurant. Smaller ferries still ply back and forth across the river from here.

Local information
● **Accommodation**

D *Midway*, Indus River Bank, T 2900, a/c, TV, phone, restaurant, waterfront location makes

this the most pleasant place to stay; **D** *Bloom Star*, E Circular Rd, T 710913, a/c rooms, also very good value non a/c rooms (**F** category), restaurant, friendly staff, parking; **D** *De Hilton*, E Circular Rd, T 710478, F 710380, a/c, TV, phone, restaurant, newly built and clean but a little noisy; **D** *Jan's*, N Circular Rd, T 710913, a/c rooms, restaurant; **D** *Royal*, Tank Rd, posh lobby, reasonable rooms, conveniently located for Tank/Daraban bus stands; **F** *Taj Mahal*, E Circular Rd, T 710834, very basic, converted Hindu temple; **F** *Gulf*, Topan Wallah Bazaar, T 710578, basic; **F** *Al-Habib*, Topan Wallah Bazaar, T 711306, basic, pleasant courtyard.

● **Places to eat**
The *Neelab* in the Midway Hotel is the best restaurant. *Indus View* is pleasantly located overlooking the Indus. The Bloom Star, De Hilton and Jan's hotels also have reasonable restaurants, as well as the Taj Mahal (more basic). Cheaper places are in the old town, particularly Topan Wallah Bazaar.

● **Banks & money changers**
National Bank of Pakistan and Muslim Commercial Bank, both in Topan Wallah Bazaar, are able to do foreign exchange, cash and TCs.

● **Hospitals & medical services**
Civil Hospital: (emergency), T 711408.

● **Post & telecommunications**
Area code: (0961).

● **Useful phone numbers**
Commissioner: T 6413.
Deputy Commissioner: T 811274.

● **Transport**
Air *PIA Booking Office*, 7-A Aziz Bhatti Rd, Cantonment, opp DC's office, T 6971. *Spinzer Travels*, Circular Rd, T 4814, can also book flights. **Peshawar**: daily flights (2 on Fri). **Quetta (via Zhob)**; 2 flights weekly (Mon, Sat). **Multan (via Zhob)**; 4 flights weekly (Tues, Thur, Fri, Sun).

Road Bus: the GTS Bus Stand is situated by the Bloom Star Hotel. Buses operate from here to Bannu/Kohat/Peshawar, Mianwali, Muzzaffargarh/Multan and Dera Ghazi Khan. The **Flying Coach Stand**, just off Bannu Rd at the northern edge of the town, has Hiace minibuses to Bannu, Kohat and Peshawar, as well as Mianwali. A third stand, known as the **Tank Adda** or **Daraban Adda**, has buses to Tank

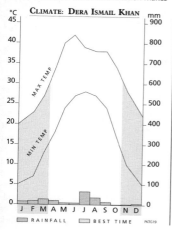

°C **CLIMATE: DERA ISMAIL KHAN** mm

MAX TEMP

MIN TEMP

J F M A M J J A S O N D

☐ RAINFALL   ☐ BEST TIME   PKTG19

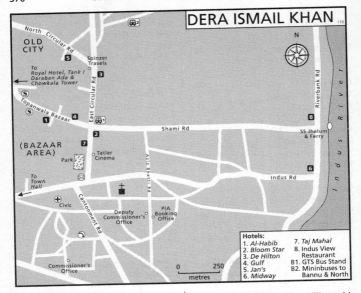

and Jandola and to Daraban and Zhob. There are also several long-distance buses operating services to Rawalpindi and Karachi; ticket offices and departures from E Circular Rd, N of Bloom Star Hotel.

ROUTES Several routes radiate from DI Khan. One road leads NE following the Indus and crosses it on the Chashma Barrage, S of Mianwali. Another crosses the Indus just W of DI Khan on a new bridge, giving access to the main N-S route between DI Khan and Multan, along the E bank of the Indus (see page 263). A third route follows the W bank of the Indus S to Dera Ghazi Khan; this road is in poor condition and often subject to flooding, particularly between DI Khan and Taunsa, although work is in progress on a section of the Indus Highway along this route (see page 190). All these routes are open to foreigners without a permit. The route SW from DI Khan, to Zhob and Quetta in Baluchistan, is unfortunately through a restricted area requiring permits. See page 191 for details of this route. The road NW to Tank is similarly restricted.

The fertile plains N and W of Peshawar form the heartland of the Peshawar valley and are of enormous agricultural and industrial importance, being the centre of tobacco and sugarcane cultivation and processing. They are also of great historical significance, rich in archaeological remains from the Gandharan Buddhist period. They are well worth exploring in their own right, either in short visits from Peshawar or en-route to Swat/Chitral. Alternatively, the road via Mardan and Swabi provides a slower but much more interesting and scenic route to Islamabad. In contrast to the busy GT Rd, lined for much of the way with heavy industrial factories, the small tree-lined roads to the N pass through a green, fertile landscape of fields and canals, with isolated bare brown hills rising out of the flat plains; the first outliers of the ascending ranges to the N. *Best time to visit*: Oct to Apr are the ideal months to visit, when the climate is pleasantly cool during the day. Summer temperatures climb well into the forties. The area is ideal for cyclists with the many canals making for excellent traffic-free cycle routes. Facilities for tourists are however generally poorly developed.

Charsadda

28 km NE of Peshawar is the town of Charsadda. This is the site of the ancient city of **Pushkalavati** (the lotus city), capital of Gandhara from around the 6th century BC to the 2nd century AD. The city later moved to Peshawar, but Pushkalavati, with its large shrine, remained an important centre of Buddhist pilgrimage. The city, first mentioned in the Hindu epic **Ramayana**, was founded by *Bharata*, Rama's brother, as a twin city of Taxila (both were named after Bharata's sons). Throughout its history,

Charsadda has been subject to continually changing river courses, giving rise to the various different sites and finally forcing the move to Peshawar.

Despite its historical importance, there is not much for the visitor to see, with the important sites being marked only by mounds which give little idea of the ancient settlements they conceal. 1 km W of the town, where the road turns sharply right (coming from Peshawar) before crossing a river, a track leads N to the two largest mounds, known as **Bala Hisar**, probably because they were used as a fort in the 18th-19th centuries. The mounds were excavated by Sir John Marshall in 1902 and by Sir Mortimer Wheeler in 1958. All the important finds were removed to Peshawar and Lahore museums, but there are countless pottery shards still scattered all over the site. Across the river to the NE of Bala Hisar are the mounds of the later city of **Shaikhan Dheri**, excavated by Peshawar University in 1963 and revealing a city founded by the Bactrian Greeks in the 2nd century AD. The contemporary village of **Rajur** (from *'Rajaghar'* or royal palace) is built on some low mounds which almost certainly contain the remains of an extensive city. Little has been excavated, although Indo-Greek, Scythian and Kushana coins have been found. The whole area is surrounded by an ancient graveyard, protecting much of the ground from excavation. Where unprotected, many of the mounds have been dug away by local villagers for use as topsoil and fertilizer. Just N of Rajur are the mounds of **Shah-e-Napursan** (literally 'neglected city') and **Mir Ziarat**, perhaps the site of the legendary stupa built by Asoka and said to contain the remains of the Lord Buddha. **Prang**, to the S of the main crossroads in Charsadda, has more mounds and probably once lay at

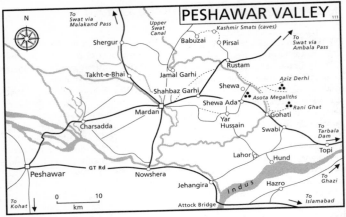

the confluence of the Kabul and Swat rivers. The name is a corruption of *prayag* or *prayang*, the sacred town at the confluence of the Jumna and Ganges rivers near Allahabad in India, suggesting that Charsadda perhaps once held a similar religious significance.

From Charsadda there is a pleasant short cut that leads directly to Takht-e-Bhai (see below); coming from Peshawar, turn left at the crossroads in the centre of the village and take the first right. This quiet road runs through fertile countryside for 22 km and joins the main Mardan-Takht-e-Bhai road about 1 km S of the town. The main road runs E from Charsadda directly to Mardan.

Mardan

The present town of Mardan has been an important military base for the last 200 years. It was the home of the elite British Guide Corps, formed in 1846 "to guide regular troops in the field, collect intelligence and keep the peace on the Northwest Frontier". Today the large Cantonment area is home to their successors, the Punjab Regiment. It lies S of the main Swabi road and is marked by small bastion gates to the spaciously laid out grounds with their wide boule-

vards. There is the old Catholic church and cemetery inside, although access is restricted. South of this is the Mall and Saddar area, Bank Rd etc. On the E side of the river is the old town of Mardan, known as **Hoti Mardan**, *Hoti* being a prominent family name going back many generations. There is an old Hindu temple and a Sikh Gurudwara here, both now homes.

The **Memorial Arch** is dedicated to the "memory of Sir Louis Cavagnari KCSI, officers and men of the Guides who fell in defence of the Kabul residency on 3 Sep 1879". Built in Gothic-Mughal style, it stands at the main intersection near the centre of the new town. Steps lead up inside each of the towers. **Mardan museum** has a small collection of Gandharan pieces gathered from the various sites in the area. If it is closed within office hours, ask for the Director, whose office is in the same building. Otherwise, Mardan is of little interest in itself; its main value is as a base from which to explore the surrounding area.

● **Accommodation** Accommodation in Mardan is limited and basic. About 4 km S of the town, down a poorly marked turning W off the road to Nowshera (impractical without

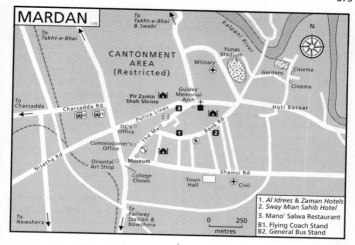

MARDAN 115

To Takht-e-Bhai & Swabi

To Takht-e-Bhai

Kalpani River

N

CANTONMENT AREA (Restricted)

Yunas Stadium

Military

Gardens

Cinema

Cinema

To Charsadda

Charsadda Rd

Pir Zamin Shah Shrine

Guides' Memorial Arch

DC's Office

Police Lines

Hoti Bazaar

Commissioner's Office

The Mall

Bank Rd

Nisatha Rd

Oriental Art Shop

Museum

College Chowk

Town Hall

Shamsi Rd

Civil

To Nowshera

To Railway Station & Nowshera

0   250
metres

1. Al Idrees & Zaman Hotels
2. Sway Mian Sahib Hotel
3. Mano' Salwa Restaurant
B1. Flying Coach Stand
B2. General Bus Stand

your own transport) there is the **C** *Jamal Guest House*, Sher Maltun Town, T (0531) 68048, a/c and non a/c (**D** category) rooms, pleasant garden, restaurant. In the town itself there are 3 hotels along Bank Rd; **F** *Al-Idrees*, T 3339, basic but clean, restaurant; **F** *Sway Mian Sahib*, pleasant courtyard, restaurant, unfriendly; **F** *Zaman*, basic rooms, restaurant. There are also several noisy hotels around the bus station, which are probably best avoided. All the above serve reasonable food, or there are lots of basic restaurants around the bus station. There is a more up-market a/c restaurant on the Mall, the *Mano' Salwa*, T 62163, serving Pakistani dishes.

● **Shopping** The *Oriental Art Gallery & Old Coin Shop*, College Chowk, T 62102, owned by Fazli Mabook Zahid has an unique collection of antique artefacts and coins from Afghanistan and Pakistan, some of which would be more appropriately housed in a museum.

● **Transport** Local transport around the town is still mostly by horse-drawn tonga, making the centre slightly less frenetic than comparably sized places. **Road Bus:** the General Bus Stand, and Flying Coach stands, are on Charsadda Rd, E of the main town. There are regular buses and Hiace mini-buses to Peshawar, Islamabad and Mingora. Buses to Chitral are best caught in Peshawar or Mingora, where they originate, but also pass through here en-route from Peshawar. There

are numerous local services to nearby villages. For Takht-e-Bhai, take any Mingora-bound transport. There are also mini-buses to Pir Baba from here.

ROUTES Mardan acts as a transport hub for the surrounding plains, with roads radiating out from the town. A fast dual carriageway leads S from Mardan to Nowshera (22 km) on the GT Rd (see Islamabad to Peshawar). A main road runs E towards Swabi and Tarbela. Another leads NW to Takht-e-Bhai and onto the Malakand Pass and Swat valley.

Takht-e-Bhai

The small town of Takht-i-Bhai, famous for its Gandharan Buddhist monastery, is 14 km NW of Mardan on the road to Swat. There is also a direct road from Charsadda (see above). The monastery is 3 km to the E of the main bazaar. The turning is in the centre of town and is well signposted. Tongas are readily available for hire. Unfortunately there is no accommodation, short of a charpoy at one of the restaurants. 4 km from Takht-i-Bhai on the road to Charsadda, there is the *Chopal Tourist Spot*, an a/c restaurant with the possibility of

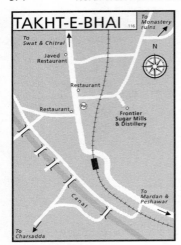

TAKHT-E-BHAI

To Monastery ruins

To Swat & Chitral

Javed Restaurant

N

Restaurant

Restaurant

Pol

Frontier Sugar Mills & Distillery

To Mardan & Peshawar

Canal

To Charsadda

dorm-style accommodation. Contact Sarhad Tourism in Peshawar for details and booking.

Takht-i-Bhai (literally 'spring on a flat terrace') was probably the largest of more than 1,400 monasteries which thrived in lower Swat and the plains of Peshawar during the Gandharan Buddhist period. The earliest settlement was founded around 40 AD, the main peak of activity was during the Kushana period of the 1st-4th centuries AD, and the last stage dates from the 5th and 6th centuries. The monastery is perched strikingly on the side of a bare ridge of rock rising up from the fertile plain and is certainly the best preserved and most impressive piece of Gandharan architecture in Pakistan. The sophistication and quality of the building work is clear from the beautifully fashioned walls with their well preserved brickwork. During summer, an early start is recommended as there is little in the way of shade against the sun.

The path climbs steeply up to the monastery, passing a 2-storey block with monks' cells, before entering the central **Court of Stupas**, enclosed by 8m high walls and surrounded by small alcoves, each of which would have contained a plaster Buddha, the largest possibly 10m high. The bases of some 38 votive stupas are scattered around the centre of the court, built as offerings by pilgrims. The walls were originally lime plastered and decorated with paintings. The statues themselves may have been gilded.

To the left is the **Court of the Main Stupa**, housing the monastery's original stupa which was about 10m high. To the right is the **Monastery Court** lined on three sides by monks' cells. An upper storey once housed more cells. There is an ancient water tank and to the left through a doorway the remains of the kitchen and refectory area. Straight ahead is the **Open Court**, beneath which are 10 vaulted chambers probably used either for meditation or as granaries. To the right of the open court, enclosed by high walls, is the **Assembly Court** where the monks would meet. The water tanks here were built during excavation work this century. To the left is a covered area with a sign saying 'museum', enclosing the remains of two small intricately worked stupas and displaying pieces of sculptures and fragments from the site.

On the way up to the monastery, a new path leads off to the left and climbs to a some more buildings, less intact but with an excellent view over to the main monastery. The early morning light is perfect for photography from here. The remains of other buildings are scattered on the hillside.

North of Takht-e-Bhai, the main road continues up to the Malakand Pass and Swat valley, passing first through Shergarh, Skapur and Dargai. At Shergur there is a turning E towards Jamal Garhi.

Jamal Garhi

The ruins of another Buddhist monastery near the village of Jamal Garhi are less complete than those at Takht-e-Bhai but still impressive and well worth a visit. The views from the hilltop over the surrounding plains, including across to Takht-i-Bhai, are particularly stunning at dawn when the air is clear, and in the evening light. The site can be easily visited as a daytrip from Mardan.

The turning N to Jamal Garhi is 1 km E of Mardan, across the river on the road to Shahbaz Garhi and Swabi. After 14 km there is a turning left signposted 'Jamal Garhi archaeological remains' leading to the village of Jamal Garhi, from where you can climb up to the ruins. Buses from Mardan run fairly frequently on the route past Jahmal Garhi up towards Katlang and Babozai. It is 3 km from the turning to the village (tongas run a shuttle service for a few rupees) and then a gentle ½-hr walk in a long zig-zag on a good path up to the monastery.

The path leads in past a long wall, striking for its near perfect brickwork, and into the monastery. On the highest point is a well preserved circular courtyard surrounding the base of a large stupa. You can look down from here onto the main buildings and courtyards filled with stupa bases. Outside the main complex are some small monks cells built into the side of the hill, some of which are still intact. Illegal digging in various parts of the site is spurred by local legends of gold buried in the ruins.

The road leading W from the staggered junction on the main road at Jamal Garhi comes out at Shergarh, on the Mardan-Malakand road. The road N leads past the village of Katlang, followed by a turning E to Shamozai and and later another to Babozai, before reaching Mian Khan, at the foot of the hills separating Mardan from Buner. From Babozai there is a pilgrim path that climbs a narrow valley to **Kashmir Smats** (or cave), a holy site to Hindus and Buddhists.

East from Mardan

The road E from Bagh Dada Chowk crosses the Kalpani River and passes the turning N to Jamal Garhi. After passing through the edge of the old town on the E side of the river turn left at the T-junction and follow the road for 13 km to Shahbaz Garhi. There is a turning N here, leading to the village of Rustam and then into Swat via the Ambela Pass. This is the route to Pir Baba (see below).

Shahbaz Garhi

The small village is surrounded by three important sites and is thought to be the location of the ancient city of **Varusha**. The city lay at the intersection of two major trade routes, from China by way of the Indus and Swat valleys, and from Europe and Afghanistan by way of Bajaur and Swat, crossing the Indus at Hund.

Just S of the village on the edge of a hill, visible from the road, are **Asoka's Rock Edicts**, two large boulders inscribed with 14 edicts in the *Kharoshthi* script of Gandhara. There are steps leading up to the rocks and a shelter over them. Having inherited a full-blown empire, Asoka extended it further by conquering Kalinga (modern day Orissa in India), before repenting at the destruction and suffering caused by his military campaigns and preaching the virtues of Buddhist pacifism. He left a series of inscriptions on pillars and rocks across the subcontinent (there are more in Pakistan at Mansehra, see page 438) in which he urged people to follow the code of *Dharma*, encouraging a social order based on tolerance, non-violence and respect for authority.

On a hill to the N of the village, reached from the road leading up to Rustam and the Ambela Pass, are the ruins of **Mekha Sanda** stupa and monastery. Local legend tells how Prince Visvantura, an incarnation of the Buddha, inherited a holy white elephant which brought rains whenever needed. The prince, in a demonstration of generosity designed to inspire his subjects, gave it to a neighbouring kingdom which was hostile but suffering from a drought. His people however disowned him and he was banished to Mekha Sanda with his wife and children. He was only accepted back years later after giving away his children to be sold in the market; the ultimate act of self denial. The two rocks on the hill supposedly resemble a pair of water buffalo, giving the site its name. Nearby are the caves where Prince Visvantura and his family took refuge.

A little further along the road to Rustam, down a track leading off to the left, is the site of **Chanaka Dehri** stupa and monastery commemorating the legendary white elephant. There is little to see there today. Back on the main road to Swabi, past the rock edicts, is the site of **But Sahri** convent and stupa, dedicated to the gift of the two children. The mound is covered by later Muslim graves and is unexcavated.

Asota megaliths

At Shewada (literally 'Shewa junction'), 40 km from Mardan, there is a crossroads. The turning N leads to the village of Shewa. To the right of the road, before the village, there is a small circle of stone megaliths. The standing stones, reminiscent of Stonehenge and other sites in Britain, are thought to have once formed a circle with 30 gates, perhaps representing days of the month. Their origins are far from clear. A local legend relates how a party of women on their way to attend a wedding were waylaid by robbers. One of the women prayed out loud, asking that they should be saved from being raped by the robbers; her prayers were answered after a fashion when the women were all turned to stone. One theory suggests that the site is perhaps a Zoroastrian temple dating from 6th century BC.

Aziz Derhi

Excavations in 1993-4 of a low mound near the village of **Gangu Dher** revealed extensive remains of a Buddhist Monastery. The site covers four periods; Scytho-Parthian, Kushan, Sassanian and Hindu Shahi. Some distinctive sculptures (not yet displayed) recovered from the site will be useful in determining its exact chronology. The carved stairs with their elaborate relief found here are comparable only to those found at the Saidu Stupa in Swat. Large terracotta pots remain on the site, standing still full with earth where they were found amongst the excavations.

The low mound overlooks a flat expanse of fertile land ringed to the N by mountains. The site can be reached either from the village of Gohati on the Mardan-Swabi road, or via Asota to the W. From Gohati, follow the E bank of the Upper Swat Canal N (the turning is signposted to Aziz Derhi) for 14 km and then turn right (also signposted). Bear right at a fork and the mound is signposted to the left after 2-3 km. From Asota you can continue N, bearing right at a fork and crossing a bridge before passing through the village of Shewa. The road then crosses the canal; follow it S to the turning to Aziz Dehri.

Rani Ghat

After 1 km on the track N from Gohati to Aziz Derhi, there is a turning E which after around 7 km arrives at the village of Nogram. Excavations nearby have revealed the archaeological site of Rani Ghat (literally 'queen's rock'), a monastery dating from the Kushan period, complete with stupas and a beautiful gate built of stone blocks.

ROUTES The main road continues E from the junction at Gohati to the town of **Swabi**. From here, one road goes to **Topi** and then crosses the base of **Tarbela Dam**. Local buses from Mardan generally go as far as Topi, from where there are buses to Tarbela, on the other side of the dam. From Tarbela there are buses to Haripur via Lawrencepur and Hasan Abdal, and direct to Islamabad.

The other road heads S to the village

of **Amber**. At the junction in the village the turning left rejoins the Tarbela road just before Topi. The right turn heads SW towards Jehangira on the GT Rd (see page 255). Just SW of the junction is a turning to the village of Hund on the banks of the Indus.

Hund

Although today only a small village reached by a dirt track, Hund was once an important crossing point on the Indus. Its Sanskrit name was *Wada Bahanda Pura* meaning 'city of the water pots', in reference to the large up-turned ceramic pots that were used to cross the river. It was also known as *Vada Bahind Pur* meaning 'city by the river', and as *Wahind*; 'the way to India'. It became the winter capital of the Hindu Shahi rulers of Gandhara after they defeated the Turki Shahis in Kabul in the 9th century AD. Alexander the Great, the Scythians and Kushanas, the Chinese pilgrims, Mahmud of Ghazni, Timurlane, Babur and many others crossed the Indus here on their journeys. The walls, bastions and gates of the 16th century **Akbar's Fort** still survive, surrounding the village. There are also traces of the cobbled road leading down to the river, marking the crossing point. The traces of diaper masonry in the cliff by the river's edge are probably the remains of the earlier Hindu Shahi fort.

The Muslim traveller *Muqaddasi* described the city in the 10th century AD as "a capital city of great glory. Situated on a square open plain, it has many gardens, clean and attractive. The fruits of both summer and winter seasons are plentifully available. Around the city are gardens full of walnuts, almonds, banana and date. Prices are low; three mounds of honey can be bought for one dirham, bread and milk are very cheap. The houses are built of timber covered with dry grass...it could match with the best cities of Iran".

The road to Swat via the Ambela Pass

An alternative to the main route to Swat over the Malakand Pass is the route via the Ambela and Buner passes. Passing through Buner District, it then crosses the Karakar Pass to rejoin the main Swat valley road at Barikot. There is also the option of a detour to the popular shrine of Pir Baba.

The quiet, tree-lined road heads NE from Shahbaz Garhi through green, fertile countryside to the village of **Rustam** where there are basic restaurants and tea stalls. The left turn in the village leads to Pirsai, from where there is a steep pilgrim track up to Kashmir Smats. The right turn leads up to the **Ambela Pass**.

This pass was the scene of the famous Ambela Campaign in 1863 in which the British set out to punish a tribe of 'Hindustani fanatics' from the village of Malka in the hills E of Buner who had been carrying out raids into British controlled territory. They attempted to march across the Ambela Pass without permission of the Pathan tribes of Buner. This provoked them into launching a *jihad* against the British which rapidly gained momentum, leading to the confrontation on the pass. The campaign grew into a major military operation involving around 10,000 men on either side and lasting for 2 months. Eventually the British won a partial victory and were allowed to carry out token retribution on the people of Malka in return for a truce with the Pathan tribes which guaranteed them their independence.

There are excellent views down onto the plains of Peshawar on the climb up to the pass. The road passes through a landscape of boulder-strewn hills scattered with low scrub and patches of cultivation, before descending into a small, well wooded basin. The main road takes a left fork to skirt round the village of Amber, then climbs to the much lower **Buner Pass** which leads over to a larger basin.

After crossing a river, the road passes through the village of Chinar. Soon after is the larger town of **Swari**. Turn left at the T-junction in the town and follow the road to **Daggar**. Shortly after the village, by a small hillock with an old colonial building and a newer fort nearby, there is a fork. The left fork is the direct route to Barikot, passing through the town of Jowar before crossing the Karakar Pass. The right fork leads to Pir Baba; after taking it, turn left at a T-junction and then bear left at a fork. The road passes a turning left which rejoins the road to Barikot at Jowar, then passes through Pacha before arriving in Pir Baba.

Pir Baba (Syed Ali)

Situated in beautiful countryside with Mount Ilam (2,811m) to the E dominating the surrounding mountains, the shrine of Pir Baba is very popular, attracting huge numbers of pilgrims, particularly during the *Urs* which is held at the begining of Sep. Pir Baba, whose real name was Syed Ali Shah (*Pir Baba* is a title of veneration, literally meaning 'great holy man') was reputedly the grandson of the Mughal Emperor Babur, although other sources suggest that his father came from Afghanistan in the service of Babur. To reach the shrine, cross the river in the village and walk up to the large mosque. A path lined with beggars and stalls selling jewellry and perfumes leads directly up to the shrine from inside the mosque.

From Pir Baba it is a ½-hr walk to **Chilla**, the cave on a hillside above the village of Narbatwal where Pir Baba lived his life of meditation. There are attendants who will show you around inside. They will expect a small offering of money.

There are several basic hotels in the village with little to choose between them. Buses and Hiace mini-buses run from here back to Mardan or on to Barikot and Mingora. The drive to Barikot is very scenic. Turn right just S of Pacha and follow the road to **Jowar**, a small town with a bazaar and restaurants etc. Turn right at the T-junction in the town and follow the road up to the **Karakar Pass**. The road climbs up through well wooded hills, with views of Mount Ilam to the right, and then descends to Barikot.

SWAT VALLEY

The Swat valley is one of the most fertile and easily accessible in northern Pakistan. The main attraction is its scenic beauty – lush green valleys with thick pine forests, surrounded by snowy peaks – and pleasant climate in summer. In addition, the area is rich in historical sites dating back to the Gandharan Buddhist period and earlier. Swat is one of the most popular hill destinations for Pakistani tourists, after Murree and the Galis. The downside of this is that some of the hill resorts have been heavily developed, with new hotels springing up rapidly in a haphazard fashion. The main resorts can also get extremely crowded during the peak summer season. However, there are still plenty of beautiful spots, quiet and unspoilt, just that little bit away from the main tourist centres.

Despite its popularity as a tourist destination, the people of Swat valley, who are Pathans and markedly tribal, are distinctly conservative in their outlook. Tourism is tolerated in the valley, and for many is the main source of income, but it sits slightly uneasily alongside the traditional Islamic tribal structure of the society. Away from the larger towns, women may feel slightly uneasy if travelling unaccompanied; they should avoid walking alone in the hills altogether.

The peak tourist season is generally from mid-Jun to mid-Aug, when the climate in the upper sections of the valley is at its best, although lower down it remains very hot. This is also when the valley receives most of its rainfall. If you want to avoid the crowds, the spring (Apr/May) and early autumn (Sep) are the best times to visit, although you should be prepared for chilly nights higher up. The road above Bahrain is sometimes still blocked in May.

Geography

Rising in the **Shandur Range**, the three principle sources of the Swat River – the Gabral, Bahandra and Ushu – unite at Kalam (2,013m) into a single hill torrent which then drops 18m/km in a narrow gorge for 39 km before reaching **Madyan** (1,312m). Here the river broadens out, liberally fed by both monsoon seasonal rainfall and summer snowmelt. Below Mingora the river becomes a huge braided stream up to 5 km wide and rich in silt deposits. The broad riverine flats are the richest and most populous areas in Swat. The river is controlled by a complex system of canals and river cuttings, combined with terracing. Known throughout the NWFP as the '*Maize Granary*', Swat also grows rice, wheat and barley as well as fruits. More recently honey collecting has become popular. Local industries include woollen Swati caps and shawls, blankets, silverware and tribal jewellery. Forestry is also an important source of income with timber being floated down the river to the railhead at Dargai.

However, forest reserves are dwindling rapidly. As well as the activities of logging contractors, there is added pressure from nomadic groups and from a population which has shot up from about 93,000 in 1884 to nearly 2 million in 1994. The joint Pak-Swiss Kalam Integrated Development Project (KIDP) enjoys a high profile and has been remarkably successful in involving local communities in initiatives aimed at ensuring a sustainable pattern of development in the valley.

People

The people of Swat Valley are mostly **Yusufzai Pathans**, displaced from the Peshawar valley by the related *Mandnar Yusufzais* late in the 16th century. The Yusufzais in turn forced the

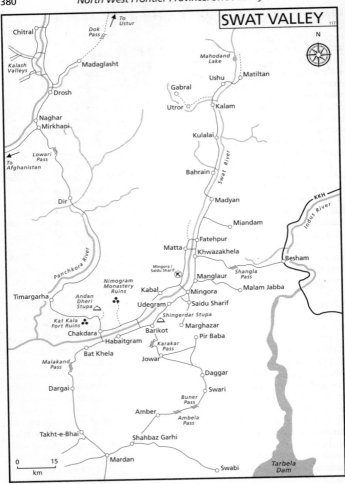

SWAT VALLEY

Dardic speaking *Dilazaks* further up the Swat Valley into the remoter parts of Kohistan and North Hazara. Today, Upper Swat, or Swat Kohistan, is inhabited by two language groups, the *Torwal* and *Gawri*, both Dardic, the former found between Madyan and Kalam, the latter above Kalam up to the Shandur range. In addition there are two nomadic groups, the *Gujars* who mainly herd cattle and the *Ajars* who rear sheep and goats. The Ajars practise extreme forms of *transhumance*, involving annual movements of whole village communities from 600m up to 4,500m, accomplished in 4-5 moves between appropriate seasonal altitude belts.

History

The Swat Valley's favourable environment for settlement has been compared with that of the **Zagros Mountains** in present day Iran, the traditional 'Cradle of Civilization'. The earliest evidence of settlement goes back at least 10,000 years to the early '*Grave Cultures*', so called because the primary evidence of settlement comes from graves. The first written reference to the valley comes from the Vedic literature of the Aryans who called it "*Suvastu*".

Later in 327 BC Alexander the Great passed through the valley when he came through Afghanistan, by way of Bajour and Dir. He captured the ancient fort of **Bazira** in present day **Barikot**, and **Ora (Udegram)** before he went on to the plain of Peshawar.

At the height of the Buddhist Gandharan civilisation in the 1st century AD there were at least 1,400 monasteries in Lower Swat alone. The *Tantric* and the *Mahayana* schools of Buddhism were developed here, spreading throughout the subcontinent. The valley is still rich in Buddhist monastery ruins, stupas, sculptures and rock carvings.

From about the 7th century AD the Swat Valley became the refuge for a much reduced Buddhist culture. Hinduism grew and the **Hindu Shahi** rulers extended their control into the valley during the 8th and 9th centuries AD until they were supplanted by the Muslim, **Mahmud of Ghazni**. Later, under the Mughals, both **Babur** and **Akbar** fought to control the Yusufzai Pathans of Swat, the former marrying into the tribe in 1519.

During the British period, Swat was the scene for the famous Malakand Campaign of 1897 against the **Sayyid Hajji Shoaib Baba** who preached *jihad* against the British and was dubbed the '*Mad Mullah*', an event covered by the young Winston Churchill for the Daily Telegraph.

Swat Valley was consolidated into an independent state in 1926 by the **Wali** or ruler, **Miangal Gulshehzada Abdul Wadood**, the grandson of the *Akhund* of Swat, a famous Sufi ascetic and religious leader (Akhund meaning teacher). His son **Miangal Jahanzib** took over in 1940 until 1969 when Swat was integrated into NWFP. They were competent leaders who achieved internal political integration and promoted the building of roads, hospitals and a free school system.

ROUTES The Swat valley is easily reached from both Peshawar and Islamabad. In either case, it is neccessary to pass first through the Peshawar valley.

From Peshawar, one can either travel E on the GT Rd as far as Nowshera, then head N through Mardan and Takht-e-Bhai and across the Malakand Pass to Swat, or else head NE through Charsadda and join the road N at Mardan or Takht-e-Bhai.

From Islamabad, one can follow the GT Rd W to Nowshera and then head N, or else branch off N at a number of points earlier to join the road running W through Tarbela and Swabi to Mardan.

An alternative route into Swat from Mardan is across the Ambela, Buner and Karakar passes. For details of the routes through the Peshawar valley, see page 371; for details of the route W from Islamabad on the GT Rd, see page 253.

From Takht-i-Bhai, the road continues N through fertile countryside. Factories for processing tobacco, one of the major cash crops in the region, line the route. Soon after the small town of **Shergur** there is a checkpost marking the border between Mardan and Malakand Districts. **Dargai**, the next major town, is the railhead for the narrow-guage line from Nowshera. The railway opened up the area for logging, which is still a major industry.

From here the road climbs steadily up to the **Malakand Pass**. On the way up there are good views S onto the Peshawar valley. The **Upper Swat Canal**, which carries water from the Swat River on the other side of the pass by way of a tunnel, can be seen snaking its way down towards the plains in a series of rapids. The pass itself is topped by a fort, built by the British following the Malakand Campaign in 1897. A small village has grown up around it, and there are simple restaurants serving tea, cold drinks and food. A little further on there is the *District Council Resthouse*, although getting permission to stay here is difficult.

The road descends gently from the pass, arriving at the town of **Bat Khela**, which is spread out over a large area. There is a bus stand here and a few very basic hotels. The ruins of a Hindu Shahi fort are visible up on a ridge to the E. The countryside around is green and fertile, and the road lined with trees. Further on there is a bridge across the Swat River to Chakdara, marking the border with Dir District, and the start of the route to Dir and Chitral (see below). Thana, the next village, with its small bazaar, also spreads up the hillside overlooking the road. Further on is **Habaitgram**, with the ruins of a huge and impressive Hindu Shahi fort above. Below the ruins is the well preserved Buddhist **Top Dara Stupa** and nearby, the ruins of a monastery. The road climbs over a shoulder of the hills and passes **Landakai Checkpost** which marks the start of Swat proper.

Nimogram

7 km beyond Landakai, a turning left leads across the river, giving access to **Nimogram Monastery and Stupas** (pronounced "Neemogram"). Cross to the N side of the river and turn left at the T-junction. At the village of **Dedawar** (2 km), there are the remains of a stupa above the road. After 7 km the road fords the wide stream of the Nimogram valley, and immediately after is the turning N to Nimogram, in the village of **Zarakhela Shamozai**. The first 4 km are metalled, then the road turns to a dirt track and follows the stream bed (for short periods after heavy rains this route becomes impassable). Do not cross over to the right bank. The village of Nimogram is 8 km up the valley. It is a short steep climb up to the ruins, which are amongst the best preserved in Swat. There

are commanding views back down the valley. Although it is not easily accessible, Nimogram is well worth a visit; if you do not have your own transport, the most practical way of doing so is as an excursion from Mingora, where a car can easily be hired. Alternatively, the valley can be reached from Chakdara, to the W. Public transport up the valley is minimal and erratic.

ROUTES The road along the N bank of the Swat River reaches W as far as Chakdara. Going in the opposite direction, it passes through Kabal, with its golf course, the turning right across the river to Mingora, and then Mingora airport. Further on at Matta, there is bridge which gives access to the main road up the Swat valley just N of Khwazakela. At Fatehpur another bridge carries the road back to the E bank.

From the bridge turning to Nimogram, the main road continues past **Birkot Hill**. Ongoing excavations by an Italian acheological team have uncovered part of what is thought to be the ancient town of **Bazira**, conquered by Alexander the Great in 327 BC. The excavations have revealed evidence of continuous occupation for 1,000 years between the 5th century BC and 5th century AD.

The small town of **Barikot** is 1 km past the excavations. A road leads SE from here, across the Karakar, Buner and Ambela passes, and back down onto the plains of Mardan (see page 377).

3 km further along the main road, the ruins of the huge **Shingerdar Stupa** are clearly visible to the right. Local legend attributes the building of this stupa to a king named Uttarasena, who is said to have housed relics of the Buddha inside.

At **Ghalagai**, 2 km futher on, there is a large Buddha carved into the cliff-face beside the road; once in perfect condition, the head has now been completely defaced. Next to it, a set of concrete steps leading to a small cave with more Buddhist carvings, now hardly discernable.

After 7 km, 1 km before the village of Udegram, there is a large rock face known as **Gogdara Rock**, to the right of the road, covered in ancient petroglyphs dating back 3,000 years, depicting stick men riding in chariots and numerous animals. There are also Buddhist carvings dating from around the 6th century AD. More recently, locals have added their names to the rock. (Is it art or is it graffitti?)

Udegram

Udegram is a site of major historical importance. There is a signposted turning right in the village leading to the excavations, which have been identified as the bazaar area of the ancient city of **Ora**, site of one of Alexander the Great's battles as he passed through the valley in 327 BC. Nothing is labelled however and the excavations themselves are not particularly impressive. A path to the right leads up through a large graveyard to the shrine of **Pir Khushab**, one of Mahmoud of Ghazni's generals who died in the seige of **Raja Gira's Fortress** on the hilltop above. The climb up to the fortress is worthwhile. Half way up are the well preserved remains of a mosque. Higher up, a flight of steps lead up to the main citidel of the fortress. The huge crumbling walls stretch out along the ridge, enclosing numerous ruined buildings. Most of the visible remains dates from the Hindu Shahi period, although the site was first occupied as early as 1000 BC. There are excellent views from here in all directions.

According to a local legend, Mahmoud of Ghazni managed to capture the fort by depriving some of his horses of water for several days. When they were released, they quickly found the source of the fortress's water supply, where Mahmoud then concentrated his attack, eventually cutting off the supply to the fortress.

From Udegram it is 8 km on to Mingora. The road enters what is now the suburb of Rahimabad, and passes a turning left which leads directly to the twin-town of Saidu Sharif. The main road enters Mingora from the E, passing the general bus stand on the right and crossing the river into the town itself.

Mingora/Saidu Sharif

The twin-towns of Mingora-Saidu Sharif have now all but merged into each other. Mingora is the old bazaar town, with most of the cheaper hotels, and all the main markets, while Saidu Sharif, to the S across the river, is the administrative centre. Together they form the largest urban centre in Swat, and Mingora in particular has become heavily congested.

Places of interest

Swat Museum Open summer 0830-1730, winter 0830-1600. Refurbished in 1994 with the help of a 'cultural grant' from Japan, the museum now has a much improved display. As well as a collection of Gandharan Buddhist statues and freizes, carved in blue schist and green phyllite, and various terracotta and stucco pieces, there are also knives, arrowheads, pieces of grave pottery etc dating back as far as the 4th century BC. The ethnographic section has some particularly fine examples of traditional silver jewellry and embroidery work.

Shrine of the Akhund of Swat The small colourful shrine to the Akhund of Swat (also known as Saidu Baba) is housed in the marble courtyard of a mosque in Saidu Sharif. It is tucked away amongst the narrow alleys between Marghazar Rd and Aqba Rd.

Saidu Stupa and Monastery Consisting of a lower terrace with the remains of the main stupa, and a higher terrace with the monastery remains, this site is the most easily accessible. Excavations were carried out over a period of 2 decades between 1963 and 1972 by an Italian archaeological team. Take the turning E from the road behind the Central Hospital. A metalled road climbs steeply up to the Stupa. Bear right where it forks.

Butkara 1 Identified as the monastery of T'a-lo, mentioned by the Chinese

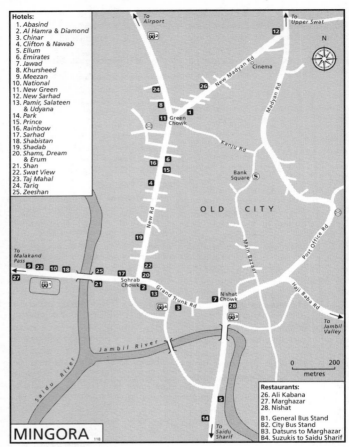

Hotels:
1. *Abasind*
2. *Al Hamra & Diamond*
3. *Chinar*
4. *Clifton & Nawab*
5. *Ellum*
6. *Emirates*
7. *Jawad*
8. *Khursheed*
9. *Meezan*
10. *National*
11. *New Green*
12. *New Sarhad*
13. *Pamir, Salateen & Udyana*
14. *Park*
15. *Prince*
16. *Rainbow*
17. *Sarhad*
18. *Shabistan*
19. *Shadab*
20. *Shams, Dream & Erum*
21. *Shan*
22. *Swat View*
23. *Taj Mahal*
24. *Tariq*
25. *Zeeshan*

Restaurants:
26. Ali Kabana
27. Marghazar
28. Nishat

B1. General Bus Stand
B2. City Bus Stand
B3. Datsuns to Marghazar
B4. Suzukis to Saidu Sharif

MINGORA 118

pilgrim Sung Yun in 520 AD, this site (also known as Gulkada, or simply But-kara) is the most important of those around Saidu Sharif, and yielded a vast array of artefacts. The Italian archaeologist G Tucci identifies the site as part of the ancient city of Uddiyana. The main stupa, thought to have been started by Asoka in the 3rd century BC (at the same time as Dharmarajika in Taxila) perhaps to house some of the ashes of the Buddha, was over the next 12 centuries completely encased by a new, larger stupa no less than five times. Surrounding it are the remains numerous smaller stupa bases, viharas and columns, as well as various stone sculptures, including the lion statues made famous in PTDC posters. During its long period of occupation, the site was subject to repeated flooding and earthquakes, and the different building techniques and styles of each era are clearly identifiable. The successive building phases are reflected

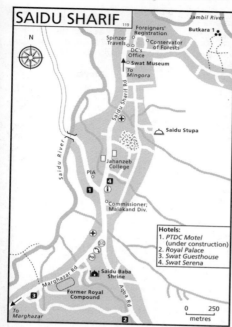

SAIDU SHARIF

Hotels:
1. *PTDC Motel* (under construction)
2. *Royal Palace*
3. *Swat Guesthouse*
4. *Swat Serena*

side of the stream, crossing to the centre where it divides and passing a small mosque on the right, then bear right across a small patch of flat land. The remains are hidden in a cleft below.

Panr The ruins at Panr (pronounced "pahn"), situated on the N side of the Jambil River, consist of a stupa court and monastery. the site is thought to date from the 1st-7th century AD. It is perhaps the least impressive of the sites, and more difficult to reach than the others. There is a crossing point to the N side of the Jambil River about 1 km beyond the turning for Butkara 3, or else follow Hajji Baba Rd SE from Mingora. A path leads off to the left from this road, by a small quarry. Follow the path along the course of a small stream for about 500m, bearing right where it forks, and soon afterwards climb up the left bank on a small path to the site.

also in the haphazard, cluttered layout of the structures surrounding the main stupa. To reach the site, take the turning E off Saidu Sharif Rd, opposite the playing fields. It is N of this road, reached by a narrow, easily missed path leading off to the left, just past the turning right up to He'ra School.

Butkara 3 In some ways this site is the most atmospheric, being tucked away in a small, wooded ravine. There is an open stupa court surrounded by small chambers housing stupas, a couple of which are still fully intact. Excavations were carried out between 1982 and 1985 by Dr Abdur Rahman of Peshawar University. The site is thought to have been occupied from 2nd century BC to 7th century AD. To reach the site, continue along the road for about 500m past Butkara 1 to a culvert; follow the path leading off to the left, up the left

Local information
● Accommodation
The best hotel is the **A** *Swat Serena*, Saidu Sharif, T 710518, F 710402, housed in the old Residency, a/c, heater, TV, fridge, best rooms upstairs overlooking gardens, PTDC Tourist Information Centre, squash, golf (at Kabbal), children's play area, handicraft shops, airport courtesy car, parking, the *Suvastu Restaurant* serves excellent food, heavily discounted summer deals for families.

In Mingora, the best is the central but perhaps overly plush **B** *Pameer*, GT Rd, T 720201, F 720206, a/c, heater, TV/satellite, restaurant, parking.

Away from the centre, the **C** *De-Shahzad*, Canal Rd, Mingora, T 2484 (head N on Madyan Rd and turn left into Canal Rd; hotel is signposted), is quiet and has a pleasant courtyard, a/c and cheaper (**D** category) non a/c rooms, phone, hot water, restaurant (TV/dish), parking, PTDC a/c coach service to Rawalpindi; the **C** *Royal Palace*, Aqba Rd, Saidu Sharif, T 720239, is the old residence of the Wali of Swat, situated up on a hillside overlooking the town, it makes for a good value and restful retreat, a/c and cheaper non a/c rooms, garden, restaurant, parking; **C** *Swat Guest House*, Marghazar Rd, Saidu Sharif, T 720050, also away from centre, a/c and cheaper non a/c rooms, TV/dish, hot water, parking, restaurant, pleasant courtyard and garden; **C** *Swat View*, New Rd, Mingora, T 720886, central, newly built, a/c and cheaper non a/c rooms, heater, TV/dish, fridge, restaurant, car rental, parking. Shopping arcade below; **C** *Zeeshan*, GT Rd, Mingora, T 720325, a/c and cheaper non a/c rooms, hot water, car rental, restaurant (TV/dish); **C** *Al-Hamra*, GT Rd, Mingora, T 710966, a/c, heater, fridge, TV/dish, restaurant, car rental, parking.

There are a great many **E** and **F** category hotels, all of them in Mingora; opp the bus stand and along GT Rd, New Rd, Airport Rd, New Madyan Rd and Madyan Rd. A selection of the better ones are listed here; more are marked on the map.

Opp the General Bus Stand: the **F** *National*, T 4122 and **F** *Taj Mahal*, T 5794, are better. The latter also has some a/c rooms; all of them are noisy.

On GT Rd: are the **E** *Chinar*, T 4456, carpet, clean rooms, restaurant; **E** *Dream*, T 711321, hot water, restaurant (TV/satellite), parking; **E** *Erum*, T 6419, hot water, also some **D** category a/c rooms with TV/satellite, restaurant; **F** *Shan*, T 4206, restaurant; **F** *Udyana*, T 5076, restaurant, good value.

On New Rd: are the **F** *Clifton*, T 720968, restaurant; and next door the **F** *Nawab*, T 720575, also 'duluxe' rooms with carpet and TV/satellite, restaurant; **F** *Mehran*, T 710882, basic but friendly, restaurant; **F** *Rainbow*, T 720573, clean rooms, good value, restaurant, pleasant courtyard, parking, reasonably quiet, rec.

On Airport Rd: the **F** *Khursheed*, T 720469 and **F** *Tariq*, T 6228, both with restaurants, are reasonable though a little out of the way.

On New Madyan Rd: are the **E** *Abasind*, T 710961, pleasant courtyard with parking, and some **C** category a/c rooms, restaurant; **F** *Ali*, T 710964, also some **E** category a/c rooms and rec *Ali Kabana Restaurant* opp; **F** *Shezan*, T 2186, restaurant, basic.

On Madyan Rd: N of People's Chowk, are the **D** *Dilson*, T 2520, a/c and cheaper (**E** category) non a/c rooms, hot water, restaurant (TV/satellite), parking, TDCP a/c coach service to Rawalpindi; **F** *Iqbal*, T 3473, reasonably quiet rooms around a small courtyard, restaurant.

● **Places to eat**
Almost all of the hotels have restaurants; at the top of the range, the *Serena's Suvastu* is rec; it has a good value evening buffet and does an outdoor BBQ on Fri. The restaurant in the *Swat View Hotel* is of a high quality and rec. The cheaper and simpler *Ali Kabana*, opp the *Ali Hotel*, serves good kebabs, karai and tikka, and has a roof-top terrace. The *Nishat*, by Nishat Chowk, is basic but clean, and serves good food. Mingora is an excellent place to sample grilled kebabs, tikkas, karai, and braised liver or *kadahi*, all of which are available from numerous local-style restaurants or road-side stalls, particularly along New Madyan Rd, and also New Rd and GT Rd.

● **Banks & money changers**
National, **United** and **Habib** banks are able to change foreign currency and TCs. All 3 are in Bank Square on Main Bazaar, rates must be phoned through from Karachi so go after 1000, and be prepared for a wait. The *Serena* and *Pameer* hotels do foreign exchange, but rates are significantly below bank rates.

● **Hospitals & medical services**
Chemists: there are chemists in the vicinity of both hospitals and many more in Mingora.

Hospitals: there are 2 hospitals in Saidu Sharif, the *Central* and *Saidu Sharif*.

● **Post & telecommunications**
Area code: 0936.

Post office: there are 2 Post Offices in Mingora; the main one is hidden away in a small alley off New Rd, while the other is on Post Office Rd. The GPO in Saidu Sharif is on Marghazar Rd, nr the junction with Aqba Rd.

Telegraph Office: (Pak Telecom) is next to the Saidu Sharif GPO, open 0800-2030, 7 days.

● **Shopping**
The best buys are the beautiful hand-embroidered shawls, waistcoats, frontpieces etc. There are many shops in Mingora along New Rd and GT Rd. Handicraft shops also sell intricately carved wooden furniture, traditional silver jewellery and precious/semi-precious stones. The maze of tiny alleys between Main Bazaar and New Rd are worth exploring for handicrafts and jewellery.

● **Sports**

The *Serena* has badminton courts, and there is a golf course nearby at Kabbal. PTDC can also arrange pony trekking. Swat has some excellent trout fishing, although the best is higher up the valley.

● **Tourist offices**

The PTDC Tourist Information Centre is in the *Serena Hotel* in Saidu Sharif, T 711205, they are helpful and well-informed, they can organize car hire (with driver). In 1995 the following rates were being charged for return trips; Marghazar Rs 400, Malam Jabba Rs 800, Madyan Rs 800, Miandam Rs 800, Kalam Rs 1,200, Besham Rs 1,200. They also do a good value guided tour of the main Buddhist sites in lower Swat (3-4 hrs, Rs 400). PTDC Motels in Miandam and Kalam can be booked here.

● **Useful addresses**

Police: the police station in Saidu Sharif is on Marghazar Rd, S of the junction with Aqba Rd, T 4051. **Foreigners' registration**: can be processed by the Senior Superintendent of Police (SSP), in the compound off Jambil Rd, T 4291. In special circumstances he may also be able to issue **Visa Extensions**. **Deputy Commissioner (Swat)**: office in same compound as above, T 4668. **Conservator of Forests**: also in the same compound, T 4888.

● **Transport**

Local Car hire: (with driver) can be arranged through PTDC. A number of the more expensive hotels also offer car hire. Alternatively you can negotiate your own from the taxi stand at Sohrab Chowk. **Suzukis** operate between the junction by the Udyana hotel in Mingora and the S end of Saidu Sharif. **Auto-rikshaws** are widely available and the most practical means of getting around.

Air PIA Booking Office, Faizabad, Saidu Sharif, T 711092, open 0800-1700. There are also numerous travel agents, concentrated around New Rd and GT Rd in Mingora, most of which are able to make bookings with PIA. The airport is across the river, about 9 km to the NW.

Road Bus: most services operate from the General Bus Stand, T 5175, on the GT Rd. Regular buses and Hiace mini-buses to Kalam and all towns en-route, as well as Miandam. Services also to Dir and Chitral. Regular buses and mini-buses to Mardan, Peshawar and Rawalpindi. PTDC operate an a/c bus service to Rawalpindi departing 1600 from *De Shazad Hotel* during the summer (May-Aug).

Excursions from Mingora/Saidu Sharif

Jambil Valley

This valley, running SE from Mingora, is rich in archaeological remains. As well as the sites of Butkara 1, Butkara 3 and Panr, mentioned above, there are excavated sites at **Butkara 2, Leobanr** and **Matelai**, further up the valley.

Marghazar/Mount Ilam

14 km from Saidu Sharif, at the head of the Saidu Valley, is Marghazar (1,280m), the former summer palace of the Wali of Swat. The palace has now been converted into a luxury hotel, the **B** *White Palace*, T 2008 (reservation office in Saidu Sharif, T 710848, F 4405), which is beautifully situated, with rooms on 3 levels up the hillside and pleasant gardens with ponds and running water. The restaurant serves Pakistani, Chinese and Continental food. There is a seating area under a large shady tree below the hotel, and in summer a few handicraft shops.

From Marghazar there is a trail up to the summit of Mt Ilam, considered sacred by Muslims, Hindus and Buddhists alike, and until recently attracting considerable numbers of Hindu pilgrims each year. It is a rewarding full-days walk to the top and back. PTDC recommend taking a guide.

During summer there are fairly regular pick-ups from the small yard just S of Nishat Chowk, and occasional buses, or you can hire a taxi. It is a pleasant 30-min drive up through terraced fields and small villages, the acacia-lined road running alongside Saidu stream.

Mingora to Kalam

Leave Mingora on the Madyan Rd, heading N, past Fizagat Park, following the river which flows past rapidly in a wide, shallow, braided course. A number of invitingly located hotels line the route for the first several kilometres. A path leads from the head of the valley across to Gokand in Buner District.

At **Manglaur** the main road crosses a bridge and there is a signposted turning right, up to Malam Jabba, 33 km away at the head of a picturesque valley. 3 km up the valley, on the opposite bank of the river, is the well preserved 7th century **Jahanabad Buddha**, carved on the face of a huge boulder. The carving, directly opposite the village of Malakpur, is visible from the road, although you really need to climb up to it to get a good view and a sense of its scale (it is 4m tall). A small footbridge crosses the river below the village, or there is a larger bridge, passable in a car, a little further on at the village of Jahanabad. The road continues up the valley, climbing steeply through small villages with places to stop along the way for cold drinks or tea. Higher up, the hillsides become more densely wooded with tall pines.

Malam Jabba

At an altitude of over 3,000m, Malam Jabba has snow until May. It was identified as the ideal location in which to develop a ski resort. With Austrian funding a chairlift was built, along with a large luxury hotel. However, due to disputes between the federal and provincial governments over ownership, the chairlift stands idle and the hotel, empty for the last 10 years, is delapidated and heading steadily for dereliction.

There are excellent views down into the main Swat valley and some pleasant walks in the area. The resort is a popular picnic venue in the summer. Hidden in a depression to the left as you face up the chairlift, there are the ruins of a **Buddhist Stupa** and other buildings, although little now remains to be seen.

There are various tea and snack stalls just below the hotel at the road head. Simple but clean accommodation in wooden huts (quilts provided, but no toilet facilities) can be arranged; ask at the tea stalls.

During summer, one bus comes up here once a day from Mingora, leaving around 1000 and returning around 1600; it is very slow, taking approximately 3 hrs, stopping frequently and struggling along in first gear for most of the climb from Manglaur. Datsun pick-ups run more frequently, though irregularly, from Mingora and are quicker. Both leave from the bus stand N of People's Chowk, on Madyan Rd. It is also easy to catch Malam Jabba bound traffic from the junction at Manglaur, although vehicles are often packed full, with people hanging from the roof and sides.

From Manglaur, the main road continues up the Swat valley. The next village, Charbagh, has a small bazaar. The countryside is rich and fertile, with paddy fields and small scattered settlements along the road. At the small town of **Khwazakhela**, a signposted road forks right, leading over the **Shangla Pass** (2,134m) to Besham (see page 447). This route is very scenic, climbing through fertile terraced fields and rich forests. On top of the pass there is the *Shangla Top Rest House*, bookable through the Conservator of Forests in Saidu Sharif. There are also Forestry Dept resthouses at *Yakhtangi* and *Alpurai*, on the way down from the pass. There is a bridge across to the W bank of the Swat River at Khwazakhela and a couple of simple hotels, the best being the **F** *Awami*, basic but clean, restaurant.

The main road continues N up the valley, passing through the village of Fatehpur, where another bridge crosses to the W bank of the Swat River. Shortly after the town there is a signposted turning E to Miandam. There are several small tea shops by the junction.

Miandam

Miandam, 9 km from the junction on the main road, is a popular resort and can get very busy. *Best time to visit*: is just before or after the peak season (usually Jul and Aug), when it is quieter. Situated

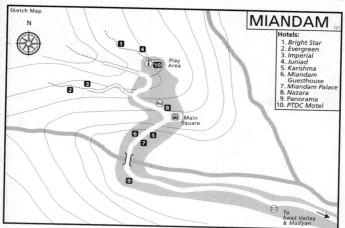

Sketch Map
N

MIANDAM

Play Area

Pol

Main Square

To
Swat Valley
& Madyan

Hotels:
1. *Bright Star*
2. *Evergreen*
3. *Imperial*
4. *Juniad*
5. *Karishma*
6. *Miandam Guesthouse*
7. *Miandam Palace*
8. *Nazara*
9. *Panorama*
10. *PTDC Motel*

at an altitude of 1,820m it is pleasantly cooler in summer. There are nice walks in the surrounding valley.

● **Accommodation** Price categories are for the peak season, when it may be neccessary to book in advance; prices are very negotiable off-season. The standard of accommodation is generally good in terms of cleanliness. **C** *Imperial*, T 780600, 3-storey, newly built with a mirror extravaganza of a lobby, VIP, duluxe and normal rooms, hot water, TV/satellite, parking, direct dialling, restaurant; **C** *Juniad*, T 17, situated behind the *PTDC Motel* with nice views down into the next valley, large rooms, some wood panelled, hot water, TV/satellite, small garden, restaurant; **C** *PTDC Motel*, T 10, expensive, but still the most pleasant for its mature shady gardens; as well as the main complex, there are 2 rm 'cottages' below, hot water, camping, restuarant, tourist information; **D** *Miandam Guest*, T 7320, next door to the *Juniad*, hot water, good views, restaurant; **D** *Evergreen*, T 780600, VIP, deluxe, ordinary rooms, hot water, comfortable, not such good views, restaurant; **D** *Miandam Guest House*, expensive for what you get, hot water, restaurant with TV/satellite; **D** *Miandam Palace*, T 4, good views, hot water, car park, restaurant; **D** *Panorama*, T 14, across bridge from main village, newly built, good value, hot water, parking, restaurant; **E** *Karishma*, T 4, good views, clean, hot water; **F** *Nazara*, T 5, overlooking main square/bus stand, reasonable, dubious sewage plumbing upstairs.

Soon after the turning E up to Miandam, the main road up the Swat valley reaches the town of Madyan, 56 km from Mingora. The valley begins to narrow here, and one gets a sense of being amongst the mountains.

Madyan

Madyan (1,320m) is a small, lively town with a bustling bazaar, situated on the banks of the Swat River where a side valley drains in from the E. The town has plenty of hotels, although it does not get as busy as Miandam or Kalam, and retains something of its traditional character. It is popular amongst backpackers, in part due to Muambar Khan's long-standing reputation (see below), and also as a quieter alternative to the busier resorts. There are several shops in the main bazaar with an interesting selection of antique jewellery, coins, furniture etc, as well as carpets, rugs and locally embroidered woolen shawls; prices generally compare favourably with the more popular resorts. The wooden mosque in the old village, down by the river, is worth a visit. There are plenty of pleasant walks in the area.

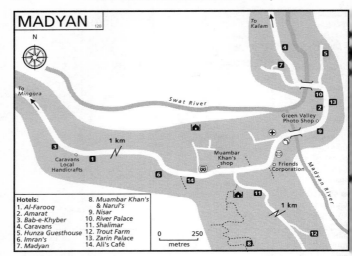

MADYAN 120

N

To Kalam

To Mingora

Swat River

Green Valley Photo Shop

Muambar Khan's shop

Friends Corporation

Madyan River

1 km

Caravans Local Handicrafts

1 km

Hotels:
1. Al-Farooq
2. Amarat
3. Bab-e-Khyber
4. Caravans
5. Hunza Guesthouse
6. Imran's
7. Madyan
8. Muambar Khan's & Narul's
9. Nisar
10. River Palace
11. Shalimar
12. Trout Farm
13. Zarin Palace
14. Ali's Café

0   250
metres

Local information

● Accommodation

C *Madyan*, T 780031, F 780035, away from the centre, across the bridge on the road to Bahrain. Good views, comfortable rooms, hot water, around courtyard/gardens, also deluxe rooms (**B** category) with river view, TV, phone, sitting room, restaurant, parking.

D *Nisar*, T 789241, rooms a little dirty, cold water, as well as the main block overlooking the bazaar, there is one behind overlooking a courtyard, restaurant, GPO/PCO below; **D** *River Palace*, T 780242, 3 storeys overlooking river, hot water, carpet, restaurant; **D** *Zarin Palace*, T 780321, large (54 rm) newly built hotel, clean, some rooms with TV/dish, phone and hot water, upstairs balcony area, function room, restaurant, handicraft shops below.

E *Caravans*, across bridge on road to Bahrain, basic but clean, cold water, established by a Danish Muslim, Michael, but forcibly bought out in 1994 and still using the *Caravans* name; Michael meanwhile has re-established himself with a house in the village (see below).

F *Hunza Guest House*, on riverside nr bridge, recently established by a British refugee couple from Kashmir, simple and friendly, 6 rm and 2 shared bathrooms, self catering, plans for a restaurant; **F** *Imran*, T 780263, nr bus stand, simple but clean rooms, hot water, nice balco-nies, restaurant; **F** *Shalimar*, Chail Rd, T 780040, reasonable rooms, cold water, pleasant quiet garden/courtyard.

House rentals: the tradition started by Muambar Khan in the 1960s of providing overland travellers with local style accomodation still continues. Muambar Khan's spartan but idyllic house in the village above the bazaa is now complemented by Michael's **E** *Caravans Guest House*, a comfortable traditionally furnished room (sleeps 4, more under construction), peaceful with nice views. Booking and information from the *Caravans Handicraft Shop* on the main road, just past the petrol pump 1 km S of Madyan; **F** *Muambar Khan and son Riaz*, the original house rental, simple rooms with shared facilities, immediately be-low Michael's *Caravans Guest House*, booking at Muambar Khan's shop, N of the bus stand. Another son meanwhile is building *Nooru Amin's Western Guest House* next door, a similar setup, but more comfortable, with hot water and self-catering facilities. Between them, Michael and Muambar Khan's family offer very pleasant alternative budget accommodation with a friendly, relaxing atmosphere.

Out of town: 1 km S of Madyan, opp the petrol station, is the **E** *Bab-e-Khyber* T 780441, F 780368, comfortable rooms, hot water, TV/dish, good value, parking, restaurant; and nearby the friendly **F** *Al Farooq*

780443, clean rooms, hot water, small garden at rear, restaurant with TV/dish. 2 km N of Madyan, on the road to Bahrain, there are 3 E category hotels; *Jamal Guest House*, 780490, overlooking river, hot water, nice balcony, restaurant and more rooms under construction, TV/dish, parking; *Mountain View*, T 780572, rec, comfortable rooms (full-size beds!) around a courtyard/garden, cold water, restaurant; *River Breez*, T 780588, hot water, better rooms with river view, small restaurant, TV/dish.

As well as the hotel restaurants in Madyan, there are a few simple Pakistani-style eating places in the bazaar. *Ali's International Cafe*, opp the Bus Stand, is friendly, if not sparkling clean.

● **Shopping**

Caravans handicraft shop, on the left about 1 km before the main town coming from the S, has a good selection of local handicrafts and antiques. The *Friends Corporation*, in the main bazaar have a similar selection; they also have a shop N of the town, next to the *Mountain View Hotel*, with probably the largest selection of antique carved wooden furniture available in Swat.

● **Transport**

Local Bus: services (buses and Hiace mini-buses) N to Bahrain and Kalam, and S to Mingora leave from the Bus Stand in the main bazaar, departing when full. Services also to Miandam.

The main road crosses to the W bank of the Swat River at Madyan, and continues N to Bahrain. The valley meanwhile steadily closes in and begins to climb more steeply. At Bahrain the river is a muddy, fast-flowing torrent, dotted with rapids.

Bahrain

This town is busy with hotels, although most of the Pakistani tourists seem to stop only to shop at the equally numerous antique and handicraft shops. The town is spread out along the road, on either side of the roaring Darel Khwar as it flows into the Swat River from the W. Away from the road, along the banks of the Darel, there are some interesting old houses with intricately carved woodwork.

● **Accommodation** C *Marina*, 780168, overlooking river, deluxe (TV/dish), moderate and economy (roadside) rooms, hot water, expensive, restaurant, parking; D *Delux*, T 780115, nice location, clean rooms with balconies overlooking river, hot water in morning, restaurant, parking; D *Swat Valley*, T 780152, overlooking Swat River, hot water, restaurant; E *Abshar*, T 780122, on the N bank overlooking the roaring Daral Khwar, hot water in morning, food on order; E *Bahrain*, T 780533, above Muslim Commercial Bank, hot water, restaurant; E *Bollan*, T 780126, rather dirty, hot water, restaurant; E *Dimsun*, T 780047, overlooking Swat River, hot water, restaurant; E *Jabees*, T 780023, next to *Abshar Hotel*, expensive, hot water, restaurant; E *Lachine*, T 780300, hot water, restaurant, parking. About 1 km N of Bahrain there is the D *Liberty*, T 780045, hot water, *Shandana Restaurant* opp; next to it is the simple F *Daman-e-Koh*, no phone, 9 rm.

It is a further 30 km to Kalam from Bahrain. Opposite the village of **Kulalai**, the Mankial valley drains in from the E. A footpath leads up the valley and over into Kandia valley, which drains into the Indus N of Dasu on the KKH; this route crosses into Indus Kohistan and is not safe without a reliable local guide. There is a *Forestry Rest House* in Kulalai, bookable through the Conservator of Forests in Saidu Sharif. The peak of Mankial mountain (5,726m) can be seen at various points from the road. Beyond Kulalai, the road deteriorates to a rough track in places; during winter it is often impassable around here. At the village of Pishmal there is a mosque by the roadside with its wooden minaret, in typical Swati style, still intact.

Kalam

This popular Pakistani holiday resort has seen phenomenal growth in the last decade, and now boasts more than 60 hotels, with many more under construction. Its great attraction is its altitude and therefore cool climate during the summer months, as well as the beauty of the surrounding valleys and mountains. The new town itself is all hotels; incongruously down-country and urban in style, built in concrete and often damp from the long winter. Along the road into town it is like a competition in extravagance. There are now quite a number of handicraft shops and various restaurants and food stalls along the main bazaar.

Across the wooden suspension bridge is the old village of Kalam. The old **mosque**, with its massive carved wooden pillers and scrolls and intricately worked doors, is worth a visit. During summer a favourite is to sit on charpoys placed in the shallow edges of the river with the cool mountain water flowing underneath, sipping cold drinks or tea and chattng. Nearby is a mini fairground.

To the N of Kalam there are several very beautiful valleys, accessible by jeep, which offer endless opportunities for day-trips as well as trekking (see below).

Local information
● **Accommodation**

Most of the better hotels are up on the hillside to the E. The cheaper places along the main bazaar, and the posh ones on the road in, are generally noisy, although in the rooms right down by the roaring river you can drown out everything. 'Load shedding' is something of a nonsense here as there is rarely electricity and at night the resort reverberates to the sound of generators. Price categories are for the high season; out of season prices are extremely negotiable. A selection of hotels is given below.

B *Honey Moon*, booking in Mingora T 4725, on main road, extravant building and decor, TV/dish, *Zafran Restaurant* outside, banquet hall upstairs, parking, will change US$ cash, overpriced; **B** *PTDC Motel*, T 14, up on hillside overlooking town, rooms in main block or seperate 'huts', restaurant, garden, parking, expensive, good views, foreigners may be allowed to camp for a couple of nights at a time, will change US$ cash; **B** *Royal Regency Inn*, T 22 (in Mingora T 710848), on main road, similar style to *Honey Moon*, though slightly less ostentatious, TV/dish, restaurant (Chinese, Continental, Pakistani), will change US$ cash, hope to have direct dialling by end 1995, parking; **B** *Walnut Heights*, T 60 (reservations T 0531 68544), situated 2 km above Kalam, past the village of Jalban, this luxury hotel with its excellent views, large, comfortable and tastefully furnished rooms and homely atmosphere, is Kalam's best kept secret

and far and away the best value luxury hotel available. Restaurant, parking.

C *Bagh-e-Bala*, good view, hot water in morning, rooms basic but clean, upstairs best, restaurant; **C** *Heaven Breeze*, T 19, up on hilltop, good views, hot water in morning, restaurant with TV/dish; **C** *Marco Polo Tourist*, newly-built wooden lodge style hotel on main road, hot water 24 hrs, food service, parking; **C** *Pameer*, T 9, on main road, hot water 24 hrs, expensive, restaurant; **C** *Sangam*, T 15, up on hillside, good location/view, comfortable well-run hotel, good value, rec, *Shahzad Restaurant*, parking.

D *Manano Inn*, T 40, on main road, hot water in morning, good clean rooms, posh restaurant, parking; **D** *Seeside*, T 26, in main bazaar by footbridge, overlooking river, hot water in morning, restaurant with TV/dish/VCR.

E *Al-Hamood*, up on hilltop, hot water, restaurant; **E** *Daryal*, T 29, in main bazaar nr footbridge, overlooking river, hot water in morning, restaurant; **E** *Delux Inn*, T 51, in main bazaar, hot water in morning, Lahori restaurant with TV/dish; **E** *Hill Top*, T 43, up on hillside, reasonable views, hot water in morning, restaurant, good value budget hotel; **E** *King's Valley*, T 20, on main road, hot water in morning, reasonably clean rooms, restaurant; **E** *Shangreela*, set slightly back from main road, small garden, hot water, restaurant with TV/dish, parking;

F *Khalid*, T 6, in main bazaar, one of the first hotels in Kalam, hot water in morning, office for Dardistan Trekking (see under tour operators).

● **Places to eat**

Most of the hotels have restaurants. There are also some simple Pakistani-style restaurants in the main bazaar.

● **Banks & money changers**

There are no banks offering foreign exchange in Kalam; the nearest is in Mingora. PTDC, Sangam and Royal Regency hotels can however change US$ cash only.

● **Hospitals & medical services**

There is a mini hospital, the Habib Medical Centre, up on the hillside, near Hill Top hotel, which can offer basic treatment.

● **Post & telecommunications**

Area code: 0936; to phone a number in Kalam you must first call the telephone exchange, T 780001, and then ask to be put through to the relevant number which is in effect an extension.

Post Office: there is no post office in Kalam; the letter box is across the wooden bridge, nr the old mosque.

● **Shopping**

There is now quite a selection of handicraft and souvenir shops, although prices are generally higher than in the towns lower down the valley.

● **Sports**

The rivers N of Kalam offer excellent trout fishing. Permits (Rs 50/day) can be obtained from the Fisheries Dept, opp the police station.

● **Tour companies & travel agents**

Dardistan Trekking Co, Khalid Hotel, run by Aslam Khan; reliable and knowledgeable; *PTDC* are able to arrange jeep hire and can also rec reliable guides for trekking; *Tourist Information Centre*, run by Shah-e-Room, jeep hire, English speaking guides, tents and trekking equipment. Most of the hotels will also offer to arrange for any treks or outings from Kalam.

● **Tourist offices**

The PTDC Motel has a small Tourist Information Centre; they are mainly useful for arranging jeep hire or finding reliable guides.

● **Useful addresses**

Police: the police station is up on the hill, past the PTDC Motel. Contact through the telephone exchange (T 780001).

● **Transport**

Jeep hire: prices for jeep hire tend to fluctuate according to demand, escalating when it gets busy. In summer 1995 it cost around Rs 800 for a day trip to Mahodand or Gabral.

Road Buses and Toyota Hiaces (much quicker) operate from the bus stand in the bazaar to Bahrain, Madyan and Mingora, leaving when full.

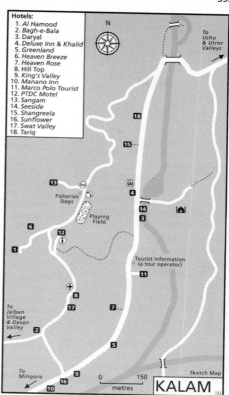

Hotels:
1. Al Hamood
2. Bagh-e-Bala
3. Daryal
4. Deluxe Inn & Khalid
5. Greenland
6. Heaven Breeze
7. Heaven Rose
8. Hill Top
9. King's Valley
10. Manano Inn
11. Marco Polo Tourist
12. PTDC Motel
13. Sangam
14. Seeside
15. Shangreela
16. Sunflower
17. Swat Valley
18. Tariq

To Ushu & Utror Valleys

Fisheries Dept

Playing Field

Tourist Information (a tour operator)

To Jalban Village & Desan Valley

To Mingora

0   150
metres

Sketch Map

KALAM

Around Kalam

The mountains and valleys around Kalam are extremely beautiful, many of them still thickly wooded, with fast-flowing trout-filled streams, waterfalls and glaciers cascading down from the mountains and numerous lakes and meadows. Locals fondly refer to their "Switzerland of Pakistan".

Socially though it is no Switzerland. Swat *Kohistan*, 'land of mountains', is almost by definition lawless and tribal, or rather governed only by tribal law. The recently removed signs saying "Do not go beyond this point as the area is dangerous and the woods are dense" have been replaced by an uneasy truce between a tribal society which is also very conservative and traditional, and the middle class Punjabis fuelling the tourist mini-boom here. The ubiquitous guns, today mostly automatic weapons, which form so fundamental part of the society now also earn Rs 10 for each bullet fired by the tourists. **NB** Whether you are going for a day-trip to one of the valleys around Kalam or intend to trek N to Laspur or E to Dir, it is essential that you take a reliable local guide. Permits are required for fishing in any of the rivers around Kalam.

A bridge crosses the Swat River at the N end of Kalam. Shortly afterwards the road forks; left to Utror and Gabral; right to the Ushu valley and Mahodand.

Ushu valley and Mahodand

Following the right fork, the road passes through thick pine forest and climbs up the **Ushu valley** to Ushu village. Beyond the village it crosses the river and immediately after is the pleasant **D** *Ushu Hotel*, beautifully situated right down by the fast-flowing river, with a small trout farm adjacent. The road then passes through Matiltan village with its old wooden mosque. There is a *Forestry Rest House* here, bookable through the Conservator of Forests in Saidu Sharif. Beyond the village, the road, previously metalled, becomes a rough jeep track. It climbs through terraced fields of potatoes, corn and maize, and then crosses the snouts of various small seasonal glaciers before reaching Mahodand, 35 km NE of Kalam. The glaciers have generally retreated sufficiently by late May/early Jun to be passable. On the way up there are excellent views of Mt Falaksir (6,259m) to the E.

Mahodand, meaning 'Lake of Fishes' in Pashto, is in fact a stretch of the Ushu River where it runs across level terrain, allowing it to widen out and giving the appearance of a lake. The 'lake' is surrounded by pine trees and beautiful open grassy meadows; its calmer waters make for excellent trout fishing. Mahodand is a very popular picnic spot in summer, and can get quite busy. A trail continues N from here, and a choice of three trekking routes lead over into the Chitral and Gilgit valleys.

Utror and Gabral

The left fork follows the Utror River for 16 km to Utror village. The road is metalled for about the first 9 km before becoming a rough track. From Utror, it is a further 8 km on to Gabral village. There is a *Forestry Rest House* in both villages, bookable through the Conservator of Forests in Saidu Sharif. There are numerous picnic spots amongst the pine trees by the river, and endless opportunities for walking, although you should take a guide with you, even for a short stroll. The walk up to Kundalu Lake, 2 hrs to the N of the jeep track between Utror and Gabral, is supposed to be particularly beautiful. The trout fishing in the area is excellent. From Utror, a trekking route leads W towards Dir.

Desan Valley

The Desan valley, which climbs up from behind the *Walnut Heights Hotel* above Kalam, through pastures and woods, is also very beautiful. There is no jeep track here, although the hotel can organize ponies for an outing or longer trek up the valley.

There are more than half a dozen lakes in the valleys around Kalam; if you have the time, it is well worth exploring the area with a knowledgeable local guide to find the nicest and most secluded spots.

CHITRAL VALLEY

Chitral is an area of outstanding natural beauty, with some spectacular opportunities for trekking and climbing. It is also home to a variety of peoples, including the non-Muslim Kalash and the semi-nomadic Wakhi. Like Hunza, the people of upper Chitral are Ismaili Muslims and much more open in their outlook. Compared with the Northern Areas, Chitral receives very few tourists.

Culturally and physically it is the most isolated region of NWFP. Only two roads connect it with the rest of Pakistan. The main route through Dir and over the **Lowari Pass** (3,118m) is closed by snow from late Nov until May while the lengthy route from Gilgit on a rough jeep track over the **Shandur Pass** (3,734m) generally closes earlier and for longer. In winter, the Fokker Friendship flights between Peshawar and Chitral are the region's main link with the outside world. They are subject to frequent cancellation due to bad weather, even in summer. The only land route into Chitral passable in winter is the route detouring into Afghanistan around the Lowari pass, unfortunately closed to foreigners.

Geography
The **Hindu Kush** range, averaging 4,500m and dominated by Tirich Mir (7,787m) and Istora Nal (7,327m) marks the watershed between the valleys draining the Oxus and the Indus Basins. S and E, the **Shandur** mountains (also known as the Hindu Raj or Mashabar) separate Chitral from Gilgit, Swat and Dir.

The **Chitral River**, known by four different names at various stages along its course, rises in the area of the **Chiantar glacier**, a 40 km sheet of ice which is also the source of the Oxus and Gilgit rivers. Here, as the **Yarkhun**, it flows down from an altitude of over 5,000m to be joined by the **Laspur River** which drains most of the N slopes of the Shandur range. It is then known as the **Mastuj** until joined by the Lutkoh branch, draining the Tirich Mir region, where it becomes the Chitral River for much of its course until, close to Afghanistan, it becomes the **Kunar**. In total the river valley runs to over 300 km. Below Chitral town the river plain widens to over 4 km in width and runs in a broken pattern of cultivated alluvial fans right down to **Nagar**, 10 km S of Drosh.

Historically the Chitral Valley was one of the main arteries of the Silk Rd, across the **Boroghil Pass** to Yarkand and Kashgar, but was later replaced by the more southern routes along the Indus and through Kashmir and Ladakh due to persistent banditry and feuding in the region.

Agriculture
Agriculture in Chitral is irrigation based, and highly developed in places, involving up to 15 km of gravity flow channels. The main crops are barley, wheat and *jowar* (millet), followed by rice, vegetables and fruit, and pulses on the *barani* land. Due to the low elevation of much of the river plain, double-cropping is extensively practised. Nevertheless, the region experiences a deficit in food grains each year and relies heavily on the surpluses imported from down-country. There is also widespread cultivation of opium and cannabis along the Afghan border, aggravating the deficit in food grains. Soil erosion is a major problem since most cultivation is on steeply sloping, cleared forest tracts. The Chitrali word for 'level ground' refers to any land at less than a 45° angle!

Flora and fauna
Chitral has a wide range of plant species, particularly higher up amongst the summer pastures; wild geraniums, hemlock, buttercups, edelweiss, blue

anemonies, delphiniums, wild onion and garlic and many others can all be seen. Most flower between May and Jul, depending on the altitude. Forest reserves are limited to about 120 km of the valley between 1,900m and 2,300m. Species include the Deodar (Indian Cedar), Blue Pine, Chiligoza Pine and Silver Fir, of which Deodar represents 90% of the forest cover and the only viable source of timber, although slow growing (125 years to maturity) and susceptible to cracking. At higher altitudes there are stands of Willow and Birch and some Juniper scrub.

Markhor, Ibex, Brown Bears and Snow Leopards were all once found in the higher valleys in considerable numbers but their populations have been much reduced by hunting. Wolves, foxes, jackals, hyenas and marmots are still common. A number of migratory birds, including the Black Throated Thrush, Golden Oriole, Grey Heron, Mallard and Oriental Turtle Dove, pass through the valleys en route between Central Asia and India. The hunting of these birds, ducks in particular, is a major problem. In many of the valleys of upper Chitral, large artificial ponds by the river's edge and at the junctions with side valleys are used to attract the migrating ducks. On landing they become an easy target for shooting. The practice is deeply rooted in Chitrali culture and remains popular today; the advent of shotguns meanwhile has radically increased the numbers killed. The Sakar Falcon is also hunted, although primarily for capture and sale in the Middle East, where falconry is a popular sport amongst the wealthy. A good female Saker Falcon can fetch as much as US$ 50,000.

History

The early history of this region is very unclear. The **Tibetans** are known to have forged a close alliance with Chitral in the 8th century AD having invaded Yasin to the E. They were driven out by the **Chinese**, who captured Chitral in 750 AD, only to be themselves defeated by the **Arabs**. According to a Sanskrit inscription found carved on a rock near the village of Barenis in Mastuj, around 900 AD the region was Buddhist and ruled by an Afghan king. Local legend talk also of attacks on Chitral by the **Mongols** under **Ghengis Khan**.

Chitral is known to have existed as an unified independent kingdom from at least the 14th century, when **Shah Nadir Rais** established himself as overall ruler. According to some sources Shah Nadir Rais was descended from the Trakhan rulers of Gilgit, others suggest that he came from Badakhshan. Certainly, the Rais Dynasty paid tribute to the rulers of Badakhshan. Prior to the arrival of Shah Nadir Rais, the region was divided amongst a number of petty rulers. Rais was successful in uniting the area by allowing each of these rulers some degree of autonomy, while at the same time playing them off against each other in order to limit their individual power and prevent them from uniting against him.

Following the death of **Sangin Ali**, a powerful advisor to the Rais rulers, in 1570, two of his four sons managed to oust the Rais Dynasty, establishing what became known as the **Kator Dynasty** which ruled right up until the 1960s. The **Adamzada** clan, which form most of the upper class in Chitral, are descended from Sangin Ali's grandsons. The **Khushwaqt** family, who later emerged as rulers of Mastuj, Yarkhun and the Gilgit valley, are similarly descended from this family. The history of the region from this time is an intricate web of intrigue and conspiracy amongst the various families of the ruling classes, further complicated by almost continual warring with neighbouring kingdoms.

In 1857, **Aman-ul-Mulk** emerged as Mehtar of Chitral, and by 1880 had exended his rule to include the semi-independent kingdom of Mastuj. The British meanwhile, fearful of the possibili-

of the Russians gaining a foothold here, had already sent a mission to Chitral under **Lockhart** in 1855-6. In 1889, following the establishment of Gilgit Political Agency, they provided him with a subsidy of Rs 6,000 per annum, which they doubled in 1891 on the condition that he accepted British advice on all matters connected with foreign policy and the defence of the frontier. By 1889 the **Trans-Caspian Railway** linking the European provinces of Tsarist Russia with Tashkent, had been completed. Russian exploration parties visited Hunza in 1889 and Chitral in 1891, and British speculation at the threat of Russian expansion into S Asia began to appear well founded.

The sudden death of Aman-ul-Mulk of a heart attack in 1892, leaving no less than 16 sons to dispute the succession amongst themselves, compounded by British attempts to influence the course of events in their favour, unleashed a particularly bloody chapter in Chitral's history. His second son, **Afzal-ul-Mulk**, who happened to be in Chitral town at the time, immediately seized power and began killing off his brothers and half-brothers so as to eliminate any challenge to his authority. **Nizam-ul-Mulk**, the eldest son, fled to Gilgit and took refuge there. **Umra Khan**, the ruler of Dir at this time, took advantage of the dissarray in Chitral and invaded, taking control of Chitral Fort. At the same time, **Sher Afzal**, the exiled brother of Aman-ul-Mulk, attacked from Afghanistan with a small army. In the ensuing chaos (Afzal-ul-Mulk was ready at this point to launch a counter-attack), Sher Afzal managed to take the fort, while Afzal-ul-Mulk was killed. Nizam-ul-Mulk then returned from Gilgit, and Shah Afzal, believing that he had the support of the British, fled back to Afghanistan. Thus Nizam-ul-Mulk regained the Mehtarship, to the relief of the British, who lost no time in establishing a Political Agency in Chitral.

The siege of Chitral 2 years later, in Jan 1895, he too was murdered, this time by **Amir-ul-Mulk** (one of his half-brothers), who took over the Fort. Umra Khan meanwhile once again marched on Chitral, taking Drosh after 1 month's seige. The British, no doubt bewildered and confused at the rapidly changing events in Chitral, which had by now assumed enormous strategic significance in their eyes, sent a force from Gilgit under **Major George Robertson** to investigate. On their arrival, they forcibly occupied the fort, a classic piece of British heavy-handedness guaranteed to turn all the parties against them. Shah Afzal, now in open allegiance with Umra Khan, duly attacked from Afghanistan. The remaining ruling class families joined them and even Amir-ul-Mulk made overtures before being confined to the Fort. For the British, the situation was begining to look desperate. Umra Khan succeeded in capturing two British Officers at Buni, annihilating their contingent of men and taking over 40,000 rounds of ammunition in the process, while another detachment of 100 men of the 14th Sikh regiment under **Captain Ross** were annihilated at Reshun. The seige of Chitral lasted for over a month. Major Robertson managed to hold out until at last a detatchment of reinforcements sent from Gilgit under the leadership of **Colonel James Kelly** prompted the Chitrali forces to retreat. Kelly's march across the snowbound Shandur Pass in early Apr, complete with two cannons, was recognized as a major achievement, and certainly took the Chitralis by surprise. Soon after, a much larger relief force (the British were taking no chances) arrived by way of Malakand and Dir. The British placed **Shuja-ul-Mulk** (Amir-ul-Mulk's brother), a boy of 14, on the throne and thereafter kept a close eye on the kingdom, supplementing the Political Agent there with a large back-up force in Drosh. Major Robertson, arguably responsible for triggering the fiasco through his indiscretion, was subsequently knighted for his "gallant bravery".

The Imperial Gazeteer records how; "Since then [the Siege of Chitral] Chitral has enjoyed an unwonted peace ... Hospitals have been opened ... Cultivation has been extended and the Methar's revenue continues to increase, while at the same time his mental horizon has been much enlarged by his visits to Calcutta, Delhi and Peshawar." In fact the British did very little; notwithstanding its strategic significance, they showed minimal interest in the province and made no real effort to develop it.

At Independence, the Mehtar of Chitral acceded to Pakistan, but remained in charge of all internal affairs of the former Princely State. The Pakistani government was represented by a Political Agent, an arrangement that almost exactly mirrored the system under British rule. However, in 1954 there was an internal revolt against the Mehtar, and the Political Agent took over direct control until 1969, when the state was formally merged into Pakistan, becoming a district of the newly formed Malakand Division of NWFP.

People

The Chitrali people, who call their land *Kho*, are not Pathan. Although their language, *Khowar*, belongs to the Dardic group, it has strong connections with the languages of the Pamir and Wakhan regions to the N, and with Iran. In addition there are two minorities; the **Kalash**, who number about 3,000 and inhabit the valleys of Birir, Bumburet and Rumbur, just S of Chitral, and the **Wakhi**, a nomadic group occupying the Pamir (literally 'upland grazing zone') and the neighbouring Wakhan Corridor, a thin wedge of Afghan territory separating the former Soviet Union and Pakistan.

Population and development

Chitral is one of the most sparsely populated and least developed districts of NWFP. It covers over one-fifth of the land area of NWFP, and yet accounts for just 1% of the total population. It was not until the 1970s that any real efforts at developing the region were made. The road from Chakdara to the Lowari Pass was paved, flights between Peshawar and Chitral initiated and electricity provided to at least the major villages. At the same time, subsidized wheat and fertilizers began to be made available along with improved healthcare and education, leading to marked improvements in income levels, nutrition and literacy. Nevertheless, Chitral remains politically and economically marginalized; per capita expenditure in 1994-5 was just Rs 358, compared to Rs 1,500 in the Northern Areas.

The Road to Chitral

The route to Chitral is the same as for Swat as far as Chakdara. Here a road crosses the Swat River and passes through **Dir District**. Dir, like Chitral to the N, existed as an independent kingdom for many centuries, before being incorporated into Pakistan following independence. The people of Dir are predominantly Yusufzai Pathans, and the region is not particularly friendly. There is little to stop for along the road up through the district, and most tourists pass straight through en-route for Chitral. Dir town is the last urban centre before the road climbs over the Lowari Pass into Chitral. It makes a convenient place in which to break the long road journey.

Chakdara

The bridge across the Swat River at Chakdara marks the start of Dir district. After the bridge, to the right of the road is **Chakdara Fort**, built by the British in 1896, on the site of an earlier Mughal fort, built in 1586 following Akbar's campaigns in the area. It is now occupied by the Dir Scouts and closed to the public. To the left of the road is **Damkot**

Hill, site of **Churchill's Picket** and **Shishi (mirror) Guard**.

Excavations on and around Damkot Hill have revealed evidence of settlement as early as the 2nd millenium BC when **Aryans** occupied the site, leaving behind distinctive black and grey pottery, wood, stone and iron utensils and copper and gold jewellery. An Aryan graveyard was also discovered at the foot of the hill, on the N side. The site then appears to have been abandoned until around the 1st century AD. With the flowering of **Gandharan** culture in the region, the site became an important **Buddhist** centre, and a monastery and stupa were built on the hill. This was destroyed by **White Huns** in 528 AD, and in the 8th century AD the **Hindu Shahis** built an extensive fort on the ruins. This fort appears to have housed a fully-fledged town, with stables, blacksmiths' forges, shops and houses. Hindu Shahi rule lasted for over 250 years until the fort was destroyed by **Mahmoud of Ghazni**, who invaded Swat in 1001. Damkot Hill itself then appears to have remained unoccupied until the arrival of the **British**, although Chakdara came under the loose control of the **Mughals** who, not withstanding their initial conquering of the area, gave the recently arrived **Yusufzai Pathan** tribes virtual autonomy. The hill is now occupied by the military and closed to the public.

The main bazaar at Chakdara is 2 km further on, across a second bridge. Chakdara is a small village, and the only place of interest is the small museum, by the junction with the road which runs along the W bank of the Swat River. **Chakdara Museum** Officially open 0730-1730 in summer and 0900-1600 in winter, with an hour for lunch; in practice you may have to track down the chowkidar. This small museum has some beautiful pieces and deserves the same presentation as at Saidu Sharif. The central hall contains many small statues and small and medium-sized

freizes, some very beautifully carved and well preserved. There are also some stucco pieces and one terracotta figure very similar to those found at Mehrghar in Baluchistan. However there is no attempt to date or locate any of the pieces. The hall to the left contains impressive traditional embroidered costumes, antique guns and swords, tribal jewellery of silverwork and semi-precious stones and a display of funeral burial items, all gathered from sites around lower Swat. In 1995 the hall to the right was empty.

● **Accommodation** 1 km beyond the main bazaar on the road to Dir there is the **E** *Jamal*, T 761063, also some **D** category a/c, rooms with TV/dish and fridge, restaurant, small garden.

● **Transport** There is no bus stand in Chakdara. You can pick up through traffic heading up to Chitral or down to Peshawar; if you are heading down to the plains it may be better to cross the bridge and pick up the more frequent transport coming from Mingora. Pick-ups run locally (to Mingora or Timargarha) and there are also some Suzukis.

There are a number of Buddhist sites around Chakdara, although little remains of them today. **Chat Pat**, to the W of the road, between Chakdara bridge and village, is the site of a Buddhist monastery. Where the road crosses a stream, follow a path for about 1½ km past a small village to the site. 8 km beyond Chakdara there is a turning right which leads to the to the ruins of **Andan Dehri Stupa**, less than 1 km from the main road. Only the base remains, but the stupa is reckoned to have been 24m tall and one of the most important in Swat. The turning continues on to the village of **Shewa**. Beyond this village, on the range of hills marking the northern border of Dir, are the ruins of the Hindu Shahi fort of **Kamal Khan China**.

The main road bears W soon after the turning for Andan Dehri, entering the Talash valley. To the S of the road, on the low pass seperating the two river valleys, there are the ruins of the Hindu Shahi fort of **Kat Kala**, identified by Sir Olaf

Caroe as the site of the ancient city of **Massaga**, captured by Alexander the Great in 327 BC. The road then bears N again, joining the Panjkora River. Across the river are the Tribal Areas of Bajour Agency. The *Bajouris*, along with other tribal groups from surrounding areas, particularly the *Mohmands*, *Malazai* and *Kohistani Pathans*, were infamous to the British for their lawlessness. The present road was built by the British close to the ridge to avoid sniping gunfire from across the river. As recently as 1977 the Pakistan Air Force was strafing 'Pathan irregulars' in a dispute over timber rights, and even today the hills of Dir and Bajour are considered a hideout for bandits and thieves.

Timargarha

Situated 48 km from Chakdara, Timargarha is the headquarters of Dir District. Across the river at **Balambat** there is an archaeological site which has revealed evidence of continuous occupation since 1500 BC by Aryans, Buddhists, Hindus and Muslims. Fire alters were also discovered, on which juniper would have been burned. Despite its administrative importance (there is also a district hospital here), the town is small and unassuming, and apart from the excavations at Balambat, there is little to stop for here.

● **Accommodation** If neccessary, there is good clean accommodation available at the newly built **E** *Al-Imran*, T (0935) 821343, at the S end of town, nr the bus stand, hotel sign in Urdu only, hot water, restaurant, parking, friendly, well run hotel. Next door is the more basic **F** *New Khyber*, T 2713, also with restaurant.

● **Transport Local** The large bus station at Timargarha has regular Hiace vans to Mingora, Mardan, Peshawar (it is sometimes neccessary to change at Mardan) and Dir, as well as buses and coaches. There are pick-ups available N of the bus stand in the main bazaar, past the turning across the river. Suzukis operate locally through the town and across the river to Balambat.

The main road continues N, following the river and passing through various small bazaars, including **Khal** (18 km), where a new bridge crosses the river. **Wara** (32 km), **Sahi Baha** (41 km), with its large new mosque and bridge across the river, **Darora** (48 km), **Bibaware** (56 km) and **Chutiatan** (72 km), before arriving at Dir (78 km), by which time the valley has become narrow and thickly wooded. From Timagarha to Dir is approximately 2 hrs on public transport. From near Chutiatan, a jeep track leads E as far as the village of **Thal**, from where it is possible to trek over into the Swat valley. This trek passes through fairly wild tribal territory; a guide, and permission from the DC in Dir, is essential.

Dir Town

Although not the district headquarters, Dir seems to have more political significance than Timagarha. This was the seat of power of the Nawab of Dir, whose palace stands on the hillside above the town, still occupied by his descendents during the summer. Below it, the royal guesthouse is now the *Dir Hotel*. It is a small, lively town, and an obvious place to break the journey between Peshawar and Chitral. Dir is famous for its homegrown knife industry, producing distinctive small pen-knives as well as larger knives and daggers. There is the potential for some pleasant walks around Dir, although a reliable guide is recommended as the area is tribal.

● **Accommodation** **E** *Al Manzar*, T 2707, hot water, popular with tour groups, restaurant, able to change US$ cash; **E** *Dir*, T 2869, former royal guesthouse, cool, airy rooms, hot water, pleasant garden, parking, rec; **E** *Yassar Palace*, T 2499, Main Bazaar, central but noisy (rear overlooks main bus stand), clean rooms, hot water, restaurant; **F** *Abshar*, T 2757, newly built, situated across the bridge, overlooking the river, clean rooms, balconies, hot water, restaurant, good value, rec; The *Al Hayat Tourist Hotel* has now been converted into offices for the education department; the manager, Taj Mohammad, still has a shop nearby, near the bridge, and is a useful source

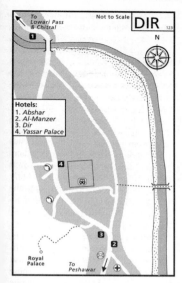

To Lowari Pass & Chitral

Not to Scale

DIR 123

N

Hotels:
1. Abshar
2. Al-Manzer
3. Dir
4. Yassar Palace

Royal Palace

To Peshawar

of local information. As well as the hotel restaurants, there are a lots of local-style restaurants serving, karai, chapli kebab, dal etc.

● **Post & telecommunications Area code**: 0934. **Telegraph Office**: there is a small Telegraph Office opp the *Yassar Palace Hotel*. More expensive, but more convenient is the *International Choice PCO*, T 880377, with IDD. The **Post Office** is on the main road, S of the Al Manzar Hotel, identifiable only by the post box outside.

● **Transport** The main bus station is in a large yard in the centre of town. Hiace vans leave for Timagarha and Peshawar from a small yard by the Dir Hotel. There are regular pick-ups heading N across the Lowari Pass to Chitral (approx 5 hrs) or it may be possible to get a seat on a Hiace coming through from Peshawar.

The main road crosses the river at Dir and continues N. After about 10 km the road becomes a rough track and begins its long climb up to the Lowari Pass, passing first through the village of Qalandar. At 3,118m, the **Lowari Pass** is generally only open from late May/early Jun through to Oct, becoming blocked by snow during winter. A tunnel, visible from the road near the foot of the pass, marks the start of an unfinished project which originally aimed to make the route a year-round one; questions about the technical feasability of the tunnel, and its cost, have put the project on hold. The rough track climbs up to the pass in a long series of switchbacks. Near the summit on the Dir side there are a few tea stalls which also serve simple food.

The descent down the Chitral side is even more tortuous. Near the foot of the pass there is a checkpost at **Ziarat** where foreigners must register. The road continues past another checkpost at the small village of Ashriat, before arriving at **Mirkhani**, with its fort occupied by the Chitral Scouts. Here a road forks off to the left, following the Kunar River to the Afghan border at Arandu. During winter, under a special arrangement, Pakistanis are able to travel by this route in order to bypass the Lowari, passing through the Afghan province of Nuristan before re-entering Pakistan via the Nawa Pass and rejoining the Chitral road just S of Dir, at Chutiatan. Foreigners are not allowed to travel by this route. It is possible however to cross the pass by foot when it is still closed to vehicles. It is a long hike and you should check first with locals as to the depth and condition of the snow.

Naghar

A short distance after Mirkhani there is a bridge across to the fort at Naghar. The fort was built in 1919 by Shuja-ul-Mulk, the then Methar of Chitral, for one of his sons, Jhazi-ul-Mulk. Today it is still occupied by the descendents of the royal family, who have opened a small hotel, the **C** *Old Fort Tourist Resort*, T (05333) 450 (or book in Islamabad, T 826423), 6 rm, more planned, camping, restaurant. The fort is an almost magically idyllic place to stop for a night and it is even worth contriving to do so just to spend an evening enjoying the setting and the hospitality. Most travellers enthusiastically write of Naghar as a "paradise" in the visitors' book. The hotel has a small, delightful garden and the rooms overlook the wide swirling waters of the Chitral River, which sweep round the outcrop of Naghar in a huge U bend. Behind the fort there are large, well maintained gardens and orchards of peaches, apples, plums, pears, apricots and cherries.

10 km on from Naghar is the town of **Drosh**, with its large fort; the headquarters of the Chitral Scouts. The fort is closed to the public and there is little else of interest in the town. Reasonably clean accommodation is available in the **E** *Javed Palace*, T 388, restaurant. There are a few other more basic hotels in the bazaar.

Just beyond Drosh is the **Shishi Valley** which climbs up to the NE. This steep, thickly wooded valley is jeepable as far as the village of **Madaglasht**, and there are opportunities for trekking beyond, although a guide is essential.

The main road continues N. Shortly before the village of Gahiret an old steel girder bridge crosses the river, giving access to Birir, the most southerly of the three Kalash valleys. Further on there is a turning left and a bridge across to the large village of Ayun, the gateway to the Kalash valleys of Bumburet and Rumbur. (For details of the Kalash Valleys, see page 406). **NB** To visit the Kalash valleys you must first have registered in Chitral (see below). From the turning to Ayun, it is a further 18 km to Chitral Town. A turning left leads to a small one-lane bridge (a larger one is under construction) which crosses the river S of the town. The main route into town is via the bridge further N.

Chitral Town

Chitral town has experienced little of the phenomenal growth seen in Gilgit to the E, and remains a small town, strung out along its one main bazaar.

What growth there has been has come mainly in the form of Afghan refugees who, as in Peshawar, have come to dominate much of the transport industry, as well as various other service sectors. It is nevertheless the district headquarters and largest urban centre in Chitral. Situated on a large alluvial fan on the E bank of the Kunar River, the town is surrounded by high mountains, with Tirich Mir to the N dominating the skyline in all its majestic splendour. The main bazaar is lively and colourful, with plenty of atmosphere and there are some excellent local handicrafts, jewellery, stones and antiques to be found in the many tourist shops.

NB Foreign tourists arriving in Chitral are required to register with the Superintendent of Police (see below under Useful Addresses), a straightforward process taking no more than 30 mins.

The town gained its importance from the trade that passed through, on its way between Afghanistan and China. It was also the seat of power of the Mehtars of Chitral. The **Chitral Fort**, situated by the bank of the river was the site of the 1895 Siege of Chitral, and focus for the bloody intriguing which characterized Chitrali politics; whoever held the Fort in effect held power in the kingdom. Today much of the Fort is a crumbling ruin, although parts of it have been restored, and are still occupied by the descendents of the royal family. Officially it is closed to the public, although if you ask you may be allowed to look round the abandoned parts. Inside, there are five cannons, two dating from WW1. The best views of the Fort are on the way into town from the N, or from across the river. Next to it is the recently restored **Shahi Masjid**, dating from the time of Shaja-ul-Mulk.

To the S of the main bazaar is the **polo ground**, one of the largest in Pakistan. Games are played here on most weekends between Mar and Oct; check with PTDC for exact dates.

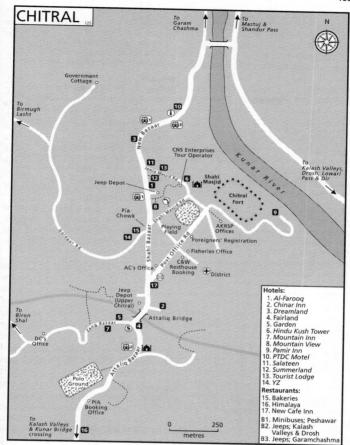

CHITRAL 125

To Garam Chashma

To Mastuj & Shandur Pass

N

Government Cottage

To Birmugh Lasht

Kunar River

To Kalash Valleys, Drosh, Lowari Pass & Dir

New Bazaar

10

3

CNS Enterprises Tour Operator

11 13
Jamia Masjid Rd
12
6 Shahi Masjid
Jeep Depot 1

Chitral Fort

Pia Chowk

Shahi Masjid Rd

Playing Field

AKRSP Offices

15

14

Goldur Rd

9

Foreigners' Registration

Fisheries Office

AC's Office

Post Office Rd

C&W Resthouse Booking

District

17

Jeep Depot (Upper Chitral)

2

To Biron Shal

DC's Office

Zang Bazaar

5
7 4

Attaliq Bridge

2

Attaliq Bazaar

Polo Ground

PIA Booking Office

To Kalash Valleys & Kunar Bridge crossing

16

0   250
metres

Hotels:
1. Al-Farooq
2. Chinar Inn
3. Dreamland
4. Fairland
5. Garden
6. Hindu Kush Tower
7. Mountain Inn
8. Mountain View
9. Pamir Inn
10. PTDC Motel
11. Salateen
12. Summerland
13. Tourist Lodge
14. YZ

Restaurants:
15. Bakeries
16. Himalaya
17. New Cafe Inn

B1. Minibuses; Peshawar
B2. Jeeps; Kalash Valleys & Drosh
B3. Jeeps; Garamchashma

Local information
● Accommodation

B *Pamir Inn*, Noghor Gardens, T 2525, comfortable rooms (normal or duluxe), hot water, peaceful riverside location, nice gardens, restaurant, camping, overpriced.

C *Mountain Inn*, T 2112, F 2781, nicely furnished rooms set around a courtyard with beautiful, mature gardens, restaurant, friendly staff, best hotel in town, rec; **C** *PTDC Motel*, New Bazaar, T 2683, comfortable rooms, hot water, good restaurant, garden,

Tourist Information Centre, expensive.

D *Dreamland*, Airport Rd, T 2615, F 2770, best rooms on upper 2 flrs, common balcony area, cheaper rooms (**E** category) on lower floors, restaurant; **D** *Fairland*, by Attaliq bridge, T 2768, clean rooms (cooler/shady at rear), hot water, restaurant, expensive.

E *Al-Farooq*, New Bazaar, T 2726, centrally located and noisy, some rooms with hot water, balconies (good views at rear, quieter), restaurant; **E** *Chinar Inn*, Shahi Rd, by Attaliq bridge, 4 rm, clean, hot water, simple restaurant, set back from road, small garden, quiet and pleasant, good value, rec; **E** *Hindu Kush Tower*, Shahi Masjid Rd, T 2888, newly built, basic but clean rooms, hot water in winter, best rooms upstairs (more expensive, good views of Tirich Mir, restaurant; **E** *Tourist Lodge*, Jamia Masjid Rd, T 2452, hot water in winter, courtyard, restaurant.

F *Garden*, opp Mountain View, very basic, charpoy beds, outside toilet, wash in stream, but pleasant, shady garden; **F** *Mountain View*, New Bazaar, T 2559, basic, ugly building, restaurant; **F** *Salateen*, New Bazaar, basic, share toilet, restaurant; **F** *Summerland*, off Jamia Masjid Rd, T 2337, reasonably clean rooms, basic.

Hindu Kush Trails are building a luxury hotel to the N of the main town, nr the airport.

● **Places to eat**

The restaurant in the *PTDC Motel* has a well-deserved reputation for the best food in Chitral; book in advance if you are not staying here. Most of the other hotels also have restaurants. There are several local-style eating places in the main bazaar. The Afghan-run *New Cafe Inn*, on the corner of Shahi Bazaar and Post Office Rd, serves good Afghan food. The *Himalaya Restaurant*, S of town, on Attaliq Bazaar past the polo ground, is too far from the centre to attract much custom, and is usually empty.

● **Banks & money changers**

The **National Bank of Pakistan**, by the junction S of Attaliq bridge, is the only place licenced to deal in foreign exchange.

● **Hospitals & medical centres**

The *District Headquarters Hospital* is off Post Office Rd. There are a several chemists shops nearby.

● **Post & telecommunications**
Area code: 0933.

Post Office: is situated on Post Office Rd, nr the junction with Shahi Bazaar.

Telecommunications: the **PCO**, in a small office off Shahi Masjid Rd, has national and international telephone, fax, telex and telegram facilities. Open 0800-1600, 7 days.

● **Shopping**

Shu, or *Patti* cloth, is a soft handwoven woollen material which is made into intricately embroidered gowns (*chunghas*), rugs, bags, Chitrali hats etc. There are dozens of tourist shops along Shahi Bazaar offering these items, along with wide range of Afghan rugs, jewellery, semi-precious stones (particularly Lapis Lazuli from Afghanistan), carved wooden items and other handicrafts and antiques. Also a couple of good shops Goldpur Rd, opp the *YZ Hotel*.

● **Sports**

Fishing: there is excellent fishing in many of Chitral's rivers. For permits and more information, contact the Fisheries Office, off Post Office Rd.

Polo: is played regularly at the polo ground in Chitral, see above.

● **Tour companies & travel agents**

CNS Enterprises, Shahi Masjid Rd, T 2461, F 2516, are able to organize jeeps and treks (incl porters and guides). They have a small 'department store' selling basic supplies and some tinned and dried foods. They also have some equipment (tents, sleeping bags etc) available for hire. *Hindu Kush Trails*, the main tour company in Chitral (run by members of the former royal family), has a liaison office at the *Mountain Inn*; their head office is in Islamabad; Hs 37, St 28, F-6/1, T 821576, F 215031. They are a good, reliable company, with extensive experience of organising trekking expeditions and jeep safaris in Chitral and elsewhere.

● **Tourist offices**

PTDC Tourist Information Centre is located in the *PTDC Motel*, T 2683. They have little in the way of useful information; the staff at *Mountain Inn*, or one of the tour companies are likely to be of more use.

● **Useful addresses**

C & W Sub Divisional Officer: off Post Office Rd, T 2103; apply here for C & W Rest House bookings.

District Forestry Officer: off Post Office Rd, T 2101; enquire here about visits to Chitral Gol National Park.

Foreigners' registration: Superintendent of Police, Post Office Rd, T 2553; register here for your stay in Chitral.

Police: T 2913.

● **Transport**

Air PIA Booking Office, nr Polo Ground, T 2963, open 0900-1700, 7 days; Airport, T 2547. 3 flights daily to Peshawar (except Sun, Thur; 2 flights). Flights are weather dependent.

Road There is no central bus station in Chitral. **Peshawar** (via Dir and Mardan); Hiace minibuses (Rs 200) leave from various depots along

New Bazaar; one depot is between *Dreamland Hotel* and *PTDC Motel*, another nr *Al-Farooq Hotel*. However, with the exception of the former they seem to get moved around frequently, although the associated ticket touts make them hard to miss. **Garam Chashma**; passenger jeeps (and occasionally mini-buses) run fairly regularly from by the PSO petrol station opp *PTDC Motel* for Rs 25. **Kalash Valleys**; passenger jeeps leave early in the morning from Attaliq Bazaar, next to the *Shabnam Hotel*, to Ayun, the starting point for Rumbur and Bumburet. There are sometimes direct jeeps to Bumburet. Jeeps also to **Drosh** from here. **Upper Chitral**; The jeep depot off Shahi Bazaar, at its S end, has passenger and cargo jeeps heading for Upper Chitral; most are bound for Mastuj (Rs 100), although some go to Sor Rich and other road-heads; all are very irregular, depending on demand; enquire at least a day before and be prepared to hang around on the day. **Shandur Pass/Gilgit**; there are no regular passenger services to Shandur or Gilgit. In the run-up to the annual polo match on Shandur there are numerous jeeps heading for the pass; most will have been hired on a private basis, but there is more chance of finding a passenger/cargo jeep around this time. Ask at the Upper Chitral depot. Similarly, this is the best time to find onward transport from Shandur to Gilgit. **Jeep hire**: If there are no passenger/cargo services to your destination, the only alternative is to hire a jeep; enquire at the Upper Chitral or Garam Chashma depots. Another depot worth trying is off New Bazaar, nr the *Al-Farooq Hotel*. Alternatively, ask at *Mountain Inn* (there are usually several jeeps waiting around outside), or go through *Hindu Kush Trails* or *CNS Enterprises*. Prices vary according to demand; bargain hard. The following rates were being charged in summer 1995; Garam Chashma Rs 700 return (plus Rs 200 for overnight), Bumburet Rs 700 return (Rs 400 one-way), Buni Rs 1,000 one-way, Shandur Rs 3,500 one-way (incl overnight stop en-route), Gilgit Rs 6,500 one-way (incl overnight stops).

Around Chitral Town

Birmugh Lasht The Methar of Chitral had his summer palace at Birmugh Lasht, situated high above the town on a small plain. The building is semi-derelict and occupied only by the chowkidar's family.

The plain used to be thickly wooded with walnut trees (Birmugh Lasht translates as 'place of walnuts'), but today only a few isolated trees remain. Higher up, on top of the mountain, there is a Wildlife Department Rest House, bookable through the District Forestry Officer in Chitral. There are excellent views in all directions, and some trees offering shade, making this an ideal picnic spot.

A steep, rough jeep track zigzags its way up to the top. Head E out of town along Goldpur road past the YZ Hotel. After the first hairpin bend the jeep track forks off to the left (there is a well-hidden signpost). It is a strenuous 3 hr walk with no shade on the way up.

Chitral Gol National Park The small side valley that climbs steeply up from Chitral town has been designated a National Park, covering 7,745 hactares. Snow Leopards, Black Bears, Markhor and Urial are reportedly still found in the upper reaches of the valley, and in theory protected under the legislation governing national parks; in practice hunting still continues, and it is debatable as to how much of the wildlife still survives. **Biron Shal**, the Mehtar's former hunting lodge is situated a little way up the valley. A permit and guide is required if you wish to trek up the valley (there is no jeep track); apply to the District Forestry Officer. It takes around 4 hrs to reach Biron Shal from the start of the path behind the DC's office. There is also a path leading into the valley from the summit above Birmugh Lasht.

Garam Chashma

Situated 45 km NW of Chitral, Garam Chashma is famous for its hot sulpher springs (hence the name). From Chitral, head N along the E bank of the Kunar River, past the airport. A little further on, the jeep track follows the **Lutkho River** branch NW, while the Mastuj River valley climbs NE towards Mastuj. The track passes the spring and pipeline supplying water to Chitral town. Further on, where the valley swings round to the W, a bridge crosses to the village of **Shogore** on the opposite bank. Here the **Karimabad Gol** climbs NE up towards the **Owir Pass**, a trekking route leading over to the Barum valley (see Trekking chapter). The valley is jeepable as far as the village of **Sasoom** (15 km). Immediately W of the Karimabad Gol, the **Arkari Gol** drains in from the N. This valley is jeepable as far as the village of **Ower** (40 km). The main jeep track continues E, following the S bank of the Lutkho River through several small villages, before crossing to the N bank. The track passes an old fort, still occupied by descendents of the Chitrali royal family, the civil hospital, a police post, where foreigners must register (take a close look at the headings in the book....) and the fisheries department office, before arriving in the main village of Garam Chashma.

There is one proper hotel here, the **D** *Injigaan*, T 14, comfortable rooms, also dorm beds (**F** category), meals to order. The hotel's main attraction though (and the main reason for coming to Garam Chashma), is its own private, spring-fed **hot water swimming pool**, a blissful way to soothe aching limbs after trekking. There is a **E** *Government Rest House* nearby; it may be possible to get rooms here through the Deputy Commissioner in Chitral. There are also a couple of very basic Afghan-run hotels in the bazaar. The public hot baths, situated up a turning to the right before the main bazaar, have six small cubicles where you can bathe, although they are dirty and poky.

At the far end of the village one jeep track continues along the N bank of the Lutkho River towards the **Dorah Pass** (4,510m) leading into Afghanistan. During the Soviet occupation, this was the route by which the mujahideen went back and forth, carrying drugs and semi-precious stones into Pakistan and returning to Afghanistan with American-supplied weapons. This route is closed

to foreigners, who are turned back at the checkpost just beyond the bazaar. A second jeep track crosses the river on a wooden bridge and follows the **Bigosht Gol** towards Nuristan in Afghanistan. There is excellent trout fishing in the area; permits can be obtained from the fisheries office on the road before the village.

Kalash Valleys

The Kalash, numbering approximately 3,000, are the smallest group amongst the religious minorities of Pakistan. Unlike the other minorities, they live exclusively in a particular geographical area; the three valleys of **Birir**, **Bumburet** and **Rumbur** situated in the Hindu Kush between the Afghan border and the Chitral valley. Muslims label the Kalash 'Kafirs' ('non believers') and their area Kafirstan. Until 1896 Kafirstan also included present-day Nuristan in Afghanistan, inhabited by the 'Red Kafirs', whereas the Kalash were called the 'Black Kafirs'.

History

Kalasha myths tell that the Kalash originally came from **Tsiam**, thought to be near Yarkand. The Kalasha oral tradition also tells that the Kalash are descended from Alexander the Great's brave general **Shalak Shah** of Tsiam, to whom Alexander gave the Chitral valley as a reward. Kalasha language is of great interest to linguists as it belongs to the ancient Dardic branch of the Indo-European languages, suggesting a Central Asian origin. Around 1500 AD the Kalash were dominant throughout southern Chitral; the Kalasha oral tradition mentions eight great Kalasha kings. Local people outside the valleys often find remnants of buildings revealing evidence former Kalash settlements.

After this Kalasha period Islam became dominant in Chitral. According to the Kalasha oral tradition Islam at first seems to have been adopted by the kings who then converted their subjects more

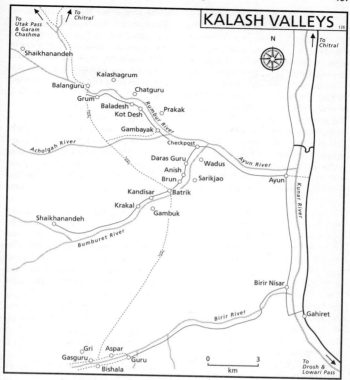

KALASH VALLEYS

To Utak Pass & Garam Chashma

To Chitral

N

Shaikhanandeh

Kalashagrum

Balanguru

Chatguru

Grum

Baladesh

Prakak

Kot Desh

Rumbu River

Gambayak

Acholgah River

Checkpost

Ayun River

Daras Guru

Wadus

Anish

Brun

Sarikjao

Ayun

Kandisar

Batrik

Kunar River

Krakal

Gambuk

Shaikhanandeh

Bumburet River

Birir Nisar

Gahiret

Birir River

Gri

Aspar

Gasguru

Guru

Bishala

0   3

km

To Drosh & Lowari Pass

To Chitral

or less forcibly. The most persistant of the Kalash took refuge from conversion in the less accessible side valleys. As a result the Kalash became marginalized; subjugated people bound to pay tributes and corvée labour to the Mehtars, economically exploited and subject to frequent raids from their neighbours in what is now Nuristan.

When the British established the Durand Line the Kalasha valleys became part of British India and so part of present day Pakistan. This protected the Kalash from the forcible conversions to Islam carried out by the Afghan king Abdur Rahman in 1896. Groups of Red Kafirs fled these conversions into

Chitral. The refugees were given land in the upper parts of the Kalasha valleys and still have their villages there. Ironically they all later gradually converted to Islam. In 1969 the kingdom of Chitral became part of Pakistan. To the Kalash this meant a lifting of their serfdom and the enshrining of their constitutional right to practice their religion.

Economy

The Kalash practice *transhumance* – a combination of agriculture and pastoralism with annual migrations of shepherds, goats and sheep between the valley bottom, the lower and the high pastures. The Kalasha religion influences the distribution of labour in such a way that the goats are exclusively tended by the men. The men also do the hard field labour; they remove the stones that have been brought down by winter weather and by floods or earthquakes, they construct and maintain the irrigation channels, they plough with oxen, they harrow and sow. The women take over the strenuous weeding and irrigation work. Both help with the harvest.

The fields need to be irrigated at 3-5 day intervals. The area a family can irrigate depends on the number of women, which limits the degree of inequality. A family with too few women will have problems, making women essential for agriculture.

In the village zone two crops are harvested; wheat as a winter crop and maize, beans and patches of vegetables as summer crops. Barley and millet used to be important, but are vanishing nowadays. A wide range of fruit trees – walnuts, mulberries, apricots, apples, pears and *jujube* – provide food and relieving shade. Old vines cling to the hollyoak trees and provide grapes for the production of wine, permitted for non-Muslim minorities like the Kalash in the Muslim state of Pakistan. Water mills grind the grain. Dominant in the diet is the bread baked on an iron plate on open fires, or on top of iron stoves. Dried fruits are an important addition to the diet in the winter.

In May the families shift to the summer pastures higher up the valley, where only one crop can be grown. The women take care of the fields and the few cows. Later, most of the men take their big herds of goats and a few sheep to the highest pastures at 3,500m or more, before returning to the lower pastures in Oct.

The pasture vegetation is transformed into meat, dairy products and manure. Meat is mainly eaten at sacrifices or feasts. The meat is distributed among the community, although meat from sacrificed male goats is only eaten by the men. Therefore the goat cheese produced during the summer is an essential protein source. The forest and alpine zones are also used for hunting animals such as marmot. The hunting of Markhor is frequently mentioned in myths but is no longer allowed.

During the winter season the goats and sheep stay in the cattle houses situated at the edge of the village and field zone. Each day the goats are taken to browse on the evergreen hollyoak trees, while sheep and cows are fed on dried weeds and hay from the summer pastures. In the spring the goats' droppings are carried out as manure to the fields, ensuring high yields and enabling even large households to subsist on a single acre of cultivated land.

Walnuts, cheese and goats used to be bartered with the surrounding world. Now a cash economy has entered and influenced the community. Some of the men have government jobs such as border police, chowdikars, health staff and a teacher. Others are involved in private enterprizes like commerce, jeep driving, hotels and tourist guides. The women sometimes succeed in selling their handicrafts to tourists, which provides them with cash. In the most touristed valleys the women even sell their culture by taking money for dancing and for being photographed.

Religion

The Muslims label the Kalash 'Kafirs' in the misapprehension that they do not believe in God and worship only idols. In fact the Kalash do believe in God, *Khodai* (the Persian word for Allah) or *Dezao*, who is the creator and can be worshipped everywhere. In case of a natural disaster or serious illness, the Kalash try to reconcile God by prayers and sacrifices.

Male and female *Dewalok* (sacred spirits) are responsible for particular parts of daily life and are addressed when necessary through prayers, offerings or sacrifices. The Kalash may ask the *Dewalok* to give their prayers to *Dezao* (in the same way as the Catholics

DRESS

Kalash women are stikingly colourful in their unique costumes. Their hair is plaited, both at front and back. On their heads they wear the *shu'shut*, a small headdress like a ring around the head with a long piece hanging down the back. On top of that the big headdress or *ku'pas* is worn for protection against the sun and for ceremonial occasions. Both headdresses are heavily decorated with cowries, buttons, beads and brass. The decorations reflect the valley of origin and the status of the woman, but nowadays, on the *shu'shut* in particular, local new fashions gain the greatest influence. When a person dies the close female relatives wear the *ku'pas* alone for the period of mourning.

The black baggy dress is tied with a broad scarf, or *patti*. Both used to be woven from home-spun wool. With the cash economy, cloth, borders and yarn from the shops have gained great popularity, allowing the women to be more colourful. For weaving a red *patti* however, the work is the same as before, because the synthetic knitting yarn still has to be spun before being woven. Huge numbers of glass bead necklaces cover the neck and breast of the woman. They are only taken off altogether by a widow during periods of mourning.

Nowadays the men wear the practical *shalwar kameez* suit, as well as the Chitrali cap. During the cold winter, decorated woollen leggings are commonly tied around the shalwar. The traditional woollen pants are still are used by some of the elders for ceremonial purposes, and are given to 4-6 year old boys for their initiation ceremony during the winter festival of *Chaomos*. This is also when the small girls receive their first *ku'pas*. The men used to wear woollen jackets or skin vests during the winter but now modern coats and jackets as well as Chitrali coats are taking over. The former traditional turban is still used for a dead man and for small boys during their initiation ceremony. The traditional men's dress is also seen on the *Gandauws* – the graveyard statues raised on the anniversary of an influencial man. (Many *Gandauws* can be seen in Peshawar Museum.)

ask the saints to do so). It is important to know and respect that the places of the *Dewalok* belong to the pure sphere, where only men are allowed to go. Exceptions are the temples representing *Jestak*, who protects the families. During menstruation and childbirth, Kalash women stay in the *Bashali* houses where *Dejalik* is represented by a carved piece of wood.

In the Kalasha perception, Nature belongs to other beings than themselves. Through offerings, sacrifices, purifications and prayers, they have to ask for permission to let the animals graze in the high pastures or cut down trees for example.

The pure-impure dualism is central to the Kalasha religion. *Onjesta* (pure, sacred) and *Pragata* (impure, profane)

are frequently mentioned in connection with locations as well as with acts, persons and objects. Basically the Kalasha world is divided into complementary spheres of *Onjesta* and *Pragata*, with the divine, the high pastures, the men and the goats belonging to the *Onjesta* sphere, and the women belonging to the *Pragata* sphere, in particular during menstruation and childbirth. For the women, their confinement to the *Bashali* during menstruation provides a monthly holiday from the daily routine of hard work. Anybody entering, or touching anybody there, must be totally washed before returning to the rest of the world.

Tourists should stay away from the *Bashali*. If a female tourist has her period she should keep quiet about it and not leave any sanitary towels or tampons for people to find, as they are considered a strong pollutant in the religious sense (take them out of the valleys, bury them at the 'shitting ground' or burn them secretly, but not in a family house).

The family houses are divided into zones. The fireplace and the area behind it are *Onjesta*. Therefore a woman is not permitted to step over these places, but only to reach with her arms and the top of her body into the area. Inside the house, women have to pour drinking water (considered *Onjesta*) from the common glass into the mouth through her left hand. The valley also is divided into zones – the higher up, the more *Onjesta*.

As women, and also Muslims, are *Pragata*, they can never go to the altars and other places of the *Dewalok* or to the goats' stables above the villages when the goats are down, as these places are *Onjesta*. Acts such as washing the body and braiding the hair are also considered *Pragata* and have to done at a certain distance from these places.

Purifications are an essential element in the Kalasha religion. These may be done by circling burning juniper or hollyoak, by rinsing the hands in pure river water, by sprinkling goat's blood or by holding something made of iron. Of particular importance is the purification of boys during their gradual transition from the *Pragata* women's sphere into the *Onjesta* male community. Only after several purifications (after the traditional trousers dressing ceremony) at the age of about 7 years, are the boys sufficiently *Onjesta* to go to the altars and to the high pastures. When still virgins they are very *Onjesta* and have special religious tasks.

Festivals

Three big festivals are of particular importance and are the milestones of the year. The spring festival *Joshi* in May honours the fairies and so safeguards the goats and shepherds before they go to the pastures. During *Utjao*, in late Aug,

the harvest of goats' cheese is celebrated At *Chaomos*, lasting most of Dec, the divine, the living and dead relatives, the crops and the goats are safeguarded, while the community, the village and the valley are purified prior to the coming year. There are also minor religious functions during the agricultural year like for instance the ploughing offering In summer tourists attracted by the vivid sound of drums may have the chance of seeing the nightly dances known as *Ratnat*, performed by the young girls and boys in order to safeguard the maize crop.

To the Kalash these festivals are the culminations of religious life and, like the big funerals, they unite the people. Tourists should behave respectfully if visiting the valleys during one of these big functions. As the entire community gathers for festivals, politicians often take advantage of the opportunity to use the occasion Joshi in particular, as a forum for political propaganda, confusing the religious dances with an ordinary feast.

Social structure

Family relations are extremely important; people rarely call each other by their name, but rather address each other in terms of their relationship to the eldest child of the family. This means that children are very important and everybody know their names. After receiving the proper dress a child is considered a full member of the community. However, the young are expected to behave respectfully towards their elders, listening and obeying their commands.

Households generally consist of the extended family, encompassing many relations and several generations, and forming an integrated economic unit. People belong to their father's clan (even married women) which is very important in terms of identity, and involves sharing the economic responsibility in case of big expenditures such as funerals and the collection of bride price.

As the women are excluded from the *Onjesta* sphere their living space is smaller than the men's. Women mostly stay below the highest water channels in the field and village areas. In the summer they go to the fields of the lower summer pastures. After their return to the villages in the autumn, these areas are purified and closed to the women. Although women are considered *Pragata*, they are not at all looked down upon; they are considered the common pride of the valley, and for instance have to walk first in the procession when coming to another valley for a funeral. The men talk proudly about "our women" meaning all women from the valley or clan. They have total self-determination in all personal matters. Thus, within the strict rules for incest and periods of abstention, a woman is able to decide whom to marry and with whom to make love (if the man agrees of course). Men frequently complain of 'women's choice' saying "What can we do?" If a man dares to pull the plaits of his wife or talk rudely to her, she normally leaves the house. She can then take a lover, and nobody can force her back again. After disputes over fields, women's elopements are the main reasons for community conflicts.

Important to the Kalash are the codes of honour that first of all emphasize generosity, living according to their religion, honesty in work and speech (quality of speech is better than quantity) and diligence. Greed is looked down upon – many myths tell how greed leads to disaster.

The Kalasha society has no formal internal leadership. Disputes are settled and decisions made by the male clan elders in common. There are also strong personalities among the women who give their opinions and are heard. Politically the community is split into factions – traditionally around competing clan elders, but nowadays increasingly around competing politicians from outside running for the minority seat in the National Assembly. The Kalasha elected minority member of the District Council in Chitral functions as a representative and mediator with the surrounding world. The Kalash have not yet succeeded in winning the minority seat in the Provincial Assembly.

The Kalash in the 20th century

The Kalasha community is at a stage of transition. The building of roads linking the valleys with the outside world has brought with it development; schools, a health system, money, commercial goods, new ideas, electricity and tourism. In particular the Kalash are a major tourist attraction and so of great economic importance for the tourist industry. Tourism is mainly outside Kalasha ownership and control, which leads to concern and frustration among the Kalash; not unanimously, but dependent on the degree to which individuals feel harassed by or benefit from the tourists.

In general the Kalash welcome visitors, if they behave with respect to the people and the culture. Less welcomed are the foreign groups who come just for a brief visit, taking pictures and behaving as if in a zoo. Least welcomed are the gangs of young men from the lowlands; confusing the women's freedom from Purdah with sexual promiscuity, they frequently harass the girls.

The Kalasha culture has always responded to and evolved along with the surrounding world. Some outside tourist interests want the Kalasha culture to be 'frozen' into a museum of the living past. Consequently they complain about modern innovations like electricity. This reflects different perceptions of what 'Kalasha culture' actually is. When asked to define Kalasha culture, a Kalash may reply "Homa Dastur!" – "our tradition" – in brief mainly words and ways, determined by the Kalasha religion. This is not what matters to most of the tourists. In general they come to *see* the 'culture' and catch it with their camera. Thus tourist interests emphasize the spectacular; the big communal rites and the material culture of dresses, houses and technology, leading to complaints about material changes.

The Kalasha religious rites and traditions are central to the unity of the community. As these rites become reified as tourist objects (in the way that dancing has been taken out of the religious context and is done for money in Bumburet and Birir), the basic functions of the rites are eroded along with the unity of the world they sustain.

So far however, contact with other ways and norms has made the Kalash very aware of their own culture. Indeed, there is a growing cultural pride among the Kalash, partly because the interest shown by tourists has made the Kalash aware of the unique nature of their culture. Also, the religious heads tend to interpret disasters like diseases among the goats as caused by cultural slackness, which encourages the people to keep their traditions alive.

Perhaps the greatest threat to the Kalash is the deforestation going on in the valleys. The Kalash valleys are among the few forested areas in Pakistan. Timber is used in increasing quantities for construction of houses for a fast growing population, while firewood is still the main fuel source for domestic use. Far more damaging however is the logging carried out by external contractors. Without their forest cover, the steep-sided valleys with their large catchment areas are exposed to heavy erosion and flash floods, both of which are occuring with increasing intensity and frequency.

Visiting the Kalash Valleys

The Kalasha valleys are easily accessible by jeep from Chitral. Bumburet and Rumbur are both reached via the village of **Ayun**, situated on a large alluvial fan on the W bank of the Kunar River, approximately 15 km S of Chitral town. Head S from Chitral along the main road. After about 12 km there is a turning left which leads down to a bridge across the river and on to Ayun. The main square/jeep stop is across another small bridge over the river draining the Kalash valleys. Passenger jeeps leave for Ayun in the early morning from S of the bridge in the Chitral Bazaar. Alternatively, take any transport heading S from Chitral and walk from the bridge turning (there is also a footbridge a few kilometres further S giving more direct access to Ayun). In Ayun one normally has to wait for another jeep. Most passenger jeeps are bound for Bumburet, the most popular valley (it may be possible to find one going direct from Chitral). If there is nothing going to Rumbur, take a Bumburet jeep as far as the checkpost and then walk (2-3 hrs to Brum/Balanguru).

There are no regular services to Birir valley, to the S of Rumbur and Bumburet, although occasional jeeps do go from Ayun, following a jeep track along the E bank of the Kunar River. The main route is via the bridge at Gahiret, 7 km S of the bridge turning for Ayun.

All of the jeep tracks up the valleys are subject to frequent blockages due to floods, landslides and earthquakes. In such cases the track to Bumburet is usually repaired within a few days. The track to Rumbur was blocked for almost 3 years following heavy flooding in 1991 (it is now open again). In 1995 the track up the Birir valley was blocked half way up following heavy flooding in March.

Permits Visitors to the Kalash valleys must purchase a permit (Rs 50, or Rs 10 for Pakistanis, valid for all three valleys) from the checkpost at the junction of Bumburet and Rumbur valleys. The permit is more accurately a toll, the proceed of which are in theory channelled back into the valleys. **NB** You must first have registered in Chitral town in order to obtain this permit; i you cannot produce your registration document, you will be turned back. Registration in Chitral should not be confused with Foreigners' Registration (see *Information for Visitors*); it is a separate formality required of all foreigners, irrespective of whether they have registered elsewhere. The permit is valid for up to a week. If staying longer, a permit must be obtained from the DC in Chitral. The latter is primarly aimed at those intending a long-term visit (anthropoligists and the like); don't worry if you overstay by a few days.

Rumbur Valley

The jeep track up the Rumbur valley continues straight on past the checkpost and turning left to Bumburet. At the village of Gambayak, the Acholgah valley branches off to the left, leading up to summer pastures. Further on the track passes through Kot Desh and Baladesh before arriving at Grum where the jeep track ends. This is the only village in the valley with any hotels. A footpath leads through the village and across the river to Balanguru, a picturesque and typically Kalash village shaded by large walnut and mulberry trees, with wooden houses built up the hillside, the roof of one forming the front yard of the next. Beyond Balanguru, there are beautiful walks up the valley, past the hydel plant supplying electricity to the village. Higher up the valley is the Muslim (Nuristani) village of Shaikhanandeh (literally 'village of converters'). It is also possible to trek across to Chitral town and Garam Chashma (see below).

● **Accommodation** F *Ex-Lant* (Excellent!), 10 basic rm, share bath, pleasant garden area opp with camping, restaurant; F *Green Kalash*, 4 basic rm, share bath; F *Kalash Hilton*, 7 basic rm, share bath, restaurant. Another hotel, the *Kalash Garden*, situated about 500m before the main village of Grum, was under construction in 1995. In Balanguru there is the E *Saifullah's Guest House*, 6 rm, shower/toilet block adjacent, meals incl in

room rent. Saifullah Jan was the first Kalash man to receive an education outside the valleys. He speaks fluent English and acts as a spokesman for the Kalash.

Bumburet Valley

The valley of Bumburet is the most popular in terms of tourism and has most of the hotels. In some ways it is also the most picturesque, being the widest of the three valleys, with villages and long, fertile stretches of cultivation strung along most of its length. Bumburet is the most easily accessible valley; the majority of the cargo jeeps at Ayun are bound for here. From the checkpost at the foot of the valley, the jeep track climbs up through the villages of Wadus, Daras Guru, Gadiandeh, Anish, Brun, Sarikjao, Batrik, Kandisar, Krakal and Gambuk. At the top of the valley there is another Muslim (Nuristani) village known, as in Rumbur, as Shaikhanandeh. The village itself is to the left of the main jeep track, piled steeply up the side of a rocky outcrop. Next to the C & W Resthouse at the end of the jeep track, there is a trout hatchery. Permits to fish in the river can be obtained from here for Rs 50. **NB** Some locals suggest that this last village is not safe for foreigners; there have been a couple of incidents in recent years involving muggings and thefts which are generally blamed on Afghan refugees living in the area.

● **Accommodation** Hotels are listed below in the order they appear along the road. Most are able to prepare food to order, even if they do not have a restaurant. Those owned and run by Kalash people are indicated, although some of the Muslim-run hotels are owned by Kalash, who lease them out. **Anish**: E *Jinnah Kalash*, set back from road, opp hydel station, Kalash owned, upstairs rooms with att bath, pleasant quiet location, restaurant, camping; D *Benazir* on main road, 4 rm in new block with att bath, cheaper (F category) rooms in old block with shared bath, restaurant, large pleasant garden, camping, shop. In 1995 a *PTDC Motel* was under construction, on the left as you enter the village. **Brun**: along the main road there are the E *Foreigner's Tourist*

Inn, good clean rooms, restaurant, shop, nice garden; **F** *Kalash Hilton*, Kalash owned, basic rooms, share toilet, restaurant; **F** *Frontier*, fairly clean, pleasant, shop, restaurant. Above the main road, in the village up on the hillside to the right, are 2 Kalash owned hotels, the **F** *Kalash Guest House* and the **F** *Kalash View*, both very basic but friendly, with excellent views, food prepared to order. **Batrik**: **F** *Peace*, just above road, to the right, clean pleasant rooms, hot water, restaurant. Another hotel, the *Kalash Continental*, was under construction in 1995. **Krakal**: **E** *Lahore Campsite*, 7 canvas tents with beds, clean toilet block with showers, lawn area, good restaurant (Pak/Continental dishes), dining hall with TV/dish; **E** *Jahangir*, opp Lahore campsite, 3 rm with att bath, 2 share bath; **E** *Kalash Mountain View*, Kalash owned, share bathroom, pleasant garden (camping) and views, food prepared to order; **E** *Alexandra*, 5 rm with att bath, hot water in buckets, pleasant garden (camping); **D** *KKH Krakal Kalash*, 2 rm with att bath and western-style toilets, main block (**F** category) with 8 rm share bath, big garden (camping), restaurant, shop; **F** *Kalash Heavan View*, Kalash owned, 6 rm with shared bath, garden, food prepared to order. **Shaikhanandeh**: **E** *C & W Rest House*, comfortable rooms, pleasant garden, book through C & W Dept in Chitral.

Birir Valley

Situated to the S of Rumbur and Bumburet, Birir valley is the least visited of the Kalash valleys. It can be reached either from Ayun, or via a bridge crossing at the village of Gahiret, further S along the road to Drosh and the Lowari Pass. From Ayun, a jeep track branches off to the left just above the main square and follows the W bank of the Kunar River to the foot of the valley. In 1995, the jeep track was blocked by landslides about 8 km up the valley. Guru is the main village and the only one with any hotels.

● **Accommodation** The 2 hotels in Guru are both on the S bank of the river. Both will prepare food to order. **E** *Paradise*, 8 rm, share bath; **F** *Mehran*, (no sign) 10 rm, share bath, friendly, better value. There is also a **E** *C & W Rest House*, reasonable rooms, pleasant garden, bookable through C & W Dept in Chitral town.

Treks

Trekking routes connect the three valleys. The trek between the Birir and Bumbure valleys can be done in one (long) day. It i a steep, hot climb over a 3,000m ridge wit little shade along the way. Carry plenty o water and start early. A guide is recommended as it is easy to get lost (particu larly going from Birir to Bumburet). From Birir valley, the path starts at the villag of Gasguru and descends into Bumbure valley at Batrik.

The trek between Bumburet and Rum bur takes 2 days, crossing a 3,000m ridge into the Acholgah valley, and then a sec ond ridge over into Rumbur. From Bum buret the track also starts from Batrik ending at Balanguru village in Rumbu A guide is strongly recommended.

From above Bumburet in the Rum bur valley, the trek across to Chitral tow is a fairly easy 2 day trek, although with out a guide it is easy to get lost. The trek across the Utak Pass (4,656m) to Garar Chashma is said to be a strenuous on taking at least 3 days and involving difficult river crossing; a local guide wh is familiar with the route is strongly recommended.

Upper Chitral

The mountains to the N and E of Chitra town are amongst the most spectacular i NWFP, easily matching any in the North ern Areas; a visit to Chitral is really no complete without at least a brief fora into this beautiful area. Awesome, rock mountains twisted and eroded into fantas tic shapes rear up on all sides, giving occa sional glimpses of majestic snowy peak beyond. The villages along the way appea as isolated oases of rich green irrigate farmland, contrasting strikingly with th surrounding barren rock. The trekking i this region, much of which has recentl been changed from a closed to a restricte zone, is particularly beautiful. Further de tails of the treks mentioned below are give in the Trekking chapter (see page 562).

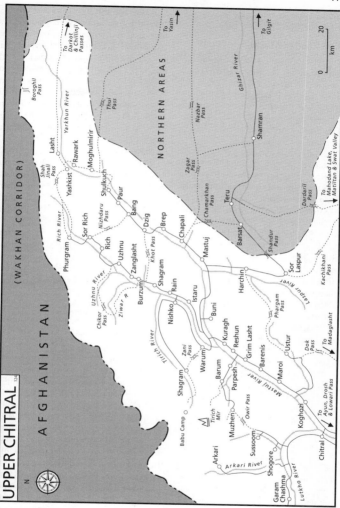

Upper Chitral is also where the majority of Chitral's Ismailis live, making the area far more open and welcoming than the valleys to the S, particularly for women. The diet is simple, centred around dairy products and wheat.

Chitrali bread, either in the form of *Khasta Shapik* or *Chapouti*, is baked in thick round loaves and makes a pleasant change from chapatis or nan. *Machir* is a thin, watery yoghurt-like drink which can be thickened into *Shetu*, or yoghurt, and is in turn is used to make *Shupinak*, a delicious thick, creamy cheese.

The Road to Mastuj

The road to Mastuj is undergoing steady improvement; the first stretch is now metalled in places, and even where still unsurfaced, it is relatively smooth. Beyond Buni it begins to deteriorate, becoming rougher but still easily passable. The journey to Mastuj village can now be made in around 5-6 hrs.

From Chitral town, cross to the E bank of the river and turn left, heading N before bearing NE along the **Mastuj River** (the Lutkho river valley, described above), drains in from the NW. Shortly after the junction of the two rivers, the road passes through the village of **Koghozi**, with its post office and a few basic shops.

About 1 km beyond Koghozi, the **Golen Gol** drains in from the SE. A jeep track leads up this valley as far as the village of **Ustur** 14 km). From there it is possible to trek NE and then either bear N across the **Shakuh Pass** to Reshun, or continue in an easterly direction across the **Phargam Pass** to Harchin. Another trek leads S from Ustur, over the **Dok Pass**, and then SW to Madaglasht at the head of the Shishi valley.

The main road continues along the Mastuj River, passing through the villages of Maroi, Barenis, Grim Lasht and soon after Reshun.

Between Grim Lasht and Reshun, the **Barum Gol** drains in from the NW. There is a bridge across to the opposite bank and the village of **Parpesh**. The Barum Gol is jeepable as far as the village of Barum and then on to Muzhen (bridge along this last section are often broken), the start of the trek across the **Owir Pass** and down to the Lutkho valley.

Back on the main road, shortly after Reshun, the **Turikho valley** (see below) can be seen draining into the Mastuj River, the two valleys running almost parallel at this point. Almost opposite the junction of the two rivers is the

village of **Kuragh**. There is a small hotel here, the **F** *Kohistan*, basic, food available, garden (camping). Just beyond the next village, **Charun**, the road crosses to the N bank of the river on a bridge. The old jeep track into the Turikho valley branches left just after the bridge; these days it is often blocked by landslides. The main road heads E and passes through the village of **Khandan** with its petrol pump, and a turning left which is the start of the new jeep track up the Turikho valley.

Further on there is a bridge across to the village of **Buni**, a large, fertile settlement (the largest in upper Chitral) spread out over a wide alluvial fan. The main jeep track continues straight on, passing through the village of **Parwak** before crossing once again to the S bank of the river. Soon after is the junction of the **Laspur River** with the Mastuj, the former draining in from the S. The jeep track crosses to the E bank of the Laspur River and then forks; left leads into Mastuj village, 3 km away, while the right fork is the route to the Shandur Pass.

Mastuj Village

Mastuj was once the seat of power of the independent Kushwaqt principality, which in its heyday reached across into the Gilgit river valley. **Mastuj Fort**, similar in style to the one in Chitral town, is still occupied by Colonel Khushwaqt-ul-Mulk, the son of Shuja-ul-Mulk, who was made Mehtar of Chitral by the British in 1895, following the siege of Chitral fort. The setting is particularly beautiful, with the village spread out across a large alluvial fan. Bubbling streams and irrigation channels run through golden fields of wheat and barley lined with towering poplar trees, shimmering in the sun and wind, while in the village apricot and *jujube* trees are scattered all around. There is a small bazaar, fairly well stocked with basic supplies (trekkers can stock up on flour, rice, lentils, tea, sugar etc here), a telephone exchange and a post office. The latter was established by the British and was considered to be the most far-flung post office in the empire.

● **Accommodation** The nicest place to stay in Mastuj is the **D** *Mastuj Fort*, situated N of the main village, between the jeep track and the river, 2 rm or camping in the grounds, toilet/shower block, hot water. Book in advance through *Hindu Kush Trails*, either in Chitral or Islamabad. In the village itself, there is the friendly **F** *Foreign Tourist Paradise*, 2 rm, basic but comfortable, furnished local-style, small pleasant garden, food prepared to order. There is also a *C & W Rest House*, though getting permission to stay there is difficult; try in Chitral or Buni.

Shandur Pass

From Mastuj village, the jeep track to the Shandur Pass heads S along the E bank of the Laspur River, passing through the village of **Harchin**. Further on, at **Sor Laspur**, the jeep track bears E and begins the climb up to Shandur Pass, the highest polo ground in the world at 3,734m and the site of the annual polo match between Chitral and Gilgit. For details of this section of the route, and the Gilgit river valley to Gilgit, see page 458.

North of Mastuj; Yarkhun valley

North of Mastuj village, the Mastuj River becomes known as the Yarkhun. A rough jeep track follows the E bank of the river as it climbs NE towards the Wakhan Corridor. The jeep track passes first through the village of **Chuinj**, where there is a small hotel, the **F** *Khyber*, basic. A little further on is **Chapali**, where a small side valley climbs up to the E, the start of the trek across the **Chamarkhan Pass** to Barsat, just E of the Shandur Pass. An alternative route branches off to lead across the **Zagar Pass**, and then either down to the Ghizar River at Shamran or on across the **Nazbar Pass** to Yasin.

The jeep track continues NE, passing through the village of **Brep**, before crossing to the W bank of the river. Shortly after is the small village of **Dzig**, the start of the trek over the **Khot Pass** and into the Turikho valley. Further on is **Bang**, consisting of a number small villages spread out over several km. Here, the **Bang Gol** drains in from the NW, marking the start of the trek over the **Nizhdaru Pass** to Sor Rich in the Turikho valley.

Beyond Bang, the track passes through the village of **Pitrangaz**, followed closely by **Paur**, before arriving at **Shulkuch**. In 1995 the jeep track reached only 1 km or so beyond the village before petering out.

The Yarkun valley continues NE, before eventually swinging round to the E. A long, strenuous but spectacular trek (around 3 weeks) follows the Yarkhun valley and crosses the **Karumbar** and **Chillinji** passes into the Chapursan valley, emerging on the KKH near Sost; alternative routes branch S across the **Darkot Pass**, giving access to the Yasin and Ishkoman valleys which drain into the Ghizar River (part of the Gilgit river valley). An alternative trek branches NE off the Yarkhun valley, across **Shah Jinali Pass** and down into the Turikho valley.

Turikho Valley

The Turikho valley is particularly green and fertile, the irrigated patches of settlement blending into each other for most of its length. The lower section of the valley is known as the **Mulkho**, the middle section as the **Turikho** and the upper section as the **Rich** valley.

From the turning just E of Khandan, the jeep track climbs steeply up to a shoulder of mountain seperating the Turikho and Mastuj rivers. On top is a small plateau with pasture known as **Kagh Lasht**, scarred by several jeep tracks which have cut through the ground cover and exposed the sandy soil underneath to erosion. The track descends to the village of **Istaru**, followed soon after by **Warkup**. Further on there is a bridge across to the village of **Nishko** on the W bank.

This bridge gives access to the **Tirich Gol** which drains in from the W, joining the Turikho River higher up, above the village of Rain. The Tirich Gol is jeepable as far as the village of **Shagram** (there are two Shagrams, the second is higher up the Turikho valley). From Shagram a trek leads SE over the **Zani Pass** and back into the Mulkho (Turikho) valley near **Warum**, to join the old jeep track along the N bank of the river. Another trek leads W towards **Tirich Mir Base Camp**.

The main jeep track up the Turikho valley continues NE through **Rain** (pronounced "ra-een"), **Shagram** and across a small side valley draining in from the E (the start of the trek over the Khot Pass to Dzig in the Yarkhun valley), to **Burzum**. There is a footbridge across to the W bank of the Turikho River here, giving access to the **Ziwar Gol**, which drains in from the NW. Further

along, at **Zanglasht**, another footbridge gives more direct access. A trek follows the Ziwar Gol, branching NW over the **Chikor Pass** and down the **Uzhnu Gol** to rejoin the Rich (Turikho) valley at Uzhnu.

The main jeep track crosses to the W bank of the river at **Uzhnu** for a short stretch, then recrosses to the E bank to arrive at **Rich**, a scattered settlement of several villages with a shop selling basic supplies. Further up, beyond **Sor Rich**, the jeep track crosses once again to the E bank to arrive at **Phurgram**. This last stretch of the track, crossing and recrossing the river, is frequently blocked as the bridges here are particularly rickety and easily broken during rains or floods. In 1995 the jeep track extended for a few kilometres beyond Phurgram before petering out. Beyond is the start of the trek over the Shah Jinali Pass and down into the Yarkhun valley.

KARAKORAM HIGHWAY AND THE NORTHERN AREAS

CONTENTS

Introduction	420
Hazara Section	432
Kaghan Valley	439
Kohistan Section	445
Gilgit District	454
Gilgit to Chitral	468
Baltistan	479
Lower Hunza and Nagar Section	500
Central Hunza/Nagar Section	507
Nagar Valley	515
Gojal (Upper) Hunza Section	516
Khunjerab Pass to China Section	524

MAPS

Northern areas	421
Karakoram Highway	429
Hazara	433
Abbottabad	435
Mansehra	437
Kaghan Valley	439
Balakot	440
Naran	442
Kohistan	446
Besham	448
Dasu and Komila	450
Chilas	452
Gilgit District	455
Gilgit Town	460
Gilgit to Chitral	469
Baltistan	480
Skardu	486
Deosai Plateau	491
Shigar	494
Khaplu	497
Hunza and Nagar	501
Chalt region and Chaprot Valley	504
Karimabad	511
Gulmit	516
Gojal (Upper) Hunza	517
Passu	519
Old Sust	521

New Sust	522
Sust to Kashgar	524
Tashkurgan	527
Kashgar	532

INTRODUCTION

To the N of Pakistan lie the Northern Areas, a mountainous region containing some of the world's most incredible scenery, a fascinating mixture of different ethnic populations, and some superb trekking and walking routes. The building of a road through the region – the **Karakoram Highway** – linking Pakistan to China has opened up a spectacular overland route between the two countries, passing through some of Pakistan's most beautiful mountain areas, and providing onward access to Central Asia's historic cities. The opening of this route to foreigners in 1986 provides adventurous travellers with the opportunity of a unique and exhilarating travel experience.

Best time to visit: the exact opening and closing times of the Khunjerab Pass between Pakistan and China are weather dependent, though it is officially open from 1 May-30 November. Areas such as Hunza are at their best in spring (Apr) and autumn (Oct), when the trees are at their most colourful. The main tourist season is Jun, Jul, Aug, Sep, although Jul can get very hot in Gilgit and the Indus canyon, and rainy Septembers can lead to landslides and blockages on the KKH. Jul and Aug are the main trekking/climbing months.

Editorial logic In its lower reaches, the Karakoram Highway passes through districts such as Hazara and Kohistan that are, in fact, administratively part of the **North West Frontier Province** (NWFP). However, since these regions form part of a natural route along the highway, the editorial logic is to include them in this **'Karakoram Highway and Northern Areas'** chapter. Excursions and diversions to valleys off the main highway are dealt with at the relevant departure point from the KKH.

Further, since the history, geography and culture of the huge area dealt with in this chapter is highly fragmented, these issues will often be dealt with separately at the relevant stage of the journey through the region.

Land and life

The administrative division known as the Northern Areas of Pakistan lies between 32° and 37° N, and 71° and 75° E, and covers 43,781 sq km. The Northern Areas have contiguous borders with Indian occupied Kashmir to the E, China to the N, Afghanistan to the NW, and the Pakistani state of NWFP to the W, SW and S. The landscape is dominated by high peaks, rivers, glaciers, plateaus and narrow valleys linked by a network of passes. Historically the political system of the region was one of small kingdoms, with shifting political alliances and boundaries, and dominated by internecinal disputes. Despite their perceived isolation, the people of the region have had traditional cultural and commercial links with their neighbours, with a strand of the old Silk Rd passing through the region. In recent years, improved access to parts of the region has brought about a transformation in the socio-economic structures in place, bringing development but exposing the vulnerability of traditional systems to the intrusions of modernity. Tourism is one of the fastest growing growth industries in the Northern Areas.

Geography

The Northern Areas of Pakistan is the meeting point of four of the world's great mountain chains, the **Himalayas**, **Karakorams**, **Pamirs and Hindu Kush**, contains the largest concentration of high peaks anywhere in the world, and is home to the longest glaciers outside the polar regions. The region consists largely of the **Kohistan Island Arc** (see page 445), a mass of displaced metamorphosed sedimentary rocks, wedged between the Eurasian and Indian plates. Two great sheer lines (*sutures*) run through the region; the N Suture separates the Kohistan Island from the Hindu Kush and Karakoram ranges to the E and N, and the Main Mantle Thrust, which separates Kohistan from the Himalayas and Indian plate to the S and SE. The pivotal point is the **Pamir Knot**, an enormous tangle of high mountains and plateaus in the N straddling Pakistan, Afghanistan, the former Soviet Central Asian states and China. All the major mountain ranges –Alai, Himalaya, Hindu Kush, Karakoram, Kunlun, Pamir, Tian Shan – run from this central feature, bifurcating into numerous sub ranges.

Although the details of the valleys and ranges are the work of glacial action, weathering and erosion, the formations as a whole are primarily the result of recent uplift. The interaction of these processes results in a highly unstable and dynamic landscape, where earthquakes and landslides are frequent.

Mountains

The Northern Areas has many of the world's highest peaks, with five over 8,000m, 25 over 7,500m and almost 100 over 7,000m. In **K2** (8,611m), Pakistan can boast a mountain second only to Everest in height, whilst **Nanga Parbat** (8,126m), graveyard to 47 climbers, can surely be acknowledged as the largest solid lump of rock anywhere on earth.

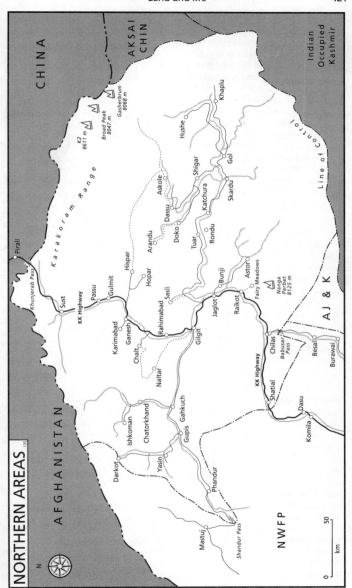

Glaciers

The Karakoram chain contains some of the longest glaciers outside of the polar regions, including **Siachen** (72 km), **Biafo** (62 km), **Hispar** (61 km), **Batura** (58 km), **Baltoro** (58 km), **Gasherbrum** and **Chogo Lungma** (both 38 km). Ice cover in the Karakoram is estimated at 23-25% as opposed to 8-10% in the Himalaya and 2.2% in the Alps. The region's glaciers provide both a creative and destructive force, being responsible for loss of agricultural land and damage to road networks through encroachment, but also providing the source for irrigation in a region where rain-fed agriculture is not possible.

Rivers

The dominant river system in the region is the **Indus**, which cuts a deep gorge trending first E-W and then N-S. With rare exceptions, such as Chilas and Skardu, habitation along the Indus' river banks has not been possible, with populations tending to stick to minor tributary valleys and mountain slopes where river and glacial water is more manageable. Numerous other rivers drain the region, forming part of the Upper Indus Basin, including the Shyok, Shigar, Astor, Gilgit, Karumbar, Hunza, Shimshal and Khunjerab rivers.

Other geographical features

There are numerous other important geographical feature in the Northern Areas, including numerous **passes** between valleys, some of which are easily crossed (eg Shandur), and others which have fearsome reputations and are closed for most of the year (eg Karakoram). The enormous plateau known as the **Deosai Plains**, lying W and NW of Skardu, is a spectacular illustration of the effects of glacial action and environmental change on the landscape.

Climate

Climatically, the Northern Areas is a region of extremes. Temperatures fluctuate between the mid to late 40°s in the furnace of the gorge around Chilas, down to -30°C at higher altitudes. The main valleys such as Gilgit, Hunza and Skardu generally have annual temperature ranges between 0°C and 30°C. Many parts of the Northern Areas are snow bound between Nov and Apr.

The Northern Areas are largely outside the monsoon belt and receive only minimal rainfall of about 100 mm annually, most of which occurs at high altitude feeding snow-fields and glaciers. The lower sections of the Kaghan Valley and Hazara lie on the edge of the SW Monsoon and receive upwards of 800 mm of rainfall annually. In Aug, the main trekking season, rivers are swollen with summer snow-melt and difficult to cross. Spring (Apr-May) and Autumn (Sep-Oct) are particularly beautiful seasons although cold at night.

History

Prehistory

The earliest known inhabitants, hunter-gathering '**Rock Art Peoples**', inhabited rock shelters and worshipped the forces of nature. At some stage there appears to have been an influx of more advanced megalith builders, perhaps from Iran, who practised ritual pit burials and were probably fire worshippers. Carvings suggest the keeping of domesticated horses, cattle, sheep and goats, as well as settled agriculture. In addition iron, bronze, copper, silver and gold appear to have been used in tool-making, weaponry and jewellery.

Early records

In the 6th century BC the Northern Areas became part of the 7th Satrapy of the **Achaemenid** Empire under Darius the Great. Interest was generated by fabulous tales. Herodotus recounts how: "Here in this desert (Baltistan/Deosai Plateau) there live amid the sand great ants, in size somewhat less than dogs, but bigger than foxes. These ants make their dwelling underground and throw up sand-heaps as they burrow. Now the sand which they throw up is full of gold...". However exaggerated, gold was certainly present and was used as a form of tribute – a practice which continued into the 20th century.

From 321 BC the **Mauryan** Empire made significant inroads. *Asoka's* Rock Edicts can be found near Mansehra, and Sanskrit texts relate how he subjugated the *Khasas*, a tribal group based around Chilas. Thus Buddhism began to penetrate. Between the 1st century BC and 1st century AD, *Kharoshthi* rock inscriptions from Chilas and Thalpan show definite artistic influence from the cultural centre of Taxila and also further afield from Iran. Bullocks, horses and chariots are depicted and there appears to have been an influx of Buddhist pilgrims.

Kanishka extended **Kushan** power in the 1st century AD as far as Xinjiang and Tibet. During this period evidence of rock carvings is restricted to areas further N, at Alam Bridge and the Sacred Rock of Hunza, suggesting an earthquake and flooding of the Indus around Chilas. Agriculture was extended and new fruits and crops introduced. Buddhism flourished and the **Silk Rd** came into effective use, bringing trade and prosperity to the major river valleys.

Towards the end of the 3rd century the **Sassanian** Empire of Persia extended into the N Areas from the Trans-Pamir region and the Sogdian and Bactrian cursive scripts were introduced, visible on the Sacred Rock of Hunza and at Shatial.

The White Huns invaded between the 5th and 6th centuries AD, and they appear on numerous rock carvings, always on horseback shooting arrows. They became converted to Hinduism and worshipped Siva. However numerous semi-independent kingdoms flourished.

Baltistan was known as **Great Bolor**. It remained largely independent, although at times strongly influenced by Tibet. The kingdom of **Little Bolor** was centred around Gilgit and Chitral and ruled by the *Patola Shahis*. Both were Buddhist and only minimally influenced by the Huns.

Mediaeval history

Sometime in the 7th century there appears to have been an influx of Turkic peoples into the Gilgit region. These Turks were probably Zoroastrians and perhaps the founders of the *Trakhan Dynasty* in Gilgit. In the 8th century Muslim Arabs advanced through Central Asia, and Tibetans moved W through Ladakh and Baltistan. Meanwhile the Chinese T'ang Dynasty, which was anxious to keep open the economically vital Silk Rd, forged alliances with the rulers of Gilgit and Kashmir and succeeded in forcing back the Arabs and eventually defeating the Tibetans in 751 AD.

By the 11th century some scholars identify a state of **Dardistan**, centred around Gilgit. The internal situation was complex, a region described as "noisy with kingdoms" by Marco Polo in the 13th century. From the 11 th century onwards the region was Islamicised by Sunnis from the S, Shi'ites (Shias) from Kashmir and Ismailis from Afghanistan. The major river valleys flourished by taxing trade along the Silk Rd and slavery was an integral part of the economy.

The **silk routes** to China brought great prosperity to the kingdoms of the N Areas. Gilgit in particular benefitted from its position at the junction of the various routes from the Iranian Plateau, and from the plains of the Punjab up the Indus River. Baltistan meanwhile commanded the old trade route along the Indus from Ladakh and Kashmir.

Throughout its history, the N Areas have been influenced socially and culturally by the silk route trade. The Balti people, although now predominantly

Shia Muslims, still show a cultural and racial affinity with Tibet, and in places even retain some traces of Buddhism, adopted after the 3rd century and blended with the existing animism and shamanism of the people.

The British period

The various small kingdoms feuded repeatedly among themselves, but periodically succeeded in repelling the Dogras and the Sikhs. In 1846 the British appointed **Gulab Singh** as the first Hindu Maharaja of the Princely State of Jammu and Kashmir. It was subsequently understood that Gilgit and Baltistan were to come under his suzerainty, but his control over the N Areas remained entirely nominal.

Towards the end of the 19th century, British interest was heightened by Russian expansion into Central Asia. The 'Great Game' between the two regional powers followed. In 1877 the first **British Agency** was established in Gilgit, but it was abandoned in 1881 after a major revolt of Kohistani tribes. In 1889 a second British Agency was established, this time with improved road and telegraph links as well as a permanent British military presence. Throughout the 1890s, a tenuous control was maintained. Later the **Gilgit Scouts** were established as a well trained force which could keep internal order and respond to any external aggression.

Independence and partition

In Aug 1947 the Muslim majorities in Gilgit and Baltistan revolted against Kashmir, declared independence, and acceded to Pakistan. The cease-fire line agreed in Jan 1949 between India and Pakistan became the de-facto international boundary. By 1973 the old autonomous states and political districts had been fully absorbed into Pakistan.

Recent developments

The most significant recent develop-ment in the history of the Northern Areas has probably been the construction of the Karakoram Highway (see below). However, although this has speeded internal communication, and helped integrate further the region within the modern state of Pakistan, it is just one of a number of factors that have brought change. It cannot alone account for the socio-economic development, the changing patterns of land use, agricultural practise and settlement patterns that have occured in recent years. Rapid population growth, increased opportunities in education and government service, labour migration (including both work in the Gulf and down country Pakistan), evolving class structures, are all amongst the dynamic processes that are changing the face of the Northern Areas.

Various cultural and social habits which were dictated by environmental constraints have also been eroded. For example, the people of Hunza and Baltistan have abandoned their seasonal raw fruit diet and no longer refrain from cooking during the summer to preserve scarce wood-fuel resources, leading to acute shortages of firewood.

However, standards of living have undoubtedly improved, with the spread of schools and hospitals into the remotest areas. Local populations often demand new roads and the benefits they bring, while foreign tourists decry the spoiling of a 'paradise', which they often seem to regard as theirs to enjoy.

Development programmes in the region are relatively enlightened. The **Aga Khan Rural Support Programme** (AKRSP) is particularly successful in Ismaili areas. The project encourages local populations to set up village organizations and identify small income generating projects. In return they receive financial and technical assistance from AKRSP. Schemes include land reclamation, irrigation, roads and bridges and training selected village representatives to upgrade their skills in various fields. The programme, involving about 800,000 people, has been particularly successful in involving women. According to a 1986 World Bank report it has "produced outstanding results". The Aga Khan Foundation is also highly active, and very successful, with its health (AKHS) and education (AKES) programmes.

Culture

People

A wide variety of different peoples live in the isolated valleys of the Northern Areas. The people of the Kaghan Valley, the *Swati*, *Sayyid* and *Gujar* nomads and the *Dilazak* and *Tanaolis* tribes further S were 17th and 18th century refugees from Swat and Buner who fled from the *Yusufzai Pathans*, who in turn had been displaced from the plains of Peshawar. Baltistan, known as '*Tibet-i-Khurd*', shows strong Tibetan influence. *Balti* is an archaic Tibetan dialect very similar to Ladakhi.

Around Gilgit, the main ethnic group are the Shina speakers. Historically a feudal society, the *Shins* represent the ruling class, with the *Yashkuns* (landowners), *Kamins* (craftsman) and *Doms* (minstrels) below them. The system of values associated with these classes remained different from the class stratification of Hinduism, although it was modelled upon it. Occupying a central position at the junction of two arteries of the ancient Silk Rd, Gilgit has absorbed Swatis and Chitralis, as well as Kashgaris, Wakhis, Kyrghiz and Tshins from Central Asia.

In the Hunza Valley, the *Hunzakuts* claim descent from Alexander's armies, but despite their fair complexion, their origins are certainly much older. Their language, *Burushaski*, is aboriginal, and apparently unrelated to any other. In Upper Hunza, or Gojal, the *Wakhi* speaking people are related to nomadic groups from Xinjiang (Chinese Turkestan) and the Pamir region.

Language

The ethnic mix of people in the Northern Areas is reflected in the number and variety of languages and dialects spoken. Indeed, some linguists suggest that the region shows the most intricate pattern of languages in the whole of Pakistan. The recent incorporation of the Northern Areas within Pakistan, and the subsequent exposure to new systems of administration, trade and education, means that Urdu, English and even Punjabi are becoming more widely spoken.

The traditional regional breakdown of languages is as follows: in Gilgit, mainly Shina, with some Burushaski; in Yasin and Ishkoman, Shina, Khowar (Chitrali), Burushaski, and Wakhi; in Hunza, predominantly Burushaski, but some Domaki; in Gojal Hunza, Wakhi; in Nagar, Burushaski, with some Shina; in Baltistan, Balti; in Chilas, Shina; in the Indus Valley below Chilas, Shina and 'Kohistani' (Maiyan, Chiliss, Gauro et al).

Prof Fussman (in Dani, 1991) suggests the origins of these languages are as follows: "**Wakhi** is an Iranian language; **Balti** is Tibetan; **Burushaski** is quite isolated; **Khowar**, **Kalasha**, **Shina**, the **Kohistanis** together with **Kashmiri** and some languages of the neighbouring Afghanistan form the **Dardic** branch of languages; **Domaki** is Indo-Aryan, heavily overlaid with Dardic and Burushaski elements". However, as Fussman points out, this terminology refers strictly to linguistics, and expressions such as Iranian, Tibetan, Indo-Aryan and Dardic refer to languages and not to countries or people.

Literature

Most of these languages rely heavily on the oral tradition, with story-telling being the main vehicle for communicating ancient history. However, a wide variety of modern literature is available that provides a detailed insight into the Northern Areas.

For contemporary accounts of the 'Great Game': Durand, A, 1899 '_The Making of a Frontier_'; Knight, EF, 1894 '_Where Three Empires Meet_' (rec); Younghusband, F, 1896 '_The Heart of a Continent_' (rec). For excellent overviews of the entire 'Great Game', and reviews of all the literature on the subject try: Hopkirk, P, 1990 '_The Great Game_' (rec) and Keay, J, 1977 '_When Men and Mountains Meet_' and 1979 '_The Gilgit Game_' (rec). Dr AH Dani's 1991 '_The History of the Northern Areas_' provides an authoritative and definitive background to the region. Most are available in Islamabad and Gilgit bookshops.

Religion

Before Islam replaced Buddhism and Hinduism in the N Areas, complex indigenous religions were practised. **Ra** or **Aftab**, the solar deity, was an archetypal figure from whom the rulers of **Little Bolor** traced their descent. Spiritual guarantors performed a variety of seasonal religious festivals ensuring the overall fertility of the land and the people. Some of their beliefs still survive.

Zones of spirituality

Dani identifies 'altitudinal zones of spirituality'. All the major peaks, such as Nanga Parbat and Rakaposhi, are considered the abodes of 'clean spirits', mostly female, which inhabit fairy castles. Below this is the zone of _Mayaro_, domain of the Markhor and Ibex, both considered sacred and tended by fairies (_Ranchi_ or _Peri_). The agricultural zone is considered neutral, man's home. Last is the the demonic sphere, a realm reserved for dangerous invisible things; demons lurking near the mouths of glaciers, in dark crevasses or by the raging torrent of a gorge.

Such animistic pantheons are common to the whole of N Pakistan and the Greater Himalaya, and in the Northern Areas remain, deeply rooted in local folklore. First they became adapted to

Buddhism, the two becoming inextricably intertwined, and later existed either secretly, or alongside Islam. Even today, _Shamans_* of an almost Siberian type and closely related to the _Ladakhi_ and _Tibetan Oracles_, sometimes act as the voice of public opinion, inhaling the smoke of juniper branches in order to induce a trance.

Islam

The initial Muslim contact came from the S, from the _Yusufzai Pathans_ of **Sunni** faith who were displaced N by other tribal migrations from the plains of Peshawar. In Gilgit the '6 venerable men' arrived in the 12th century during the _Trakhan Dynasty_, and **Buddhism** was largely replaced by the Sunni faith. Meanwhile, in Baltistan, the _Makpon_ rulers, under _Ali Sher Khan Anchan_ developed close ties with Kashmir and adopted the **Shi'ite** (Shia, or Shia Ithna' Sharis) faith, thus becoming Islamicised from the E. For a while Gilgit also became Shi'ite under _Mirza Khan_. Bloody feuding between the Sunni and Shi'ite factions continues to this day.

The Ismailis

The Ismaili Muslims arrived from Badakshan in Afghanistan during the 13-14th century. A Mongol prince, in legend _Taj Mughal_, spread the Ismaili faith in Chitral, Punial, Yasin and Hunza. The Ismailis are a reform branch of the Shi'ite (locally called _Maulavi_, sometimes referred to as Shia Imani Ismailis) which developed in the 9th century in Iraq. They are followers of the _Aga Khan_, a direct descendant of Mohammad, through Mohammad's daughter Fatima, who married the Prophet's cousin Ali.

According to the 1981 census, the religious split in the Northern Areas was as follows: Shia Imani Ismailis (Ismaili) 43%; Shia Ithna' Sharis (Shia, Shi'ite) 39%; Sunni 18%.

Government and administration

Following Partition the fate of the Northern Areas has remained tied to the dispute between Pakistan and India over the status of Kashmir, and thus the region has remained in something of a state of limbo. The UN sponsored resolution following the cease-fire in 1949 envisaged a plebiscite in all territories of Kashmir (including the Northern Areas) where the local population could choose between joining Pakistan or India (or possibly independence). The plebiscite is yet to be held. As a consequence, although the area is administered by Pakistan, it has not been formally integrated within the federal state because Pakistan does not accept the unnatural division of Kashmir.

After independence, the region was administered by the Ministry of Kashmir Affairs and Northern Areas from Islamabad. Although still directly managed by the Federal Government, over the years there has been a gradual devolution of power towards local representatives. In 1994 a new package of administrative reforms was unveiled, expanding the Northern Areas Council to 24 members, and reserving two seats for women. The Chief Executive is a government appointee, although the Deputy Chief Executive is elected by the council members. A sub level of administration allows electoral participation by the people of the Northern Areas, but although the system of administration shows the same basic features as that of a provincial government, the region is by no means integrated within the political system of Pakistan.

Economy

Agriculture

Cultivation is mostly irrigation based, and the chronic shortage of cultivable land greatly inhibits agriculture. Traditional crops include wheat, barley, millet, buckwheat and legumes, later supplemented and partly replaced by maize and potatoes. Fruits, and in particular apricots, form an important part of the local diet and grow very well at higher altitudes. Irrigation is highly developed, involving ambitious and precarious feats of engineering to channel water many miles from springs and streams along steep valley sides to terraced alluvial fans.

Some of the valleys are rich and fertile, especially to the S on the **Pahkli** and **Rash** plains of Mansehra and Abbottabad. The Kaghan Valley is thickly wooded as far up as Naran (2,440m), and extensively terraced. Cultivation is primarily a single *kharif* crop of maize, which due to the single cropping and use of manure gives very high yields. Beyond Naran cultivation dwindles. Semi-nomadic tribes of *Gujars, Sayyids* and *Swatis* take advantage of the high summer pastures to graze cattle, sheep and goats, having planted crops of maize in isolated settlements lower down.

The thick fir and pine forests of Kaghan and also the **Haripur** and **Gali Hills** to the S have been extensively logged in recent years due to their easy accessibility, contributing to greatly increased soil erosion.

The Yusufzai Pathans who migrated into the Northern Areas brought with them the **wesh** system of land-ownership. Plots of land were rotated amongst families of a common clan, allowing each family access to the best quality land for a given period. The system is still practised in certain areas of Hazara and Indus Kohistan. Although eminently democratic, it has been criticised for its disincentive to make permanent improvements on the land.

Goats are an integral part of the local economy at higher altitudes. The plentiful supplies of fodder in the altitude zone of the evergreen Holm Oak (*Quercus ilex*) allows nomadic tribal groups to support large herds at lower altitudes in winter and move up to the higher pastures in summer. In many places the semi nomadic tribes have developed a close interdependence with settled farmers, though they are of much lower social status.

Resources and industry

Timber is extensively logged in the lower valleys to the S under the *wesh* system of collective ownership. In addition, large scale commercial logging operations often buy off or ignore land rights and have flourished unchecked with the opening of the KKH. Many minerals, including gold, are common in very small quantities. Lack of reliable power supply and high transportation costs has inhibited the development of any real industrial base.

Cottage industries have traditionally centred around the production of handwoven woollen cloth and clothing, and wood carved items. However, in many areas the traditional techniques are in decline, as cheaper imports have been allowed to undermine the industry.

Tourism

The opening of the entire length of the KKH to foreigners has led to a steady flow of tourists along this route. In addition to specialized mountaineering groups, increasing numbers of trekkers, backpackers, and more recently, tour groups are using this route. The government of Pakistan estimate that around 30,000 foreign tourists visit the Northern Areas each year, and although this figure is quite modest, it is growing at an average rate of 7.5%/year. More and more local people are taking advantage of the income generating opportunities within this sector of the service industry, although some concerns are being expressed over the impact on traditional society of exposure to outside influences.

The Karakoram Highway

On its 1,300 km journey from Islamabad, Pakistan's modern capital on the plains of the Punjab, to Kashgar, the Central Asian market town in China's most westerly province, the **Karakoram Highway** (KKH) threads its way through some of the most dramatic mountain scenery in the world.

As the KKH weaves its way between the peaks, the modern traveller comes across villages and communities that less than a 100 years ago were independent principalities, where the main source of income was relieving passing travellers of their possessions. Nowadays tourism is replacing looting as a key sector of the economy.

Yet the modern day tourist is just the latest in a long line of visitors passing this way. The armies of Alexander the Great, early pilgrims taking Buddhism to China, caravans on a strand of the famous Silk Rd, and mysterious explorer-cum-spies playing out the 'Great Game' of imperial rivalry between the Russian and British Empires have all trod this path.

Modern history of the KKH route

In 1959 work on the Indus Valley Rd began. This was to be a 840 km all weather road to link Gilgit to the rest of Pakistan. At Gilgit, the road would join with the old Hunza track making feasible access across the Karakorams to Kashgar. The terrain was so difficult that by 1965 only a natural surface road had been completed.

China and Pakistan, in Oct 1967, announced an agreement to build a highway linking Gilgit to Kashgar. Several routes were suggested, including one through the Mintaka Pass, although the final route was built through the Khunjerab Pass. Seven battalions of Army Engineers from the Pakistan Army and 10,000 men from the Frontier Works Organization worked on the road, with heavy machinery having to be airlifted in after construction of improvised airstrips. The road was formally inaugurated on 16 February 1971.

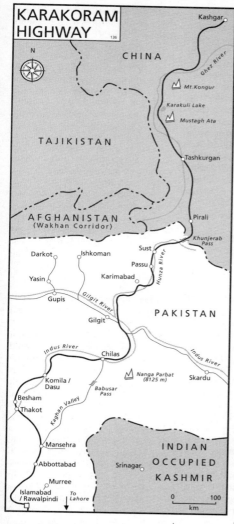

KARAKORAM
HIGHWAY

between Thakot and Hunza alone. The road was fully completed in 1978 and opened to third-country travellers in May 1986.

Liu Mahunqing, chief Chinese engineer on the KKH project, stated that "no road anywhere has been more difficult to build than the Karakoram Highway", and the construction details are impressive: 24 major bridges, 70 smaller ones; 1,708 high class culverts; 8 million kg of dynamite to move 30 million cubic metres of earth and rock; 80 million kg of cement used; 1,000 trucks consumed in the endeavour; and 400 dead and 314 seriously injured amongst the workforce, although some sources claim that the true figure is significantly higher (figures from Ispahani MZ 1989, 'Roads and Rivals: The political use of access in the borderlands of Asia', Cornell University Press).

In 1995, the government of Benazir Bhutto announced the allocation of Rs 500mn for upgrading the KKH into a 'modern, all-weather road' that would provide access to the warm water port of Karachi for Pakistan's landlocked Central Asian neighbours. There is already talk of pushing an extension of the KKH

The decision to convert the existing routes into an international highway was taken in 1973. At the peak of construction 25,000 people were at work on the highway, with over 9,000 Chinese employed through the Ishkoman Valley, and Afghanistan's Wakhan Corridor, into Tajikistan (see page 471), or of linking the Chinese section of the highway through the Tourgat Pass into Kyrghizstan.

Stated objectives of the KKH

At the time of construction, Pakistan's leaders claimed the KKH to be the tool of economic development in the Northern Areas. Following construction of the road, border trade between the two contiguous countries was expected to receive a major boost. Since 1968, 16 border trade agreements have been signed, with the main goods traded between Gilgit and Xinjiang comprising cotton textiles, hosiery goods, medicinal herbs, dry fruits, cigarettes, nylon fabrics and razor blades. Goods flowing from China to Pakistan tend to be at a higher stage of production, reflecting the relatively mature nature of the Chinese economy, with the balance of trade generally in China's favour.

However, border trade is still conducted on a very limited basis, probably with an annual value of less than Rs 50mn. The main constraint keeping the value of border trade low is that the production points in both Pakistan and China are located so far from the border trade points.

That is not to say, though, that the construction of the road has not had a major economic and social impact upon the Northern Areas of Pakistan. The Mir of Hunza states that "the Karakoram Highway has changed our lives and brought us into Pakistan ... we now get whatever we need and things are much cheaper" (Ispahani MZ 1989). In fact, areas that were previously self-sufficient in food are now dependant upon food imports, and the old egalitarian system of land distribution has been disrupted now that land has become a marketable commodity. New technology has come to the area, such as the introduction of a new telecommunications system, and the general opening of the area has encouraged inhabitants to enter the service industries, eg tourism, or to migrate to Pakistani cities in search of employment opportunities. Exposure to new customs and practises has occurred, as contact with foreign tourists and downcountry Pakistanis has become more regular, and thus traditional cultures have become more vulnerable to the intrusions of modernity. Further, mountain land use has become a function of access to nearby roads, and thus the settlement pattern of dense nucleated villages has changed to the *strassendorf* model with new structures strung out along the road.

However, despite the multiplier effects that the road has had on these mountain communities, the enormous costs of the road, both in terms of original investment and yearly maintenance costs, could never be rationalized as mere economic-development projects. In a similar manner to the period when these northern regions of Pakistan represented the frontiers of British India to be guarded, economic or political development was not the major concern. In fact the economies and societies of areas such as Hunza remained unaffected until the last quarter of this century, and thus when changes did come, they were the result of military and political goals. Therefore, the motivation behind building the Karakoram Highway must be assumed to be political.

Political objectives of the KKH

The KKH is one of several transmontaine roads built since the 1960s in S Asia that are 'manifestations of geopolitical alliances on the mountain landscape' (Allan NJR 1989). China's strongest ties in S Asia are with Pakistan, the KKH being the key piece of Chinese development aid to the region. Between 1956 and 1979 Pakistan received 13%, or $620mn of China's aid to Asia and the Middle East, and the building of roads is a relatively inexpensive way for China to deliver economic and military aid to Pakistan. Some commentators refer to this as China's policy of 'stadium diplomacy'.

The KKH is also linked to China's other main geostrategic lines of access in the region, connecting Xinjiang and Tibet, and thus the aims of China's foreign policy are inseparable from those of China's domestic security policy.

With closening economic and political ties emerging between India and the Soviet Union in the 1960s, as well as American support for India during the Sino-Indian War of 1962, Pakistan increased its efforts to closen links with China. The border agreement of 1963 marked improving economic and political relations between Pakistan and China, and the joint collaboration on projects such as the Indus River Rd, later the Karakoram Highway, greatly enhanced Pakistan's internal communications. In the same way that China developed transport networks within Xinjiang and Tibet to bring them under central control, Pakistan attempted to integrate the Northern Areas into the fabric of the country.

The government's main programme for the Northern Areas was to establish a network of routes. The constraints of the physical environment meant that for centuries access to peripheral areas of the borderlands was greatly restricted. However, with the perceived proximate danger from India in Kashmir, and the Soviet Union just a short distance away, the construction of routes in the area not only extended central control and lessened the physical distance to the rest of Pakistan, it also contrived, in the form of the Karakoram Highway, to lessen the physical distance to Pakistan's regional ally in China.

In an area that has managed to retain its autonomy for centuries, where inhabitants do not recognize arbitrary borders that intersect their territory, and where 'nation-state' and 'sovereignty' are meaningless concepts, Pakistan desperately needed to integrate the Northern Areas into modern Pakistan. The development of communications infrastructure was the logical way of achieving this.

Another Pakistani consideration behind the decision to build the Karakorum Highway has been to put their regional rival, India, on the psychological defensive in Kashmir. India fears that the highway allows Chinese access to their lines of communication between Srinagar and Leh, and allows China to complete a pincer movement around Kashmir via the Aksai Chin road. The highway is also seen by India as an endorsement by China of Pakistan's stand on Kashmir. The Indian government has described the road as being offensive in nature, and suggests that China has expansionist goals in the subcontinent. In 1978, the Soviet press agency TASS referred to the road as "the road of danger" and stated that it "linked with Peking's plans of military interference in Asia" (Ispahani MZ 1989). From a Pakistani viewpoint, the joint Sino-Pakistani route building programme has not only complicated India's intentions in the area, but it has also brought China into the Kashmir dispute on their side.

In terms of practicality the Karakoram Highway is greatly flawed. The nature of the terrain makes it vulnerable to air attack, and should this be successful, as a military supply route there are no terrestrial alternatives. (Even during peace-time the route is regularly blocked by rockfalls and landslides). Being so vulnerable to attack it is not suited to the movement of supplies and troops during a period of war. However, despite this, the perceived potential of the highway in militaristic terms far outweighs its physical ability to deliver, and thus the Karakoram Highway has had a profound effect upon the political manouvering in the region.

HAZARA SECTION

Environment

The KKH's journey begins in the **Hazara** district of the North West Frontier Province. The leading physical features of Hazara are the mountain ranges that define the boundaries on each side. To the E the main chain is a long ridge of outlying Himalayan spurs that flank the Jhelum and Kunhar rivers, terminating in the hills around Murree. To the NE, in the Kaghan Valley, another small range marks the boundary between Hazara and Kashmir, and includes the 5,291m Malika Parbat. To the W, Hazara is separated from the Swat Valley by the Black Mountains. Between these ranges, the region comprises a series of level tracts of varying size and character. The **geology** of Hazara reflects its position within the area of Himalayan disturbance.

The **climate** of Hazara also shows varied characteristics, with a marked N-S divide in levels of rainfall. Thus, the environment shows marked alterations between the hills and plains, dry soils and moist, and areas of vegetation and barrenness. In the S, the **flora** shows marked similarity to the Punjab, although there is evidence that suggests that prior to environmental change, the region was covered by *chir* forests. The forest tracts of the region are rich in *deodar* and *biar* (blue pine).

History

The ancient name of the region was 'Urasha'; perhaps the 'Uraya' of the *Mahabharata*. The first written account of the district is **Ptolemy's** description, written at the time of **Alexander's** invasion. The region came under Buddhist rule in the 3rd century BC, and some interesting archaeological sites date from this period, including **Asoka's** Rock Edicts at Mansehra (see below). The region is also mentioned by the 8th century Chinese traveller **Hiuen Tsang**, who referred to the district as the kingdom of *Wu-la-shi*.

The name 'Hazara' is thought to date to the 15th century, following the invasion by the Turkic speaking forces of **Timur** (Tamerlane). The word 'hazara', meaning 'thousand' is a translation of the Turkic word *ming*, meaning a regiment of a thousand men. Hazara then came under the control of the **Mughals**, for whom it formed part of the strategic route to Kashmir, but during the decline of their empire it was repeatedly invaded by Pathans from Swat (**Swathis**). In 1752, Hazara eventually came under the control of the Afghan emperor, **Ahmad Shah Durani**.

The **Sikhs** extended their influence into the region at the beginning of the 19th century, and following the conclusion of the First Sikh War in 1846, much to the resentment of the local population, the area was ceded to **Gulab Singh**, the Maharaja of Kashmir. In 1847, however, Hazara was transferred to the Lahore Darbar; effectively British rule and **James Abbott** was appointed as administrator (see below). During the Second Sikh War, the local ruler **Sardar Chattar Singh** was eventually defeated by a predominantly local army headed by Abbott, who was then made Deputy Commissioner of the district. Hazara remained in British hands until independence.

Culture

There are a number of different tribal groups in the Hazara district, many of whom arrived from the neighbouring valleys within the last 300 years. Most numerous are probably the **Jaduns**, descendants of the Yusufzai Pathans of Swat who migrated to Hazara in the early 17th century. The **Swathis** also share a common background. Other important groups include the **Gakhars**,

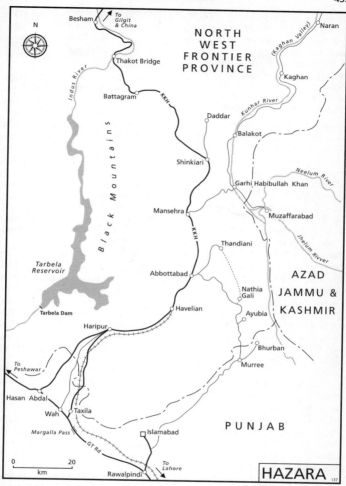

Besham
To Gilgit & China
Thakot Bridge
Battagram
Daddar
Shinkiari
Mansehra
Thandiani
Abbottabad
Nathia Gali
Havelian
Ayubia
Haripur
Bhurban
Murree
To Peshawar
Hasan Abdal
Wah
Taxila
Margalla Pass
Islamabad
GT Rd
To Lahore
Rawalpindi

Indus River
Black Mountains
Tarbela Reservoir
Tarbela Dam

NORTH WEST FRONTIER PROVINCE
Naran
(Kaghan Valley)
Kaghan
Kunhar River
Balakot
Garhi Habibullah Khan
Neelum River
Muzaffarabad
Jhelum River
AZAD JAMMU & KASHMIR
PUNJAB

KKH

N

0   20
km

HAZARA
137

found predominantly in the S. These traditionally warlike people came to the region with **Mahmud of Ghazni** around 1000 AD, and subsequently fought repeated battles with the Mughals. Another interesting group are the **Mishwanis**, who formed the backbone of Abbott's army in the Second Sikh War. The N of the Kaghan Valley is populated mainly by **Sayyids**, also descendants of the Swathis – the main ethnic group in the lower Kaghan Valley. The oldest inhabitants are probably the **Gujars**, a semi-nomadic group of pastoralists who generally farmlands in the S of the district, and migrate with their flocks in the summer to the northern pastures of the Kaghan Valley, into Swat, and even as far as the Darel and Tangir Valleys near to Chilas.

The main language of Hazara is **Hindko**, a branch of Punjabi, although Pashtu is spoken in the main Pathan areas, and the Gujars have their own language, Gojri.

To reach the beginning of the KKH, one must travel W from Islamabad/Rawalpindi on the Peshawar bound GT Rd (see page 253). Having passed through the Margalla Pass, it is possible to turn N either at **Taxila** (31 km), or to continue through **Wah** and turn N at **Hasan Abdal** (16 km). The latter route is quicker, but the former is marginally quieter. Both routes lead to **Haripur** (34 km).

Situated in the lush green Dor Valley, **Haripur** (64 km, 1 hr from Ism) was founded in 1822 by Sardar Hari Singh, one of Ranjit Singh's ablest generals. Just to the E of the town lie the remains of the Harkishangarh Fort, a formidable stronghold built by Hari Singh. Following the building of Abbottabad, Haripur declined in strategic significance, and nowadays is just a small, bustling market town. Haripur is the starting point for visits to the Tarbela Dam (see page 241).

A further 20 km on is **Havelian**, the terminus for the narrow gauge railway from Taxila, and the official starting point of the Karakoram Highway. Beyond the town the road crosses the Dor River, and then rapidly climbs through denuded hills, before dropping down into **Abbottabad**.

Abbottabad

Established in 1853 as a new cantonment town, **Abbottabad** was named after the British soldier turned administrator **James Abbott** (see box). In addition to its role as District Headquarters, Abbottabad has maintained its military tradition, and is today the base of the elite Frontier Force (The 'Piffers'),

Baluch Regiment, Army Medical Corps and the Army School of Music. It is also home of some of Pakistan's most prestigious public schools.

Places of interest

Being less than 150 years old, there is little of historic interest in Abbottabad, although the town does have a relaxed, easy going feel to it. The cantonment area has tree lined avenues, parks, large bungalows with lush gardens, some old churches, and a morbid Christian cemetery. The bazaar area is crowded, lively and very colourful.

Local information
● Accommodation

C *Comfort Inn*, Shahrah-e-Resham, T 5542, a/c, heating, dish TV, rent-a-car, a/c restaurant serves Pak, Chinese and continental; **C** *Royal*, KKH, N of town, T 6492, a/c, plus good Chinese restaurant; **C** *Sarban*, The Mall, T 4877, a/c and deluxe rooms, (with some cheaper standard room), room service, laundry, car rental, Pak and continental restaurant plus rooftop terrace, bathrooms with tubs; **C** *Springfield*, The Mall, T 4834, a/c, (some cheaper non a/c rooms), TV, phone, restaurant, takes bookings for *Springfield* guest hse and cottage at Naran.

D *New Palm*, The Mall, T 5190, some cheaper class rooms, friendly but run-down; **D** *Ramlina*, KKH nr bus stand, T 5431, also has cheaper non deluxe rooms, restaurant, terrace and garden, excursions and cultural shows arranged, friendly and good value, takes bookings for *Swiss Cottage* in Naran.

E *Alzar*, Jinnah Rd, T 31671, restaurant; **E** *Al-Zahra*, Havelian Rd, T 30155; **E** *Bolan*, Fowara Chowk, The Mall, T 4623, close to bus stand, restaurant and parking, quite good value; **E** *Cantt View*, Jinnah Rd, T 31346, restaurant; **E** *Kohsar*, Jinnah Rd, T 31583; **E** *Park*, Havelian Rd, T 6175, undergoing renovation in 1995, but has snooker table; **E** *Zarbat*, The Mall, T 5508.

F *Asia*, Eid Gah Rd, T 5212, good value; **F** *Al Mehran*, Kutchery Rd, very basic; **F** *Faisal* and *Falcon*, The Mall, both reluctant to take foreigners; **F** *Marhaba*, Eid Gah Rd, basic; **F** *Mount View*, Eid Gah Rd, T 30818, clean and friendly, rec; **F** *Pines View*, Jinnah Rd, T 6139, basic.

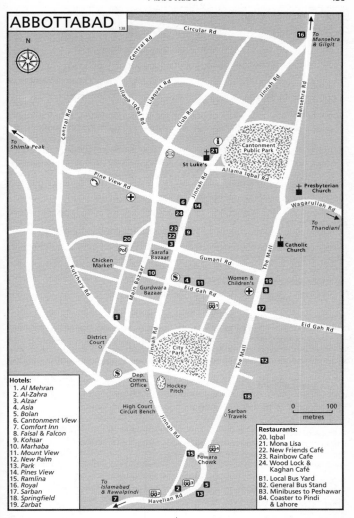

ABBOTTABAD

Hotels:
1. Al Mehran
2. Al-Zahra
3. Alzar
4. Asia
5. Bolan
6. Cantonment View
7. Comfort Inn
8. Faisal & Falcon
9. Kohsar
10. Marhaba
11. Mount View
12. New Palm
13. Park
14. Pines View
15. Ramlina
16. Royal
17. Sarban
18. Springfield
19. Zarbat

Restaurants:
20. Iqbal
21. Mona Lisa
22. New Friends Café
23. Rainbow Cafe
24. Wood Lock & Kaghan Café

B1. Local Bus Yard
B2. General Bus Stand
B3. Minibuses to Peshawar
B4. Coaster to Pindi & Lahore

● **Places to eat**

Most of the hotels have their own restaurants, and there are a selection of cafes, such as *Rainbow*, *New Friends*, *Woodlock* and *Kaghan* on Jinnah Rd. The *Mona Lisa*, nr to PTDC, is quite good, with a nice terrace. There are several upmarket places, incl *Milano Pizza*

Parlour, on the Mansehra Rd/KKH to the N of town.

● **Banks & money changers**

Muslim Commercial Bank, Jinnah Chowk, Eid Gah Rd. **National Bank**, nr to District Ct. **United Bank**, Pine View Rd.

JAMES ABBOTT

Born in England in 1807, and a schoolfellow of Disraeli, James Abbott received a commission in the Bengal Artillery in 1823 and travelled to India. He later saw action at Kandahar, and served in Herat as an assistant to Major D'Arcy Todd before being deputed to the 1839 British mission to Khiva. The object of this mission was to effect the release of Russian prisoners and slaves that were being detained by the Khan of Khiva, and despite some resistance, including an incident in which a sabre blow severed $1\frac{1}{2}$ fingers from Abbott's right hand, he was largely successful in negotiating the release of the Russians. He later wrote a lively two volume narrative of his adventures.

Upon his return to India, he worked on the survey and demarcation of the boundary between Punjab and Kashmir, and in 1847 became an administrator in Hazara District. When the Second Sikh War broke out the following year, Abbott found allies amongst the Mishwani Pathans of Hazara, and with Colonel John Nicholson, helped defeat the local Sikh ruler Chattar Singh. In 1849 he was appointed the first Deputy Commissioner of Hazara.

Described as "sanguine, chivalrous, warm-hearted and generous", and reputed to be known as Kaka (Uncle) Abbott by local children because of his habit of distributing sweets, Abbott proved to be a good and popular administrator. The local population revered him as their liberator from Sikh and Dogra rule, and it is said that when he left the post in 1853, he was followed to Hasan Abdal by "a weeping and lamenting crowd". It was his successor, Herbert Edwardes, who established the town of Abbottabad.

Abbott retired to the Isle of Wight, and died in 1896.

● **Hospitals & medical services**
Cantt General, Pines View Rd. *Women and Children's Hospital*, The Mall. The huge, modern *Ayub Hospital and Medical Complex* is just N of Abbottabad, on the Mansehra Rd/KKH.

● **Post & telecommunications**
GPO: is at the junction of Club Rd and Allama Iqbal Rd, just N of the bazaar. The Central Telegraph Office is W, on Pines View Rd.

● **Places of worship**
Catholic and *Presbyterian* churches are on The Mall, St Luke's *Protestant* church is at Jinnah Rd/Allama Iqbal Rd.

● **Tour companies & travel agencies**
Sarban Travels, Iqbal Shopping Complex, The Mall, T 5011 handles tickets for PIA, Aero Asia and Shaheen.

● **Tourist offices**
PTDC, Jinnah Rd, T 4946, has little information.

● **Transport**
Local Suzukis run to local destinations, incl Thandiani (1 hr), from the bus yard on Eid Gah Rd.

Air Abbottabad now has the PPP Government's much heralded, but effectively inconsequential, daily helicopter service to/from Islamabad. Depart Islamabad: 0800 1720; Depart Abbottabad: 0850 1810. Flight time 30 mins, Rs 900.

Road Bus: the chaotic **General Bus Stand** is to the S of town. Apparently there are schedules, but in reality, most buses work on a 'depart when full' system. Services run to **Rawalpindi** (3 hrs), although there are faster, more comfortable coasters from a yard outside the *Al Zahra Hotel*, and opp Fowara Chowk, continuing to **Lahore**; **Mansehra** (1 hr), with faster minibuses from Iqbal Shopping Complex on The Mall; **Murree** (5-6 hrs); **Muzaffarabad** (4 hrs); **Besham** (5 hrs). For destinations in the **Kaghan Valley**, go to Mansehra. Both government and private services from Rawalpindi to **Gilgit** pass through Abbottabad, but they are difficult to flag down, and are often full. A better option is to travel to Besham and change. Minibuses also run to **Peshawar** from the yard outside the *Al Zahra Hotel*.

Excursions from Abbottabad

Thandiani The most northerly of the Galis chain of hill-stations, **Thandiani** is currently reachable by road only from Abbottabad. The winding road climbs the 26 km (1 hr) from Abbottabad through fragrant pine forests. At the summit, a group of shacks serve as restaurants/hotels, incl *Green Hills* and *Shalimar*. Some have small 1 or 2-bedroom sheds attached, but unless you bargain very hard, they are vastly over priced. The *Shalimar* is clean, with an attached toilet (hole in floor), but ludicrously priced at Rs 250.

The road at the summit forks left, past St Saviour's Church to **E** *Far Pavilions*, (500m downhill). There are two pleasant cottages, a restaurant, plus plenty of camping space on the attractive lawns.

Further along the ridge from the *Shalimar* is the *C&W Inspection Bungalow*, and some fine walks through shady pine forest. A shingle (jeepable) road is being built to **Nathia Gali**, although at present the journey can only be done as a 2-day hike. There are *Resthouses* enroute at Biran Gali (1,920m) and Palakot (2,720m). The Asian Study Group (see under local information, Islamabad) have produced a route map of the walk.

The KKH continues N from Abbottabad, through the satellite settlement of Sikanderabad, and passing the impressive new Ayub Hospital and Medical Complex. There are several hotels on the KKH here, including the **C** *Abbottabad/Greens Gardens* and **D** *Paradise*.

The KKH itself actually by-passes **Mansehra** (26 km), although two link roads run up into the town. The southern road turns off next to the large **D** *Karakoram Hotel*, and the second road turns off next to **Asoka's Sacred Rocks**. The main bus terminus is several km N of Mansehra, on the KKH itself.

Mansehra

Prior to Partition and the unnatural division of Kashmir, **Mansehra** developed as a trading centre on the route to Srinigar, and as a Sikh garrison town. Despite being by-passed by the KKH, the town remains an important transport junction between Muzaffarabad in Azad Kashmir, the Kaghan Valley and points N along the KKH.

Hotels:
1. Al Naz
2. Al Junaid
3. Batgram
4. Errum
5. Moon
6. Parabat
7. Taj Mahal
8. Zam Zam

MANSEHRA

Mansehra's main attraction are **Asoka's Rock Edicts**, which date from the 3rd century AD. Inscribed on three large boulders adjacent to the KKH, (and now protected by modern roof structures), the edicts give King Priyadarsin's (Asoka) opinions on 'merits of piety', 'prompt dispatch of business', 'true glory', and vegetarianism, amongst other things. However, the *Kharaoshthi* script is so weather-beaten as to be all but invisible.

There are still remains of the Sikh occupation of the town, including a relatively recent Gurdwara (temple) that now serves as the police station, but the old fort has virtually disappeared under the new prison.

Mansehra has a large Afghan refugee population, many of whom speak good English and are keen to engage you in conversation.

● **Accommodation** D *Errum*, Shinkiari Rd, T 36245, very clean, some rooms with TV, attached hot/cold bath, carpeted rooms, very friendly, restaurant rec; E *Parbat*, Kashmir Rd, T 2179, fan, attached hot/cold bath, dish TV in restaurant, friendly, good value; F *Zam Zam*, (alley off) Shinkiari Rd, T 2127, basic, but friendly, some very cheap rooms without bath, restaurant rec, there are a number of very cheap hotels on Abbottabad and Kashmir Rds, most with no English sign, and some reluctant to take foreigners; incl, on Kashmir Rd: F *Al Junaid*, T 2810, *Moon*, *Battagram*, and on Abbottabad Rd: F *Taj Mahal*, T 2096, *Al Naz*, T 2481 and *Afghan Mahajir Spolmay*.

● **Transport** The main transport terminus is on the KKH, several km N of Mansehra (Suzuki Rs 1). Almost all the services to **Islamabad/Rawalpindi, Peshawar, Muzaffarabad, Abbottabad, Besham** and **Balakot** (Kaghan Valley) operate on a 'depart when full' basis. *Flying Coach* to **Lahore**, 0800, 0900, 1000, 1100, 1900, 2000, 2200 (Rs 130, 8 hrs) and, if you're mad, *Flying Coach* to **Karachi**, 1000, 1400 (Rs 300, 30 hrs +). **Road** There are no direct services to **Gilgit**, and passing buses are hard to flag down (go to Besham). Some minibus services, incl Pindi, Haripur, Abbottabad and Kaghan Valley operate from the minibus stand on Abbottabad Rd. *PIA* booking office, T 36747, is on Abbottabad Rd (just off map).

From Mansehra it is possible to make a diversion to the beautiful **Kaghan Valley**. Not only does this trip offer some of Pakistan's most attractive alpine scenery, it also offers a challenging alternative route N, across the **Babusar Pass**, rejoining the KKH at Chilas.

KAGHAN VALLEY

In a country of outstanding natural beauty, the Kaghan Valley must rank as one of Pakistan's most beautiful regions. The 161 km long valley offers stunning alpine forests, deep blue high altitude lakes, lush green meadows and distant snowy peaks, whilst the Kunhar River that flows through the valley provides some of the best trout fishing in Pakistan.

NB As with other regions that are popular with Pakistani tourists (eg Murree and Swat), hotel prices in the Kaghan Valley tend to inflate in the high season, at weekends, and when the manager feels like it. It is worth bargaining, especially out of season. If you wish to stay in the better hotels at peak times, it is recommended that you book in advance.

Best time to visit: during the winter months (Nov-Mar), heavy snowfall means that it is generally impossible to go any further N than Kaghan village. The Babusar Pass is usually only open to jeeps from Jul until early Sep, although it is possible to cross on foot a little before and after these dates. The summer months, May, Jun and Jul show the Kaghan Valley at its best, allowing an escape from the heat of the Punjab plains, although the valley is more crowded with visitors. Late Jul sees the onset of the monsoon. Autumn can be pleasant, though cold at night.

KAGHAN VALLEY 141

N

NORTHERN AREAS

To Islamabad
KKH
Indus
Chilas
To Gilgit

Babusar

Babusar Pass (4529 m)

Lake Lulusar
Gittidas

Besal

N W F P

Battakundi (2713 m)
Naran (2440 m)
Burawai

Bhogarmang Peak (4945 m)
Lake Saiful Malik (3215 m)
Lalazar Plateau (3200 m)

Danna Meadows
Kaghan (2038 m)
Khanian
Jared
Malika Parbat (5290 m)
Sharan
Shinu
Kawai
Paras
Shogran (2362 m)

AZAD KASHMIR

KKH
Kunhar River
Balakot
Makra Peak (3885 m)

Shinkiari
Garhi Habibullah Khan

Mansehra
Muzaffarabad

0   15
km

Balakot

The gateway to the Kaghan Valley, **Balakot** can be reached from Abbottabad in 2 hrs on a good quality winding road. The road passes the bridge at **Garhi Habibullah Khan**, the junction for **Muzaffarabad** in Azad Kashmir.

There is little of interest in Balakot itself, although the town was the scene of an important battle between the Sikhs and the Muslims in 1831. Ahmed Shah Bereli, leader of the Muslim forces, is buried in the small, green-tiled tomb down by the river.

● **Accommodation** B *Pine Park*, (across river, on road to Naran), T 7323, good views, but very run down (balconies to the point of being dangerous) and grossly overpriced. However, the other hotels in the *Pine Park* chain are in a differ-

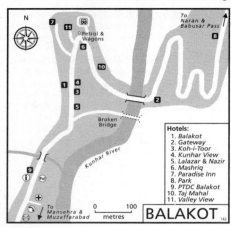

BALAKOT 142

Hotels:
1. Balakot
2. Gateway
3. Koh-i-Toor
4. Kunhar View
5. Lalazar & Nazir
6. Mashriq
7. Paradise Inn
8. Park
9. PTDC Balakot
10. Taj Mahal
11. Valley View

beautifully located settlement. Kawai (1,463m) is the junction for the jeep track up to the resort of **Shogran**, and a quiet, peaceful place to stay. **Accommodation F** *Tourist Hotel*, is very good value. **F** *Faisal Hotel*, under construction 1995. Jeeps run the 10 km up the old logging track to Shogran (Rs 200 hire, negotiable), although for those who want to walk, there is a shorter, but very steep, footpath (the manager at the hotel can point you in the right direction).

ent class entirely, offering high quality accommodation, albeit at high prices. Bookings can be made here for the other *Pine Park* hotels in Kaghan Valley at Shogran, Naran, Danna Meadows and Khanian, or from the head office, Pine Parks Resorts, House 11a, St 47, F-7/1, Islamabad. **C** *PTDC Balakot Motel*, spacious rooms with terrace, set in nice garden, quite good value, restaurant, plus helpful PTDC office. Bookings taken for PTDC Hotel at Naran and Pine Park Hotel at Shogran. **C** *Taj Mahal*, T 321, over priced, Chinese restaurant; **D** *Balakot*, T 482, large, carpeted rooms, friendly, best in category; **D** *Gateway*, T 210294, set on hill across river, good views, still under construction in 1995; **D** *Koh-i-Toor*, T 263. **D** *Kunhar View*, T 229, dark, small, overpriced rooms; **E** *Mashriq*, sleazy, noisy and overpriced rooms with shared bath; **E** *Paradise*, T 210315, friendly, quiet, with good views; **E** *Valley View*, prices according to floor, but all noisy; **F** *Lalazar* and *Nazir*, no English signs, both very basic and reluctant to take foreigners.

• **Transport Pick-ups and minibuses:** N (as far as Naran) run when full from the bus yard next to the petrol station. Although there are some services S to Rawalpindi and Abbottabad, you will probably have to go to Mansehra and change.

From Balakot, the road up the Kaghan Valley climbs quite rapidly, high above the Kunhar River. This very scenic route winds its way to **Kawai** (24 km, 1 hr), a small,

Shogran

Shogran (2,362m) is one of the loveliest locations in the Kaghan Valley, and despite recent hotel construction, remains remarkably unspoilt. Indeed, for many visiting Pakistanis it is the *Pine Park Resort* itself that offers the greatest attraction! The views from Shogran, however, are unsurpassed, especially if you walk up for 2 hrs through the forest to the high summer pastures at **Seri Paya**. The camping here is superb. To the S are views of Makra Peak (3,885m), whilst to the N is **Malika Parbat** (5,291m), the highest mountain in the Kaghan Valley. The peak was first climbed in 1890 by CG Bruce, and then by the N face by Capt BW Battye in 1920. More sedate visitors prefer to wander through the fragrant pine forest or stroll through the flowers in the lush green meadow.

• **Accommodation A** *Pine Park Resort*, open Apr-Dec, main block (double rooms), Rs 1,300; Swiss Cottages (1 double rm), Rs 2,120; Pine Villas (2 double rm), Rs 4,240; Dbl VIP Suite (2 double rm and sitting rm), Rs 4,240; Sin VIP Suite (1 double rm and sitting room), Rs 2,120; Tourist block (double rooms), Rs 650, Pak and Chinese restaurant, souvenir shop, car rental, excursions arranged, large garden; **B** *Lalazar*, a large cottage, with 4 rm opening onto a communal lounge, kitchen, fine views; **C** *Faisal*, rather expensive, restaurant; **D** *Punjab Hazara*, basic and grossly overpriced.

The road from Kawai continues high above the E bank of the Kunhar River, before passing through **Paras** (1½ hrs from Balakot). On public transport this is generally a chai-stop, although it may be possible to stay overnight on a charpoy at the **F** *Bismillah Hotel* if desperate. Beyond Paras the road drops down to the valley bottom, adjacent to the river. Jeep tracks turns off right for Malakandi and Shogram, and left for **Sharan** (16 km), set in deep forest. A *Youth Hostel* here is currently being renovated.

The next small settlement is Fareedabad, and then **Shinu**, with its trout hatchery, before the road again climbs above the valley floor. A narrow bridge crosses a tributary of the Kunhar River at **Mahandri** (46 km from Balakot), and the road continues to **Khanian**. *Pine Parks* have a **B** category hotel under construction here that is due to serve as a transit stop on the way to **Danna Meadows**. Approachable by a jeep road 1 hr W of Khanian, Danna is situated in a remote side valley, surrounded by virgin forest. The location of the **A** *Pine Park* cottage, with 3 double rm, dining room, kitchen and enclosing verandah (open May-Oct) is superb, set in the shadow of Bhogarmang Peak (4,945m).

A further 5 km beyond Khanian is the settlement of **Kaghan** (2,038m) that gives its name to the whole valley, and the most northerly point that you can generally reach in winter. During the rest of the year, most visitors continue on to Naran (24 km). **Accommodation** **D** *Lalazar*, **E** *New Punjab*, **E** *Sabza zar*.

Naran

The centre-piece of the tourism industry in Kaghan Valley, **Naran** is a combination of stunning scenery and haphazard, unplanned development. The location is beautiful, but the main bazaar is a jumble of unattractive hotels, restaurants and numerous 'handicraft' shops. However, the views are excellent, and a 10 min walk in any direction from the town centre will lead you to peace and tranquillity.

Places of interest

Lake Saiful Malik

Naran's prime attraction is the stunning **Saiful Malik Lake**, 10 km to the E. Located at an altitude of 3,215m, and ringed by an amphitheatre of snow-capped mountains, large blocks of ice can often be seen floating on the sapphire waters. The lake is delightful in summer, when the meadows of alpine flowers are in bloom, and the water is reflecting the peak of **Malika Parbat**. It is absolutely de rigeur for visiting Punjabis to be photographed here, preferably with a Westerner also in the shot. Sadly, it also seems de rigeur to scatter as many empty biscuit packets, drink cartons and general litter over as wide a space around the lake as possible. All foreign tourists seem to comment on the nonchalance with which visiting Pakistani's litter this spot.

Local legends speak of princes, fairies and jealous demon's who visit the lake at night to dance and bathe. Woe betide any mortal who encounters them. Never mind the fairies, this spot could do with a visit from the Wombles.

The lake can be reached in a stiff 3-hr climb from Naran, or by hired jeep (generally Rs 600 return), although the drive across the glacier is exhilarating/petrifying. The lake is impossibly crowded on Fri, Sat and holidays. There are a number of small snack and cold drinks stalls at the lake, and horses and ponies can be hired.

Lalazar Plateau

Another pleasant ½-day jeep excursion from Naran is up to the **Lalazar Plateau**. A jeep track climbs up to the plateau

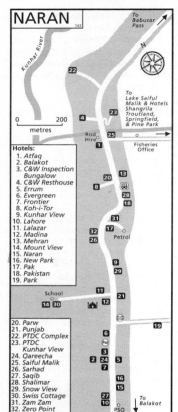

Trout Hatchery in Naran (Rs 50), and rods can be hired in the town (Rs 30/day).

Local information

● **Accommodation**

NB Most room rates in Naran are open to negotiation, although at the top hotels it is advisable to book rooms in advance.

B *Pine Park*, (1 km up road to lake), T 23, double rooms in 3 self-contained blocks, fine views; **B** *PTDC*, large grounds contain standard rooms (Rs 1,014), Surti Cottage (Rs 1,226) and some excellent value economy rooms (Rs 350), there are also some separate, self-contained cottages; Hill Top Cott (Rs 1,680), View Cott (Rs 1,680) and Kunhar Cott (Rs 3,430), book in advance in Islamabad T 819384; **B** *Shangrila Troutland*, (1 km up road to lake), due to open by 1996, looks very impressive with good views and well landscaped garden; **B** *Springfield Guesthouse*, (2 km up road to lake), suites and VIP rooms available, good location, book through *Springfield Hotel* in Abbottabad.

C *Errum*, T 28, spacious, clean carpetted rooms, but noisy generator, restaurant rec; **C** *Lalazar*, T 1, huge, noisy and unsightly, also operates VIP cottage on road to lake, with 3 double rm, kitchen and lounge (Rs 1,500) and 2 cottages at Lake Saiful Malik (Rs 1,500, no electricity); **C** *Swiss Cottage*, T 19, formerly run by TDCP, quiet and friendly, best rooms upstairs.

D *Mountview*, T 30, quiet, some cheaper rooms without bath, camping in garden; **D** *Naran*, T 8; **D** *New Park*, T 23, attached hot bath (24 hrs), restaurant, office of *Zeb Travels*, (Karachi); **D** *Park*, (behind GPO), quiet, but basic; **D** *Qareecha Gul*, small rooms, overpriced.

E There are numerous hotels in this category, most of which are pretty similar. They incl: *Balakot, Frontier, Koh-i-Toor, Kunhar View, Madina, Pakistan, Punjab, Saiful Malik, Saqib, Sarhad, Shalimar, Snow View, Zam Zam* and *Zero Point*.

F *Mehran* and **F** *Parw* are both very basic.

● **Places to eat**

Almost all the hotels have their own restaurants, plus there are several cheap meat and chapati places on the main street.

● **Transport**

Local Road Most of the transport activity is from the yard next to the *Shalimar Hotel*. Minibuses and pick-ups run when full to Mansehra

---

from Battakundi, some 16 km N of Naran. Located at 3,200m, this beautiful meadow is awash with colourful alpine flowers in spring and summer, and set amongst the cool pine forests. A footpath leads from Lalazar Plateau down to Lake Saiful Malik, taking 5-6 hrs.

Fishing

Kaghan Valley has some of Pakistan's best trout fishing, and there are six authorized reaches in the Naran locality. Permits are available from the NWFP Fisheries Dept Fisheries Office and

and occasionally **Abbottabad**. Sometimes it is possible to join a private hire vehicle to **Rawalpindi** and even **Lahore**. The yard is also the centre for hiring jeeps N, and for trips to Lake Saiful Malik (Rs 600) and Lalazar Plateau (Rs 600).

It is also possible to hire a jeep to go over the **Babusar Pass** to **Chilas** for about Rs 3,500 one way, although the route is generally only open to vehicles from late Jun to early Sep (depending on the weather). Walkers can make the crossing slightly earlier or later, although there may well be snow on the pass. The route is generally impassable from Nov-Apr.

Warning Take local advice before embarking on this trip (see page 443).

Beyond Naran, the road becomes a jeep track, passing through some sublime scenery as it traces the course of the Kunhar River. There are some excellent trout fishing reaches here.

The track begins to climb high above the river, through isolated summer settlements that are located amongst fields of peas and potatoes. Gujar shepherds can be seen leading their flocks W, across high passes to pastures in Swat Kohistan.

Shortly before **Battakundi** (16 km) a jeep track leads 5 km E, up to the **Lalazar Plateau** (3,200m). The main road drops down to the small settlement of **Battakundi** (2,713). There are 4 or 5 small, basic **F** hotels – usually a charpoy in a communal kitchen/sleeping area. The **F** *Garaib Nawaz Hotel* (no English sign) at the N end of the village has separate bedrooms. A *Youth Hostel* here is being refurbished.

A *PWD Resthouse* can be found at **Burawai**, 13 km N of Battakundi, as well as a very basic charpoy place. There is a marked change in scenery here, with the silver fir and blue pine trees becoming scantier. There are fine views of the snow-capped **Dabuka** ridge however (4,859m).

Beyond Burawai the hills become barer, and as the valley opens out at **Besal** (18 km), the landscape has been likened to a 'bleak Scotch moor'. Accommodation is available in very basic 'hotels', although the camping at nearby **Lulusar Lake** is superb.

Shaped like an irregular crescent, 2½ km long, 250m wide and 50m deep, Lulusar Lake is the source of the Kunhar River that flows through the Kaghan Valley. The water is deep green in colour, and with the sheer mountains rising directly up from the lakeside, it is certainly more beautiful than Saiful Malik. Remote, and at 3,350m, there are far fewer tourists too. A legend relates that a blind daughter of Emperor Akbar bathed in its waters and her sight was restored.

The last village before the pass, **Gittidas** (12 km), is a Kohistani village, and not the best place to stay without a local guide. A path from here heads W along the Aphuta Pani Katha (stream) to Jalkot, on the KKH in Kohistan, although it is far too dangerous to attempt to visit this area.

From Gittidas it is a steady climb of 7 km to the summit of **Babusar Pass** ('Babusar Top'), at 4,529m. The actual pass is shaped like a saddle, and the best views are to be had by climbing either flank of the saddle for a further 200m or so. The view of Nanga Parbat to the E is incredible.

From the top of the pass it is a difficult 13 km zig-zagging descent down to **Babusar** village. There is a **E** *NAPWD Inspection Bungalow* here (bookable in Gilgit if coming from the N) and some basic charpoy hotels, but if you are coming in a jeep from Naran, most drivers prefer to push on to **Chilas**. Irregular public cargo jeeps run in either direction between Babusar and Chilas, but it is rare to find cargo jeeps going all the way across the pass. Private jeeps can be hired in Chilas or Naran, although at Rs 3,500 one way, the trip is not cheap.

The section of the road between Babusar Top and Chilas is particularly rough, and it can take up to 4 hrs to cover the 37 km by jeep. Cyclists mention this same journey taking up to 12 hrs.

Warning In recent years there have been a number of incidents where walkers and cyclists have been either robbed, or threatened by armed Kohistani men whilst crossing the pass, or travelling between Babusar and Chilas. Other travellers, whilst not having been actually assaulted, speak of having been made to feel very 'uncomfortable'. Take advice, either in Naran or Chilas, before making the trip, and if necessary hire a local guide. Cyclists note, the road is extremely rough, and is only really passable on a lightly loaded mountain bike. Because you will be travelling so slowly, you will be particularly vulnerable to Kohistan's legendary stone throwing kids.

KOHISTAN SECTION

The section of the KKH that passes through Kohistan is probably one of the most dramatic, as the road clings to increasingly vertical sides of the narrow Indus gorge. This is also one of the wilder areas of Pakistan, with little government control beyond the main highway. The Kohistani people have a warlike history, and are not known for their hospitality to outsiders. Thus it is not recommended that you attempt to visit any of the tempting side valleys off the main route.

Environment

Literally meaning 'Land of Mountains', Kohistan is one of the most geologically fascinating places on earth. As the KKH follows the course of the deep Indus gorge, the rock formations take you on a journey from the centre of the earth to its outer crust. Just to the N of Besham, at **Jijal**, the greenish and dark red rocks along the roadside are the result of materials formed 30 km below the earth's surface, and as the KKH continues to **Chalt**, to the N of Gilgit, all the earth's layers are exposed.

Approximately 140 million years ago, a giant landmass floating on the fluid earth mantle broke away northwards from the Gondwanaland supercontinent that forms the modern day continents of Africa, Australia and Antarctica. About 70 million years later, this **'Indian Plate'** began a slow motion collision with the Laurasian landmass, or **'Asian Plate'**, that continues today. At the margins of the collision the Indian Plate is subducting beneath the Asian Plate, with the resulting pressure being responsible for the mountain building process that created the Himalaya and Karakoram ranges. Trapped in the middle of the two plates is the small ocean plate that previously supported the **Sea of Tethys**, a shallow sea that used to lie between the Laurasian and Gondwanaland land masses. In the course of the collision between the plates, a narrow chain of volcanic islands that stood in the Sea of Tethys – the **Kohistan Island Arc** – were compressed and contorted, with the result that the metamorphic rock formed at great depth below the oceanic plate has been pushed to the surface, and revealed around Jijal. The younger sedimentary and volcanic materials can be seen at the northern margins of the Kohistan Island Arc, where it joins the Asian Plate near to Chalt. Between the two, the intermediate rock stratas are revealed at the surface. As several signs along the KKH claim, 'Here Continents Collided'.

History

The history of the region is equally fascinating. Although referred to as Kohistan, the region has also been known as *Yaghistan*, or 'Land of the Ungovernable'. British influence in the region was minimal, and even today, Pakistani control beyond the Karakoram Highway is questionable. It is for this reason that tourists are advised **not** to attempt to visit the numerous side valleys away from the main KKH route.

The pattern of settlement in Kohistan has been the occupation of the numerous small valleys, where glacial streams and rivers are more controllable, as opposed to habitation in the Indus Valley itself. The mountain ranges between these valleys proved a barrier to communication, allowing the evolution of numerous independent kingdoms – effectively mini republics. The system of government was by *jirga*, or tribal assembly, but many commentators have noted that the independence of thought of the Kohistanis made the area virtually ungovernable. With the

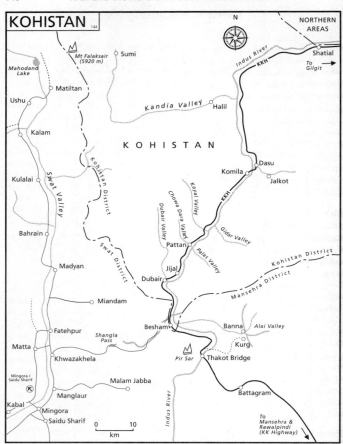

exception of Chilas, the British never really established any control over the numerous side valleys.

The situation remains pretty much the same today. Although nominally part of Pakistan, the federal government wields very little influence away from the main road. The societies are very inward looking, fiercely traditional, and reluctant to expose themselves to outside influences. One such example is in the role of women.

In some of the valleys female literacy levels are as close to zero as it is possible to get. The current concern of the federal government in the region is the agitation for the introduction of the full Shariat, or system of Islamic law.

Culture

Kohistan is an ethnically mixed area, reflecting its history of isolated valleys, with periods of hostile incursions from rival kingdoms. The main ethnic group are descended from the **Shins**, but also linked with **Swathis** and **Yusufzai Pathans** from the Swat Valley. Pushto, Shina, and a language collectively known as 'Kohistani' (various dialects incl Maiyum, Chiliss, Gauro) are mainly spoken. The area is almost exclusively Sunni Muslim.

Beyond Mansehra the Karakoram Highway gradually begins to climb through a series of switchbacks, and crosses the Siran River near to Shinkiari (25 km). From here it is possible to follow the course of the river up to **Daddar**, from where there are fine views of Bhogarmang Peak (4,945m) in the Kaghan Valley.

The KKH proceeds N through the fertile bowl of Chattar Plain (named after the Sikh general), passing the small town of **Battagram**, with the **D** *PTDC Motel* and **F** *Al Fakhar Hotel* before reaching the **Indus River** at **Thakot Bridge** (33 km). The bridge, built by the Chinese, marks the boundary of Hazara and Kohistan. The decorative lions on the bridge's balustrade have long since disappeared. For the next 350 km or so, the KKH virtually follows the course of the Indus, with the river rarely out of sight.

About 8 km S of the bridge at Thakot, the small hillock called **Pir Sar** to the W of the river has been associated with Aornos, site of one of Alexander the Great's battles. However, recent investigations by archaeologists refute this claim.

Excursion from the KKH

Alai Valley

From the small roadside town of Thakot on the right bank of the Indus, a reasonably good jeep road travels E, up the **Alai Valley**. Pick-up trucks from Thakot climb steeply up the mountain road, through terraced rice fields, offering fine views of long stretches of the Indus below. In summer it is particularly hot, and the pick-ups stop at every small stream to fill their radiators. The road passes through **Kanai** (19 km), where it

begins to deteriorate, before dropping down to **Kurg** (29 km), where the ride terminates (1½ hrs, Rs 25). Below the bazaar is the main village, a cluster of square, flat-roofed houses near to the Alai River. A partially damaged bridge crosses the river to **Banna**, a newer settlement of mainly breeze-block and tin roof buildings.

Although this is one of the few valleys off the KKH in Kohistan that it is possible to visit, you should ask yourself if it is really necessary to come here. If you are conservatively dressed, you will probably be cordially greeted, but you should bear in mind that the valley's traditional Pathan residents certainly don't invite outsiders into their community. You should not proceed beyond Banna without the support of the former Nawab, and now MNA, Ayub Khan. Nevertheless, the Alai Valley can certainly boast some of the finest henna beards in the whole of Pakistan.

Having crossed the Indus over Thakot Bridge, the KKH passes through the village of **Dandai**, with the **F** *Sapari Hotel* before continuing to **Besham** (28 km).

Besham

Although Besham has been identified with the site of the Chinese pilgrim Fa-Hien's crossing of the Indus in 403 AD, there is little of interest in Besham to detain passing tourists. Most visitors see Besham as a meal stop on the N bound journey between Islamabad/Rawalpindi and Gilgit, or as a place to change vehicles on a journey W across the **Shangla Pass** to/from Swat.

The town itself is very much a product of the KKH, showing the changing pattern of land use that is associated with road building in mountain environment, with construction taking place on a linear (*strassendorf*) pattern along the road. Although there are several hotels, allowing you to break the journey between Islamabad and Gilgit, the town

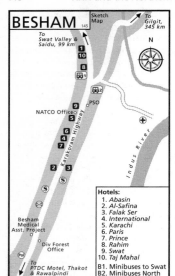

BESHAM Sketch Map

To Gilgit, 345 km

To Swat Valley & Saidu, 99 km

N

Karakoram Highway

NATCO Office

PSO

Indus River

Hotels:
1. Abasin
2. Al-Safina
3. Falak Ser
4. International
5. Karachi
6. Paris
7. Prince
8. Rahim
9. Swat
10. Taj Mahal
B1. Minibuses to Swat
B2. Minibuses North

Besham Medical Asst. Project

Div Forest Office

To PTDC Motel, Thakot & Rawalpindi

is noisy with traffic at all hours. From Besham it is 7 hrs by bus to Islamabad/Rawalpindi, and 9 hrs to Gilgit.

● **Accommodation** C *PTDC Motel*, (2 km S of town), T 98, comfortable rooms, restaurant rec, quiet, reception has some tourist information, souvenir shop has a reasonable book selection; **E** *Abasin*, Mingora Rd, T 38, quite good value, quieter than hotels on KKH; **E** *Paris*, KKH, 10, clean, carpetted rooms, good value if you bargain; **E** *Prince*, KKH, T 18, rooms open onto noisy courtyard; **E** *Taj Mahal*, Mingora Rd, T 82, restaurant; **F** *Al-Madina*, KKH, remote, S of town; **F** *Al-Safina*, KKH, T 64, basic, and none too friendly; **F** *Falak Ser*, KKH, T 130, basic; **F** *International*, KKH, T 65, cheap and good value, staff helpful, rec; **F** *Karachi*, KKH, very basic charpoy place; **F** *Rahim*, KKH, basic; **F** *Swat*, KKH, T 67, very basic.

● **Transport Road** Main minibus stand is at N end of town, where the road divides left to Swat, and right to Gilgit. Minibuses run when full across the Shangla Pass to **Khwazakhela** and **Mingora** in Swat (Rs 45, 4 hrs). Travelling N, most minibuses only go as far as **Komila/Dasu** (Rs 30, 2 hrs) via **Pattan** (Rs 15,

½ hr), although some go as far as **Chilas** (Rs 90, 5 hrs). Minibuses S to **Mansehra** run from the fly-blown *Karachi Hotel*, and a very early morning minibus sometimes runs to **Gilgit** from here. *NATCO* has a 0500 bus to **Rawalpindi** (Rs 59), and 1100 bus to **Gilgit** (Rs 103) It may be possible to flag down private coasters, as well as passing NATCO services, enroute between Pindi and Gilgit, although generally they are pretty full.

Almost 20 km N of Besham, the Dubair River joins the Indus. The KKH crosses this tributary at **Dubair**, a cluster of small wooden shops and houses lining the road and sandwiched on terraces between the river and the highway. The well appointed **F** *Rest Point Hotel*, T 6, is just below the bridge. The restaurant here is very popular

A trip up the **Dubair Valley** to the original settlement of Dubair (15 km) looks very enticing, but this is one of those Kohistani valleys that is definitely off-limits to tourists. The Dubair Valley continues due N for some 64 km or so, with tracks leading off from the head of the valley into both Swat and Kandia Valley.

Travelling N of Dubair, the Indus canyon closes in somewhat, with the KKH perched on a narrow ledge some 300m above the river. This section of the Indus gorge is described in graphic detail by the Chinese traveller Fa-Hien, travelling in the early 5th century: "The road was difficult and broken with steep crags and precipices in the way. The mountain-side is simply a stone wall standing up 10,000 ft. Looking down, the sight is confused, and on going forward there is no sure foothold. Below is a river called Sint u-ho (Indus). In old days men bored through the rocks to make a way, and spread out side-ladders, of which there are 700 (steps) in all to pass. Having passed the ladders, we proceed by a hanging rope bridge and cross the river".

Fa-Hien is in effect describing the forerunner of the Karakoram Highway, where men had to be lowered down from above by rope, in order to place explosive charges that would blast a path out of the mountainside. This section of the

KKH is said to have been the most difficult to construct, costing more lives per m of road built than any other, and where daily progress was measured in metres rather than kilometres.

The road continues through **Jijal**, before the valley opens out into a wide fertile bowl as the Chowa Dara River joins the Indus shortly before **Pattan** (20 km). This stretch of the highway is geologically fascinating; the contact point between the Indian and Eurasian tectonic plates, the latter here exposing layers usually buried 30m below the earth's surface (see page 445).

Pattan

The KKH passes above Pattan, although a feeder road runs down to the village at the N end. Biddulph described Pattan as being "the largest and most flourishing place in Kohistan", and commented on the fertility of the soil and richness of the crops. Pattan remains at the heart of this fertile bowl, although the region was devastated in 1974 by a massive earthquake centred on Pattan. Entire villages were buried by the resulting rockfalls, and it is thought that over 5,000 were killed and 15,000 injured.

Accommodation There are 3 basic hotel/restaurants on the KKH at Pattan, **F** *Pak Kashmir*, **F** *Khangrab*, **F** *Kohistan*, and 1 very basic hotel down in the village itself, **F** *Feroz*.

A suspension bridge at Pattan crosses the Indus, providing access to the **Palas Valley**. The valley stretches in a south-easterly direction, with easy access at its head to the Alai Valley. For the 40,000 or so Palasi inhabitants of the valley, the forests represent the only resource, and as Biddulph pointed out, the abundance of this resource attracted the envious gaze of the Pathans of the Alai Valley. Today, this threat remains from down country timber merchants. In 1995, the European Community committed 4.8 million ECU (Rs 191mn) towards the conservation and sustainable development of forestry resources in the Palas Valley.

Warning The office of the Assistant Commissioner (AC) in Pattan, Raja Gastasab Khan, was insistent that tourists should not attempt to visit the side valleys of **Chowa Dara** and **Palas** that join the main Indus canyon at Pattan, nor the **Kayal** and **Gidar Valleys** slightly further N along the KKH.

Beyond the Pattan bowl, the canyon narrows once more, forcing the KKH high on the valley side. A further 10 km N of Pattan, the Kayal River joins the Indus, and the KKH temporarily detours several km up the **Kayal Valley** until a bridging point on the river is reached. The highway then drops down nearer to the Indus, although there are still some impressive rock overhangs on the near side, before running into **Komila** (35 km).

Komila/Dasu

The twin settlements of Komila and Dasu sprawl along either bank of the Indus, connected in the middle by the bridge over the river. Komila, on the W bank, is little more than a small bazaar, with a number of hotels, restaurants and transport connections N and S. Dasu, on the E bank, is the administrative centre, with a police station, Dy Commissioner of Kohistan's offices, Ass Com of Dasu's offices, and NWFP C&W Ex Engineer's office. A jeep road from Dasu leads E to Jalkot, and eventually to the Babusar Pass and Kaghan Valley, although you should not attempt to follow this ancient communications route.

By bus, Komila/Dasu is more or less the half-way point between Islamabad/Rawalpindi and Gilgit.

● **Accommodation** Easily the best hotel in town is the **E** *Green Hills*, T 632, in the main Komila bazaar, although there isn't much competition. Even this place can be noisy because it is often used as a meal stop on the Gilgit-Rawalpindi bus route. The restaurant is quite good though. Other very basic places in Komila Bazaar incl: **F** *Al-Mashriq*, *Ameen*, *Azeem*, *Indus Kohistan Haz*, *New Abasind* and the *Moor* across the river, just N of Dasu. The

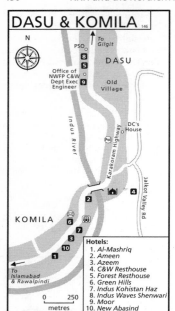

DASU & KOMILA 146

N

To Gilgit

PSO

DASU

Office of NWFP C&W Dept Exec Engineer

Old Village

DC's House

Karakoram Highway

Indus River

Jalkot Valley Rd

KOMILA

To Islamabad & Rawalpindi

Hotels:
1. Al-Mashriq
2. Ameen
3. Azeem
4. C&W Resthouse
5. Forest Resthouse
6. Green Hills
7. Indus Kohistan Haz
8. Indus Waves Shenwari
9. Moor
10. New Abasind

0   250
metres

E *Indus Waves Shenwari*, T 968, 1 km N of Dasu, is rather quieter.

● **Transport** Minibuses run from a yard outside the *Indus Kohistan Haz*, although N bound, few go beyond **Shatial** (Rs 30, 1½ hrs), or **Besham** S bound.

Just to the N of Dasu the KKH passes over a temporary girder bridge that seems to have become permanent. It certainly creaks as vehicles cross it. After 30 km, the Indus is joined from the W by the Kandia River. A suspension bridge over the Indus provides access to the extensive **Kandia Valley**, which runs due W before sharply bending to the N. A jeep track runs tantalisingly along the left bank, to Sumi at the head of the valley, from where a track then leads N around Mt Falaksair (5,920m) into the upper Swat Valley. A further track gives access to the valley of Tangir. This was a well worn Buddhist pilgrim route in the first century AD, but is strictly off-limits to visitors today.

The people of the Kandia Valley speak **Maiyan**, (also known as Kohistani), although little is known about the 'Manzari' dialect of the language that is used here.

The Indus Valley turns sharply to the E, with plenty of spectacular overhangs on the near side of the KKH, before the canyon walls gradually step back, the river widens and slows, and the North West Frontier Province gives way to the **Northern Areas of Pakistan**.

The first settlement of the Northern Areas on the main KKH is **Shatial**, although don't let this miserable collection of shacks put you off the delights to come. There are two very basic **F** 'hotels' in Shatial, *Ittefaq* and *Swat*. If your public transport terminates in Shatial, there is usually transport available N to **Chilas** (Rs 50, 60 km) and S to **Komila** (Rs 30, 1½ hrs).

A sign just beyond Shatial reminds you that there are 'Petroglyphs for the next 70 km'. These rock carvings are part of a chain of inscriptions that reflect historic and prehistoric lines of communications. Concentrations of this rock art are found along the KKH from Shatial to Chilas, along the old Buddhist pilgrim routes through Tangir and Darel to Yasin and Ghizr, at the confluence of the Gilgit and Hunza rivers, on the Sacred Rocks of Hunza near Karimabad, at Passu and Sust in Upper Hunza, along the Gilgit to Chitral route, and also throughout Baltistan.

A rope suspension bridge to the left crosses the Indus, providing access to the infamous **Tangir** and **Darel Valleys**. Do not be seduced by the azure blue of the Darel River – these two valleys are definitely out of bounds to the casual tourist. This is a great pity since both valleys are rich in archaeological remains, dating particularly from the early centuries AD when Buddhist pilgrims such as Fa-Hien used these routes to travel between China and the great Buddhist sites of S Asia.

TANGIR AND DAREL VALLEYS

In describing the people of the Tangir and Darel Valleys, Schomberg suggests that they "know nothing of law and order; the one interest of their lives, their one obsession, is murder." Both valleys were left alone by the British when this area was known as **Yagistan**, 'Land of the Ungovernable', and even today, Pakistani central government control is negligible. However, with both valleys being extremely fertile, the heads of the valleys in particular being thickly forested, it would seem logical for the valley inhabitants to fiercely protect their resources from predatory neighbours. Schomberg's analysis in the 1930s that the people "want to be taken over (by the British administration) and they hope to force the Government to do so by making themselves troublesome" hardly seems credible. Today, the forest tracts are under threat of over-logging, the evidence of which can be seen in the huge timber dumps along the KKH at the entrance to the valleys.

Tangir has many links with Yasin, a function of the ease of communication between the two valleys. Indeed, Yasini rulers used to claim a nominal allegiance and a small tribute from Tangir, although any attempts by Yasin to exercise authority here were fiercely resisted. However, the valley did gain something of a reputation as a place of refuge for princes from Yasin who were seeking asylum.

Similarly, Darel paid a nominal tribute to Kashmir following the invasion of Dogra troops in 1866, although the soldiers did not remain long enough to attempt to impose any rule of law in the valley. In fact, Schomberg claims that only one man, Pakhtun Wali (son of Mir Wali, see page 474), ever managed to dominate this region, and that was only because he was well qualified as "a blackguard, a treacherous, lawless tyrant, and an accomplished and unflagging intriguer."

Both states remained independent until being incorporated into Pakistan in 1956.

The KKH follows the course of the Indus, having made a huge easterly bend at Shatial. In contrast to its passage through the lower reaches of Indus Kohistan, the river here is wide and gentle, frequently flanked by enticing sandy beaches. These beaches will appear particularly seductive if you are crammed into a local bus, because this whole stretch of the journey is particularly hot in summer. Sand dunes border the KKH in what is effectively a high altitude desert, and as you drive into Thore, with its petrol station and abandoned looking settlements, the impression is more of arriving in a Mexican desert town. The only splash of colour is provided by the vivid green cultivation around Hudor, across the Indus via a 650m rope suspension bridge. 15 km beyond the bridge turn off is a police check-post (foreigners must enter passport details) at **Chilas**.

Chilas

District headquarters of Dyamar (Diamar), which includes the tehsils of Tangir, Darel and Astor, Chilas is referred to as Silavata (a sort of Sanskrit cum Shina word meaning 'rock or hill of stones') on a nearby 6th century AD rock inscription. Other local inscriptions refer to Chilas as Somanagara, or 'Heroic City of the Moon'.

The incredible collection of **rock art** in the local vicinity is the main attraction of Chilas. It is the main source of information on the early history of the region, left by pilgrims, missionaries, merchants and conquerors, as well as early inhabitants and depict various

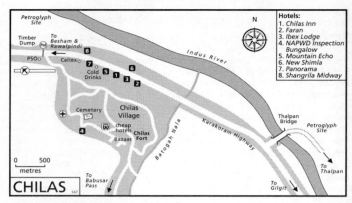

animals, human figures, Buddhist designs etc. The best sites are probably 'Thalpan I' and 'Thalpan V', on the right side of the Indus across the bridge to Thalpan, 'Chilas I' that straddles the KKH next to the Thalpan Bridge, 'Gondophares Rock', the hillock at the mouth of the Batogah Nala, and 'Chilas II to X' to the W of the checkpost on the KKH. For a full discussion consult Dr AH Dani's *'Chilas: City of Nanga Parbat'* and Karl Jettmar's *'Rock Carvings and Inscriptions in the Northern Areas of Pakistan'*, both available in Islamabad.

It was the extraordinary character Dr GW Leitner who first brought Chilas to the attention of Europeans. Having visited Chilas in 1866, ostensibly to study the language and customs of Chilas, Leitner later published in 1877 'The Languages and Races of Dardistan', a monumental volume that included such gems as vernacular greetings in prominent use by the Chilasis. These included, according to Keay ('The Gilgit Game', 1977), "we kill all infidels" and "beat him now, kill him afterwards".

The Chilasis gained a reputation as fanatical Sunni Muslims, also making frequent raids into the adjacent Kashmir, Neelum, Astor and Gilgit valleys. Following the Sikh occupation of Kashmir, an punitive expedition was sent against Chilas, only to sustain a disastrous defeat. In 1851 the Sikhs returned, and captured the fort at Chilas.

Chilas drew the attention of the British during the era of the 'Great Game', when the British were attempting to consolidate their position on the NW frontier of the British Empire. Col Algernon Durand, the British Agent at Gilgit, saw the unpredictable Chilasis as a threat to the recently opened British supply line across the Babusar Pass to the Punjab. In 1892 a situation was engineered that allowed the British to march on Thalpan, opposite Chilas, and after naturally rising to the provocation, the Chilasis were subsequently defeated in battle and their town occupied. Indeed, Keay notes that during the battle, the Kashmiri troops of the British army "pulled off their trousers the better to give chase."

However, in 1893, in what is referred to as the Indus Valley Rising, the fort at Chilas was attacked, and one third of the garrison was killed or wounded in what was probably the British Army's most disastrous battle fought in Dardistan. For some reason, possibly the lack of food supplies, the Chilasis did not press their advantage, and the garrison was relieved. Durand eventually recognized his tactical error in attempting to occupy the Indus Valley death trap; something the Dogra troops of the Maharaja of Kashmir were to experience 54 years later at Partition (see page 482).

Few tourists stop for long in Chilas; those who do are generally making the trip across the Babusar Pass to/from Kaghan Valley (see page 443). The actual town is some 3 km above the KKH, and retains something of a reputation for not welcoming outsiders. Yet despite this fearsome reputation, it's not unusual to see groups of Chilasi men sitting playing Ludo!

● **Accommodation** **B** *Shangrila Midway House*, KKH, T (211) 235, best in town, with soon to be installed central a/c, plus restaurant, coffee shop, gift shop, bookings in Rawalpindi, T 73006; **C** *Chilas Inn*, KKH, T 349, all rooms a/c, some suites, conference hall, restaurant, bookings in Rawalpindi, T 553374; **C** *Panorama*, KKH, T 340, carpetted rooms with air cooler, attached bath, good restaurant, used by tour groups, discounts available; **D** *Mountain Echo*, KKH, T 315, attached bath, restaurant, garden; **D** *NAPWD Inspection Bungalow*, Ranoi Rd, the new bungalow is quite plush, although often full, book in Gilgit; **D** *New Shimla*, KKH, T 212, clean, carpetted, but overpriced rooms; **E** *Ibex Lodge*, KKH, T 247, good value rooms with attached bath. **F** There are several **F** hotels in the main bazaar, incl *Bismillah*, *Hamala International* T 36, *Khunjrab*, T 290, some of which do not have English signs. The *Delux* is marginally the best (or least bad). There are several very basic charpoy places down on the KKH.

● **Transport** Minibuses S to **Komila** (3½ hrs) and **Besham** (5 hrs) run when full from the main bus yard, as do buses N to **Gilgit** (3½ hrs). Transport to **Babusar**, and across the Babusar Pass to the **Kaghan Valley** is unreliable. There are no regular times for cargo jeeps that make the 35 km, but 4-hrs' trip to Babusar village. Further, there is no guarantee that there will be any jeeps available at Babusar to make the trip across the pass. The cheapest price quoted in Chilas for a private hire jeep to **Naran** was Rs 3,500 (from the *Panorama Hotel*). For details of this trip and **Warning**, see page 443.

GILGIT DISTRICT

The Gilgit Agency was an administrative division created by the British in 1877 in an attempt to increase their influence in a region seen as being vulnerable to Russian incursions. The Agency, based at Gilgit, was closed in 1881, and control was returned to the Maharaja of Kashmir. However, the Agency was reopened and revitalized in 1889 with the appointment of Algernon Durand as British Resident. Although the Maharaja of Kashmir retained authority of the Gilgit Wazarat, it was the British who were responsible for policy in the overall Agency. The British signed a lease to continue to rule the area in 1935, and continued to do so right up until Partition. The Agency is now referred to as Gilgit District, and along with Baltistan, Diamar and Ghizr, now forms one of the administrative divisions of the Northern Areas of Pakistan.

The KKH continues N through Gunner Farm (30 km), with its police fort, petrol station and *NAPWD Inspection Bungalow*, and then through the tiny settlement of Jalipur (10 km) (*NAPWD Inspection Bungalow*).

Some 57 km N of Chilas is a troublesome area around Tatta Pani that is plagued by landslides that often block the KKH. 2 km beyond here the KKH crosses to the W bank of the Indus over the **Raikot Bridge**. There is a police check-post and the *Shangri-La Motel*. A recently constructed jeep track runs up to **Fairy Meadows** (15 km), and a new jeep road to Astor is under construction behind the motel. Distances from Raikot Bridge: Gilgit 78 km N, Dasu 179 km S, Pattan 215 km S, Rawalpindi 520 km S.

Fairy Meadows

Situated at the base of Nanga Parbat, **Fairy Meadows** (approx 3,200m) truly is a place of outstanding beauty. The meadows are flower-strewn high altitude alpine pastures situated amongst pine forest, with an imposing backdrop of the massive N or Raikot face of the world's ninth highest mountain. It is a wonderful place to camp, has endless possibilities for short walks, and is incredibly photogenic.

The most spectacular walks from Fairy Meadows include a 5-6 hr walk up to the base camp of Nanga Parbat. There is a memorial here to the members of the German-Austrian expedition who were killed on the mountain in 1937. You can camp here at about 4,000m. From the base-camp it is possible to climb up to the base of Gilipur Peak and camp there (about 4,200m). A more challenging alternative is a long day-trip, climbing up to Gilipur Pass to the W (about 4,900m) and continuing to the top of Gilipur Peak (5,029m), before returning to basecamp. **NB** Read the Health Information section on trekking at altitude, and the potential dangers, before attempting these excursions.

Local information
● **Accommodation**

For at least the last 5 years there has been constant talk of the *Shangri-La* chain building a luxury hotel at Fairy Meadows. A large hotel, particularly with a tacky red pagoda-style roof, is probably the last thing that Fairy Meadows needs, and fortunately, up until now, the conservationists have won the day. However, not before a large area of forest was clear-cut for the site.

At present it is possible to stay at the **E** *Raikot Serai*, a camp site with 2 and 4 person tents, plus a kitchen and semi-permanent dining area, the site is open from mid May until the end of Oct, and bookings can be made through various Gilgit travel agents, or through the head office in Islamabad (House 1, St 15, Khayaban-e-Iqbal, F 7/2, T 216117.

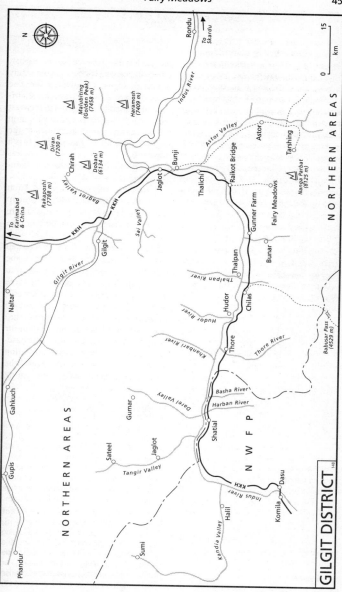

NANGA PARBAT

The local name for this 8,125m giant is Dyamar (correctly Diva-Meru), meaning 'Heavenly Mount', although the mountain is almost exclusively referred to as Nanga Parbat. Kashmiri for 'Naked Mountain', this name is a reference to the massive 4,500m wall of the SE face that is too sheer for snow to stick. However, such is the awesome reputation of the peak that it has been nick-named 'Killer Mountain'.

The mountaineering history of Nanga Parbat begins in 1895 when a British expedition attempted the peak. The leader of the expedition, the famed climber Mummery, along with two Gurkha porters, reached almost 7,000m before disappearing without trace. Locals blamed the fairies, spirits, and giant snow snakes that are said to inhabit the mountain, although another explanation may be one of Nanga Parbat's unpredictable avalanches.

In the 1930s no fewer than five separate expeditions attempted the peak. The 1934 Austro-German expedition is believed to have got within several hundred metres of the summit before bad weather forced them back. Four Germans and six Sherpas died in the descent. Just three years later another German party was within striking range of the summit before being wiped out by an avalanche. A later expedition found most of the men lying dead in their tents, as if asleep, their watches all stopped at 1220.

In 1950, a small British expedition attempted the mountain. A member of the party was Tenzing Norgay, later to find fame with Sir Edmund Hillary on the first successful ascent of Everest. However, the expedition were poorly prepared, and Tenzing was later to describe the decision of the British officers to attempt a full ascent as "craziness". Despite a rescue attempt by Tenzing and one of the British officers, the other two members of the expedition died high up on the mountain.

It was not until 1953, less than five weeks after Tenzing and Hillary had 'conquered' Everest, that Nanga Parbat was finally defeated. Hermann Buhl, a noted Austrian climber, eventually stood where no other person had ever been.

The current death toll on Nanga Parbat is thought to be 47. Not only is the mountain's sheer size a huge challenge-its N face slopes down an incredible 7,000m down to the Indus – its position as an exposed sentinel at the western end of the Himalayas has led to the formation of its own highly unpredictable micro-climate. Weather conditions change rapidly, and avalanches are common and violent. Yet from the KKH, particularly at sunset, the ethereal beauty of the mountain is sublime.

F 216116), however, few people have anything good to say about the site or the manager who runs it, greed runs rampant here, with a bed in a tent costing an incredible Rs 250, a basic meal Rs 150, and a charge of Rs 200 to pitch your own tent in the compound, if you attempt to bargain, some visitors report that the manager just laughs in your face, a far better solution is to bring your own equipment (readily available for purchase or hire in Gilgit), and camp further up in the forest.

● **Transport**
Considering the distance (less than 100 km),

at Rs 1,800, the cost of hiring a jeep from Gilgit to Fairy Meadows is pretty expensive. The travel companies in Gilgit claim this is due to a Rs 500 surcharge imposed on each jeep by the local people who built the private road up from the KKH to Raikot Bridge (78 km S of Gilgit) and walk. It is a hot, dry 4-5 hr walk up the jeep track to Thato, and a further 2 hrs to Fairy Meadows. The total distance from the KKH is about 15 km. Private jeeps can be hired at Raikot Bridge for extortionate prices. To return to Gilgit, or points S, return to Raikot Bridge and flag down any passing traffic.

Just to the N of Raikot Bridge, the Indus is joined by a minor tributary from the E, the **Liachar Nala**. In 1841, a massive landslip, probably triggered by an earthquake, completely dammed the river, creating a giant lake that stretched almost 50 km back to Gilgit. The dam, several hundred metres thick, is said to have raised the water up to 300m above its normal level. When breached in early Jun 1841, having held for several months, the resulting flood is said to have washed away an entire Sikh regiment camped downstream at Chach (although the image of a massive wall of water rushing down is said to be something of an exaggeration). Durand claims that the pile of driftwood left by the flood provided a source of firewood for the local people for almost 50 years.

If the weather is clear, this stretch of road has some of the best views on the entire length of the Karakoram Highway. Directly to the N is the magnificent **Rakaposhi** massif (7,788m), flanked by **Dobani** (6,134m), with the serrated ridges of **Haramosh** (7,409m) to the NE. Directly behind you, to the S, is the massive N (Raikot) face of **Nanga Parbat** (8,125m). A small sign at the settlement of Thalichi (*NAPWD Inspection Bungalow*) reminds you to look. Across the Indus from Thalichi is the entrance to the **Astor Valley**, gateway to a trekking route round to the naked SE Rupal face of Nanga Parbat.

At **Jaglot** (87 km from Chilas, 50 km from Gilgit), a suspension bridge crosses the Indus, and a jeep track runs back S through **Bunji** to the **Astor Valley**.

Excursion from the KKH

Bunji

Strategically placed at a crossing point of the Indus, and guarding the entrance to the Astor Valley, the small, nondescript settlement of Bunji has played a remarkably significant role in the recent history of the Northern Areas. The fur-

thest outpost of the Kashmir state, beyond which lay 'Yaghistan', this is the point at which Leitner crossed the Indus in 1866 on his celebrated visit to Dardistan.

The British built a fort at Bunji in order to protect the route across the Burzil Pass into Kashmir- the main supply line between British India and the outpost of the empire at Gilgit. During the Gilgit uprising at Partition, when the people of the Northern Areas fought to throw off the Dogra rule of the Maharaja of Kashmir, Bunji's strategic importance at the head of the pass into Kashmir was re-emphasized. In fact, Col Hasan Khan, one of the key players in the military action, suggests that the capture of Bunji was "the deciding factor in the whole game of Gilgit's freedom struggle" (Dani, 1991). Such was the terror that the advancing Chilas Scouts struck into the hearts of the Dogra and Sikh garrison at Bunji, that the Maharaja's troops fled during the night, allowing the fort and a huge supply of arms and ammunition to be captured without a shot being fired.

Although the route across the Burzil Pass into Indian occupied Kashmir is closed, Bunji still maintains its strategic significance controlling a vital supply line to Pakistani troops stationed in the Northern Areas. It is also the headquarters of the Northern Light Infantry; the successors to the Gilgit Scouts.

Astor Valley

Although the route between Gilgit and Srinagar is now firmly closed, the Astor Valley provides a starting point for trips across the Deosai Plains (see page 490) to Baltistan, and for a number of excellent treks around the eastern and southern sides of Nanga Parbat (see page 555).

Astor village is about 4 hrs from the KKH on a hot, dry and rough jeep road. There are 3 basic **F** hotels, although the best accommodation is in the **E** *NAPWD Inspection Bungalow* that can be booked in Gilgit. The bazaar is fairly small, so those planning on trekking are advised to buy their provisions in Gilgit. The same applies to those heading across the Deosai Plains. There is public jeep transport between Gilgit, the KKH at Jaglot, and Astor, but it is unreliable and crowded. A privately hired jeep costs around Rs 2,000 one-way.

From Astor it is possible to trek up to the beautiful **Rama Lake**, about 4 hrs away through dense pine forest. The camping here is superb, although it is possible to stay at the *NAPWD Inspection Bungalow* about half-way between Astor and the lake (bookings in Gilgit).

Following the Astor Valley to the S, at Gurikot a track leads E across the **Deosai Plains** to Baltistan. Beyond Gurikot, the head of the valley turns W to the small village of **Tarshing**, starting point for the excellent Rupal Valley and Mazeno Base Camp trek around Nanga Parbat (see Trekking section).

Returning to the KKH, several km N of Jaglot is the confluence of the Indus and Gilgit Rivers. Here, 38 km from Gilgit, the KKH leaves the Indus and branches along the W bank of the Gilgit River. The **Skardu** road crosses the Gilgit River here on the Alam Bridge, and follows the course of the Indus Valley E to **Baltistan** (see page 479). A sign marks this place as a 'unique spot', at the confluence of two rivers and three mountain systems.

The KKH continues through another police check-post, before turning N shortly before the confluence of the Gilgit and Hunza Rivers. The KKH crosses the river on a long suspension bridge, and proceeds N for **Hunza** and **China**, whilst the left fork enters **Gilgit** through its eastern suburb of Jutial.

Gilgit

The administrative capital of the region, Gilgit has retained its strategic importance at the centre of transport and communications in the Northern Areas of Pakistan. Keay described it as "the hub, the crow's-nest, the fulcrum of Asia" ('The Gilgit Game', 1979), and today, Gilgit is the key junction in the N for travel to all points of the compass.

The town has a long and varied history, but each event reflects Gilgit's strategic location. From the numerous territorial disputes between the rival petty kingdoms in the surrounding valleys, through the imperial rivalry of the era of the 'Great Game', up until the Partition war between Pakistan and India and the continuing antagonism between the two states, Gilgit has held its place at the centre of local history.

In recent years Gilgit has undergone rapid social and economic change, as the upgrading of an ancient trading route in the form of the Karakoram Highway has brought greater integration between the N and the rest of Pakistan, as well as revolutionising patterns of trade and employment.

Most tourists visiting the Northern Areas spend some time in Gilgit, whether preparing or recovering from a trek, shopping, or just connecting with onward transportation.

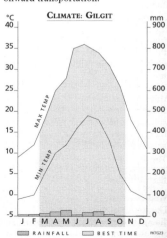

CLIMATE: GILGIT

NB Those wishing to escape the oppressive summer heat of the plains by travelling up to Gilgit are in for a disappointment. The albedo of Gilgit's brown, barren hills is high, and the heat from the sun just seems to bounce around the bowl that the town sits in; temperatures in the 40s are not unknown. Further, at only 1,500m above sea-level, there are none of the cooling effects of altitude.

Ancient history

With a few exceptions, the rock art that features so prominently in other parts of the Northern Areas is lacking around Gilgit, and thus this area 'still remains *terra incognita* as far as the prehistory period is concerned' (Dani, 1991). There are some remains dating from the Buddhist era, including the 7th or 8th century carved Buddha at Kargah, just to the W of the town, and there is strong evidence to suggest links between Gilgit and the great **Kushan** Empire centred at Taxila in the 1st to 3rd centuries. Later evidence suggests that the **Huns** were active in the region, perhaps by the mid 5th century.

The earliest written references to places in the region are made by Chinese Buddhist pilgrims travelling between Central and South Asia (eg Fa-Hien and Hieun Tsang). In the 6th, 7th and 8th centuries, Gilgit was ruled by the Buddhist **Palolas**, who's kings maintained good diplomatic relations with the Chinese T'ang Empire. Chinese accounts refer to the area as *Pa-lo-lai*, or *Bolor* in Muslim sources, and *Little Bolor* is thought to refer to Gilgit. Tibetan advances into the area were rebuffed by the T'angs, but the Chinese influence diminished following their defeat in Central Asia in 751 AD by the **Arabs**. The period that followed, referred to by Dani as 'Mediaeval History', is not well documented.

Medieval history

The source of information for the mediaeval history of Gilgit is primarily the oral tradition, and thus nothing can be stated with absolute certainty. The last Buddhist ruler of Gilgit was **Sri Badad** (or Sri Badat), although some sources claim he was a Hindu. He is remembered in a number of local legends, primarily for his cruelty, and it is said that he developed such a taste for the flesh of young children, that he ate nothing else.

The Shah Rais Dynasty to which Sri Badad belonged was followed by the rule of the **Trakhans**, the dominant dynasty in the mediaeval history of Gilgit. The Trakhans ruled Gilgit through eight distinct phases, from some time in the 8th century right up until 1840 (for intricate detail see Dani's 'History of the Northern Areas', 1991), and it is from this line that the rival ruling families of Hunza and Nagar evolved, (Ayash in the former, Maglot in the latter), sometime in the third period of the Trakhan Dynasty (1241-1449). The Trakhan era was a period of both chaos and stability- hardly surprising given the length of their rule-and the history of these times is a catalogue of wars, truces, alliances and further wars with the neighbouring kingdoms.

Modern history

Towards the end of the Trakhan Dynasty, both **Sikh** and **British** influence was growing in the region. In 1842 a Sikh army from Kashmir, at the request of the beleaguered ruler of Gilgit, Karim Khan, succeeded in driving the murderous **Gohar Aman** back to his stronghold in Yasin. Gohar Aman continued to harass Karim Khan and the Sikh garrison, and eventually succeeded in recapturing Gilgit in 1852. He ruled there unopposed until his death in 1860, by which time he is alleged to have sold half of the local population into slavery.

In the meantime, following the decisive victory in the First Anglo-Sikh War of 1846, the British had 'sold' Kashmir to the Dogra Raja of Jammu, **Gulab Singh** after he had footed the bill for the Sikh's war reparations. Following Gohar Aman's death, the Dogras returned

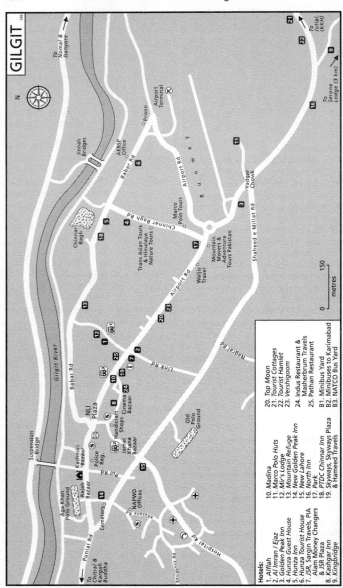

GILGIT

To Normal & Danyore

To Jutial, (KKH)

Gilgit River

Jinnah Bridges

AKRSP Office

Babar Rd

Prison

Airport Terminal

Chinnar Bagh

Babar Rd

Suspension Bridge

Kashmiri Bazaar

Police Reg.

NLI Plaza

Jamat Khana Bazaar

Cinema Bazaar

Handicraft Shops

Aga Khan Polo Ground

Rajah Bazaar

Cemetery

NAPWD Offices

Khazana Rd

Old Polo Ground

Punial Rd

Pul Rd

Hospital Rd

Residency Rd

To Chitral & Kargah Buddha

Chinnar Bagh Rd

Marco Polo Tours

Trans Asian Tours & Himalaya Nature Tours

Runway

Airport Rd

Wallis Travel

Mountain Movers & Adventure Tours Pakistan

Airport Rd

Link Rd

Nagral Rd

Shaheed e Millat Rd

Yadgar Chowk

To Serena Lodge (3 km)

metres

0   150

Hotels:
1. Afflah
2. Al Imran / Ejaz
3. Golden Peak Inn
4. Hunza Guest House
5. Hunza Inn
6. Hunza Tourist House
7. JSR, Sargin Travels, PIA, Alam Money Changers & JSR Plaza
8. Kashgar Inn
9. Kingbridge
10. Madina
11. Marco Polo Huts
12. Mir's Lodge
13. Mountain Refuge
14. New Golden Peak Inn
15. New Lahore
16. North Inn
17. Park
18. PTDC Chinnar Inn
19. Skyways, Skyways Plaza & Hameed Travels
20. Top Moon
21. Tourist Cottages
22. Tourist Hamlet
23. Vershigoom
24. Indus Restaurant & Masherbrum Travels
25. Pathan Restaurant

B1. Minibus Yard
B2. Minibuses to Karimabad
B3. NATCO Bus Yard

to Gilgit under the direction of Gulab Singh's successor Ranbir Singh. Thus, for the first time since the rule of Sri Badad some 11 centuries earlier, Gilgit found itself under the yoke of a non-Muslim ruler.

It was around this time that the British were beginning to penetrate the region. Vigne and Moorcroft had reached close to Gilgit in the late 1830s, and in 1866 the amazing Leitner had brought back the first written account of the town, albeit after a stay of less than 24 hrs. British concern was growing over the perceived threat of a Russian invasion through the unmapped passes to the N, and the vulnerability of the Kashmir frontier became a major issue. John Biddulph was appointed on 'special duty' at Gilgit between 1877 and 1881 in a move that is interpreted by some as either a prelude to direct annexation of the territory by the British government, or as an attempt to bring them under the control of their feudatory, the Maharaja of Kashmir (Dani, 1991). Russian intriguing, as well as British anxiety, (and maybe a touch of paranoia), led to the reappointment of a Political Agent in 1889. Although in theory just a representative of the British government on the frontier, **Col Algernon Durand** was the defacto military commander of the region, and as such was the key policy maker. A system evolved by which the Political Agent was responsible for the area of the Agency, reporting to the British Resident in Kashmir, whilst the Maharaja's representative was only answerable for Kashmir State Territories, which at this stage included the district (Wazarat) of Gilgit.

This system of 'dual control' was not seen as acceptable by the British, but it was not until 1935 that an alternative was agreed upon. In 1925 **Raja Hari Singh** had become Maharaja of Kashmir, but within several years of his accession he was facing serious agitation from the majority Muslim population of the state, demanding representative government. Recognising his weak position, with the threat of British 'intervention' hanging over him, Hari Singh had little option but to sign a document 'leasing' the Gilgit Wazarat to the British for 60 years. The 'lease', signed on 29 March 1935, authorized the British government to "assume the civil military government of the Wazarat of Gilgit subject to the condition that the territory would continue to be included within the dominion of His Highness the Maharaja of Jammu and Kashmir". This is how the position of Gilgit stood at the partition of the sub-continent in 1947, and the creation of the state of Pakistan.

Partition

A radical reinterpretation of the 1935 lease agreement meant that when British paramountcy over India lapsed on 3 June 1947, the whole of the Gilgit Agency was handed over to the Maharaja of Kashmir. His representative, **Brig Ghansara Singh**, took over as governor of the area on 1 August 1947, 2 weeks before the date set for the independence of India and Pakistan. This was despite the fact that all the civil and military officers had expressed a preference to the British to join Pakistan. The local population had not been consulted at all.

It is difficult to find an objective chronicle of what became known as the **Gilgit Uprising**, as all the key players attempt to overstate their individual role. However, Dani's account in his comprehensive 'History of the Northern Areas' (1991) is perhaps the best record of the events as they occurred.

On the night of 26 October 1947, Maharaja Hari Singh announced his accession to India. How much this decision was influenced by the arrival of Pathan Afridi tribesmen from NWFP on his doorstep proclaiming a *jihad*, is open to historical debate, but in Gilgit plans for this eventuality had obviously already been made. A small group of army officers serving in the Gilgit Scouts had already secretly pledged their allegiance to Pakistan, and made plans for the liberation of Gilgit. In the early hours of the morning of 1 November 1947, Brigadier Ghansara Singh was arrested at his home, and placed under custody. He was made to sign a surrender document, and the Pakistani flag was raised over Gilgit. Within 4 days the Chilas Scouts had captured the fort at Bunji, thus gaining control of the vital line of communication, and potential counter-attack, with Srinagar. Meanwhile, in Gilgit, a Provisional Government had been set up, headed by Shah Rais Khan, a descendant of the former ruling family of Gilgit. Assistance was requested from Pakistan, although this fledgling state's meagre resources meant that the support given was generally moral as opposed to tangible. Major (later Brig) Mohammad Aslam Khan, winner of the Military Cross on the Burma front in 1941 and now proprietor of the *Shangrila* chain of hotels, was flown in to coordinate the military defence of the country so far acquired, and to 'liberate' as much territory as possible. He formed three forces, nicknamed 'Tiger', 'Ibex' and 'Eskimo', that not only succeeded in holding the territory gained, but also managed to liberate Baltistan and occupy parts of Kashmir.

In Jan 1948 a UN sponsored ceasefire ended the war, leaving the Line of Control as the defacto border between Pakistan and India.

Recent events

The key event in the recent history of Gilgit has been the development of transport infrastructure in the region, in particular the construction of the Karakoram Highway. Gilgit is now a major staging post in the border trade with China, and potentially with Central Asia in the future. It is also a key market for goods from both China and down country Pakistan, as well as a local centre for labour.

In recent years, Gilgit has had more than its share of sectarian violence. The population is roughly split between Sunni and Shia Muslims, with a sizeable community of Ismailis. Tensions between the Sunni and Shia communities are at their highest around key religious dates, particularly *Ashura* and the end of *Ramadan*. In 1988 several hundred were killed in gun battles in the Gilgit area, and again in 1993 greater casualties were only avoided by the imposition of a 24-hr curfew. Although there was no trouble in 1995, the town is probably best avoided at these times.

Places of interest

In terms of tourism, Gilgit's greatest utility is as a base to visit nearby attractions, arrange transport to other places in the Northern Areas, or prepare for a trekking expedition. Although a major tourist centre, there is not really that much to see in Gilgit itself.

There are a number of monuments dedicated to the Gilgit Uprising, including a memorial in **Chinar Bagh**, the municipal gardens down by the river, where the graves of two of the key players are located. The redevelopment of the Northern Light Infantry's former barracks into a shopping plaza means that you can now visit the **Oath Hall** where the officers of the Gilgit Scouts pledged their allegiance to Pakistan, and the **Drill Hall** where Brig Ghansara Singh was imprisoned. However, neither are particularly inspiring. The shopping plaza redevelopment also means that you can now see the sole remaining tower of the **fort** that Gohar Aman built in the 1850s.

European cemetery

On Khazana Rd, to the W of town, is the cemetery in which the British explorer **George Hayward** is buried. The graveyard is also the final resting place of a Captain in the Sikh Pioneers who 'accidently drowned in the Indus near Bunji' in 1929, some members of the 1959 Batura Muztagh Expedition, and a young British school teacher who died in a fall near Sust in 1989. The key to the cemetery can be obtained from Mohammad Ali in the tailor's shop opposite.

Kargah Buddha

Thought to date to the 7th or 8th century, and showing marked similarities to Tibetan carvings found in Baltistan, this large image of a standing Buddha is found on a cliff face at Kargah, several km W of Gilgit. There is an excellent local legend that provides a far more amusing explanation for the carved figure. The image is actually that of a giant who used to terrorise the local population. A passing saint was enlisted by the terrified villagers to deal with the menace, and he succeeded in pinning the giant to the rock face. The saint explained that the giant would remain pinned there for as long as he was alive, and they would continue to be safe if they buried the saint at the foot of the cliff upon his death. The resourceful villagers killed the saint there and then, and buried him at the foot of the cliff!

Several 100m upstream of the Buddha are the remains of a monastery and several stupas, whose excavation revealed a number of Sanskrit Buddhist texts. Kargah is about 8 km from Gilgit, and can be reached on foot, or by hiring a Suzuki.

Local information
● **Accommodation**

Hotel Classifications			
AL	Rs4,000	**A**	Rs1,800-4,000
B	Rs900-1,800	**C**	Rs450-900
D	Rs300-450	**E**	Rs150-300
F	up to Rs150		

A *Serena*, Jutial, T 2330, F 2525, luxurious rooms, all with private terrace but small and hot in summer, heating, dish TV, phone, room service, *Dumani* restaurant, *Jutial* coffee lounge, conference facilities, travel agents, shopping, badminton and tennis, foreign exchange, accepts credit cards, best in town.

B *Oasis International*, Jutial, T 2797, under construction in late 1995, but plans 200 beds on 5 storeys, plus pool.

C *Hunza Tourist House*, Babar Rd, T 3788, light and airy rooms around a nice garden, often used for visiting AKRSP staff, restaurant rec; **C** *Mir's Lodge*, Link Rd, T 2875, new, friendly hotel, excellent restaurant, group rates and discounts available; **C** *PTDC Chinnar Inn*, Babar Rd, T 2562, luxury rooms, restaurant, large garden, shopping and PTDC office. **C** *Park*, Airport Rd, T 2379, F 3796, clean rooms with hot/cold, optional TV, and some cheaper rooms, generator is very noisy, restaurant quite good; **C** *Tourist Hamlet*, Jutial Rd, T 2934, Gilgit's first hotel with a swimming pool (very cold), has friendly service, a large garden, plus some very good value dorms in the **F** price range, rec.

D *Hunza Inn*, Babar Rd, T 2814, popular hotel run by the entertaining Abdullah Baig, has luxury rooms with hot/cold bath, simple, cheaper rooms, and some cheap dorm beds in the annex, quiet, shady garden, 10% discount on best rooms to users of this book, rec; **D** *Kinbridge*, Khomer Chowk, Jutial Rd, T 2298, Chinese run, has large, clean carpetted rooms, with dish TV, a/c and hot/cold bath, the place is usually empty, so some real bargains can be had. Chinese restaurant is very good, and you may get a beer; **D** *Mountain Refuge*, Chinnar Gardens Rd, dorms are cheap, but other rooms overpriced; **D** *North Inn*, Khomer Chowk, Jutial Rd, T 2887, rooms overpriced, but restaurant is quite good; **D** *Younas*, Shah-e-Resham Rd, Cantt, Jutial, T 3776, 7 km from town centre, but quiet with good views, large, carpetted rooms, dish TV, restaurant, garden, and plans for a pool.

E *Alflah*, Link Rd, T 3447, restaurant; **E** *Alpine*, Jutial, T 2641, 5 km from town; **E** *JSR*, JSR Plaza, Airport Rd, T 2308, carpetted rooms, some cheaper with separate bath, restaurant good for breakfast; **E** *Marco Polo Huts*, nr Yadgar Chowk, T 2783, quiet, relaxing garden, camping, restaurant; **E** *Skyways*, Skyways Plaza, Airport Rd, T 2742, central location, but very noisy music shop downstairs.

F *Al Imran/Ejaz*, Ejaz Plaza, Airport Rd, T 3468, quite basic, *Ejaz* section looks structurally unsound; **F** *Friendship*, Airport Rd, very basic; **F** *Golden Peak Inn*, Yadgar Chowk, T 3685, the original, run by very helpful and informative Latif Anwar Khan, doubles, singles, dorms, tent-beds and camping in shady garden, treks, tours and pony trekking organized; **F** *Hunza Guest House*, Chinnar Bagh Rd, T 2229, formerly the *Chinese Lodge*, rather run down; **F** *Kashgar Inn*, Cinema Bazaar, T 2326, basic; **F** *Madina*, NLI Chowk, hugely popular, and one of Pakistan's few real 'traveller' hang-outs, cheap rooms and dorms, good dinners, the staff work hard to make your stay a success, improves each year, rec; **F** *New Golden Peak Inn*, Khazana Rd, T 2235, not a patch on the original, although the Chinese restaurant is very good; **F** *New Lahore*, Hospital Rd, T 3327, bit dingy, although garden is nice and staff friendly; **F** *Vershigoom/Peshawari*, Airport Rd, very basic annex to restaurant of same name; **F** *Top Moon*, Airport Rd, T 3828, new hotel and restaurant, but undistinguished; **F** *Tourist Cottages*, Khomer, Jutial Rd, a travellers' favourite, was run by the excellent Mashroof Khan (and his Japanese wife Keiko), until his tragic death in Aug 1995, has cheap rooms, dorms and a lovely shady garden, built in traditional local style, the rooms remain cool in summer and warm in winter, excellent dinner served at 1930, rec; **F** *Tourist Hamlet*: see under **C** category.

NB Gilgit is the only place that you can make bookings for the *NAPWD Inspection Bungalows* in the surrounding area. In some of the more remote areas, particularly to the W between Gilgit and Chitral, this is the only accommodation available. Tourists take the lowest priority behind visiting dignitaries and NAPWD employees, and your booking can be cancelled without notice if someone higher in the pecking order turns up unannounced. If you do not have a booking, (very likely if coming from Chitral side), you will generally be able to use the rest house if it is unoccupied.

Villages that have *Inspection Bungalows*, but limited alternative accommodation include Chilas, Babusar, Imit, Gahkuch, Gupis, Yasin, Darkot, Phandur, Singal and Gulapur. Those in particularly choice locations, eg Naltar, seem permanently full. Bookings should be made through Administrative Officer (Mr Aktar Hussain), Office of Chief Engineer, NAPWD, Khazana Rd, T 3375. Fees are generally Rs 160 for a double room, Rs 200 for a VIP room, and the receipt must be given to the chowkidar at the bungalow. Bedding is provided and the chowkidars are usually able to arrange basic meals, although it is certainly worth taking your own supplements.

● **Places to eat**
The higher grade hotels all have good restaurants, especially **Serena, Hunza Tourist House, Mir's Lodge** and **PTDC Chinnar Inn**, good, filling, budget dinners are served at the **Madina Hotel** and **Tourist Cottages** each evening. By far the most popular restaurant with the local population is the **Pathan Hotel** opp Skyways Plaza. The chicken karahi is excellent here. The theme is meat, and this is not the place to order nut cutlets and tofu surprise.

● **Airline offices**
PIA, JSR Plaza, Airport Rd, T 3390. The certificates for the 2 tourist allocated seats on each flight to Islamabad should be obtained from the PTDC office at the Chinnar Inn. Book as far in advance as possible.

● **Banks & money changers**
National Bank of Pakistan, Khazana Rd and **Habib Bank**, next to GPO, both offer foreign exchange (incl TCs) at rates slightly inferior to those down country. *Alam Money Changers*, PIA Plaza, T 2605, offers quicker, more efficient foreign exchange (TCs and cash).

● **Hospitals & medical services**
General Hospital is on Hospital Rd. A *Women's Hospital* is nearby. *Aga Khan Health Services Maternity Home*, Khomer, Jutial Rd.

● **Libraries**
There is a small *Municipal Library* on Khazana Rd. There is an excellent 'development' library at the AKRSP office on Babar Rd, T 2480.

● **Post & telecommunications**
The General Post Office (GPO) is in Saddar Bazaar. The Poste Restante is in a room right round the back. The Central Telegraph Office is on Hospital Rd. International calls must be routed through Islamabad. Some callers wait minutes for their connection, others hours. PCOs will also make international calls, with a Rs 20/min surcharge.

● **Shopping**
The largest collection of *local handicrafts* are in the shops at the junction of Cinema Bazaar/Jamat Khana Bazaar. *GM Baig & Sons*, Jamat Khana Bazaar, T 2409, has a good selection of books and maps of the local area, plus daily newspapers (flights permitting). **Trekking equipment** can be bought or hired from *Mountaineering Equipments* and *Gown House* on Airport Rd, (tents Rs 70/day, sleeping bags from Rs 30/day etc).

● **Sports**
Horse riding is available at the *Danyore Horse Club*, Danyore, nr Gilgit, T 30 (Mr Mir Aman, or

through most hotels), incl the chance to play polo. Charges: 1 hr, Rs 200; all day Rs 600; polo lessons Rs 350. No insurance provided.

Polo: the national sport of the Northern Areas, exciting games are held both in the *Aga Khan Polo Stadium*, W of the main mosque in Raja Bazaar, or more regularly at the 'Old Polo Ground' (little more than a street), off Hospital Rd. There is a big tournament in early Nov, as part of the independence day celebrations, sometimes one on 14 Aug (Pak Independence Day), and frequent matches prior to the big Shandur Pass tournament at the end of Jun.

● **Tour companies & travel agents**
Reflecting its position as the hub of transport and tourism in the Northern Areas, Gilgit has numerous tour companies and travel agents offering **trekking**, **jeep hire**, **guides** and many other services. One of the most reputable, and Pakistan's oldest, is *Waljis*, Airport Rd, T 2665. Typical jeep hire fares are as follows: Kargah Buddha Rs 350 (return); Naltar Rs 1,000 (return); Karimabad Rs 1,200 (1-way), Rs 1,600 (same-day return); Fairy Meadow Rs 1,800 incl Rs 500 local 'tax' (1-way); Tarshing Rs 2,500 (1-way); Khunjerab Pass Rs 3,960 (3 day return); Islamabad Rs 6,500 (1-way). For other destinations, a rough rule of thumb is Rs 8/mile on metalled roads, Rs 12/mile on non-metalled roads, plus Rs 200 day charge, and Rs 200 for overnight stops. *Waljis* also offer **white-water rafting** in season. Other travel agents incl: on Airport Rd, *Adventure Tours Pakistan*, T 2663 and *Mountain Movers*; on Chinar Bagh Rd, *Marco Polo Tourist Transport*, T 3074 and *Himalaya Nature Tour*, T 2946, the latter of whom offer **mountain bike** hire (Rs 400/day).

● **Tourist offices**
The main **PTDC** office is at the *Chinnar Inn*, although there is a sub-office in JSR Plaza.

● **Useful addresses**
Aga Khan Rural Support Programme (AKRSP): Babar Rd, T 2480.

The **Foreigners Registration Office**: is next to the GPO.

● **Transport**
Local Suzukis run between Jutial and Saddar Bazaar (Rs 2), and along Babar and Chinar Bagh Rds. Some of the more remote hotels offer minibus services into town, and to/from the airport. **Jeep hire**: for details of jeep hire prices, see under Tour companies & travel agents.

Air Islamabad Mon 0615, 0645, 1115; Tues 0615; Wed 0615, 0915; Thur 0615, 0930, 1230; Fri 0615, 0645, 1115; Sat 0615, 0915; Sun 0615 0930 1230.

Road Bus: the *NATCO* (Northern Areas Transport Corporation) yard and booking office is in a new location at NLI Chowk, opp the Madina Hotel. Tickets can normally be bought 1 day in advance. Student card holders can get a 50% discount (except on 'deluxe' Rawalpindi services). **Rawalpindi** 0400 ('normal', Rs 180, 18 hrs +) 1100 ('normal') 1400 ('deluxe', Rs 220, 16 hrs +) 1700 ('deluxe') 2000 ('deluxe'). **Sust** 0800 (Rs 70, 6 hrs) via **Ganesh** (for **Karimabad**, 3 hrs), **Gulmit** (4 hrs), **Passu** (4½ hrs). **Skardu** 0530 (Rs 81, 8 hrs). The *NATCO* bus to **Gupis** and **Yasin** (Rs 50, 6 hrs) leaves from the *NATCO* office on Punial Rd. *Masherbrum Travels*, behind Indus Hotel on Cinema Bazaar, run a number of services. **Rawalpindi** (Pir Wadhi Bus Station) 1300, 1700 ('deluxe', Rs 220) 1600 ('normal', Rs 180). **Skardu** 0700 ('big bus', Rs 81) 0800, 1000, 1200 (minibus, Rs 115). *Hameed Travels*, Skyways Plaza, T 3181, run coasters to **Rawalpindi** (Mashriq Hotel) 1500, 1700 (Rs 250, 16 hrs). *Sargin Travels* also run coasters to **Rawalpindi** (Novelty Cinema) 1500, 1700 (Rs 250, 16 hrs). Minibuses to **Karimabad** depart when full in the morning and early afternoon from Jamat Khana Bazaar. The minibus stand on Link Rd serves the following destinations, unless otherwise specified, on a 'depart when full' basis. **Chilas** (3½ hrs), **Nomal** (1 hr), **Jaglot** (1½ hrs), **Naltar** (1300, 4 hrs) and **Besham** (9 hrs).

Excursions from Gilgit

Naltar Valley

The road to Naltar Valley leaves Gilgit by the Jinnah Bridge, but turns N (left) at the Frontier Constabulary post, rather than crossing the suspension bridge to Danyore and the KKH. This route used to form part of the Old Hunza Rd prior to the construction of the KKH. The route is dry and dusty until you reach the extensive cultivated area of **Nomal**. There is a *NAPWD Inspection Bungalow* here, as well as a dubious looking footbridge across the Hunza River to the KKH.

At Nomal a rough jeep track turns W, up the Naltar Valley. As Schomberg (1933) points out, this entrance to the Naltar Valley is an "unprepossessing means of access to the lovely valley behind". After 10 km you reach 'Lower' Naltar, or Naltar Paen. 'Upper' Naltar is a further 10 km up the valley.

Upper Naltar

The lower reaches of the Naltar Valley are confined within a hot, rocky, narrow canyon, but at 'Upper' Naltar the valley opens out to reveal lush green alpine pastures and pine forests surrounded by spectacular snowy peaks. In winter, the scene is entirely different, and it is here that the Pakistan Air Force maintain a winter survival school.

● **Accommodation E** *Pasban Inn* has large room with attached bath, restaurant with a good menu and dish TV; **F** *Hilltop* has a 4 bed dorm and a 3 bed dorm, both with attached bath, restaurant, karaoke machine and walnut garden with flashing lights; **F** *Prince* has a couple of triples, with separate open air toilet, restaurant, and garden without flashing lights.

● **Transport** Naltar's cargo jeep drivers have a well deserved poor reputation, and are keen to fleece visiting tourists. You may be asked to pay for a 'special booking' only to find another 16 passengers sharing your jeep. If travelling from Gilgit, it is essential to establish whether the fare is to 'Lower' or 'Upper' Naltar. The fare from Gilgit to 'Lower' Naltar is Rs 50, and you may be asked for the same again to continue to 'Upper' Naltar. Cargo jeeps leave from Gilgit's Rajah Bazaar, and from nr the minibus stand on Link Rd. A private jeep from Gilgit to 'Upper' Naltar costs Rs 500. Return jeeps leave 'Upper' Naltar early in the morning.

Naltar Lake

The beautiful Naltar Lake is a gentle 12 km walk beyond 'Upper' Naltar, and can be reached in 3½-4 hrs. The path passes through pleasant meadows and scattered pine forests, although there is some scrambling over loose scree and boulders at the start of the trek. The gradient is quite modest though. It is worth noting if you are returning the same day, however, that the numerous streams that you have to hop across are considerably higher by late afternoon. There are actually several lakes in the upper part of the Naltar Valley, although the first one that you come to is probably the most attractive. Set in a hollow of terminal moraine deposited by a long since retreated glacier, Naltar Lake is a stunning vision of colour, with exquisite aquamarines, electric blues and vivid greens. In places it is unbelievably clear. Potential swimmers should note that it is very deep and genital-shrivellingly cold. Diving in may cause unhealthy rapid changes in body temperature. It can also take longer to climb out than you think, so don't leave it until you are turning blue before attempting to scramble out. Upon closer investigation, male swimmers may have the impression of having undergone a sex change.

It is quite possible to camp at this idyllic spot, or to use the tents provided by the **F** *Lake View Hotel*, or *Red Stone Huts*. Both also serve food. The two other lakes beyond Naltar Lake are said to offer the best fishing.

Beyond the series of lakes, there are two strenuous trekking opportunities. One route travels over the 4,267m Naltar (or Pakor) Pass into the Ishkoman Valley (see page 558), and the other crosses the Daintar Pass (4,800m) to Chalt (see page 556).

Bagrot Valley

Located to the E of Gilgit, the Bagrot Valley runs roughly SW-NE for 20 km or so, before turning E and providing a route into the Haramosh Valley. In addition to offering fine views of the S face of the Rakaposhi Massif, this little visited valley offers some excellent walking.

The highly cultivated entrance to the valley is usually reached from Danyore, on the KKH, although public cargo jeeps are irregular. It may be possible to take a very crowded cargo jeep from Garhi Bazaar in Gilgit- otherwise you will have to hire a vehicle. All food supplies should be purchased in Gilgit before setting out for the valley.

The first few km of the valley are rocky and barren, as the jeep track winds its way through the lateral moraine, but this soon gives way to intensively cultivated agricultural land. The jeep track runs as far as Chirah, where the run-down **E** *NAPWD Inspection Bungalow* provides the valley's only accommodation. Beyond Chirah there are walks up to the summer pastures, and a demanding trek across the Burche Glacier into the Haramosh Valley. A guide is necessary for this trek.

The 6,134m Dobani (Bilchar) Peak at the centre of the valley is said to be inhabited by fairies, and the belief here in the power of shamans is strong. The population of the valley are Shia Muslims, and traditionally provided the backbone of the army raised in times of war by the rulers of Gilgit. When Durand visited the valley in 1889, he found evidence of an earlier raid by Gohar Aman, a prince of Yasin, in which it is estimated that two-thirds of the population had been killed or carried off into slavery. Schomberg, naturally, has his usual quota of negative opinions about the people of this valley, claiming that Bagrotis are 'famous for their stupidity'. It would be interesting to find out what they thought of him.

Few people visit this valley, although in recent years a large number of anthropologists (many attached to the joint German-Pak 'Culture Area Karakoram' project) have been studying the rapidly changing social structures within the valley.

GILGIT TO CHITRAL

The journey W from Gilgit towards Chitral is one of the most beautiful and challenging trips in Pakistan. The route follows the Gilgit River upstream, providing access to the fascinating side valleys of Ishkoman and Yasin, both of which have almost inexhaustible trekking potential. The scenery at Phandur is sublime, before the road crosses the famous Shandur Pass -scene of the most spectacular polo event in the world. The jeep road can be rough, and in places dangerous, but this is a journey you will remember for a long time.

Local information
● **Accommodation**

If you are equipped to camp, this trip offers some great overnight resting places. Particularly rec are the lake just after Gupis, the Phandur region, Langar and the Shandur Pass itself. If you require hotel accommodation, then some advanced planning is worthwhile. The *NAPWD Inspection Bungalows* at Gulapur, Singal, Gahkuch, Chatorkhand, Imit, Gupis, Yasin, Phandur and Teru all offer comfortable accommodation, albeit with very basic food. However, they can only be booked in Gilgit (see 'Accommodation', Gilgit) – not much use if you are coming from Chitral. Most will accept casual callers if unoccupied. Singal, Gilmiti, Gahkuch, Gupis, Phandur, Sor Laspur and Mastuj all offer some form of basic **F** accommodation.

● **Transport**

Local Your enjoyment of this journey will be directly affected by the mode and style of transport that you select. If you are travelling on a tight budget, then this is the one trip in Pakistan where it is worth splashing out on a private hire jeep. Although the journey is perfectly feasible in a cargo jeep, the public vehicles on this route are very heavily loaded, and it is not unusual to find 20 other passengers also clinging to the back of the jeep. The road can be quite rough in places, and Pakistani cargo jeeps seem to have a disproportionate number of strategically placed sharp metal objects which your swaying body will regularly find. It is difficult to enjoy the scenery under these circumstances. Further, this route offers some sublime camping spots, whereas cargo jeeps tend to stop for the night in relatively uninteresting villages. If you are travelling by cargo jeep, it is rec that you take your time over the trip, travelling in short bursts, and alighting at points that take your fancy. Jeeps can be privately hired in Gilgit through most hotels, although the reputable travel agents such as *Waljis* are no more expensive, and far more reliable. Expect to pay around Rs 5,000 to Mastuj, Rs 6,000 to Chitral for a 2 to 3-day trip. Jeeps seat 4 comfortably, 5 or 6 at a push, and thus the cost is not excessive when shared.

Cargo jeeps: leave from Gilgit's Punial Rd, although it's unusual to find a vehicle going the whole way to Chitral. Chitral based jeep drivers, who would otherwise be returning back empty, often tour the cheap hotels such as the *Madina* offering competitive prices for the trip.

For details of transport from Chitral to Gilgit, see the Chitral section.

Gilgit to Gahkuch

The road to Chitral leaves Gilgit to the W, passing the turn off to the Kargah Buddah. In 1995 the road was only sealed for a few km beyond Gilgit, before changing into a reasonably good jeep road. However, plans are underway to upgrade the road, initially laying tarmac as far as Gahkuch, and eventually sealing the road all the way along the route to Chitral. If and when this occurs, it is bound to greatly affect the volume and pattern of transport across the Shandur Pass.

The jeep road passes along the S side of the Gilgit River, through the small village of **Shenote** that marks the boundary between Gilgit and **Punial District**.

The road continues through **Gulapur**, with its E *NAPWD Inspection Bungalow*, with the green and fertile village of Rashmal across the river, connected by a new bridge. At the next village, Goharabad, there is a small chai stop.

Being a relatively fertile and well watered strip of land on either side of the

Gilgit River, the former independent kingdom of **Punial** became a bone of contention between the rulers of Yasin and Gilgit. Both states possessed the region in turn, until it was annexed by the Maharaja of Kashmir in 1860. Part of the desire to control Punial was due to the strategic location of the fort at **Sher Qila**.

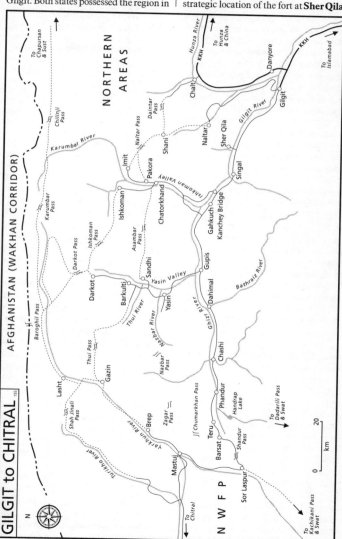

SHER QILA WOMENS' ART GROUP (S.W.A.G)

The Sher Qila Women's Art Group is a recently established women's cooperative that produces "art that reflects the women's first tentative explorations into self-expression, self-esteem and financial independence". The women received intensive training from a professional Canadian artist, Vicki Mattice, and are now producing attractive, quality paintings on handmade paper. The inexpensive prints are available from the S.W.A.G. studio at the residence of the former Raja of Punial in Sher Qila (visitors welcome), and from a number of handicraft shops in Karimabad. Profits will provide essential income for the community, with long term goals including the establishment of a permanent Arts Centre for the women. For further information contact Ms Nilusha Bardai, c/o Pilot School Sher Qila, BPO Sher Qila, Ghizr, NA, Pakistan.

On the N side of the river, connected to the main road by a suspension bridge, Sher Qila (33 km from Gilgit, 1½ hrs by bus) controls the western approach to Gilgit. The word 'Sher', a Dogra corruption of the Shina word 'Cher', means 'an impregnable rock', whilst 'Qila' means 'fort'. All that remains of the fort today is one 150-year-old watchtower, close to the river. Sher Qila's most impressive building now is the Aga Khan High School for Girls.

At **Singal** (48 km from Gilgit, 2 hrs by bus), you must enter your passport details at the police check-post. Singal is the site of a very plush Aga Khan Medical Centre, a *NAPWD Inspection Bungalow*, and the basic **F** *Ghizer Hotel*.

The road then passes through the small village of **Gilmiti** (7 km), where there is a PSO petrol pump and the basic **F** *Nadir Hotel*. Kuwait, the village on the opposite side of the river, is famed locally for its wine! Indeed, Schomberg notes how the people of Punial are "inordinately pleasure-seeking", and how "they love the juice of the grape, either as wine or, preferably, in the form of that trebly distiled liquor, potent and unrefined, which would make any Western head ache for weeks." Perhaps Schomberg's judgement was also impaired, for having described the people of Punial as "shrewd and intelligent", in the next breath he is referring to them as "unenterprising and dirty".

Shortly before Gahkuch, the recently built Chinese **Kanchey Bridge** (65 km from Gilgit) crosses the river, offering one of two alternative routes to the **Ishkoman Valley**. This route passes along the N side of the Gilgit River, through the village of Silpi. The old rope suspension bridge that the Kanchey Bridge replaced was dismantled, and moved up-river to connect Silpi to Gahkuch. The jeep track, shortly to be upgraded, then runs up the E side of the Ishkoman Valley to Chatorkhand.

Gahkuch (73 km from Gilgit), the district headquarters, has a large police check-post where you enter passport details. This is the most westerly settlement in the Punial District. An important fort previously stood at Gahkuch, commanding both the entrance to the Ishkoman Valley, and the Gilgit-Chitral road. It was whilst occupying this fort in 1893 that Durand learnt of the Indus Valley Uprising.

Local information
● **Accommodation**

The *NAPWD Inspection Bungalow* is very luxurious, although you are likely to be turned away if you do not have a booking from Gilgit.

F *Snow Drop Inn*, Main Bazaar, T 73, has 1 grotty, basic and not very private room, the restaurant is often a meal stop on the Gilgit-Yasin bus trip; **F** *Ghizer Tourist House* (left off main bazaar) is quite basic, but has a good restaurant; **F** *Shandur Tourist House* (right off main bazaar) has reasonable triples with attached bath.

BETWEEN THE OXUS AND THE INDUS

Amongst all the accounts of travel in the Northern Areas of Pakistan by British military types, that of Colonel RCF Schomberg is one of the most extraordinary. Published in 1933, and received as an authoritative study of the lands and peoples of the region between the two great rivers, "Between the Oxus and the Indus" must be one of the most bigoted pieces of colonial writing ever published. Amongst excellent descriptions of the physical terrain, and the local political scene and social structures, are dotted with highly disparaging remarks about the capabilities of the local people. Referring to the people of one particular valley, Schomberg remarks: "It is difficult to describe the luscious beauty of a walk through this countryside when summer is ablaze. The people, stupid, dirty, and but indifferent imitations of monkeys, cannot mar the noble prospect." The only people that Schomberg admired were the Hunzakuts, and only then because they were the best porters, and could tie a load onto a horse.

Although not wishing to give a platform to Schomberg's views, selected quotes have been included in this text in order to give some idea of the British attitudes to the various ethnic groups in the region.

● **Places to eat**

Gahkuch is currently the only place between Gilgit and Chitral where you are likely to be able to get a Coke.

● **Transport**

The *NATCO* bus to Gilgit passes through Gahkuch around 0930.

A further 10 km beyond Gahkuch, a 100m suspension bridge crosses the river to the **Ishkoman Valley**. From this point it is 83 km E to Gilgit, 27 km W to Gupis, and travelling N up the Ishkoman Valley, 20 km to Chatorkhand, 55 km to Imit and 100 km to the Pamir Border with Afghanistan. Currently, there is more traffic to the Ishkoman Valley via this route than the alternative Kanchey Bridge. Cargo jeeps from Gahkuch (Rs 25, 1 hr) are particularly crowded.

Ishkoman Valley

Although the whole valley is generally referred to as the Ishkoman Valley, the major river that runs through the valley is the **Karumber** (which descends from the Karumber Glacier to the NE), and some texts refer to the valley as the Karumber Valley. The actual Ishkoman River is a small tributary that joins the Karumber from the NW, from a valley

that is referred to as 'Ishkoman proper'.

The language pattern of the valley reflects the history of migration into the area and conquest by the neighbouring states of Chitral, Yasin and Gilgit, with Shina, Khowar (Chitrali), Burushaski and Wakhi all being spoken.

Our old friend Schomberg visited the area, and as usual, he was not impressed by the people: "The more I saw of the inhabitants of Ishkoman, the more was I struck by their degeneracy; they were poor in physique and lacking in brains." Working himself up into an apoplexy, Schomberg refers to the indigenous population as "absurd pygmies", "no better than cretins", before finally concluding with "I am afraid that the people of Ishkoman represent as low a type of humanity as any in the North-West of India"!

Few foreign visitors, bar the odd trekking groups, visit the Ishkoman Valley, which is a great pity because the local people are very friendly and welcoming. However, the entire valley may soon be subject to dramatic change. In 1995, the federal government of Benazir Bhutto launched a feasibility study looking into the possibility of pushing a major road through the Ishkoman Valley to link the KKH, and hence Islamabad, with

Central Asia. Bhutto's government is pursuing a vigorous campaign to sell the idea to the land-locked countries of Central Asia that Karachi is their logical warm water port outlet. A number of transit trade agreements have already been signed, and all that remains is for the infrastructure to be provided.

In its favour, the relatively flat nature of the terrain means that the road is technically feasible. Further, the Ishkoman route has a very powerful lobbyist in the Deputy Chief Executive of the Northern Areas Council, who is from Chatorkhand. On the debit side, however, the road would have to pass through both Afghanistan and Tajikistan – two countries currently in the grip of civil war. It is also thought that potential funders of the project are more in favour of an improved access route through the Lowari Pass and Chitral, rather than the time consuming KKH route via Gilgit. Either way, the long term fruition of this project is still many years off.

At the entrance to the Ishkoman Valley is a wide alluvial fan, upon which the green and well cultivated fields of the village of Hatoon stand. The jeep road runs along the W side of the valley, before crossing the river on the 75m suspension bridge at Hasis (8 km). Here, the jeep road joins the alternative route S via Silpi to the Kanchey Bridge. The road N up the valley continues to Chatorkhand (12 km).

Chatorkhand is the largest settlement in the valley, and was described by Schomberg as being "famous for its pir and its bugs". The Ismaili community venerate their pirs, (a hereditary position as a religious leader), and many attain considerable power and social status. The current pir, Syed Karim Ali Shah, is Deputy Chief Executive of the Northern Areas.

The *NAPWD Inspection Bungalow* has three VIP doubles, with eccentric plumbing, plus two standard rm set in a large garden. Basic meals are available

through the chowkidar, although you may well want to bring your own supplements. There are several chai shops in the village.

Several km N of Chatorkhand is the village of **Pakora** (marked on some maps as Phakor or Pakor). A *nala* joins from the E, and it is through the narrow opening to this valley that you can trek E across the **Pakor Pass** (4,267m), sometimes marked Naltar Pass, to the **Naltar Valley** (see page 558).

Immediately beyond the Jamat Khana in Pakora, the road divides, although both forks rejoin several km further N. A steep path several hundred metres along the left fork leads down to a rope suspension bridge across the Karumber River. This route leads along the W side of the valley to **Ishkoman**. It also leads to the valley joining from the W that provides a relatively easy 5-day trek across the **Asambar Pass** (4,432m) to **Yasin**.

Ishkoman 'proper' comprises a series of small villages along the Ishkoman River, including Jalalabad, Dalti Thupushkin, Mominabad, Faizabad, Ishkoman Bala and Gotolti (scene of a major smallpox epidemic in 1965). All claim to be the original settlement of Ishkoman 'proper'. The valley continues NW across the 3,600m **Ishkoman Pass** to the **Yasin Valley**, right at the foot of the Darkot Pass (4,744m). There is no accommodation in Ishkoman 'proper', and transport is very irregular.

The jeep track along the E side of the valley, hugging the base of the cliffs, continues to **Imit**. During the summer months it is best to cross the river at this point since the high level of the water can make it difficult to cross directly between Ishkoman and Imit further up the valley.

Imit is the starting point for another trek across into the Naltar Valley. It is also possible to cross the Karumber Glacier, and then head W across the Chillinji Pass towards Chitral, although this is a difficult trek through a restricted area and a guide is essential.

There is reputed to be a sulphurous hot spring near to Imit, although local people claim that it has now disappeared. Schomberg's comment on Imit was that it has two claims to distinction, 'the flies and dogs'.

There is an **E** *NAPWD Inspection Bungalow* at Imit. Public transport to Imit is very limited. Extremely crowded cargo jeeps from Gilgit pass through Chatorkhand between 1500 and 1600 each day, and return from Imit early the next morning.

Gahkuch to Gupis

Returning to the main jeep road between Gilgit and Chitral, **Gupis** lies a further 37 km W of Gahkuch (2 hrs by bus). There is a *NAPWD Inspection Bungalow*, **F** *Snow Leopard Inn* and in 1995 a PTDC Motel was under construction. The settlement also has a Civil Hospital, Post Office and a newly built fort.

Several km W of Gupis is the recently Chinese constructed 96m **Gupis Bridge**, at the entrance to the **Yasin Valley**. From this point it is 112 km to Gilgit, 42 km to Gahkuch, 54 km to Phandur, 104 km to the Shandur Pass, and 25 km N up the Yasin Valley to 'Central' Yasin.

Yasin Valley

The Yasin Valley, and in particular the characters it produced, has played a leading role in the history of the region. Continually fought over by the rulers of both Chitral and Gilgit, the history of the rulers of Yasin reads like a catalogue of patricide, fratricide and avunculicide. Yasin came to the attention of Victorian Britain following the murder of British explorer George Hayward in the upper reaches of the valley.

Biddulph classifies the original inhabitants of the valley as Yeshkuns, although they refer to themselves as Boorushi. The majority of the valley are Ismaili Muslims, speaking Burushaski, although it is a more archaic dialect than the Burushaski spoken in Hunza and Nagar. The ruling class, however, speak Khowar (Chitrali), reflecting their origins in the valley to the W. Today, many residents of Yasin Valley are bilingual. The valley is sometimes referred to as Woorshigum ('Valley of the Boorushi').

The valley is well watered, and in the lower reaches in particular, there is extensive cultivatable land. Yasin is probably seen at its best in late Aug, as the wheat and maize are approaching harvest. Locally, Yasini women have a reputation for great beauty, although it is not uncommon to find that women who originally belonged to the Khushwakht families of Chitral, practise purdah.

The entrance to the Yasin Valley is relatively dry and stony, until you reach the first green settlements at Damalgan and Gindaie. The road continues through the terminal moraine to the suspension bridge at **Noh**. The *NATCO* bus from Gilgit (7 hrs) terminates at this point, although a new bridge capable of taking heavier traffic is currently under construction. From the bridge you can either walk, or hitch a lift on a cargo jeep/tractor the 3 km to 'Central' **Yasin**.

Yasin

'Central' Yasin is a long, sprawling series of settlements collectively known as Yasin. There are still remains of the fort built by **Gohar Aman**, one of the valleys most celebrated rulers. A member of the Khushwakte ruling family, he is remembered as much for his "cruelty of disposition" as his ability as "an able and energetic Soldier" (Biddulph). Naturally, Schomberg is more caustic in his analysis, referring to Gohar Aman as "a mighty murderer and strapping tyrant". Gohar Aman was the father of Mir Wali, the man generally held responsible for the murder of George Hayward.

Antagonistic towards Shias, Gohar Aman made many raids on Gilgit, and later had great success against the Dogra

GEORGE HAYWARD

Of all the players in the 'Great Game', George J Whitaker Hayward must rank as one of the most extraordinary. Little is known about his early life, and even the details of his place of birth are uncertain. To add to the mystery, there only appears to one photograph of the man, currently in the possession of the Royal Geographical Society (RGS) in London. Recent investigations by Charles Timmis suggest that Hayward was born in Headingly, Yorkshire, and not Ireland as initially thought, after which he attended school in Snaresbrook, just E of London.

His movements are uncertain after he resigned his commission in the Cameron Highlanders, yet in 1868 this relatively unknown man was sponsored by the RGS to undertake a journey to the Pamirs, in search of the source of the Oxus. After being pretty much given up for dead, Hayward re-emerged in 1869 to a hero's welcome, following his extensive surveys in the Pamirs and visits to the great Central Asian cities of Yarkand and Kashgar. He was awarded the R.G.S.'s coveted Gold Medal.

Within a year, Hayward had returned to this dangerous and unmapped region. As Hopkirk suggests, "to a man like Hayward, the risks merely made it more attractive", and a greater insight into the man is revealed in a line that Hayward wrote to a fellow explorer: "I shall wander about the wilds of Central Asia possessed of an insane desire to try the effects of cold steel across my throat." This line was to prove prophetic. On 18 July 1870, he was murdered at Darkot, in the Yasin Valley.

The reasons for Hayward's murder have never really been established, nor the instigator of the crime identified. One prime suspect is the Maharaja of Kashmir, embarrassed by Hayward's revelations in a newspaper of a massacre committed by his Dogra troops several years earlier in Yasin. Another prime candidate is Mir Wali, the local ruler, with whom Hayward is said to have argued with in public just days before his death. Whatever the facts of the matter, it was Mir Wali who fled from Yasin, himself meeting a grisly end some years later.

Today, Hayward's body lies buried in the graveyard in Gilgit.

forces. However, following the eventual Dogra victory in 1863, a punitive expedition was sent to Yasin Valley to extract revenge, and it is the details of this massacre at nearby Muduri that Hayward described so graphically in _The Pioneer_ newspaper: "They (Dogra troops) threw the little ones in the air and cut them in two as they fell. It is said that the pregnant women, after being killed, were ripped open and their unborn babies hacked to pieces. Some forty women who were not yet dead were dragged to one spot, and were there burnt by the Dogra sepoys. With the exception of a few wounded men and women who ultimately recovered, every man, woman and child within the fort, and, in all,

1,200 to 1,400 of these unhappy villagers, were massacred by the foulest treachery and cruelty" (Keay, 1979 'The Gilgit Game').

Yasin Fort stands on the W side of the river, although you may have to enlist some local help to find it. Within the courtyard is a large tree and a new mosque, although the old mosque, complete with carved pillars, remains. One tower still stands, and although the door remains locked, it is possible to scramble inside where part of the wall has fallen away. Down by the river, near to the small plank bridge, is the grave of Gohar Aman. It is a simple Muslim shrine, surrounded by a low, jagged tooth wall.

Another place of interest close to Yasin is what is referred to as **Hayward's Rock**. Perhaps sensing that he was in some danger, Hayward carved his initials, 'GWH', the figure '20' (the distance in miles to Darkot), and an arrow pointing in the direction he intended to travel. The rock is about 1 km from Yasin, on the Nazbar Rd, and the chowkidar at the *Inspection Bungalow* can show you where it is.

● **Accommodation** Set in a large garden, the well furnished **E** *NAPWD Inspection Bungalow* has 1 single and 1 double, both joining a communal dining rm, and private bathrooms. There is also a 3-rm VIP block. The chowkidar can fix meals but they are very basic. Best to bring your own food.

● **Transport Bus:** *NATCO* run a bus from Gilgit to Noh, 3 km S of Yasin (Rs 56, 7 hrs), each day at 0900 from their yard on Punial Rd (not from the main *NATCO* yard). The bus returns to Gilgit from the bridge at Noh at 0700. Very crowded cargo jeeps leave early most mornings from Punial Rd in Gilgit, and, on the return leg, from nr to the *Insp Bungalow* in Yasin.

Travelling N from Yasin, the new concrete bridge across the river is unfinished. The central spans are in place, but the approaches are unbuilt. Small Yasini school children seem able to scramble up the wire netting with ease; large-footed Westerners will probably find it safer to continue 200m downriver, and cross by the old wooden plank bridge.

The first village N of Yasin is the sprawling settlement of **Thaous** (various spellings). The valley here is wide, flat and well irrigated, providing extensive wheat and maize cultivation. Beyond Thaous, the terrain becomes barren and stony. The only greenery is provided by the settlement of Sandhi, across the river.

The small village of **Muduri**, above Sandhi, has been identified with the site of the Dogra massacres that Hayward wrote about. Visiting the scene 7 years after the massacre, Hayward noted "I have myself counted 147 still entire skulls, nearly all of those women and children. The ground is literally white with bleached human bones and the remains of not less than 400 human beings are now lying on the hill" (Keay 1979). The *nala* above Sandhi runs E across the **Asambar Pass** (4,432m) to the **Ishkoman Valley**.

The river bed N of Thaous is wide and stony, with water running through only one or two main channels. The flow of the river is augmented by that of the Thui River, that joins the main river some 12 km N of Yasin at **Barkulti**. The **Thui Valley** provides a popular and spectacular trekking route across the **Thui Pass** (4,499m) to the Yarkhun Valley in Chitral District.

Beyond the large agricultural settlement of Barkulti, it is a further 6 hrs' walk to **Darkot**. Public transport is very irregular.

Darkot

Infamous as the scene of Hayward's murder, the small village of Darkot stands at the head of the narrow gorge that leads to the Darkot Pass. It was this pass that Hayward was about to cross when he was murdered. Ostensibly on his way to the Pamirs and the source of the Oxus, possibly to 'bag' them for the British, it was no coincidence that the information that Hayward would bring back would be vital in assessing the feasibility of a Russian invasion of India through these unmapped passes.

Many accounts have been written of the circumstances of Hayward's death, the most fanciful of which was a cheesy poem by Sir Henry Newbolt that somehow found its way into the official report of the Gilgit Mission of 1885-6, headed by Col Lockhart. This tells how, upon his capture and facing certain death, he asks to be allowed to ascend a mound and gaze upon the rising sun one final time. An alleged eye-witness to the murder paints a scene that would appeal to such Victorian romanticism, describing Hayward as he walked up the mound:

"as tall against the morning sky, with the rising sun lighting up his fair hair as a glory; he was beautiful to look at." Hayward is then said to have returned, said "I am ready", and was then killed.

Subsequent investigations by Drew, who recovered the body and buried it at Gilgit, and later by Schomberg, suggest that Hayward was seized during a meal, and along with his servants, was bound and dragged to the mouth of a small nullah where all were killed. The actual scene of the murder is at the base of a cliff, where a small nullah joins the main Nia Bar. It is a sort of natural arena, although the large boulder that stood over the scene has been washed away. If you ask at the shop of the one-armed man (honest!) on the path towards the Ishkoman Valley, he will show you the site.

● **Accommodation** There is a basic **E** *Resthouse* in Darkot, although it does not see many visitors.

The approach to the **Darkot Pass** (4,744m) from the S side is particularly steep. Having crossed the pass into the Chapsuran Valley, you are now in a restricted area for which a permit is necessary (although there is no check-post).

Gupis to Shandur Pass

The districts between Gupis and the Shandur Pass are referred to as **Ghizr** (sometimes Ghizer) and **Kuh**. Up until Phandur, the majority of the population of the main valley speak Shina, and beyond Phandur it is Khowar that prevails. Between Gupis and Phandur, there are numerous rock carvings, many on boulders that can be easily viewed from the road. Dani (1991 'History of the Northern Areas') suggests that these art forms illustrate the lives of pastoral nomads who may have moved here in early Christian times, and show great continuity with similar designs found in the Pamir region. Many show mounted horsemen, solar motifs, hunting scenes, and long horned ibexes.

About 5 km W beyond Gupis is the large, natural **Khalti Lake** that has remained since a major flood about 8 years ago. It makes a great place to camp. A small hotel is under construction nearby.

Beyond Gupis, the river is referred to as the **Ghizr River**, and at **Dahimal** (22 km) it is joined from the S by the emerald green **Bathraiz River** flowing from Swat Kohistan. The Bathraiz Valley leads S towards the Tangir Valley, although you should not attempt to follow this route. This was one route that the early Buddhist pilgrims used on their journeys from China to Gandhara, Swat and other pilgrimage sites in S Asia, as well as the means of access for invading armies from Chitral and the kingdoms to the N.

As the jeep track continues W, look out for the numerous petroglyphs on the rocks just past the village of **Pingul**. Sure enough, Schomberg has an anecdote with which to disparage the people of Pingul. Upon asking the villagers why they live in such run-down houses, bearing in mind that heavy snowfall forces them indoors for long periods of the winter, they are alleged to have replied: "We are too lazy. We like comfort and hate exertion, so are content to live in these houses. They are bad and miserable but we cannot be bothered to build better ones"!

At **Chashi**, the valley widens greatly, and the main river is augmented by tributaries from both the N and S, the latter of which provide access to Tangir and Darel Valleys. When Schomberg saw the small houses at Chashi, with their open skylights in their roof, "the temptation to lob stones into some of them was hard to resist"!

Beyond Chashi is **Phandur** (36 km from Dahimal), where the jeep track crosses to the N side of the river, as it passes through some of the loveliest scenery in the whole of Pakistan. At the top of a hill created by the terminal moraine of a long since receded glacier, there is a superbly located *NAPWD Inspection Bungalow* and the **F** *Viewspoint*

Hotel. PTDC are constructing a hotel at Phandur. The view down to the deep blue **Phandur Lake** is magnificent, with the Ghizr River meandering through the green, and highly cultivated flood plain. The lake, situated at an altitude of about 2,800m, is said to be well stocked with trout.

A little to the W of Phandur, a side valley leads S to **Handrap Lake**, also renowned for its trout fishing. It is possible to trek S from here across the **Dadarili Pass** into Swat.

The jeep track continues through **Teru** (22 km) at 3,065m, (*NAPWD Inspection Bungalow*), and **Barsat**, the final settlement in the district, before entering a beautiful glen. The camping here at **Langar** is superb, with fresh springs, a trout stocked river, and a lush green meadow set in a natural amphitheatre of snow capped peaks.

Shandur Pass to Chitral

The track then begins to climb up to the **Shandur Pass** (28 km from Teru). The pass is not particularly high at 3,734m,

and is generally described more as a plateau, with two large lakes lying on it. The polo ground is said to be the highest in the world, and is venue for the celebrated annual Gilgit vs Chitral match. At the centre of the pass, the Northern Areas give way to the **North West Frontier Province**.

The most famous crossing of the pass was perhaps that by Col James Kelly in 1895, at the head of an expeditionary force sent to relieve the British forces besieged in the fort at Chitral. Crossing in Apr, and faced by shoulder deep snow, the decision to bring artillery pieces looked as if it would doom the entire expedition, although they were to prove crucial later as the force battled towards their goal. Inspired by their commander, Lt Cosmo Stewart, the native regiment dismantled the guns and carried them through the snow. As one British officer pointed out: "Nothing can be said too highly in praise of this splendid achievement. Here were some 250 men, Hindus and Mussulmans, who, working shoulder to shoulder, had

---

SHANDUR PASS POLO

In recent years, the 3,735m Shandur Pass has become the annual venue for the most spectacular polo event in the world, although the first ever tournament was held here as far back as 1936. Each year, the teams of Gilgit and Chitral compete as the highlight of a 3-day festival when Shandur Top becomes a huge tent city. In addition to the polo, there are golf and fishing tournaments, cultural shows, as well as the opportunity for the elite of Pakistan to 'be seen'. When it comes to the polo, forget Prince Charles and Windsor Great Park, this is how the game was meant to be played. It's fast, exciting and dangerous.

On the downside, the organisation of the festival is invariably a monumental cock-up. For years the Tourism Department have been trying to fix an annual date for the event, but their attempts are frequently scuppered by the politicians who change the dates at short notice to fit in with their own plans. In 1995 the dates were rearranged with just one month's notice, and the final was played on the first day of the festival because that was the only day that the President of Pakistan could make it. The 500 jeep traffic jam that develops as everyone leaves at the end of the festival isn't much fun either.

Accommodation, food and transport can be arranged in Gilgit just before the festival begins. Shop around for the best deal. Alternatively, bring your own equipment.

brought two mountain guns, with their carriages and supplies of ammunition, across some 20 miles of deep soft snow, across a pass 12,300 ft high, at the beginning of Apr, the worst time of the year".

In 1990, another Cosmo – a young British man called Cosmo Lush – also made an Apr crossing of the Shandur Pass. Battling through chest deep snow, and travelling during the freezing night to make walking on the snow easier, he was on his way to Mastuj to meet his girlfriend. Conditions were so bad, that it wasn't until mid morning that his water-bottle thawed sufficiently to provide a drink. After taking the best part of a week to walk from Gupis across the Shandur Pass, and not having seen another sole, he arrived in Mastuj. His girlfriend never showed up!

The first village in NWFP, as you descend from the Shandur Pass, is **Sor Laspur**, starting point for a trek across the **Kachikani Pass** (4,766m) into Upper Swat. There is a basic **F** hotel in Sor Laspur. It is a further 22 km from here to **Mastuj**.

BALTISTAN

Baltistan lies right at the heart of the Karakoram mountains, and possesses a landscape that is as spectacular and exhilerating as it is forbidding, inhospitable and isolated. Apart from the weather-dependent flights, the region's only link with the rest of Pakistan is via the 764 km of tortuous road from Skardu to the KKH and on to Islamabad.

Baltistan's main attractions are the opportunities it offers for climbing and trekking. Skardu, the regional capital, is the starting point for expeditions up to **K2**, the second highest mountain in the world at 8,611m, and three other 8,000m peaks in the immediate vicinity; **Gasherbrum I** (8,068m, also known as Hidden Peak), **Broad Peak** (8060m) and **Gasherbrum II** (8,035m). There are dozens of 7,000m peaks and literally hundreds of 6,000m ones, the majority of them unnamed. For the trekker there are numerous options, from easy day-hikes to demanding high-altitude treks.

But the region also has much to offer the non-trekker. Some of the most beautiful areas are easily accessible by jeep (you can even view the mountains from the comfort of a Boeing 737 on a roundtrip 'air safari' with PIA from Islamabad). There is excellent fishing in many of the rivers. There is a wealth of history and culture stretching back to Buddhist times and earlier, much of it still in evidence in the local architecture, language and traditions of the people. Or if all you want is to indulge yourself, to relax and enjoy the views and scenery, then Baltistan is the place to do it. *Best time to visit*: is from mid-May to mid-Oct; the trekking season lasts from early Jun to late Sep.

Geography

To the N, the **Karakoram** mountains dominate the region, a huge tangle of rock and ice with 12 of the 30 highest recorded peaks in the world. At its core is the **Baltoro** glacier (1,200 sq km) and four peaks exceeding 8,000m, including K2. To the S is the **Deosai** plain, an enormous expanse of high plateaux, all above 4,000m. Flowing through the middle of Baltistan and dividing these two main features is the **Indus** River. Entering the region from the S across the ceasefire line with India, it then trends NW, at one point spreading out over a wide glacial plain around Skardu, before raging through a narrow gorge till it loops sharply S to emerge near its confluence with the Gilgit River. Joining it from the E is the **Shyok** River, while near Skardu the **Shigar** River flows in from the N. Although lesser in terms of size, the latter two are of crucial important in terms of the opportunities for settlement which they afford.

History

Pre-history

Very little is known about the early history of Baltistan, although as elsewhere in the Northern Areas, evidence of early hunter-gatherers is to be found in the rock carvings of the region. The earliest rock carvings in Baltistan, depicting hunting scenes and animals such as Ibex and Markhor, probably date from around the 2nd century BC. Later carvings depict the grazing of livestock, followed by simple symbols and later by stupas and Buddha figures.

Early history

Buddhism first emerged in Baltistan during the Kushan period, around the 3rd or 4th century AD. Around the 5th and 6th centuries AD, White Huns are known to have reached into Baltistan. Later, in the 8th century AD, the Tibetans invaded, leaving numerous carvings and establishing Buddhism as the main religion once again. The first references

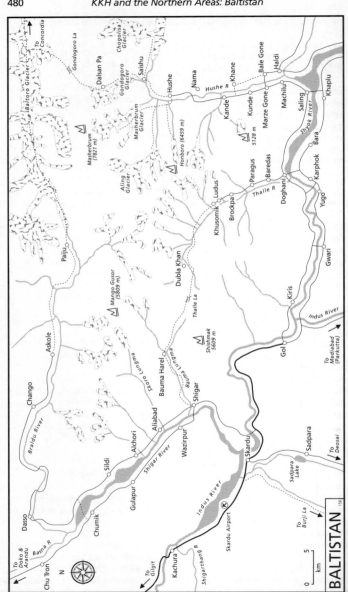

to Baltistan as a distinct region date from around the 5th century when it was known as **Great Bolor** in Arabic literature, or *Po-lu-lo* in Chinese accounts. Internally the region was divided into eight kingdoms, Skardu forming the most important central power, followed by Khapalu, Shigar, and Rondu. Finally there were the lesser kingdoms of Kiris, Parkutta, Tolti and Kharmang, each a 'fortress principality' guarding the approaches to Ladakh along the Indus. Astor, along with the sparsely populated Deosai Plateau, was at times loosely connected with Baltistan.

Makpons

It was not until after the decline of Tibetan power around the beginning of the 10th century that the region established some degree of independence. The most important dynasty to emerge in Baltistan was the Makpon Dynasty, centred on the Indus River around Skardu. Its origins are uncertain. One legend relates how the dynasty was founded by a man named **Ibrahim Shah** somewhere around the 12th-13th century, thought by some to have come from Kashmir, while others hold that he originally came from Egypt. Another tradition identifies the dynasty as having descended from the White Huns. The term 'Makpon' on the other hand translates literally from Tibetan as 'commander of a frontier region' or 'commander in chief', suggesting Tibetan origins

By the start of the 16th century, Baltistan was united as a kingdom under the ruler **Makpon Bokha**, with Skardu as the capital. He was suceeded by **Sher Shah I** (1515-1540), by which time the dynasty was strong enough to repel the invasion of the Central Asian Mughal **Sultan Abu Said Khan** in 1532. The Makpons continued to extend their rule and by the time of **Ali Sher Khan Anchen** (1595-1633), considered the greatest of the Makpon rulers (the *Anchen* was a title added later, meaning

'great'), they exercised control over all the minor kingdoms of Baltistan. Ali Sher Khan waged war with the Ladakhis, at one point invading their capital. He also attacked Gilgit, Chilas and Astor, and even reached as far as Chitral. However, only the valley of Haramosh was annexed, being integrated into Rondu. He brought back many prisoners from his campaigns, putting them to work on numerous building projects.

Close relations were established between the **Mughals** and the Makpon rulers following Akbar's conquest of Kashmir in 1586. According to local legend, a Mughal princess by the name of **Gul Khatoon** was given in marriage to Ali Sher Khan, although historical sources suggest that he married a Ladakhi princess. Whoever his wife was, she was responsible for building the aquaduct which still survives in Skardu, and for laying out a Mughal-style gardens (no longer remaining) fed by the waters of the aquaduct. The strong influence of the Mughals can be seen in the carved marble steps of the Raja's Palace at Skardu. The Raja's Palace at Khaplu also shows Mughal architectural influence. It was during his reign that the dam at Sadpara was built.

Ali Sher Khan's death was followed by a period of feuding which resulted ultimately in the Mughals establishing suzerainty over Baltistan. However, they hardly interfered at all in the internal affairs of the region, to the extent that the semi-independent kingdoms were left to fight amongst themselves. This they did with a vengence, and at one stage the Mughals, fearful of the instability of their northern border, undertook a campaign against Ladakh and Baltistan. Even after this, they appear to have been happy to maintain subsidiarly local authority. The rule of **Shah Morad Khan** in Skardu (1660-1680) was considered to be another golden age, equal to that of Ali Sher Khan's; fortresses and palaces were built, craftsmen brought from Kashmir and trade extended as far as Tibet and Kashgar. Campaigns were also undertaken against the other Balti kingdoms, and on two occasions Morad Khan attacked Gilgit.

The 18th century was marked by invasions, internecine wars between the kingdoms, as well as campaigns against Kashmir and Ladakh. Skardu was captured and plundered by the Afghan **Haji Karim Dad Khan** in 1779, and a year later it was absorbed by the powerful ruler of Shigar, **Azam Khan**, who held it for the next 5 years. At the start of the 19th century there was a long and bitter war between Skardu and Khaplu, in which the former enlisted the help of the Sikh rulers of Kashmir.

Sikhs and Dogras

The Sikhs, who took power in Kashmir in the second half of the 18th century, extended their control also into Ladakh by the start of the 19th century. At this time, **Ahmed Shah** (1800-1840) was the ruler of Skardu. He had already repelled one Sikh attack on Skardu, engaging their troops for long enough to ensure that the majority died in the bitterly cold weather and vicious snowstorms during their subsequent retreat across the Deosai. When the British explorer **GT Vigne** visited Skardu in 1835, Ahmed Shah was convinced that his mission was a diplomatic one and that the British would offer him protection against the Sikhs. However Vigne, officially at least, had no such brief and in 1840 the Raja of Jammu **Gulab Singh**, a Rajput Hindu and member of the Dogra tribe, again attacked, this time taking Skardu and subjugating Baltistan. Following the death of Ranjit Singh, Gulab Singh, who had previously paid tribute to the Sikh rulers of Kashmir (themselves practically independent of Ranjit Singh), was successful in forging close links with the British, even siding with them in the Sikh Wars. For his loyalty he was awarded the whole of Kashmir

and left to his own devices. Although he taxed Baltistan heavily, the indigeneous rulers were allowed to remain in place, watched over only by a *Kardar*, a kind of politcal agent, and a small force of 100 men. In 1842 Ahmed Shah led a rebellion against the Dogras which Gulab Singh quelled, destroying Karpochu fort in the process and thereafter trebling the number of troops in Skardu. Administration of Baltistan however still remained under the various Rajas.

Independence and Partition

At Independence the people of Baltistan followed the lead taken in Gilgit and revolted against their Dogra rulers. While the battle was a swift one in Gilgit (which was able to formally accede to Pakistan in Nov 1947), in Baltistan the Dogra army resisted until 1948 before being finally driven out. It was not until Jan 1949 that a ceasefire was declared between India and Pakistan, with the line of control becoming the de-facto border between the two countries. The line of control divided a geographically and culturally integrated area and severed an important trade route from Kashmir through Baltistan to the Punjab.

Political development

Initially Baltistan was administered as an Agency under a Political Agent. By 1974 this had been converted to a District headed by a Deputy Commissioner and the official status of the various Rajas abolished. Baltistan remains under the direct administration of the federal government through the Ministry of Kashmir Affairs and Northern Areas, although like the rest of the Northern Areas it has never been formally integrated into Pakistan. The region remains a sensitive one; in 1984 hostilities once again flared with India, this time over the Siachen Glacier, where unknown numbers of Pakistani troops are still stationed. Their plight is a sorry one; ill equipped for a war of nerves in sub-zero conditions at altitudes exceeding 6,000m, the majority of casualties

AN ICY ROMANCE

The irrigation water which sustains agriculture in Baltistan comes almost entirely from glacier-melt. For the people of Baltistan, glaciers are therefore fundamental to their survival; the body of folklore which has grown up around these life-giving sources of water is fascinating. Glaciers are believed to be either male or female, their gender influencing the fertility of the land they irrigate, as well as the characteristics of the people who cultivate the fields. Thus male glaciers are believed to produce higher yields and a more virile male population, but less attractive women. Female glaciers meanwhile produce lower yields, less 'manly' men, but particularly beautiful women. Not surprisingly, there is little or no consensus between villages as to the gender of the relevent glaciers.

More importantly however, the people of Baltistan believe that they can induce glaciers to 'mate' and produce offspring, thus creating new sources of irrigation water. First a suitable site for the new glacier is selected. Large chunks from two glaciers, one male and one female, are then carried to the spot. According to tradition, the chunks of glacier must be transported in one go, with the bearers observing strict silence along the way. During winter, snow accumulates around the fledgeling glacier, increasing its size. During summer, it must be carefully tended and a canopy of hay is built and kept continually moist to protect it from the melting rays of the sun. Given the right conditions, the new glacier gains a momentum of its own after around 7 years, thereafter providing a permanent source of irrigation water.

The practice of breeding glaciers appears to be dying out, with no new ones known to have been created in the last 30 years or so. However, according to village elders, there are dozens such glaciers scattered around Baltistan, a testament to the ingenuity and resourcefulness of the people in the face of their harsh, marginal environment.

are the result of hypothermia, frostbite and altitude sickness.

Economy

Agriculture is irrigation based and centred around wheat, barley and millets such as *jowar* and *bajra*. A variety of fruits are grown, including apricots, apples and oranges. Livestock are also of major importance. Yaks and cows, *dzo* (a cross between a Yak and a cow), sheep and goats are all kept in significant numbers, providing important sources of dairy products and meat; the *dzo* are also used for ploughing fields, threshing and as beasts of burden.

The building of the road linking Skardu with the KKH and the initiation of flights from Islamabad have been of major importance to the development of the region. **Tourism** has grown over the years to be-

come of vital importance to the economy of the area. Agriculture meanwhile has continued to decline in importance. This can in part be attributed to the effects of tourism; a porter or guide can earn huge sums of money during the climbing and trekking season, which unfortunately coincides with the harvesting of the spring crop and sowing of the autumn crop. Subsidized imports of food-grains from down country meanwhile have undermined the agricultural economy. However, certain initiatives such as the export of dried apricots have shown remarkable success. New sulpher drying techniques have improved the marketability of the fruit and resulted in a 10-fold increase in their value. Similarly, in a region where forests are scarce, growing trees on a sustainable basis for their timber could prove very profitable.

Religion, culture and society

The majority of people in Baltistan are **Shia** Muslims. According to local legend, the Shia faith was brought to Baltistan by a man named **Amir Kabir Syed Ali Hamadani**, who is said to have arrived in Shigar around 1379 AD. He is said to have come originally from Iran, by way of Kashmir. Nearly 150 years later a second Muslim missionary, **Mir Shamsuddin Iraqi**, arrived in Baltistan around the time of Makpon Bokha and Buddhism finally died out. The **Nurbakshi** faith of the people of Khaplu and Hushe is traditionally attributed to **Hazrat Syed Mohammad Nur Baksh**, the vice-regent of the son of Amir Kabir, who preached between 1438-1448. It is closely linked to the Shia faith, and according to some sources, Nur Baksh was himself a pious Shia whose teachings were in fact later spread in somewhat adapted form by Mir Shamsuddin Iraqi and subsequent missionaries, thus giving rise to the Nurbakshi sect.

The Shia faith as practiced in Baltistan today is very strict, and apart from in Nurbakshi areas, one is very unlikely to see any women at all. However, this is a relatively recent phenomenon. The spread of Islam, which at the time had a strong Sufi element to it, originally involved a synthesis of the Muslim faith with the cultural heritage of the region. Traces of Sufism can still be seen in the old mosques of Shigar and Khaplu for example, which are known as *Khanqahs* or monasteries, and include special cells for meditation and prayer. Traditions of music, dance and folk literature meanwhile remained very much alive in Baltistan until very recently. Dances depicted different aspects of everyday life and the surrounding environment, songs and music were used to mark religious and social festivals, while epics such as the *Gesar* recounted the Buddhist history of the Baltis. Most observers link the transformation with the revolution in Iran which coincided with the politicisation of religion and the emergence of more militant sectarian groups in Pakistan as a whole.

While Baltistan's cultural traditions and the overall status of women have certainly suffered as a result, there have also been certain benefits. Surprisingly, Baltistan has proved particularly open to family planning and there is an increasing eagerness amongst communities to educate their women. The literacy rate in Baltistan was estimated at 13.8% at the time of the 1981 census. This concealed a massive disparity between men and women; 23.8% for men as against just 2.1% for women. A survey of six villages in Baltistan, carried out in 1994 by AKRSP, suggested a significant increase in the overall literacy rate (37.9%), and at least some reduction in the male-female disparity (men 58.3%, women 15.2%). Nevertheless, the strictures of Purdah and the associated absence of women teachers remains a major obstacle to female education.

Gilgit to Skardu

The journey from Gilgit to Skardu takes approximately 7 hrs by public bus. The right side of the bus gives the best views, but is definately not for vertigo sufferers! It is worth taking your own supplies as the food along the way is generally poor. The route is a spectacular one following the narrow gorge of the Indus as it cuts its way through sheer rock mountains. In technical terms the road is in many places even more of an engineering triumph than the KKH; certainly the most difficult sections claimed more lives/km built than any section of the KKH.

From Gilgit, rejoin the KKH and head S for 33 km to the turning E across the Indus at **Alam Bridge**, where the Skardu road leaves the KKH. There are several rock carvings and inscriptions by the turning. After crossing the Indus, the road first bears NW, giving excellent views of the Nanga Parbat massif followed by a glimpse of Rakaposhi, and then bends sharply SE at **Sasli** (27 km, also known as Sassi). There are tea shops and a petrol pump here. At the bend in the river, a steep side valley enters from the N, leading up towards the N face Base Camp of **Haramosh**. From here the road enters a narrow gorge and the Indus roars past.

The gorge begins to widen at **Tuar** (or Thowar). A little further on is **Rondu**, capital of the former kingdom of the same name, perched high up the steep valley side on a flat shelf, across the river. There is an **E** *NAPWD Resthouse* here, bookable through the Administrative Assistant of the Chief Engineer in Skardu. Further E, the road crosses to the S bank of the Indus on a large suspension bridge. The mountains fall back, and the river, released from its narrow gorge, spreads lazily across a wide open plain with rolling sand dunes.

Just W of the bridge the road passes through Kachura village, where there is a signposted turning to **Kachura Lake**, reputed to be good for trout fishing. Orchards surround the lake and there is the luxury *Shangrila Tourist Resort* (see under Excursions from Skardu). From Kachura it is a further 32 km on to Skardu, across the parched and sandy plain. The road first passes **Skardu Airport**, 13 km W of the main town.

Skardu

Skardu's setting is a dramatic one, dominated by the huge rocky outcrop of Karpochu on the banks of the Indus as it flows lazily through a wide open plain. Bare rolling sandunes stretch out to the W; from the S the wide stony course of the Satpara Nullah, an irrigated oasis scattered with trees and fields, fans down from Satpara Lake, while all around an amphitheatre of imposing rock mountains, dry and barren (or capped with snow after rain), hide the vast tangle of high

Karakaram to the N, and the equally vast high plateaux of the Deosai to the S.

In summer Skardu is usually quite hot, with temperatures reaching well above 30°C, and even touching 40°C on occasion. Temperatures however drop considerably if there is cloud or rain. Nights are generally pleasantly cool. During winter it is bitterly cold, with temperatures dropping to as low as -30°C.

Places of interest

The main town itself is dusty and uninteresting, strung out along College Rd, Naya (new) Bazaar, Hameed Garh Rd and Hospital Rd; more a place to set off from and return to than a destination in itself, and indeed this is the starting point for some of the most spectacular trekking and mountaineering that Pakistan has to offer.

Purana (old) Bazaar, which runs in a short arc to the S of Naya Bazaar, gives something of the flavour of the town before the arrival of jeeps and concrete, with its wooden houses and shops selling basic supplies, clothes, shoes and household goods. The large **Polo Ground**, just E of the old aquaduct, is usually deserted though it is a lively social focal point during the summer when occasional polo matches are held. You can climb as far as the remains of the old Dogra Fort on the eastern slopes of **Karpochu** on a good footpath from near the aquaduct. The Dogra fort replaced one built by Ali Sher Khan Anchan in the 17th century, although some date the first fortress here to the time of Makpon Bokha in the early 16th century. The views from here down onto Skardu are excellent. To reach the top you need to start from the western end, near the Sadpara International hotel. It is a long, dry, exposed climb, and very difficult in places (not recommended unless you have at least a rudimentary knowledge of rock climbing), although the views from the top are spectacular. There are further ruined fortificatons here of uncertain origin.

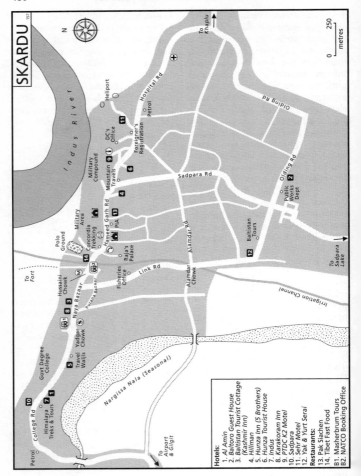

SKARDU

N

0   250
metres

To Khaplu

Indus River

Heliport

Hospital Rd

Petrol

DC's Office

Foreigner's
Registration

Military
Compound

Mountain
Travels

Sadpara Rd

Olding Rd

Public
Works
Dept

Military
Area

Hameed Garh Rd

PIA

Concordia
Trekking

Baltistan
Tours

Polo
Ground

Raja's
Palace

Link Rd

Fisheries
Office

Alamdar Rd

Alamdar
Chowk

To Fort

Hussaini
Chowk

Naya Bazaar

Purana Bazaar

Yadgar
Chowk

Irrigation Channel

To
Sadpara
Lake

Govt Degree
College

Nargissa Nala (Seasonal)

Petrol

College Rd

Himalaya
Treks & Tours

Travel
Waljis

To
Airport
& Gilgit

Hotels:
1. Al Amin
2. Baltoro Guest House
3. Baltistan Tourist Cottage
   (Kashmir Inn)
4. Hillman
5. Hunza Inn (5 Brothers)
6. Hunza Tourist House
7. Indus
8. Karakoram Inn
9. PTDC K2 Motel
10. Sadpara
11. Sehr Motel
12. Yak & Yurt Serai

Restaurants:
13. Pak Siachen
14. Tibet Fast Food

B1. Masherbrum Tours
B2. NATCO Booking Office

Excursions

Sadpara Lake and Buddha

Situated 8 km S of Skardu, Sadpara
Lake is a beautiful, tranquil spot and
well worth a visit. The lake is fed by the
mountain torrent which flows down
from the Deosai plateau to the S, and
dammed on its northern edge. It is a
comfortable walk to the lake, or you can
hire a suzuki/jeep, or try hitching. By
foot the most scenic option is to follow
the aquaduct from the centre of town
before joining Link Rd by Alamdar
Chowk. Continue S along Link Rd and
then either follow the rough track heading S from the corner where Yak and Yurt
Serai is situated, or turn E and then S
again at the next crossroads. A short

detour across Sadpara stream takes you also to the **Sadpara Buddha**, a meditating *Maitreya Buddha* surrounded by *Bodhisattvas* carved into a large boulder, thought to date from around 900 AD. Immediately after leaving Skardu's suburbs, the main Sadpara Rd turns to a jeep track. Below the lake is a hydro-electric power station. By the lake are 2 hotels; **D** *PTDC Sadpara Hut*, book through PTDC in Skardu, reasonable rooms, expensive restaurant, rowing boat for hire; **E** *Lake View Motel*, basic, pleasant garden, restaurant, boat hire. **Fishing permits** can be obtained from the Fisheries Office by the lake or from the office in Skardu. The general consensus seems to be that though the lake is well stocked with trout, some of them very large, they are far too clever to bite on a hook! It is a further 7 km to the picturesque Sadpara village above the lake. The people of Sadpara are Shina speakers, known in Balti as *Brokpas* (literally 'settlers of high places'). They are descended from the prisoners brought back by Ali Sher Khan Anchan following his campaigns against the people of Chilas, Gilgit and Astor. There is a checkpost on the road by the turning to the village marking the start of the Deosai Wilderness Park (see below).

Deosai Plateau

The spectacular high plateau of the Deosai can be visited as a full-day excursion from Skardu if you have your own transport. With an early start, a reasonable day-trip would be to drive up onto the plateau either as far as the river fording, or to the wooden bridge further on. See below for full details about the Deosai.

Shigar Village

The picturesque village of Shigar can also be reached as a day-trip from Skardu with your own transport. It is feasable by public transport, but be sure to check when the last jeep is likely to return to Skardu. See below under Shigar valley for more details.

Kachura Lake

32 km from Skardu on the road to Gilgit, this picturesque lake is best known for the luxury **A/AL** *Shangrila Tourist Resort*, T 2970 (or book in Karachi; I Clifton Centre, Khayaban-e-Iqbal, Clifton, T 571146, F 578052, or Rawalpindi; 143-N Murree Rd, T 73006, F 553075), a complex of red pagoda-roofed cottages, pool, and also a curiosity – a double en-suite room in the converted fuselage of a DC-3 plane. There is also the less extravagant **D** *Tibet* nearby. While the Shangrila extravaganza may be of dubious aesthetic value, the lake itself is very beautiful and there are plenty of interesting short walks in the area. The **Shigarthang Nullah**, which drains into the Indus just E of the lake, is the starting point for treks up onto the Deosai plateau (see Trekking Chapter).

Local information
● Accommodation

C *Hunza Tourist House*, Hameed Garh Rd, opp K2 Motel, T 2515, set back from road, light airy rooms, pleasant garden, restaurant, parking; **C** *K2 Motel*, Hameed Garh Rd, T 2946, F 3322, the traditional focal point for mountaineering and trekking groups, and a good place to get current information or link up with other trekkers/climbers, pleasant garden and excellent views over Indus, restaurant, camping, parking, PTDC Tourist Information Centre; **C** *Pioneer*, Airport Rd, nr Airport (10 km from Skardu), comfortable but arkwardly situated unless you have your own transport, good views, restaurant, parking; **C** *Sehr Motel*, off Hospital Rd, nr Heliport, T 2841, closed during 1995 season – no information available about its future, had good reputation for food and service, excellent views over Indus; **C** *Yak and Yurt Serai*, Link Rd, T 2856 (or book through Karakoram Tours, Islamabad, T 829120), luxury Mongolian style yurts, restaurant, away from centre (erratic public transport), closed during 1995 season due to snow damage during winter; repairs were in progress.

E *Al-Amin*, College Rd, T 2798, hot water, simple rooms, clean and friendly, shared balconies with good views towards Sadpara, restaurant; **E** *Baltoro Guest House (NAPWD)*, hot water, comfortable, good value but away from centre (erratic public transport), book through Administrative Officer, Skardu District

Chief Engineer, T 2788, 2 doors along; E *Indus Motel*, College Rd, T 2608, hot water, best rooms at back with views, clean, restaurant; E *Karakoram Inn*, Chowk Yadgar, T 2449, slightly oppressive interior, hot water, also 4 deluxe rm (D category, comfortable, good value), restaurant; E *Sadpara International*, College Rd, T 2951, hot water, courtyard, reasonable rooms, restaurant, parking at rear, temporary PIA booking office downstairs.

F *Baltistan Tourist Cottage (Kashmir Inn)*, Chowk Yadgar, T 2707, popular though rooms are not up to much, some dorm beds, restaurant; F *Hillman*, Hameed Garh Rd, newly-built, set back from road, simple rooms, pleasant garden (camping), restaurant, parking; F *Hunza Inn (5 Brothers)*, College Rd, T 2570, rooms around pleasant garden/courtyard at rear, some sharing bathroom, good value, rec, basic restaurant.

Camping: as well as the gardens of the *K2 Motel* (certainly the nicest place to camp) and *Hillman Hotel*, the *Pak-Siachen*, next to the new PIA office, has a walled yard behind the restaurant with basic toilet/shower facilities.

● **Places to eat**
Skardu is not exactly a gourmet's paradise. If you are vegetarian, choice is particularly limited. The restaurant at K2 Motel is open to non-guests. When there are 30 or more people staying there is also an evening buffet; book in advance if you are not staying. The restaurants at the *Sehr Motel* and *Yak and Yurt Serai* have good reputations though both were closed during the 1995 season. Most of the other hotels have their own restaurants offering reasonable but uninspiring food. There are several cheap local-style restaurants in Naya Bazaar. *Tibet Fast Food* is rec, particularly for soups, although some travellers question the hygene standards.

● **Banks & money changers**
National Bank of Pakistan, Naya Bazaar, is the only bank in Skardu able to change TCs. Rates are obtained from head office, usually not before 1000-1100, and tend to be a few rupees below those offered in Islamabad/Rawalpindi. They require photocopies of the relevant pages of your passport and of the cheques to be cashed. K2 Motel is able to change dollars cash, or there are plenty of unofficial money changers in Naya Bazaar on the lookout for dollars; don't expect more than a rupee above the bank rate, if that.

● **Hospitals & medical services**
Chemists: there are several chemists opp the hospital, and some in Naya Bazaar.

Hospitals: *The District Headquarters Hospital* is situated E of the main town, beyond K2 Motel, on Hospital Rd.

● **Post & telecommunications**
Area code: 0575.

Telegraph Office: is just E of the aquaduct, on Hameed Garh Rd, open 0600-2300, 7 days.

Post office: is a little further along, down some steps leading off from the main road.

● **Shopping**
There are several souvenir/jewellery/gemstone shops along Naya Bazaar, incl *Topaz Gems*, below Karakoram Inn, T 3196, *Baltistan Gems*, nr Baltistan Tourist Cottage and *Pakiza*, next to National Bank. Hameed Garh Rd and Hospital Rd. Precious and semi-precious stones available incl Ruby, Amethyst, Emerald, Topaz, Garnet, Turquoise, Aquamarine (mined locally around Baltistan), Tourmaline and Lapis Lazuli amongst others. Some of the antique jewellry and other artefacts are quite striking. *Concordia Handicrafts*, Hameed Garh Rd, just E of the aquaduct, has a good selection of post-cards, T-shirts, gifts and handicrafts.

Purana Bazaar is the best place to shop for basic trekking supplies. All staple foods, biscuits etc are readily available, as well as cooking implements (incl pressure cookers) and kerosene stoves. High-energy and freeze-dried foods are more difficult to come by, although left-overs from previous expeditions sometimes find their way into stores; College Rd and Naya Bazaar are the best place to look for these.

● **Sports**
During the summer there are occasional **polo** matches (usually on Thur or Sun) at the large polo ground just E of the aquaduct; check with PTDC for dates. There is good **trout fishing** on many of the rivers in Baltistan. Permits can be obtained from the Office of the Assistant Inspector of Fisheries on Link Rd. Otherwise you are surrounded by thousands of square kilometres of climbing and trekking territory.

● **Tour companies & travel agents**
Baltistan Tours, PO Box 604, Link Rd, Satellite Town, T 2626, F 2108 (Liaison Office, PO Box 1285, Hs 14, St 44, F-6/1, Islamabad, T 220338, F 218620), one of the larger trekking companies, local handlers for *Karakoram Experience* (see under trekking companies in

the Trekking chapter), good, reliable service, but a little expensive; *Concordia Trekking Services*, PO Box 626, T 3440, run by Mr Abbas Kazmi, one time manager of the *Baltistan Tourist Cottage*, a local scholar specialising in Baltistan's pre-Islamic history and culture, wide range of organized/tailor-made treks and jeep safaris; *Himalaya Treks and Tours*, College Rd, T 2528 (Liason Office; 112 Rahim Plaza, Murree Rd, Rawalpindi T/F 563014, mountain-eering/trekking expeditions, jeep safaris, equipment hire available for up to 50 people, good reputation, close links with *American Himalayan Foundation* and *Himalayan Green Club*, 2 organizations working specifically in Baltistan to promote sustainable tourism; *Mountain Travel*, Hameed Garh Rd, T 2750; *Siachen Travels and Tours*, PO Box 622, Hus-saini Chowk, T 2844 (Postal address: PO Box 2014, GPO, Islamabad, T 264213, F 260469), a reliable company with a good reputation and guides such as Rozi Ali Hushe, veteran of numerous mountaineering expeditions with many of the climbing world's great names; *Travel Waljis*, College Rd, T 3468 (Head Of-fice: PO Box 1088, 10 Khayaban-e-Suhrawardy, Islamabad, T 214345, F 210762), Pakistan's largest tour operator, it is probably best to organize treks and tours through their head office in Islamabad.

● **Tourist offices**

PTDC Tourist Information Centre, K2 Motel, T 2946, F 3322, services incl jeep rental – rates in 1995 were as follows: Sadpara Lake (incl visit to Buddha) Rs 300, Deosai Rs 2-3,000, Astor (2 days) Rs 6,000, Katchura Lake Rs 500, Gilgit Rs 3,000, Shigar Rs 600, Dassu Rs 1,200, Askole Rs 3,000, Khaplu Rs 1,600, Hushe Rs 3,000 (**NB** One-way/return rates are the same). PTDC have 2 seats/flight reserved for foreign tourists; they will issue you with a letter to present to PIA. Also able to book seats on NATCO/Masherbrum Tours buses.

● **Useful addresses**

Deputy Commissioner's Office: Hospital Rd, T 2955, apply here also for **Visa Extensions**; if you look set to over-run on your Visa due to flight cancellations/road blockages/illness, he will issue you at least with a letter of explanation to present to the visa extension office in Islamabad.

Foreigners' registration: Superintendent of Police, Hospital Rd, T 2424.

NAPWD: Link Rd; **Administrative Officer**: Skardu District Chief Engineer, T 2788;

Administrative Officer: Ganche District Chief Engineer, T 2406 (for booking NAPWD Res-thouses in Skardu/Ganche Districts respectively).

● **Transport**

Local Suzukis: ply E-W along College Rd, Naya Bazaar, Hameed Garh Rd and Hospital Rd during the day, but stop after dark. There are now a few **Taxis** available for hire in the main bazaar.

Air PIA Booking Office, *Sadpara Interna-tional Hotel*, College Rd, T 2491, open 0800-1400, 7 days. A new office, situated on Hameed Garh Rd, E of the town centre (see map) is scheduled to open early 1996. **NB** All flights, being weather dependent, are effec-tively on a stand-by basis. To confirm your seat, deposit your ticket at the booking office by 1230 on the day before your flight and collect it after 1400 the same day. If the flight is cancelled, you need to repeat the process to reconfirm your seat for the next flight. Passen-gers from cancelled flights are given priority on the next available flight. **NB** With a few days bad weather, a large back-log quickly builds up; leave time to take the bus if you have a tight schedule/onward connections. The air-port is situated 13 km W of Skardu; on arrival there are usually vans or buses ready to pick up passengers, or jeeps/taxis for hire. There is no regular public transport to the airport from town; the safest option is to hire a suzuki or jeep. **Islamabad** 1 flight daily (Boeing 737), 1130, 1 hr (**NB** These flights continue on to Lahore/Karachi); Fri, additional flight (Fokker Friendship F-27 en-route from Gilgit), 0915, 1¼ hrs. **Gilgit** 1 flight weekly (Fokker Friend-ship), Mon, 0825, 30 mins.

Road Bus: there are two bus companies op-erating from Skardu, the government-run Northern Areas Transport Company (NATCO), and the private Masherbrum Tours. **Cargo Jeeps**: are the cheapest way of getting to places not served by public bus. Finding a cargo jeep going to your destination can be difficult, particularly as everyone will try to persuade you to hire a private jeep (a 'special' or 'booking'), but they do run on an irregular basis up the Shigar valley at least as far as Dassu or Chutron, across the Deosai to Astor and E towards Khaplu and up to Hushe. The most regular are to Kachura, Shigar town, Doghani (at the start of the Thalle valley) and Khaplu. Most depart from opposite the NATCO office, where there is also a cargo booking office. **Jeep hire**: is available from NATCO and PTDC (see above). Most of the tour operators and many of the hotels in Skardu can also arrange jeep hire, or you can negotiate directly with drivers in the bazaar. Rates are generally negotiable. Those given for PTDC are fixed, and on the high side. If bargaining, bear in mind factors such as the number of people/amount of luggage. **Masherbrum Tours**: T 2616; **Gilgit**, 4 buses/minibuses daily, dep 0600 (bus), 0700 (minibus), 1000 (minibus), 1200 (minibus), **NB** later minibuses are sometimes cancelled if there are not enough passengers; **Rawalpindi**, 1 bus daily, dep 1600, 22 hrs; **Khaplu**, 1 bus daily, dep 0800, 4 hrs. **NATCO**, Booking Office: T 3313, Station Manager's Office: T 2534; **Gilgit**, 1 bus daily, dep 0600, 7 hrs; **Rawalpindi**, 1 bus (deluxe) daily, dep 1500, 22 hrs; **Khaplu**, 1 bus daily, dep 0700, 4 hrs; **Shigar**, 1 bus daily, dep 1500, 1½ hrs; **Wazirpur/Gulapur** (half way up Shigar valley, W bank), 1 pick-up daily, dep 1300-1400, 2½ hrs. Jeep hire also available.

The Deosai Plateau

Covering an area of over 400 sq km, all of it above 4,000m, the Deosai plateau is stunningly beautiful. In Shina the word translates literally as 'giants abode', and it isn't hard to see how a landscape on such a massive scale could have inspired stories of giants. In Balti, the region is known as *Bhear Sar*, meaning 'place of flowers', an apt description during summer. Closely resembling the Tibetan plateau in its topography and environment, it contrasts sharply with the ring of jagged rocky mountains that surround it on all sides. Gently rolling hills extend into the distance as far as the eye can see, clothed in a soft cladding of vegetation and carpeted with brightly coloured flowers in summer. The plateau's rivers flow past crystal clear and icy cold. There is an unmistakable sense of the elevation in the huge expanse of horizon, the wide open space and the clarity of light and colour typical of such high altitudes.

The Deosai is of enormous significance in hydrological terms, acting as a huge water store. As it gradually melts, the snow that has built up here over the winter accounts for over 5% of the total discharge of the Indus. The data from weather stations monitoring snow-fall on the Deosai are used to predict the peak flow of the Indus later in the year.

Fauna and flora

Frozen beneath a deep blanket of snow for much of the year, the Deosai is surprisingly rich in plants and animals, bursting into life during the brief spring and summer months. The plateau is home to the **Himalayan Brown Bear** (*Ursus arctos Isabellinus*), a species of bear unique to this part of the world, and under serious threat due mostly to illegal hunting. Rough estimates place the total number still surviving in Pakistan at around 30-40, with perhaps 25 inhabiting the Deosai. The remainder are found in the Biafo glacier area and in Khunjerab National Park. Other mammals found on Deosai include the Golden Marmot (in large numbers), Tibetan Wolf, Tibetan Red Fox, Himalayan Ibex, Ladakh Urial and various small rodents, including voles and shrews.

Reptiles include lizards such as the Himalayan Agama, Ground Skink and Glacial Skink. The trout found in rivers lower down are replaced by Snow Carp up on the Deosai. Below 3,000m, in the nullahs leading down off the plateau, the Himalayan Otter feeds on the snow carp. This altitude zone and habitat is also home to some Snow Leopords and Musk Deer, particularly amongst birch and juniper forests. The recently discovered Alpine Toad looks set to qualify as a separate species.

The plateau provides spring and summer breeding grounds for many of Pakistan's birds, including the Himalayan Golden Eagle, Lammergier (bearded vulture), Northern Hobby (a falcon), Kestrel and Long-legged Buzzard, as well as larks, wagtails, warblers and sand plovers. It also lies on the flight path of a number of migratory birds which can be seen in late Sep on their return from Central Asia to the plains

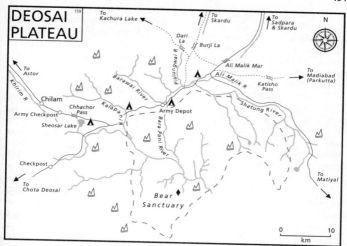

of the subcontinent. Species include the Osprey, Damoselle Crane, Little Turn, Great Black-headed Gull and ducks such as the common Teal, Pintail, Shoveller and Marganzer.

More than 100 species of plants and grasses are found on the Deosai, including colourful flowers such as Aconitum, Rheum, Iris, Astragalus and Spiraea. There is also a wealth of herbs and medicinal plants, including Ginger, Primula, Geranium, Mint, Artmesia, Rubus and Barberry. At lower altitude on the peripheries wild rose is found, as well as trees such as Juniper, Blue Pine, Spruce, Pencil Cedar, White Birch, Himalayan Poplar and Chinese Salix.

Deosai Wilderness Park

In an attempt to provide some sanctuary to the remaining Brown Bears, and to monitor them and learn more about their behaviour and habitat, the Deosai Wilderness Park was established in 1993. The park has a semi-official status and an important part of the management plan involves gaining official recognition and ensuring proper implementation of recommendations for the protection of the Brown Bear and its habitat. One problem is the inflexible nature of existing regulations for National Parks. The Deosai is vital to the livelihoods of many people, providing important pastures for livestock during the spring and summer. The lesson learnt from similar projects in Pakistan, such as the Khunjerab National Park, is that all-or-nothing measures such as the complete banning of grazing are generally unworkable and serve only to alienate local people. The priority for Deosai has been very much to encourage local support and involvement, and to formulate a set of rules that are flexible enough to take account of existing land-use patterns without compromising the integrity of the park area.

There is a checkpost at Sadpara village, and another one near Sherkuli village on the way down from Chhachor Pass to Chilam. The hunting of bears or other wildlife and carrying of firearms is forbidden in the park area (line-fishing is allowed). Vehicles are not allowed off the main jeep tracks. People are asked to camp at the recognized camp-sites, or within 60m of the track. Entry into the 'Bear Sanctuary' area (see map) is restricted and permits must be obtained, either from the District Forestry Officer in Skardu, or from the Conservator of Wildlife in Gilgit.

If you are interested in seeing a Brown Bear, the best way is through the staff of the Wilderness Park, who are properly trained, familiar with the terrain and experienced in tracking the animals (safely). There is a seasonal camp near the sanctuary (Bara Pani), used by the monitoring team, where visitors can stay and be taken for excursions into the sanctuary area. To organize a visit, contact the *Himalayan Wildlife Project*, Centre One, House 1, St 15, Khayaban-e-Iqbal, F-7/2, Islamabad, T (051) 220061, F 216116. Alternatively, it may be possible to arrange a visit by contacting the staff at the checkposts at Sadpara or Sherkuli, depending on who is available at short notice.

The jeep route across Deosai; Skardu to Astor

There is a jeep track from the Sadpara side all the way across the Deosai to Astor (Skardu-Astor 115 km), and down to the KKH at Bunji. Cargo jeeps do make the journey from Skardu as far as Chilam on an irregular basis, and from Chilam there are fairly regular cargo/passenger jeeps to Astor, which is linked by public transport with the KKH and Gilgit. Renting a private jeep is fairly expensive (Skardu to Astor was around Rs 5-6,000 in 1995), but worthwhile, particularly if you can split the cost between several people.

The best time to make the journey is from mid-Jul to late Aug. **NB** The rivers of the Deosai can be impassable in a vehicle when in spate (usually during Jun and early Jul). Take local advice and find out about the current state of the jeep track before setting out. Mosquitoes are

a major problem during the early part of the season and strong repellent or mosquito nets are essential. This is also when the plains are in full flower.

There is very little in the way of food available, so bring all your own supplies. Whether walking or going by jeep, take enough to cover unexpected delays. While the weather can be glorious in daytime during summer, temperatures drop dramatically at night and the weather can turn nasty very quickly. Intense wind-storms often sweep across the plateau. I is essential that you are properly equipped for high altitudes. If you have flown directly up from the plains and are planning a visit to the Deosai, acclimatisation is an important consideration.

From Skardu the jeep track climbs up past Sadpara Lake (see above – Excursions from Skardu) to Sadpara village. There is a **checkpost** on the road by the village marking the start of the Wilderness Park area. There is a spare tent here which is able to sleep up to four people (bring your own bedding), or you can pitch your own tent. The checkpost is recommended as an overnight acclimatisation stop. Above the checkpost where a small nullah joins the main stream, there is an area of cultivated land on the hillside, strewn with several enormous boulders covered in rock inscriptions from pre-historic, Buddhist and Islamic times.

Beyond the checkpost the jeep track climbs steeply up the Sadpara Nullah. After the track crosses to the W bank o the stream, the course of the old jeep track which continued along the E bank can still be seen in places; if the new track feels scary in places, you can comfort yourself with the realisation that it is infinitely less hair-raising than the old one. At the top is **Ali Malik Mar** (4,080m), the pass marking the start of the Deosai proper. The track descends for a short way to a camping site with a seasonal 'hotel', the *Deosai*, consisting of a couple of tiny tents. Tea and basic food can usually be obtained here when it is open. Below there are some shepherds' huts.

After about 30 mins, the jeep track forks; the right fork is the main route to Chilam and Astor, while the left fork heads SE towards Matiyal. The latter route is closed to foreigners. Further on there is a second camping site close to where the Ali Malik Mar and Shatung streams converge. There is another simple seasonal 'hotel' here, the *Deosai Cottage*, consisting of 2 tents for sleeping and a kitchen tent. If you are planning on relying on either of these 'hotels' for food/accommodation, check first that they are up and running. The track next fords the two streams, a tricky process at the best of times, and then continues along the main river to the bridge-crossing at **Bara Pani**. There is an army depot across the bridge. If you continue past the bridge for a short distance without crossing it, you reach the main summer camp of the Wilderness Park staff. There is good camping on either side of the river in the vicinity of the bridge.

After crossing the bridge, the track climbs gently but steadily over a watershed and down to the Kalpani River. There is another camping site situated here. The track crosses the river and after around an hour, forks. The right fork is the Chilam/Astor route, while the left fork leads to the area known as **Chota (small) Deosai**, currently closed to foreigners and guarded by an army checkpost. The main track continues on to the Beautiful **Sheosar lake**, where there is good camping. Immediately after is the **Chhachor pass** (4230m), and then a descent down to Chilam.

Situated near the top of the Khirim valley, **Chilam** is a small village and army post. There is a clinic and primary school, as well as a couple of simple restaurants and shops. It is usually possible to find public transport from here to Astor (see page 457).

Treks There are a number of spectacular but strenuous trekking options on the Deosai, or the above route can be covered from Skardu to Chilam on foot in 5 to 7 days. See the Trekking chapter for more information. **Horses** are also available for hire in Skardu (try at *Karakoram Tours*) and Chilam.

Shigar River Valley

The Shigar River flows into the Indus just N of Skardu. The valley is wide and fertile, carpeted by gently terraced fields of wheat, barley and maize and rich orchards of apricot, mulberry, peach, plum, apple and pear. Once a powerful independent kingdom, this easily accessible valley is the gateway to some of the most spectacular treks in N Pakistan, including the famous Baltoro trek up to Concordia and K2 base camp (see Trekking chapter).

There is daily bus service to Shigar village from Skardu and a daily pick-up service to the villages of Wazirpur and Gulapur, further up the valley on the W bank (see above). Cargo jeeps are fairly frequent, and during the summer season there are often private jeeps returning from dropping trekkers at Askole.

The turning left for Shigar is signposted about 10 km E of Skardu on the road to Khaplu. From the turning onwards the road is unmetalled, though in fairly good condition. The old wooden suspension bridge across the Indus has now been supplemented by a brand new Japanese-built bridge right next to it. After crossing the river, the track runs N across a level plain before climbing over a shoulder of mountain giving excellent views back down onto the Indus and up the Shigar valley. The track then descends to Shigar village (32 km).

History

Shigar was one of the most powerful semi-independent kingdoms after that of the Makpon rulers of Skardu. A local legend traces the ancestry of the ruling family to a man named **Cha Tham** (or Shah

kingdom of Shigar. It appears to have changed little, and today retains much of its charm, with many of the houses still built of wood, with intricately carved doorways and windows. The largely destroyed ruins of the **Raja's Fort** stand on a sharp outcrop of rock overlooking the village. Below it is the former **Raja's Palace**, in the same style as those at Baltit and Altit in Hunza. By the roadside there is an impressive wooden **mosque** with a 3-tiered roof built by Kashmiri craftsmen, the largest of several in the village. Unfortunately, entry is forbidden to non-Muslims. The mosque is generally attributed to the Muslim missionary Mir Shamsuddin Iraqi. Scattered around a low ridge to the SE of the main village are numerous **rock carvings** depicting ibex, Buddhist stupas and other symbols. The ruins of a **Buddhist monastery** have also recently been excavated in the area.

Tham), who was deposed as the ruler of Nagar during the second period of the Trakhan Dynasty in Gilgit. He crossed over to Shigar by way of the Hispar and Biafo glaciers and soon established the *Amacha* Dynasty which continued to rule right up until the Dogra period. It was to Shigar that the Muslim missionaries Amir Kabir Sayed Ali Hamadani and Mir Shamsuddin Iraqi are first said to have come, in the 14th and 16th centuries respectively. Following Sultan Abu Said Khan's invasion of Baltistan in 1532, which brought him by way of the Braldo pass to Shigar, strong links were forged with Yarkand to the N. Later these were replaced by ties with the Mughals of Kashmir. **Imam Quli Khan** (1634-1705) is considered the greatest of Shigar's rulers. He forged close links with the ruler of Skardu, Shah Morad Khan, helping him with his campaigns against Khaplu, Kadakh and Gilgit. It was during the rule of his son **Azam Khan** that Skardu fell under the control of Shigar for a short period.

Shigar Village

This picturesque village, shady and green, was once the capital of the ancient

● **Accommodation** The only hotel in Shigar is the **E** *NAPWD Resthouse*, pleasantly situated by the Bauma stream, 2 rm, clean and comfortable, good value, nice garden (good camping), food on order, book through Administrative Officer, Skardu District Chief Engineer in Skardu, or else try just turning up; the chowkidar seems quite happy to let people stay without a booking, provided there is space (which there usually is). A second hotel, the *Shah Nisar Inn* was under construction in 1995, 4-5 rm planned.

● **Places to eat** There are a few very basic restaurants, incl the *Mohammadi* and *K2* offering simple food, and bedding for the night if you don't mind roughing it on the floor along with whoever else is passing through.

Bauma Lungma

The side valley climbing up to the E from Shigar village is known as Bauma

Lungma (*lungma* meaning 'stream'). A jeep track leads up as far as the hydro-electric plant that provides Shigar with electricity. This is the start (or finish) of the Thalle La trek (see Trekking chapter). It is possible to walk up as far as the settlement at **Ol** (about 2 hrs), or continue on to the bridge across the stream and double back to the settlement of **Anisgal** on the opposite bank.

Basna Valley

A bridge at Shigar crosses the river and a jeep track leads up the W bank, giving access to the Basna valley which branches off to the NW. A NATCO jeep service operates as far as Gulapur, and cargo jeeps run fairly regularly at least as far as Chumik. At **Chu Tron**, 8 km into the Basna valley, there are hot sulpher springs with separate bathing huts for men and women. There is also a *NAPWD Resthouse* adjacent, bookable in Skardu (also worth trying without a booking). The jeep track continues up the valley as far as the beautiful village of **Doko** (20 km). It is a long day's walk (or 2 fairly easy days) to **Arondu**, a tiny village at the snout of the awesome 38 km **Chogo Lungma glacier**. North of the village, the glaciated Kero Lungma valley leads up to the extremely difficult and deeply crevassed Nushik La, and over to the Hispar glacier. The pass was once used as a route connecting Nagar with Baltistan, but is today considered to be impassable by locals.

Road to Askole

The main route up the Shigar valley continues up the E bank, passing through several green and fertile villages along the way. At the confluence of the Basna and Braldu valleys, a series of bridges provide an alternative point of access to the Basna valley, although after heavy rains the crossing is often not possible. **Dasso**, 11 km into the Braldu valley where the jeep track crosses to the N bank, is the first village. This was

originally the starting point for the trek to K2, but the jeep track has now been extended as far as **Askole**. This last section of jeep track is still unstable in places and subject to frequent closures due to landslides. A little way beyond the village of **Chango**, above the jeep track, there are hot sulpher springs suitable for bathing.

East to Khaplu

The road E from Skardu to Khaplu is metalled for the first section as far as Gol. After crossing the Indus it becomes a compacted gravel track, rough in places but generally in good condition. After passing the bridge-turning to Shigar (see above), the road bends SE across a stony plain to **Gol** (30 km). Just before the village several large boulders have weatherbeaten inscriptions in Tibetan and carvings of Buddhist stupas, tridents and other symbols.

A bridge at Gol crosses the Indus giving access to a rough jeep track running along the N bank of the **Shyok River**, parallel to the main route along the S bank. The track along the N bank gives access to Kiris and the Kiris Valley (use this bridge to reach here), the village of Daghoni at the foot of the Thalle valley, and then leads directly into the Hushe valley. With the new bridge at Khaplu, the quickest route into the Hushe valley is now along the S bank. There is a *NAPWD Resthouse* at Kiris (book in Skardu).

A few km beyond Gol the Shyok River drains into the Indus from the E, while the Indus continues SE, passing the villages of **Mediabad** (formerly Parkutta), **Totli** and **Kharmang**, once centres of tiny independent kingdoms, and leading towards the Line of Control (effectively the border) with India. **NB** This route along the Indus is closed to foreigners.

The main route E crosses the Indus on a suspension bridge just S of its confluence with the Shyok River and follows the

S bank of the Shyok. This first stretch of the river was once the home of the tiny kingdom of **Kiris** (the village is on the opposite bank). Beyond was the powerful kingdom of Khapalu, second only to Skardu, guarding the old route to Ladakh.

At **Gwari** there is a bridge across to the N bank of the Shyok. Between the villages of **Yugo** and **Karphok** there is a second bridge giving easy access to the village of **Doghani** at the foot of the Thalle valley. Above Karphok there is a large lake fed by glacier water. Further on, beyond Karphok, there is a bridge under construction, which, when complete, will provide much more direct access to Doghani. For details of the Thalle valley and the trek across to Shigar, see the Trekking chapter.

The main road continues along the S bank of the Shyok, passing through **Bara**, a cluster of villages stretching for several kilometres, before arriving at Khaplu town (2,600m), 103 km from Skardu.

Khaplu

Khaplu is beautifully situated, spread across a wide alluvial fan which slopes steeply down from an amphitheatre of mountains to the S. It is surprisingly green, numerous irrigation channels feeding terraced fields and orchards which abound in apricots, apples and even oranges (harvested late Aug/early Sep), and pleasantly cooler than Skardu in summer. There are numerous walks along tree-lined paths and irrigation channels and good fishing in the calmer bits of the Shyok River. Like the village of Shigar, it is a picturesque place where you can experience something of the flavour of traditional Balti culture. The people belong to the **Nurbakshi** sect of Islam, similar to the Ismailis of Hunza and Chitral in their more progressive outlook on life. They are warm and friendly and the women go about their business freely, without observing purdah. As throughout most of Baltistan

however, years of exposure to mountaineering and trekking expeditions have generated a persistent 'one pen' culture amongst the children.

History

Khaplu formed the third major kingdom of Baltistan. It is interesting in that the ruling dynasty, known as the **Yabgu**, are thought to have come from Central Asia, possibly from Yarkand via the Saltoro pass. The term *Yabgu* is certainly of Turkic origin, being a well known Turkish title. It was during the rule of **Bahram** (1494-1550) that the Muslim missionary Mir Shamsuddin Iraqi is known to have visited Khaplu. According to some sources it is he who was responsible for establishing the Nurbakshi sect. Many folktales talk of the great theological debates which took place at this time. Khaplu was subject to repeated attacks from Skardu, although at a later stage, under the rule of **Hatim Khan** (1650-1715) who was considered the greatest of the Yabgu kings, Khaplu in its turn attacked Skardu. The gates of the Raja's palace in Khaplu are said to have been taken from Skardu at this time. Later, in the early 19th century, Ahmed Shah of Skardu once again attacked Khaplu, installing his own governor, or *Kharpon*. The divisions this caused amongst the people ultimately paved the way for the Dogra invasion of Baltistan.

Places of interest

Raja Mahal Overlooking the village is the Raja Mahal, or Raja's Palace. The palace is thought to be around 400 years old, built by Kashmiri craftsmen for the rulers of the Yabgu Dynasty. It was occupied until recently by three brothers of the old ruling family. Today it is a somewhat delapidated building occupied only by the *chowkidar's* family, but the impressive 4-tiered carved wooden balcony still survives, and there are intricately carved doorways and lattice windows. You can look around inside and climb up onto the roof, although

KHAPLU

Shyok River

← *To Skardu*

To Hushe →

N

NATCO

Hydro Power Station

Playing Field

Khankha Masjid

Polo Ground

Raja Mahal (old palace)

Chakchan Masjid

Sketch Map

Hotels:
1. Ganche Inn
2. K7
3. Khaplu Inn
4. NAPWD Resthouse
5. PTDC Motel (under construction)
6. Siachen

care should be taken as parts of the building would appear to be structurally unsound.

Chakchan Masjid The beautiful carved wooden mosque in the village of Chakchan is worth a visit, although unfortunately non-Muslims are not allowed to enter. The **Khankha Masjid** is in a similar style, and also closed to non-Muslims. It is not actually visible from the road. Behind it is a smaller, older shrine, with a model of the larger mosque inside it.

Hanjore SE of the main village, up on the shoulder of mountain reaching down to the river, is an area of summer pasture with sheperds' huts known as Hanjore. From here there are excellent views of Masherbrum (7,821m) above the Hushe Valley to the N. Further up, towards the glacier above the pasture, there is a lake. To reach Hanjore, follow the old jeep track which branches off by

the polo ground (before the construction of the riverside road, this was the main route across to Surmo, SE of Khaplu. It is a long and fairly strenuous climb.

Local information
● Accommodation
The best place (though overpriced) is the new **C** *K7 Motel*, situated above the main village nr the Raja's Palace (a 30 min walk from the main road) with excellent views out across the valley, 4 rm each with own mini verandah, hot water not yet installed in 1995, restaurant, small garden and pond, camping. In the main village there is the **E** *Khaplu Inn*, some rooms with hot water, clean, friendly and helpful staff, popular, good restaurant, rec; nearby is the **F** *Siachen*, 5 rm, basic but OK; down on the main road, E of the turning up to the village, there is the **E** *NAPWD Resthouse*, comfortable rooms, bookable through the Administrative Officer, Ganche District Chief Engineer, in Skardu; further along is the **F** *Ganche Inn*, 4 rm, basic and not very clean, simple restaurant, small garden (camping), best budget accommodation.

There is also a *PTDC Motel* under construction between the *Ganche Inn* and *NAPWD Resthouse*, scheduled for completion in 1997.

● Transport
Local The NATCO bus to Skardu leaves from the main village between 0900-1000. There is also 1 regular passenger jeep which leaves around this time. There is usually a Hiace minivan which leaves for Skardu around 1630-1700 and if there is sufficient demand, further passenger jeeps leaving around the same time. There are no regular passenger services up to Hushe; cargo jeeps pass through irregularly enroute from Skardu, but are often already full. In 1995 a private 'booking' to Hushe in a jeep cost Rs 800-1,000. Similarly there are no regular services to Doghani/Thalle valley. Cargo jeeps to here are best caught from Skardu, or wait by the bridge crossing between Yugo and Karphok. A private booking is Rs 1,000 or more. **NB** Foreigners are not allowed to proceed SE from Khaplu further than **Surmo**, the second bridge across the Shyok which gives access to Haldi on the E bank of the Hushe River.

Hushe Valley

North of Khaplu, the Hushe valley (pronounced Hooshay) climbs gently up to Hushe village, gaining just 450m in the

30 km. A rough jeep track, difficult in places, reaches as far as Hushe village, leading past spectacular views of snow-capped peaks on all sides, with Masherbrum to the N dominating. As in Khaplu, the people are predominantly Nurbakshi.

Being the only approach route to Masherbrum, as well as numerous other major peaks in the area, the Hushe valley has for a long time attracted mountaineers. With the discovery of the Gondogora La route across to Concordia and the Boltoro glacier, the valley has become of major importance, at least in terms of mountain tourism; trekkers can now make the 10-12 day trek from Askole to Concordia, and then instead of doubling all the way back, climb up over the Gondogoro La (a very strenuous 5,500m with snow traverse and glacier, but with the most awesome views of K2 and surrounding peaks) and down into Hushe valley. Children in the valley can be particularly hard work.

Originally locals would cross the Shyok River from Khaplu on rafts known as *dzaks*, made of inflated goatskins, walking several kilometres upstream before paddling their way furiously across the fast-flowing river. Until very recently this was continued, with inner-tubes replacing the goatskins, but the regular fatalities, particularly when the river was swollen, finally convinced the authorities to build a bridge. The bridge, completed in 1992, crosses the Shyok 4 km E of Khaplu to the village of **Saling**, supplementing the bridge 10 km further upstream at Surmo, which gives access to the track leading up the E bank of the Hushe River to Haldi.

From Saling, the track climbs up into the valley. A bridge is under construction across to Gurtse on the E bank. At the village of **Machilu** there is a *NAPWD Resthouse*, bookable in Skardu. Opposite is the village of **Haldi**, on the banks of the Saltoro River as it enters from the E.

The **Saltoro River Valley** is currently closed to tourists due to the border dispute with India over the Siachen glacier. The valley is particularly stunning in parts with sheer granite pinacles rising to nearly 1,000m above the valley floor. Higher up, the valley divides, the N fork being the **Kondus valley**, while that to the S keeps the name of Saltoro (*giver of life*). Both valleys have the potential for some beautiful trekking and climbing.

The main track up the Hushe valley passes through **Thallis**, to **Marze Gone**, where a bridge crosses to the E bank village of **Bale Gone**. From Bale Gone a jeep track leads S back to Haldi. In 1995 the track N along the E bank was impassable except on foot due to landslides.

The main track continues N, passing the village of **Khane** on the E bank, reached only by a footbridge, before arriving at **Kande**, a reasonable sized village with a small hotel, the **F** *K6 Motel*, with 1 double rm and 1 'dorm' (sleep on the floor) room, restaurant and small shop opp. If you are walking up to Hushe (a long though not too steep haul in 1 day), this is a good place to break the journey. Above Kande, the jeep track continues on for a while before crossing to the E bank on a wooden bridge and climbing the final stretch up to Hushe village

Hushe Village

The village is beautifully located on a small hillock, surrounded by rocky peaks and pinnacles, with Masherbrum to the N dominating, visible from here in all its splendour. The village is steadily gearing itself up to the increased flow of trekkers and climbers, with new camping sites and shops opening each year, and a considerable selection of equipment available for hire. For information on trekking from Hushe, see the Trekking chapter.

● **Accommodation** Hushe's 1 hotel, the basic **F** *Masherbrum Inn*, has 3 double rm, seperate bathroom, kitchen and store room. The oldest running camping site is the

F *Gondogoro*, owned by Ashraf Hussain, a small walled yard with a simple toilet, kitchen/dining room and a store room. The other camping sites offer similar facilities – they are the **F** *Gondogoro La*, (Farhat Ali); **F** *K6-K7*, (Mahmood Hassan); **F** *Leyla Peak*, (Hamza Ali). All are able to provide simple food. Biscuits, snacks etc (often incl foreign chocolate and other goodies) can be found in the small stores. There is also an open campsite (no charge) just beyond the village, down nr the spring, but don't expect any privacy or respite from boisterous, inquisitive and demanding children.

● **Transport Local** If you are willing to wait around in Hushe, cargo jeeps do come up as far as here, and occasionally there are passenger jeeps. It is also often possible to negotiate something with private jeeps heading back down to Khaplu/Skardu, having dropped their group at the roadhead. Otherwise, it's a case of start walking.

Around Hushe

For the non-trekker, there are some very pleasant and easy walks that can be done from Hushe. The walk to **Saisho** is very pretty, passing through lots of greenery with wild roses, willow and birch in abundance. It can be done in around 3-4 hrs one-way, making it possible as a day-trip, though better as an overnighter. There is good camping, and now even a couple of seasonal 'shops' offering some food. There is also a pit latrine and rubbish pit, built by a team from Cambridge University in 1992. Alternatively, you can walk as far as feels comfortable towards Aling or Masherbrum.

LOWER HUNZA AND NAGAR SECTION

With the exception of Chalt, and the Chaprot and Bar Valleys to the W, Hunza occupies all the territories N of the Hunza River, whilst Nagar occupies the land to the S. Although the former is larger, Nagar actually has more cultivable land and can thus support the greater population.

The two states emerged as separate independent kingdoms sometime from the 11th century onwards, and have remained as rivals ever since. Although the exact origins of the Hunzakuts and Nagaris are unknown, it is thought that they come from a separate stock, they follow different branches of Islam, and are very different in their outlooks.

Myth-making in Hunza

Many commentators suggest that Hunza has always been the dominant partner in this often bitter rivalry, but this may just be because Hunza has evolved a powerful mythopeiatic force, promulgating many half-truths and legends. Despite a prolonged history of contact with outsiders, the legend of Hunza's perceived isolation remains. It was through the Hunza Valley that Buddhism first reached China, and by 200 AD a branch of the Silk Road connected the region with Central Asia and China. By the time Islam became established here in the 11th century, Turks, Mongols, Persians, Afghans, Taimunis, Dogras and Chinese had all passed through, as soldiers, pilgrims, traders and adventurers. Inscriptions on the Sacred Rocks of Hunza, near Karimabad, bear testament to 2,000 years of travellers' graffiti. Yet current holiday brochures still advertise the Hunza Valley as being "famed for its isolation". Part of this idealization has been inspired by Hilton's 1933 novel "*Lost Horizons*", whose 'Shangri-la' is supposedly based

on Hunza. Again, some tour companies still advertise Hunza as "a real Shangri-la".

The myth-making process continued into the latter part of this century, with stories of a society free from illness and famed for the longevity of its people. In 1964, Hoffman produced a book titled "*Hunza: 15 Secrets of the World's Healthiest and Longest Living People*". This romanticization of Hunza continues in some quarters today, with another current tourist brochure claiming that the Hunzakuts are "a robust people famed for their ageless long life and good looks. Their secret elixir seems to consist of isolation and a spartan diet".

In reality, this idealization is far from the truth. A WHO report in 1985 estimated that 60% of the population of the Northern Areas suffers from iodine deficiency, resulting in cretinism in as much as 7% of the population. Although somewhat less in Hunza, infant mortality rates in the Northern Areas remain high, and it is only within the last 20 years or so that TB and dysentry have been contained.

Brief history

Both Hunza and Nagar were formerly princely states, each ruled by an unbroken line of *Thums* (kings) for almost 1,000 years. The present ruling families occupied their positions some time during the fourth period of Trakhan rule in Gilgit (1241-1449), and both houses (Ayash in Hunza, Maglot in Nagar) are descended from a pair of brothers. Like many of the other semi independent kingdoms in the Northern Areas, internecine was the usual mechanism of succession. Despite periodic intermarriages between the two houses, a great rivalry, frequently resulting in open hostility, has continued between the two kingdoms, yet as the British found out when they annexed the region

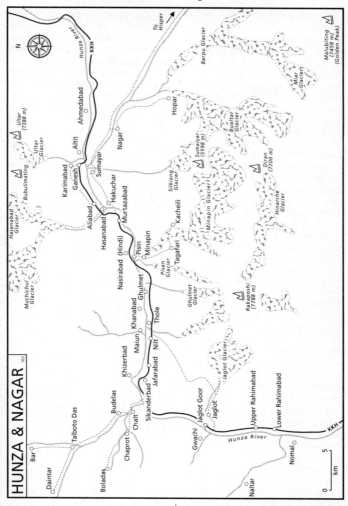

in 1891/92, the two were prepared to unite against a common enemy.

Hunza in particular emerged as a powerful kingdom in the region, establishing relations on equal terms with both China and Kashmir, whilst they, in the words of Durand, "impar-

tially plundered caravans to the N and kidnapped slaves to the S". It was partly this persistent caravan raiding, and partly perceived closening links between Hunza and Russia during the era of the 'Great Game' that precipitated the 1891/92 'Hunza

Campaign'that resulted in the British annexation of the two states.

Hunza and Nagar both retained a semi-autonomous status in British India until Partition, and then became independent princely states within Pakistan. Prime Minister Zulfiqar Ali Bhutto's reforms of 1973 and 1974 eventually abolished the feudal authority of the Mirs, and incorporated the princely states within the Northern Areas of Pakistan, so ending the long standing year hereditary rule of the two families.

The recent construction of the Karakoram Highway has brought great changes, particularly to Hunza, although the implications of this are discussed elsewhere. In recent years, the various development networks of the Aga Khan Foundation (Aga Khan Rural Support Programme, Education Services, Health Services, Cultural Services) have been highly active in the region, being particularly successful in Hunza.

Culture

The origins of the people of Hunza and Nagar are not certain, but it is safe to say that the Hunzakuts are **not** the descendants of Alexander the Great's army, despite their often fair hair and blue/green eyes. The Nagaris are Shia Muslims, whereas the Hunzakuts are almost exclusively Ismaili. Hunza women do not observe purdah and dress colourfully, wearing distinctive embroidered hats draped with light shawls. Although female education in Hunza has come on in leaps and bounds in recent years (with female literacy probably being 10 times as high in Hunza as in Nagar), this still is a very traditional society, and female employment away from the household or fields is still extremely rare.

The ancient folklores which centre around demon and fairy worship still have a deep hold on the people here; neither Buddhism in the past, nor Islam today have really succeeded in eroding such beliefs.

The dominant language of the region is Burashaski (see Northern Areas introduction), although there are some subtle differences in the dialects spoken in the two valleys. Domaki is a minority language spoken in parts of Hunza, with Shina being used in parts of lower Nagar.

Gilgit to Hunza and Nagar

Travelling N to Hunza there are two roads out of Gilgit. Jeeps and Suzukis leave Gilgit by the Jinnah Bridge across the Gilgit River, and then run parallel to the river, before encountering a spectacular suspension bridge across the Hunza River. Vehicles to **Nomal** and **Naltar Valley** continue along the W side of the Hunza River, whilst those travelling to **Hunza** cross a suspension bridge that disappears into a tunnel in the cliff face. The tunnel emerges into the village of **Danyore**.

Larger vehicles travelling N leave Gilgit via Jutial, on the road leading to the KKH. Several km beyond Jutial, the KKH forks right (S) for Islamabad and left (N) for Hunza and China. Travelling N, the KKH crosses the confluence of the Gilgit and Hunza Rivers, and continues along the E bank of the Hunza River. 6 km N of Gilgit is the village of **Danyore**.

Danyore has the **E** *Travel Lodge*, KKH, T (3999) 30, rooms with attached bath, shady garden and quiet location. Camping available. This is the HQ of the Danyore Horse Club (see Gilgit sports info).

Beyond Danyore, the landscape is quite barren on either side of the KKH. Across the river, running like a long scar along the mountainside, you can make out the Old Hunza Rd.

The first real splash of green is the village of *Jutal* (15 km), through which the KKH passes. On the opposite side of the river is the sprawling agricultural lands of the village of **Nomal**, gateway to the **Naltar Valley** (see page 465). There is a footbridge across the river several km N of Jutal village, although the footpath down to the bridge from the KKH is very steep. Several km further along the KKH is a memorial to the 103 Corps of Engineers 'who preferred to make the Karakorams their permanent abode'.

The next village on the KKH is **Ra-himabad** (60 km from Aliabad), situated on either side of a small bridge. The **F** *Hassan Shah Hotel*, in Upper Rahimabad, is often used as a meal stop on N bound buses.

Beyond Rahimabad the canyon wall closes in on the right side, and a 'slide area' begins. At the end of the slide area is a Frontier Constabulary Checkpost where foreigners are required to enter their passport details.

At **Jaglot Goor** (5 km) there are a number of chai and cold drink stalls, incl the *New Krakoram Hotel* (sic) that serves excellent meat and grisle pies. The **F** *New Hunza Hotel* is basically a restaurant, although it is possible to stay on a charpoy here. Jaglot is also a base for one of the many KKH road maintenance crews.

Beyond one of several potential 'slide areas' N of Jaglot Goor, Gilgit District ends and the KKH enters **Hunza and Nagar**. A very small stone high above the KKH to the right bears the inscription 'Here continents collided'; a reference to the 'Kohistan Island Arc' geological phenomenon (see page 445). Ironically, a larger, roadside metal sign bearing the same message has been destroyed by landslides triggered by the very action it described. In fact, when Biddulph visited the area in 1876, himself being an experienced Himalayan explorer, he was moved to say: "I suddenly found myself confronted with a more difficult and dangerous piece of ground than I had ever traversed in a tolerably large experience of Himalayan sport. For nearly half a mile it was necessary to scramble over rocky ledges, sometimes letting oneself down nearly to the water's edge, then ascending 300 or 400

ft above the stream, holding on by corners of rock, working along rocky shelves 3 or 4 ins wide, and round projecting knobs and corners where no 4-footed animal less agile than a wild goat could find a path."

As the KKH leaves Gilgit District and enters **Nagar**, the highway takes a sharp bend to the right, following the Hunza River. To the left, a jeep road drops down to the river and crosses a bridge to the village of **Chalt**.

Chalt and the Chaprot Valley

Despite being the gateway to the beautiful Chaprot and Ghashumaling Valleys, Chalt receives remarkably few visitors. In fact, a report by the Aga Khan Rural Support Programme in 1995 found that less than 50 foreign tourists visit Chalt each year. As such, Chalt and the Chaprot Valley can claim to be the Northern Areas best kept secret, for even Schomberg was moved to say "the Chaprot Valley is lovely, more beautiful than any other in the whole of the Gilgit Agency."

The whole area has a wonderfully rustic feel to it, reflecting the availability of fertile, well irrigated agricultural land. It is partly for this reason that the Chaprot Valley was a source of contention for so long between the rival kingdoms of Gilgit, Hunza and Nagar. Further, the fort at Chalt has strategically controlled the main southern approach to both Hunza and Nagar. As Keay notes: "to both states the control of Chaprot and Chalt represented the difference between being besiegers and besieged" (1979, 'The Gilgit Game'). In 1886 the then Mir of Hunza, Ghazan Khan, was so desperate for the restoration of Chaprot to his control that he begged of Col Lockhart, "Give me Chaprot and my people shall carry you through the Killik snows as if you were women", adding that the forts at Chalt and Chaprot were "as dear to him as the strings which secured his wives' pyjamas" (Keay).

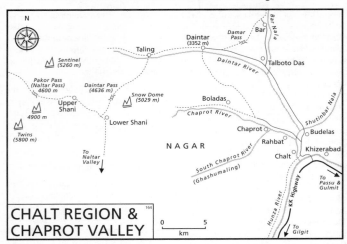

CHALT REGION & CHAPROT VALLEY

0   5
km

Today, the valley belongs to Nagar, and the population are predominantly Shia. Although remarkably friendly, the local people have less experience of dealing with foreign tourists than the people of, say, Hunza, and it is vital that visitors show a sensitivity to local customs, particularly in terms of modest dress. The only accommodation is in Chalt itself, although there is some good camping in the upper reaches of the valleys.

● **Accommodation E** *NAPWD Inspection Bungalow*, set in pleasant garden, has 2 carpeted rooms with attached bath, book in Gilgit (although casual callers may be able to stay if rooms are vacant); **F** *Baltar Cottage*, 2 very basic rm; **F** *Soni Pakosh Inn*, basic, separate bath, restaurant.

The small village of Chaprot in the **Chaprot Valley** is about an hour's walk beyond Chalt. Continuing for a further 4-5 hrs, the track leads to the summer pastures above Boladas, from where there is an excellent but demanding trek across a 4,636m pass into the Naltar Valley. An alternative is to take the path NW just after Chaprot village, and join the trek over the Daintar Pass to Naltar (see page 556).

Another option is to head up the **Budelas** or **Bar Valley** from Chalt (follow the Bar signpost). Several km beyond Budelas there is a hot, sulphurous spring, said to have healing qualities. At Talboto Das the path divides, with the right fork continuing to Bar (18 km from Chalt), and the left fork leading to Daintar – starting point for the strenuous trek across the 4,800m Daintar Pass into Naltar Valley (see page 556).

As the Hunza River and the KKH make a 90° bend, marvellous views of Rakaposhi come into view straight ahead. Although the KKH continues on the Nagar side of the valley, across the river, the first **Hunza** village (Khizerabad) can be seen. Significantly, the rope bridge between **Sikanderabad** on the Nagar side, and **Khizerabad** on the Hunza side, was burnt in mid 1995 during the first Shia-Ismaili clashes.

The KKH passes through the small Nagar village of **Jafarabad** (previously known as Tondas). **E** *NAPWD Inspection Bungalow* and **F** *Jafarabad Tourist Inn*.

Beyond Jafarabad is the small settlement of **Nilt** (1,425m), scene of the

---

BATTLE OF NILT, 1891

Although relatively insignificant amongst the many great battles that the British Army fought during their period of conquest of South Asia, the battle for the fort of Nilt on 1 December 1891 is remembered in British military history as an action in which two Victoria Crosses were won. In fact, such was the bravery on display that one local ruler is reported to have commented "This is the fighting of giants, not of men."

Having crossed the Hunza River, the British expeditionary force was stopped in its tracks by the seemingly impregnable stone fortress at Nilt. With the seven pound guns making no impression on the fort walls, the defenders were able to pick off the British troops at will through the narrow peepholes. In fact, the British commander Col Durand, who refused to take cover by crouching behind a rock, received a bullet in a delicate part of his anatomy that meant he had to do quite a lot of crouching in the future!

With casualties mounting, the order was given to blow the main gate. The special *Times* correspondent EF Knight who witnessed the battle, (and later wrote an excellent, if unintentionally hilarious, account of this period of history in "Where Three Empires Meet"), described what happened next as "one of the most gallant things recorded in Indian warfare." Rushing through a hail of bullets to the gate, Captain Fenton Aylmer, two subalterns and a Pathan orderly laid an explosive charge, lit the fuse and retreated along the wall to await the explosion. Aylmer was hit by a bullet at such short range that the powder charge singed his uniform, and then to make matters worse, the fuse went out. Risking what Knight thought was certain death, the wounded Aylmer returned to the gate, trimmed the fuse and relit it. Whilst doing this, a heavy rock dropped from above by the fort's defenders crushed one of his hands. This time the fuse was good, and with the gates blown, the three British officers and six Gurkhas dashed into the fort. Unfortunately, the rest of the British force did not realise that the walls had been breached, and for many minutes the storming party were isolated. It wasn't until Lt Boisragon, one of the subalterns, dashed back to the breech, thus exposing himself to the fire from both sides, that the British realised their colleagues were inside. Within minutes the reinforcements had stormed the fort and the battle was over. For their gallantry, both Aylmer and Boisragon received the Victoria Cross.

---

pivotal battle in the 1891 Hunza and Nagar Campaign, although next to nothing remains of the famous fort (see box).

The green, fertile lands on the Hunza side of the river belong to the small villages of **Maiun** and **Khanabad**. To the left of the KKH at **Thole** is the small, green domed roof tomb of **Sayyid Shah Wali**, a 16th century preacher from Badakhshan who settled in the area.

At the village of **Ghulmet** (not to be confused with Gulmit in Upper Hunza), several entrepreneurs have set up small cafes and camping grounds to take advantage of the stunning views up the Ghulmet Glacier to the peak of **Rakaposhi** (7,788m). The **F** *Rakaposhi View Point*, for some inexplicable reason, suggests that "sometimes a hot cup of tea is more welcome when it comes with sympathy". It is possible to trek up to the Japanese Base Camp from Ghulmet in a hot, dry 4 hrs (2 hrs return).

At **Pisin**, on the KKH, a jeep track branches right to **Minapin** (4 km); the starting point for the magnificent trek to the base camps of **Rakaposhi** (7,788m) and **Diran** (7,200m), see page 506.

Minapin

There is no reliable public transport from the KKH to Minapin. The best you can probably manage is to be dropped off at Pisin on the KKH, and walk the 4 km from there. If you are carrying a lot of equipment for an expedition, you will probably have to hire a jeep all the way from Gilgit or Karimabad.

● **Accommodation** The new **D** *Diran Guest House*, under construction in 1995, will offer excellent facilities, incl a planned pool. The existing **E** *Diran Guest House* offers excellent value, incl accommodation in a traditional style house set in a very attractive garden, camping also available, the friendly staff can also assist with guides, porters and equipment for the Rakaposhi/Diran base camp trek, rec; **F** *Alpine Camping* has 2 doubles with attached bath, restaurant and camping facilities.

Returning to the KKH, a little beyond Pisin the road crosses the river by way of a Chinese built bridge into **Hunza**. From here, it is 80 km S to Gilgit, and 21 km N to Aliabad.

The first village in Hunza on the KKH is **Hindi**, now known as **Nasirabad** (1,500m). The *Eden Gardens* cold drinks stand offers great views of Rakaposhi and Diran from its flower filled garden. Just beyond Hindi is one of the worst 'slide areas' on this section of the KKH.

The KKH passes through **Murtazabad**, with its **F** *Eagle's Nest Hotel* (not to be confused with the hotel of the same name in Duicar). Beyond the village, a jeep road crosses a rope suspension bridge to **Sumayar** (8 km) on the Nagar side. Here, marginal terraced fields cling to the steep hillside. On the Hunza side of the river, there are magnificent views of the daunting **Ultar Peak** (7,388m).

The KKH swings into the mouth of the Hasanabad Valley, created by the Hasanabad and Hachindar Glaciers. The valley offers some excellent treks. This is one of the most treacherous 'slide areas' on the entire length of the KKH, and consequently a road maintenance depot is permanently located nearby. The recently improved Norwegian Hydel power station provides a regular supply of electricity to the Karimabad/Central Hunza region. The village of Hasanabad(2,010m) is located just below the KKH. Foreigners are required to enter passport details at the Frontier Constabulary Checkpost on the highway.

Just beyond the checkpost, a link road to the left runs the 10 km up to **Karimabad**. The main KKH continues through **Aliabad** (incorrectly signposted as being at 2,500m).

Aliabad

With Karimabad offering better views and a quieter atmosphere, few tourists stop off in what is in effect a typical KKH road-side village (albeit with friendlier people and a nicer atmosphere than those further S in Kohistan). Aliabad does, however, pre-date the building of the KKH, and was the base used by EO Lorimer when researching her 1939 book 'Language Hunting in the Karakoram'.

Significantly, Aliabad was the scene in 1995 of the first sectarian tensions between the Shia and Ismaili communities, as opposed to the regular confrontations between Sunnis and Shias in Gilgit. The Shia community objected to the planned redevelopment of land upon which a disused mosque was standing. In fact, rather than allow the mosque to fall into a state of total disrepair, the Shias wished to rebuild the structure. A further rumour circulating

in 1995 suggested that the Shia community of Nagar wanted the annual Ashura procession (10th day of Muharram, when the martyrdom of Hussain is commemorated) to pass through parts of Hunza. The Ismaili community were opposed to both plans. For the time being the confrontation seems to have subsided, although at its height, a bridge connecting Hunza and Nagar was burnt. Commentators are unsure as to whether this is a dangerous new escalation of sectarianism in the Northern Areas, or a revival of the traditional Hunza-Nagar rivalry.

● **Accommodation D** *Aliabad Rakaposhi Inn*, T (450) 96, large rooms, great views of Rakaposhi; **E** *Village Guest House*, T 16, traditional Hunza style house, sleeps 6, plus 2 doubles; **F** *Dumani, Prince, Shishper, SR* all pretty basic.

Shortly after **Haiderabad** is the **C** *PTDC Hunza Motel*, T 69, until the completion of a number of hotels under construction in Karimabad (due mid 1996), this is probably the most luxurious hotel in Hunza, with large carpeted rooms, restaurant, jeep rental and laundry, group and corporate discounts available, bookings in Islamabad T 819384. Opposite is the **D** *Golden Peak Inn*.

The KKH enters a large S bend around the settlement of **Ganesh**, the only Shia village on the Hunza side of the river. North and S bound NATCO buses drop and pick up passengers by the KKH memorial, next to the **E** *Karakoram Highway Inn*, T (470) 72. (For bus timings see under Karimabad 'Transport' section).

At Ganesh, a recently constructed jeep track ('New Ganesh Rd') runs up to **Karimabad** (2 km). The jeeps waiting at Ganesh to take you up will charge whatever they think they can get away with. On a hot day, it's a steep climb with a back-pack. Half-way up, the right fork leads via the small settlement of

Mominabad to **Altit** (1 ½ km). The road (and bridge) is due for completion in early 1996.

Karimabad

The centre-piece of the Northern Areas' tourism industry, Karimabad is a delightful village set in a wonderful location. Panoramic views around the Hunza and Nagar Valleys incorporate three snow-capped peaks over 7,000m (Rakaposhi 7,788m, Diran 7,200m and Ultar 7,388m), providing a contrast to the colourful natural environment of Karimabad that includes 30,000 fruit trees, 18,000 poplars and 10,000 other trees. The view of the Hunza Valley from Karimabad in autumn is incredible. Karimabad is the base for a number of short walks and excursions, as well as being a popular place with visitors to relax and unwind.

History

The village now known as Karimabad has absorbed the *khun*, or cluster of households around the fort at Baltit, as well as the Khurukushal and Dhirimshal khuns, and has expanded greatly from being just the settlement around the new palace of the *Mir*, (King), that was built in 1923.

The state of Hunza was ruled by the same family for 960 years, with their seat of power being the **Baltit Fort**. Famous for their incessant caravan raiding, and constant wars against the rival state of Nagar, the modern history of the Hunzakuts of Karimabad begins in 1891/92 when the British occupied the fort at Baltit. Hunza became a princely state within British India, and then retained a similar status within Pakistan following Partition. The administrative reforms of Zulfikar Ali Bhutto's government abolished the feudal authority of the Mir in 1973, and incorporated Hunza within the Northern Areas of Pakistan.

The People

More than 95% of the population of Karimabad belong to the Ismaili, with His Highness, Shah Karim al-Husayni Aga Khan IV as their spiritual head. Traditionally there were only two classes in Hunza: the Mir's family and courtiers, and, the agriculturalists. There is no hereditary occupational class structure (except for the Dom -see Mominabad), with the village hierarchy cutting across a segmentary system of clans of different origin, and no obligation to marry within the clan. Unlike the Nagar subdivision to the S, there is no purdah system in Karimabad, and women work alongside the men in the fields. Some may argue that the women do all the work. Local myths and folklore that pre-date Islam- particularly belief in wizards (*bitten*), fairies (*paris*) and the power of the shaman- are an important cultural aspect of Hunza life.

The population according to the 1981 census was 2,947, although a survey taken in 1990 put the population at 4,596, comprising 616 households at an average size of 7.5 members. A standing joke suggests that the average household composition in Karimabad comprises 1 grandparent, a husband and wife, 4 children, a cow, 2 goats, 5 chickens and an anthropologist.

The predominant language in Karimabad is Burushaski, although increasing opportunities in education and government service means that Urdu and English are widely spoken. The people of Karimabad are justifiably proud of their achievements in the field of education, and with 95% of all children attending school, the implications for future literacy rates are encouraging. The Aga Khan Academy for Girls is the showpiece school.

Foreign tourists find the Hunzakuts of Karimabad amongst the most friendly and welcoming people in Pakistan.

Economy

The nature of the terrain has paid a large part in determining the social economy of Karimabad. With annual precipitation below 150 mm, rain fed agriculture is not possible, and thus an intricate network of glacier fed irrigation channels serve the limited agricultural land. Previously a subsistence economy based upon agriculture and pastoral activity, but producing no surplus, evolved. The most pressing social necessity for a household in Karimabad was to be self-sufficient in every way.

The improvement of access to the area, in association with other processes of socio-economic change, has had a major impact upon the economy of Karimabad. Previously self sufficient in food, albeit through a system that entailed frequent winter famines, Karimabad is now dependent upon food imports, particularly cheap subsidized food grains imported from down-country. Conversely, new opportunities have been created for exporting crops, particularly fruit, as cash cropping becomes the major system of agriculture. However, attempts to move production to a higher stage to gain value added, eg processing fruit into jam locally, is compounded by problems of transport costs (jars) and power supply.

Recent socio-economic change

The influence of improved access to the region, education, introduction of the cash economy, consumerism, land reform and social change has led to the end of the self-sufficiency outlook. A new middle class has emerged, and now about 70% of all families have some family member engaged in trade, commerce, tourism related activity, artisanal work, or in government service. Earnings in administrative sectors, service sectors (including tourism) and in trade and commerce are seen as far more lucrative and requiring less physical work than farming, with the result that interest in agriculture has declined. With the population growing so rapidly, and the emergence of an educated class, more and more young men are seeking employment down-country.

Tourism in Karimabad

Tourism has become an important, and highly conspicuous sector of Karimabad's economy. In fact, some visitors would argue that it has become too conspicuous. With Karimabad's scenic beauty being the main attraction drawing tourists, there is the danger that the infrastructure that is being built to cater to these tourists is making the village less attractive, with the long term consequence being that tourists will move elsewhere. However, despite the fact that there have been some real monstrosities built lately, much of this view that Karimabad is "too touristy" or "has been spoilt", is down to the snob mentality of backpacker tourism. Many 'travellers' who claim that Karimabad is "too touristy" have decamped to the nearby village of Altit, presumably to repeat the process there. The ultimate irony is to listen to 40 or so 'travellers' at the Kisar Inn in Altit explaining that they are escaping the tourist ghetto of Karimabad, when in fact all the hotels there are empty.

Little attention appears to be paid to the fact that it is local people, albeit a relatively small elite, who are encouraging the development of tourism infrastructure in Karimabad. Larger and more upmarket hotels are being built because the people want to attract higher spending tourists. Likewise, new link roads are being built to serve the needs of the local community and as such, is a form of development encouraged by local people. Yet many tourists see the development of access as "spoiling" the region. Dichotomous views of the environment is a common phenomenon: host communities rarely see themselves or their everyday environmenta sa 'tourist attraction', whereas for the tourist it is an integral part of the travel experience.

NB Numerous studies have been undertaken into perceptions of tourism amongst the people of Hunza, and Karimabad in particular (including research by both authors of this book). A reoccuring theme amongst local people is the **inappropriate dress** that many visitors wear. Tour groups are the worst offenders, although some backpackers who have remained modestly dressed whilst visiting the rest of Pakistan, suddenly abandon all sense of modesty here. Unfortunately, most Hunzakuts are too polite to register their complaint, but it must be emphasized that the people **are** offended by shorts, singlets, revealing or tight clothes **on both men and women**. Italians in particular please note.

Places of interest

Baltit Fort

Located on a large rocky outcrop at the base of the Ultar Nala, Baltit Fort dominates Karimabad, and the view of the Hunza and Nagar Valleys from the roof is superb. The exact origins of the fort are unclear, although the foundations are thought to be around 600 years old. It was seemingly built as part of a dowry accompanying a Baltistan princess who came to marry the Mir, with the architecture reflecting Baltistan's ancient links with Tibet. It is primarily built of mud plaster, stone and timber beams. The balconies and bow windows were added later, and the fort remained in use as the official residence of the Mir of Hunza until the 1960s.

The fort has been closed to visitors since 1991 in order to complete vital restoration work. However, a grand reopening ceremony and spectacular cultural festival is due to take place in mid 1996. Prior to the commencement of the maintenance work, the fort was in grave danger of collapse. The solid rock upon which it stands is subject to the constant attention of the shifting Ultar Glacier, and the subsequent movement had made the fort highly unstable. The entire structure has been completely repinned, in addition to major cosmetic refurbishment.

Formerly in the possession of the Mir the fort has been donated to the Baltit Heritage Trust- a semi government organization entrusted with the running and maintenance of the building.

Walks around Karimabad

In addition to sitting around admiring the view, you can undertake a number of short walks around Karimabad. More sedate strolls can be taken along the numerous water channels, or down to the neighbouring village of **Altit** (see below). More energetic visitors may wish to visit the summer pastures below the Ultar Glacier

Ultar Glacier

The view from the pastures sited below the imposing Ultar Peak is one of the highlights of a visit to Karimabad. The main Ultar Peak, at 7,388m (and 73rd highest mountain in the world), is one of the lowest unclimbed peaks. It also has a fearsome reputation, and has claimed three Japanese lives in the last few years. Bubulimating, the granite spire to the left, is so sheer that it cannot hold snow. For those camping at the meadow, prepare to have your sleep interupted by the creaking Ultar Glacier, and the sound of distant avalanches.

Although the nala, or canyon, that leads to the Ultar Glacier from just behind Baltit Fort looks quite narrow at the entrance, a strenuous climb of 3-4 hrs along the lateral moraine reveals a wide grassy bowl, surrounded by a spectacular mountain amphitheatre. Shepherds occupy the stone huts during the summer, and are keen to sell chai and fresh dairy products to visitors. It's possible to camp here (at about 3,000m) although if you are too close to the hut and the corals holding the 600 or so sheep and goats, you may wake up the next day scratching.

KARIMABAD 165

To Ultar Glacier

Barber Kool

Baltit Fort (2438 m)

N

Jamat Khana

Aga Khan

Polo Ground

School

Aliabad Rd

To Hotels Hillview & Village, Village Guest House & Aliabad

6

Hunza Antiques

KPSS

Village Jewelers

Karimabad Gems

Original Hunza Jewellery

Hunza Weaving Centre

Antique Shop

15

2

4

9

14

Hunza Gift House

19

To Altit, (1 km)

Concordia Expeditions

3

18

Alam Money Changers

5

11

12

Cemetery

Mir's Palace

Women's Welfare Centre Handicrafts Shop

1

16

17

S

7

13

10

8

To Mominabad & Altit (1km)

Old Ganesh Rd

To Ganesh

To Ganesh

New Ganesh Rd

0   100
metres

Hotels:
1. Baltit Inn
2. Garden Lodge
3. Hill Top
4. Hunza Lodge
5. Karakoram
6. Karim
7. Karimabad
8. Mountain View
9. New Golden Lodge
10. New Hunza Inn
11. New Hunza Tourist
12. New Karakoram (1996 under construction)
13. Old Hunza Inn
14. Park & Shuq Restaurant
15. Rainbow
16. Rakaposhi View
17. Serena Lodge (unbuilt)
18. Tourist Park
19. Ultar Restaurant

It is not essential to take a guide up to Ultar, although if you feel more comfortable taking one, they are not difficult to find in Karimabad. Expect to pay about Rs 300. An early start is advised, and you should carry plenty of water.

A further 4 hrs up the Hons ridge to the left of the shepherd's huts offers even better views, although there is no water on this route, and it should only really be tackled if you are overnighting at the meadow.

Local information
● Accommodation

B *Hunza View*, under construction in 1995, this huge monstrosity on the 'New Ganesh Rd' threatens to dominate the scenery for miles around, boycott this one; **B** *Rakaposhi View*, a one-time project of the Mir of Hunza, this massive hotel has been under construction since at least 1992, currently only the Chinese restaurant is operational, this hotel also threatens to dominate the scene.

C *Baltit Inn*, currently best in the village, carpeted rooms with attached hot bath, good views and restaurant, operated by Tourism Promotion Services (Pakistan) Ltd, who run the *Serena* chain, bookings through Gilgit (0572) 2330, Rawalpindi (051) 592386, Lahore (042) 5761834 and Karachi (021) 5873812, the nearby remains of a half-built hotel have been around for at least the last 10 years, although there are plans to demolish them and built a luxury, but traditional style hotel; **C** *Mountain View*, T (470) 53, used mainly by tour groups, 24-hr hot water, restaurant, some suites.

D *Golden Lodge*, T 94, some rooms with hot bath, other cheaper rooms with cold only, nice terrace barbecue; **D** *Hill Top*, T 10, large rooms, with attached bath, hot water twice a day, restaurant, cultural shows arranged; **D** *Karakoram*, currently has 4 rm with attached bath, restaurant, a new 20 rm hotel that will carry the *Karakoram* name is under construction nearby, and the current premises will reopen with a new name; **D** *Tourist Park*, T 45, large, unattractive extension under construction.

E *Garden Lodge*, T 93, shady garden, camping, restaurant; **E** *Hunza Lodge*, T 61, best value in class, rooms with attached bath, terrace and good views of Rakaposhi. *Moon* restaurant is popular, but food variable.

F *Hunza Inn (Old)* and *Hunza Inn (New)*, one of Karimabad's original hotels, the *Old Hunza Inn* (further up the hill) has very cheap dorms and a big evening Hunza-style dinner, unfortunately, the original owner never registered the name *Hunza Inn*, so when the new hotel was built next door in 1993, its owner 'stole' the name *Hunza Inn* and cashed in on the popularity of Karimabad's longest established hotel, although the newer hotel (lower down the hill) is in better condition, visitors should vote with their feet; **F** *Hill View*, Aliabad Link Rd, friendly, but basic, restaurant with dish TV, garden; **F** *Karim*, T 89, very friendly, 6 rm plus large Hunza-style rooms, great views from the terrace, rec; **F** *Karimabad*, basic, 2 cheaper rm with separate bath; **F** *New Hunza Tourist*, cheap rooms, dorm, restaurant; **F** *Rainbow*, T 49, basic, restaurant with dish TV is popular in the evening with local men; **F** *Village Guest House No 1 (Karim Baig)*, opp *Hill View*, Aliabad Link Rd, T 90, an excellent alternative to hotel accommodation, the *Village Guest House* scheme allows tourists to stay in a traditional Hunza-style house in the heart of the local community, you certainly get an authentic 'village feel', although visitors need to be even more sensitive to local feelings, particularly in terms of dress and behaviour. Main rooms sleeps 6-10 with attached bath, rec; **F** *Village*, Aliabad Link Rd, attached bath, restaurant, but remote.

On the road between Karimabad and the nearby village of Altit, set in a spectacular location, is the **F** *Ideal View Hotel*, currently only camping is available, although there are plans to build some rooms.

● **Places to eat**

Most of the hotels serve food, although the big evening dinner at the *Kisar Inn* at Altit is particularly good. Simple, predominantly vegetarian food is available at the *Shuq Cafe*, *Ultar Restaurant* and *Moon Restaurant*. The *Pak Cafe* is more of a place to sit and watch satellite TV.

● **Banks & money changers**

National Bank of Pakistan changes foreign currency and TCs, at rates slightly inferior to banks down-country (eg Islamabad). **Alam Money Changers**, opp *Hill Top Hotel*, offers the same services.

● **Hospitals & medical services**

Chemists: there is a chemist on the Aliabad Link Rd. Many visitors to Karimabad get stomach problems, and it is not rec that you drink the cloudy, mica filled local water supply. The chemist frequently runs out of the drug *Flagyl*.

Hospital: *Civil Hospital* is just below the village, on the 'Old Ganesh Rd'.

● **Post & telecommunications**

Area code: 470.

Post Office: has moved to a new location on the main bazaar. Gilgit is the nearest place from which to make international calls.

● **Shopping**

There are numerous handicraft shops in Karimabad catering to tourist demands. Unfortunately, the indigenous Karimabad handicraft business is in something of a crisis, with few new students learning traditional craft industries. Thus, many of the handicrafts are imported from other parts of the country.

● **Tour companies & travel agents**

Travel Waljis have their office at the *Tourist Park Hotel*. *Concordia Expeditions* are at the *Hill Top Hotel*. Both offer jeep safaris, guides, trekking, and general tourist info. A return jeep trip to *Hopar*, in Nagar, generally costs Rs 800. A rec local guide is Illias Khan, who can be contacted through *Hunza Lodge*.

● **Transport**

Gilgit: A minibus (Rs 50, 3 hrs) departs at 0500 from outside the *Rainbow Hotel*. It doesn't hang around, so arrive early. The *NATCO* bus from Sust passes through **Ganesh** at about 0800 enroute for Gilgit. If you miss either of these services, unless you hire a vehicle, you may be stuck there for the day.

Services N are more regular, and you may get a minibus or Suzuki if you miss the *NATCO* bus. The *NATCO* bus from Gilgit passes through **Ganesh** at about 1130-1200, calling at **Gulmit** (Rs 15, 1 hr), **Passu** (Rs 20, 1½ hrs), **Sust** (Rs 45, 2½ hrs).

Altit

A 1½ km walk to the E of Karimabad (follow the sign) leads you to the charming village of Altit. A sort of scaled down, quieter version of Karimabad, the village is becoming increasingly popular with visitors as a place to spend time relaxing. There are a number of pleasant walks around the neighbourhood, and a fort dramatically positioned on the cliff, 300m above the Hunza River.

Altit Fort is thought to be about a 100 years older than the one at Baltit, and prior to the annexation of the Gojal, or Upper, part of Hunza, marked the northern most extremity of the state. The fort is approached through an apricot orchard, where the chowkidar usually meets you with the key (Rs 10-entrance). The fort is a intricate maze of rooms connected by small doorways, ladders and trapdoors, built on three levels. The dungeon, said to be the scene of one of the many cases of fratricide that litter the history of the ruling families of Hunza and Nagar, has been sealed off. From the balcony of the modern royal apartments there is a tremendous view down to the cluster of houses of old Altit village. Because the densely packed rooftops are regularly used by women for drying fruit and washing, photography of this very appealing scene is forbidden.

It is possible to climb the 16th century watch-tower, (surmounted by a carved wooden goat complete with ibex horns), for a grand view down the Hunza Valley. A glance down the 300m vertical cliff face to the river below is not recommended for sufferers of vertigo.

● **Accommodation** C *White Apricot Lodge*, T (470) 74, large carpetted rooms, with attached hot bath, restaurant, and rooftop terrace with great views, Concessions available; E *Village Guest House No 1 (Amir Jan)*, T 24, probably the best of Altit's *Village Guest Houses*, Amir Jan offers friendly service in a very quiet setting, room rates negotiable, rec; E *Village Guest House No 3 (Wilayat Ali)*, T 39, run by the village post-master, 2 quiet rm set in well cultivated garden; E *Village Guest House No 4 (Ghulam Murtaza)*, T 23, run by village lumbadar (head-man), has 2 rm and 1 traditional Hunza-style house; F *Kisar Inn*, T 41, Altit's longest established hotel, the *Kisar Inn* is a popular and relaxing 'traveller' hang-out, cheap doubles, dorms and an excellent Rs 50 evening dinner, rec, free pick-up/drop off to Ganesh, the friendly owner, Ali Madad, also runs the *Eagle's Nest Hotel* in the spectacular location of **Duicar**, high above Altit.

● **Transport** A recently constructed jeep road links Altit to the KKH at Ganesh (1 ½ km) via Mominabad. A road also links Altit to Karimabad (1 ½ km). A minibus to **Gilgit** leaves from outside the *Kisar Inn* most mornings at 0830.

Duicar

For some of the finest views in the whole of the Hunza Valley, a climb up to Duicar (pronounced 'Dweecar') is highly recommended. On a clear day, the scenes at sunrise and sunset are unrivalled, particularly late on a summer's afternoon when the rays of the setting sun illuminate the 7,458m Malubiting Peak far to the W. It is easy to see why the local people refer to this mountain as Golden Peak.

Ali Madad, owner of Altit's *Kisar Inn*, has grand plans for the *Eagle's Nest Hotel* that he is building at Duicar. Currently it is just a single room traditional Hunza house, sleeping up to 10, with an attached hot shower. In the future he plans to add further rooms, a camping area, and even a swimming pool. He promises not to build a monstrosity that will dominate the hillside (breakfast, hot meals and cold drinks are available, rec).

Duicar is reached in a stiff 1 ½ hr climb above Altit, although it is possible to hire a jeep up the rough track for about Rs 500. The road up to Duicar begins at Sultanabad, the small settlement halfway between Altit and Karimabad. The local villagers have requested that the government build a proper link road up to Duicar, so in future it may be possible to make the trip by Suzuki.

From Duicar, a pathway to the W provides a good 2 hr walk to **Hosht**, the spectacular ridge high above Baltit Fort.

Another interesting village between Altit and Karimabad is **Mominabad**, a community of 65 or so houses. The occupants of Mominabad are the Dom, or Berichos, the hereditary lower caste members of the Hunza society who occupy the lower professions, such as those of blacksmiths, cobblers and musicians. They have their own language, Domaki, although the higher cast Burushaski speakers refer to this language in a derogatory way as Beriski.

However, linguists studying Domaki fear that this language may be dead within one generation. The elders of the village believe that they will continue to be discriminated against as lower class citizens if they continue to use their own language, and thus the younger generations are being encouraged to use Burushaski, Urdu and English. Many 5 and 6 year olds now have a very narrow Domaki vocabulary. This is an interesting reversal of the normal pattern of a language going out of general usage, where it is the younger generations who make the decision to dispense with the traditional language.

Just after Ganesh, the KKH crosses the Hunza River and a jeep track bears off SE up the Hispar Valley. After 6 km the track forks; the left fork continues up the E bank to Hora, 10 km on, while the right fork crosses the river and follows the W bank up to the fertile villages of Nagar. Formerly a powerful independent kingdom, often locked in conflict with Hunza, Nagar included all the territory on the S side of the Hunza River, as far W as Chalt, as well as the Chaprot and Bar Valleys. Despite being smaller than Hunza, it possessed more fertile land and thus supported a larger population. The region is famous for its apricots, which are dried and exported to the Punjab in considerable quantities and the streams are supposedly rich in gold. Today the people still differ markedly from the Hunzakuts, being darker in complexion and strict Shi'ite Muslims.

In Nagar village there is the **Mir's Residence**, a private compound complete with polo ground, audience pavilion and a carved wooden mosque.

Hopar

15 km further on the jeep track ends at **Hopar**, set in an impressive wide, fertile bowl ringed by high peaks.

● **Accommodation** Competition between the 2 hotel owners in Hopar is so fierce, you may find them literally fighting each other for your custom, or attempting to lure you with the offer of three (as opposed to two) eggs in your omelette! **F** *Hopar Hilton*, several large, 4 bed tents, complete with table and chairs, plus 2 double rm, restaurant; **F** *Hopar Inn*, similar tent accommodation.

Nearby, below a ridge of moraine, is the **Bualtar Glacier** which can be traversed to reach the larger and pristine white **Barpu Glacier**. Paths follow the W edge of the glacier up to high summer pastures at Hamdar and Miar. Clearly visible up ahead is the towering Golden Peak. Another more difficult route crosses to the E side of Barpu Glacier and climbs up to the higher pastures at **Girgindil**, several days walk away. **Warning** This route involves some difficult stretches of glacier walking and a guide is essential.

If on ascending the Hispar Valley you continue along the E bank to Hora, where the jeep track ends, you can trek up to Hispar village (20 km) at the snout of the **Hispar Glacier**. The Hispar joins with the **Biafo Glacier** and leads down into the **Braldu Valley** in Baltistan. This trek is extremely demanding and technical in parts, covering some 115 km, often actually on the glacier.

For further details of walks in Nagar, see the Trekking section, see page 553.

GOJAL (UPPER) HUNZA SECTION

The upper part of Hunza is referred to as Gojal (Guhjal), and is populated by Wakhi speaking communities who settled here several generations ago. Originally nomads from the grazing pastures of the Upper Oxus, they are thought to have arrived through the Irshad Pass which connects the Wakhan, Yarkun, Ishkoman and Chapsuran Valleys, and settled down to sedentary agriculture. They were previously ruled by their own Raja, but later came under the suzerainty of the Mir Of Hunza. The people are almost exclusively Ismaili.

For the tourist, the Gojal Hunza region offers good trekking, and some excellent walks, usually within easy range of the Karakoram Highway.

Just N of Ganesh, the KKH crosses onto the S side of the Hunza River, where there is also a turning for the jeep track to Nagar. Just after the turning, to the left of the KKH, are the **Sacred Rocks of Hunza**, and beyond this is the Chinese built and run brick factory.

The Sacred Rocks of Hunza

Carved onto a number of boulders at a place known locally as 'Haldikish, or Place of Rams', are a series of petroglyphs that date from the 1st century AD right up until modern times. Generally referred to now as the Sacred Rocks of Hunza, a more detailed explanation of the inscriptions on show can be found in Karl Jettmar's '*Rock

Carvings and Inscriptions in the Northern Areas of Pakistan, or AH Dani's '*Human Records on the Karakoram Highway*', both available from Islamabad bookshops.

The KKH recrosses the Hunza River just N of Nazimabad and continues to the police checkpost 2 km before **Gulmit**. Foreigners have to record their passport details.

Gulmit

Former summer residence of the Mir of Hunza, Gulmit (2,370m) is a sleepy village set amongst productive agricultural land, and offers some easy short walks. The main village is centred around the old polo field several minutes walk above the KKH. There is an excellent, if somewhat eccentric **Cultural Museum**,

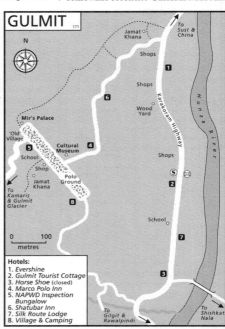

GULMIT 171

To Sust & China

Jamat Khana

Shops

Shops

Wood Yard

Karakoram Highway

Hunza River

Mir's Palace

'Old' Village

Cultural Museum

School

Shop

Jamat Khana

Polo Ground

To Kamaris & Gulmit Glacier

Shops

School

0   100
metres

To Gilgit & Rawalpindi

To Shishkat Nala

Hotels:
1. *Evershine*
2. *Gulmit Tourist Cottage*
3. *Horse Shoe* (closed)
4. *Marco Polo Inn*
5. *NAPWD Inspection Bungalow*
6. *Shatubar Inn*
7. *Silk Route Lodge*
8. *Village & Camping*

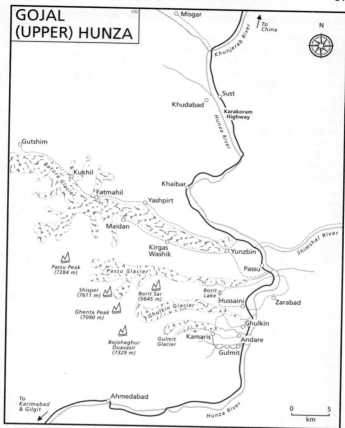

GOJAL (UPPER) HUNZA

170

including the gun that is said to have caused Col Durand to walk in such a funny way (see Battle of Nilt).

Next to the Mir's former palace is the original settlement of Gulmit, a labyrinth of alleyways running between the old stone, mud and wooden houses. There is an 'Old House' museum that is open to visitors (Rs 15), and an even older Shia mosque.

● **Accommodation** C *Marco Polo Inn*, T (461) 7, rooms with attached hot bath, verandah, in attractive flower garden, restaurant, best value in class; C *Shatubar*, T 19, hot bath, restaurant; C *Silk Route*, KKH, T 18, best in village, carpeted rooms, hot bath, room service, restaurant, bookable in Gilgit (T 3956); E *Tourist Cottage*, KKH, some doubles, dorm, restaurant, large extension under construction; E *Village Guest House*, Polo Ground, T 12, best value in village, very quiet and relaxing set in heart of village, camping in shady garden, some cheaper rooms with separate bath, rec; F *Evershine*, KKH, rundown, but cheap rooms and dorms, restaurant with dish TV, there is also a *NAPWD Inspection Bungalow* on the Polo Ground.

Short walks around Gulmit

Gulmit Glacier

It is possible to walk up to the **Gulmit Glacier** above the village as a long day trip, or as an overnight. The track behind Gulmit climbs steeply to the small village of **Kamaris**, from where a footpath continues for some 4 hrs or so to shepherd's huts on the S side of the Gulmit Glacier. On your return, it is possible to take the path leading down to the E of Kamaris, past the insubstantial remains of the 200 year old **Andare Fort**, and back to Gulmit.

Ghulkin, Ghulkin Glacier and Borit Lake

The small village of **Ghulkin** can be reached by either crossing the snout of the Gulmit Glacier, or from a link road off the KKH, 500m N of Gulmit. There is an **E** *Village Guest House* at Ghulkin, and the **E** *Al-Rahim Hotel* at the link road turn off on the KKH. From Ghulkin a footpath crosses the snout of the **Ghulkin Glacier**, before climbing up the lateral moraine. If you are unsure about crossing the glacier, ask for local advice, or hire a small child as an inexpensive guide. A further 2½ hrs' walk brings you to **Borit Lake**, a large brackish glacial lake. There is a basic **F** *Borit Lake Hotel* here. From the lake you can either return to Gulmit (4 hrs), or continue on to Passu (5 hrs- route described in Passu section). To walk from Gulmit, via Borit Lake, to Passu all in 1 day is quite a slog.

Warning Both glaciers are active and highly unstable, especially in summer.

NB From Gulmit it used to be possible to take a pleasant ½-day walk by crossing the bridge below the *Horse Shoe Motel*, walking past the **Shishkat Nala** on the opposite side of the river, before rejoining the KKH at the bridge at Nazimabad. However, in 1995, the path along the E bank of the river had been pretty much swept away. It was a landslide in this area in 1974 that is said to have dammed the Hunza River for several years.

1 km N of Gulmit on the KKH is a jeep road turn off for **Ghulkin**. At the junction is the **E** *Al-Rahim Hotel*. Several km further on, the KKH passes the small village of **Hussaini**, where you can cross the river on one of two spectacular rope bridges (see Passu section).

Passu

The region around Passu (2,543m) offers some of the best walking in the entire Northern Areas, from ½ and full day trips, to short, multi day walks, right up to long, strenuous treks- and all within easy reach of the KKH.

The actual village of Passu is situated to the E of the KKH, on a wide alluvial fan, with houses scattered among the irrigated fields and orchards. Flooding that follows periodic damming of both the Shimshal and Hunza rivers has done irreparable damage to the agricultural system in Passu, and greatly reduced the amount of land available for cultivation.

To the S of the village, the KKH bridges a stream of the **Passu Glacier**, strikingly white in contrast to the dirty grey morainal glaciers common to this region. To the N of Passu is a wide stony plain, once the site of the Chinese KKH construction headquarters, but now slowly being brought under cultivation with technical assistance from the AKRSP. Also to the N of the village is the immense **Batura Glacier**, stretching some 58 km from the Batura Muztagh group of peaks to the W, right down to (and sometimes through) the KKH. Across the river is a huge and ruggedly beautiful multi-pinnacled ridge of crumbling granite spires.

● **Accommodation D** *Passu Inn*, KKH, T (461) 01, some large rooms with attached hot bath, plus much cheaper rooms with cold bath, restaurant; **E** *Shisper View*, KKH, 1 km S, good value doubles with attached bath, dorm, restaurant, rec; **E** *Village Guest House No 1 (A Karim)*, (follow path opp *Passu Inn*),

PASSU
172
Sketch Map

To
Sust &
China

N

Karakoram Highway

2

4   Passu
General
Store
Shop   ○

3

Panorama
Treks & Tours   ○ Jamat
Khana

Aga Khan
School   1

*Path to
Passu Lake
& Yunz Valley*
←

Hotels:
1. *A Karim Village
   Guesthouse*
2. *Batura Inn*
3. *NAPWD Inspection
   Bungalow*
4. *Passu Inn*
5. *Shisper View*

*Path to
Passu Gar,
& Borit Lake*
←

5   To
Karimabad
& Gilgit
→

0   250
metres

Passu Gar

This day trip follows the S side of the Passu Glacier to some shepherd's huts at **Passu Gar**, plus a number of detours enroute. Due to the Sep 1992 rains, the path is not always obvious, so a certain amount of backtracking is inevitable. The path leaves the KKH just to the S of the *Shisper View Hotel*, and continues for about 4-5 hrs steady climb up to the shepherd's huts. There are good views down onto the glacier, and of Passu Peak straight ahead.

A further option is to take the steep path to the left (S) at the foot of the glacier, and drop down to **Borit Lake**. From here you can continue to Ghulkin (see Gulmit section), or take the jeep road back down to the KKH.

Twin suspension bridges

Probably the most popular day hike from Passu, this trip crosses and then recrosses the Hunza River on two dramatic suspension bridges, passing through some delightful Upper Hunza villages, and affording fine views of the Passu Glacier. Frequent comparisons are made whilst crossing the river with a certain series of movies starring Harrison Ford. **NB** This trip is quite hot and dry, so take plenty of water.

South of the *Shisper View Hotel*, at the first hairpin out of Passu, follow the path down from the KKH (it may be marked by some white cairns). Follow the path, and don't be tempted to drop down to the river too early. About ¾ of an hour downstream, you come to the first bridge. Irregular planks and branches, in places up to metre apart, supply the footholds, whilst two rusty metal cables provide a handrail. The bridge sways as you walk across it, even more so on a windy day or if more than one person attempts to cross at a time. Having crossed the river, continue straight ahead across the rocky, alluvial fan, and aim to cross the ravine to your right as

beautifully located in heart of tiny Passu village, dorm in traditional Hunza-style house is excellent value, 1 double with attached hot bath, plus cheaper rooms with separate bath, best value in village, rec; **F** *Batura Inn*, KKH, 1 km N, previously used as accommodation for KKH builders, now showing its age greatly, but cheap and friendly, communal dinner at 2000. There is also a **E** *NAPWD Inspection Bungalow*.

Short walks around Passu

NB Catastrophic heavy rains in Sep 1992 greatly affected the landscape of Northern Pakistan, particularly in the Passu region. As a result, any trekking routes described before this time are now unreliable. Take local advice before attempting even short routes (hotel managers are good sources of information), and check the 'rumour book' in the *Batura Inn* for recent travellers' tips.

high as possible. Near the top, to the left, is the route to Abdegar (see below).

The village of **Zarabad** to the right, is well cultivated, and the people are very friendly. It is particularly photogenic in autumn, when the crops are ripening against the distant white background of the Passu Glacier. Follow the path through the village, and then descend by way of the path and steps cut in the cliff-face to the second bridge. There are two bridges here, although the one furthest downstream is too dangerous to use. Across the river is **Hussaini**, another small village, situated below the KKH. Near to the bridge are some hot springs, with segregated bathing times for men and women. From Hussaini it is about 8 km to Passu along the KKH, although you should be able to hitch-hike quite easily.

Yunz Valley

The 1 day, but hot, dry and strenuous walk through the **Yunz Valley** offers good views of the Passu and Batura glaciers. The route passes behind Skazart, the massive yellow rock that looms over Passu, and takes between 6 and 8 hrs depending upon how many of the 'viewpoints' you make it to. There is a beautifully painted map of the route, complete with cut-aways and highlights, in the 1995 'rumour book' at the *Batura Inn*, although all the text is in Japanese. **NB** This is one of the routes that was affected by the Sep 1992 rains.

Walk S through Passu, beyond the *Passu Inn*, until you reach some stone huts near to the KKH bridge across the Passu Glacier stream. Head up towards the Passu Glacier until you reach the small lake. Walk around the right side of the lake, ignoring the old route along the water channel high to your right (this now ends in a precipitous drop). Follow the cairns (small, route-marking piles of rock), and climb up the steep path into the Yunz Valley (the route is not always obvious). A couple of hours

along the valley is a detour to the right, which leads to a 'viewpoint' above the Hunza Valley. This will add 1½ hrs to your journey. At the N end of the valley, descend the moraine to **Yunz Bin**, and follow the path of the Batura Glacier back down to the KKH.

Abdegar

The walk up to **Abdegar** is one of the most strenuous short trips from Passu, and although the views are rewarding, it is only for the very fit. From the 4,900m ridge across the river from Passu, there are incredible panoramic views back towards the entire Batura Muztagh cluster, including Passu Peak (7,284m), Batura Muztagh itself (7,785m), numerous other 7,000 and 7,500m peaks, plus the Passu and Batura glaciers. For those wanting an idea of the view, there is a panoramic photo of the scene on the reception counter at the *Batura Inn*.

This is really an overnight trip for which you should be fully prepared. Whatever the day time temperature, it will be freezing cold at night so a good sleeping bag and a tent are essential. You may be able to hire these in the shop near to the *Passu Inn*. It is also worth bearing in mind that you will be sleeping some 2,000m higher than you were in Passu, and the dangers of altitude sickness problems are very real. There is water at the camp-site, and at the foot of the hill, but none imbetween. And finally, the route up the scree to the camp-site is not always obvious, and in order to avoid needless, energy sapping backtracking, it may be wise to hire a local guide. Having said all this, the views on a clear day truly are magnificent.

Having crossed the rope bridge to Zarabad, bear left towards Kharamabad village, and then head up to the bottom of the main hill. There is a freshwater spring emerging out of the cliff next to the waterfall pool. Cross the stream, and the path upwards begins 100m downstream of the waterfall. It is a pretty vertical 3½ hrs to the camp-site (6 hrs in total from Passu). The following morning you can climb for a further 3 hrs up to the viewpoint, although if you don't really feel up to it, take some consolation in the fact that the view from the camp-site is 90% as good. It takes 1½ hrs to descend from the ridge to the camp-site, and then 4 hrs back to Passu. Good luck.

The details of the **Batura Glacier** trek, and trips to the **Shimshal Valley** can be found in the Trekking section.

Beyond Passu, the KKH crosses the snout of the Batura Glacier; an ever present threat to the road. A bridge crosses the Hunza River here, and a new jeep track proceeds a short distance up the difficult gorge of the **Shimshal Valley**. This remote valley was at one time used by the Mirs of Hunza as a penal colony, although its primary usage was as a secret route by which the Hunzakuts could raid the Kashmiri and Ladakhi caravans. The area was extensively explored and mapped by the indefatigable Younghusband in 1889.

The KKH continues northwards, passing the small settlements of **Khaibar** (**F** *Khyber Inn*), **Murkhon** (9 km from Sust) with the **D** *Greenland Hotel*, and **Sartez** on the outskirts of Sust (**D** *Hunza Dreamland Hotel*).

Sust

The Pakistani border town of Sust has changed beyond all recognition within the last 2 years. Since the construction of a new Customs and Immigration House 2 km to the N of the original village, a whole new town has sprung up around it. Built entirely to cater for the cross border trade, it is a jumble of hotels, restaurants and shops selling imported/smuggled goods.

Local information
● Accommodation
'Old' Sust: **C** *Khunjerab*, S exit of Sust, T (462) 19, carpeted rooms with attached bath, restaurant; **E** *Tourist Lodge*, T 9, very poor value, miserable pre-fab tin rooms, very hot, but restaurant good.

F There are numerous **F** category hotels in 'Old' Sust, with varying degrees of sleaze, but you may only need to use one if the excellent *Mountain Refuge* is full. The *Mountain Refuge* has cheap dorms and doubles with attached bath, plus some more upmarket carpeted rms with hot showers. This place is the best option in both 'Old' and 'New' Sust. A big communal dinner is served each night at 2000. The owner, Ibriham Baig, can also help with transport arrangements S, and to China.

'New' Sust: **B** *PTDC Motel*, under construction in 1995, will have best facilities in town.

C *North Star*, under construction 1995; **C** *Skybridge Inn*, large carpeted rooms with

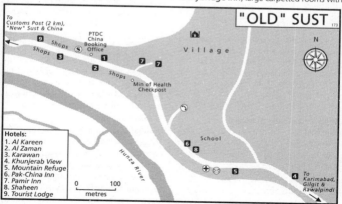

"OLD" SUST

```
To
Customs Post (2 km),
"New" Sust & China
        9  Shops                PTDC
                              China
      Shops 3           (S) Booking
                           Office
              3         2  1          Village        N
                  Shops
                       2
                          7    7
                     o Min of Health
                       Checkpost
                                                     School
                                              6
                                              8
                    Hunza River          +        5      4  To
                                                            Karimabad,
                                                            Gilgit &
                                                            Rawalpindi
Hotels:
1. Al Kareen
2. Al Zaman
3. Karawan
4. Khunjerab View
5. Mountain Refuge
6. Pak-China Inn
7. Pamir Inn
8. Shaheen
9. Tourist Lodge

0        100
   metres
```

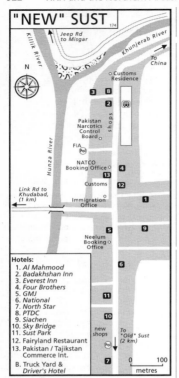

"NEW" SUST

Jeep Rd
to Misgar

Killik River

Khunjerab River

To
China

N

Customs
Residence

shops

Pakistan
Narcotics
Control
Board

FIA
(Pol)

Hunza River

NATCO
Booking Office

Customs

Link Rd to
Khudabad,
(1 km)

Immigration
Office

Neelum
Booking
Office

Hotels:
1. Al Mahmood
2. Badakhshan Inn
3. Everest Inn
4. Four Brothers
5. GMJ
6. National
7. North Star
8. PTDC
9. Siachen
10. Sky Bridge
11. Sust Park
12. Fairyland Restaurant
13. Pakistan / Tajikistan
Commerce Int.
B. Truck Yard &
Driver's Hotel

new
shops

To
"Old" Sust
(2 km)

Pol

0   100
metres

attached hot bath, some cheaper rooms, good restaurant, used by tour groups, *Waljis* have their office here.

E Hotels incl *Al Mahmood*, *Four Brothers*, although the *Badakhshan* is the best of the **E** category, with carpetted rms, attached hot bath, a good restaurant, and plans for a pool.

F Incl: *Everest*, *GMJ*, *National*, *Siachen*, *Sust Park*, but you're much better off walking the 2 km up the road to the *Mountain Refuge*.

● **Banks & money-changers**

National Bank of Pakistan, operating from a shed in 'Old' Sust changes foreign currency, but **not** TCs. When you arrive from China, they are likely to be closed in any case. Some of the hotels nr to the bank will change TCs, but at poor rates. Unofficial money changers around the Customs House will buy or sell excess Rupees and Chinese Yuan, in addition to hard

currencies, although it is worth asking around amongst other travellers as to the proper exchange rate.

● **Transport**

China: The *NATCO* booking office for China is in the Customs House in 'New' Sust. Tickets to the Chinese customs and immigration post at the town of **Tashkurgan** can be bought up to a day in advance. The fare of Rs 740 incl a 'tax' for crossing the Khunjerab Pass. *NATCO* run Chinese built 'big buses', coasters and landcruisers for the same fare, although before you request a seat in the landcruiser, bear in mind that on this journey it holds 10 passengers plus driver! However, sometimes you may get lucky and find that only 3 or 4 of the seats are occupied. The official departure time for all services is at 0900, although sometimes it takes up to 3 hrs to clear customs and immigration. The journey time to Tashkurgan is about 7-8 hrs, quicker in a landcruiser.

PTDC also run coasters to **China** (same fare) for foreigners only, although it is a less regular service. Tickets from *PTDC China Booking Office* in 'Old' Sust.

Gilgit: The S bound *NATCO* bus to **Gilgit** (Rs 70, 6½ hrs), via **Passu** (Rs 25, 1 hr), **Gulmit** (Rs 30, 1½ hrs), **Ganesh** (for **Karimabad** Rs 45, 2½ hrs) leaves from 'Old' Sust at 0500. Tickets bought on board. If you're staying at the *Mountain Refuge*, Ibriham may be able to ensure that the bus stops outside as it passes.

Minibuses and Suzukis: run S later in the day, although there's no fixed schedule. *Nellum Transport* claim to run buses to **Gilgit** from 'New' Sust at 0600 until 1600. If you arrive from China in the late afternoon, if there are enough passengers, you can generally hire a minibus to Karimabad or Gilgit for a reasonable price.

NB Cyclists should note that it is a pretty tough climb up to the pass, although some complain that if the wind is against you, it is even tougher cycling down. Tashkurgan, the next place from Sust at which you can buy any food, is for most cyclists **at least** 2 days away, probably 3.

Day trips to the Khunjerab Pass

Because transport is so unreliable to/from the pass, and buses passing through are invariably full, this trip is only really feasible if you have your own transport (eg bicycle), or if you hire a vehicle (about Rs 800 for a Suzuki that holds up to 8). You have to tell Immigration that you are going, and they generally hold onto your passport until you return. If you are camping the night, bear in mind that it will be very cold, and there is nowhere to get any food. Officially you require a permit, but if you stay away from the Chinese checkpost on the road, you should be okay. **NB** Do not attempt to by-pass the Chinese checkpost, or attempt to enter China.

Crossing the border

Arriving in Pakistan

If you have a visa before arriving at the border post, your crossing will be a much smoother operation. Unfortunately, the immigration post at Sust enjoys a fair deal of autonomy, and rules that apply to visa requirements elsewhere in Pakistan, are at the whim of the immigration official on duty. For example, according to the Pakistan High Commission in London, holders of a British passport do not require a visa for Pakistan if staying for less than 30 days. However, they choose to ignore this rule in Sust, and if you arrive without a visa (whatever your nationality) you will be told that it is a "big problem". However, persistence pays off, and eventually you will be given a piece of paper authorising you to enter and stay for up to 15 days. If you wish to remain longer, you will have to go to Islamabad within the 15 day period, and extend the visa there (see Islamabad section). Women arriving at the border without a visa seem to have to endure more hassle than men. Also, the immigration officers never seem to have, or voluntarily offer, this mysterious Form 'C' (see page 19) that some nationalities seem to require. On the positive side, customs checks for arriving foreigners are usually only cursory and very quick.

Therefore, to conclude, it is possible for most nationals of Western countries to get a 15 day transit visa on arrival, although it will save hassle if you get a visa beforehand. **NB** Currently, you cannot get a Pakistani visa in Kashgar, and the only Pakistani embassy in China is in Beijing.

Leaving Pakistan

It can take several hours for the entire bus to clear Pakistani customs when leaving the country, although Westerners' luggage is rarely checked in any detail. **NB Do not attempt to smuggle illegal drugs into China- the penalties are severe**. Make sure you get an exit stamp from Pakistani Immigration, otherwise you will not be able to enter China (Chinese officials will check for an exit stamp at the various checkposts enroute to Tashkurgan). **NB It is not possible to get a Chinese visa on the border**. Almost all nationalities need a visa for China. The nearest Chinese embassy is in Islamabad. It is not possible to bring private vehicles into China, unless arranged in advance (and this can take months). The Chinese officials are so used to seeing cyclists pedalling this route, they no longer attempt to force them onto buses. However, please note that on the visa application form at the Chinese embassy in London, for example, it specifically states that it is not permitted to take bicycles into China.

KHUNJERAB PASS TO CHINA SECTION

The KKH to China travels N, entering a narrow canyon about 1 km above Sust. Here, the Hunza River is joined from the W by the Chapsuran Valley. This is the gateway (or terminus) of one of the Northern Areas most spectacular trekking routes, running along Pakistan's border with the Afghan Wakhan Corridor, and providing access to Chitral Valley to the W, (as well as the Yasin and Ishkoman Valleys imbetween). For details, see the Trekking chapter.

A further 17 km along the canyon, a jeep road leads off to the W along a side valley to **Misgar** (3,708m). An ancient strand of the Silk Rd trading route used to run N from Misgar, crossing into Chinese territory by way of either the Mintaka Pass (4,709m) or the Killik Pass. These two passes were of great strategic concern to the British who feared a Russian invasion of India in the 19th century, particularly when they received a report in 1874 claiming the Killik Pass to be "remarkably easy of access". However, Lockhart's Mission of 1885 found the pass to be a nightmare, losing two porters through exposure, with all the party suffering from snowblindness, and by 1893 the Pamir Boundary Commission had concluded "we have no reason to fear a Russian advance through the passes" (Keay, 1979). When the KKH was being constructed, the route through the Mintaka Pass was considered, but rejected as lying too close to the Afghan and Soviet borders.

Above the junction of the Chapsuran and Killik valleys, the Hunza River is referred to as the Khunjerab River. The KKH follows this narrow gorge in a NE direction, before turning N at the Khunjerab River's confluence with the Ghujerab. At the Pakistani checkpost of **Dih** (35 km from Sust), exit stamps are examined, and foreigners must make an entry of passport details in the book. The Khunjerab National Park begins at Dih, although it is highly unlikely that you will see any of the endangered Marco Polo sheep that the park is designed to protect. As the road climbs up a series of 12 tight switchback bends, however, it is likely that you will catch a glimpse

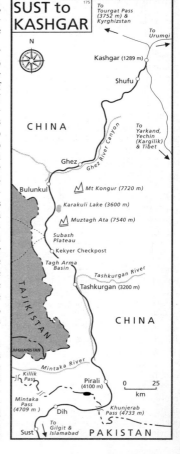

SUST to KASHGAR

175

N

To Tourgat Pass (3752 m) & Kyrghizstan

To Urumqi

Kashgar (1289 m)

Shufu

CHINA

Ghez River Canyon

To Yarkand, Yechin (Kargilik) & Tibet

Ghez

Bulunkul

Mt Kongur (7720 m)

Karakuli Lake (3600 m)

Muztagh Ata (7540 m)

Subash Plateau

Kekyer Checkpost

Tagh Arma Basin

Tashkurgan River

Tashkurgan (3200 m)

CHINA

TAJIKISTAN

AFGHANISTAN

Mintaka River

Killik Pass

Pirali (4100 m)

0   25
km

Mintaka Pass (4709 m)

Dih

Khunjerab Pass (4733 m)

Sust

To Gilgit & Islamabad

PAKISTAN

of some Himalayan marmots.

Having climbed significantly, albeit gently, through the series of hairpin bends, the KKH reaches the **Khunjerab Pass** (86 km from Sust). Although no two sources seem to agree on the exact altitude of the pass (although 4,733m is probably the most accurate of a series of estimates that range from 4,602 up to 4,877m), it is still thought to represent the highest paved-road international border crossing in the world. Also referred to as Khunjerab Top, the pass is a broad, grassy valley, flanked on all side by snowy peaks. How close to the road the snow reaches depends upon the time of year that you cross.

The pass is significant in terms of physical geography in that it marks the continental watershed, (with rivers to the S flowing down towards the Indian Ocean, and rivers to the N flowing into the Tarim basin), as well as a convenient junction between two major mountain chains (the Pamirs and the Karakorams). Further, the physical terrain varies considerably on either side of the pass, with the tight, narrow canyon valleys that have been the main feature of the KKH on the last 650 km of its journey through Pakistan, giving way to wide, grassy high altitude plateau on the Chinese side.

A number of stone markers indicate the international border between the two countries, and it is not unusual for S bound Pakistani traders returning from Kashgar to hop off the bus in order to piss on the Chinese side, before entering Pakistan. The bus drivers make a dramatic swerve here, from left-hand drive Pakistan to right-hand drive China. There is a small Chinese checkpoint where exit stamps from each respective country are checked.

NB On crossing into China, you move into a different time-zone; something that seems to confuse most visitors for the duration of their stay in Xinjiang province. The whole of China runs on

Beijing time, which is 3 hrs ahead of Pakistan time. However, due to daylight-saving (also known as summer time), from May to Sep, Beijing time is 4 hrs ahead of Pakistan time. The problem is further compounded by the fact that Xinjiang works on an unofficial Xinjiang time, sometimes referred to as 'local time'. In summer this is 2 hrs ahead of Pakistan time and 2 hrs behind Beijing time (the rest of the year the differences being 1 hr ahead of Pakistan, and 1 hr behind Beijing). Unfortunately, whenever you are quoted departure times for planes, trains and buses in Xinjiang Province, it is never quite specified which time is being used, unless you ask.

A further 30 km on is **Pirali** (4,100m), the former Chinese immigration and customs post, but now just an exit stamp checkpoint. A jeep road to the W leads off to the Killik Pass. Beyond Pirali the KKH gives the impression of being straight and flat, although at speed it is remarkably bumpy. The scenery on the road is a mixture of green pastureland, being grazed by yaks, dzou (a yak/cow crossbreed), cattle, sheep and goats, followed by long stretches of high altitude sandy desert. Twin-humped Bactrian camels are a common sight, as are the spectacularly dressed nomadic Kyrghiz horsemen. The route is lined to the distant W by the Pamirs.

Several hours beyond Pirali, via the relatively large Kyrghiz settlement of Dabdar, the KKH reaches the Chinese Customs and Immigration House on the outskirts of **Tashkurgan** (120 km from Khunjerab Pass).

Entry/Exit Formalities

Chinese entry and exit formalities are completed at the Immigration and Customs House 1 km S of town. **NB Please note that no visas are granted upon arrival, and that it is not permitted to bring private motor vehicles into China.** The Chinese authorities are now so used to seeing cyclists entering and exiting the country through this route, that they no longer attempt to force them onto buses. However, it is worth noting that on the visa application form at the Chinese Embassy in London, it states specifically that it is not permitted to bring bicycles into China.

Entry For those arriving in China, you will first have to fill out a health declaration form, and then a landing card. If you arrive from Pakistan on a bus full of Pathans, the chances are that you will have to fill out all their cards for them too. You then pass through Immigration, before having to fill out a customs declaration form detailing your foreign currency and expensive consumer items. You should keep the stamped copy until you depart China. Westerners rarely have their bags checked.

As you leave the Customs Hall, directly ahead is a Uigyur run bank that does foreign exchange (but **not** TCs) at reasonable rates. The Bank of China, next door, is said to change TCs, but rarely seems open.

To the left, behind the Customs House, is a separate building where you can buy tickets for the following day's bus to Kashgar. People who buy their tickets here the day before have priority over those who buy them the following day at the main ticket office at the *Traffic Hotel*. The foreigners' fare to Kashgar is an extortionate Y77 (the locals pay Y18), which seems illogical when the foreigners' fare in the opposite direction from Kashgar to Tashkurgan is Y40. Holders of tickets for the following day's bus are given a lift the 1 km into town; others have to walk.

Exit The exit formalities rather depend upon where you boarded the bus. If you boarded the Pakistan bound bus at the *Chini Bagh Hotel* in Kashgar, and paid the Kashgar-Sust fare of Y265, customs procedures will have been completed at the hotel in Kashgar. If the passenger manifest (list) matches the passports of those on board, you can clear Customs and Immigration fairly quickly. If, however, any passengers have

been picked up enroute, or at Tashkurgan, the process of putting them on the passenger manifest can delay your departure for hours.

If you are unable to get a place on a Pakistan bound bus in Tashkurgan, it may be worth walking out to the Customs Hall and trying to arrange transport from there. The *NATCO* landcruisers and buses generally return to Pakistan empty, although they are not allowed to take passengers unless the uncooperative Chinese Immigration officials give their permission. You are not generally allowed through Immigration unless you have S bound transport arranged.

Exchange rates

The Chinese unit of currency is the Yuan (¥), sometimes referred to in the slang term as Kwai (like the English 'quid' or American 'buck'). The two currency system, with RMB for locals and FEC for foreigners, has now been abandoned, although the policy of charging foreigners double, treble, quadruple and beyond for goods and services has been retained. Banks in the major cities (incl Kashgar) change TCs, generally with small commission charges. In 1995, the approximate exchange rates were as follows: £1= ¥13; $1=¥8; ¥1=Rs 4.

Tashkurgan

For a town that everyone has to stop in, Tashkurgan (around 3,200m) has remarkably little to offer besides some disgusting hotels and rip-off restaurants. Capital of the Tajik Autonomous County, within the Xinjiang Uiygur Autonomous Region of the People's Republic of China, Tashkurgan is a town of around 6,000 predominantly Tajik people, although there are representations of other minorities such as Uiygurs, Kỷrghiz, Uzbeks and of course, Han Chinese.

The town has a long history and is said to have been mentioned in the 2nd century AD by Ptolemy. The word

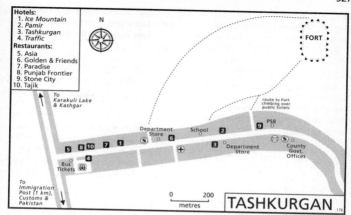

Hotels:
1. *Ice Mountain*
2. *Pamir*
3. *Tashkurgan*
4. *Traffic*
Restaurants:
5. *Asia*
6. *Golden & Friends*
7. *Paradise*
8. *Punjab Frontier*
9. *Stone City*
10. *Tajik*

TASHKURGAN

Tashkurgan means 'Stone Tower' or 'Stone City', although the town, little more than one main street, hardly lives up to the billing given to it under this title by the Chinese tourism department. Its one attraction is the ancient crumbling **fortress**, mentioned by the Chinese traveller Hieun Tsang when he passed through 13 centuries ago. Much of the outer walls and battlements are intact, and the views of the surrounding plains are good, but it is hardly worth paying the Y5 to go inside and look at a pile of rubble.

● **Accommodation** Travelling between Pakistan and Kashgar you will almost certainly have to spend a night in Tashkurgan. This means experiencing some of the most disgusting hotels in China (and there's quite some competition). The *Pamir Hotel*, T (0998) 421085, is used mainly by tour groups, with luxury doubles with attached bath for Y180, there are triples for Y30/bed and a Y15 dorm, but these share some pretty filthy toilets with no showers. The *Traffic Hotel* is almost certainly where the public bus will drop you, welcome to the worst of China, the reception staff seem unable to deal with large groups arriving at the same time, and are prone to saying that the hotel is 'full' when you know that there are at least 100 empty beds, the downstairs corridor is usually flooded, which is ironic because there never seems to be any

water in the taps, the toilets are usually full of shit, and if they are not when you arrive, they almost certainly will be after everyone has moved their bowels the following morning, there are some reasonable doubles on the top floor for Y120, with attached bath, but most accommodation is in 4 bed dorms at Y15 pp, the rooms and bed linen is usually clean, but those toilets will live in your memory for a long time. The *Ice Mountain Hotel*, T 421134, is a better bet, with a more regular water supply and friendly Pakistani management, doubles for Y60, plus dorm beds with shared toilet for Y20 and Y15 (depending on whether you require carpet), you can also pay in Pakistani Rupees. The superbly named *Hotel of Tashkurgan Food and Oil Trade Corporation* does not seem interested in foreigners.

● **Places to eat**
There are numerous small cafes and restaurants along Tashkurgan's main street, but this is the sort of town where you have to negotiate the price of everything before you order. The Tajik place opp the *Traffic Hotel* is popular, but the staff are not adverse to charging Y3 for a piece of bread that should cost Y0.5. Expect to pay Y5 for a bottle of beer that costs Y3.5 in Kashgar. The place is probably best avoided. Next door is the Pakistani run *Punjab Frontier Restaurant*, where you can get Pakistani food for four times the price you would pay across the border. The *Friends Restaurant* further down the street serves good food, but set the prices before you order. Tashkurgan's altitude may mean that the first beer may hit you more than you expected.

● **Transport**

Bus: The main bus ticket office is just inside the gate of the *Traffic Hotel*, and it only opens about 1 hr prior to bus departures. Unless you have the latest Chinese student card (or a fake), it is all but impossible to avoid paying the foreigners' fare.

Pakistan (Sust): The through-service bus from the *Chini Bagh Hotel* in Kashgar leaves from the *Traffic Hotel* in Tashkurgan around 0800 Xinjiang (local) time. However, it is often full, and the ticket office will not sell tickets. If there are empty seats, or the driver thinks he can fit you on (you may have to sit on the floor), it may be possible to get on. You have to pay the full fare to Sust (¥220) even if you don't get a proper seat. There may be delays at Immigration whilst your name is added to the passenger manifest, (and the fare is paid once this is completed).

Sometimes there is a bus service to Sust that originates in Tashkurgan (as opposed to Kashgar), in which case the ticket office at the *Traffic Hotel* will sell you a ticket (¥220, departure 0800 local time). You may also be able to hitch a ride on a bus privately hired by Pakistani traders. The journey time to Sust is about 8 hrs, excluding Immigration delays.

Kashgar: Those who buy tickets at the Immigration and Customs Hall the previous day (see **Entry/Exit Formalities**) have priority on the bus to Kashgar the following morning. However, there is generally more than one bus on this service, and tickets are available from the ticket office at the *Traffic Hotel* from about 0700 local time. Fare Y77, departure time 0800 local time. Even though the ticket states that you are allowed one piece of luggage up to 10 kg, you will almost certainly be charged an additional Y2/piece of roof luggage. Refusal to pay seems to delay the bus departure indefinetely. The journey time to Kashgar is about 7 hrs, but the bus does not normally stop for a meal break until the town of Shufu, just 1 hr short of Kashgar. Load up with food and drink in Tashkurgan. Because most tourists are heading to Kashgar's Sun Market, this route is particularly busy on Thur and Fri.

Karakuli Lake: It is possible to buy a ticket from the office at the *Traffic Hotel* that allows you to break your journey for a day or more at Karakuli Lake (2 hrs), on the way to Kashgar. However, there is no guarantee of a seat when you resume your journey, or that the passing bus will even stop when you try to flag it down. For those going up to Kashgar and then re-turning to Pakistan, transport is easier to arrange if you stop at the lake on the return leg.

Cyclists: should note that it is 285 km to Kashgar, with nowhere to buy food supplies imbetween. The journey generally takes 2-3 days, plus whatever time you spend at Karakuli Lake.

Tashkurgan to Kashgar

Improvements on the road N to Kashgar (285 km) means that the journey generally only takes 7-8 hrs, although there is one point in particular where you may be delayed by landslides. The scenery, however, is amongst the most spectacular anywhere in the world.

Travelling NW from Tashkurgan, the KKH passes through the marshy pasture of the Tagh Arma Basin. Having been through the checkpost at Kekyor, the road climbs in a barely discernible way up to the Subash Plateau. To the W, tantalisingly close, the Pamirs mark the boundaries with the Wakhan Corridor of Afghanistan, and of Tajikistan. A number of jeep roads lead W towards passes that thread their way through these mountains into the two states, although at the time of writing both are off-limits to tourists.

To the E, the spectacular 7,540m **Muztagh Ata** (Father of Ice Mountain) comes into view. Possibly the most attractive peak in he entire Pamir range, Muztagh Ata was first mapped in 1886 by the British explorer Ney Elias, although the name he gave it, Mt Dufferin, did not stick. The geological age of the Pamirs, considerably older than its Himalayan and Karakoram neighbours, accounts for the rounding of the peaks, with Muztagh Ata being no exception. The mountain is popular with 'ultimate skiing' enthusiasts, and a great source of revenue for the Chinese government, although this commercial exploitation does not sit well with the local Kyrghiz who revere the holy spirits that are said to live on the summit.

Karakuli Lake

Sitting below Muztagh Ata, and flanked by 7,720m **Mt Kongur** to the NE, is the beautiful Karakuli Lake. Without doubt, this is one of the most stunning places on the entire length of the Karakoram Highway, as the dark, deep waters of the lake reflect the giant peaks that flank two sides. It is a photographers dream, with the local Kyrghiz population being as photogenic as the remarkable scenery.

It is a good 5 hr walk around the lake, with the soggy marsh terrain to the SE of the lake adding time to the journey. Another popular walk is N along the KKH, to two other smaller lakes, and a friendly Kyrghiz village. Donkey, horse and camel rides are also available at the lake. At 3,600m, you may well feel the effects of the altitude, particularly if you have come from Kashgar, and it is essential to wear plenty of sunblock. The blistered and weather beaten features of the local children will serve as a painful reminder. The kids here don't beg for pens or money, but moisturiser. The weather is very changeable, and you should prepare for all eventualities if going on a long walk. It gets very cold at night, although the yurts are provided with thick duvets.

- **Accommodation and places to eat** One of the attractions of Karakuli Lake is the opportunity to stay in a traditional Kyrghiz **yurt**, or circular nomad's tent. The Chinese have recognized this desire, and consequently the cost of accommodation in the yurts at Karakuli has gone up 400% in the last 2 years. It now costs ¥40 pp/night. Similarly, the food situation is also a total rip-off, with the main restaurant charging ¥20 for a plate of food, ¥5 for rice, complete with service with a scowl. The prices are marginally cheaper in the restaurant in the blue tin shacks. If you can arrive at Karakuli with your own tent, and are self sufficient in food, your enjoyment of your stay will be greatly enhanced. Having said that, it truly is beautiful here, and certainly worth a visit. In theory, a travel permit from the PSB is required to stay at the lake, although nobody seems to bother getting one and no one ever asks to see it.

- **Transport** Onward transport from Karakuli works on the principal of standing by the road and flagging down any passing vehicle. Hitch-hiking is an unknown concept, so trucks and private vehicles will expect to be paid. Agree the fee in advance. It seems easier to flag down S bound (Tashkurgan) buses, rather than those heading to Kashgar. The 'local' Tashkurgan bound bus passes through at about 1200 local time, the 'international' bus from the *Chini Bagh Hotel* in Kashgar at about 1600-1700 local time. It is 2- 2½ hrs S to Tashkurgan. North bound buses to Kashgar (about 5-6 hrs) pass through between 1000 and 1300 local time.

An hour or so N of Karakuli Lake is the Kyrghiz settlement of **Bulunkul**, where there is a police checkpost. Cold drinks and snacks, incl delicious parathas stuffed with spicy fried vegetables, are usually available, although you have to be quick because the bus doesn't stop for long.

Continuing N, the KKH leaves the pastures of the plateau, and descends into the rocky canyon of the **Ghez River**, sometimes referred to as Tiger's Mouth Gorge. The road here is rough in parts, and subject to rockfalls and landslides. The enclosing mountains are highly folded, with stratas of multicoloured sandstone providing a dramatic impression. Some of the deep burgundy reds are particularly striking.

After 70 km or so, the KKH leaves the canyon and continues for the last 80 km to Kashgar along a wide, flat plain. Trees line the road that effectively links a chain of smaller oasis to the major city of the region. Frustratingly, the bus always seems to stop for a meal break at Shufu, just 1 hr short of **Kashgar**.

Kashgar

The oasis city of Kashgar (1,289m) has been strategically important for the last 2,000 years. Lying on the ancient trans-Asian trading route later dubbed the Silk Rd, the list of visitors and conquerors is long and varied. Today, the city of Kashgar remains a major Central Asian market town, but has also developed into a thriving tourist attraction. Despite what you may read in other publications, Kashgar is very much on the tourist trail. It has, however, managed to retain some of its original character, and its prime attraction, the weekly Sunday Market, remains a spectacular sight.

Early history

By the 1st century AD, the **Han Chinese** had grabbed control of Kashgar, following the extension of the Great Wall westwards, and the construction of a chain of beacons that warned of attack by marauding raiders. However, following the collapse of the Han Dynasty in the 3rd century, Kashgar was sacked by the Huns, and a great period of instability ensued. It wasn't until the end of the 7th century that the **T'ang Dynasty** reimposed Chinese rule in the region, although they were to be defeated by an alliance of Western Turks and Arabs in 752 AD. The **Arabs** had the upper hand in this one-sided alliance, and subsequently Islam became the dominant religion in the region.

In 1219 the city fell to the great Mongol ruler **Genghis Khan**, as he established an empire that stretched from Asia to eastern Europe. Ironically, the fear generated by the Mongol Horde brought great stability to the whole region, and trade along the Silk Rd flourished. In 1265 **Marco Polo** visited Kashgar, and registered his comments on the city.

As the power of the Mongol Empire waned towards the end of the 14th century, the city was sacked by **Tamerlane**. However, his death in 1405 marked the beginning of another era of instability that was to last almost 350 years.

Middle history

In the middle of the 18th century, the Manchu Dynasty of the **Ching** returned to the Tarim Basin, ending the isolation from China that was imposed by the insular Ming Dynasty. The Ching rule over the region was tenuous however, and in 1865 the Turkic leader **Yakub Beg** crossed the Pamirs, and having seized control of 'Kashgaria', declared it independent.

In 1868 the first British visitor, a tea planter cum adventurer named Robert Shaw, arrived in Kashgar, followed closely behind by George Hayward (see page 474). Although they were held under virtual house arrest for 3 months by Yakub Beg, they fared better than the earlier European traveller Adolf Schlaginweit, who in 1857, was tortured and beheaded in the main bazaar.

The Great Game

In the era that followed, Kashgar became the furthest extension of the rival British and Russian empires, acting as a listening post in the great game of imperial rivalry. A British mission headed by Sir Douglas Forsyth, and including John Biddulph, had been received at Kashgar in 1873 by Yakub Beg. However, in 1877 the Ching army put down Yakub Beg's rebellion, and Kashgar was incorporated within the Xinjiang ('New Frontier') Province of China. As a snub to the British for their dealings with Yakub Beg, in 1882 the Chings allowed the Russians to open a Consulate in the city, not sanctioning a British presence there until 8 years later.

The first British representative was the 24-year-old **George Macartney**, who was to remain in Kashgar for the next 28 years. A shrewd tactician and 'Great Game' player, Macartney is remembered as one of the most extraordinary characters from the latter era of Kashgar's history. In 1898 he returned from brief home leave with a young wife, **Catherine Theodora Borland**, and so begun the dramatic transformation of the consulate building, the Chini Bagh (Chinese garden), into a little island of Britain in the heart of Central Asia. Catherine was later to write a book, *An*

English Lady in Chinese Turkestan, detailing such exploits as culinary disasters with soggy Christmas puddings.

In 1908 the Chinese finally recognized the British representative in Kashgar as a Consul, although within 3 years the Manchu government had fallen and China was declared a republic. In the resulting upheaval, the Manchu appointed ruler, the Taotai, was subsequently murdered, and Kashgar threatened to descend into another period of savagery. Order was only restored at the intervention of Russian troops.

As the 1917 Russian Revolution spread slowly eastwards towards Kashgar, the Russian Consulate there remained briefly as a refuge for White Russians. By 1924, however, the Bolsheviks had taken over. Kashgar, meantime, continued to be ruled from Urumqi by Governor Yang until his assassination at a banquet in 1928. In the resulting bloody conflict between the Han Chinese and the **Tungans** (Chinese Muslims), Kashgar was briefly captured in 1934 by the Tungans, although they were soon driven out by a local warlord backed by the Soviets.

The warlord, **General Sheng Shih-tsai** appointed himself as Governor of Xinjiang, and ruled until 1944 when he was pensioned off by the Chinese.

Recent history

Following Indian independence, and the creation of Pakistan, the last British Consul-General, Eric Shipton, left Kashgar. Within a year, **Mao Zedong** had declared the foundation of the People's Republic of China, and a major modernisation of Kashgar began. Much of the old city, including the 500 year old city walls, have been bulldozed to make way for uninspiring concrete blocks, although a few pockets remain. In recent years there have been reports of Uiygur uprisings in Kashgar, although news of such incidents is suppressed. A building opposite the *Seman Hotel* was supposedly blown up, although it has since been rebuilt, but foreigners who hang around there asking questions and taking photos seem to end up down at the PSB answering questions themselves.

The People

Like the rest of Xinjiang Province, Kashgar is predominantly populated by **Uiygurs** (pronounced 'Weegur'), a Turkic Muslim race thought to have arrived in the area around 700 years ago. There are significant numbers of minority groups in Kashgar, including Tajiks, Kyrghiz, Uzbeks, Kazakhs and of course ever expanding numbers of Han Chinese. Although Mandarin Chinese is the official language, Uiygur (written using the Arabic script) is the most widely used in the bazaar. It is not unusual to meet Pakistani traders who are well versed in both languages.

Places of interest

Sunday Market

Without any doubt Kashgar's prime attraction is the weekly **Sunday Market**, and the city seems to fill with tourists in the days leading up to the event, and empty shortly afterwards. No doubt some will claim that the market is "too touristy", but the sheer scale of it, particularly the livestock market, still seems able to accommodate the number of visitors. **NB** The volume of tourists is considerably lower outside the May-Oct period when the Khunjerab Pass route to Pakistan is closed.

The main market grounds are within a walled area to the E of the old town, but on a Sun the entire surrounding area is one enormous donkey-cart and pedestrian traffic jam. Along a side road, just to the W of the main market, is the most fascinating part of the whole spectacle-the livestock enclosure. Throughout the morning, from 0600 onwards, the enclosure gradually fills with sheep, goats, donkeys, horses, bullocks, cows, buyers, sellers, hangers-on, sightseers and tourists (although in the last 6 years I've

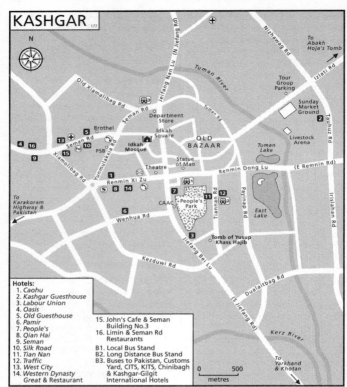

KASGHAR

Hotels:
1. Caohu
2. Kashgar Guesthouse
3. Labour Union
4. Oasis
5. Old Guesthouse
6. Pamir
7. People's
8. Qian Hai
9. Seman
10. Silk Road
11. Tian Nan
12. Traffic
13. West City
14. Western Dynasty Great & Restaurant
15. John's Cafe & Seman Building No.3
16. Limin & Seman Rd Restaurants

B1. Local Bus Stand
B2. Long Distance Bus Stand
B3. Buses to Pakistan, Customs Yard, CITS, KITS, Chinibagh & Kashgar-Gilgit International Hotels

never seen a camel), until there's no more open space bar the run where men test-drive the animals. It truly is a photographer's dream, with a sea of fascinating faces, and a superb collection of old bearded men. The livestock deals are so important, and the negotiators so intent upon their bargaining, that they hardly seem to register the presence of several hundred thousand pounds worth of Japanese photographic technology on display.

The main enclosed market grounds contain an astonishing array of goods, from avenues of brightly and elaborately coloured cloth, through to fruit and vegetables, to primitive radio cassette players and electrical goods. There are also traditional Uiygur handicrafts such as elaborately carved knifes and daggers, as well as numerous types of hats. Unfortunately, fur is widely prevalent, and there are many complete pelts of the endangered snow leopard. Potential purchasers should note that most civilized countries impose hefty fines, and the threat of jail, for importing many fur products. The area behind the main market, outside the walls, is where the poorer dealers trade, some of whose stock merely comprises several odd shoes. It's quite depressing. Equally depressing is the way in which the land around the market has been allowed to be developed, into a modern but unused business park.

It's best to arrive at the market as early as possible, (before most of the tour groups), in order to watch it gradually filling up. Shared rickshaw taxis can be hired from outside the main hotels (about ¥4 pp from the *Seman*), and it is not recommended that you take a bicycle. Beware of pickpockets.

Old City, bazaars and city walls

With the exception of the livestock market, a mini version of the Sun Market seems to occur everyday within the old city area. To the E of the main bazaar lies the old city, a narrow labyrinth of mud-brick built houses, shops and mosques built on traditional Islamic city design of enclosed courtyards, tight passages and numerous cul-de-sacs. On the edge of this old town lie the bazaars, selling all manner of products, and covering all possible occupations. The hats, knifes and handicrafts are probably a better bargain here than at the Sun Market.

On Seman Rd, not far from the *Seman Hotel*, two short stretches of the ancient city walls remain.

Idkah Mosque

When the original **Idkah Mosque** was built in 1442, it was located on the edge of town, but Kashgar's gradual expansion means that the mosque is now pretty much at the centre of town. The mosque currently standing is considerably larger than the original, and has been rebuilt or repaired many times. The main features are the now restored yellow-tiled tower gate, a victim of the excesses of the Cultural Revolution, and the large 16,800 sq m courtyard, said to be capable of holding 20,000 people. Visitors are welcomed if respectfully dressed (arms, legs, and women's heads covered), and the quiet atmosphere in the shady courtyard is certainly worth the ¥3 entrance fee.

The main Idkah Square outside the mosque, and the surrounding street markets, are enormously interesting.

Abakh Hoja's Tomb

To the E of the town, several km beyond the Sun Market grounds, is the beautiful **Tomb of Abakh Hoja**. Probably dating to the 18th century (although some sources place it earlier), the mausoleum shows a distinct Persian influence in its use of green and blue tile work on its facade and dome. Although there are some 70 graves in the main domed chamber, the tomb is named after a local Uiygur aristocrat, Abakh Hoja, sometimes referred to as the 'patron saint of Kashgar'.

The tomb is also claimed to be the burial place of Abakh Hoja's grand daughter, popularly known as **Xiangfei**, or Fragrant Consort. Legend suggests that she was the leader of a failed Uiygur uprising in 1759, and was subsequently carried off to the imperial court of the Qing Emperor Qian Long to be a concubine. The Emperor is said to have become so besotted by his new acquisition, that his mother, fearing the growing influence of Xiangfei, ordered her to commit suicide.

The tombs are best reached on a pleasant bicycle journey (¾ hr from the *Seman Hotel*). The large Muslim graveyard located behind the tomb is particularly attractive during the late afternoon, although the main tomb may be closed by then.

Tomb of Yusup Khass Hajib

Built during the Song Dynasty c 1130, the Tomb of Yusup Khass Hajib was superbly rebuilt and restored in 1993. An 11th century Uiygur poet and philosopher, **Yusup Khass Hajib** was the author of what is considered to be the most important Uiygur text ever produced, '*The Wisdom of Royal Glory*'. He was born near to the Central Asian city of Tokhmahk in 1019, when it was the summer capital of the Karakhanid Dynasty, but later moved to study at the Royal Islamic College in Kashgar. He wrote his 13,290 line "didactic lyric epic" in 18 months between 1069 and 1070, and presented his work to the Great Khan of the E Karakhanid Dynasty, Talughach Bughra Khan Abdul Ali Hasan bin Sulaiman Arslankhan (!). He was rewarded with the title of 'Khass Hajib', or Privy Chamberlain (King's adviser). Yusup Khass Hajib died in 1085 and was buried in Kashgar, although when the tomb was destroyed by a natural disaster, he was reburied at the present site.

A political, economic and cultural history of the Karakhanid Dynasty, the original manuscript of '*The Wisdom of Royal Glory*' has never been found, although three ancient copies survive in Vienna, Cairo and Namangan in the Fergana Valley.

The shrine is entered through the large tiled N gate. The main facade of the tomb features superb blue and white tile work, and is topped by a tall, blue tiled dome. The restoration work really is first rate. Inside the chamber, the sarcophagus stands on a large plinth. The walls are engraved with fine calligraphy, and excerpts from the Qu'ran in Arabic, Chinese and Romaniced Uiygur. In the surrounding cloistered courtyard is a small exhibition detailing the life and work of Yusup Khass Hajib.

Parks

There are a number of pleasant public parks in Kashgar, including one set around the **East Lake** to the E of the city. The central **People's Park**, opposite the incongruous giant Mao statue, is a great place to watch the Chinese and Uiygurs at leisure. The **zoo**, however, must rank alongside the cruellest and most depressing in the world. To my personal knowledge, the totally insane Himalayan bear has been pacing that same tiny cage for 6 years.

Café society

Kashgar is also a fine place to relax, and many visitors do little more than sit around the three restaurants outside the *Seman Hotel* enjoying the food and drink. Recent arrivals from Pakistan revel in the availability of cheap Chinese beer whilst being shocked at the lack of clothes work by tourists and Chinese women alike. Despite being a predominantly Muslim town, there is little reaction to tourists (including women) wearing shorts – hardly surprising when most young Han Chinese women are wearing shorter and shorter miniskirts.

Local information
● Accommodation

Classifying hotels in Kashgar according to price is rather difficult since most offer the full range of accommodation from luxury doubles to simple dormitory beds. Thus, the hotels below are listed in order of their popularity and usage by foreign tourists.

Seman, Seman Rd, T (0998) 222001, F 222361, most visitors to Kashgar stay somewhere in the *Seman Hotel*, 'Block A' caters almost exclusively for pre-booked tour groups, in carpetted doubles with attached hot bath, 'Block 1' is the best maintained part of the old Russian Consulate, with ultra-luxury suites with antique furniture, TV, phone, fridge and bath tubs for ¥500, the main block of the hotel has all variety of rooms, from ¥120 doubles with TV and attached bath to ¥15 dorm beds, the dormitories are variable, with some having 12 beds, whilst others have only 2!, each floor has a toilet block and hot showers (morning and evening), in the more dilapidated section of the old Russian Consulate, there are some 2 bed dorms with attached hot bath, the hotel also has a pool, laundry service, clinic, barbers, Uigyur theatre for cultural shows, Muslim restaurant, *Merryland* nightclub, several souvenir shops, bicycle-hire, taxi service, airport bus (1930 Beijing time) and travel agent; *Seman Building No 3*, opp Seman Hotel, T 222129. Dbles with fan, TV and attached bath for ¥40, ¥60 and ¥80; *Chini Bagh (Qiniwake)*, Seman Rd, T 222103, built on the site of the old British Consulate, this hotel is the most popular amongst Pakistani traders, some Western women have complained of harassment here, doubles with TV and attached hot bath from ¥164, and dorm beds for ¥15, restaurant, self-service cafeteria, foreign exchange, next to Customs Hall and departure point for buses to Pakistan, many of the buses from Tashkurgan arrive here. **Kashgar Gilgit International**, Seman Rd, T 223842, F 223842, this recently opened joint China-Pakistan venture caters mainly to tour groups, and benefits greatly from the friendly and cooperative Pakistani management, large, luxury suites (Y500), plus comfortable doubles with TV, phone, fridge, room service, and great views of Kashgar (Y240), good restaurant with Pak, Chinese and continental food, cultural hall/disco, laundry, international business centre with IDD phones, fax and typing, can be booked through Pak-China Border Trade, Gilgit (T 2645), rec; **Tian Nan**, Tiannan Rd, T 222211, convenient to the bus station, has very cheap dorm (Y8), doubles for ¥30 with shared bath, and 'deluxe' rooms up to ¥160; **Traffic**, at bus station, T 225208, 3 bed dorms from ¥25 each, up to 'special' doubles for ¥80 each, very noisy; **Silk Road**, Seman Rd, T 222004, good value triples and doubles from ¥25/bed, upper floors have TV and attached bath, pleasant roof-top restaurant/coffee house, some visitors complain of lack of water in plumbing; **Renmin (People's)**, Jctn Renmin Dong Lu and Jiefang Nan Lu, T 224890, doubles from ¥160; **Kashgar Hotel**, Tauhuz Rd, conveniently located for the Sun Market, but inconveniently located for everything else, rooms from ¥120; **Qian Hai**, Renmin Xi Lu, T 222922, very smart and friendly, with rooms from ¥320-800, but nobody speaks English; **Labour Union**, Jiefang Nan Lu, T 221147, 3 bed dorm with attached bath ¥45/bed, doubles with separate bath ¥30.

There are several other hotels in Kashgar that are either closed, undergoing renovation, or unwilling to accept foreigners, incl **Oasis**, **West City**, **Pamir**, **Old Guesthouse**, **Caohu**.

● **Places to eat**
By far the most popular places to eat amongst Kashgar's not inconsiderable backpacker community are the adjacent **Limin** and **Seman Road** cafés, opp the *Seman Hotel*. Both places serve good food, incl breakfast, and are popular for a beer or two in the evening (or afternoon!). The beauty of one of the flirtatious waitresses in the *Limin* is legendary the length of the Silk Route. **John's Café**, outside *Seman Hotel Building No 3* is a good place to meet for a beer and a chat, although you may soon be bored by the interminable "is Tibet open?" conversations. For good Uiygur food, try the numerous stalls around the main bazaar outside the Id Kah Mosque, particularly during the night market.

● **Airline offices**
CAAC, Jiefang Nan Lu, T 222113.

● **Banks & money changers**
Bank of China, W end of Renmin Xi Lu, offers foreign exchange (incl TCs) at nominal commission rates (1000-1400; 1530-1930 Beijing time). Uiygur money changers hang around the *Chini Bagh* and *Seman Hotels*, but their rates are not particularly exciting.

● **Entertainment**
Nightclub/disco: the *Merryland* nightclub at the *Seman Hotel* offers tacky decor, karaoke, ballroom dancing, expensive beer, a possible hefty cover-charge, and by the end of the night has the atmosphere and appearance of a brothel. There is a rather interesting Chinese *disco* nr to the People's Park.

Cultural shows: a number of hotels, incl the *Seman*, put on Uiygur cultural shows for tour groups. Ask at reception.

● **Hospitals & medical services**
People's Hospital, Airport Rd, T 222337. *Uiygur Medical Hospital*, Seman Rd. There is a clinic at the *Seman Hotel*.

● **Post & telecommunications**
Area code: 0998.

Post Office: the main Post Office is on Renmin Xi Lu. Poste Restante and international mail services are upstairs (1000-1400; 1530-1900 Beijing time). The Central Telegraph Office is opp. It is also possible to make international IDD calls, and to send faxes from the *Seman Hotel* and *John's Café*, although it's not cheap.

● **Shopping**
With the exception of livestock, most products that tourists will be interested in buying, such as hats, decorated knifes, and handicrafts, can probably be found at cheaper prices in the bazaar to the E of Idkah Sq, than at the Sun Market. Connoisseurs of crap may be keen to peruse the numerous department stores in the centre of town. Colour print, and some slide **film** is readily available in Kashgar, although it is probably better to stock up at home. Print film is cheaper in Pakistan, and B&W is difficult to find.

● **Tour companies & travel agents**
China International Travel Service (CITS), Chini Bagh Hotel, Seman Rd, T 222103, F 223087, can take care of all your travel needs, incl travel permits, guides, transport, hotel

bookings, visa extensions, etc- but at a price. The *Kashgar International Travel Service (KITS)*, part of *CITS*, and operating from the same address, offer similar services (for similar prices) incl tours to Karakuli Lake, Yarkand, the 'Silk Route', 'Footsteps of Marco Polo', Taklamakan Desert etc. The Manager, Muhammad Ali Yimin is helpful and speaks good English. The *KITS*, however, in some of its tourist literature, does attempt to claim that 'Qorir' (K2 ?), the second highest peak in the world, is 'located in Kashgar!' John Hu of *John's Information Centre*, Seman Hotel Building No 3, T 224186, F 222861, is a good source of travel information, and can supply bus, train and air tickets, visa extensions and permits from the PSB, as well as permits to cross the Tourgat Pass into Kyrghizstan.

● **Tourist offices**
See *CITS* and *KITS* above.

● **Useful addresses**
Public Security Bureau (PSB), Yunmulakxia Rd, for visa extensions and travel permits. (Typical 30 day extension fees: UK ¥65; Aus ¥60; Jap ¥120; Can ¥110; Ity ¥45; Others ¥25).

● **Transport**
Local Bus: there is a network of buses along Kashgar's main streets, although they are very crowded, and unless you can read or speak Chinese, it is unlikely that you will find the one you want. **Bicycle**: easily the most civilized way of getting around town is on a bicycle, that can be hired from outside the *Seman Hotel* or at *John's Café*. You will have to leave some security as deposit, and should thoroughly check the condition of the bike before leaving. **Taxi**: taxis are readily available in Kashgar, usually outside the main hotels, although it is considerably cheaper to take one of the **motorcycle rickshaws** (up to 10 passengers), or **motorcycle/side-car combination** (seats 2). Typical fare from *Seman Hotel* to bus station is ¥10/vehicle.

Air *CAAC* have evening flights to **Urumqi** (2 flights on Wed, Thur, Fri, Sun) for ¥1265. There is an airport bus (¥10) from the *Seman Hotel* at 1930 (Beijing time) every night.

Road Bus: the long distance bus stand is on Tiannan Rd, E of the People's Park. Tickets can be bought at least 1 day in advance, although if you want to travel on a popular route at a peak time (eg to Urumqi immediately after the Sun Market), it is best to book early. When buying a ticket, ascertain as to whether the departure time is Beijing or Xinjiang (local) time. **Urumqi**: There are at least 5 different options available on the trip to Urumqi. Most comfortable is the non-stop, 36 hr 'sleeper bus', which has semi-reclining beds as opposed to seats. Upper berths are ¥322, Lower ¥378. Departure times vary, although there's generally an early morning and early evening bus each day. There are several other buses, with varying degrees of comfort/misery, for ¥188, ¥214, ¥253, some of which take 3 days, stopping at revolting hotels for the night where you have no access to your roof luggage. Urumqi tickets from windows 5 and 6. **Tashkurgan**: Daily, 0700 local time, ¥40, 7 hrs. This is the bus for Karakuli Lake (5 hrs), although you generally have to pay the full Tashkurgan fare. Ticket window 7. **Yarkhand (Shache)** and **Yecheng (Kargilik)**: 6 daily buses serve both destinations, every 2 hrs from 0700 local time. **Khotan (Hotan)**: Daily, 0630 1900 local time. Ticket windows 5, 6, 7.

Travelling on from Kashgar

Urumqi/Kazakhstan/rest of China

See Transport section above for details on how to reach Urumqi. Although there is now a recognized border crossing and train service between Urumqi and Kazakhstan, visas are not available on the border or in Urumqi. A Kazakhstan embassy has recently opened in Islamabad.

Tibet

The subject of inumerable boring conversations in the cafés around the *Seman Hotel*, the dramatic southern route along China's Western Military Rd into Tibet is the goal of many travellers. The situation concerning travel in Tibet changes so quickly, and is subject to so many rumours, that it is only possible to describe the situation as it stood in late 1995.

It appears that the journey is considerably easier to arrange when travelling from Lhasa to Kashgar, than in the opposite direction. The PSB in Lhasa is prepared to issue the relevant travel documents to groups as long as they book through a travel agency. The normal mode of transport is a truck, taking about 1 month to complete the journey (including a visit to Mt Kailash), and costing around US$1,000 pp.

In Kashgar, however, the PSB do not seem to issue the necessary travel documents. Rather than actually refuse to issue the permit, they claim that the road is 'under-repair', or 'temporarily closed'. Even John Hu, who seems to be able to 'fix' most things in Kashgar, cannot arrange this permit. For those attempting the trip without the necessary documents should note that there is a checkpost 15 km beyond Yechin (Kargilik) and a second one shortly before Ali. You may be fined, turned back, or allowed to pass; the response is not consistent. The journey is difficult, crossing some very high passes and passing through remote areas. You should be well equipped, and prepared for all eventualities.

Kyrghizstan

The PSB in Kashgar point out that the border crossing across the **Tourgat Pass** (3,752m) into Kyrghizstan is a trade route, as opposed to a tourist route, and thus they are reluctant to issue the necessary travel documents. The Chinese side of the border is a restricted military zone, so it would be unwise to attempt this journey without the relevant paperwork. Further, there is no public transport to the border, although a jeep (seats 5) can be hired for around ¥1,400. The road to the pass (160 km, 6 hrs) is pretty poor, although it is being improved. Arriving from Kyrghizstan, you will not be permitted to enter China without the travel permit that allows you to use this road. John Hu can generally organize both transport and permits for travel in either direction (see Kashgar 'Tour companies and travel agents'), as can the *CITS* and *KITS*. There is 5 km of no man's land at the head of the pass, and it is not permitted to walk across, so transport must be arranged in advance. Visas for Kyrghizstan are not available in Kashgar, or at the border. Chinese visas are not available at the border either.

NB This was the situation in late 1995. As demand increases to use this route, the regulations are likely to change.

TREKKING

CONTENTS

Types of trekking	540
Choosing a trek	542
Organising a trek	544
Baltistan	549
Gilgit	556
Hunza	559
Upper Chitral	562

MAPS

Baltistan	550
Deosai Plateau	555
Gilgit to Chitral	557
Gajal (Upper) Hunza	561
Upper Chitral	563

Pakistan offers some of the best trekking in the world. The Karakoram, Himalaya and Hindu Kush ranges which dominate the Northern Areas and NWFP are truly spectacular. They encompass soaring mountains of rock, ice and snow, huge sweeping glaciers, plateaux and high pastures carpeted with grass and flowers in summer, valleys of contrasting bare rock and fertile irrigated settlements, and rich pine forests lower down. In terms of sheer scope and variety, the region arguably surpasses any other, offering a range of opportunities to cover all tastes and inclinations, with everything from easy day-walks to demanding treks of up to 3 weeks or more. For the climber there is heaven and hell.

Yet the potential of this region remains for the most part undiscovered. With the exception of one or two areas (the trek to the base camp of K2 in particular is far and away the most popular in Pakistan, and experiences many of the problems found in the Everest region of Nepal), trekking in Pakistan is generally completely free of crowds and pollution. The days when European explorers set out to fill in the 'blanks on the map' may be past, but this region remains one of the least comprehensively mapped in the world and is still full of adventure and excitement.

Aside from the natural beauty of the mountains and the peaceful, unspoilt solitude they offer, perhaps the most rewarding aspect of trekking in Pakistan is the contact it brings with the people who inhabit this beautiful and yet harsh environment. With one or two notable exceptions (see below), the people of northern Pakistan are friendly, hospitable and open in a way which seems to be characteristic of mountain people throughout the world. In Pakistan this is complemented by a fascinating variety of cultures; moving from one valley to the next it is often possible to witness a complete change in the traditions, lifestyle, language and ethnic origins of the people.

Trekking in Pakistan is more demanding than in countries such as Nepal and even India, where facilities are so far developed that luxuries such as 'tea-shop trekking' are an option. In Pakistan this is not the case. Any trek involves having all the supplies and equipment, as well as the physical stamina, to be completely self-sufficient if need be. On many treks it is perfectly possible to go for several days at a time without encountering any permanent settlements, and even in areas that are settled, agriculture is usually at subsistence level, making it impossible (and unfair) to rely on them for food. Most treks, if crossing a pass, rise to a minimum of 4,000m and can reach anywhere up to 5,500m. The terrain can be very demanding, crossing glaciers, glacial moraine, scree slopes and fast-flowing rivers, and involving numerous steep ascents and descents in the course of even a gradual overall climb. In this context, physical fitness, proper acclimatisation and careful planning are crucial to both your enjoyment and safety on a trek.

NB This chapter aims to provide a general overview of the opportunities for trekking in Pakistan and detailed practical information on how to set about planning and organising a trek. The notes on specific treks aim only to give a general insight into what to expect (those treks which have been covered first-hand by the editors are indicated and treated in more detail, the remainder have been compiled from other sources).

Indeed, any step-by-step descriptions of trekking in Pakistan should be treated with a healthy degree of scepticism. Mountain topography changes rapidly; avalanches, landslides, glacial action, flooding and erosion all conspire to make a mockery of the concept of a fixed route. Bridges may be destroyed; paths washed away and rerouted along the opposite sides of valleys, or rendered completely impassable; glaciers inevitably shift, and with them the best routes across them. Other variables such as the season, specific weather conditions and even the time of the day, can make the difference between the route across a pass being easily followed or waist-deep in snow, and rivers being easily fordable or impassable raging torrents.

There is simply no substitute for up-to-the-minute, first hand information about a particular area or route. Local tour operators are often a good source of information and can be very helpful. Talk to other trekkers and climbers; in Chitral, Gilgit and Skardu they are easily found, often congregating in specific hotels. Talk to local people; this is invariably the best source of information, although it can be misleading and must be carefully sought. The language barrier is the most frequent source of misunderstandings and crossed lines; it is essential to establish how much the person you are talking to understands of what you are asking. Related to this is the problem of leading questions. Most

people when asked for information genuinely feel obliged to help; if they don't know the answer, or do not fully understand the question, they are most likely to say what they think person wants to hear, or agree with what they are suggesting in their question. "Which path leads to .....?" will reveal far more than "Is this the path to ....?". The concept of 'local' also needs to be treated carefully; specific information, unless given by an experienced guide, is only likely to be accurate if the person giving it is actually from the particular valley. If they are from elsewhere then you are talking to the wrong person.

Ecology and conservation

The mountains of northern Pakistan, as well as being very beautiful, also represent an extremely fragile environment. The growth of mountaineering and trekking undoubtedly poses serious threat to the ecology of the region. Unfortunately, climbers and trekkers often appear to be the least aware, or least concerned, about the dangers.

Firewood

For many, part of the romance of trekking is associated with 'wilderness' images of sitting around campfires under a starlit sky. While certainly appealing, the cutting and burning of firewood is perhaps the most immediate and dramatic cause of environmental degradation. Forests are all too scarce in most of northern Pakistan and are under serious threat. There is no justification for trekkers and climbers to light fires; they have (or should have) their own stoves and fuel.

More importantly, they should ensure that their porters are likewise equipped. Existing forest and scrub is already under heavy pressure from local people and all of it is allocated on a collective basis to local communities. A contingent of porters arriving in another valley and collecting firewood to cook their evening meal are eating into the stock of firewood which will be collected and used during the harsh winter that follows the tourist season. It is ultimately up to you to ensure that your porters have kerosene stoves, and use them.

Pollution

Litter is perhaps the most needless legacy of trekking and climbing groups. For some inexplicable reason, having spent small fortunes employing porters to carry their precious supplies for them, most people appear to be think it perfectly acceptable to leave the associated waste in the mountains. Why not pay that little bit extra to have it carried out?? (Or carry it out yourself.) With a just a bit of forethought it is possible to significantly reduce the amount of waste that your supplies will generate in the first place; discard any surplus packaging beforehand; decant as much as possible into reusable containers (generally lighter and more practical anyway). Paper can be burnt, but not plastics. Remember that even biodegradable items take a long time to degrade in cold, dry, high altitude conditions. Dig a pit for shitting in (at least 30m from water supplies and above the high water mark of rivers). Avoid contaminating rivers, streams and water channels with detergents; they are likely to be someone's drinking water supply lower down. Burn toilet paper or better still, get used to using water instead. Anyone who has trekked the Annapurna "Andrex Trail" in Nepal will appreciate the outcome of 'my little bit...' attitudes.

Types of trekking

Organized treks

There are a large number of foreign and local 'adventure travel' tour operators offering specialized trekking services in Pakistan. Foreign tour operators are the most expensive. Their main advantage is that everything is done for you; pay your money and you will be looked after from the airport until you return, with everything in between, short of actually walking, taken care of. If you can afford it and have limited time, this is undoubtedly the best way of avoiding the inevitably time consuming process of planning and organising a trek. Reputable foreign companies generally offer an excellent service, with carefully planned treks and experienced overseas staff and local guides combining to minimize the possibility of a hitch.

There are now also a large number of local tour operators, some of which are extremely competent and easily able to match the services of foreign companies, for less money. They are also generally very flexible, allowing you to plan your own itinerary and change it if necessary. However, liaising with local companies from abroad can (though not necessarily) be more difficult. If going through a smaller company it is essential to ensure that all the details regarding jeeps, guides, porters etc are clear beforehand. It is worth shopping around between the various companies to find the best deal.

NB A list of major overseas and Pakistani tour operators offering trekking services is included in the Information for Visitors chapter. Smaller local trekking agencies are included in the Local Information sections of Chitral, Gilgit and Skardu.

Self-organized treks

By choosing to join an organized trek, all the responsibility for hiring porters and guides, buying supplies, arranging transport etc, is passed to the tour operator. The second option is to undertake all these aspects of the planning and preparation yourself. The main advantage of this is that it generally works out cheaper. The main disadvantage is that the planning and preparation is a time consuming process and ultimately you will have to deal with any problems which may arise yourself. Be prepared to invest a few days at least organising your trek. Read the information below on organising a trek.

Independent trekking

The third option is the simplest and by far the cheapest. Hiring porters and guides is an expensive business. For 2 people for anything more than a few days, you soon encounter the logistical realities of having to hire porters to carry food for the porters, and enter a steep spiral of costs. If you are travelling on a budget, trekking independently is likely to be the only option. It is essential however that you have at least some experience of trekking, as it involves carrying all your own equipment and supplies, and finding your own way along the route. Trekking alone is not advisable. Many trekking areas in Pakistan are extremely remote and isolated, sparsely populated and without any reliable system of rescue; if you sustain an injury or get lost, you are on your own. The main disadvantage of this form of trekking is that, since you must be completely self-sufficient, your range is greatly limited. Assuming a maximum load of around 20 kg (which is a hefty weight to lug around at high altitude), you are likely to be able to trek for no more than 5 days at a time. The great advantage is that you do not have a retinue of porters following you around everywhere, and are free to camp where you choose, as oppose to being tied to the porters' recognized overnight stops.

One approach is to aim for a compromise which may either involve hiring a free-lance guide to accompany you, carrying an equal load, or to hire 1 or 2 porters en-route. If you hire porters in the area in which you are trekking, they will have a good knowledge of routes and their condition, and extend your range considerably. Hiring on an informal basis is easily done; it is often possible to set out without any porters or guides and then simply hire a local farmer or shepherd for a section of the trek, to get you across a difficult pass for example.

Classification of treks

A 'trek' is officially defined as any route which does not exceed 6,000m in altitude. Treks are classified into 'open', 'restricted' or 'closed' zones, according to the sensitivity/safety of the area.

Open zone

The majority of treks fall into the open zone category, meaning that you are free to undertake the trek without a guide and without first gaining any official permission.

Restricted zone

Treks in restricted zones require that you obtain an official trekking permit for the particular trek you wish to undertake (see below) and that you employ a government-registered guide. Restricted areas include a 48 km zone approaching any of Pakistan's international borders (16 km in Azad Kashmir), parts of Chitral and the most popular treks in Baltistan (ie Baltoro Glacier to the base camp of K2). A list of government-approved treks in restricted zones is given below.

Baltistan

Baltoro Glacier, including Vigne, Masherbrum and Gondogoro passes and Panmah Glacier (5 treks).
Katisho Pass between Deosai plains and Mediabad (Parkutta).
Ganse Pass between Kharmang and Khaplu.

Chitral

Utak Pass between Rumbur (Kalash valley) and Garam Chashma.
Garam Chashma to Shishgol.
Owir Pass between Shoghor and Barum.
Barum to Tirich Mir.
Zani Pass to Tirich Mir.
Chikor Pass between Ziwar Gol and Uzhnu Gol.
Shah Jinali Pass between Yarkhun valley and Turikho (Rich) valley.

Chitral/Gilgit/Hunza

Karumbar and Chillinji Passes between Yarkhun and Chapursan valleys (including route via Lupghar Pass).

Darkot Pass between Yasin and Yarkhun valleys.

Thui Pass between Yarkhun and Yasin valleys.

NB A number of the above treks have only recently been reclassified from closed to restricted; it is likely that there will be further relaxation of restrictions on trekking in the future, so it is worth checking with the Ministry of Tourism regarding the latest situation.

Closed zone

These areas are generally the most sensitive in political and military terms, for example the Siachen area close to the disputed Line of Control with India. They are off-limits to trekkers unless they are able to obtain special permission, which is very rarely granted. If you wish to trek in a closed zone you really need to have contacts in high places. Alternatively, try applying through one of the major local trekking agencies, which is more likely to have the relevant contacts and so give your application at least some chance of success.

Mountaineering

Anything above 6,000m is classified as 'mountaineering', for which a separate permit is needed. Mountaineering expeditions must pay a 'royalty' according to the altitude of the peak they are attempting and be accompanied by a government-appointed liaison officer. Expeditions are governed by a series of rules and regulations as laid down by the Tourism Division of the Ministry of Culture, Sports and Tourism. They are outlined in a booklet entitled "Mountaineering Rules and Regulations", the latest edition being 1993 although an updated version was due to be published in late 1995.

Choosing a trek

There is a huge variety of treks in Pakistan, with enormous variations in the level of difficulty. Choosing the right trek is extremely important. Most obviously, the trek you undertake should match your level of fitness; unless you are fairly fit and used to walking, setting off on a long, hard trek is likely to be an exhausting experience, and so not particularly enjoyable. Likewise, if you have flown directly to Chitral, Gilgit or Skardu, it is essential that you acclimatize properly before undertaking any strenuous treks. If you have the time, the best approach is to do one or two shorter, easier treks first, before attempting anything more strenuous. It is well worth undertaking a programme of physical fitness training before you go. Bear in mind also that some treks do involve a certain level of technical difficulty – be it traversing glaciers, walking on snow, or fording rivers – which can be dangerous unless you (or your guide) have the experience and equipment to deal with the conditions. **NB** If you wish to trek independently, you must trek in an open zone, where a permit and registered guide are not required.

'Dangerous' areas

A number of areas in northern Pakistan, despite being in open zones, are inherently dangerous. These are invariably 'tribal' areas where banditry has been the norm for centuries, and remains so even today. The main areas where this is the case are **Indus Kohistan** (which includes all the side valleys leading off from the KKH in the area; the Jalkot, Tangir, Kandia, Darel and Thor valleys, as well as the route between Chilas and Babusar Pass), **Daimer District** (the approaches to the N side of Nanga Parbat from the KKH, also inhabited by Kohistanis), **Swat Kohistan** (the valleys N of Kalam leading over into the Gilgit river valley) and **Dir Kohistan** (the routes leading E from around Dir into Swat).

This does not mean that trekking is not possible in these areas, but that you need to take extra care. It is strongly advised (and in some cases officially required) that you trek with a reliable local guide and first inform the local authorities of your intended itinerary. The Deputy or Assistant Commissioners of each of these areas are the best people to turn to; they will be able to vet your guide, or help find one, and also advise you as to whether a particular area is safe at a given time.

Female trekkers

Women are advised not to trek alone in Pakistan. Even in the areas which are otherwise safe for women travellers, the spectacle of a woman walking through the mountains on her own is likely to cause serious offence and result in misunderstandings and problems. News of your presence would certainly spread like wildfire and be likely to attract more than just idle curiosity from local people.

The only real option for solo women travellers is either to link up with other groups, or to hire a reliable guide to accompany you. In the latter case, going through a recognized company with a reputation to uphold is the best way to ensure your safety. Alternatively, make sure that a competent authority is informed as to the trek you are undertaking, and the identity of your guide (make sure the guide is aware of this also).

Health

Read the Health section in Information for Visitors for detailed information on staying healthy. Pay particular attention to the sections on acclimatisation, altitude sickness and hypothermia. The golden rule is to allow plenty of time for acclimatisation and to descend carefully to a lower altitude if the symptoms of altitude sickness manifest themselves. Avoiding hypothermia is largely a question of being properly equipped and observing basic common sense while trekking.

Getting sick is unpleasant at the best of times; while trekking it can also be dangerous in that you might be several

days walk from the nearest medical facilities, which are likely to be fairly basic anyway. The most common problems are stomach upsets due to contaminated food and water. *Giardia lambia* is widespread, and one of the most common causes of diarrhoea in northern Pakistan. The best insurance against any form of diarrhoea is to take meticulous care over personal hygiene and the preparation of food, and to purify any water which has not been collected directly at source from a spring. However pure and crystal clear a mountain stream might appear, there is no guarantee that there is not a rotting carcass higher up its course. If you have hired a cook, it is essential that he understands the importance of hygiene and proper preparation food; most locals have a far higher tolerance than foreigners, so it is usually necessary to directly supervise their cooking, initially at least. See the Health section regarding the medical treatment of diarrhoea and the purification of water.

The other main risk while trekking is of injury. Trekkers are strongly advised to learn about the basics of first aid; there are various courses available in Europe and North America. All trekking groups in restricted areas are officially required to have at least one member with some knowledge of first aid. In addition to the comments regarding first aid kits outlined in the Health section, items such as elastic bandages for binding sprains and providing added support to ankles and knees, blister and corn plasters, Metronidazole for treating Giardia and amoebic dysentery and antibiotics for the treatment of bacterial diarrhoea should also be taken.

Maps

Maps of northern Pakistan are fairly limited and vary greatly in their accuracy and reliability. Even the best available trekking maps are really only reliable on the main trekking routes. Within Pakistan there is little or nothing which is of any use to trekkers, so it is essential to obtain all your maps before leaving home.

The **US Army Map Service (AMS) U502 series** covers most of northern Pakistan at a scale of 1:250,000 in a series of 8 sheets (2 further sheets covering the border with Afghanistan are restricted). Published in the 1950s and '60s, most existing roads and jeep tracks are not shown, while village names are woefully inaccurate. However, they do on the whole give accurate information as to the topography and are useful in planning a trek (**NB** Each map has a 'reliability' diagram dividing the map into poor/fair/good areas). Published in colour, they are also the most detailed in terms of contour information. International boundries are not marked.

A book entitled **Mountaineering Maps of the World; Karakoram, Hindu Kush, Pamir and Tien Shan** published in Japan in 1978 at a scale of 1:200,000 also covers most of northern Pakistan. Although the text is in Japanese, the maps themselves are labelled in Roman script. They are on the whole reasonably accurate. The main disadvantage is that this hefty volume is very expensive and quite difficult to find.

For the Karakoram range, the **Swiss Foundation for Alpine Research** 'orographical sketch map' in 2 sheets at a scale of 1:250,000, or the 'trekking map' in 3 sheets at a scale of 1:200,000 are the best available. Published in 1990, they are generally the most accurate, at least in terms of village names, trails and mountain topography (newer jeep tracks are often not marked). International boundries with India and China are not marked. **Leomann** also publishes a good set of 4 trekking maps of Gilgit, Hunza and Baltistan at a scale of 1:200,000.

There are also several more detailed maps. The excellent **Deutsche Himalaya Expedition** 1:50,000 maps in 2 sheets, 1 covering Nanga Parbat and the other Minapin Glacier were published in 1934 but updated in 1980. The Chinese **Institute of Glaciology, Cryopedology and Desert Research, Acedemia Sinica** published an excellent map of the Batura Glacier at a scale of 1:60,000 in 1978. There is also a Japanese map of the Baltoro Glacier at a scale of 1:100,000, published on the basis of the 1977 Japan-Pakistan K2 Expedition.

Buying maps

Most of the maps mentioned above can be obtained from the following places: *Cordee Books*, 3A De Montford St, Leicester LE1 7HD, UK, T (0116) 2543579, F (0116) 2471176; *Edward Stanford Ltd*, 12-14 Long Acre, London WC2E 9LP, UK, T (0171) 8361321, F (0171) 8360189; *Geo Buch Verlag*, Rosental 6, D-800, Munchen 2, Germany; *ILH Geo Center*, Schockenriestrasse 40A, Postfach 800830, D-700 Stuttgarte 80, Germany; *Libreria Alpina*, Via C Coronedi-Berti, 4, 40137 Bologna, Zona 3705, Italy; *Maplink*, 25 East Mason St, Santa Barbara, CA 93101, USA; *Michael Chessler Books*, PO Box 2436, Evergreen, CO 80439, USA, T (800) 6548502; *Travel Bookshop*, Rindermarkt 20, 8001 Zurich, Switzerland; *US Library of Congress; Geography and Map Division*, 101 Independence Av, Washington, DC 20540, USA.

Organizing a trek

Permits

Permits for the restricted treks listed above are relatively straightforward to obtain. In theory you can do it yourself, provided that you have found a government-registered guide, but in practice it is easiest to go through a local trekking agency. Most however charge a hefty fee for obtaining the permit, which is a rip-off as the permit is issued by the authorities more or less on the spot and completely free of charge.

At present all trekking permits must be applied for in Islamabad, from the Tourism Division, 13-T/U, College Rd,

Markaz F-7, T 816932, F 824173 (a regional office in Skardu was recently closed). Unless you are going through a local trekking agency, you must first have found yourself a guide. Applications (in duplicate) must identify the relevant trek, give exact dates and a list of all people going on the trek, including passport details and 2 photos pp. A trekking 'fee' (US$20/head in 1995) is charged. Insurance must also be provided for all porters and guides (it is in this respect that going through a local trekking company is easiest, since arranging insurance in Pakistan is a predictably lengthy process). The guide and group leader must also present themselves at the offices of the Tourism Division for a briefing beforehand.

Applying for a permit to trek in a restricted zone on a route not listed above is more difficult. Applications (as above) must be made through a recognized trekking agency and also include a detailed route map. Permission is then granted or rejected in theory within 15 days. A liaison officer is assigned to any authorized trek.

A booklet entitled Trekking Rules and Regulations is available from the Tourism Division, giving further details. The latest edition of the booklet is 1987, although an updated version was due to be published at the end of 1995.

NB The above information was correct at the time of going to press. However, there are concerted efforts to reduce the bureaucratic red tape associated with trekking in Pakistan and there are likely to be changes to the rules in the near future.

Guides

The guide is undoubtedly the most important component of any organized trek, and can make the difference between a trek being a highly enjoyable and rewarding success, or a complete disaster. The best guides will have experience of organising and leading treks, and an understanding of the peculiarities of foreigners; particularly with respect to health, hygiene and fitness, but also in terms of their interest and motivation towards trekking (for example wanting time to enjoy and camp in the most picturesque spots). They will also have detailed knowledge of the particular trek you are setting off on.

It is crucial that you are able to communicate satisfactorily with your guide; in most circumstances this is determined by their grasp of English. Hiring a guide who is from the specific area in which you are going to trek is an enormous advantage. As well as being very familiar with the trek itself, your guide will also be in a position to introduce you to the local people (invariably family, friends or relations) along the way. This can make a trek infinitely more rewarding and open up a whole new world which would otherwise be far more difficult to connect with. The best guides will also take the main responsible for hiring porters, ideally dealing with people with whom they are already familiar. This can be of enormous importance when it comes to dealing with any disputes which may (and often do) arise concerning porters.

Given the profitability of the profession it is not surprising that there is no shortage of people offering their services as guides. The main distinction is between government-registered guides, who are officially permitted to lead trekking groups, and unofficial guides. Government-registered guides are generally either working for one or more of the foreign/local trekking companies, or on a freelance basis, or as is commonly the case, a combination of the two. They are generally reliable, although there is a great deal of variation in their level of competence. All will have a certificate confirming their status as registered guides (if someone is unable to produce one they are probably not registered). With unofficial guides, there is a much greater element of chance.

Both registered and unofficial

guides, if they are any good, will have built up a collection of letters of recommendation from previous clients. This is invariably the most revealing indicator of their competence, and with those who have genuinely built up a solid reputation over the years, it is the best insurance against opportunistic rip-offs. Ultimately however, and particularly in remoter areas, choosing a guide is largely a matter of intuition; at the least, you should get a sense of whether you feel comfortable putting yourself in that person's hands, and whether you are prepared to spend the duration of your trek with them. Local trekking companies will have their own register of guides; if you explain that you wish to organize your own trek they are usually willing to recommend an available guide.

It is usual practice to pay guides on a daily basis, as oppose to by stages (see below). Rates vary a great deal between different areas and according to the experience/competence of the guide, whether they are registered and the difficulty of the trek to be undertaken. In 1995, the daily wage for guides generally ranged from around Rs 350 up to Rs 700. As a rule it is worth paying more for a guide with a proven reputation and experience; often it can end up saving a great deal more in the long run.

Porters

The terms and conditions on which porters are hired are the most frequent source of disputes and misunderstandings. If you have a good guide they will hopefully be able to foresee and avoid such difficulties. But however good your guide, it is crucially important that you involve yourself with the hiring of porters and are able to satisfy yourself that all the terms and conditions of their employment have been discussed, understood and agreed.

Porters are traditionally paid by the stage. Stages are more or less established, again according to tradition, along each

particular route. Most disputes arise out of the fact that an average day's trek will usually cover at least 2 porter's stages, meaning that the rate of payment you agree with your porters is not per day, but per stage. At lower altitudes this can end up being very expensive; over flat terrain, a porter's stage may be no more than a couple of hours walk. Make sure that it is crystal clear as to whether you are paying your porters by the day or by the stage, and establish beforehand the number of stages on a particular trek. The official line on porters is that they should cover between 10-13 km/day, although in practice this has little or no relevance. One option is to negotiate a fixed payment for the porters for the whole trek. Other related points to clarify before setting off include payment on rest days or in case of forced halts due to bad weather (officially full pay), payment for the return trip (officially half pay) and transport arrangements if the porters will be returning home by road. A good idea is to write out an informal 'contract' for your porters, covering all details of payment, transport, food and clothing. It is also well worth making a list of your porters so that you can get them to sign against their names (or tick them off) after paying them.

Food and clothing

There are a number of government regulations regarding food and clothing for porters. Again it is essential to establish exact arrangements beforehand. Officially you are required to provide each porter with the following rations:

	grams/day
Atta (wheat flour)	624
Ghee (cooking oil)	71
Dal (lentils)	85
Meat	100
Sugar	57
Tea	14
Milk	57
Salt	14
Onions (dried)	7
Curry powder	7
Cigarettes	10
Matches	1 box/week

On this basis, each porter requires around 1 kg of food/day. In practice porters often prefer to be paid a daily rate in lieu of their food ration and to make their own arrangements for food, particularly if trekking through their own areas where they can eat with relations and friends. Make sure though that porters take adequate food if you are heading beyond any settlements.

Government rules stipulate that each porter must be equipped with rubber shoes, gloves, sunglasses and two pairs of socks, as well as a stove/fuel and tarpaulin sheet per 8 porters. At higher altitudes they require in addition a jacket, and if walking on snow, proper boots. Again in practice little of this is adhered to, although the rubber shoes are often expected. However, each year a number of porters die in accidents, usually related to inadequate equipment. If you are going to be trekking across ice or snow, it is your responsibility to ensure that porters have the right equipment; rubber shoes are not adequate. Indeed, rubber shoes must be the most grotesquely inappropriate kit for porters wherever they are walking; canvas shoes are not that much more expensive and are far more comfortable.

Clothing and equipment

Proper clothing and equipment is essential for trekking in northern Pakistan. It is possible in summer at lower altitude treks to get away with surprisingly little, but if the weather turns bad you could find yourself in serious trouble. At higher altitudes weather conditions can get extremely nasty very suddenly at any time of year. The following is not a comprehensive list, but covers the main essentials.

Clothing

In terms of warmth, a good combination is to have a high quality 'fleece' type jacket and a waterproof/windproof jacket to go over it in extreme conditions. Full thermal underwear is also very warm and relatively light. It is through the extremities of the body however that most heat is lost, so good gloves, socks and a woollen hat are vital. In most circumstances it can get quite hot during the daytime so light, loose-fitting, cotton clothing is the most practical. Many people swear by the traditional Pakistani *shalwar kamiz* as the ideal loose-fitting, light-weight, quick-drying attire. A broad-brimmed sun hat is invaluable for protection against the sun.

Footwear

Footwear is largely a question of personal preference. The most important thing is to have adequate ankle support, for which boots are essential. Good quality leather boots with a metal *shank* in the sole are the most robust and supportive, but some people prefer to go for lighter-weight canvas or synthetic boots. Trainers can be very comfortable and perfectly adequate on many treks, but they do not give any ankle support and therefore increase the likelihood of a sprained ankle or worse. They are however very pleasant to change into after a days walking, and invaluable for fording streams.

Equipment

A good sleeping bag (minimum four-season, preferably five; a cotton sleeping bag liner will increase the warmth of a sleeping bag considerably), a sleeping mat and a tent able to withstand strong winds (domed or tunnel tents are generally the best) are essential. If you are carrying your own load, a good framed rucksack is vital and worth spending money on. Women should choose a rucksack specially designed for wider hips. If you are taking porters, a day pack is still neccessary (your porters will rarely be in the same place as you en-route). Other essentials include a first-aid kit (see above and main Health section), a water bottle to carry with you while walking, torch, sun cream (minimum factor 15) and sun block, lip cream (sunburnt lips are no fun), sunglasses (note that cheaper sunglasses can seriously damage your eyes by encouraging your pupils to dilate without actually filtering out harmful rays) and snow glasses if you are likely to spend much time above the snow-line. In an emergency, a 'survival blanket' (insulating silver sheet) and 'bivvy bag' (reinforced plastic sack large enough to crawl into) are potential life-savers; be sure to carry them with you if trekking with porters. A telescopic ski pole is useful for balance when fording rivers, traversing scree slopes and if walking on snow or ice. Other more specialized equipment such as ice-axes, crampons, ropes etc are only of value if you have experience in using them in the relevant conditions.

Cooking

Cooking equipment is an important consideration. Kerosene or petrol stoves are most practical in that fuel is readily available, even in fairly remote areas (a fine-gauze strainer is very useful for filtering out impurities). High tech stoves such as the MSR are the lightest and most efficient. Older designs or locally made kerosene stoves have the advantage of being more readily serviceable, particularly the latter, for which spares are available in any bazaar. Make sure that you have spares of all the main components before setting out; most failures are related to the pump (make sure it is properly oiled) and to blockages in the vaporizing jets (take lots of needle 'pokers'). Aluminium 1 litre fuel containers are best, but large groups will need a larger plastic jerry can (the latter are readily available in most bazaars in 5, 10 and 25 litre sizes). Butane/propane gas (Gaz) stoves are lighter, but finding refills is difficult (though not impossible) and you face the problem of getting them onto flights. They also generally have less heating power than kerosene/petrol. The best are those that re-seal themselves automatically when dismantled. A pressure cooker is a good idea, particularly at higher altitudes where it can save significant amounts of fuel and is the only way to force water up to 100°C. A large foldable plastic water container saves numerous trips to collect water at camp.

Hiring/buying equipment

It is becoming increasingly possible to hire equipment in Pakistan. Many of the local trekking agencies have built up a comprehensive range of equipment from previous expeditions, including sleeping bags, tents, ice axes, crampons, ropes etc. Some agencies are in a position to fully equip a large group for even the most demanding treks. Apart from Islamabad, where the larger trekking agencies have their head offices, Skardu and Gilgit have the widest range; Chitral has relatively little. Details of what is available and from whom is given are the regional sections.

Rawalpindi and Gilgit are the best places to buy equipment, although there is a certain amount available in Skardu and Chitral. Most readily available are army surplus items such as sleeping bags, groundsheets, jackets etc, although all tend to be heavy. Left over expedition equipment is sometimes available and trekking agencies are sometimes willing to sell equipment.

Whether hiring or buying second-hand equipment, be sure to check that it is in good condition. Hiring ropes is not a good idea unless you are sure of their condition. Boots are much better brought from home. Buy new boots well in advance and take time to break them in properly.

Food

The most important thing is to ensure a balanced diet (proteins, fats, vitamins, minerals, carbohydrates and fibre) and an adequate intake of calories (anywhere between 3,000 and 4,500 depending on your weight, metabolism and level of activity). Vitamin and mineral deficiencies are the most likely when trekking. Vitamin supplements are a good idea (many vitamins quickly deteriorate in even relatively fresh fruit and vegetables). Salts are rapidly lost from the body through perspiration and must be replaced. Carbohydrates (eg wheat, rice, sugar) are your main source of instant energy and need to be consumed in increased quantities; pasta is the most easily and efficiently converted carbohydrate energy source.

The main consideration in planning what food to take on a trek is whether you intend to rely on what is available in Pakistan or to bring your own supplies from home. A combination of the two gives the most flexibility and variety. The standard porters' fare of chapatis, rice, dhal, vegetables and tea (with lots of milk and sugar) is actually very nutritious and is readily available in any bazaar. The fastest cooking varieties of lentils are *mung* and *masoor*. It is often possible to obtain fresh dairy products from shepherds when trekking through summer pastures, but don't rely on it (remember also that milk and cheese will not have been pasteurized). Other items readily available all over Pakistan include pasta, biscuits, porridge, dried fruit, nuts and fresh seasonal fruits and vegetables, dried milk, tea, sugar, salt and spices. Items such as tinned and freeze-dried foods, stock cubes, coffee, honey and jam, yeast extract, tomato ketchup and other condiments are more readily available in major cities such as Islamabad/Rawalpindi, but can sometimes be found in Chitral, Gilgit and Skardu.

The most useful items to bring from home include freeze-dried/dehydrated foods (packet soups, though available in Pakistan, are generally pretty foul), instant noodles, high-energy foods such as chocolate bars, glucose tablets etc. **NB** Many of these items can often be found in Chitral, Gilgit and Skardu, having been left behind by previous expeditions; it is a matter of luck though as to what is actually available.

BALTISTAN

Treks from Hushe

The village of Hushe marks the end of the jeep track and the start of treks N towards the glaciers of Aling, Masherbrum, Gondogoro and Chogolisa, and numerous peaks in the area. For details of the route up from Khaplu, and camping and accommodation in Hushe, see page 498. The village is basically very well set up to handle trekkers and climbers. Unless a large group have hired everyone and everything (fairly unlikely), it is usually possible to turn up in Hushe and organize guides, porters, equipment and food for any of the treks to the N.

Guides, equipment and supplies

Each of the camping sites in Hushe is owned by a government-registered guide (see under Hushe), and there are several others from Hushe, including Firma Ali, Mohammad Nazir and Anwar Ali, a free-lancer with plenty of experience and good humour. There is a considerable amount of equipment available for hire, including tents, sleeping bags, crampons, ice axes, ropes etc (**NB** Check the condition of equipment before setting off; most climbers avoid using second-hand ropes of uncertain age/history). Hamza Ali (Leyla Peak Camping) has a good selection of equipment, as does Ashraf Hussain (Gondogoro Camp Site), and the *K2 Shop* claims to have enough to equip a party of 12. The latter, and also a couple of other stores, usually have a reasonable selection of high-energy, freeze-dried and tinned foods left over from previous expeditions, though it depends on who has passed through recently.

Gondogoro La

Open zone. Maximum elevation 5,500m. Jun to Sep. Maps: Swiss Foundation are the best; U502 series, NI 43-3 Mundik, is adequate as far as Dalsan Pa. Trek researched first hand. **NB** This trek is in an open zone as far as the top of Gondogoro

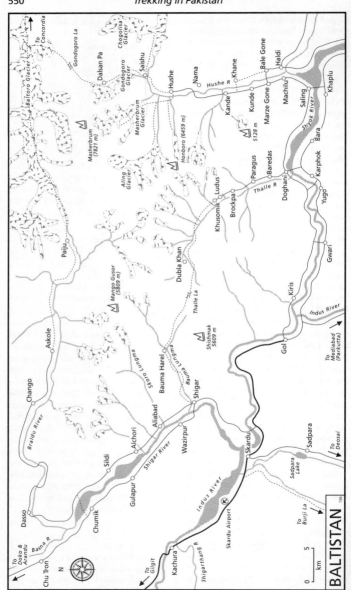

La, but trekkers are not allowed to descend to the Baltoro glacier and Concordia without a permit. On previous occasions, those caught on the Concordia side without a permit have been helicoptered back to Skardu at their own expense (around US$4,000).

This is a very beautiful trek, and if you go all the way up to the top of Gondogoro La, you have the benefit of some of the best close-up views of K2 and a host of other high peaks in the fore-ground. The panorama is breathtaking. It is also an extremely strenuous climb (particularly without the benefit of a couple of weeks walking and acclimatising that you get if you come from the Baltoro side), with the top of the pass being at an altitude of 5,500m (another 500m and it would qualify as a mountain, requiring a permit etc), and involving a climb along the glacier and a snow traverse. A guide and proper equipment (high-altitude clothing/bedding, crampons, rope) is essential if going this far. It is perfectly possible to trek as far as Dalsan Pa (the last stop before heading onto the glacier) without a guide, and for the less determined this is still a very beautiful and worthwhile trek.

From Hushe it is 6 stages up to Dalsan Pa (3-4 days), and a further three to the top of the pass (2 days). The path heads N along the E bank of the river through fields and stands of willow and wild rose. It then bears E along the S bank of the **Charaksar River**, passing through a summer camp used by shepherds. Just beyond where the Gondogoro River joins from the N, a bridge crosses to the N bank to reach **Saishu**, where there is good camping. A rubbish pit and latrines have been dug here, and in season there are even a couple of simple 'shops'. The path then climbs up the E side of Gondogoro River and glacier, following lateral moraine and stretches of ablation valley. There are several possible camping places, with the main one being at **Gondogoro summer settlement**. Above here there is a difficult stretch down beside the edge of the glacier before climbing back onto the lateral moraine and then passing through a beautiful meadow area and up to **Dalsan Pa**. Dalsan Pa is particularly beautiful, with two small lakes and a meadow that is carpeted with flowers in spring. The last 3 stages from Dalsan Pa – onto the glacier, up to Gondogoro base camp and then to the top – is where the going gets tough. An alternative route crosses the extremely difficult and technical Masherbrum La.

Chogolisa and Charaksar Glaciers

From Saishu a route continues E along the N bank of the Charaksa River and then along the N side of the Charaksar glacier to its junction with the Chogolisa glacier. The valley is more barren than the Gondogoro or Masherbrum, and the main attractions are the opportunities for climbing K6 and K7.

Masherbrum Base Camp

Open zone. Maximum elevation optional (up to 4,200m). Jun to Sep. Maps: as for Gondogoro La.

This trek bears off to the NW above Hushe and follows the left side of the Masherbrum glacier up to the base camp. Cross the footbridge just N of Hushe village to the W bank of the river. The path crosses the Honboro River, passes through a seasonal settlement and then crosses the Aling River. Higher up is **Dumsung**, and a little further on is **Parbisan**, both good camping spots. As far as Parbisan (1 stage) is easy and pleasant, passing through fields and stands of wild rose, willow, juniper and tamarisk. Above Parsiban, there is a difficult section up onto the lateral moraine, for which a guide is recommended. Once on top, it is a beautiful walk along the lateral moraine to **Brumbrama**, situated on a wide sandy area between the lateral moraine and the mountains. It is possible to reach this far in a day (2 stages). A little higher up is **Chogospang**, with a few stone huts where in summer women tend large flocks of sheep and goats, as well as yaks, cows and *dzo*. Above Chogospang the path follows the lateral moraine before dropping down onto the glacier itself to reach Masherbrum Base Camp (c 4,200m). A guide is recommended also for this last stretch.

Aling Glacier

A trekking route follows the N bank of the Aling River as far as the summer settlement of Ghazala, on the N side of the Aling glacier. Allow 2 days to trek as far as here.

Thalle La

Open Zone. Maximum elevation 4,572. Jul to Sep. Maps: Swiss Foundation are the best; U502 series, NI 43-3 Mundik, is reasonably accurate topographically, though place names are mostly redundant. Trek researched first hand.

This trek is easily accessible from Skardu and makes an excellent trek if you are looking for something not too demanding, or wish to acclimatize and improve your fitness. It can be done in either direction; the ascent to the pass is gentler from Shigar side, though if you cannot afford to organize jeeps to pick you up at the end of the trek, it is probably best to finish in Shigar, where public transport back to Skardu is readily available (on the Thalle side you are likely to have to walk all the way down to **Doghani** before finding any public transport). The trek is here described from Doghani to Shigar. If you are fit and determined, the trek can be done in 3 days; 4 days is more manageable, or 5 if you wish to go slowly and have time to relax and explore at the end of each day's walking.

For details of getting to Doghani, at the foot of the Thalle valley, see page 495. From Doghani, the jeep track continues up the Thalle valley as far as **Khusomik**, the last permanent village. Up until about 50 years ago, the side valley that drains from the E at Khusomik was used as a route across to Kande in the Hushe valley. However, glacial advance and deep crevasses have made this route no longer passable.

From Khusomik the trail crosses the side valley on a foot bridge and climbs gently past two small areas of fields and pasture and then crosses to the W bank of the valley. The side valley that leads off to the SW from here is a trekking route across to Kiris, on the N bank of the Shyok near where it joins the Indus. The trail continues up through beautiful summer pastures with rich green meadows, flowers (Jul and early Aug), fields and scattered seasonal settlements of tiny stone houses and animal enclosures. There are numerous places to camp along this stretch. Higher up, near **Metsik Pa**, which consists of two animal enclosures with huts, the valley forks. The left fork is the route up to Thalle La, while the right fork leads up to the much higher and more difficult **Tusserpo La** (5,048m) which provides an alternative route over to Shigar. *Metsik Pa* means 'place of fire' in Balti, and according to locals this area was thickly wooded until around 100 years ago, when a huge fire which raged for more than a month completely destroyed the forests.

The trail continues along the left bank of the stream to **Dumsum** (literally meaning 'junction'), where there are shepherds' huts, before crossing to the right bank. There is one more potential camping place higher up at **La**, again a small seasonal settlement of shepherds' huts, before the final ascent up to **Thalle La** (4,572m). From the top of the pass it is a long steady descent along the right bank of the stream. The pastures on either side of the pass abound in Marmots. Lower down, the vegetation gradually gives way to stunted woods of pine, Juniper and wild rose. There are three small settlements in close succession, offering good camping places, before reaching **Bauma Harel**, at the junction of the Thalle La and Tusserpo La valleys, again a good camping spot. From Bauma Harel it is a steep descent down the **Bauma Lungma**, which is a narrow, rocky and dry gorge for much of the way. The path follows the right bank, crosses to the left and then back to the right bank. Beyond the second bridge, on the left bank, is the picturesque settlement of **Anisgal**. Further on, the trail passes the similar settlement of **Ol**, before finally reaching the hydro-electric power station at **Chaupi Ol**, from where it is a short walk along a jeep track down to Shigar village.

Baltoro Glacier; Concordia & K2

Restricted zone. Maximum elevation optional (5,000m plus). Jun to mid Sep. Maps: Swiss Foundation are the best; Leomann's sheets 2 and 3 are also good; U502 series, NI 43-3, Mundik and NI 43-4, Chulung are adequate; the excellent 1977 Japanese-Pakistan K2 1;100,000 map covers the Baltoro glacier only.

Since this trek is in a restricted zone and therefore requires a permit and registered guide, no detailed route description is given here. In practice it is only possible to obtain a permit through a recognized trekking agency. It is far and away the most popular trek in Pakistan, attracting large numbers of trekking groups (all the major trekking agencies bring groups here) as well as numerous mountaineering expeditions en-route to peaks around Concordia. As a result it can get seriously crowded and some of the main campsites have become heavily polluted.

However, the popularity of this trek is also an accurate reflection of its attractions. The trek in along the **Braldu** and **Biaho** rivers, and then onto the Baltoro glacier is a long and extremely demanding one. The reward on the other hand is spectacular, taking you right into the heart of the Karakoram mountains at **Concordia**, where the **Godwin-Austin glacier** descends from **K2** to join the Baltoro. Surrounding these huge expanses of ice are some of the highest peaks in the world, with seven of them – K2, Broad Peak, Gasherbrum IV, Mustagh Tower, Golden Throne, Chogolisa and Masherbrum – clearly visible.

Notwithstanding landslides and blockages, the jeep track now extends as far as **Askole**. See page 495 for details of the route from Skardu up the Shigar and Braldu valleys to Askole. The trek from Askole to Concordia takes around 8 days, not including rest days. Porters on this trek can be difficult, often striking for increased pay, or refusing to go beyond the lower stages of the trek. There are 20 recognized stages between Askole and Concordia. It takes a full day to trek up to the K2 base camp from Concordia. Count 4-6 days for the return trip.

Another option which is becoming increasingly popular is to trek out of Concordia into the Hushe valley over the Gondogoro pass (see above). At 5,500m the route across this pass is extremely strenuous. An alternative route across the Masherbrum pass is slightly lower (5,364m), but extemely difficult, involving technical sections on the descent through an icefall on the far side and requiring ropes, crampons and ice axes.

Biafo-Hispar; Askole to Nagar

Open zone. Maximum elevation 5,150m. Jul to mid Sep. Maps: Swiss Foundation are best; U502 series, NI 43-3 Mundik, NJ 43-15 Shimshal, NJ 43-14 Baltit, reliability poor but adequate. See map, page 421 for reference.

Although this trek is in an open zone, it is extremely strenuous, involving long stretches of glacier walking along this 115 km ice corridor; a guide is essential, as well as crampons and ropes. Most people recommend doing the trek from Baltistan to Nagar rather than vica-versa since porters in Nagar have a bad reputation. The trek takes you far from any permanent settlements and is rich in wildlife, including Himalayan Brown Bears. It begins at **Askole**, following the K2 trek for a short way before branching up the Biafo glacier. The first part of this trek, up the lower sections of the Biafo glacier are particularly difficult. Above the junction of the Sim Gang and Biafo glaciers, off to the N approaching Hispar Pass, is **Snow Lake**, a huge expanse of ice covering around 80 sq km. Known locally as Lukpe Lawo, it was named Snow Lake in 1892 by the British explorer Martin Conway. The 5,150m **Hispar Pass** provides stunning views in good weather; W down the Hispar glacier towards Hunza and E back to the peaks surrounding Snow Lake and Sim Gang glacier. The trek down to Hispar village along the N edge of the Hispar Glacier is difficult in places, crossing 4-side glaciers en-route. Between these there are several beautiful ablation valleys (small valleys running parallel to the glacier), rich in alpine flora and with plentiful water. **Hispar village**, the first permanent settlement after leaving Askole, is at the head of the jeep track which runs up past Nagar village from the KKH opposite Karimabad. There is no regular public transport up to Hispar, so unless you have organized a jeep to meet you at Hispar, it is still another 2 days' walk down to Nagar, where you can count on finding public transport. The trek between Askole and Hispar villages takes around 12 days (not including rest days) and involves around 16-18 porter stages (definite porter stages on this route have not been established).

Deosai Plateau

Open zone. Maximum elevation optional (4,080-4,820m). Aug. Maps: the U502 series, NI 43-3 Mundik and NI 43-2 Gilgit are not accurate enough to be relied on for treks on Deosai. Partially researched first hand. **NB** Foreigners are not permitted to go S or E of the jeep track between Ali Malik Mar (pass) and Chachhor Pass without a permit.

The Deosai plateau offers several opportunities for trekking and is easily accessible from Skardu. The route along the jeep track across the Deosai, from Skardu to Astor, is described in detail in the Baltistan section. It can also be done as a trek; allow around 5 days between Skardu and Chilam, where public trans-

port is generally available on to Astor.

Burji La

The most popular trek is a short loop from Skardu, climbing up past Sadpara Lake, across Ali Malik Mar, then doubling back across Burji La and down to Skardu. This takes around 4 days. It is advisable to do the trek in this direction as the ascent from Skardu to the 4,820m Burji La is extremely steep and involves an altitude gain of nearly 2,500m in just 2 days. In either direction, it is essential to acclimatize properly first; do not be tempted to do this trek if you have just flown into Skardu. The approach to Burji La from the S does not follow any clear path and the route across the pass itself can be difficult to determine. A guide is strongly recommended (**NB** There is no shortage of people in Skardu claiming to be guides; only go with someone who has references proving they have done the trek).

If walking from Skardu, the best place to camp for the first night is by the checkpost on the jeep track above Sadpara village. The second day takes you over **Ali Malik Mar** (4,080m) to the shepherds' huts and camping ground just beyond the pass. From here follow the jeep track on for a short distance and then branch off sharply to the right to head due N towards Burji La (if you reach the main fork in the jeep track you have gone too far). The approach to the pass leads past two small lakes with options for camping wherever there is water. The pass itself gives spectacular views of the Karakoram mountains to the N, and S back onto the Deosai. It is feasible to reach Skardu from the top of the pass in 1 day, although an overnight stop half way down at some shepherd's huts is more realistic.

Shigarthang Valley

From near Kachura Lake trekking routes lead up the Shigarthang valley onto the Deosai. Higher up, the valley divides. The left fork climbs SE over the

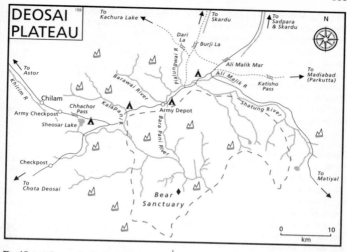

Dari La and on to the Deosai. From here you can angle sharply NE over the **Burji La** and drop down towards Skardu, or else join the rough Skardu-Astor jeep track to the S. The right fork continues SW up the main stream, crosses the **Alam Pir La**, and then follows first the **Bubind** and then the **Das Khirim** valley down towards Astor. An alternative route branches W above the first fork in the valley, across the **Banak La** and descends the Parishing River directly to Astor. The editors have not covered these routes, but a survey of the literature reveals some confusion as to names and exact routes; a guide familiar with the area is strongly recommended.

Around Nanga Parbat

The Astor valley provides the main access for treks around Nanga Parbat. For details of the route to Astor village, and the walk up to Rama Lake, see page 458. Another approach to Nanga Parbat is from the N side, leaving the KKH at Raikot Bridge and climbing up past Fairy Meadows. For details of Fairy Meadows, see page 454.

Rupal Valley
Open zone. Maximum elevation optional (4,000-5,377m). Jun to Sep. Maps: the Deutsche Himalaya Expedition of Nanga Parbat is excellent; U502 series, NI 43-2 Gilgit also good. See map, page 455.

This trek is a popular with trekking agencies. It is fairly easy and perfectly possible without a guide. There is regular public transport from Gilgit as far as Astor. From Astor it is usually neccessary to hire a jeep, or walk. It is sometimes possible to get a lift as far as Gurikot with jeeps heading for Chilam. The jeep track reaches as far as the village of **Tarashing**, where there is a basic hotel with a garden. There are always plenty of guides and porters available here, as well as horses and donkeys for hire. It takes around 4 days to reach Mazeno Base Camp and return by the same route.

The trail climbs the lateral moraine of **Tarashing glacier** before crossing the glacier on a good path to reach the settlement of **Rupal**, divided into upper and lower villages. There is good camping beyond the upper village, or further on at **Bazhin**, an ideal spot with woods, flowers and clear spring water. The path then crosses the Bazhin glacier (again, this is an easy glacier crossing; there is also a fairly regular flow of locals going back and forth if you don't feel confident on your own). On the far side, below the lateral moraine, is another good camping place known as **Tupp Meadow**, surrounded by summer settlements where sheep, goats, dzo and horses are brought to graze. An alternative route from Rupal village crosses to the S bank of the river on a good bridge and skirts the snout of the Bazhin glacier to arrive at Tupp Meadow. From here the trail continues up the Rupal valley, passing several possible campsites, to **Shaigiri** which offers the best camping and excellent views of Nanga Parbat's S face. The trail then follows lateral moraine as it climbs up to **Mazeno Base Camp**. Beyond the trail bears sharply N and begins its steep ascent to Mazeno Pass (5,377m). About a third of the way up is Mazeno High Camp.

It is possible, instead of returning to Tarashing, to trek over Mazeno Pass and descend into Daimer valley, which gives access to the KKH via the Bunar valley. However, the descent on the Daimer side is technical in places, requiring crampons and ropes, and not recommended unless you are experienced. The area on the Daimer side is also not considered safe in terms of banditry, so a reliable local guide is neccessary; see under 'Dangerous' Areas above.

Chungphar Valley

From Tarashing village, a very pleasant 1 day or overnight trek leads up the Chungphar valley to N. It takes around 4 hrs to reach the summer pastures and settlements on the S flank of Chongra mountain, where there is good camping.

GILGIT

Naltar Valley

The Naltar valley to the N of Gilgit gives access to two possible treks, one leading over the **Daintar Pass** and via the Daintar valley to Chalt in the Chaprot valley, the second leading over the **Naltar Pass** into the Ishkoman valley. Although in an open zone, a guide is recommended for both treks since the routes across the Daintar and Naltar passes are not obvious and it is easy to get lost. Both treks are quite strenuous, although they offer excellent views and welcome relief from the heat of Gilgit. The Naltar valley, as well as being significantly cooler higher up, receives considerably more rainfall than Gilgit and is thickly wooded. There are plenty of Gujar nomads in the upper reaches of the valley. **NB** The Daintar/Chaprot valleys are Shia areas (part of the former kingdom of Nagar), where women are likely to feel less welcome. Allow at least 6 days for the Daintar Pass trek, and 5 days for the Naltar Pass trek (not including rest days). For details of Nomal village and the Naltar valley as far as Naltar village, and of the lakes higher up, see page 465.

Daintar Pass

Open zone. Maximum elevation 4,636m. Jul to Sep. Maps: Swiss Foundation are good; the U502 series, NJ 43-14 Baltit is not adequate for this trek.

From Naltar it is a 3½-4 hr walk up to **Naltar Lake**. The jeep track is sometimes though rarely passable as far as the main lake, which offers the best camping. North of Naltar Lake the path crosses to the E bank of the river and climbs through pastures and moraine to **Lower Shani**. There is good camping along the way, and at Lower Shani. This is where the paths for Naltar and Daintar passes fork.

Climb up onto the ridge to the E of Lower Shani and head N to a flattish shoulder of mountain known as **Daintar Base Camp**. From here the path climbs steadily, following the shoulder, up to Daintar Pass (4,636m). A thick snow cornice forces you to bear off to the right following the crest to its highest point. A little further on it becomes possible to descend a very steep shale gulley to a large snowfield. Lower down there is a large summer pasture offering camping in good weather. The recognized camp-site is further down at the shepherds' settlement of **Tolibari**. From here the path along the S bank of the river runs through woods and pastures, fording

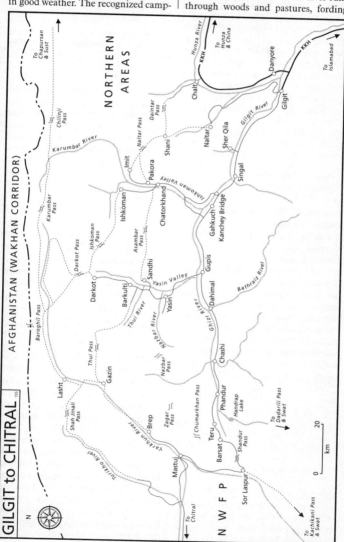

GILGIT to CHITRAL 555

AFGHANISTAN (WAKHAN CORRIDOR)

NORTHERN AREAS

To Chapursan & Sust

To Hunza & China

To Islamabad

Hunza River

KKH

KKH

Gilgit River

Gilgit

Danyore

Chalt

Naltar

Sher Qila

Chilinji Pass

Karumbar River

Daintar Pass

Naltar Pass

Shani

Singal

Imit

Pakora

Ishkoman Valley

Karumbar Pass

Ishkoman

Chatorkhand

Asambar Pass

Ishkoman Pass

Gahkuch

Kanchey Bridge

Darkot Pass

Sandhi

Gupis

Bathrait River

Baroghil Pass

Thui River

Barkulti

Yasin Valley

Dahimal

Darkot

Yasin

Nazbar River

Ghizr River

Chashi

Thui Pass

Nazbar Pass

Gazin

Lasht

Shah Jinali Pass

Yarkhun River

Brep

Zagar Pass

Chumarkhan Pass

Phandur

Handrap Lake

To Dadarili Pass & Swat

Turikho River

Teru

Barsat

Shandur Pass

Mastuj

Sor Laspur

To Chitral

N W F P

To Kachikani Pass & Swat

km

0   20

N

two side streams and then enters a narrow gorge before arriving at the village of **Taling**, where the Daintar River flows down from the N. There is a polo ground above the village. Taling is at the head of the jeep track, although it is often blocked lower down and jeeps rarely come up this far (if you are planning to arrange for a jeep to pick you up from here, check first as to the condition of the track). It takes around 3 hrs to walk down to Talboto Das, from where there are fairly regular passenger jeeps. At Daintar just past Taling, a path on the opposite (S) bank of the river climbs up to the ridge behind and leads down to Chaprot village, 3 km above Chalt.

Naltar (Pakor) Pass

Open zone. Maximum elevation 4,600m. Jul to Sep. Maps: as for Daintar Pass.

From Lower Shani (see above) the path heads W on a good path alongside Shani glacier to **Upper Shani**, a large area of summer pasture at the foot of the pass. Higher up there is another area of summer pasture on a plateau, also good for camping. Naltar (or Pakor) Pass (4,600m) is wide and flat topped, with no definite path across it. Shortly after the summit the route bears off to the right (N) across crevassed snowfields, crosses a small side glacier and then follows the crest of lateral moraine before arriving at a meadow surrounded by trees, known as **Kruibokht**. From here the path follows the Phakora River, passing through pastures, woods and summer settlements, crossing the river three times. The lower section of the valley enters a narrow gorge for a while before opening out as it approaches Pakora village, at the junction with the Ishkoman valley. For details of the Ishkoman valley, see page 471.

Ishkoman Valley to Yasin Valley

There are two trekking routes leading W from the Ishkoman valley into the Yasin valley, one via the Asambar Pass and the other via the Ishkoman Pass.

The easier of the two treks, over the Asambar Pass, is outlined here. There is often plenty of snow on the Ishkoman Pass even in late Aug, and it should not be attempted much earlier.

Asambar Pass

Open zone. Maximum elevation c 4,400m. Jul to Sep. Maps: U502 series, NJ 43-14 Baltit and NJ 43-13 Mastuj are the only ones readily available and are fairly good.

This is a relatively easy trek passing through villages and summer settlements along the way. It can done without a guide. From **Pakora** village (see page 472), cross to the W side of the valley. A good path heads E along the S bank of the Asambar River, passing through stands of willow and silver birch, fields and small settlements. **Chalinj**, a large settlement situated at the junction of a side valley draining in from the SW, makes for a convenient overnight stop. From Chalinj it is possible to cross the Asambar Pass and reach suitable camping on the far side in one long day, or there is an area of pasture good for camping at the foot of the pass, beyond the last settlement. There are in fact two passes, seperated by a rounded hill. The Asambar is the easier of the two. The path over it climbs steadily and then branches off to the right, around the hill. There are magnificent views from the top. On the other side, the path descends to the first settlement of **Jiji Shawaran** and then crosses to the S bank of the river. A little further on is a beautiful campsite by a small lake. If you have walked all the way from Chalinj, this is the obvious place to camp. The walk down to the Yasin valley is a pleasant one, passing through woods and settlements, with places to camp all along the route. The path crosses to the N bank of the river to arrive at the permanent village of **Chuchuanotik**, and then follows the jeep track to join the Yasin valley at the village of **Sandhi** (see page 475).

Rakaposhi South Face

There are two possible treks starting near to Gilgit which lead up towards the S face of Rakaposhi, giving excellent views of the mountain. The first runs from Danyore village up to the glacier at the head of the Danyore valley. The second runs E from the village of Chirah at the head of the jeep track up the Bagrot valley, along the Burche glacier and over the Rakhan Pass (4,548m) into the Haramosh valley, to emerge on the Skardu road near Sasli (or Sassi). Details of this trek are not given as there is no reliable information as to the exact route. For details of the Bagrot valley, see page 466.

Danyore valley

Open zone. Maximum elevation c 4,000m. Jul to Sep. Maps: Swiss Foundation good; U502 series, NI 43-2 Gilgit and NJ 43-14 Baltit are adequate. Trek researched first hand.

This trek is an excellent way of getting in shape for more strenuous treks; it does not involve crossing any passes, and although the lower sections of the valley are hot and dry, higher up there are beautiful alpine woods and pastures in the ablation valley alongside the glacier flowing down from Rakaposhi. Allow 2 days (3 going slowly) to reach the head of the valley, and 2 (or 1 very long day) to return.

The path into the valley climbs up through **Danyore village**, heading towards the "Danyore Hydel Project" on the right bank of the river. It takes 4-5 hrs in a baking hot, bare rock canyon to reach the first spring water. The path then crosses the river three times before climbing steeply over a shoulder and descending once again to the river. Further on, across a wide stony plain, a rock cairn marks the point where a small spring emerges at the base of the low cliffs by the river. The path then climbs steeply up to **Barit village**, situated on a small plateau. Rich green terraced fields extend up the side valley flowing in from

the W. The path crosses the side valley on a wooden bridge and then climbs steeply to rejoin the main valley, running along an irrigation channel. It then continues past three bridges giving access to cultivated summer settlements on the E bank before climbing up through pine forests to a small summer settlement high above the river. There is spring water available here. After descending back to the river level, cross to the E bank of the river. The path, marked by stone cairns, runs through lightly wooded, rocky terrain. It crosses a small side stream and then climbs onto the ridge of glacier's lateral moraine. Follow the ridge until the ablation valley to the right widens out into an large area of alpine pastures, woods and streams, offering numerous idyllic camping spots. It is well worth spending a day or 2 here to explore and take in the awesome scenery.

HUNZA

The Hunza region offers some excellent trekking, with the added advantage that all of it is easily accessible directly from the KKH. For women, this is also one of the best areas to trek (along with Upper Chitral) as the people are predominantly Ismaili and therefore more liberal in their outlook. The exception to this is the Shia areas of the former kingdom of Nagar (Chalt/Chaprot valley and Nagar valley).

Rakaposhi/Diran

Open zone. Maximum elevation optional (2,400-4,000m). Apr to Oct. Maps: Deutsche Himalaya Expedition of Minapin is excellent; Swiss Foundation good; U502 series, NJ 43-14 Baltit is reasonable. See map, page 501 for reference.

This is a fairly easy, ideal first trek offering excellent views of the N face of Rakaposhi. Its only disadvantage is that the porters in the area have a reputation for being greedy and expensive (they usually try to charge for 6 stages and insist that you hire new porters for the return trip). It takes 2 days (or 1 long day) to reach Tagafari, and one to return. Beyond Tagafari you must cross the glacier and a guide is recommended. For details of getting to Minapin village, 4 km from the KKH, see page 506.

From **Minapin village** the path follows the irrigation channel and crosses the river on a good bridge. It then follows the right bank of the river before ascending steeply through woods to a summer settlement known as **Bungidas**. Higher up is the smaller summer settlement of **Hapakun** with good camping. The path continues through woods and pastures, climbing steeply to the crest of lateral moraine which until now has hidden the huge Minapin glacier to the left. There are spectacular views from here of Diran peak (7,266m). The narrow path then traverses a scree slope which drops away steeply down to the glacier before descending to **Tagafari**, a narrow field between the lateral moraine and Rakaposhi. If this is as far as you intend to go, it is well worth spending a day here to explore and take in the scenery. From Tagafari, it is possible to cross the Minapin glacier to **Kacheili**, a summer pasture with superb views of Rakaposhi. Take a guide.

Treks from Passu

There are numerous trekking options from Passu ranging from easy day walks to strenuous treks. Two are covered here; the relatively easy Batura glacier trek and the more difficult and demanding Shimshal trek. For details of Passu, and some of the shorter walks in the area, see page 518.

Batura Glacier

Open zone. Maximum elevation optional (up to 4,000m). Early Jun to late Sep. Maps: the Chinese Institute of Glaciology map of Batura is excellent; Swis foundation is good; U502 series, NJ 43-14 Baltit is adequate. Trek researched first hand.

The Batura glacier trek is a popular one

and relatively easy, apart from the crossing of the glacier at the beginning of the trek. It can be completed in 6-8 days, although you may want longer to explore higher up the glacier.

There are two ways to start the trek, either via the **Yunz** valley (see under Short Walks from Passu), or by following the S side of the Batura glacier from the KKH to the N of Passu. If taking the latter route it is well worth trying to find transport to drop you off by the Batura glacier itself. Both ways lead to the shepherds' hut at **Yunzbin**, where you can camp. From here the main route crosses to the N side of the Batura glacier, although it is possible to continue along the S side a far as **Kirgas Washik** and then cross near there. The exact route across the glacier from Yunzbin changes each year and is marked by small stone cairns set up by the locals at the beginning of the season. A guide is recommended for the crossing unless you have experience of glaciers; the most difficult part is getting off the glacier again from its northern edge. Once off the glacier, the path climbs through a series of lightly wooded ablation valleys to **Yashpirt**, the main summer settlement for the people of Passu. There are spectacular views from here of the glacier and surrounding mountains; it is also a beautiful place to spend a day or two exploring. The path continues up through the summer pastures and settlements of **Fatmahil**, **Kukhil** and **Shelmin** to **Gutshim**, the last summer settlement. All of these are good for camping. Higher up at the pasture of **Lupdor**, the ablation valley ends and the only way to continue further is on the glacier. The return journey is back along the same route.

Shimshal Valley

Restricted zone, maximum elevation optional (4,700m if going all the way to Shewert), Jul to Aug (Apr to Oct for Shimshal village only). Maps: Swiss Foundation is good; U502 series, NJ 43-14 Baltit and NJ 43-15 Shimshal are adequate. Trek researched first hand. **NB** Although not officially listed as being in a restricted zone, you are required to take a local guide for all treks from Shimshal village. This was largely the result of a British climber trekking across into China from Shimshal, which led initially to a permanent police post in the village. Shambi Khan, the village headman, subsequently negotiated a deal whereby all foreigners would be accompanied by guides. It may also be neccessary to get a permit from Gilgit; enquire with the DC there.

The information given here is based on research carried out in 1991. At that time, the jeep track which the Shimshalis were fighting so hard to have built reached only 6 km or so into the valley, as far as **Jurgur**. Since then, it has apparently been extended all the way to the **Molunguti glacier**, and may now even reach as far as the village. However, the valley is a narrow gorge for most of the way, and extremely unstable. It is likely to be subject to frequent (and potentially dangerous) landslides and blockages,

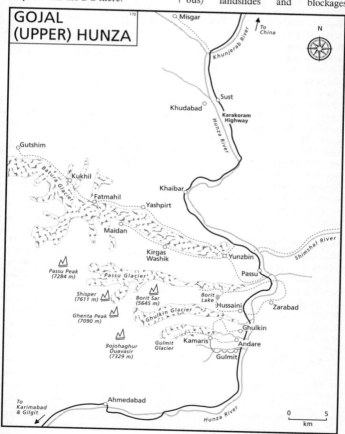

GOJAL (UPPER) HUNZA

170

To China

N

Misgar

Khunjerab River

Sust

Khudabad

Hunza River

Karakoram Highway

Gutshim

Batura Glacier

Kukhil

Fatmahil

Khaibar

Yashpirt

Maidan

Kirgas Washik

Yunzbin

Shimshal River

Passu Peak (7284 m)

Passu Glacier

Passu

Shisper (7611 m)

Borit Sar (5645 m)

Borit Lake

Ghenta Peak (7090 m)

Ghulkin Glacier

Hussaini

Zarabad

Bojohaghur Duavasir (7329 m)

Gulmit Glacier

Kamaris

Ghulkin

Andare

Gulmit

Ahmedabad

To Karimabad & Gilgit

Hunza River

0   5
km

particularly during rains. Check first as to the current situation.

Shimshal village (3,150m) is a refreshing and beautiful oasis of green after the stark and barren gorge that preceeds it. In 1991 there was one basic 'hotel', the *Distaghil Cottage*. Others may since have opened. If you are with a local guide, he will probably be able to arrange accommodation.

The trek from Shimshal to Shujerab is a demanding one, crossing three passes, and takes 3 days. It is also very beautiful. Porters charge for 5 stages. The path leads E from the village (entering the Khunjerab National Park) and then crosses to the N bank of the river on a good bridge. Further on it climbs steeply N up the W bank of the **Zardgarbin** valley before crossing to the E bank and climbing E to an area of pasture with good camping by a large boulder below **Wyeen Pass** (4,560m, also referred to as Zardgarbin Pass).

Another route continues up the Zardgarbin River, across the **Boesam Pass** (5490m) and follows the Ghujerab River to rejoin the KKH to the N of Sust. This is difficult trek, primarily due to the repeated crossings of the Ghujerab River, and can only be undertaken after late Sep, when the water level is lower.

The climb over Wyeen Pass is strenuous and, immediately after the steep and difficult descent from the pass, it climbs once again, zigzagging steeply up the mountainside, to cross the **Shachmirk Pass** (4,350m), marked near the summit by a wooden gateway. On the far side there is camping at the foot of the pass by a side river which flows into the Shimshal River from the N. If neccessary it is possible to camp between the two passes. The path then runs along barren plateau, through an area which was once well wooded, following the Shimshal River to arrive at the shepherds' settlement of **Shujerab** with its complex of small stone huts. From here, the path climbs up to the **Shimshal Pass**

(4,700m), a beautiful open plateau with two lakes. A little further on is the main summer settlement of **Shewert**.

Here huge numbers of sheep, goats and yaks are tended by the women of Shimshal, who collect the milk to produce butter and cheese. The spectacle of the animals returning to their night enclosures in the dying light of the sun is a spectacular one. Lovingly referred to by Shimshalis as their "Pamir" (upland grazing area), this area is incredibly beautiful, though extremely harsh as well. The minute the sun drops below the mountains, temperatures fall dramatically. In winter, the yaks are taken to the Shorlik pastures on the Oprang River, while the sheep and goats are brought down to Shimshal.

It is possible to continue SE from Shewert and then follow the Braldu River S onto the Braldu glacier and over the **Lupke Pass** to Snow Lake, joining the Biafo-Hispar glacier trek. This is an extremely difficult and technical route which should only be attempted by properly equipped, experienced mountaineers and with an experienced guide familiar with the route.

UPPER CHITRAL

Upper Chitral offers endless and spectacular opportunities for trekking. It is also one of the least visited areas of the mountainous N. Unfortunately, all the treks in the area, with the exception of the Chamarkhan Pass between the Yarkhun and Gilgit valleys, and the Khot Pass between Turikho and Yarkhun valleys, are restricted and therefore require permits. Just a few of the possible treks in this region are outlined here; others are mentioned in passing in the section on Upper Chitral. **NB** Porters can be difficult to find in Upper Chitral during Sep and Oct, when the majority of the men are busy collecting firewood for the winter.

Owir Pass

Restricted zone. Maximum elevation 4,338m. Aug to mid Sep. Maps: the U502 series sheet covering this trek is restricted; Mountaineering Maps of the World, P 268 Tirich Mir and Buni Zom is reasonable.

The jeep track from **Barum village** in the Barum valley (see page 416) is in theory jeepable as far as **Muzhen** (pronounced 'Mujen'), although the bridges along the way are often broken. Alternatively it is a 7 km walk, steep at first but gentle after

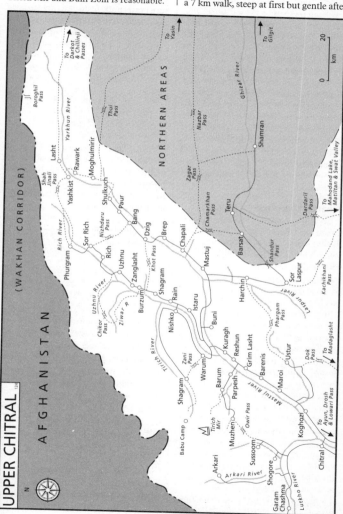

the village of **Shungosh**, just over halfway. Beside the path above Muzhen there is good camping by the stream, with trees for shade. Above Muzhen the route climbs through open pastures up towards Owir Pass (4,338m). There are plenty of potential camping spots on the way up. Be prepared for bitterly cold nights and high winds. The best views of Tirich Mir and Buni Zom, are from a small hillock to the N of the pass itself. On the far side the descent is steep, crossing loose slate, before arriving at pastures with good camping. Further down the path passes through small settlements before arriving at **Sussoom**, the most important village in the Karimabad (previously Ozher) valley, and the head of the jeep track up from Shogore, in the Lutkho valley between Chitral and Garam Chashma. The valley below Sussoom is very narrow with sheer slate cliffs on the S side.

Chamarkhan Pass

Open zone. Maximum elevation 4,344m. Jun to Oct. Maps: U502 series, NJ 43-13 Mastuj is good; Mountaineering Maps of the World, P 212 Central Hindu Raj is better.

This is a relatively easy trek taking 2 days (3 going slowly) and offering an alternative route from Chitral into the Gilgit valley, bypassing the Shandur Pass. A guide is not neccessary, although you need to be fully acclimatized if coming from the Chitral side as there is a height gain of over 1,500m on the trek.

From the village of **Chapali** (see page 417), the path climbs E up the S bank of the small side valley before crossing to the N bank and arriving at a stone shelter at **Malo**. Here the valley forks. The path crosses the stream flowing down from the NE and follows the right hand branch SE, climbing through woods of birch and willow and traversing a scree slope. Higher up the valley forks again.

The valley draining in from the E is the Zagaro, which leads up to the **Zagar Pass** (c 5,000m). It is possible to con-

tinue E across this pass and then across the **Nazbar Pass** (4,977m) to arrive at Yasin. Between the two passes it is also possible to descend the Bahushtaro Gol to the Ghizar (Gilgit) River at Shamran.

The main track crosses the Zagaro River and heads S up the Chamarkhan Gol. There is good camping and beautiful views at the small shepherds' hut at **Shal**. From here it is a long steady climb up to the Chamarkhan Pass through beautiful pastures carpeted with flowers in summer. The pass itself is wide and flat-topped, and also covered in pasture. Stone cairns mark the route. On the other side, the path descends along the E bank of the river, with plenty of good camping spots along the way, to the junction with the Ghizar (Gilgit) River. There is a police post consisting of a couple of tents by the main Chitral-Gilgit jeep track. **NB** Public transport is infrequent in either direction from here, so be prepared to wait around for a day or 2, or walk.

Shah Jinali Pass

Restricted zone. Maximum elevation 4,259m. Jul to Sep. Maps: U502 series NJ 43-13 Mastuj is good, though some place names are misleading; Mountaineering maps of the World, P 236 Eastern Hindu Kush is good. Trek researched first hand.

This is a particularly beautiful though strenuous trek and well worth the expense associated with trekking in restricted areas. Most people recommend doing it from the Turikho (Rich) to Yarkhun valley due to the steep climb towards the pass coming from the other direction. This depends though on whether you prefer your ascents to be short and sharp, or longer and gentler. The trek is described here going from the Yarkhun to Turikho valley. Allow 4-5 days (not including rest days). Porters charge for a minimum of 6 stages.

The first section from **Shalkuch** (see page 417) is an easy walk climbing gently along the E bank of the Yarkhun River, crossing the Gazin Gol flowing in from the E (the route up to the Thui Pass across to Yasin), and passing through settlements and green, lightly wooded terrain to **Moghulmirir**, where there is good camping.

Above Moghulmirir the main path zigzags steeply up a shoulder of mountain to the village and fields of **Rewak**, situated on a beautiful small plateau with excellent views. On the other side it descends steeply through deep meadows of flowers and wild rose. An alternative route follows the river around the shoulder, but involves fording to a shingle bank and back, and is not always passable. Further on a bridge leads across the Yarkhun River and the path doubles back before climbing up to the village of **Yashkist**. It is possible to camp in the village, although flat ground is very limited.

Above the village the path enters the Seru Gol, crosses to the S bank of the river, recrosses further up and doubles back to enter the narrow gorge of Isperu Dok Gol. The climb up the gorge is very steep, gaining more than 800m before arriving eventually at the summer settlement and pastures of **Isperu Dok**. There is a excellent camping on a small grassy patch by the river below the main cluster of stone huts. The setting is a spectacular one and it is well worth spending a day here to explore. It is possible to cover the section from Moghulmirir to Isperu Dok in 1 long day if you are fit.

Above Isperu Dok the valley divides, the left fork being the route to Shah Jinali. Cross to the opposite bank of the river and climb over a shoulder, ascending steadily to the top of the pass. The Shah Jinali (King's Polo Ground) Pass is a beautiful area of rolling pasture, covered in flowers in early July. The greenery is broken in places by snowdrifts, small ponds and crystal clear streams. All around is an amphitheatre of icy peaks. It is a steady descent to **Shah Ghari**, another beautiful spot deep with wild geraniums, onion, hemlock and buttercups.

The next section, down to the village of **Darshal** is subject to frequent change and can follow either bank of the river. In 1995 the bridge across to Darshal had been destroyed, although it was possible to camp in the narrow stretch of woods opposite. Further on, following the right bank after Darshal, there is a precariously perched tiny camp with a rock shelter. A gulley fed by a waterfall runs down from the N. The path then descends steadily, crossing to the left bank and rounding a gradual bend. On the opposite bank, where the Rahozon Gol drains in from the N, there is an area of level ground and trees known as **Moghlong**. Further round the bend, by a fording of a side stream, there is a possible campsite. The valley steadily opens out from its narrow gorge to a wide plain. Further on the path crosses to the right bank of the river on a good bridge and eventually joins the head of the jeep track shortly before **Phurgram village**.

Karumbar/Chillinji Passes

This spectacular but demanding trek continues along the Yarkhun valley from where the trek to Shah Jinali branches W (see above). The Yarkhun valley swings round gradually to the E to run parallel with Afghanistan's Wakhan Corridor to the N. It passes the route N over the **Boroghil Pass** into Afghanistan, then crosses the Karumbar Pass (4,300m), crowned by a string of lakes, into the Karumbar valley. After crossing the snout of the **Chatteboi glacier**, it then climbs up over the glaciated Chillinji Pass (5,290m) and crosses into the Chapursan valley to eventually emerge on the KKH to the N of Sust. For more information about this trek, contact either Karakoram Experience in UK or Hindu Kush Trails, who between them lead groups on this trek.

USEFUL URDU WORDS AND PHRASES

Pronounce
ā as in ah   ī as in bee
ō as in oh   u as oo in book
nasalized vowels are shown as **an un** etc
Note These marks to help with pronunciation do not appear in the main text.

Useful words and phrases

Hello, good morning	*alsalām aleikum*
Goodbye	*hudā hāfiz*
Thank you/ no thank you	*shukriyā / nahīn shukriyā*
Excuse me, sorry	*mihrbānī*
Yes/ no	*jī hān / jī nahīn*
never mind/ that's all right	*koi bāt nahīn*
Very wel/ I see/ OK	*āccha*
What is your name?	*āpkā nām kyā hai?*
My name is	*merā nām .... hai*
Do you speak English?	*āp kō angrezī āti hai?*
a little	*thorī -sī*
How are you?/ are you well	*kyā āp kaise hain?*
I am well, thanks, and you?	*main thīk hun, aur āp?*
I am not well	*main thīk nahīn hun*
Where is the ....?	*.........kahān hai?*
Who is ....?	*......... kaun hai?*
What is this?	*yeh kyā hai?*
I like/ I don't like	*mujhe pasand hai / mujhe pasand nahīn*
What time is it?	*Yeh kitnī baaje hai?*
Please sit down	*tashreef rakhiye*
Please come	*tashreef lāiye*
Please tell me	*farmāiye*
God willing	*inshallah*
As quickly as possible	*jitni jaldi ho sake*

Shopping

How much is this?	*kitnā / iskā kitnā paisa hai?*
That is very expensive!	*yeh bahut mahangā hai!*
Make it a bit cheaper!	*thorā kam kījiye!*

The hotel

What is the room charge?	*ek din kā kirāyā kitnā hai?/*
	ek kamlō kitnā paisa hai?
Please show me the room.	*zarā mujhe kamrā dekhāiye*
Is there an airconditioned room?	*kyā a/c kamrā hai?*
Is there <u>hot water</u>?	*kyā kamre men <u>garam pānī</u> hai?*
... a bathroom/ fan/mosquito net	*...<u>ghusal khana/ pankhā/ machhar dānī</u>*
Is there a large room?	*barā kamrā hai?*
The room is not clean	*yeh kamrā sāf nahīn hai*
Please clean the room	*yeh kamrā sāf karwā dījiye*
Are there clean sheets/ blanket?	*sāf chādaren/kambal hain?*
This is OK	*yah thīk hai*
Please give the bill	*mihrbānī, bill dījiye*

Travel

Where's the <u>railway station</u>?	*<u>railway station</u> kahān hai?*
How much is the ticket to <u>Karachi</u>?	*<u>Karachi</u> kā ticket kitnā paisa hai?*
When does the <u>Karachi</u> bus leave?	*<u>Karachi</u> bus keb jāegī?*
How much to go to the (Fort)?	*<u>killa</u> jāne ke liye, kitnā?*
Will you go for <u>10</u> rupees?	*<u>das</u> rupiye lenge?*
Is it far?	*kyā yeh dur hai?*
left/right	*bāien/dāhinā*
go straight on	*sīdhā chaliye*
nearby	*nazdīk*

Is it near the station?		station ke nazdīk hai?
Please come here at 8		āth bajai yehān ānā
Quickly		jaldi
stop		rukiye
train		rel gari
north		shimal
south		junub
east		mashriq
west		mahgreb

Restaurants

Please show the menu	menu dekhāiye
No chillis please	mirch nahīn dālnā
....sugar/ milk/ ice	chīnī/ doodh/ baraf....
i do not like meat	mujhe gosht pasand nahīn
I do not want chicken	mujhe murghi chāhiye nahīn
I don't like the food	khānā mujhe achhā nahīn lagta
...do not open it	......kholnā nahīn
sweet/ savoury	mīthā/ namkīn
spoon, fork, knife	chamach, kāntā, chhurī

Time and days

right now	abhī		**Numbers**	
morning/ early morning	suba/ suba saveray		1	ek
Midday	dopahar		2	dō
afternoon/ evening	shām		3	tīn
night	rāt		4	chār
today	āj		5	pānch
tomorrow/ yesterday	kal/ kal		6	chhai
day	din		7	sāt
week	haftā		8	āth
month	mahīnā		9	nau
year	sāl		10	das
quarter to	paune		11	gyāra
half past	sarhe		12	bārāh
quarter past	sava		13	terāh
eg ¼ past 7	sava sāth baaje		14	chaudāh
eg ½ past 7	sarhe sāth baaje		15	pandrāh
eg ¼ to 8	paune āth baaje		16	solāh
nb half past 1	desh baaje		17	satrāh
nb half past 2	dhaj baaje		18	athārāh
			19	unnīs
Sunday	itvār		20	bīs
Monday	pir		100/ 200	sau/ do sau
Tuesday	mangal		1000/ 2000	hazār/do hazār
Wednesday	budh		100,000	lākh
Thursday	jum'erāt			
Friday	jum'ā		**Ordinals**	
Saturday	haftā		first	pahla
			second	dussa
			third	tissa
			fourth	chaudtha
			fifth	pānchvan
			sixth	chhata
			seventh	sātvan
			eight	āthvan
			ninth	nauvan
			tenth	dasvan

Basic vocabulary

airport, bank, bathroom, bus, doctor, embassy, ferry, hotel, hospital, juice, police, restaurant, station, stamp, taxi, ticket, train (these are used locally though often pronounced differently eg *daktar, haspatāl*)

and	*aur*	sick (ill)	*bīmār*
after	*ke bād*	silk	*reshmī/ silk*
alone	*akela*	sister	*bahīn*
bathroom	*ghusl khānā*	small	*chhotā*
beautiful	*hūbsūrat*	sometimes	*khabī khabī*
before	*se pahle*	student	*talib-ilm*
behind	*ke piche*	summer	*garmiyān*
big	*barā*	tea	*chai*
brother	*bhai*	tea-shop	*chai-khānā*
chemist	*dawāi kī dukān*	that	*woh*
Christian	*isai*	thirst	*pyas*
clean	*sāf*	this	*yeh*
cold	*thandā*	tourist	*sayyah*
day	*din*	town/ city	*shahar*
delicious	*lazeez*	water	*pānī*
difficult	*mushkil*	what	*kyā*
dirty	*gandā*	when	*kab*
English	*angrezi*	where	*kahān/ kidhar*
excellent	*bahut achhā*	which/who	*kaun*
food/ to eat	*khānā*	why	*kiun*
hot (spicy)	*jhāl*	wife	*bivi*
hot (temp)	*garam*	winter	*sardiyan*
hunger	*bhūk*	with	*ke sāthh*
luggage	*samān*		
marriage	*shadi*	**Fruit** (*phal*)	
medicine	*dawāi*	apple	*seb*
Muslim	*musalman*	banana	*kelā*
name	*nām*	coconut	*nāriyal*
newspaper	*akhbār*	green coconut	*dāb*
of course, sure	*zaroor*	lemon	*nimbu*
old	*puranā*	lychee	*lichi*
pen	*qalam*	mango	*āmb*
post (office)	*dāk khānā*	orange	*santrā*
road/ route	*rāstā*	pineapple	*anānās*
room	*kamrā*	**For Food and Drink see page 28**	
shop	*dukan*		

Index

Figures shown in bold indicate a map

A

Abakh Hoja's Tomb 533
Abbott, James 436
Abbottabad 434, **435**
Abdegar 520
Abdul Gaffar Khan 340
Abdul Latif Shah 81
Abdul Rahim Khan-e-Khanan 118
Abdur Rahman 343
Achaemenid Empire 242
Adamzada 396
Adi Granth 80
Aga Khan Foundation 502
Aga Khan Rural Support Programme 424
Ahmad Shah Durrani 89, 118, 171, 220
Ahmadis 71
Ahmadzai Khans 171
Aitchison College 283
Ajars 380
Akbar 89, 118, 219, 272, 320
Akbari Mosque 155
Akhund Darweza Baba 352
Akra Mounds 367
Alai Valley 447
Alam Bridge 484
Alam Pir La 555
Alexander the Great 86, 117, 170, 219, 242, 268, 338, 381
Ali Malik Mar 492
Ali Sher Khan Anchen 481
Aliabad 332, 507
Aling Glacier 552
All Saints Church 352
Allama Iqbal, Mausoleum of 277
All-India Muslim League 90
Alor 155
Altit Fort 513
Altit 512
Aman-ul-Mulk 396
Ambela Pass 377
Amir Kabir Syed Ali Hamadani 484
Amir Khusrau 81

Amri-ware 157
Anarkali's Tomb 282
Andan Dehri Stupa 399
Andare Fort 518
Andarshah Bazaar 351
Archaemenid 338
Arghun 89, 118, 171
Army of the Indus 340
Arondu 495
Asambar Pass 472, 475, 558
Ashoura 74
Asian Plate 445
Asif Zardari 99
Askole 495
Aslam Khan, Major Mohammad 462
Asoka 86, 117, 219, 242, 338
Asoka's Rock Edicts 375, 438
Asota megaliths 376
Astor Valley 457
Athmuqam 327
Attock 254
Aurangzeb 89, 219, 339
Avitabile, Gen 352
Awami League 96
Awami National Party 345
Aylmer, Captain Fenton 505
Ayub Khan, General 95
Ayub National Park 233
Ayubia 252
Ayun 412
Azad Jammu and Kashmir 318, **319**
Aziz Derhi 376

B

Baba Farid-ud-din Ganj Shakkar 292
Bab-i-Khyber 359
Babur 89, 272, 339
Babusar Pass 443
Bactrian Greeks 86, 219, 338
Badal 342
Badshahi Mosque 277
Bagh 331

Bagrot Valley 466
Bahawalpur 304, **305**
Bahrain 391
Baisakhi Festival 254
Bajosa 331
Balakot 439, **440**
Balambat 400
Baleji Beach 129
Balti 425
Baltistan 479, **480**
Baltit Fort 510
Baltit 508
Baltoro Glacier 553
Baluch 77, 172, 173
Baluchistan 166, **167**
 Archaeological Museum 179
 Black Bear 168
Banak La 555
Banbhore 139
Bangladesh 97
Banna 447
Bannu 367
Bar Valley 504
Bara 496
Barian 251
Barikot 382
Barkulti 475
Barpu Glacier 515
Barsat 477
Basna Valley 495
Bat Khela 382
Bathraiz River 476
Battagram 447
Batura Glacier 518, 560
Bauma Lungma 494
Bazira 382
beaches
 Baleji 129
 Clifton 129
 Gaddani 130
 Hawkes Bay 129
 Paradise Point 129
 Sandspit 129
Bedi Dat 211
Besal 443
Besham 447, **448**
Bhit Shah 150
Bhong Mosque 311
Bhong 311
Bhurban 248
Bhutto, Benazir 99, 121
Bhutto, Zulfikar Ali 96, 121
Biafo Glacier 515, 553

Bibi Jalwindi, Tomb of 307
Biddulph, John 473, 530
Bir Mound 243
Birir Valley 414
Birkot Hill 382
Birmugh Lasht 405
Biron Shal 405
Boesam Pass 562
Boisragon, Lt 505
Bolan Pass 193
Borit Lake 518
Borland, Catherine Theodora 530
Boroghil Pass 395
Boroghil Pass 565
Bradford 333
Brahmanabad/Mansura 151
Brahui 77, 172, 173
Braldu Valley 515
Bride Price 173
British East India Company 89
Bualtar Glacier 515
Budelas 504
Bukkur Island 155
Bumburet Valley 413
Buner Pass 377
Buni 416
Bunji 457
Burawai 443
Burji La 554
Burnes, Alexander 339
Burushaski 425
Burzil Pass 457
But Sahri 376
Butkara 1 383
Butkara 3 385

C

Central Brahui Range 167
Central Makran Range 208
Central Makran 167
Chach 117
Chachro 149
Chagai Hills 167
Chakchan Masjid 497
Chakdara Museum 399
Chakdara 398
Chakkar Rind Fort 196

Chakor 168
Chakoti 329
Chakwal 256
Chalt 445, 503, **504**
Chaman 198
Chamarkhand Pass 417, 564
Chanaka Dehri 376
Chananian 330
Chandragupta Maurya 86, 169, 242
Chandragupta 219
Chapali 417
Chappar Rift 185
Chapri 364
Chaprot Valley 503, 504
Chapsuran Valley 524
Charaksar glacier 551
Charra Pani 247
Charsadda 371
Chashi 476
Chashma Barrage 315
Chasma Barrage 262
Chat Pat 399
Chatorkhand 472
Chattar Bagh 247
Chaudhuri Rahmat Ali 92
Chaukundi tombs 139
Chautair 187
Chenab 115
Chhachor pass 493
Chhanga Manga 291
Chhangla Gali 251
Chikar 329
Chilam 493
Chilas 443, 451, **452**
Chilla 378
Chillinji 417
Chillinji Pass 472, 565
Chiltan Markhor 168
Chiniot 316
Chirah 467
Chitral Fort 402
Chitral Gol National Park 405
Chitral River 395
Chitral Town 402, **403**
Chitral Valley 337, 395
Choa Saidan Shah 256
Chogo Lungma glacier 495
Chogolisa glacier 551
Cholistan Desert 115, 218
Chowa Dara River 449
Chowk Yadgar 351
Christian 74

Chu Tron 495
Chuinj 417
Chungphar Valley 556
Churchill's Picket 399
Clifton Beach 129
Command and Staff College Museum 179
Concordia 553
crabbing 130
Cunningham Clocktower 351
Cyrus the Great 169, 206, 242

D

Dabarra 368
Dadarili Pass 477
Dadhar 195
Dagbir Mosque 141
Daggar 378
Dahimal 476
Daintar Pass 466, 504
Dalbandin 200
Dalsan Pa 551
Daman-e-Koh 226
Dandai 447
Dani Baqaian 329
Danna Meadows 441
Danna 330
Danyore valley 559
Danyore 502
Daptar Shah 173
Daraban 192
Darel Valley 451
Dargai 381
Dari La 555
Darius I 169, 242
Darius the Great 116, 338
Darkot Pass 417, 472
Darkot 475
Darra Adam Khel 360
Dasht River 208
Dasht 168
Dasu and Komila **450**
Dasso 495
Debal 139
Delhi Sultanate 88, 339
Demetrius 117
Deosai Plateau 490, **491**, 554
Dera Ghazi Khan 189
Dera Ismail Khan 368, **370**
Dera Nawab Sahib 309
Derawar, Fort 309
Dharmarajika 244
Dhirimshal 508
Dhirkot 332
Dih 524

Dil Sor 188
Dir District 398
Dir Town 400, **401**
Dir valley 337
Diran 505
Diran 508, 559
Dobani (Bilchar) Peak 467
Dobani 457
Doghani 496
Dok Pass 416
Doko 495
Domaki 425, 514
Domanda 192
Dorah Pass 406
Dost Mohammad 339
Dowarian 327
Drazinda 192
Drosh 402
Dubair Valley 448
Duicar 513
Dunga Gali 252
Dungian 329
Durand line 340
Durand, Col Algernon 452, 461
Durranis 339

E

Earthquake Recording Office 179
Edwardes College 354
Eid ul-Ajha 74
Eidgah 302
Eid-ul-Fitr 74

F

Fa-Hien 448
Fairy Meadows 454
Faisal Masjid 225
Faisalabad 313, **315**
Falaksair, Mt 450
festival, Baisakhi 254
fishing 442
Fort Munro 189
Frere Hall 131

G

Gaddani Beach 130
Gahkuch 470
Galapur 468
Galis, The 250
Gandharan kingdom 219
Ganesh 507
Garam Chashma 405
Garhi Habibullah Khan 439
Gawri 380

Genghis Khan 88, 272, 339, 530
Ghalagai 382
Ghansara Singh, Brig 461
Gharo 139
Ghashumaling Valley 503
Ghazal 81
Ghazan Khan 503
Ghaznavid empire 339
Ghaznavid Empire 87
Ghez River 529
Ghizr 476
Ghora Gali 247
Ghorid empire 339
Ghotki 153
Ghulam Mohammad Barrage 143
Ghulam Shah Kalhora 118
Ghulam Shah Kalhora 144
Ghulkin Glacier 518
Ghulmet 505
Gidar Valley 449
Gilgit District 454, **455**
Gilgit to Hunza and Nagar 502
Gilgit Uprising 461
Gilgit 458, **460**
Gilmiti 470
Girja Ghar Hindu Temple 302
Gittidas 443
Gobind Singh 220
Godwin-Austin glacier 553
Gogdara Rock 383
Gohar Aman 459, 473
Gohar Aman 467
Goharabad 468
Gojal (Upper) Hunza 516, **517**
Gojri 322
Gol 495
Golden Mosque 282
Gondogoro La 549
Gondophernes 243
Gondrani Caves 205
Gor Khatri 351
Grand Trunk Road 264
Great Bolor 481
Green Turtles 129
Gujar Khan 265
Gujars 380
Gujranwala 270
Gujrat 268
Gulab Singh 320, 459, 482

Gulmit Glacier 518
Gulmit **516**
Gunner Farm 454
Gunz 214
Gupis Bridge 473
Gurdwara of Arjan
  Dev 279
Gurikot 458
Guru Nanak 254
Gwadar 212
Gwari 496

H

Hab 168
Habaitgram 382
Hachindar Glacier 507
Hajj 72
Hala 150
Haldi 498
Haleji Lake Bird
  Sanctuary 140
Halmat 328
Hamun-i-Lora 167
Hamun-i-Lora 200
Hamun-i-Mashkel
  167
Han Chinese 526,
  531
Handrap Lake 477
Hangu 364
Hanjore 497
Hanna Lake 179
Haramosh Valley 466
Haramosh 457
Harappa 219, 293,
  294
Haripur 434
Harnai Gorge 185
Hasan Abdal 253,
  434
Hasanabad Glacier
  507
Hasanabad Valley 507
Hasanabad 507
Hasis 472
Hatoon 472
Havelian 434
Hawkes Bay 129
Hayatabad 354
Hayward, George
  462, 473, 474, 530
Hayward's Rock 475
Hazara 432, **433**
Hazerganji Chiltan
  National Park 180
Hazrat Ali Akbar Shah,
  Shrine of 302
Hazrat Haji Bahadar
  Rahmat Ali, Tomb
  of 363
Hazrat Imam Ali ul
  Haq 269
Hazrat Lal Shahbaz

Qalander 158
Hazrat Musa Pak
  Shaheed, Shrine of
  302
Hazrat Syed
  Mohammad Nur
  Baksh 484
Hazuri Bagh 277
Hermann Buhl 456
Himalayan Brown
  Bear 490
Hindi 506
Hindko 322
Hindko 77
Hindu Kush 337, 395
Hindus 74
Hingol River 208
Hingol 168
Hispar Glacier 515,
  553
Hispar Pass 554
Hispar Valley 515
Hiuen Tsang 117,
  156, 243, 264, 272,
  432, 527
Hons 511
Hopar 515
Hora 515
Hoshab 211
Hosht 513
Hoti Mardan 372
Houbara Bustard
  143, 168
Hub Chowki 205
Hujra 342
Humayun 272
Hund 377
Huns 86
Hunza and Nagar
  501, 503
Hunza 500
Hunzakuts 500
Hushe Valley 497
Hussaini 520
Hyderabad 143, **145**

I

Ibrahim Lodi 272
Idkah Mosque 533
Iltutmish 88
Imit 472
Imran Khan 262
Indian National
  Congress 90
Indian Plate 445
Indus Flyway 66
Indus River Dolphin
  67
Indus River 114
Indus Valley
  Civilization 116,
  219
Indus Valley Rd 428

Indus Valley Rising 452
Indus valley 337
Indus Waters Treaty
  115, 218
Iqbal Park 285
Iqbal, Mohammad
  80, 91 221, 270
Ishkoman Pass 472
Ishkoman Valley 471,
  558
Ishkoman 472
Islam 69
Islamabad Museum
  226
Islamabad National
  Park 239
Islamabad 223, **224,
  225, 227**
Islamakot 149
Islamia College 354
Islamic Jamhoori
  Ittehad 99
Ismailis 71

J

Jacob, Gen John 197
Jacobabad 197
Jafarabad 504
Jaglot Goor 503
Jaglot 457
Jahanabad Buddha
  388
Jahangir 89, 219
Jahangir's Tomb 285
Jain Temple of Gori
  149
Jalipur 454
Jallo Park 291
Jamal Garhi 374
Jambil Valley 387
Jami Masjid 205
Jamrud Fort 359
Jandial 245
Jangal Khel 363
Jaulian 245
Jhang 314
Jhelum Valley 329
Jhelum 115, 268
Jijal 445, 449
Jinnah, M A 92, 119
Jirga 342
Jiwani 214
Jowar 378
Juniper forests 168
Jutal 502

K

K2 420, 553
Kabir 80

Kach 185
Kachhi plain 194
Kachikani Pass 478
Kachura Lake 487
Kaghan Valley 337,
  439, 442
Kaghan **439,** 441
Kahuta 265
Kalabagh Dam 115,
  263
Kalam 391, **393**
Kalash Valleys 406,
  407
Kalasha 425
Kalat 202
Kalatuk 211
Kalhora Tombs 146
Kallar Kahar 259
Kamal Khan China
  399
Kamaris 518
Kanai 447
Kanchey Bridge 470
Kandahar 198
Kandia Valley 450
Kanishka 86, 117,
  219, 243, 339
Karachi 124, **126-7,
  132, 134**
Karakar Pass 378
Karakoram Highway
  and the Northern
  Areas 419
Karakoram Highway
  428, **429**
Karakuli Lake 529
Karez Fort 200
karez 174
Kargah Buddha 463
Karimabad 508, **511**
Karphok 496
Karpochu 485
Karumbar Pass 565
Karumbar 417
Karumber Glacier 472
Karumber 471
Kashgar 529, **532**
Kashmir Dispute 103
Kashmir Smats 375
Kashmir 318
Kashmiri 322, 425
Kat Kala 399
Kator Dynasty 396
Kawai 440
Kayal Valley 449
Kazakhs 531
Kazakhstan 536
Keamari Harbour 130
Kech valley 208
Kelly, Col James 397,
  477
Keran 327
Ketas 258
Khadeji Falls 143

Khaibar 521
Khairpur 151
Khaljis 89
Khalti Lake 476
Khanabad 505
Khanian 441
Khanispur 252
Khankha Masjid 497
Khanozai 188
Khanpur 310
Khaplu 496, **497**
Kharan 200
Kharian 268
Kharmang 495
Kharoshthi 347
Khawaja
   Nazim-ud-Din 94
Khel 328
Khewra Salt Mine 257
Khirgi Post 368
Khizerabad 504
Khojak Pass 198
Khot Pass 417
Khowar 425
Khudabad 159
Khudai Khidmatgars
   341
Khunjerab National
   Park 524
Khunjerab Pass 522,
   525
Khurukushal 508
Khushab 317
Khushal Khattak
   Khan 343
Khushwakht 473
Khushwaqt 396
Khuzdar 203, **204**
Khwazakhela 388
Khyber Bazaar 349
Khyber Pass 358
Killik Pass 524
Kinhhar Lake 142
Kiris 496
Kirthar Mountains
   115
Kirthar National Park
   143
Kirthar Range 167
Knight, EF 505
Koghozi 416
Kohat Fort 362
Kohat 361, **363**
Koh-e-Bahtil 213
Koh-i-Murad 209
Kohistan Island Arc
   420, 445, 503
Kohistan 445, **446**
Kohistanis 425
Kohori 327
Kolpur 193
Komila/Dasu 449
Kondus valley 498
Kongur, Mt 529

Kot Diji Fort 151
Kotla Mohsin Khan
   Gate and Tombs
   352
Kotli 334
Kotri Barrage 142
Kuch Lak 188
Kulalai 391
Kunala stupa 245
Kundal Shahi 327
Kunhar River 439
Kuragh 416
Kurg 447
Kurram valley 364
Kushan 219, 339
Kutton 327
Kuwait 470
Kyrghiz 526, 531
Kyrghizstan 537

L

Lahore 272, **275, 281**
Lahore Central
   Museum 283, **284**
Lahore Fort **278,** 279
Lahore Resolution of
   1940 91, 276
lakes
   Borit 518
   Haleji Lake 140
   Hamun-i-Lora 167
   Hamun-i-Mashkel
      167
   Handrap 477
   Hanna 179
   Kachura 487
   Karakuli 529
   Khalti 476
   Kinhhar 142
   Lulusar 443
   Manchar 159
   Mangla 265
   Naltar 466, 556
   Phandur 477
   Rama 458
   Rawal 227
   Sadpara 486
   Saiful Malik 441
   Snow 554
Lal Musa 268
Lal Suhanra National
   Park 306
Lalazar Plateau 441
Lalkani Checkpost
   382
Landi Kotal 359
Langar 477
Larkana 164, **165**
Las Bela 204
Lasharis 169
Lashkar 342
Laspur River 416
Lassi 204

Lea Market 129
Lea market 129
Leepa Valley 330
Leitner, GW 452
Liachar Nala 457
Liaqat Ali Khan 94
Liaqat Memorial Hall
   233
Line of Control 321
Lockhart Fort 364
Lockhart 397
Lockhart, Col 475
Lodis 89
Lok Virsa Museum
   226
Loonbagla 329
Loralai 188
Lorimer, EO 507
Lowari Pass 401
Lower Hunza and
   Nagar Section 500
Lucknow Pact 91
Lulusar Lake 443
Lupke Pass 562
Lyall, Sir James 313

M

Macartney, George
   530
Mach 193
Machilu 498
Madaglasht 402
Madyan **389**
Mahabat Khan
   Mosque 352
Mahandri 441
Maharaja Hari Singh
   321
Maharaja of Kashmir
   94
Mahmud of Ghazni
   87, 169, 219, 272,
   339
Mahodand 394
Maiun 505
Makhdum Syed
   Mohammad Yusuf
   Gardezi, Shrine of
   300
Makli Hill 140
Makpons 481
Makran Coastal
   Range 167, 208
Makran 206, **207**
Makrani 173
Malakand Pass 381
Malam Jabba 388
Malika Parbat 440
Malot 259
Manchar Lake 159
Mand 211
Mandra 265
Manghopir 133

Mangla Dam 218,
   265
Mangla Lake 265
Mangla 115
Manglaur 388
Manikyala Buddhist
   stupa 264
Manora Point 131
Mansehra **437**
Mao Zedong 531
Marco Polo 530
Mardan 372, **373**
Margalla Hills 239,
   240
Margalla Pass 253
Marghazar/Mount
   Ilam 387
Masherbrum Base
   Camp 551
Masjid-e-Tooba 131
Massaga 400
Mastuj Village 416
Mastuj 478
Mastung 202
Maulana Sufi
   Mohammad 344
Mauryan Empire 86,
   117, 219
Mauryan 338
Mausoleum
   Baba Sheikh
      Abdullah 213
   Gen Mohammad
      Haroon 204
   Shah Khairuddin
      Jilani 153
Mediabad 495
Meena Bazaar 351
Mekha Sanda 375
Melmastia 342
Memon Mosque 131
Merhgarh 194
Mian Mohammad
   Nawaz Sharif 99
Miandam 388, **390**
Miani 150
Mianwali 262
Minapin 506
Minaret of Masum
   Shah, The 153
Mingora 383, **384**
Mintaka Pass 524
Mir Chakar Rind 169
Mir Nur Mohammad
   Kalhora 118
Mir Shamsuddin Iraqi
   484
Mir Wali 474
Mir Ziarat 371
Miran Jani 252
Miri Kalat 211
Mirkhani 401
Mirpur Khas 147
Mirpur 333

Misgar 524
Mithi 149
Moenjo Daro 159, **161**
Mohajir Qaumi Movement 121
mohajirs 119
Mohammad bin Qasim 87, 117, 139, 219
Mohammad 69
Mohana fisherman 155, 159
Mohatta Palace 130
Mominabad 513
Moro 151
mosques
  Akbari 155
  Badshahi 277
  Bhong 311
  Dagbir 141
  Faisal Masjid 225
  Golden 282
  Idkah 533
  Memon 131
  Phulhattan Wali 302
  Shah Jahan 141
  Wali Mohammad 302
  Wazir Khan 280
Mount Khalifat 187
Mountbatten, Lord 93
mountains
  Central Brahui Range 167
  Central Makran 167
  Chagai Hills 167
  Hindu Kush 337
  K2 420
  Kirthar Range 167
  Kirthar 115
  Makran Coast Range 167
  Pab Range 167
  Pamir 337
  Ras Koh 167
  Safed Koh 337
  Salt Range 218
  Shandur range 337
  Siahan 167
  Sikeram 337
  Suleiman Range 167, 218, 337
  Takatu 198
  Tirich Mir 337
  Tobar Kakar Range 167
  Waziristan hills 337
Muduri 475
Mughal Dynasty 89
Mughal Khot 192
Mu'izzu'd Din 88
Mulkho 417
Mullah Mohammad 209

Multan 297, **301**
Mummery 456
Murkhon 521
Murree 247, **249, 251**
Murtazabad 506
museums
  Baluchistan Archaeological 179
  Chakdara 399
  Command and College 179
  Islamabad 226
  Lahore Central 283
  Lok Virsa 226
  Mardan 372
  National Museum of Pakistan 132
  Peshawar 352
  Quaid-e-Azam House 128
  Shakaparian 226
  Sibi 195
  Swat 383
  Taxila 243
Muslimbagh 188
Mutiny 90
Muzaffarabad 324, **325**
Muztagh Ata 528
Myth-making in Hunza 500

N

N and S Waziristan 368
Nagar Parkar 149
Nagar 500, 515
Nagaris 500
Naghar 401
Naltar (Pakor) Pass 466, 558
Naltar Lake 466, 556
Naltar Valley 465, 502, 556
Namak Mandi 349
Nanawati 342
Nang 342
Nanga Parbat 456, 457, 555
Napier, Sir Charles 118
Naran 441, **442**
Nasir Khan I 171
Nasirabad 211, 506
Nathia Gali 252
National Museum of Pakistan 132
national parks
  Ayub 233
  Kirthar 143
  Chitral Gol 405
  Hazerganji Chiltan 180
  Islamabad 239

Khunjerab 524
Lal Suhanra 306
Naukot 148
Naushero 194
Nazbar Pass 417, 564
Nearchus 141
Neelum Valley 327
Newbolt, Sir Henry 475
Ney Elias 528
Nicholson, General John 253
Nilt 504
Nimogram 382
Nizhdaru Pass 417
No Objection Certificate 323
Nok Kundi 201
Nomal 465
Noonbagla 329
North West Frontier Province 335, **336**
Northern areas **421**
Nouseri 327
Nowshera 255
Nur Jahan's Tomb 286
Nur Mahal Palace 305
Nurbakshi 71, 484, 496
Nurpur Shahan 226
Nushki 199

O

Okara 292
Old Hunza Rd 465
Olive Ridley Turtles 129
Ora 383
Owir Pass 416, 563

P

Pab Range 167
Padag 200
Pagaro Pirs 152
Pahari 322
Pakistan Muslim League (PML) 97
Pakistan's Peoples' Party 96, 121
Pakor Pass 472
Pakora 472
Pakpattan 292
Palas Valley 449
Pamir mountain 337
Panah 342
Panch Pir 363
Panjnad Headworks 309
Panr 385
Parachinar 366
Paradise Point 129
Paras 441

Parinagar 149
parks
  Iqbal 285
  Jallo 291
Parsees 75
Parthians 86, 219, 339
Pashto 77, 343
Passu Gar 519
Passu 518, **519**, 560
Pathans 77, 343
Patikha 327
Patriata 248
Pattan 449
Peepul Mundi 351
Pennell Missionary Hospital 367
Peru 268
Peshawar **348, 350, 353, 354**
Peshawar valley 337, 371, **372**
Petroglyphs 450
Pezu 368
Phandur Lake 477
Phandur 476
Phargam Pass 416
Phulhattan Wali Mosque 302
Piderak 212
Pind Dadan Khan 258
Pingul 476
Pir Baba 378
Pir Ghaib 194
Pir Khushab 383
Pir Mangho 133
Pir Mohammad Suleiman Shah 190
Pir Sar 447
Pirali 525
Piri Chat 212
Pirjo Goth 152
Pishin 198
Pishkurgan 214
Pisin 505
polo, Shandur Pass 477
Porali 168
Potwar Plateau 218, 264
Prahladpuri Temple 299
Prang 371
Ptolemy 526
Pukhtuns 343
Pukhtunwali 342
Punial District 468
Punjab 216, **217**
Punjabi 76
Pushkalavati 371

Q

Qadam Gah of Hazrat Ali 146

Qawwali 81
Qazi 344
Qila Abdullah 198
Qila Saifullah 188
Qissa Khawani
Bazaar 350
Quaid-e-Azam House
Museum 128
Quaid-e-Azam's
Mausoleum 129
Quais 343
Quetta 177, **178,**
181, 186
Qutb u'd Din Aibak 88

R

Radcliffe Boundary
Commission 93
Radcliffe, Sir Cyril 93
Rahim Yar Khan 310
Rahimabad 503
Rahman Dheri 368
Rai Bahadur Sardar
Soojan Singh 233
Raikot Bridge 454
Raja Gira's Fortress
383
Raja Hari Singh 461
Raja Mahal 496
Rajah Bazaar 233
Rajputs 117
Rajur 371
Rakaposhi 457, 504,
505, 508, 559
Rama Lake 458
Ramadan 75
Ramayana 272
Rani Ghat 376
Ranikot Fort 156, **157**
Ranjit Singh 320, 339
Ras Koh 167
Rashmal 468
Rawal Lake 227
Rawalkot 331
Rawalpindi 232, **234,**
235, 236
Razmak 364
Red Fort 324
Reshian Pass 330
Reti 153
Rich 417
Rig Veda 80
Rinds 169
rivers
Chenab 115
Chitral 395
Chowa Dara 449
Dasht 168, 208
Ghez 529
Ghizr 476
Hab 168
Hingol 168, 208
Indus 114, 115

Jhelum 115
Kech 208
Kunhar 439
Laspur 416
Mangla Dam 218
Mastuj 416
Porali 168
Shyok 495
Tarbela Dam 218
Zhob 168
Riwat 264
Robertson, Major
George 397
rock art 451
rod-kohi 346
Rohri 155
Rohtas Fort 265, **267**
Rondu 485
Rose and Jasmine
Garden 227
Rumbur Valley 413
Rupal Valley 555
Rustam 377

S

Sacred Rocks of
Hunza, The 516
Sadda 364
Sadequain 131, 265
Sadhbella 153
Sadpara Lake 486
Safed Koh mountains
337
Sahiwal 292
Saidpur Village 226
Saidu Sharif 383, **385**
Saidu Stupa and
Monastery 383
Saiful Malik, lake 441
Saishu 551
Sakas 219
Sakhi Sarwar 189
Sakkas 86
Salat 72
Saling 498
Salkhata 327
Salt Range 218, 256
Saltoro River Valley
498
Sami 211
Sammas 118
Samnas 89
Sandeman, Sir Robert
172
Sandeman's Grave
204
Sandhi 475
Sandspit 129
Sandy Desert 168
Sann 156
Sargodha 316
Sartez 521

Sasli 485
Sassanian 86, 117,
339
Satghara Hindu
Temples 258
Sathbahin Jo Maskan
155
Sawm 72
Sayyid Shah Wali 505
Schlaginweit, Adolf
530
Schomberg, Colonel
RCF 471
Scylax of Caryanda
116
Scythians 117, 339
Sea of Tethys 445
Second Sikh War 268
Sehwan 158
Seleucus Nicator 206
Semiramis 206
Seraiki 77
Sethi St 351
Shachmirk Pass 562
Shagai Fort 359
Shah Abdul Latif 118
Shah Abdul Latif 150
Shah Daula of
Baghdad 270
Shah Jahan Mosque
141
Shah Jahan 89, 219
Shah Jinali Pass 417
Shah Jinali Pass 564
Shah Karim al-Husayni
Aga Khan IV 508
Shah Makkai Fort 145
Shah Morad Khan
481
Shah Nadir Rais 396
Shah Rais Khan 462
Shah Rukn-e-Alam,
Shrine of 300
Shahada 72
Shahbaz Garhi 375
Shah-e-Napursan 371
Shahi Masjid 402
Shah-ji-ki-Dheri 347
Shaikhan Dheri 371
Shakaparian
Museum 226
Shalimar Gardens
286, 349
Sham-i Tabriz, Shrine
of 300
Shandur Pass 417,
477
Shandur range 337
Shandur 395
Shangla Pass 388,
447
Shangri-la 500
Sharan 441
Sharda 327

Shariat Law 344
Shatial 450
Shaw, Robert 530
Sheikh Abdul Qadir
Gilani 203
Sheikh Budin 368
Sheikh Farid Shakar
209
Sheikh Mohammad
Makkai 145
Sheikhupura 291
Sheng Shih-tsai,
General 531
Shenote 468
Sher Qila 469
Sher Shah Suri 253,
254, 265, 272
Shergarh Fort 157
Shergur 381
Shia 70, 484
Shigar River Valley
493
Shigar Village **494**
Shigarthan Valley 554
Shimshal Pass 562
Shimshal Valley 521,
560
Shina 425
Shingerdar Stupa 382
Shinu 441
Shipton, Eric 531
Shishi Valley 402
Shishkat Nala 518
Shogran 440
Shree Ratneswar
Mahdevi Hindu
Temple 130
Shrines
Abdullah Shah
Ghazi 130
Akhund of Swat
383
Data Ganj Baksh
282
Hazrat Bahauddin
Zakaria 300
Pir Makki 282
Shyok River 495
Siahan Range 208
Siahan 167
Sialkot 269, **271**
Sibi 195, **196**
Sikanderabad 504
Sikeram 337
Silpi 470
Simla Agreement,
The 321
Sind 113, **114**
Sindhi 77
Singal 470
Sipah-e-Mohammad
Pakistan (SMP) 221
Sipah-i-Sahaba
Pakistan (SSP) 221

Sir Sayyid Ahmad Khan 90
Sirkap 245
Sirsukh 245
Skardu 485, **486**
Snow Lake 554
Sohbat Serai 196
Sor Laspur 478
Soudhan Gali 329
Southern NWFP 361
Sphola Stupa 359
Sri Badad 459
SS Jhelum 369
St John's Cathedral 354
Stewart, Lt Cosmo 477
Sufi 120
Sufism 71
Sukkur Barrage 152
Sukkur 153, **154**
Suleiman Range 167, 218, 337
Sumas 89
Sumayar 506
Summit Minar 285
Sumra 118
Sun Temple 299
Sunday Market 531
Sunni 70
Sunny Bank 247
Suntsar 212
Surab 203
Sust 521, **521, 522, 524**
Swabi 376
Swari 378
Swat Museum 383
Swat valley 337, 379, **380**
Syed Karim Ali Shah 472

T

Taftan 201
Tajik Autonomous County 526
Tajiks 531
Takatu Mountain 198
Takht-e-Bhai 373, **374**
Takht-e-Suleiman 192, 340
Talboto Das 504
Taliban 104
Tamerlane 339
Tamerlane 530
Tanai Scout Post 368
Tangir Valley 451
Tank 368
Tappa 81

Tararkhel and Pallandri 331
Tarashing 555
Tarbela Dam 218, 241
Tarbela 115
Tarkhans 89, 118
Tarshing 458
Tashkurgan 526, **527**
Tattapani 331
Taunsa Barrage 190
Taunsa Sharif 190
Taxila Museum 243
Taxila 242, **244**, 253
temples
   Girja Ghar Hindu 302
   Jain Temple of Gori 149
   Prahladpuri 299
   Rai Bahadur Sardar Soojan Singh 233
   Satghara Hindu 258
   Shree Ratneswar Mahdevi Hindu 130
   Sun 299
Tenzing Norgay 456
Teru 477
Thakot Bridge 447
Thal 364
Thalichi 457
Thalle La 552
Thandiana 252
Thandiani 437
Thaous 475
Thar Desert 115, 147
Thatta 141
Thole 505
Thui Pass 475
Thui Valley 475
Tibet 536
Timargarha 400
Timur (Tamerlane) 89, 272
Tirich Mir Base Camp 418
Tirich Mir 337
TNSM 344
Toba Kakar range 191
Tobar Kakar Range 167
Tombs of the Talpur Mirs 146
Top Dara Stupa 382
Torkham 359
Torwal 380
Totli 495
Tourgat Pass 537
Trakhans 459
Trans-Caspian Railway 397
Transit Trade

Agreements 472
Treaty of Amritsar 320
Treaty of Gandamak 172
Trekking 538
Trimmu Headworks 314
Tripartite Treaty 340
Tuar 485
Tughluqs 89
Tump 211
Tungans 531
Turbat 210
Turikho Valley 417
Tusserpo La 552

U

Ubauro 153
Uch Sharif 307
Udegram 383
Uigyur 526, 531
Ultar Glacier 510
Ultar Peak 506
Ultar 508
Umarkot 148
University Town 354
Upper Chitral 414, **415**
Upper Naltar 466
Upper Swat Canal 381
Urak Valley 179
Urdu 76
Urumqi 536
Ushu valley 394
Ustur 416
Uthal 205
Uzbeks 526, 531

V

Varusha 375
Vigne, GT 482
Vijnot 153
Virawah 149

W

Wah Cantonment 253
Wah Mughal Gardens 253
Wah 434
Wakhi 425
Wali Mohammad Mosque 302
Wana 368
Warsak Dam 359
waterlogging 123
Wazir Khan Mosque

280
Wazir Mansion 128
Wazirabad 269
Waziristan hills 337
West Wharf Harbour 131
Wheeler, Sir Mortimer 294
White Huns 117, 339
Wyeen Pass 562

X

Xiangfei 533
Xinjiang Uiygur 526

Y

Yabgu 496
Yagistan 451
Yahya Khan, General 96
Yakmach 200
Yakub Beg 530
Yarkhun valley 417
Yasin Fort 474
Yasin Valley 558
Yasin 473
Younghusband, Sir Francis 248, 521
Yugo 496
Yunz Valley 520
Yusufzai 379
Yusup Khass Hajib 533
Yusup Khass Hajib, Tomb of 533

Z

Zagar Pass 417
Zagar Pass 564
Zahedan 201
Zakat 72
Zam zama 285
Zani Pass 418
Zarabad 520
Zhob River 168
Zhob valley 191
Zia ul-Haq, General 97, 305
Ziarat Rahman Baba 352
Ziarat 186
Zikri 71, 209
zoo, Lahore 285
Zoroastrians 75

WILL YOU HELP US?

We do all we can to get our facts right in the **PAKISTAN HANDBOOK**. Each section is always thoroughly revised, but the country is large and our eyes cannot be everywhere. If you have enjoyed a tour, trek, train trip, beach, museum, temple, fort or any other activity and would like to share it, please write with all the details. We are always pleased to hear about any restaurants, or hotels you have enjoyed. When writing, please give the page number referred to. In return we will send you details of our special guidebook offer.

Thank you very much indeed for your help.

TRADE & TRAVEL
Handbooks

Write to The Editor, *Pakistan Handbook*, Trade & Travel,
6 Riverside Court, Lower Bristol Road, Bath BA2 3DZ. England
Fax 01225 469461   E mail 100660.1250@compuserve.com

TRADE & TRAVEL
Handbooks

Trade & Travel *Handbooks* are available worldwide in good bookshops. They can also be obtained by mail order directly from us in Bath (see below for address). Please contact us if you have difficulty finding a title.

South American Handbook

Mexico & Central American Handbook

Caribbean Islands Handbook

India Handbook

Thailand & Burma Handbook

Vietnam, Laos & Cambodia Handbook

Indonesia, Malaysia & Singapore Handbook

Morocco & Tunisia Handbook
with Algeria, Libya and Mauritania

East African Handbook
with Kenya, Tanzania, Uganda and Ethiopia

Egypt Handbook
with excursions into Israel, Jordan, Libya and Sudan

Tibet Handbook
with Bhutan

Sri Lanka Handbook

Pakistan Handbook

New in September 1996
South Africa Handbook
with Swaziland and Lesotho

Zimbabwe and Malawi Handbook
with Mozambique, Botswana and Zambia

Keep in touch. If you would like a catalogue or more information about the new titles please contact us at :

Trade & Travel, 6 Riverside Court, Lower Bristol Road, Bath BA2 3DZ. England
Tel 01225 469141   Fax 01225 469461   Email 100660.1250@compuserve.com